CRITICAL SURVEY
OF
SHORT FICTION

CRITICAL SURVEY
OF
SHORT FICTION

Second Revised Edition

Volume 7

Essays

Research Tools

Indexes

Editor, Second Revised Edition

Charles E. May

California State University, Long Beach

Editor, First Edition

Frank N. Magill

SALEM PRESS, INC.

Pasadena, California Hackensack, New Jersey

Managing Editor: Christina J. Moose
Research Supervisor: Jeffry Jensen
Acquisitions Editor: Mark Rehn
Photograph Editor: Philip Bader
Manuscript Editors: Lauren M. Mitchell
Melanie Watkins
Research Assistant: Jeff Stephens
Production Editor: Cynthia Beres
Layout: Ross Castellano

∞ The paper used in these volumes conforms to the American National Standard for Permanence of Paper for Printed Library Materials, Z39.48-1992(R1997).

Library of Congress Cataloging-in-Publication Data

Critical survey of short fiction / editor, Charles E. May.—2nd rev. ed.
7 v. ; cm.
First edition edited by Frank Northen Magill.
Includes bibliographical references and index.
ISBN 0-89356-006-5 (set : alk. paper) — ISBN 0-89356-007-3 (v. 1 : alk. paper) — ISBN 0-89356-008-1 (v. 2 : alk. paper) — ISBN 0-89356-009-X (v. 3 : alk. paper) — ISBN 0-89356-010-3 (v. 4 : alk. paper) — ISBN 0-89356-011-1 (v. 5 : alk. paper) — ISBN 0-89356-012-X (v. 6 : alk. paper) — ISBN 0-89356-013-8 (v. 7 : alk. paper)
1. Short story. 2. Short story—History and criticism. 3. Short story—Bio-bibliography. I. May, Charles E. (Charles Edward) 1941 - . II. Magill, Frank Northen, 1907-1997.

PN3321 .C7 2001
809.3′1—dc21 00-046384

Fourth Printing

PRINTED IN THE UNITED STATES OF AMERICA

CONTENTS

Complete List of Authors ci

Theory of Short Fiction

Theory of Short Fiction 2599
The Detective Story 2613
The Fable Tradition 2625
The Science-Fiction Story 2632
The Supernatural Story 2643

History of Short Fiction

Short Fiction in Antiquity 2657
The Saga and Tháttr 2669
The Early Middle Ages 2680
The Medieval Romance 2691
The Renaissance Novelle 2700
The Sixteenth and Seventeenth Centuries . . . 2708
The Eighteenth Century 2726
The Early Nineteenth Century: 1800-1840 2736
The Late Nineteenth Century: 1840-1880 2752
The Turn of the Twentieth Century: 1880-1920 2786
The Mid-Twentieth Century: 1920-1960 2803
The Late Twentieth Century: 1960-2000 2826

Short Fiction Around the World

African Short Fiction 2845
African American Short Fiction 2857
Asian American Short Fiction 2871
Australia and New Zealand Short Fiction . . . 2888
Canadian Short Fiction 2898
Chinese Short Fiction 2908
Irish Short Fiction 2914
Japanese Short Fiction 2928
Latin American Short Fiction 2936
Latino Short Fiction 2949
Native American Short Fiction 2960
South Asian Short Fiction 2972

Research Tools

Major Awards 2981
The Best American Short Stories 2983
The O. Henry Awards, 1919-2000 3015
Short-Fiction Chronology 3044
Terms and Techniques 3056
Bibliography 3069

Geographical Index CLIX
Category Index CLXV
Subject Index CLXXXIII

COMPLETE LIST OF AUTHORS

Volume I

Abbott, Lee K. 1
Achebe, Chinua 4
Adams, Alice 9
Addison, Joseph 14
Agee, James 19
Agnon, Shmuel Yosef 22
Aichinger, Ilse 28
Aiken, Conrad 32
Akutagawa, Ryūnosuke 37
Alarcón, Pedro Antonio de 41
Aldrich, Thomas Bailey 46
Aleichem, Sholom 50
Alexie, Sherman 55
Algren, Nelson 58
Allen, Woody 62
Allende, Isabel 67
Andersen, Hans Christian 70
Anderson, Sherwood 76
Angelou, Maya 83
Apple, Max 86
Arreola, Juan José 89
Asimov, Isaac 95
Asturias, Miguel Ángel 102
Atwood, Margaret 108
Auchincloss, Louis 116
Austen, Jane 123

Babel, Isaac. 128
Baldwin, James. 135
Ballard, J. G. 141
Balzac, Honoré de 147
Bambara, Toni Cade 152
Bank, Melissa 156
Banks, Russell 160
Baraka, Amiri 165
Barnes, Julian 169
Barrett, Andrea 173
Barth, John 176
Barthelme, Donald 182
Barthelme, Frederick 190
Bass, Rick 194
Bates, H. E.. 197
Bausch, Richard 203
Baxter, Charles 207
Beattie, Ann 210
Beckett, Samuel 218
Beerbohm, Max 225
Bell, Madison Smartt. 230
Bellow, Saul 233
Bender, Aimee 239
Benét, Stephen Vincent 242
Berriault, Gina 248
Betts, Doris. 252
Bierce, Ambrose 257
Blackwood, Algernon 262
Boccaccio, Giovanni 266
Böll, Heinrich 272
Bombal, María Luisa. 278
Bontemps, Arna 281
Borges, Jorge Luis 285
Borowski, Tadeusz 295
Bowen, Elizabeth. 300
Bowles, Jane 306
Bowles, Paul 311
Boyle, Kay 317
Boyle, T. Coraghessan 325
Bradbury, Ray 331
Brautigan, Richard 341
Brecht, Bertolt 348
Brodkey, Harold 354
Brown, Larry 360
Broyard, Bliss 363
Buck, Pearl S. 366
Bunin, Ivan 372
Butler, Robert Olen 377
Buzzati, Dino. 381
Byatt, A. S.. 387
Byers, Michael 390

Cable, George Washington 394
Cain, James M. 400
Caldwell, Erskine 404
Calisher, Hortense 409
Callaghan, Morley 415

Volume II

Calvino, Italo 423
Camus, Albert 429
Canin, Ethan 434
Čapek, Karel 437
Capote, Truman 441
Card, Orson Scott 446
Carey, Peter 451
Carleton, William 455
Carpentier, Alejo 460
Carr, John Dickson 464
Carter, Angela 469
Carver, Raymond 472
Cassill, R. V. 481
Cather, Willa 485
Cervantes, Miguel de 491
Chabon, Michael 499
Chandler, Raymond 505
Chang, Lan Samantha 511
Chappell, Fred 514
Chaucer, Geoffrey 518
Cheever, John 532
Chekhov, Anton 540
Chesnutt, Charles Waddell 549
Chesterton, G. K. 556
Chopin, Kate 562
Chrétien de Troyes 567
Christie, Agatha 572
Cisneros, Sandra 579
Clark, Walter Van Tilburg 585
Clarke, Arthur C. 590
Colette 597
Collier, John 605
Congreve, William 611
Connell, Evan S., Jr. 614
Conrad, Joseph 620
Conroy, Frank 628
Coover, Robert 632
Coppard, A. E. 638
Cortázar, Julio 644
Cozzens, James Gould 649
Crane, Stephen 654

Dahl, Roald 664
Dante 670
Daudet, Alphonse 676
Davenport, Guy 681
Davies, Peter Ho 691
Davies, Rhys 694
Dazai, Osamu 699
de la Mare, Walter 704
Delany, Samuel R. 709
Derleth, August 714
Dick, Philip K. 719
Dickens, Charles 725
Diderot, Denis 731
Dinesen, Isak 737
Disch, Thomas M. 745
Dixon, Stephen 749
Doerr, Harriet 752
Donoso, José 756
Dostoevski, Fyodor 760
Douglas, Ellen 766
Dovlatov, Sergei 769
Doyle, Arthur Conan 775
Dreiser, Theodore 783
Dubus, Andre 789
Dunbar, Paul Laurence 793
Dunsany, Lord 797
Dybek, Stuart 803

Edgeworth, Maria 807
Eliot, George 816
Elkin, Stanley 820
Elliott, George P. 825
Ellison, Harlan 831
Ellison, Ralph 837
Endō, Shūsaku 841
Erdrich, Louise 847

Volume III

Farrell, James T. 851
Faulkner, William 856
Fitzgerald, F. Scott 864
Flaubert, Gustave. 872
Ford, Richard. 880
Forster, E. M.. 886
Fowles, John 891
France, Anatole 897
Franklin, Benjamin. 903
Freeman, Mary E. Wilkins 908
Friedman, Bruce Jay 914
Friel, Brian 920
Fuentes, Carlos. 924

Gaines, Ernest J. 930
Gaitskill, Mary 936
Gallant, Mavis 939
Galsworthy, John. 945
García Márquez, Gabriel. 950
Gardner, John. 956
Garland, Hamlin 963
Garrett, George. 969
Gass, William H.. 975
Gates, David 980
Gautier, Théophile 984
Gautreux, Tim 988
Gilchrist, Ellen 991
Gilliatt, Penelope. 997
Gilman, Charlotte Perkins 1003
Glasgow, Ellen 1007
Godwin, Gail 1013
Goethe, Johann Wolfgang von 1016
Gogol, Nikolai 1022
Gold, Herbert 1030
Goldsmith, Oliver. 1033
Gordimer, Nadine. 1039
Gordon, Caroline 1046
Gordon, Mary 1052
Gorky, Maxim. 1055
Goyen, William 1060
Grau, Shirley Ann. 1065
Greenberg, Joanne 1069
Greene, Graham. 1074
Greene, Robert 1081
Grimm, The Brothers 1086
Guimarães Rosa, João 1092

Hale, Nancy 1096
Hall, Lawrence Sargent. 1101
Hammett, Dashiell 1104
Hannah, Barry. 1108
Hardy, Thomas 1112
Harjo, Joy 1118
Harris, Joel Chandler 1121
Harrison, Jim 1127
Harte, Bret 1133
Hawkesworth, John 1139
Hawthorne, Nathaniel. 1143
Head, Bessie 1152
Hearn, Lafcadio. 1156
Heinlein, Robert A.. 1159
Helprin, Mark. 1164
Hemingway, Ernest 1172
Hempel, Amy 1180
Henry, O. 1183
Hesse, Hermann. 1187
Highsmith, Patricia 1193
Hildesheimer, Wolfgang 1201
Himes, Chester 1204
Hoch, Edward D. 1210
Hoffmann, E. T. A. 1216
Homer. 1222
Hospital, Janette Turner 1228
Houston, Pam 1231
Howells, William Dean 1234
Hughes, Langston. 1238
Humphrey, William. 1243
Hurston, Zora Neale 1249
Huxley, Aldous 1255

Ihara Saikaku 1261
Irving, Washington 1268

Jackson, Shirley. 1274
Jacobs, W. W.. 1279

Volume IV

James, Henry 1283
James, M. R. 1291
Jewett, Sarah Orne 1296
Jhabvala, Ruth Prawer 1302
Johnson, Charles 1306
Johnson, Denis 1310
Johnson, Samuel 1314
Joyce, James 1319

Kafka, Franz 1328
Kaplan, David Michael 1336
Kavan, Anna 1339
Kawabata, Yasunari 1344
Keillor, Garrison 1350
Kiely, Benedict 1356
Kincaid, Jamaica 1362
King, Stephen 1368
Kingsolver, Barbara 1374
Kingston, Maxine Hong 1378
Kinsella, W. P. 1382
Kipling, Rudyard 1388
Kiš, Danilo 1397
Kleist, Heinrich von 1400
Knowles, John 1406
Kundera, Milan 1412

Lagerkvist, Pär 1420
Lahiri, Jhumpa 1424
Landolfi, Tommaso 1427
Lardner, Ring 1434
Laurence, Margaret 1438
Lavin, Mary 1443
Lawrence, D. H.. 1449
Lawson, Henry 1458
Leavitt, David 1463
Le Fanu, Joseph Sheridan. 1469
Le Guin, Ursula K. 1476
Lem, Stanisław 1481
Leskov, Nikolai 1488
Lessing, Doris. 1494
Lewis, Wyndham 1501
L'Heureux, John 1509
Lind, Jakov 1513
Lispector, Clarice 1517
London, Jack 1522
Longstreet, Augustus Baldwin 1527
Lordan, Beth 1531
Lovecraft, H. P. 1535
Lu Xun 1541

McCarthy, Mary 1551
McCullers, Carson 1556
McEwan, Ian 1562
McGahern, John 1566
Machado de Assis, Joaquim Maria 1569
Machen, Arthur 1574
McKnight, Reginald 1577
McPherson, James Alan 1581
Mahfouz, Naguib 1586
Major, Clarence 1591
Malamud, Bernard 1595
Malory, Sir Thomas. 1603
Mann, Thomas 1607
Mansfield, Katherine 1617
Marie de France. 1625
Mars-Jones, Adam 1630
Marshall, Paule 1634
Mason, Bobbie Ann. 1639
Maugham, W. Somerset 1645
Maupassant, Guy de 1652
Meckel, Christoph 1659
Melville, Herman 1664
Mérimée, Prosper 1671
Michaels, Leonard 1675
Miller, Sue 1679
Millhauser, Steven 1682
Minot, Susan 1686
Mishima, Yukio 1690
Moore, George 1695
Moore, Lorrie 1699
Moravia, Alberto 1702
Morris, Wright 1710
Mphahlele, Ezekiel 1717

Volume V

Mukherjee, Bharati 1721
Munro, Alice 1730

Nabokov, Vladimir 1738
Nahman of Bratslav, Rabbi 1745
Narayan, R. K. 1750
Nerval, Gérard de 1756
Nin, Anaïs. 1760
Norris, Frank 1765

Oates, Joyce Carol 1771
O'Brien, Edna. 1780
O'Brien, Fitz-James. 1786
O'Brien, Tim 1790
O'Connor, Flannery. 1794
O'Connor, Frank 1802
Ōe, Kenzaburō 1809
O'Faoláin, Seán. 1816
Offutt, Chris. 1822
O'Flaherty, Liam 1826
O'Hara, John 1832
Okri, Ben 1838
Olsen, Tillie. 1843
Onetti, Juan Carlos 1849
Ovid. 1852
Oz, Amos 1860
Ozick, Cynthia 1865

Paley, Grace. 1872
Pardo Bazán, Emilia 1878
Parker, Dorothy 1883
Pasternak, Boris. 1887
Pavese, Cesare 1893
Perabo, Susan 1898
Perelman, S. J. 1901
Peretz, Isaac Leib 1906
Petronius 1911
Petry, Ann. 1916
Phillips, Jayne Anne 1923
Pirandello, Luigi 1927
Plath, Sylvia. 1933
Plomer, William. 1937
Poe, Edgar Allan 1940
Porter, Katherine Anne 1949
Powers, J. F.. 1957
Price, Reynolds 1961
Pritchett, V. S.. 1968
Prose, Francine 1977
Proulx, E. Annie 1980
Pu Songling 1984
Purdy, James 1990
Pushkin, Alexander 1997
Pynchon, Thomas 2004

Queen, Ellery 2011
Quiroga, Horacio 2017

Rasputin, Valentin 2023
Reid, Elwood 2027
Rhys, Jean. 2031
Richler, Mordecai 2036
Rivera, Tomás. 2041
Robbe-Grillet, Alain 2045
Roberts, Elizabeth Madox 2049
Robison, Mary 2052
Roth, Philip 2059
Rulfo, Juan 2064
Rushdie, Salman 2068

Saki 2072
Salinger, J. D.. 2076
Sansom, William 2084
Saroyan, William 2090
Sartre, Jean-Paul 2095
Sayles, John. 2102
Schulz, Bruno 2106
Schwartz, Delmore 2112
Schwartz, Lynne Sharon 2117
Scott, Sir Walter 2120
Shalamov, Varlam. 2126
Shaw, Irwin 2131
Silko, Leslie Marmon 2135
Sillitoe, Alan 2142
Simms, William Gilmore 2147
Simpson, Mona 2153

Volume VI

Singer, Isaac Bashevis 2157
Sinyavsky, Andrei. 2165
Slavin, Julia 2171
Smiley, Jane. 2174
Smith, Lee. 2182
Solzhenitsyn, Aleksandr 2187
Sontag, Susan 2193
Spark, Muriel 2196
Spencer, Elizabeth 2202
Stafford, Jean 2208
Steele, Richard 2213
Steele, Wilbur Daniel 2217
Stegner, Wallace 2220
Stein, Gertrude 2225
Steinbeck, John 2233
Stern, Richard G. 2239
Stevenson, Robert Louis 2245
Stockton, Frank R. 2250
Stone, Robert 2254
Stuart, Jesse 2258
Sturgeon, Theodore 2264
Svevo, Italo 2269
Swift, Graham. 2272

Tallent, Elizabeth 2276
Tan, Amy 2279
Tanizaki, Jun'ichirō 2283
Targan, Barry 2288
Taylor, Elizabeth 2291
Taylor, Peter. 2294
Thackeray, William Makepeace 2300
Thomas, Dylan 2306
Thurber, James 2312
Tilghman, Christopher 2317
Tolstaya, Tatyana 2320
Tolstoy, Leo 2326
Toomer, Jean 2335
Trevor, William 2340
Tuohy, Frank 2347
Turgenev, Ivan 2352
Twain, Mark. 2359
Tyler, Anne 2365

Unamuno y Jugo, Miguel de 2371
Updike, John 2375

Valenzuela, Luisa 2386
Vanderhaeghe, Guy 2390
Verga, Giovanni. 2393
Vergil 2398
Viramontes, Helena María 2403
Vizenor, Gerald 2406
Voltaire 2410
Vonnegut, Kurt 2416

Wain, John 2424
Walker, Alice 2428
Walser, Robert 2437
Wang Anyi 2443
Warner, Sylvia Townsend. 2449
Warren, Robert Penn 2456
Weidman, Jerome 2462
Welch, Denton 2466
Weldon, Fay. 2472
Wells, H. G.. 2476
Welty, Eudora 2482
Wescott, Glenway. 2490
West, Jessamyn 2495
Wharton, Edith 2500
White, E. B.. 2506
Wideman, John Edgar 2509
Wiggins, Marianne 2516
Williams, Joy 2520
Williams, Tennessee 2524
Williams, William Carlos. 2530
Wilson, Angus 2535
Woiwode, Larry. 2538
Wolfe, Thomas 2544
Wolff, Tobias 2549
Woolf, Virginia 2554
Wright, Richard. 2560

Yeats, William Butler. 2566

Zamyatin, Yevgeny 2572
Zhang Jie 2578
Zola, Émile 2584
Zoshchenko, Mikhail 2589

CRITICAL SURVEY
OF
SHORT FICTION

Theory of Short Fiction

THEORY OF SHORT FICTION

The common critical assumption is that the short story was first recognized as a literary genre with unique characteristics in the 1840's with Edgar Allan Poe's discussions of a "unified effect" of "the tale proper." However, Poe did not develop these ideas out of thin air; short prose fiction was a topic of critical discussion in Germany in the decades preceding Poe's influential assertions.

Friedrich Schlegel was the first to theorize generically about short fiction, which, in keeping with the precedent established by Giovanni Boccaccio and Miguel de Cervantes, he called *novelle.* Schlegel says the form usually focuses on the oral telling of a new, unknown story, which should arouse interest in and of itself alone, without connection to "the nations, the times, the progress of humanity, or even the relation to culture itself." Schlegel also suggested that although the anecdotal basis of short fiction may be trivial or its subject matter slight, its manner or way of telling must be appealing. One corollary of this focus on "manner" rather than "matter," Schlegel noted, was that the narrator takes on a more significant role in short fiction—a shift related to the general trend in Romantic poetry toward a lyric point of view. The first effect of this trend, in such writers as Washington Irving, was an increased emphasis on the style of telling; later with Poe, it shifted emphasis to the direct involvement of the narrator in the tale that he or she tells.

German author Ludwig Tieck reiterates Schlegel's paradoxical idea that because events in short fiction should be strange and yet commonplace they should be described as objectively taking place. However, Tieck's most controversial idea is his notion of a *Wendepunkt*, a "twist in the story" or turning point from which it unexpectedly takes a different direction and, argues Tieck,

> develops consequences that are nevertheless natural and entirely in keeping with characters and circumstances; this extraordinary and striking turning point, which persists in many short stories throughout the form's history, distinguishes short fiction from every other narrative form.

Poe owes much of his influential theory of the unified effect in short fiction to Schlegel's concept of a "totality of interest." Poe argued in several of his early reviews that whereas in long works one may be pleased with particular passages, in short pieces, the pleasure results from the perception of the oneness, the uniqueness, the overall unity of the piece—on the adaptation of all the constituent parts, which constitutes a totality of interest. Poe distinguished between the usual notion of plot as merely events that occur one after another to arouse suspense and his own definition of plot as an overall pattern, design, or unity. Only pattern can make the separate elements of the work meaningful, insisted Poe, not temporal or realistic cause-and-effect events. Moreover, Poe argued that only when the reader has an awareness of the overall pattern of the work will seemingly trivial elements become relevant and meaningful.

Poe's 1842 review of Nathaniel Hawthorne's *Twice-Told Tales* (1837, expanded 1842) contains the central statements of his theory of the short story. What is most important in the literary work is unity, says Poe; however, unity can only be achieved in a work that the reader can hold in the mind all at once. Poe claims only the short tale has the potential for being unified in the way the poem—the highest form of literary art—is. The effect of the tale is synonymous with its overall pattern or design and thus its theme or central idea. Poe was always more interested in the work's pattern, structure, conventions, and techniques than its reference to the external world or its social or psychological themes.

Brander Matthews and the Handbooks

In 1901, in the first full-length study of the short story (*The Philosophy of the Short-Story*), Brander Matthews noted the "strange neglect" of the form in histories of prose fiction and set out to justify Poe's suggestive comments about the form made sixty years earlier and to establish what he called the "art of the short-story." However, instead of Matthews's opinion—that the short story is a unique art form differing from the novel in substantive ways—most critics of the time felt that the short story was a smaller, simpler, easier, and less important form of the novel. Not only did Matthews's book fail to encourage new and creative artistic work in the short story, but also it had the opposite effect of further popularizing the form in the pejorative sense. As a result, the short story in the early twentieth century came to be considered a question of cold-blooded rules of composition.

The appeal of Matthews's account, along with the popularity of the formulaic stories of O. Henry, gave rise to a number of books in the first two decades of the twentieth century that proposed anyone could write short stories if they only knew the rules. Joseph Berg Esenwein's *Writing the Short Story: A Practical Handbook on the Rise, Structure, Writing, and Sale of the Modern Short Story* (1909), Carl Henry Grabo's *The Art of the Short Story* (1913), and Blanche Colton Williams's *A Handbook on Story Writing* (1917) are only three of numerous such books. By the 1930's, serious readers and critics called for an end to it, filling the quality periodicals with articles on the "decline," the "decay," and the "senility" of the short story. Even Edward Joseph Harrington O'Brien, probably the greatest champion of the form America has ever had, wrote his book *The Dance of the Machines* in 1929, censuring the mechanized structure of American society and the machinelike short story that reflected it.

THE EARLY HISTORIES

Soon after Matthews's study of the short story, the first histories of the form and some new scholarly studies began to appear. Henry Seidel Canby's *The Short Story in English* (1909) is an especially helpful study of the form that traces the development of short prose narrative from Boccaccio's *Decameron: O, Prencipe Galetta* (1349-1351; *The Decameron*, 1620) and Geoffrey Chaucer's *The Canterbury Tales* (1387-1400) up through O. Henry. Barry Pain's small 1916 pamphlet *The Short Story* contains still-useful comments on its essentially romantic nature. Early histories attempted to delineate what constituted the "newness" of the short story beginning with Poe. In *The Short Story in English*, Canby argued that all writers have used the short narrative to "turn a moral, as in fable, or to bring home, in a fabliau, an amusing reflection upon life, or to depict a situation." The difference between the nineteenth century short story and previous short narratives, claimed Canby, is not a difference in kind but one of degree; the nineteenth century form shows a higher measure of unity. The conscious purpose of the short story, says Canby, a purpose that throws so much emphasis on the climax of a story, is "a vivid realization for the reader of that which moved the author to write, be it incident, be it emotion, be it situation . . . ; thus the art of the short story becomes as much an art of tone as of incident."

Both Fred Lewis Pattee (*The Development of the American Short Story*) and O'Brien (*The Advance of the American Short Story*) in their 1923 histories of the American short story place the birth of the form with Washington Irving's combination of the style of Joseph Addison and Richard Steele's essays with the subject matter of German Romanticism. Pattee says that in Irving's *The Sketch Book of Geoffrey Crayon, Gent.* (1819-1820) "the Addisonian Arctic current was cut across by the Gulf Stream of romanticism" and thus was born the American short story, "a new genre, something distinctively our own in the world of letters." Focusing more on the classical "Arctic" than the Gulf Stream romanticism, Edward O'Brien says that the short story begins with *The Sketch Book* when Irving detached the story from the essay, especially the personal essay of the eighteenth century which arose from the need to chronicle the "talk of the town."

Poe's contribution, insisted Canby in his *The Short Story in English*, was to do for the short story what Samuel Taylor Coleridge and John Keats were doing for poetry—that is, to excite the emotions and to apply an impressionistic technique to his materials to hold his stories together. Hawthorne, he argued, who uses a moral situation as the nucleus to hold his stories together, was the first American story writer to build a story on a situation, an "active relationship between characters and circumstances." Fred Lewis Pattee agreed that Hawthorne was the first to "touch the new romanticism with morals," and that both

Hawthorne and Poe differ from E. T. A. Hoffmann's and Tieck's "lawless creative genius" and "wild abandon" by exercising deliberate control and art. Pattee suggested that Poe's important contribution was his realization that the tale is akin to the ballad form and, like lyric poetry, was dependent on an emotional, rather than a conceptual unity.

Bliss Perry in a departure from usual studies or histories of prose fiction at the turn of the century devoted a chapter to the short story in his 1902 *A Study of Prose Fiction*. He noted that because of the shortness of the form, a character must be "unique, original enough to catch the eye at once." The result of this necessity for choosing the exceptional rather than the normal characters is that the short story is thrown upon the side of romanticism rather than of realism. Perry also pointed out another aspect of the short story that has remained constant in the form since its inception: "Sanity, balance, naturalness; the novel stands or falls in the long run, by these tests. But your short-story writer may be fit for a madhouse and yet compose tales that shall be immortal."

The Short Story as a Romantic Genre

The basic romantic nature of the short story, both in its focus on unusual events and on the subjectivity of the author, was strongly voiced during the later part of the nineteenth century when Ambrose Bierce entered into the argument then raging over the romance versus the novel form. In his attack on the William Dean Howells school of fiction in his essay "The Short Story," Bierce said, "to them nothing is probable outside the narrow domain of the commonplace man's commonplace experience."

Other short-story writers have noted this same romantic characteristic of the form. Henry James said he rejoiced in the anecdote, which he defined as something that "oddly happened" to someone. More recently Flannery O'Connor has claimed the form makes "alive some experience which we are not accustomed to observe everyday, or which the ordinary man may never experience in his ordinary life." Short stories, says O'Connor, "lean away from typical social patterns, toward mystery and the unexpected." Of her own work she says, it takes its character from "a reasonable use of the unreasonable," a quality that both Poe and Hawthorne would have echoed about their stories. "The peculiar problem of the short-story writer," O'Connor says, is "how to make the action he describes reveal as much of the mystery of existence as possible . . . his problem is really how to make the concrete work double time for him."

The only extended discussion of this romantic element in the short story is Mary Rohrberger's 1961 study on Hawthorne and the modern short story (*Hawthorne and the Modern Literary Short Story: A Study Genre*). Rohrberger notes that Hawthorne and many modern short-story writers share the romantic notion of a reality that lies beyond the extensional, everyday world with which the novel had been traditionally concerned. Consequently, the short story shares characteristics with the romance in being symbolic and romantic. "The short story derives from the romantic tradition . . . the metaphysical view that there is more to the world than that which can be apprehended through the senses."

The Short Story and Social Reality

Many critics have noted the fact that the short story does not deal with generalized social reality or abstract social values. In fact, the form seems to thrive best in societies where there is a diversity or fragmentation of values and people. This geographic and social fragmentation of peoples and values has often been cited as one reason why the short story quickly became popular in nineteenth century America. In 1924, Katherine Fullerton Gerould said that American short-story writers have dealt with peculiar atmospheres and special moods, for America has no centralized civilization. "The short story does not need a complex and traditional background so badly as the novel does." Ruth Suckow in 1927 also suggested that the chaos and unevenness of American life made the short story a natural expression. Life in America was so multitudinous that "its meaning could be caught only in fragments, perceived only by will-of-the-wisp gleams, preserved only in tiny pieces of perfection."

More recent comments on the English short story by Wendell V. Harris and Lionel Stevenson suggest somewhat the same reason for the difference between the English short story and the American form. Stevenson points out that as soon as a culture becomes more complex, brief narratives expand or "agglomerate" and thus cause the short story to lose its identity. Throughout the nineteenth century in England, the novel predominated. Only writers, like Thomas Hardy, who depicted a relatively simple social milieu, could present a short-story sense of "reality" in his ironic verse narratives. The fragmentation of sensibility did not set in England until about 1880, at which time the short story was seen as the best medium for presenting this fragmentation.

Harris also observes that the 1890's in England was known as the golden age of the short story, noting that with the fragmentation of sensibility perspective, or "angle of vision," became most important in fiction, especially the short story, in which instead of a world to enter, as the novel provides, the form presents a vignette to contemplate. Harris has also noted that from Henry Fielding to Thomas Hardy, fiction was defined in England as a "presentation of life in latitudinal or longitudinal completeness." The "essence of the short story," on the other hand, says Harris,

> is to isolate, to portray the individual person, or moment, or scene in isolation—detached from the great continuum—at once social and historical . . . the short story is a natural form for the presentation of a moment whose intensity makes it seem outside the ordinary stream of time, or the scene significance is outside the ordinary range of experience.

Short fiction achieves real success when the realms of "real life" and the mysterious interact and reflect a balance between the rational and the irrational side of human nature. Ray Benedict West has said that naturalism made less of an impact on the short story than on the novel because the former's shortness of the form demands more preoccupation with technique than naturalistic writers were willing or able to grant. One reason the short story requires more attention to technique is that the form is romantic and therefore concerned with the unseen reality beneath the surface of life and thus requires more artifice. As Edith Wharton has said, "the greater the improbability to be overcome the more studied must be the approach, the more perfectly maintained the air of naturalness, the easy assumption that things are always likely to happen that way."

Bonaro Wilkinson Overstreet has suggested that the short stories of the nineteenth century, mainly action stories, depended on two basic faiths: that one could know right from wrong because a basic social code of values was taken for granted and that people were what they seemed to be. In action stories, one cannot be forever hunting out obscure motives; men of action have to "assume a reliable correspondence between inner character and outward behavior." In the twentieth century, says Overstreet, perhaps as a result of the war, readers have lost these faiths and consequently they are "thrown back upon a study of human nature—human motives, fears, wants, prejudices." The drama of the nineteenth century, says Overstreet, is "the drama of what goes on in the mind." The short story is an "expert medium for the expression of our deep concern about human moods and motives."

A much more extensive study of these shifts and their many implications for short fiction in the twenties can be seen in Austin McGiffert Wright's exhaustive study, *The American Short Story in the Twenties* (1961). That better stories are written by Sherwood Anderson, Ernest Hemingway, and William Faulkner than were written by Mary Eleanor Wilkins Freeman, Hamlin Garland, and Theodore Dreiser is primarily due to a loss of confidence in the adequacy of the social system and a new reliance on the individual self. Wright says that interest in moral problems in the nineteenth century focused on how to resolve the dilemma within the social system. "In stories of the twenties, on the other hand, the more fully developed moral problems have no solution, and their interest centers more directly on the question of sympathy for the bewildered individual." Wright says that while the world of the nineteenth century was relatively stable, with substantial agreement on the worth of society and social principles as moral guidance, the world of the 1920's was "fragmented both socially and morally, with each man isolated, obliged to find or make for himself his appropriate place in society and the appropriate principles to guide him."

Frank O'Connor has also related the short story to a country or a milieu's attitude toward society, claiming that in those countries where society does not seem adequate or sufficient for self-definition or the repository of acceptable values the reader finds the short story most pertinent. "The novel can still adhere to the classical concept of civilized society, of man as an animal who lives in a community—as in Jane Austen and Anthony Trollope it obviously does—but the short story remains by its very nature remote from the community—romantic, individualistic, and intransigent." These considerations lead O'Connor to formulate his famous theory that the short story always presents a sense of "outlawed figures wandering about the fringes of society." As a result, says O'Connor, there is an intense awareness of human loneliness in the short story that does not exist in the novel. The short story is more akin to the mood of Blaise Pascal's saying: "The silence of these infinite spaces frightens me."

The Short Story vs. the Novel

The short story is a narrative form that makes the reader aware of reality as perspective. Nadine Gordimer, the South African short-story writer, notes a general dissatisfaction that writers have with the novel as a means of "netting ultimate reality." The short story, she says, may be better equipped than the novel to capture ultimate reality in the modern world, where truth is perspective. Short-story writers have always known what novelists seem to have recently discovered: The strongest convention of the novel, "prolonged coherence of tone," is false to human reality in which "contact is more like the flash of fireflies, in and out, now here, now there, in darkness." The short-story writer's art, says Gordimer, "is the art of the only thing one can be sure of—the present moment." The short story aims at a discrete moment of truth, not *the* moment of truth, "because the short story doesn't deal in cumulatives."

It has often been recognized that the situations that the short story presents are quite different from separable incidents in a novel. As early as 1909, William James Dawson, a critic at the *North American Review*, suggested that incidents that are suited for novels or incidents that could be expanded into novels are not really incidents for short stories at all: "Life consists both of prolonged sequences and of flashing episodes. The first affords the material of the novelist, the second of the short-story writer." In that same year, Canby also noted that the short narrative is best used for "life-units where only brevity and the consequent unified impression will serve."

Seán O'Faoláin, on the other hand, has called the short form one vast convention. "There is in life no such thing as a short story; all life's stories are long, long, stories . . . to chop up life is to pretend that life is not continuous but spasmodic or intermittent." O'Connor would probably agree, but with significant differences in focus. O'Connor says that in the novel time is the novelist's essential asset: "The chronological development of character or incident is essential form as we see it in life, and the novelist flouts it at his own peril." There is no essential form for the short-story writer, O'Connor says. Because the short-story writer must select a point at which he can approach life, each selection he makes contains the possibility of a new form.

The novel as a composite of experiences is not a composite of the kinds of experiences that make up short stories. The flow of experience in the novel is determined by some concept of the "totality of experience," or as Alberto Moravia says, some skeletal framework of philosophic outlook. The individual experiences that make up the short story are determined by some confrontation that breaks up the totality of experience. The novel presents life as it really is experienced only in the sense that life is usually experienced as perception of a set of categories. Moravia suggests that if the reader accepts the view that art presents experiences that cannot be conceptualized, then it follows that the novel is the most conceptual and therefore the least artistic literary form.

The Pattern of the Short Story

In 1916, Barry Pain suggested that the length of the form creates in the short story something very rarely found in the novel "in the same degree of intensity—a very curious, haunting, and suggestive quality." This haunting quality, this intensity that manifests itself in the short story, however, does not come from the incident chosen alone; it comes from a tight dramatic patterning of the incident in such a way that its dramatic tension is exposed and felt. Danforth Ross in his study of the American short story says that the major contribution that Poe makes to the short fiction form is that he brings tension, long a characteristic of poetry, to the story form. Whereas Irving's stories meander, Poe attempted to present a story as a dramatist does in a play. In an article in 1943, Gorham Bert Munson says that the O. Henry story at the turn of the century marked a degeneration of the Poe short story. "Poe aimed not at a transcription of actuality, but at a patterned dramatization of life." For this, says Munson, he needed a "storyable incident," an anecdote in the Jamesian sense of something that "oddly happened," an anecdote with a hard nugget of latent value.

The nugget, however, must be laid bare of its latent value. By metaphor and condensation the latent must be made manifest in whatever seeming artificial manner. Even W. Somerset Maugham, whose story preference was for one that could be told in a drawing room or smoker, insisted on stories as a "dramatization" of life, not simply a transcription. This "artificial" patterning of the short story, this heightening of intensity and deepening of significance has often been a point of controversy among critics. Canby argued in 1909 that whereas the novelist aims at a natural method of transcription, "the author of the short story adopts a very artificial one. His endeavor is to give a striking narrative picture of one phase of the situation or character, disregarding much that a cross section might show." Such a process, says Canby, is very artificial, but also very powerful. A few years later, Elsworth Corey condemned this very compression in the short story as pathological: "Its unity is abnormally artificial and intense" and leads to titillating the nerves in pathological moments. Not only does the technique seem abnormally intense and pathological to some critics, but also it seems to lead to a sterile art for others. Falcon O. Baker said in 1953 that the concern of the New Critics for form and unity leads toward the dullness of geometry in the short story.

THE LIMITATIONS OF THE SHORT STORY

The highly formalistic nature of the short story has also been criticized by those critics and novelists who have affirmed the value of naturalistic presentation and social involvement and awareness. It was criticized by the naturalist writers in the nineteenth century and has been scorned by the Marxist writers and critics since the 1930's. James T. Farrell criticized the form in two essays in the 1930's for its sterile formality and its failure to be a vehicle for revolutionary ideology. Maxwell Geismar in 1964 lashed out at *The New Yorker* school of short-story writer, which included J. D. Salinger, Philip Roth, Bernard Malamud, and J. F. Powers, for the narrow range of their vision and subject matter and their stress on the intricate craftsmanship of the well-made story.

Another reason why the short story has not been popular or has not maintained its place in modern literature is that readers prefer the novel precisely because it does not demand anything more than perseverance in a continuous flow of reading, becoming one with the sustained rhythm and tone of the work. William Dean Howells noted in 1901 that although the short story may be attractive when one runs across one singly in a magazine, the short story in a collection seems most repellant to the reader. The reason stems from the very intensity and compression and suggestiveness of the form itself. Reading one story, says Howells, one can receive a pleasant "spur to his own constructive faculty. But if this is repeated in ten or twenty stories, he becomes fluttered and exhausted by the draft upon his energies; whereas a continuous fiction of the same quantity acts as an agreeable sedative." V. S. Pritchett has said much the same. The length, inclusiveness, and shapelessness of the novel creates a "bemusing effect," says Pritchett.

> The short story, on the other hand, wakes the reader up. Not only that; it answers the primitive craving for art, the wit, paradox and beauty of shape, the longing to see a dramatic pattern and significance in our experience, the desire for the electric shock.

THE SUBJECTIVE IMPULSE IN THE SHORT STORY

In addition to the kind of event or situation it deals

with and the tight dramatic patterning of that event, another element of the short story that creates unity and compression is the subjective and lyrical impulse of the writer. Elizabeth Bowen has said that the

> first necessity for the short story, at the set out, is necessariness. The story, that is to say, must spring from an impression or perception pressing enough, acute enough, to have made the writer write. . . . The story should have the valid central emotion and inner spontaneity of the lyric; it should magnetize the imagination and give pleasure—of however disturbing, painful or complex a kind. The story should be as composed, in the plastic sense, and as visual as a picture. . . . The necessary subject dictates its own relevance. . . . The art of the short story permits a break at what in the novel would be the crux of the plot: the short story, free from the longueurs of the novel is also exempt from the novel's conclusiveness—too often forced and false: it may thus more nearly than the novel approach aesthetic and moral truth.

Eudora Welty has said that all stories by a writer come from some source within: "All of one writer's stories must take on their quality, carry their signature, because of one characteristic lyrical impulse of his mind—the impulse to praise, love, to call up, to prophesy." Something in the outside world, some person, place, thing leads back to the emotions in a specific way, says Welty; it is the "break of the living world upon what is stirring inside the mind, and the answering impulse that in a moment of high consciousness fuses impact and image and fires them off together." William Carlos Williams has said that the short story consists of one "single flight of the imagination, complete: up and down."

Many writers have said they feel the form is a subjective medium. Seán O'Faoláin calls it an "emphatically personal exposition." William Carlos Williams says he thinks it a good medium for "nailing down a single conviction. Emotionally." V. S. Pritchett says the good short-story writer knows he or she is putting on a personal individual act, catching "a piece of life as it flies" and makes "his personal performance out of it." Katherine Mansfield has said that what is essential for the short-story writer is to "penetrate one's subject, not to take a flat view of it; thus feelings, and objects as well, must be contemplated—or rather 'submitted to'—until one is truly lost in them."

The detachment from circumstances in the short story makes it necessary to have every word exactly right. For if it is not circumstances the writer is concerned with, except that these circumstances are resonant with meaning and signification, then the words chosen have to be exactly right to convey or capture the writer's subjective impression of the significance of the event, character, thing, being described. This means that the short story must be rigorously executed; it must tend, says Herbert Gold to "control and formalize experience" and "strike hot like the lyric poem." Because of the subjectivity of the form, editor Herschell Brickell has noted, it requires technical accomplishment. "The whole thing is delicate and subtle, a matter of nuances, and the style itself must have both beauty and exactness, must partake of the esthetic and the functional, if the full effect is to be achieved."

One very important implication of the subjectivity of the short story is the concomitant importance of tone in the story, a force that more than narrative seems to hold the story together. Canby said very early in the history of the short story that the art of the form is as much that of tone as incident. The work of the author in the story is "harmonized into one tone, as if narrative were a painting." This perfection of tone is necessary to emphasize the climax, that central core for which the story was written. Irving Howe has said, "If the short-story writer is to create the illusion of reality, he must sing mostly aria and very little recitative. As a result, he uses a series of technical devices, often quite simple inflections of style, the end effect of which is called the story tone. A novel written in one dominant tone becomes intolerable; a story too often deviating from it risks chaos." However, Howe notes the same problem of this dependence of the story on tone that writer Edith R. Mirrielees had noted eight years earlier, that is several writers either write from the same tone so often that the stories seem identical (the same tone held too long becomes toneless) or else because tone can so easily be wrenched from its necessary context that it can become a stereotype and destroy a writer's individuality. Howe says, in the novel the "second-rater tends to parrot a vision of life; in the story, he tends to echo a tone of voice."

Leaving Things Out in the Short Story

Another aspect of the lyric nature of the story is its tendency to "leave things out." Hemingway once said, "I always try to write on the principle of the iceberg. There is seven-eighths of it underwater for every part that shows." Rudyard Kipling suggested, "A tale from which pieces have been raked out is like a fire that has been poked. One does not know the operation has been performed, but everyone feels the effect." Anton Chekhov once wrote to I. L. Shcheglov, "In short stories it is better to say not enough than to say too much, because,—because—I don't know why." In another letter Chekhov says that it is compactness that makes small things alive. "Alive" here must be understood to be life at the remove of art, of life more alive for being compressed. Chekhov once wrote to Maxim Gorky that he lacked restraint and thus grace. "When a man spends the least possible number of movements over some definite action, that is grace." Another implication of this need for compression is that for a story to be good, it must be perfect, a demand made on the form that is never made upon the novel.

This lyric nature of the short story has led some critics, such as Sister Mary Joselyn Baldeshwiler, to argue that although all stories have a mimetic base, some have additional elements that are usually associated with verse. Some of these poetic elements she notes are: "(1) marked deviation from chronological sequence (2) exploitation of purely verbal resources such as tone and imagery (3) a concentration upon increased awareness rather than upon a completed action, and (4) a high degree of suggestiveness, emotional intensity, achieved with a minimum of means." Most interestingly, Baldeshwiler says that the lyric story often has a dual action: a syllogistic plot that rests on the onward flow of time, and a secondary action that expresses "man's attempt to isolate certain happenings from the flux of time, to hold them static, to probe to their inwardness and grasp their meaning." British short-story writer and novelist Elizabeth Taylor has also suggested that the short story by its lyrical nature, its sustaining of one mood throughout, can give an impression of "perfection" and give the feeling of "being lifted into another world, instead of rather sinking into it, as one does with longer fiction." The German short-story writer Martin Walser also sees the short story as a form that presents not reality but "transcendence of reality," a counterpoint to reality. Other writers have noted the same paradox of the short story. Maurice Shadbolt says that the challenge of the form is to pull as much of life as the story can bear into the fewest pages and therefore produce "if possible, that hallucinatory point in which time past and time future seem to co-exist with time present, that hallucinatory point which to me defines the good or great short story."

Character in the Short Story

Since its beginning, the short story has been criticized for its failure to present character in a full and convincing way. Pattee said in 1923 that short-story characters are strangers flashed only momentarily; their tragedy affects readers as if they had seen an unknown man run over in an accident, a moment's thrill of horror. "If it had been our brother or our son we should feel it." Pattee unknowingly hits an important point here about the form, a point that O'Connor has made his own in *The Lonely Voice* (1963). It is precisely the point of the short story that it presents readers with characters they do not have time to get to know intimately; however, this alone no more relieves the readers of responsibility for them than a brief acquaintance relieves them in real life. Many critics and writers have noted that what readers remember about the short story is not the person but the predicament of the story. Howells says readers can scarcely even remember by name any of the people in the short story.

Frank O'Connor claims that in the novel the reader is bound to be involved in a process of identification with the character. One character must represent the reader in some "aspect of his own conception of himself . . . and this process of identification invariably leads to some concept of normality and to some relationship—hostile or friendly—with society as a whole." However, in the short story, says O'Connor, there is no one the reader can identify with, and no form of society that the character (or the reader) can attach himself to and regard as normal.

Writing in 1958, Granville Hicks said that plot had not counted in the short story for a long time, "and now character, though important, is more often a means to an end rather than an end in itself. More and more commonly, the end is an emotional experience for the reader. Both events and characters are used to create a specific emotion, and the climax, to provide a release for it." In 1965, George P. Elliott, reviewing several short-story collections of that year, also noted the loss of character and warned that "the worse pitfall a writer dealing in extremes must watch out for is depersonalizing his characters. At the brink, people are apt to behave much alike, less according to their personal natures than according to human nature generally." However, it is the emotional reaction to the mystery of personality at which Flannery O'Connor says the short story excels. Character in the short story does not give in to the illusion that the novel does that readers "know" this character simply because they have lived with him or her for a period of time. Character in the short story is not revealed or presented either by social context or familiarity, for after all, those are abstractions that can never reveal the totality of personality. Such a totality itself is an illusion and an abstraction.

THE SHORT STORY AND THE NEW CRITICS

Professors did not really begin to consider the short story seriously in college classrooms until Cleanth Brooks and Robert Penn Warren's 1943 short-story textbook *Understanding Fiction* made analysis of individual examples of the form respectable. Arno Lehman Bader's essay made the formalist approach to the form quite explicit in 1945. Confronting the common complaint that the modern literary short story has no structure, he tries to show that although a narrative structure is still present in the form, its presentation and resolution are so indirect that the reader must work harder to find the perceived relationships of the parts of the story. John Walter Sullivan developed this rather simple and general assessment into a more rigid formalist methodology in 1951. Using Mark Schorer's comment that the short story is an art of "moral revelation," Sullivan asserts that the fundamental methodological concept of the short story is a change from innocence to knowledge—a change that can be either "inter-concatenate" (occurring within the main character) or "extra-concatenate" (occurring within a peripheral character). In 1956, Theodore Albert Stroud, extending Bader's and Sullivan's New Critical approaches, focused more on aesthetic than on narrative pattern, arguing that the best way to discern pattern in the short story is to examine how the completeness of a story results from the units or episodes in a work combining to make credible a change in one of the characters or to create a sense of realization in the reader.

General comments about the nature of the short story as a genre were sparse in American criticism during the 1940's and 1950's because the formalist approach of the New Critics focused primarily on individual readings of individual works. One notable exception is Norman Friedman's attempt to answer the basic question, "What Makes a Short Story Short?" Taking his approach from Chicago critic Elder Olson's "Outline of Poetic Theory" which itself is taken, in part, from Aristotle's *De poetica*, c. 334-323 B.C.E. (*Poetics*, 1705), Friedman argues that a short story is short because the size of the action is short, because the action is static or dynamic, because the author chooses to present in a contracted scale by means of summation and deletion, or because the author chooses a point of view that lends itself to brevity.

NEW THEORIES OF THE SHORT STORY

Since the late 1970's there has been a revival of interest in the short story by literary critics, partially sparked by the publication in 1976 of *Short Story Theories*, in which Charles E. May argued that what was needed was a theory of the form derived from the "underlying vision of the short story, its characteristic mode of understanding and confronting reality." In that same year, in an essay in the journal *Studies in Short Fiction*, May suggested an initial definition of the short story's underlying vision and argued that

Poe's description of the form's "unique effect" was consistent with philosopher Ernst Cassirer's concept of "mythic perception." In several essays written during the 1980's, according to critic Susan Lohafer, May has become one of the most consistent proponents of the notion that there is an inherent relationship between a characteristic short-story structure and its theme.

It is this very issue—whether a unified generic definition of the short story is possible—that divided short-story theorists in the 1980's into two groups. The difference between those critics and writers who doubt that a definition of the short story is possible and those who argue for such a definition revolves around two different concepts of generic definition. The antidefinition group insist on a positivist definition that includes characteristics common to all examples of the short story that will distinguish it from the novel; the prodefinition group are more interested in trying to find a network of similarities and relationships within examples of the form. As long as they can find some characteristics shared by examples of the short story they do not need to find a definition that satisfies necessary and sufficient conditions to distinguish the short story from the novel.

One of the most emphatic proponents of this group is Allan H. Pasco, who believes that the work of defining a genre succeeds when the definition corresponds to general practice and understanding. He is therefore not concerned with finding a single touchstone for the form but rather looks for clusters of traits common to it. The best a genre definition can do, he says, is to draw attention to the dominant aspects of genre, which may indeed include elements that one can find in other genres.

One of the most influential of those who did not think such a generic description is possible was Mary Louise Pratt, who disagreed with those who argued that the short story is a primary form, claiming that since the novel has always been more prestigious and powerful as a genre, the development of the short story has been secondarily conditioned by the novel. Pratt concluded that she did not think that a generic determination of the characteristics of a genre like the short story will ever be possible.

Books on the short story in the 1980's only unevenly dealt with specifically generic issues. For example, Walter Ernest Allen's 1981 survey is a traditional discussion valuable for providing a framework for understanding the development of the form, but it does not attempt to formulate a generic approach. Valerie Shaw's desultory discussion of the form in 1983 disparaged any attempt at a unified approach. Helmut Bonheim's 1982 study of narrative modes of the short story, based on a statistical study of the form, particularly short-story endings, focused on only a limited set of short-story techniques. John C. Gerlach's 1985 analysis of the concept of closure in the American short story is a helpful study of an important element of the form but is somewhat narrowly focused both theoretically and in the number of stories examined. John Bayley's 1988 discussion of typical poetic techniques and devices common to the form from Henry James to Elizabeth Bowen and Clare Hanson's 1985 study of the authority of the teller in the form between 1880 and 1980 are both suggestive contributions but also focus only on limited historical periods. The most important book on the short story published in the 1980's was Susan Lohafer's *Coming to Terms with the Short Story* (1983), a sophisticated discussion of how the narrative rhythm of the short story uniquely engages the reader's attention. In this book, Lohafer introduced her concept of "preclosure" which she has further explored and developed in a number of important essays in the 1990's.

Collections of essays on the short story published during the 1980's include *The Teller and the Tale: Aspects of the Short Story* (1982), edited by Wendell Aycock, and *Re-Reading the Short Story* (1989), edited by Clare Hanson, both of which include original essays on a number of aspects of the form. The most important collections of theoretical essays on the form in the 1980's were the special issue of *Modern Fiction Studies* published in 1982 and *Short Story Theory at a Crossroads*, edited by Susan Lohafer and Jo Ellyn Clarey in 1989. The *Modern Fiction Studies* special issue is especially notable for two suggestive essays: Suzanne Hunter Brown's discussion of two readings of a section from Thomas Hardy's *Tess of the D'Urbervilles* (1891), which argues that identical texts are read differently depending on what genre frame of expectations is brought to them, and Suzanne Ferguson's argument that the modern short story is not a discrete genre, different from the sketch and tale that went before it, but rather a manifestation of the techniques and assumptions of literary impressionism.

Both Brown and Ferguson also have essays in Lohafer and Clarey's *Short Story Theory at a Crossroads*—Ferguson showing how social factors influenced the rise and fall of the prestige of the short story, and Brown providing a helpful analytical survey of research being done by psychologists of discourse on the nature of storyness and cognitive responses to literature. Also included in this volume are essays by critics already mentioned in this survey: Norman Friedman, who reviews and critiques a number of contemporary theorists; Mary Rohrberger, who disagrees with Friedman's strictly scientific approach to a definition of the form; Austin Wright, who argues for a formalist view of the genre as a cluster of conventions; and Charles May, who discusses the shift from mythic to metaphoric motivation in the early development of the form during the American romantic period.

Karl-Heinz Stierle reminds readers that there are two different ways in which narrative texts produce systematic texts—by means of the fable and of the exemplum. By fable, Stierle means roughly the same thing that Robert Franklin Marler means by tale; by exemplum, he means roughly the same thing Marler means by the short story. For although fable and exemplum create meaning in quite different ways—the fable presenting the general as the particular, while in the exemplum the general appears in the particular—at a certain historical point at the end of the eighteenth century, it became less easy to determine the meaning lying beyond the events depicted in the short story. The whole history of the development of the short story can be seen as a constant interplay between the exemplary nature of story and its realistic presentation of characters in time and space.

Twayne Publishers has provided a significant boost to the revival of critical interest in the short story in the 1980's with two book series: Critical History of the Short Story and Studies in Short Fiction. While the first series features historical/critical survey essays on English, American, Russian, Irish, and Latin American short fiction, the second series focuses on the short fiction of individual authors. Each volume in this series includes an extended original essay on the short-story writer as well as a few selected previously published essays by other critics.

By and large, the burgeoning of interest in literary theory since the 1960's has not had a significant effect on criticism of the short story, in spite of the fact that the highly formal nature of the genre would seem to lend itself to formalist, structuralist, and poststructuralist theory. Frederic Jameson, in one of the best early surveys of formalism and structuralism, suggested that structuralism would find the short story more amenable to its own brand of analysis than the novel, for whereas the novel has no preexisting laws that govern its form, the short story or tale is "characterized by a specific and determinate kind of content" and thus its laws can be the object of investigation. However, although narratologists such as Roland Barthes and Tzvetan Todorov have focused on short forms, this is due less to their generic interest in the form than to the fact that their intensive analyses of grammatical structure are too burdensome to sustain over the long haul of the novel. Representative examples of the sometimes tedious thoroughness of the structuralist or linguistic approach to short fiction that made it die of its own weight are Seymour Benjamin Chatman's essay "New Ways of Analyzing Narrative Structure," with its detailed analysis of James Joyce's story "Eveline," and Gerald Prince's *A Grammar of Stories: An Introduction* (1973), which attempts to account for the structure of all syntactical sets that readers intuitively recognize as stories.

In 1993, a special issue of the journal *Style* was devoted to the modern short story, featuring essays by Susan Lohafer, Charles May, and several others on oral narratives, the epiphany, and the nature of reality in the modern short story. In 1997 and 1998, respectively, two collections of essays by various critics were devoted to the short story: *Creative and Critical*

Approaches to the Short Story, edited by Noel Harold Kaylor, Jr., and *Tales We Tell: Perspectives on the Short Story*, edited by Barbara Lounsberry, Susan Lohafer, Mary Rohrberger, Stephen Pett, and R. C. Feddersen. In these books, the best-known short-story critics and theorists, such as Lohafer, May, Suzanne Ferguson, Austin Wright, and Mary Rohrberger were joined by several other critics specializing in the short story, such as John Gerlach, Ian Reid, Susan Rochette-Crawley, Hilary Siebert, and Suzanne Hunter Brown.

The journal *Studies in Short Fiction* published a special issue on the theory of the short story in 1996, with essays on the theory of the short story by Charles May, on preclosure by Susan Lohafer, and on the short story and the novel by Suzanne Ferguson, as well as essays on temporality and the short story and the nature of minimalism by short-story critics Michael Trussler and Cynthia Hallett. Also featuring a special issue on the short story in 1996 was the *Journal of Modern Literature*, which reprinted selected papers presented at the 1994 Third International Conference on the Short Story. The issue included essays on the short story by such writers as Isabel Allende, Bharati Mukherjee, Amiri Baraka, and Wilson Harris, as well as discussions of gender, cultural, and social issues in the form.

A number of significant book-length studies of the short story appeared in the 1990's. Dominic Head's book *The Modernist Short Story: A Study in Theory and Practice* (1992) discusses the modern short story from a Bakhtinian approach, arguing that the form's stress on literary artifice makes it most amenable to modernist experimentation. Andrew Levy in *The Culture and Commerce of the American Short Story* (1993) explains how the short story has reflected American values throughout its historical development. Kirk Curnutt's *Wise Economies: Brevity and Storytelling in American Short Stories* (1997) is an extended study of the issue of brevity in the short story, with chapters on a number of important American writers, discussing how stylistic economy is an important evolving aesthetic tactic in the short story that continually redefined how readers had to form interpretations of the short story.

Charles May's 1976 collection *Short Story Theories* was reissued in a new, extensively revised edition in 1994, entitled *The New Short Story Theories*. The collection included important essays on the theory of short fiction by Mary Louise Pratt, Wendell V. Harris, Robert F. Marler, Susan Lohafer, and Suzanne Ferguson, as well as discussions of the form by such writers as Julio Cortázar, Nadine Gordimer, Elizabeth Bowen, and Raymond Carver. The following year, May's historical/generic study of the development of the short story *The Short Story: The Reality of Artifice* was published.

As an indication of the continuing interest in the short story both by practicing writers and by classroom teachers, two books of interviews and practical essays appeared in the late 1990's. *Speaking of the Short Story: Interviews with Contemporary Writers* (1997), edited by Farhat Iftekharuddin, Mary Rohrberger, and Maurice Lee, featured interviews with Isabel Allende, Bharati Mukherjee, Leslie Marmon Silko, Richard Ford, and Rudolfo A. Anaya. *Short Stories in the Classroom* (1999), edited by Carole L. Hamilton and Peter Kratzke, includes brief essays by a number of teachers and critics providing practical suggestions about teaching the short story from a wide variety of critical and pedagogical perspectives.

Modern Genre Theory and the Short Story

Much of the critical resistance to short-story genre theory in the past has resulted from two basic misapprehensions. First, short-story critics have often failed to distinguish between two different meanings of the term "genre." Either they have treated historical genres as if they were theoretical concepts and then gleefully pronounced genre theory a failure because historical genres change or they have assumed that one generic approach should fit all narrative genres and then triumphantly surrendered when a theory based on the novel does not clarify the characteristics of the short story. The short story deserves a generic theory based on the characteristics of the form recognized both by authors and readers throughout its history, a theory that should be judged on its explanatory power in understanding the form's historical changes without insisting that the short story is a "pure" form or that its history has been "evolutionary."

The basic generic question that must be confronted by critics of the short story is, What are the significant theoretical and historical implications of shortness in narrative? If narrative is one of the basic means by which one comes to know the world, then how does short narrative "know the world" differently than the novel knows the world? The question that short-story critics must confront is, what methods and means of seeing and conceptualizing reality are accessible to prose fictions that are short?

One of the most persistent implications of the short story's shortness is that it creates the illusion that understanding of the whole precedes understanding of the parts, first proposed by Poe. Indeed, Poe's most significant contribution to the development of the short story as a new genre in American literature was his creation of an alternative definition of narrative "plot." Instead of "simple complexity" or "involution of incident," Poe adapted from Schlegel a new meaning of the term: "that from which no part can be displaced without ruin to the whole." By this one stroke, Poe shifted the reader's narrative focus from mimetic events to aesthetic pattern. Poe argued that without the "key" of the overall design or plan of a work of fiction, many points would seem insignificant or unimportant through the impossibility of the reader's comprehending them. Once the reader has the overall design in mind, however, all those points that might otherwise have been "insipid" or "null" will "break out in all directions like stars, and throw quadruple brilliance over the narrative."

What Poe's approach to the shortness of story reflects is the basic paradox inherent in all narrative: the writer's restriction to the dimension of time juxtaposed against his or her desire to create a structure that reflects an atemporal theme. Because of the shortness of the short story, the form gives up the sense of real time, but it compensates for this loss by focusing on significance, pattern, meaning. The central problem, says C. S. Lewis, is that for stories to be stories, they must be a series of events; yet at the same time it must be understood that this series is only a net to catch something else. This "something else," which, for want of a better word, is called theme, is something "that has no sequence in it, something other than a process and much more like a state or quality." The result is that the means of fiction are always at war with its end.

Lewis says, "In real life, as in a story, something must happen. That is just the trouble. We grasp at a state and find only a succession of events in which the state is never quite embodied." E. M. Forster has called attention to the same paradox in a famous mock lament in *Aspects of the Novel* (1927), reminding the reader that even as he or she agrees that the "fundamental aspect of the novel is its story-telling aspect," the reader voices his or her assent sadly: "Yes—oh, dear, yes—the novel tells a story."

Both Forster and Lewis agree that the problem stems from the sense of time. Forster notes that in addition to the time sense in daily life there is something else, something not measured by minutes or hours but by intensity, something called value. Story as such can only deal with the time sense. Story, the "naked worm of time," is an atavistic form that presents an appearance both "unlovely and dull," says Forster. Yet novelists flout it at their peril. As soon as fiction is "completely delivered from time it cannot express anything at all." The problem is that one cannot abolish story unless one abolishes the sequence between sentences, which in turn cannot be done unless one abolishes the order of words in a sentence, which then necessitates abolishing the order of letters or sounds in the words. A novel that attempts to destroy the time sense and only express the sense of value, reminds Forster, "becomes unintelligible and therefore valueless." The desire to liberate the novel from time is a noble one but one doomed to failure. Thus the reader says sadly, "Yes—oh dear, yes—the novel tells a story."

The problem is, from the point of view of the writer's task, how to convert mere events, one thing after another, into significance. The problem for the writer's relationship to the reader is, once the reader is encouraged to keep turning pages to find out what happens next, that some way must found to make the reader see that what happens next is not what is important. This basic incompatibility, noted by many critics, is more obvious in the short form, which, in its frequent focus on a frozen moment, seems atemporal. Julio Cortázar says, "The short-story writer knows that he can't proceed cumulatively, that time is not his ally. His only solution is to work vertically, heading up or down in literary space."

The most difficult problem the aesthetic nature of the short story poses for critics at the end of the twentieth century is that it necessitates approaching the short story from the currently discredited formalist point of view characteristic of romanticism and modernism. In one of the several book-length theoretical studies of the short story published in the last decade of the century, Head complained that short-story theory has largely been determined by an oversimplified perception of modernist practice and urges critics to go beyond what he calls the "visual artifact aesthetic" or the "unity aesthetic" that has dominated criticism of the form since Poe.

However, although Head makes valuable contributions to short-story theory, his insistence on some nebulous connection between literary form and social context and his consequent effort to apply currently fashionable sociological theories to the short story prevent him from developing an approach consistent with the short story's unique generic characteristics. It is not helpful to dismiss all previous commentary on the short story by authors and critics as wrong simply because the commentary is not currently fashionable. What the short story requires is a thorough analysis of previous short-story criticism as well as short-story practice in order to develop a theory that does justice to this most ancient and yet most distinctly modern form.

Charles E. May

BIBLIOGRAPHY

For further information about the most important books and articles mentioned in this survey see "Bibliography" in this volume.

THE DETECTIVE STORY

Though Edgar Allan Poe generally is considered the father of detective fiction, some historians of the genre go as far back as ancient Greece and Herodotus's tale of King Rhampsinitus or to the biblical story of Susanna and the Elders for the origins of this popular literary form. These putative sources share elements with mystery fiction—natural cunning, the cross-examination of witnesses, false clues—but lack major essentials. The same can be said about many other claimants, such as the popular crime narratives and rogue pseudomemoirs of eighteenth century England and also Voltaire's *Zadig: Ou, La Destinée, Histoire orientale* (1748; originally as *Memnon: Histoire orientale*, 1747; *Zadig: Or, The Book of Fate*, 1749), in a chapter in which the hero uses analytical deduction to reach conclusions about things he has not seen. François-Eugène Vidocq's *Mémoires de Vidocq, chef de la police de sûreté jusqu'en 1827* (1828-1829; *Memoirs of Vidocq, Principal Agent of the French Police Until 1827*, 1828-1829; revised as *Histoire de Vidocq, chef de la police de sûreté: Écrite d'après lui-même*, 1829), however, is a forerunner that was a direct influence on Poe and his successors. A former criminal who became the first head of the French police, Vidocq later set himself up as a private detective.

Edgar Allan Poe

Poe's "The Murders in the Rue Morgue"—which takes place in Paris, as do his other mystery stories—is the seminal work from which all subsequent detective fiction descends. It is, first of all, the archetypal locked-room mystery, a subgenre in which a body is discovered in an apparently sealed room. Second, C. Auguste Dupin, the first fictional private detective, solves crimes that perplex the police and is the prototype of many later brilliant men (including Sherlock Holmes, Ellery Queen, and Hercule Poirot), whose activities are described by admiring chroniclers. Third, in this and the other two stories in which he appears ("The Mystery of Marie Roget" and "The Purloined Letter"), Dupin reaches solutions through what Poe called ratiocination, the process of logical and methodical reasoning. Finally, in "The Mystery of Marie Roget," Dupin is a prototypical armchair detective, working from newspaper accounts to deduce a solution. In two other detective tales—"The Gold Bug" and "Thou Art the Man"—Poe also introduces devices that would become commonplace in the genre: false clues, the use of ballistics, a deciphered code, the detective as narrator, and the least likely suspect as culprit.

In the decades following the publication of these innovative stories, crime and detection were favorite subjects of the popular press in England, notably the sensational "penny dreadfuls" periodicals and Charles Dickens's *Household Words* articles about the London police detective department, particularly its Inspector Field, who was the inspiration for Inspector Bucket of Dickens's *Bleak House* (1852-1853). Another detective department member, Inspector Jonathan Whicher, is the source of Sergeant Cuff, Wilkie Collins's methodical sleuth in *The Moonstone* (1868), the first English detective novel. Similar to Cuff is American Anna Katharine Green's city detective Ebenezer Gryce, who debuted in *The Leavenworth Case: A Lawyer's Story* (1878). These works and other crime literature soon were overshadowed by Arthur Conan Doyle's mystery novels, *A Study in Scarlet* (1887) and *The Sign of Four* (1890), whose success led editor Herbert Greenhough Smith of London's new *Strand Magazine* to ask Doyle for six Holmes stories, the first of which, "A Scandal in Bohemia," appeared in July, 1891. They were so popular that Smith commissioned another series, and three mass-circulation American periodicals–*Munsey's Magazine*, *Ladies' Home Journal*, and *McClure's Magazine*—also began to publish them.

Sherlock Holmes

With Dr. John Watson's casebook of Sherlock Holmes, the detective story finally came into its own as a distinct genre. Building upon the example of Poe, a debt he acknowledged, Doyle created the genre's indelible pattern: a crime attempted or committed, a sleuth either working independently or aiding the baffled police, and a solution arrived at by the detective. Significantly, he added a vital element. Whereas Poe's Dupin is an undeveloped, shadowy figure, Doyle's Holmes is a real person, and in his fifty-six stories, Doyle presents a myriad of information about the character, whose activities add details to his persona. A Nietzschean superman, Holmes not only acts superior to others but also actually is so. He is an intriguing eccentric, uses drugs, plays the violin, is a master of disguise, is almost passionless, is an expert in anatomy, chemistry, the law, and mathematics, and has written many scholarly monographs on such varied topics as bees, tobacco, and the Cornish language. Holmes puts his far-ranging intellect to practical use in the stories, which tends to personalize the narratives. Also serving this function is the narrator, Dr. Watson, Holmes's obsequious physician friend. An honest, likable man of average intellect, he is one with whom the reader can identify. While some tales, particularly later ones, are marred by improbabilities, contradictions, and inexplicable lapses in Holmes's deductive acuity, the detective's mythic personality and the singular appeal of the milieus make such faults insignificant. Holmes is not only the exemplar of the fictional detective but also the world's best known literary character.

Doyle wrote four long Holmes tales: *A Study in Scarlet* (1887), *The Sign of Four* (1890), *The Hound of the Baskervilles* (1901-1902), and *The Valley of Fear* (1915). He collected the short stories in five volumes: *The Adventures of Sherlock Holmes* (1892), *The Memoirs of Sherlock Holmes* (1894), *The Return of Sherlock Holmes* (1905), *His Last Bow* (1917), and *The Case-Book of Sherlock Holmes* (1927). The dozen tales in the first collection rank among the best in the genre. Among them, "The Speckled Band" is the standard by which later locked-room mysteries are measured and is of interest, too, because it shows Holmes's willingness to risk his life at the scene of a crime; "A Scandal in Bohemia" is memorable because of the detective's confrontation with the seductive Irene Adler, a singer who dupes him but who remains, in memory, the one woman in his life; and "The Red-Headed League" shows Holmes preventing a crime—a bank robbery—from being committed. The first tale in *The Memoirs of Sherlock Holmes* is "Silver Blaze," whose centerpiece is "the curious incident of the dog in the night-time," which provides Holmes with perhaps the most singular clue of his career. The volume also includes "The *Gloria Scott*," which Watson says was Holmes's first case; "The Greek Interpreter," in which his older brother Mycroft is introduced; and "The Final Problem," intended to be the last Holmes story, and in which he apparently is killed in a confrontation with his archrival, the criminal Dr. Moriarty. In response to public outcry, Doyle cleverly resurrected Holmes, and the thirteen stories in *The Return of Sherlock Holmes* include some of the best in the canon: "The Adventure of the Six Napoleons," "The Adventure of the Abbey Grange," and "The Adventure of the Priory School." The stories in the final collection, *The Case-Book of Sherlock Holmes*, are generally inferior to Doyle's earlier ones, and the group is of interest primarily because Dr. Watson tells only nine of the twelve, the novelist functions as narrator of one, and Holmes himself relates two.

In the Wake of Holmes

Holmes's popularity spawned other sleuths who either share some of his major traits or are almost polar opposites. Among the supermen-detectives, for example, is Professor Augustus S. F. X. Van Dusen, the creation of Jacques Futrelle, an American from Georgia. Van Dusen, an eccentric genius with many university degrees, is the omniscient sleuth in two collections, *The Thinking Machine* (1907; also known as *The Problem of Cell Thirteen*) and *The Thinking Machine on the Case* (1908; also known as *The Professor on the Case*). Futrelle's best-known story is "The Problem of Cell Thirteen," a locked-room mystery in which Van Dusen escapes from prison, disproving the challenge that "no man can *think* himself out of a cell." Another superman in the same mode is Max Carrados, Ernest Bramah's blind detective, who relies not only upon his deductive skills but also upon his superior sensory perception. For instance, he can tell that someone is wearing a false mustache because he smells adhesive and can read newspaper headlines by an acute sense of touch that enables him to distinguish areas of printer's ink. Carrados also has what Bramah labels an elusive sixth sense, actually just a keen understanding of human psychology. In the Doyle pattern, Bramah provides a myriad of details about Carrados's life, so he is a convincingly credible character, and the extent to which he has overcome the limitations of his affliction makes him engaging and likable. Accompanied on rounds by his Watson, Louis Carlyle, a private investigator who refers cases to him, independently wealthy Carrados epitomizes the gentleman sleuth, choosing problems that interest him and refusing fees. Like Holmes, Carrados sometimes solves cases before they cross the line to serious criminality, including at least one ("The Clever Mrs. Straithwaite") that is little more than a domestic farce embellished by an alleged jewel theft and phony insurance claim. Unlike most of his peers, Bramah sometimes used contemporary issues as the linchpin of his stories, such as "The Knight's Cross Signal Problem" (anti-British feelings in India) and "The Missing Witness Sensation" (an Irish Sinn Fein kidnapping). Also atypical is the fact that few of Carrados's cases involve murder. Ellery Queen described Bramah's first collection of mysteries, *Max Carrados* (1914), as "one of the ten best volumes of detective shorts ever written," and they remain eminently readable.

Holmes Contemporaries and Successors

In deliberate contrast with the Holmes pattern, Arthur Morrison, a Doyle contemporary who also published in *The Strand Magazine*, wrote eighteen stories featuring law clerk Martin Hewitt, a determinedly ordinary man whose cases a journalist friend narrates. G. K. Chesterton's Father Brown also seems to be unexceptional but proves to be otherwise in fifty witty stories (published from 1911 to 1935) that are constructed around paradoxes. A prototype for later clergymen-sleuths, Father Brown relies on intuition and insight more than on deduction and clues, but like Holmes is a keen observer, trying to get inside the mind of a suspect and noticing what others overlook, as in "The Invisible Man," in which the culprit disguises himself as a mailman, someone so familiar that people disregard him. Sympathetic toward criminals, the priest sometimes lets them go free so they can repent their sins and reform. Another detective who, like Father Brown, appears to be unexceptional, is M. McDonnell Bodkin's Paul Beck, who also was deliberately conceived as the opposite of Holmes. Beck claims to muddle his way through cases, and other professionals scorn him, but his native wit serves him well. Similar to Holmes as a master of disguise but otherwise very different is A. J. Raffles, a gentleman burglar, safecracker, amateur cricketer—the brainchild of E. W. Hornung, Doyle's brother-in-law. Supposedly created as an intentional contrast with Holmes (Hornung unequivocally describes his sleuth as a villain), Raffles is crime fiction's first antihero and was so popular that for a half century after Hornung's death, Barry Perowne produced almost two dozen more volumes of Raffles stories and novels. Sherlock Holmes often used his extensive scientific knowledge as a tool to solve cases, and following in these procedural footsteps is Dr. John Evelyn Thorndyke, the creation of R. Austin Freeman, a British physician like Doyle. Beginning in 1907 and continuing for more than three decades, Dr. Thorndyke (barrister, physician, forensic scientist) reigned as the genre's premier "scientific detective" in convincingly realistic novels and stories narrated by another doctor, Christopher Jervis, with whom Thorndyke shares his lodgings. Often shown delving into a green box filled with chemicals and instruments, Thorndyke is a pure scientist who focuses upon things rather than people and thus is the opposite of Father Brown and a refinement of one aspect of Holmes. Freeman's other major contribution to the genre is his invention (in *The Singing Bone*, 1912) of the inverted mystery, a form in which the reader witnesses a murder being committed and then follows the detective's deliberate process of discovery as he moves toward solving the case. Later noteworthy examples of this technique are Francis Iles's novels *Malice Aforethought* (1931) and *Before the Fact* (1932) as well as the *Columbo* television series, created by William Link and Richard Levinson.

By calling some of his Holmes stories adventures,

Doyle made clear that the sleuth's modus operandi involved physical as well as intellectual labors. Some of Holmes's descendants, however, treat crime solving almost solely as an intellectual exercise. The prototype of these armchair detectives is Baroness Orczy's Old Man in the Corner, featured in thirty-eight tales between 1901 and 1925. While sitting in a London tearoom drinking milk and unraveling knots in a piece of string, the slight old man reviews newspaper reports and listens to journalist Polly Burton recount puzzling crimes. Noting details the police overlook and making deductions based on ratiocination and intuition, he works cases backward until he arrives at solutions. Decades later, Rex Stout's sedentary Nero Wolfe donned the Old Man's mantle. Baroness Orczy made another significant contribution to the genre: attorney Patrick Mulligan, whose cases were collected in *Skin o' My Tooth: His Memoirs by his Confidential Clerk* (1928). Like Erle Stanley Gardner's Perry Mason years later, Mulligan is absolutely loyal to his clients and engages in all that is necessary, even skirting the law, to free them. Another unscrupulous hero that influenced Gardner is Melville Davisson Post's New York attorney Randolph Mason, whose creed is that his guilty clients must avoid punishment, and he labors mightily toward either their acquittal or a circumvention of the law. Post's other major crime fiction character is the antithesis of Mason: Uncle Abner, a pre-Civil War Virginia country squire who is a Bible-quoting man of absolute integrity. Ellery Queen ranked the Post collection *Uncle Abner: Master of Mysteries* (1918) second only to Poe's tales in the corpus of American detective short fiction. Of these stories *Uncle Abner* is a stellar locked-room whodunit.

American Pulp Magazines

During the decades covered thus far of the developing crime fiction genre, the short story was the dominant form, though most authors also wrote novels. Novels became the preferred form after World War I because of social, economic, and other developments, not the least of which was the rise of lending libraries in the United States and Great Britain, but many magazines in both countries continued to provide outlets for mystery stories.

Among them were the American "pulps," which flourished between the world wars and published all kinds of popular fiction. The first crime fiction pulp magazine, *Detective Story*, debuted in 1915, and by the 1930's many different pulps were devoted solely to the genre. Initially, most of their stories had Holmes-like Victorian settings, but soon an increasing number featured contemporary American milieus. *Black Mask*, which first appeared in 1920, quickly became the preeminent pulp, and its most prominent detective was Race Williams, whose 1923 debut story was "Knights of the Open Palm," in which he infiltrates the Ku Klux Klan. The brainchild of Carroll John Daly (who earlier had created a sleuth dubbed Three-Gun Mack), Williams became the first popular hard-boiled sleuth in a long line of such private investigators, including Mickey Spillane's Mike Hammer and Lawrence Block's Matt Scudder. A superb gunman, Williams is a fearless, snarling tough guy who engages in whatever seems necessary—violence, brutality, even murder—to administer his instinctive kind of justice. The stories sometimes cross the line to melodrama, and Williams is closer in ancestry to an American cowboy hero than to Dupin or Holmes.

A few issues after Williams's debut, Dashiell Hammett introduced *Black Mask* readers to the San Francisco-based Continental Op in "Arson Plus." A hard-boiled private eye who generally is considered the prototypical one, he is credible, unheroic, and thoroughly professional, quite unlike the swashbuckler Williams. Drawing from his own experiences as a private investigator, Hammett created a detective devoted to his craft and usually successful at it, more concerned with getting facts than with engaging in violent confrontations, not at all motivated by the lure of money (as Williams is), and willing to cooperate with the police when necessary. He is a deliberate and careful worker, patiently gathering details, shadowing suspects for hours at a time, reviewing newspaper files and company records, and staking out houses. When necessary, the Op wields a gun effectively, but does not engage in Williams-like heroics, and though feelings sometimes dictate his responses to people and situations, he realizes that "emotions are nuisances during business hours." With their realistic urban American settings, terse style, and often cynical tone, the Continental Op stories pretty much set the pattern for subsequent American private-eye fiction. Hammett, then, is the first author in a continuum that includes Raymond Chandler, Ross Macdonald, Robert B. Parker, and Bill Pronzini. Some eight decades had passed after Poe's seminal stories of the 1840's before a full-fledged American detective hero would be introduced.

In 1933, Raymond Chandler published his first story in *Black Mask*, "Blackmailers Don't Shoot." A slower writer and more conscious craftsman than his peers—he published just nineteen pulp stories between 1933 and 1939, when his first novel, *The Big Sleep* (1939) came out—Chandler endowed his detective, variously, Mallory, Dalmas, Malvern, Carmady, and unnamed, before he eventually settled upon Philip Marlowe, with an overt compassion that in the Continental Op had been merely implicit. A college-educated chess player who listens to classical music and quotes poetry, Chandler's introspective private eye is a brave loner with a strong moral streak, a twentieth century knight who says that trouble is his business. Resisting the corruption, spawned by money and power, that surrounds him, he tries to restore decency to his milieu, the mean streets of Los Angeles. (Years later, Ross Macdonald would turn to Chandler's Marlowe as the pattern for his series detective Lew Archer.) In a classic essay, "The Simple Art of Murder," Chandler says,

> Hammett gave murder back to the kind of people that commit it for reasons, not just to provide a corpse; and with the means at hand, not with hand-wrought dueling pistols, curare, and tropical fish. He put these people down on paper as they are, and he made them talk and think in the language they customarily used for these purposes.

The words also serve as Chandler's credo, which is apparent, too, in his novels, among the best of which are *The Big Sleep*, *Farewell, My Lovely* (1940), *The Lady in the Lake* (1943), and *The Long Goodbye* (1953). Interestingly, the books to a considerable extent blend and elaborate upon previously published Chandler stories—"cannibalization," he called the process. These four novels and many of his stories, with their enduring thematic relevance, transcend the genre category and rise to the standard of mainstream literature.

GUILTY VICARAGE CRIME FICTION

While Daly, Hammett, Chandler, and their pulp peers were honing a distinctively American innovative approach to crime fiction, most American whodunit writers were still producing stories and books in the so-called Guilty Vicarage mold, basically English in setting and attitude, with detectives and plots that were almost as eccentric and aristocratic as those of Doyle and his followers. The phenomenally successful Philo Vance books by S. S. Van Dine, Mary Roberts Rinehart's equally popular novels, and the early Ellery Queen are prime examples. In Great Britain, the successful old formula remained the order of the day, though with significant variations.

A landmark event in British crime fiction was the 1913 publication of E. C. Bentley's *Trent and the Last Case*, which he intended as a gentle burlesque of detective conventions. It introduced the fallible sleuth and ironically is widely considered to have inaugurated the golden age of the English detective novel. (John Franklin Carter, a 1930's journalist and White House official who wrote such mysteries as "Diplomat," called Bentley the father of the contemporary detective story.) As Bentley explained his approach, it was

> a more modern sort of character-drawing. . . . The idea at the bottom of it was to get as far away from the Holmes tradition as possible. Trent . . . does not take himself at all seriously. He is not a scientific expert; he is not a professional crime investigator. He is an artist, a painter, by calling, who has strayed accidentally into the business of crime journalism. . . . He is not superior to the feelings of average humanity; he does not stand aloof from mankind, but enjoys the society of his fellow creatures and makes friends with everybody. He even goes so far as to fall in love. He does not regard the Scotland Yard men as a set of bungling half-wits, but has the highest respect for their trained abilities. All very unlike Holmes. . . .

Another departure from what Bentley saw as the artificiality and sterility of the Holmes pattern is his adherence to the fair-play doctrine, with the reader being given all of the evidence, taken into Trent's confidence, and learning what he thinks. *Trent Intervenes* (1938) is a gathering of stories about Philip Trent in which these principles are at work, a dozen tales generally more complex than most detective short stories. Among the best are "The Genuine Tabard," "The Sweet Shot," and the humorous "The Inoffensive Captain."

Peter Wimsey and Mr. Fortune

Dorothy L. Sayers said that she based her detective, Lord Peter Wimsey, in part on Philip Trent, and in fact, both are friendly, tactful, and gently humorous human beings. Historian and critic as well as practitioner of the craft, Sayers is considered by some to be a stellar writer of detective fiction, with imaginatively conceived, carefully wrought plots, and original means of murder; but to others she is verbose, writes peripheral and lengthy dialogues, and has a pompous snob, Lord Peter Wimsey, as her detective. Indeed, some of her stories and novels are more manners narratives than whodunits. Wimsey appears in twenty-one short stories, most of which proceed more briskly than do the novels, and in the later ones he is less a dandy and more a sleuth. The first collection *Lord Peter Views the Body* (1928) has a dozen stories, of which "The Abominable History of the Man with the Copper Fingers" is the among the most effective in its build-up of suspense. Of the twelve stories in *Hangman's Holiday* (1933), Wimsey is in just four, and six of them feature another Sayers amateur sleuth, wine salesman Montague Egg. Of special interest in the volume is "The Man Who Knew How," which has no detective. *In the Teeth of the Evidence, and Other Stories* (1939), the third collection, has two Wimsey stories, five Egg, and ten nonseries, one of the best being "The Inspiration of Mr. Budd." In sum, Sayers's nearly forty stories are characterized by variety, cunning plots, a tempering infusion of wit, and expansive development of a social milieu, traits that combine to make them classics of the genre. Lord Peter, who traces his pedigree to William the Conqueror, is the prototype for other aristocratic sleuths, including Margery Allingham's Mr. Campion (who renounced his noble tag), John Creasey's The Toff, Martha Grimes's Melrose Plant (who declined his earldom), and Elizabeth George's Inspector Thomas Lynley (eighth Earl of Asherton).

Reggie Fortune, H. C. Bailey's amateur detective, who is a physician, surgeon, and forensic pathologist, has the same aristocratic affectations and prejudices as Albert Campion and Lord Peter Wimsey, but this genial and sensitive man, whose cases often have him helping mistreated and endangered children and who works closely with Scotland Yard, also descends from Dr. Thorndyke and Father Brown. In the introduction to a group of Fortune stories, Bailey wrote about his sleuth being described as having an "old-fashioned" mind.

> Insofar as this refers to morals it means that he holds by the standard principles of conduct and responsibility, of right and wrong, of sin and punishment. He does not always accept the law of a case as justice and has always been known to act on his own responsibility in contriving the punishment of those who could not legally be found guilty or the immunity of those who were not legally innocent.

Bailey's fair-play mysteries were very popular between the world wars (his first collection, *Call Mr. Fortune*, was published in England in 1920, and over a quarter century he produced almost one hundred), their length reflecting the complexity of the plots and his substantive characterizations. Among the best are "The Angel's Eye," with its rare twist at the end; "The Thistle Down," in which murder is disguised as suicide; and "The Long Barrow," which shows Fortune, the intuitive detective and judge of character, at his best.

Agatha Christie

Agatha Christie, a Bailey and Sayers contemporary, began writing when Sherlock Holmes took "his last bow" in 1917. The world's most widely read whodunit writer, and one of the most prolific, she turned out more than eighty novels and short-story collections. Her first novel, *The Mysterious Affair at*

Styles: A Detective Story, was published in 1920; four more novels plus a Hercule Poirot collection of stories followed in the next five years, and in 1926, she produced *The Murder of Roger Ackroyd*, which was both widely popular and highly controversial since the Watson-like narrator turns out to be the murderer. Although Christie built most of her narratives for half a century upon a standard template, she often springs Ackroyd-like surprises, but however much the deceptions perplex readers, she always plays fair. Dorothy L. Sayers's 1928 defense of *The Murder of Roger Ackroyd* is applicable to most Christie whodunits: "All the necessary data are given. The reader ought to be able to guess the criminal, if he is sharp enough, and nobody can ask for more than this. It is, after all, the reader's job to keep his wits about him, and, like the perfect detective, to suspect *everybody*."

Christie's early works usually have the tripartite Doyle pattern of a private sleuth (Holmes/Poirot) and a foil (Watson/Hastings) helping the police (Lestrade/Japp), but within a decade she sent ignorant Hastings back to Argentina, and Poirot subsequently worked on his own with occasional assistance from a valet or secretary. Poirot and Christie's other sleuths—with the exception of husband-and-wife team Tommy and Tuppence Beresford—fundamentally are loners, detached emotionally and intellectually even from those closest to them, much in the manner of Holmes and the Old Man in the Corner. Nevertheless, she often shows them with families, for many of her crimes take place at family gatherings or have family members as suspects. Also, a recurrent Christie crime scene is a village that apparently is a model of stability and respectability but in which dirty secrets lurk beneath the surface. As her sleuth Miss Marple puts it: "Human nature is much the same everywhere, and, of course, one has opportunities of observing it at closer quarters in a village." Since old Miss Marple relies on parallels to solve crimes, St. Mary Mead must be quite different from the bucolic place it seems to be. Observation, as Miss Marple demonstrates in stories and novels, is a key to solving a Christie mystery, but unlike Doyle and Freeman, this writer does not require her readers to know all manner of arcane things, only that they pay close attention to details. At the same time, Christie is a skilled perpetrator of red herrings, distracting readers and leading them to focus upon irrelevancies. She also surprises by fingering sympathetic characters as criminals and apparent victims as villains, as in "Three Blind Mice" (the source of her play *The Mousetrap*, pr. 1952), "The Bloodstained Pavement," and "Triangle at Rhodes."

Poirot Investigates (1924), Christie's third Poirot book, is her first collection of stories, fourteen in all, each of which is narrated by Captain Hastings. They illustrate Poirot's dictum that the little gray cells in his head are all he needs to solve cases. "With logic," he believes, "one can accomplish anything!" Nevertheless, he is not at all an armchair detective, since he often travels far afield, including to Egypt in "The Adventure of the Egyptian Tomb." An armchair detective in the Old Man tradition is Miss Marple in *The Thirteen Problems* (1932; pb. in U.S. as *The Tuesday Club Murders*, 1933), a collection in which people describe cases to her. Knitting by her fireplace, she listens to the tales of murders, smuggling, and other diversions; draws her parallels; considers suspects; and without moving far afield, comes up with solutions.

Unlike Sayers, Christie is not a prose stylist, has no literary pretensions, and does not linger over character development. She provides only those personal facts and traits necessary to illuminate a situation. Even her sleuths become three-dimensional people only over time, through an incremental accumulation of details—bits and pieces—in a series of works. The others—villains, victims, bystanders—remain shallow types. To Christie, the mystery itself is what matters.

In the collection *Partners in Crime* (1929), Tommy and Tuppence Beresford, husband-and-wife sleuths from the 1922 novel *The Secret Adversary*, are involved in espionage and international intrigue, having learned their new trade through Tommy's reading of detective novels. The stories parody the styles and methods of writers Tommy has read—Baroness Orczy, Chesterton, Freeman—and are generally successful pastiches. They thus are an early manifestation of Christie's inclination to experiment while not straying far from the genre's traditional bounds. In 1930, she again departed from the commonplace with *The Mysterious Mr. Quin*, twelve stories about murder, disappearances of jewelry and people, and reuniting former lovers. The nominal sleuth is Mr. Satterthwaite, but strange Mr. Harley Quin serves as guide and catalyst, helping his inadequate friend unravel the mysteries. The tales are a tentative Christie attempt at creating an unreal, almost supernatural atmosphere, something to which she sporadically returned throughout her career, with mixed results. For example, three years later, in 1933, she published *The Hound of Death and Other Stories*, a salmagundi of assorted tales of the macabre, occult, and supernatural, that also includes what may be her best story, "Witness for the Prosecution." Another collection featuring a minor Christie sleuth is *Parker Pyne Investigates*, 1934 (pb. in U.S. as *Mr. Parker Pyne, Detective*), a dozen stories about a "happiness consultant," who advertises his services in the newspaper. After hearing people's woeful tales, Pyne turns to a stable of helpmates for assistance in restoring clients' happiness, jewels, whatever. A variation on the armchair detective form, this unexceptional group is of interest primarily because it introduces (as a member of Pyne's stable) Mrs. Ariadne Oliver, a whodunit writer (Christie's alter ego) who is the sleuth in *The Pale Horse*, a 1961 novel. Christie's prime collection is *The Labours of Hercules: Short Stories* (1947; pb. in U.S. as *Labours of Hercules: New Adventures in Crime by Hercule Poirot*), twelve Poirot cases that are modern correspondences to the challenges with which the mythological Hercules was confronted. Though it echoes somewhat other works by Christie and her peers, this varied set of problems is filled with clever twists, and a nice touch is the increasing difficulty of Poirot's labors as he moves through the dozen.

Productive short-story writer that Christie surely was, her bibliography seems lengthier than it actually is, because her publishers sometimes changed story titles, often gave different titles to the same volumes for American and British markets, and regularly compiled new collections from old pieces. Christie herself frequently engaged in more substantive recycling. For example, the plots of *Death on the Nile* (1937) and *Evil Under the Sun* (1941) are almost the same, and the latter is an expansion of the idea of "Triangle at Rhodes" from four years earlier. "The Incredible Theft" is an elaboration of "The Submarine Plans," which itself is indebted to Arthur Conan Doyle. Two more examples of recycling: *The Mystery of the Blue Train* (1928) has its source in "The Plymouth Express," and "The Yellow Iris" is the inspiration for the 1945 novel *Remembered Death* (1945; pb. in U.S. as *Sparkling Cyanide*). To record such recycling is not to diminish Christie's fertile imagination that produced a vast body of novels, stories, and plays with unexpected variations on familiar situations. With rare exceptions, the reader must cope with cardboard characters, flat style, and predictable settings, but these weaknesses become unimportant when one gets hooked, in her best works, by a typically intricate Christie puzzle.

Ellery Queen

During the height of Christie's popularity on both sides of the Atlantic, Ellery Queen became the best known American name in the genre as both a crime fiction sleuth and the pseudonym of Frederic Dannay and Manfred B. Lee. As Queen, they wrote novels and stories; in 1941 founded *Ellery Queen's Mystery Magazine* (*EQMM*), which rejuvenated detective short fiction and remains an indispensable outlet for novice and established writers; edited anthologies that helped shaped the canon; and served as the genre's unofficial bibliographers. Created in imitation of Philo Vance, an American Peter Wimsey, the Queen character (in his early manifestations) is a pseudosophisticate and pseudointellectual dandy with a pince-nez. The first book of Queen stories, *The Adventures of Ellery Queen*, was published in 1934, and its subtitle–*Problems in Deduction*—unequivocally places it squarely in the Holmes tradition, as does "The Adventure of . . . " start to each title. Central to the stories is how young Queen solves sometimes bizarre riddles, such as finding a kidnapped banker in "The Adventure of the Three Lame Men." Notable, too, is "The Adventure of the Mad Tea Party," a clever narrative whose events parallel those in Lewis Carroll's *Alice's Adventures in Wonderland* (1865). A collection of nine stories, *The New Adventures of Ellery Queen*, appeared in 1940. Of four with sports backgrounds, one is a classic, "Man Bites Dog," in which Queen is a kind of armchair detective, solving a murder while watching a baseball game. Though Queen as short-story writer—there are five more volumes—did not advance the genre, he has left a number of imaginatively conceived puzzles that a delightful sleuth solves by credible reasoning and analysis.

Ellery Queen's Mystery Magazine has launched, nurtured, and sustained many careers, among them that of Edward D. Hoch. In addition to several novels, he has written about eight hundred short stories since his 1955 debut, and in 1973 began a decades-long run of at least one story in every issue of *EQMM*. Among his many series characters are Rand, a cipher expert and spy; Nick Velvet, a thief who steals odd things for a fee (water from a pool, a baseball team); Simon Ark, supposedly two thousand years old, who uses logic to solve supernatural crimes; and Ben Snow, an 1880's cowboy who solves a murder during a stagecoach ride. The stories are traditional whodunits seasoned with unusual characters and situations.

Perhaps the most unforgettable *EQMM* story ever published is Stanley Ellin's first story, "The Specialty of the House." Like his other carefully wrought tales (which he produced at a rate of about one a year and which won many awards), it is not a traditional whodunit but rather a macabre horror tale and was one of a number of Ellin stories dramatized on Alfred Hitchcock's 1950's television series. Julian Symbols credits Ellin, whose "ingenuity is turned to ends which produce the authentic shiver," with having brought imagination back to the crime short story. His best, according to Symbols, "go beyond the usual limits of the genre and turn into fables, occasionally tender but more often sharp, about the grotesque shapes of urban society and the dreams of the human beings who live in it."

Ross Macdonald

Also transcending the limits of the genre, but very differently from Ellin, is Ross Macdonald, whose career ran from the 1940's to the 1970's. Having begun as a spy novelist, Macdonald in 1947 published *Blue City* (as Kenneth Millar), his first hard-boiled novel in the Hammett-Chandler tradition. In it and his later works, the fully realized characters and atypically complex plots are vehicles for such recurring themes as the Oedipal search for a father and variations on how people corrupt the American dream by greed and lack of vision. Each Macdonald novel is a tragedy wherein destruction is wrought from within the characters, who unleash avenging furies whose disastrous forces endure through generations. Through the efforts of private eye Lew Archer, the moral center of almost all the tales, evil finally is purged, and those who remain can look ahead to normal lives.

Macdonald wrote only nine stories, mainly early in his career. Two were published in *EQMM*, and all were collected, with some revisions, in *Lew Archer, Private Investigator* (1977). They are set in Southern California, like most of the novels, and echo them. One of the *EQMM* stories, "Find the Woman," opens with what would become a familiar Macdonald motif: a parent hiring Archer to search for a missing child. "Wild Goose Chase," the second *EQMM* story, is a domestic tragedy built around entangled relationships and greed and has an ironic twist of fate at the end In other words, it has the standard mix of Macdonald's novels: posturing and duplicitous people, young victims, troubled women, and arrogant yet insecure and unhappy rich people unable to shake their pasts. Several other stories in the volume, though simpler in concept and less nuanced than his later novels, also have intergenerational themes.

Macdonald Followers

Indebted though he was to Hammett and Chandler, Macdonald moved beyond their influence, shaping more complex plots that exemplified his moral and social themes, writing in a more polished and allusive style, and muting the hard-boiled traits of his compassionate and introspective private eye. Among Macdonald's descendants in the hard-boiled Hammett-Chandler tradition are Robert B. Parker, Bill Pronzini, and Lawrence Block. Of the trio, only Pronzini has produced volumes of short stories,

Casefile (1983) and *Graveyard Plots: The Best Short Stories of Bill Pronzini* (1985), both of which feature a private eye known as Nameless who first appeared in a 1968 *Alfred Hitchcock's Mystery Magazine* story, "It's a Lousy World." There is a wistful, nostalgic quality to Nameless. Like Hammett's Continental Op, he is middle-aged, overweight, and based in San Francisco. After working in Army intelligence and the San Francisco police department, he became a private eye and now lives alone in a dirty apartment whose only orderly area is where he keeps thousands of old pulp magazines. Nameless dreams about early pulp detectives, fantasizes about being one of them, and always carries a magazine to read at odd moments. Emotional, compassionate, and a worrier, he does not carry a gun and is closer to Philip Marlowe and Lew Archer than to Race Williams, Sam Spade, or Mike Hammer. Pronzini's method also has an affinity with traditional crime writers because of his focus upon clues and the development of puzzles with surprising resolutions. Like Chandler, he has expanded stories into novels.

Dick Francis

In the last third of the twentieth century, *EQMM* was one of the few remaining general circulation magazine outlets for crime short stories, and because the economics of publishing favored the novel over the shorter form, most major writers of the period—such as Dick Francis, P. D. James, Elmore Leonard, Martha Grimes, Tony Hillerman, and Ed McBain—produced relatively few stories. Francis, for instance, began as a novelist in 1962 (*Dead Cert*), and produced thirty-five more before publishing his first story collection, *Field of Thirteen*, in 1998. Eight of the stories date from 1975 to 1980 and five previously unpublished ones Francis calls "recent." Like the novels, all have horse-racing backgrounds or themes, but there the resemblance pretty much stops. Absent are the novels' admirable young men, narrator-heroes who reluctantly are caught up in life-threatening challenges for which they are temperamentally unprepared but who nevertheless excise corruption and restore the code of honor and normal tranquillity to their world, whose locus usually is the Jockey Club. On the other hand, the stories, such as "Raid at Kingdom Hill" and "The Day of the Losers" generally do not have such a moral core, are peopled by rogues rather than criminals, often lack violence and death, and frequently have a whimsical tone. The aforementioned stories, as well as "Haig's Death," "Blind Chance," "Nightmare," and "Song for Mona" end in an O. Henry-like ironic manner, quite unlike the typically straightforward and fast-paced conclusions of the novels. Only the last of these stories, one of several about a parent-child relationship (a recurring motif, too, in the novels), develops a major character with the emotional complexity and intensity common to the novels. The stories, in sum, are skillfully plotted entertainments that modestly engage the reader's puzzle-solving abilities.

Rumpole of the Bailey

The surprise twists with which Francis wraps up his carefully wrought plots also are standard devices in John Mortimer's stories featuring London barrister Horace Rumpole, whose international popularity rivals that of Holmes. Since his first appearance in *Rumpole of the Bailey* (1978), the self-described Old Bailey hack has demonstrated his wit, compassion, knowledge of William Shakespeare and William Wordsworth, and sometimes even legal acumen in dozens of stories (and a short novel) gathered in ten collections and dramatized for television. In "Rumpole and the Younger Generation," which opens the 1978 book, he introduces himself in the following manner:

> "I, who have a mind full of old murders, legal anecdotes, and memorable fragments of the *Oxford Book of English Verse* (Sir Arthur Quiller-Couch's edition) together with a dependable knowledge of bloodstains, blood groups, fingerprints, and forgery by typewriter; I, who am now the oldest member of my Chambers, take up my pen at this advanced age during a lull in business. . . . "

Though he has not risen to Queen's Counsel and most of his cases are ones his colleagues shun, Rumpole is satisfied with his lot, perhaps because he almost always bests nominal superiors, including judges and the boorish head of his chambers. Typically, a Rumpole story has two complementary plots, courtroom and personal, the latter either a domestic crisis between Rumpole and his wife Hilda (referred to as "She Who Must Be Obeyed") or a problem in the courts or among the aging barrister's colleagues and is thematically related to the primary plot. The subplots not only entertain but also further characterize this unlikely hero, who selflessly rescues the personal reputations and careers of ambitious younger barristers, and whose insights and slyness enable him to shape people and situations to his own purposes. These traits also serve him well in the courtroom, where his orations are deft combinations of emotion, wit, and legal legerdemain, and normally carry the day. Confessing in his first adventure that he only feels "truly alive and happy in Law Courts," Rumpole also admits to "a singular distaste for the law." Indeed, his advocacy on behalf of mainly worthless clients (frequently, one of the Timson clan of petty criminals whose escapades have helped support Rumpole through much of his career) relies not so much upon legal knowledge as upon detection skills and the ability to judge character. These talents link him to Holmes, from whom Rumpole often quotes, and many of the stories follow the Holmes pattern; however, Rumpole's moral sense, liberalism, and comic voice distinguish him from Holmes. The humor takes the form either of improbable occurrences, which Rumpole cleverly initiates and nurtures, or misunderstood statements and actions.

A 1990 collection of six tales, *Rumpole à la Carte*, is a typical mix. In the title story, the barrister unhappily confronts *nouvelle cuisine* in a three-star London restaurant to which his wife's expatriate cousin takes them. Ironically, the owner-chef, whose food and establishment Rumpole had roundly insulted, later hires Rumpole to defend him in a case that may destroy his business. In "Rumpole at Sea," Hilda books the couple on a two-week cruise over her husband's objections, and among the passengers, unhappily, is one of Rumpole's high court nemeses, Mr. "Miscarriage of Justice" Graves. These adversaries become involved in a shipboard mystery that Graves bungles but that Rumpole solves. In "Rumpole for the Prosecution," as the title reveals, the old barrister becomes, for the first time in his career, a prosecuting attorney, but even in this atypical role his shrewd instincts prevail, and in a curious turnabout he secures an acquittal for the accused. Though his character remains fundamentally the same through his career, he regularly is confronted with new experiences. The 1995 *Rumpole and the Angel of Death*, for example, has a story about hunters and animal rights ("Rumpole and the Way Through the Woods") and another that takes the Old Bailey barrister to the European Court of Human Rights ("Rumpole and the Rights of Man"). In an epistolary nod to Dr. Watson, Mortimer in this collection also uses, for the first time, a narrator other than Rumpole. "Hilda's Story" is in the form of a letter from Mrs. Rumpole to a friend, "the story Rumpole will never tell."

Thus, within his format of mystery mixed with humor, Mortimer presents an insider's view of England's legal system, with hypocritical barristers and biased, even ignorant, judges. Rumpole, an iconoclast fighting the establishment, sometimes is a nonconformist upholding his own interests but more often struggles on behalf of a kindred soul, an unrepentant outsider of some sort.

Building upon the model of Edgar Allan Poe's four stories of the 1840's, Arthur Conan Doyle in the late nineteenth century brought the crime story to its fullest fruition, and as the twentieth century was drawing to a close, John Mortimer was creating a body of tales whose international popularity came to rival most of those that preceded them. Among the many American and British sleuths that have advanced the genre while entertaining generations of readers since the mid-nineteenth century, these authors' three creations stand apart and above: Auguste Dupin for being the progenitor of all that follows, Sherlock Holmes as the most brilliant exponent of the mind-boggling arts of detection, and Horace Rumpole, as smart as his predecessors but more realistically and humanely portrayed within a provocative thematic context.

Gerald H. Strauss

Bibliography

Barzun, Jacques, and Wendell Hertig Taylor. *A Catalogue of Crime*. New York: Harper & Row, 1989. A classic compendium by two voracious readers of crime writing, this book is more useful as a bibliography than as a guide to its authors' likes and dislikes.

DeAndrea, William L. *Encyclopedia Mysteriosa*. New York: Prentice Hall, 1994. Not as comprehensive as its title suggests, this very personal book by a writer of crime fiction thoroughly covers radio, film, and television detection in addition to the print medium.

Herbert, Rosemary, ed. *The Oxford Companion to Crime and Mystery Writing*. New York: Oxford University Press, 1999. Essays and brief entries by hundreds of authorities span every conceivable aspect of the genre, making this an invaluable reference work for the student, casual reader, and scholar.

Keating, H. R. F., ed. *Whodunit? A Guide to Crime, Suspense, and Spy Fiction*. New York: Van Nostrand Reinhold, 1982. Tilted somewhat toward British crime fiction, this nevertheless is an informative and entertaining gathering of essays by various hands and "a consumer's guide" to works by writers from the 1840's to the 1980's.

Queen, Ellery. *Queen's Quorum: A History of the Detective-Crime Short Story as Revealed in the 106 Most Important Books Published in this Field since 1845*. New York: Biblo and Tannen, 1969. Though the passage of time has rendered a number of the judgments questionable, this study remains valuable as a historical guide as well as a bibliographical source.

Symons, Julian. *Bloody Murder.* New York: Mysterious Press, 1993. By a leading critic and mystery-fiction writer, this is one of the most thorough, balanced, and readable histories and critical analyses of the genre ever published. It is indispensable both for the fan and student of crime fiction.

THE FABLE TRADITION

The most primitive desire underlying the impulse to tell a story is the need to account for things. Primitive stories, often called myths, that account for basic mysteries of existence, such as the creation of the earth or the origins of human life, were once basic explanatory models, much like scientific theories are in modern times. Since their truth could not be tested by checking them against external reality, such stories were judged "true" if they were coherent, that is, if they held together in a plausible and convincing way. In addition to these broad myths, local mythic stories, often called legends, were created to explain some mysterious event unaccounted for by pragmatic criteria or buried in the distant past and thus inaccessible.

The basic motivation underlying both grand cosmic myths and local legends is to create or to represent conceptual ideas in narrative form. When writers begin with the intention of explaining something or illustrating a set of ideas or values, they are most likely to allow the concept to determine the nature of the fiction. Consequently, fables, myths, and allegories are more formal and conventional than realistic stories, for they are governed by the logic of the conceptual ideas that underlie them. The basic difference between fabular narrative and realistic narrative is that the writer of a realistic story is more apt to allow the event or the psychological nature of the characters to determine the structure of the story.

Writers who create realistic stories are usually more concerned with characters who seem to be like real people in the real world, people who have inner thoughts, historical backgrounds, and unpredictable ways. However, writers who construct fables and allegories are so concerned with the idea they wish to illustrate that characters are most often two-dimensional functions of the plot. Angus Fletcher, in a study of allegory, has said that if the reader was to meet an allegorical character in real life, the character would act as if he or she were obsessed, having only one idea in mind, for the allegorical character can be only that emotion, fear, desire, or personality trait that he or she represents.

Although it is impossible to trace the genre of the fable to a single source or a first writer, it is known that the fable tradition has its roots far back in ancient history; in fact, the fable is perhaps one of the earliest forms of the short story. Although readers have most often come to associate the fable with Aesop, even to the extent of attributing to Aesop fables written at a much later time, the fable tradition actually flourished in many cultures other than that of ancient Greece, as proven by the existence of fables in diverse ancient writings.

From the time of its very inception, the fable seems to have entailed the notion of allegory. According to the definition of the ancient Greeks, whose fables are most familiar to the Western world, the fable is a story, a tale, a narrative; the Greeks made clear the fable's fictional nature by terming it μυθος (from which comes the word "myth") and thus distinguishing this sort of tale from the historical tale, which was termed λογος or ιστορια. Nevertheless, although the tale was fictive, its intent was to portray allegorically a reality of some kind, and this basic assumption concerning the fable's nature has characterized the fable throughout centuries of varied treatment.

As it most commonly appears, the fable personifies animals, or occasionally plants, or sometimes even the elements of nature, so as to reveal some truth; ordinarily that truth concerns a particular aspect of human behavior, although some fables that are etiological (such as how the turtle got its shell) have come to be attached to the genre. The use of animals to represent human truth may have come about in part because people are familiar with animals, often living in close association with them. Moreover, certain animals have been perceived as displaying various attributes or patterns of behavior that have come to be associated with them, such as the wiliness of the fox and the rapaciousness of the wolf. Although it is difficult now to determine whether the animals actually possess such traits or whether the fable has taught the reader to perceive the animals as possessing such traits, the fact is that certain animals have come to embody an identifiable symbolic meaning. Human familiarity with both the animals themselves and with their distinguishing characteristics makes animal particularly well suited to metaphorical or allegorical uses.

Even though the early fables occasionally included gnomic lines, the fables were not written with specific morals attached but relied instead on implication and inference. The practice of adding epimythia, statements that overtly present the fable's moral purpose, became very popular in the Middle Ages when the fables were used for moral instruction. Since these medieval fables are the ones that are known best, the fable has come to be identified with moral didacticism; in its genesis, however, the fable's purpose seems to have been merely to contain wisdom.

The most famous writer of fables is Aesop. By the time of the Middle Ages, his fables existed in many variant forms—in verse and in prose, and in many languages such as French, German, Latin, and English. Although Aesop was not the only source of medieval fables, many of the most popular are traceable ultimately to Aesop, by means of such redactors as Demetrius Phalereus, Phaedrus, Bebrius, Avianus, and Gualterus Anglicus. Since Aesop probably did not write his fables down, the reader is obliged to rely on the testimony of these later writers who claim that their collections are based on Aesop's work. The extent to which Aesop is responsible for all the fables attributed to him cannot be finally determined, but it is known that he is associated with the beginning of the genre as it developed in Greece.

There were earlier users of the fable than Aesop, but their work, for the most part, has been lost. Archilochus, a Greek poet believed to have lived on the island of Paros in the seventh century B.C.E., composed a number of fables concerning the fox and the monkey, the fox and the eagle, and the fox and the hedgehog, but unfortunately his work survives only in fragments. Another early fable is that of Hesiod, a Greek poet who wrote around 700 B.C.E. His fable of the hawk and the nightingale, contained in the poem *Erga kai emerai* (c. 700 B.C.E.; *Works and Days*, 1618) is one of the oldest known of the Greek fables:

> A hawk catches a nightingale and carries her in his claws high up to the clouds. In response to her pitiful wailing the hawk asks why she screams, since her master has her and she will therefore go wherever he wishes to take her; if he wishes to eat her he will, or if he wishes to let her go, he may do so. The hawk points out that one who tries to match strength with someone stronger will not only lose the battle but also be hurt as well by shame.

Hesiod claims that his fable is for the barons, who will understand it.

Even older is the fable in Judges 9:8-15, concerning the trees which seek a king:

> The olive tree, when asked to reign over the other trees, responded by inquiring if it should leave its rich oil, which honors gods and men, so as to sway over the trees. The fig tree, also asked, similarly inquired if it should leave its good fruit in order to reign. In like manner the vine inquired if it should leave its good wine, which cheers gods and men. The bramble, when asked, responded that if the trees were in good faith anointing it as king they should take shelter in its shade, but if they were not, that fire should come out of the bramble and burn up the cedars of Lebanon.

Despite such earlier fables as these, however, it is Aesop, who is believed to have lived in the sixth century B.C.E., with whom the fable has come to be most closely associated. Much of Aesop's life remains a mystery, although tradition has it that he was a Phrygian slave who was owned by Iadmon of the island of Samos, that he was ugly and deformed, and that he was killed by the people of Delphi. How much of this legendry is true one cannot know. From the testimony of Herodotus, Aristophanes, Xenophon, Plato, and Aristotle, scholars today have concluded that Aesop did exist and that he was known as a fabulist who concerned himself with moral and satirical lessons; Plato, for example, tells of Socrates amusing himself during the last days of his life with Aesop's tales. Beyond this, however, there is no real way of verifying "facts" about Aesop's life.

Similarly there is a lack of absolute information about Aesop's canon. The first collector of Aesop's fables of whom there is knowledge is Demetrius Phalerus, who was reported to have assembled Aesop's fables in prose in the fourth century B.C.E. This collection is not available, although it was, apparently, the source used by the later fabulists Phaedrus and Babrius. Phaedrus, a Roman who lived in Greece in the first century C.E., wrote a collection of fables in Latin verse that included Aesopic tales as well as new fables that Phaedrus himself wrote concerning contemporary social and political events. While Phaedrus states in his prologue that he is merely putting into verse stories that Aesop invented, he does in some instances attribute a particular fable to Aesop, such as the tale of the dog and the meat:

> A dog carrying a piece of meat in his mouth while crossing a river sees his reflection in the water; believing that he sees another dog also carrying meat, he snatches for the reflection, letting fall the meat he held in his mouth. In addition to failing to get that which he coveted, he also loses that which he already had.

In its simplicity, its brevity, and its implied meaning, this fable is typical of the early Aesopic tradition.

Babrius, like Phaedrus, was a Roman who is believed to have lived in the second half of the first century; also like Phaedrus, Babrius added to the Aesopic fables tales of his own composition, in the collection he wrote in Greek verse. Again like Phaedrus, Babrius refers to Aesop in his prologue, explaining that his intent is to soften and sweeten Aesop's sometimes hard or stinging iambic lines. One of the best known of the Aesopic fables is that of the fox and the grapes, which is included in the Babrius collection:

> A fox, seeing several bunches of grapes hanging from a vine, leaped in vain to pick the fruit, which was ripe and purple. Being unable to reach the grapes he went away, remarking as he went that the grapes were sour, and not ripe at all as he had thought.

To these two sources, Phaedrus and Babrius, and through them to Aesop, are traceable most of the fables that were popularized in the Middle Ages and that have become part of fable lore.

Along with Phaedrus and Babrius, another writer of the first century C.E. to whom readers are indebted for a particular popular fable is Horace, a Roman poet who included in his *Satires* (35 B.C.E., 30 B.C.E.; English translation, 1567) the fable of the town mouse and the country mouse. Horace explains that this fable's purpose is to illustrate the care that accompanies wealth:

> When the country mouse entertains his city friend, the city mouse scorns the meal of peas, oats, and bacon rinds. Since life is so short, the city mouse explains, one should seek pleasure, which can be found in the city. Once there, the country mouse finds that indeed luxuries abound and delicious food is available, but when the watchdogs are let loose, frightening the country mouse half to death, he decides that his quiet home and simple food are quite sufficient for him.

This fable was used repeatedly by later writers to demonstrate the virtue of the simple life and the wisdom of keeping one's proper place in the social hierarchy.

Both the Phaedrus and the Babrius collections were used extensively by later writers. The Babrius collection was put into Latin verse, perhaps around 400 C.E., by Avianus, a Roman writer of whom little is known. The Avianus fables, because of their simplicity, were popular in medieval schools as exercises in grammar and composition; fables had been recommended for this purpose as early as the first century C.E. by Quintilianus, a rhetorician who prized the Aesopic fables as aids in memorizing, reciting, and composing. The Avianus fables were also used by Alexander Neckham for his *Novus Avianus* of the late twelfth century, on which a number of later French versions rely. The Phaedrus translation of the fables was the basis for the tenth century *Romulus* collection in Latin prose, which circulated widely in manuscripts of varying contents. This collection, which was said to be directly derived from Aesop, was extremely popular. In the twelfth century, Gualterus Anglicus (Walter the Englishman) translated this *Romulus* collection into Latin verse; it is also from Walter's translation, known in the Middle Ages as *Esopus, Ysopet*, or *Isopet* (or the *Anonymous Neveleti*, since the collection was published anonymously by Nevelet in 1610), that many later French and Italian versions are derived.

Also writing fables in the twelfth century was Marie de France, who drew on both the *Romulus* collection and the *Roman de Renart* (c. 1175-1205), the tales of Reynard the fox, for her fables, many of which referred to contemporary society. Another French writer, whose fables were influenced by the work of Marie, by the *Romulus* collection, and by Hebrew lore, was Rabbi Berechiah ben Natronai ha-Nakdan, who, toward the end of the twelfth century, wrote his *Mishle shu'alim* (*Fables of a Jewish Aesop*, 1967), which was a translation of *Fox Fables*. In spite of the title, however, not all the fables concern the fox, as, for example, the fable of the mouse who overeats:

> A mouse who was black and thin went through a hole into a granary where he ate until he was immensely fat. When he was ready to leave he discovered he could not fit through the hole. A cat informed him that unless he vomited up what he had eaten and grew thin, he would never be able to leave and would never see his father again. This story is for one who covets the wealth of others but who eventually loses what he gains.

Like other writers and collectors of fables in the Middle Ages, Berechiah attached an epimythia, a brief concluding passage that makes explicit the fable's moral application.

This custom of using fables specifically for didactic purposes became in the Middle Ages part of the fable tradition. Fables were used by medieval preachers as exempla, to illustrate scriptural or doctrinal points and to portray moral and immoral behavior. Such churchmen as Jacques de Vitry, who included fables in his collection of exempla, and Odo of Cheriton, who collected fables specifically to be used in sermons, helped to popularize the moralization of fables. As a consequence, the fables possessed today almost uniformly have morals attached.

In addition to being used by medieval preachers as exempla and by medieval teachers as exercises in language and composition, fables were used by medieval poets for both didactic and aesthetic ends. Geoffrey Chaucer, writing in the last half of the fourteenth century, immortalized in "The Nun's Priest's Tale" the fable of Chauntecleer, the proud cock who lets himself be tricked and captured by the fox but who then in turn tricks the fox into permitting him to escape. This same fable was also used by Robert Henryson, a Scots poet working approximately a century later, who reworked a number of well-known tales for his volume of *The Morall Fabillis of Esope, the Phrygian* (1570; also known as *Fables*). In Henryson's hands the fable was a vehicle not only to point out a moral but also to convey social and political commentary. Typical of Henryson's treatment of the genre is his fable of the sheep and the dog:

> A dog who is poor falsely claims before the ecclesiastical court that a sheep owes him a loaf of bread. The court, composed of the sheep's natural enemies, is presided over by a wolf as judge. Although the sheep makes a noble defense, pointing out the prejudicial atmosphere and the unfairness of the court, he loses the case and must sell his wool to pay the dog.

The *moralitas* that follows explains the fable's allegorical significance: The poor shivering sheep is like simple folk who are oppressed on all sides but who suffer particularly from the corruption in the civil and ecclesiastical courts. The sheep plaintively asks God why He sleeps so long and permits such evil to go unchecked in the world. The large part which the *moralitas* plays in Henryson's fables is evident in such poems as this, wherein Henryson devotes sixteen stanzas to the fable itself and nine stanzas to the explanation of the moral. Henryson's collection of thirteen fables, to which are appended such extended *moralitas*, perhaps develops to its poetic extreme the convention of the epimythia.

Working at approximately the same time as Henryson in the fifteenth century was Heinrich Steinhöwel, who, using the prose *Romulus* collection, published a reworking of the Aesopic fables around 1480. Steinhöwel added to the fables promythia, statements at the beginning of the fables concerning their moral purposes. It is believed that Steinhöwel's *Äsop*, or a French translation of Steinhöwel, or both, were used by William Caxton when he began, in 1483, to print his *Aesop*, which was one of the first of the fable collections printed in English.

The Middle Ages was clearly one of the great periods of growth and popularity for the fable, a time during which the form was widely and successfully used for such diverse purposes as instruction and entertainment. The fable experienced similar major revivals of interest in the late seventeenth century and in the eighteenth century, when it was taken very seriously as a literary genre.

The seventeenth century revival of interest in the fable was due in large part to the work of the Frenchman Jean de La Fontaine, who published twelve books of fables between 1668 and 1694. He is perhaps more responsible than anyone else for moving the fable into the realm of poetry. Although he claimed to be unoriginal, to be merely translating and adapting from Aesop and Phaedrus, his originality was made manifest in the lyrical and dramatic verse with which he transformed his material. Followers of La Fontaine included such writers as John Gay and Robert Dodsley, the Spanish writer Tomás de Iriarte, the German writer C. F. Gellert, and Ivan Krylov, a Russian writer of the late eighteenth and early nineteenth centuries.

La Fontaine's innovative treatment of the genre did, however, provoke a countermovement. In response to what he perceived as La Fontaine's revolutionary and inappropriate poeticizing of the form, Gotthold Lessing, writing in Germany in the eighteenth century, initiated an opposing trend for fabulists. His intent, as indicated in his 1759 collection, *Fabeln nebst Abhandlungen* (*Fables*, 1773), was to return to the original conventions of the Aesopic fable, to make the fable not poetic but philosophical. His fables, accordingly, were short, simple, and pithy. An interesting example is that of the nightingale and the lark: "What can be said to poets who go on flights above their readers' understanding? As the nightingale inquired of the lark, does one soar so high deliberately, so as not to be heard?"

The controversy in the eighteenth century over the nature of the fable was of great interest to writers and critics; in contrast to scholars of other times who dismissed the form as suitable primarily for the purposes of teaching and preaching, eighteenth century scholars considered the fable to possess genuine literary respectability. After this great flowering of interest, however, the fable fell into disuse as a literary form.

The fable tradition plays an important role in the early nineteenth century development of the short story. In America, where the form got its most influential beginning, writers such as Edgar Allan Poe, Washington Irving, Nathaniel Hawthorne, and Herman Melville combined the old fable and folktale tradition they inherited from Germany with the realistic tradition developed throughout the eighteenth century in England. The result was that in such stories as Poe's "The Fall of the House of Usher," the narrator of the story seems to have an internal psychology much like a real person in the world, whereas Roderick Usher seems more like a two-dimensional character from an old romance fable. Similarly, characters such as Rip Van Winkle and Ichabod Crane in Washington Irving's two most famous stories seem to be real characters in a fully realized social world changing historically and culturally, but at the same time, they seem two-dimensional embodiments of the mythic German folktales Irving borrowed from.

Poe was the most self-conscious experimenter with the combination of psychological realism and fabulistic gothic romance; his greatest narrative innovation was transferring the seemingly obsessive characters of the old fable and allegory to the psychological obsession of individual characters. Similarly, the famous ambiguity of Hawthorne's most famous short story, "Young Goodman Brown," is a result of Brown's being both like a realistic character, who has scruples and reservations about going into the forest, and like an allegorical character compelled to make his journey because of his Everyman status in an allegory. Finally, the mid-nineteenth century story that most strikingly shows the integration of the fable and the realistic tradition is Melville's "Bartleby the Scrivener," whose enigmatic central character is a purely two-dimensional and representative figure introduced into the story to create an existential and moral challenge to the realistic narrator.

Since in the nineteenth century world action no longer gets its sanction from transcendent reality, as it did in the Middle Ages, it can now be substantiated only by subjective feelings. Whereas the characters of the old mythic and fabulistic story were functions of primordial events in a transcendent reality, archetypal characters in the nineteenth century story are projections of individual emotions. The short story as a new nineteenth century form begins with the demythologizing of the outer world and the remythologizing of the inner self.

In insisting that his work was not of Germany, but of the soul, Poe was emphasizing that although his stories do not come from folktale and fairy tale, the "new" situations he creates are similar to the old stories because psychic extremes always participate in archetypal repetition—in ultimate confrontations with the self and the world that transcend the immediate social situation of everyday reality.

Nevertheless, in the twentieth century the genre may be experiencing a revival, or perhaps a rebirth in a new form; the work of such writers as Donald Barthelme, John Barth, Kurt Vonnegut, Jorge Luis Borges, and Gabriel García Márquez has been said to be, in various ways, akin to the fable. These writers may, however, be redefining the genre as they explore, through it, the notion of story. For the most part, fabulists prior to the twentieth century used the fable as a vehicle for transmitting a specific message and kept its form discrete. In contrast, some twentieth century writers of short fiction employ the fable not because of the form's didactic abilities but because of the form's magical essence—its enchantment as an older form of story. Such contemporary writers frequently blend the fable form directly into a narrative and do not, in consequence, make a clear definition between the two genres. In such works there often results a mix of the fantastic and the realistic; fabulous narrative elements which abrogate scientific laws are blended with firmly realistic narrative elements. Other contemporary writers, however, keeping the form of the fable discrete, include fable segments within a larger narrative framework; John Barth, for example, in a self-conscious use of the form, uses wisdom figures within a narrative to tell tales within tales, and García Márquez uses fablelike short-story elements within his narrative form.

While many contemporary writers of short fiction do not use the fable form didactically—Kurt Vonnegut, for example, seems to indicate that the moral is that there is no moral—other conscious fabulists such as James Thurber have deliberately sought a didactic end. Part of the appeal of Thurber's satire is that the form serves as a commentary upon the content; part of his fables' humor and irony depends upon his use of what many see as a childish form to convey sophisticated ideas. Consequently, in contrast to those contemporary writers of short fiction who use the fable to convey a nebulous worldview and who move into the fable's magical world as a retreat from the realistic world, Thurber is more in the tradition of Aesop in using the fable form purposefully to convey a sharply satiric commentary upon human behavior.

The tradition of the fable, then, persisted in the twentieth century world, although in a seemingly changing form. Originally a "short story" which usually depended upon elements of narrative, drama, and dialogue, the form in its infancy used fantasy, usually in the shape of personified animals, to convey human reality. The form's roots were thus firmly located in the psychological desire to remove human truths to a simpler realm, specifically the world of animals. This desire to simplify and simultaneously mythify human experience is surely basic to much imaginative writing. At the same time, the early form of the fable was concise and pithy, readily engaging the mind and achieving the immediate effect of an understanding on one plane—that is, on the plane of the supernatural or the extraordinary—which could be transferred to and which would inform another plane—the plane of reality and human experience. The form's ability to achieve this immediate understanding made it perfectly suited to didactic ends.

In the twentieth century, however, except when used by such consciously traditional fabulists as Thurber, the fable seems to have changed in two important ways: One rarely sees a direct one-to-one correspondence wherein the fabulous world and the real world are juxtaposed, wherein a fictive creature reveals truth about real human beings; and similarly one rarely finds a direct moralization. Whereas the fable developed as an apologue, a fiction created to edify, in contemporary usage the fable has become primarily a device of fantasy, a fictional technique used to evoke a magical world. The contemporary fabulist, then, in refocusing the genre upon fantasy, uses the form for the effect of creating enchantment, thereby preserving and continuing one of the earliest purposes of the story.

The story takes its origin from the religious, broadly considered. However, while the old story could be measured against truths based on cosmic or transcendent reality, a loss of the cosmic ground or of the value based on social codes or reason demanded a new kind of truth against which the moral content of the story could be measured. This new truth in post-Romantic literature was the personal truth of the individual soul in all its ambiguity; it was not the truth of absolute morality, but rather that of a relativist morality, thus making the epiphany a psychological rather than a religious phenomenon.

For these reasons, the short story has always been the preferred form for unrealistic or fantastic events that represent mysterious human fears and desires, for no matter how fantastic a novel may be, the reader is apt to accept it as reality for the time span involved, if for no other reason than length alone. Fantasy for an extended time span is apt to become allegory, as in John Bunyan's *The Pilgrim's Progress from This World to That Which Is to Come* (1678), or satire, as in Jonathan Swift's *Gulliver's Travels* (1726; originally entitled *Travels into Several Remote Nations of the World, in Four Parts, by Lemuel Gulliver, First a Surgeon, and Then a Captain of Several Ships*)—that is, it is apt to require a substructure of ideas or concepts, to give it structure. However, in the short story, the brief illusion of dream can be maintained; thus the fiction seems to exist in a realm different from that of the everyday world.

Evelyn Newlyn, updated by Charles E. May

BIBLIOGRAPHY

Aizenberg, Edna, ed. *Borges and His Successors*. Columbia: University of Missouri Press, 1990. Collection of essays by various critics on Borges's fables and philosophy and his relationship to such writers as Italo Calvino, Umberto Eco, and Peter Carey.

Brown, Suzanne Hunter. "The Chronotope of the Short Story: Time, Character, and Brevity." In *Creative and Critical Approaches to the Short Story*, edited by Noel Harold Kaylor, Jr. Lewiston, N.Y.: The Edwin Mellen Press, 1997. An important discussion of the critical assumption that short stories deal with characters as eternal essences and that novels deal with characters who change over time.

Fletcher, Angus. *Allegory: The Theory of a Symbolic Mode*. Ithaca, N.Y.: Cornell University Press, 1964. Fletcher develops a theoretical model for allegory, showing its development from magic and ritual forms, its relationship to other forms such as folktale and fable, and its analogy to psychological obsession and compulsion.

Kenney, Catherine McGehee. *Thurber's Anatomy of Confusion*. Hamden, Conn.: Archon Books, 1984. Discusses Thurber's *Fables for Our Time* (1940), as well as "The Secret Life of Walter Mitty." Argues that the latter examines the impotent world of modern urban America, embodying all of the elements of Thurber's fictional world.

May, Charles E. "Obsession and the Short Story." In *Creative and Critical Approaches to the Short Story*, edited by Noel Harold Kaylor, Jr. Lewiston, N.Y.: The Edwin Mellen Press, 1997. Discusses the relationship between psychological obsession and aesthetic unity in the fables of Poe, Hawthorne, and Melville as a generic characteristic of the short story.

Patteson, Richard, ed. *Critical Essays on Donald Barthelme*. New York: G. K. Hall, 1992. A collection of critical essays that deal with Barthelme's use of language, his fragmentation of reality, his fabular method, and his montage technique.

THE SCIENCE-FICTION STORY

Although the term "science fiction" did not come into common usage until the late 1920's—having been briefly preceded by other terms that never quite gained currency, including "scientific romance"—it is possible to identify many earlier works to which the label might be applied.

The Origins of Science Fiction

It was in the eighteenth century that the word "science" acquired its modern meaning. The scientific method and the discoveries it produced were key elements of what is now looked back on as the Enlightenment. The new definition of science represented the realization that arguments from authority are worthless and that reliable knowledge is rooted in the evidence of the senses, carefully sifted by deductive reasoning and the careful testing of generalizations. As soon as the new image of science was established writers began producing speculative fictions about new discoveries and new technologies that might come about as a result of the application of the scientific method.

The earliest short fictions of this kind were accommodated within the ready-made narrative frameworks of the anecdotal traveler's tale, the dream story and the moral fable, sometimes embedding painstaking attempts to dramatize philosophical propositions within frameworks that had usually been employed for more frivolous endeavors. The argument in favor of the Copernican theory of the solar system advanced by Johannes Kepler's dream story *Somnium* (1634; English translation, 1965) includes an ingenious attempt to imagine how life on the moon might have adapted to the long cycle of day and night. Voltaire's *Le Micromégas* (1752; *Micromegas*, 1753) employs a gargantuan native of Saturn to pour witty but devastating scorn on human delusions of grandeur.

Early American Science Fiction

The potential of science fiction as an imaginative tool for repeated and varied use was first tested by Edgar Allan Poe. Poe's early poems include "Sonnet—to Science" and the cosmic vision "Al Aaraaf" and his career culminated in *Eureka: A Prose Poem* (1848), an extraordinary poetic essay on the nature of the universe revealed by astronomical telescopes. In the meantime, the visionary thread connecting these works was woven into a number of tales, including "The Conversation of Eiros and Charmion," whose protagonists recall the destruction of Earth by a comet and "Mesmeric Revelation." Although the prefatory essay on verisimilitude that Poe attached to the lunar voyage story "The Unparalleled Adventure of One Hans Pfaall" is not intended to be taken too seriously, it constitutes the first tentative manifesto for science fiction. Poe's interest in hoaxes also led him to experiment with tales cast in the mold that eventually produced the modern "scientific paper," including "The Facts in the Case of M. Valdemar."

Poe's contemporary Nathaniel Hawthorne also imported scientific experiments into some of his moral tales. Whereas Poe was only slightly ambivalent about the wonders of science, Hawthorne was deeply suspicious of its firm exclusion of ethics and aesthetics from the realm of reliable knowledge. His tales in this vein—especially "The Birthmark" and "Rappaccini's Daughter"—are among the foundation stones of a skeptical tradition that has always seemed to literary men to be the worthiest kind of science fiction because it rails against the presumed excesses of what is nowadays stigmatized as "scientism."

Most of the science-fiction stories to be found in the canons of American writers influenced by Poe and Hawthorne belong to this suspicious subspecies. The most notable include Fitz-James O'Brien's "The Diamond Lens" and Ambrose Bierce's "Moxon's Master." Several nineteenth century U.S. writers of science fiction who continued in Poe's footsteps, in the sense that they wrote for locally circulated periodicals and newspapers, never contrived to collect their work in book form. It was left to the science-fiction historian Sam Moskowitz to assemble works from the 1870's and 1880's by Edward Page Mitchell in *The Crystal Man* (1973) and works from the 1880's by Robert Duncan Milne in *Into the Sun and Other Stories* (1980). Some writers who did contrive to collect their work remained equally obscure; W. H. Rhodes's *Caxton's Book* (1876) was consigned to obscurity for a century before Moskowitz reprinted it.

Another strand of nineteenth century American science fiction emerged from the strong tradition of utopian speculation. Although formal utopian design is ill-fitted to short fiction, utopian thought involves philosophical speculations that can easily be embedded in moral tales and brief satires. Edward Everett Hale produced "The Brick Moon" and "Hands Off!," the former being the first story about an artificial satellite and the latter the first significant alternative history. Edward Bellamy produced capsule accounts of exemplary societies in "The Blindman's World" and "To Whom This May Come." Most of Mark Twain's contributions to the genre—many of which remained unpublished in his lifetime—are also affiliated with the utopian tradition, albeit skeptically. They include "The Curious Republic of Gondour" and "Captain Stormfield's Visit to Heaven."

Early European Science Fiction

Poe's works were translated into French by Charles Baudelaire, and this helped to ensure that his influence in France outweighed his influence in the English-speaking world. The most important pioneer of French science fiction, Jules Verne, loved Poe's work, but he wrote only a handful of short stories. Poe's influence is more obvious in the work of J. H. Rosny the elder, whose best short stories include "Les Xipéhuz" ("The Shapes") and "Un Autre Monde" ("Another World").

British speculative fiction received its first important boost in 1871 when *Blackwood's Magazine* published George T. Chesney's account of "The Battle of Dorking." This provoked the establishment of a genre of future-war stories that remained prolific until the outbreak of the World War I in 1914. Growing awareness that the advancement of military technology would utterly transform the business of war made accounts of the coming conflict increasingly lurid, but relatively few of them were couched as short fiction, even when the explosive growth of new middlebrow magazines like *The Strand* in the 1890's opened up vast territories of literary space ripe for colonization.

It was while these new magazines were in an experimental mood—a mood which lasted little more than ten years—that the British genre of "scientific romance" first appeared. It was foreshadowed in the work of Grant Allen, in such stories as "Pausodyne" and the utopian parable "The Child of the Phalanstery," but its most important pioneer by far was the young H. G. Wells, who quickly realized that the ideas in the brief speculative essays he was writing for the *Pall Mall Gazette* could be milked for a second time.

Although Wells was an enthusiastic utopian and one of the most clear-sighted contributors to the future-war genre, the exuberant adventures of his imagination, which he undertook in a spirt of pure inquisitiveness, set the most important precedents. It is a great pity that he virtually gave up on them—in order to set his mind to more serious tasks—after the turn of the century.

Wells's most important short science-fiction stories include numerous encounters with strange lifeforms, which range from the relatively trivial "Aepyornis Island" and "The Flowering of the Strange Orchid" to profound lessons in humility such as "The Sea Raiders" and "The Empire of the Ants." Other attempts to dramatize the folly of human delusions of grandeur include "The Star" and his two most famous moral tales, "The Man Who Could Work Miracles" and "The Country of the Blind." Two of his anticipations of future technological development, "The Argonauts of the Air" and "The Land Ironclads," were soon overtaken by history, although the more daring thought-experiment in "The New Accelerator" was not. Wells's visionary fantasies include "The Remarkable Case of Davidson's Eyes," "Under the Knife," and "The Crystal Egg."

Where Wells led others followed, but not to anything like such wondrous effect. The writer whose career flourished most abundantly in the new magazines was Arthur Conan Doyle, but scientific romance was always a minor strand in his canon, although it did include the notable science-fiction horror stories "The Los Amigos Fiasco" and "The Horror of the Heights." The most extravagant writer of future-war stories, George Griffith, wrote a number of Wellsian short stories, including the political fantasy "A Corner in Lightning" and "From Pole to Pole," but none is of much distinction. C. J. Cutcliffe Hyne was far more prolific, under his own name and the pseudonym Weatherby Chesney, but many of his science-fiction stories recycle a standard formula in which a new invention proves troublesome and has to be destroyed.

William Hope Hodgson and J. D. Beresford were far more serious in their endeavors than Griffith or Hyne but had the misfortune to arrive on the scene after the turn of the century when the wave of fashion had left science fiction adrift. Both struggled to find publishers for their work, although Hodgson's "The Voice in the Night" subsequently became one of the most widely reprinted science-fiction horror stories. The decline of scientific romance became a sharp fall when World War I broke out, and its fortunes did not revive until 1930.

PULP SCIENCE FICTION

The first pulp magazines appeared in America in the 1890's. They were so named because they took advantage of new technologies that produced cheap paper from wood pulp. After Frank Munsey converted *The Argosy* to an all-fiction magazine in 1896 the kind of fiction most typical of the pulp magazines—garish melodramas aimed at unsophisticated readers—attracted the dismissive name of "pulp fiction." Much early pulp fiction consisted of serial novels, and the first kind of science fiction to gain a firm foothold in the pulp arena was the extraterrestrial adventure story pioneered by Edgar Rice Burroughs in 1912.

The pulp magazines proved far more hospitable to science fiction than more respectable U.S. magazines like *Harper's* and *Cosmopolitan*, as well as offering far more space, but the heavy emphasis they placed on action/adventure stories made it difficult for writers to develop science-fiction ideas in short fiction. The short forms most readily assimilated to pulp fiction were tales of rapidly aborted inventions, travelers' tales, and horror stories using science-fiction motifs. Moral tales were considered too highbrow and dream stories too unsophisticated.

The U.S. pulps imported a certain amount of British scientific romance, including work by Griffith, Hyne, and Hodgson, but much of it was fiction by writers best known as writers of "boys' books." These included Francis H. Atkins, who wrote as Frank Aubrey and Fenton Ash, and George C. Wallis, whose "The Last Days of Earth" was perhaps the most extravagant of all the early British scientific romances. Home-grown pulp writers who began to work in the same area included the astronomer Garrett P. Serviss, and George Allan England. Burroughs's success attracted many others, including Ralph Milne Farley and Ray Cummings, but the pulp magazines published hardly any short science fiction of note before 1920. Although *Weird Tales* (launched in 1923) initially published a good deal of science fiction, and subsequently played a major role in the evolution of the science-fiction horror story, the first pulp magazine specializing in science fiction was *Amazing Stories*, founded in 1926 by Hugo Gernsback.

Gernsback had been publishing short "scientifiction" stories in such popular science magazines as *The Electrical Experimenter* and *Science and Invention* for some years. Although scientifiction was extremely crude in literary terms, it was significant because it was forced to develop its own distinct forms in order to fulfill its didactic purpose, which was to advertise and dramatize new technological possibilities. The form its writers found most useful was the tall tale, as featured in Gernsback's own accounts of "Baron Munchhausen's New Scientific Adventures" and Clement Fézandie's Doctor Hackenshaw series. These series paid little attention to matters of plot and style, but they established a method of using a playful mask for the earnest exposition of extravagant ideas that was carried forward into *Amazing Stories*.

THE EVOLUTION OF THE IDEA-AS-HERO STORY

The emphasis of the early science-fiction pulps was as firmly placed on novels and novellas as that of any other pulp fiction magazine, but the environment provided by a specialist magazine allowed writers of short fiction to take far more for granted than they had been able to do in the general fiction pulps. General readers had had to be carefully introduced to the notion that a story was to be set in the future or an alien world, and the narrative labor required to establish the world-within-the-text could easily cripple the pace and economy of the story. Readers of specialist magazines not only expected exotic settings but also could be assumed to be familiar with a series of basic templates, thus relieving the short-story writer of the necessity to begin explanations from scratch.

This benefit was balanced by the cost that much science fiction written for "connoisseur readers" became quite opaque to readers unfamiliar with the genre's basic templates. It was probably inevitable that the science-fiction magazines would become isolated from the remainder of the pulps in a kind of ghetto and that science-fiction fans would acquire a reputation for weirdness. The pulp ghetto did, however, provide an ideal environment for the evolution of the kind of short story that was to become typical of modern science fiction.

Many of the most effective short stories published in *Weird Tales* and the science-fiction pulps during their first decade were visionary fantasies, conspicuous early examples being "Twilight" and "Night" by "Don A. Stuart" (a pseudonym of John W. Campbell, Jr.). It was not long, however, before attempts to cultivate briefer and brisker versions of the planetary romance began to bear fruit, paradigm examples being established by Stanley G. Weinbaum during a hectic career which lasted only from 1934 until his death in 1936 and whose work is collected in *A Martian Odyssey* (1962). The most profitable development was, however, the gradual evolution of the kind of didactic tall tale pioneered by Gernsback's early magazines into a cleverer and more overtly earnest kind of story.

Although the newer stories of this kind remained tightly focused on some central novelty glimpsed through the lens of scientific or technological possibility, they employed careful ingenuity in extrapolating those ideas in logical but unexpected ways, using the element of surprise to formulate more satisfactory plots. Such stories became increasingly common, and by the time the pulps finally gave way to the far less gaudy digest magazines they had already displaced action/adventure novels and novellas at the core of the genre. Kingsley Amis, looking back from the vantage point of the 1950's—by which time the form had attained a slick optimum—labeled this kind of tale "the idea-as-hero story."

The extrapolation of the pivotal idea of a science-fiction story in such a way as to produce seemingly inevitable but unexpected consequences became a literary game akin to the planning of ingenious murder mysteries. Whole subgenres of such stories quickly became established, notably the time paradox story, in which writers used the basic hypothesis of time travel to tie ever-more-complicated knots in patterns of cause-and-effect. Early exponents of the idea-as-hero story tended to write stories that seemed even cruder, stylistically speaking, than the general run of pulp fiction, but they had a special imaginative appeal that seemed to many readers to be uniquely fitted to their era. Such stories as Edmond Hamilton's "Evolution Island," David H. Keller's "The Revolt of the Pedestrians," and Miles J. Breuer's "The Captured Cross-Section" are barely readable today, but they paved the way for the development of more sophisticated variations on their basic themes: the relentlessness and profligacy of progress, humankind's increasing dependence on technology, and the difficulty of negotiating sudden encounters with the unexpected and the alien.

The Campbellian Crusade

Science fiction crossed an important threshold in 1938 when the best-selling science-fiction pulp *Astounding Stories* was delivered into the charge of John W. Campbell, Jr. Campbell believed that science fiction had the potential to become an important medium for the conduct of socially valuable thought-experiments. He wanted writers to be much more careful than they had previously been to make certain that their stories were scientifically consistent, but he saw that as a beginning rather than an end. The narrative thrust of any science-fiction story, in his view, had to involve the extrapolation of its speculative ideas as well as the projects and troubles of its characters.

Campbell's editorial prospectus firmly established the idea-as-hero story as the primary template of science fiction, and he insisted that it ought to be employed as a means of intellectually disciplined inquiry. His cause was immediately taken up by a stable of young writers whose imaginations had already been schooled by pulp science fiction and who were eager for further education. The stable included L. Sprague de Camp, Lester del Rey, Theodore Sturgeon, Clifford Simak, Henry Kuttner, C. L. Moore, and A. E. van Vogt, but its most important members were Robert A. Heinlein and Isaac Asimov.

Heinlein's "Blowups Happen," which examines the social and psychological stresses associated with the establishment of an atomic power plant, now seems remarkably prescient—as does del Rey's "Nerves," which describes the struggle to contain a meltdown in a nuclear reactor before it causes an environmental disaster—but such anticipatory hits were not the point of the exercise. In order to promote a new consciousness of the multitudinous possibilities that the future contained, and to emphasize that the adaptations that individuals and societies would have to make to future change would be complicated and problematic, it was necessary to write about all possible futures and all imaginable worlds. Forecasting the actual shape that the future would take was not necessary and certainly could not have been sufficient to fulfil the most elementary ambitions of Campbellian science fiction.

In the two years before Heinlein was recalled to military service in the wake of the bombing of Pearl Harbor, he provided a series of paradigmatic examples which revolutionized the science-fiction story, setting new standards in narrative realism. "Requiem" is a Hemingwayesque tale gushing with understated sentimentality in which the weak-hearted man whose entrepreneurialism first made space travel economically viable finally makes his own fatal voyage to the moon. In "The Roads Must Roll," public transport in an overcrowded metropolis is paralyzed by a labor dispute. "Coventry" describes life in a reservation to which dissidents from a formal social contract called the Covenant are banished; the inhabitants have stubbornly reproduced all the ideological divisions and violent conflicts that the new contract has negotiated away.

Isaac Asimov's moral tale "Nightfall," about a world with six suns where darkness falls only once in two thousand years, remained the most popular pulp science-fiction story for at least two decades after its appearance, providing a key encapsulation of the science-fiction myth of "cosmic breakthrough." More typical of his subsequent work, however, was a series of stories exploring the logical and moral puzzles generated by not-too-obvious applications of the Three Laws of Robotics built into future machinery as safeguards. The extension and gradual philosophical complication of this series continued throughout Asimov's exceptionally busy life, its highlights including "Reason," "Little Lost Robot," "That Thou Art Mindful of Him," and "The Bicentennial Man."

The bedrock established by Asimov's robot stories underlies many other robot stories by other writers, including the "City" series and "All the Traps of Earth" by Clifford D. Simak, "With Folded Hands" by Jack Williamson, "The Quest for Saint Aquin" by Anthony Boucher, and "Second Variety" by Philip K. Dick. Viewed as a collective, these stories constitute a wry and perceptive commentary on the problem of humankind's evolving relationship with machinery. Their literary method was, however, far more flexible; Asimov was later to apply it even more prolifically to the writing of scientific essays, becoming the past master of the idea-as-hero science nonfiction story.

The idea-as-hero story offers a unique combination of intellectual and artistic challenges, demanding in its purest form that a writer should not only be able to extrapolate the possible consequences of an imaginary discovery or technology but also be able to set them out in such a way that the climax of the story reveals something that is not obvious but is profound. Perfect examples of the format are rare; the most famous examples include "Flowers for Algernon" by Daniel Keyes and "Light of Other Days" by Bob Shaw.

BEYOND THE PULP GHETTO

Campbell's *Astounding Stories* became a "digest" magazine in 1943 but its competitors clung as stubbornly to the larger pulp format as they did to the norms and values of pulp fiction. None of them recovered fully from wartime economies, and the next phase in the evolution of magazine science fiction was led by a new wave of digest magazines, headed by *The Magazine of Fantasy and Science Fiction* and *Galaxy*. The smaller format encouraged more prolific use of short forms, and these diversified rapidly in the 1950's in directions of which the increasingly narrow-minded Campbell did not approve.

The first science-fiction writer to break out of the magazine ghetto to achieve wider fame was not Heinlein or Asimov, although Heinlein did his utmost to avoid the down-market magazines when he returned to science fiction after the war, concentrating his efforts on slick magazines, television, and juvenile fiction, and Asimov established himself as a significant popularizer of science. The first science-fiction writer to win any real literary acclaim was Ray Bradbury, who paid no attention at all to matters of scientific plausibility in the tales collected in *The Martian Chronicles* (1950), and flatly refused to celebrate the march of progress, preferring to indulge in heavily sentimentalized nostalgia for the world that progress had obliterated and which the atom bomb now threatened to destroy. His tales were certainly idea-as-hero stories, but they celebrated the idea of space travel as an escapist dream rather than a social project.

Literary critics found it far easier to love Bradbury than any writer interested in the increasingly esoteric world of scientific theory and technological development—and in fairness, even committed science-fiction readers found it difficult to get on with writers such as Hal Clement, who were so obviously the best players of the game of reasoned extrapolation, that their work tended toward relentless exposition and painstaking abstruseness. The task of developing an idea based in real science while keeping explanatory exposition to a minimum is very difficult, and the few writers who eventually mastered it, including Poul Anderson, Larry Niven, and Gregory Benford, have rarely received appropriate critical recognition for their achievements. *Time and Stars* (1964) is one of many collections displaying Anderson's expertise, while Niven's most archetypical collection is *Tales of Known Space* (1975) and Benford's early work is assembled in *In Alien Flesh* (1986).

The literary people who loved Bradbury were equally delighted, in a later phase of science fiction's development, to discover the work of Philip K. Dick, whose work expressed the suspicion—and, ultimately, the conviction—that the entire world of empirical experience (and therefore everything science might have to say about it) was a cruel delusion. With admirable cunning, however, the critics began to heap praise on Dick only once he was safely dead, thus avoiding the risk of increasing his confidence in material rewards.

Dick's posthumous fame allowed his short fiction, initially published between 1952 and 1982, to receive the ultimate accolade of comprehensive assembly in *The Collected Stories of Philip K. Dick* (1987). Another who received similar posthumous treatment was Theodore Sturgeon, who began writing for John Campbell but did not hit his stride until the 1950's. Sturgeon's work required ten volumes, which began to appear at yearly intervals in 1994. The emotional intensity of Sturgeon's work was even more exaggerated than Bradbury's or Dick's, and he too focused on the desperate need to preserve human identity and human integrity in a world doubly threatened by imminent atomic destruction and the slow erosion of our capacity to put ourselves in the shoes of others by the supposed demands of objectivity.

SATIRE AND SOCIAL COMMENTARY

Another element shared by the work of Bradbury, Dick, and Sturgeon was a ready wit. All three were more accomplished tragedians than comedians, and their humor was often rather black, but each had a well-developed sense of irony. The same was true of many of the other writers who rose to prominence within the genre in the 1950's, although the only really prominent writer of outrightly humorous science fiction in that era was Robert Sheckley.

Frederik Pohl and Cyril M. Kornbluth were singled out for particular praise by Kingsley Amis because of their accomplishments in "satire," although the idiosyncratic kind of social criticism they practiced in their work is sufficiently distinctive to resist ready subsumption under that label. Their best early novels were written in collaboration, but they wrote their best short fiction solo, classic examples including Kornbluth's "The Little Black Bag" and "The Marching Morons" and Pohl's "The Midas World" and "The Tunnel Under the World."

Pohl and Kornbluth were core members of a group styling themselves the Futurians, who constituted a younger generation determined not to pay more reverence than was due to their Campbellian forebears. The group's senior member, Donald A. Wollheim, became an editor who played a leading role in guiding science fiction out of its magazine ghetto into the brave new marketplace of paperback books, and Virginia Kidd became a leading agent within the field, while other members who became successful writers included Judith Merril, James Blish, and Damon Knight.

Judith Merril was the second notable female science-fiction writer to emerge from the magazine genre, although her predecessor, C. L. Moore, had written most of her work in collaboration with her husband Henry Kuttner and had hidden the bulk of it behind a bewildering assortment of pseudonyms. It was not until Donna Haraway published her "Cyborg Manifesto" that Moore's "No Woman Born" was recognized as a significant protofeminist work, although Merril's outlook was obvious from the outset in such masculinity-questioning stories as "Dead Center." The best-of-the-year anthologies that Merril edited from 1956 to 1968 played an important role in defining the range and ambition of the science-fiction story. Katherine MacLean, whose oft-anthologized "Pictures Don't Lie" offers a perfect example of the manner in which idea-as-hero stories can be used to set up surprise endings, was also peripherally associated with the Futurians; another influential female science-fiction writer, Kate Wilhelm, subsequently married into the group.

James Blish was the most earnest of the Futurians, and the one who adapted himself most easily to Campbell's cause. He wrote several significant philosophical tales, including "Beep" and "A Work of Art," although his most popular story was "Surface Tension," a parable of conceptual breakthrough to rival Asimov's "Nightfall," in which microbe-sized humans discover that what they think of as the sky is only the first and narrowest barrier separating them from their universal heritage.

As a writer of dark, socially critical science fiction Damon Knight was overshadowed by Frederik Pohl, although "The Country of the Kind" is an outstanding example of that kind of story. Knight set a more significant precedent with the apocalyptic comedy "Not With a Bang," which appeared in one of the earliest issues of *The Magazine of Fantasy and Science Fiction*. It added a slyly cynical gloss to an idea that Fredric Brown's "Knock" had borrowed from Thomas Bailey Aldrich and launched a whole series of variations on the theme whose tone and manner became characteristic of an important subset of the magazine's product, equipping it with a veneer of urbane sophistication that other science-fiction magazines conspicuously lacked. Like Pohl, Knight went on to be a zealous editor of short science fiction, but his most enduring influence was in importing the methods of the Iowa Writers' Workshop into the annual "conferences" he hosted (later in association with Kate Wilhelm). In the late 1960's, these conferences became the inspiration of the Clarion workshops and many similar enterprises, which gradually hammered out an analysis of the special problems involved in constructing science-fiction stories and the best methods of solving them that is now virtually canonical.

British Science Fiction

American science fiction flooded into war-devastated Europe after 1945, overwhelming native traditions of speculative fiction that had already been enfeebled by World War I. British speculative fiction had revived in the 1930's but it consisted almost entirely of doom-laden prophecies of a renewal of conflict that would complete the demolition of civilization. There was no room for such dark material in the popular magazines, so those new writers of scientific romance who dabbled in short fiction—including

Neil Bell and J. Leslie Mitchell—quickly gave it up and concentrated on novels. The only significant science-fiction story collection published in the United Kingdom between the wars was S. Fowler Wright's vitriolic *The New Gods Lead* (1932).

Several British writers had become familiar with the U.S. pulps before the war (out-of-date copies were sold cheap in department stores, having allegedly been used as ballast by transatlantic liners) and had become frequent contributors in the 1930's, most notably Eric Frank Russell and John Beynon Harris (who later became famous as John Wyndham). Others, however, especially after World War II, became disenchanted with the quasi-imperialist vision of galactic conquest that had become enshrined in the magazines as a broadly consensual image of future history.

It is arguable that the real reason for the establishment of galaxy-wide cultures at the heart of the science-fiction enterprise was its utility as a framework for the location of any and all imaginable hypothetical societies, and new British writers like Brian Aldiss were perfectly happy to use it in that way, but others were enthusiastic to take up a slogan coined by J. G. Ballard, to the effect that "Earth is the only alien planet."

As a teenager Ballard had been interned by the Japanese during World War II and had been a helpless witness to the collapse and obliteration of what had passed for civilization in the international enclave of Shanghai. The science fiction he began writing in the late 1950's was saturated with images of collapse and creeping desolation dispassionately observed by helpless onlookers. Ballard was fascinated by surrealism and the avant-garde writing of William Burroughs, which seemed to him to offer useful insights and methods for the analysis of this kind of process, and he began to borrow from them in such mold-breaking stories as "The Voices of Time" and "The Terminal Beach." His casual denial of everything that American science fiction espoused was at its most subversive in "The Cage of Sand," which looked forward—seven years before the first moon landing—to the day when the space program would be a forgotten folly and Cape Canaveral a graveyard of dreams.

By 1974 Ballard's assertion that the space age was over and all its dreams of conquest lost began to seem far more plausible. By that time, however, the "new wave" of science fiction he had inspired, which had obtained an outlet when Michael Moorcock took over the editorship of the British science-fiction magazine *New Worlds* in 1964, had also begun to seem like a thing of the past. Moorcock's declared intention to import modern literary methods and values into science fiction, and to banish the lingering echoes of pulp that still infected it, attracted far more attention than sales. *New Worlds* was relaunched in a glossier format with the support of an Arts Council grant, but its commercial fate was sealed when Britain's largest distributor, W. H. Smith, refused to handle it because of its use of offensive language. Ironically, the four-letter words in question were deployed by one of several American writers attracted by the magazine's subversive ambitions, Norman Spinrad.

Spinrad and his fellow Americans Samuel R. Delany, John T. Sladek, and Thomas M. Disch all went on to enjoy more successful careers than Moorcock's domestic protégés, who included Barrington J. Bayley, Langdon Jones, David I. Masson, and M. John Harrison. Christopher Priest and Ian Watson also published early work in Moorcock's *New Worlds*, while Josephine Saxton made her debut in its companion *Impulse* and Keith Roberts also published his finest work there. These writers did, however, produce a good deal of first-rate short fiction, displayed in such collections as Masson's *The Caltraps of Time* (1968), Roberts's *Pavane* (1968), Bayley's *The Knights of the Limits* (1978), Priest's *An Infinite Summer* (1979), Watson's *The Very Slow Time Machine* (1979), and Saxton's *The Power of Time* (1985). Such writers as Priest and Roberts actually had stronger links with the venerable tradition of scientific romance than the new wave, and the fading out of the avant-garde coincided with the emergence of the even more traditionally inclined Richard Cowper—the pseudonym of the similarly named son of the famous literary critic John Middleton-Murry—who published three stylish collections of short science fiction, beginning with *The Custodians, and Other Stories* (1976), under the name Richard Cowper.

Avant-Garde Science Fiction

The British new wave was enthusiastically supported in the United States by Judith Merril, but Harlan Ellison created a home-grown version with his pioneering anthology of "taboo-breaking" stories *Dangerous Visions* (1967). Ellison had put his early days as a prolific hack behind him when he broke through into writing television scripts in the early 1960's, and from then on his literary output was concentrated on intense, vivid, and surreal short fiction. "'Repent, Harlequin!' said the Ticktockman" won him the first of many awards, "I Have No Mouth and I Must Scream," "The Deathbird," and "A Boy and His Dog" all adding to the list.

Dangerous Visions called attention to the fact that there were American science-fiction writers who had been producing avant-garde science fiction for some time, mostly in the obscurity of minor magazines. Fritz Leiber had begun to produce stylistic and taboo-testing science fiction as long ago as the early 1950's, in such tales as "Coming Attraction," "Nice Girl with Five Husbands," and the early items in the groundbreaking series collected in *The Change War* (1978). David R. Bunch's bizarre fables of a world in which human beings forsake their "fleshstrips" for mechanized bodies were collected in *Moderan* (1971). Another highly distinctive fabulist, R. A. Lafferty, enjoyed a brief moment of success before he became the first of many science-fiction writers to be relegated to the uncommercial world of the small presses. Fabulists working in the margins of the science-fiction genre like Kit Reed, or wholly outside it, like Donald Barthelme, made such good use of science-fiction motifs in the 1970's that the critic Robert Scholes was moved to suggest a new expansion of the acronym in *Structural Fabulation* (1975).

Several U.S. writers centrally or peripherally related to the new wave wrote brilliant short fiction while under its partial influence, although they did not all continue breaking new ground thereafter. After writing "Time Considered as a Helix of Semi-Precious Stones" Samuel R. Delany decided that his efforts would be more profitably devoted to novels, and Roger Zelazny gradually retreated from the startling virtuosity of such stories as "A Rose for Ecclesiastes" and "The Doors of His Face, the Lamps of His Mouth" to the production of commercial sword-and-sorcery books, but Thomas M. Disch blurred the bounds of the genre even more effectively than Ellison in the excellent *Getting into Death* (1973) and its successors. The blackness of Disch's humor and the scathing quality of his sarcasm did not endear him to all readers, but he became the deadliest and most brutal of the genre's satirists (in the truest sense of the word). Barry N. Malzberg also contrived to combine a keen satirical eye with a stylistic verve all too rarely seen within the genre, although only a fraction of his short fiction was ever assembled into such volumes as *The Man Who Loved the Midnight Lady* (1980). The more orthodox Robert Silverberg, by contrast, managed to collect almost all of his more polished short fiction, the most admirably intense of which is to be found in *The Reality Trip, and Other Implausibilities* (1972) and *Beyond the Safe Zone* (1986).

It was within the context formed by the new wave that some American interest was developed in science fiction from Eastern Europe, much of which was based in local satirical traditions. The leading beneficiary of this interest was the Polish writer Stanisław Lem, whose most notable short fictions were the "robot fables" collected in *Cyberiada* (1965; *The Cyberiad: Fables for the Cybernetic Age*, 1974) and *Bajki robotów*, 1964 (partial translation; *Mortal Engines*, 1977), although the Czech writer Josef Nesvadba—a sampler of whose short works was issued in the United States as *The Lost Face* (1970)—is equally ingenious.

The Contemporary Scene

Science fiction ceased to be a magazine-based genre in the 1960's, when paperback books became its primary commercial engine. Attempts to shift science fiction's magazine culture into the new medium, involving such paperback anthology series as Damon Knight's *Orbit*, Terry Carr's *Universe*, and Robert Silverberg's *New Dimensions* flourished briefly but died out as conventional editorial wisdom embraced the theory that because novels always outsold collections of short stories there was no point in publishing any short fiction except for the occasional collection by a best-selling writer.

By the beginning of the 1990's most people who identified themselves as science-fiction fans were mainly or exclusively interested in television and cinema science fiction, and the most commercially successful books carrying the label were television and film tie-ins. The meaning of the term—which is routinely diminished to "sci-fi"—has shifted so dramatically, giving rise to "science-fiction shops" that sell videos, games, comics, toys, and "collectibles" but carry no books at all.

In view of these developments, it is perhaps surprising that short science-fiction stories still exist at all, and it is a remarkable testimony to the hardihood of the form that several commercial science-fiction magazines still exist in a world from which all-fiction magazines have all but disappeared. The last surviving monthly fiction magazine in the English language is the British *Interzone*, although several U.S. science-fiction magazines are still in existence.

Most of the leading names in modern science fiction have done their best work in novel form, but there are a number of them who seem more comfortable working at shorter lengths and who have produced outstanding work of the idea-as-hero kind. Moral fables and philosophical tales have become increasingly common, widely featured in the work of such prolific short-fiction writers as Michael Bishop, whose best work is collected in *One Winter in Eden* (1984) and *Close Encounters with the Deity* (1986); Gene Wolfe, whose best collection of enigmatic futuristic fables is *Endangered Species* (1989); and James Tiptree, Jr.—the principal pseudonym of Alice Sheldon—the best of whose mischievously garish futuristic visions can be found in the sampler *Her Smoke Rose Up Forever* (1990). Ursula K. Le Guin has found short formats ideal for many of her exercises in imaginary anthropology, which are among the finest philosophical tales ever written; they can be found in a series of collections ranging from *The Wind's Twelve Quarters* (1975) to *Four Ways to Forgiveness* (1995). Ardent feminist Joanna Russ also found short science-fiction ideal for didactic accounts of routes to political and psychological liberation, in such tales as those collected in *Extra (Ordinary) People* (1984).

The pioneers of the "cyberpunk" movement, which was taken up with great enthusiasm by postmodernist critics and philosophers, produced some exceptionally fine short fiction, a representative selection of which is assembled in Bruce Sterling's best-selling anthology *Mirrorshades* (1986). Sterling's own reputation was sealed by the "Shaper/Mechanist" series of stories included in the collection *Crystal Express* (1989), while William Gibson laid the groundwork for *Neuromancer* (1984) in the short stories collected in *Burning Chrome* (1986). Other writers central to the movement were John Shirley and Pat Cadigan, while mathematician Rudy Rucker was co-opted even though his short fiction—collected in *Transreal!* (1991)—is highly idiosyncratic. The same might be said of Howard Waldrop, the co-inventor of "steampunk": a curious subgenre of stories which employs an ultra-modern sensibility to reassess—and often to rewrite—history; his early work is assembled in *Strange Things in Close Up* (1989).

The persistence of *Interzone* has provided a useful forum for the latest generation of British science-fiction writers, including Stephen Baxter and Paul McAuley. One especially fine writer of short fiction is Ian McDonald, whose *Empire Dreams* (1988) is an outstanding collection. *Interzone* also served as an important market for the Australian writer Greg Egan, who is undoubtedly one of the most perceptive and most versatile contemporary writers of stories based in cutting-edge science. His second collection *Luminous* (1998) features the sharp moral tale "Cocoon" and the brilliant philosophical tale "Reasons to be Cheerful."

For as long as the last science-fiction magazines can cling to their precarious existence the flow of short science fiction will continue, bearing moral fables focusing on the ethical issues raised by new technologies, visionary fantasies more elaborate and grandiose than any previously seen, and—perhaps most important—idea-as-hero stories which attempt to anticipate all the problems of social and psychological adaptation with which the rapid march of technology might confront generations to come.

Brian Stableford

Bibliography

Amis, Kingsley. *New Maps of Hell: A Survey of Science Fiction*. London: Gollancz, 1960. A slightly superficial study by a critic whose relative ignorance of the genre's history is amply compensated by his insights into the distinctive forms and merits of short sf.

Ashley, Michael. *The History of the Science Fiction Magazines*. 4 vols. London: New English Library, 1974-78. A comprehensive history of magazine sf; each volume covers ten years and includes representative samples of stories from the decade plus bibliographies of the works of leading writers.

Carter, Paul A. *The Creation of Tomorrow: Fifty Years of Magazine Science Fiction*. New York: Columbia University Press, 1977. An intelligent and well-informed history of the genre, which pays more careful attention than most of its rivals to short fiction.

Clute, John, and Peter Nicholls. *The Encyclopedia of Science Fiction*. London: Orbit, 1993. By far the most comprehensive guide to the genre's history, practitioners, and themes.

Scholes, Robert. *Structural Fabulation: An Essay on Fiction of the Future*. Notre Dame, Ind.: University of Notre Dame Press, 1975. Scholes argues that fabular futuristic fictions are more pertinent to present concerns in a fast-changing world than any present-set fiction can be.

Wilson, Robin Scott, ed. *Those Who Can: A Science Fiction Reader.* New York: Mentor, 1973. An anthology of stories with attendant commentaries by the authors; although primarily intended as a guide for would-be writers it provides an excellent analysis of the ways in which short story formats need to be adapted for genre deployment.

THE SUPERNATURAL STORY

To the modern reader, the stories that make up the mythology and folklore of ancient cultures are largely supernatural. Whether the storytellers originally responsible for composing, adding to, and passing on these stories necessarily thought in terms of "natural" and "supernatural" is debatable, yet the existence of such classical works as *Metamorphoses* (c. 8 C.E.; English translation, 1867) by Ovid suggests that such a distinction eventually became clear. Ovid's stories in verse are based upon Latin mythology and deal with transformations—metamorphoses—of humans into plants and animals, a theme destined to become common in what came to be recognized as supernatural literature.

Much later collections in the same general vein include *Alf layla wa-layla* (fifteenth century; *The Arabian Nights' Entertainments*, 1706-1708). Drawn from much earlier sources in Persia and Arabia, this mammoth collection has been the inspiration for innumerable other works and was translated in its most complete English version (1885-1886) by explorer Sir Richard Francis Burton. Rivaling *The Arabian Nights' Entertainments* in scope and surpassing them in influence in the Western world are the tales that make up the cycle about the (perhaps) legendary King Arthur and his Knights of the Round Table.

The stories, characters, and themes preserved in these and many other collections have proven to be a treasure trove for later writers, although science and rationalism have frequently consigned them to a kind of literary underground. Yet the emotions they deal with—from fear of death on one hand to religious ecstasy on the other—have continued to animate writers and readers alike. In mid-eighteenth century England such emotions would erupt in a most memorable way.

The Gothic School

Although little gothic literature is read today, the movement and the impulse behind it have significantly affected modern literature. Ostensibly an eighteenth century revival of interest in medieval architecture and related matters, the movement involved a reintroduction of mystery, awe, and wonder into literature and life. The movement was born with *The Castle of Otranto* (1765), Horace Walpole's wildly extravagant tale of a haunted castle riddled with secret passages and riven with dark plots. This short novel stood in direct contrast to the domesticated and emotionally desiccated literature of the period, and gave vent to feelings routinely denied and suppressed at the time. The work quickly attracted imitators, most of whom excelled at novel-length works.

One of the first writers to exploit the gothic in short forms was Count Jan Potocki, a Polish nobleman who wrote in French and who is said to have ended his long and accomplished life by shooting himself in the head with a silver bullet blessed by his chaplain. Potocki's great work is *The Saragossa Manuscript*, parts of which were circulated in manuscript as early as 1805 but which appeared in a complete English translation only in 1995 (as *The Manuscript Found in Saragossa*). This phantasmagoric work is a long series of interwoven stories, ostensibly collected by a Walloon soldier in the Sierra Morena mountains of Spain in 1739. The stories—supernatural and erotic by turns—are narrated by a variety of roguish storytellers. The narratives often overlap, and one story is humorously framed four-deep within a series of others.

More influential were the tales of German writer, artist, and composer E. T. A. Hoffmann, who more than any gothic figure before him located the fantastic in contemporary life. Ironically enough, modern readers may find Hoffmann's early nineteenth century European settings and his fascination with such subjects as automatons and *Doppelgängers* (doubles) equally quaint, yet the nervous energy and satirical bent of his works assure their readability. Hoffmann's best-known story is probably "The Sandman," in which a student falls fatally in love with a mechanical woman.

Early American Masters

Washington Irving was the first American writer of any distinction and wrote many supernatural stories. A few, such as "The Adventure of the German Student," about a young man in Paris who spends the night with what turns out to be a guillotined corpse, are clearly in the gothic tradition. More familiar are two stories from *The Sketch Book of Geoffrey Crayon, Gent.* (1819-1820): the justly influential "Rip Van Winkle," an Americanized version of European folktales of a man bewitched into sleeping for decades, and "The Legend of Sleepy Hollow," which pokes fun at supernatural conventions. Ironically enough, Irving also translated an episode from *The Saragossa Manuscript* by Potocki as "The Grand Prior of Minorca," but the story was assumed by readers to be by Irving himself.

Nathaniel Hawthorne is celebrated for his novels *The Scarlet Letter* (1850) and *The House of the Seven Gables* (1851), both of which contain supernatural elements but which perhaps fail to exploit them fully. His story "The Wedding Knell" enlarges upon the tradition of the specter-bridegroom by describing the ceremony a long-jilted lover arranges for his equally aged bride-to-be. Hawthorne's most successful supernatural story is "Young Goodman Brown," in which an upright Puritan journeys into a forest to observe—to his horror—a witches' coven involving not only the most reputable members of his community but also his own wife. Brown, suggests Hawthorne, may simply have had a nightmare, but his life is blighted nevertheless. Here Hawthorne's ambivalence toward the supernatural results in a masterful study of morbid human psychology.

Edgar Allan Poe's name is easily the most famous in supernatural literature, and his work represents a literary subcontinent all its own. During his four decades of life, Poe transformed the European gothic tradition, bringing an intensity and a kind of word-drunk enthusiasm to the most horrific themes and situations. Despite Poe's reputation, most of his works are not strictly supernatural, although their claustrophobia and their obsessive concern with madness, death (especially that of beloved and beautiful women), and premature burial mark them as gothic. Indeed one of Poe's most famous stories is entitled simply "The Premature Burial," and the theme is also treated in the frequently reprinted "The Cask of Amontillado."

"The Fall of the House of Usher" manages to combine almost all Poe's morbid concerns, with the "house" of its title suggesting the family dwelling place, the near-extinct family itself, *and* the central character's tottering sanity. Madeline Usher has apparently succumbed to a wasting illness and has been entombed by her twin Roderick, who himself suffers from a preternatural sensitivity to sounds and other sense phenomena. While Roderick's acute hearing registers the frantic attempts of his reawakened sister to escape the tomb, he lacks the moral stamina to go to her aid. During a furious storm Madeline finally breaks free, seeks out her brother, and with her last breath collapses upon him. He in turn dies instantly of fright, and the mansion collapses.

Allied with Poe's stories of premature burial are those of individuals hypnotized (or "mesmerized") prior to death, with the result that their souls are imprisoned in their bodies. Poe's most famous treatment of this theme is "The Facts in the Case of M. Valdemar," in which the unfortunate M. Valdemar's body disintegrates instantly and loathsomely when the hypnotic spell is lifted.

Poe was an industrious writer whose success was undercut by his own intolerance and by disastrously bad luck. His young wife succumbed to tuberculosis after an agonizing five-year struggle, and Poe himself died in delirium some two years later—a death for years blamed on alcoholism but now suspected to have been brought on by disease.

The Victorian Period

Famed and prolific English novelist Charles Dickens wrote a number of supernatural works, the most famous of which is certainly the short piece *A Christmas Carol* (1843). A shorter supernatural story is "No. 1 Branch Line, the Signal-Man," about a railway worker who receives repeated spectral warnings prior to accidents. Equally prolific but nearly completely forgotten, Dickens's contemporary Edward Bulwer-Lytton wrote one of the very best haunted-house stories in "The Haunted and the Haunters: Or, The House and the Brain."

Avoiding the more extravagant clichés of the gothic school, Irish novelist and short-story writer Joseph Sheridan Le Fanu explored the psychological states of his protagonists, locating the seeds of horror and terror within their psyches rather than in external agents. According to his son, Le Fanu wrote his most frightening stories late at night by candlelight as he sat in bed, drawing upon his dreams and nightmares.

Le Fanu's most important works include the collections *In a Glass Darkly* (1872) and the posthumously published *The Purcell Papers* (1880), which reprints earlier material. The former volume, regarded as one of the most important in the history of the genre, includes the story "Green Tea" and the novella *Carmilla*, both presented as "cases" of one Dr. Hesselius.

"Green Tea" is routinely recognized as the prototypical story of the supernatural and recounts the ordeal of one Reverend Jennings, who is haunted—stalked might be a better word—by a malevolent monkey invisible to all but the victim himself. Although many critics have supplied "explanations" for Jennings's predicament, the truth is that he has done nothing to deserve the creature's attentions but drink quantities of green tea—a beverage not coincidentally favored by Le Fanu himself. That is, like the protagonists of later stories by such writers as M. R. James and H. P. Lovecraft, the Reverend has done nothing to deserve his fate. Despite Hesselius's attentions, Jennings's ordeal progresses by increasingly disturbing degrees to the point at which he kills himself.

Besides excelling in his exploration of what would now be characterized as extreme psychological states, Le Fanu was a master of disturbing, often grotesque details—details that in another context could be absurd or even funny. In "Madame Crowl's Ghost" the wizened old woman of the title spends much of her time in bed dressed in the splendor of another age, complete with tall powdered wig, long false teeth and equally (and unnaturally) long finger nails cut to points. In "The Child That Went with the Fairies," whose action is summarized in its title, an even more gruesome detail stands out. One of the two women responsible for carrying off the child in question is so taken with what appears to be mirthful anticipation of the victim's fate that she stuffs fold after fold of her voluminous handkerchief into her mouth to stifle her laughter.

Le Fanu influenced succeeding writers in a number of ways. M. R. James was so impressed with his work that he reintroduced the Irish master to the reading public with the collection *Madam Crowl's Ghost and Other Stories* (1923). Le Fanu's use of the character Dr. Hesselius, a medical doctor concerned with the psychological states of his patients, marked the first appearance of the occult investigator—a figure developed more fully by Bram Stoker in the novel *Dracula* (1897) and by Algernon Blackwood and William Hope Hodgson in many of their stories. As the *other* outstanding fictional work about vampires in English, *Dracula* itself is thematically indebted to *Carmilla*, as are most of the many stories and novels about vampires that have been written since.

European Writers

Over the years writers from several European countries contributed stories to the body of supernatural literature. In France these included renowned authors Prosper Mérimée and Guy de Maupassant. Mérimée is known to readers and music lovers as the author of the novella *Carmen* (1845), but produced a masterpiece of supernatural fiction in *Lokis* (1869), a novel about a were-bear set in Lithuania. More famous still is the prolific Maupassant, whose best-known supernatural story is "The Horla," about a man who finds himself haunted by an invisible and seemingly indestructible being whom he tries to kill by burning his house—but does he succeed?

Pitched at a somewhat lower level of creativity were the works of French writers Émile Erckmann and Alexandre Chatrian, whose best supernatural stories include "The Man-Wolf" and the widely translated and reprinted "The Crab Spider." The latter features an escaped South American spider that has grown to enormous size.

Russian novelist Nikolai Gogol produced a number of fantastic works, including "The Nose," a famous story describing in deadpan manner the dilemma of a man whose nose has disappeared. Perhaps more striking is "Viy," an account of a seminarian's wildly horrifying sexual obsession and his ultimate destruction. Fellow Russian Alexis Tolstoi produced a classic vampire story in "The Family of a Vourdalak," which is set in Serbia.

Much later Czech writer Franz Kafka (who wrote in German) produced the famous and chilling novella *Die Verwandlung* (1915; *The Metamorphosis*, 1936), in which an innocuous salesman is transformed into an enormous insect, only to be disowned by his family. As in many European works, the supernatural element here is little more than a mechanism that allows the author to explore other concerns.

A Golden Age

The four decades preceding World War I are now recognized as a kind of golden age not only of supernatural fiction but also of the supernatural story in particular. Its key figures were Arthur Machen, Algernon Blackwood, and M. R. James—dissimilar figures who nevertheless so thoroughly dominated the field in Great Britain that only in the second half of the century did a definite break occur in the genre's development.

Machen and Blackwood wrote what noted American supernatural writer H. P. Lovecraft termed "cosmic horror," establishing a worldview that disturbingly redefined the elements of horror to include all of creation. Lovecraft himself wrote in a similar philosophical vein, as did fellow American Robert W. Chambers and, in his novels at least, Englishman William Hope Hodgson. Cosmic horror would resurface later in the twentieth century in many of the works of Ramsey Campbell, Clive Barker, Stephen King, Peter Straub, and T. E. D. Klein.

Arthur Machen was at one time or another in his life a journalist and actor as well as novelist and short-story writer. His first success was the novella *The Great God Pan* (1890), which recounts in characteristically indirect fashion the gruesome results of a brain operation designed to allow its subject to "see" Pan—that is, to experience the true malignity of the universe. The novella's horrific climax actually surpasses the final scene of bodily disintegration in Poe's "The Facts in the Case of M. Valdemar." Several of Machen's most successful stories appeared soon after in *The Three Impostors* (1895), which weaves several narratives into an elaborate if not wholly convincing framework. These "embedded" stories include "Novel of the Black Seal" and "Novel of the White Powder," both frequently reprinted minus their misleading labels as "novels."

Raised on the English-Welsh border in a countryside punctuated with ruins of the ancient Roman occupation, Machen believed that a greater "reality" underlay the mundane events of modern life. As dramatized in his works, the reality was sometimes horribly intrusive, sometimes beguilingly elusive. The former tendency is illustrated in "The White People." This remarkable work, which recounts in a naïve, sing-song narrative a young girl's seduction into witchcraft, is often cited by critics as the best supernatural story ever written. Machen's belief that a stunted, malignant race of beings may have survived into modern times, giving rise to the folklore of elves and fairies, is dramatized not only in this story but also in *The Three Impostors* and *The Shining Pyramid* (1923). A less terrifying aspect of Machen's work is exemplified in the late story "N," a leisurely narrative whose various characters realize that a beautiful, transfiguring garden is sometimes to be encountered in a sleepy and otherwise wholly unremarkable suburb of London.

Along with Machen's "The White People," Algernon Blackwood's stories "The Willows" and "The Wendigo" are recognized as high points of supernatural literature. Like Machen, Blackwood wrote of experiences and states of being that are ecstatic or thrilling, although they seldom include the former writer's touches of physical horror. Blackwood wrote prolifically and although his novels are diffuse by modern standards, he excelled at the long story, a form that allowed him to develop his dramatic effects in a leisurely manner.

Blackwood's best stories take place in the remote wilderness, for which he held and conveyed a mystical regard. "The Willows" is set on a tiny, lonely island in the Danube River increasingly overgrown with willows; two canoeists trapped in a flood sense that they are victims of malevolent forces from another dimension. "The Wendigo" is set in Labrador, Canada, and dramatizes a Native American legend concerning a supernatural creature which steals human beings and conveys them across the sky, at the same time burning their feet—sensations that, not coincidentally, signal frostbite.

Nearly as dramatic is "The Camp of the Dog," set on a Swedish island in the Baltic Sea and dealing with a werewolf. This story also features a recurring character named John Silence, an occult detective. Other notable John Silence stories include "Ancient Sorceries," set in a French village whose inhabitants assume the form of cats to attend a witches' Sabbath, and "Secret Worship," about a sect of Devil worshipers in the Black Forest of Germany (where Blackwood himself was educated). Most of this occult detective's cases appeared in *John Silence, Physician Extraordinary* (1908).

M. R. James was a noted academic and scholar who wrote and told ghost stories for the amusement of his friends and students, often at Christmas. His scholarly works are now largely forgotten, but his stories—issued in *Ghost Stories of an Antiquary* (1904), *More Ghost Stories of an Antiquary* (1911), *A Thin Ghost and Others* (1919), and the deliciously titled *A Warning to the Curious* (1925)—are the best of their kind, elegantly and concisely told and all the more chillingly effective for their deceptively offhand manner.

As the titles of his first two collections indicate, James wrote for the most part about antiquaries, amateur seekers after ancient inscriptions, old books, and the like. His most famous story may be "The Mezzotint," in which a print of an old house inexplicably reveals the successive stages of a ghastly crime—the kidnapping of an infant by a shrouded, skeletal figure. In this case James suggests a motive, but in most of his stories supernatural intrusion is occasioned by little more than meddling on the part of the "curious." In "Oh, Whistle and I'll Come to You, My Lad," an antiquary uncovers an ancient whistle, and, intrigued by its Latin inscription (in translation, "Who is this who is coming?"), unwisely decides to find out.

Like Le Fanu, James was a master of the telling detail, however briefly glimpsed. In "Oh, Whistle and I'll Come to You, My Lad," the presence summoned has a face resembling "crumpled" linen. "The Ash-Tree" involves creatures living in the tree of the title, and the first glimpse the reader catches of one in the moonlight carries the chilling impression that it is running up the trunk on more than four legs—an image more powerful than the detailed view James subsequently gives us. The vampire story "An Episode of Cathedral History" is enlivened by equally suggestive details.

So effective were James's seemingly straightforward techniques that several of his friends—particularly E. G. Swain and R. H. Malden, both of whom dedicated volumes to him—wrote stories in a similar vein, producing material with suitably antiquarian themes but little originality. James's works are now recognized as prototypically English ghost stories but have proven difficult to imitate effectively.

Other British Writers

Three British figures stand apart during this period for their originality: M. P. Shiel, William Hope Hodgson, and Lord Dunsany. Shiel wrote prolifically in a variety of forms and genres—science fiction, the detective story and novel, the adventure novel—displaying a rich vocabulary and a taste for the arcane that often appealed more to other writers than to the general public. His most remarkable stories include "Xélucha" and "Vaila" from *Shapes in the Fire* (1896), works indebted to Edgar Allan Poe but written in an even more ornate style than Poe's. "Xélucha" is a fantasy of necrophilia set in a bizarre, wildly imagined London. "Vaila" (to some extent a retelling of Poe's "The Fall of the House of Usher") takes place on a remote, wind-swept island in the North Sea and involves a brass house literally chained to the island and doomed by a family curse.

Shiel rewrote "Vaila" as "The House of Sounds" and included it in *The Pale Ape and Other Pulses* (1911), along with "Huguenin's Wife." Set on a Greek island recreated with as little regard for "reality" as was the London of "Xélucha," this story concerns a murdered wife who returns to life as a huge, feathered, winged cat. Shiel's most haunting work is "Dark Lot of One Saul," about a sailor thrown overboard in a barrel and sucked down by a current to an air-filled cave far beneath the surface of the sea. The sensations of utter solitude and—oddly enough—spiritual awe conveyed by this story have seldom been equaled in print.

William Hope Hodgson's best works are his novels, but he wrote two series of exceptional supernatural stories as well. One series featured an occult detective somewhat reminiscent of Algernon Blackwood's *John Silence*. *Carnacki the Ghost Finder* (1913) collected several of these cases, while an expanded edition of 1948 added three more. Typical is "The Whistling Room," about a house haunted in a most horrendous and original fashion. Other, more loosely connected stories were set at sea (where Hodgson spend eight years), and appeared for the most part in *Men of the Deep Waters* (1914) and the posthumous compilation *Deep Waters* (1967). One of the best of these is "The Voice in the Night," in which a marooned, fungus-covered couple approaches a ship by night in a rowboat to beg for food. Hodgson was one of the most original writers of his generation, and his death at an early age during World War I may have robbed supernatural fiction of its most talented modern writer.

Edward John Moreton Drax Plunkett, better known as Lord Dunsany, began publishing during this period, and although he wrote prolifically until the mid-1950's, his works continued to reflect the period in which he found his voice. Dunsany produced works in a variety of forms, including drama and the novel, although his first stories—collected in *The Gods of Pegãna* (1905) and *Time and the Gods* (1906)—have proven to be his most influential. These volumes create a new, fanciful pantheon. Its ostensible ruler was Mana-Yood-Sushai, who in turn created a host of gods, who in turn created something like the modern world.

Many of Lord Dunsany's subsequent stories evoke equally magical worlds. An outstanding example is "The Fortress Unvanquishable, Save for Sacnoth," a mock-heroic yet powerful fantasy about the banishment of an evil being who visits the earth every 230 years on a comet. Dunsany also wrote a series of entertaining volumes concerning the fanciful adventures of a sailor named Joseph Jorkens.

Another odd man out was Hector Hugh Munro, known to the reading public as "Saki." Saki's many stories are brief and sardonic—very English equivalents of Ambrose Bierce's tales. A typical example is "Gabriel-Ernest," a werewolf story whose calculated cleverness and coldness are more horrifying than many more conventional horrors. Several of Saki's frequently reprinted stories are not literally supernatural. "Sredni Vashtar," for example, concerns a put-upon little boy who worships a pet ferret which subsequently disposes of the boy's despised female guardian. "The Open Window" turns upon a frightening practical joke. Like William Hope Hodgson, Saki died in the World War I.

A number of British writers famous for other achievements nevertheless contributed important work to the supernatural field. An outstanding and unsettling story from prolific Anglo-Indian writer Rudyard Kipling is "The Mark of the Beast," in which a foolish Englishman profanes an Indian temple and is transformed by its leper guardian into a werewolf. Best known for his stories about private detective Sherlock Holmes, Arthur Conan Doyle wrote in a variety of genres, including the supernatural. One of his most memorable contributions to this field is "The Captain of the 'Pole Star.'" The story of a ship sailing through the Arctic winter and commanded by a captain who longs for his dead fiancé, it achieves a chilling unity of setting and theme.

Several other British writers are known to readers for one or two works only. In "The Seventh Man," about a party of six desperate men who sense that there is a seventh among them, Arthur Quiller-Couch wrote a story of the Arctic as striking as Doyle's. During his short life Richard Middleton produced only a handful of stories, among them the humorous and frequently reprinted story "The Ghost Ship" and the shocking "On the Brighton Road." By contrast W. W. Jacobs lived a long and productive literary life but is remembered solely for "The Monkey's Paw." This story's carefully paced narrative and its theme—the terrible price to be paid for challenging fate—make it one of the best of any genre in the language. In "How Love Came to Professor Guildea," Robert S. Hichens wrote of an emotionally sterile academic haunted by a love-sick and apparently imbecilic spirit. Although his writing career extended to mid-century, Oliver Onions produced his best-known work, the novella *The Beckoning Fair One*, in 1911. A carefully paced study of a writer fatally possessed by his own creation, it has been rated one of the classic works of the supernatural.

America at the Beginning of the Nineteenth Century

The two most important writers of supernatural fiction in the United States around the beginning of the nineteenth century were Ambrose Bierce and Robert W. Chambers. A veteran of the U.S. Civil War turned journalist, Bierce produced stories and sketches ranging from the sardonic to the cruel to the horrifying. His collection *Tales of Soldiers and Civilians* (1891; also known as *In the Midst of Life*, 1898) includes the classic and frequently reprinted stories "An Occurrence at Owl Creek Bridge" and "The Damned Thing." The former re-creates the final desperate fantasy of a hanged man, while the latter deals chillingly with a bloodthirsty but invisible carnivore. "The Death of Halprin Frayser" is a maddeningly convoluted story of incest and murder from beyond the grave—a necrophilial mixture so disquieting that Bierce may not have been able to deal with it more directly. A tired and embittered man, Bierce disappeared in Mexico in late 1913, ostensibly on his way to report on the Mexican revolution.

One of Bierce's most haunting stories is "An Inhabitant of Carcosa" in which the narrator awakens in a ruined city and only gradually realizes that he has long been dead and that the ruins are those of his beloved city. This story was to influence the younger American writer Robert W. Chambers, who incorporated the dreamlike Carcosa into several of the stories in his landmark collection *The King in Yellow* (1895).

Included in *The King in Yellow* are five fantastic stories that display a dreamlike—or more accurately nightmarish—logic, most of them involving a play that drives readers mad. Perhaps the most effective story in the collection is "The Repairer of Reputations," an unsettling amalgam of themes and ingredients. Set in what was then the future—the United States in 1920—it posits a benevolent dictatorship in which suicide has been institutionalized. Narrating the story is a dilettante who believes that his cousin is heir to an American monarchy and who plots to usurp the throne and serve the King in Yellow. There are clear indications that the narrator is mad, and yet the apparently accurate details of the narrative are themselves so suggestive that the issue is unclear. Unfortunately Chambers wrote little else in this vein, and the rest of his vast output has been forgotten.

Two highly esteemed American mainstream writers from this period produced notable ghost stories. These were Henry James and Edith Wharton, friends and mutual admirers who spent much of their time abroad and whose works were influenced by English and European models. James wrote the most ambiguous and thus most debated (if not most read) work of supernatural fiction in the language, the novella *The Turn of the Screw* (1898). Equally haunting are such stories as "The Jolly Corner," in which a figure much like James himself returns from a long period abroad to confront his double—who never left home. Edith Wharton's most striking stories of the genre are "Afterward" and "Pomegranate Seed," both psychologically acute studies of married relationships threatened from beyond the grave.

Other American writers of the supernatural from this period include Ralph Adams Cram and F. Marion Crawford. Cram was an authority on gothic architecture and became an important architect himself. His single collection, rich in European color, is *Black Spirits and White* (1895), and its most notable story is "The Dead Valley," about a malevolent piece of landscape that anticipates similar works by Algernon Blackwood.

Like Chambers, F. Marion Crawford wrote prolifically in other veins but is remembered almost exclusively for his few supernatural works. Crawford's most important collection was *Wandering Ghosts* (1911; published in Great Britain as *Uncanny Tales*), which included "For the Blood Is the Life," an atmospheric and frequently reprinted vampire story. "The Upper Berth" is an atypically restrained story about the haunted berth of a steamship.

Great Britain Between the Wars

The period after World War I found a number of prominent British writers specializing wholly or in part in supernatural fiction. By this time a number of themes had become standard: ghosts, haunted houses, vampires, werewolves, and so on. Readers knew what to expect from stories on such themes, and writers (and the periodicals and publishers for whom they worked) were able to tailor their stories to the public's expectations. As always, however, the most creative among them were able to breath new life into what had become old formulas.

A prominent exemplar of this trend was the urbane and highly prolific E. F. Benson, whose career began before the war. Many of Benson's supernatural nature stories recall the visionary works of Algernon Blackwood, although they lack the sense of personal belief that distinguishes Blackwood at his best. "The Man Who Went Too Far" involves Pan and "The Temple" an ancient ruin in Cornwall; both recall similar works by Arthur Machen, although once again minus the intensity of the earlier writer. Benson is perhaps most familiar to readers of the supernatural for "Mrs. Amworth," one of the best vampire stories ever written. Several other, perhaps more original stories such as "Caterpillars" (1912) feature strikingly loathsome crawling creatures—in the case of "Caterpillars" as begetters of disease.

Another prolific writer, H. Russell Wakefield, suffered much the same fate as Benson—to have been born too late to help shape the genre at which he so clearly excelled. Wakefield's best works include two noted haunted house stories, "The Red Lodge" (based on the writer's personal experience) and the dramatically brief "Blind Man's Buff." "He Cometh and He Passeth By" includes a character based on the infamous occult practitioner Aleister Crowley. Wakefield continued writing until 1961, but his most representative works were produced much earlier.

Throughout this period a few highly individualistic British writers produced works so unusual that it is difficult to fit them comfortably into any tradition. The most outstanding was Walter de la Mare, who wrote frequently for or about children, often in the form of novels and poetry. One of his best and best-known stories is "Seaton's Aunt," an ambiguous and disturbing study of psychological vampirism worthy of Henry James. "Miss Jemima" describes a young girl who avoids the fate described by Le Fanu in "The Child That Went with the Fairies." In "The House" Mr. Asprey takes one last look around the house from which he is being evicted; only gradually does the reader realize that Asprey is dying and that the house is his life.

Another original figure was John Metcalfe, who produced troublingly ambiguous stories that often defy logical explanation. "The Double Admiral," for instance, involves a retired and ailing Navy man who sets out with two friends to investigate a mysterious island that he insists lies just on the horizon. Yet the party never reaches its goal; instead, they pass another boat very much like their own, at which point the admiral dies. Suddenly and inexplicably the party finds itself sailing back toward land, where subsequently the admiral—or is it his double?—is found to be very much alive, and joins them to discuss a most disturbing dream.

Although he spent the years after World War II in Hollywood as a screenwriter, John Collier was born in Great Britain and produced his most memorable work before the war. His stories recall Saki's in their brevity and urbanity. Typical is "Evening Primrose," in which a young man attempting to live in a department store after hours discovers that he is not alone.

America Between the Wars

Although Edward Lucas White apparently wrote many of his stories before World War I, most were published later in *Lukundoo and Other Stories* (1927). The powerful title story—detailing a physiologically grotesque instance of retribution upon an explorer in Africa—is often reprinted. Stranger still are "The Snout," about a baboon-headed dwarf who collects artistic representations of those similarly afflicted, and "Amina," about a race of were-beings in Persia. White claimed that many of his vivid stories had their origins in the nightmares from which he suffered all his life.

The major American writer of supernatural fiction in the post-World War I period was H. P. Lovecraft, a reclusive writer who nevertheless maintained many friendships by correspondence. Lovecraft was fascinated by the past and cultivated an archaic, adjective-rich style that many readers find tiresome. Initially influenced by Lord Dunsany, he in turn influenced many of his contemporaries and successors.

Lovecraft's major contribution to supernatural literature is the "Cthulhu Mythos," a pantheon of imaginary beings inspired to some extent by Dunsany's more benign creations. Introduced in the story "The Call of Cthulhu" and elaborated in such stories as "The Dunwich Horror" and "The Shadow out of Time," the mythos is an imaginative reconstruction of history that posits the existence of malignant entities—Yog-Sothoth, Azathoth, Nyarlathotep, and the like—driven from our planet in ancient times but eternally striving to gain reentry. Like the protagonists of M. R. James's stories, Lovecraft's characters are forever stumbling upon some abominable "truth"—to their detriment.

There were few outlets for horror or fantasy fiction in the United States during this period, and Lovecraft and similar writers found themselves consigned to low-paying, sometimes poorly produced markets such as the magazine *Weird Tales*. The result was that supernatural fiction was cut off from the development of "mainstream" fiction in the United States, to the ultimate detriment of both camps.

Fellow writers August Derleth and Donald Wandrei were so impressed with H. P. Lovecraft's work that they founded Arkham Press with the purpose of preserving his works in book form. The press's first volume was the collection *The Outsider and Others* (1939), regarded as a landmark in the history of supernatural fiction. Arkham went on to publish a number of significant works, including many more Lovecraft volumes, but the press's very success among a small if avid readership further isolated what was becoming a distinct genre. Dozens of other writers—including Derleth himself—subsequently took up Lovecraft's rich and suggestive mythical framework for one or more stories, but, like the imitators of M. R. James, they seldom produced memorable work.

Four other writers—Clark Ashton Smith, Robert E. Howard, Seabury Quinn, and Henry S. Whitehead—were also closely identified with *Weird Tales*. Clark Ashton Smith wrote several series of darkly fantastic tales set in such mythical locales as Hyperborea and Zothique, realms evoked with the fervor but not the skill of Poe and Shiel. Robert E. Howard wrote adventure stories in a more robust, straightforward mode—a subgenre that would come to be known as "sword-and-sorcery"—and is remembered primarily for his larger-than-life character Conan, a prehistoric adventurer. Like Lovecraft, Howard was to be exploited by other writers anxious to adopt his themes and complete the stories he left unfinished at his early death. Seabury Quinn produced a long series of colorful but crude stories and novels about occult detective Jules de Grandin.

Standing somewhat apart from these three in terms of literary quality was Henry S. Whitehead. Whitehead wrote stories of West Indian voodoo based on long experience in the Virgin Islands, including several—"Passing of a God" and "Cassius"—reminiscent of White's "Lukundoo" and apparently based on similar folkloric material.

Late in the 1930's Fritz Leiber initiated a series of earthy, light-hearted heroic fantasies with "Two Sought Adventure" (later retitled "The Jewels in the Forest"). Featuring two characters named Fafhrd and the Gray Mouser, the story and several sequels appeared in the magazine *Unknown*, a short-lived competitor to *Weird Tales*. Leiber revived the series after the war, and it stands in interesting contrast to Robert E. Howard's cruder series.

The Later Twentieth Century

The outstanding writer of short supernatural fiction in postwar Great Britain was probably Robert Aickman, who called his psychologically rich works "strange stories." Although a few fall into recognizable categories—the award-winning "Pages from a Young Girl's Journal," for instance, is about an initiation into vampirism—most resemble John Metcalfe's works in refusing to provide easy answers. The outstanding example is perhaps "The Trains," in which two girls lodging in a strange house near a railway experience a series of disorienting and wholly inexplicable events. In "Ringing the Changes" a recently married couple discover that the bells disturbing their honeymoon are awakening the dead.

Aickman's first collection was *We Are for the Dark* (1951), which he wrote with Elizabeth Jane Howard. Howard would subsequently establish a reputation as a highly regarded mainstream novelist, but one of the stories she contributed to this volume—"Three Miles Up," about a party of boaters on a canal who suddenly and frighteningly discover that they are no longer landlocked—equals Aickman's best. Like Howard, a number of other mainstream British writers produced memorable supernatural stories from time to time. These include Graham Greene, Elizabeth Bowen, Muriel Spark, and John Fowles.

Two other prolific and widely read British writers—Ramsey Campbell and Clive Barker—have worked largely within the supernatural genre, although the visceral content of their stories shows a clear American influence. Campbell has written many novels, although his flat style works most effectively in the claustrophobic stories collected in such volumes as *The Height of the Scream* (1976) and *Dark Companions* (1982). Like Campbell, Clive Barker has frequently utilized urban settings, most notably in his *Books of Blood* (1984-1985; 6 volumes). One of the most memorable stories collected here is "The Midnight Meat Train," in which a New York subway train is utilized to supply human carcasses to the "City Fathers" living far below the surface. Despite his grotesque subject matter, Barker writes with a bright and fluid style.

British writer Angela Carter drew inspiration from sources as disparate as fairy tales and surrealism, producing a fantastic mixture displayed in such collections as the appropriately titled *Fireworks: Nine Profane Pieces* (1974). Her most famous story is "The Company of Wolves," in which a girl who clearly grasps the subtext of the fairy tale of Little Red Riding-Hood eagerly climbs into bed with the wolf.

Prolific American writer Ray Bradbury has been active in a number of genres, but his reputation rests on his science fiction and fantasy—categories that in Bradbury's case frequently overlap. Bradbury began publishing in the mid-1930's, hitting his stride with *The Illustrated Man* (1951) and *The October Country* (1955). Stories such as "The Small Assassin," about a pregnant woman who senses the evil nature of the baby she is carrying, display Bradbury's pessimistic side, but his later works are gentler, imbued with nostalgia for a kind of Midwestern American golden age.

The most famous figure in modern American supernatural fiction is Stephen King, a phenomenally popular author who has pioneered a rebirth of public interest in the genre. While King writes primarily in longer forms, several of his American contemporaries and near-contemporaries—T. E. D. Klein, Thomas Ligotti, and Dennis Etchison—have excelled at the short story. Klein's story "The Events at Poroth Farm" is indebted to both H. P. Lovecraft and Arthur Machen and was expanded into the outstanding novel *The Ceremonies* (1984). His collection *Dark Gods* (1985) reveals the same influences, making him one of the few writers to have profited from exposure to Lovecraft. Etchison's stories in *The Dark Country* (1982) reflect the contemporary American landscape of highways and strip malls and drifters. Justly famous is "It Only Comes out at Night," a nightmarish account of late-night events at a rest stop. Ligotti's densely poetic and surreal stories have appeared in *Songs of a Dead Dreamer* (1989) and *Noctuary* (1994).

In the decades after World War II several prominent mainstream American writers produced outstanding supernatural stories, bridging to some extent the gap that had arisen before the war. These include Paul Bowles, who has acknowledged his indebtedness to folktales, hallucinogenic drugs, and his own subconscious. Among his most effective stories are "You Are Not I" and "Allal," both involving the transfer of a protagonist's personality into another body, in the latter story that of a snake.

Argentinean Jorge Luis Borges was undoubtedly one of the preeminent fantasists of the nineteenth century, a prolific writer obsessed with mazes and mirrors. Borges's imaginative universe was vast—he drew inspiration from sources as disparate as *The Arabian Nights' Entertainments* and the work of H. P. Lovecraft—and his influence has been worldwide. Although he began writing fiction in the 1930's, his best works appeared in the following decades, and he did not reach an English-speaking audience until the 1960's. In one of his most famous stories, "Tlön, Uqbar, Orbis Tertius," an entry in a unique volume of an encyclopedia suggests the existence of another, exotic world—one that henceforward begins to infiltrate the reader's. "The Aleph" concerns a tiny iridescent sphere, accidentally discovered in a cellar, that encompasses infinity. "Everything and Nothing" deals with one of Borges's favorite themes, the mystery of identity, in the form of a confrontation between William Shakespeare and God. *Manual de zoología fantástica* (1957; with Margarita Guerrero; *The Imaginary Zoo*, 1969, revised as *El libro de los seres imaginarios*, 1967, *The Book of Imaginary Beings*, 1969) is a fantastic and delightful bestiary.

Grove Koger

BIBLIOGRAPHY

Barron, Neil, ed. *Fantasy Literature: A Reader's Guide*. New York: Garland, 1990. An extensive guide to primary and secondary works, most of them annotated.

Bleiler, E. F. *The Guide to Supernatural Fiction*. Kent, Ohio: The Kent State University Press, 1983. Bleiler's guide describes 1,775 books published from the mid-eighteenth century to 1960 and concludes with author, title, and motif indexes.

________, ed. *Supernatural Fiction Writers: Fantasy and Horror*. New York: Charles Scribner's Sons, 1985. A two-volume collection of substantial survey articles covering nearly 150 writers. Each entry concludes with a bibliography.

Cavaliero, Glen. *The Supernatural and English Fiction*. Oxford, England: Oxford University Press, 1995. A survey from the rise of the gothic to important late twentieth century figures. Includes notes and a select bibliography of supernatural novels, collections, and critical works.

De Camp, L. Sprague. *Literary Swordsmen and Sorcerers: The Makers of Heroic Fantasy*. Sauk City, Wis.: Arkham House, 1976. A noted writer in the field, De Camp provides informal essays on several writers discussed above, including Dunsany, Lovecraft, Howard, Smith, and Leiber.

Joshi, S. T. *The Weird Tale: Arthur Machen, Lord Dunsany, Algernon Blackwood, M. R. James, Ambrose Bierce, H. P. Lovecraft*. Austin: University of Texas Press, 1990. Joshi's essays on six key writers are trenchant, although his judgments often differ from those of other critics. Also included are primary and secondary bibliographies.

Sullivan, Jack. *Elegant Nightmares: The English Ghost Story from Le Fanu to Blackwood*. Athens: Ohio University Press, 1978. Besides the authors named in his title, Sullivan also discusses M. R. James and his imitators. Sullivan concludes with notes and a generous bibliography of "ghostly fiction" and secondary sources.

History of Short Fiction

SHORT FICTION IN ANTIQUITY

The urge to tell stories, and the concomitant desire to listen to them, are ancient and universal in human beings. Because stories are pleasurable, they require no motive beyond that of entertainment, but for the same reason they are extremely useful in celebrating the past, in inculcating moral principles, in explaining religious doctrine, and in various other endeavors. As far back as narrative storytelling can be traced, it has been used for such purposes, as well as for pure pleasure.

A story told for the purpose of keeping alive the memory of past events—a purpose that predates literacy—will inevitably be altered in the process of retelling as the teller perceives ways of improving it. One may doubt that it really took anyone ten years to return home from the Trojan War, as it took Odysseus, or that such a person was diverted and detained by supernatural beings such as Circe and Calypso, but there probably was something like a Trojan War, and there may well have been somebody like an Odysseus who had great troubles arriving home again afterward. Because scholars now attempt to preserve carefully the distinctions between history and fiction with a historical setting, they tend to regard the *Odyssey* (c. 800 B.C.E.; English translation, 1616) as a good story but as bad history. Such generic distinctions would not have occurred to audiences in antiquity. Long after Thucydides, the first rigorous historian, wrote his *Historia tou Peloponnesiacou polemou*, 431-404 B.C.E. (*History of the Peloponnesian War*, 1550), storytellers saw no harm in altering history for artistic purposes. They altered freely the kinds of facts now regarded as worthy of respect; they were much less likely to tamper with the legendary characters of their heroes. Homer was more interested in preserving the truth of Odysseus's shrewdness and resourcefulness than in the chronology of his travels.

What the modern world regards as literature—the very word implies writing—invariably has its origins in an oral culture. Stories existed long before anyone devised a way to write them down. Even after a people become literate, they are much more likely to use their newfound language for nonliterary purposes, most often for business; later, they may begin to write down their poetry and fiction. Because people today think of "real" literature as written, they often suppose the efforts of preliterate people to be primitive and unworthy of attention. The modern preliterates with whom people are familiar, after all, are young children and the culturally subordinated. The idea of preliterates including sophisticated artists and mature audiences now seems odd—but it is nevertheless true.

Folktales

Probably the earliest form of fiction is the folktale in its various forms, including ballad and folk song. A folktale is a short narrative that is transmitted orally, with various tellers introducing modifications as the tale is passed along to a contemporary audience and down to succeeding generations. It is clearly impossible to come into direct contact with this oldest form of narrative as it existed in antiquity, but it is possible to know with considerable assurance what ancient folktales were like. For one thing, folktales still persist; for another, a comparison of extant folktales from around the globe reveals striking similarities and suggests that paleolithic audiences doubtless enjoyed the same fictive themes and patterns that continue to engross their descendants.

Folktales are popular stories that can be understood by most people in a society, whatever their social status and level of specialized knowledge. Though folktales in pure form are difficult to find in ancient writing, they are frequently embedded within seemingly historical narratives. This is true of two tales from ancient Egypt. The tale of Sinuhe (c. 1900 B.C.E.) involves the adventures of an Egyptian who is exiled from his native country. As Donald B. Redford points out in *Egypt, Canaan, and Israel in Ancient Times* (1992), though the story of Sinuhe reflects plausible historical conditions, it is not certain whether or not it is fictional. In any event, the story of Sinuhe, a high-level bureaucrat at the royal court who flees after the ruler he has served is killed, goes off to the desert, where he lives and prospers among less 'cultured' peoples, and then triumphantly returns to Egypt in old age, welcomed by the new king, embodies motifs of adventure and wish-fulfillment often to be found wherever stories are told.

The story of Wen-Amon (eleventh century B.C.E.) is, or appears to be, an autobiographical account of an Egyptian merchant who attempts to trade with the nations of the eastern Mediterranean coast. This short narrative contains a distinct historical background, as Egypt has declined in political power, and the name of Egypt no longer inspires awe in its inhabitants. Wen-Amon wanders forlornly, begging the Prince of Byblos, Zakar-Baal, to give him some wood to bring back to Egypt. The prince finally consents, but not before reminding Wen-Amon that the mountain slopes are littered with the tombs of former Egyptian traders. Wen-Amon finally returns home, though the final parts of the story have not survived in manuscript. The Wen-Amon story's idea of travel and return, combined with the suspense as to its outcome and the vulnerability of its protagonists, is a splendid example of how narrative works in deploying concrete incidents that can be read in the light of general meanings.

Another interesting early narrative is the story of Idrimi (c. 1400 B.C.E.), a minor king of the realm called Mitanni or Hanigalbat, located around what is now the border between Syria and Iraq. This story traces the life of an exiled prince who, starting out as a young boy, eventually rallies the support of his people and attains his throne, under the patronage of a more powerful ruler. Although this could well have happened historically, the story also contains folktale elements, such as the theme of the rise of the powerless boy to a position of power. This theme is found through the ancient world—in the stories of the Hebrew leader Moses as an abandoned baby in the bulrushes, of the Akkadian king, Sargon, left in a boat as a baby, of the Roman kings Romulus and Remus, suckled by wolves. All of the above were semi-historical figures for whom folktales filled gaps in their lives that history could not illuminate.

The story of Moses, the young baby endangered by Egyptian persecution of the Hebrews and saved by a benevolent Egyptian princess, is a good illustration of how the Bible is permeated by the folktale genre. Folktale strands persist in the biblical narrative of Moses and the Exodus, often coexisting with far more "sophisticated" modes. The tale of David and Goliath, although embedded in the larger political narrative of David, also has obvious folktale elements. The story of the young boy slaying the giant enemy champion and redeeming his people's fortune has the inspirational air of a story told around the campfire. The idea of the unlikely hero, winning out against all odds, defying the greater strength of the opponent, has an obvious and perennial appeal. It also features the frequent folktale motif of wit winning out over sheer brawn. Not only is the David and Goliath story enjoyed by children today without any linkage to the rest of David's saga, but also it is certainly plausible to think that the David and Goliath story was written as an independent unit and only later connected to the general narrative of David's accomplishments. In other stories, David is a prince, a king, a warrior, just as the adult Moses is a leader and a lawgiver. In the folktalelike stories told about them as children, David and Moses are seemingly ordinary children, placed in grave danger at an early age and rescued only by the hand of God.

In general, folktales are more likely to be told by and about the common people, whereas myths and epics tended, in the ancient world, to pertain to the priestly and warrior classes. This means folktales often are more difficult to preserve; yet what has endured testifies that folktales indeed played a pivotal role in how the ancient world practiced the art of storytelling.

Fairy tales, myths, fables, and legends are forms of folktale distinguishable by their purposes and emphases. In literate cultures, folktales are likely to pass into written form, thus ceasing to be folktales. When Jacob and Wilhelm Grimm, early in the nineteenth century, collected and published the fairy tales with which their name has become synonymous, they were both preserving and destroying the tales in the process. When the tales are written down, they become standardized, they do not change with tellers, and they come to their audiences in a different form. Even a very young child, listening to a parent read a fairy tale, knows that it is coming from the pages of a book. Only since the time of the Brothers Grimm, or roughly a half century earlier in the case of folk ballads, have printed texts competed with and, in most cases, replaced oral transmission. When educated people such as Bishop Thomas Percy, the first great ballad collector, and the Brothers Grimm become involved, folktales become contaminated by the literary culture—much more so in the twentieth century with its radio, television, and recording and playback devices. Children will not listen to grandmother's stories if they can listen to (and watch) video presentations, and her stories will die with her. Meanwhile, the entertainment media choose, reject, and edit folk materials for their own, usually commercial, purposes, a process quite unlike the one that brought the folk material down through the centuries.

Myth

"The narratives of literature," wrote Northrop Frye in *Words with Power: Being a Second Study of "The Bible and Literature"* (1990), "descend historically from myths, or rather from the aggregate of myths we call a mythology." While perhaps too sweeping a generalization, this statement by a major critic demonstrates how important the study of myth has become. Myths are stories about gods, which humans devise to explain creation, existence, death, and natural phenomena of all sorts. From one point of view, myths are religious truths; from another, they are fictions. These viewpoints are often assumed to conflict, although they do not if it is conceded that fictions can convey truths. Some of the most profound truths can perhaps be conveyed only indirectly. It is sometimes alleged that myths recede as scientific explanations of natural phenomena advance.

The Egyptians and the Mesopotamians were the first literate civilizations to produce imaginative tales that were written down as formal narratives. In Egyptian literature, mythic narratives, insofar as they are available to the modern world, existed largely to explain how the gods manifested themselves within nature. For instance, the story of the sun god Ra and his voyaging in both a day boat and a night boat is an explanation of the workings of the solar cycle and the alternation of light and darkness. Myth often has this conceptual, protoscientific side, where stories are used as modes to explain and speculate upon the cosmos. In Egypt as in other cultures, fictions conveyed truths.

The relation between myth and story in Mesopotamian literature is more complicated. Mesopotamia, the once-fertile land between the Tigris and Euphrates rivers in present-day Iraq, produced the first literate civilization in about 3000 B.C.E. Ancient Mesopotamian literature actually comprises several literatures, that of the Sumerians, the earliest literate Mesopotamian people whose language cannot reliably be linked to any other group, and the Akkadians, Babylonians, and Assyrians, all of whom spoke Semitic languages somewhat similar to Hebrew and Arabic. Most of the ancient Mesopotamian narratives that survive are in Akkadian or Babylonian and were unearthed by archaeological digs in the nineteenth and twentieth centuries.

Self-contained, relatively realistic stories like those of Sinuhe and Wen-Amon are rare in Mesopotamian literature. What is more typical is something like the Atrahasis epic. As Thorkild Jacobsen puts it in *The Treasures of Darkness* (1976), this is a story of beginnings, a story of the creation of mankind by the gods. The gods create mankind because they are tired of working and feel exploited by their supervisor-god Enlil. Man will take up the slack of laboring. Man does well at his task, so well that he reproduces a hundredfold, and there are so many men that there is a cacophony of noise, disturbing the rest of the gods. To reduce the noise, the gods send successively, plague, drought, and finally a terrible flood. Atrahasis, a wise man, appeals to the gods to end these torments, but each time his success is followed by a worse natural disaster. Finally, the gods agree to employ demons to reduce the human birthrate, and gods and mankind settle down to an uneasy truce. As in the Egyptian story, narratives are used to explain the ways of nature, but specifically human themes, such as the need for population control, are threaded within the cosmic frame.

Greek myth is, to the modern reader, the best known body of ancient mythology. Greek myths are important to the evolution of the short-story form in that the myths themselves, though constituting a massive body of work, are, in individual terms, not that long. Greek myths served to instruct, to explain, but also to entertain their original audience. This is in line with most ancient narrative, which had a compound purpose, and was for the most part not purely 'artistic' in intent. In the myth of Tantalus, a man of only half-divine parentage is allowed to partake of the food and drink of the gods, only to think that that privilege makes him one of the gods himself. His punishment consists of being imprisoned in the underworld with appealing food and drink seemingly within his reach but perpetually evading his grasp, thus illustrating that human pride cannot accomplish anything on its own, without the good will of the gods. Tantalus's punishment, in itself, illustrates the nature of his misdeed. This short, self-contained tale, even though interrelated to many other stories, involves a limited cast of characters and has a determinate point that the reader may interpret in different ways. Most Greek myths are like this; although displayed against a chronological story of the development of gods, heroes, and men, they are segmented narratives consistent with each other only in a very general way. Different versions provided by different poets and playwrights (Homer and Hesiod, Homer and Aeschylus) may supply very different endings or emphases. The fact that we derive the ordinary word "tantalize" from the story of Tantalus shows how thoroughly the body of Greek mythology has permeated contemporary language and culture; even people who have never read a word of Greek myth have used a word or a concept derived from it. Thus its literary impact remains long after the end of its religious or scientific role.

Greek mythology permeates Western literary forms as far back as they can be perceived, though differently in different genres. Epics, for example, allude to myths, but rather than retell familiar myths they tend to employ mythological characters, with their well-known attributes, to interact in various ways with human characters, as to assist them in crises or thwart them if they turn impious. Thus, in the *Iliad* (c. 800 B.C.E.; English translation, 1567), Achilles's goddess mother Thetis restrains him from imprudent retaliation against Agamemnon, who has appropriated a woman whom Achilles earlier gained as a prize during the Trojan War, while in the *Odyssey*, the sea god Poseidon frustrates Odysseus's attempt to reach his homeland of Ithaca after the war because the latter has blinded Poseidon's son Polyphemus the Cyclops. In later romances, the gods continue to perform such functions, less often by direct intervention in human shape, more often through the prayers of the hero or heroine, characteristically directed to icons in sacred places.

The first collector of Greco-Roman myths to endow them with high literary polish was the Roman poet Ovid in his *Metamorphoses* (c. 8 B.C.E.; English translation, 1567). This work weaves together a large number of more or less unrelated stories in one continuous narrative. He begins with an account of the ordering of a primal Chaos and continues by describing an early golden age from which the earth has declined, after which he proceeds to the doings of the Olympian gods. In the eleventh of his fifteen books, Ovid turns his attention to "history," especially the legendary events leading to the establishment of the Roman Empire under Augustus in Ovid's own time. In unifying this disparate material, he used the technique of seizing upon a frequent, though not inevitable, feature of the old myths—the transformations or metamorphoses of characters into other forms of being: trees, animals, springs of water, and the like. In addition to this thematic unification, Ovid links the myths by associative devices, by stories within stories, and sometimes by quite arbitrary but ingenious transitions. Ovid avoids monotony by a modulation of tone from eloquently grand all the way to quietly informal. Enormously popular in the Middle Ages and Renaissance, Ovid influenced writers of fiction for centuries.

Fables and Parables

Of the ancient narrative forms devised to serve a nonliterary purpose, the fable is perhaps the most ingratiating. The fable is usually short, often features animals that portray human weaknesses and vices, and is told to illustrate a moral truth, which may or may not be explicitly stated at the beginning or end. Fables have been found on Egyptian papyruses, among the birth tales of Buddha, and in Sanskrit literature. The fables best known in the Western world, however, come chiefly from Greece, the earliest known being the story of the hawk and the nightingale in Hesiod's *Erga kai Emerai* (c. 700 B.C.E.; *Works and Days*, 1618). About two centuries later, a slave named Aesop composed fables, according to Herodotus (a Greek historian who himself told wonderful stories, sometimes of dubious factual value). Subsequently, Aesop came to be regarded as the originator of virtually all ancient fables, the charm of which, along with their utility in promoting virtuous and sensible behavior, earned for them a popularity that they have retained throughout the centuries. It is a rare child who does not know the story of the fox and the grapes or that of the dog in the manger. Many proverbs are essentially fables in outline form.

Fables have been cultivated by professional writers since classical times, though Greek and Roman writers were inclined to work them into larger literary contexts, an example being the Roman poet Horace who, as part of his book of satires in the first century B.C.E., gave posterity the story of the town mouse and the country mouse. The medieval Persian poet ʿUbaid Zakani told a cat-and-mouse fable with a satiric twist. A cat, conscience-stricken after eating mice, finds religion. All the mice in the neighborhood rejoice but later find that the cat devours more of them than ever—as a religious duty. Fables persist in Europe in Geoffrey Chaucer's "The Nun's Priest's Tale," and notably in the fables of Jean de La Fontaine and in the characteristically modern ones of James Thurber.

Another type of story with a nonliterary purpose is the parable. The details of a parable, such as Jesus Christ's parable of the laborers in the vineyard, present a moral lesson, usually implicitly but nevertheless pointedly. Parables are common in religious prose around the world; they are, for example, a frequent feature of Hindu scriptures. The famous thirteenth century Persian poet Saʿdi of Shiraz, in his *Gulistan* (1258; *The Rose Garden*, 1806) combines poetry and prose parables. One of the latter tells of a great wrestler who teaches a young protégé all of his holds except one. The overconfident protégé challenges the master to a match, but the latter uses that one hold to throw him. Parables are usually considered a species of allegory, in which the characters and actions make literal sense but point to another, usually moral, level of meaning. As a fictional form, allegory did not otherwise develop very far in antiquity but became extremely popular in the Christian Middle Ages.

Although fables and parables are created for nonliterary purposes, they hold a secure place in the hearts of story lovers. Furthermore, since fables such as Aesop's and the parables of Christ are so well known, many subsequent writers have used them both structurally and allusively in making longer fictional works.

Epic

The Babylonian poem called *Gilgamesh* (c. 2000 B.C.E.; English translation, 1917), based on a Sumerian original, is the earliest work to be called an "epic" by modern literary historians, although it is rather short for an epic. The story of a hero, his self-definition, and his search for immortality, *Gilgamesh* contains a series of episodes that each illustrates a discrete point, though bound together by the overall theme of the epic. The story of how Gilgamesh meets his friend, Enkidu (whose death spurs Gilgamesh's quest for immortality), symbolizes the divide between nature and culture, as Enkidu, a wild man, is enticed into entering the walls of the city through the wiles of a seductive prostitute. This short episode uses narrative to create an impression in the mind of the reader, and can stand on its own despite its emplacement in the larger story.

Modern readers often think of Homer as standing at the beginning of Western literature; anthologies of ancient classics usually begin with those extended heroic narratives, the *Iliad* and the *Odyssey*, traditionally assigned to the blind poet. In an important way, however, the Homeric epics represent the end of a literary tradition, or at least an important turn in the literary road, for they came into being (or at least into the form familiar to posterity) around the time that the Greek alphabet was being devised and Greek literacy was becoming possible. A long oral tradition lies behind these folk epics. They could have been written down not long after they were composed, but initially they were listened to, not read, and they were transmitted orally like any other type of folk narrative.

There are important differences between the kind of story that Homer told and the others mentioned above. Anyone can learn a ballad or song or short fable, but the development of longer oral narratives required the memorization of stories as long as some modern novels. Inevitably, professional performers arose to meet this need. These rhapsodists, as they were called, accomplished the remarkable feat of memorizing whole epics. They would not have been able to achieve these mnemonic feats, however, without the assistance of techniques such as systematic meter and verbal formulas that could be plugged into metrical lines at strategic points. Thus epic narratives were embodied in beautiful rhythms that became available to reading audiences of later times only if they could read Homeric Greek, although skillful translators can imitate the effects of the original poems to a certain extent.

The many repeated lines and phrases and the fixed epithets attached to the names of characters in Greek epics are not affectations or signs of imaginative weakness but essential features both for rhapsodist and audience. Although later "literary" epic poets, such as Vergil, had considerably less need of such devices, the attractiveness of the hexameter line used in the *Iliad* and *Odyssey* led him and other Roman poets to adapt it to Latin, as well as other features originally devised for practical purposes in an oral culture. Vergil wrote his epic, the *Aeneid* (c. 29-19 B.C.E.; English translation, 1553), and expected people to read it, but in an age when people did not often have the privilege of holding that rare and expensive thing, the book, these oral features continued to enhance the memorability of the epic.

The Homeric epics purport to treat of a heroic era several centuries before the time of their composition (around the eighth century B.C.E.). Scholars disagree over whether the same poet actually composed both poems, but each is, in its own way, a narrative masterpiece. The *Iliad* focuses on a struggle of wills between two stubborn Greek kings, the commander in chief, Agamemnon, and the great warrior Achilles, whose refusal to take part jeopardizes the effort to seize Troy and return Helen, Agamemnon's sister-in-law, to her Greek husband. The story develops systematically to the point at which the Trojan prince Hector's killing of Achilles' close friend Patroclus and subsequent dishonoring of his body drives Achilles to exact revenge on Hector. The fact that the *Iliad* does not deal at all comprehensively with the war but ends with the Trojan king Priam's reclaiming of his son's body from Achilles suggests the likelihood of other epics detailing other aspects of the conflict, especially its climax, which the *Iliad* stops short of recounting. Indeed, fragments of Trojan War epics from a somewhat later period do exist.

Whereas the *Iliad* focuses on the events of a few days outside the gates of Troy, the *Odyssey* covers ten years and takes its hero all over the Mediterranean world. It too is admirably constructed, paralleling the simultaneous experiences of son and father, Telemachus and Odysseus, then allowing Odysseus to describe his decade of adventures to a friendly people with whom he had taken temporary refuge, and finally bringing Odysseus and Telemachus together to plan and execute retaliation against the suitors of the former's wife (Penelope), who have invaded Odysseus's house and besieged her relentlessly during his absence. The device of allowing Odysseus to tell his own, often improbable, story serves the important purpose of preserving Homer from charges of lying—a handy protection that other writers of fiction were not slow to imitate. From the reader's perspective, Odysseus's narrative, covering four of the twenty-four books, fills in the prior adventures that the *in medias res* beginning (that is, beginning in the middle of things) has left hanging; it also delays and thus enhances the climax.

The Homeric epics, though much longer than *Gilgamesh*, follow the earlier work's pattern of short episodic adventures within a larger narrative frame. Even though the *Odyssey* is unified by the theme of Odysseus's quest to return home, each episode, each individual strand in his adventures, is self-contained, and it may be speculated that characters such as the Cyclops or Circe originally existed in legend outside Homer's narrative and might have been brought in by the poet to add color to his hero's narrative. These semiembedded narratives keep the reader motivated as the suspense of Odysseus's ultimate fate is played out. In the *Iliad*, the episode in Book 10 involving the young, inexperienced hero Dolon, who is outwitted by two far more veteran heroes, Odysseus and Diomedes, has no overall relevance to the outcome of the work, yet is invaluable in its study of character and motivation. Swift-footed Dolon volunteers to spy for the Trojans on the Greeks, his motive being to steal the horses of the great Achilles. Dolon, an insignificant man, is killed by the two Greeks on the spot, and his death is not given any great weight; and yet the insignificant and the great here come into contact and complement each other, setting the tone for much future story writing in its braiding of the ordinary and the extraordinary. Another aspect of Homeric epic that performs this joining of the mundane and the majestic is the epic simile, in which the feelings or doings of a warrior on the battlefield are likened to a motif in nature or in ordinary life. For instance, at the beginning of Book 10 of the *Iliad* the psychological tumult of the king, Agamemnon, is compared to hail or a raging thunderstorm. Two realms—nature in all its unpredictability and the uncertainty of the military leader in the midst of battle—are brought together in one phrase to shed light upon each other. This has always been one of the roles of short fiction—to contrast and bring into dialogue disparate spheres of existence.

The lost Greek epics include a cycle on the legends of Thebes (given dramatic treatment by the Greek tragedians) and a *Persica*, or epic on the Persian Wars of the early fifth century B.C.E., by Choerilus of Samos. Extant is a third century *Argonautica* by Apollonius Rhodius, an Alexandrian Greek whose narrative of Jason and the Argonauts takes the gods and religion much less seriously and puts a new emphasis on love, relatively unimportant in Homeric epic but central in the romances to come.

Roman writers imitated the Greek achievement in epic as in other forms of both literary and nonliterary art. The earliest original Roman writer of an epic, Gnaeus Naevius, composed an epic on the First Punic War (254-241 B.C.E.), in which he served as a young man, but only a few lines survive. Quintus Ennius wrote a more ambitious epic on the history of Rome up to his time, the *Annales* (c. 250-205 B.C.E.; *Annals*) in eighteen books, of which about six hundred lines survive. The most important Roman epic poet was Vergil (70-19 B.C.E.), who took as his subject the legendary career of Aeneas, one of the numerous sons of King Priam, who gathered remnants of the defeated Trojans and set out for Latium, the site of the future Rome. The *Aeneid* is in twelve books, the first six of which have been called Vergil's *Odyssey*, or account of Aeneas's journey to Latium, while the last six resemble the *Iliad* in concentrating on the war that Aeneas and his companions must wage to secure this site of future Roman glory. Epics commonly celebrate the supposed virtues of a people, and Aeneas embodies the Roman ideal of piety and civic duty. Vergil paints an unforgettable picture of a man who relishes war not at all but is obliged to prosecute one. Vergil would doubtless have been amazed at the influence that Book 4 of his *Aeneid* (his story of the Carthaginian queen, Dido, who expressed her love for Aeneas, and Aeneas's dutiful rejection of her offer of herself and share of her African kingdom) had on subsequent fiction.

After Vergil, the most important Roman epics are those of Lucan (39-65 C.E.), whose *Bellum civile* (60-65 C.E.; *Pharsalia*, 1614) deals with the civil war between Julius Caesar and Gnaeus Pompey, and Statius, who went back to the Theban legends for his *Thebais* (c. 90; *Thebiad*, 1767). After these poets of what is called the Silver Age of Roman literature, the heroic ideal passed into prose romances as indicated below.

The folk epic reappeared in other cultures for centuries thereafter, usually with many features similar to those of the Homeric epics. The Old English *Beowulf*, composed around the eighth century, seems to derive in large measure from fairy tales like the *Odyssey*; the Old French *Chanson de Roland* (eleventh century; *The Song of Roland*, c. 1100) resembles the *Iliad* particularly in its magnification of a relatively small martial incident, in this case one from the conflicts between Carolingian barons, into heroic proportions; the German *The Nibelungenlied* (c. 1200), like both Homeric epics, shows signs of a long development from earlier oral narratives. All these epics memorialize feats of a heroic age from the perspective of a people who are tacitly confessing that the era of heroes has ended. Between these epics and the Scandinavian sagas, the chief difference is formal: The latter are normally in prose rather than in verse. Of the many sagas, one of the best is the Icelandic *Grettis saga* (*The Saga of Grettir*, 1869), which dates from about 1300 in its present form. It incorporates many folklore motifs, including the hero's battles with ghosts and trolls. Literary epics generally persist longer in a culture, with John Milton's *Paradise Lost* (1674) arguably the last great epic in English.

Eastern peoples also have their epics. Iranians, for example, treasure the *Shahnamah* of Firdusi, who composed his epic around the year 1010. It begins with the creation of the universe and proceeds through forty thousand lines to the rise and subsequent glories of the Iranian people. The great epics of India, the *Rāmāyana* (c. 350 B.C.E.; *Ramayana*, 1870-1874) and *Māhabhārata* (c. 400 B.C.E.-200 C.E.; *Mahabharata*, 1834), while resembling the Homeric ones in a number of respects, are, unlike the *Iliad* and *Odyssey*, sacred books. Only about one fifth of the *Mahabharata* is taken up by the main story, but the narrative portions are still longer than the two great Greek epics combined. Long as such works are, they incorporate many episodes and incidents, which are in effect short stories.

Comic and Satiric Fiction

Satire, which ridicules individuals, institutions, and sometimes other literary works for the sake of promoting better ones, also took narrative form in antiquity. Often, satire seems clearly allied with fables and parables in that the story is not told for its own sake, but some satirists are accomplished storytellers. In fact, Northrop Frye, in his influential *Anatomy of Criticism: Four Essays* (1957), identifies Menippean satire as one of the four characteristic forms that fiction has taken in Western literature. It is named for a Greek writer of the third century B.C.E., Menippus, whose works influenced a succession of Greek and Roman writers. The *Saturae Menippeae* of the Roman author Marcus Terentius Varro (116-27 B.C.E.) exists only in fragmentary form. It is the work of a moralist who viewed Roman life critically in the tumultuous era leading to the establishment of the Empire. The chief Greek follower of Menippus, Lucian (c. C.E. 120-after 180), wrote *Alēthōn diēgēmatōn* (*A True History*, 1634), which parodies travelers' tales, including the *Odyssey*, by describing a voyage that begins on the sea, continues in the sky, and even visits the Elysian Fields. Doubtfully ascribed to Lucian is *Onos* (*The Ass*, 1684), important as the basis of Apuleius's masterpiece described below.

Satyricon (c. 60; *The Satyricon*, 1694), by Petronius (c. 20 C.E.-c. 66), is a long prose narrative interspersed with verse; only a substantial fragment survives. It is regarded as the ancestor of the picaresque fiction that arose in sixteenth century Spain, spread quickly over Europe, and remains viable today. Encolpus, the narrator, and Ascyltus are two young men wandering about the Italian peninsula living by their wits. In the most famous section, that of Trimalchio's dinner party, the two take part in an elaborately ridiculous party given by a tasteless rich man. In the Trimalchio episode, Petronius is not primarily a satirist but a devotee of the art of purely entertaining fiction—an activity that professional writers of the ancient world scorned. Not only is the party, marked by a drunken brawl and even a dogfight, one of the liveliest works of the Latin Silver Age but also Petronius even manages to incorporate two ghost stories for good measure.

A century after Petronius, Rome produced its other genius of comic prose, Lucius Apuleius (c. 124-probably after 170). His *Metamorphoses* (second century; *The Golden Ass*, 1566) alone among Latin prose narratives has survived the centuries complete. Like so many Roman artistic achievements, it imitates an earlier Greek work, but Apuleius's adaptation is superior to its original. The hero, Lucius, fascinated by sorcery and enchantment, is by a miscalculation transformed into an ass, in which shape he remains for most of the eleven books. Apuleius greatly expands the episodes of his source and adds numerous stories of his own: adventure stories, tragedies, fairy tales, erotica—an enormous variety of types. Sometimes they support the main narrative, sometimes they are tonally inappropriate; they are there because Apuleius recognized them as good stories. He missed no opportunity to add action and surprises, and he excelled at vivid and dramatic details. Of the interpolated narratives, his story of Cupid and Psyche is the most celebrated. Psyche is a woman so beautiful that the jealous goddess Venus orders Cupid to make her fall in love with an ugly creature, but instead Psyche and Cupid become lovers. After a string of adventures brought on by Venus's vindictiveness, Psyche, deified, becomes Cupid's bride. Here Apuleius has reworked mythological material freely to produce a highly original narrative.

Even when incongruous in their context, Apuleius's stories increase the pleasure of the literary journey and prolong the suspense. Eventually, Lucius finds an opportunity to eat roses, the one act that will return him to human form. As a whole, *The Golden Ass* foreshadows the rogue or picaresque novel, but in its particulars this work can be seen as one of the earliest collections of short—and not so short—stories. Because Apuleius could in his time exploit comically the mythological characters and motifs that Ovid, an exploiter himself by temperament, still took with relative seriousness, he created a highly original fictive work that would open new vistas for later satirists and comic writers.

Romance

Epic was "displaced"—to use W. P. Ker's term (*Epic and Romance*, 1897)—by romance in the medieval world, but the distinction between them sometimes blurs, especially in the transitional romances of the early Christian era. The hero of a romance is likely to rival the epic warrior in such traits as strength, courage, and resourcefulness, but he is unlikely to serve as an idealized representative of a people or nation in the manner of, say, Vergil's Aeneas. Rather, he is a private individual whose adventures do not culminate in the establishment of a state or the winning of a war but in winning a beautiful heroine—a character not generally found in epic. The titles of the early Greek romances–*Chaereas and Callirhoe* (second century C.E.; English translation, 1764), *Leucippe and Clitophon* (second century C.E.; *The Loves of Clitophon and Leucippe*, 1597), *Daphnis and Chloë* (third century C.E.; English translation, 1587)—signify the emergence of a female character equal in interest to the male hero. Although Vergil might accurately have titled the fourth book of his epic "Aeneas and Dido," Dido disappears thereafter, only turning up briefly in the underworld after her suicide. Dido is not a woman to win or to please but an obstacle to be overcome. Although Odysseus does strive to be reunited with Penelope, neither Homer nor his audience would have dreamed of reducing even this less serious of his epics to "Odysseus and Penelope." The later romances blend the beauty and passionate spirit of Dido with the loyalty and perseverance of Penelope to make heroines who become the be-all and end-all of the heroes' existence.

Whereas epics perpetuate legends and old traditions and thus are bound in certain respects by what their devisers understood as history, romances are historical only in the manner of their modern counterparts; the authors are free to invent characters and adventures to suit their plot and, with the same end in mind, to devise fictional roles for their "historical" characters. Insofar as romancers work clear of allegiance to legend and create an unhistorical milieu, they create a distinctive genre. Another important difference is formal: the Greco-Roman epics are in verse—the literary form of the time—while the early romances are in prose.

The surviving Greek romances, which, in suitable modern translations, have finally been gathered conveniently by B. P. Reardon (*Collected Ancient Greek Novels*, 1989), feature lovers who are buffeted about in an alien world. Though usually of noble blood, they are often reared as foundlings. The heroine is likely to retain her virginity through a succession of captivities by pirates, lustful potentates, and others yet more savage. These romances' concern with chastity often seems no more than deference to respectability of the sort that constrained Victorian novelists.

In the face of Fortune, both hero and heroine often remain passive, and Fortune remains stubbornly bad until the happy ending. Prescient dreams, strange coincidences, presumed deaths (later explained away either naturally or supernaturally), and escapes from seemingly impossible predicaments abound. The hero and heroine are always ready to die rather than confront the prospect of the other's extinction or marriage to someone else. Unlike both epic and satire, romance has no moral or historical lessons to inculcate, but it aspires to spiritual edification in its idealization of character.

Although fragments of earlier Greek romances exist, the first complete specimen is the *Chaereas and Callirhoe* of Chariton. It begins simply and straightforwardly: "My name is Chariton, of Aphrodisias, and I am clerk to the attorney Athenagoras. I am going to tell you the story of a love affair that took place in Syracuse." Actually this narrative, slightly more than one hundred pages in modern translation, jumps briskly around the Mediterranean world. The hero and heroine, actually married early in the story, are separated by Callirhoe's presumed death, and both she and her husband endure many perils before their reunification. Despite many quotations from, and allusions to, Homer, this work was probably scorned by intellectuals of the day. It is well constructed, however, and uses dialogue effectively. Although it exists in but a single manuscript, scattered fragments found on Egyptian papyruses suggest popular appeal. (It must be remembered that even a "popular" reading public was tiny compared to that of today.)

In *An Ephesian Tale of Anthia and Habrocomes* (c. 100-150 C.E.), attributed to one Xenophon of Ephesus, roughly contemporary with Chariton, a similar plot draws in several episodes of folk origin. Graham Anderson, in *Ancient Fiction: The Novel in the Greco-Roman World* (1984), has shown similarities between Greek and Oriental tales in this and other romances, which illustrate how widely such folktales were disseminated. Stylistically, *An Ephesian Tale of Anthia and Habrocomes* is rather crude and monotonous.

A more miscellaneous romance is *Leucippe and Clitophon*, composed by Achilles Tatius. In the first few pages, the author describes a meeting with his hero, Clitophon, who is then allowed to tell his story in the first person—though Clitophon becomes more or less omniscient in the process. Clitophon is unusual among romantic protagonists in failing to remain completely loyal to Leucippe during their lengthy separation; circumstances force her to become the consort of a foreign potentate for a time, but their goal is nevertheless eventual reunion. The style ranges from poetic to prosaic. Achilles Tatius can manage realistic descriptions of a storm at sea, psychological portraits of his characters, elaborate puns, and melodramatic incidents.

Around 200 C.E., a writer known as Longus composed the pastoral romance *Poimenika ta kata Daphin kai Chloen* (third century; *Daphnis and Chloë*, 1587) thus blending elements from a poetic tradition whose monuments are the eclogues of Theocritus and Vergil with prose narrative. Longus shows considerable ingenuity in accomplishing the difficult feat of combining features from the static, halcyon world of pastoral with the mobile and frequently menacing milieu of romance. The young lovers' staunch relationship is traced from the time of their childhood as goatherds and shepherds through their sexual awakening and ultimate union. The story does not leave the island of hLesbos, famed as the home of the first great lyric poet (certainly the first great female poet) Sappho. Whereas the innocent Daphnis and Chloë must prevail over the wiles of more sophisticated enemies and even well-intentioned friends, this plot keeps them close to home, and unlike the noble lovers of other romances, these two desire nothing more than a fruitful marriage and the opportunity to continue tending their flocks.

The longest and best known of the Greek romances is Heliodorus of Emesa's *Aethiopica* (C.E. 225; *An Ethiopian History*, 1569; also known by several other titles, including *The Story of Theagenes and Charikleia*, after its protagonists). It is an ambitious work by a sophisticated writer who was obviously eager to put romance on a footing with the still-venerated epics. Whether or not he succeeded, at times he loses interest in Theagenes and Charikleia as a result of his preoccupation with elaborate stories within stories and the fierce battles he stages among Egyptians, Persians, and Ethiopians. There is also a mystery to be solved about Charikleia's parentage; she turns out to be an Ethiopian. Heliodorus is one of the greatest of Greek prose stylists, and he influenced such towering figures as Miguel de Cervantes, Sir Philip Sidney, and Jean Racine.

An excellent general account of the Greek and Roman romances is Ben Edwin Perry's *The Ancient Romances: A Literary-Historical Account of Their Origins* (1967). Romance is a form that has flourished in many parts of the world. An Arabic example that has become especially well known in Europe and the United States is *Alf layla wa-layla* (fifteenth century; *The Arabian Nights' Entertainments*, 1706-1708). Transmitted orally for centuries, it is a collection of stories that has existed in some form for more than a thousand years. Like many later literary works, the tales themselves (not always a thousand) are set within a frame story, in this case one about a misogynistic king who has vowed to kill all women. Two young women avoid his wrath by telling him a different unfinished story each evening, thus postponing their fate until he hears the end. Immediately upon finishing, they launch upon another story; the tactic goes on until the king finally abandons his homicidal program. The stories themselves—those of Aladdin, Ali Baba, and Sinbad the Sailor, for example—have spread all over the world since publication in various languages in the eighteenth and nineteenth centuries. Clearly the work of various hands, they have been traced to India, Iran, Iraq, Egypt, and even Greece. The interested reader may consult M. I. Gerhardt, *The Art of Story-Telling: A Literary Study of the Thousand and One Nights* (1963). The combination of sophisticated technique and yarn-spinning dexterity that marks *The Arabian Nights' Entertainments* collection makes it a milestone in the early development of the short story. Many college courses on the history of the short story in premodern times begin with this work.

THE NEAR AND FAR EAST

Medieval Persian poets developed a verse form called *mathnavi* for long narratives. Niẓāmi of Ganja, who flourished late in the twelfth century, composed several of these, including *Leyli o-Mejnun* (twelfth century; *Lailí and Majnún*, 1836; also known as *The Story of Layla and Majnun*, 1966), a tragic poem akin to the courtly European romances of the same era.

Murasaki Shikibu (c. 978-c. 1030) prevails as the most illustrious of early Japanese romancers. Her *Genji monogatari* (*The Tale of Genji*, 1925-1933), composed c. 1004, has been called the oldest novel in the world. It includes a series of delicately crafted love stories and forcefully depicts Japanese court life of her time, an atmosphere that Murasaki knew well. Since its translation into English by Arthur Waley in 1935, it has gained recognition in English-speaking countries.

Luo Guanzhong (c. 1320-1380) gave coherent form to cycles of legends long popular in China. His *Sanguo yanyi* (fourteenth century; *Romance of the Three Kingdoms*, 1925) is based on historical events of the third century C.E., while *Shuihu zhuan* (translated as *All Men Are Brothers* by Pearl Buck, 1933) also has gained a following in the West.

Columbia University Press has done much to introduce English-speaking readers to Asian fiction, as well as other literary forms, with a series of translations and "approaches." One example is *Approaches to the Oriental Classics: Asian Literature and Thought in General Education*, edited by William Theodore De Bary (1959).

Robert P. Ellis

BIBLIOGRAPHY

Albrecht, Michael von. *A History of Roman Literature: From Livius Andronicus to Boethius, with Special Regard to Its Influence on World Literature*. New York: E. J. Brill, 1997. An exhaustive survey of Roman literature and culture and its influence on modern letters, this volume includes bibliographical references and an index.

Cairns, Douglas L. *Aidos: The Psychology and Ethics of Honour and Shame in Ancient Greek Literature*. New York: Oxford University Press, 1993. A historical and critical look at Greek literature and psychology in literature. Includes bibliographical references and an index.

Canepa, Nancy L., ed. *Out of the Woods: The Origins of the Literary Fairy Tale in Italy and France*. Detroit, Mich.: Wayne State University Press, 1997. A historical study of the fairy tale as it developed in Italy and France. Includes bibliographical references and an index.

Dover, K. J., ed. *Ancient Greek Literature*. New York: Oxford University Press, 1997. A historical and critical study of literature in the ancient world, this work includes bibliographical references and an index.

Foley, John Miles. *Immanent Art: From Structure to Meaning in Traditional Oral Epic*. Bloomington: Indiana University Press, 1991. Examines the oral, epic, and folk traditions in literature. Includes bibliographical references and an index.

Harris, Joseph, ed. *The Ballad and Oral Literature*. Cambridge, Mass.: Harvard University Press, 1991. A collection of lectures, some of which were given at a symposium on the Child ballads held at Harvard University in November of 1998. Includes bibliographical references and an index.

Jackson-Laufer, Guida M. *Encyclopedia of Literary Epics*. Santa Barbara, Calif.: ABC-CLIO, 1996. A useful compendium of information about the epic tradition. Includes bibliographical references and an index.

Lazzari, Marie, ed. *Epics for Students: Presenting Analysis, Context, and Criticism on Commonly Studied Epics*. A good resource for the beginner, this volume includes a foreword by Helen Conrad-O'Brian, bibliographical references, and an index.

Putnam, Michael C. J. *Virgil's "Aeneid": Interpretation and Influence*. Chapel Hill: University of North Carolina Press, 1995. Examines the place of the character of Aeneas in literature and the influence of Roman culture on modern literature. Includes bibliographical references and an index.

Rosenberg, Bruce A., ed. *Folklore and Literature: Rival Siblings*. Knoxville: University of Tennessee Press, 1991. This study of folklore in medieval literature includes bibliographical references and an index.

THE SAGA AND THÁTTR

The term "saga" (pl. sögur) is Old Norse in origin and means "a saw" or "saying." After written language supplemented oral language in the North, the word "saga" was extended to include any kind of legend, story, tale, or history written in prose. As a literary term, "saga" refers more specifically to prose narratives written in medieval Iceland. The sagas are traditionally classified according to their subject matter. The main types of sagas are *Konungasögur* (kings' sagas), *Íslendingasögur* (sagas of the Icelanders or family sagas), *Sturlunga saga* (saga of the Sturlungs), *Byskupasögur* (bishops' sagas), *Fornaldarsögur* (sagas of past times), *Riddarosögur* (sagas of chivalry), and *Lygisögur* (lying sagas). In general, family sagas and kings' sagas are of highest literary merit. Their excellence ranks them among the finest work of the European Middle Ages.

Closely associated with the saga in medieval Icelandic literature was the tháttr (pl. thættir), a shorter prose form which is related to the saga in roughly the same fashion as a short story is to a novel: The most evident difference between the two is length. Tháttr literally means "a single strand," as of rope. The Icelanders early extended this meaning metaphorically to refer to parts of written works. Episodes of narratives, chapters of histories, or sections of law were thus known as thættir. Icelandic short stories came to be called thættir because many of them are preserved as anecdotes or strands in sagas, particularly in the kings' sagas.

While the term "saga" has made its way into popular modern nomenclature as a label for an epiclike narrative, the word "tháttr" has no cognate descendant in English and has but recently been accorded attention as a genre with its own governing rules. The common habit of embedding short stories in the sagas suggests why the Icelandic thættir have either been overlooked or absorbed into a general discussion of saga literature. Enough versions of single stories exist both as separate manuscripts and as episodes in the sagas to indicate that the stories had a recognizable identity of their own, more or less independent of the host texts. Genre distinctions in medieval Icelandic writing were not particularly definitive. Terms such as "frásaga" (story, narrative), "æfentyri" (adventurous exploits), and "hlut" (part) mingle with "saga" and "tháttr" as reference terms in the literature. On occasion a narrative referred to in one place as a tháttr is called a saga in another. Although more sophisticated and telling differences between saga and tháttr were established through practice of the arts, the boundary between stories and sagas remained fluid.

Origins of the saga and tháttr forms

Evidence of the strong ties and shifting boundaries between the saga and tháttr forms has provoked ongoing speculation about the original relationship between the two. The once-held belief that thættir were oral tales recorded by scribes and then linked into sagas has been discarded. Sagas and thættir represent a sophisticated confluence of numerous sources both written and oral and are dependent as well on the genius of their individual authors. While the origin of saga and tháttr writing is a matter of speculation, it can be said that the two are related emanations of the deeply rooted storytelling traditions of Northern Europe.

Storytelling, poetry recitation, and their descendant written forms have historically been the most favored of all arts in Scandinavia and particularly in Iceland. This affection for and mastery of the literary arts in Iceland has been attributed to strong urges of an emigrant culture to preserve knowledge of its European ancestral history. Medieval Icelandic manuscripts are the single preserve of certain heroic Germanic myths and tales which were part of a shared tradition of the Northern peoples. The old literature was lost in Germany and England, where Christianity arrived early. In Scandinavia, where Teutonic mythology and religion held sway for centuries longer (Sweden did not have a Christian bishop until the twelfth century), some of the old myths and stories were preserved, mainly in two Icelandic texts known as the

Eddas. The *Poetic Edda* (ninth to twelfth century; English translation, 1923) contains heroic, didactic, and mythological poems which allude to events, legends, and beliefs of the Teutonic tribes. The *Prose Edda* (c. 1220; English translation, 1916) relates mythological and heroic stories of the pre-Christian North and provides an elaborate poetics for the poetry associated with the legends.

Medieval Icelanders had material as well as patriotic motives for their literary efforts. Those who note the preponderance of writing and the relative absence of other artistic endeavors in Iceland point out the lack of native materials necessary for practicing other arts. Those who engaged themselves in such vigorous literary activity on a remote and rural island several hundred miles from the European mainland were by majority Norwegian emigrants who came to Iceland during the reign of Harald I. Harald's ambitious rise to power during the later decades of the ninth century clashed with the Norwegian landed gentry whose livelihoods and properties were threatened by the young monarch's expansion. Rather than suffer servitude or death many chose emigration westward. Various other causes, including hope for a better life and need to escape the law, brought more settlers.

From all accounts, the Icelanders were industrious and enterprising farmers, exceptionally literate and particularly skilled in self-government and law. Those who could argue the law and bring cases to just settlement were highly regarded. The Icelandic pioneers organized assemblies called "Things" which ruled the country by democratic process. They elected to their head not a monarch, but a lawspeaker, part of whose job it was to recite the entire body of law every three years. The first law of the land was a customary one, added to and refined at the annual assembly and passed by memory between generations. An old law formula recited in *Grettis Saga* (c. 1300; *The Saga of Grettir the Strong*, 1869) gives evidence that alliterative techniques aided in memorization and so rendered law into a poetry of sorts. This law system, suggested by district assemblies in Scandinavia, was unlike any other the world had known. Democratic assemblies ruled the entire country of Iceland for more than eight hundred years before such an idea began to infect Western history on a larger scale. Although the system was far from utopian in practice, it commanded the respect and loyalty of the people. Words were the recognized bond of the body democratic; they were to replace force as the *modus operandi* of government. Against this vision of rational and peaceable government struggled old revenge codes from the heroic tradition. Conflicts between law and violence and the law's frequent incapacity to stop violence became major themes in the Family Saga literature.

Christianity was adopted by assembly vote in the year 1000. One of the most important legacies of the new faith was the access its missionaries provided to written language. Icelanders quickly learned the Latin the churchmen brought and became familiar with its texts. They also put the new alphabet to most vigorous use in the practice of vernacular and sometimes secular literatures. Young Icelanders furthered their educations in Europe or at home. By the early twelfth century there were two bishoprics in Iceland, at Skalaholt and Holar. Both sees supported schools where chieftains sent their sons. At Holar, Icelandic farm boys learned Gregorian chant and Latin versification from a French clergyman. Class distinctions were few, thus allowing the new learning to spread rapidly.

Christianity, with its attendant teachings and written language, initiated Iceland into European traditions. Biblical lore and Christian ethics were added to the Icelanders' stock of old Germanic stories and myths without replacing the older literature. Confident of the value of their own history, Icelanders gave over their enlarged knowledge to the service of the stories of their own peoples. Possibilities for preservation became virtually unlimited. Stories, law, and history had found their harbor on vellum. Before the era closed, Iceland produced a prodigious amount of hagiography, historiography, homiletics, astronomy, grammars, laws, romances, and stories, much of it in Icelandic.

The oldest manuscripts, which are preserved in Iceland, are from the twelfth century; the earliest text is thought to have been a legal code. Ari Thorgilsson (c. 1067-1148) is regarded as the father of Icelandic vernacular history. His *Libellus Islandorum*, commonly called *Íslendingabók* (c. 1120; *Book of the Icelanders*, 1930), comments on the settlement of Iceland, on exploration voyages to Greenland and Vinland (America), and on other important political data associated with the founding of the island republic. *Book of the Icelanders* well reflects the respect for historical data and interest in biography which continued to be evident in the later Kings' Sagas and Family Sagas; it is written in a style free from embellishment; it is sober and thorough but not without touches of human interest.

Of more central importance to the evolution of the distinctly literary sagas and thættir is *Landnámabók* (c. 1140; *Book of Settlements*, 1973), which was also first written in Ari Thorgilsson's time and is sometimes attributed to him. *Book of Settlements* is a rich repository of historical and legendary anecdotes about four hundred of Iceland's first settlers. The work documents land claims, describes farmsteads, and gives accounts of feuds, law cases, and marriages. It lavishes special care on genealogy, naming the pioneers' descendants and ancestors as fully as the author's knowledge allows. The author weaves dramatic incident and brief character sketches in with the more sober demographic and historical data. About Ingolf, who was Iceland's first settler, *Book of Settlements* reports that as soon as he saw Iceland he threw his high-seat pillars into the sea and made settlement where they landed. Details of ordinary life, both comic and domestic, interlace the carefully prepared documentary. One section describes a dale named for a cow, and another tells about a man who lost his life in battle when his belt broke and his britches fell. In the *Thórdarbók* version of *Book of Settlements*, the author justifies his compilation, noting that civilized peoples are always eager "to know about the origins of their own society and the beginnings of their own race." Historians continued to expand and revise *Book of Settlements*, issuing it in various editions during the thirteenth and fourteenth centuries.

KINGS' SAGAS

The first document to which the name "saga" is attached is the fragmentary *Oldest Olafs saga helga (St. Olaf's saga) from about 1180. Although primarily a hagiographic account of King Olaf Haraldsson (St. Olaf, c. 995-1030), the saga does contain several thættir made lively by verbal exchanges. Oldest Olafs saga helga* was likely composed at the Benedictine monastery in northern Iceland. Such monasteries carried on a wide range of literary activities, not all of them religious in nature. Translations of European histories were undertaken and biographies of kings were written with an eye to more than the kings' saintly virtues. Most of these early works are lost.

The popularity of sagas about kings is evidenced by the compilation of the *Morkinskinna* (rotten skin) c. 1220. *Morkinskinna* is a collection of biographies of eleventh and twelfth century Norwegian kings which incorporates thirty thættir, among them "Halldor Snorrason," "Ivar's Story," and the most famous tháttr, "Audun and the Bear," one of the most beautiful pilgrimage stories in world literature. When the Icelandic biographers of kings set to documenting the lives of long-dead Norwegian monarchs, they turned to the skaldic verse which celebrated their subjects. The fixity of the verse patterns and the conventionality of the kennings (elaborate metaphors) made the poetry a more reliable medium for accurate preservation of the kings' lives than oral tales.

Skaldic verse had its origins in Norway, but Icelanders became its greatest practitioners. Several of Iceland's pioneers were skalds, including the most famous of all skaldic poets, Egill Skallagrimsson, whose two beautiful poems, *Hofuðlausn* (c. 948; *The Ransome of Egill, the Scald*, 1763) and *Sonátorrek* (c. 961; lament for my sons), are centerpieces in *Egils Saga* (c. 1220; *Egil's Saga*, 1763). Many kings' sagas are liberally interspersed with skaldic poems, but it would be a mistake in most cases to think of kings' sagas as merely prose expansion of the tighter verse forms. The numerous histories which grew out of the skaldic tradition seem to have directed attention to the art of biography for its own sake. These kings' sagas, especially those found in the *Morkinskinna* and *Flateyjarbók* manuscripts, are also host to dozens of thættir which feature as their subject a meeting between an Icelander and a Norwegian or Danish king. These short stories probably gave rise to techniques, characters, and themes more purely fictional than the histories which embody them. The subject matter of the thættir is not often traceable to skaldic verse.

Practitioners of skaldic poetry became favorite subjects for both saga and tháttr writers. A number of heroes of the great family sagas—Egill, Gisli, Grettir, and Gunnlaug among them—are also famous poets. The kings' sagas contain many stories which feature a Norwegian king and his skald. Even heroes who are not poets can grace a scene with a skaldic verse when the occasion warrants.

Side by side with the newer written forms, stories continued to be recited; such performances also provided subject matter for the writer of sagas and thættir. In *Morkinskinna* is recorded the story of a young Icelander visiting a European court. It is Yuletide, and the boy makes the court company merry each night with his stories. As Christmas draws near the boy's spirits fall, for his stock of stories is nearly spent. He tells King Harald he has but one final story, the story of Harald's own adventures abroad. The king is delighted by this unexpected attention and arranges it so the story lasts for the twelve nights of the festival.

Medieval Icelanders told stories about stories and stories about poems. They recorded poems about past events which were made into stories with poems embedded in them; they celebrated those who recited and wrote verse and tale. Clearly the literary arts and its practitioners were accorded a position of honor, and what the bards praised in their ancestors they put into practice themselves.

The medieval Icelander who has most clearly come to embody the Icelandic desire to preserve antiquarian literature is Snorri Sturluson (1179-1241), a historian and poet who simultaneously practiced the more pragmatic arts of law and diplomacy. Snorri's work is impressively diverse. He is the author of the so-called *Prose Edda*, which is a compendium of Germanic mythology, a catalog of kennings and a poem of more than one hundred stanzas authored by Sturluson. The poem is accompanied by a commentary on the stanzaic and metric forms of each verse. Other works attributed to Sturluson include the masterful collection of kings' sagas known as *Heimskringla* (c. 1230-1235; English translation, 1844), one part of which is the distinguished *St. Olaf's Saga*. Sturluson has been called the author of *Egil's Saga*, although that is a matter of conjecture.

During the thirteenth century, the powerful Sturluson family dominated Icelandic political affairs. Sturluson undertook diplomatic missions to Norway and was powerful in Icelandic politics, serving twelve years as lawspeaker. His talents as historian, literary critic, antiquarian, sagaman, and poet rank him as the most prominent literary figure of his age. He was also an influential and wily chieftain who was deeply involved in the internecine struggles of the day and who was neglectful of family obligations. It was his own estranged son-in-law who, leading sixty men, murdered Sturluson in an ambush in response to an order from the Norwegian king.

This incident serves to point up the state of general lawlessness which plagued the Icelandic Republic in the thirteenth century. (The Saga of the Sturlungs gives lurid account of these days.) While the old democratic system of assembly rule had never matched in practice what it held in theory, legend at least had it that for several generations the country was, for the most part, at peace. The prestigious assemblies had continued to function, and respect for the law had kept violent family feuds from turning into general lawlessness. By the first decades of the thirteenth century, however, Iceland's political and social life had become a welter of competing factions. The Norwegian crown, the assemblies, and the church bishops vied to impose a gaggle of rules and counter-rules. The lines of authority were so indistinct that no group hesitated to use force to advance its position.

Family Sagas

It was during these last chaotic days of the Icelandic Republic (Norway assumed jurisdiction over the country in 1262) that the most sophisticated of all the sagas, the family sagas, were written. These sagas of Icelanders owe important debts to the centuries of interest in law, history, and kings' lives which preceded them. Yet the blend of national history, genealogy, local legend, and character anecdote gathered into stories with structures and aesthetic values of their own is quite unlike earlier sagas or Continental literature of the same period.

Nowhere else in Europe (excluding the British Isles) had prose been adopted for such clearly literary purposes: The medium of the Continent's literature was still verse, and the subject matter was heroic and traditional when it did not take up prevailing Christian motifs. In Europe, the thirteenth century was the age of scholasticism, and its literature was written mainly under the inspiration of the Christian faith. Dante's *La divina commedia* (c. 1320; *The Divine Comedy*, 1802) stands as the age's crowning achievement.

The Icelanders knew the heroic tradition well. This hoard of common experience, which found voice in works as diverse as *Beowulf* (c. 1000), the *Poetic Edda*, and *Nibelungenlied* (c. 1200; *The Nibelungenlied*, 1848), was kept alive mainly by Icelanders. Nor were the Icelanders unaffected by the Christian literature of courtly romance. Thomas of Brittany's *Tristan* (c. 1160) was translated into Old Norse as *Tristrams saga ok Ísöndar* in 1226, and numerous other translations followed.

Such material engaged the imaginations of the family saga writers and supplied them with a storehouse of conventional stories, cosmological schemes, and codes of heroic behavior, but the subject matter and the ethos of the family sagas spring from a native source. Sagamen took their ancestors' history and their own knowledge of the Icelandic landscape and transformed the Icelandic experience into narratives and stories which, in retrospect, read remarkably like novels and short stories. The high literary merit of the family sagas has made them widely known outside of Iceland and linked the name "saga" with their particular subject matter. The more than 120 sagas and thættir thought to have been written during the thirteenth century provide a remarkable fictional portrait of the tenth and the first third of the eleventh centuries. The sagamen rendered their histories in human terms. They were interested in individual men and women and the drama their lives provoked. By aesthetically arranging these incidents, which often range over a century and involve scores of characters, the sagamen aroused interest in the moral dimensions of their ancestors' acts and the larger questions which they raised about human destiny in general.

The saga writer's techniques are those which are often associated with modern realistic fiction. Verisimilitude is of primary importance. Characters are not drawn as types but are faithful portraits of individuals. Characters speak as people do to one another and are revealed through action. Description is minimal and lyrical effusion is absent. The imagery is spare, homely, and solid, free of affectation and exaggeration.

Presumably the authors of the family sagas did not have in mind a literary experiment when they wrote their stories. More likely they sought to reduplicate the actual features of life as they thought it had existed for their ancestors and as they had come to know it. For a long time it was thought that the sagas provided reasonably accurate histories of the Icelandic pioneers and their descendants. Research conducted in the past thirty years, however, has shown that the sagas are not reliable as histories nor as indices to local geography, although they take historical events and lives of historical persons as their subject. It is far more accurate to describe the sagas as well-composed fiction. The manner of presentation is the historian's, but the effect is literary. Pertinent genealogies are recorded, local customs explained, and place names accounted for as the stories unfold. Use of the authorial "I" is almost totally absent, and point of view is established by selection of detail and juxtaposition of scenes rather than by interpretive commentary.

Saga language also suggests the historian's objective tone. Concrete nouns are its hallmark. Verbs tend to be generalized and clauses strung loosely by means of parataxis. Interpretive adverbs and adjectives are avoided, and, when employed, they are determining rather than descriptive. Descriptions of landscapes or of persons are consequential. If a river is filled with floating chunks of ice, someone will surely jump from one to another or swim between them. When fantastic elements or dreams break into a realistic account, verisimilitude is not lost. For example, the same language is employed in *Grettis saga* when the monster Glam attacks Grettir as when the opponent is human or the scene less dramatic.

Language spoken in the family saga is terse and laconic. It is never rhetorical or stylized. Dialogue typically occurs at dramatic moments and so increases tension and reveals character. Forceful and felicitous language is accorded the highest respect: Lawspeaker, poet, and wit have the day. To die with a quip on one's lips is a measure of heroic stature. Vesteinn dies complimenting his assailant on his effective blow, and Attli falls noting that "broad spears are becoming fashionable nowadays."

Family sagas tend to be episodic. Individual scenes begin and end in rest. They are related to one another by movement through time as well as by cause and effect patterns generated by the action. Characteristically a saga closes decades or even centuries after it begins, and this remorseless passage of time is often associated with fate. The saga's episodic structure attains its unity through juxtaposition and symmetry among its lesser parts. Reliance on techniques of short fiction is apparent: The scene is the basic unit of the family saga, and the larger effects of the narrative rely on the successful realization of each scene and the arrangement of those scenes.

Although bound into a close family by the commonality of the Icelandic historical milieu and shared method of construction, the family sagas support a range of character types and thematic interests broader than other medieval literatures. *Laxdœla Saga* (c. 1200; English translation, 1899) has as a main theme the decline of the generous habits which prevailed during the pioneer generations. Unn the Deep Minded, who gave wise counsel until the day of her death, is mother of the Laxdaela clan and emblem of pioneer largesse. *Laxdœla Saga*'s central story is of the imperious Gudrun who forces her third husband to kill Kjartan, her former lover and her husband's cousin. Kjartan is a hero in the old tradition and also one of the first to practice Christianity in Iceland. His death ushers in a more violent era; Gudrun takes control and sets off revenge killings which disrupt the entire district. Peace is finally won but in an atmosphere less luminous and expectant than that of the pioneer age. *Eyrbggja saga* (c. 1200) also has a district's history as its subject and shares some characters with *Gísla saga súrssonar* (c. 1200; *The Saga of Gisli*, 1866). The powerful Sturluson figure, known for his strength and wiliness in a number of sagas, figures in many scenes, and his attempts to advance his career by means of shrewd planning and outright trickery provide focus in the otherwise diffuse history of the Snaefelsness region. *Eyrbggja Saga*'s author had a strong antiquarian interest. Hauntings and old religious rites figure prominently in the saga. Strict adherence to the heathen viewpoint does not admit the romantic and heraldic details which decorate the latter half of *Laxdœla saga*.

Several of the finest sagas are biographies. *Egil's saga* preludes the story of the famous warrior-poet with a long and well-wrought section about Egil's father, grandfather, and uncle and their conflicts and alliances with Harald Fairhair. Egil himself is portrayed as a Viking with a lusty appetite for brawling and ransacking. He has a series of confrontations with European royalty, managing in the most extreme situation to save himself from Eirik Bloodaxe's wrath by composing and reciting a poem in praise of the king. In his mature years, Egil settles in Iceland and is one of the few saga heroes to die of old age. In his last years Egil becomes old and blind and is mocked by servants, but his contrariness exerts itself to the last. He takes his treasure and buries it without a trace.

The Saga of Gisli and *Grettis saga* are biographies of two of Iceland's great outlaws. Both heroes are poets. Gisli is a man obsessed by the desire to protect family honor; he kills his sister's husband to avenge the killing of his wife's brother. He is found out and outlawed, and his enemies pursue him and drive him to take up undignified poses and disguises to save his life. He is also terrorized by bloody, prophetic dreams, which appear in the saga as verses given him by dream women, one bright and one dark. Gisli makes brave defense and is portrayed as a far greater man than those with whom he does battle. *The Saga of Gisli* distinguishes itself by its intensely concentrated telling. A foreboding and tragic tone sounds throughout.

Grettir's outlawry is longer and less ominous than

Gisli's. Like Egil, Grettir is a precocious and taciturn child. After a brilliant youthful career as a land-cleanser, Grettir's great strength is arrested by a curse placed on him by the monster Glam. The battle scene between Grettir and Glam is one of the finest in saga literature. The reckless young hero hears how Glam has ravaged the Vatnsdale district and is anxious to test his strength against such an opponent. He is warned from such opportunism, but he pays no heed. Grettir defeats Glam but is cursed by the dying monster to a life of fear and solitude. Grettir's outlawry, which follows this battle, is the result of a false charge. He is eventually forced into the interior of the island where he lives as a solitary, fending off those who come to kill him for bounty. Despite his perilous situation, Grettir becomes a gentler and more dignified man during his nineteen years of outlawry. He dies a tragic death, but the saga ends with the lucky adventures of Grettir's half-brother, which are presented in the "Spés tháttr."

Njáls saga (c. thirteenth century; *The Story of Burnt Njal*, 1861) is called the greatest of all the family sagas. It encompasses the two biographies of Gunnar of Hlidarendi and Njal, which are followed by the story of Kari's vengeance. This intricately designed triptych is woven into a whole by the author's imaginative grasp of every feature of his narrative. Gunnar lives his life within the framework of the old heroic code, but he is not a lucky man. He arouses the envy of lesser men and has a wife who steals. He is unable to stop a chain of events which leads him to kill three members of the same family, a situation which Njal has predicted will lead to his death. Gunnar is hunted down and murdered in his own house, a victim of lesser men. His wife, Hallgerd, a sinister force in the saga, betrays him. Gunnar's friend and mentor, Njal, is a lawyer and a prophet of sorts who devotes his life to an attempt to replace the old revenge codes with justice and law. His attempts are insightful and trusting but finally fruitless. His own sons kill Njal's foster son, and after other violent developments, Njal and his family are burned in their house by Flosi. Njal's son-in-law Kari takes revenge. Reconciliation is finally achieved after Kari and Flosi are both absolved in Rome. The reconciliation is confirmed when Kari marries Flosi's niece, the young woman who instigated the burning of Njal. On a larger plane this saga takes as its subject the upheaval and redefinition of values associated with the coming of Christianity to Iceland. Njal himself has certain characteristics of the Christian martyr. *Laxdœla saga* and *Grettis saga* contemplate this same theme from different points of view.

The great age of family saga writing seems to have ended about 1300, a time just postdating the passing of the Icelandic Republic into Norwegian control. Of the major family sagas only *Grettis Saga* is thought to have been written later. Authors of the later era turned their attention to mythic and heroic themes drawn from the Germanic heritage. They wrote what are known as sagas of past times, which have as their subjects fantastic, heroic, and supernatural events of the remote past.

Sagas of Past Times

The most notable of the sagas of past times is the *Völsunga saga* (c. 1270; *The Saga of the Volsungs*, 1930), which opens by recounting the earliest days of the tribe of the Völsungs. The flower of the clan is Sigurd, the most popular of all Northern heroes. Sigurd kills the dragon Fafnir and comes into possession of the Nibelungen wealth. Later he is betrothed to the Valkyrie Brynhild, but the affair comes to tragedy when Sigurd, under a witch's spell, forgets Brynhild and marries another woman. Brynhild is married into the same family and eventually urges her husband to kill Sigurd. When the deed has been accomplished, Brynhild throws herself on Sigurd's funeral pyre. The remainder of the saga follows the life of Sigurd's widow, Gudrun, and the revenge killings her children carry out. Stories and characters of the *Völsunga Saga* are common to all Germanic peoples; *The Nibelungenlied* is based on the same tales which also form the basis for Richard Wagner's opera *Der Ring des Nibelungen* (1874; *The Ring of the Nibelungs*).

The author of the *Völsunga Saga* relied heavily on the eddic poems which include all the elements of his story. The prose in *Völsunga Saga* is notably passionless and lacks the verisimilitude that the solid presence of the Icelandic landscape and historical personages gave to the family sagas. The sagas of past times in general do not retain the high literary standards of their predecessors, although sagas such as *Ragnars saga Lodbrókar* (c. eleventh century; *The Saga of Ragnor Lodbrok*, 1930), *Örvar-odds saga* (eleventh century; *Arrow-Odd*, 1970), and *Hrólf saga kraka* (c. 1280-1350; *The Saga of Hrolf Kraki*, 1933) are popular as swashbuckling adventure stories. Icelandic romances of chivalry (*Riddarasögur*) and the fairy tale or lying sagas (*Lygisögur*), which were based on foreign models, captured the interest of fourteenth and fifteenth century writers. These outlandish adventures are written in an ornate and verbose style. The day of the family saga had passed; although family sagas were collected and copied during the fourteenth and fifteenth centuries, and were doubtlessly read, they were no longer written.

Away from the European mainstream, Icelandic writers created a literature of psychological realism worthy of comparison with nineteenth and twentieth century fiction. At the same time, the family sagas found a unique place within the humanistic tradition of the Middle Ages. Sagamen were Christian. The importance of an individual life, the emphasis on selflessness, forbearance, and conciliation as well as other Christian values exert quiet force when they appear as qualities of fine men and women, whether they are pagan or Christian. The pagan heroic code, with its stringent and violent demands, comes to clash with these gentler ideas. Such conflicts may be within an individual, between family members, or argued in the courts. Whatever the dramatic forum, the importance of the immediate conflict is never sacrificed to point up an abstract principle. Family sagas are primarily good stories well told. The best of them retain allegiance to district history and genealogy without allowing antiquarian interests or Christian creed to obscure their aesthetic designs.

The family sagas number around thirty-five and are anonymous. They vary in length from a few pages to more than four hundred. *Njál's Saga* is the longest, and both *Egil's Saga* and *Grettis Saga* are more than three hundred pages long. Most of the longer sagas deal with heroes and families in the Northern and Western regions of Iceland. *Njál's Saga* is set in the South. The sagas which are set in Eastern Iceland are fewer in number, and they are shorter. Among them are two fine sagas, *The Vapnfjord Men* and *Hrafnkels saga freysgoða* (c. 1200; *Hrafnkel's Saga*, 1935). *The Vapnfjord Men* is the story of a friendship between two brothers-in-law which disintegrates when they are alienated by a Norwegian merchant and quarrel over a box of silver. After one friend casts off his sick wife, who is the other friend's sister, a feud opens and continues into a second generation. Reconciliation is achieved only after a young man kills his best-loved uncle in answer to an earlier killing. Half-hearted battles between the inheritors of the quarrel convince them that it is more honorable to end the fighting.

Hrafnkel's Saga is a masterpiece of short fiction. It relates the story of the precocious son of an Icelandic pioneer who rises quickly to district prominence. Hrafnkel kills his shepherd for riding his horse and is brought to trial by the shepherd's family. Judgment is passed against Hrafnkel, and he loses his wealth and is tortured at the confiscation trial. Later, after abandoning his heathen practices, Hrafnkel rises again to district renown. He takes revenge on his opponents by killing an innocent man, and this time there is no retort. Hrafnkel remains in control and enjoys great prestige. The saga makes exceptionally fine use of landscape features to forward its plot, and the dialogues spoken at the National Assembly are among the best in family saga literature. Characters in this tightly woven saga are finely and individually drawn.

Short sagas stand midway between the saga and the tháttr genres. *Hrafnkel's Saga*, for example, is a saga, although in the main it tells a single strand story. In English collections it is often placed among Icelandic stories. At thirty-five pages, it is longer than a tháttr and much shorter than the generational sagas. Such commonality of subject matter and similarity of technique do bind saga and tháttr and might well indicate that they are shorter or longer redactions of the same prose form. As noted earlier, boundaries between saga and tháttr are not explicit. Despite the wide common ground, however, certain provinces belonging only to the tháttr reveal its closer affinities to the modern short story.

Thættir

One hundred short stories are usually named as thættir. Approximately forty-five of these fall into a group which features an Icelander as protagonist, and among this group are the most distinguished of the stories. Tháttr length runs from a single page to about twenty-five pages, the average being between ten and twelve standard printed pages.

While the family sagas typically take as heroes famous men or families, the thættir usually choose a common man. Thættir about Icelandic farmers cluster around the lives of saints, historic heroes, folklore heroes, or kings. By far the most popular subject matter is the Icelander who travels to the court of a European king; these thættir outnumber all others by approximately five to one. Such a predominance of one sort of short story may be an accident of preservation, but it is more likely that the kings' sagas, which host them, provided a kind of yeast for the development of such short stories. One suspects they are fictional and imaginative, even fanciful outgrowths associated with the serious business of relating kings' biographies.

A tháttr tends to focus on a single character. At first the hero may appear to be a fool, who later proves himself to be inventive and insightful. Many tháttr heroes are poets, and some are simple, anonymous travelers. These protagonists are usually young men strayed away from home, equipped with a native wit or goodness which is hidden under an offhanded ingenuousness. In a typical tháttr of the king and Icelander type, the Icelander speaks with one or more monarchs, often alienates himself in the initial meeting, and leaves court intent on proving his true worth to the king. The moments of recognition and reconciliation tend to be complimentary to both king and Icelander; a spirit of equality unites the common man from the North with the powerful monarch. The effect is clearly patriotic, revealing the pride the Icelanders took in the most ordinary among their ancestors.

Hreidar the Fool is one such story. Hreidar is the younger of two brothers and said to be barely able to care for himself, but it is apparent almost immediately that he is a very canny fool. Hreidar traps his brother into taking him abroad with him, where he manages to meet King Magnus. Magnus is charmed by his eccentricity and invites Hreidar and his brother to stay at court. The king predicts that Hreidar will lose his even temper and learn to be clever with his hands.

When he is rudely teased by some of King Harald's men, Hreidar does lose his temper and kills a man. He seeks asylum with an upland farmer, and while in hiding, tries his hand at metal-smithing. When Harald and his men arrive to capture Hreidar, he is well enough hidden to escape detection. He is willing to risk his life for a joke, however, and bursts into Harald's presence handing him a gilded silver pig he has made. Before Harald realizes the pig is an insult, Hreidar races away and returns to King Magnus, for whom he recites a poem and is rewarded with an island. Hreidar gives the island back at Magnus's suggestion and returns to Iceland where, as the text says, he put aside his foolishness and became a successful farmer.

In brief, the lowly Icelander has his way with everyone. His foolish cleverness reveals Harald to be a harsh and tempestuous man and Magnus to be a good ruler and counselor. For his own part, Hreidar has an entertaining series of adventures and returns home a wise and more mature man.

The tone in such a story is noticeably lighter than in the family sagas. Thættir are infused with the optimistic outlook of the Christian Middle Ages, in contrast to the family sagas, whose scope tends to be epic and serious. While there are many comic moments in the family sagas, the burden of bringing alive the ethos of an age imposes epic obligations on an author. The tháttr writer is free from such weighty obligations. While a character like Hreidar shares nobility of spirit with a saga hero like Hrafnkel, the tháttr author is not burdened by the long-term consequences of his hero's deeds except in the most general way. The tháttr writer, for example, need not confront his hero's death. The tháttr form may well have encouraged writing stories which were more fictional than historical. The interchange between Icelander and king typically has far more moral and psychological consequence than historical importance. Ivar in

Ivar's Story is an Icelandic poet residing at the court of King Eystein. Ivar asks his brother to tell Oddney back in Iceland that he wishes to marry her. Ivar's brother does not deliver the message; instead he marries Oddney himself. Ivar hears the news and becomes downcast. The king cannot understand his sorrow and calls Ivar to him and offers him land, gifts, and other women, but Ivar is not solaced. The king can think of nothing else to offer except his companionship. Ivar accepts Eystein's offer of friendship. Each day before the tables are cleared, Ivar joins the king and speaks of Oddney to his heart's content. Soon the poet's happiness returns, and he remains with King Eystein.

The tháttr writer seems to have enjoyed a greater imaginative freedom because he was not bound to make aesthetic sense of a vast amount of time. Since he wrote about a moment often unmarked in history and about an Icelander whose life was not particularly noteworthy, he could turn his attention to the creation of a fictional environment. The thættir are not analyses of historical deeds whose consequences are national in scope; they are tributes to the characters of kings. The stories also celebrate the characters of common Icelanders who call forth the true natures of the kings they visit. Likely the Icelandic writers knew little about life in Norway or about its landscape, so focus tended to remain on character and dialogue, which were explored and exploited to the exclusion of other features. The thættir characters found themselves in realistic dilemmas and extricated themselves through dint of their imaginations, or, as in the famous case of Audun, told in *Audun and the Bear*, by innocence and goodness.

Audun and the Bear

Audun is a Westfjord man of very modest means who gives all of his money for a Greenland bear that he wishes to present to King Svein of Denmark. When Audun lands in Norway, King Harald, having heard about the precious bear, invites Audun to court, hoping to buy it or have it given to him. In a graceful show of honesty and naïveté, Audun tells Harald he wishes to deliver the bear to Svein. Harald is so startled by the man's innocence that he sends him on his way even though Norway and Denmark are at war. Audun finally makes his way to Svein, but not without begging for food and selling half of the bear to do so. Svein is pleased and supplies Audun with silver for a pilgrimage to Rome. When Audun returns to Svein's court after his journey south, he is reduced to a beggar, and the kings' men mock him. Svein recognizes Audun and richly rewards him, praising him as a man who knows how to care for his soul. Audun refuses a position in Svein's court in order to return to Iceland to care for his mother. On his way home, he visits once more with Harald and at the Norwegian monarch's request tells him about the gifts Svein has given him. Among those gifts is an arm ring which Svein has instructed Audun to keep unless he can give it to a great man to whom he was obligated. Audun gives the ring to Harald, because, as he says, Harald could have had his bear and his life but took neither. Audun sails back to Iceland and is considered a man of great luck. In the few scenes of this story, the tháttr author gathers peace, goodwill, generosity, and integrity around this modest Icelander, who, without consciousness, becomes a model of the medieval pilgrim.

The thættir as a group, although they are restricted in subject matter, tend to take the shape of modern short stories; they develop character swiftly and pointedly through action. They are dramatic rather than narrative. Genealogy is curtailed if it is used at all. The ominousness of fate and the burden of history are usually dispensed with. Language is terse and witty, often with a lightness appropriate to its subject.

During the fourteenth century, the themes of the sagas of past times were also taken up by tháttr writers. These stories tend to lack the tension, the energy, and the comic juxtaposition of earlier thættir. The old patterns are visible but without the solidity that the stories of Icelanders in the kings' courts have. The setting shifts to prehistoric Europe, and the plots often read as bawdy folktales. In the story *Gridr's Fosterling, Illugi* (c. 1300), for example, the young prince's playmate, Illugi, wins royal favor by killing a revenant and is allowed to accompany the prince on an ocean voyage. When Illugi swims to shore for fire to save the ship's crew from freezing, he wanders into the cave of an ogress who tests his courage before allowing him her daughter's favors. The monster is a queen under an evil spell. Illugi destroys the spell and marries the daughter. The queen marries the prince and all live happily ever after.

When this sort of subject matter replaced the realistic action and individual characters of the earlier thættir, the stories became less distinguishable as a genre and certainly less akin to modern fiction.

This shift in subject matter indicates a stronger bonding with the European literatures. The popularity of the adventure and the fantastic tale were prompted by the Continental interest in romance. Certain of the later thættir are strong and resemble the best *fabliaux*. The strongest stories of this group are usually reliant on historical matter and the learned tradition, as their predecessors were, rather than on folktale. "Spes Tháttr," which concludes *Grettis Saga*, is an example. Because of their optimistic character, thættir do have natural affinities to *fabliaux*, but the tháttr's strengths are particularly its own. The use of realistic characters, few and vividly dramatized scenes, vigorous dialogue, and definitive imagery give the medieval Icelandic short story a distinct place in the history of European short fiction.

Helen Menke

BIBLIOGRAPHY

Andersson, Theodore M., and William Ian Miller. *Law and Literature in Medieval Iceland: "Ljósvetninga saga" and "Valla-Ljóts saga."* Stanford, Calif.: Stanford University Press, 1989. Written by a literary critic and a legal historian, this study combines methodologies to the study, translation, and annotation of two relatively unknown family sagas. Includes a bibliography and an index.

Clover, Carol J. *Óláfs Saga Helga, Runsivals Tháttr, and Njáls Saga: A Structural Comparison*. Berkeley: University of California Press, 1972. Clover compares three sagas in this historical study. Includes a bibliography.

Durrenberger, E. Paul. *The Dynamics of Medieval Iceland: Political Economy and Literature*. Iowa City: University of Iowa Press, 1992. Durrenberger touches upon a number of important and complex issues in the study of Icelandic society and its sources. Includes a bibliography.

Hollander, Lee Milton. *Víga-Glúms saga and "The Story of Ögmund Dytt."* New York: Twayne, 1972. Includes a discussion of *The Story of Ögmund Dytt*, which is a translation of *Ögmundar Þáttr Dytts*, part of the *Óláfs saga Tryggvasonar.* Includes a bibliography.

Molan, Chris. *The Viking Saga*. Austin, Tex.: Raintree Steck-Vaughn, 1985. Based on modern translations by Magnus Magnusson and Herman Pálsson of *Groenlendinga saga* and *Eirik's saga*, this work describes how the Vikings came to discover Vinland and their settlements in the New World.

Stitt, J. Michael. *Beowulf and the Bear's Son: Epic, Saga, and Fairytale in Northern Germanic Tradition*. New York: Garland, 1992. An informative study comparing texts within the tradition, including a chapter entitled "Epic, Saga, and Fairytale." Includes an index.

Tucker, John, ed. *Sagas of the Icelanders: A Book of Essays*. New York: Garland, 1989. A collection of essays by noted authors in the field, including a general introduction by Tucker entitled "Sagas of the Icelanders." Includes a bibliography and an index.

Víga-Glúms Saga, with the Tales of Ögmund Bash and Thorvald Chatterbox. Chester Springs, Pa.: Dufour Editions, 1987. Text includes a translations of *Ögmundar Þáttr dytts* and *þorvalds þáttur tasalda*. Includes bibliographical references.

THE EARLY MIDDLE AGES

The early Middle Ages (for the purposes of this discussion c. 476-1050) represent a time of transition and readjustment from the declining Roman, classical era to a culture that more and more clearly defined itself as a new age in the West (medieval scholars considered themselves modern men). This period saw the gradual development of the romance languages from Vulgar Latin and, especially as social conditions stabilized in the late eighth and early ninth centuries, the development of an increasingly varied body of literary work.

It is only fair and necessary to assume literary continuity in this transitional time. The great Latin writers, Ovid for example, were recopied as well as imitated, and Latin versions of the fables of Aesop continued to be produced and read. There was a considerable body of oral fiction, but this study will be confined to such exemplars of short fiction that have survived in written form. It will be necessary, especially for the early centuries of the period, to abstract our exemplars from works that are not fictional as such. Many of the writings of the late classical and early Christian periods were grammatical or historical, and early Christian writings were primarily dogmatic treatises. Furthermore, the Church fathers tended to distrust pagan literature even when their own writings betrayed their classical educations in every sentence, as an examination of the works of St. Jerome or St. Augustine easily shows. Later, although the Church was responsible for the suppression of much pagan literature, notably the Germanic heroic works, remnants of which survive in Old Icelandic (Old Norse) versions, the accommodation of the literary impulse to the Christian ethos would produce a significant body of hagiographical literature and, in the later Middle Ages, the various romance cycles in which the didactic element does not overwhelm real literary merit.

The *Etymologiae* (partial translation in *An Encyclopedist of the Dark Ages*, 1912) of Saint Isidore of Seville, provides a contemporary definition of story (*fabula*): Story does not speak of things done (*res factae*) but of things created in speech (*res fictae de loquendo*). The emphasis in this study will be on the latter point, "things created," because even in historical or quasi-historical works, authors such as St. Gregory the Great or Gregory of Tours would break the flow of their narratives to develop or expand upon a striking episode, making of it more a vignette than a mere recital of details. What one finds, in other words, are coherence of focus and intensity of presentation that make of such an episode a totality of intrinsic narrative interest. One looks for fictive *form* and not necessarily fictive *content*. The writer imposes his or her creative skill upon the incidents, factual or not, so that they become almost independent of the historical, narrative matrix in which they are found.

These early works of "short fiction" should possess as well the sharp, intense focus of the lyric or the *lai* as opposed to the broader scope and grander scale of the epic or extended romance. Most of the works considered in this study will range from 250 to 500 words, but length is less of a concern than focus, scale, or ambiance: *Beowulf* (early eighth century?) is not lengthy, but it fits the definition of epic very obviously when compared with the unity of conflict to be found in the late ninth century *Waltharius* or the Irish tale *The Exile of the Sons of Uisliu*, also written in the ninth century. These two works are better termed heroic lays or tales than epics. Other generic categories of short fiction include the vignette or anecdote, both of which tend not to be found independently of some larger narrative framework; the saint's life or miracle tale whether in verse or prose; and later, the romantic tale, even when it still possesses a strong heroic or mythic content.

The period under discussion extends from 476 C.E., the date of the deposition of the last Roman emperor in the West, to c. 1050, a time when it was manifest that political and economical stability, along with an influx of new knowledge and the rise of the great cathedral schools, had led to the beginnings of the high Middle Ages. The historical events relevant for this study go back to 375, the death of Ermanaric, the Ostrogothic emperor whose deeds, filtered

Historical and Literary Events

Historical		Literary	
375	Death of Ermanaric		
435	Defeat of Gundaharius by the Huns		
451	Defeat of Attila by the Burgundians		
453	Death of Attila		
476	Odovacar king in Italy (deposition of the last Roman ruler)		
493	Theodoric the Ostrogoth conquers Italy		
		520	Cassiodorus's *History of the Goths* (lost)
		c. 591	Gregory of Tours's *History of the Franks*
		c. 550	Jordanes's *Getica* (abbreviated version of Cassiodorus's work)
		593	Gregory the Great's *Dialogues*
		622-623	Isidore of Seville's *Eytmologies*
		731	Bede's *Ecclesiastical History of the English People*
		750-785	Cynewulf; *Elene*
		8th century	*Andreas*
		after 787	Paul the Deacon's *History of the Lombards*
768-814	Reign of Charlemagne		
		c. 800	The *Hildebrandslied*
842	The Strasbourg Oaths		
843	The Treaty of Verdun		
		9th century	Irish tales: *Exiles of the Sons of Uisliu*; *Wooing of Etain*
		c. 850-890?	The *Waltharius*
		c. 880	The *Cantilena of St. Eulalia*
987	Hugh Capet crowned	9th and 10th centuries	Icelandic tales: *Atlakviða*; *Hamðismál*
991	The Battle of Maldon (poem composed soon afterward)		
		10th century	Welsh tales: *The Mabinogion*
		1040	The *Life of St. Alexis*

through the lost chronicle of Cassiodorus and its condensation written by Jordanes, figure in the Old Icelandic *Hamðismál* (tenth century; *Poem of Hamðir*, 1923). A similar process occurred with the stories of Attila and Theodoric the Ostrogoth as history was transmuted into heroic legends that spread from their places of origin near Rome or the Rhine as far west as Iceland.

As important to this study as historical personages are events marking the development of European national units, such as the Treaty of Verdun (843) that created France and Germany, and of the major European languages, such as the Strasbourg Oaths (842), which testify to the necessity of using both Old French and the Germanic dialects so that all witnesses of the proceedings might understand the oaths of peace between Charles the Bald and Louis the German. A history of literary development in the early Middle Ages is also a history of the development of the major European languages as tools of creative expression as well as of day-to-day communication. Indeed, for some time, many of the works to be discussed in this study were analyzed chiefly as linguistic monuments rather than as literary exemplars. Twentieth century studies, however, have repeatedly established their literary merits.

A chronological look at the works illustrates the increasing variety of forms in the literature of the early Middle Ages as well as the linguistic variety that characterizes the latter part of the period. The apparent consistency of literary forms of the pre-Carolingian period is somewhat misleading since the vignettes and anecdotes found in the various works differ widely in content and presentation. Consider, for example, the Munderic episode in Gregory of Tours's *Historia Francorum* (c. 594; *The History of the Franks*, 1927) and one of the dialogues from the first book of *Dialogi* (c. 593; *Dialogues*, c. 887) of Gregory the Great.

MUNDERIC

The story of Munderic is actually an episode in the reign of Thierry I, son of Clovis. Munderic, a relative of Thierry I, revolts against his king, claiming that his blood makes him equally entitled to the throne. He gains followers and is besieged by Thierry I. His defense is strong enough that Thierry I resorts to guile, luring Munderic from his stronghold with false pledges of good faith and having him executed once he is vulnerable.

This episode has multiple functions in Gregory's narrative: It is one of the historical events he is bound to include in his work, but it is also one of a series of episodes portraying the ruthlessness and administrative ingenuity of Thierry I. Although Gregory deplores Thierry I's tactics, this attitude is mixed with some admiration for Thierry I's strength of character. Furthermore, the Munderic episode offers an opportunity for Gregory to exercise his skill as a storyteller. The events are not complicated, but the episode stands out because of Gregory's use of two motifs—good faith and bad faith—that are intensified by repetition. Munderic is a traitor, but he has a loyal following; Thierry I, the rightful ruler, does not hesitate to use deceit, and his envoy, Aregyselus, is able to persuade the strangely guileless Munderic that Thierry I will honor the oath sworn on the altar in his name. Aregyselus promptly betrays Munderic to Thierry I's forces, and Munderic, finally aware of treachery, kills the messenger and dies, honorably defending himself. With no real description of his personality, one still can perceive a rather simple, straightforward man who is destroyed as much by his ambition as by the machinations of his opponent. The techniques of fiction, especially the coherence provided by the emphasis of two major motifs, elevate the episode from a mere sequence of events to the status of story.

GREGORY THE GREAT

The anecdotes of Gregory the Great are more easily identified as fiction because the narrator himself describes them as tales he has heard from others and will now relate to his interlocutor, Peter. One such story, found in Book 1 of the *Dialogues*, is a conventional exemplum describing the powers of a holy man and the chastising of a thief. The latter has stolen vegetables from the monastery garden, so the prior commands a snake to guard the path. The thief, startled by the snake, tries to escape but finds himself entangled in the fence, hanging head downward. The prior dismisses the snake with a blessing and rebukes the thief, giving him the vegetables he had tried to steal.

Many scholars have commented on the naïveté Gregory shows toward these stories. He relates tale after tale, seeming to give critical acceptance to even the most preposterous. This may be, but Gregory saw as a function of the anecdote or exemplum the edifi-

Literature Chronology

Author	Work	Date	Language	Form
	PRE-CAROLINGIAN C. 500-750			
Cassiodorus	*History of the Goths* (lost)	520	Latin	History/Vignettes
Jordanes	*Getica*	c. 550	Latin	History/Vignettes
Gregory of Tours	*History of the Franks*	c. 575-594	Latin	History/Vignettes
Gregory the Great	*Dialogues*	593	Latin	History/Vignettes
Bede	*Ecclesiastical History*	731	Latin	History/Vignettes
Paul the Deacon	*History of the Lombards*	after 787	Latin	History/Vignettes
	CAROLINGIAN AND ANGLO-SAXON c. 750-1000			
Cynewulf	*Elene*	750-785	Old English	Heroic miracle-tale
	Andreas	8th century	Old English	Heroic miracle-tale
	Hildebrandslied	c. 800	Old High German	Heroic verse-narrative
	Waltharius	late 9th century	Latin	Heroic verse-narrative
	Cantilena of St. Eulalia	c. 880	Old French	Verse hagiography
	Battle of Maldon	early 10th century	Old English	Heroic verse-narrative
	Life of St. Alexis	mid-10th century	Old French	Verse hagiography
	CELTIC AND ICELANDIC c. 800-1050			
	Voyage of St. Brendan	9th century	Latin	Prose hagiography
	Exile of the Sons of Uisliu and *Wooing of Etain*	9th century	Old Irish	Heroic\romantic prose-narrative
	Atlakviða; *Hamðismál*	9th/10th centuries?	Old Icelandic	Heroic verse-narrative
	The Mabinogion	10th century	Welsh	Heroic\romantic prose-narrative

cation through pleasure of the least sophisticated of his audience. What appears to be naïveté, a quality one can ascribe to a politician and religious leader such as Gregory only with difficulty, is actually an absence of ironic overtones. The snake obeys a command made in the name of Christ; this is simply one of the conventions of the miracle tale. The miracle is the focus and *raison d'être* of the story and is the one element that cannot be called into question if the tale is to succeed.

Bede the Venerable

The anecdotes and miracle stories told by Saint Bede the Venerable in his *Historia ecclesiastica gentis Anglorum* (731; *Ecclesiastical History of the English People*, c. 887) are of a more sober variety than those of Gregory the Great. They are generally biographical, such as the story of Caedmon, and the focus of the miracles is on personal help—healing or the conferring of some special gift such as Caedmon's gift of song. A good example of Bede's narrative skill is his description of Caedmon's painful reluctance even to remain in the hall when others were drinking and singing lest he be required to sing; this realistic touch heightens the effect of the miraculous bestowal of musical talent. Likewise, Bede's usual narrative restraint enhances the effect of such stories, as one comes upon them as gems in a plainer matrix.

Bede and Gregory have in common their use of hagiography as the controlling convention for the stories they incorporate into their works. With Paul the Deacon, readers return to the more secular, heroic cast of story that was observed in the work of Gregory of Tours. One much-praised episode, the story of Alboin, was reworked in various versions as late as the Elizabethan period. Alboin's career is developed at length in the first two books of Paul the Deacon's *Historia Langobardorum* (after 787; *History of the Lombards*, 1907), but it is the story of his winning his weapons and a man's place in his society that deserves critical consideration. Alboin must receive his weapons from the king of a foreign nation, and the king he chooses, Turisind, is the father of a man Alboin has just killed. Turisind, mindful of the oath of peace extended to all guests, restrains his men, gives Alboin his weapons, and allows him to depart unharmed. It is the tension between Alboin's audacity and Turisind's honorable restraint that gives the episode its power. Paul allows the story to stand on its own merits, which are considerable, but in other instances such as the story of Lamisso, he feels free to comment if the details of the story strain the readers' credulity too much. His doubts and disclaimers appear as storyteller's asides which do not hamper the progress of the narrative; the asides do not prevent him from giving all the details of the story, however improbable.

To suggest that the most prominent literary monuments of the sixth through the eighth centuries were, for the most part, Latin secular histories that incorporated short tales rather misrepresents the fictive activity of that period. Much has been lost, for example, of stories in Old High German. It is also safe to assume oral versions for the stories that have been dated as eighth century or later. When stories are connected, however tenuously, with historical events, one can assume that some version of those events entered the storyteller's realm soon afterward. One of the best sets of examples involves the heroic tales concerning the Huns, the Burgundians, and the Goths; there is enough of the historical to tempt scholars to link each character with a historical personage yet enough events that are patently contrary to established fact that one is forced to see the storyteller's hand and judgment at work.

Ermanaric

The first example of the evolution of story from history concerns the death of the Ostrogothic ruler, Ermanaric, in 376, an event attested by a contemporary historian, Ammianus Marcellinus, and in the later histories of Jordanes and thus presumably in the lost history of Cassiodorus. Ermanaric had executed Sunnilda, the wife of a treacherous member of his following, having her torn apart or trampled by wild horses. Her brothers attempted to avenge her death but succeeded only in wounding Ermanaric so that he was permanently incapacitated. Later, this story becomes linked with the legends of the Nibelungs and the Völsungs and forms the background for the Old Icelandic *Hamðismál*. Gudrun, a well-known figure in the Nibelung and Völsung legends, urges her sons, Hamðir and Sorli, to avenge the death of Svanhildr, their sister. As in the earlier account, the death of the sister is not part of the action of the story proper but forms a powerful motivation for her brothers. The *Hamðismál* departs from its sources in the introduction of Erpr, an illegitimate half brother, killed by Hamðir and Sorli when he offers, with taunting speeches, to accompany them. The brothers succeed in mutilating Jomunrekkr (Ermanaric) but are destroyed by his men, realizing too late that, if they had allowed Erpr to assist them, they would have killed Jomunrekkr and survived the encounter. The focus of the lay has shifted from simple revenge to a tragedy of hubris and folly as the brothers' wrongful violence against Erpr destroys them. The *Hamðismál*, an excellent example of the stark narrative of the lays in the collection known as the *Poetic Edda*, is brief and tightly constructed, with no word or incident that is irrelevant to the plot. The author has as well a gift for understatement, especially in Sorli's rebuke to Hamðir: "You'd have had a brave heart [Erpr's], Hamðir/ if you'd had a wise one:/ a man lacks much/ when he lacks a brain."

Ermanaric figures in several heroic tales, such as the *Völsunga Saga* (c. 1270; *The Saga of the Volsungs*, 1930), the Old English *Widsith* (seventh century?), and the Old Icelandic *Þiðreks* saga (seventh century?). He is usually depicted in negative situations, although some versions of the Ermanaric stories show some sympathy for his plight. The *Þiðreks Saga* links him, in a totally nonhistorical fashion, with another figure of history and legend, Theodoric the Ostrogoth, who was known in legend as Dietrich von Bern (Dietrich of Verona) and as *Þiðrek*. Theodoric's literary development is much more involved than that of Ermanaric; his fame as a conqueror and a ruler made him the focus of many legends. One of the earliest tales in which he figures, although not as a character, is one of the best, the fragmentary *Hildebrandslied* (c. 800; *The Hildebrandslied*, 1914), the only extant example of Old High German heroic tale.

Hildebrand, returning to Italy with Dietrich from exile, is confronted by the army of his enemy, Odoaker (Odovacar). The conflict is to be decided by a duel, and Hildebrand's opponent is his own son, Hadubrand, who had been a very young child when his father was exiled. Hildebrand identifies himself, but Hadubrand, convinced that Hildebrand had died long before, refuses to believe him. Hadubrand insists on fighting, even when his father begs him to reconsider. The poem breaks off, but the outcome is certain to be tragic: Either the father will kill the son as in the case of Rustum and Sohrab, or the son will kill the father as Oedipus does Laius. In fewer than seventy lines, however, the poet has presented an episode that is powerful and deeply moving—almost a drama since much of the poem is in dialogue. The two characters reveal their personalities in their speeches. Hadubrand is all adolescent pride and truculence; Hildebrand is desperate as he realizes the futility of his pleading, seeing that his paternal affection must yield before the demands of his honor as a warrior.

Although events in the *Hildebrandslied* can be located in the historical context of Theodoric's conflict with Odovacar, the poet has chosen the father-son conflict as the focus of his work and has even altered historical fact for the sake of his story. Theodoric defeated Odovacar; the latter did not drive him out of his kingdom. This nonhistorical detail is a kind of "name-dropping," a storyteller's device to attract and hold the attention of his hearers as he proceeds to tell a story of his own making. Furthermore, the motif of exile works well for the conflict in the *Hildebrandslied* and, in fact, becomes a part of the Theodoric legend. Theodoric's and Hildebrand's exile also allow the poet to allude to another character, Attila the Hun, with whom they presumably resided for a time.

The impact of Attila on Western civilization is undeniable, and the legends of the races he encountered attest his impact on their fiction as well. The "Scourge of God" was also the benevolent patron of Walther in the ninth century *Waltharius* and received positive treatment as Etzel in the thirteenth century *The Nibelungenlied* (c. 1200; *The Nibelungenlied*). The negative portraits of Attila are to be found in the Old Icelandic tales of the Nibelungs and the Völsungs such as the *Atlakviða* (ninth century?; *Lay of Atli*, 1923). Later medieval stories would link him with the other legendary figures from the time of the migrations, making him the contemporary not only of Theodoric, born twenty years after his death, but also of Ermanaric, who lived and died long before Attila's time. These complexities are of less importance than the tales themselves, two of which, the *Waltharius* and the *Atlakviða*, will be discussed here.

WALTHARIUS

The *Waltharius* contains the stuff of epics. Attila has taken hostages from three of the kingdoms he has encountered: Walther, a prince of Aquitaine; Hildegund, a Burgundian princess; and Hagen, a Frankish nobleman. The *Waltharius*, however, is not the story of war but of the ingenuity and martial prowess of Walther himself as he extricates himself from various dilemmas. Moreover, Walther is not an Odysseus; his struggles are with men, not with gods. He wishes only to free himself and Hildegund, his beloved, from the benevolent captivity of Attila, who considers him one of his best warriors. The lovers escape when Attila and his men are all intoxicated after a feast given by Walther. They reach the kingdom of the Franks only to be attacked by Gunther, the Frankish king who covets the treasure Walther has brought from his Hunnish captivity. Among Gunther's men is Hagen, who had escaped earlier from Attila. Hagen is forced by his allegiance to Gunther to join him in a two-against-one combat with Walther, who before this was his friend, but he rationalizes his acquiescence to Gunther's demand by means of the vengeance he must seek for a nephew killed by Walther during the battle. All three fighters survive the conflict, although Walther loses his right hand, Gunther loses a leg, and Hagen loses one eye; at the end, Walther mocks Hagen for joining Gunther against him.

The poet uses all the techniques of the epic—scholars have suggested the influence of Vergil's *Aeneid* (c. 29-19 B.C.E.; English translation, 1553)—while maintaining his focus on personal conflicts, especially that between Walther and Hagen. In this respect, the poet of the *Waltharius* resembles the poet of the *Hildebrandslied*. The great events and personages of the migrations and the fall of the Roman Empire are simply contest and background for the central conflicts of the tales. Both the *Hildebrandslied* and the *Waltharius* are heroic lays that achieve their narrative power by concentrated focus on potentially tragic confrontations.

Atlakviða

In the *Atlakviða*, Attila is given the negative role which is more familiar to most readers. Gunther and Hagen appear as the brothers of Gudrun, the wife of Atli (Attila). Atli has persuaded the brothers to come to his court, and, once they are there, he tortures them to force from them the location of the great treasure of the Nibelungs. Hogni (Hagen) is killed, and Gunther eventually dies in a pit of snakes. Gudrun takes vengeance in Aeschylean fashion; she kills her sons by Atli and serves him their flesh. She then sets fire to the hall, and all perish. The *Atlakviða* is as terse and stark as the other example of the Eddic lay, the *Hamðismál*. The poet attends to the basic matter of the conflicts—Atli's avarice, the heroic resistance of the brothers, and the total vengeance of Gudrun.

The tales of the Goths, the Burgundians, and the Huns are primarily interesting because of their literary style, which combines narrative simplicity with compelling, dramatic situations that in and of themselves serve the purposes of characterization. The other aspect of their importance involves the way in which important figures and events of history find their way into fictional narrative, a process much more complex than this study can indicate, but one which demonstrates the interaction between fact, tradition, and the creative impulse.

History and fable (or story) come together also in one of the major Old English heroic works, the *Battle of Maldon* (c. tenth century). The poem has been much admired for the clarity with which it illustrates both the glory and the tragedy of the heroic ethos in confrontation with the reality of war. Byrthnoth, the leader of an English troop, permits an invading party of Norwegians to cross, at low tide, a causeway that at any other time would be impassable. His heroic and hubristic generosity dooms him and his men in the subsequent battle. They die to a man, one of the last survivors rendering in epigrammatic fashion the code by and for which they lived and died: "Heart must be braver, courage the bolder/Mood the stouter as our strength grows less!"

Battle of Maldon

The *Battle of Maldon* exists for us without the opening lines, but the point at which the story begins is nevertheless lyrical in force: A young knight frees his falcon, and this, the poet says, is a sign that he will not fail his leader; the poem maintains this elegiac note throughout. Scholars have established nearly all the details concerning the historicity of the battle, but it is the work of the poet—his skill in depicting Byrthnoth's *ofermoð*, hubris, and the dogged courage of his men—that makes the *Battle of Maldon* unequaled in tragic impact within its scope except by the *Hildebrandslied*.

An early passage in this study mentioned the accommodations that Christian literary sensibilities made to some of the modes of secular literature. The various hagiographical stories of the early Middle

Ages are a good index to this accommodation. One might argue that the tales of saints and martyrs are not, strictly speaking, fiction, yet their narrative form quickly becomes standardized—miraculous birth, early piety, many miracles, much self-denial, fortitude under oppression, and painful martyrdom or blissful death—and, of greater significance, these tales participate in one of the major fictional modes, that of romance. No matter how gruesome the details of a martyrdom might be, the tale has, in the Christian context, the requisite "happy ending" of romance. The saint's life or miracle is yet another aspect of the wish fulfillment that underlies the mode of romance.

One must make distinctions among the various forms of medieval hagiography. The Old English *Andreas* (eighth century?) or the *Elene* (750-785), or the Irish *Navigato sancti Brendani abbatis* (ninth century; *The Voyage of St. Brendan*, 1928), are quite different from such Old French works as *Cantilène de Sainte Eulalie* (c. 880; *The Prose of St. Eulalie*, 1912) sequence or *La Vie de Sainte Alexis* (1040; *The Life of St. Alexis*, 1912). The Old English tales have a strong heroic element and have a wider scope of action than the Old French tales. The *Voyage of St. Brendan* takes the form of a quest and has been linked with the Old Irish voyage tales (*Imramma*) such as the *Voyage of Brân* (seventh century) or the *Voyage of Maeldune* (seventh-ninth centuries). It is as much a tale of the wonders witnessed by St. Brendan and his companions as it is the story of a holy ascetic.

Voyage of St. Brendan

The *Voyage of St. Brendan* relates the quest of the abbot St. Brendan and several of his monks for a fabled "Promised Land of the Saints," an earthly Paradise. The journey is a series of encounters with strange creatures and enchanted places, but it is also a spiritual journey. Some scholars have argued that the various islands or sailing conditions, such as the Coagulated Sea (the Sargasso?) can be identified and that the *Voyage of St. Brendan* suggests actual journeys perhaps even to the Americas. This hint of possible veracity accounts in part for the popularity of the work all through the medieval period, but its popularity resulted as well from the writer's descriptions of the beautiful and the strange, from the way in which monastic spirituality is unified with the quest for marvels (centuries before the Old French *La Queste del Saint Graal* (1225-1230; *The Quest of the Holy Grail*, 1926), and from the person of St. Brendan himself. His calm faith sustains his monks through all of their fantastic adventures, and even the presence of a sea monster, the leviathan Jasconius, does not disrupt the tranquil tone of the work.

The Andreas and the Elene

In contrast to the *Voyage of St. Brendan*, the spirituality and piety of the *Andreas* and the *Elene* seem more vigorous and active. Andreas (the apostle Andrew) must rescue his fellow apostle Matthias from a race of cannibals. The poem graphically describes the torments suffered by Andreas once he rescues both Matthias and the youth of the cannibal race chosen to die in Matthias's stead. Among the best passages of the poem are those that describe Andreas's sea journeys with a mysterious boatman who catechizes him on matters of faith and who is, as Andreas slowly realizes, Christ himself. Andreas's role as deliverer and missionary crystallizes in the image of the water from the rock, a flood Andreas invokes to destroy his enemies. He relents so much as to pray for the resurrection of the youths of the cannibals, and, having converted them to Christianity, he departs. For all of his passivity, Andreas is a fighter, a thane of Christ, and a Moses figure. He is timid when first confronted with his task, but the dominant impression left by this heroic miracle tale is the forceful personality of its protagonist.

The same evaluation applies to Cynewulf's *Elene*, the story of the recovery of the True Cross by St. Helena, mother of the emperor Constantine. Confronted by the obstinacy of the elders of Jerusalem, she incarcerates a wise man who is known to hold the key to the mystery of the rebel teacher executed in that city. The wise man, named, oddly enough, Judas, yields before Elene's harshness and reveals not only the identity of the rebel but also the place of His crucifixion. Only one of the crosses found there can resurrect a dead youth, and Elene claims it as the long-sought relic. Judas converts to the Christian faith and receives the name Cyriacus, and Elene returns to her son in a triumph of healing miracles.

The *Elene* and the *Andreas* have been described here as heroic miracle tales because they emphasize the power of their protagonists (and their protagonists' Patron). Andreas, although broken by torture, can nevertheless invoke an enemy-destroying miracle, and Elene uses the power of her imperial rank, usually a negative element, in the service of the faith. Indeed, the *Elene*, from its first episode, the triumph granted Constantine by the sign of the Cross, deals with the *power* of the new Faith. This emphasis on militant Christianity is in marked contrast to the hagiographic narratives of the *Cantilena of St. Eulalia* and the *Life of St. Alexis*.

Cantilena of St. Eulalia

The *Cantilena of St. Eulalia* is the first literary monument of the French language. In addition to its linguistic significance it also attests the adaptation of the liturgical sequence (an extended embellishment of a line of text) to the uses of lyric poetry. The poem is very brief and tells the story of Eulalia's martyrdom in the simplest manner. Eulalia, a young Christian noblewoman, refuses to give up her faith; brought before Maximian, she persists in her resistance and is given over to be burned. When the flames do not harm her, Maximian orders her beheaded. Her soul flies to heaven in the form of a dove.

For all its brevity, the *Cantilena of St. Eulalia* presents a complete dramatic action that builds in intensity from Eulalia's resistance through the torturing and martyrdom and is resolved in her soul's flight. As stated above, this tale differs from the Old English tales here described in its emphasis not on Eulalia's active power but on her endurance and her helplessness to resist, physically at least, her tormentors. Also, the focus of the tale is on the personal rather than the social effects of the miracles.

Life of St. Alexis

The *Life of St. Alexis*, another early French monument, deals again with the struggles of an individual. Alexis, a wealthy young man, decides on his wedding night to reject all—wife, riches, and family—to devote himself to prayer and self-denial. After a lengthy self-exile, he returns to his home and lives, unrecognized by his family, as a poor holy man under the staircase of his former home. His family only learns of his true identity by means of a letter that they find after his death. The poem ends proclaiming Alexis's joy in Heaven where he is reunited with his maiden bride. The *Life of St. Alexis* follows the conventions of the flight-from-the-world, which is one of the many varieties of saints' lives. Its compact narrative and careful handling of rhythm and assonance show the French language in the process of becoming one of the major literary languages of the West.

Exile of the Sons of Uisliu

The saints' lives have been described as participating formally in the mode of romance in a period in which, for the most part, heroic tales dominated. The great age of medieval romance would begin in the early decades of the twelfth century, but as early as the ninth century and possibly even earlier, there were Celtic precursors to many of the major romances. The Irish *Exile of the Sons of Uisliu* has been linked with the development of the Tristan legend, and the *Wooing of Etain* (ninth century), also Irish, with the legend of Lancelot and Guinevere at least insofar as the abductions of Guinevere are concerned.

The *Exile of the Sons of Uisliu*, sometimes called the story of Deirdre, describes the fate of those sons of Uisliu who accompany Noisiu, their brother, into exile after he elopes with Deirdre, who has been promised to Conchobar, king of Ulster. The outcome is tragic for both lovers: Noisiu is treacherously slain, and Deirdre, who signs two poignant laments for her lover, later commits suicide rather than be given to one she despises. One can see the details that later became part of the Tristan story—the illicit love affair, the lovers' flight, and their tragic demise—but the work has its own inherent interest. One sympathizes with Deirdre, fated from before her birth to cause dissension among men, when she chooses Noisiu in defiance of the arrangement that makes her the property of the aging Conchobar. Likewise, Noisiu draws the reader's sympathy as he is taunted by Deirdre into accepting her, an act that seals his fate.

WOOING OF ETAIN

The *Wooing of Etain* is the story of how King Eochaid Airem wins Etain, a princess of the fairy folk, loses her to her former mate and regains her by besieging the fairy mounds and eventually succeeding in the trials set before him there. This tale reappears in many guises, not only in the *Lancelot: Ou, Le Chevalier à la charrette* (c. 1168; *Lancelot: Or, The Knight of the Cart*, 1913) of Chrétien de Troyes but also in *Pwyll, Prince of Dyved*, one of the tales included in *The Mabinogion* (1838-1849; tales from *The White Book of Rhydderch*, 1300-1325, and *The Red Book of Hergest*, 1375-1425), a group of Welsh tales dating from the very end of the period under discussion here. Like the *Exile of the Sons of Uisliu*, the *Wooing of Etain* is important as a good piece of fiction in its own right, from the lavish description of Etain with which it begins to the moment of surprise when Etain is magically abducted despite the hapless Eochaid's attempts to guard her.

SUMMARY

In bringing together an extended discussion of the forms of short fiction in the Middle Ages, a danger exists of oversimplification or of a too-pat schematic view of diverse developments. The period of the early Middle Ages was an unsettled time. Necessary social and economic adjustments to the collapse of Roman domination in the West threatened the preservation of the classical tradition of education. The number of surviving works of fiction seems small beside the compendiums of rhetorical, historical, or doctrinal works, but at no time did the art of fiction lapse, certainly not as far as oral transmission and development was concerned, as the complicated history of the Goths, Burgundians, and their heroes clearly shows. Often, however, "story" was put to work in sermons or in histories without losing the essential crafted nature that sets a work of fiction apart from mere sequential reportage. Many of the independent stories never ceased to engage their audiences, and storytellers adapted them by retelling or forging ever more complex combinations of the tales, some with the range and scope, for example, of the Theodoric stories. Although many of the gems of early medieval fiction remain buried in little-read histories or in collections primarily of interest to scholars, others, some of which have been discussed here, are now receiving the scholarly and critical attention they have deserved as literary works.

Amelia A. Rutledge

BIBLIOGRAPHY

Hasty, Will, and James Hardin, eds. *German Writers and Works of the Early Middle Ages, 800-1170.* Dictionary of Literary Biography 148. Detroit: Gale Research, 1995. This comprehensive reference source includes information on Old High and Middle High German literature. Includes biographies of the major writers of the period, bibliographical references, and an index.

Gantz, Jeffrey, trans. *Early Irish Myths and Sagas.* New York: Penguin, 1981. Each chapter of this survey is devoted to a different Irish myth or saga. Includes a discussion of the *Exile of the Sons of Uisliu*. Also includes an introduction and notes by Gantz, bibliographical references, and an index.

Griffiths, Bill. *The Battle of Maldon: Text and Translation.* Hockwold-cum-Wilton, Norfolk, England: Anglo-Saxon Books, 1996. This translation from the Old English includes bibliographical references.

Jackson, William T. H., ed. *Prudentius to Medieval Drama.* Vol. 1 in *European Writers: The Middle Ages and the Renaissance*, edited by George Stade. New York: Charles Scribner's Sons, 1983. An exhaustive study of the major forms of medieval fiction, with chapters written by prominent scholars. Includes discussion of medieval fiction forms, such as the epic, the ballad, the allegory, the satire, and the saga.

Ludlow, John Malcolm. *Popular Epics of the Middle Ages of the Norse-German and Carlovingian Cycles.* 2 vols. London: Macmillan, 1865. A thoughtful analysis of the major epics of the medieval period. Each chapter is devoted to a study of a different epic. Includes two overview chapters, entitled "Some Words on the Growth of Legend" and "The Great Cycles of Middle Age Romance."

Murdoch, Brian, trans. *Walthari: A Verse Translation of the Medieval Latin "Waltharius."* Glasgow: Scottish Papers in Germanic Studies, 1989. This translation of Waltharius includes bibliographical references.

Odenkirchen, Carl J. trans. *"The Life of St. Alexius" in the Old French Version of the Hildesheim Manuscript: The Original Text Reviewed, with Comparative Greek and Latin Versions, All Accompanied by English Translations, and an Introductory Study, a Bibliography, and Appendices.* Brookline, Mass.: Classical Folia Editions, 1978. Includes Johann Wolfgang von Goethe's retelling of the tale in original German and English translation.

Schreiber, Lady Charlotte, trans. *The Mabinogion.* Mineola, N.Y.: Dover Publications, 1997. Translations of a number of Arthurian romances and medieval Welsh tales, including *Pwyll, Prince of Dyved*. Includes bibliographical references and an index.

Twaddell, William Freeman. *The Hildebrandlied.* Providence, R.I.: Brown University, 1976. This English translation includes a commentary by Twaddell.

Watanabe-O'Kelly, Helen, ed. *The Cambridge History of German Literature*. Cambridge, England: Cambridge University Press, 1997. This history of German literature includes two chapters devoted to the Middle Ages, in which critical issues are debated and discussed. Includes bibliographical references and an index.

Webb, J. F., ed. *The Age of Bede*. Harmondsworth, Middlesex, England: Penguin, 1998. Includes discussions of Bede's *Life of Cuthbert* and *Lives of the Abbots of Wearmouth and Jarrow*, Eddius Stephanus's *Life of Wilfrid*, and the anonymous history of Abbot Ceolfrith with *The Voyage of St. Brendan*. Includes bibliographical references and an index.

THE MEDIEVAL ROMANCE

The Middle Ages witnessed the flowering of one of the most important predecessors of the modern short story, the romance. By the late Middle Ages, this genre had become an extremely popular literary form. During the genre's inception in the eleventh century, the term "romance" referred exclusively to a composition written in French—a "Romance" language. During the literary history of the Middle Ages, however, the term came to denote a fictional narrative of a particular type: The romance is an adventure story focusing upon the experiences of love, honor, terror, and adoration. It is daringly unrealistic in conception and frequently employs remote settings but nevertheless strives for psychological realism. Conventional motifs of the romance include a mysterious challenge, love at first sight, a lonely journey through a wilderness or hostile landscape, and a battle with the enemy, sometimes a monster, often resulting in the rescue of the beloved.

Origins of the Romance

Although the romance assumed a generic identity and acquired a defined form during the Middle Ages, it had its roots in a much earlier tradition. The genre's development was significantly aided by the infusion of material from classical sources. Medieval romances are to some degree analogous to narrative prose tales, known as Greek romances, written from the first century B.C.E. to the third century C.E. by such authors as Chariton, Xenophon, Heliodorus of Emesa, and Longus. Although medieval writers probably had no direct contact with the original Greek tales, the stories, often about faithful lovers separated and reunited after perilous adventures, were carried on in the oral tradition. The tale of Apollonious of Tyre, a story of Greek origin but only extant in a third or fourth century Latin version, became one of the most widely retold stories of the Middle Ages.

Clerks, the professional writers of the twelfth century, had been trained in the cathedral schools in the arts of Latin grammar and rhetoric. Such Latin works as Ovid's *Metamorphoses* (c. 8 C.E.; English translation, 1567) and *Ars amatoria* (c. 2 B.C.E.; *Art of Love*, 1612) provided not only more material for the early writers of romance but also a style of exposition which encouraged a systematic development and a symbolic framework in which to elaborate their tales. Rhetorical embellishments with elaborate descriptions of surroundings and procedures and lists of everything from dishes at a feast to flowers in a field decorate the romances as details in an intricate tapestry.

Classical epics such as the *Odyssey* (c. 800 B.C.E.; English translation, 1616) and the *Aeneid* (c. 29-19 B.C.E.; English translation, 1553), sagas such as *The Nibelungenlied* (c. 1200), *chansons de geste* such as *The Song of Roland* (c. 1100), and the early chronicle accounts of Arthur all contain the elements of love, mystery, adventure, and psychology that have now come to be associated with romance. These earlier works, however, differ from romance in being consciously nationalistic and either historical or pseudohistorical, whereas romance, even while striving for verisimilitude, is consciously and deliberately fictional. During the Middle Ages the romance became a distinct literary type in part because writers wished to free themselves from the restrictions of the epic form and in part because the developing interest in new themes and ideas required new modes of expression.

Many of these new ideas and themes concerned the four historical "matters" we have come to associate with romance: the matter of Rome, which consists of romances based upon classical material, whether legendary or historical; the matter of France, which focuses upon the adventures of Charlemagne and his peers; the matter of Britain or Brittany, which concerns stories from Arthurian legend; and the matter of England, which treats native English heroes or heroes whose lives and adventures in some way concerned England.

Medieval romance, then, can be seen to differ from epic—a term that includes saga and *chanson de geste*—in content, form of presentation, and emphasis. Whereas the epic usually concerns a serious subject of national importance and a warrior-hero whose actions have national implications, the romance often has a plot that concerns a matter of personal importance, such as a love affair and its attendant problems or a chivalric adventure. The plot of the epic serves to reveal the hero's character and to establish his national importance, while the plot of the romance serves to reveal motivation, to delineate psychological processes and responses, and to explore intellectual and emotional dilemmas. Although many romances deal with the four "matters" of Rome, France, Britain, and England, which would lead one to believe they were historical in nature, their purpose was nevertheless primarily entertainment, and they often contained elements of the mysterious and the supernatural. Further contrasting the epic, which is usually sharply focused and unified, the romance is often of much looser structure; the plot is often episodic, and the episodes are both undeveloped and yet usually embellished by picturesque and detailed descriptions. The romance hero often fights for the sake of fighting or to prove his worth to his lady, while the epic hero ordinarily fights only for a highly significant or exalted purpose. Finally, while the epic very often is tragic, ending with the hero's death, the romance frequently has a happy ending.

The Matter of Rome

Although medieval romances concerned with the matter of Rome had as possible subjects the adventures of Alexander the Great, the Trojan War, the siege of Thebes, and the adventures of Aeneas, stories of Alexander and of Troy seem to have been the most popular. *Kyng Alisaunder* (fourteenth century), the best of the Alexander romances, first tells of Alexander's begetting through the magical powers of the Egyptian king Nectanebus, who contrives to mate with Olympias, the wife of Philip II of Macedon, and thereby fathers Alexander. The romance also details Alexander's rise to power and his various military accomplishments, particularly his wars with Darius the Great of Persia. The second part of the romance, treating Alexander's conquest of India and the many adventures he experienced in the Far Eastern countries, relies heavily on the excitement of the unknown and the distant in its description of mythical beasts and other wondrous sights.

The Alexander romances, although concerned with a historical figure, had as little basis in history as did the romances based upon the Troy theme. Since Homer was unknown to Western Europe in the medieval period, Troy romances were based not on the *Iliad* (c. 800 B.C.E.; English translation, 1616) but on two later accounts of the Trojan siege by Dictys of Crete and by Dares Phrygius. Their works concern the story of Jason and the Argonauts in their quest for the Golden Fleece, the siege of Troy, and the Greeks' return home. Among the Troy romances that make use of these accounts are *The Gest Historiale of the Destruction of Troy* (thirteenth century); the *Laud Troy Book* (c. 1400), which selectively treats the material of *The Gest Historiale of the Destruction of Troy*; John Lydgate's *The Hystorye, Sege and Dystruccyon of Troy* (1513; better known as *Troy Book*); and, most notably, Geoffrey Chaucer's poem *Troilus and Criseyde* (1382), the finest execution of this theme. Chaucer uses the Trojan War, however, merely as a backdrop for an examination of chivalric love and the complex psychologies of his two main characters; his concern is with human love, human relations, and human idealism, and the student of romance could do no better than to study Chaucer's poem in order to obtain a thorough understanding of the genre of romance.

The Matter of France

Those romances concerned with the matter of France—the Charlemagne romances—are closest in kind to the epic form. They concern themselves less with love and psychology and more with warfare and heroism. The Charlemagne romances have as their ultimate source *Chanson de Roland* (eleventh century; *The Song of Roland*, c. 1100), the Old French epic detailing Roland's heroism, Oliver's wisdom, Ganelon's treachery, and Archbishop Turpin's bravery and piety. The Charlemagne romances (early fourteenth century) fall roughly into two groups: One group, concerning the story of Otuel, contains such romances as *Otuel*, *The Sege of Melayne*, and *Roland and Vernagu*, while the other group, concerned with the story of Ferumbras, contains such romances as *The Sowdone of Babylone* and *Sir Ferumbras*. The earliest Charlemagne romance in English, *Otuel*, contrasts with the original Old French epic by diminishing the stature of Roland in order to elevate that of the hero Otuel. After detailing Otuel's conversion to Christianity in the midst of his combat with Roland, who had killed Otuel's uncle Vernagu, the romance describes Otuel's performance as a Christian knight in battles against the Saracens. *The Sege of Melayne*, another romance in the Otuel group, is notable for its depiction of Archbishop Turpin as a heroic figure in battle and for its presentation of religious visions and miracles. *Roland and Vernagu* makes use of the Latin legend that Charlemagne went to the Holy Land and received there such relics as St. Simeon's arm, Mary's smock, and the crown of thorns; the romance also tells of the invasion of Spain and of Roland's battle with Vernagu. Unfinished, the romance was perhaps intended as an introduction to *Otuel*. The Charlemagne romances, in their treatment of the religious conflict between Christians and infidels, are in some ways akin to Arthurian romances concerned with the Grail theme, in that in both sorts of romances religious faith provides a significant motivating force.

In the second group of romances, which concern the Ferumbras theme, *The Sowdone of Babylone* tells of Laban, Sultan of Babylon, and his twenty-foot-tall son Ferumbras, who sack Rome and, having obtained the relics of the Passion—the cross, the crown of thorns, and the Crucifixion nails—remove them to Spain. When Charlemagne's army comes to recover the relics, many adventures ensue. Oliver meets Ferumbras in single combat, conquers him, and converts him, after which Ferumbras fights with the Christians against the Saracens. This romance has a noteworthy love story that concerns Floripas, the Sultan's daughter, who falls in love with Guy of Burgundy, one of Charlemagne's knights. Her ingenuity and determination, which are inspired by her love, are ultimately significant to the victory of Charlemagne's forces and the rescue of the relics; consequently, after being baptized, she is married to her lover. A number of the incidents in the second part of this romance form the substance of *Sir Ferumbras*, a consciously and carefully crafted romance, perhaps the best of the English Charlemagne romances.

The Matter of Britain

The most popular of the four matters was the Arthurian theme, the matter of Britain, which was treated extensively by writers in England and on the Continent. The treatment accorded the story of Arthur, surely one of the most famous figures in European literature, well exemplifies the change in literary expression from epic to romance. The earliest accounts in which Arthur appears portray him as a historical hero who comes to assume national importance. By the twelfth century he has been transformed by courtly writers from a historical and national hero to a hero of romance.

Apparently the first historian to mention Arthur is Nennius, whose ninth century *Historia Brittonum*, a redaction of previous chronicles from the seventh and eighth centuries, describes Arthur as *dux bellorum*, "the leader of battles," who slaughters many pagans. Carrying the image of the Virgin Mary on his shield and invoking the name of the Mother of God as a battle cry, Arthur is said to have single-handedly slain 960 men in one day. A similar but much briefer account of Arthur's prowess in battle is found in the *Annales Cambriae*, the tenth century work of a Welsh writer who states that Arthur, having carried the cross of Christ on his shoulders for three days and three nights, was victorious in the Battle of Badon. Around 1125, William of Malmesbury, in his *Gesta regum Anglorum* (*The Deeds of the Kings of the English*, 1847), attests Arthur's historicity while he simultaneously acknowledges that myth-making concerning Arthur is taking place; he differentiates between the Arthur of truthful histories and the Arthur of false myths produced by the Britons. In fact, the Arthurian legend expanded greatly during this time, both in Britain and on the Continent; with every crossing of the English Channel the legend accumulated more and more material, so that the actual historicity of Arthur became increasingly difficult to verify.

These historical and pseudohistorical accounts provided the basis for the more deliberately imaginative Arthurian writings, the major sources of contemporary Arthurian legend, which begin to appear in the twelfth century. In that century there is a shift from the treatment of Arthur as a historical figure to the treatment of him as a figure of mythic proportion. Much Arthurian material was carried orally by Breton *conteurs*. The widespread influence of these bilingual (Breton and French) storytellers was in no little way aided by the military and political success of their patrons, the Normans. As Anglo-Norman power spread by conquest and marriage, the *conteurs* found welcome in courts in Britain, France, Scotland, Germany, Spain, and Italy. The nature of the Arthurian tales was modified as they traveled.

Traditions and motifs from Celtic legend and folklore were the earliest accruals to the legend of Arthur. The Welsh invested Arthur with the trappings of kingship. Prominent in the early verse is his position at the head of a band of heroes renowned for their skill at slaying monsters. Among these heroes listed and described in *Culhwch ac Olwen* (c. 1100) are some who survived into later legend including Cai (Sir Kay), Bedwyr (Sir Bedivere), and Mabon, son of Modron. The quest motif became an integral part of the Arthurian legend in Welsh tradition. One version of the quest is told in *Culhwch ac Olwen* when Arthur travels to the Otherworld to steal a cauldron, reputed to be able to restore the dead to life. The theme of a hero traveling to far-off lands, even into the Otherworld, to bring back gifts to his people, is also a basic story in folklore and myth worldwide. That the Welsh tales are the prototypes for the Grail quest has been the matter of much argument, but at least it can be said that here the theme of the questing hero was first connected to Arthurian legend. Jeffrey Gantz, translator of the *Mabinogion* (1976), connects the quest in *Culhwch ac Olwen* to similar raids in the other tales in which a hero ventures forth to capture an object—a bowl, a cauldron, or a woman—which is symbolic of female regenerative power. The most prevalent contest is between two men for a woman. This triangle motif is present throughout the *Mabinogion* and survives in the Arthur-Guinevere-Lancelot and Tristan-Iseult-Mark triangles of later Arthurian romances. The movement by a woman back and forth from one man to another in Celtic literature is frequently connected with abduction. Arthur's queen, Guinevere, appears first in Welsh traditions, and from the earliest sources, she is the heroine of such an abduction story.

Incorporating material from Celtic tradition, classical sources, and even biblical material, Geoffrey of Monmouth's *Historia regum Britanniae* (c. 1136; *History of the Kings of Britain*, 1718) consciously builds upon the scant writings of Nennius to create a national hero for Britain. Geoffrey added to Arthur's primary historical characterization as a fighter and a leader of warriors the coloration of chivalry, thus combining both epic and courtly traditions. Geoffrey adds to the legend the descent of Arthur from Aeneas of Troy, the begetting of Arthur by Uther Pendragon, the figures of Merlin and Mordred, and the courtly entourage that was necessary in order to reshape Arthur from a local chieftain into a great king. Indications of courtliness are displayed in the notions that a woman could be an incentive for a knight to excel and that a knight's bravery and nobility could be an incentive for the woman to be pure.

This transformation of the Arthurian story from epic to romance was continued in Wace's *Roman de Brut* of 1155. Wace adds to the written legend the tradition of the Round Table, dramatizes the Arthurian story through the addition of dialogue and action, and portrays Arthur as more courtly and less barbaric, as possessing other than martial attributes and abilities. Layamon's *Brut*, written around 1200, makes further additions to the legend of an extraordinary and supernatural nature, such as the fays who nurture the infant Arthur and the mysterious ladies who take Arthur away to Avalon. As other writers drew upon and developed the Arthurian material, the story of Arthur, the national hero, eventually became merely a backdrop or a departure point for stories which focused on such corollary themes as the quest for the Holy Grail and on such other knights as Perceval, Lancelot, and Gawain. By the time *Sir Gawain and the Green Knight* was written late in the fourteenth century, Arthur had been completely transformed from the epic hero he had been at his inception to the chivalric hero of romance.

As time passed and more and more material accrued to the legend of Arthur, the knights of the Round Table superseded Arthur as the focus of the romances; Gawain, Tristan, Lancelot, Galahad, and Perceval are all the subject of stories in which Arthur is only a minor or a corollary figure. Chrétien de Troyes, writing in the last half of the twelfth century, produced several romances for the court of Marie de Champagne. Of those five extant, the unfinished *Perceval: Ou, Le Conte du Graal* (c. 1180; *Perceval: Or, The Story of the Grail*, 1844) is notable as a spiritual romance concerning the quest for the Holy Grail, which was used by Wolfram von Eschenbach for his romance *Parzival* (c. 1200-1210; English translation, 1894), and which inspired as well a number of later romances concerning the Grail legend; this romance overtly links chivalry and religion in the romance form.

Chrétien's *Lancelot: Ou, Le Chevalier à la charrette* (c. 1168; *Lancelot: Or, The Knight of the Cart*, 1913) is significant for its development of the ideal that love requires an absolute and unhesitating devotion. Although Chrétien received the material for this romance from his patron, Marie de Champagne, his emphasis on psychological analysis and his examination of the parameters of human commitment to a code of conduct make his treatment of the material unique. In the course of the romance Lancelot sets out to rescue the queen who, as a result of Arthur's rash promise, has been taken captive. Having been unhorsed by the captor, Lancelot is walking disconsolately behind a cart when the driver tells him to get in if he wishes to learn about the queen. Although Lancelot's love for Guinevere is great, his pride and his dismay at having to ride in a fashion so unbefitting a knight cause him to take two more steps behind the cart before getting into it. After this act, although he triumphantly passes a number of tests of his devotion to his queen which require him to resist a seduction attempt, to crawl painfully over a bridge made of swords, to fight backward so as to keep his eyes fixed on the tower where his lady watches, and to play the coward in a tournament, Lancelot is nevertheless treated disdainfully by the queen because of the incompleteness of his devotion, indicated by those two additional steps which he had taken behind the cart before climbing in. This romance clearly demonstrates the absolute necessity of total commitment to the loved one.

Sir Thomas Malory, one of the most influential writers of Arthurian material, pulled together for his *Le Morte d'Arthur* (1485) many of the romances into a more or less unified whole. Although most of Malory's work is certainly a redaction of earlier writings, it is much more than that, in large part because of Malory's reshaping of the material into a body of writing that has coherence and purpose. Many later treatments of the story of Arthur are based upon Malory's work. The enduring popularity of the Arthurian theme is evident in such twentieth century works as Thomas Berger's *Arthur Rex* (1978), Richard Monaco's *Parzival: Or, A Knight's Tale* (1977), T. H. White's *The Once and Future King*, 1958 (a tetralogy including *The Sword in the Stone*, *The Witch in the Wood*, *The Ill-Made Knight*, and *The Candle in the Wind*) and *The Book of Merlyn: The Unpublished Conclusion to "The Once and Future King"* (1977), *The Mists of Avalon* (1983) by Marion Zimmer Bradley, and the several treatments of the theme by Mary Stewart.

The Matter of England

The romances said to concern the matter of England for the most part differ in some important ways from the other medieval romances discussed. They are often much less courtly and less sophisticated than the other romances, and they advance and support humble and simple virtues rather than the aristocratic virtues of chivalry and the courtly life. The inherited material of these romances, whether of native or foreign origin, having been adapted to the lower-class taste, is consequently often spare and realistic, with little of descriptive set pieces and other courtly elements. Action is preferred to introspection and analysis, and the poems are usually vigorous and balladlike in their concision.

Among these romances concerning the matter of England are *King Horn* (c. 1225), which uses the exile and return theme; *Bevis of Hampton* (c. 1200-1250), which begins with a variation on the Hamlet theme; *The Tale of Gamelyn* (c. 1350), from which

Shakespeare drew for *As You Like It* (c. 1599-1600); and *William of Paleme* (early fourteenth century), which uses the popular werewolf theme. Perhaps most reflective, however, of the spirit and the values of England's peasantry and its growing middle class is *Havelok the Dane* (c. 1350), a romance concerning a hero who is wrongly excluded from his kingdom in Denmark by an untrustworthy guardian. When the poor fisherman who reared Havelok can no longer support him, Havelok obtains work as a kitchen helper, soon earning renown locally for his ability to putt the stone; while such activities seem the very antithesis of courtly endeavor, they are nonetheless solidly representative of middle-class virtues. In time Havelok marries an orphaned English princess, Goldeboru, who, like Havelok, was betrayed by a guardian; when one night Goldeboru sees a luminous mark on Havelok's shoulder that indicates his royalty, she is overjoyed. After returning to Denmark and claiming his throne, Havelok conquers England and rewards all who have treated him well. The emphasis throughout the poem is on adventure, justice, and homely but traditional virtues, an emphasis that clearly distinguishes this romance and the other romances on the matter of England from those romances of the period which emphasize courtliness.

Courtly Love

The ideals of chivalry and courtly love, hallmarks of the romance, were signs of a revolutionary change in Western culture. Although debate continues as to whether or not a "system" of courtly love was recognized as such in the Middle Ages, historians do know for certain that courtly attitudes existed, that people aspired to courtly ideals, and that those courtly attitudes and ideals influenced people's conduct. One of the reasons for the importance of these attitudes undoubtedly is attributable to the patronage of artists and writers by such influential women as Eleanor of Aquitaine, queen first of France and then of England, and her daughter Marie de Champagne. In conjunction with the cult of the Virgin, the courtly mystique elevated noble women to morally and spiritually superior beings who could inspire admirers to transcend human limitations and rise to new heights of nobility; courtly love made a religion of male devotion to a lady, and courtly idealism demanded a high degree of civilized and sophisticated behavior in its adherents.

The courtly idealism so characteristic of the romance form during the Middle Ages first appeared in the eleventh century Provençal poetry of the trouvères. The originality of the Provençal poets, led by Guillaume X of Aquitaine (Eleanor's grandfather), lay not only in their use of vernacular language but also in their concept of a passion characterized by love at first sight, friendship between the lover and his lady, humility in wooing the lady, graciousness on the lady's part in granting her favor to the lover, and secrecy in concealing the love. The new poetry spread swiftly throughout Europe. From Aquitaine and Provence, the troubadours of central France took up the songs; at Eleanor's court at Poitiers, Bernard de Ventadour wrote his best poetry. The German *minnesänger* brought courtly love to Germany, inspiring the prose romances of Gottfried von Strassburg and Wolfram von Eschenbach. In Italy poets embraced *la stil nuova*, the sweet new style, which culminated in Dante's fusion of courtly love and mystical vision, first in *La vita nuova* (c. 1292; *Vita Nuova*, 1861, better known as *The New Life*) and most sublimely in *La divina commedia* (c. 1320; *The Divine Comedy*; 1802).

From France the courtly ideal spread throughout Europe, advanced in part by the enormously influential work of André Le Chapelain. A chaplain to the court of Marie de Champagne, Capellanus, in the latter quarter of the twelfth century, codified the system of courtly love in his three-volume work *Liber de arte honeste amandi et reprobatione inhonesti amoris* (c. 1185; *The Art of Courtly Love*, 1941). The work's first two books define love, establish its rules, and detail the appropriate conduct for its devotees, while the third book, curiously, serves as a retraction which seems to contradict everything said before. The first two books, emphasizing the ennobling nature of passionate love, explain the incompatibility of love and marriage; in fact, Capellanus states that love has no place in marriage since love requires secrecy, jealousy, apprehension, and difficulty in attainment. Marriage is not, however, an excuse for not loving;

rather the beloved must be someone other than one's spouse. Capellanus also states that the lover's whole mind is on the beloved and, in consequence, the lover will suffer greatly, will exhibit paleness, and will experience sleeplessness, heart palpitations, and loss of appetite.

The influence of this codification of courtly love on medieval romance, on the later romance tradition, and indeed on Western society, is immeasurable, since the work of Capellanus is both descriptive in recording existing attitudes and prescriptive in establishing those attitudes as the ideal. The emotional concept which we now call "romantic love" is thus invented during the Middle Ages, when love was separated from marriage; marriage, after all, was based on such things as property and politics and was, therefore, practical and mundane, whereas courtly love, as depicted by Capellanus, is spiritual and passionate. Thus, in its establishment of love as an ennobling social influence, in its delineation of the rules for the conduct of love, and in its development of the notion of feminine worth, the work of Capellanus influenced to a great extent both literature and society. Many of the deepest patterns of behavior which today govern relations between the sexes have their genesis in the code which Capellanus describes.

If Capellanus provided a formulation of the rules of courtly behavior, both Chrétien de Troyes and Marie de France, poets of the latter part of the twelfth century, provided extremely influential artistic celebrations of the courtly system. The approximately fifteen extant lais that are attributed to Marie are all short, simple, and direct, and were probably intended to be sung to harp accompaniment; emphasizing love rather than warfare, the poems reflect courtly sentiment in their focus upon courtesy, chivalry, and loyalty in love. Typical of Marie's themes and treatments is the lai of "Lanval." In disfavor with his king, Lanval one day rides into the country; lying down to rest, he is approached by two beautiful maidens who take him to their lady in a nearby pavilion. The lady, obviously a supernatural being, gives Lanval her love and a bottomless purse but warns him that if he speaks of her to anyone, he will never see her again. When Guinevere accuses Lanval of being false to his lord, of having secret sins, and of despising women, he defends himself by stating indignantly that in fact he has a lover and that the lowliest of her servants excels Guinevere in every way. Denounced by Guinevere to Arthur, Lanval is directed to produce his lady and prove his statement but he is unable to summon her. Saved from prison only by the surety of his friends, he is about to be sentenced to exile when a procession of beautiful maidens arrives, the last of whom is Lanval's mistress. When Arthur agrees that she is indeed more beautiful than the queen, Lanval's supernatural lover takes him away with her to Avalon.

Marie claimed that her intent in her work was merely to turn traditional tales into romance, and clearly she uses in her lais many conventional topics: The woman scorned motif draws upon the theme of Potiphar's wife; the idea of the supernatural lover comes either from Celtic fairy lore or from the classical myth of Cupid and Psyche; and the bottomless purse and the outcast who becomes favored above all are elements common in folktale. Marie has, however, imbued these thematic strands with the coloration of courtly love, so that the lai serves as an exemplum illustrating one of the courtly love tenets—the necessity of keeping love secret.

Influence of the Medieval Romance

In sum, then, medieval romances can be seen to encompass a wide variety of subjects and to represent various cultural attitudes. In the medieval age the form drew upon a broad spectrum of sources, including history, legend, folktale, saints' lives, exemplum, fairy lore, and classical materials. After its beginning in the twelfth century, the romance was widely adapted throughout the next three centuries by writers of many countries whose works influenced one another to the extent that establishing direct lines of descent for particular themes or subjects is generally impossible. The pervasiveness of those ideas in later fiction results in part from the genre's use of themes that transcend temporal limitations; the motifs of the wicked guardian, the disinherited hero, the scorned admirer, the wronged lover, and the love triangle, which are found in such abundance in medieval romances, continue to inform later works of short and long fiction. The medieval romance, like myth and folktale, thus draws on archetypal situations and figures for the presentation of its themes, but at the same time it satisfies the reader's desire for the unusual, the strange, and the alien.

Romance also transcends time in its presentation of the idealized world; the impulse to depict such a world, seen continually in medieval romances, persists in contemporary fiction. Similarly, the medieval romance's insistence on seeing women as admirable creatures and as sources of inspiration enabled the genre to posit the validity of love as a motive for and a cause of nobility, an idea which continues to govern much modern writing. Clearly, the importance of medieval romance in contributing form, material, and attitude to the development of modern prose fiction can hardly be overestimated; the romance provided a broad imaginative scope while it simultaneously bequeathed a legacy of rich material for plot and characterization.

In the late seventeenth and early eighteenth centuries the romance as a literary form declined in popularity, making way for neoclassical forms. In the late eighteenth century the gothic romance became popular, but this was a variation on the traditional romance form that relied heavily on sensational material and the evocation of emotions heightened to a painful degree. In the nineteenth century, romance ceased to be primarily a generic distinction and became instead an attribute or a characteristic or an attitude, which was frequently juxtaposed to realism; whereas realism meant the objective literary consideration of ordinary people in ordinary situations, romance came to mean the subjective literary consideration of the unusual. Nathaniel Hawthorne, in his preface to *The House of the Seven Gables* (1851), illustrates this perception of the genre as he states that romance implies for the author a latitude in content and expression that permits the manipulation of the atmosphere and the delicate and judicious inclusion of the marvelous.

In modern times, romance has undergone yet further alterations. When hearing the term in the twentieth century, one usually thinks either of "confessional" love stories found in women's magazines or of popular love stories in novel form. This form of romance has clearly deteriorated from that of the Middle Ages, but the characteristics of romance are deeply ingrained in our literary heritage. Both science fiction and fantasy stories must be considered modern forms of the romance, as are stories of the American West—whenever heroes venture out into the unknown to confront hostile or mysterious forces, the reader is in the territory of romance. Any literature that is other than firmly realistic, which strives for psychological analysis, which conceives of a world as it ought to be rather than as it is, which sees love as a motive force for nobility, or which is imaginative in simultaneously portraying an unreal world with unreal characters who nevertheless reveal human truths, owes its very essence to the romance tradition.

Evelyn Newlyn, revised by Jane Anderson Jones

Bibliography

Barron, W. R. J. *English Medieval Romance*. Longman Literature in English Series. London: Longman, 1987. A comprehensive study of Middle English romance which starts with the European roots of romance and its evolution in twelfth century France. The bulk of the book focuses on a detailed study of English romances—the variety of forms and the grouping of story material into the four historical matters of romance.

Clogan, Paul Maurice, ed. *Medieval Hagiography and Romance*. New York: Cambridge University Press, 1975. An introductory study of the medieval romance, including a discussion of Christian saints in literature. Includes a bibliography and an index.

Field, Rosalind, ed. *Tradition and Transformation in Medieval Romance*. Rochester, N.Y.: D. S. Brewer, 1999. A historical and critical look at the Medieval Romance, including an examination of Medieval rhetoric. Includes bibliographical references and an index.

Kelly, Douglas. *The Art of Medieval French Romance*. Madison: University of Wisconsin Press, 1992. Kelly discusses the distinction between author and narrator, the question of literary terminology in Old French, the relationship between Latin rhetoric and vernacular literature, and the definition of the romance genre itself.

Kreuger, Roberta L., ed. *The Cambridge Companion to Medieval Romance*. Cambridge, England: Cambridge University Press, 2000. Fifteen essays describe the origins of early verse romance in twelfth century French and Anglo-Norman courts and analyze the evolution of verse and prose romance in France, Germany, England, Italy, and Spain throughout the Middle Ages. Fresh perspectives are offered on the relationship of romance to other genres, popular romance in urban contexts, romance as a mirror of familial and social tensions, and the representation of courtly love, chivalry, 'other' worlds, and gender roles.

Meale, Carol M., ed. *Readings in Medieval English Romance*. Rochester, N.Y.: D. S. Brewer, 1994. A historical look at the English romance in the Middle Ages. Includes a bibliography and an index.

Mills, Maldwyn, Jennifer Fellows, and Carol M. Meale, eds. *Romance in Medieval England*. Rochester, N.Y.: D. S. Brewer, 1991. A collection of essays given at a 1988 conference on Medieval Romance in England, held at the University of Wales Conference Centre in Gregynog, Newtown; discusses Medieval romance and poetry. Includes bibliographical references and an index.

Stevens, John. *Medieval Romance: Themes and Approaches*. New York: W. W. Norton, 1973. This book stresses the continuity between medieval and later literature and declares that the subjects of medieval romance are the great and permanent concerns of literature.

THE RENAISSANCE NOVELLE

It is difficult to come to an exact definition of the Renaissance *novella* (plural–*novelle*) because of the rapid development of prose fiction in the late Middle Ages and Renaissance. The *novella* is defined as a short, prose narrative, usually realistic and often satiric in tone. *Novella* is an Italian word deriving from the feminine form of the word for "new." The quality of newness in the *novella* is, perhaps, best associated with the subject matter of the stories–*novelle* are based on current local events—with a viewpoint that ranges from amorous to humorous and satirical to political or moral. The characters in a *novella* are placed in a realistic setting, complete with the rhythms of everyday life and conversation. In counterpoint to medieval romances that present an idealized world peopled with noble characters in grand adventures, *novelle* narrate common incidents in the lives of ordinary townspeople. These incidents become uncommon as they are flavored with exaggeration and caricature, sometimes stretching the limits of the imagination.

Scholars generally agree that the genre of the *novella* originated in thirteenth century Italy as a brief, well-structured prose narrative. The genre includes stories of action, experience, brief anecdotes, and accounts of clever sayings with plots of amorous intrigue, clerical corruption, and clever tricks. *Novelle* were often gathered together in collections, using a frame tale to unify the stories with a common theme. While the teller of a *novella* may claim a moral intention for the story, the underlying purpose of the Renaissance *novella* is to entertain. The moral intent claimed by some authors or narrators of Renaissance *novelle* is most often connected to the frame that encloses the collection of *novelle*.

Origins of the Novella

Short narratives originated with the beginning of humankind—the impulse to tell a story must be one of the earliest of human impulses. The ancient civilizations of the Middle East and Egypt recorded short narratives, heroic and didactic, in both prose and poetry as early as the second millennium B.C.E. Greek, Roman, Hebrew, and Indian cultures all contributed to the growing body of ancient fictional prose narratives. These usually didactic stories were told to idealize certain behaviors, to teach moral attitudes, and to illustrate the rewards for good choices and the punishments for bad ones.

In the European Middle Ages, short tales came from a variety of sources to fill a growing hunger for enlightenment and entertainment. The sagas of Scandinavia and Iceland recorded the rough founding of a new society in a barren landscape. Celtic tales reveled in the imaginative romance and magic. Moral *exempla*, in the form of saints' lives and tales of martyrs, were told to model behavior for uneducated or newly converted Christians. Among the common folk, a new kind of tale arose—one grounded in the incidents of everyday lives, preferring humor and common sense and sensuality to idealism. The *fabliau*, a short metrical tale, satirized marriage, women, and the clergy. Vivid detail and realistic observation enhanced the plot, usually centered on an adulterous triangle, comic and often bawdy.

The Renaissance *novella* drew inspiration from all of these sources but was most specifically grounded in two: tales from the Orient and Christian *exempla*. The Oriental tales had been collected and collated in frame tale collections by Arabic storytellers and diffused in Greek, Latin, and Hebrew translations well known throughout Europe by the twelfth century. Such widely known Oriental texts as the *Panchatantra* and *Alf layla wa-layla* (fifteenth century; *The Arabian Nights' Entertainments*, 1706-1708) offered models for Renaissance authors.

The *Panchatantra*, a collection of tales that originated in India as early as the second century B.C.E., were translated from Sanskrit into Arabic in the eighth century. The outer frame for the tales probably was crafted in the Middle East and then translated back into Sanskrit (the original Sanskrit versions are lost) and into European languages. It is a simple frame: Three sons of a king refuse to be educated until a wise man comes along and proposes to teach them by telling stories. The princes agree and in a short time learn all the wise man has to offer about statecraft, friendship, war and peace, loss and gain, and impetuous actions. Nearly all of the stories in the *Panchatantra* emphasize intelligence and clear thinking as the most valuable qualities for survival and leadership. Despite the fact that many of the tales are beast fables, the underlying virtues are human ones—especially the emphasis on friendship, a secular value that idealizes bonds among members of society.

Likewise, in *The Arabian Nights' Entertainments*, the frame emphasizes the humanizing quality of the storytelling. Scheherazade offers herself as victim-wife to King Shahryar, who has determined to kill each wife after the bridal night in vengeance for his first queen's betrayal. However, through her storytelling, Scheherazade not only piques the curiosity of the king but also teaches him the virtues of forgiveness and friendship. As Scheherazade is reborn every day in the postponement of her death, so the theme of renewal—the possibility of beginning over and over again runs through the narrative. The frame, as is typical of Arabic practice, is a loose one—the thousand and one signifies an unlimited number in Arabic—not a finite closure. So as long as the storytelling continues, life goes on.

The Christian *exemplum* (example; plural *exempla*), a didactic tale, presents an example of behavior, which if positive is praised or if evil is criticized. Medieval preachers incorporated these short tales into their sermons to illustrate moral points. Collections of these stories, such as Jacques de Vitry's *Exempla* (c. 1200), were gathered and disseminated to assist preachers in composing their sermons. Secular writers, including Geoffrey Chaucer in his "The Pardoner's Tale," often used *exempla* as inspiration for more elaborate tales in verse or prose. The source of these *exempla* was not strictly of Judeo-Christian origin, however. A famous collection, Johanes de Capua's *Directorium humanae vitae* (twelfth century), was developed from the Indic fables of Bidpai via an eighth century Arabic translation and a subsequent Hebrew translation.

Exempla and Oriental frame tales merged in the earliest European collection of framed tales, the twelfth century *Disciplina clericalis* by Petrus Alfonsi. Alfonsi, born Moses Sefardi, a Jew from Aragon, had been a rabbi, an Islamic scholar, and a physician before he converted to Christianity in 1106. In 1110, he traveled to England to serve as royal physician to King Henry I. After his conversion, he composed the *Disciplina clericalis*, first in Arabic, and then translated it into Latin. As narrator, Alfonsi claims that he has gathered his material partly from Arab proverbs, fables, and poems and partly from bird and animal tales. His *exempla* appear within the frame of a dialogue between a dying Arab father and his son; the father desires to impart his wisdom on friendship, conniving women, and death—practical lessons of living in a social world. The influence of the *Disciplina clericalis* reached through all social classes, and its importance can be gauged by the number of extant Latin manuscripts (more than sixty) and the reappearance of its stories in the *Gesta Romanorum*, the *lais* of Marie de France, John Gower's *Confessio Amantis* (1386-1390), Chaucer's *The Canterbury Tales* (1387-1400), Giovanni Boccaccio's *Decameron: O, Prencipe Galetto* (1349-1351; *The Decameron*, 1620), and the works of such Spaniards as Juan Ruiz and Don Juan Manuel.

Critics generally agree that the transformation of *exempla* into *novelle* occurred in Tuscany in the thirteenth century as the *exempla* were elaborated and fused with existing tales, saints' lives, verse *fabliaux* and *lais*, and regional and classical legends. Composed between 1281 and 1300, the anonymous *Il novellino* (*Il Novellino: The Hundred Old Tales*, 1928) is considered to be the first real Italian work of fiction. This collection of *novelle* exists in two versions: *Le cento novelle antiche* contains a hundred *novelle*, and *Il libro di novelle et di bel parlare gientile*, probably a later version, contains one hundred and fifty *novelle*. Many of the *novelle* are extremely short, little more than anecdotes or clever sayings. Stories of action and experience engage such historic and legendary characters as Hercules, Hector, Alexander, Aristotle, David, Solomon, Jesus Christ and his disciples, Seneca, Charlemagne, Arthur, Richard the Lion-Hearted, and Emperor Frederick

II—figures from the far and near past—all dressed in contemporary costumes and practicing contemporary customs. Beyond the famous, the *novelle* are peopled with citizens from all classes: knights and ladies, peasants and townsfolk, clerics and minstrels, professors and students, angels and rascals. While there is a didactic bent in the tales, they also celebrate wit and intellect and are told with a hearty dose of everyday humor and some salaciousness. The *Novellino* has no discrete frame to enclose its *novelle*, but the author's style of clever and direct storytelling with few embellishments gives the work a unifying element. This collection of *novelle* with its Oriental, biblical, classical, medieval, and historical sources undoubtedly was the most important piece of inspiration for Boccaccio's *Decameron*.

Boccaccio and the Italian Novelle

Born in 1313, Boccaccio was brought up in a merchant's family in Certaldo, near Florence. As a young man, he studied commerce and canon law in Naples, where he began his literary career and fell in love with the woman he would call Fiammetta. He returned to Florence in 1341, held various positions in Ravenna and Forli, and was settled again in Florence by 1348 when the Black Death devastated the city.

Although deeply inspired by the work of Dante and influenced by his elder contemporary and friend, Petrarch, Boccaccio's literary output throughout his life was highly versatile and original. He composed the first Italian hunting poem (*La caccia di Diana*, c. 1334), the first Italian prose romance (*Il filocolo*, c. 1336; *Labor of Love*, 1566), the first Tuscan epic (*Teseida*, 1340-1341; *The Book of Theseus*, 1974), the first Italian prose romance with pastoral elements (*Ameto*, 1341-1342), the first Italian psychological romance (*Elegia di Madonna Fiammetta*, 1343-1344; *Amorous Fiammetta*, 1587, better known as *The Elegy of Lady Fiammetta*), the first Italian idyll (*Il ninfale fiesolano*, 1344-1346; *The Nymph of Fiesole*, 1597), allegories, lyric poetry, and *The Decameron*.

The Decameron is a bit of an anomaly among Boccaccio's other works, which tend, on one hand, to be romantic and adventurous tales told for the aristocratic class and, on the other hand, to be sober, learned works for the scholars. *The Decameron* is at once a collection of diverting *novelle* for a wide, newly literate bourgeois audience and a glimpse into the increasingly realistic and observational art of the Renaissance. The setting for the frame of *The Decameron* is contemporary Florence, a city in the midst of the Black Plague. The framing tale is a remarkable piece of writing that heralds much of the Renaissance spirit to come. It is, undoubtedly, a grim introduction to the lighthearted tales to follow, but the circumstances of the Florentine plague allow for the extraordinary gathering of the young tale-tellers in a suburban villa.

Boccaccio's description of plague-stricken Florence is one of the earliest European eyewitness accounts of a disaster that neither exaggerates nor allegorizes the events. His descriptions of the physical symptoms of the disease are scientific: "The said deadly buboes began to spread indiscriminately over every part of the body; and after this, the symptoms changed to black or livid spots appearing on the arms and thighs, and on every part of the body, some large ones and sometimes many little ones scattered all around. . . . a very certain indication of impending death." Likewise, his analysis of the effect of the plague on the citizenry of Florence has an almost sociological ring. He observes that because of the high death rate, such customs as female modesty before doctors and elaborate funeral rites, which had been commonplace, were abandoned out of necessity. Women stricken with the disease were grateful for the attention of any manservant, and dead family members were interred in mass burials. He notes that citizens resorted to a variety of means to ensure their survival—some fled the city, others practiced asceticism in the hope of warding off the deadly fumes, while still others abandoned themselves to the *carpe diem* pleasures of drinking and carousing away their last days. Anarchy reigned for "like other men, the ministers and executors of the laws were either dead or sick or so short of help that it was impossible for them to fulfill their duties; as a result, everybody was free to do as he pleased." In this framing, Boccaccio depends neither upon authority nor on any other account than his own eyewitness evidence of the material facts—here is a factual rendering of contemporary events that sets the tone for the subsequent outpouring of the one hundred *novelle* of *The Decameron*.

Boccaccio gathers his seven young women together in a church—each has been, the narrator hastens to report, a faithful attendant to family members now deceased. They decide that the wisest course for them to follow is to leave Florence and seek refuge in the countryside. Feeling the need for male protection, they invite three young men to accompany them. The ten young people, all well-born, intelligent, charming, and ranging in age from seventeen to twenty-seven, pack up their belongings and servants and retreat to first one and then another suburban villa for two weeks. To provide some order for their days and amusements, a schedule of wandering in the gardens, picnicking, singing, dancing, and late afternoon storytelling is instituted. On each of ten days, each of the companions tells a story, following a theme set by the one chosen as king or queen for the day. Although the companions have their own individual traits and quirks, they are not highly individuated. Conversations and commentary go on between the stories, but Boccaccio, unlike Chaucer in *The Canterbury Tales*, does not connect the character of his narrators with the tales they are telling. He is less interested in the dynamics among the characters than in the stories themselves.

Critics agree that the *novelle* in *The Decameron* are skillfully constructed, filled with clearly visualized settings, well-developed characterizations, good dialogue, and well-directed narratives that arouse suspense and curiosity. The stories are peopled with the entire range of contemporary Italian humanity, motivated by a desire for pleasure, self-interest, and an understanding of both the forces of nature and society. Although the frame lays out a different theme for each day's storytelling, the tales actually fall into five broad categories: stories of trickery, stories of adventure, stories of verbal wit, stories of tragedy, and stories of generosity. The changes in mood are swift and frequent, and despite the pervasive atmosphere of humor, there are moments of intense seriousness and even pathos. The humor ranges from gentle amusement to bawdy guffaws—there is no room for prudery in the world of *The Decameron*.

In the epilogue Boccaccio claims that the audience of *The Decameron* might learn from his stories:

> If anyone should study them usefulness and profit they may bring him, he will not be disappointed. Nor will they ever be thought of or described as anything but useful and seemly, if they are read at the proper time by the people for whom they are written.

However, his intent was hardly didactic. In the *proemio* (prologue), he declares that the book was written to distract those—especially ladies—in torment, whether from disappointed love or other circumstances. He apologizes for the unpleasantness of the introductory description of the plague but maintains it a necessary prelude to the gathering of his storytellers. Indeed, it is their desire for diversion that occasions the tales. Boccaccio's *novelle* reveal a secular world coming to an appraisal of its humanity, not through divine revelation, but with an understanding of the importance of wit, intelligence, and most of all, compassion.

The influence of *The Decameron* was far-reaching. It was the model for story collections not only in Italy but also in Spain, Germany, and France. During the fifteenth century, translations of the entire work appeared in Catalan, French, Castilian, and German. Translations and adaptations of individual stories spread even more quickly and widely. Among the most well known of the novelle are "The Three Rings," "Isabella and the Pot of Basil," "Federigo and the Falcon," "A Garden in January," and "The Patient Griselda." A few of the English writers who used stories from *The Decameron* include Chaucer, William Shakespeare, Ben Jonson, Aphra Behn, Jonathan Swift, Alexander Pope, John Keats, and Alfred, Lord Tennyson. Ernest Hatch Wilkins describes *The Decameron* as "the central point of an hourglass through which, converging from many sources, the sands of narrative pass, to be dispersed into the vast field of later fiction."

The Decameron directly inspired Italian writers for three hundred years. Among such derivative works are the *Trecentonovelle* by Franco Sacchetti

(c. 1330-1400), an untitled collection by Giovanni Sercambi (1348-1424), *Il pecorone* ("the numskull," c. 1378-1385; *The Pecorone of Ser Giovanni*, 1901) by Ser Giovanni, *Il novellino* (1475; *The Novellino*, 1895) by Masuccio Salernitano, *Novelle* (*The Novels of Matteo Bandello*, 1895) by Matteo Bandello, *Le piacevoli notti* (1550-1553; *The Facetious Nights of Straparola*, 1901) by Gianfrancesco Straparola, and *Gli ecatommiti* (*The Hundred Stories*, 1565) by Cinthio Giambattista Giraldi. Bandello's *Novelle*, 214 stories published in four volumes (1554-1573), is particularly interesting for the number of tales borrowed from it by both Italian and Elizabethan dramatists. Shakespeare's *Much Ado About Nothing* (pr. c. 1598-1599), *Romeo and Juliet* (pr. c. 1595-1596), and *Twelfth Night: Or, What You Will* (pr. c. 1600-1602), Philip Massinger's *The Picture* (pr. 1629), John Webster's *The Duchess of Malfi* (pr. 1614), and William Rowley and John Fletcher's *The Maid in the Mill* (1623) and *The Triumph of Death* (c. 1612) all borrowed plots or themes from translations of Bandello's collection.

Chaucer and The Canterbury Tales

Although Chaucer's *The Canterbury Tales* has many resemblances to *The Decameron*, most critics are unwilling to admit that Chaucer was familiar with Boccaccio's book. The connections between Chaucer's book and Boccaccio's are stylistic and thematic, not directly verbal. Although "The Clerk's Tale," the story of patient Griselda, is derived from *The Decameron*, Chaucer used Petrarch's retelling of the tale as his model. Both Chaucer and Boccaccio present a variety of tales from the perspectives of different narrators; both use frame tales to set up a situation in which tales will be told to divert and entertain the company; and both authors have an enigmatic attitude toward the nature of language and reality. Chaucer's frame, however, is more intricately and dramatically developed than Boccaccio's.

Bound for a pilgrimage to the Canterbury shrine of Thomas à Becket, a group of about thirty citizens including a knight, a variety of religious figures, guildspeople, country folk, and Geoffrey, Chaucer's affable and naïve avatar, gather at the Tabard Inn across the Thames from London. Encouraged by Harry Bailly, the host of the inn, the pilgrims agree to a storytelling contest on their journey. In the prologue Geoffrey introduces each of the pilgrims in a vivid and character-revealing sketch, and interspersed between the twenty-four tales are lively dramatic scenes involving the host and one or more of the pilgrims. The character of each of the pilgrims and the dynamics that evolve from their relationships with one another have a direct effect on the impact of each tale. Although each story can stand on its own as a narrative, the overall impression of the whole of *The Canterbury Tales* is theatrical.

Unlike *The Decameron*, Chaucer's work did not result in the development of a strong tradition of short fiction in England. Arguably, Chaucer's *Canterbury Tales* may not be considered *novelle* at all since all but two of the tales are written in verse rather than prose. Certainly the tales resemble *novelle* as psychologically subtle and tightly structured short stories gathered together in a collection, but Chaucer's inclusion of such genres as the *lai*, the courtly romance, the saint's life, the allegorical tale, and the sermon anchor *The Canterbury Tales* in the Middle Ages rather than the Renaissance. The dramatic and realistic interplay of the pilgrims, on the other hand, hints at the outpouring of dramatic activity that was to come in sixteenth century Renaissance England.

French Nouvelles and Marguerite of Navarre

Throughout the Middle Ages, French writers from Chrétien de Troyes and Marie de France to the Chevalier de La Tour Landry and Christine de Pizan to countless anonymous authors of romances, *exempla*, and *fabliaux* exhibited skill and mastery in short fictional forms, both in verse and prose. At the end of the fourteenth century, the first vernacular collection of *exempla*, the *Les Contes moralisés*, compiled by Nicole Bozon, appeared in France. Nevertheless, it was the circulation of Italian *novelle* that provided a model for the development of French *nouvelles* in the fifteenth century.

The appearance of *Les Cent Nouvelles nouvelles* (1456-1461; *One Hundred Merrie and Delightsome Stories*, 1899), whose anonymous author declares that he consciously penned his work in imitation of *The Decameron*, occasions the first French collection of stories with no didactic overtones. However, it is the form of Boccaccio's collection, not the stories, that are imitated. The frame for the tales is lightly developed—the storytellers are named, but there is little interaction or characterization. Some of the tales have analogues in Italian collections, but most are retold with original twists, and all have French settings. Oral sources probably supplied much of the material, as the author claims they are of *fresche memoir.*

The *novella* in France reached its peak in the sixteenth century in response to the growing bourgeois audience's demand for an art based not on aristocratic fancies but on everyday life. The basic narrative technique depended upon a brief exposition, a humorous denouement dependent on a twist ending or trick, and a swift conclusion. The clear connection between the audience and the narrator and the dependence on oral sources is revealed in the use of repetitive devices, stereotyped reactions to events, and the use of verbal irony and understatement. A rather static and cynical view of human nature with a tendency to divide people into stereotypical categories leads to an emphasis on action over character or thought.

Nevertheless, the settings of the *nouvelle* are highly realistic: The audience demanded *vérité*—truthfulness—and the authors responded by asserting that their stories really happened and by providing such specificity of everyday life that the *nouvelle* remains one of the most reliable sources about how people actually lived in fifteenth and sixteenth century France. There is practically no use of the marvelous, miraculous, supernatural, or exotic—the authors are self-consciously and patriotically French. Dialogue reflects accurate patterns of speech with dialectical and regional variations.

The world of the *nouvelle* is highly materialistic yet informed by a psychological awareness of human machinations, especially regarding the powers of manipulation. Adultery, corruption of clergy, and the *bon tour*–the good trick—are the major themes. The stories of adultery usually focus on unfaithful wives, reflecting the pervasive misogyny of the times, but the tales also reflect a growing dissatisfaction with social mores that decreed arranged marriages, often between young girls and much older husbands. Likewise, the stories of corrupt clergy are implicit criticisms of a system in which younger sons were often forced into a religious life with no vocation. The stories of good tricks often have as protagonist a wise fool—an individual who survives and succeeds because of his own ingenuity.

The stories in Philippe de Vigneulles's *Les Cent Nouvelles nouvelles*, unpublished during his lifetime, are told by a group of gentlemen spending time in a garrison during a truce. Although the stories reflect a high degree of familiarity with Italian originals, they are reset in a French town and reflect the local color. *Le Grand Parangon des nouvelles nouvelles* (1535-1557) by Nicolas de Troyes, a harnessmaker, presents a realistic depiction of French peasantry and dialogue with good character delineations and clear prose. His *nouvelle* contains a genuine concern for the poor and desire for social justice. In the *Baliverneries* (1548), Noël Du Fail entangles the frame and narrative. The three protagonists are more interested in discussing their own experiences and commenting on others' experiences than actually telling stories, which are little more than anecdotes or examples—the storytelling is beginning to be replaced by conversation. The reputation of Bonaventure Des Périers, a serious Renaissance humanist in the service of Marguerite de Navarre, was preserved by the posthumous publication of *Les Nouvelles Récréations et joyeux devis* (1558; *The Mirrour of Mirth and Pleasant Conceits*, 1583). His literate and witty stories depend on less rigid forms than those of his predecessors—some even start *in medias res*. He is more interested in human eccentricities than plot devices, and his lighthearted tone is enhanced by Rabelaisian verbal wit.

The most important and influential sixteenth century French collection of nouvelles is *L'Heptaméron* (1559; *The Heptameron*, 1597) by Marguerite de Navarre. Marguerite de Valois, sister to King François I of France, duchess of Alençon (married in 1509 to Charles, Duc d'Alençon) and queen of Navarre (married in 1526 to King Henri II of Navarre), was at the center of the brilliant French court, introducing refinements which would lead to the literary salon society of the seventeenth century. As patron of such literati as François Rabelais and Des Périers and protector of religious reformers, she participated in the major intellectual movements of her time. Marguerite commissioned the first French translation of *The Decameron* by Le Maçon in 1545. The French court and Marguerite herself had long considered a French version of Boccaccio's masterpiece. After her brother died, Marguerite spent more time at her husband's estates and began to put together the work that would become *The Heptameron*, a collection of seventy-two stories told by ten aristocratic *dévisants*, or storytellers. Like Boccaccio's collection, Marguerite's is occasioned by a natural disaster, in this case a flood. While they await the building of a bridge replacement, her travelers decide to tell stories to pass the time—but restrictions are put on the tales: Each must be a tale of something the narrator either witnessed or heard from a reliable source, and the stories must be told without literary rhetorical devices. Marguerite's storytellers are all based on members of her circle, including herself and her husband, and the discussions that ensue reflect a variety of philosophical and moral positions. Unlike most of her contemporaries, Marguerite took the institution of marriage seriously, and she understood the complexity of the human condition. The theme of love is intertwined with social and religious concerns, not simply an occasion for bawdy laughter. Indeed, love, marriage, and the relationship between the sexes are more often problematic than pleasurable in *The Heptameron*. Marguerite's influence was central in fostering French humanism, and *The Heptameron* served as a stylistic, if not thematic, model for such seventeenth century collectors of tales as Charles Perrault and Jean de La Fontaine.

Cervantes and the Spanish Novelle

The earliest influence on the development of the prose tale in Spain was, undoubtedly, Arabic. The eight hundred years of Moorish presence in Spain fostered the diffusion of Arabic learning and culture. When the Spaniards recaptured Toledo, it became a center for translation from Oriental sources. In the thirteenth century, Kalilah wa dimnah, the translation of an Arabic beast fable, and *Sendebar*, an adaptation of the Oriental Seven Sages tales, were the first examples of storytelling in Spanish. Translations of other collections of Eastern stories found their bridge into Europe through Spain. Don Juan Manuel's *Libro de los enxiemplos del conde Lucanor et de Patronio* (1328-1335; *Count Lucanor: Or, The Fifty Pleasant Stories of Patronio*), a collection of *exempla*, draws on Arabic sources but exhibits an originality that marks it as an important harbinger of Spanish fiction.

Miguel de Cervantes's claim that he wrote the first collection of novellas in Castilian is probably justified. His *Novelas ejemplares* (1613; *Exemplary Novels*, 1846), composed after *Don Quixote*, contains twelve tales that vary in style and tone but mainly fall into the two categories of romance-based stories and realistic stories. The focus of the tales is neither didactic nor simply entertaining; Cervantes here, as in *Don Quixote*, is interested in the nature of man's existence in the world. Cervantes dispensed with the frame tale as did most of the Spanish novella writers of the 1620's and 1630's.

One notable exception is María de Zayas y Sotomayor, who wrote two collections of novellas set in the same frame: *Novelas amorosas y exemplares* (1637) and *Desengaños amorosos* (1647). In both collections, Lisis, a young noblewoman, is suffering from *mal de amor* (the malady of love), and her female friends gather around to tell tales about love, desire, and male treachery. All the tales are told by women for women, and the tone is cautionary—in a patriarchal, macho society women are often at the mercy of male treachery. Popular in her own day, Zayas's frankness and openness about sexuality relegated her to the ranks of scandalous writers in the views of later literary critics. In the last of half of the twentieth century, however, her works have been rediscovered and have garnered a canonical status in the literature of the Spanish Golden Age.

Influence of the Renaissance Novella

The emergence of the novel in the seventeenth century, the resurgent popularity of drama and poetry, and a preference for journalistic sketches and travel literature led to a decline of short fiction for about two hundred years. Nevertheless, Renaissance drama, especially in England, was highly indebted to novella collections for plots. It was the realism introduced by the Renaissance novella, along with the keen psychological insights about human behavior, that fostered the techniques that led to the development of the novel. The audience of female readers courted by novella writers was the same audience that writers of novels would tap to ensure the success of their endeavors. As the short story emerged in Europe and America at the turn of the nineteenth century, such pioneers of the realistic story as Johann Wolfgang von Goethe and Friedrich Schlegel acknowledged the debt to Boccaccio. The novella, with its fusion of Eastern and Western elements, is a cornerstone in the development of modern literature.

Jane Anderson Jones

BIBLIOGRAPHY

Bergin, Thomas G. *Boccaccio*. New York: Viking Press, 1981. An approachable and comprehensive study of Boccaccio's life and works.

Caporello-Szykman, Corradina. *The Boccaccian Novella: The Creation and Waning of a Genre*. New York: Peter Lang, 1990. Caporella-Szykman argues that the true novella genre existed only between the publication of Boccaccio's *Decameron* in 1349-1951 and Cervantes's *Novelas ejemplares* in 1613.

Cholakian, Patricia, and Rouben Cholakian. *The Early French Novella: An Anthology of Fifteenth and Sixteenth-Century French Tales*. Albany: State University of New York Press, 1972. A collection of French Renaissance *nouvelles* with an introduction discussing the history, themes, characters, and realism of the genre.

Clements, Robert J., and Joseph Gibaldi. *Anatomy of the Novella: The European Tale Collection from Boccaccio and Chaucer to Cervantes*. New York: New York University Press, 1977.

Forni, Pier Massimo. *Adventures in Speech: Rhetoric and Narration in Boccaccio's "Decameron."* Philadelphia: University of Pennsylvania Press, 1996. A study of rhetorical tools used by Boccaccio in his development of vernacular realism.

Gittes, Katherine S. *Framing the "Canterbury Tales": Chaucer and the Medieval Frame Narrative Tradition*. Westport, Conn.: Greenwood Press, 1991. A study of the Eastern and Western traditions of the frame narrative from the eighth to the fourteenth century that illuminates the methodology of *The Canterbury Tales*.

Greer, Margaret Rich. *Desiring Readers: Maria de Zayas Tells Baroque Tales of Love and the Cruelty of Men*. University Park: Pennsylvania State University Press, 2000. A comprehensive study of Zayas's prose that explores the relationship between narration and desire—the desire for readers and the sexual desire that drives the telling of the novellas.

Menocal, Maria Rosa. *The Arabic Role in Medieval Literary History*. Philadelphia: University of Pennsylvania Press, 1987. A discussion of the influence of Arabic culture and literature on medieval and Renaissance literature.

Thompson, Nigel S. *Chaucer, Boccaccio, and the Debate of Love: A Comparative Study of the "Decameron" and the "Canterbury Tales."* Oxford, England: Clarendon Press, 1996. Thompson uses connections between the two works to argue that Chaucer was familiar with *The Decameron*.

Wilkins, Ernest Hatch. *A History of Italian Literature*. Rev. ed. Cambridge, Mass.: Harvard University Press, 1974. A chronological history of Italian literature from the thirteenth century to the twentieth with chapters on Boccaccio and his contemporaries.

THE SIXTEENTH AND SEVENTEENTH CENTURIES

Modern scholars have disagreed sharply over whether Renaissance prose fiction can best be seen as taking tentative steps toward the eighteenth century novel or whether it marks the end of the medieval tradition. As with most academic debates, both approaches are useful and depend on the critic's perspective. In fact, in some limited but important ways, the state of prose fiction between the first use of movable type in England (1485) and the last decades of the seventeenth century is comparable to that in modern times. It was an era of deep-rooted sociocultural change: A traditional mode of literature was slowly dying or being adapted to an apparently less discriminating audience; also, a bewildering variety of literary experiments, many of which were uncertain or outright failures, was accompanied by an uncertainty about the conventions and the value of prose fiction. To read the works of George Gascoigne, Thomas Deloney, or Aphra Behn is certainly to receive notions about the nature of prose fiction radically challenged. Yet a useful comparison of their strangeness to the modern reader can be made with the reader's increasing familiarity with the postmodern experiments in fiction. There is also the awareness that although the world they describe is, largely, one that is now lost, they do nevertheless articulate important aspects of modern cultural heritage and so of modern self-understanding.

The period marked by the English revolution, the Restoration, and the Settlement of 1688 is one of the vital watersheds in history, and its effects can be sensed in the age's prose fiction. By the late seventeenth century, many of the European literary fashions that England had belatedly adopted were taking root, and as socioeconomic balance shifted radically, so a new form of prose fiction developed. Historical changes of such magnitude, however, rarely occur overnight, and the whole era, in particular between 1570 and 1640 when the period's social, intellectual, and cultural turmoil was at its most concentrated, provides anticipations and experiments of enormous interest. In any period of unusual turbulence, writers and texts tell the reader more than they know, and the role of the critic is more than that of deconstructing the obvious surface referentiality of texts, as the reader searches for evidence of deeper implicit, but eventually enormously important, changes in a society's culture.

So far as "short" fiction is concerned, the Renaissance, unlike later periods, had no coherent theory of prose fiction in general, let alone for distinguishing between shorter and longer forms. The period inherited a huge variety of shorter forms from its past—jests, anecdotes, fables, exempla, romances, *fabliaux*, homilies, folktales, *récits*, novelle—but few writers seem to have given conscious attention to questions of length. Instead, they seem to have been anxious to justify the art of fiction-making itself—"poetry" was their usual term—alongside other human activities. Much Renaissance fiction is uneasily claimed to be "history" and contains elaborate justifications of the teller's veracity. Although George Gascoigne and John Barth are worlds apart in sophistication of technique, both show a self-conscious uneasiness about their craft that points not merely to the uncertain quality of fiction but, beyond, to the nature of their societies. If one looks to France, Italy, or Spain, one finds evidence of a more self-conscious concern with shorter as opposed to longer forms of fiction and, indeed, in France between about 1560 and 1600 and again between 1660 and 1700, various short forms dominated fashions in prose fiction. In England, however, no such self-consciousness seems to have existed, and in order to get an adequate sense of what forms of short fiction did exist, it will be necessary to stretch and at some points to ignore the limits of the topic.

Notwithstanding uncertainty over the nature of prose fiction (and this is not simply an English phenomenon), an increasing amount was written and published as the new technology of moving type coincided with the expansion of the reading public. Among the earliest books printed by William Caxton and Wynkyn de Worde were editions of medieval romances, and by 1600, approximately one-quarter of the books printed in England were prose fiction. The expansion of a literate, book-buying class was a complex business, and one of its most relevant aspects was the growing fear observable among the dominant and educated classes that the more the reading public grew, the more literary standards and—by association—social and political order, would be threatened. Authors who preferred the traditional role of court entertainer slowly adapted to the new commercial market, often with some reluctance, as new economic relationships developed between authors, entrepreneurs, and readers that would eventually radically transform the nature and status of the craft. Whereas Sir Philip Sidney's primary audience was his sister, his family, and his friends, and John Lyly saw his fiction as a means of social advancement, Robert Greene, Thomas Nashe, Deloney, and, by the mid-seventeenth century, most writers of fiction had abandoned the traditional role. While still archaically addressing their readers in continual parentheses as "gentles" and "fayre ladies," in approved courtly manner, writers increasingly found themselves related commercially to their audiences and usually conceived their role as purveying and reinforcing what they saw as their audience's normative values. Any emergent values or techniques observed, in hindsight, in Nashe, Deloney, or Behn are expressed indirectly in their works.

The major emergent literary form of the period was the drama of the public theater. Like prose fiction, the drama went through a period of uncertainty and experimentation and had to reconcile a long tradition of communal entertainment with new intellectual pretensions and the new demands of the marketplace. While the best of Elizabethan prose fiction is manifestly the expression of the same energies that produced the Elizabethan drama, it is striking that while in the theater an art form developed which expressed the energies of the period in a remarkable fusion of popular entertainment and philosophical and psychological profundity, fiction-writing remained a minor and peripheral form. One cannot simply say that the energies that later ages gave to the novel and short story were directed into the drama: The theater seems uniquely equipped to explore the bewildering variety of problems the age felt regarding contingency and change. The role-playing of the theater, its inherent relativism, its juxtapositions of opposing philosophies and moods, and its fierce demands on emotional involvement, all seem, in hindsight, to have captured the needs and confusions of the age better, perhaps, than the age itself knew.

The theater had, as well, the advantage of developing subtle forms of independence of court values (although not of court patronage or censorship). By making the fascination of human actions its central interest, it opened the possibilities for audiences to contemplate themselves, their society, their world. More than any other literary or art form, the drama articulated the age's struggle to free itself from archaic and residual intellectual, social, and political forces and to release the emergent drives of a new world. Readers look back to *Hamlet, Prince of Denmark* (pr. c. 1600-1601), *Doctor Faustus* (pr. c. 1588), *The White Devil* (pr. C. 1609-1612), and *The Tempest* (1611) as embodiments of energies and insights that were to form and direct subsequent history. By contrast, the greatest work of prose fiction of the age, Sidney's *Arcadia* (1590, 1593, 1598; originally entitled *The Countess of Pembroke's Arcadia*), looks back nostalgically to an earlier world of order and stasis. What seemed to Sidney's contemporaries to be the shoring up of standards was eventually to be seen as retrogressive and nostalgic, and so far as prose fiction is concerned, the real growing points—for the eighteenth century novel and beyond—were peripheral and obscure parts of Renaissance culture.

Having identified somewhat the place of prose fiction in the sociocultural dynamic of the age, it is now appropriate to examine specifically the characteristics of short prose fiction. Notwithstanding the difficulty of defining "short" forms for the period, there is a variety of interesting works and points of potential growth for later ages. First to be dealt with will be those forms of fiction to which Renaissance authorities would have given greatest approval, those directly associated with the aesthetic demands of the court—adaptations of medieval romances, translations, and imitations of Continental modes (especially the *novella*, the *conte*, and the various picaresque forms). Second, the forms of prose fiction which, explicitly or not, modified or challenged the dominance of the court will be covered. These included the middle-class adaptation and eventual transformation of romance, fiction, which bore the marked impact of Protestantism, and the various forms of short fiction that emerged from sociopolitical realities on the periphery of or outside the dominant culture. These forms—folk stories, anecdotes, jests, tales of ordinary and seemingly trivial experience—however excluded by the hegemonic forms, nevertheless constitute a crucial part of the cultural life of England and point beyond to the life and literature of later periods.

During the sixteenth century, literature and the arts generally became increasingly subject to the control and values of the age's dominant institution, the court. As the Tudor state took a more confident shape, it systematically—although on a European scale, belatedly—attempted to use the arts as an instrument in its policy of centralization and control. Epic and lyric poetry and the masque particularly felt its pressure, and the development of these modes show the power of the court over its subjects. The most important works of prose fiction in the European Renaissance—those by François Rabelais, Miguel de Cervantes, Ángel de Saavedra, and Sidney—all articulate directly or in reaction the new buoyancy and aggressiveness of the Renaissance court. Most writers of any kind were either courtiers or financially dependent on court patronage; until late in the sixteenth century, most conceived of themselves as court entertainers. As the court hegemony broke down over the succeeding century, writers were forced to find alternative social roles and audiences and to change their modes of writing to express the new social realities.

The dominance of the court in the Tudor period meant that the works written or translated were heavily influenced by court taste. The majority of early works of prose fiction drew on traditional medieval chivalric material—stories of romantic love, Arthurian adventures, and the like. Even as early as 1500, their values were fast becoming archaic so far as actual social practices are concerned, but their increasingly escapist aura continued to appeal to readers for the next two centuries by means of an intriguing mixture of nostalgia and practicality. Their settings, characters, and actions are essentially escapist—enchanted islands, captured ladies, gallant knights, monsters, miracles, coincidences—but they are invariably heavily moralistic.

Indeed, it is one of the strengths of the late Elizabethan flowering of prose fiction that even the most tedious and confused tale can suddenly break into an earnest moral argument between author and reader. Prompted by marginal notes and directly addressed by the author (who in the most unpredictable and seemingly postmodern manner can drop objectivity at any moment), the reader may be asked to enter an intense moral debate. Walter R. Davis has argued that central to Elizabethan romance is an attempt to test traditional moral and intellectual beliefs, embodied in the romance world of pure, idealized motives opposed to reminders of a harsher reality in which the reader uncomfortably lived. He points further to the higher interest in ideas in English romances than in their European counterparts; one witnesses the earnest adaptation to pragmatic ends of a set of values essentially idealistic, escapist, and archaic.

In most cases, however—the earliest signs of a countermovement are not found before the works of Deloney in the 1590's—the reified values of the romances are the traditional chivalric ones, and any real possibility of debate, like that afforded by the drama–*Hamlet*, *Troilus and Cressida* (c. 1601-1602), *The White Devil*, for example—is lost. Nevertheless, aristocratic readers of the typical romance tale in 1590 make a fascinating case history: Surrounded by the uneasiness of a world increasingly threatened by strange new sociocultural forces, they turned to prose fiction as they turned to Edmund Spenser's *The Faerie Queene* (1590, 1596) or, a decade later, to the Jacobean court masque, for the reassurance of values and habits long archaic and unlike the reality outside their chambers. Perhaps a few miles away, however, in a dank public theater, a new play about a German necromancer was alluring or disturbing audiences from very different social groups with the thrill of blasphemy, ambition, and the possibility (reassuringly, to most of the audience, unsuccessful) of avoiding a just damnation.

When turning to the examples of short prose fiction from which the Renaissance reader had to choose (especially those few occasions when writers seemed more conscious of writing "short" forms), one discovers that the prose fiction of the English Renaissance was dominated by continental models. Most important for the period's short fiction was the Italian *novella*, best exemplified by Giovanni Boccaccio in the fourteenth century, a form able to use a variety of serious, romantic, and satiric elements to transmit a sense of vivid, immediate life from teller to hearer. Various novelle by Boccaccio himself were translated or imitated and published in sixteenth century England, including, quite early, the anonymous, lively *Frederyke of Jennen* (1509), derived through various intermediaries from Boccaccio's *Decameron: O, Prencipe Galeotto* (1349-1351; *The Decameron*, 1620). Later in the period, many of the 214 novelle by Matteo Bandello, richly melodramatic stories of love and violence, were translated or imitated. In 1567, William Painter published *Palace of Pleasure* (1566, 1567, 1575), taken from François de Belleforest's French version of Bandello's work. Subtitled "Pleasant Histories and excellent Novelles," Painter's work was described rather disapprovingly by the humanist educator, Roger Ascham, in *The Scholemaster* (1570) as "fond books, of late translated out of Italian into English, sold in every shop in London." Painter includes more than one hundred short tales, including the contemporary story of the Duchess of Amalfi (later adapted by John Webster), all combining rich melodrama and dogged, simplistic moralization. Painter offers them as demonstrations that the world is "a stage and theatre" providing "diversitie of matter pleasant and plausible" as well as being "for example and imitation good and commendable." Titillating scandal exists side by side with moral lectures—a typical combination in the English collections of novelle.

A similar combination, even more diverse in its elements, can be found in Geoffrey Fenton's adaptions of Belleforest and Bandello in his *Certain Tragical Discourses* (1567), thirteen short tales, mainly about the evils of lust, combining prurient details and long moralizing harangues on the inevitability of divine punishment. George Pettie's *A Petite Pallace of Pettie His Pleasure* (1576) also adapts twelve novelle, but their direct brevity is swamped, again, by coy moralizing and also—a new element which shows how the form was being adapted to genteel courtly taste—by a self-consciously elegant prose style, heavy-handed allegory, stylized debates, stolid abstractions, and sly asides to members of the courtly audience. Despite the sycophantic tone, however, Pettie's work does show a strong sense of its audience, as does Barnaby Rich's *Farewell to Militarie Profession* (1581), eight stories adapted from various novelle and addressed to the "righte courteous Gentlewoman" of the court with the usual mixture of titillation and moral commonplaces. All these examples of framed novelle and others—Edmund Tilney's *A Briefe and Pleasant Discourse of Duties in Mariage, Called The Flower of Friendship* (1568) or George Whetstone's *An Heptameron of Civill Discourses* (1582)—seem unaware that the novella's power lies precisely in its brevity and directness; they aspire to longer, leisurely, more courtly forms of prose fiction. It was left to later dramatists such as William Shakespeare and Webster to use the concentration of the *novella* in a different medium.

Similarly sophisticated in its handling of a short form—and providing an instinctive contrast with England—is the tradition in France. Until the reign of François I, France, like England, remained dominated by Italian or Spanish models. From the 1530's, however, and as part of the sudden rebirth of secular and religious literature associated with the Pléiade and the court *salons*, there grew up an impressive tradition of prose fiction. Its longer forms were dominated by Rabelais, its shorter forms (the *conte, novella*, or *récit*) by Marguerite de Navarre (in the *L'Heptaméron*, 1559; *The Heptameron*, 1597) and her circle, including Bonaventure Des Périers, Henri Estienne, and Belleforest. The vogue for short fiction, either as part of a collection told by a variety of *dévisants*, or storytellers, who frequently offered diverse interpretations of similar situations and so involved the readers in a moral debate, or else in separate unlinked examples, resulted in great advances in the art of short fiction. One can see a dramatic thematic widening, an unprecedented sophistication of style and technique, and an important contribution to the expressive powers of French prose. By the end of the century, short fiction in France was not merely highly popular but had become a major literary form in a way that English prose fiction did not until the eighteenth century. English writers adapted material from the French collections of stories but seemed to learn little about the sophisticated possibilities of the form.

The third major source—and, again, it provides a contrast with English fiction writers—is Spain. As in Italy and France, the Iberian peninsula developed a varied tradition of fiction, seen at its greatest in Cervantes's *El ingenioso hidalgo don Quixote de la Mancha* (1605, 1615, *The History of the Valorous and Wittie Knight-Errant, Don Quixote of the Mancha*, 1612-1620; better known as *Don Quixote de la Mancha*). Sentimental novels, pastoral romances, picaresque tales, and rogue fiction are all evidence of vigorous interest in shorter forms of fiction in Spain and Portugal. David Rowland translated the *Lazarillo de Tormes* (1553) in 1576, "strange and mery reports, very recreative and pleasant," and James Mabbe in 1622 *The Rogue: Or, The Life and Adventures of Guzmán de Alfarache* (1599, 1604), thus bringing two notable examples of the picaresque into English. Margaret Tyler's *The Mirror of Princely Deeds* (1578) and Anthony Munday's *Palmerin of England* (1581) and many others adapted the rambling, idealized adventure-romance. These chivalric works—which Cervantes attempts to "demolish" for their "ill-founded structure" and absurdities—were enormously popular in England, but as long works, they underline how the English taste turned inevitably to such leisured, essentially escapist, fiction.

One further foreign influence, although one hardly contemporary with Sidney, Lyly, and their fellows, should be mentioned. English writers were usually aware that their literary inheritance included a number of distinctive stories written in pre-Christian Greece. Usually referred to as "the Greek romances," these included Heliodorus's *Aethiopica*, Longus's short tale *Daphnis and Chloë* (third century c.e.; English translation, 1587) and Achilles Tatius's *Clitophon and Leucippe* (second century c.e.; *The Loves of Clitophon and Leucippe*, 1597), all of which were translated into English in the 1560-1590 period. All are elaborate in incident, intricate in plot, and held together by a graceful, sensual melancholy, and all stress the fickleness of human affairs. Greene's prose romances and Shakespeare's dramatic romances are among English works which show a careful study of their attractive atmosphere and incident-packed plots.

Between about 1570 and 1610, then, occurred what can justly be seen as a most interesting flowering of prose fiction. A great variety of short and long fiction—much derived from Italian, Spanish, and French sources—was translated, adapted, or imitated. Medieval romances, English and continental alike, were revived in prose versions; the new writers of the Elizabethan younger generation—Gascoigne, Sidney, Greene, Thomas Lodge, Nashe, Deloney, Emmanuel Forde—produced a variety of native examples. Although it is, once again, difficult to sort out distinctively "short" forms—and in some cases impossible if one wishes to get a rounded picture—one can nevertheless note some of the most important trends and illustrate them largely from short examples. Interestingly, one of the best pieces of prose fiction in English was written early in the period and is sufficiently contracted—about thirty-two thousand words long—to almost qualify as "short" fiction. It is the court poet-translator George Gascoigne's *The Discourse of the Adventures Passed by Master F. J.* (revised as *The Pleasant Fable of Ferdinando Jeronimi and Leonora de Valasco*), first published in 1573 and ostensibly set in some unnamed Northern castle, and then republished in 1575, somewhat rewritten, retitled, and set in a typical Italianate court, accompanied by a denial that the early version had been, as had been alleged, a *roman à clef*. The work appeared as part of a miscellany of court entertainments by Gascoigne entitled *A Hundreth Sundrie Flowres Bounde Up in One Small Poesie* (1573) and included poems and translations, all "gathered partely . . . in the fyne outlandish Gardins of Euripides, Ovid, Petrarcke, Ariosto, and others: and partly by invention, out of our own fruitful Orchardes in Englande." *The Discourse of the Adventures Passed by Master F. J.* itself is described as "a pleasant discourse of the adventures of master F. J. conteyning excellent letters, sonnets, Lays, Ballets, Rondlets, Verlays and verses."

Alongside most other examples of prose fiction, short or long, between 1500 and 1700, *The Discourse of the Adventures Passed by Master F. J.* is an unusually coherent and skillful piece of fiction. Put in a European perspective, it appears as a typical product of a sophisticated court society, an antiromantic *novella*. It depicts the affair between a young man, saturated with the rhetoric of courtly love, learning something of his own naïveté and the archaic nature of his ideals, and a highly manipulative young married woman. *Amour courtoise* was, by the 1570's, long dead in practice, except in the archaic rituals revived in the Elizabethan court; Gascoigne's tale is an amusing scrutiny of its irrelevance to the actual experience of human love—as opposed to its value for social allegiance to the Queen. Within a very limited sphere, Gascoigne is doing for the courtly tale, and the ethos behind it, what Cervantes was to do for longer chivalric romances.

During the late 1570's and 1580's, there was a concentrated attempt, largely initiated by Sir Philip Sidney and his circle, to bring about a renaissance of English letters. Sidney's own *Astrophil and Stella* (1591, pirated edition printed by Thomas Newman; 1598, first authorized edition), *Defence of Poesie* (1595, also published as *An Apologie for Poetry*), *The Psalmes of David, Translated into Divers and Sundry Kindes of Verse* (1823, with Mary Sidney Herbert, Countess of Pembroke), and Spenser's *The Faerie Queene* are all parts of this movement. In prose fiction Sidney also led the way with the age's most important prose work, *Arcadia*. Sidney's work epitomizes the dominance of the court over Elizabethan culture but, interestingly, it also betrays something of the intellectual and sociocultural strains that were to challenge the hegemony of the court over the next fifty years. Unlike most other prose fiction of the period, the *Arcadia* presents a complex and challenging model for aristocratic living, for action in and comprehension of the world. The debate Sidney takes the reader into may, finally, be settled by archaic and regressive ideas, but it is infinitely more complex and disturbing than any other work of prose fiction, and far more interesting. Motivation and moral insight are rooted in cultural and intellectual values. Technically, too, Sidney's work is far in advance of any other work of prose fiction, short or long, before the eighteenth century. While the *Arcadia*'s plot is appropriately elaborate (especially in the revised version), it is nevertheless unified by a coherent and subtle vision, all the more interesting because one senses that, like Spenser, Sidney increasingly felt the pressure to explore and question the values of his class and age. It is arguable, indeed, that the revised *Arcadia*, like *The Faerie Queene*, is an unfinishable work, its elaborate display and complexity an epitome of its author's uneasiness before the questions his work raised for him and his society and one that he sensed would never be settled within his lifetime.

Sidney's work was the most admired piece of prose fiction in English before Samuel Richardson's *Pamela: Or, Virtue Rewarded* (1740-1741). It was imitated, completed, translated, summarized, and, in part, dramatized; it increasingly became regarded as a storehouse of lost moral wisdom. The *Arcadia* was a mine of plots and situations for dramatists and for later writers of prose fiction; only the collections by Pettie, Painter, and their like were used so much by the following century's writers. The most popular tale within the complex fabric of Sidney's work was that of Argalus and Parthenia, which was probably at least as familiar to English readers as the story of Romeo and Juliet, and which inspired poems, plays, and a variety of cheap chapbook condensations or summaries of the *Arcadia*. Some versions, late in the seventeenth century, add characters, such as a villainous mother and a tricky maid, and vastly increase the melodramatic violence and suspense. None of the imitations, short or long, approach the intellectual richness or formal mastery of Sidney's work. Indeed, so great was the power of Sidney, as an ideal even more than as a person, that the *Arcadia* might well be seen as hindering developments in prose fiction over the next century or so.

The other major writer of the 1570's and 1580's who, although not strictly a writer of "short" fiction, nevertheless deserves mention is John Lyly. His works, *Euphues, the Anatomy of Wit* (1578) and *Euphues and His England* (1580), provide excellent examples of the pressure of the court upon the role of fiction writing and the style and scope of his work. Whereas by his position as an aristocrat, Sidney had both the freedom and security to challenge or at least severely qualify court values, Lyly was an eagerly aspiring court follower, anxious for preferment and happy to write according to court taste. *Euphues, the Anatomy of Wit* is court fiction *par excellence*, a courtly game designed primarily to provide stylish entertainment with a minimum of intellectual substance. Although occasionally ironical in intent, Lyly is concerned less with the substance of ideas than with their manipulation as part of a demonstration of wit and sophisticated cleverness. His audience is almost exclusively the ladies and gentlemen of the court, and his intention is to flatter, titillate, and reassure; what moral insights he offers are incidental to the use of stylistic devices as witty display. Yet beneath the glittering surface of Lyly's prose there can be clearly sensed the unresisted pressure of the court: Contrary ideas are balanced to "prove" that moderation and judicious reasoning coincide with the commonplaces of the Elizabethan regime. Commonplace didacticism is presented, through the formal and mellifluous structure of the prose, as universal truth. In other words, Lyly is not simply offering his elegant style for admiration: He is asserting against the chaos of the world outside the mannered beauty of the court and the order of the courtly ideal. His style creates an emblem of harmony, a sense of formalized security, completely controlled so that the harsher realities of the outside world cannot invade. The constant use of superlatives—"the sweetest wine turneth to the sharpest vinegar"—has often been commented upon for its formal beauty, but it is more than decorative: It is a device designed to suggest that the whole possible range of experience has been considered and, through art, is being controlled and ruled. Lyly's style is thus a flattering mirror of the court, and the readers of his books are invited to enter and take their places in that world. Almost as much space is given to such invitations, flattering the reader, as to dialogue: "Euphues had rather lye shut in a Ladyes casket, than open in a Schollar's studie" is Lyly's own gloss on his work.

Sidney and Lyly epitomize different aspects of the court aesthetic's hold over prose fiction, although it was not just over prose fiction, nor was it simply an aesthetic. Hardly any prose fiction, short or long, during the 1580's or early 1590's escaped their influence. Euphuism gave writers such as Greene, Lodge, Brian Melbancke, and William Warner an elegant mode of presenting characters and ideas as part of a tapestry of stylistic effects; Sidney gave his followers an emphasis on moral seriousness and, interacting with the influence of Greek romance and Spanish chivalric romances, an emphasis on the unpredictability and the infinite complexity of human events.

It is with Lodge and Greene that one can see the romance tradition being adapted to shorter fictional forms. Although Stephen Gosson's *The Ephemerides of Phialo* (1579), Anthony Munday's *Zelauto* (1580), and Brian Melbancke's *Philotimus* (1583) are all medium-length adaptations of Lyly's mode, with exemplary dialogues and debates and a self-conscious elegance of style, Greene and Lodge provide readers with the best evidence for the popularity and the adaptability of the court-dominated forms. Lodge is the more influenced by Sidney. In *Rosalynde: Or, Euphues Golden Legacy* (1590), for example, the major source for Shakespeare's *As You Like It* (pr. 1599-1600), the typical (although not exclusively) Arcadian motif of the contrast between court and country is used to test the ideals of conduct and style on which the court prided itself. *A Margarite of America* (1595) is similarly Sidneyan in its mellifluous pastoral atmosphere and delicate moral touches. Between 1579 and 1592, Greene (who was probably the best-selling short-fiction writer of the whole period, with some seventy editions of his romances published before 1640), published about thirty pieces of fiction and, in fact, derived much of his income from what he termed his "trifling Pamphlets . . . and vaine fantasies." He continually adjusted his work to prevailing fashion, writing Euphuistic fiction (*Mamillia: A Mir-*

ror or Looking Glass for the Ladies of England, 1583, 1593), love-tales, low-life and criminal stories, moral exempla–*The Mirror of Modesty* (1584) shows that "the graie heades of dooting adulterers shall not go with peace into the grave"—and adventure stories. Of his shorter works, *Pandosto: The Triumph of Time* (1588) is an especially interesting use of the Greek romance tradition. Used by Shakespeare for the main source of the plot of *The Winter's Tale* (pr. c. 1610-1611), it is a tale of lost love, unpredictable fortune, and unexpected joy and sorrow, all designed to stress the illogicality and unpredictability of fortune, but unlike Shakespeare's play, revealing, in Walter Davis's words, an "almost cynical or Calvinistic assumption of the inconsequentiality of human purposes." Another example of Greene's adaptability in a brief form is *A Quip for an Upstart Courtier* (1592), a calculated criticism of the waste and self-deception of pretentious gentility, written from the conservative viewpoint of a cautious bourgeois. The ethos of this and of his lively "conny-catching" rogue-fiction pamphlets, which display something of the vigorous anarchy of the low-life and the criminal subculture of London, show the gradual adaptation of the romance to a wider audience and, eventually, to anticourt sentiments. As Davis comments, Greene "began his career as the staunchest of the young Euphuists, but by the end of it he had neglected everything Lyly stood for." As such, he epitomizes the revolution that was coming over much of the literature of the age by the time of his death in 1592.

Before looking in some detail at the distinctive features of the short fiction of the 1590's, it is perhaps important to sense something of an overview of the courtly fiction that dominated the 1570's, 1580's, and early 1590's, and which in increasingly adapted forms continued to be overwhelmingly popular through the seventeenth century. As can be seen from looking at its two dominant writers, Sidney and Lyly, courtly fiction is essentially conservative in intellectual outlook: Originating in the values of the court, it harks nostalgically back to a world of order, harmony, and mystery. Essentially escapist in its values, it therefore tends to avoid or else to romanticize the pressures and contradictions of material life. Its characters are abstractions and types. Its settings are exotic and romantic, its plots episodic, coincidental, melodramatic, and unsurprising in their continual unexpectedness. Its style, if rarely as explicitly as in Lyly, tends to reinforce the ethos of nostalgia. It is rhetorically heightened, static and emblematic, and self-conscious in its use of rhetoric and ornament to convey the experience of participation in a ritual of comfort and wish fulfillment. In its origins, courtly fiction grew from a tradition of oral entertainment, its tellers subservient (although aspiring) members of the court whose values it espoused. Its narrative techniques go back to those courtly origins. They still show marks of the storyteller, the court entertainer, conscious always of the audience and of the roles he or she must therefore play. Although there is no clear break with the writers of the 1590's, readers do start to become aware of new forces threatening and disconcerting the dominance of the court. Even Lyly betrays something of an unease before a crucial transition that had, in fact, been under way since the invention of printing: the creation of a larger, more impersonal, and more diverse audience created by the printing press. This was a literate although not necessarily a learned audience eager for entertainment and the reinforcement of its own very different and rapidly changing values and experiences.

In many areas of literature, the 1590's saw disturbing formal and thematic developments—in satire, in a pared-down rhetoric in both poetry and prose, in the public theater, in the influx of new ideas, and in the virtual invention of new literary forms. So far as prose fiction is concerned, the developments have often been described as the surfacing of a new strain of realism, anticipating, clumsily, developments in the eighteenth century novel. The confusions and the achievements of the 1590's deserve better than that. They are both important crystallization of the enthusiasms and anxieties of their time and indicative of wider and more long-term cultural changes. Erich Auerbach's observation that "courtly culture was decidedly unfavorable to the development of a literary art which should apprehend reality in its full breadth and depth" has real point here. It is seen, very clearly, in the ways in which the public theater of Shakespeare's time responded to and in part created the tastes and self-consciousness of a new audience, and how its new modes of perceiving reality were in part dependent on its growing independence and rejection of the values of the court—paradoxically even while it was ostensibly responsible to and dependent on the court. Only spasmodically does one see such possibilities develop in prose fiction.

The 1590's show some of the few signs. The later works of Greene, written just before his death in 1592, show him turning to the raw energies of contemporary London life for the material of fiction, and the possibilities of a new, disturbing realism can be seen in another transitional writer, Thomas Nashe. Like Greene, Nashe adapted his considerable talents to both traditional courtly tastes and to a new, wider, less discriminating audience. He attacked the "idle pens," "fantasticall dreams," and "worne out impressions of the feyned no where acts" of the chivalric romances and saw his *The Unfortunate Traveller: Or, The Life of Jack Wilton* (1594) as written in a "cleane different vaine." Using an impressive range of satire, parody, burlesque, and realistic observation, Nashe's work is a picaresque biography of one Jack Wilton, an adventurer who observes warfare, travel, and various aspects of contemporary life. Nashe's plot is unsophisticatedly episodic, and the straightforwardness of his hero, a roguish outsider able to inhabit a variety of recognizable milieus, affords him an unusual degree of realistic observation. *The Unfortunate Traveller* is a typical 1590's work, akin to experiments in poetry and drama, mixing the characteristics of a variety of traditional literary modes, held together by the restless persona of its author, and betraying signs of emergent cultural experiences straining at the restrictions of older artistic forms.

Some of Nashe's other works, including *Nashe's Lenten Stuffe* (1599) and *Have with You to Saffron-Walden* (1596), are on the boundary (not easy to draw in the 1590's) between fiction and disputation. In these two works, he fictionalizes his enemy Gabriel Harvey, pouring scorn on his learning and affectations and complaining that true learning and wit go unrewarded. In his complaint, one senses less the iconoclast than the aspiring court entertainer, harking back to older, more traditional ways, idealized in Thomas Nashe's *Pierce Penniless His Supplication to the Divell* (1592) by the Sidneys. He bewails that a gentleman like himself should have to make himself "a gazing stock and a publique spectacle to all the world for nothing." Like many of his generation—restless, ambitious Inns of Court or University men—Nashe is self-indulgent, insecure, and despite his astringent style, still seeing his fiction as a means to preferment in a world where advancement seems increasingly denied. While he has the true performer's delight in rhetoric and a vivid sense of his audience—"Readers, be merry; for in me there shall want nothing I can doo to make you merry," he cries in *The Unfortunate Traveller*—his qualities of realistic observation and pointed commentary remain incidental to his residual conception of the role of fiction, and they point forward to later developments despite his own intentions.

Nashe, Greene, and Lodge all show signs of a vital transition in the nature and function of prose fiction. Even in the *Arcadia*, in so many pivotal ways the age's most significant work, there are signs of the incipient breakdown, even at its apparent height, of the cultural hegemony of the court. Any culture contains, as has been shown, residual elements of an earlier phase of society—frequently embodied in the dominant and therefore more conservative tastes of society—and emergent cultural values and experiences, which often appear unknown to authors and which the modern reader identifies as culturally significant. The confusion and experimentation of the 1590's is not unique to prose fiction writers, but in their searches for social and literary identity one can certainly sense something of the age's most important cultural shifts.

Raymond Williams, commenting on the *Arcadia*, points to the irony that the work which gave its name to a central facet of the English pastoral tradition should have been written on a real country estate whose wealth had been created by upsetting traditional bonds between people and their land, and then ruthlessly exploiting the enclosures thus acquired. Sidney certainly seems unaware of the irony, and the reader may notice, perhaps a little uncomfortably, that he seems supremely indifferent to the pressures of the real-life values or problems of tenants, peasants, or any class below the level of his admirable, if erring, heroes and heroines. What, as was seen with Greene and Nashe, the 1590's bring is a gradual transformation of the forms and function of traditional fiction by an audience and an incipient structure of values, beliefs, and habits that would eventually transform not only prose fiction but also the sociocultural fabric of England. It is therefore fascinating to see the court romance invaded and subverted increasingly in the years following the 1590's. What are usually termed "bourgeois romances" can be seen as early as the 1580's. At first they are simply adaptations of the traditional fantastic adventures, except that their heroes are not aristocratic but middle-class knights errant. In works such as Lodge's *The Life and Death of William Long Beard* (1593), Henry Roberts's *Pheander the Mayden Knight* (1595), and Richard Johnson's *The Most Pleasant History of Tom a Lincolne* (1607), the quests of the heroes are to protect values that express the world not of Arcadia but of Southwark or Eastcheap.

The bourgeois romances are cautious and decorous to the point of incongruity, however, calling into question their courtly antecedents by implication only and explicitly intent on appealing still to the values of "the gentleman reader," although the term is taking on a meaning far broader than Baldassare Castiglione, Sidney, or even Nashe would have approved. The most successful writers of this form of fiction are Emanuel Forde and Thomas Deloney, whose works, like Gascoigne's or Greene's, are somewhat awkwardly located between "long" and "short." Forde's enormously popular *The Most Pleasant History of Ornatus and Artesia* (1595?) and *The Famous and Pleasant History of Parismus* (1598-1599) are works of moderate length which add to an explicitly although romanticized bourgeois setting an interest in the motivation of humble people exploited by overbearing aristocrats. Deloney was almost as popular a writer and even more interesting in his mixture of realism and traditional romance. In 1596 he was accused of "bringing in" the Queen to one of his works, "to speak with her people in dialogue in very fond and undecent sort," which would never have done for Sidney (or Spenser). His heroes typically rise from being lowly apprentices or servants to becoming wealthy clothiers or Members of Parliament. His settings are still idealized but are recognizably related to England rather than Arcadia and are peopled with a variety of merchants, shoemakers, citizens, and goodwives, whose natural loyalties are more patriotic, Deloney constantly asserts, than those of the aristocracy. In *Thomas of Reading: Or, The Six Worthy Yeomen of the West* (c. 1600) after an especially jovial interview with the king, Hodgekins the clothiers' spokesman "affirmed on his faith that he had rather speak to the king's majesty than to many justices of peace." With such a revolution in the content of his work, Deloney is, however, disappointingly traditional, even archaic, in the structure and mode of his fiction. His work is still chivalric romance, adapted for a new class anxious to see its newfound respectability and power idealized in the way its superiors continued, more uneasily, to idealize theirs.

One can, however, find fiction (and significantly, specifically short fiction) that escapes the dominance of the residual court modes if one looks even further from Whitehall than Hodgekins and his like afford. The recovery of popular, especially lower-class, literature in the period is beset with extraordinary difficulties. Much, if not most, has been lost simply because it was not or could not be written down and printed; much that has survived in print has been laundered for a more genteel audience. From various written sources, often very indirect ones, however—commonplace books, letters, and the like, as well as some printed sources—one can piece together a vivid tradition of folk and popular art that never escaped the force of the dominant sociocultural pressures, but which nevertheless constituted a rich tradition in its own right and which surfaced, increasingly, in the seventeenth century in the Commonwealth and in works such as John Bunyan's *The Pilgrim's Progress: From This World to That Which Is to Come*, Part I (1678). Difficult as it may be to pin down a visible tradition of folk stories actually published in the period, one can nevertheless from indirect sources (letters, brief mentions in plays, and other works) see how the stories of traditional folk heroes, such as Robin Hood, served as outlets for the frustrations and ambitions of the underprivileged and unlettered.

Indeed, perhaps the most pervasive form of short fiction, written or oral, in the period is the short, homely anecdote or tale. Hundreds of examples are found, often tucked away in other literary forms (in Shakespeare's *Henry IV, Part I*, pr. c. 1597-1598, for example) or assembled in the enormously popular collections of jest-books. Jest-books were accumulations of varying length of tales and jokes, most centered on a clinching or witty *riposte* designed to provoke laughter or admiration (or a free drink); the tales used a variety of typical characters—faithless wives, rapacious clergy, corrupt lawyers—that simultaneously drew on traditional wisdom and sharp observation. A typical example is the anonymous *The Sack Full of Newes* (1558), a collection of twenty-two miscellaneous jests, some with dialogue, some with brief, pithy morals, but all meant for entertainment. Some of the jests are developed into short capsule-biographies and become picaresque tales of a rogue or practical joker whose exploits demand the reader's sympathy. Examples include George Peele's *Merrie Conceited Jests of George Peele* (1607), *Dobson's Dire Bobbes* (1607), and *The Life of Long Meg of Westminister* (published 1620, probably written thirty or more years earlier). The atmosphere is usually colloquial and vulgar, and the basic narrative structure is episodic, with a rapid focus on a succession of individual incidents.

Anecdotes, jest-books, and jest-biographies all bring the reader much closer to the world that court romances were deliberately written to exclude and control. They constitute an undercurrent of short fiction that, while surfacing as much indirectly in other forms of literature as in their own right, nevertheless constitute a genuine alternative to the dominant cultural forms. The sources of energy in key works of the age—again, Bunyan provides an important example—coincide with and reinforce the tradition the reader must next consider. That tradition, Protestantism, on the surface seems antithetical to the dominant characteristics of prose (or any) fiction, and it is usually ignored in histories of the prose fiction of the period. This neglect is unfortunate, since in many ways Protestantism constituted the most important forward-looking movement of the whole age.

Except for occasional references, one group of Renaissance writings neglected as examples of prose fiction are the popular theological tracts. Many, admittedly, are among the most memorably unreadable works ever written—with exceptions such as John Foxe's *The Book of Martyrs* (1563), which is a masterwork of propaganda, of religious devotion, and, it might be suggested, of fiction. At its greatest moments—in the account of the deaths of Latimer and Ridley, for example—Foxe sets the reader down as an eyewitness (even ear- and nostril-witnesses) to events purportedly historical, revealing the details of which only the victims themselves could have been aware. Facts are redoubled, hearsay becomes fact, rumor is given tongue, and Foxe's rhetoric above all else directs his readers to participate in the revulsion against the persecutions of Bloody Mary.

In short, Foxe, self-consciously or otherwise, takes over the rhetorical duplicity and inherent depravity that pious Protestants mistrusted in literature, art, and above all prose fiction. During the 1570's, indeed, as the new movement in prose fiction gathered impetus, Protestant moralists shifted their traditional attacks on medieval verse romances to the new prose examples. Ascham, no extremist, regretted that the Bible was banished from the court and "Morte Arthure received into the Princes Chamber." Philip Stubbes, Gosson, and Perkins described the prose romances as "idle tales," "dreams merely to amuse the idle," "bookes of love, all idle discourses and histories," "nothing else but enticements and baites unto manifold sinnes." In the 1630's, the sophisticated Nicholas Ferrar spoke for a century of Protestant condemnation when he stated that romances and tales could not be allowed "to passe for good examples of vertue among Christians." Protestant theologians such as William Prynne in the 1630's or John Milton a decade later saw prose fiction as "profane discourses," or "baits for sin and corruption."

Behind such condemnations lies a suspicion of the autonomy of the human imagination, expressed in Saint Augustine's oft-cited definition of a tale or fable as "a lie, made for delectation sake." Yet, although Protestants attacked their society's increasing tolerance of books "whose impure Filth and vain Fabulosity, the light of God hath abolished utterly," as one Puritan pamphleteer put it, there is nevertheless a sense of the gradual fusion of fiction writer and theologian in a tradition of popular theological pamphlets heavily influenced by Foxe. As C. S. Lewis noted, while most of the attacks on prose fiction were by Protestants, so were most of the defenses. Sidney's *Arcadia* was praised by such stern moralists as his friend Fulke Greville for its moral seriousness, and it has been made apparent how consistently English readers and writers alike were most comfortable when their fiction was reassuringly moralized. In Europe, the Council of Trent was attempting to create a religious literature to replace the secular forms that dominated genteel and popular taste, and its influence can be seen in both the devotional lyric and in a fashion for explicitly Christian romances. The movement is especially associated with Jean-Pierre Camus, Bishop of Bellay, whose *Dorothée* (1621) and *Palombe* (1624) are examples of the genre. Each is a Christianized pastoral romance designed to teach, respectively, the purity of marriage and the duties of parents. The typical romance features that have been observed are all present—dreamlike atmosphere, idealized characters, complicated plots—all held together by an explicitly theological drive.

Even more interesting are works that, while explicitly rejecting any fictional status, nevertheless show the marked influence of fictional techniques. Thomas Beard's *The Theatre of Gods Judgements* (1596, and many subsequent editions) is a case in point. Beard's aim is to survey the whole course of human history to demonstrate the inevitability of God's revenging judgments over a world which is "nothing else but an ocean full of hideous monsters or a thicke forest full of theeves and robbers." Apart from its highly colorful interpretation of God's nature, Beard's work is distinctive for its reliance on an endless succession of anecdotes, tales, and gossip—in short, on a variety of short fictions. Beard's style has the dash and crudity of Greene's conny-catching pamphlets and the vividness of Nashe or Bandello: Of the eighty-seven chapters in his first edition, eighteen are concerned with lust, whoredom, and uncleanness, twelve with the crimes of great men, and eleven with murder. Even within chapters dealing with offenses against less spectacular commandments—such as blasphemy, false witness, idolatry, and perjury—his examples are chosen for their lurid powers of persuasion. Many of his examples are taken from Foxe and significantly elaborated by techniques drawn from the sources in popular culture that provided the strength of the best Elizabethan fiction. Yet another unusual hybrid is John Reynolds's *The Triumphs of Gods Revenge, Against the Crying, and Execrable Sinne of Murther* (1621), in which quite explicitly the enemy is not merely sin but fiction. Reynolds attacks the popularity of the amorous romance which, he says, panders to humankind's bare appetites by their "Perfuming, Powdering, Croping, Paynting, Amarous kisses, Sweet Smyles, Suggered speeches, Wanton embracings, and lascivious dalliance."

When one thinks of the importance of prose fiction in succeeding centuries, one might well look back to Beard and Reynolds (or to Bunyan's self-chastisement for reading lewd romances) as misguided opinions bypassed by history. Paradoxically, however, it was the Puritan dynamic, with its emphasis on self-understanding and the conscience of the individual before God, that came through into the eighteenth century to provide the intense moral concerns of Daniel Defoe, Richardson, and others. Protestant books of devotion and moral treatises turned inevitably to fictional portraits to exemplify worthy behavior. The classical genre of the character-book was revived and infused with a distinctive moralistic cast and again stressed not idealized characters in unrealistic settings but the temptations and contingencies of the world and the correct inner attitudes to cultivate. In short, the intense moral seriousness of the Protestant dynamic started, through the seventeenth century, to constitute a genuine countercultural movement that radically transformed the whole tone of English (and, by the 1620's, North American) life. Part of that transformation is the effect not only on forms of popular literature but also on the creation of a sensibility which would look to fiction with a new concentration on realistic motivation, recognizable settings, verisimilitude of characterization, and intense and complex moral dilemmas. Protestant polemics against fiction may have, in the period, distorted or helped prevent the maturing of an audience for prose fiction, but ultimately they provided crucial elements to make it possible.

Of the native works, the most popular were reprints of Sidney, Forde, Johnson, Munday, and Deloney. Overall, the English fiction of the whole century presents a depressing picture. Continental fiction, by way of contrast, continued to dominate, especially the long French heroic romances such as Honoré d'Urfe's *L'Astrée* (1607-1628, 1925; 5 volumes; *Astrea*, 1657-1658), which was imitated in England in the 1640's and 1650's, and the Spanish picaresque such as the old *La Celestina*, first published anonymously in 1499 as the *Comedia de Calixto y Melibea*. It reappeared several years later in a series of expanded versions entitled *Tragicomedia de Calixto y Melibea*, in which there is textual evidence that the author of at least the major part of the work was Fernando de Rojas. It was subsequently retitled *La Celestina*, after the main character.

Cervantes's *Novelas ejemplares* (1613; *Exemplary Novels*, 1846), one of the landmarks in the development of the European short story, was partially translated into English by James Mabbe in 1640 but was not widely influential in England. The tentative beginnings of a new realism foreshadowed in Greene and Nashe come to fruition in these experimental tales, which turn their focus squarely on the life of secular characters in contemporary social settings. Cervantes himself explicitly recognizes in the preface that he is breaking new generic ground in Spanish literature: "I am the first who has written novels in the Spanish language, though many have hitherto appeared among us, all of them translated from foreign authors. But these are my own, neither imitated nor stolen from anyone . . . ." He does, however, retain distinct ties to the earlier courtly romance and didactic moral treatise: His protagonists are typically of noble birth, and the tales are explicitly presented as "exemplary" because, as he remarks in his preface, "there is not one of them from which you may not draw some useful example." These elements of the escapist aristocratic romance are combined in many of the tales with a dedication to verisimilitude and realism and are frequently grafted onto plots and social milieus drawn from the picaresque tradition.

Furthermore, the putative exemplarity of the stories often seems highly problematical upon close examination. While the first story in the collection, "The Gypsy Maid," does end with the harmonious union of a virtuous young couple of noble birth, even here the setting for most of the action is picaresque: the outcast (and officially outlawed) society of gypsies. Later tales in the collection yield morals that are ambiguous at best. In *The Jealous Extremaduran*, even the narrator expresses his bafflement at the failure of the heroine to dispel her husband's conviction that she has behaved dishonorably. The final two stories of the set, *The Deceitful Marriage* and *The Dialogue of the Dogs*, seem to defy any simple attempt at moralistic interpretation. The former depicts the reciprocal treacheries and betrayals of a couple who marry under false pretenses with the intention of stealing from one another. The husband, having contracted a venereal disease from his wife (who has since abandoned him), overheard a dialogue between two dogs while recuperating in the hospital, which he then relates as an embedded narrative within the story of the marriage. The dogs deliver a thorough (and hilarious) denunciation of virtually every aspect of contemporary Spanish society, ending with the (unfulfilled) promise of a sequel. As this example of embedded narrative and non-human point of view suggests, the tales are highly innovative at the level of narrative technique. Cervantes eschews both the autobiographical first-person narration of the picaresque novel and the omniscient third-person narration of the romance for a limited third-person mode heavily reliant upon characters' speeches and, especially, dialogues, reflecting his long-standing interest in writing for the theater and opening up the texts to a multiplicity of dramatized voices.

A durable critical tradition has divided the twelve tales into two subgroups. The first comprises a series of relatively conservative and conventional idealistic romances (*The Two Damsels*, *The Force of Blood*, *The Lady Cornelia*, *The Generous Lover*, and *The Spanish-English Lady*). A second group consists of more realistic and experimental tales, which break from conventional patterns and foreshadow the future of narrative fiction in the genre of the novel (*Rinconete and Cortadillo*, *The Licentiate Vidriera*, *The Jealous Extremaduran*, *The Deceitful Marriage*, and *The Dialogue of the Dogs*). The remaining two, *The Gypsy Maid* and *The Illustrious Scullery-Maid*, have proven less easy to assign to either group and are often considered transitional or mixed in form. This interplay between idealism and realism (or, as it came to be characterized by modern critics, between the romantic and the novelistic) in Cervantes's work, noted as early as 1633 by Charles Sorel in his *L'Anti-Roman: Ou, L'Histoire du Berger Lysis* (*The Anti-Romance: Or, The History of the Shepherd Lysis*, 1654), begins to be codified in Mabbe's 1640 English version. Mabbe offers a clear index of contemporary English taste in literature by translating only six of the tales: all five from the list of melodramatic romances, plus *The Jealous Extremaduran*. By way of historical contrast, Rodríguez Marín, in 1914, similarly translates only six of the tales for his influential Clásicos Castellanos edition. In accordance with much different early twentieth-century critical tenets, he takes four of them from the list of novelistic tales, the two from the "mixed" list, and none from the list of romances. Either of these implicit schemes of evaluation consigns at least half of the tales to the status of artistic embarrassments, whether it be as crude examples of debased popular and folkloric forms or as failed attempts by Cervantes to mine the historically outworn genre of the Byzantine romance.

Under the (probably unconscious) influence of evolutionary thinking, modern critics long viewed Cervantes's career under the latter of these two models. His overall artistic trajectory was considered to be itself exemplified by the *Exemplary Novels*, which were thought to demonstrate his development from a backward-looking writer of artificial romances early in his career to a forward-looking precursor of the modern novelist in his more realistic mature works. Over time the wide factual disparity between this oversimplified characterization of his oeuvre and the chronological history of his publications worked to question and eventually overturn the pseudo-evolutionary view that every genre must succeed and render extinct its predecessors. The discovery and study of the early versions in the Porras manuscript (usually dated 1604 or 1606) of the picaresque *Rinconete and Cortadillo* and the bawdy *The Jealous Extremaduran* established that Cervantes became interested in the "modern" realistic tales relatively early in his foreshortened career. Conversely, bibliographic study of his last two major works, Part 2 of *Don Quixote de la Mancha*, typically read as the deathblow to traditional romance writing, and *Persiles and Sigismunda* (1617), a textbook example of traditional romance writing, establishes that he must have been working on both of them at the same time.

More recent studies of the themes and techniques of Cervantes's writings have led to the recognition that he found much of value in a wide range of styles and genres and freely mixed elements of all of them together, forging artistic links between the spiritual and secular worlds. The alternation of genres in the *Exemplary Novels*, as well as in other works throughout his career, is more plausibly the result of a conscious artistic juxtaposition of the codes of pastoral romance and the demands of verisimilitude rather than evidence of a pivotal change in his own attitudes toward literature. Cervantes's hybridization of colorful depictions of low-life gypsies and picaresque scoundrels with sentimental aristocratic love stories has come to look less like artistic miscalculation and more like the habitual succession of comic and elevated scenes in the plays of his exact contemporary Shakespeare. Critics are now disposed to rank the romantic and realistic stories as of comparable merit and interest, opening up the opportunity for a more balanced appreciation of the novelle than has perhaps been available since Cervantes wrote them. Consideration has also begun of the integrity of the work as a whole, circling back to a hint at a larger unity that Cervantes had offered in his preface: "Were I not afraid of being too prolix, I might show you what savory and unsavory fruit might be extracted from them, collectively and severally." Critical assessment of the literary achievement of the collection has become increasingly positive, and current estimates of the *Exemplary Novels* have placed it at the point that it cannot be fairly compared with any other body of short fiction of its period.

In subsequent English fiction, one can, nevertheless, certainly pick out both interesting trends and a variety of fictional forms. The best short fiction in the sixteenth and seventeenth centuries, then, was written in this period of transition, between about 1570 and 1620, when it looked as if the tradition established by Sidney, Gascoigne, Lyly, Lodge, Greene, and Nashe, and then modified by Deloney and Forde, might produce a flowering in fiction akin to that in France, Italy, or Spain. This did not happen, however. R. A. Day has described the period between the death of Elizabeth and the early eighteenth century as a "wasteland" so far as fiction is concerned. It is a pardonable exaggeration. Continental fiction continued to dominate, especially the Spanish picaresque such as the old *La Celestina* (1499), which was first translated into English in 1631, and the long French heroic romance such as Honoré d'Urfé's *Astrea*.

Nevertheless, one can certainly pick out both interesting trends and a variety of fictional forms. Of the shorter kinds of fiction—tales of sentiment and love, collections of novelle in the manner of Boccaccio (who was first translated in 1620), didactic and exemplary fiction, jest-books, cautionary tales—all continued to be published. By and large, however, C. C. Mish's summary is an apt one: The course of short fiction during the years 1600-1660 was a "downward decline; the bright promise went down in sterile entertainment and preciousness." While (as Mish and others have shown) it is possible to put together an anthology of entertaining pieces from the period, most of the work is derivative, nostalgic, uncertain in style, and vitiated by inconsistency of technique and uncertainty of aim. The best continues to be translation—from the French, Italian, or classical sources which continued to dominate European taste in fiction—or short, popular tales and anecdotes in the jest-book or jest-biography tradition such as Hugh Peters's *The Tales and Jests of Hugh Peters* (1660) and Nathaniel Crouch's *English Jests Refined* (1687), or picaresque fiction such as the anonymous *Murther upon Murther* (1684), *Sir John* (c. 1700), and *Bateman's Tragedy* (c. 1700). It is in the later seventeenth century, in fact, that the folklore and folktales, of which there was only spasmodic evidence a century before, start to surface in published works. Stories of Robin Hood, Fortunatus and his Magic Purse, and the like were clearly the main fictional diet of the lower classes and had been for centuries. Only gradually were they becoming part of the mainstream of English culture. Other fiction remained firmly in the tradition of improbable, elaborate romance, often with exotic settings expressing the public's interest in newly discovered or fashionable parts of the world such as the United States, Turkey, or Surinam.

Major historical transitions do not occur overnight, and although in post-Restoration England there is little to change the picture of what short fiction was written there, nevertheless from the 1680's on there are signs of a new impetus in prose fiction that would lead to the re-creation of the genre as central to English culture during the following two hundred years. One sign is the indirect but crucial impact of the Protestant emphasis on soberly meeting and contemplating oneself as an individual and learning what it was, in this world, that might make for one's salvation. Indicative of this new importance of self-analysis was the gradual rise of epistolary fiction, stories in the form of letters, which was eventually to lead to Richardson's *Pamela*. In the seventeenth century, epistolary fiction was typically focused on the personal lives of wellborn or respectable women, and, while hardly (to modern taste) penetrating beneath the genteel surfaces, in retrospect these attempts represent an enormous breakthrough toward psychological realism. Telling a story in letters, as in the anonymous *Lettres portugaises* (France, 1669; translated as *Five Love-Letters from a Nun to a Cavalier* in 1678), allows the reader to focus on and partly inhabit the self-consciousness of the narrator. Gradually, prose-fiction writers were discovering what the dramatists had almost a century before—the need to let the reader participate in the making of the work's meanings. Another important change was the growing insistence, already anticipated by Nashe or Deloney, on a degree of external verisimilitude in fiction. Details of setting became more functional, characters were introduced as part of the ongoing plot, motivation was more carefully linked by logic and circumstance, and speeches became more colloquial.

Particularly in France, there was a rapid growth in the variety and sophistication of short fiction. The long romance, *le roman de longue haleine*, gradually became less important in France and a variety of shorter, more realistic forms, became more dominant. The crucial difference between the earlier tales of Bandello, Cynthius, or Marguerite de Navarre and those of Madame de La Fayette, such as *La Princesse de Montpensier* (1662 as Segrais; *The Princess of Montpensier*, 1666) or *La Princesse de Clèves* (1678, published anonymously; *The Princess of Clèves*, 1679), and others is precisely the movement toward some degree of *vraisemblance* in setting and, especially, in psychology. In England the development was slower, but a growing verisimilitude of setting at least appears in some of the tales of roguery such as John Davies's *Scarron's Novels* (1665), translated and adapted from the diverse short pieces in Paul Scarron's *Le Roman comique* (1651-1657, 3 vols.; English translation, 1651, 1657; also as *The Comical Romance*, 1665).

In the various kinds of fiction written after the Restoration, too, a new solution slowly developed for a problem that had clearly worried Elizabethan prose fictionists—the role of the narrator within the work. In collections such as Boccaccio's, Cynthius's, or Painter's, there is usually a close relationship maintained between the narrator and the author in the introductory or "frame" material that links the individual tales together. At other times, as in Gascoigne or Sidney, the narrator will directly address his reader, at times be seemingly omnipotent, and at other times be disarmingly frank about his ignorance of his characters' motives, actions, or origins. In short, there is a shifting and often arbitrary relationship between the different narrative voices of the work; there is a characteristic opaqueness which continued into the eighteenth century in Laurence Sterne and which, interestingly, has reappeared in such fictionists as John Barth, Robert Coover, Raymond Federman, and Ronald Sukenick.

Gradually, however, especially after the Restoration, one can sense in fiction, first in France and then in England, the rise of fictional illusionism. The question of the author's access to the states of mind of his characters, especially if they were portrayed as historically real, which by the time of Jane Austen or William Makepeace Thackeray or Henry James was seen as jejune, was for Madame de Scudéry or Aphra Behn a most awkward one. The diverse solutions—the claims of having seen letters, read diaries, spoken to the persons involved—seem naïve to later eyes, but the questions being asked gradually produced the belief in the illusionism of fiction, the omnipotence of the narrator, and the self-contained autonomy of the world of the novel or tale. Without such developments, the so-called realistic novel of later centuries would not have been possible.

Of all the shorter fiction written in England after the Restoration, the most significant, and still readable, is that by the female dramatist-novelist Aphra Behn, who wrote a dozen or so pieces of short fiction. Most are interesting mixtures of traditional romance with a few rather genteel hints of the new realism. Her stories are melodramatic, generalized, and elevated, but nevertheless—as in *The Nun: Or, The Perjur'd Beauty* (1697), *The History of the Nun: Or, The Fair Vow-Breaker* (pr. 1689), or the longer and posthumously published in 1688 *The Fair Jilt: Or, The History of Prince Tarquin and Miranda* and *Oroonoko: Or, The History of the Royal Slave*—reach unusual levels of intensity. *The History of the Nun* compresses into twenty-one pages the complicated love affairs of five men and women, including one, the beautiful and unpredictable Ardelia, who falls in love with three men, causing the death of all three, the sister of one, and her own. Superficial, exploitative, and psychologically improbable, the work nevertheless has some energy and concentration that make it more approachable than the longer works of the period, such as the Earl of Orrery's labored *Parthenissa* (1654-1669), which drags its reader lugubriously through six volumes nostalgically looking back to the world of Sidney's *Arcadia*.

In 1692, near enough to the end of this study's period to constitute a landmark, an indication at least of slowly changing tastes and of the deeper sociocultural currents beneath, William Congreve published his *Incognita: Or, Love and Duty Reconcil'd* (1692). Written when Congreve was twenty-two, the work—a charming, well-plotted, amusing Scarronian tale, a not altogether unsympathetic attack on the romance tradition—contains a preface which was to set out many of the issues for prose fiction in the next decades. He comments on the incredibility of the romance tradition: Romances, he argues, are "generally composed of the Constant Loves and invincible Courages of Hero's, Heroins . . . where loftly Language, miraculous Contingencies and impossible Performances, elevate and surprise the Reader into a giddy Delight." Novels, by contrast, "are of a more familiar nature; come near us . . . with . . . Events but not such as a wholly unusual or unprecedented." Congreve's terminology was not new—Jean Regnault de Segrais in 1656 had distinguished the *novelle* from the *roman* by its greater *vraisemblance*—but in England, Congreve's explicit statement marks an important turning point in the development of fiction, as he bids farewell to the archaic world of romance and looks to the already emergent modes of short and long fiction that were to dominate the next century.

Looking back over this survey of short prose fiction between the impact of printing in the late fifteenth and the late seventeenth centuries, one can see that the changes in literary taste are inevitably the expressions of complex but definable structures of idea and feeling in the life of the whole society. In England the period was one of political and social energies for radical change, concentrated, thwarted, and then overwhelmed by forces closely tied to the new dominance of entrepreneurial capitalism. At the beginning of this period, the sociocultural power was slowly slipping from the older feudal aristocracy to classes more in harmony with the new forces of secularism, industrialism, and dominance over the world, nature, and one another. The cultural development of England between 1500 and 1700 is too complex to summarize thus, but one can see how the fiction of the period responds to and articulates such pressures—the slow replacement of an increasingly archaic mode of romance narrative, the slow growth of a confident new illusionism ("realism" is far too question-begging a term), an uncertainty not merely about the mode of fiction but about the very place of fiction in such a society, the spasmodic surfacing of repressed cultural modes of living in folktale, jest, or other popular forms—through the otherwise dominant cultural forms. Such changes can be discussed in literary terms, but they are not simply literary changes.

In particular, this is the case with the so-called growth of realism. The triumph of realistic prose narrative in the eighteenth century is the triumph of a way of seeing the world, which provides an illusion that chosen events are linked causally, that details can be selected from human events and be perceived as inevitable, given, and irreducible. Realism, however, like the social system that it expresses, stresses the product and its consumption by the reader, not the production. Just as capitalist society represses the mode of production of any article and stresses the product's marketable value, so realism (produced, in fact, by a certain use of language) stresses only the final illusion of reality and the harmonious final effect on the reader-consumer. The writer's concern throughout this period with the place of the narrator in his text reflects more than a technical problem; in the eighteenth century, both Jonathan Swift and Laurence Sterne mercilessly satirize the notions that language is simply instrumental and reading is simply consumption. They look back, angrily or whimsically, to the earlier period when the writer-narrator was on more arbitrary but nevertheless intimate terms with his reader, and the writer did not feel obliged to believe that language was identical with the real world. The gradual triumph of the illusion of realism is undoubtedly the single most important development in this period—which, as we have seen, does contain (despite many modern scholars' opinions) a goodly variety of amusing, interesting fiction—but its triumph is not simply a passing fashion. Realism, with all its apparent naturalness, is the exact, and in many ways limited and limiting, articulation of the dynamic of a new age. In England (in America, a very different pattern was starting to emerge triumphantly) readers had to wait another two hundred years for an equivalent literary change—and for the complex cultural changes intertwining with and expressed by it.

Gary F. Waller, updated by William Nelles

BIBLIOGRAPHY

Atkinson, William C. "Cervantes, El Pinciano, and the *Novelas ejemplares*." *Hispanic Review* 16 (1948): 189-208; reprinted in *Critical Essays on Cervantes*. Ruth El Saffar, ed. Boston: G. K. Hall, 1986. Reads Cervantes's collection as a series of literary experiments in the aesthetics of the new genre of short fiction, heavily influenced by the Italian literary theorist El Pinciano's *Philosophía antigua poética*.

Avalle-Arce, Juan Bautista. "*Novelas ejemplares:* Reality, Realism, Literary Tradition." In *Mimesis: From Mirror to Method, Augustine to Descartes*. Edited by John D. Lyons and Stephen G. Nichols, Jr. Hanover, N.H.: University Press of New England, 1982. 197-214. Locates the *Exemplary Novels* in relation to the main currents of the Spanish literary tradition and argues that Cervantes was consciously setting out to invent a new literary genre with the collection.

Clamurro, William H. *Beneath the Fiction: The Contrary Worlds of Cervantes's "Novelas ejemplares."* New York: Peter Lang, 1997. Argues that each of the novellas in the collection illustrates the inherent tension between the ideal values of the ostensibly dominant social mores and the more complicated realities of a rich and diverse cultural community. Cervantes's ostensibly conservative affirmations of the social order simultaneously dramatize the range of conflicting and often disorderly behavior that goes on within it.

El Saffar, Ruth. *Novel to Romance: A Study of Cervantes's "Novelas ejemplares."* Baltimore: The Johns Hopkins University Press, 1974. Argues that the novellas, when read in the order of their composition, reveal a trajectory in Cervantes's production from early realistic stories to later idealistic stories. The full meaning of the overall pattern of the published collection can best be evaluated against this chronological ordering, which implicitly contradicts much modern discussion about the development of Cervantes's aesthetic principles.

Forcione, Alban K. *Cervantes and the Humanist Vision: A Study of Four Exemplary Novels*. Princeton, N.J.: Princeton University Press, 1982. Locates four of the *Exemplary Novels–The Jealous Extremaduran, The Gypsy Maid, The Licentiate vidriera*, and *The Force of Blood*—within the mainstream of the Christian Humanist tradition of Western European thought. Forcione argues specifically for the influence of Erasmus on Cervantes's tales.

Ricapito, Joseph V. *Cervantes's "Novelas ejemplares:" Between History and Creativity*. West Lafayette, Ind.: Purdue University Press, 1996. Explores the manifold connections between the novellas and their historical contexts. Includes detailed analyses of social, religious, economic, and political backgrounds as they relate to individual stories.

Riley, E. C. "Cervantes: A Question of Genre." In *Medieval and Renaissance Studies on Spain and Portugal in Honour of P. E. Russell*. Edited by F. W. Holcroft et al. Oxford, England: Society for the Study of Mediaeval Languages and Literature, 1981. 69-85. A concise and balanced overview of the long history of critical discussion about the "novelistic" and "romance" elements in Cervantes's works, including the *Exemplary Novels*.

THE EIGHTEENTH CENTURY

The eighteenth century did not produce the first modern short story as it is known today as an art form, a clearly defined genre. Seldom during the century did a story have the firm story line and economy of effect that would justify labeling it a short story in the modern sense; a story was concerned with how an experience is valued and what difference it makes to someone, not merely what is said and done. A surprising number of literary historians agree that the birth of the genre did not occur until the early nineteenth century, in *The Sketch Book of Geoffrey Crayon, Gent.* (1819-1820), by Washington Irving.

As Benjamin Boyce states in his essay "Eighteenth-Century Short Fiction," however, for "the present discussion . . . 'short fiction' includes any kind of imaginative writing about people that contains or implies action and that does not exceed in length 12,000 words." Within this definition can be found the vast variety of forms of short fiction that were produced by writers of the eighteenth century. These include fairy tales, Oriental tales, satirical adventure tales, the *conte*, epistolary fiction, rogue literature, *sueño* (or dream) fiction, essays, moral tracts, character sketches, the German *Novelle*, and the *nouvelle* or novelette (considered by some critics to be merely a stepchild of the novel, simply a short, uncomplicated novel; for this essay's purposes, the novelette qualifies as eighteenth century short fiction). As will be seen, the great periodical of the eighteenth century, *The Spectator* (1711-1712, 1714), was the chief vehicle for most of these forms. In the latter part of the century, with the advent of Romanticism, gothic fiction and psychological tales became immensely popular.

It is quite apparent from the foregoing list that if the birth of the distinctly defined genre of the short story did not occur until the nineteenth century, then the eighteenth could fairly be said to be its gestation period. It saw a time in which fragmentary but excellent characteristics of the short story were refined until they coalesced into a superb whole. The seeds that allowed the growth of the genre were planted in the eighteenth century.

To appreciate fully the merits of authors or their writings, it is necessary to throw a searchlight on the period in which they wrote. The eighteenth century was, after all, one of the great pivotal and transitional eras of all time. It saw a severe dichotomy of thought. The century opened with the Enlightenment (also called the Age of Reason), then moved through the beginning of the Industrial Age with the invention of the steam engine in 1765, and then saw the American and French revolutions, before closing under the strong and lasting influence of the age of passion, Romanticism. This essay will examine briefly the events of the age when considering each individual nation. The short fiction of the Western world is the focus here: England, America, France, Germany, Spain, and Italy.

England

England in 1700 was possibly the most advanced nation in Europe, yet the English scene of 1700 was darkened by political and religious corruption and injustice. Literature was strictly for aristocrats—those "to the manor born." Public schools were slowly being instituted, but they were few, and most people were unable to read or write. The cities, however, were growing, and the well-to-do were spending less time in their countryseats and more in the cities—more specifically, in the coffeehouses, discussing the latest news from abroad, from Parliament, from society.

Within these conditions was found the germ of the eventual short story proper. The need for a new social expression against the excesses of the Restoration created the personal essay, which attempted not only to address the conflicts of the time but also to chronicle the "talk of the town." Fictional "talkers" were created by the authors of periodicals. In *The Tatler* (1709-1711), created by Joseph Addison, and later in the superior *The Spectator*, created by both Addison and Richard Steele, were found the highest quality of fictional talkers, reflectors of their times. *The Spectator* was one of the most important periodicals of the century, greatly influencing writers throughout Western Europe and America. The best-known of the characters about whom Mr. Spectator "talks" in *The Spectator* is Sir Roger de Coverley, a good-natured gentleman who represents surviving feudalism and through whom the vehement opposition between town and country was expressed.

The mixture of fashionable contempt for book learning, blended with shrewd wit, is well represented in the character of amiable, simpleminded Will Wimble, one of Sir Roger's friends. His character is amazingly fleshed out with gentle satire in the de Coverley papers. Poor Will, younger brother to a baronet, has no estate and naturally no business sense, but he has mastered the craft of idleness. The depiction of English homebred life formed the basic nature of the early eighteenth century story: a graceful realism and the criticism of manners in an attractive satirical style, found especially in Addison's stories.

The Tatler and *The Spectator* were the first organs attempting to give form and consistency to the opinions rising out of the social context. Through Addison and Steele, public opinion was founded by a conscious effort of reason and persuasion. *The Spectator* and its predecessors, with their dual purposes to instruct and/or entertain, were true children of the Enlightenment. Reason and instruction were foremost considerations, and often this made for severe didacticism. Happily, though, the vehicle for instruction was fictional entertainment. That philosophy, consistently followed, is put best in Mr. Spectator's own words: "The mind ought sometimes to be diverted, that it may return to thinking better" (*The Spectator*, 102). Short fiction, still dubious and generally unfamiliar as a form of entertainment, played an important role in the success of *The Spectator*, and in a smaller way, *The Tatler*, which preceded it.

Through character sketches such as those in the de Coverley papers, the short story began tentatively to detach itself from the essay. *The Spectator*, unlike earlier periodicals, presented dialogue not merely as a device to present two viewpoints but as a give-and-take between two generally believable characters. Although the short fiction in *The Spectator* is not always technically well drawn, it did provide embryonic examples of modern narration and developed characters.

Perhaps the best narrative is Addison's "The Vision of Mizrah" (*The Spectator*, 159). Oriental tales became enormously popular after Antoine Galland's translation of *Alf layla wa-layla* (fifteenth century; *The Arabian Nights' Entertainments*, 1706-1708). *The Spectator*, not surprisingly, capitalized on the form's influence in Oriental-flavored moral tales such as "The Vision of Mizrah." Other forms of Oriental tales appeared as "letters" from the Orient, as in Charles de Montesquieu's *Lettres persanes* (1721; *Persian Letters*, 1722) and Oliver Goldsmith's *The Citizen of the World* (1762), and as romances—moral, philosophical, or satirical—such as Voltaire's popular *Zadig: Ou, La Destinée, Histoire orientale* (1748; originally as *Memnon: Histoire orientale*, 1747; *Zadig: Or, The Book of Fate*, 1749) and Samuel Johnson's similar *Rasselas, Prince of Abyssinia: A Tale by S. Johnson* (1759).

"The Vision of Mizrah" displays a pleasing mixture of elements—Oriental material, allegory, and dream vision—and showcases Addison's ability to construct a narrative around a consistent mood and condensed action. A good narrator also controls a story by presenting a scene in its varied details. Addison excels in imaging a scene, and in "The Vision of Mizrah," the reader is taken successfully by the second paragraph to enjoy the air on the mountaintops above Baghdad.

In Steele's sketch "The Matchmaker" (*The Spectator*, 437), realistic details and several characters in motion make it a delightful narrative story. From the beginning words, the emphasis is on minute details of movement and gesture and on conversation with real people. "The Biter" (*The Spectator*, 504), though technically a simple character sketch, contains the record of actual spoken words, presented in such a way as to convey a conversational tone and the sting of wit, and is an excellent short narrative episode.

Whether directly by description or indirectly through action, the authors come close, in a number of cases, to achieving the conflict, unity of mood, and character interplay necessary for the short story proper, as in "The Envious Man" (*The Spectator*, 19). Sir Roger and his friends acted and talked in accordance with their imagined personalities. Human figures so naturally drawn had not appeared in English prose fiction before. The smooth, easy flow of words and natural conversational tone overlaid with brevity throughout *The Spectator* is worth a study for any short-fiction enthusiast.

The custom of didacticism restricted the range of short fiction in the eighteenth century to a certain extent. The tones in Johnson's didactic essays in *The Rambler*, though of high quality, approach dictatorial instruction. Anyone comparing the light and rhythmical periods of *The Spectator* to the ponderous sententiousness of *The Rambler* will perceive that the spirit of preaching was gaining ground on the genius of conversation. Hannah More's *Cheap Repository* tracts also reflect the limitations of didacticism. Brought up from childhood on *The Spectator* and *The Rambler*, which introduced new and lofty conceptions of the principles of morality, the characters in More's tracts and her fifty tales and ballads are merely pegs on which to hang principles. The principles are stated with considerable skill in her case, but there is little development of character to help the case of short fiction at the time.

Didacticism of the period did reap benefits, though. The didactic morality influenced other writers such as Daniel Defoe and Jonathan Swift. The satire was generally directed against the upper classes, which, through writers such as Defoe, began a sympathetic understanding of poverty and the travails of the underprivileged. Truth and realism were the watchwords of Defoe, a professed moralist. He brought to his short fiction a journalistic sense of truth and clarity. Indeed, Defoe's *A True Relation of the Apparition of One Mrs. Veal* (1706), long considered fiction, is merely a piece of expert reporting. His writing skills are evident, and the account has the same clear and simple delineation of scenes and the same lucid factual tone that compels the reader's belief, possessed by Defoe's later famous works, such as *The Life and Strange Surprizing Adventures of Robinson Crusoe, of York, Mariner, Written by Himself* (1719; commonly known as *Robinson Crusoe*).

What Defoe tries to do in the story is retain the significance of the old legends, ballads, and folktales in a culture in which those beliefs were no longer tenable. *A True Relation of the Apparition of One Mrs. Veal* looks backward to the most traditional form of short narrative—the fable presented to teach a moral lesson—and forward to the realistic story presented for its own sake as an account of an actual event. What makes the story so interesting is that it foregrounds this duality so emphatically.

A True Relation of the Apparition of One Mrs. Veal can be taken in several different ways at once. First of all, although it is presented as a moral tale, it is much more detailed and specific than other "moral tales" or illustrative essays of the early eighteenth century, in which the sincerity of the teller alone was sufficient to persuade the reader of the truth of the event. It little matters, in terms of the technique of the tale, whether the apparition actually appeared to Mrs. Bargrave or not, nor does it matter that Defoe takes the incident from an actual account by Mrs. Bargrave. What does matter is the process by which the relation becomes a story. Whether an event actually took place or whether a central character or narrator is "crazed" and has simply hallucinated the event is one of the most common foregrounded concerns of short fiction later in the nineteenth century.

Another English writer admired for his simplicity, lucidity, and reasonableness is Goldsmith, the most noteworthy successor of Johnson in the art of the didactic short story. He writes with a range of humor, from subtle irony to broad farce, and the impulse to tell a good story carried his imagination far beyond the scope of so-called good sense. The best-known eighteenth century character sketch/essay with moral purpose is Goldsmith's "The Disabled Soldier." The narrator's reflections center on the difference between the misfortunes of tragic and epic sufferers, who are usually considered to be fit subjects for artistic presentation, and the misfortunes of socially insignificant sufferers, who are usually ignored. The frame reflections suggest a radical difference between the epic form that gave rise to the novel and the folktale form that gave rise to the short story. In the former, the epic or tragic structure depends on the hero's high stature and the incongruity of his consequent fall.

For the ordinary person, however, for whom distress is the usual course of things, calamity poses no incongruity and thus no reason for his life to be the subject of a tragic or epic form. There is no obvious irony in the oral teller's story. The irony exists tacitly in the fact that the litany of events is presented to readers who perceive the gap between the soldier's situation and their own. "The Disabled Soldier" neatly illustrates the tale within the essay, differences between history and story, and some basic distinctions between the oral and written story. It also centers on the prototypical nineteenth century short-story character, the little man whose identity resides only in the story of adversity he tells.

Perhaps the most important eighteenth century short fiction to influence the nineteenth century short story is Horace Walpole's gothic romance, *The Castle of Otranto* (1765), for in it, Walpole self-consciously combined conventions of both realism and romance. In his famous preface to the second edition, Walpole says his work is an attempt to blend the ancient and the modern in which, while

> leaving the powers of fancy at liberty to expatiate through the boundless realms of invention, and thence of creating more interesting situations, he wished to conduct "the mortal agents in his drama according to the rules of probability; in short, to make them think, speak, and act, as it might be supposed mere men and women do in extraordinary positions."

However, because Walpole's ordinary people are placed in extraordinary situations, his characters do not remain "ordinary." For even though they seem to be motivated by individual psychology, placing them in extreme situations transforms them into psychological embodiments. The basic story of *The Castle of Otranto* is the family romance—the mystery of paternity and the problem of who shall rule, all of which is "displaced" and emphasized by the multiplication of character roles. There are, for example, three "fathers" (Manfred, Frederick, and Jerome), two "sons" (Conrad and Theodore), and two "daughters" (Isabelle and Matilda). In structure, *The Castle of Otranto* is a story in which all characters and thus all motifs are closely and obsessively related.

In the middle years of the eighteenth century, the novel is prominent among literary forms in England. Ultimately, the great novelists in England exerted a deep influence on Europe. Therefore, while the *nouvelle* in France emerged as a popular art form in the late seventeenth and early eighteenth centuries, the novelette and other similar fictional forms in England were quite overshadowed by the novel. Some of these included travel accounts, secret histories, memoirs, and biographies (each of these forms were usually thinly disguised romances of passion). Eliza Haywood, who wrote, among other short fiction, *Secret Histories, Novels, and Poems* (1725), is an example of an author who acquiesced to the decreasing demand for the above-mentioned fictional forms and wisely moved on to produce good quality novels.

Because of the emergence of the novel in England, then, the short story generally remained tied to the essay, chiefly in the periodical. Within this small range, its success was remarkable, and its impact kept the seeds of short fiction, though dormant in many ways by the end of the century, still alive.

America

In America during the eighteenth century, all roads did not lead to the novel, as in England. As literary historian Edward J. O'Brien (*The Advance of the American Short Story*, 1931) theorizes, the answer lies in the difference of temperament and environment between the English (and Europeans) and the Americans. The more impatient and restless temperament of the pioneers, settling the relatively new and largely unexplored nation, and their view that there was little place for leisure in their rough and difficult environment (compare hardworking wealthy landowners in America to the Court and aristocracy of England and Europe in the 1700's) made the short story much more appealing—being brief and able to condense emotion into a figurative moment as it flies.

The essays of Benjamin Franklin covered a broad range of subject matter, in form and in purpose; it can be said that they kept short fiction creatively alive in the 1700's in America. He wrote gracefully and urbanely yet could write equally well in the rough school of realism fathered by Defoe. The earthy realism of Franklin's style is vividly exemplified in one of his essays, "Reflections on Courtship and Marriage," in which he describes the picture that some women present in the morning, with "frowsy hair hanging in sweaty ringlets, staring like Medusa with her serpents . . . teeth furred and eyes crusted. . . ."

Influenced by the great periodicals in England, humor and satire were increasingly being given more stress in American essays. Franklin's "Silence Dogood Essays" demonstrate his vivid imagination and his sense of the ridiculous. They resemble in style the colloquial manner of *The Spectator*, with one major difference, more typical of the aggressive pioneer spirit of America: The learned allusions and literary anecdotes of *The Spectator* were replaced by homely sayings and by comic, even earthy stories. They also show remarkable empathy for women and their problems, as Franklin sees through the eyes of the widow Silence Dogood; many are related to women's affairs and problems.

In 1732, Franklin wrote a series of three character sketches: of Anthony Afterwit, an honest tradesman with an extravagant wife; of Celia Single, a sketch with considerable dialogue as a forum to discuss women's rights; and of Alice Addertongue, whose words, through Franklin's pen, speak facetiously about scandal yet scrupulously avoid making his newspaper *The Pennsylvania Gazette* a scandal sheet, as were some of the other papers of the day.

Franklin's "The Bagatelles," lighthearted or humorous essays, are classics in short fiction that cover a great emotional range. Here, Franklin momentarily lays aside his constant watchword "utility." For once, his essay becomes not a mere means to an end. "The Elysian Fields," for example, is an excellent piece that shows considerable similarities to modern short stories—with a clearly discernible beginning, middle, and end, with elements of surprise and balanced irony. He was a writer clearly ahead of his time. Franklin established a tradition of humor and journalistic writing that was peculiarly American and that can be found in the best of modern short fiction.

France

In France, as well as America and England, the formal short story—with its exacting demands of narrative structure, content, and development—did not fully develop until well into the nineteenth century. From France, though, at the end of the seventeenth century and through the first half of the eighteenth, came the highest-quality short fiction in Europe and America. Voltaire and the Encyclopedists, leaders in Enlightenment thinking, were producing high quality *contes philosophiques*, and the *nouvelle* had replaced the heroic romance in popularity. A short fiction centered on a love intrigue, the *nouvelle*, though generally longer than most short fiction, showed the move toward shorter pieces and is considered integral to the development of the short story.

The first work of fiction in the 1700's actually to comply with the theory of the *nouvelle* is Robert Challes's *Les Illustres Françoises* (1713; *The Illustrious French Lovers*, 1727). The work is a collection of *nouvelles* or *histoires*, joined together within a narrative frame, so it belongs to the fictional genre that also contains Giovanni Boccaccio's *Decameron: O, Prencipe Galetto* (1349-1351; *The Decameron*, 1620) and Geoffrey Chaucer's *The Canterbury Tales* (1387-1400). Challes's *nouvelle* is revolutionary in the way in which it focuses more closely on the texture of experience than earlier fictions, but at the same time it places heavy stress on the elements that restrain and shape emotional and impulsive elements in human character.

Montesquieu, a forerunner of Voltaire, deserves further mention in this essay for his vastly entertaining *Persian Letters*, fictional letters written home by two Persians traveling in France. One can enjoy them for their subtle irony and urbane style, and one can faintly hear the first criticisms of the artificiality of the French aristocracy.

Voltaire, in the early eighteenth century, stood as a symbol of the Enlightenment, and he is now considered an intellectual precursor of the French Revolution. He used—as did Franklin, who manifested the same spirit and ideals in America before the American Revolution—the weapon of humor to correct human folly. The bizarre adventures in *Candide: Ou,*

L'Optimisme (1759; *Candide: Or, All for the Best*, 1759; also as *Candide: Or, The Optimist*, 1762; also as *Candide: Or, Optimism*, 1947) are the best examples of his skill in persuading with a smile, to carry the reader along on an even flow, even while he uses satire's fierce energies to challenge readers' complacencies. He reveals the underside of the Enlightenment ideal of reason: that the much-praised reason of human beings can also expose their weaknesses.

Voltaire at once invented the *conte philosophique* and brought it to such perfection that only few writers have dared to imitate him. *Le Micromégas* (1752; *Micromegas*, 1753), *Zadig*, and *Candide* all show Voltaire's ability to cover ground with complete lucidity in a small number of words. The first page of *Candide* offers a wonderful example. Without the slightest sense of haste or compression, the scene is set, the chief characters are introduced, and the tone and feeling of the story are established.

To complete a view of eighteenth century short fiction in France, it is necessary to observe the revolutionary effects, to observe how the disintegrating work of Voltaire and the Encyclopedists was followed by the constructive work of Jean-Jacques Rousseau, the dreamer. The earlier writers, such as Voltaire, worked to expose, even to destroy, the existing system; the later writers, such as Rousseau, were hopeful constructors, dreamers of ideal commonwealths and societies. Rousseau, at first alone, and seconded only later in life by the enthusiasm of a new school of Romanticists, imparts a touch of poetic fire to French thought in the latter half of the eighteenth century. Rousseau's *Julie: Ou, La Nouvelle Héloïse* (1761; *Eloise: Or, A Series of Original Letters*, 1761; also as *Julie: Or, The New Eloise*, 1968) marks the beginning of the new period. The essential idea is of life as an organic whole and human beings as creatures essentially connected with the rest of nature by virtue of their emotions—this is the very center of Romantic theory. Rousseau's *nouvelle* marked the shift in writing to an increase of subjectivity, which was ultimately painful and stressful (eventually, intense subjectivity became, as Johann Wolfgang von Goethe described it, a form of sickness). The new, free intensity of feeling of Romanticism, however, opened the floodgates of creativity, and the short story flourished in the nineteenth century because of it.

Even before Rousseau and full-blown Romanticism, there was an interest on the Continent in highly developed emotional responsiveness. In Germany, Goethe's work *Die Leiden des jungen Werthers* (1774; *The Sorrows of Young Werther*, 1779) was immensely influential in establishing the image of the introspective, self-pitying, melancholy Romantic hero. In fact, it was the German Romantic school that developed most quickly and thoroughly in Europe.

Germany

Although it was the novel that became the most popular fictional form in Germany during the "Romantic" end of the eighteenth century, excellent short fiction was produced as well because of the stronger emphasis on the narrative, rediscovered interest in fables, and the relaxed formal structures allowing increased freedom of expression.

The German *Novelle*, an original romance form of short fiction, was cultivated by the German Romanticists as well. Noteworthy is Goethe's *Unterhaltungen deutscher Ausgewanderten* (1795; *Conversations of German Emigrants*, 1854), with its escapist motif, written for the German periodical *Die Hören*. It is a framework series of stories intended primarily to entertain and to instruct, written in much the same manner as Boccaccio's *Decameron*. As in the Italian work, there is a background of suffering and death contrasted with the relative calm among the small group of aristocrats involved in the storytelling.

The German Romanticist Ludwig Tieck was a prolific writer of *Novellen*, but his best work was in the realm of Romantic fairy tales. The excellent *Der blonde Eckbert* (1797; *Fair Eckbert*, 1828) is a product of dreams and fancies which spin a web of varicolored moods and atmospheres. It delves into the depths of the subconscious. The awe-inspiring potency of Romantic writing is seen here at its best. Tieck succeeds quite well in giving poetic form to his mystic feeling for nature and in making nature a sort of allegory for the vague strivings and imaginings of humankind. True to his fatalism, which told him that human beings are at the mercy of higher powers, the horrible is seen as residing in nature itself and overpowering humankind.

The problem with *Fair Eckbert* is not only that the story makes use of such fairy-tale motifs as a magical bird, a grotesque old lady, and a child who runs away from home to enter an enchanted world but also that characters seem to do things without any reason, and there does not seem to be any logical connection between the events in the tale. Bertha's tale within a tale is dominated by a dream logic that makes it seem predominantly like a fairy tale. However, Bertha's story differs from fairy tales because, presented as a story of a personal experience, it becomes a self-conscious embodiment of psychological processes.

Because Bertha's story is about the child's retreat from the external world into the world of fantasy or fairy tale, the specific motivation for her leaving home cannot be made clear; she leaves the house scarcely realizing what she is doing, for truly her departure is an unconscious one, both in the manifest story and in its latent meaning. Her journey into the mountains that reveal no sign of human habitation, her encounter with the strange old woman whose face twitches so that Bertha is never sure what she really looks like and with the bird that lays an egg each day with a pearl or gem inside are all characterized as if they were a dream—even a dream within a dream, says Bertha. As the dream events become familiar to her, the dream reality takes on the appearance of the only reality there is.

When the reader returns to the frame, which is Eckbert's story, he or she enters into a different realm of motivation and logic of events, for the reader is, comparatively speaking, "back to reality." Eckbert's anxiety about the telling of the secret story to his friend, Walther, can be accounted for consciously rather than unconsciously, just as his original motivation for urging Bertha to tell the story can be accounted for as an irresistible impulse to tell a friend a secret to make him a closer friend. However, after the story is told, Eckbert regrets the confidence, fearing that it is human nature that the listener will misuse the secret. This anxiety transforms the "real" story of Eckbert into a fairy-tale story, as Eckbert unconsciously kills Walther and thus mysteriously "causes" the death of Bertha. This double loss of wife and friend makes Eckbert feel that his life is "more like a strange fairy-tale than an actual mortal existence."

The Romanticists' aversion to rationalism is exemplified in Tieck's famous short-fiction works in the three-volume *Volksmärchen* (1797), characterized by childlike feeling, unrestrained imagination, and satire against the Enlightenment. Here, reason is held up to ridicule, and winsome miraculous happenings come into their own. Tieck and other early German Romantics sought the elements of wonder and horror in old fairy tales and in old German chapbooks and found far-off colorful lands of poesy, miracles, and dreams.

Spain

Both Romanticism and the Enlightenment came late to Spain, which was weakened from divisions and the loss of much territory at the beginning of the eighteenth century as a result of the War of the Spanish Succession. Additionally, throughout the century, government censors and inquisitors were vigilant. As late as 1793, for example, a group of intellectuals who wanted to publish a periodical called *El Académico* made a promise that shows the power of censorship over the press at that time. They proclaimed, "We will say nothing, quote nothing, and become involved in nothing which might cause offence and would rather pass for ignorant in the eyes of some than for men of new ideas." It was a situation unique to the rest of the Western world at that time.

Although censors and inquisitors might have kept much of the Enlightenment out of print, however, they could not keep it out of Spain. For example, in the 1770's, the bishop of Plasencia complained to the king of the ease with which he had procured the irreligious and subversive writings of Voltaire himself. Even if such works could not be published in Spain, it was difficult to avoid their discussion at private gatherings and in the coffeehouses.

By the middle of the century, increasing contact with the rest of Europe led Spanish writers to explore international literary forms. One of the first to adopt an obviously European style was José Clavijo y Fajardo, whose periodical *El Pensador* began to appear weekly in 1762. The model for this was clearly *The Spectator.* Seven whole speculations are translated, and there are direct imitations of at least six others. Clavijo y Fajardo adopted many of *The Spectator*'s fictional forms. Some of his fictional devices, however, have purely Spanish sources.

The periodicals encouraged the development of short forms and rapid, even casual reading habits in readers. Enlightenment topics occupied the majority of space in Spanish periodicals and fueled such dangerous prose works as *Cartas marruecas* (wr. 1774, pb. 1793), by José de Cadalso y Vásquez (the most original of the literary Enlightenment thinkers of the day), which accepts the morality of the Moors as well as the Christians. Works such as Cadalso's often fell victim to the Inquisition.

A preperiodical short fiction form that was to become a staple of Spanish periodicals in the late eighteenth and early nineteenth centuries was the fictional dream or *sueño*. Diego de Torres Villarroel's *Sueños morales* (1727 and 1728) and later those of Ramirez de Gongora are the best examples of the dream fiction that later found its way in the form of short *sueños morales* into the periodicals.

In the light of eighteenth century repression in Spain, it is understandable that through most of the century, Spanish writers restrained their imagination. Even Spanish satires were more closely related to the everyday in Spain than, say, Jonathan Swift's *Gulliver's Travels* or Voltaire's *Candide*. The Peninsular War in the middle of the century was instrumental in opening the way for Romantic thought with its non-*hidalgo* officers, which made for the first real breach in the status system. The middle and lower classes had found a voice. Finally, in the 1790's, with the publication of Mor de Fuentes's *La Serafina* (1796)—a novel of love in the provinces told in the form of letters and singing the virtues of country life and simple people—it was obvious that Romanticism was arriving.

ITALY

If in Italy, the seventeenth century, a period of the iron despotism of Spain, was a time of stagnation, then the eighteenth was a period of recovery, for Italy was one of the territories lost by Spain in the War of the Spanish Succession. The ancient luster of literature, indeed, was but feebly rekindled, but an invigorating breath pervaded the nation as Spanish dominion disappeared from Italy. People wrote and thought in comparative freedom.

The extinction of the free spirit of the Renaissance was the more unfortunate for Italy, as it arrested the development of speculative and scientific research, which had seemed to be opening up there. Therefore, it was natural that the thrust of Italian literature was toward those directions in the eighteenth century, not toward fiction in its many forms experienced throughout the Continent. Certainly no novelist of reputation wrote from Italy during the century. Italy could have easily degenerated into mediocrity but for the tremendous literary convulsions at the end of the century. Only in drama did Italy stand apart and supreme during nearly the whole of the age.

By the middle of the century, a strong wave of foreign influence, particularly from France, and more indirectly from England, aided markedly in the awakening of Enlightenment thinking reflected in Italian literature. As one might assume by now, it was the periodical that hurried the spread of liberal ideas in Italy and kept various forms of short fiction active. It should also be no surprise that *The Spectator* was the model for most Italian periodicals, such as *Il Caffe* (1764-1766) and Gasparo Gozzi's *La Gazzetta veneta* (1760-1761), which included imaginative original sketches and stories with acute but gentle satire and humor directed at the Venetian scene. Gozzi continued the tradition in 1761 and 1762 with *L'Osservatore venuto*, a journal of manners and customs very similar to Addison's *The Spectator.*

Gozzi's younger brother Carlo was a writer of note with considerable ability. The popularity of his works show the slow move to Romanticism that blossomed at the end of the century in Italy. Carlo Gozzi's best-known works are his fairy tales. The most successful one of his famous scenic stories is the exotic and fantastical theatrical fable *L'Amore delle tre malarance* (pr. 1761; *The Love for Three Oranges*, 1949). His stories were intensely popular throughout the Romantic period and beyond.

Italy was one of the last countries to feel the effects of Romanticism, but as the cosmopolitan drift became more and more powerful toward the end of the century, writers such as Goethe and Sir Walter Scott excited the curiosity of Italian readers. Italy joined late but joined entirely the movement, impatient with the prosaic present and enamored of the neglected Middle Ages.

As the eighteenth century drew to a close, Spain and Italy were playing literary catch-up, while the focus in Germany, France, and England was on the novel. The geographic isolation of America made it a separate entity as far as literature was concerned, almost an anomaly. Given the state of short fiction in England and on the Continent by the end of the eighteenth century, perhaps it is not surprising that the short-story genre emerged strong and distinct in America. In England, great periodicals such as *The Spectator* had lost considerable influence in the face of the proliferation of low-quality magazines, penny dreadfuls, and chapbooks because of cheaper printing methods and a growing working-class readership.

The news for short fiction, however, was not all bad. Gothic themes were found not only in cheap magazines but also in high-quality novels. Also, the element of suspense and tension in the gothic theme found its way into the modern short story, elements that had been lacking throughout the eighteenth century. Additionally, the coming of the popular magazine established a market for brief prose pieces, however inferior those pieces might be. The way was kept open for the exceptional creativity of nineteenth century writers and for the emergence of the distinct short-story genre.

The debt that these writers owe to the Enlightenment periodicals is not small. The vast array of fictional forms produced in these publications paved the way for the cohesive short forms that evolved in the nineteenth century.

The Spectator was the model for most of the periodicals of the age. For good reason, it was the most widely read and the best periodical of the century. The purpose of *The Spectator* was not only to instruct but also—and this is perhaps its most significant contribution to the short-story genre—to entertain. The motto for the first edition of *The Spectator* was successfully followed by Addison and Steele and has the kind of staying power that makes it a worthy goal for fiction of any age: "Not smoke after flame does he plan to give, but after smoke the light, that then he may set forth striking and wondrous tales."

Marilyn Schultz, updated by Charles E. May

Bibliography

Anderson, Douglas. *The Radical Enlightenments of Benjamin Franklin*. Baltimore: The Johns Hopkins University Press, 1997. Discusses the literary and intellectual career of Franklin in his early years; provides a close reading of a number of Franklin texts.

Brooks, Christopher K. "'Guilty of Being Poor': Oliver Goldsmith's 'No-Account' Centinel." *English Language Notes* 36 (September, 1998): 23-38. Argues that "Private Centinel" in *The Citizen of the World* is one of the most profound uses of a poor, homeless character in eighteenth-century literature.

Howells, Robin. *Disabled Powers: A Reading of Voltaire's Contes*. Atlanta, Ga.: Rodopi, 1993. An interpretation of the Contes of Voltaire in the light of Mikhail Bakhtin's concept of the "carnivalesque." Part I focuses on the theme of disablement. Part II contains carnivalesque readings of two tales, "Le Monde comme il va" and "Candide." The third part considers the historical changes in consciousness represented by the later tales. Includes bibliographical references.

_______. "Pleasure Principles: Tales, Infantile Naming, and Voltaire." *The Modern Language Review* 92 (April, 1997): 295-307. Suggests that one of the characteristics of the eighteenth century French prose tale is repetition typical of young children.

Hunter, J. Paul. *Before Novels: The Cultural Contexts of Eighteenth-Century English Fiction*. New York: W. W. Norton, 1990. Examines the background for the development of the modern novel, including discussions of literacy, popular culture, and society in the eighteenth century.

Knight, Charles A. *Joseph Addison and Richard*

Steele: A Reference Guide. New York: G. K. Hall, 1994. An exhaustive reference source containing works written about Addison and Steele between 1729 and 1991. Includes summaries of major scholarship about the authors. Includes an index.

_______. "*The Spectator*'s Moral Economy." *Modern Philology* 91 (November, 1993): 161-179. Examines Addison and Steele's principles of moral economy in *The Spectator* to control dreams of endless financial gains. Argues they found a secular basis for moral behavior, which emphasized the common good over individual gain.

THE EARLY NINETEENTH CENTURY: 1800-1840

By the year 1800 various Western literatures could boast isolated examples of works which, if they were published today, would almost certainly be called short stories in the modern sense of the term. These works are in one sense rather like those hypothetical Phoenicians or Greeks who stumbled onto America before Columbus. In the final analysis Columbus is celebrated not so much for being the first as for being the first to make much historical difference. By the same token, the originator of the modern short story is the writer whose first short story made the most dramatic difference to the genre and to subsequent literary history. By 1800, although well on the way, that person had not yet arrived. What was found then in short fiction throughout the Western world was a dizzying variety of forms, traditions, genres, and subgenres that sometimes approached quite closely the modern short story, which in fact seemed to have produced splendid isolated examples, as in Richard Steele's *The Spectator*, but which—although generating fine literature according to other criteria—finally fell short of a consistent vision, a full conception of the short story as it is thought of today.

This short narrative current in the year 1800 can be arbitrarily divided in as many different ways as might a custard pie, but the most meaningful division would seem to be into the broad categories of work in the tale tradition on the one hand and in the essay-sketch tradition on the other.

The Tale Tradition

The tale tradition had by far a longer and more complex history than the essay-sketch tradition. Virtually every anthropologist, linguist, and literary historian would agree that tales in one form or another are approximately as old as language, and if language is the distinguishing feature of human beings, then tales must have originated at almost the same time as human beings. Judging from what is known of human nature, one can assume that the first tales took the form of either lies or gossip, which remain among the most seductive categories of narrative today. People must have soon varied the literary fare with the sort of oral tales which seem to have flourished then and which still flourish today among preliterate peoples in just about every culture on the face of the earth: myths, legends, folktales, jokes, anecdotes, and so on—and subsequently with the sorts of refinements and variations of these forms that develop in diverse guises in various cultures at various times. Among the terms (often overlapping) for specifically oral tales with which Stith Thompson deals in his classic study, *The Folktale* (1851), are *Märchen*, fairy tale, household tale, *conte populaire*, novella, hero tale, *Sage*, local tradition, local legend, migratory legend, *tradition populaire*, explanatory tale, etiological tale, *Natursage, pourquoi* story, animal tale, fable, jest, humorous anecdote, merry tale, *Schwank*, and so on.

Such genres invariably alter, sometimes quite subtly, sometimes fundamentally, when the means of transmission become not the more or less dramatic human voice (with accompanying facial expressions and physical gestures) of a person immediately present but the impersonal pen and ink. Earlier sections of *The Folktale* describe some of the forms of written tale that have spanned the centuries since the paleolithic oral tale: Geoffrey Chaucer's *fabliaux*, saints' legends, beast fables, and Chivalric romances, for example.

About the year 1800, as for many decades before and after, there were basically three avenues by which these works in the tale tradition reached the public. The first is the oldest, the most widespread, and in many ways the most important—oral storytelling. It is safe to say that, until television metastasized so dramatically in the 1950's, almost everyone on the planet was introduced to literature by way of tales such as "Snow White" and "Jack and the Beanstalk." Even the Saturday morning television programs so many children watch are fundamentally in the same tale tradition. The second means of transmission was books. European children had long enjoyed chapbooks like *Jack the Giant Killer*, and adults titillated their own imaginations with fare as varied as jest books and saints' legends. Countless European fairy tales had appeared in print, among them Charles Perrault's *Histoires et contes du temps passé, avec des moralités* (1697), but a powerful new influence entered with Antoine Galland's first European translation (into French) of *Alf layla wa-layla* (fifteenth century; *The Arabian Nights' Entertainments*, 1706-1708). Something of the international character of these stories may be inferred from the fact that the English translated the French translation which was itself an Arabic (largely Persian) translation of stories primarily derived from India and China. Where the stories ultimately originated and how old they really are no one will ever know. The magnificent example of *The Arabian Nights' Entertainments* and the growing interest in the past and in primitives which helped stimulate the rise of Romanticism led to Jacob and Wilhelm Grimm's *Kinder- und Hausmärchen* (1812, 1815, revised 1819-1822; *German Popular Stories*, 1823-1826; better known as *Grimm's Fairy Tales*) and to a host of similar folkloric collections in the early 1800's.

The tales in books tended to be one step from the traditional oral tales, but by 1800 a third medium, periodical publications—chiefly newspapers and magazines—offered a bewildering variety of forms of tale. Many were quite traditional; magazines published forms such as fables, anecdotes, fairy tales, and legends. Many, however, were quite different forms; many were much closer to what would be recognized as the modern short story. James Louis Gray lists, among the many subgenres of short fiction in late eighteenth and early nineteenth century periodicals, forms he calls tales of character, moral tales, histories, dialogues, sentimental tales, adventure tales, and allegories of the heart.

By the year 1800 all these antecedent forms continued to exist—orally or in print—and inevitably had a tremendous impact on the mind of anyone concerned with short fiction.

THE ESSAY-SKETCH TRADITION

The second grand tradition dominating short prose works in the year 1800 was that of the essay, especially the periodical essay or sketch. One can trace full-fledged tales back to the evolution of language, but the essay or sketch can hardly have existed before the creation of a fairly sophisticated system of writing. In one form or another essays must have existed from the time the first writer attempted (the word "essay" comes from the French word meaning to try or to attempt) to capture in prose thoughts or feelings about some subject; alternately, the sketch must have begun when the writer attempted to characterize or to describe some subject in prose.

Most historians of Western literature recognize as the first great writer of sketches the Greek philosopher Theophrastus, who, around 319 B.C.E., composed a book called *Charactēres ethikōi* (*The Moral Characters of Theophrastus*, 1616; best known as *Characters*); the work was composed of several short prose pieces, each representing some basic character or personality type. Theophrastus's sketches had a tremendous influence on later writers of sketches, especially those in the seventeenth century: Joseph Hall, John Earle, Sir Thomas Overbury, and Jean de La Bruyère. These writers in turn influenced Joseph Addison and Richard Steele, who in *The Tatler* and *The Spectator* developed a number of more or less typical characters; the most important was Sir Roger de Coverley, a good-natured provincial squire with whom the sketch approached the sort of sophistication with which subsequent novelists were to treat character. In the decades preceding 1800 various writers, such as Benjamin Franklin and Oliver Goldsmith, inspired by the example of Sir Roger, carried the character sketch further and further from idealized abstraction, closer and closer to the sort of uniqueness and individuality associated with character in fiction. With the gradual waxing of Romanticism and the slow shift of emphasis from thought to feeling, the character sketch had evolved into a form only slightly removed from the modern short story.

The essay has a similar lengthy history. From the beginnings of the form, the subject discussed seems to have held precedence over the individual mind acting on that subject, but in 1580 a minor literary revolution occurred when the Frenchman Michel Eyquem de Montaigne published his *Essais* (1580-1595; *The Essays*, 1603). Wishing to explore the nature of humanity and convinced that each person was a microcosm of the whole, he determined to plumb his own mind in detail ("I myself am the matter of my book. . . . It is myself that I depict"). Few subsequent essayists ever achieved a style or tone approaching Montaigne's charming intimacy, but his intensive compelling introspection helped others, even writers such as the relatively formal Sir Francis Bacon, shift their own focus more in the direction of personality. Again Addison and Steele played a crucial role; in *The Tatler* and especially in *The Spectator*, they popularized what had been a relatively esoteric form and established a most successful model for a periodical series; these periodical series offered a variety of brief compositions on a dizzying miscellany of topics, unified by little but the persona of the essayist, the anonymous Tatler or Spectator. Benjamin Franklin and other followers cultivated a richer personality in the essayist; and by the year 1800, with the rise of sentimentality and Romanticism, the personality of the essayist became dramatically more important, to reach a plateau shortly in the familiar or personal essay as practiced by Charles Lamb and his contemporaries and followers.

Absolutely pure prose forms are approximately as rare as unicorns. Although the essay takes the natural form of exposition and the sketch inherently, irresistibly gravitates toward description, some narrative did invade both forms. Narrative essays and sketches that are almost stories are familiar to the modern reader; these were popular phenomena long before the birth of the modern short story.

WASHINGTON IRVING

Precisely when did the modern short story begin? The question is like asking precisely where it is that the blue shades into violet in a rainbow. The more specific and dogmatic the answer, the less reliable it is likely to be. It is known, however, that by the early 1800's in America and to various degrees throughout the Western world, two distinct traditions existed side by side: one, the tale tradition full of narrative bursting with drama and incident, extraordinary situations and settings, and rather flat characters depicted for the most part externally; the other, the essay-sketch tradition, more subtly developed, largely ignoring striking incidents to focus on the vagaries of character, preferring the more normal and usual (in one sense more realistic) characters, situations, events, and settings, depending more on sharply observed detail, introspection, and thoughtfulness than on drama. The union of these two traditions was to mark the creation of the modern short story—but precisely when did that happen?

Literary historians, although less than unanimous, show a surprising degree of agreement that the modern short story began in America and that the American with whom it began was Washington Irving. The finest scholar of the American short story, Frederick Lewis Pattee, wrote that the form began in October, 1807, with Irving's publication in the periodical series *Salmagundi* of "The Little Man in Black." The piece is short and a story but has decidedly too little sophistication, too little psychological depth, and too little successful imagery really to succeed as a modern short story. At least as good, if not better, a case could be made for "Sketches from Nature" (perhaps by Irving or by his collaborator James Kirke Paulding, although in fact more likely by both), which appeared a month earlier in the same periodical series. Here there is a focus on mood and psychological subtleties, on sharply observed imagery, and on interior states. The problem is that finally the psychic change on which the piece ends does not add up to very much. The solution seems simple now: Merely blend the virtues of "The Little Man in Black" (those of the tale tradition generally) and the virtues of "Sketches from Nature" (those of the essay-sketch tradition); but the evolution which had waited several thousand years after the introduction of writing to the Western world, tens and perhaps hundreds of thousands of years after the invention of storytelling, was in no hurry to occur.

No one, with any degree of certainty, can point to any given work as indisputably the world's first modern short story. One can with confidence, however, point out the first truly great modern short story produced in the Western world: "Rip Van Winkle," which appeared in the May, 1819, debut of Irving's periodically published book, *The Sketch Book of*

Geoffrey Crayon, Gent. Earlier writers had managed various blends of the tale and essay-sketch traditions before Irving, but none managed so brilliantly to blend the best of both traditions as to create from these two an irresistibly successful example of a wholly new form. How did Irving do it?

The most memorable parts of the story, the striking incident pattern involving Rip's experience with the dwarfish sailors of the *Half-Moon* and his two-decades-long nap, Irving based on a tale about a goatherd taken from Germanic folklore. In another bow toward the tale tradition, within the text itself, Irving's narrative persona, Diedrich Knickerbocker, relates that he heard the tale told orally by Rip himself and by other old Dutch settlers in the Catskill Mountains. The supernatural motifs of encountering the crew of Henrick Hudson's *Half-Moon*, who return every twenty years to tipple and to play ninepins in the mountains, and Rip's long sleep also derive from the traditions of oral narrative.

In one form or another, however, all these elements existed long before Irving. His genius consisted in the brilliance with which he transmuted the elements that the tale tradition offered to him and to every other writer of his time. Irving transformed those basic elements by treating them as he might have treated the essential matter of a periodical essay or sketch. He developed Rip not as the flat character so common in tales, not as a kind of cardboard marker to be pushed from square to square in a board game but as a rich, full, complete human being. Rather than merely assert certain abstract qualities in his character, Irving shows the reader through rich details a Rip who is good-natured, lovable, feckless, irresponsible, and (inevitably, given the above qualities and a wife, too) terribly henpecked. The details with which Irving develops Rip are realistic, credible, and concrete—precisely the kinds of details with which the contemporary sketch-developed characters descended from Sir Roger de Coverley. Few if any previous prose tales could boast a character so effectively developed in terms of a credible human personality.

For many, the most characteristic aspect of the modern short story is its quality of psychological analysis, and the short prose form most inclined to intimate personal revelation came from the essay-sketch tradition, the familiar or personal essay. It is no accident that *The Sketch Book of Geoffrey Crayon, Gent.*, generally credited with containing the first great American successes in the personal essay, also contained a minutely detailed analysis of Rip Van Winkle's slowly dawning recognition of the immense changes twenty years made in himself and in his environment. Rarely if ever in a prose tale before Irving's masterpiece has the reader spent so much time minutely analyzing a character's mind.

Yet in "Rip Van Winkle," Irving pays quite as much attention to setting as to personality and psychology. With the rise of Romanticism, verbal sketches of nature achieved the same sort of popularity as those in the visual arts. Unlike almost any previous tale, "Rip Van Winkle" opens not by introducing a character or by outlining an incident or a situation, but with a subtle, sensitive, and thematically quite relevant description of a setting: the Catskills and a sleepy Dutch village within them. The careful arrangement and coloring, the sharp detail, and the attention to atmosphere in "Rip Van Winkle" help set it apart from earlier prose tales, which tended either to ignore setting or to dismiss it in brief, idealized summary.

Some define the modern short story in terms of its realism, another quality much more characteristic of the essay-sketch tradition than of works in the tale tradition. For many readers the supernatural tipplers and Rip's incredible twenty-year sleep absolutely destroy any of the story's claims to realism—as they should if these elements reflect the mood of the story as a whole; but they do not, for three reasons. First, the great mass of the story (all but about six paragraphs) takes place in a densely realistic environment, in a setting developed with detail rich and credible enough to be all but photographic; few stories, for example, picture a scene more powerfully realistic than the long account of Rip's homecoming. Second, Irving gives the reader every reason to disbelieve that anything supernatural ever occurred. For one thing, most of the townspeople themselves refuse to believe Rip's story; for another, the reader learns that

Rip himself told several versions of his story before finally fixing on one. A third point (one that cannot be appreciated if readers consult only anthologies' butchered reprintings of the story) is that Irving chooses to tell the story not through an omniscient narrator, not through the reliable Geoffrey Crayon, who supposedly authors *The Sketch Book of Geoffrey Crayon, Gent.* as a whole, but through the credulous dunderhead Diedrich Knickerbocker, purported author of Irving's ridiculous *A History of New York* (1809). In a note at the end the reader learns that even Knickerbocker realizes how unbelievable Rip's story is and feels obliged to offer corroborating evidence. The evidence is he has heard of equally incredible stories supposed to have occurred in the Catskills, and, for the clinching argument, he heard the story from Rip Van Winkle himself, who even (and before a rural justice of the peace) signed, with an "X," a document testifying to the tale's accuracy. In a technical strategy as old as time, Irving allows the reader a choice between alternative explanations: The story is literally true or, if one prefers, Rip ran away from his henpecking wife and, hearing that after twenty years she died in a fit of anger at a peddler, he promptly returned with an outrageous lie to explain his long absence, a lie which only the most naïve will believe in the least. For those inclined to look closely, behind the facade of fantasy Irving displays an architecture grounded in solid reality.

It was particularly the confluence of these elements from the tale (plot and striking incident) and from the essay-sketch (character, psychological depth, setting, realism) that created the modern short story. Certain other, rather more unique, factors of "Rip Van Winkle" pioneered various subsequent trends in the short story. The intense focus on a unique place—the physical surroundings, the habits, customs, and peculiar modes of thought of a subculture—showed the way for the local color movement which dominated Western literature in the second half of the century. In the bookish outsider Diedrich Knickerbocker, bamboozled by a backwoods native's outrageous tall tale (and in "The Legend of Sleepy Hollow" the outsider Ichabod Crane's unhappy experiences with the native frontiersman Brom Bones), there is found an early example of frontier humor, a mode that burst on the scene in the 1830's and eventually gave rise to Mark Twain and the *Adventures of Huckleberry Finn* (1884) and in later decades to much of William Faulkner's work. Other important aspects of "Rip Van Winkle" are the story's toying with conventions of literary realism—its claim to truth based on a statement taken before a notary public, its layering of narrators (from Irving to Crayon to Knickerbocker), its recycling of Knickerbocker from *A History of New York* and *Salmagundi*, and its reference to one of Rip's cronies, Peter Vanderdonk, and to his ancestor, Adriaen Van der Donck, who actually lived and who wrote an actual description of New Netherland (New York), to which Irving also refers in the story. This "deconstructive" technique of calling into question the essential "reality" of the narrative itself looks forward to O. Henry and beyond to the postmodernists.

Irving's literary earthquake, "Rip Van Winkle," was followed by a series of aftershocks that began the new decade of the 1820's for the short story. "The Spectre Bridegroom," "The Legend of Sleepy Hollow," and "The Adventure of the German Student," all read with pleasure today, show an increasing tendency toward the gothic mode, which Nathaniel Hawthorne, Edgar Allan Poe, and Herman Melville were to employ to create some of the finest short stories in world literature. There are some other American stories of the 1820's read with genuine pleasure in later years—William Austin's "Peter Rugg, the Missing Man," for example—but most of the decade was given over to melodrama, to sentimental romance, or to didacticism. The popular reputations of the literary lions of the day have biodegraded quite as thoroughly as most of the paper on which they imposed their writings. Even the best among them—James Kirke Paulding, Catharine Sedgwick, Nathaniel Parker, John Neal, Timothy Flint, James Hall—are now little more than historical footnotes.

Point of view may be as important in literary history as in literature. In America the decade of the 1820's represented a tremendous falling off if the standard of comparison is the best of Irving's *The Sketch Book of Geoffrey Crayon, Gent.* On the other hand, if the standard is all other short narrative of the immediately preceding decades, then the 1820's represented a period of regular, if unhurried, advances in the skill and sophistication with which writers approached short fiction in general and this new form, the modern short story, in particular.

The true decade of advance for the genre—in America and, as shall be seen, in Europe—was the 1830's, which saw three different kinds of revolutions, one authored by Hawthorne, one by Poe, and one by Augustus Baldwin Longstreet.

NATHANIEL HAWTHORNE

Hawthorne's career began in a kind of imitation of the development of the modern short story. His earliest works were rather old-fashioned tales—"The Hollow of the Three Hills" and "Sir William Phipps"—and he also produced an early sketch, "Sights from a Steeple," which was much vaunted in his day; but these early works are finally insignificant. Hawthorne created the kind of artistic success destined to stand time's most stringent tests only when he combined the best of these two antecedent traditions in "My Kinsman, Major Molineux." Here, on one hand, is a form close to the local New England legends he so loved to read and to compose—he opens with a paragraph of history referring to a real historian, sets the scene in historical Boston, gives a rough time for the event, builds his climax around the kind of episode (tarring and feathering a minor Tory official) which might have earned a brief footnote or inspired some oral tale. To this frame, however, Hawthorne adds the sort of rich imagery, the close psychological analysis, and the compelling specific detail that characterized his many experiments in the essay-sketch tradition. The result is neither essay, sketch, nor tale, but one of the finest modern short stories anyone ever wrote.

Similar patterns dominate "Young Goodman Brown." Many mistakenly try to read the story as a kind of simplistic parable, but Henry James, among others, emphatically disagreed: "This, it seems to me, is just what it is not. It is not a parable, but a picture, which is a very different thing." As in "My Kinsman, Major Molineux," Hawthorne here relies on intensive imagery and detailed psychological analysis to move well beyond the traditional tale and to create a truly modern short story. Here, as in many other short pieces, he borrows much from the tale tradition—striking incident, dramatic situation, gothic motifs, and so on. In his best work he does not, however, borrow plot in the strict sense of the term—that is, plot in the sense of a causal sequence of events leading to a climax. J. Donald Crowley and many other critics have described a "processional mode" that Hawthorne tends to substitute for plot. In these two stories, as in many others, Hawthorne develops the central experience through a series of tableaux or vivid scenes which occur in front of the character's eyes. The mode, which tends to be much more passive than active, seems to have been instinctive with Hawthorne, but a case could be made that he borrowed the technique from the contemporary descriptive sketch. Certainly the pattern dominated his own sketches; and, oddly enough, until he published *The Scarlet Letter* in 1850, it was these works firmly in the essay-sketch tradition rather than the short stories (or "tales" as his contemporaries would have called them) for which Hawthorne was principally recognized. In various personal comments, such as the 1851 preface to *Twice-Told Tales* (1837), Hawthorne alluded to the public conception of himself as "a mild, shy, gentle, melancholic, exceedingly sensitive, and not very forcible man," generally, that is, as the author of such popular pieces as "Little Annie's Ramble," "A Rill from the Town Pump," and "The Toll-Gatherer's Day." What R. H. Fogle called "a general nineteenth-century mistrust of plot" helped cause many of those works least read in the twentieth century to be among the most popular in his own. A contemporary, Henry T. Tuckerman, noted a "melodramatic" and a "meditative" strain in Hawthorne's fiction, and, like a great many contemporary readers and critics, revealed a decided preference for the latter, those more akin to the essay-sketch tradition.

EDGAR ALLAN POE

One tends to think of the early nineteenth century as the heyday of the "traditional" short story—that is, the short story dominated by plot—but in fact experimental or innovative or plotless short fiction was at least as popular in the time of Hawthorne and Poe as it was in the twentieth century. Perhaps the most important reason for twentieth century myopia is that in May, 1842, Edgar Allan Poe's highly laudatory and immensely influential review of Hawthorne's *Twice-Told Tales* was published; Poe's essay is almost universally recognized as the very first attempt to develop a cogent formal theory of the modern short story. Most critics today recognize that Poe's theory applies much more closely to his own work than to that of Hawthorne, who himself wrote Poe in June, 1846, that he admired Poe more "as a writer of tales than as a critic upon them. I might often—and often do—dissent from your opinions in the latter capacity, but would never fail to recognize your force and originality in the former." In an 1847 review for *Godey's Magazine*, five years after his first attempt, Poe was still refining his theory, but in essence he still held that a story must be judged wholly on the basis of the effect it creates; he further insisted that only the most finely adapted and consciously applied technical skill could ensure the desired effect. The technical skill itself should focus tightly on incident and arrangement of incident (in 1847 he added "tone" to his blueprint).

Poe's theory of short fiction is based on the concept of unity as the fundamental principle of existence. As a result, for Poe, the purpose of literature is not to mirror the external world but to create a self-contained realm of reality that corresponds to the basic human desire for total unity. For Poe, "plot" is not merely a series of sequential events to arouse suspense but rather overall pattern, design, or unity. Only pattern, not realistic cause and effect, can make the separate elements of the work meaningful. Moreover, Poe insists that only when the reader has an awareness of the "end" of the work, that is, the overall pattern, will seemingly trivial elements become relevant and therefore meaningful.

In his famous 1842 Hawthorne review, Poe argues that although unity is the most important characteristic of the literary work, unity can only be achieved in a work that the reader can hold in the mind all at once. After the poem, traditionally the highest of high literary art, Poe says, the short tale has the greatest potential for being unified in the way the poem is. The effect of the tale is synonymous with its overall pattern or design, which is also synonymous with its theme or idea.

One of the most significant of Poe's contributions to the development of the tight aesthetic unity of the short story form derives from one of his most typical themes: the theme of psychological obsession embodied in a first-person narrator. Poe transforms the ironically distanced and discursive first-person narrator familiar to readers of the sketches of Washington Irving to the voice of a narrator so obsessed with the subject of his narration that the obsession becomes the thematic center of the story and thus creates the story's tight aesthetic unity. As with obsession, not only are all irrelevant things excluded, but also seemingly trivial things are magnified or transformed into meaningful motifs relevant to the central theme. When a character is motivated by an obsession, the motivation cannot be presented realistically in terms of ordinary cause and effect.

The most significant contribution Poe's detective stories make to the development of the short story consists of their basing a story's central theme and structure on the very process by which the reader perceives that unifying structure and pattern. They are Poe's most explicit examples of works in which questions of interpretation are not outside the story but are involved in every stage of the narrative development. Poe was self-consciously aware that he was embodying both the creator and the explicator in his so-called stories of ratiocination, for the stories are indeed about creating patterns. It is a matter of accepting a text as a mystery, a contextual pattern made up of motifs or clues, which have meaning precisely because of the role they play within the pattern.

Many scholars credit Poe's theory with an immense influence on the subsequent development of the short story. Certainly Poe's disciple Fitz-James O'Brien (c. 1828-1862) and many others would seem to have constructed their houses of fiction brick by brick according to Poe's blueprint; but how well does the blueprint describe antecedent fiction, such as Hawthorne's? According to Hawthorne and according to the best critics among his contemporaries, not very well. How well does the blueprint fit Poe's own fiction? Again, not very well. Poe does often have a climactic scene at the conclusion of his stories, but he most often and most successfully prepares for that conclusion not by developing a strong plot, a strong series of tightly integrated actions, but by intensely, powerfully, mercilessly overwhelming his readers with a dizzying atmosphere of sensually powerful imagery. As countless critics have commented, even in his most dramatic stories, in "The Fall of the House of Usher," in "Ligeia," and in "The Masque of the Red Death," Poe relies on a minimum of incident and on a maximum of imagery to prepare for his final effect.

Poe seems to have intuitively realized the fact and to have acknowledged its truth in the text of his most popular and perhaps his finest short story, "The Fall of the House of Usher." The story's epigraph keys the reader to the significance of an intensely sensitive awareness, and the story's first paragraph depicts a narrator powerfully affected not by any incident or arrangement of incident but by imagery—the aspect of the house he describes so powerfully. Poe as book reviewer focuses on effect created by consciously manipulated patterns of incident; Poe's narrative protagonist focuses on effects created by the subconscious powers of imagery: "There *are* combinations of very simple natural objects which have the power of thus affecting us, still the analysis of this power lies among considerations beyond our depth." The reader who falls under Poe's spell in the story can only agree. Poe does have some stories more dependent on incident—"The Black Cat," for example, and "The Pit and the Pendulum"—but strangely enough he has other works, which he called "tales," that have practically no incident whatever and that most readers would be much more inclined to consider sketches than true stories—"The Elk" is an example.

What conclusions should one draw? Poe's description of the intensively plotted story of effect described Hawthorne's best fiction and Poe's own best relatively poorly. Much more was going on than reasoned analysis could master. On the other hand, Poe might be said to have outlined his analysis as more an ideal to be sought (various desirable but unattainable ideals form the constant focus of his poems and stories) than as a reality already achieved. In this sense—that is, as a call to greater artistry in a genre too often considered a subcategory of journalism rather than as a nascent art form—Poe's theory seems to have been much more successful. Earlier writers treated structure, form, and technique with a rather cavalier disregard; N. P. Willis, for example, had a habit of writing a loose introductory descriptive sketch and following it with an only marginally related incident. Poe's insistence on applying the kind of unremitting attention to technique that conventional wisdom associated only with lyric poetry demanded for the short story a respect as literature that it had never before achieved.

Augustus Baldwin Longstreet

Irving created the modern short story by combining the inherent narrative interest of incident and plot (which already existed in the tale) with a tendency toward fully developed character, realism, specific detail and vivid imagery, and close psychological analysis (which characterized work in the essay-sketch tradition). Hawthorne brought to the form an intellectual commitment and a profound moral depth, which raised the short story above mere entertainment and endowed it with the high worth associated with the finest poems, novels, and plays. In his criticism, Poe demanded on one hand that readers acknowledge the new form's right to be considered as true literature and, on the other, insisted that writers must bring the sorts of technical, artistic resources that alone could justify such a claim. In his own fiction, Poe demonstrated the power and subtlety possible when a writer marshaled the vast array of resources at hand.

Had these pioneering giants left anything out? Evidently many of their contemporaries believed so, for, quite independently of the short-story tradition which these men conspired to create, a quite different mode of short fiction was inventing itself.

Irving, Poe, Hawthorne, and their associates considered themselves among the cultured elite. Each took many of his most fundamental literary values from the Eastern establishment, which borrowed its own from Europe, particularly from England. Meanwhile, below and beyond the Appalachian Mountains, in the barbarous regions of the "southwestern frontier," in Tennessee, Georgia, Alabama, Mississippi, Arkansas, and other relatively unsettled areas of what then constituted the United States, relatively primitive living conditions had reduced the cultural level of the pioneering settlers below that of the established section of the Eastern seaboard. Down there, literature consisted not of delicate sensibilities written in Latinate phrasings but in a vigorous telling of exaggerated oral tales. Scholars such as Constance Rourke and Bernard De Voto consider this oral tradition of outrageous storytelling to be the true original American art form and feel that it is as old as America.

Scholars usually identify as the first appearance of this mode in written literature Augustus Baldwin Longstreet's *Georgia Scenes, Characters, Incidents, Etc. in the First Half Century of the Republic* (1835), but three years earlier Longstreet had begun publishing these treatments of the barbarous Georgians native to the Augusta area. A year before that, in 1831, William T. Porter had begun publishing the *Spirit of the Times*, a national magazine that soon began publishing narrative letters and other contributions from its widely distributed readership. The popularity that Longstreet and Porter achieved inspired a number of later frontier humorists, among them George Washington Harris (1814-1869), Joseph Glover Baldwin (1815-1864), Johnson J. Hooper (1815-1862), and Harden Taliaferro (1818-1875). In the opinion of many, the two great individual masterpieces of the genre are "The Big Bear of Arkansas" by Thomas Bangs Thorpe (1815-1878) and "The Celebrated Jumping Frog of Calaveras County" by Mark Twain.

Longstreet and his peers tended to isolate the more literary and sophisticated elements of the essay-sketch tradition in a gentleman (or a dude) who dominated frame material bracketed at the beginning and at the end. Within this frame, as Walter Blair long ago explained, the reader finds a "mock-oral tale," a story designed as nearly as possible to capitalize on the virtues of the orally rendered stories any traveler could hear on the frontiers of the polite establishment.

One important element was humor, a feature with which Irving succeeded but with which Poe, Hawthorne, and most of their polite contemporaries seem to have failed miserably. These writers from the frontier based much of their humor on violence, physical grotesqueness, and cruelty, and much of their material is offensive to modern sensibility. Another element important to the genre was an almost exaggerated realism. Except for his two great stories, Irving's fiction tended to drift toward the same Romantic environments that so often seduced Hawthorne and Poe. The frontier humorists wrote of immediate life, full of spavined horses, ripped trousers, spilled liquor, and hostile husbands; they wrote of their farms, shops, quiltings, revivals, militia meetings—of all that was most vivid, vital, and real to them.

In many ways the most significant element of southwestern humor, and perhaps its greatest gift to Mark Twain and his finest gift to subsequent American literature was the sense of a genuine speaking voice. The writing style of the established writers to the Northeast was emphatically artificial and valued highly for that very quality. No one ever really spoke as Poe and Hawthorne wrote, and their artificiality was central to their art. The frontier humorists delighted in introducing gifted folk storytellers and, so far as possible, allowing them to exploit on the page the priceless virtues of a concrete, unaffected, vital, and vivid oral narrative. Nothing quite like it had ever been seen before. In its finest form, *Adventures of Huckleberry Finn*, it would never be bettered by anything in American literature.

England and the Modern Short Story

By 1840, then, in the modern short story, American literature could boast the triumphs of southwestern literature as well as masterpieces by Irving, Hawthorne, and Poe, even though as an independent country America could measure its existence only in decades. What was being produced in the great European literatures, especially in English literature? Curiously enough, the country with the greatest literary heritage on earth, although it could boast much excellent short fiction, had not yet produced creditable modern short stories. Many of England's finest writers experimented, often unsuccessfully, with shorter forms: Sir Walter Scott (1771-1832), who had helped give Irving's career a great boost, produced some fine ghost stories and an interesting tale, "The Two Drovers," which develops from an essay framework. Beginning in 1820, Charles Lamb (1775-1834) published his *Essays of Elia* (1823) in the *London Magazine*; these were a series of brilliant familiar essays with everything required of a short story—psychologically rich character, sharply imaged setting, at least a minimal narrative flow—everything but a focus on a unique, particular experience meaningful for its own sake (the only likely exception might be "Dream Children," published in 1822, which is sometimes anthologized as a short story).

"Dream Children," with its narrative movement and its management of time between present and past, is a precursor to a central nineteenth century short story convention, for it depends on a surprise ending in which what the reader took to be an actual event is ultimately revealed to be mere reverie. As in the eighteenth century essay form generally, no one really exists in "Dream Children" except the teller; characters and events merely serve his rhetorical purpose. The climax comes when the teller sees the dead mother in the face of one of the children and begins to doubt "which of them stood there before me." Irving's character Rip Van Winkle has the same ambiguous response when he awakes and sees his own son as himself. Variations of the motif occur throughout the century whenever there is some ambiguity within the narrative as to the psychological or phenomenological status of characters or events.

The best-known example of the literary transformation of the oral folktale in early nineteenth century British literature is Sir Walter Scott's insert tale in *Redgauntlet* (1824), often anthologized as "Wandering Willie's Tale." Told by the blind fiddler Willie Steenson, "Wandering Willie's Tale" manifests the typical ambiguity of the nineteenth century short story as to whether the events recounted are supernatural or psychologically realistic. "Wandering Willie's Tale" forms an interesting bridge between the traditional folk tale, in which supernatural confrontations were the stock-in-trade and the later British mystery story in which the seemingly supernatural encounter is justified in a grotesque but realistic way.

Both the supernatural and the natural are presented side by side in the tale to create a pattern of motifs that mocks the Lord of the manor, Sir Robert, even as it also mocks supernatural explanations for the mysterious disappearance of the rent money and Steenson's consequent visit to hell to obtain the receipt he needs to prove he paid the rent. Because of the ambiguous tone of the teller, "Wandering Willie's Tale" marks a transition from the supernatural tale of the folk variety to the modern short story in which the seemingly supernatural events have either realistic or psychological explanations.

Again and again, as T. O. Beachcroft points out, the best English writers seemed inclined to treat the kind of material most appropriate to a short story only as an episode in a novel or as a brief narrative poem. Countless examples of short stories *manqué* from the early nineteenth century might be drawn from Jane Austen's novels or from certain narrative poems of such poets as William Wordsworth or George Gordon, Lord Byron. William Makepeace Thackeray published a series of condensed novels, summary parodies of popular contemporary genres, and a handful of other short fictions, mostly old-fashioned series of incidents unified chiefly by the life of a central character.

England's great popular and artistic success in short fiction during this period was unquestionably *Sketches by Boz*, which Charles Dickens published in 1836; yet the fact that the greatest book of British short fiction from 1800 to 1840 hardly stands comparison with the least of that writer's novels gives one some sense of the way the British imagination scaled its proprieties. The *Sketches by Boz*, Dickens's first great success, owes much more to the essay-sketch tradition than to the tale. The young journalist who authored these sketches devoted his time, considerable energies, amazing powers of observation, and incomparable imagination to representing in brief prose pieces some of the multifarious scenes, characters, and activities he encountered in his endless jaunts through the London streets. In these pieces his sentimentality and melodrama are at (for him) a minimum, and his comic appreciation of color, contrast, and human oddity under no perceptible restraint. The book is absolutely delightful, but contains no real short stories. Some of these narratives have something of a plot, but in none does the author focus on creating a tightly focused, genuinely meaningful human experience of the sort expected from the modern short story. It is senseless to try to fault Dickens for failing to achieve something he never attempted, but many writers much inferior to Dickens in all but a sense of form have produced much finer short fiction.

Why is it that, working from essentially the same literary traditions, the Americans produced so many very fine modern short stories by 1840 when the English had produced none? There have been many half-baked theories to explain British predominance in the novel and American precedence in the short story during the period in question (and in fact it was well into the 1880's before a writer born and bred in England produced a respectable—not outstanding—volume of short stories, Thomas Hardy's *Wessex Tales* in 1888). Some suggest that the rushed pace of American economic life and its business morality equating time and money forced American writers to generate works that might be read in short snatches of time, the physically slower pace of British life promoting longer narratives. This is nonsense. For one thing, during the period in question the rush-quotient did not differ appreciably from one side of the ocean to the other. For another, a great many British magazines flourished because of serialized novels, each monthly segment approximating a short story in length. Thus the consideration of physical length or of reading time seems finally an irrelevant consideration.

Much more important, and more commonly accepted as a reason for the national tendencies toward novels or toward stories, were the contemporary copyright laws, or the lack of them. In essence writers' works were protected by copyright only in their own countries. As a result American publishers could reprint any British novels they chose without paying a penny in royalties. The relatively higher status of British writers, and the fact that their works were freely available, made American publishers reluctant to publish novels by Americans. Economic conditions thus forced, or at least strongly encouraged, American writers to focus on publishing short fiction in magazines and gift books (books usually of prose, poetry, and artwork which were published annually and intended largely as Christmas gifts), where payments to authors were minimal. Even the copyright theory should be taken with a grain of salt. For one thing, it does not explain the fact that the English, novelists of brilliance, failed to produce higher quality short fiction for their own magazines (which published discrete fictions as well as serialized novels). For another, it ignores the triumphs of James Fenimore Cooper and others who, long before the copyright laws were altered at the turn of the century, demonstrated that American novels could reward American publishers (and readers) quite handsomely. The contemporary copyright laws were a factor but should not be overrated.

Another factor, as Hawthorne, James, and other American writers have lamented, is that the novel as a form seems best adapted to a complex social environment, one in which manners, classes, and traditions carry enormous weight. The short story as a form has traditionally had a focus more psychological than sociological, more individual than social. Those cultures or those individual minds that pay relatively more imaginative attention to society than to the individual would seem naturally to have more affinity for the novel than for the short story.

Of more importance seems to have been a quite distinct factor, one which helps explain not only why the British turned to novels during the period and the Americans to stories but also why so many individual writers who have attempted both forms are able to achieve real success only in one or in the other. Although many individual exceptions exist, in general the novel as a form tends to emphasize evolutionary changes which take place over a long period of time; the short story as a form tends to focus on a sharp change which occurs in a brief period of time, sometimes no more than a moment. Americans as a people are notorious for a mentality which demands immediate results and which focuses on the short term; Britons as a people are famous for their historical sense which emphasizes the part each smaller unit plays in some much longer evolutionary change. (It was a

Briton who first proposed the biological theory of natural selection occurring over eons, an American who first measured the speed of light.) In some way the British mind seems predisposed to the kind of gestalt a novel represents; the Americans seem more predisposed to that of the short story. For whatever reason, the best short stories in English in the nineteenth century were not written by the English.

GERMANY AND THE MODERN SHORT STORY

Previous discussion has shown how the early nineteenth century American short story developed essentially from a synthesis of the best that two divergent traditions offered. The Americans' model for the essay-sketch tradition came primarily from England; for contemporary Americans and Englishmen, however, the dominant written model for the other strain, that of the tale tradition, consisted chiefly of the literary *Märchen* (folktales) and *Novellen* (longer and relatively more realistic stories) of then-fashionable German writers. As was earlier noted, for example, the Brothers Grimm, Jacob and Wilhelm, achieved vast and immediate popularity by publishing short narratives based on their researches into Germanic folklore. Irving based "Rip Van Winkle" on a tale in a similar collection by Otmar. Such stories are called "fairy tales" in English, although often they contain no fairies at all but witches, trolls, giants, or ogres. What they all do contain is emphasis on a striking incident or series of incidents that take precedence over character, setting, and all other elements. In addition, as true folktales, they share a common origin in folk traditions; each, in this sense, is (despite the inevitable variations incorporated by each individual narrator) a very old story.

In contrast to these traditional folktales there developed in Germany a tradition of *Novellen*. The term *Novellen* derives from the Italian term *novella*, which signifies "a small new thing." The sense of the word "new" in *Novellen* and *novella* (and in the French term *nouvelle*) might be taken to mean "unusual or surprising," but in fact it seems most probably to have developed to distinguish a basically or at least largely original story from an essentially traditional story. The *Novellen* do tend to have a relatively more complex and realistic social background, but otherwise any artificial distinction between *Märchen* and *Novellen* becomes quite problematic when there is in both genres of German tale a fondness for particular settings (often isolated and grotesque), a frequent use of type characters (young lovers, bellicose aristocrats, sinister intellectuals), a focus on dramatic incident (some define the *Novellen* in terms of a requisite surprising "turning-point" or *Wendepunkt*), and so on.

Historically, the German form itself, like its name, owes an imposing debt to the largely Latin tradition of short tales involving—to mention only a few of the very best among many other works—Giovanni Boccaccio's *Decameron: O, Prencipe Galetto*, 1349-1351 (*The Decameron*, 1620), Marguerite de Navarre's *Heptameron* (1558), and Miguel de Cervantes' *Novelas ejemplares* (1613; *The Exemplary Novels*, 1640). Apparently the first German author to use the term *Novelle* was Christopher Martin Wieland, a particular favorite of Poe, who in 1772 offered the following brief description:

> The term "Novelle" is applied especially to a kind of narrative [tale] that differs from long novels by the simplicity of [its] plot [plan] and the small bulk of [its] fable, or, the relationship between them [the *Novellen* and novels] is like that of a small play to a great tragedy or comedy.

A. G. Meissner, who published a German translation of Boccaccio's *The Decameron* in 1782, published a volume of original stories, *Novellen des Rittmeisters Schuster*, four years later. The first genuine artistic climax in the German form, however, came in 1795 with Johann Wolfgang von Goethe's *Unterhaltungen deutscher Ausgewanderten* (1795; *Conversations of German Emigrants*, 1854), a series of frame tales told within a contemporary setting, which reflects the troubled political situation of the times. The relatively more rational social and moral emphases in Goethe's *Conversations of German Emigrants* in the later history of the *Novelle* altered in the direction of irrationality and exploration of personal and more specifically imaginative concerns.

Among the more important and more widely influential early nineteenth century writers of the

Novelle were E. T. A. Hoffmann, Ludwig Tieck, Heinrich von Kleist, and Friedrich La Motte-Fouqué, and among the form's prominent critics (whose influences on Poe's theories are problematic) were Friedrich Schlegel and his brother August Wilhelm Schlegel. The Schlegels' intensive emphasis on the artistic importance of unity of effect seems to have captured Poe's critical imagination much as the German fiction writers' dramatic, surprising, emotional, mysterious, often fantastic, and at times quite grotesque stories popularized the mode Anglo-American writers called gothic, a mode which dominated much of the best short fiction in English until the 1850's, and some even beyond that. Yet various theorists of their time and of today would remind us that despite a heavy emphasis on fantasy, on the irrational, and on the supernatural, there was also a contrary impulse toward realism, one that entered the form in embryo when the *Novelle* initially divorced itself from the *Märchen* and that gradually grew throughout the nineteenth century until in the later decades, up to about 1890, the form's dominant mode was "poetic realism." This impulse to acknowledge the actualities of coherent environment and at the same time to emphasize irrationality and chaos, the antithetical impulses toward amoral narcissistic self-analysis on one hand and toward moral imperative on the other, the vacillation between the asocial individual and the socially dominated individual, and the loyalties divided between the comic and the tragic—these and other tendencies of the early nineteenth century *Novelle* have been variously exploited in myriad patterns into the twentieth century.

Russia and the Modern Short Story

The origins of the Russian short story, like those of Russian literature itself, most scholars trace to Alexander Pushkin. Before Pushkin, in prose as in verse, there were two predominant "literary" strains in Russia: on one hand, a vigorous tradition of oral folklore and, on the other, a written tradition dominated by foreign models, especially by the French. In fact, during Pushkin's time, French was the language affected by the elite; Pushkin's education was essentially French, his early reading emphasized French literature, and, startling though the fact may be, the father of Russian literature began his career as a writer in the French language.

As with the great American and European short-story writers, however, although his formal education emphasized polite written literature, Pushkin was informally introduced to a rich folkloric tradition of oral tales bursting with sharply defined characters, improbable incidents, and marvelous settings—the Russian *narodnye skazki* (folktales) and *volsebnye skazki* (fairy tales).

Pushkin began as a poet, and a long-verse narrative, *Ruslan i Lyudmila* (1820; *Ruslan and Liudmila*, 1936), was his first great success. He went on, however, to produce masterpieces in all the major genres—the play *Boris Godunov* (wr. 1824-1825, pb. 1831; English translation, 1918), the brilliant verse novel *Evgeny Onegin* (1825-1832, 1833; *Eugene Onegin*, 1881), and, most important for the purposes of this discussion, *Povesti Belkina* (1831; *Russian Romance*, 1875; better known as *The Tales of Belkin*, 1947), a framed group of five dramatic and romantic short stories—but his masterpiece of short fiction is *The Queen of Spades*. By Poe's standards the piece is long (about ten thousand words, it is divided into chapters) and rambling, with a need for tighter focus, but it may be considered the first great short story in Russian literature.

Normally considered the second great Russian writer, although actually much more of a contemporary, Nikolai Gogol brought to the form emphases that magnificently complemented those that dominated Pushkin's work. Pushkin was drawn relatively more to the Byronic mode of Romanticism, to European models, and to aristocratic characters and backgrounds. The much earthier Gogol began his career with a group of stories strongly based on Ukranian folklore, *Vechera na khutore bliz Dikanki* (1831, 1832; *Evenings on a Farm Near Dikanka*, 1926). Here the folk models and backgrounds are as important to Gogol as the aristocratic and European are to Pushkin. The following years saw Gogol's great innovative fantasies "Diary of a Madman," "The Nose," and finally the masterpiece on which he worked for a number of years, "The Overcoat." The latter work brilliantly combines three distinctive elements of Gogol's work—first, a humor quite alien to the short story as Pushkin imagined it; second, a marvelous strain of fantasy akin to but finally quite distinct from that of the folklore he so loved; and third, a marvelous sense of realism.

As is typical of the development of the short story in the early nineteenth century, Pushkin combined previous generic conventions with his own self-conscious experimentation with prose. Like many other early nineteenth century stories by Hawthorne, Poe, Hoffmann, and Gogol, all of whom have been given credit for originating the short-story genre, the problem with Pushkin's most famous story, *The Queen of Spades*, is that Pushkin combined so many different existing fictional conventions within it that readers have always been somewhat puzzled about how to read it.

Basically, the plot of the story is motivated by a secret; the attempt to discover the secret generates the plot, the story ending when the secret is discovered. In this case, the secret, the possession of which would eliminate chance, revolves around a game of cards. The engineer Hermann's fascination with the secret of the three cards introduces another typical romantic short-story element later explored so thoroughly by Poe—a character's powerful obsession that makes all reality contract around the object of the obsession itself. Self-consciously aware that he was experimenting with the conventions of narrative fiction, Pushkin has, in *The Queen of Spades*, created a story, which in parodying narrative conventions, is about the basic desire that underlies all fiction—the romantic desire to impose one's own will on the world of fact, contingency, and chance.

To Fyodor Dostoevski and Ivan Turgenev and various other Russian realists has been applied the quip, "We all came out from under Gogol's overcoat." Paradoxical as it may seem, the humorous tale of an insignificant clerk, who wreaks revenge as a ghost, did contain the seeds of precisely observed detail, of a specific social group's mores and behavior, and of a fidelity to life as the mass of his readers would recognize it that led directly to the fictions, short and long, of the giants of Russian literature, Ivan Turgenev, Dostoevski, Leo Tolstoy, and even beyond to Anton Chekhov and to various others, to the social criticism in Yevgeni Zamyatin's fantasies, Mikhail Zoshchenko's mild satires, and to much of the very best of modern Russian fiction.

France and the Modern Short Story

Anomalies and paradoxes abound in the short story. One is that the French, celebrated for their emphasis on logic and rationality (or alternately reviled for their penchant for contentious rationalization), have spent much less energy defining their basic critical terms for short fiction, *conte* and *nouvelle*, than people such as the Germans and the Americans have expended analyzing their own. Yet the French have among the world's richest traditions in short fiction generally and in the short story in particular.

Conte, apparently the older French term, seems quite close to the word "tale"—on one hand connoting emphasis on a dramatic (often supernatural or fantastic) central incident or incidents and on the other hand forming part of numerous compound terms: *conte de fées* (fairy tale), *conte moral* (moral tale), *conte oriental* (Oriental tale), and so on. *Nouvelle*, which in one sense means "news," would seem a literary term derived from the Italian term *novella* and the Spanish *novela* to indicate works such as the short fictions of Boccaccio and Cervantes, which tend to be more realistic than *contes*, more integrated with a social milieu, and which often have more narrative complications.

The French critic Ferdinand Brunetière distinguished between the forms by setting the *conte* and the *roman* (the novel) as two poles with the *nouvelle* in between. The *roman* he considered the most realistic, the *conte* the least realistic. The *nouvelle* he believed dealt with subjects that might be extraordinary, unusual, or quite rare but between the poles represented by the other two. Alfred Engstrom recognized the same polar arrangement but distinguished among the three primarily on the basis of length and of narrative complexity, with the *conte* limited to a single and tightly integrated focus, the *nouvelle* limited to a single line of development (which may involve several linked incidents, no one of which is the story's primary focus), and the *roman* with plural lines of development. The *nouvelle* Engstrom equates with the English term novelette, the *conte* he considers the true short story, and he exiles from the genre any work with unrationalized supernatural elements, that is, works that contain incidents that cannot be considered "realistic" in the common sense of the term.

One may assume, in fact should assume, that neither scheme is really definitive, for both *conte* and *nouvelle* are quite elastic and even overlapping terms. One may assert, however, that a quite new and distinct sort of *conte* or *nouvelle* developed in France in the early decades of the nineteenth century and that this new form may be identified with the modern short story. In many ways the finest candidate for the first true French short story is "Mateo Falcone," which Prosper Mérimée published in the *Revue de Paris* in May, 1829. In this brilliant, powerful story and in three others published later that year, "La Vision de Charles XI," "Tamango," and "L'Enlévement de la redoute," Mérimée showed the ability to compress his action and to focus on a single incident, to create through closely observed detail a sense of a real environment, and to develop characters who possess genuine psychological depth.

With "Mateo Falcone," Mérimée electrified a folk legend with the same kind of unified effect that Poe described in his famous *Twice-Told Tales* (1837, expanded 1842) review, thus originating the formal French short story by moving French short fiction away from the eighteenth century *conte philosophique* of Voltaire. The final scene when the boy says his prayers, begs for forgiveness, and makes a last desperate attempt to cling to his father's knees, is horrible because neither Falcone nor Mérimée give in to sentiment or comment. The irony is that the boy must die by the hands of the father for acting according to the bandit nature of the world in which his father lives. What makes the story so powerful is not simply the final horror but rather the stark simple world Mérimée creates—a world of crime, punishment, betrayal, cunning, pride—in which moral issues are simple and therefore terrifying.

The following year, 1830, saw the first short stories of France's great colossus of the nineteenth century novel, Honoré de Balzac: "El Verdugo," "Une Passion dans le désert," "Un Episode sous la terreur," and in the following years several more, many of the later ones figuring as integral elements of his vast complex of novels, *La Comédie humaine* (1829-1848; *The Comedy of Human Life*, 1885-1893, 1896). Balzac constantly favored the more dramatic, more romantic materials, compulsively highlighting violence and strong emotions and at the same time constantly exploiting the novelist's predilection for questions of social forces and of social identity.

Balzac's "La Grande Bretèche" ("The Grande Bretèche") is an important story which marks the transition from the plot conventions of short fiction used by Boccaccio and Cervantes to the psychological conventions characteristic of gothic obsession and romance. The story begins with the convention of the mysterious house and the secret of its past. Like the narrator in Poe's "The Fall of the House of Usher," the teller is mystified by the effect of the house and creates various stories to account for this "monumental embodiment of woe." Vowing he will find out the whole story, the protagonist is determined to get it from the maid Rosalie, even if he must seduce her for the secret.

The plot complications focus on various reversals in which the Count has the closet walled up, the Countess has a crack left, and the Count catches her chipping away at the mortar and stays with her for twenty days while her lover dies in the closet. "La Grande Breteche" is a prototypical story of the shift from the Boccaccio type of story of intrigue, infidelity, and jealousy to the nineteenth century gothic story in which jealousy becomes a projected obsession.

Théophile Gautier, the third important French writer to figure prominently in the short story's early history, published "La Cafetiére" in 1831 and a handful of others at irregular intervals in the following years. Of the three, Gautier is indubitably the most like Poe (although, in fact, Poe did not publish his first short story, "Metzengerstein," until 1832), favoring idealized type characters, fantastic incidents, and exotic settings; in fact, as in the work of Poe, Gautier's powerfully suggestive imagery often carries the burden of emphasis, meaning, and power in his short stories.

Other French writers produced significant short fiction before 1840—Charles Nodier, Gérard de Nerval, and others—but it was these three early masters who provided French literature with a new kind of short fiction, a story which tended to concentrate its interest tightly on a single, focused narrative event rather than dissipating its energies in a long train of incidents, a story that valued the psychological dimension of its characters quite as much as it valued their predilection for fantastic situations, and a story that replaced summary background with a sharply observed imagery designed to create a powerful and often suggestive environment in which the characters and incidents could credibly exist.

The grounds had been laid for one of the world's greatest short-story traditions, although the form's greatest writers, among them none greater than Guy de Maupassant, were yet to arrive on the scene.

Walter Evans, updated by Charles E. May

BIBLIOGRAPHY

Aderman, Ralph M., ed. *Critical Essays on Washington Irving*. Boston: G. K. Hall, 1990. A collection of essays on Irving's art and literary debts, the relationship of his stories to his culture, and his generic heritage.

Bunge, Nancy. *Nathaniel Hawthorne: A Study of the Short Fiction*. New York: Twayne, 1993. Discusses Hawthorne's major short stories in three categories: isolation and community, artists and scientists, and perspective, humility, and joy.

Canby, Henry S. *The Short Story in English*. New York: Holt, Rinehart, and Winston, 1909. Canby argues that the romantic movement gave birth to the modern short story and that Poe is its first important figure. The rest of the nineteenth century applied Poe's theory of single effect to new subjects.

Curnutt, Kirk. *Wise Economies: Brevity and Storytelling in American Short Stories*. Moscow: University of Idaho Press, 1997. A historical analysis of the short story's structuring of the tension between brevity and storytelling. Shows how stylistic brevity as an evolving aesthetic practice redefined the interpretive demands placed on readers.

Levy, Andrews. *The Culture and Commerce of the American Short Story*. Cambridge, England: Cambridge University Press, 1993. A historical survey showing how the short story became an image of American values through political movements, editorial policies, and changes in education. Devotes chapters to Poe's efforts to create a magazine that would accommodate his particular kind of story.

May, Charles E. *Edgar Allan Poe: A Study of the Short Fiction*. Boston: Twayne, 1991. An introduction to Poe's short stories that attempts to place them with the nineteenth century short narrative tradition and within the context of Poe's aesthetic theory. Suggests Poe's contributions to the short story in terms of his development of detective fiction, fantasy, satire, and self-reflexivity.

Pain, Barry. *The Short Story*. London: Martin Secker, 1916. Pain claims that the primary difference between the short story and the novel in the nineteenth century is that the short story, because of its dependence on suggestive devices, demands more of the reader's participation.

Perry, Bliss. *A Study of Prose Fiction*. Rev. ed. Boston: Houghton Mifflin, 1920. Perry argues that the short story differs from the novel by presenting unique and original characters, by focusing on fragments of reality, and by making use of the poetic devices of impressionism and symbolism.

Terras, Victor. "Pushkin's Prose Fiction in an Historical Context." In *Pushkin Today*, edited by David M. Bethea. Bloomington: Indiana University Press, 1993. Discusses Pushkin's importance in the ascendancy of prose fiction in Russia in the nineteenth century. Comments on the basic characteristics of Pushkin's prose style.

THE LATE NINETEENTH CENTURY: 1840-1880

Beginning in the mid-twentieth century, American literary critics have become increasingly concerned with what Aristotle termed the art of literature in general as well as its various species. As a result of René Wellek and Austin Warren's *Theory of Literature* in 1949, the revival of the Aristotelian tradition encouraged by R. S. Crane's *Critics and Criticism: Ancient and Modern* in 1952, and Northrop Frye's *Anatomy of Criticism: Four Essays* in 1957, as well as the American discovery of early Russian formalism and modern European structuralism, books on poetics and literary theory roll off commercial and university presses in growing numbers. Particularly energetic have been efforts to establish a poetics for that species of literature which seems most resistant to theory—that is, prose fiction or narrative. Studies on the nature of narrative, the rhetoric of fiction, the theory of fiction, and the poetics of prose dominate the field both in number and importance.

On making even the most casual survey of these studies, however, one soon discovers an assumption so pervasive that it is seldom announced, much less questioned. When critics use the terms "prose fiction" and "narrative," they mean that relative latecomer to the hallowed realms of art and academic concern—the novel. They seldom mention, except as an afterthought, the form of prose fiction that has developed with sophistication and vigor alongside the novel—at least since the beginnings of the nineteenth century—the short story. This attitude toward the short story, an attitude which hardly makes the form worth mentioning in the rarefied atmosphere of current criticism about "serious" literature, is not new in Anglo-American literary studies; it is, in fact, as old as criticism of the short story itself. In 1884, when Brander Matthews published the first discussion of the short-story genre since Edgar Allan Poe's famous 1842 review of Nathaniel Hawthorne's *Twice-Told Tales* (1837), he noted the "strange neglect" of the short story in histories of prose fiction.

The reasons for this neglect, which has persisted up to the present, are too complex to recount here. One of the most basic reasons, however, is the general devaluation of genre theory in Anglo-American criticism until recently; a truly critical history of a literary form is simply not possible without a generic theory of that form. Fifty years separate Frederick Lewis Pattee's *The Development of the American Short Story* (1923) and Arthur Voss's *The American Short Story: A Critical Survey* (1973), but their similarities sum up histories of the American short story. Both are surveys, filled with names, titles, dates, and sketchy considerations of influence, but neither is critical or theoretical and neither is informed by a generic theory of the form. R. S. Crane, in his *Critical and Historical Principles of Literary History* (1971), insists that the inductive development of distinctions of species is an essential task before one can write a narrative history. Wellek and Warren suggest that one of the most obvious values of genre study is that it calls attention to the internal development of literature; Wellek even goes so far as to say that the "history of genres is indubitably one of the most promising areas for the study of literary history."

The Story as Genre

Most comments about the short story focus on the form's midway position between the novel and the lyric poem. Edgar Allan Poe himself placed the short story next to the lyric as offering the opportunity for the highest practice of literary art. Most critics since have not really disagreed and have, in fact, compared the short story to the lyric in various ways. Except for the fact that the short story shares with the novel the medium of prose, there is a fundamental difference between the two forms: Although the short story is committed to prose fictional representations of events, it makes use of the plural signification of poetry—using metaphoric, overdetermined language because of the basically subjective nature of the form or its *multum in parvo* necessity to use the most suggestive but economical means possible.

The Russian formalist critic B. M. Ejxenbaum says that the novel and the short story are not only different in kind but also "inherently at odds." The novel is either developed from collections of stories or complicated by the incorporation of "manners-and-morals" material. The short story, on the other hand, is a "fundamental, elementary (which does not mean primitive) form." The difference between the two, says Ejxenbaum, is one of essence, "a difference in principle conditioned by the fundamental distinction between big and small forms." According to Ejxenbaum, the important implication arising from difference in size has to do with the difference between the endings of short stories and novels. Because the novel is structured on the linking of disparate materials and the paralleling of intrigues, the ending usually involves a "point of let-up." The short story, however, constructed on the basis of a contradiction or incongruity, "amasses its whole weight toward the ending." This built-in necessity of the form has been the source of much of the popular appeal of the short story and also the cause of the resultant scorn by the critics. Not all short stories depend on the kind of snap ending that O. Henry mastered, yet shortness of the form does seem inevitably to necessitate some sense of intensity of structure that is lacking in the novel.

Another suggestion about the implications of the shortness of the form has been made by Georg Lukács in his pre-Marxist *Die Théorie des Romans: Ein geschichtsphilosophischer Versuch über die Formen der grossen Epik* (1920; *The Theory of the Novel: A Historico-Philosophical Essay on the Forms of Great Epic Literature*, 1971). Although Lukács has since repudiated this early attempt to formulate a general dialectic of literary genres, his comments on the short story here offer some fruitful bases for further consideration. Perceiving that the short story is a fictional form which deals with a "fragment of life," lifted out of life's totality, Lukács says that the form is thus stamped with its origin in the author's "will and knowledge." The short story is inevitably lyrical because of the author's "form-giving, structuring, delimiting act." Its lyricism lies in pure selection. Yet, regardless of this lyricism, the short story must deal with event; and the kind of event it focuses on, says Lukács, is one that "pin-points the strangeness and ambiguity of life," the event that suggests the arbitrary nature of experience, whose workings are always without cause or reason. The result of the form's focus on "absurdity in all its undisguised and unadorned nakedness" is that the lyricism is concealed behind the "hard outlines of the event" and thus the view of absurdity is given the "consecration of form: meaninglessness *as* meaninglessness becomes form; it becomes eternal because it is affirmed, transcended and redeemed by form." Consequently, says Lukács, the short story is the most purely artistic literary genre.

When Lukács says that the short story is the most purely artistic form, he means that it is the least conceptual form—that it deals with experiences which refuse to be reduced to a concept or to be integrated into a larger conceptual system. Such experiences can only be selected. This is what Frank O'Connor means in *The Lonely Voice* (1963) when he says that whereas the novel makes use of the essential form of the development of character or incident as seen in life, for the short-story writer there is no such thing as essential form. "Because his frame of reference can never be the totality of a human life, he must forever be selecting the point at which he can approach it, and each selection he makes contains the possibility of a new form as well as the possibility of a complete fiasco." Thus the basic difference between the two forms is the difference between pure and applied storytelling, and the pure storytelling that is found in the short story is more artistic than the applied storytelling that is found in the novel. Lukács says that the short story expresses the "very sense and content of the creative process." The result is that the short story is a highly self-conscious, even a self-reflexive, form that often tends to be about the nature of story itself.

The fact that the short story pinpoints the strangeness of life is due precisely to the fact that the short story focuses on fragments that not only are detached from the conceptual framework of what is called the totality of life but also reveal the absurdity of that conceptual framework, even, as Albert Camus would put it, the absurdity of hoping for a meaningful conceptual framework. Because the individual experience thus detached is always meaningless, it can have nothing but form; the only possible integration for it is the integration within itself. To focus on the fragment of experience is to necessarily sense absurdity or meaninglessness, or else its polar extreme, meaningfulness that transcends the "normal," the conceptual, the everyday. It is a clear indication of the modern temperament that a contemporary short-story writer such as Donald Barthelme can say, "Fragments are the only forms I trust."

The revelation in the short story is, as Robert Langbaum describes the revelation of nineteenth century poetry in his *The Poetry of Experience* (1957), not a formulated idea that dispels mystery but a perception that advances in intensity to a deeper and wider, a more inclusive mystery. When Mark Schorer said that the short story is an art of "moral revelation" and the novel an art of "moral evolution," he was assuming the nonconceptual character of the experience depicted in short stories and the conceptual nature of experience in the novel. Evolution is a linear process manifested as cause and effect—the essence of the conceptual experience. Revelation is, by its very nature and definition, without cause. Something shows forth that was hidden before. Evolution implies a teleology, an evolving toward some end; revelation has no such end.

The short story's method, however, is to present a glimpse through external meaninglessness to essential and immanent meaning. At least since James Joyce, it has been recognized that the short story's way of meaning is by means of the epiphany. Moreover, the "whatness" of the object that Joyce describes in aesthetic terms is equivalent to the "thouness" Martin Buber describes in moral terms. As Langbaum suggests, the epiphany is a way of knowing or apprehending value when value is no longer objective. This simply means that the epiphany mode is a radical return to the primitive mythic mode when there was no such thing as objective value, when all value by its very nature was subjective. The modern return to this mode begins in the early nineteenth century when external values are discredited and the short fictional form and the short lyric form become the most appropriate genres for the new milieu. The short story has always been an antisocial form, either in its adherence to mythic relationships or in its adherence to secularized psychological replacements of the lost mythic relationship. The short story as a modern artistic form seeks to replace the lost mythic perception with intense subjectivity and a revival of archetypes.

Short stories thus present synchronic invariants of human action, not the diachronic variants of social interaction. Since the short story does deal with such universals regardless of social surroundings, there was a need to hear stories long before there was a need to read the mimetic depictions of everyday reality. It is the liminal nature of human existence, even the religious nature of human existence as Philip Wheelwright and William James have described it, that gives rise to the short story. The English short-story writer Christina Stead says: "The belief that life is a dream and we the dreamers only dreams, which comes to us at strange, romantic, and tragic moments, what is it but a desire for the great legend, the powerful story rooted in all things which will explain life to us and, understanding which, the meaning of things can be threaded through all that happens." Human beings need to hear stories for the same reason they need to experience religion, says Canadian writer Hugh Hood. "Story is very close to liturgy, which is why one's children like to have the story repeated exactly as they heard it the night before. The scribe ought not to deviate from the prescribed form. That is because the myths at the core of story are always going on."

This notion of the story as liturgy is also suggested by Indries Shah in his discussion of the Sufi teaching story. Such stories do not teach by concept but rather by some more intuitive method of communication, by rhythm, or, as the structuralists would say, by a deep structure that lies beneath the conscious level of concept. Readers must go back to an early stage to prepare themselves for story, says Shah, a stage in which readers regard story as the "consistent and productive parallel or allegory of certain states of mind. Its symbols are the characters in the story. The way in which they move conveys to the mind the way in which the human mind can work."

The fact that the short story does not deal with social reality means that it tends to thrive best in societies where there is a diversity or fragmentation of values and people. This diversity has often been cited as one reason why the short story became quickly popular in the nineteenth century in America. In 1924, Katherine Fullerton Gerould said that American short-story writers have dealt with peculiar atmospheres and special moods, for America has no centralized society. "The short story does not need a complex and traditional background so badly as the novel does." Ruth Suckow also suggested in 1927 that the chaos and unevenness of American life made the short story a natural expression. The life in America was so multitudinous that "its meaning could be caught only in fragments, perceived only by will-of-the-wisp gleams, preserved only in tiny pieces of perfection." The more firmly organized a country is, says Seán O'Faoláin, "the less room there is for the short story—for the intimate close-up, the odd slant, or the unique comment." Frank O'Connor also notes that in those countries in which society does not seem adequate or sufficient for the repository of acceptable values one finds the short story to be the most pertinent form. "The novel," says O'Connor, "can still adhere to the classical concept of civilized society, of man as an animal who lives in a community . . . ; but the short story remains by its very nature remote from the community—romantic, individualistic, and intransigent."

These considerations lead O'Connor to formulate his famous theory that the short story always presents a sense of

> outlawed figures wandering about the fringes of society. . . . As a result there is in the short story at its most characteristic something we do not often find in the novel—an intense awareness of human loneliness. Indeed, it might be truer to say that while we often read the novel again for companionship, we approach the short story in a very different mood. It is more akin to the mood of Pascal's saying: *Le silence éternel de ces espaces infinis m'effraie.*

The antisocial nature of the short story is one of its most predominant features. To understand this aspect of the short story, one might use, *mutatis mutandis*, a description T. S. Eliot once made of Henry James's fiction:

> The general scheme of James's fiction is not one character, nor a group of characters in a plot or merely in a crowd. The focus is a situation, a relation, an atmosphere to which the characters pay tribute. The real hero in any of James's stories is a social entity of which the men and women are constituents.

The focus of short fiction is also an atmosphere or situation to which the characters pay tribute and of which they are constituents. Because the short-story situation, however, is like that of dream or myth, indeed, because the short story is always more atmosphere than event, its meaning is difficult to apprehend. As Joseph Conrad's Marlow understands when he attempts to tell the story of Mr. Kurtz and the journey into the heart of darkness, the meaning of an episode is not within like a kernel, "but outside, enveloping the tale which brought it out only as a glow brings out a haze." Marlow impatiently asks, "Do you see the story? Do you see anything? It seems to me I am trying to tell you a dream—making a vain attempt. No relation of a dream can convey that notion of being captured by the incredible which is the very essence of dreams."

The atmosphere that plays about the short story is not the social atmosphere or social entity of James's fiction, or by extension, of the novel generally; rather, it is an antisocial entity. If it is religious or numinous, one must remember that Herbert Otto in his study of the holy has pointed out that the numinous can have a violent and frightening Dionysian aspect as well as a Christlike one. Regardless of which aspect it takes, the short story, like the mythic aura of Christ and Dionysus, represents both the human and the divine; for both Christ and Dionysus are gods of showing-forth, of revelation, of epiphany. Both demand of their followers strange and paradoxical requirements: that they lose themselves to find themselves, that they plunge into the irrational, the incredible, into all that is against social law and human order in the everyday world.

THE SHORT STORY BEFORE POE

There is no such phenomenon as a totally new genre. Genres that appear to be new, such as the

American short story in the 1840's, are the results of reactions against and integration of preexisting literary forms. The short story drew primarily from five such forms: the folktale, the medieval romance, the eighteenth century essay or sketch, the eighteenth century novel, and the romantic lyric. From the folktale, the short story takes its focus on a single event, usually an event that cannot be explained in terms of everyday reality. From the eighteenth century essay or sketch, it takes its focus from a personalized point of view—a definite teller whose attitude toward the story is as important as the story itself. Washington Irving's famous tales are perfect examples of this combination of folktale and point of view. Although Irving borrowed his plots from German folklore, he borrowed his teller's tone from Joseph Addison and Richard Steele. Irving himself drew attention to his concern with tone and point of view in a letter:

> For my part, I consider a story merely as a frame on which to stretch my materials. It is the play of thought, and sentiment, and language; the weaving in of characters, lightly, yet expressively delineated; the familiar and faithful exhibition of scenes in common life; and the half-concealed vein of humor that is often playing through the whole—these are among what I am at, and upon which I felicitate myself in proportion as I think I succeed.

From the medieval romance and the eighteenth century novel, the short story gets its focus on a symbolic or projective fiction, but one in which real people are involved. This experiment in fiction began in the late eighteenth century with Horace Walpole's *The Castle of Otranto* (1765). Walpole said that *The Castle of Otranto* was an attempt to "blend the two kinds of romance, the ancient and the modern." That is, he wished to retain the imagination and improbability of the medieval romance but make use of the convention of verisimilitude of character found in the novel. As Walpole says in his preface,

> Desirous of leaving the powers of fancy at liberty to expatiate through the boundless realms of invention, and thence of creating more interesting situations, he wished to conduct the mortal agents in his drama according to the rules of probability; in short, to make them think, speak, and act as it might be supposed mere men and women would do in extraordinary positions.

The result in the gothic story is essentially a projective fiction embodying emotional states, yet a fiction in which characters with their own thoughts, fears, and anxieties—in short, psychologies—are enmeshed. The effect, to use Mary Shelley's *raison d'être* of another famous gothic fiction, *Frankenstein* (1818), is a fiction that, however impossible as a physical fact, "affords a point of view to the imagination for the delineating of human passions more comprehensive and commanding than any which the ordinary relations of existing events can yield."

This is a basic Romantic view that also infused the epoch-making *Lyrical Ballads* (1798) and which underlies an important distinction between the Romantic lyric and the eighteenth century poetry that went before it. The basic Romantic fascination with medievalism and folk material springs from a realization of the basic religious or spiritual source of both the old romance and the folk ballad. The Romantics' fascination with the old ballads and tales was part of their effort to recapture the primal religious experience, to demythologize it of the dogma that had reified the religious experience and to remythologize it by internalization and projection. In order to preserve the old religious values without the old mythological trappings, they secularized the religious encounter by perceiving it as a basic psychic process, by taking it back from the priests who had solidified it and experiencing it in stark uniqueness and singleness. This is indeed the focus in the preface to the *Lyrical Ballads* and in Samuel Taylor Coleridge's discussion of his and William Wordsworth's dual tasks in *Biographia Literaria* (1817). The uniting of the old ballad material with the lyric voice of a single individual perceiver in a concrete situation gave rise to the Romantic lyric. Robert Langbaum has discussed this creation of a subjective point of view in a concrete dramatic situation in his *The Poetry of Experience*. The positioning of a real speaker in a concrete situation encountering a particular phenomenon which his own subjectivity transforms from the profane into the sacred is the key to the Romantic breakthrough.

The ballad story previous to Wordsworth and Coleridge existed detached from a teller, a projective fiction independent of teller and tone. In the nineteenth century it became infused with the subjectivity of the poet and projected on the world as the basis for a new mythos. The thrust was dual. As Coleridge says, his own task was to focus on the supernatural, "yet so as to transfer from our inward nature a human interest and a semblance of truth sufficient to produce for these shadows of imagination that willing suspension of disbelief for the moment, which constitutes poetic faith." Wordsworth was to choose subjects from ordinary life and "excite a feeling analogous to the supernatural by awakening the mind's attention from the lethargy of custom and directing it to the loveliness and the wonders of the world before us." Clear examples of this dual project are Coleridge's lyrical story *The Rime of the Ancient Mariner* (1798) and Wordsworth's lyrical story "Resolution and Independence." The poems are representative of two primary modes of fiction—what Carl Jung calls the "visionary" and the "psychological," respectively. In Northrop Frye's terminology, they correspond to the basic difference between the romance mode and the novel mode, and therefore the basic difference between the tale and the short story. In the first, the characters are psychic archetypes; in the second they are primarily social personae.

The moral values in these poems are those of sympathy, identification, and love—the primary values of romantic axiology, most explicitly delineated in Percy Bysshe Shelley's *A Defence of Poetry* (1840). They later become the primary values of Nathaniel Hawthorne's stories in America. In the *Lyrical Ballads*, the ballad or "story" element, the hard outlines of the event, are subsumed by the lyrical element, which is foregrounded. For Hawthorne and Poe, however, in America it is the story element that is foregrounded. The lyrical element exists as the personal voice of the teller, a teller who responds personally to the event but whose tone is somewhat delyricized by the influence of the "talk-of-the-town" tone of the eighteenth century essay and sketch.

Both Fred Lewis Pattee and Edward J. O'Brien in their 1923 histories of the American short story place the birth of the form with Washington Irving's combination of the style of Addison and Steele with the subject matter of German Romanticism. Pattee says about Irving's *The Sketch Book of Geoffrey Crayon, Gent.* (1819-1820): "It is at this point where in him the Addisonian Arctic current was cut across by the Gulf Stream of romanticism that there was born the American short story, a new genre, something distinctly our own in the world of letters." O'Brien, focusing more on the classical Arctic than the Gulf Stream Romanticism, says that the short story began when Irving detached the story from the essay, especially the personal essay of the "talk-of-the-town." It is obvious that Irving's Diedrich Knickerbocker is more like the eighteenth century Roger de Coverley than he is the anonymous folk storyteller of the ancient ballad.

H. S. Canby has also noted Addison's influence on Irving, which resulted in a classical restraint and a gentle humor in his stories, but it is with Hawthorne's and Poe's mutations and development of the romantic impulse that the short story more properly begins. Poe's contribution, says Canby, was to do for the short story what Coleridge and John Keats were doing for poetry: to excite the emotions and to apply an impressionistic technique to his materials to hold his stories together. Hawthorne, however, uses a moral situation as the nucleus to hold his stories together. Hawthorne was, in fact, the first American story writer to build a story on a situation, an "active relationship between characters and circumstances." Pattee agrees that Hawthorne was the first to touch "the new romanticism with morals" and that both Hawthorne and Poe differ from E. T. A. Hoffmann's and Ludwig Tieck's "lawless creative genius" and "wild abandon" by exercising deliberate control and art. Pattee also suggests that Poe's important contribution was his realization that the tale is akin to the ballad form, but that like the lyric, it was dependent on an emotional, rather than a conceptual unity. For Poe, says Pattee, the story was a "lyrical unit, a single stroke of impressionism, the record of a moment of tension." Alfred C. Ward, in his 1924 study of the modern American and English short story, is quite right in noting that what links Hawthorne's stories to those of writers of the twentieth century is that they both "meet in the region of half-lights, where there is commerce between this world and 'the other-world.'" The difference between short-story writers before Hawthorne and those after him, however, is that while this region of half-lights for the pre-Romantic existed in the external world of myth and the religious externals of allegory, for writers after the Romantic shift the realm exists within what James has termed Hawthorne's "deeper psychology." Many critics since Ward have agreed with him that the brief prose form "affords a more suitable medium than the novel for excursions into the dim territory of the subconscious." In the first "theory" of the short story after Poe, Brander Matthews makes a brief suggestion that the short story has always been popular in America because the Americans take more thought of things unseen than the English. Matthews was also the first to notice, although he does not develop the point, that although Poe depicts things realistically or objectively, a shadow of mystery always broods over them. The subtle movement from Hoffmann's and Tieck's fairy-tale-like unrealities and supernatural events to Poe's psychological stories which push psychic responses to such extremes that they *seem* supernatural marks the beginnings of the short story.

Bliss Perry, in an unusual departure from usual histories of prose fiction at the turn of the century, devotes a chapter to the short story in his 1902 study entitled *A Study of Prose Fiction*. He notes that because of the shortness of the form, if the story is concerned with character, the character must be "unique, original enough to catch the eye at once." The result of this necessity for choosing the exceptional rather than the normal character is that the short story is thrown upon the side of Romanticism rather than realism. Perry also notes another point about the short story that has remained constant since its inception:

> Sanity, balance, naturalness; the novel stands or falls, in the long run, by these tests. But your short-story writer may be fit for a madhouse and yet compose tales that shall be immortal. . . . The novelist has his theory of the general scheme of things which enfolds us all, and he cannot write his novel without betraying his theory. . . . But the short-story writer, with all respects to him, need be nothing of the sort.

Both Alberto Moravia and Richard Kostelanetz have noted this characteristic of the short story in opposition to the novel.

This insistence on the basic romantic nature of the short story, both in its focus on unusual events and on the subjectivity of the form, was strongly voiced in the late nineteenth century when Ambrose Bierce entered the argument then raging between William Dean Howells and Henry James over the romance versus the novel form. In his attack on the Howells school of fiction, Bierce says, "To them nothing is probable outside the narrow domain of the commonplace man's commonplace experience." The true artist, says Bierce, is one who sees that life is "crowded with figures of heroic stature, with spirits of dream, with demons of the pit. . . . The truest eye is that which discerns the shadow and the portent, the dead hands reaching, the light that is the heart of darkness." Even James says that he rejoices in the anecdote that he defines as something that "oddly happened" to someone. More recently, Flannery O'Connor has placed the short story within the modern romance tradition, a form in which the writer makes alive "some experience which we are not accustomed to observe everyday, or which ordinary man may never experience in his ordinary life."

The only extended critical discussion of this romantic element in the short story is Mary Rohrberger's *Hawthorne and the Modern Short Story: A Study in Genre* (1966). Comparing Hawthorne's comments in his prefaces with comments by modern short-story writers, Rohrberger notes that both share the romantic notion that reality lies beyond the extensional, everyday world with which the novel has always been traditionally concerned. "The short story derives from the romantic tradition," says Rohrberger.

> The metaphysical view that there is more to the world than that which can be apprehended through the senses provides the rationale for the short story which is a vehicle for the author's probing for the nature of the real. As in the metaphysical view, reality lies beyond the or-

dinary world of appearances, so in the short story, meaning lies beneath the surface of the narrative.

Poe, Hawthorne, and Gogol: The Beginnings of the Short Story

Poe's romantic allegiance to poetry and his debt to Wordsworth and especially Coleridge for his theories about the nature of poetry and the imagination is made clear in his many reviews and critical essays. For Poe, the highest genius can be best employed in the creation of the short rhymed poem; it is poetry that elicits the poetic sentiment—"the sense of the beautiful, of the sublime, and of the mystical." If one wishes to write in prose, however, Poe says, "the fairest field for the exercise of the loftiest talent" is the tale; for the tale is the closest one can get to poetry when writing mere prose. The basic difference between poetry and the tale form for Poe is that while the tale is concerned with truth, the poem is concerned with beauty and pleasure; and truth, Poe makes quite clear in his discussion of Hawthorne's *Twice-Told Tales*, means the presentation of a theme by means of the author's ability to use a "vast variety of modes or inflections of thought and expression." Furthermore, what Poe admires in Hawthorne in addition to the central attribute of the short story—"Every word *tells* and there is not a word that does *not* tell"—is that Hawthorne not only displays a novelty of theme but also a novelty of tone as well.

The most troublesome element of Poe's theory of the short story, however, lies in his remarks on the tale's "single effect," for these comments led in the early twentieth century to a misplaced concern with the tricks a writer may use to construct a story for effect rather than with how a story complexly affects the reader. A further consequence of misreading Poe has been that many critics have taken the phrase "single effect" to mean "simple effect." Part of the problem is the critical bias against the very "shortness" of prose narrative that Poe most insisted on. The usual assumption is that narrative by its very nature is concerned with movement and therefore character development and change. Since change is a complex phenomenon influenced by a multitude of forces, it follows that the novel can more plausibly present change than the short story. As Thomas Gullason has pointed out (*Studies in Short Fiction*, 1973), Mark Schorer's famous distinction between the short story as the "art of moral revelation" and the novel as the "art of moral revolution" does seem to contribute to various stereotypes that have deadened the response of readers to short fiction. The distinction is damaging to the short story, however, only if one accepts the prevailing bias that the nature of narrative is to present change plausibly and that the novel is thus the narrative norm. Unfortunately, Gullason does accept this, asserting that "it is mainly in terms of 'moral evolution' or growth that a fiction becomes organic—lifelike, plausible, multidimensional, and long-lived. Moral revelation alone usually leaves a fiction artificial, unrealistic, one-dimensional, and short-lived." In short, Gullason attempts to defend the short story by suggesting that it is really more like the novel than previous stereotypes have led one to believe—that it is realistic and has an "everyday quality" applicable to general reality. The best way to redeem the short story from previous critical neglect is not to ignore its unique characteristics but rather to focus on how the very shortness of the story compels it to deal with a different mode of reality and knowledge from that of the novel and therefore how it has a different effect on the reader. One way to achieve this and better understand what Poe meant by "single effect" is to make use of approaches developed by philosophy and anthropology to the nature of myth. The most helpful are those of Ernst Cassirer. What is being suggested is that the short story, although separate stories may indeed structure myths as different constitutive units, is primarily a literary mode that embodies and recapitulates mythic perception itself.

Once one hypothesizes this as a central characteristic of the short story, one can better defend Poe's insistence on the unique or single effect of the form; one can better combat the bias against it which, confusing novel with story and history with myth, insists that the short story have a plausible, everyday quality; and one can better justify the comments already made that the short story is centered around emotion, intuition, and fleeting perceptions that consequently give it its mysterious, dreamlike quality. In short, one can begin to see that the bias for the novel as narrative norm and the consequent neglect of the short story is the same bias that Cassirer describes as modern man's preference for theoretical thinking over mythical thinking.

Not only is mythic perception impregnated with emotional qualities and surrounded by a specific atmosphere, but also it is characterized by a focus on the immediate present. Cassirer says, thought is "captivated and enthralled by the intuition which suddenly confronts it. It comes to rest in the immediate experience, the sensible present is so great that everything else dwindles before it." From this point of view, Poe's stress on the "immense force" of the short story "derivable from *totality*" and the great importance of "unity of impression" to make possible the "deepest effects" becomes more significant. The short story, more than other modes of narrative, requires complete absorption. Moreover, it is the only form of narrative with which the reader can be completely absorbed for the *totality* of the narrative experience. As Poe says, "During the hour of perusal the soul of the reader is at the writer's control. There are no external or extrinsic influences—resulting from weariness or interruption." Similarly, Cassirer says, when one is under the spell of mythic thinking, "it is as though the whole world were simply annihilated; the immediate content so fills his consciousness that nothing else can exist beside and apart from it." Cassirer says the characteristic of such an experience is not expansion but an impulse toward concentration; "instead of extensive distribution, intensive compression. This focusing of all forces on a single point is the prerequisite for all mythical thinking and mythical formulation."

The short-story form manifests this impulse toward compression and demands this intense focusing for the totality of the narrative experience primarily because it takes for its essential subject the mysterious and dreamlike manifestations of what Cassirer calls the "momentary deity." The production of these deities, the first phase of the development of theological concepts, does not involve investing them with mythic and religious images. Rather, Cassirer says:

> It is something purely instantaneous, a fleeting, emerging and vanishing mental content. . . . Just let spontaneous feeling invest the object before him, or his own personal condition, or some display of power that surprises him, with an air of holiness, and the momentary god has been experienced and created. In stark uniqueness and singleness it confronts us . . . as something that exists only here and now, in one indivisible moment of experience, and for only one subject whom it overwhelms and holds in thrall.

Many, perhaps most, short stories present characters thus overwhelmed and enthralled by something within or without them which they invest with mythic rather than logical significance. Roderick Usher's obsession with the horror of the house that he can neither name nor understand, Goodman Brown's compulsion toward the witches' Sabbath, Bartleby's absorption with the wall that makes him prefer to do nothing—none of these experiences can be accounted for logically; neither can they be presented in terms of everyday reality. In fact, they are characterized by their removal from everyday reality. Thus, the short story is the form best able to embody this mythic experience. As Cassirer says:

> It is as though the isolated occurrence of an impression, its separation from the totality of ordinary, commonplace experience produced not only a tremendous intensification, but also the highest degree of condensation, and as though by virtue of this condensation the objective form of the god were created so that it veritably burst forth from the experience.

Hawthorne's critical comments about art are less developed than Poe's and confine themselves primarily to prefaces in which he discusses the nature of the romance form. Hawthorne, however, no less than Poe, is concerned with the mythic and the mysterious. Hawthorne's comments about the romance can be applied equally to the short tale, for as Northrop Frye has pointed out, the romance bears the same relation to the tale form as the novel does to the more developed short story. In the former, the characters are archetypes that serve the function of the mythic plot; in the latter, the characters are wearing their social masks. The romance and the tale are visionary forms, while the novel and the short story tend more toward psychologizing and verisimilitude. Hawthorne, although he may have expressed a longing to master the techniques of realism, found such techniques impossible to reconcile with his own vision of the superiority of moral truth over physical truth. In fact, Hawthorne's technique is to spiritualize the material and thus, in true romantic fashion, discover true or "sacred" reality always immanent in the "profane" physical world. As he notes in his preface to *The House of the Seven Gables* (1851), Hawthorne finds that the romance, while governed by its own laws, is not bound by the laws of fact and is therefore freer than the novel. Hawthorne's stories, like Poe's, follow the laws of their own conventions rather than the laws of external reality. Thus, to use Northrop Frye's term, they are less "displaced" than the novel; they do not try to conceal their conventions under the cover of verisimilitude.

Another central element of fiction for Hawthorne, one that accompanies Poe's emphasis on tone, is the importance of atmosphere. In the preface to *The Blithedale Romance* (1852), Hawthorne laments the loss of the "old world" conventional privileges of the romance. Among American writers there is no "Faery Land" which has its own rules that govern it so that it can be placed equally alongside nature, no realm of reality that is so much like the real world in its truth and laws that in its "atmosphere of strange enchantment," the "inhabitants have a propriety of their own." Without such an atmosphere, Hawthorne says, the characters of the imagination "must show themselves in the same category as actually living mortals." It is precisely this atmosphere of fantasy in which real people dwell, however, that begins to make itself felt as central to the genius of the short story. It is that "neutral territory somewhere between the real world and fairy-land, where the Actual and the Imaginary may meet and each imbue itself with the nature of the other."

One final element in Hawthorne's fiction which further contributes to the development of the short story as a genre is a thematic view also shared by Poe—the importance of sympathy. For Hawthorne, as it was for Shelley in *A Defence of Poetry*, sympathy was the great secret of morals. Shelley says, "A man, to be greatly good, must imagine intensely and comprehensively; he must put himself in the place of another and of many others; the pains and pleasures of his species must become his own." It is obvious that in Hawthorne's fiction, isolation and alienation exist for those who, like Ethan Brand and Giovanni, lack "the key of holy sympathy." Poe's fiction, because it seems less obviously concerned with moral themes than that of Hawthorne, appears to lack the element of sympathy; this is not, however, the case. Poe's first-person narratives, such as "The Tell-Tale Heart," "The Black Cat," and others, demand of the reader a sympathy and participation in much the same way that Robert Langbaum says is required for the narrators of Robert Browning's monologues. Moreover, the nature of sympathy becomes a metaphysical principle for Poe in *Eureka: A Prose Poem* (1848), in which he points to a universal brotherhood of atoms themselves. It is a cosmology which for Poe has a moral implication: "No one soul is inferior to another."

Lest one might think these combinations of elements—the fantastic and dreamlike with the real, a focus on sympathy, an emphasis on unity, and a concern with the story following its own laws—are an isolated American occurrence, it is best to now turn to a development in Russian literature in 1842—the same year as Poe's famous review—the publication of Nikolai Gogol's "The Overcoat." Frank O'Connor, in his study of the short story, has suggested that Ivan Turgenev's famous remark, "We all came out from under Gogol's 'Overcoat,'" not only is applicable to Russian writers but is a general truth as well. O'Connor points to this story as marking the origin of the short-story form. For O'Connor, "The Overcoat" is like nothing in the world of literature before it.

> It uses the old rhetorical device of the mock-heroic, but it uses it to create a new form that is neither satiric nor heroic, but something that perhaps finally transcends both. So far as I know, it is the first appearance in fiction of the Little Man, which may define what I mean by the short story better than any other terms I may later use about it.

O'Connor goes even further and suggests that if one wanted an accurate key description of what is central to the short story, one could do no better than quote Akaky Akakyevitch's plaintive tacit cry to those who harass him: "I am your brother." The phrase indicates both the isolation of Akaky and his need for sympathy. In Akaky, O'Connor finds a central type of figure in the short story because always in the short story, O'Connor says, there is a "sense of outlawed figures wandering about the fringes of society. . . . As a result there is . . . an intense awareness of human loneliness."

This cry for human sympathy, this sense of isolation and loneliness, however, is not the only thing that characterizes "The Overcoat" and makes it stand out as a unique new fictional creation. The passage from which O'Connor quotes is referred to in Russian criticism as the "humane passage." Indeed, the classical Russian view of the story in the nineteenth century is it is one of the first Russian works about the "little man" oppressed by the crushing regime of the czars, that the story is a realistic one with social significance; its only blot is the introduction of the fantastic at the end. In the 1920's, however, in what has now become a significant contribution to the Russian formalist movement, the critic Ejxenbaum discovered the technical and formal genius of Gogol's story. Ejxenbaum says that "The Overcoat" is a masterpiece of grotesque stylization in which Gogol takes the basic narrative technique known in Russian criticism as *skaz* (the oral narrative of a lowbrow speaker) and juxtaposes it against the sentimental rhetoric of the tone to make the reader uneasy about whether to sympathize with Akaky or laugh at him. The "humane passage" exists not simply to make the reader feel the oppression of the "little man" but rather to create a contrapuntal tension between comic *skaz* and sentimental rhetoric. "This pattern," says Ejxembaum, "in which the purely anecdotal narrative is interwoven with a melodramatic and solemn declaration, determines indeed the entire composition of 'The Overcoat' as a grotesque." The effect of the story is a "playing with reality"—a breaking up of the ordinary so that the unusual logical and psychological connections of reality become, in this constructed world of the story, unreal.

This is precisely the kind of play with reality, although admittedly with a different tone, in which Hawthorne was engaged; it is also similar to the tone of combined mock seriousness and sarcasm in which Poe delighted. Ejxenbaum says that the structure of a short story always depends in large part on the kind of "role which the author's personal tone plays in it."

Hawthorne's stories are obviously very close to their folklore and gothic origins. The genius of Hawthorne that sets him apart from the anonymity of folklore and the plot focus of the gothic, however, is not only his own personal tone but also his awareness that the conventions of folklore and the gothic are really the embodiments of unconscious, even mythic, reality. Moreover, although many of his stories seem allegorical, they are less allegorical in the traditional sense than they are early attempts to perform in prose fiction the function that romantic poetry had served: to find the spiritual and moral meaning beneath the external physical and social reality of human life and events. The result, says Hyatt H. Waggoner, is that there is no name for Hawthorne's type of story—not quite allegorical, not quite symbolic but somewhere in between. In fact, Hawthorne's type of story is the result of a merging of the representative fiction of allegory and the mimetic fiction of the novel. Thus, the stories seem to be both determined by the characters within them and at the same time determined by the story of which the characters are only functions. This focus tends to make the short story more aware of its own artifice and illusion than the novel, therefore more aware of its own process of ordering. The result is often a dreamlike story that is aware of itself as dream.

The problem of the dream nature of "Young Goodman Brown" is related to its modal situation halfway between realism and romance. If one asks whether the story is a dream told as if it were reality, or whether it is a reality told as if it were a dream, one realizes that that determination cannot be made. The story begins with a concern with the oneiric as Faith tells Brown that she has been troubled by dreams; he wonders if a dream has warned her of his journey on this one night of the year. At the end of the story, Hawthorne teases the reader with the question: "Had

Goodman Brown fallen asleep in the forest and only dreamed a wild dream of a witch meeting?" The problem of the story is: If it is a dream, when did the dream begin and who is dreaming it? There is certainly no point in the story at which Brown falls asleep, as is typical of the traditional dream-vision story. Moreover, if the forest meeting is a dream, then the whole story must be dream, for Brown knows where he is going from the beginning; and indeed from the point of view of the story as a projective fiction, both Faith and Brown are merely functions of a dreamlike folklore allegory—that is, Hawthorne's "dream."

Because Brown seems to have his own consciousness and seems at times to be uncertain about what lies before him in the forest, the story has its mimetic aspect as well. The crucial moment in the forest when Brown calls out to Faith to resist the evil one is clearly a breakthrough moment when he manifests his own will and becomes a psychological character rather than a parabolic function. This uncertainty as to the nature of reality in the story is intrinsically related to the moral-thematic impact of the story. "Young Goodman Brown" is not a simple initiation story of a youth becoming aware of evil, but rather a mimetic-symbolic story of the movement from *faith* that reality is simply its surface appearance to *knowledge* that reality is complex and hidden; it is a movement from an unquestioned sense of community to a realization that community must be constantly developed. In this sense it is a romantic story of the fall in perception from a unified sense of reality to the awareness of separation and the realization of the necessity of healing that separation. Instead of making the effort of sympathy and love to unite himself with others, however, Brown turns from them forever; having lost the absolute, he cannot live with ambiguity.

Another Hawthorne story that seems part parable and part mimetic representation is "The Minister's Black Veil." Although the minister has his own psychology and thus much of the story depicts his personal suffering, Hawthorne transforms the veil (rather the minister himself makes this transformation) into a symbolic object and the story into a parable—not a parable in the usual sense of a simple story to illustrate a moral but rather a parable in the basic root sense of the word; that is, a story that probes basic mystery. The minister does not hide his face to conceal some secret personal sin (as he might in a realistic story) but rather to objectify his metaphysical awareness that the meaning of sin is separation. The thematic thrust of the story is similar to that in "Young Goodman Brown"; the minister, made aware of basic human separation, now tries to perform his ministerial function by teaching others that same awareness through the emblem of the veil. The moral implication of this awareness, as it often is for Hawthorne, is that life must be lived with the realization of separation so that the individual will see the need to have sympathy for the other—the need to project the self into the other, penetrate behind the social veil that everyone wears. The story is also similar to Herman Melville's "Bartleby the Scrivener" in that the minister's black veil is like Bartleby's wall: an emblem of all that stands in the way of human communication. What makes Hawthorne's story more than a simple allegory is not only the complex meaning of the veil but also the fact that the minister is consciously aware of the meaning of the veil. His "madness" in the mimetic world of the story, which makes him treat a simple object as if it were its metaphysical meaning, is a function of his symbolic role in the parabolic world of the story.

The loss of the absolute and the entrance into ambiguity is also depicted in "My Kinsman, Major Molineux," a story which combines actuality (this time a historical transition that takes place in America) with myth and dreamlike reality. Young Robin, the rustic youth on his first visit to town just after his eighteenth birthday, has all the characteristics of the conventional folktale initiate setting out to seek his fortune in the world. His evening of ambiguity as he searches for his kinsman from whom he seeks preferment is a symbolic journey in which he encounters figures of human ambiguity: sexuality in the form of the young girl with the scarlet petticoat, death in the elder man with his "sepulchral hems" which evoke the "thought of the cold grave," authority in the night watchman who warns Robin he will be in the stocks by daylight, and ultimate duality in the Janus-faced man who suggests both a fiend of fire and a fiend of darkness.

Each time Robin is rebuffed in his quest for his kinsman, he tries to rationalize an explanation; finally reason is rebuffed so often that he begins to doubt not only reason but also the state of his present reality. He recalls his father and home and asks: "Am I here or there," and his mind vibrates between fancy and reality. When a stranger comes by, he cries, "I've been searching half the night, for one Major Molineux; now, sir, is there really such a person in these parts, or am I dreaming?" Indeed, at this point in the story the reader may well feel that Robin's encounters have been so grotesque and mysterious that the story *is* the embodiment of a dream or a myth. Also at this point, however, the mystery is explained by reality itself as Robin sees the crowd coming down the street with the tarred-and-feathered kinsman; the historical framework—of the colonists rejecting governors appointed by the king—supplies the realistic motivation to account for all the seemingly mythical events of the night. Hawthorne, however, never completely "naturalizes" his fictions; the realistic explanation does not dislodge the mythic aura of the events. Furthermore, the stranger with Robin at the end is not realistically explained; he is solely a function of the parabolic story—a mythic elder companion to Robin's new awareness, a denizen of the fable element of the story.

The same kind of fantasy-and-reality integration constitutes the nature of Hawthorne's most difficult story, "Rappaccini's Daughter," probably Hawthorne's most complex treatment of reality, fantasy, fairy tale, myth, legend, and symbol. In the preface to the story (which Hawthorne attributes to M. de l'Aubépine), Hawthorne recognizes his own ambiguous situation between the transcendentalists, who are concerned with the spiritual and the metaphysical, and the great body of writers who address the "intellect and sympathies of the multitude," that is, the realists. Aubépine, says Hawthorne, "generally contents himself with a very slight embroidery of outward manners—the faintest possible counterfeit of real life—and endeavors to create an interest by some less obvious peculiarity of the subject."

Giovanni, like Goodman Brown and Robin, is primarily an inhabitant of the real world (that is, the mimetic aspect of the fiction) who is confronted with a dreamlike or fablelike fantasy. This encounter is complicated by the fact that the story is a maze of inversions of usual expectations of good and evil, spirit and body, innocence and experience. Beatrice, like Dante's guide, is a spiritual figure of allegory; but she is also, like Mary Shelley's Frankenstein monster, a creation of nineteenth century science. When Giovanni first sees Rappaccini in the garden walking through the flowers as if they are malignant influences, his imagination connects the garden with the mythic story of the Garden of Eden. "Was this garden, then, the Eden of the present world?" Giovanni thus both creates and walks innocently into the stuff of myth itself; however, it is the Eden story turned upside down. Rappaccini is both god figure who created the garden and serpent figure who sets up the downfall of Giovanni, who is indeed the new Adam. Beatrice is Eve, brought up without contact with the fallen world. Giovanni is fallen man who must be seduced back into paradise again. The result of the story is that Giovanni, like Goodman Brown, cannot live with the mysterious mixture of spirit and body that Beatrice seems to represent: "Am I awake?" he cries. "Have I my senses? What is this being? Beautiful shall I call her, or inexpressibly terrible?"

Thus, instead of a story of the fall from grace into reality, this is instead a story of how fallen Adam tempts Eve into reality, even as she tries to tempt him into the fall back into grace again through faith and love. Giovanni's efforts to bring Beatrice into the "limits of ordinary experience" is evidence of his lack of acceptance and love; it means the death of the denizen of the romance world of fiction and thus the end of the story. "Rappaccini's Daughter" is about the conflict between reality and fantasy, materiality and spirit, empiricism and faith; and thus it is about the very conflict between characters like Giovanni, with psychological verisimilitude, and characters like Beatrice, who exist for the sake of the story as parable. The conflict is an inevitable one for the short story, taking as it does elements both from the old parable and romance form and from the conventions of the realistic eighteenth century novel. The classic example of a Poe story which involves this same kind of interaction is "The Fall of the House of Usher," in which the realistic narrator confronts Roderick, who by his very obsession has been turned into a purely symbolic figure. Melville exploits the mixture of the two fictional conventions even further in "Bartleby the Scrivener" as the short story moves more within the realistic tradition of the late nineteenth century.

The European mind has always been more hospitable to Poe than has been the American mind. Charles Baudelaire led the French in a discovery of Poe while Poe was still being scorned as a hack and a misfit in America. Recently, the French structuralists have resurrected Poe from many years of critical condescension by considering his stories from a point of view of both new theories in psychoanalysis and new theories of narrative. American empiricism has simply been unconcerned with the basically phenomenological point of view of Poe's works. One of the most basic criticisms of Poe's stories, and an influential one because it is by W. H. Auden, is that Poe's stories have one overriding negative characteristic: "There is no place in any of them for the human individual as he actually exists in space and time." Poe's characters, says Auden, are "unitary states" who cannot exist except operatically. Yvor Winters's famous criticism of Poe as a classic case of obscurantism is based on a similar assumption—that Poe is not concerned with human experience, only emotion, and that he exhibits a "willful dislocation of feeling from understanding." In fact, says Winters, "Poe is interested in the creation of an emotion for its own sake, not in the understanding of experience." These views of Poe are common in American and English criticism. They result from a common genre error when a critic approaches a short story and scorns it because it does not follow the mimetic conventions of the novel. One can certainly admit that many of Poe's characters are unitary states without at the same time admitting that Poe is unconcerned with human understanding. As has already been shown, the short story from its beginnings is more closely aligned to projectionist fiction and a lyrical point of view than to the realistic fiction and rational point of view of the novel.

The best place to begin a consideration of the nature of Poe's stories is with a relatively unassuming story depicted in a basically realistic technique: the simple revenge story of "The Cask of Amontillado." The key to understanding the story is to perceive it as a monologue with a listener within the story. The narrator at the beginning addresses a definite "you" who he says "well know the nature of my soul." At the end of the story the reader discovers that the present telling-time of the story takes place fifty years after the told event. The final line of the story—"*In pace requiescat*"—thus refers both to Fortunato, whose bones have never been discovered, and to Montresor, who is making the present confession, the reader assumes, to a priest. The entire story is a complex tissue of irony; just as Montresor has made sure that none of his servants will be home by ordering them not to leave, so does he lure Fortunato into the catacombs by urging him to go home. Moreover, the irony takes on a structure of mocking and grotesque echo-action. As Fortunato begs Montresor to release him and screams in despair, Montresor echoes his words and screams. The central irony of the mock action in the story, however, turns on a reversal of Montresor's dual requirements for the perfect revenge and an ironic inversion of the symbolic meaning of Montresor's family coat of arms. Montresor says: "A wrong is unredressed when retribution overtakes its redresser. It is equally unredressed when the avenger fails to make himself known as such to him who has done the wrong." When the reader realizes, however, that the mocking screams of Montresor border on hysteria, when the reader realizes that he is not making confession of his crime, when the reader notes that his heart grew sick after walling up Fortunato, and when the reader remembers that Montresor does not let Fortunato know that his murderous act is indeed an act of revenge—then it becomes clear that Fortunato has more closely fulfilled the revenge criteria than has Montresor. The coat of arms—a human foot which crushes a serpent whose fangs remain embedded in the heel—is equally ironic. If the Montresor family is represented by the foot that crushes the serpent Fortunato, then the reader notes that the serpent still clings to the heel. The family motto—No one harms me with impunity—thus applies to Fortunato as well as it does to Montresor. Every element in the story contributes to this single but certainly not simple, ironic effect. Tone is the key to the story's meaning. There is, however, one more ironic turn of the screw in the story; although Montresor is now confessing, and thus, presumably, is repentant for his crime, the very fact that the reader enjoys the clever ironic ways he tricked Fortunato indicates that by his very tone of telling, Montresor is enjoying it again also and is thus not repentant. Even though he is on his deathbed, he relives with glee the experience; and although he confesses, his tone damns him completely.

Although Poe disliked allegory, calling it the lowest form of art, his "The Pit and the Pendulum" and "The Masque of the Red Death" are both forms of allegory; however, they are more complex than the traditional conceptual allegorical fiction because of their dreamlike nature and because their elements symbolize complex metaphysical and psychological reality. "The Pit and the Pendulum" is very close to a self-contained dream story, but, like Franz Kafka's stories, it has enough of verisimilitude to give it the feeling of reality experienced as if it were nightmare. The entire story is a dream and Poe is the dreamer; it is pure projective fiction from the beginning, when the narrator says "I was sick—sick unto death" until the end when the loud blast of the trumpet marks his rescue from the dream by awakening him. The story is marked by many considerations of dream phenomena in the beginning, as if the dreamer could consciously consider the curious epistemological and ontological status of dream itself. "Arousing from the most profound slumber," he says, "we break the gossamer web of *some* dream. Yet in a second afterward (so frail may that web have been) we remember not that we have dreamed." Moreover, the story is marked by a struggle to control the actions of the dream instead of being controlled by them; throughout the story the narrator undergoes a constant struggle to escape the machinations of the dream mechanism that controls him, but each time a danger is thwarted, a new danger is thrown in his way, for there is no way to escape the dangers that threaten one in a dream except to awaken from the dream itself. The events that threaten the narrator—the pit, the pendulum, the walls that close in on him, the rats—are thus all of his own making; yet they are outside his control at the same time, for they are products of his own unconscious. The dilemma of the narrator is an objectification of the dilemma of all characters in this kind of self-conscious fiction—the dilemma of making one's story and being trapped by the story at the same time. The thematic content of the dream, however, is universal rather than personal; for it is a dream of being trapped by time (the pendulum), being prey to the nausea of body itself (the rats), and being threatened by the unknown and unnameable (the pit). As Harry Levin says of this story, it is an existential allegory that transcends the conceptual nature of allegory and becomes oneiric symbolism.

"The Masque of the Red Death" is allegorical fiction also, but again it is more complex than allegory is usually assumed to be, both because it is tempered by Poe's characteristic irony and because it is infused with his concern to symbolize the nature of art itself. Prince Prospero is, like William Shakespeare's master magician in *The Tempest* (pr. 1611), a representation of the desire not simply to escape from death but to escape from life into a replacement world of fantasy and art. The story is an objectification of the attempt to escape from dynamic life (which inevitably results in death) into the static life of the art work (which means eternity). The first key to this understanding of the story lies in the title. The avatar of the pestilence death in the story is red, the color of blood, and blood is the symbol of life; however, it is Poe's view that life itself is the curse because it leads inevitably to death. Thus, Prospero shuts himself up within the castle and surrounds himself with clowns, improvisatori, dancers, musicians, actors; in short, figures who mimic life rather than participate in it. What Prospero in effect does is to enclose himself within the hermetically sealed art work itself, which says, as all romantic art works do: "The external world can take care of itself." The masked figure dabbled with blood is Poe's image of death masquerading as life, for it suggests that the sign of blood is always a masque for the death that lies beneath life or is inherent within it. When the revelers try to seize the figure, they find that it has no tangible form; for death that is inherent in life is a nothingness that can be neither grasped nor escaped.

Poe deals with the problem of trying to escape death in another story that is not so much allegory as it is surrealistic and symbolic psychological fiction. "The Tell-Tale Heart" presents a narrator who is mysteriously obsessed with the eye of the old man with whom he lives. The key to this unexplained obsession lies in the double meaning of the title of the story and in the pun Poe plays on the word "eye" itself. Although the title seems to refer to the end of the story, when the narrator thinks that the old man's beating heart has "told on him," that is, exposed his crime to the police, more generally the title refers to the only tale the heart can tell: the tale of time, as each heartbeat echoes the tick of the clock bringing one closer and closer to death. This is the tale that the narrator wishes to escape, and his obsessive concern to slow down and stop time altogether in his spying on the old man indicates this. The narrator's obsession with the eye is related to his identification with the old man. As he spies on him, the narrator delights that the old man is "listening just as I have done." He comments on the old man's groan of fear, "I knew the sound well." He then chuckles, "I knew what he felt and pitied him." The madness of the narrator is a metaphysical madness, for he hates the eye because it has come to mean "I" to him. The irony of the story is that the narrator wishes to escape death by destroying the "I"; that is, his own ego. He wishes to escape the tale the heart tells by destroying the self he has projected on the old man. The narrator's attempts to destroy the "I" by destroying the "eye" are ironically fulfilled at the end when he hears the beating of his own heart and thinks it is the old man's. The story consistently mixes up external and psychological reality to reveal a metaphysical meaning. Its refusal to separate the inner reality from the outer one is a typical device of Poe, and it is an influential one that characterizes the short story as a genre.

Poe's "The Fall of the House of Usher" presents a character configuration and a plot development that is typical of the short story from its beginnings up to the present day. It is the story of an actual or mimetic character, the narrator, who encounters a character who has been transformed into a parabolic figure by his own obsession with metaphysical mysteries. The story begins with the narrator's entrance into a world of ambiguity and myth; it is an entrance into the realm of story itself. It looks backward to Rip Van Winkle's entrance into the world of legend even as it looks forward to the encounter the narrator has with the ambiguous Bartleby in Melville's famous story. That the narrator enters the world of the art work itself is emphasized by his unsuccessful attempts to account for the feeling of gloom the house creates in him. He notes that while "there *are* combinations of very simple natural objects which have the power of thus affecting us, still the analysis of this power lies among considerations beyond our depth." What he is considering here is the romantic notion of the mystery of the imaginatively constructed art work—that it is not the elements but their combination that constitutes the mysterious unexplainable effect the art work has on the reader.

Usher himself is best known as one who is fascinated by art, especially the intricacies of music—that art form which Poe thinks to be the highest, because the most mysterious, source of the poetic sentiment. The effect of "The Fall of the House of Usher," however, is that of the poetic sentiment carried to its disastrous logical extreme—the poetic sentiment that has distanced itself so completely from material reality that it no longer has contact with the actual. Roderick Usher lives completely within the house of art, so detached from physicality that his senses cannot tolerate anything but the most insipid food, can stand only certain kinds of clothing, cannot bear odors, can bear only the faintest light. His music is wild and abstract; his paintings are not of things but ideas. When the narrator tries to determine what Usher fears, Usher can only suggest that it is fear itself. Indeed, Usher is afraid of nothing, but it is a nothing similar to that experienced by the old waiter in Ernest Hemingway's "A Clean, Well-Lighted Place"—a felt nothing that he knows too well. It is the *nada* that waits for the artist who so pursues his quest of pure art that he cuts himself off from any external reality and thus can only feed on his own subjectivity. Roderick's twin sister Madeline functions to embody (as the old man's eye does in "The Tell-Tale Heart") a projection of Roderick's gradual withdrawal. His attempt to bury his own obsession returns to destroy him. Roderick's dilemma of being caught between the world of the art work and the real world—in which the art work gradually displaces the real world—is objectified in the scene in which the narrator reads to Usher from a gothic romance; the actions of the fiction are echoed by the actions of Madeline as she breaks out of her entombment. At the end of the story when Madeline enters the room and collapses onto Roderick, she symbolically collapses back into him. Then in a compressed symbolic climax, Roderick collapses back into the house and the house collapses back into the nothingness that is the story. The ultimate end of the artist who cuts himself off from actuality to live in the realm of the art work is the nothingness that results from devouring the self.

This is the Poe in whom Baudelaire saw the genius, and this is the Poe who contributes so much to the genius of the short story as a form—a form that combines mimesis and romance, myth and actuality, and that is supremely conscious of its own processes of doing so. The narrator of "The Fall of the House of Usher" is left with the memory of the encounter and thus with an obsessive tale to tell. The end of the events of the story is the beginning of the endless telling of it. As Randall Jarrell says about stories, "we take pleasure . . . in repeating over and over, until we can bear it, all that we found unbearable."

Before moving on to Melville's *The Piazza Tales* (1856), which mark a transition, especially in "Bartleby the Scrivener," toward a more realistic emphasis in the short story, the romantic stories of the 1840's and 1850's in France and England, as well as the beginnings of poetic realism in Russia, will be briefly examined.

Romantic Short Fiction in Europe and England

Albert George, in his book *Short Fiction in France: 1800-1850* (1964), notes that the history of short fiction has been mostly ignored in France because of its oral origins and plebeian associations. In the 1820's and 1830's, however, the short story began to be popular in France in the magazines even though the Romantics continued the long tradition of the short tale in the folktale and the oral anecdote. Almost all critics agree that the formal short story, as Poe defines it, came into being in France in 1829 with the publication of Prosper Mérimée's "Mateo Falcone." Honoré de Balzac's "Passion in the Desert" and "La Grande Bretèche" appeared in 1830 and 1832, respectively. Yet regardless of this introduction of a new formal control in short fiction, the short story, or *conte*, during the romantic period of the 1840's and 1850's in France is a combination of romantic fantasy, the supernatural, and a whimsical or satirical tone.

Typical of romantic whimsy and the supernatural is Théophile Gautier's "The Mummy's Foot," published in 1840. It is a story which derives from the earlier gothic fiction of Hoffmann but is presented in a new lightness of tone by a first-person narrator whom the reader cannot take seriously. The narrator buys the foot of an Egyptian princess in a bric-a-brac shop and then later dreams of returning the foot and traveling with the princess to a mummy afterlife; he awakes to find the foot gone. The plot is, as the narrator says of the foot itself, "charming, bizarre, and romantic," but it is ultimately silly; however, the plot is the least of the story. Tone, in fact, is everything here, as the romantic, dilettantish narrator confronts in mock seriousness the absurdity of a one-footed princess and later is introduced to "the mummies of her acquaintance." What the story represents in the development of short fiction is a movement toward the sophistication of the supernatural and a satire of the dream-vision convention itself; it both develops the romantic dream vision and ironically undercuts that vision at the same time; it signals a trivializing of a convention and a self-parody which is the first step toward the establishing of a new convention, in this case the convention of realistic verisimilitude.

Gérard de Nerval's story "Pandora," although presented in more brittle satiric tones, is similarly a sign of the naturalizing of romanticism. Published in 1854, it integrates mythical and dream reality into the sophisticated social setting of the realistic convention of Balzac. If Gautier's inspiration is Hoffmann, Nerval's is Johann Wolfgang von Goethe; and his story, embodying the tension between the sensuous and the supernatural, has a more significant metaphysical thematic base than does Gautier's. The central character, in his adoration of Pandora, elevates her to a symbolic status even as he transforms himself into the tormented Prometheus. The dream of hallucinatory vision embodied here is more believable than in "The Mummy's Foot," because it is inextricably intertwined in the story rather than set apart from it. In this way, Nerval anticipates the style of Kafka by confusing reality and dream so purposefully that dream takes on an ontological status equal to that of phenomenal reality. Moreover, the narrator in "Pandora," a writer self-consciously aware of his own work, notes in the story that "Pandora" is a continuation of an earlier work and also inserts a confidential letter into the narrative addressed to Gautier himself in which the narrator and the writer of the letter are the same man. This self-reflexive technique confuses the point of view quite purposely to entangle elements of fiction and reality within the fiction itself. Again, when a work of fiction becomes self-consciously aware of itself as fiction and thus parodies the very conventions upon which it depends, the reader knows he or she is on the brink of a shift to another generic convention.

It has often been noted that Mérimée's later stories do not match in impact and artistic control his earlier ones such as "Mateo Falcone." One of his best-known stories, however, published in the 1840's, "The Abbé Aubain," marks a complete break from the romantic supernaturalism and self-parody of Gautier and Nerval and establishes the short story as a realistic and radically ironic form. On one hand, the story is reminiscent of the early Italian novellas of Giovanni Boccaccio in its satire on human vanity; on the other hand, because of its ironic reversal at the end, it points toward the kind of trick story that Guy de Maupassant made so popular in the latter part of the century in France. The story is told almost entirely in the form of letters from a wealthy, sophisticated society woman (who has moved to the country) to a friend in the city. As is typical of such a radically first-person form (which is actually transcribed monologue), much of the pleasure of the story lies in the reader's opportunity to mock the lady for her superficiality, which she reveals unawares. Her condescension toward the parish priest throughout the story allows the reader to laugh at her foolishness at the end. For although she fancies that the priest is in love with her (an infatuation that she finds amusing and which she uses to entertain herself), the reader discovers in the last letter (which the priest writes to his old professor) that he has instead been using her to gain preferment and thus escape the country to a higher position in the Church. The concealment of this information, which is the only thing that makes this a story at all, is possible by the use of the letter convention. At the end of the piece, the reader is left with two unappealing characters who have not only underestimated each other but also remain self-deceived. The story contributes nothing to the short story except to move it toward the kind of ironic plot reversal that Maupassant perfected in "The Necklace."

The fact that the short story did not fare well in England in the nineteenth century seems partial support for Frank O'Connor's thesis that the short story deals with the individual detached from society. Lionel Stevenson has drawn attention to the Victorian assumption that any serious work of literature should offer a well-integrated view of society—an assumption that made English authors ignore the short-story form as trivial. Not until the 1880's, when the "fragmentation of sensibility" set in England, did the short story begin to be seen as the most appropriate form for representing such a sensibility. As has already been noted, the romantic impulse in England found its form primarily in poetry, especially the romantic lyric moving toward the dramatic monologue. The short story is a fictional parallel to such forms because they, like the short story, depend on a particular point of view, usually of a single event. In certain ways, Coleridge's "The Rime of the Ancient Mariner" is a model short story, as is Browning's "Andrea del Sarto" and "Fra Lippo Lippi." The fictional embodiment of romanticism in nineteenth century England was only an undercurrent to the development of the Victorian novel, taking its direction from the gothic fiction of Horace Walpole, Ann Radcliffe, William Beckford, and Matthew Gregory Lewis. That short fiction in England during this period often dealt with strange and unexplainable (or at least seemingly unexplainable) events springs partially from the old folktale tradition of dealing with such events and partially from the influence of the darker side of German Romanticism. The English way to deal with the supernatural, however, is to explain it away naturalistically or play it for its simple shock effect, rather than, as in America, to exploit its metaphysical and psychological implications.

A typical example is Wilkie Collins's "The Traveler's Story of a Terribly Strange Bed." The story is about a single narrator who begins winning at gambling prodigiously and is encouraged and seemingly protected by a dirty and wrinkled old man with vulture eyes. After breaking the bank at the gambling house, the narrator is almost killed in a four-poster bed when the top is lowered down to crush him. The story has the kind of plot and character potential of which Fyodor Dostoevski could have made metaphysical capital, or that Poe could have developed into a psychological nightmare. For Collins, however, the story is a simple one of a thwarted murder attempt, in which the mysterious old man turns out to be the owner of the gambling house and the perpetrator of the plot to kill the narrator. The story is not without its suspense and not without its elements of mysterious hallucination. The bed, however, turns out to be not very "terribly strange" at all—only a smooth-running mechanism for murder. The story is indeed short and self-contained, but it is told more in a novelistic manner that focuses on realistic motivation and verisimilitude than in the true short-story manner which focuses on psychological and metaphysical mysteries.

Edward Bulwer-Lytton's story "The Haunted and the Haunters: Or, The House and the Brain" is a ghost story with a ratiocinative twist. The narrator of the story is a dilettantish ghost hunter who spends a night in a mysterious house in order to disprove, or at least to explain, the strange phenomena that have been reported there. Indeed, mysterious manifestations do take place during his night in the house: A child's footprints are seen, ghastly exhalations are felt, and ghostly voices are heard. The narrator discovers clues that the previous residents of the house had been involved in mysterious events of love and death—events that somehow had given rise to the phenomena. The narrator, however, is little interested in the lives that seem perpetuated in the house; his only concern is to explain the events and to prove his theory that the supernatural is only a natural law about which he has been previously ignorant. The final solution involves not the elaborate ratiocinative devices of Poe's detective figures nor does the haunting of the house suggest the sort of psychological hallucination and dream reality of Poe's horror stories. In fact, the discovery of a powerful lodestone, some amber and rock crystal lumps, and a magic symbol in a secret chamber do little to explain anything. The final discovery is that a famous charlatan who once lived in the house has left behind a mechanism which preserves his own powerful will and affects the occupants of the house. The motivation for his action, however, is left vague and unexplored. A more typical short story would have involved the narrator in the story in some crucial way; but here, he only exists to explain, in pseudoscientific ways, the mystery of the phenomenon. How the events take place is all that is important, not why they happen or what they mean.

A more pertinent example of the failure to exploit the particular characteristics of the short-story genre in England can be seen in a tale by Charles Dickens. One would think that Dickens, with his focus on the outcast figure on the fringe of society and his mastery of the grotesque and extreme situation, would have found the short story a most viable vehicle. In "The Signalman," however, Dickens has all the plot and character elements of a successful short story but fails to use them in an intense and revealing way. The narrator of the story, who identifies himself as a "man who had been shut up within narrow limits all his life, and who being at last set free, had a newly awakened interest" in the world around him, encounters a railway signalman. The narrator descends through an extremely deep cutting of clammy stone, that becomes oozier and wetter as he goes down, to the signalman's post; it is solitary and dismal and has an earthy, deadly smell and so much cold wind rushing through it that the narrator feels as if he had "left the natural world." The signalman himself has the potentially symbolic task of watchfulness and exactness; in fact, he seems to exist only for this purpose and has learned a language of telegraphic communication that sets him apart from the phenomenal world.

The story, however, is a structure of potential elements that are never realized. The signalman's function and his cavernous location down the ravine, which the narrator finds "easier to mount than to descend," seem the materials of symbolic fiction; the narrator himself, who has been confined within narrow limits, seems the stuff of psychological drama; the central events of the story—the signalman's perception of a specter with the left arm across the face and the right one waving violently as if to say, "For God's sake, clear the way"—has all the elements of the *Doppelgänger* motif; and the final event in the story, when the signalman has been killed and the narrator sees an actual embodiment of the specter make the waving gesture, has the potential of involving the narrator in the story. All these elements could have come together in a story about the nature of isolation, concretely realized and vividly symbolized. Instead, it is a simple demonstration of the psychic phenomenon of precognition. The potential of the story, either psychologically or morally, that a Poe or a Hawthorne could have developed is never fulfilled or even suggested in a unified way. For Dickens, these elements are interesting in themselves, but they do not come together in the single and unified complex effect that marks the mastery of the short-story genre.

For whatever reason, because of individual poetic genius or because of the difference in social milieu, Ivan Turgenev could have transformed the Dickens material into a unified, lyric, and symbolic story. There is no question that *Zapiski okhotnika*, 1852 (*Russian Life in the Interior*, 1855; better known as *A Sportsman's Sketches*, 1932) is one of the great collections of short fiction in the nineteenth century. Frank O'Connor says it may well be the greatest book of short stories ever written. Turgenev is a distinctly romantic writer but a romantic writer moving toward realism. Strongly influenced by the German Romantics—Hoffmann, Tieck, Novalis—Turgenev had a strong sense of the irrational and an adherence to the mysterious saving power of love. Marina Ledkovsky, in her 1973 study entitled *The Other Turgenev*, describes the characteristics of Turgenev's tales in a way that could be a description of the short-story form itself: "The peculiarity of the structure of the mysterious tales consists in the alternating and at times fusing of extremely realistic, prosaic events with fantastic episodes. . . . Thus the irrational and illogical are woven into banal reality to create a grotesque setting on two planes." As is true for the short story generally, Turgenev's realism is not an indication of a philosophic acceptance of the primary reality of the physical and phenomenal world; rather, it is simply a technique for involving everyday reality with the immanently mysterious world of the irrational. This is why the short story often involves the grotesque, and why the form, as exemplified in Turgenev, suggests the entanglement of the physical world with the dreamlike world of story itself. Turgenev's two best-known stories—"The Country Doctor" and "Bezhin Meadow"—are exemplars of the short story as a form; so completely do they represent the short story that their subject matter is the world of story itself.

"The Country Doctor" is a framed story in which the sportsman narrator, taken by a fever, calls in a district doctor who tells him a "remarkable story" which the sportsman then relates to the reader in the doctor's own words. The story is one about the doctor's trip to tend a beautiful sick young girl in the home of her poor but cultivated mother. The girl's slow death over a period of days is ironically the doctor's one moment of life—life elevated from his everyday routine. The tale the doctor tells of his falling in love with the girl and her falling in love with him reaches its climax and crux when the doctor realizes that she loves him only because she is going to die. The doctor says he understands that "if she had not believed herself on the point of death, she would never have given me a thought; but say what you like, there must be something appalling about dying at twenty-five without ever having loved; that was the thought that tormented her, and that was why, in despair, she seized on me." What adds another excruciating turn of the screw is that the girl, having proclaimed her love for the doctor, is desperate to die. When she begs the doctor that she must die, that he promised her that she would die, he says, "It was a bitter moment for me, for many reasons."

The conception of the story is a stroke of genius, for it combines for the doctor a moment of the highest fulfillment, yet at the same time a moment of the deepest despair precisely because of the fulfillment itself. Yet the real genius of the story lies in the telling itself, as the doctor in his hurried yet halting way tries both to justify the experience and to understand it. It is a typical Turgenev device, as it was later to be for Anton Chekhov, to have the story end in understatement. After the story is told and the narrator takes the doctor's hand in unspoken sympathy, the doctor suggests a game of Preference and offhandedly says he has since married a woman as common as he is, "a spiteful hag, I must say, but luckily she sleeps all day." The last paragraph of the story is: "We got down to Preference for copeck stakes. Trifon Ivanich won two and a half roubles from me—and went home late, very pleased with his victory." Such an ending is not to suggest that the reader has been tricked into a sympathy for the doctor which he does not deserve. On the contrary, it is an indication of the depth of his significant loss that he is content with the trivial win. For the central irony of the story is that if he had won, that is, if the girl had lived, he would have lost. His only win is the memory, the story itself, and that is a constant source of both joy and torture for him. There is no sentimentality in the story, nor is there cynicism. It is simply the recounting of a moment in time when the evanescent possibility to be elevated from the everyday occurred—a recounting which indeed suggests that the only possibilities for such transcendence are, by their very nature, evanescent. Transcendence is a strange and lyrical moment surrounded by the mundane and the ordinary; it is one of the functions of the short-story form to depict such moments in all their bittersweetness.

"Bezhin Meadow" is an even more complex story about the transition from the ordinary phenomenal world into the extraordinary world of dream, wish, and thus story itself. The tale begins with the sportsman getting lost; as he experiences a sense of disorientation, he cries, "Where on earth am I?" and the reader realizes, as he or she does with Rip Van Winkle's strange trek up the mountain, with Young Goodman Brown's journey into the forest, and with the narrator in "The Fall of the House of Usher" as he approaches the ominous house, that the sportsman is nowhere on earth, that he or she has moved from the terrestrial into a realm of folktale and dream. The landscape traveled through is a familiar one in romantic poetry and the short-story genre:

> The hollow was like an almost symmetrical cauldron with sloping sides. At the bottom of it rose, bolt upright, several large white stones, which seemed to have crept down there for a secret conclave, and the whole place had such a deaf-and-dumb feeling the sky hung so flatly and gloomily above it, that my heart shrank. Some little creature was squeaking faintly and plaintively among the stones.

Floundering through this mythic landscape, the sportsman comes upon a group of peasant boys tending horses. As he pretends to sleep, he hears the five boys tell the following stories. Fedya tells the first story of a ghost in a paper mill which frightened him and some of his friends and then made a sound of choking and coughing like a sheep. Kostya tells the story of a carpenter who confronts a water sprite in the forest and crosses himself in fear that it is the devil; at this act she begins to cry and tells him that if he had not crossed himself he could have lived with her merrily forever; since that time the carpenter goes about grieving. Ilyusha tells a story of the kennel man Ermil, who, seeing a lamb on the grave of a drowned man, strokes it and says "Baa-lamb, baa-lamb," to which the lamb bares its teeth and answers him back. Pavel tells a story of the coming of Trishka, the Antichrist, who turns out to be only the barrel maker who had bought himself a new jug and had put the empty jug over his head. Finally, Kostya tells of a little boy who drowned in the river near where the boys are and whose mother has not been right in the head since. At the end of this story, Pavel, who has told the only "supernatural" story with a naturalistic explanation, comes back from the river and says that he has heard the drowned boy call to him from under the water.

The story has no plot, is not *about* a single event except for the narrator's encounter with the realm of story itself. "Bezhin Meadow" projects a basic romantic image of man; like Shelley's poet who is a nightingale singing in the darkness, the boys tell their stories and light up a small place. The stories themselves are kernels of short stories—folk legends of mysterious encounters with hope, wish, pathos, madness. Pavel is central in the narrator's consciousness because of his attempts to find some rational explanation for the supernatural events; but he too is drawn into the dream world of story until the virtual world itself is transformed and he hears the voice of the drowned child. The irony of the story is the irony of all the stories people tell of those things that frighten them, for they tell them as a way of dealing with their fears. It is a story of the storytelling impulse as an example of Sigmund Freud's repetition compulsion, a basic urge to control the uncontrollable by managing it in the form of story itself. For Turgenev, as for all great storytellers, the nature of reality lies not in hard events but rather in human emotions that construct those events and make them meaningful. Story is a primal form of expressing the emotion-made nature of reality—a primal form of expressing the reality of wish, of dream, of feeling, of the ultimately unexplainable, that yet must be integrated and coped with.

Although Dostoevski is often praised as a prophetic voice of the twentieth century existential sensibility, and his novels are often cited as exemplars of the philosophical novel, little has been said of his use of, and contribution to, the short-story form. Indeed, in his short fictions, the focus is less on the formal perfection of a lyrical form to penetrate psychological and metaphysical mysteries than it is on the presentation of a conceptual philosophic position. Among his stories, "The Crocodile" is a satire of civil service bureaucracy and "The Dream of a Ridiculous Man" is a parable which sets forth his own Christian existentialism. Even the two stories singled out for *Zapiski iz podpolya* (1864; *Letters from the Underworld*, 1913; also known as *Notes from the Underground*) and "The Peasant Marey"—have been analyzed mainly for their conceptual or parabolic content. What is to be suggested is that, both formally and thematically, the stories fall within the tradition of short fiction in the nineteenth century.

First of all, the Underground Man is a clear example of that isolated individual which Frank O'Connor suggests is central to the short-story form. He is a "characterless creature" who has cut himself off from the social world and feeds instead on his own subjectivity. Like Melville's Bartleby, he has confronted a wall before which he is impotent. In his story "Apropos of the Wet Snow," he recounts the experiences that have led him to the underground and thus to his philosophic monologue. Basically, "Apropos of the Wet Snow" recounts his attempts to involve himself in real life, attempts to love and be loved; but they are attempts that fail because of his morbid self-consciousness and his bookish posturing and artificiality. The Underground Man's relationship with the characters in the story are basically the same as his relationship with the readers in the monologue: He tries to win them over even as he mocks them. The Russian critic Konstantin Mochulsky sums up this dilemma and the theme of the story in a way that marks its similarity to the theme of many of the stories of Hawthorne: "A strongly developed person recoils from the world, desperately defends his own autonomy, and, at the same time, is attracted to others and understands his dependence on them." The tragedy of "Apropos of the Wet Snow" is, Mochulsky says, the tragedy of human communication. Mochulsky notes that this tension also dominates the monologue section of the story, for it is a monologue which is in the nature of a dialogue. Although the Underground Man insists that he needs no reader, each statement is intended to make an impression on the reader.

Although the monologue has received the most critical attention, it is the story "Apropos of the Wet Snow" that constitutes the center of the work. The monologue is, as Ralph Matlaw has suggested, a false start, leading the reader away from the real subject of the work. Before he can recall and reveal, the narrator evades and attempts to build up an image of the self through philosophic speculation. It is the story that depicts his encounters with "the real thing" and his failures both because of his confusion between real life and artistic life and his own self-consciousness. His situation in the two parts of the stories are echoed in the monologue of J. Alfred Prufrock and in James's story of John Marcher in "The Beast in the Jungle" a generation later.

"The Peasant Marey" is a story within a story that depicts the relationship of a remembered or storied past event to an intolerable present situation. The present time of the story is Easter week, and the narrator is in prison. Disgusted by the violence and disorder of his surroundings and affected by a hissed whisper to him by a political prisoner—"I hate these scum"—the narrator loses himself in memories of when he was nine years old and heard a shout of "wolf" but was comforted by one of his father's peasants, Marey, who told him that the shout was in his fancy only. After the narrator resurrects this incident (which he says must have lain hidden in his soul for twenty years), he looks on his fellow prisoners with more sympathetic eyes; for now he feels that the very criminal he had found so disgusting may be the very Marey who had comforted him as a child.

The parabolic nature of the story is simple enough: that one must recognize the basic humanity of all people regardless of their external appearances. The mode of the story—in which a memory is revived and relived as a key to a present situation—is more complex. For the story of Marey and the boy who heard "wolf" is a play with the folktale of the boy who cried "wolf." Whereas the folktale is about a boy who so often presents a fantasy as if it were a reality that when he confronts the reality no one believes him and he is devoured by it, Dostoevski's story is about a fantasy (or memory or story) which reminds the narrator that the external reality he perceives around him is appearance only—that the significant reality resides in the story—the very story that he remembers and constructs. Thus, as often in the short-story form, the fiction becomes more real than the external reality.

The Well-Made Story and the Advent of Realism

After the era of Hawthorne and Poe in America, the short story ceased to be a distinctive form until Henry James revived it as a serious art form in the 1880's. This does not mean, however, that important changes in the form did not take place in the 1850's, 1860's, and 1870's—changes that have affected the development of the form up to the present day. The primary movement in this period was the shift toward realism; and realism is neither a philosophic assumption nor a literary convention that is conductive to the basically romantic and psychological/metaphysical nature of the short-story form. Herman Melville's "Bartleby the Scrivener" is an exception, because even as it points forward to the highly polished psychological tales of Henry James, it points backward to Poe's psychological hallucinations and Hawthorne's moral parables. Beyond Melville's distinctive contribution to the short story in the 1850's, the other two movements in the development of the form that dominate the period up to the 1880's are the stories of local color and the so-called well-made stories. Of the many examples of local-color stories that dominate the period, the short stories of Bret Harte and Mark Twain have been chosen to comment on. Of the well-made story, the best-known stories of Fitz-James O'Brien, Thomas Aldrich, and Edward Everett Hale have been selected for commentary.

Frederick Lewis Pattee, in his 1923 study of the short story, has noted the avalanche of female authors that followed Hawthorne and Poe in the 1850's and filled the magazines with sentimental stories. Hawthorne himself said in 1855, "America is now wholly given over to a d—-d mob of scribbling women. I should have no chance of success while the public taste is occupied with their trash—and should be ashamed of myself if I did succeed." Besides Melville, the only other figure in the 1850's to contribute (for better or worse) to the future of the short story was Fitz-James O'Brien. His 1859 story, "What Was It?," makes use of the fantasy and supernatural elements that Poe perfected, but it also points ahead to the journalistic style of O. Henry. "What Was It?" is a well-made, formally constructed story far superior to similar stories by Wilkie Collins and Edward Bulwer-Lytton but very much inferior to the intricate blending of fantasy and reality that Poe achieved.

Character development in the story is slight; Harry, the narrator, serves primarily to tell the story of his capture of an invisible ghoulish figure. He is a writer and a smoker of opium and somewhat of an amateur expert on supernaturalism. The central event takes place in a boarding house, reputed to be haunted, on a night after he and a friend, Dr. Hammond, have been smoking opium and talking. On this particular night, instead of talking about the light or Ariel side of life, as was their custom, they discuss the darker or Caliban side. Hammond brings up the philosophic question to Harry: "What do you consider to be the greatest element of terror?" Dr. Hammond thinks of various effects in the works of Brockden Brown and Edward Bulwer-Lytton and thinks that if only he were master of a literary style he could write a story like Hoffmann on this particular night.

After retiring, the narrator of "What Was It?" tries to get the horrible thoughts of the discussion out of his mind; he feels something drop from the ceiling onto his chest and try to strangle him with bony hands. After a struggle, he subdues the thing and turns on the light, only to find nothing. In contrast to the usual such dream-vision awakenings, however, the thing is still there; it is invisible, but it is still a concrete "thereness." Later when they call in a doctor to chloroform the thing and make a cast of it, what is revealed is a four-footed, manlike creature with muscular limbs; the narrator describes it only as something that surpasses figures from Gustave Doré or Jacques Callot. Now the creature becomes a burden—something they can neither release, nor keep, nor kill. Finally the creature dies, seemingly having starved to death, and is buried. What the story is, given O'Brien's fascination with *The Tempest*, is an objectification of fantasy—the intrusion into reality of an abstract yet emotionally created object of terror that the narrator and doctor have been discussing. In fact, the entire house of boarders has been infected psychologically by dark fantasies, for they have been reading a book entitled *The Night Side of Nature* before the creature appears. Thus within the fantasy entitled "What Was It?" the reader has an actual objectification of the fantasies of the fictional characters. Such a self-reflexive motif, while not as expert as similar motifs in Poe, is more polished than stories of other supernatural writers in the 1850's and 1860's.

Herman Melville's short fiction has been little appreciated until recently. Pattee only briefly mentions him in his 1923 study of the short story. Of the mass of criticism that has been published on Melville's short stories in the last twenty years, the story that has received the most attention (and rightfully so) is "Bartleby the Scrivener." In nothing else that Melville wrote, says Newton Arvin, "did he achieve by the accumulation of details themselves commonplace, prosaic, and humdrum, a total effect of such strangeness and even madness as this." The story has been discussed by numerous critics as an autobiographical parable of Melville's feeling of artistic failure, as a case study in schizophrenia, and as a social allegory of how the system crushes the little man. The one discussion that approaches the story as a short story is an article by Robert Marler (*American Literature*, May, 1974), which argues that "Bartleby the Scrivener" marks a transition from the "tale" form, in which characters are unitary figures or archetypes, to the true "short story," in which characters have their own psychologies and are wearing their social personae. Marler says that "Bartleby the Scrivener" is a fully developed short story because it is embedded in a social context and is a reflection of the narrator's mind. It is not Bartleby's story, says Marler, but a story of the narrator's movement from a state of ignorance to a state of knowledge.

There is not sufficient space here to argue with all of Marler's points which indicate that the story is the first true short story and therefore radically different from the "tale" form that preceded it; it is not a point worth belaboring. The difference between "Bartleby the Scrivener" and the stories of Hawthorne and Poe is indeed a result of a step toward realism. Even though Melville focuses on the prosaic and the commonplace in the story, however, the effect is as psychologically mysterious as a story by Poe and as morally complex as a story by Hawthorne; for the prosaic and the commonplace are transformed here into symbol. Although the story takes place in an actual setting—an office on New York's Wall Street—as the story develops, the reader gradually discovers that Wall Street serves less as a social situation than as a symbolic backdrop to Bartleby's story. Indeed, it is a story filled with walls—both blank walls which Bartleby faces and dividing walls that separate him from others. The story is symbolic in the sense that Bartleby himself, for no discernible reasons, has transformed the physical walls around him into metaphors for all the psychological and metaphysical walls that stand between people and an understanding of the world. If Bartleby is mad, his madness is that of one who, like Dostoevski's Underground Man or Hawthorne's minister with the black veil, has understood too clearly that nothing can be understood at all. By his transformation of a real object—the wall—into a symbolic object and his consequent reaction to the object as if it were the significance he has projected on it, Bartleby himself is transformed into a symbolic figure. Bartleby then becomes a "wall" for the narrator, something opaque and mysterious, something that cannot be explained rationally. Indeed, the story *is* the narrator's story; it is his effort to "replay" the experience with Bartleby both as a means of justifying his actions and of understanding what the experience meant.

The basic conflict between Bartleby and the narrator is, as pointed out by Norman Springer, that while the narrator is a man of assumptions, Bartleby is an embodiment of preferences. Thus, Bartleby exists to demonstrate the inadequacy of all assumptions. The narrator perceives, as does the narrator of "The Fall of the House of Usher," that the mysterious figure before him has "nothing ordinarily human about him." When the narrator asks Bartleby during one of his "dead-wall reveries" why he will do no more copying, Bartleby replies, "Do you not see the reason for yourself?" His reference is to the wall he stares at. Even if the narrator could see in the metaphysical yet mad way that Bartleby sees and were to ask him why the wall makes him withdraw from life, Bartleby could answer only that the wall means "nothing." It would be a nothing that is a tangible, felt reality in the way Hemingway's old waiter understands it in "A Clean, Well-Lighted Place," a *nada* that butts all heads at last. The frustration that the narrator feels at not being able either to understand Bartleby or to help him is a result not only of the narrator's safe and secure position, which Bartleby comes to challenge, but also of the impossibility of what Bartleby tacitly demands. For what Bartleby presents is the radical challenge to charity and love that Jesus Christ requires. Bartleby tacitly asks to be understood although he refuses to aid in that understanding; he asks to be loved although he infuriatingly rebuffs all efforts the narrator makes to help him. Bartleby is indeed a particularly painful case of the inability of one to penetrate to the core of the other and say "I-Thou," for he is the "other *par excellence*" who comes solely to challenge the narrator's easy assumptions.

The relationship between Bartleby and the narrator is different from the relationship between Roderick Usher and his narrator only in that the focus shifts. In "The Fall of the House of Usher," the symbolic figure Usher is foregrounded, and the reader knows little of the narrator's mind except his puzzlement and inability to understand. In "Bartleby the Scrivener," it is indeed the narrator's inability to understand, and by extension the basic human inability to understand, that is foregrounded into the subject matter of the story. Although there are no immediate heirs to this shift of emphasis in the short story in America, it does dominate the form from Henry James and Joseph Conrad on up through the twentieth century. The reader now sees in Flannery O'Connor, Eudora Welty, Bernard Malamud, and other contemporary writers short-story situations in which an ordinary person in the phenomenal world confronts some mysterious character or figure who throws him or her out of an often-uneasy placidity into the mystery of human communication and love (or the impossibility of either), and the reader sees the loneliness that inevitably results.

Fred Lewis Pattee points out that the gradual rise of realism and the magazine *The Atlantic Monthly* dominated the short-story form in America in the 1860's. Of the many stories published in *The Atlantic*

Monthly during this period, commentary will be kept to the most famous, Edward Everett Hale's "The Man Without a Country," a tremendously popular story at the time, which remains worthy of note because of its so-called realism. The story is told by a first-person narrator, and the tone is that of a cautionary tale for young military men. Philip Nolan, the man without a country, is presented as a "real" man involved in an actual event (Aaron Burr's attempted overthrow of the country), but the historical framework serves only the purpose of establishing the event as having really happened and of motivating Nolan's unique sentence—the carrying out of which is the main material of the story. Nolan's character is not explored, and his personal motivation is not developed. The traitorous act itself is described rather in terms of some sort of a satanic temptation. Burr is described simply as a "gay deceiver" who "seduces" Nolan "body and soul."

When Nolan damns the United States at his trial and vows, "I wish I may never hear of the United States again," the court sentences him to fulfill his wish. He is transferred back and forth on Navy vessels for fifty years, never closer than one hundred miles to United States soil. All officers and crewmen on the ships are forbidden to make any reference to the United States; his reading material is carefully censored, even to the deletion of references to the United States in foreign books and newspapers. The story is primarily narrative, with only a few scenes that indicate Nolan's growing loneliness and awareness of the extremity of his situation. The actual thematic thrust of the story, for all its realistic plot detail, is of a man tempted into a traitorous act by a figure who has become legendary in American history. The result of Nolan's act is that not only is he forced to have his wish fulfilled—a wish he discovers to be a curse—but also he himself is turned into a legendary figure in a cautionary tale. Just as the early short story concerns a mythic figure presented as a man, Hale's story presents a man being transformed into a mythic figure—the stuff of continuing story. Regardless of whatever surface verisimilitude a short story may manifest, its so-called realism is always mixed with the mythic and the storylike.

Bret Harte is not a realist in any sense except for the fact that he situates his stories in a specific locality for which he establishes a Western atmosphere and a set of social customs. His characters are types who serve the ironic function of his stories. Moreover, Harte's "local color" is primarily romantic, for he creates his own self-contained little world in which he stylizes the customs, caricatures the characters, and romanticizes the surroundings. Although his effect was strongly felt at the time his first stories appeared in the *Overland Monthly* in 1868, his reputation has not fared well since. In his best story, "Tennessee's Partner," his humorous and ironic point of view and his carefully controlled technique make a definite contribution to the short-story genre; for here he creates a story that, as all good stories do, seduces the reader into a response quite contrary to what the actual events of the story suggest on the surface.

Arthur Hobson Quinn has said that Harte taught nearly every American writer of short stories some of the essentials of his art. Quinn suggests that Harte's sense of humor "preserved in him that sense of proportion which was one of his great gifts to the development of the short story." Harte would have been happy to accept this as his major contribution, for in his *Cornhill* article of 1899, he singles out humor as the factor that finally diminished the influence of English models on the short story in America and helped create a distinctly American form:

> It was *Humour*—of a quality as distinct and original as the country and civilization in which it was developed. It was first noticeable in the anecdote or "story," and after the fashion of such beginnings, was orally transmitted. It was common in the barrooms, the gatherings in the "country store," and finally at public meetings in the mouths of "stump orators."

According to Harte, it is the storyteller's tone and point of view that determine the meaning of a short story, for it is his moral perspective that should direct the reader's response to the story. "Tennessee's Partner" has a dramatically defined narrator with a voice and purpose of his own. After relating how Tennessee's partner went to San Francisco for a wife and was stopped in Stockton by a young waitress who broke at least two plates of toast over his head, the narrator says that he is well aware that "something more might be made of this episode, but I prefer to tell it as it was current at Sandy Bar—in the gulches and barrooms—where all sentiment was modified by a strong sense of humor." It is this barroom point of view, in fact, that dominates the whole story; and once the reader is willing to accept this tone, the story takes on a new and not-so-pathetic dimension. The narrator fully intends for this story to be not the occasion for tears but for sardonic laughter.

When Tennessee's partner invites the men to Tennessee's funeral, the narrator says, "Perhaps it was from a sense of humor, which I have already intimated was a feature of Sandy Bar—perhaps it was from something even better than that, but two thirds of the loungers accepted the invitation at once." That "something better," which sentimental readers have always been willing to accept as an indication of sympathy and perhaps regret on the part of the men for their condemnation of Tennessee, might be seen instead as the final necessary act in the ritual of complicity between the partner and the town in their vigilante justice on Tennessee. The "popular feeling" that had grown up against Tennessee in Sandy Bar could end no other way. At the trial, the narrator makes it abundantly clear that Tennessee's fate was sealed, that the trial is only to justify "the previous irregularities of arrest and indictment." The men have no doubt about his fate; they are "secure in the hypothesis that he ought to be hanged on general principles." It is this very knowledge that they are going to hang Tennessee not so much for a concrete wrong as on general principles that makes them begin to waver, until the partner, who *has* suffered a concrete wrong by Tennessee, enters the game with his attempted bribe of the judge. As a result of his taking a hand, the town helps Tennessee's partner avenge himself on Tennessee for stealing his wife, and the partner helps the town get rid of a bothersome blight on the body politic. The economical use of detail in the story, as well as its combination of sardonic humor and moral complexity, is similar to Poe's masterpiece, "The Cask of Amontillado." In its use of a narrator who quietly and cleverly controls his satiric intent, it is surely as well done as Ring Lardner's "Haircut" or Mark Twain's "The Celebrated Jumping Frog of Calaveras County."

In contrast to Harte's humorous story, about which little has been said, Mark Twain's jumping frog story has come in for much critical commentary. The story has been called a multilevel satire pitting the simplicity of the West against the cunning of the East in which, although the Westerner Jim Smily is bested in the contest by the Easterner, the West gets its revenge on the East by imposing Simon Wheeler's long-winded story on the Easterner, Mark Twain. The story itself is a clear example of Twain's own definition of the humorous in his 1895 piece, "How to Tell a Story." The humorous is told gravely, says Twain; "the teller does his best to conceal the fact that he even dimly suspects that there is anything funny about it." The humorous story always depends on the manner of the telling rather than on the matter, says Twain; and Simon Wheeler tells his story with such earnestness that "so far from imagining that there was anything ridiculous or funny about his story, he regarded it as a really important matter, and admired its two heroes as men of transcendent genius in finesse." The irony of the story is that although an Easterner beats the inveterate gambler Jim Smily, the Western story itself is the champion. The genius in finesse is Simon Wheeler (or rather his creator Mark Twain—not his auditor Mark Twain), and the framed story triumphs over the frame itself. Truly, as Bret Harte has said, the genius of the American Western story is the tone of the telling; the tone in Twain's tale is one that hovers uneasily between seriousness and triviality and between reality and parable.

T. B. Thorpe's "Big Bear of Arkansas" is a classic example of the frame tale or dual narrator convention, in which a pompous passenger on a Mississippi River steamboat describes and then introduces Jim Doggett, a rambunctious tall-tale storyteller. Walter Blair points out that the frame separates the world of the intelligent, educated observer from the world of the frontiersman. The outer sophisticated narrator calls attention to what he knows will be the central interest of the story, the inner narrator's style: "His manner was so singular, that half of his story consisted in his excellent way of telling it." The story itself is not significant, told solely as an excuse for exhibiting the style of the teller; when it is over, the outer narrator notes the sort of superstitious awe the tall-tale teller has about the bear, but the story never really becomes either the mythic story that William Faulkner later creates in "The Bear" or the comic story of the frontiersman having a bit of fun with the innocent easterner that Mark Twain sets up in his famous jumping frog story. What makes "The Big Bear of Arkansas" work is that it is an ambiguous mixture of both mythic and comic.

Sut Lovingood, the frontier tall-tale character in George Washington Harris's sketches, published in *Sut Lovingood: Yarns Spun by a "Nat'ral Born Durn'd Fool" Warped and Wove for Public Wear* in 1867, is a central example of the frontier humor that Bret Harte felt gave the short story its uniquely American voice. It was a mode that was "often irreverent" and "devoid of all moral responsibility," said Harte, but it was "original! . . . the parent of the American 'short story.'"

Sut Lovingood is not the heroic natural man, such as the reader encounters in Thomas Bangs Thorpe's "Big Bear of Arkansas," nor is he a simple comic rogue like Johnson Jones Hooper's Simon Suggs; instead he is a nonconformist disrupter of the body politic. In the eight sketches in *Sut Lovingood*, Sut is not merely a trickster, but a trickster with the iconoclastic purpose of undermining the genteel assumptions that support social life. Sut does not attack easy targets, such as the simple hypocrisy of the camp meeting, as does Captain Suggs. Instead he attacks and subverts the foundations of the social establishment. He sees not only through hypocrisy but also through social convention itself. In "Mrs. Yardley's Quilting" and "Sicily Burns's Wedding," the two best-known sketches in the book, Sut exposes and undermines two of society's most cherished communal rituals—weddings and funerals.

Sut specializes in disruption, which Harris is careful not to present as aimless destruction, but, as has been the case of short fiction since Boccaccio, disruption that is poetically and symbolically appropriate. For example, in "Sicily Burns's Wedding," a cow blindly stumbling about with a basket over her head, knocking over a dozen stands of bees, and a bull who throws old man Burns on his back create a wild chaotic scene that reflects the primal sexual violence that underlies the genteel ceremony of the wedding. The image of the blinded cow with the basket over her head is echoed by the image of the bride squatting in a cold spring up to her eyes with a milk crock over hers. The fact that the bees are particularly vicious in stinging the women so that they swell up is a comically grotesque image of the result of the wedding night sex.

Death is treated just as irreverently in "Mrs. Yardley's Quilting," which opens with Sut's describing how old Mrs. Yardley came to be salted down, as if she were so much smokehouse meat. When asked what Mrs. Yardley died of, Sut says, "Nuffin, only her heart stop't beatin 'bout losing a nine dimunt quilt. True, she got a skeer'd horse tu run over her, but she'd a-got over that ef a quilt hadn't been mix'd up in the catastrophe." Just as in "Sicily Burns's Wedding," Sut is responsible for the chaos in "Mrs. Yardley's Quilting." Once again using animals whose primitive nature breaks up a genteel and refined ceremony, Sut ties the prize quilts to a horse and hits him on the backside; however, he says, in spite of the death of Mrs. Yardley, his conscience is free, for he blames it all on the horse. The image of the horse as male physicality madly dashing about with the bedroom quilts connected to him is symbolically appropriate.

George Washington Cable, the first literary voice of the postwar South, also makes use of the trickster motif or confidence-man theme in one of his best-known stories, "Posson Jone." However, Cable moves the story away from the backwoods trickster by the simple fact of placing him in the city of New Orleans and giving him a French background. The story begins with Joules St.-Ange's intention to try a confidence game on the giant backwoods preacher Jimmy Jones in order to pay off his gambling debts. The characters are given tall-tale status by their caricature descriptions, including the preacher's giant servant named Colossus of Rhodes and Joules's clever little servant named Baptiste.

The key themes that dominate the story are "special providence" and theatrical pretense. The parson says it is special providence that he has met Joules. It is indeed a special providence that Colossus steals the money from his master just when he is about to loan it to Joules to gamble away. When he discovers the money is gone, Joules says it is "specious providence" that the lost money is not the parson's and that he won more than six hundred dollars. Parson Jones says, "Providence moves in a mysterious way His wonders to perform." The comedy of providence intensifies when Baptiste is knocked into the water and Colossus displays the lost money; the story ends with, "the ways of Providence are indeed strange." The central focus of the story is that the mysterious nature of confluence is what makes things happen.

Cable's best-known stories combine local color with gothic romanticism. "'Sieur George" opens, much like Poe's "The Fall of the House of Usher" and Faulkner's "A Rose for Emily," with an antique house that has the "solemn look of gentility in rags." Cable uses a number of nineteenth century short-story conventions: In addition to the decaying and mysterious old house, there is the ancient landlord, Kookoo, a sort of "periodically animate mummy," who is as punctual as an executioner, and the mysterious old tenant, known as "'Sieur George." The central narrative drive of the story, embodied in the landlord and the unopened hair-trunk, is the reader's desire to find some practical motive for the mystery of the old man; however, it soon becomes clear that practical motives, such as a duel, madness, disinheritance, and other rumors imagined by the rumor mongers are not sufficient to account for the mystery. Although time passes in the story, 'Sieur George stays the same; a character out of place, out of time.

"Jean-ah Poquelin" is probably Cable's most admired story, for it not only makes use of the gothic tradition, the well-made story, and the conventions of local color, but also symbolically embodies a social message. Beginning, as does Washington Irving's "The Legend of Sleepy Hollow," with the loss of the old European world and the introduction of the hateful new American cultural and political life, the story begins, in typical gothic fashion, with the mysterious old plantation house in ruins. Years before, the hermit-like Jean Marie Poquelin went to Africa to engage the slave trade, taking his younger brother with him. When he returns without him, many ask, "Where is thy brother, Abel?" and the name Jean Marie Poquelin becomes "a symbol of witchery, devilish crime, and hideous nursery fictions." People believe they have seen the ghost of the half brother, a figure in white, and Poquelin becomes "an omen and embodiment of public and private ill fortune." As in Faulkner's "A Rose for Emily," the city grows and encroaches on Poquelin's isolation, and a sickening odor emanates from the house as if from the ground like the smell of some old sin.

At the end of the story, when a mob comes to the house, a Negro slave carries Jean's coffin and leads the half brother Jacques into the swamp, to the Leper's Land, and they are never seen again. This surprise ending seems more symbolically significant than that which closes "'Sieur George" because of the introduction of the Cain and Abel theme and the theme of the objectification of past sin. The final irony is that the brother's whiteness suggests the decay of white society that has prospered on the slave trade of the black man.

The best-known stories of Mary Murfree subordinate local color to the conventions of the romance tradition. "Electioneering on Big Injun Mountain" focuses on "the return of the native" theme, in which a mountain man, Chad, moves to the city, becomes a lawyer, and is elected district attorney; when he returns to the mountains to run for public office, he is scorned by the mountain folk for his city clothes and ways and because he has become a ruthless prosecutor of mountain folk. However, when beaten by a bully, he reverts to the mountain code by refusing to identify his assailant; only then is he welcomed back to the mountain community. Chad decides not to identify Boker, the wife abuser, as he who beat him up in the woods after a romantic epiphanic glimpse of the sad Mrs. Boker standing in the doorway. "The sympathetic heart of the multitude, so quick to respond to a noble impulse, had caught the true interpretation of last night's scene, and to-day all the barriers of ignorance and misunderstanding were down."

With Joel Chandler Harris, the reader returns to the trickster-story convention, this time nearest its origins in the folklore of a culture. Harris presents himself not as creator but as collector and raconteur. Although there is still some critical disagreement as to whether the source of the Uncle Remus tales is Africa or Europe, it seems clear that Harris transcribed old oral tales, perhaps of multiple origins, to the written page. Several critics have noted the subversive nature of the stories, in which Brer Rabbit is a symbol of the covert resistance of the black underdog against powerful oppressors. What made the stories palatable to white audiences was Harris's use of a mythic fantasy of the white imagination in the Uncle Remus frame. The Uncle Remus stories are always about how the clever weak character overcomes the strong dominant one by irony and trickery. Critic Fred Lewis Pattee notes the key to the technique is that within the inner story Harris creates a uniform atmosphere that envelops the whole work until one is awakened at the end by a return to the real world with a start. The Uncle Remus stories are not merely anecdotes, says Pattee, but short stories that remind the reader that "the modern short story follows more of the canons of the ballad art than any other form."

The beginnings of the well-made story in America have already been noted in the stories of Edward Everett Hale and Fitz-James O'Brien. The form did not become overwhelmingly popular and influential, however, until Thomas Bailey Aldrich's "Marjorie Daw" appeared in 1873 in *The Atlantic Monthly.* Its impact was similar to that created by Harte's "The Luck of Roaring Camp," Frank R. Stockton's "The Lady or the Tiger?," or more recently Shirley Jackson's "The Lottery." Like these stories, "Marjorie Daw" has come to stand as an exemplar of the short-story form in the popular imagination. As Fred Lewis Pattee has noted, "Marjorie Daw" became a type "standing for controlled artistry, a whimsical wit, and a totally unexpected denouement that sends the reader back over the story again." Although it is often suggested that Aldrich's surprise ending is the key to the story's success, the basic thematic impulse of the story is as characteristic of the short-story form as is the characteristic turn at the end. The short story often presents a realm in which fantasy and reality are blurred or one in which fantasy becomes more real than the phenomenal world. "Marjorie Daw" is a story that takes this central characteristic as its primary theme. The epistolary form of the story, in which Edward Delaney writes letters to the laid-up John Fleming describing a beautiful young girl who lives across from him and Fleming writes back describing his growing love for the girl, is the point-of-view device that makes possible keeping the secret that there is no such girl.

The story is about the power of the writer's ability to create an "as-if" reality that is more real than a real person. Delaney wishes he were a novelist with the skill of Turgenev as he begins to weave his tale of the young girl in the hammock across the way. As the letters progress, Fleming seems to feel he has known her in some previous state of existence or has dreamed her. Indeed, she is an embodiment of dream, a shadow or chimera; and Delaney marvels that Fleming could fall in love with her, even as he writes Fleming that the chimera is falling in love with him. Thus both Marjorie Daw and Fleming are transformed into fictional figures by Delaney, "a couple of ethereal beings moving in finer air than I can breathe with my commonplace lungs"; and Delaney, caught up in his own fictional creation, begins to "accept things as persons do in dreams." The end of the story is told in Delaney's last letter to Fleming, which Fleming reads when he has finally come to see Marjorie for himself, and it catches the reader with what Mark Twain would call a "snapper": "For oh, dear Jack, there isn't any colonial mansion on the other side of the road, there isn't any piazza, there isn't any hammock—there isn't any Marjorie Daw!" The reader's surprise at this ending and his subsequent going back over the story for clues to the trick is an objectification of what every reader feels when he or she has taken a fictional character to be real. "Marjorie Daw" is a story of the storytelling function itself—a discovery that characters are made of letters only.

The final figures in the development of the short story in the period from 1840 to 1880 are the self-conscious masters of fictional technique in the nineteenth century: Gustave Flaubert and Henry James. Poe's discussion of the importance of form and the artistic nature of the short story in 1842 is echoed by James in his discussion of the art of the novel in 1884. Poe's insistence that "In the whole composition there should be no word written, of which the tendency, direct or indirect, is not to the one preestablished design" is repeated by James's insistence that the novel is a "living thing, all one and continuous, like any other organism, and in porportion as it lives will it be found, I think, that in each of the parts there is something of each of the other parts." This is indeed a new criterion for the novel, one that redeems it from the realm of the popular and includes it within the realm of the artist. Furthermore, Poe's insistence on the importance of the point of view of the teller and its predominance over a simple mimetic presentation of events is also echoed by James's assertion that experience in fiction is an "immense sensibility, a kind of spider-web of the finest silken threads suspended in the chamber of consciousness . . . the very atmosphere of the mind." It is a curiosity of literary criticism that while James's essay is hailed as marking a new direction for the novel at the end of the century, Poe's similar insistence for the short story forty years earlier has been scorned as simplistic. In spite of the similarity of the two essays, many critics seem to believe that James's discussion is the first effort to justify fiction itself as an art form.

What James and Flaubert contribute to the novel form at the end of the nineteenth century is possible because of the development of the short story from the beginnings of the century. The importance of both point of view and form and their intrinsic relation to content, which seems a new departure for fiction at the end of the century, seems so only because the short story has always taken a back seat to the novel. The so-called modern novel may begin in the twentieth century, but for fiction generally "modernism" begins with the nineteenth century short story. Albert George, in his study *Short Fiction in France, 1800-1850*, says that Flaubert's *Trois Contes* (1877; *Three Tales*, 1903) are an indication that Flaubert was the first to profit from Romantic attempts to understand short fiction; they are "the superb refinement of the accumulated knowledge of a half-century." The same might be said of Henry James's *Daisy Miller*, published in 1878. Flaubert's "A Simple Heart" and James's *Daisy Miller* constitute a new beginning for the short story, a definite movement away from the romantic tale that had dominated the century toward a new focus on realism but a realism controlled by an ironic tone, a continuing focus on sympathy, and an undercurrent of symbolism that has been unique to the short story since Gogol and Hawthorne. Flaubert's Félicité and James's Daisy are similar to Gogol's Akaky and Melville's Bartleby. They differ in that instead of being primarily functions of the story, they move to the forefront of the story and are presented as characters that can be identified with, even as they are symbolic. The kind of case that Robert Marler makes for "Bartleby the Scrivener" as marking the beginning of the true short story can be made also for "A Simple Heart" and *Daisy Miller.* In fact, Ray B. West, Jr., in his *The Short Story in America* (1952), notes that James's collection *Daisy Miller: A Study; and Other Stories* (1883) may be the first use of the term "story" in the title of a work in English. "Story" rather than "tale" has been used almost exclusively ever since.

The key to the power of "A Simple Heart," a story that Flaubert himself thought so much of that he sent it to a friend as an illustration of what he thought a story should be, lies in the complex mixture of irony and sympathy in the point of view of the teller, as well as in the use of realistic details that even in their ordinariness seem resonant with suggestive symbolism. It is the kind of technique that James Joyce brings to perfection in *Dubliners* (1914) and the kind of tone that Chekhov masters in his short stories. The interesting aspect of characterization in the story is that the only character of importance is Félicité, and she herself is characterless; she is the servant *par excellence* in that she gives herself completely to others. For all the particular detail of Félicité's life, she is finally not so much an individual character as she is representative of simplicity itself. In reading the story, one takes it incident by incident as a character study of the concrete universal, Félicité/Simplicity. It is not until the final pages of the story when she gets Loulou the parrot that the reader begins to suspect the symbolic nature of the story. For the parrot is a grotesque image of the kind of iconic figure that Félicité herself becomes. Flaubert says that by the age of fifty she was like a "woman made of wood," although she herself is hurt when people compare Loulou to a log of wood. Just as Félicité becomes deaf and her circle of ideas grows narrower, transforming her into a static iconic figure, so does the parrot become an iconic figure to Félicité after it is stuffed. While alive, the parrot is like a son and a lover to her; when dead he becomes an image of the Holy Ghost.

> They were linked in her thoughts; and the parrot was consecrated by his association with the Holy Ghost, which became more vivid to her eye and more intelligible. The Father could not have chosen to express himself through a dove, for such creatures cannot speak; it must have been one of Loulou's ancestors, surely.

Félicité begins to kneel to the parrot to say her prayers, and as she deteriorates, so does the bird. On her deathbed, he is brought to her with a broken wing, the worms having devoured him; but Félicité is blind now as well as deaf, and she kisses him. Although Félicité's devotion to the parrot throughout the last part of the story has something of the absurd about it, her simplicity and deteriorating condition prevent the reader from laughing at her. Although the tone of the story never drops from a kind of sympathetic distance, the conclusion runs the risk of dropping into bathos. In the moment of most poignancy, the reader is also confronted with the moment of most absurdity: "The beats of her heart lessened one by one, vaguer each time and softer, as a fountain sinks, an echo disappears; and when she sighed her last breath she thought she saw an opening in the heavens, and a gigantic parrot hovering above her head." The story of Félicité's treatment of the parrot is a symbolic echo of Flaubert's treatment of Félicité herself. Little more than a shadow throughout her life, Félicité can do little more than parrot others. She acts by instinct rather than rationality; she is, in the early part of the story, a representative of simplicity itself, but by her very simplicity she is transformed. In the later part of the story as the parrot becomes an iconic figure to her, so does she become an iconic figure to the reader; and that the Holy Ghost is perceived as a parrot by a peasant girl is no more absurd than that a peasant girl is perceived by the reader as a Christ figure. What Flaubert has done is what Frank O'Connor says that Gogol did so boldly and brilliantly. He has taken a mock-heroic character and imposed her image over that of the crucified Christ, "so that even while we laugh we are filled with horror at the resemblance."

Henry James also creates a figure of simplicity in *Daisy Miller*. In a work that James himself called "the purest poetry," he creates a character that becomes a type. "Poor little Daisy Miller was, as I understand her," says James, "above all things innocent. . . . She was too ignorant, too irreflective, too little versed in the proportions of things." The whole idea of the story, James concludes, "is the little tragedy of a light, thin, natural, unsuspecting creature being sacrificed as it were to a social rumpus that went on quite above her head and to which she stood in no measurable relation." When considering why he called the story a "study," James said the reasons had escaped him, unless "they may have taken account simply of a certain flatness in my poor little heroine's literal denomination. Flatness indeed, one must have felt, was the very sum of her story." The sum of Daisy's story, however, is no more flat than that of Félicité, and for the same reasons—point of view and a symbolic undercurrent. James makes use of a *ficelle* in the story, a foil and a figure on which Daisy makes her impression. Giles Winterbourne, as his cold name implies, has an attachment to Geneva, the little metropolis of Calvinism, and has thus lost his instinct in the matter of innocence; his reason cannot help him in regard to Daisy. He can only apply a formula to her, that she is unsophisticated, even as he knows that is not the answer. The story deals with the inextricable nature of innocence and guilt. Moreover, it is a story of form versus formlessness.

Daisy Miller is very similar to Hawthorne's "Rappaccini's Daughter" in its placing a creature from another world into contact with the real world. The difference is in the mode of the telling. Instead of creating symbolic settings and using supernatural events to convey such a conflict, as Hawthorne did,

James uses the realistic conflict between American innocence and European social order and sophistication. The terms of innocence and guilt, vulgarity and sophistication, formlessness and form seem natural elements of this realistic situation. Winterbourne becomes more and more angry at himself for being "reduced to chopping logic about this young lady; he was vexed at his want of instinctive certitude as to how far her eccentricities were generic, national, personal." Finally, with horror and relief, the ambiguity and the riddle of Daisy's behavior flash upon him in an ironic illumination of his own simplicity; that she was "a lady whom a gentleman need no longer be at pains to respect." Like Hawthorne's Giovanni, Winterbourne has made the mistake of judging when he should have loved; and Daisy, like Félicité, has been transformed from realistic character into icon, "a living embodiment," says Leslie Fiedler, "of the American faith that evil is appearance only." Like Bartleby, Daisy is the victim of the tragedy of being misunderstood; and like many short stories, Daisy's story is the drama of the need for the irrationality of love to transcend reason.

Conclusion

In the modern world since the beginning of the nineteenth century, when religious sanctions no longer applied, not only morality but also reality itself has become problematical, even arbitrary. Anyone who is secure in his or her own absolutist view of reality is likely to be challenged in fiction by the romantic perception of the irrational. The encounter with this mysterious deeper reality immanent in external categorical perceptions of reality can so challenge one and unsettle one's comfortable and familiar framework that he or she is unable to readjust, or at least must see that readjustment requires a radical reorientation or perspective. This is surely the significance of Goodman Brown's journey into the forest, Giovanni's encounter with Rappaccini's daughter, the narrator's encounter with Bartleby, or the guest's sojourn in the house of Usher; and in the twentieth century the irrational is confronted by Eudora Welty's traveling salesman, Flannery O'Connor's unfortunate family who meets the inevitable misfit, and Bernard Malamud's reluctant rabbi in "The Magic Barrel."

Often in the short story the reader is presented with characters who are *too* comfortable, too settled in their illusion that their lives are controlled and regular; they must be made aware of the problematic and arbitrary nature of their perceptions and the limitations of their awareness. Their unauthentic lives must be challenged. The short story does not reassure the reader that the world is as he or she usually sees it, nor does it assure him or her that leaps of faith can be made with anything but fear and trembling. It only presents one with the realization that "I-Thou" encounters are ambiguous, mysterious, and problematical. The reality the short story presents is the reality of those subuniverses of the supernatural and the fable. It presents the reality of the *mysterium tremendum* that suddenly erupts in the midst of the profane everyday. It presents those magical episodes in which the reader is torn away to what Martin Buber calls "dangerous extremes," in which security is shattered. It presents moments that make the reader aware that life is a becoming, a possibility of not-yet existence. As Flannery O'Connor says, it appeals to the kind of person who is willing to have his or her "sense of mystery deepened by contact with reality and sense of reality deepened by contact with mystery." It is both "canny and uncanny" at once.

The short story represents both desire and the frustration of desire, one's deepest wishes censored and distorted by the external reality that one must affirm every day in order to survive. It says, however, that surviving is not enough, that one must make superhuman efforts in a superhuman world that always lies immanent in the world of the everyday. The short story is the most paradoxical of all fictional forms, for it gives one reality and unreality at once—gives one both the familiar and the unfamiliar, the universal and the particular. It reminds one of the fact of separation and the possibility for unity—a unity that is not given but that must constantly be made.

Charles E. May

Bibliography

Addison, Claire. *Where Flaubert Lies*. Cambridge, England: Cambridge University Press, 1996. Focuses on the relationship between Flaubert's personal life, his historical context, and his fiction.

Allen, Elizabeth Cheresh. *Beyond Realism: Turgenev's Poetics of Secular Salvation*. Stanford, Calif.: Stanford University Press, 1992. Discusses Ivan Turgenev's development of narrative techniques in *Zapiski okhotnika* (1852; *Russian Life in the Interior*, 1855; better known as *A Sportsman's Sketches*, 1932), analyzing several of the major stories, such as "Bezhin Meadow" and "The Singers."

Ferguson, Suzanne. "Local Color and the Function of Setting in the English Short Story." In *Creative and Critical Approaches to the Short Story*, edited by Noel Harold Kaylor, Jr. Lewiston, N.Y.: The Edwin Mellen Press, 1997. Ferguson argues that the function of setting in early stories is to establish a degree of verisimilitude, but in later stories setting establishes the emotional interaction of the characters with elements of the physical environment.

Lester, Julius. "The Storyteller's Voice: Reflections on the Rewriting of Uncle Remus." In *The Voice of the Narrator in Children's Literature*, edited by Charlotte F. Otten and Gary D. Schmidt. New York: Greenwood Press, 1989. Argues that voice is the heart of Harris's stories.

Lustig, T. J. *Henry James and the Ghostly*. Cambridge, England: Cambridge University Press, 1994. Discusses James's ghost stories and the significance of the "ghostly" for James's work generally. Among the best-known James stories discussed are "The Jolly Corner" and *The Turn of the Screw*.

Parker, Herschel. *Herman Melville: A Biography, Volume I, 1819-1851*. Baltimore: The Johns Hopkins University Press, 1996. The first volume of a two-volume biography of Melville by the most distinguished authority on his life and art covers his life from birth in 1819 until the publication of *Moby Dick* in 1851.

Price, Kenneth M., and Susan Belasco Smith, eds. *Periodical Literature in Nineteenth-Century America*. Charlottesville: University Press of Virginia, 1995. A collection of essays by various scholars about how the periodical transformed the American literary marketplace between 1830 and 1890.

Scharnhorst, Gary. *Bret Harte*. New York: Twayne, 1992. A critical biography of Harte, providing analyses of stories from four different periods of his life, fully informed by critical reception of Harte's work. An afterword summarizes Harte's critical reputation.

THE TURN OF THE TWENTIETH CENTURY: 1880-1920

Until the early nineteenth century, short prose fiction was primarily a vehicle for didactic messages, often religious in nature. Romantic writers, wishing to preserve the old values without the religious dogma and mythological trappings, secularized the old stories by presenting them as basic psychic processes. The ballad tale that had previously existed as received story now became infused with the subjectivity of the teller. The famous collaboration of William Wordsworth and Samuel Taylor Coleridge in *Lyrical Ballads* (1798) marked the beginning of this shift.

Wordsworth's task was to choose situations and scenes from everyday life and by a process of defamiliarization suggest the spiritual value latent within them. Coleridge, on the other hand, was to take supernatural stories or situations and give them the semblance of reality by making them projections of the artist's psyche. Often in these "lyrical ballads," the story element was subsumed by the lyrical element because of their emphasis on the poet's subjective impression. The German Romantics, from whom Coleridge gained many of his critical assumptions, however, were more committed to stories with the lyrical element concealed behind the hard outlines of the event. American writers, also strongly influenced by the Germans, similarly turned from Romantic poetry to Romantic tale. The short story as developed by Washington Irving, Edgar Allan Poe, and Nathaniel Hawthorne was the narrative side of what Coleridge and Wordsworth were doing with the lyric poem in England.

The United States

New literary movements often begin as a reaction against whatever literary movement is predominant at the time, especially when the conventions of the existing movement become stereotyped. Realism, which dominated the writing of fiction during the latter part of the nineteenth century in Europe and the United States, was a reaction against the stereotyped sentimentalizing of the Romantic movement that prevailed during the early part of the century. The basic difference between Romantics and realists is a philosophic disagreement about what constitutes significant "reality." For the Romantics, what was meaningfully real was the ideal or the spiritual, a transcendent objectification of human desire. For the realists, what mattered was the stuff of the physical world.

One of the first results of this focus on the everyday real rather than the transcendent ideal in American fiction was the so-called local color movement; for the more a writer focused on the external world, the more he or she emphasized particular places and people, complete with their habits, customs, language, and idiosyncrasies. Whereas it seldom mattered where in the physical world the stories of Hawthorne and Poe took place (for they always seemed to take place in the mind of the characters or in some fabulist world between fantasy and everyday reality), the stories of Bret Harte were grounded in the American West, just as the stories of Sarah Orne Jewett were tied to New England. The realists wished to localize characters in a physical world and ground their lives in a social reality.

Although the realist assumption, however, began to predominate in the latter part of the century, Romanticism remained; the result was two branches of the local color movement: the earthy Western folktale and the Eastern sentimental story. Sometimes these two types merged, as they did in the stories of Harte, who managed to combine the sentimental idealism of the East with the humorous realism of the West. Sometimes the conflict between the two types was satirized, as it was in Mark Twain's famous story "The Celebrated Jumping Frog of Calaveras County," in which a Western tall-tale artist gets the better of a genteel easterner. Other well-known stories of the period, such as William Dean Howells's "Editha" and Mary E. Wilkins Freeman's "A New England Nun," expose the sterility of genteel idealism when it is cut off from the facts of everyday reality and physical life.

The clearest example of the gradual movement

from the local-color story to the well-made story in the late nineteenth century is Kate Chopin, who was more influenced by Guy de Maupassant's tightly unified stories than by the southern regionalists. Of the over forty stories published in *Bayou Folk* (1894) and *A Night in Acadie* (1897), some of the best-known are formal stories very close to Maupassant anecdotes. For example, "Madame Celestin's Divorce" is a simple story in the Maupassant mode about a lawyer, Paxton, who advises a woman to divorce her drinking, wife-beating husband. The lawyer, thinking he will then marry her, falls into the habit of dreaming of taking a wife. She meets him on the street and tells him that her husband is home and has promised to turn over a new leaf. "La Belle Zoraide" is a sentimental story about a servant who has an illegitimate child, but whose mistress, not wanting to lose her services, sends it away and tells her it is dead. The servant pines away, caring for a bundle of rags that represent the baby to her. Even when the mistress relents and brings the actual baby to her, she will have nothing to do with it and lives to be an old woman with her bundle of rags.

Chopin's best-known story is "Désirée's Baby," for in it the formal structure of the story and its Maupassant-like reverse ending is made more complex by the importance of the social issue on which it depends. This was Chopin's most successful story during her lifetime and has received renewed attention since the advent of feminist criticism. However, many recent critics feel they must apologize for or justify the story's trick ending, suggesting Chopin's most important literary forefather, Guy de Maupassant. The importance of paternal names is introduced very early, for Armand does not care that Désirée is nameless (the name her foster mother has given her suggests that she was desired), for this means he can all the more easily impose his own family name—one of the oldest and proudest in Mississippi—on her when they marry. Indeed Désirée says Armand is particularly proud that the child is a boy who will bear his name. Armand's home shows little of the softness of a woman, suggesting instead the strictness of a male monastic life, with the roof coming down steep and black like a cowl and with big solemn oaks whose branches shadow the house like a pall. The "shadow" metaphor is further emphasized by Désirée's growing suspicion that there is some air of mystery about the house and by her efforts to "penetrate the threatening mist" about her.

Mary Wilkins Freeman moves the short story further away from local-color regionalism and closer to modern impressionism and tight thematic structure by combining detailed realism with the thematic patterning pioneered by Anton Chekhov, James Joyce, Ivan Turgenev, and Sherwood Anderson. In "A New England Nun," Louisa, the central character, is a Jamesian figure shut away from the flow of everyday life. The focus of the story is her "artistic" control over the order and neatness of her solitary home, for which she rejects the masculine disorder of her impending marriage. Louisa is not romantic but realistic, attentive to detail; however, she has "almost the enthusiasm of an artist over the mere order and cleanliness of her solitary home." She worries about the disorder of coarse masculine belongings strewn about in endless litter.

Upon learning of the love between Lily and Joe, she parts with him, like a queen "who, after fearing lest her domain be wrested away from her, sees it firmly insured in her possession." She looks ahead

> through a long reach of future days strung together like pearls in a rosary, every one like the others, and all smooth and flawless and innocent, and her heart went up in thankfulness. . . . Louisa sat, prayerfully numbering her days, like an uncloisterd nun.

This sort of genteel withdrawal from life into an artistic and idealistic pattern receives harsh criticism from Howells, the so-called father of American realists, in his most famous story, "Editha." Editha extols the Romantic ideal of war so much that her fiancé George joins the army to please her. When he is killed and Editha goes to see his mother, the older woman chastises her severely for her foolish romanticism. As the story ends, however, Editha, while having her portrait done, is confirmed in her own view when she tells the artist about it and the woman says, "How vulgar!" Although the content of the story rejects the idealistic, "artistic" view typical of romanticism for a more everyday human reality, its own form, like most Romantic short stories, is a tightly organized aesthetic pattern.

In addition to the emphasis on local color, another result of the shift from Romanticism to realism in the latter part of the century was a shift from the focus on form to the focus on content. For the Romantics, pattern was more important than plausibility; thus, their stories were apt to be more formal and "literary" than the stories of the realists. By insisting on a faithful adherence to the stuff of the external world, the realists had to allow content—which was often apt to be ragged and random—to dictate form. Because of this shift, the novel, which can expand to create better an illusion of everyday reality, became the favored form of the realists, while the short story, basically a Romantic form that requires more artifice and patterning, assumed a secondary role.

Poe and Hawthorne knew this difference between the two forms well and consequently, by means of a tightly controlled form, created a self-sustained moral and aesthetic universe in their stories. Those writers of the latter part of the nineteenth century who were committed to the short-story form instead of the novel were also well aware of this fact. For example, when Ambrose Bierce entered into the argument then raging between the Romantics and the realists, he attacked the Howells school of realist fiction by arguing, "to them nothing is probable outside the narrow domain of the commonplace man's most commonplace experience." Bierce was interested in those extreme rather than ordinary moments of human experience when reality became transmuted into hallucination. His best-known story, "An Occurrence at Owl Creek Bridge," ironically focuses on a real world that seems sterile and lifeless and a fantasy world (in the split second before death) that seems dynamic and real. Tight ironic patterning is what creates the similitude of reality in this story, not a slavish fidelity to the ordinary events of the world.

Bierce's short stories deal with those moments when people act in such a way that even those closest to them cannot understand what motivates them. Bierce's most obsessive concern in the short story is not simple macabre horror but rather the central paradox that underlies the most basic human desire and fear—the desire for a sense of unity and significance and the fear that the realization of such a desire means death. Bierce's characteristic short-story tactic is to distance his characters from the ordinary world of everyday reality by presenting them in a static formal posture or picture, by putting them in a dreamlike autistic state, or by putting them on a formal stage. In a Bierce story, when this formal picture or frozen sense of reality is broken, the result is often the shock of entering another realm of reality.

"Chickamauga" is a particularly rich example of this theme of unreality presented as reality. The story opens with the child's play with toy sword as he postures in ways he has seen in pictures in his father's military books, overcoming invisible and imaginary foes. When he sees men crawling through the woods, he associates them with pictures he has seen—dog, pig, bear. However, to maintain the tension between the play reality of the child and the war reality of the adult, Bierce asserts an adult perspective on the boy's experience, noting that all he describes would not have been seen by the child but rather "by an elder observer" or "an observer of better experience." The story focuses on the two basic worlds: child and adult, fantasy and reality, innocence and experience. When the child reaches home, it is as if he has gone a long way to stay where he was; the plantation "seemed to turn as if on a pivot." The story ends with the boy's loss of his mother and the reader's discovery that he is a deaf mute, his final inarticulate and indescribable cries suggesting grief that goes beyond language.

The relationship between static reality and dynamic reality is again emphasized in "The Man and the Snake," in which Harker Brayton, while reading in bed, sees two small eyes and the coils of a snake in his room. Brayton is not afraid but rather conscious of the incongruity of the situation, "revolting, but absurd." He decides the snake is not dangerous but "*de trop*—'matter out of place,'" an "impertinence." Bierce emphasizes that as these thoughts formed in Brayton's mind, in a process called "consideration and decision," the "secret of human action" is initiated. When he looks at the eyes of the snake, the spell of the perverse reasserts itself so that even as he tries to brace himself back, he slowly advances toward the snake on his elbows. The reader's final discovery that the snake is stuffed and the eyes two shoe buttons, does not trivialize Brayton's death but rather emphasizes Bierce's typical theme of the power of imaginative reality to triumph, sometime heroically, sometimes tragically, sometimes grotesquely, over everyday reality.

Bierce's most famous narrative play with the frozen moment of time and the power of imaginative reality is "An Occurrence at Owl Creek Bridge." The story explicitly and sardonically exploits the idea of the reader being pulled up short as Peyton Farquhar comes to the end of his rope and faces the ultimate and only genuine "natural end" possible—death. However, in this story death is forestalled in the only way it can be forestalled—through an act of the imagination and an elaborate bit of fiction-making that the reader initially takes to be reality.

The first part of the story, the only part in which the realistic convention suggests that something is "actually happening," seems static and dead, a still picture, formalized and stiff. At the end of part 1, the teller tips the reader off to the narrative necessity of time: "As these thoughts, which have here to be set down in words, were flashed into the doomed man's brain rather than evolved from it the captain nodded to the sergeant. The sergeant stepped aside." The self-reflexive reference here is to the most notorious characteristic of fiction—the impossibility of escaping time. In spite of the fact that the author wishes to communicate that which is instantaneous or timeless, he is trapped by the time-bound nature of words that can only be told one after another. This rhetorical acceptance of the nature of discourse motivates the final fantastic section of the story. Rather than being a cheap trick dependent on a shocking ending, "An Occurrence at Owl Creek Bridge" is a complex narrative reflecting both in its theme and its technique the essential truth that in discourse there is no ending but an imaginative, that is, an artificial, one.

Those late nineteenth century writers who have had the most influence on the short story in the twentieth century were the ones who not only wished to present so-called realistic content but also were aware of the importance of technique, pattern, and form. For example, Henry James argued (as Poe did before him) in his influential essay *The Art of Fiction* (1884) that a fictional work is a "living thing, all one and continuous, like any other organism, and in proportion as it lives will it be found . . . that in each of the parts there is something of each of the other parts."

An important fictional treatment of the tension between the "real" and artistic technique is James's famous story "The Real Thing." The artist in the story pays so much attention to the social stereotype that his models represent that he is unable to penetrate to the human reality beneath the surface. As James makes clear, however, in his preface to the story, as an artist, what he is interested in is the pattern or form of the work—its ability to transcend mere narrative and communicate something illustrative, something conceptual: "I must be very clear as to what is in this idea and what I wish to get out of it. . . . It must be an idea—it can't be a 'story' in the vulgar sense of the word. It must be a picture; it must illustrate something . . . something of the real essence of the subject."

Although James's artist in the story insists that he cherishes "human accidents" and that what he hates most is being ridden by a type, the irony of which James himself is aware is that the only way an artist can communicate character is to create a patterned picture that illustrates something; there is no such thing as a "human accident" in a story. As he argues in *The Art of Fiction*, a work of art is not a copy of life, but far different, "a personal, a direct impression of life." James says that the supreme virtue of a work of fiction is "the success with which the author has produced the illusion of life." The emphasis for James is on "impression" and "illusion"—both of which create and derive from artistic form and pattern.

James's focus on "impression" indicates an inevitable shift from realism as merely a kind of mirror held up to external reality to what is called either naturalism or verism, in which the focus was on the writer's reaction to that external reality. As critic Mark Schorer has pointed out, Hamlin Garland's "veritism" (or verism) differs from Howells's realism chiefly in its emphasis on impressionism and its insistence that fiction develop a form based on the moment of experience. Although the artist attempts to be perfectly true to life, there is always a tone or a color that comes unconsciously into his or her work, argues Garland. Garland's reputation rests particularly on his collection of short stories, *Main-Travelled Roads: Six Mississippi Valley Stories* (1891), of which the best-known stories are "The Return of the Private," "Mrs. Ripley's Trip," and "Under the Lion's Paw." Garland differs from many other local-color writers of the period in his avoidance of sentimentalism and his outrage at social injustices. Most critics suggest that the impressionism in his stories moves readers closer to the more powerful impressionism of Stephen Crane.

Many critics have claimed that Crane marks the true beginnings of the modern short story in the United States. It is Crane's impressionism—the combination of the subjectivity of Romanticism with the so-called objectivity of realism—that does most to effect this transition. The result is not an emphasis on reality communicated by the mere description and narration of events one after the other in a temporal fashion but rather reality suggested by moments of time frozen into a kind of spatial stasis by the impression of the perceiver. For the impressionist, reality cannot be separated from the superimposition of attitudes, emotions, and feelings of the perceiver.

One of Crane's best-known impressionistic stories is "The Blue Hotel," in which complex image patterns convey the formal and mechanical unreality of the events. The real issue, however, of unreality versus reality here centers on the character of the Swede. The irony of the story turns on the precipitating fact that the Swede, as a result of reading dime Western fiction, enters the hotel feeling that he will be killed there. This obsession that he has entered into a fictional world that has become real prevails until the hotel keeper, Scully, takes him upstairs and convinces him that the town is civilized and real, not barbaric and fictional. When the Swede returns, he is transformed; instead of being a stranger to the conventions that he thought existed in the hotel, he becomes familiar and at home with them, too much at home.

Perhaps the best way to understand the Swede's situation is to see the story as being about the blurring of the lines between the fictional world and the real world. Scully has convinced the Swede that what he thought was reality—the childlike world of the dime Western—was a game after all. Thus, the Swede decides to "play" the game. Indeed the card game forms the center of the story and leads to its violent climax, when the Swede, following the conventions of the Western novel, accuses Johnny of cheating, even though the game is "only for fun." The fight that follows is a conventional device of the dime Western.

The Swede wins because of the superiority of his new point of view: He can now self-consciously play the fictional game that Johnny and the others take seriously; while they rage with impotent anger, he only laughs. The final irony takes place when the Swede, still within the conventions of the game, leaves the hotel and enters a bar. When he tries to bully the gambler into drinking with him, the gambler, being a professional who does not play for fun, stabs the Swede, who falls with a "cry of supreme astonishment." Thus the Swede's premonition at the beginning of the story is fulfilled: His initial "error" about the place is not an error at all; it is a violent and barbaric world.

Willa Cather's "Paul's Case" also derives from the naturalist/impressionist approach favored by Crane. Like "The Blue Hotel," it is a story in which the world of the everyday and the world of the art work become tragically blurred. Paul has a "bad case" because he wishes to be a character in the world of art, but he is trapped in the everyday world of ordinary reality. The theme of "Paul's Case" is the realistic one of the squashing of the artist by a middle-class, bourgeois environment.

During the local-color movement, there was also a "return to Poe" by such critics as Brander Matthews and such writers as Frank R. Stockton and Ambrose Bierce. With these writers, the focus, as in Poe, was not on the ragged reality of the everyday but on the patterned reality or ironic story. The title of Brander Matthews's book *The Philosophy of the Short Story* (1901), however, indicates that he was as much influenced by Poe's "The Philosophy of Composition" as he was by his *Twice Told Tales* review. Perhaps Matthews believed that Poe was completely serious in his famous description of how he wrote "The Raven." Most Poe critics agree that while the raven in Poe's poem is brought to life by the creative imagination, in his after-the-fact justification of the poem, it is a stuffed and lifeless affair indeed. Matthews seemed to prefer the philosophy to the creation. As a result of his misreading of Poe, the short story in the early twentieth century came to be considered merely a question of taxidermy after all.

Even then, however, Matthews's formal rules for the genre might not have had such a disastrous effect if O. Henry had not had such great popular success with his formula stories at about the same time. The writers rushed to imitate O. Henry and the critics rushed to imitate Matthews, both with the same purpose in mind: popular financial success. Anyone could write short stories if he or she only knew the rules. J. Berg Esenwein's *Writing the Short Story* (1909), Carl H. Grabo's *The Art of the Short Story* (1913), and Blanche Colton Williams's *A Handbook on Story Writing* (1917) are only three of the countless such books published in the first twenty years of the twentieth century. Finally, the serious readers and critics called for an end to it, filling the quality periodicals with articles on the "decline," the "decay," and the "senility" of the short story. One critic, Gilbert Seldes, summed up the reaction at its most extreme in *The Dial* in 1922: "The American short story is by all odds the weakest, most trivial, most stupid, most insignificant art work produced in this country and perhaps in any country."

According to many critics, the most famous source of this formalization of the American short story was O. Henry—a local-colorist writer focusing on the city of New York who so emphasized the ironic pattern of his stories that his name has become associated with the formulaic short story. O. Henry's popularity and his output were unprecedented. By 1920, nearly five million copies of his books were sold in the United States. Ironically, while he was being soundly scolded by the serious critics in the United States, who preferred the more serious slice-of-life stories of the Russian writer Anton Chekhov, in Russia others were praising O. Henry for his mastery of the complex conventions of storytelling.

O. Henry poses the same problem for a history of the short story that Harte does, for as with Harte, O. Henry's influence far exceeds his excellence as a short-story writer. However, like Harte, O. Henry was the right man at the right time, a writer who pushed the well-made formal nature of the short story to its furthest extreme.

O. Henry wrote so many short stories so rapidly that he became the quintessential example of Edward O'Brien's accusation that the short story had become a machine-made product. However, his best-known stories are those that reflect the kind of reverse ending for which he was famous: "The Gift of the Magi," "Mammon and the Archer," "The Cop and the Anthem," "The Furnished Room," and "A Municipal Report." O. Henry is the writer with which Frederick Lewis Pattee ends his classic history of the development of the short story, citing him as the master of the "that reminds me of another" story, but a writer, for all his smooth slick style, of no depth, no thought, no philosophy, no moral complexity. The problem of O. Henry is that he is a master of technique and to cite him as a representative short-story writer is simply to say that technique is more important for the short story than these other aspects.

At the turn of the century the name O. Henry was synonymous with the short story as a form. For many readers still, the notion of what a short story is derives from the kind of trick or twist ending associated with such O. Henry stories as "The Gift of the Magi," a sentimental story about the poor young couple—he who sold his watch to buy combs for her long hair and she who sold her hair to a wig-maker to buy a chain for his gold watch. Not many O. Henry stories deal with serious issues in a serious way; they are either sentimental or else they are comically ironic. "The Cop and the Anthem" is of the latter kind, but just because it does not carry a heavy theme or a serious idea does not mean that it will not repay a close study.

The character of Soapy is as important to this story as its ironic structure, in which every action that he takes creates a reaction opposite to the one he wishes. The basic irony of the story is that as long as Soapy is "free," that is, loose in the city, he is not free at all, because of the coming winter. However, if he were in prison, he would indeed be "free" to enjoy life without fear. However, Soapy does not want something for nothing; he is willing to pay for his room and board by going to some effort to commit an act that, according to the law, will get him in jail. The ultimate irony is that Soapy, who does not want something for nothing and who goes to a great deal to get thrown into jail, finally does get thrown into jail for doing precisely nothing.

Stories during the latter part of the nineteenth century that succeed in sustaining the tradition of the Romantic short story and signify the transition to modernism of the new century are those that are concerned with the inner complex jungle of the psyche, such as the stories of Henry James, or the impressionistic symbolic world of violence and sensations such as the stories of Stephen Crane—not the stories by realist writers who focused on the social world.

In order to understand the shift that takes place between the end of the nineteenth century and the beginning of the 1920's—a period that marked a rebirth of the short-story form—one must look at the loss of confidence in the social codes during the period. Literary critics of the time suggested that the short stories of the nineteenth century, mainly action stories, depended on two basic faiths: that one can know right from wrong because a basic social code of values was taken for granted and that people were what they seemed to be.

In the twentieth century, argued critic Bonaro Wilkinson Overstreet, perhaps as a result of World War I, people have lost these faiths and consequently are "thrown back upon a study of human nature—human motives, fears, wants, prejudices." The drama of the twentieth century is "the drama of what goes on in the mind," and the short story is an "expert medium for the expression of our deep concern about human moods and motives." In his study of this transition to the modern short story, Austin Wright says that while the world of the nineteenth century was relatively stable with substantial agreement on the worth of society and social principles as moral guidance, the world of the 1920's was "fragmented both socially and morally," with each person obliged to find the appropriate principles for guidance. It is this distinctly modern world that the modern short story, ushered in by the publication of Sherwood Anderson's *Winesburg, Ohio* (1919), reflects.

France

Many critics argue that realism began in Europe with the publication of the first installment of Gustave Flaubert's *Madame Bovary* (1857; English translation, 1886). Later, in his best-known short fiction, "La Légende de Saint Julien l'Hospitalier" ("The Legend of St. Julian, Hospitaler"), Flaubert returned to the medieval saint's legend or folktale to find a model for both its character and its form. Flaubert's moral fable, however, differs from its medieval source by representing the static and frozen nature of the medieval story itself. The subject matter of Flaubert's story, although it has a moral issue at its center, is the method by which the medieval tale is made moral and illustrative. The events of the story are frozen into timelessness even as the storyteller relates them as if they were occurring in time. The story poses an answer to the primal question "What is the true self?" by structuring the two basic means by which one tries to find the self—that is, by assertion or by denial.

The transition from Flaubert to Maupassant is relatively easy to chart, for Flaubert was an important influence on Maupassant, reading his early work and encouraging him. In the decade between 1880 and 1890, Maupassant published more than three hundred short stories in a variety of modes, including the supernatural legend, the surprise-ending tale, and the realistic story. Although he is best known for such surprise-ending tales as "La Parure" ("The Necklace") and is most respected for such affecting realistic stories as "Boule de Suif" (ball of fat), Maupassant also contributed to the sophistication of the traditional horror story by pushing it even further than Poe into the modern mode of psychological obsession and madness. Maupassant got his start as a writer in much the same way that Chekhov in Russia and O. Henry in the United States did—by publishing anecdotal and ironic sketches or stories in that most ephemeral of media, the newspapers.

Maupassant's first full volume of short fiction appeared in 1881 under the title of his second important story, "La Maison Tellier" ("Madame Tellier's Establishment"), a comic piece about a group of prostitutes who attend a first Communion. After the success of this book, Maupassant published numerous stories in newspapers and periodicals, which were then reprinted in the volumes of his stories that began to appear at the rate of approximately two a year. Many of his stories created much controversy among the French critics of the time because he dared to focus on the experiences of so-called lowlife characters.

In addition to the realistic stories of the lower class, however, Maupassant experimented with mystery tales, many of which are reminiscent of the stories of Poe. Instead of depending on the supernatural, these stories focus on some mysterious dimension of reality, which is justified rationally by the central character. As a result, the reader is never quite sure whether this realm exists in actuality or whether it is a product of the obsessed mind of the narrator.

In 1884, Maupassant published his most famous short story, "La Parure," ("The Necklace") which has become one of the most famous short stories in any language. Indeed, it has become so famous that it is the story that most commonly comes to mind when Maupassant's name is mentioned, in spite of the fact that most critics agree that Maupassant's creation of tone and character in such stories as "Boule de Suif" and "Madame Tellier's Establishment" is much more representative of his genius than this ironically plotted, brief trick story about the woman who wasted her entire life to pay back a lost necklace, only to discover that it was fake.

"Le Horla" ("The Horla"), a story almost as famous as "The Necklace," focuses on the central character's intuition of a reality that surrounds human life but remains imperceptible to the senses. What makes the story distinctive is the increasing need of the narrator to account for his madness as caused by something external to himself. "The Horla" is a masterpiece of horror because it focuses so strongly on the mistaking of inner reality for outer reality, which is the very basis of hallucination.

Maupassant belongs with such innovators of the short-story form as Chekhov, Turgenev, Bierce, and O. Henry. On the one hand, like O. Henry, he mastered the ability to create the tight little ironic story that depends, as all short stories do, on the impact of the ending, but on the other hand he also had the ability, like Chekhov, to focus keenly on a limited number of characters in a luminous situation. Because of his ability to transform the short mystery tale from a primitive oral form based on legend into a sophisticated modern form in which mystery originates within the complex human mind, Maupassant is an important figure in the transition between the nineteenth century tale of the supernatural and the twentieth century short story of psychological obsession.

Germany

Although the French bias was that prose fiction is committed to deal with the actual world rather than the transcendental or the immanent, just the opposite assumption was growing in the nineteenth century in Germany. Many German critics argued that short fiction was the ideal form for the movement called "poetic realism," a phrase coined by Otto Ludwig to characterize that period between Romanticism and the beginning of naturalism in Germany—the 1830's through the 1880's. Poetic realism deals with the realm midway between objective truth and the patterned nature of reality; thus, it united naturalism's focus on the multiplicity of things and idealism's focus on abstract unity underlying the multiplicity. Poetic realism in Germany is simply another name for what was being called impressionism in France and the United States. What must be communicated by the art work is not simply the subject, as in Romanticism, or the object, as in realism, but rather the tone or atmosphere that creates the communication between the subject and the object.

Although Thomas Mann, the most important German fiction writer of this period, is best known for his novels, he began his career writing short fiction. His greatest work in this genre, *Der Tod in Venedig* (1912; *Death in Venice*, 1925), is particularly modern in its transformation of the temporal events of story into spatial reality by the device of the leitmotif, which Mann claims to have used in a directly musical way and which determines the whole mode of presentation of the work. The basic motifs of the story—mock action, significant encounter, transience of time, presence of death, nature of love—are repeated throughout in various guises. Moreover, the story is a classic example of short fiction's midway point between realism and myth, between external reality and subjective reality, as embodied in Aschenbach's yearning to escape the cold and rigid artwork into the passion and the impulsive life of experience itself. The story suggests that the experience that overtakes Aschenbach is one that is necessary to transform him from his inauthentic abstract self into the concrete but "messy" life of existential reality. Throughout the complex imagistic action that propels the story, Aschenbach begins to emerge as his own creation, one who has become transformed into a character in one of his own fictions; art, not an active life, has taken over the modeling of his features.

This basic conflict between the Romantic inclination toward fantasy and dream and the realist tendency toward the external world receives one of its most successful treatments in modern short fiction in Franz Kafka's *Die Verwandlung* (1915; *The Metamorphosis*, 1936). The extreme step that Kafka takes is to make the transformation of the psychic into the physical the precipitating premise from which the entire story follows. The only suspension of disbelief required in the story is that the reader accept the premise that Gregor Samsa awakes one morning from uneasy dreams to find himself transformed into a giant dung beetle. Once the reader accepts this event, the rest of the story is quite prosaic, quite detailed, and (with the exception of leaving the description of Gregor purposely vague) fully externalized. *The Metamorphosis* is an exemplar of the typical short-fiction effort to present an inner state of reality as a fantastic but real outer event. Thematically, the story also is exemplary, for it presents the little man who, by his very grotesqueness, challenges the other to love him. In his transformation of the details of everyday life into hallucination and nightmare, Kafka is the prototype of the modern tendency in short fiction to challenge the realist assumption of what reality is by pushing it to grotesque extremes.

Russia

Although modern short fiction in Russia begins with Fyodor Dostoevski and Leo Tolstoy, it reaches its complete maturity with Anton Chekhov. Dostoevski's most influential short fiction, *Zapiski iz podpolya* (1864; *Notes from the Underground*, 1918), reflects the modern transition to an existential philosophy and an impressionistic technique by being structured in two parts to represent the two basic means by which one tries to know the self: introspection and narrative. It reverses the Socratic injunction that the unexamined life is not worth living to suggest the Hamlet theme—that the intensely examined life is unlivable. The basic theme of Tolstoy's "Smert Ivana Ilicha" (1886; "The Death of Ivan Ilyich," 1887) is made clear in the classic syllogism: "Ivan Ilyich is a man. All men are mortal. Therefore, Ivan Ilyich is mortal." In its transformation of this abstract syllogism into a concrete reality, however, the story also reflects the modern short fiction combination of the conceptual and the concrete. Indeed, it is about the transformation of Ivan himself from abstract man into concrete man.

The most influential figure in the development of modern short fiction in Russia, and in many ways in the world at large, is Chekhov. Chekhov's short stories were first welcomed in England and the United States just after the turn of the century as examples of late nineteenth century realism, but since they did not embody the social commitment or political convictions of the realistic novel, they were termed "realistic" primarily because they seemed to focus on fragments of everyday reality. Consequently, they were characterized as "sketches," "slices of life," "cross-sections of Russian life," and were often said to be lacking those elements that constitute a really good short story. At the same time, however, other critics saw that Chekhov's ability to dispense with a striking incident, his impressionism, and his freedom from the literary conventions of the highly plotted and formalized story marked the beginnings of a new or "modern" kind of short fiction that combined the specific detail of realism with the poetic lyricism of Romanticism.

The Chekhovian shift to the "modern" short story is marked by a transition from the Romantic focus on a projective fiction, in which characters are functions in an essentially code-bound parabolic or ironic structure, to an apparently realistic episode in which plot is subordinate to "as-if-real" character. Chekhov's fictional figures, however, are not realistic in the way that characters in the novel usually are. The short story is too short to allow for character to be created by the multiplicity of detail and social interaction typical of the novel.

Once it is seen that the short story, by its very shortness, cannot deal with the denseness of detail and the duration of time typical of the novel but rather focuses on a revelatory breakup of the rhythm of everyday reality, one can see how the form, striving to accommodate "realism" at the end of the nineteenth century, focused on an experience under the influence of a particular mood and therefore depended more on tone than on plot as a principle of unity—all of which led to the significant impressionistic influence.

Although Chekhov's conception of the short story as a lyrically charged fragment in which characters are less fully rounded realistic figures than embodiments of mood has influenced all twentieth century practitioners of the form, his most immediate impact has been on the three writers of the early 1920's who have received the most critical attention for fully developing the so-called modern short story: Joyce, Katherine Mansfield, and Sherwood Anderson.

The most obvious similarity between the stories of Chekhov and those of Joyce, Anderson, and Mansfield is their minimal dependence on the traditional notion of plot and their focus instead on a single situation in which everyday reality is broken up by a crisis. Typical of Chekhov's minimalist stories is the often-anthologized "Misery," in which the rhythm of the old cabdriver's everyday reality is suggested by his two different fares, a rhythm that Iona himself tries to break up with the news that his son is dead. The story would indeed be only a sketch if Iona did not tell his story to his uncomprehending little mare at the end, for what the story communicates is the comic and pathetic sense of the incommunicable nature of grief itself. Iona "thirsts for speech," wants to talk of the death of his son "properly, with deliberation." He is caught by the primal desire to tell a story of the breakup of his everyday reality that will express the irony he senses and that, by being deliberate and detailed, will both express his grief and control it. In this sense, "Misery" is a lament—a controlled objectification of grief and its incommunicable nature by the presentation of deliberate details.

The story therefore illustrates one of the primary contributions that Chekhov made to the modern short story—the expression of a complex inner state by the presentation of selected concrete details rather than either by a parabolic form or by the depiction of the mind of the character. Significant reality for Chekhov is inner rather than outer reality, but the problem he tried to solve is how to create an illusion of inner reality by focusing only on external details. The answer for Chekhov, and thus for the modern short story generally, was to find an event that, if expressed "properly"—that is, by the judicious choice of relevant details—embodied the complexity of the inner state. T. S. Eliot later termed such a technique an "objective correlative"—a detailed event, description, or characterization that served as a sort of objectification or formula for the emotion sought. Modern short-story writers after Chekhov made the objective correlative the central device in their development of the form.

Such Chekhov stories as "Sleepy" and "The Bishop" make use of another significant modern short-story technique: focusing on reality as an ambiguous mixture of the psychic and the external. "Sleepy" marks a sort of realistic halfway point between the symbolic use of the hypnagogic state by Poe and its being pushed to surrealistic extremes by Kafka. Chekhov presents a basically realistic situation of the young Varka being literally caught in a hypnagogic state between desirable sleep and undesirable reality. The two realms blend indistinguishably in her mind until the hallucination takes over completely and she strangles the baby so she can sleep as "soundly as the dead." Although the irony of the ending is obvious, it is the hypnotic rhythm of the events and the hallucinatory images blending dream and reality that make the story a significant treatment of the short-story device of dissolving the rhythm of everyday reality into the purely psychic.

Chekhov's adoption of such an impressionistic point of view is what makes him both a master of the short story and an innovator of its modernity. Critic Peter Stowell has made a strong case for understanding Chekhov's modernism as a result of his impressionistic point of view. The ambiguous and tenuous nature of experience perceived by the impressionist, says Stowell, "drives the author to render perceptually blurred bewilderment, rather than either the subject or the object." What is rendered, says Stowell, is the mood and atmosphere that exists between perceiver and perceived, subject and object. In this way, impressionism and modernism become synonymous terms.

Like Chekhov, both Anderson and Joyce focus on the central themes of isolation and the need for human sympathy and the moral failure of inaction that dominate the modernist movement in the early twentieth century; both abjure highly plotted stories in favor of seemingly static episodes and "slices" of reality; both depend on unity of feeling to create a sense of "storyness"; and both establish a sense of the seemingly casual out of that which is deliberately patterned, creating significance out of the trivial by judicious selection of detail and meaningful ordering of the parts. The result is an objective-ironic style that has characterized the modern short story up to the present day. It is a style that, even as it seems realistic on its surface, in fact emphasizes the radical difference between the routine of everyday reality and the incisive nature of story itself as the only means to know true reality. Contemporary short-story writers push this Chekhovian realization to even more aesthetic extremes.

It is with Chekhov that the short story was liberated from its adherence to the parabolic exemplum and fiction generally was liberated from the tedium of the realistic novel. With Chekhov, the short story took on a new respectability and began to be seen as the most appropriate narrative form to reflect the modern temperament. There can be no understanding of the short story as a genre without an understanding of Chekhov's contribution to the form. Conrad Aiken's assessment of him in 1921 has yet to be challenged: "possibly the greatest writer of the short story who has ever lived."

England and Ireland

The English, with the exception of modern Irish writers, have never excelled in the short-story form. The reason may have something to do with the English attitude toward a cohesive society. Critic and literary historian Lionel Stevenson has suggested that as soon as a culture becomes more complex, brief narratives expand or "agglomerate" and thus cause the short story to lose its identity. The fragmentation of sensibility necessary for the development of the short story did not set in in England until about 1880, at which time the form came to the fore as the best medium for presenting it. As another critic, Wendell Harris, has noted, with the fragmentation of sensibility, perspective (or "angle of vision") becomes most important in fiction, especially in the short story, in which instead of a world to enter, as in the novel, the form presents a vignette to contemplate. The essence of the short story, says Harris, "is to isolate, to portray the individual person, or moment, or scene in isolation—detached from the great continuum—at once social and historical. . . . The short story is a natural form for the presentation of a moment whose intensity makes it seem outside the ordinary stream of time . . . or outside the ordinary range of experience."

It is an interesting irony that the 1890's, the period which H. G. Wells called "The Golden Age" of the short story in England, derived, although in an indirect way, from Poe; for it was Poe who inspired Charles Baudelaire, who in turn inspired the Symbolist movement, which ultimately gave impetus to the development of the short story during this period. For Poe, and later for Baudelaire and the aesthetes, the "art" of the story itself was what was important in life, and life was important because of art's ability to make matter and events meaningful.

Increasingly, the view that art should deemphasize the social and emphasize the formal dominated what critics have called the "state of mind" that was the 1890's in English literature. Short fiction of the so-called *fin de siècle* exemplifies this view in various ways, from the allegory of George Gissing's "House of Cobwebs" to the parable form of Arthur Symons's "Christian Trevalga," and from the aesthetic embodiment of Ernest Dowson's "The Dying of Francis Donne" to the satiric shaft of Max Beerbohm's "A. V. Laider."

Gissing's best-known story, "House of Cobwebs," is primarily an allegory of the artist. Through the symbol of the house of decay and cobwebs, with its choking artichokes, Gissing suggests that the artist cannot survive the middle-class world of the realists. Symons's "Christian Trevalga" is a parable of the artist who carries the theories of Stéphane Mallarmé to their ultimate conclusions, for Christian reaches a state of music without sound just as Mallarmé desired to reach a state of literature without words.

Dowson's "The Dying of Francis Donne" and Beerbohm's "A. V. Laider" represent two opposite extremes of the short fiction of the *fin de siècle*. Dowson suggests the period's morbid self-consciousness, and Beerbohm reflects its final ability to mock itself satirically. The famous story to which "The Dying of Francis Donne" is likely to be compared is Tolstoy's "The Death of Ivan Ilyich." Unlike the middle-class Ivan, however, for whom the process is ironically the only "living" he has ever experienced, Francis Donne is a doctor, a "student" of life and death. Moreover, as opposed to Ivan, for whom awareness of death begins with the absurd act of bumping his side while hanging drapes, Donne's awareness begins with his diagnostic and reasoning ability. Beerbohm's "A. V. Laider" is a clever and well-constructed manipulation of the conventions of storytelling. The story is similar in its use of story-telling as the basis of a trick played on the reader to Twain's "The Celebrated Jumping Frog of Calaveras County" and Saki's "The Open Window." Such stories lay bare by means of parody one of the form's essential characteristics: the projection of an imaginative reality that can only temporarily be taken to be real.

Another short-fiction form popular in England at the beginning of the twentieth century is the ghost story or mystery story. However, as Algernon Blackwood, one of the most influential of the mystery story writers, has made clear, the primary interest of these writers was not the ghost story as such but rather stories of extended consciousness. "My fundamental interest," said Blackwood, "is signs and proofs of other powers that lie hidden in us all; the extension, in other words, of human faculty." Fiction writers who hold to such a vision are more often likely to be short-story writers than novelists and not merely writers of the so-called supernatural story. Whereas novelists are most likely to build on the assumption that everyday reality is primary reality, true reality for the short-story writer is more often a function of the imagination.

H. P. Lovecraft has called "The Willows" the foremost Blackwood tale, an opinion with which many critics of the supernatural story agree, seeing it as typical of Blackwood's thematic structure of having an average man, through a "flash of terror or beauty," experience something beyond the sensory reality of the everyday. The ambiguity, as is usually the case in nineteenth century short fiction, stems from whether one understands the experience to be external or internal—that is, whether it actually occurs in the world of the story or the events are hallucinated by the character.

The best-known story of Lord Dunsany (Edward John Moreton Drax Plunkett), "The Ghosts," is a self-conscious parody of the ghost story, for it makes explicit the conventions and rules of the genre. As is typical of such parodies, the story depends on the conventions of its generic models even as it mocks them. For example, "The Ghosts" begins with a traditional description of the conventional ghost-story setting—an old house surrounded by whispering cedars and encrusted with antiquity. The problem here is to determine what ontological status the ghosts maintain: Are they real and thus manifestations of the place, or are they manifestations of the hallucinatory state of the protagonist?

To move from the stories of Dunsany to those of Saki (H. H. Munro) is to move from the world of story as a means to parody story to a world in which story is presented as a joke, sometimes a bitter joke, but a joke nevertheless. Saki may very well mark a decided shift in Edwardian short fiction to the trick-ending story that dominates popular short stories both in England and in the United States at the turn of the century. Saki's most anthologized story, "The Open Window," is a particularly clear and simple example of foregrounding the process of story itself, for what makes "The Open Window" work is the uncertainty, felt both by the protagonist and by the reader, about the nature of the story that they are listening to or reading. The dramatized storyteller is the typical Saki artist who manipulates the reader into various possibilities about the genre of the story, only to reveal that the story is about the process of turning fantasy into supposed fact and that it is fantasy after all.

In his study of the short story, Walter Allen calls Walter de la Mare the most distinguished of the writers who made the Edwardian age a "haunted period" in English literature. Part of the reason for this is the "dignity" of the poetry of de la Mare as opposed to what is often called the "crude gothicism" of his contemporaries. Lord David Cecil calls de la Mare a Symbolist for whom the outer world is only an "incarnation of an internal drama." He says that de la Mare is concerned with the most profound human issues, particularly the central issue of whether the world has any objective existence or is a reflection of the mind, which alters, depending on the mood and character of the observer. For de la Mare, only the imagination makes reality significant, and what is called external reality itself is like a dream. All these characteristics, which are actually characteristics of the short-story genre itself, can be seen most readily in de la Mare's best-known and most anthologized story, "The Riddle," a delicate fable about the passing of youth.

It is no coincidence that the first British writer to be recognized as a specialist in the short story is also the champion of the romance form in the latter part of the nineteenth century. Nor is it coincidence that this short-story specialist was one of the first British short-fiction writers to focus, as did Henry James, on technique and form rather than on content alone. The writer is Robert Louis Stevenson, and many critics suggest that it is with his work that the true modern short story began in England. Both Lionel Stevenson and Walter Allen say that the watershed for the modern short story began in 1878 with the publication of "A Lodging for the Night," with Allen going so far as to say that the change to the specifically modern short story can be precisely dated at that point.

Like his fellow romance writer in the United States, Ambrose Bierce, Stevenson urges that literature, when it is in its most typical mode of narrative, flees from external reality and pursues "an independent and creative aim." For Stevenson, the work of art exists not by its resemblance to life, "but by its immeasurable difference from life." Such an awareness was indeed essential before what critics call the "modern short story" could become possible in the nineteenth century.

"A Lodging for the Night" is a strange candidate for a landmark story that marks the shift to modern short fiction. Although it is highly detailed and focuses on a specific time-limited situation, it poses more questions about its status than clear answers. The secret of the story's ambiguous mixture of horror and amusement depends solely on the nature of the poet Villon, who alternates between attending to the immediate concerns of life to assure his own preservation and taking an amused and distant view of reality to indicate his own broad view of life. Villon survives not only because of his concern with immediate things but also because he can take such an ironic view of life and death. What Stevenson has done here is to create a story about the artist who transforms reality into art stuff; the story is an exercise in this seeming paradox, indicating that reality must be dealt with both in terms of practical existence and in terms of the ambiguous mixture of amusement and horror, for life and death must be mocked in order to transform them into art at all.

Although Stevenson is the first British writer to build his career on the short-story form, Rudyard Kipling is the first to stimulate a considerable amount of criticism, much of it adverse, because of his short fiction. Much of the negative criticism that Kipling has received, however, is precisely the same kind of criticism that has often been lodged against the short-story form in general—for example, that it focuses only on episodes, that it is too concerned with technique, that it is too dependent on tricks, and that it often lacks a moral force. Lionel Trilling notes that the words "craft" and "craftily" are Kipling's favorites, and Edmund Wilson says that it is the paradox of his career that he "should have extended the conquests of his craftsmanship in proportion to the shrinking of the range of his dramatic imagination. As his responses to human beings became duller, his sensitivity to his medium increased."

Kipling's best-known stories—"The Man Who Would Be King," "Without Benefit of Clergy," "Mary Postgate," and "The Gardener"—are perfect representations of the transition point between the old-fashioned tale of the nineteenth century and the modern short story—a transition, however, that Joseph Conrad, because of the profundity of his vision, perhaps was better able to make than Kipling. Many critics have suggested that "The Man Who Would Be King" is one of Kipling's most Conrad-like stories but lament that Kipling evades the metaphysical issues implicit in the story and refuses to venture on the great generalizations forced upon Conrad in "Heart of Darkness." Although "The Man Who Would Be King" does not contain the philosophic generalizations of Conrad's tale, nor perhaps is it as subtle a piece of Symbolist fiction, nevertheless, it is a coherent piece of fabular fiction carefully constructed and thematically significant.

The story focuses primarily on the crucial difference between a tale told by a narrator who merely reports a story and a narrator who lives a story. The frame narrator is a journalist whose job it is to report the doings of "real kings," whereas Peachey, the inner narrator, has as his task the reporting of the events of a "fictional king," telling a story of two characters who project themselves out of the "as-if" real world of the frame tale into the purely projected and fictional world of their adventure. The fact that Peachey and Davrot are really only overdetermined double figures is indicated not only by Peachey's reference to himself as suffering Davrot's fate but also by the fact that if Davrot is the ambiguous god-man, then it is Peachey who must be crucified. Kipling finds it necessary to make this split, for not only must he have his god-man die, but also he must have him resurrected as well. Peachey is the resurrected figure who brings back the head of Davrot, still with its crown, and tells the tale to the narrator. Peachey's final madness and death and the mysterious disappearance of the crowned head climax a story that embodies a complex symbolic pattern.

Most critics agree, however, that it is Joseph Conrad who creates the true modern Symbolist tale. Conrad argued that fiction must aspire to the magic suggestiveness of music, that explicitness was fatal to art, for it robs it of all suggestiveness. This is the basis of Conrad's impressionism, an impressionism that begins with Crane in the United States and is later extended by Anderson, Mansfield, and Joyce. Conrad has said that his best stories resulted from his attempt to give a story a "sinister romance, a tonality of its own, a continued vibration that . . . would hang on the air and dwell on the ear after the last note had been struck." One of Conrad's most famous impressionistic and symbolist stories is "The Secret Sharer."

Making the psychological theme of the double plausible is the central problem in Conrad's "The Secret Sharer," for the double is not only projected outside the protagonist but also dramatized in the story as an external self who has been involved in a crime apart from the protagonist and whose crime is at the core of the moral issue facing him. The story itself is split between the plot, which focuses on the stranger and the captain's efforts to protect and conceal him, and the mind of the captain, who obsessively persists in perceiving and describing the stranger Leggatt as his other self, his double. The story also depends on metaphorical details, which suggest that Leggatt has been summoned forth from the captain's unconscious as an aspect of the self with which he must deal. Although it can be said that Leggatt represents some aspect of the captain's personality that he must integrate—instinctive behavior rather than the Hamlet-like uncertainty he experiences on his first command—it is more probable that he is brought on board to make explicit and dramatically concrete the dual workings of the captain's mind, which distract him and tear him apart. This creation of an "as-if" real character to embody what are essentially psychic processes marks the impressionistic extension of the trend that began the short-story form during the Romantic period.

Like Chekhov, whom she greatly admired, Katherine Mansfield was often accused of writing sketches instead of stories, because her works did not manifest the plotted action of nineteenth century short fiction. The best-known Mansfield story similar in technique and theme to the typical Chekhov story is "The Fly." The external action of the story is extremely slight. The unnamed "boss" is visited by a retired friend whose casual mention of the boss's dead son makes him aware of his inability to grieve. The story ends with the boss idly dropping ink on a fly until it dies, whereupon he flings it away. Like Chekhov's "Misery," the story is about the nature of grief, and like Chekhov's story, "The Fly" maintains a strictly objective point of view, allowing the details of the story to communicate the latent significance of the boss's emotional state.

Mansfield, however, differs from her mentor Chekhov by placing more dependence on the fly itself, as a symbol of the death of the boss's grief, his own manipulated son, or the trivia of life that distracts one from feeling. Moreover, instead of focusing on the inarticulate nature of grief that goes deeper than words, "The Fly" seems to emphasize the transitory nature of grief; regardless of how much the boss would like to hold on to his grief for his son, he finds it increasingly difficult to maintain such feelings. Such an inevitable loss of grief does not necessarily suggest that the boss's feelings for his son are negligible; rather, it suggests a subtle aspect of grief—that it either flows naturally or else must be self-consciously and artificially sought after. The subtle way that Mansfield communicates the complexity of the boss's emotional situation by the seemingly irrelevant conversation between the boss and his old acquaintance and by his apparently idle toying with the fly is typical of the Chekhovian device of allowing objective detail to communicate complex states of feeling.

Critics of the short story such as H. E. Bates and Frank O'Connor have suggested that the modern Irish short story began with George Moore's publication of *The Untilled Field* in 1903. Others have concurred with Moore's own typically immodest assessment that the collection was a "frontier book, between the new and the old style" of fiction. One can certainly agree with critics that the stories seem unique for their time in combining the content of French naturalism with the concern for style of the *fin de siècle* aesthetics. Moore's view is that reality itself must be understood via story. This need to understand reality by means of story can be clearly seen in Moore's best-known and most anthologized work from *The Untilled Field*, "Julia Cahill's Curse," for it is a fairly clear example of Moore's effort to use the folktale mode as a means to understand social reality.

The basic situation of the tale is that of a story being told by a driver to the first-person narrator, who, on hearing the name Julia Cahill, urges the driver to tell him her story. The story, which indeed constitutes the bulk of "Julia Cahill's Curse," is of an event that took place twenty years earlier, when the priest Father Madden had Julia put out of the parish and consequently Julia put a curse on the parish that every year a roof would fall in and a family would go to America. The basic conflict in the tale is between Julia, who in her dancing and courting represents free pagan values, and the priest, who, in his desire to restrain Julia, represents church control of such freedom.

The conflict between Julia and the priest is clear enough, but it is the relationship between the teller and the listener that constitutes the structural interest of the story, for what the tale is really about is the nature of story used to understand social reality. The story is an actual event of social reality that has been mythicized by the teller and thus by the village folk both to explain and to justify the breakdown of Irish parish life in the late nineteenth century. The teller of the tale believes that the desertion of the parish is a consequence of Julia's curse. The listener of the tale does not believe in the curse in this literal way but, as he says, for the moment he too believes it, at least in some way that is not made explicit. It is the nature of the belief that constitutes the difference and thus the significance of the story. What Moore does here is to present a story that is responded to within the story itself in both the old way and the new way—that is, as a literal story of magic and as a symbolic story to account for the breakdown of the parish life, the tension between pagan freedom and Church control.

The typically modern theme of presenting the predominance of the inner life of imagination over that of the everyday can be seen in almost a paradigmatic form in "The Clerk's Quest." Although in the "old" romance story, everyday reality is broken up by the intrusion of the supernatural, in the modern story, it is often accident, and trivial accident at that, which creates the disruption of the rhythm of everyday reality. In a self-consciously economical prose style, Moore makes it clear that it is the "slight accident" of a perfumed cheque that destroys Dempsey's "well-ordered and closely-guarded life."

Indeed, the story is a self-conscious modern version of the chivalric romance story as the clerk gives up everything to go on his sacred quest, wandering through the countryside with presents of diamonds for the ideal stimulated by a cheque which smells of heliotrope. The mood of romantic fantasy and the ironic tone of parody of chivalric romance are completely sustained and self conscious. At the conclusion of the story, the reader is torn between humor and pathos at the absurdity of the little clerk's quest as well as at its chivalric romanticism. The tragicomic result is not unlike that achieved by Chekhov, Anderson, Joyce, and Mansfield, who similarly present insignificant characters caught in a breakup of the routine of reality. The difference, here, however, is that Moore more obviously parodies the old romantic story, creating a "new" realistic version of the "old" romance form. As a result, he prepares the way for the modern technique of Joyce, who pushes the trivial and seemingly inconsequential realistic story to more subtle epiphanic extremes in the collection of short stories in Anglo-Irish literature that marks the end of the nineteenth century short-fiction tradition, *Dubliners* (1914).

Joyce's most famous contribution to the theory and technique of modern narrative is his notion of the "epiphany," which he explicitly defined in his novel *Stephen Hero* (1944):

> By an epiphany he meant a sudden spiritual manifestation, whether in the vulgarity of speech or of gesture or in a memorable phrase of the mind itself. He believed that it was for the man of letters to record these epiphanies with extreme care, seeing that they themselves are the most delicate and evanescent of moments.

In a Joyce story, and in many stories by other writers since Joyce, an epiphany is a formulation through metaphor or symbol of some revelatory aspect of human experience, some highly significant aspect of personal reality; it is usually communicated by a pattern of what otherwise would be seen as meaningless details and events.

Although any story in *Dubliners* would serve as an illustration of this epiphanic technique, Joyce's most famous story, "The Dead," makes it quite clear. The primary movement is from the objective world in part 1 to the lyrical quality created after Gabriel and his wife leave the party. This is paralleled by a movement in Gabriel himself from self-assertion to self-effacement. Concrete details predominate through the first two-thirds of the story, as everyday life seems to be fully embodied in the Christmas party. It is only in the last third, when Gabriel's life is transformed, first by his romantic and sexual fantasy about his wife and then by his confrontation with love and death, that the reader reflects on the story and perceives that the concrete life in the earlier sections repeatedly revealed hints of death. Only after Gabriel's epiphany, his true vision of his former self as death in life, does the reader perceive the concrete details and trivial remarks of the earlier portion as symbolically meaningful. The lyrical and symbol-laden language of the final section of the story casts a new light on the trivial details and comments of the earlier part. The story illustrates how in short fiction only the end makes what went before meaningful. Since the ultimate end is death, Gabriel's awareness and acceptance of it is the ultimate epiphany, the sacred realization that transforms the trivial into the meaningful.

Conclusion

The first one hundred years of the short story divides into two almost equal periods: the movement from Romanticism to realism between 1820 and 1880 and the movement from realism to impressionism between 1880 and 1920. It is less a straight line of development from Washington Irving's *The Sketch Book of Geoffrey Crayon, Gent.* (1819-1820) to Sherwood Anderson's *Winesburg, Ohio* than it is a one-hundred-year cycle, for it is a movement from the Romantic subjectifying of the old story form in the early part of the century to the realistic emphasis on objective reality in the latter part, and finally a return to the subjectifying of the objective world at the turn of the century. It is this return to Romanticism that marks the beginning of what is now known as modernism.

Charles E. May

BIBLIOGRAPHY

Bierce, Ambrose. "The Short Story." In *The Collected Works of Ambrose Bierce*. New York: Gordian Press, 1966. Bierce criticizes William Dean Howells and the realistic school for their prosaic and pedestrian realism which fails to perceive the mystery of human life.

Current-García, Eugene. *O. Henry: A Study of the Short Fiction*. New York: Twayne, 1993. Focuses on O. Henry's frequent themes, his romanticism, and his narrative techniques, such as his use of the tall-tale conventions. Includes critical excerpts from discussions of O. Henry by other critics.

Davidson, Cathy N. *The Experimental Fictions of Ambrose Bierce: Structuring the Ineffable*. Lincoln: University of Nebraska Press, 1984. Examines how Bierce blurs distinctions between external reality and imaginative reality in many of his most important short stories.

Fusco, Richard. *Maupassant and the American Short Story: The Influence of Form at the Turn of the Century*. University Park: Pennsylvania State University Press, 1994. Discusses seven different short-story forms in Maupassant's stories: linear, ironic coda, surprise-inversion, loop, descending helical, contrast, and sinusoidal. Discusses Maupassant's influence on Ambrose Bierce, O. Henry, Kate Chopin, and Henry James.

Gerber, Philip. *Willa Cather*. Rev. ed. New York: Twayne, 1995. Discusses the major themes of the experience of the artist and life in rural Nebraska in major Cather short stories.

Koloski, Bernard. *Kate Chopin: A Study of the Short Fiction*. New York: Twayne, 1996. Discusses Chopin's short stories in the context of her bilingual and bicultural imagination; provides readings of her most important stories.

Marchalonis, Shirley, ed. *Critical Essays on Mary Wilkins Freeman*. Boston: G. K. Hall, 1991. A collection of essays ranging from early reviews to a number of essays influential in starting a revival of interest in Freeman's stories.

THE MID-TWENTIETH CENTURY: 1920-1960

Because storytelling is inherent in human nature, stories have existed throughout history. For a long time, short fiction was considered the poor relation of the novel. In the nineteenth century, however, the short story and its longer relative, the novelette or novella, were shaped as distinct art forms by Heinrich von Kleist, E. T. A. Hoffmann, Edgar Allan Poe, Nathaniel Hawthorne, Nikolai Gogol, and Guy de Maupassant. A break with the traditional stress on plotting came in the late nineteenth and early twentieth centuries, particularly with the stories of Anton Chekhov and Joseph Conrad, James Joyce and D. H. Lawrence, Franz Kafka, and Ernest Hemingway.

Chekhov and Joyce can properly be called the progenitors of most twentieth century short fiction. Chekhov renders experience obliquely, by an apparently aimless arrangement of casual incidents, suggesting and implying rather than climaxing and commenting. His endings are no longer the inevitable locus of surprise or value judgment. He breaks the heroic mold with many of his characters, often dealing with lonely recluses, shy fantasists, ridiculous yet tenderhearted weaklings. Joyce sometimes places his climaxes in the middle rather than the end of his stories, during sudden moments of revelation, which he calls "epiphanies." His style is highly pictorial, presenting the reader with a series of vivid images in an incantatory, lyrical prose, sometimes hypnotically repetitive, subtly and suitably modulated. The prevailing tone of his tales is one of poetic naturalness that can transmute the drabness of common life into moments of haunting beauty and poignant compassion.

After World War I, most distinguished writers of short fiction minimized plotting, believing that a careful arrangement of events toward conflict and resolution would work against the faithfulness and expressiveness of their rendering of life. They have preferred the creation of memorable characters (William Faulkner's "A Rose for Emily," Eudora Welty's "Why I Live at the P.O."), the evocation of mood and atmosphere (Hemingway's "Hills Like White Elephants," Lawrence's "The Horse Dealer's Daughter"), the uncharted recesses of the internal landscape (Katherine Anne Porter's "Old Mortality," Colette's "Chéri"), myth and fantasy (Faulkner's "The Bear," John Cheever's "The Enormous Radio," Isak Dinesen's "The Sailor-Boy's Tale," Isaac Bashevis Singer's "The Gentleman from Cracow"), the dramatization of deep emotions (Saul Bellow's "Seize the Day," Isaac Babel's "The Death of Dolgushov," Yukio Mishima's "Patriotism"). Metaphor and symbol, point of view, and the reliability or dubiousness of narrators grow in importance as writers seek to create fiction of complexity and sophistication.

A note about the form of short fiction called the novelette or novella or simply the short novel: It is a prose narrative longer than even long short stories yet considerably briefer than a full-length novel, consisting of fifteen thousand to fifty thousand words. As a rule, the novella moves along a single line of action, whereas a novel develops an extended series of actions that often include subplots. The novella has room for only a few characters and confines itself to a short span of time, while the rhythm of its narration is tight and exclusive, concentrating on an arc of behavior that has symbolic significance. The form encourages, as in Faulkner's "The Bear," Thomas Mann's "Mario and the Magician," and Bellow's "Seize the Day," treatment of profound philosophic or ethical issues.

The United States

Sherwood Anderson's *Winesburg, Ohio* (1919) appeared almost exactly one hundred years after the publication of Washington Irving's *The Sketchbook of Geoffrey Crayon, Gent.* (1819-1820). In that hundred-year period the short-story form changed from primarily a folktale and fable genre to a form that focuses more on lyric moments of realization than linear events. Critics have noted the influence of impressionism and post-impressionism on the stories in *Winesburg, Ohio*, pointing out that the narratives are based on the flow of feeling and impressions rather than time; their structure is psychological rather than chronological. A series of thematically and symbolically related images rather than temporal plot holds Anderson's stories together and gives them their sense of reality. In his memoirs Anderson said, "There are no plot stories in life."

"Hands" is a central example of Anderson's development of what critics have called the modern lyrical story. Instead of being dependent on a straightforward plot line, the story revolves around the central image of hands in such a way that the main character is revealed by various reactions to them. The story focuses on Wing Biddlebaum, a "fat little old man" who lives alone in Winesburg and is befriended only by George Willard, a young reporter for the local newspaper who serves as the major linking device in the stories. Biddlebaum is a former schoolteacher who was driven out of another town twenty years earlier because he, quite innocently, "touched" the young boys in his class. However, as Anderson says, the real story of Wing Biddlebaum is "a story of hands."

Anderson laments throughout the story that revealing the secret of Biddlebaum's hands is a job for a poet. Thus, as a prose writer he struggles with the problem of trying to communicate something subtle and delicate with words that are coarse and clumsy, for all he has to work with are the tools of story—event and explanation. What he needs is a way to use language, the way the poet does, to transcend language. This inadequacy of language is why the central metaphor of this story is Biddlebaum's "talking with hands." However, what Biddlebaum aspires to is not hands but, as the name given to him by some obscure poet of the town suggests, "wings," which enable one, like the poet, to fly. The use of hands as a central image also suggests many other implications in the story, such as the magic of "laying on of hands," the injunction to "keep your hands off," and the need to maintain "clean hands."

At the end of "Hands," when Biddlebaum is performing the mundane task of picking up crumbs, the gesture is transformed into a spiritual act. This technique is similar to the stories of Chekhov, Katherine Mansfield and Joyce, in which intangible spiritual desires and feelings are either contaminated by the material, or the material to communicate them.

Many critics consider William Faulkner to be the greatest American fiction writer of the twentieth century. His range of effects, philosophical weight, originality of style, mythic grandeur, variety of characterization, and tragic intensity are without equal among modern authors in the United States. As a short-fiction writer, he is, however, uneven. Since his novels did not sell well until the late 1940's, he had to grind out many short stories for periodical publication to keep food on the table, and some of them are potboilers; others are, however, superb.

No land in fiction lives more vividly on the printed page than Faulkner's mythical Yoknapatawpha County, whose twenty-four hundred square miles are located in his native Mississippi and whose population spills in and out of his works, intimately known and traced through complex interrelations. This territory is not only realistically rendered but also mythically interpreted, with Faulkner considering the white settlers of the land as self-doomed by the curse of chattel slavery.

Faulkner's most celebrated story, "The Bear," is a novella that was published as the centerpiece of a collection, *Go Down, Moses* (1942). He insisted on regarding the collection as a novel, even though the book's organic unity is debatable. The narrative opens with Isaac ("Ike") McCaslin, a sixteen-year-old youth, guided by part-Indian, part-black Sam Fathers and accepted into a party of expert hunters. The tale maneuvers back and forth in Ike's life to develop and emphasize his maturation, as he measures himself against an immense, apparently immortal bear of the same age. The annual hunt of the bear, Old Ben, is a ritual, since none of the pursuers believes that he can actually kill the great animal, which embodies the wilderness. A great mongrel dog, Lion, is tamed by Sam Fathers and is taught to hunt; he manages to hold Old Ben at bay for a few moments. A year later, Lion traps the bear long enough for one of the hunters to kill him. When Ike is twenty-one, he inherits a prosperous plantation but renounces it, insisting that no man should own what is nature's. Moreover, he is horrified to discover that his grandfather has not only sired a child by one of his slaves but also thereafter committed incest with his black daughter. Ike now interprets the South's loss of the Civil War as God's punishment of a slaveholding society. Through his renunciation of ancestral property, he hopes to free himself from his family's sins.

In the final part of the tale, Faulkner takes the reader back three years, with Ike now eighteen, and Old Ben hunted down two years ago. Ike locates the graves of Lion and Sam Fathers and has a vision of nature's immortality. Yet in an ambiguous ending, the forces of exploitive greed seem to doom the wilderness. Still, Ike's resolute acts of conscience and forbearance make him one of Faulkner's most admirable protagonists.

Three of Faulkner's finest stories are "Barn Burning," "That Evening Sun," and "A Rose for Emily." The first is a miniature tale of maturation focusing on ten-year-old "Sarty" Snopes, son of a hard-bitten sharecropper, Ab Snopes, who specializes in burning the barns of landowners with whom he has quarreled. Little Sarty Snopes finds himself torn between loyalty to his criminal father and his own sense of honor. In a melodramatic ending, the boy believes—mistakenly—that his father has been killed and runs away from home.

"That Evening Sun" features the Compson family, who would become the principal characters in Faulkner's great novel *The Sound and the Fury* (1929). The heroine is Nancy, the Compson family's part-time cook, who is terrified of being killed by her husband, Jesus, for having prostituted herself to white men. The story stresses the helpless terror of a young black woman in a deeply racist, white-dominated community. It is the town's indifference to her fate that shows itself to be the essential villain.

"A Rose for Emily" is a shockingly macabre story in which Miss Emily Grierson, a southern lady of high repute, is discovered to have poisoned her lover, a Northern construction boss who betrayed her, and to have kept his body in an upstairs bedroom until her own death, forty years later. As an aristocrat, Miss Emily is admired by the townspeople; as a pathological recluse, she is laughed at; as a person of pride and independence, she cows the community. Her refusal to submit to conventional standards of conduct earns for her a victory over everyday respectability.

Part of the reason for the widespread popularity of "A Rose for Emily" is that its gothic elements make it horrifying enough to be appealing to the popular imagination and it seems so representative of Faulkner's most characteristic themes and techniques, especially his theme of the decay of the South and his experimentation with point of view and narrative time. The most common critical concern about the story is the relationship between Emily's denial of time and Faulkner's technique of breaking up the linearity of time in the telling of the story.

The story is about the denial of time as a linear series of events, both in the action of Emily's trying to deny death and in Faulkner's refusal to lay out the story in a linear fashion. The central passage occurs near the end when the narrator describes the old men who come to the funeral who confuse "time with its mathematical progression, as the old do, to whom all the past is not a diminishing road but instead a huge meadow. . . ." This spatialization of time is central, for Emily is not so much a real person as she is an icon, a sign frozen in time and space, the clue to which is that she looks frozen into an idol in her window, a sort of "hereditary obligation upon the town. . . . Dear, inescapable, impervious, tranquil, and perverse." The use of the plural narrator, a kind of choral voice of the town, supplements this notion of time as spatial and Emily as icon, for the reader does not get the sense of one voice recounting an event laid out neatly in linear time.

The style and tone of Ernest Hemingway revolutionized modern prose fiction. He sought direct pictorial contact between eye and object, object and reader. To obtain it, he trimmed off authorial explanation or comment, making every effort to keep himself out of view as he pruned descriptions and kept his dialogue sparse, abrupt, apparently casual, powerfully compressed.

Many critics have called attention to the combination in Hemingway's fiction of naturalistic detail and symbolist structure and intention. Carlos Baker says the result, especially in the short stories, is a sense of "nightmares at noonday" while Sheridan Baker says there is a kind of "objective magic" in Hemingway's fiction; both comments suggest that by focusing on mere objective things in the world Hemingway is simultaneously able to give such "mere things" a resonance and an aura of significance. In his famous iceberg analogy from *Death in the Afternoon* (1932), Hemingway says,

> If a writer of prose knows enough about what he is writing about he may omit things that he knows and the reader, if the writer is writing truly enough, will have a feeling of those things as strongly as though the writer had stated them. The dignity of movement of an iceberg is due to only one-eighth of it being above water.

Hemingway's "Big Two-Hearted River" is a paradigm of the famous Hemingway style, for in it seemingly realistic descriptive details metaphorically objectify Nick's psychic distress rather than mimetically create a sense of the external world. Thus, at the end of the story, Nick's refusal to go into the swamp has nothing to do with the real qualities of the swamp, only its metaphoric qualities as an embodiment of his own psychic state.

A classic example of this method at its most successful is "Hills Like White Elephants," in which the author refuses to relate himself to the characters yet puts before his readers a highly charged conflict of considerable consequence. The story takes place in Spain, during a forty-minute wait between trains. A young, unmarried couple discusses whether the woman should bear to term the fetus she is carrying. The man wants her to abort it, fearing that a child would be a "white elephant" for them. The woman wants to have the child, because she is tired of their brittle, rootless existence and is ready for a fuller life. The man's refusal to accept the responsibilities of parenthood dooms the couple to sterility and emptiness, as they lose their chance to change directions. The tone of the characters' dialogue changes subtly as they converse with barely restrained irritation, mockery, and bitterness.

In "The Killers," Nick Adams, the young protagonist of many early Hemingway tales, encounters the face of evil as an unavoidable and unalterable aspect of humanity. The style is succinct and flat, the sentence structure is simple, the clauses lack subordination, the characters lack complexity—all implying a dislocated, fragmented world. Two gangsters visit a diner, bind the help, and wait for the arrival of Ole Andreson, a retired heavyweight fighter whom they intend to kill. Gloved and faceless, the gangsters follow a code: They are weary, bored hired guns come to do their job. When Ole does not arrive, they leave, and Nick walks to the intended victim's rooming house and warns Ole, who lies on his bed inert and resigned. Nick entreats Ole to seek police help or flee the town; Ole will do neither. "Couldn't you fix it up some way?" Nick asks. Replies Ole: "No. I got in wrong. There ain't anything to do." Living by his code, the hunted man accepts his victimization. Nick is severely shocked by his discovery of annihilating wickedness. He will leave town.

"The Snows of Kilimanjaro," Hemingway's favorite story, takes up enough material for several novels. Hemingway uses two levels of action: A writer, Harry Street, is dying of gangrene caused by an untreated thorn scratch; he alternately talks with his wife and others around him and reflects on his life. It has been a struggle between his creative and destructive urges, and Harry, in interior monologues, admits that he has traded his talent for the luxury and sloth of his marriage to a rich woman. Toward the story's end, Harry is flown over the snow-covered peaks of Mount Kilimanjaro, a symbol of both death and absolute beauty. The author, however, has failed to integrate the three levels of the story: Harry's relationship with his wife, his communings with his soul, and the surrounding African continent. Harry's potential as a fine writer is never dramatized—only his self-pity and running quarrel with most of the world.

Some of the best modern American writers of short fiction have been southerners, with their writing distinguished for its concrete mastery of the sensory world and insistence on the elemental truths of life and death. In addition to Faulkner, the most brilliant southern authors of tales have been Katherine Anne Porter, Eudora Welty, and Flannery O'Connor.

Welty has said that by using only enough of the physical world to meet her needs Katherine Anne Porter makes the reader see the "subjective worlds of hallucination, obsession, fever, guilt." Robert Penn Warren, however, notes that Porter's stories are characterized by "rich surface detail scattered with apparently casual profuseness and the close structure which makes such detail meaningful." These two famous comments perceptively pinpoint the central quality of Porter's art—her ability to make mere physical reality resonate with moral significance. By means of a tactic that has dominated modern short fiction since Chekhov, Porter makes such stories as her most famous one, "Flowering Judas," appear to be realistic situations about people caught in specific moral dilemmas while at the same time they are spiritual allegories in which characters and objects are emblems of universal moral issues.

Although the conflict in "Flowering Judas" takes place, as Welty says about most of Porter's stories, in the interior of the protagonist's life, the story is less a psychological study of one individual's act of renunciation than it is a symbolic story of the basic nature of renunciation. Laura, named perhaps for the unattainable and thus idealistic object of Petrarch's love in his famous sonnets, is caught between her desire to embody her own ideals as a Marxist revolutionary in Mexico and her realization that the very nature of idealism is that it cannot be embodied.

The many dichotomies in the story—Laura's Catholicism and her socialism, her sensuality and her ascetic renunciation, her dedication to the people and her renunciation of genuine involvement—coalesce in the symbolic dichotomy of Braggioni, who affirms life even though it means throwing himself into the physical and becoming a "professional lover of humanity," and Eugenio, the imprisoned revolutionary who maintains his idealism but who negates life and wants to die because he is bored. The key mythic figures who embody this antithesis in the story are Judas, who gives it its title, and Christ, the one he betrayed.

Given the powerful universal significance of these dichotomies, it is little wonder that they cannot be solved in actuality but must be resolved aesthetically in a dream—typical of medieval dream visions that the story in some ways resembles. In Laura's dream she refuses to follow Eugenio to death because he will not take her hand. In a dream-distorted reversal of the Christian Communion, Eugenio gives her bleeding flowers from the Judas tree (the tree from which Judas hanged himself), which she greedily eats. However, rather than affirming the inextricable union of body and spirit as does the Christian Communion, Laura's act is a negative one of betrayal for helping Eugenio to escape life. The story ends with the "holy talismanic word" Laura always uses that keeps her from being led into evil but which also keeps her from being involved in life—"No."

Porter's very brief story "The Grave" is closer to a lyric poem than it is to traditional narrative; consequently, it communicates more by metaphor and symbol than by character and event. It is a story about a significant moment, in this case a moment of realization or passage from one state of being to another. It is a paradigm of story in that it is a memory self-consciously fashioned into meaning.

The story focuses on Miranda's reaction to the gold ring, which makes her long to put aside her childhood for the traditionally feminine world of her thinnest and most becoming dress, and the opened body of a pregnant rabbit, which introduces her to the mysterious nature of birth. When Miranda sees the unborn rabbits, it is as if she had known this all along; she now understands some of the secret formless intuitions in her mind and body which have been taking form so slowly and gradually that she had not realized she was learning what she had to know. Both perceptions suggest a traditional initiation of the young girl into womanhood.

Porter's "Old Mortality" is a three-part novella featuring Miranda, her favorite character, who appears in half a dozen of her stories. In the first section, she is eight, listening to accounts of her beautiful, vivacious Aunt Amy, especially her long courtship and brief marriage to the handsome, dashing Uncle Gabriel before Amy died of an incurable illness. Part 2 consists almost wholly of shocks dispelling many of Miranda's illusions. Now ten and in a convent school, she is taken by her father to a racetrack where she meets Uncle Gabriel for the first time. To her dismay, he turns out to be coarse, alcoholic, shabby, fat, and cruel. Part 3 shows Miranda, at eighteen, reconciling her illusions and disappointments in a union that transcends cynicism. On a train, returning from Uncle Gabriel's funeral, she encounters an older, feminist cousin, Eva, who provides her with a disenchanting view of Aunt Amy as a sexually hungry, wild, shallow woman. Miranda resolves to free herself from the past's legends and to begin her own life, her own legend. She has come to understand that human involvements tend to be ambiguous and that no secondhand version of anyone's life will serve her. Porter's irony is marked yet gentle, aware of both the human capacity for self-deception and the need for familial ties.

By focusing brilliantly on the Mississippi milieu she knows so well, Welty creates symbolic situations that transform the ordinary into the mythical. Although Welty's stories do not often focus on realistic social situations that emphasize the external life of woman in southern society, they are filled with strong and independent women who memorably assert their unique identity. Typical is Ruby Fisher in "A Piece of News," who is trapped in a marriage that allows her no sense of herself as an independent person. When she sees a story in a newspaper describing how a woman named Ruby Fisher was shot in the leg by her husband, her elaborate fantasy of her own death and burial is an ironic effort to find a sense of identity. When her husband tells her that the newspaper is from another state, she feels a puzzling sense of loss.

In "Clytie," the main character is a stereotyped old maid, exploited by her family and laughed at by the townspeople for her eccentricity. Just as Ruby Fisher sees her self in the newspaper story, Clytie achieves a similar recognition when she looks into the mirrored surface of a rain barrel and can think of nothing else to do but thrust her head into the "kind, featureless depth" of the water and hold it there. It is not simply social isolation that plagues Welty's women but rather a primal sense of separateness; and it is not mere social validation that they hunger for, but rather a genuine healing love that will give them a sense of order and meaning.

Other memorable women in Welty's stories caught in a quest for their own identity include Leota and Mrs. Fletcher who, Medusa-like in a beauty parlor in "Petrified Man," metaphorically turn men into stone; Phoenix Jackson, the indefatigable grandmother who in "A Worn Path" goes on a heroic journey to seek relief for her suffering grandson; and Livie, in the story that bears her name, who dares to leave the control and order of the paternalistic Solomon for the vitality of Cash McCord.

Welty's stories focus less on women defined by their stereotypical social roles than they are by their archetypal metaphysical being. As a result, they do not so much confront their social self as they reveal what Welty sees as their primal nature as isolated human beings.

Welty's dominant mode is comic, with the range of her effects wide: exultant celebrations of folk vitality, both delicate and astringent irony, occasionally corrosive satire, high-spirited farce, and always a probing tenderness toward her people, which is Chekhovian in its lightness and clarity. While her spectrum of characters is broad, she is particularly adept at delineating the manner and idioms of proletarian rural southerners.

One of her finest tales in this vein is "Why I Live at the P.O." Its dramatic monologuist, postmistress of the hamlet of China Grove, is cantankerous, at incessant odds with her family, and obsessively envious of her younger sister, whose marriage has shattered and who has come home to her mother. Like a Chaucerian personality, she can recall, in an unceasing flow of elliptical and baroque talk, every single slight allegedly inflicted on her. She is one of Welty's many isolated people, paranoid, vindictive and self-pitying yet possessed of irresistible gusto and a resourcefulness that prevents the reader from pitying her. In recording her protagonist's talk, Welty demonstrates eyes and ears as sharp and true as a tuning fork.

O'Connor's literary reputation has risen steeply since her death; in 1989, her collected works were published in the prestigious Library of America series—virtually formal canonization as a major writer. Her artistic virtues include subtle wit, an economical style, an eye for the maliciously revealing detail, piercingly apt imagery, a knack for sliding seamlessly between the ordinary and the sinister, an infallible sense of pace, mastery of understatement, and superlative skill in springing ironic reversals. Her few defects are a narrowness of emphasis and predictability of both technique and theme, for O'Connor prided herself on informing her tales and novels with the central teachings of Roman Catholicism. Her overriding concern with redemption impelled her, in much of her work, to impart last-moment visions of Christian belief to her main characters. Like Welty, O'Connor is a comic writer, with a Dickensian fondness for eccentric personalities as well as a gothic penchant for eruptions of disorder and violence.

Her most celebrated story, "A Good Man Is Hard to Find," presents the reader with sardonically treated, shocking events. On the surface, a homicidal maniac, called the Misfit, slaughters a family of innocent people whom he happens to encounter on the road. Read carefully, the tale becomes a commentary on general human values. The family begins a banal vacation trip on a chord of dissonance: The grandmother is self-centered and sly; her son, Bailey, is weak and surly; his wife is a dull frump; the children are snotty. Their first stop is at Red Sammy's barbecue tower, where the proprietor informs them that a good man is hard to find. Then the grandmother persuades her son to turn the car in the direction of an old plantation she had known in her childhood. He takes a dirt road to it, and she, by causing her cat to terrify the driver, is responsible for the resulting accident and the consequent confrontation with the Misfit and his henchmen. Professing goodness, the grandmother nevertheless seals the family's fate. In calling the mass murderer "one of my own children," is she surmounting her earlier vanity and expressing a Christlike grace, or is she simply selfishly pleading for her life? Is the Misfit, unmoved by his victims' appeals, a Grand Inquisitor, a psychotic, a lost pilgrim, a demon, the Devil himself? Such indeterminacy is built into this densely ambiguous, powerful text.

Paul Engles, editor of the O. Henry Award anthology when this story was selected for inclusion in 1942, said he considers Carson McCullers's "A Tree. A Rock. A Cloud" "the most perfect short story in American Literature." Although this may sound somewhat extreme for such a seemingly slight little narrative, there is something classic about the basic character configuration and theme of the story. The enclosed situation of the café in the early morning, the confrontation between the young initiate and the experienced one; the cynical and ironic observer, the silent chorus of men in the background—all this suggest a classic short story situation. Moreover, the story's focus on loneliness and the difficulty of loving fits with Frank O'Connor's famous definition of the short story in *The Lonely Voice* (1963) and thematically align it with a number of other stories in this collection.

The narrative situation of the story is simple; what needs to be understood is the notion of love that it presents. If the reader asks why it is easier to love a tree, a rock, a cloud than it is to love a person, the answer must be that love is indeed synonymous with identification with the other. The aim of love is to dissolve that which separates us and to swallow up the other. This is difficult with a person because the other is a subjective consciousness who wishes to maintain self-identity. However, as the transient tells the puzzled boy, one can gradually learn to identify with the other if one begins simply with the less threatening. This story is about that primitive sense of the sacred that constitutes true reality, the basic religious yearning of human consciousness to lose the self in the other. Leo knows the transient is right, but he also knows that such a demand is impossible for the ordinary human; the boy has yet to learn this hard fact of human reality.

The combination of reality and fantasy in which a realistic character confronts the embodiment of a *mana* figure can be seen in the stories of Truman Capote, Flannery O'Connor, McCullers, and John Steinbeck. In "The Snake," a typical story from his collection *The Long Valley* (1938), Steinbeck presents the tension between the life of science and reason and the mythic world of primal reality. The forces which oppose each other in Steinbeck's story are suggested in the first paragraph by the juxtaposition of the laboratory and the tide pool: the one closed off from nature yet built for the purpose of observing nature, the other the primal source of life itself where the mysteries of nature truly take place. The action that opens the story—Dr. Phillips's leaving the tide pool for the laboratory—creates an atmosphere that resonates with ominousness. Even when the reader discovers that the clammy sack is filled only with common starfish and that the dissection table is used for small animals, the reader is still apprehensive that something is not "natural" about the laboratory or the young doctor, who has the "preoccupied eyes of one who looks through a microscope a great deal" and whose bedroom is a book-lined cell containing an army cot, a reading light and an uncomfortable chair. The imagery is too much that of one who, having withdrawn from life, is content merely to look on, of one who does not live life but experiments with it.

Most of the description of the woman clearly and simply establishes her physical identity with the snake. Tall and lean, dressed in a severe dark suit, she has straight black hair growing low on a flat forehead. "He noted how short her chin was between lower lip and point." As she waits to talk to him, she seems completely at rest. "Her eyes were bright but the rest of her was almost in a state of suspended animation." He thought, "Low metabolic rate, almost as low as a frog's, from the looks." However, other details and actions of the woman are not so clearly related to the snake. Her eyes do not center on him; "rather they covered him and seemed to see in a big circle around him." When the doctor goes over to the rattlesnake cage, he turns to find her standing beside him. "He had not heard her get up from the chair. He had heard only the splash of water among the piles and the scampering of rats on the wire screen." Later, when the doctor puts the rat into the snake cage, the room becomes very silent. "Dr. Phillips did not know whether the water sighed among the piles or whether the woman sighed." Finally, when the woman leaves, the doctor hears her footsteps on the stairs but "could not hear her walk away on the pavement." These details do not identify the woman with the snake so much as with the sea itself. The yoking of the sounds she makes with the sound of the waves underneath the laboratory make this clear. The doctor does not hear her walk away on the pavement because she does not walk away; she goes back to the tide pool from whence she came, back to the "deep pool of consciousness" out of which she awakens when the doctor is ready to talk to her. She does not wish to look into the microscope because, being a mythic creature, her vision sees not narrowly but in a large circle that is all-encompassing.

To understand why the snake-woman or instinctual force has risen abruptly from the doctor's unconscious to confront him, the reader does not have to try to understand the "personal" contents of his unconscious any more than he or she has to try to understand or postulate a particular sexual neurosis for the woman. Indeed, the story gives the reader no basis for trying to understand either as individual characters. The doctor, embodying as he does a scientific and therefore detached existence, is simply intolerable in his one-sidedness. The woman is a threatening force to the doctor because he refuses to recognize and integrate the archetypal contents of his unconscious, which she embodies.

John Cheever, in brilliant stories beginning in the late 1930's, established a recognizable landscape that can be called "Cheever Country." In it, people hang together, or often fall apart, in Manhattan apartments, vainly awaiting their fortunes ("The Pot of Gold"), or they live in the WASPy, alcoholic suburbs of Westchester or Fairfield County. In "The Swimmer," during his summer-afternoon plunge homeward, the swimmer finds the air turning chill, flowers blooming out of season, his body weakening with age, and his home, once he reaches it, closed up. The reader is no longer in a recognizable community but in the realm of legend, with the protagonist discovering his life in ruins. In "Torch Song," a New Yorker encounters a mistreated woman over a period of years; he comes to realize that the men who insult and injure her are vainly defending themselves against the Angel of Death. Cheever's characters' sleep is troubled by nightmares as they stumble through wastelands of greed, lust, furtive frustration and coldness of heart despite their well-mannered, privileged upper-middle-class status. Cheever is essentially a mythic writer, drawing a fine tone of fable through his fiction in a lyrical prose unmatched in complexity, melody, and precision by his contemporaries.

In "The Enormous Radio," the marriage of a Manhattan couple, the Westcotts, is realistically treated. Their apartment, manners, tastes, speech, and behavior all seem typical and blandly complacent. Then, Cheever introduces the fantasy of an enormous, expensive radio that shreds the veil that not only the Westcotts but also their neighbors in the building have drawn over their secret lives: adulteries, wife beatings, thefts, insults, obscenities, stinginess, and quarrels, quarrels, quarrels. Irene Westcott protests to her husband that *their* marriage is not sordid and hateful like the marriages of the others. She proves to be mistaken, as her husband bitterly attacks her for her extravagance, duplicity, mendacity, and hypocrisy. Is the Westcotts' marriage better after this bout of truth telling? The radio's voice is "suave and noncommittal."

Of the many Jewish writers who rose to prominence after World War II, only a few excel in short fiction: Bernard Malamud, Saul Bellow, and Philip Roth. The patron saint of these authors is Fyodor Dostoevski, whose characters must always search for meaning, who cannot permit life to flow without anxious examination. Jews came to the United States with a rich tradition of devotion to learning, and when that drive detached itself from Talmudic faith, it often became passionately involved in secular ideas and moral challenges. Moreover, the horror of the Holocaust stands behind all postwar Jewish American fiction, even when not explicitly acknowledged as a patrimony. The protagonist in many texts by Jewish writers is the victim, the dangling man, the schlemiel or bungler, with both his impulse toward decency and his proneness to failure, bereft, wandering, fooled, and bewildered.

Alone among American authors, Malamud has focused on the Jew as representative man—and on the schlemiel as representative Jew: isolated, displaced, misunderstood, an apostate from society's gospel of material success. In Malamud's stories, the protagonist has frequent opportunities for suffering, submitting to loss, pain, humiliation, deception, sometimes ignominy. His characters usually triumph as human beings only by virtue of their failures in the world at large. Unashamedly romantic and moralistic, Malamud's fiction delineates the broken dreams and private griefs of the spirit, the anguish of the heart, the ungovernable course of compassion. Far from the mainstream of American culture, his work often stands guard against the temptations toward assimilation, rendering New York City as a pale or *shtetl*, a somber and often joyless world where dread and punishment are daily staples.

Although Bernard Malamud is the best-known spokesman of the Jewish experience in American literature, the Jew in his fiction is an embodiment of the complex moral experience of universal human suffering, responsibility, and love rather than a realistic representative of a particular ethnic and social situation. Although there are traces of the Yiddish tale in Malamud's stories, they also reflect the tight symbolic structure and ironic and distanced point of view associated with the modern short story. Bernard Malamud particularizes universal human suffering and the difficult human challenge to come to terms with the mysterious other in the concrete experiences of Jews and thus universalizes the Jewish experience as being wholly human. As the old tailor Manischevitz says in "Angel Levine" after accepting the Black Angel Levine as a divine messenger, "Believe me, there are Jews everywhere." Indeed, in Malamud's worldview, all who suffer are Jews.

Although Malamud is a master of both the realistic and the fantastic, he is at his best when he mixes conventions of the two styles in such stories as "Idiot's First," "Pictures of Fidelman," and his best-known story "The Magic Barrel." This mixture is not so much the straight-faced acceptance of the incredible that the reader is accustomed to in the Magical Realism of Borges or García Márquez, but rather establishes a fictional world in which moral demands seem to force the supernatural into the psychic depths of the individual character's secret need. It is the technique most responsible for the uniqueness of Malamud's stories.

Although Malamud's stories involve age-old moral dilemmas, they do not end with a moral resolution, as does the traditional folklore parable; moral dilemmas in Malamud's stories are not so much resolved as they are left frozen in a symbolic epiphany or ironic gesture. Malamud's characters are often caught in a moral quandary that they not only cannot resolve but also cannot understand, at least until it is too late. At the end of "Take Pity," for example, Rosen does all he can to help a proud widow, but when she continues to refuse his aid, he wills all his possessions to her and sticks his head in the oven. In "Black Is My Favorite Color," Nat Lime bemoans his many efforts to help black people, only to have them kick him in the teeth.

The most fantastic version of the alien stranger who demands acceptance, understanding, even love, in Malamud's fiction is the bedraggled Jewbird in the story of the same name who appears out of nowhere one day at Harry Cohen's window, seeking protection from "Anti-Semeets." Cohen puts up with the inconveniences of the Jewbird as long as he can and finally throws him out into the snow. When he is found in the spring by Cohen's son, who asks him who did this to him, the dying bird answers, "Anti-Semeets." If, as the tailor Manischevitz says in "Angel Levine," "There are Jews everywhere," this story suggests there are also anti-Semites everywhere, even among Jews.

In his best-known tale, "The Magic Barrel," Malamud's tone shuttles from the promise of a fairy tale to the sadness of a sardonic parable. Its protagonist, Leo Finkle, is a rabbinical student nearing graduation who decides to marry so he can have a good chance of winning a congregation. Finkle is scholarly and ascetic but essentially godless, and he is fearful of his inability to love anyone. He calls in a marriage broker, Pinye Salzman, half con man and half spiritual exemplar. Most of Salzman's candidates, however, bear the marks of defeat. Then Leo falls in love with a snapshot accidentally included in a packet of pictures left him by the wily Salzman. The matchmaker is horrified when Leo insists on meeting *this* woman—it is Salzman's daughter, Stella, whose sorrowful father describes her as "wild, without shame. . . . Like an animal." Leo insists on a meeting. His rapture, on seeing Stella, is both erotic and religious: "He pictured, in her, his own redemption. Violins and lit candles revolved in the sky. Leo ran forward with flowers outthrust." Malamud's ending is ambiguous and paradoxical. Will the unworldly Leo discover his salvation through loving the sinful, whorish Stella? In the story's last sentence, Salzman chants prayers for the dead. Because his daughter is lost to him? Because of his role in bringing Leo and Stella together? Because he mourns Leo's loss of innocence? Malamud leaves the reader with problems and possibilities.

Bellow, born in Canada but living in the United States since he was nine, is generally recognized as the dominant prose writer of the generation following Faulkner and Hemingway. His fiction has a European flavor in its fondness for philosophical, historical, and political debate and its stress on his characters' intense, gloomy mental lives, which often cast them adrift in seas of hallucination and guilt. One of the crucial themes of Bellow's work is the anguished attempt of his protagonists to get a grip on existence in a lonely and dehumanizing world, to try to understand an infinitely elusive, sometimes senseless, universe.

Perhaps his most accomplished text is the novella *Seize the Day* (1956), which exhibits his concentrated power at its best and curbs his natural tendency to lecture the reader. The effect is one of extreme compression along the lines of classical tragedy, with a single day of the hero's—or the antihero's—life summing up and invoking a judgment upon his entire history. Tommy Wilhelm is a middle-aged Manhattan salesman, out of a job, fat, divorced, behind in his alimony payments, scorned by his former wife, rejected by his father. He is a buffeted buffoon, humiliated before others, adrift, stumbling through the routines of life. The reader meets Tommy on a day of panic, when his world seems to be collapsing as he discovers that he has lost his remaining savings by having foolishly played the stock market under the influence of a fast-talking sharper, the psychiatrist Dr. Tamkin. The *carpe diem* injunction of the title is ironic, for Tommy has never had the courage or the drive to turn an opportunity to his advantage. At the end of the tale, the scheming Tamkin has fled, Dr. Adler coldly refuses to aid his son, Tommy's former wife has hounded him for money, and he is broke and desperate. He knows that only love can make his life bearable, but his vanity and self-pity thwart his emotions.

Then Bellow concludes with a splendid catharsis: Tommy wanders along Broadway into a Jewish funeral service and there releases his grief in a great surge at the coffin of the unknown corpse. He finds himself sharing and universalizing his suffering. In the story's last sentence, Tommy "sank deeper than sorrow, through torn sobs and cries toward the consummation of his heart's ultimate need."

Roth was to create his unmistakable schlemiel in the protagonist of his most popular novel, *Portnoy's Complaint* (1969). In *Goodbye, Columbus* (1959), the short-story collection that launched Roth's career to critical acclaim, he investigates Jewish middle-class rather than lower-class life, dealing with the tensions between assimilation into the larger American culture and ethnic identity, public image and private passion, material success and spiritual failure. While influenced by Malamud and Bellow, Roth owes a larger debt to F. Scott Fitzgerald. In the long, sharply satiric title story, he relates the defeat in love of a poor, young Jewish man by a brutally materialistic, wealthy Jewish family. In "Eli, the Fanatic," the conflict is between Hasidic and secularized Jews. In "The Conversion of the Jews," the motif suggests the validity of diverse religious beliefs, with tolerance of pluralism triumphing over closed-minded faith.

Roth's best story is "Defender of the Faith," in which Sergeant Nathan Marx, assigned to a Missouri training company after European combat, encounters over and over again the wiles of trainee Sheldon Grossbart, who cunningly uses their shared roots in the New York Jewish community to abuse Marx's humaneness, generosity, and scrupulosity. Marx's dilemma is thorny: How to be a good person, a good soldier, and a good Jew in a conniving and insensitive world. He decides that the best way to be a defender of his faith is to reject Grossbart's advantage-mongering, yet he finds that he can restore the balance of Justice's scales only by descending to Grossbart's level of lying and trickery. The tough-minded Roth affirms that a worthy end does justify unworthy means. This is a complex, powerfully imagined tale, sharply observed in its command of dialogue and characteristic gestures. Even though Roth proceeded to use the novel rather than the tale as his preferred medium, his fictive debut shows him to be a masterful storyteller.

Great Britain and Ireland

The short stories and novellas of D. H. Lawrence are usually not the forum for exploring a new set of ideas in his visionary career. While not the product of his most fertile imagination, however, the best of them are often superior in structure and more artistically realized than his novels, keeping to a minimum his tendency to exhort the reader or to repeat himself. Their recurring themes are the distortion of love by possessiveness, materialism, or false romanticism, the pressure of class feelings upon male/female relationships, and the interplay of antagonism and tenderness that marks the sexual battlefield.

In "Tickets, Please," one of the young inspectors of a train line, John Thomas, charming but promiscuous, begins to date Annie, one of the girl conductors, but he drops her when she begins to take him seriously. Annie then organizes a group revenge on him, joined by a number of the other women equally picked up and then rejected by "Coddy" Thomas. They trap him, rough him up, humiliate him, then find themselves nonplussed by their bright, maenad-like frenzy; the story thus ends on a note of uneasy irresolution, with the young women unable to understand fully their paradoxical impulses of aggressiveness and surrender. They are financially independent yet wish to fulfill themselves in marriage. "Coddy's" masculine pride and arrogance both infuriate and attract them. As soon as they have redressed the balance between the sexes, they feel lost and miserable, appalled by their victory over the macho male.

"The Horse Dealer's Daughter" opens at a moment of family crisis: Three brothers have failed in the business passed to them from their father. Their sister, Mabel, especially mourns the death of her mother as she keeps house. Lonely, sullen, isolated among her egotistical brothers, she attempts suicide as a desperate fulfillment. A young doctor rescues her from drowning in a stagnant pond, carries her back to the house, strips off her clothes, and wraps her in warming blankets. When she awakens, she asks him, directly, "Do you love me, then?" The shock of the exposure has transcended her inhibitions. He finds himself unable to withdraw from her, able only to yield and declare a reciprocal love. He and the woman have undergone a deathly baptism and have been reborn, contrary to their previous intentions. Their delivery of each other is also a crucial self-discovery. This is a totally unsentimental, compelling dramatization of the triumph of love and life.

"The Prussian Officer" is one of D. H. Lawrence's best stories, representative of his favorite theme of so-called blood consciousness and his customary narrative technique of combining the realistic with the mythic. The plot of the story is so simple and its two characters are so stark as to be archetypal. An aristocratic Prussian captain becomes obsessed with his uncomplicated young orderly but deals with the obsession by repressing it, humiliating and physically mistreating the young man. The story reaches its climax when the orderly kills the officer, destroying the world of everyday reality for the young man and launching him into an alienated psychic state that leads to his own death. Just as the officer seems driven by forces outside his control and understanding, the orderly responds in a primitive unthinking manner.

As opposed to the officer, who is bound to the rules of the aristocracy and the military, the orderly is one who seems "never to have thought, only to have received life direct through his senses, and acted straight from instinct." It is this "blind instinctive sureness of movement of an unhampered young animal" that so irritates the officer. Realizing this, the orderly feels like "a wild thing caught" and his hatred in response to the officer's passion grows; as the officer seems to be going irritably insane, the youth becomes deeply frightened.

This movement toward unreality in which the two characters become transformed by their very passion is a typical Lawrentian structural device by which conventional characters are transfigured into depersonalized representatives of states of mind. The orderly's murder of the captain, which is presented in unmistakable sexual terms, completes the young man's alienation from the ordinary world. His actual death seems an inevitable and even anticlimactic consequence of his complete distancing from the world.

In *The Fox*, a novella, Lawrence achieves a wonderfully naturalistic narrative in which, as often in his work, an outsider liberates people from convention, isolation, and repression. Two women, March and Banford, nearing thirty, are struggling to manage an isolated, small farm. March is ruddy, physically effective, dominant; Banford is frail, oversensitive, passionless. The fox who preys on the chickens represents wild nature endangering their way of life. Enter a young Canadian soldier, Henry, whose prominent cheekbones and bright eyes remind March of the fox. He, too, represents the danger and discord of an intruder. Henry kills the fox, then encounters Banford's resentment of his presence and realizes that he has no hope of successfully wooing the older March while she is still on the farm. He proposes to March, she half-consents, then relapses into indecision while with the needy Banford. In a willed accident, Henry axes a tree in such a way that one of its boughs kills Banford. Relieved and released, March agrees to marry Henry and start a new life with him in Canada. Lawrence's command of atmosphere, setting, and dialogue is classically perfect without overworking the symbolism of the fox.

Graham Greene is a master of the politics of disenchantment and sadness, dealing usually with characters who are seedy, melancholy, disloyal, fallen, and despairing. He invests his narratives with a probing moral concern, often colored by his conversion to Roman Catholicism, and dramatizes his themes in patterns of intrigue, flight, pursuit, and sometimes annihilation. While some of his tales are trivial digressions from his longer fiction, others are splendidly crafted. He came to appreciate the opportunities offered by short fiction for unified tone and precision of language and declared that he had never written anything better than the stories "The Destructors," "A Chance for Mr. Lever," "Under the Garden," and "Cheap in August."

"The Basement Room" is generally considered Greene's finest story. It is narrated by the dying, sixty-seven-year-old Philip Lane, still living with the traumatic effects of a day in his life when he was seven and entrusted, in his parents' absence, to the care of two household servants, Mr. and Mrs. Baines. Young Philip loves and admires the butler Baines while fearing his malevolent, nagging, housekeeping wife. The story focuses on Philip's meeting a young woman, Emily, whom Baines presents to him as his niece but who is clearly his mistress. Philip is now thrust into an adult world of duplicity and malice as the boy becomes a pawn in the match between the hostile couple. When Mrs. Baines returns unexpectedly and discovers her husband's infidelity, it is Philip who unwillingly betrays him. Then, after the wife falls over the banister to her death, it is again Philip who, exhausted by the pressure of events, incriminates Baines. Sixty years later, Philip still suffers from death of the heart, having led a wasteful, loveless, empty life, unable to be more than a dilettante. The story guides the reader to many of Greene's major concerns: the innocence of childhood contaminated by the adult world, the victory of betrayal over trust, and the relative impotence of good when it encounters evil.

"The Destructors," Greene's most chilling story, focuses on a brilliant but sociopathic teenager, Trevor, son of an architect who has "come down in the world" to a clerkship after World War II. Trevor gains leadership of a gang when he enthralls its members with his proposal to pull down the great and stately house of "Old Misery," a kind old man whose home was built by the great Sir Christopher Wren. Trevor achieves the status of a demonic destructive artist as he orchestrates the ruination of the house in virtuoso fashion. The tale is a parable of England's confused and impoverished society during the immediate postwar period. The elegant house, symbolizing aristocratic values, is brought to rubble by a cruelly insensitive new generation. Creativity is harnessed to destruction in a Manichaean fashion. On a political level, "The Destructors" can be understood as an allegory on the seductive appeal of power which, once unleashed, gains totalitarian momentum. The story's nightmarish implications are alarming.

The Irish writer Frank O'Connor, born Michael Francis O'Donovan, was a younger member of the distinguished Irish literary renaissance headed by William Butler Yeats. Most of his writing consists of short stories dealing with the soul of the Irish people. More entertaining, witty, and charming than his great compatriot James Joyce, O'Connor is also a more uneven craftsman, some of whose work is slight and poorly resolved. At his best, however, O'Connor has produced some of the finest short fiction of the twentieth century.

"Guests of the Nation" may be his most powerful story. Two British soldiers, Hawkins and Belcher, are held hostage by Irish guards who play cards with them, engage them in spirited arguments, and become their friends, even though their two nations are at war with each other in the early 1920's. When news arrives that four Irish prisoners have been killed by their captors, the Irish soldier in charge insists on shooting the two hostages in reprisal. The perky little Hawkins protests that they are all "chums" and declares his readiness to join his Irish friends' side—to no avail. The sweet-tempered, generous Belcher reveals his desertion by an adulterous wife, then accepts his deadly fate stoically. The narrator, revolted by the barbarity of warfare, is desolated by the loss of two warm human beings: "And anything that ever happened to me after I never felt the same about again."

"The Drunkard" shows to superb effect O'Connor's talent for mixing humor and irony with shrewd psychology. An alcoholic father looks forward to honoring the life and death of a friend, Mr. Dooley, by indulging himself at the postburial celebration. His young son, Larry (who narrates the tale), however, downs his dad's porter, gets sick, and has to be rushed home by his embarrassed father. Forced into sobriety by the circumstances, the father is unjustly scolded by his wife for corrupting their child. The next morning, however, the wife-mother expresses her gratitude to Larry for having served as his father's guardian angel, preventing him from—at least, this time—disgracing and impoverishing the household. Role reversal dominates this hilarious story, with little Larry monitoring his childlike, improvident father, and imitating him on a noisy, tipsy promenade from pub to home. Instead of composing a temperance tract, O'Connor has written an enchanting tale about human vanities and frailties.

Europe

Thomas Mann is the most representative German author of the twentieth century, ranking with the era's greatest prose masters. His work is filled with polarities and ironies: a conservative style yet boldly experimental subject matter, barbaric vitalism arrayed against decadent civilization, nationalism opposed to cosmopolitanism, and varying conceptions of the artist as hero, priest, and charlatan. Mann wrote some of the century's most distinguished short fiction. Some of the tales, such as the novella *Der Tod in Venedig* (1912; *Death in Venice*, 1925) and "Tonio Kröger," were published prior to 1920; others, such as "Unordnung und frühes Leid" ("Disorder and Early Sorrow") and the novella *Mario und der Zauberer* (1930; *Mario and the Magician*, 1930), came thereafter.

"Disorder and Early Sorrow," composed shortly after Mann had finished his titanic novel *Der Zauberberg* (1924; *The Magic Mountain*, 1927, is one of his subtlest, deftest, and most understated texts. The "disorder" is German society's ills after World War I, with prices astronomically inflated, commodities scarce, and traditional ideas and modes as deflated as the currency. The "early sorrow" is felt by five-year-old Ellie, the youngest and favorite daughter of a historian, Professor Cornelius. The girl becomes infatuated with a handsome but dull student who has jocularly danced with her at a house party. The sorrow is most painfully felt by Ellie's father, for Dr. Cornelius knows both that she is previewing the inevitable withdrawal of her affections from him to a lover and that he can in no significant way prevent the pains of life's disappointments from befalling her. Allegorically, the values of German middle-class culture are threatened by incoherent, undisciplined currents of revolutionary change. Professor Cornelius realizes that his preference for the past has become outdated.

In *Mario and the Magician*, written in 1929, Mann gives high aesthetic form to an indictment of fascism in a novella he termed "a tale with moral and political implications." The work falls into two parts: In the first, a German family visiting an Italian beach town encounters a series of increasingly unpleasant incidents, redolent of intolerance and overheated nationalism. The second division stars the hypnotist Cipolla, ill-humored, hunchbacked, chauvinistic, sadistic, sinister, and driven by his inferiority complex. He is a malevolent and demonic artist, using his talent to degrade his public. Cipolla is finally shot by Mario, a modest and ordinary waiter, whom the illusionist has mocked beyond endurance. Allegorically, Mann implies that the hypnotic spell of totalitarianism can be lifted by the forces of decency and dignity. History has usually proved him wrong.

The theme of Mann's "Railway Accident" is similar to his most famous tale, *Death in Venice*, for it suggests that the protagonist must learn that the order of art needs the disorder of reality. There is no obvious conflict for the narrator; nothing seems changed at the end. However, the problem of this story's "storyness" is indeed its central issue. Students might note that it begins with the very question as to whether what follows is a "story" or simply an anecdote. The narrator obviously thinks it does qualify as story. However, what is crucial here is the fact that the narrator is a writer. Thus, the reader may assume that the railway accident is not in itself the subject of the story but that the true theme is what the railway accident makes it possible for him to understand about writing.

Before the accident the writer's experience is presented as ordinary everyday reality in which he confidently sees the world in a comfortable stereotyped way. However, what this story is about is just that breakup of ordinary reality that all stories present in one way or another—a breakup that undermines the writer's assumptions and destroys his comfortable stereotypes. However, the tone is not as serious as this theme might suggest, for now that the event is in the past, it becomes the comfortable subject of the very story he is telling; thus, he can take a somewhat wry perspective of the event.

The Baroness Karen Blixen-Finecke, who took the pen name Isak Dinesen, is Denmark's greatest modern writer. Her tales, which she did not begin publishing until she was forty-nine, are consciously anachronistic, depending on often improbable fantasies, constant metamorphoses, enigmatic signs, elemental magic, highly mannered characterization, and mazelike patterns of stories set within stories. She likened herself to Scheherazade, making up narratives to save her life and provide her public with new visions that would change hearts and minds.

In "Sorrow-Acre," Dinesen pits against each other archaic and modern modes of feeling and thinking. The plot, derived from a Jutland folktale, deals with a peasant woman who, to save her son from execution, is required by the local lord to reap between sunrise and sunset a field of rye, which ordinarily would require four men to reap in one day. The woman fulfills the bargain but then drops dead; the superhuman feat is memorialized by the name "Sorrow-Acre," thereafter attached to the field. The action is viewed through the eyes of the lord's nephew, Adam, who has encountered new humanitarian ideas while visiting England. He threatens to leave the estate forever, unless his uncle releases the woman from the cruel compact. The uncle will not yield, replying that to do so would be to lighten the woman's exploit, to deprive it of tragic significance. Two worldviews are opposed: humanitarianism set against a manorial culture that values the law above individual suffering. The nephew is reconciled to the presence of evil in the world and decides to stay with his uncle.

In "The Blank Page," Dinesen draws an analogy between the pure white sheet of the marriage bed and a blank page of a story. Indeed, the only purpose of the story about the bed sheet is to create this analogy. The success of the story thus is dependent on how successfully an understanding of the white sheet helps the reader understand the complexity of the concept of the blank page. One possible reason that the white sheet suggests a more complex and significant story than any of the other sheets is that whereas the sheet with the bloodstain tells the simple story that the bride was a virgin, the blank sheet tells an ambiguous story that cannot be resolved: either that the bride was not a virgin on the wedding night or else that she was still a virgin on the next morning. There is no puzzle in the bloodstained sheets; however, there is a real mystery in the white sheet. Furthermore, the very nature of the white sheet permits many more possibilities than the bloodstained sheets. Although one may read the stains as if they were inkblots suggesting several possibilities—signs of the zodiac, pictures from the world of ideas—there is no limitation as to how one may read the white sheet.

"Skibsdrængens fortælling" ("The Sailor-Boy's Tale") uses marvelous elements to dramatize a young man's initiation into adulthood. A nineteen-year-old deckhand, Simon, sees a peregrine falcon entangled in tackle yarn. He rescues her but not without being hacked on the thumb. On shore, he becomes infatuated with a teenage girl and, in his anxiety to keep a tryst with her, accidentally kills a Russian sailor. Pursued by the Russian's shipmates, Simon is rescued by an old Lapp woman who shelters him, mingles her blood with his, and reveals herself as a witch who had metamorphosed herself into the falcon that he had freed. The next morning, she pushes him on his way and prophesies that he will be faithful to the sea his life long. The charm of Dinesen's fable lies in its use of fairy-tale elements to dramatize the transformation that entry into maturation constitutes.

Isaac Bashevis Singer was born in Poland of a Hasidic rabbinical family. In 1935, anticipating the German invasion of Poland, he emigrated to the United States but continued to write in Yiddish. Dipping his pen in an inkwell of demonology, he excels in dramatizing a varied, forceful, and frequently fantastic vision of Eastern Europe's vanished Jewry, finding his imagination most at home in the culture of the *shtetl*—a small Jewish ghetto village of nineteenth century Poland. The short story is Singer's natural medium, affording an appropriate vehicle for his compact, coiled, and clipped style, which reflects the Yiddish oral tradition: ironic, nervous, staccato, and proverbial. His greatest stories breathe an enigmatic moral tone, of life as a dance on the grave with both evil and death imminent. No loving God smiles His benefactions upon His chosen people. The reader catches none of the sentimental idealism of such Yiddish writers as Sholom Aleichem, none of the soft dreaminess of Marc Chagall's tailors and fiddlers floating lyrically over rooftops. Instead, Satan's forces often hold sway, with the world a moral Armageddon and people staring into the shattered ruins of their lives as if into a bottomless pit. Despite his traditional techniques, Singer has a modern sensibility, caustic, unsettling, absurdist, regarding the world as incoherent, arbitrary, and mysterious.

"Gimpel Tam" ("Gimpel the Fool"), his most famous story, is narrated by the title character who is a schlemiel as well as a holy simpleton. He is wholly gullible, eager to believe all he is told and to trust everyone, particularly his sluttish wife, Elka, none of whose six children are his. Yet Singer's characterization of Gimpel is enigmatic: Like a Shakespearean character, he may choose to play the fool so as to retain his moral sanity in an exploitive, mendacious world. When people become relativists in Singer's writings, they become tortured by doubts. Gimpel prefers an absolute faith, finding the value of his life in a total openness to suffering and ridicule. He is certain he is doing God's will; the reader may have doubts.

"The Gentleman from Cracow" is set in a poor, tiny village tempted by unaccustomed luxury when, miraculously, a wealthy, widowed doctor arrives bearing many alms. He organizes a splendid ball, providing appropriate clothes for all, spreading gold everywhere, and announcing that he will choose his new wife at the festival. At the ball, the doctor dances with the whorish Hodle, promises a dowry of ten thousand ducats to every woman who will wed, but, when denounced by a true believer, he sets the town on fire and reveals his identity as the Chief of Devils, with an eye in his chest and a tail of serpents. Hodle is discovered to be the witch Lilith, while evil spirits celebrate their unholy union. Purged of their greed and lust, the villagers, poor again, resign themselves to their small existence.

Colette is of the same generation as André Gide and Marcel Proust, and she greatly admired the latter, sharing with him a remarkable talent for acutely rendering vibrating, sensual recollections of childhood experiences. In the 1920's Colette produced a series of novellas that were masterpieces: *La Maison de Claudine* (1922; *My Mother's House*, 1953), *La Naissance du jour* (1928; *A Lesson in Love*, 1932; also known as *Break of Day*), *Sido* (1929; English translation, 1953), and, by far the most famous: *Chéri* (1920; English translation, 1929) and *La Fin de Chéri* (1926; *The Last of Chéri*, 1932).

Even though the last two were published six years apart, they form one continuous love story. They relate the liaison between Léa, an aging courtesan, and the extremely handsome but also extremely dependent Frédéric Peloux, nicknamed Chéri; the lovers' ages differ by twenty-four years. The scene is Paris, the setting, the demimonde, the period, 1906-1919. In the first novella Léa is the gracefully protective mistress, Chéri the moody, narcissistic taker of her tenderness. He will soon be married to Edmée, a beautiful, wealthy young woman. Chéri returns from his honeymoon tense and irritable, bursts into Léa's bedroom and insists that they resume their relationship. Heroically, Léa decides not to do so, instead sending him back to his wife.

The Last of Chéri continues in the postwar Paris of 1919. Chéri, now thirty-two, is unable to cope with what he regards as the frenetic busyness of his wife in a military hospital. He feels empty and apathetic, unable to take hold of life. Once more returning to Léa, Chéri discovers her to be a corpulent, gray-haired woman who has put eroticism behind her. Chéri clings to his memory of Léa as a mother-mistress, refusing to recognize the inevitability of natural changes. Disgusted with life, listless, depressed, he ends up shooting himself in the temple.

Léa is a splendidly drawn character, one of the strongest and most memorable in modern fiction. Colette uses sensory imagery with superb skill, creating potently erotic scenes without any explicit rendering of intercourse. She relies instead on oblique observations, color symbolism, and incisive notation of the intricate network of vital details and habits surrounding a relationship. She explores and accepts life's joys and pains as inevitable and fascinating aspects of existence, with no metaphysical anguish, no ideological premises, no social commitment, no estrangement and much wonder, delight, and tact.

Jean-Paul Sartre constituted himself a prodigiously creative one-man band of modern thought and literature, doing important work in philosophy, psychology, drama, biography, literary criticism, journalism, political pamphleteering, and screenwriting, as well as fiction. In 1939, he published five short stories under the title of *Le Mur* (*The Wall and Other Stories*, 1948), later to appear in England and the United States as the more provocative *Intimacy*. Each tale focuses on a particular physical or emotional experience in order to dramatize a particular philosophical concept. The body of Sartre's ideas is his version of existentialism, according to which human beings are cast into a godless world without any preordained or privileged position or "essence." Every individual must therefore invent the values by which he or she lives through doing just that—living them. Human beings' freedom can lead to exhilaration but also to anguish, since they must continually define their nature by their behavior in an irrational, absurd world. As one character says in the play *Huis clos* (1944; *No Exit*, 1947), "You are—your life, and nothing else."

The title story of the collection seeks to refute the contention of the German philosopher Martin Heidegger that individuals can live meaningfully toward their own death and thus humanize, even heroize it, as Kyo Gisors does in André Malraux's novel *La Condition humaine* (1933; *Man's Fate*, 1934). The protagonist, Pablo Ibbieta, is a Spanish Republican who has been taken prisoner by Franco's Falangists in the Civil War. Together with Tom, an Irishman from the International Brigade, and Juan, a teenage Spaniard who took no part in politics, he is condemned to death. Sartre concentrates on the feelings that Pablo has as he contemplates his impending nothingness. While young Juan goes into sobbing hysterics and Tom urinates in his pants through sheer terror, Pablo, though sweating heavily in his cold cell, does his best to confront death with Hemingwayesque stoicism, seeking to remain "terribly hard."

In the face of death, Pablo decides that nothing matters to him anymore—his mistress, his comrades, his political cause. The wall of his prison becomes a symbol of his coming annihilation, with death nullifying all meaning. In the morning, given fifteen minutes to decide whether he would be willing to save his life by revealing the whereabouts of his friend and leader, Juan Gris, Pablo decides to play a trick on his captors. He tells them that Gris is hiding in the cemetery, knowing that Gris is at his cousins' home. It comes to light that Gris, however, having quarreled with his cousins, did flee to the gravediggers' shack; when the Falangists find him there, they kill him. Hearing of this absurd coincidence, Pablo can only collapse in delirious laughter.

When Albert Camus received the Nobel Prize in December, 1957, he pledged himself to distill a literature of dignity and courage from a century often at war, beset by self-doubts, and threatened by disintegration. In the collection of six stories he issued earlier that year, *L'Exil et le royaume* (1957; *Exile and the Kingdom*, 1958), he largely fulfilled that promise. All the tales are studies in exile, all deal with people trying to find a country where they will be fully at home. Four are set in Camus's native Algeria, one in Brazil, one in France. Each work is subtly written and builds to an inevitable climax, in the manner of Maupassant or Lawrence.

In "L'Hôte" ("The Guest"), Camus admirably dramatizes his absurdist philosophy that life is difficult and lacks ultimate meaning but that nevertheless a man defines himself by the quality of his moral decisions and his courage in acting on them. The protagonist is a French Algerian schoolteacher, Daru, who has charge of a one-room school for Arab children in the middle of a bleak Algerian plateau, which he nevertheless loves as his birthplace. He is given the unwelcome duty of transporting an Arab prisoner to police headquarters at a village about four hours away. This is not part of Daru's job, but police shorthandedness in the face of an incipient Arabian revolt has thrust it upon him. A sensitive, humane, and compassionate person, Daru treats his prisoner as a guest rather than as a member of an inferior culture. He rebels against the notion of handing over the Arab, who had killed in a tribal dispute, to French authorities for a trial.

The story centers on Daru's dilemma. Should he obey a gendarme's orders and deliver the Arab to the French? Should he take the Arab to his nomadic tribe? Should he give the Arab his freedom? Daru solves his dilemma by taking his guest to a high plateau from which he gives the Arab the choice of walking either to a French prison or to his freedom. The Arab chooses prison, and Daru returns sadly to his classroom, only to find, chalked on the blackboard, the threat: "You have handed over our brother. You will pay for this." This text poignantly illustrates both the necessity and the burdensome nature of individual moral choice. In Camus's world, human beings live, choose, suffer, and die essentially alone. At the story's end, Daru finds himself isolated in every sense, perilously misunderstood, a martyr to Camus's sorrowful humanism.

The Russian author Isaac Babel remains a haunting anomaly in modern literature. This Jewish writer, who once called himself a "past master of the art of silence," left behind him, besides a few scenarios and plays, fewer than four hundred pages of published short fiction. Whatever else he might have written but was not ready to publish was lost to the world when Babel was arrested by Joseph Stalin's police in 1939, to die soon after—whether by bullet or illness—in a Soviet concentration camp. Yet his slim literary legacy has sufficed to establish his reputation as one of the twentieth century's important European writers.

As an artist, Babel is full of ambivalences and paradoxes: He is a Soviet writer who welcomes the revolution yet dramatizes its terror through the mindless, ruthless savagery of the cossacks. He is a self-consciously Jewish intellectual, a "chap with specs," who is nevertheless driven to strike blows against his cultural heritage by celebrating guiltless violence, primitive energy, and even aimless destruction. He is a traditional Russian writer, with debts to Leo Tolstoy and Chekhov, who identifies strongest with Maupassant and Gustave Flaubert, secondarily with Stephen Crane and Hemingway. The example of Flaubert seems the most compelling in Babel's monklike devotion to his art and untiring struggle with language to find exactly the right phrase or word for each nuance of statement. "No iron can stab the heart" (he writes in the story "Guy de Maupassant") "with such force as a period put just at the right place."

The crucial experience of Babel's life was his service with a regiment of cossacks in 1920, during the civil war that followed the Russian Revolution. In the superb tales that he derived from this event, collected in *Konarmiia* (1926; *Red Cavalry*, 1929), he contrasts, in story after story, the glamorous but cruel grace of the cossacks with the humaneness, physical inadequacy, and pacifism of the Jews. In "Moi pervyi gus" ("My First Goose"), the Jewish newcomer to the cossack brigade is snubbed for his intellectualism, until he ingratiates himself by killing, in particularly grotesque fashion, a goose belonging to an old woman. Now admitted to the fellowship of the group, the narrator's "heart, stained with bloodshed, grated and brimmed over," in a last sentence loaded with enigmas.

"My First Goose" is one of Babel's most famous stories because it structures the conflict between mind and body and language and physicality so starkly. Although there is something beautiful about the Cossacks—the commander's long legs like "girls sheathed to the neck in shining riding boots"—there is also something primitive and violent that underlies the soldiers. The narrator primarily aligns himself with language and thought, but he cannot escape his animal nature. Although the death of the goose can hardly be called a murder, it is motivated by a violent desire to assert one's self physically.

The primary impact of the *Red Cavalry* collection is one of shock. The stories are lean, hard, terse, intense, gorgeously colored, kinesthetic. Babel is ready to wrench language to gain nervous immediacy, even to inflict psychic wounds on the reader. He specializes in interweaving extremes of behavior. In "The Death of Dolgushov," a badly wounded cossack by that name has his entrails hanging over his knees and begs the Jewish narrator for a mercy killing; the narrator refuses, being soft and scrupulous. A comrade of Dolgushov then does the job and turns furiously on the Jew: "You guys in specs have about as much pity for chaps like us as a cat has for a mouse." He cocks his rifle to shoot the narrator, who has the courage to ride away slowly, "feeling the chill of death in my back." Another cossack diverts the executioner from double murder, catches up with the narrator, and offers him a shriveled apple. The Jew is hardly ever accepted on terms of egalitarian fellowship with the bloodthirsty cossack. Babel strains for a union of passion and tenderness but usually fails to achieve it, being honest enough to discover them tragically dissociated in modern life.

Even though Vladimir Nabokov spent nineteen years in the United States, his Russian roots and the three-fourths of his life in Europe strongly stamp him as a continental author. In his productive career, he composed about forty stories as well as novels, poetry, memoirs, and literary criticism. His early stories are set in the post-World War I era, with Germany the usual location, and sensitive, exiled Russian men the usual protagonists. Nabokov displays in these tales his abiding fascination with the interplay between reality and fantasy as well as his devotion to style, commanding a remarkable precision of language and nuanced tones ranging from grandeur to irony to parody.

In "Signs and Symbols," Nabokov wrote his most sorrowful and possibly finest story. An elderly, poor Russian émigré couple go to visit their son on his birthday; he is in a sanatorium, diagnosed as afflicted with "referential mania," whereby the patient considers all events occurring anywhere near him as veiled references to his own life. On their trip to the sanatorium, the machinery of existence seems to malfunction in a variety of frustrating ways. Once there, they are told that their son has again attempted suicide and should not be disturbed. Back home, in the story's last section, the couple decides to bring the son back to their apartment; each parent will spend part of the night with him. A telephone call, however, indicates that this time the troubled son has succeeded in escaping this world. Artistically, this story is virtually flawless: It is intricately patterned, densely textured, intense in tone and feeling. Nabokov, the literary jeweler, has here cut more deeply than his usual surfaces, has abandoned gamesmanship and mirror play to face the grimmest horrors of a sometimes hopeless world.

Alberto Moravia, born Alberto Pincherle, was Italy's leading writer of fiction for at least five decades. His novels and stories are grounds for battles of the sexes that sometimes seem as grueling as a fight to the finish, with sex a sickness and love a torment. Eroticism for Moravia, however, is only a metaphor for dealing with even deeper problems of human existence. For his protagonists, sex is never an end in itself; instead, it is an expression of will, a means to power. Moravia is fundamentally a romantic moralist who indicts egotism, greed, the bourgeois mentality that frustrates natural instincts, the social decadence that leads to fascism. The problem that most preoccupies him is the moral consequences of acts of will—or failure to act as a result of hypersensitive passivity. His prose, hard and urgent, is reminiscent of Stendhal, as is his union of cool observation with lyrical fervor.

Perhaps Moravia's most successful novelette is *Agostino* (1944; English translation, 1947). It explores the agonies, bewilderments, and frustrations of adolescence with infernal accuracy. As a sensitive boy of thirteen, Agostino finds himself powerfully attracted to his beautiful, stately mother who has recently been widowed. When she strikes up a friendship with a handsome, womanizing swimmer at the beach, Agostino attaches himself to a gang of tough, cruel working-class lads who mock him for his middle-class status and sexual innocence. At the center of this vulgar group is a six-fingered, grotesque beach attendant, Saro, whose inclinations are manifestly homosexual and whose cruises on a sailboat constitute parodies of a Homeric epic. Agostino's previous Eden of unconditional bonding with his mother is transformed into a disheartening world of anguish, aggression, and amorality. The proletarian gang unjustly accuses him of pederasty and brutalizes and exploits him. His tenderness for his mother changes into pained awareness of her erotic drives. Agostino ends up being misunderstood as well as mistreated, aware that "a long, unhappy time would have to pass" before he will reach adulthood. The story is a masterfully accurate study of the suffering that coming of age can entail.

Japan

In his forty-five years, the Japanese author Yukio Mishima, often compared by critics to either Gide or Hemingway, produced a staggering amount of literary works: forty novels, twenty plays, eighty stories, and countless essays. He became the most internationally celebrated talent among his nation's twentieth century authors, eclipsing the Nobel Prize-winning Yasunari Kawabata and the distinguished Jun'ichirō Tanizaki. Writing with a fluid Western flair, sometimes slick but often subtle, sardonic, sex-obsessed, Mishima dredges up the explosive passions and capricious violence buried in the Japanese subconscious, commenting with sharp irony and grisly humor on their modern manifestations, relating his country's feudal past to its materialistic present.

Mishima's most notorious story is "Ykoku" ("Patriotism"). It was inspired by the Army Rebellion of 1936, which he would invest with increasing symbolic significance as his own special brand of reactionary patriotism evolved. On February 26, 1936, twenty-one officers in Japan's Imperial Army attempted to overthrow what they considered an insufficiently militant government and succeeded in assassinating three cabinet ministers. When an angry Emperor Hirohito insisted on severe punishment for these mutineers, several of them committed ritual suicide—seppuku. In Mishima's tale, the hero is a young lieutenant whose comrades have kept him ignorant of the attempted coup out of consideration for his recent marriage. The following day, he is ordered to march against his rebellious friends. Unable to resolve his dilemma of conflicting loyalties, the officer purifies himself in a bath, makes love to his wife, then performs the act of seppuku. His bride thereupon thrusts a dagger into her throat.

So intrigued was Mishima by the dramatic dynamics of this story that he made a powerful, twenty-four-minute film of it in which he starred in the officer's role. Ten years later, life was made to imitate art. On November 25, 1970, accompanied by four cadets whom he had trained, Mishima visited the commandant of Japan's Self-Defense Force in Tokyo. The commandant was forced, at sword point, to assemble his regiment in the courtyard. Mishima exhorted this captive audience to rise up with him against a spineless postwar democracy that no longer revered the country's imperial tradition. Jeered and hissed at by the young men, Mishima broke off his harangue and committed seppuku (ritual suicide). Honor satisfied, one of his cadets beheaded him with a long sword, completing the ritual. His macabre death served to endow many of his works with an eerie aroma of art anticipating the extinction of the artist.

Latin America

Prior to World War II, Latin American writers relied on traditional realism in their representations. Since then, this regionalist writing has undergone a series of drastic changes to become one of contemporary literature's most imaginative and avant-garde art forms. The progenitor of this revolution is the brilliant, intricate Argentine author Jorge Luis Borges, intellectually as well as structurally one of the most sophisticated and complex of twentieth century authors. His fictive world stems from his encyclopedic and often esoteric readings in not only literature but also philosophy and theology, with his tales exuding an aura of fantastic elaboration. He loves to play out abstract intellectual games by pushing an initial situation or concept to its logical extreme, regardless of realistic plausibility or psychological consistency.

Jorge Luis Borges might well be called a writer's writer, for the subject of his stories is more often the nature of writing itself than actual events in the world. By the same token, Borges should be seen as a metaphysical writer, for his stories most often focus on the fantastic paradoxes that ensnare those who think. Because of Borges's overriding interest in aesthetic and metaphysical reality, his stories often resemble fables or essays.

One of his best-known essay/stories, "Pierre Menard, Author of the *Quixote*," deals with a French writer who decides to write *El ingenioso hidalgo don Quixote de la Mancha* (1605, 1615; *The History of the Valorous and Wittie Knight-Errant, Don Quixote of the Mancha*, 1612-1620; better known as *Don Quixote de la Mancha*), in spite of the fact that it has already been written by Miguel de Cervantes. Borges then compares the two versions and finds them identical; however, he argues that the second version is richer, more ambitious, and in many ways more subtle than Cervantes's original. In another well-known story, "Funes the Memorious," Borges presents a character who is unable to forget details of his experience, no matter how small.

If the situations of these two men seem alien to ordinary human experience, it is because Borges is interested in the extraordinary nature of metaphysical rather than physical reality. The fact that Pierre

Menard can rewrite the *Don Quixote de la Mancha* identical to the original yet create a more complex and subtle work can be attributed to the notion that one reads a present work with all previous works inscribed within it. The fact that Funes is condemned to remember every single detail of his experience means that he can never tell stories because he is unable to abstract from his experience. Funes knows that to tell the story of his life would not be a story at all but an exact recounting of every event and every nuance of every event. Thus, by the time of his death he would have barely finished classifying the memories of his childhood. What the story suggests is the fact that absolute reality in all its specific detail is unlivable: "The truth is that we all live by leaving behind."

Borges's most common technique is to take previously established genres such as the science-fiction story, the detective story, or the philosophical essay, and then to parody those forms by pushing them to absurd extremes. Thus, most of Borges's fictions are puzzling, frustrating, sometimes shocking, often humorous, but always profoundly thought-provoking. "Funes, the Memorious" is, in a way, a justification for the fantastic nature of his art, for, as Funes's experience shows, absolute reality is intolerable and inhuman. Only the fantastic is real.

Like Sartre and Camus, Borges is a philosophical absurdist—but with a difference. He does not share their commitment to social justice or to individual responsibility and freedom of choice. He subordinates his characters to the control of his plots, content to draw them as archetypal figures created solely to illustrate ideas. Borges's protagonists are usually engaged in a vain quest for knowledge, power, or salvation, since he considers all pursuits of truth as vain endeavors. His stories can often be read as parables of an ambiguous universe, rich in metaphysical implications, filled with mazes of hearsay and confusion, with dreams, mirrors, and labyrinths that destroy any assumption of stability, harmony, or progress.

In "La biblioteca de Babel" ("The Library of Babel"), Borges sketches a cosmic library with an infinite array of bookcases, lamps, hallways, and staircases, which represent the cosmos. The narrator, a tired old librarian, has spent his life vainly searching for a certain book, among countless billions of books, which will be the cipher and compendium of all the others. Unable to find it, he is yet unwilling to accept the thesis of recent skeptics who think of the library—that is, the world—as indecipherable and meaningless. The library conveys Borges's notion of modern man alienated in a mysterious world. Yet the librarian tries to seek solace in the belief that, while the human species will eventually become extinct, the universe—that is, the Library—will endure forever because it is "limitless and periodic." If an eternal traveler were to traverse its vastness in any direction, he would find it cyclical, with the same volumes repeated in the same disorder—which would amount to a kind of order. This story amounts to a virtuoso performance brooding symbolically over human beings's intellectual exertions as they pathetically try to disentangle and understand an inexplicable universe or to console themselves with dreamy speculations.

"Tlön, Uqbar, Orbis Tertius," Borges's longest and most demanding tale, expresses nearly all of his central ideas, preoccupations, and mannerisms. It opens with the narrator Borges hearing his friend, Adolfo Bioy Casares, alluding to Uqbar, an exotic land he has read about in his *Anglo-American Cyclopaedia.* Bioy's encyclopedia contains a long article on this country in Asia Minor, but other copies of this work lack the entry. Uqbar's literature is invariably fantastic in mode and set on the imaginary planet of Tlön. Two years later, the narrator comes across one volume of an encyclopedia about Tlön. The imaginary inhabitants of fancied Tlön are all idealists of the Berkeleian type, believing that the universe is a subjective projection of the mind and lacks material existence. Consequently, Tlön's language has no nouns (which presuppose a world of objects), things tend to efface themselves when they are forgotten, and materialism is inconceivable as a philosophy.

In a "Postscript, 1947" (even though Borges composed this text in 1940), a letter brought to the narrator's attention discloses that a secret society of scholars, including Bishop Berkeley, was founded in seventeenth century England to invent an idealistic country, and that, in the nineteenth century United

States, an eccentric American atheistic tycoon financed the Tlön project, which resulted in a forty-volume encyclopedia regarding this planet, whose projected title was *Orbis Tertius*. In the 1940's, Tlön's fantastic world intruded upon the real world, with the widespread distribution of the Tlön encyclopedia. People were fascinated by descriptions of this ordered, logical region, and Tlön's history and languages are now taking control of school curricula, displacing English, French, and Spanish. "Now, in all memories, a fictitious past occupies the place of any other. . . . The world will be Tlön."

Borges's partiality for philosophical idealism animates this superb story. He shows how reality depends on one's perceptions, how the mind can create, modify, or destroy both past and present. The tale's conclusion underscores Borges's skepticism: the narrator ignores Tlön's incursions to concentrate on translating into Spanish the major work of the seventeenth century English baroque writer, Sir Thomas Browne: *Urn Burial*. Eventually, Borges implies, the vogue of idealism will yield to another and that to another, ad infinitum.

Conclusion

Like all art forms, short fiction between 1920 and 1960 both reflects and shapes the culture of the period, which is dominated by modernism and postmodernism. To be sure, some of the authors discussed (Welty, Frank O'Connor, Singer, Dinesen, Colette) use traditional fictive techniques and themes to link their vision of humanity to nineteenth century perspectives. Most writers of note, however, imbue their tales with the sense of loss, alienation, and despair that characterizes their age. Short fiction is natural to modern culture's nervousness, impatience, skepticism, intensity, and preference for quickness and compression.

Most writers, from Faulkner and Hemingway to Sartre to Mishima to Borges, question the existence of a coherent and stable social order as they revolt against traditional literary forms. They elevate individual existence over society (Roth, Camus, Babel, Nabokov), unconscious feeling over conscious reasoning (Faulkner, Flannery O'Connor, Malamud, Lawrence), passion and will over the intellect and systematic morals (Porter, Cheever, Moravia), dense actuality over practical reality (Greene, Bellow, Mann). They exhibit personal urgency as well as experimental verve. In sum, theirs is a disturbing imagination of disaster, subverting previously accepted modes of existence and revealing the abyss of nothingness over which human lives are precariously poised.

Gerhard Brand, updated by Charles E. May

Bibliography

Abramson, Edward A. *Bernard Malamud Revisited*. New York: Twayne, 1993. A brief, general introduction to the short stories, divided into such categories as fantasies, Italian stories, father-son stories, and socio-political stories.

Bosha, Francis J., ed. *The Critical Response to John Cheever.* Westport, Conn.: Greenwood Press, 1994. A collection of reviews and critical essays on Cheever's novels and short-story collections by various commentators and critics.

Brinkmeyer, Robert H., Jr. *Katherine Anne Porter's Artistic Development*. Baton Rouge: Louisiana State University Press, 1993. Argues that when Porter created a memory-based dialogue with her southern past, she reached her artistic height.

Ferguson, James. *Faulkner's Short Fiction*. Knoxville: University of Tennessee Press, 1991. Discusses Faulkner's poetic and narrative impulses, his themes of loss of innocence, failure to love, loneliness, and isolation; comments on his manipulation of time and point of view.

Flora, Joseph M. *Ernest Hemingway: A Study of the Short Fiction*. Boston: Twayne, 1989. Focuses on the importance of reading the stories within the literary context Hemingway creates for them in the collections.

O'Hara, James Eugene. *John Cheever: A Study of the Short Fiction*. Boston: Twayne, 1989. A general introduction to Cheever's short stories with comments on fiction by Cheever and a few critical articles by other critics.

Rath, Sura P., and Mary Neff Shaw, eds. *Flannery O'Connor: New Perspectives*. Athens: University of Georgia Press, 1996. Mostly feminist and Bakhtinian perspectives to such stories as "A View From the Woods" and "The Artificial Nigger."

Sicher, Efraim. *Style and Structure in the Prose of Isaak Babel*. Columbus, Ohio: Slavica, 1986. A formalist study analyzing setting, characterization, narrative structure, and point of view in Babel's stories.

Thornton, Weldon. *D. H. Lawrence: A Study of the Short Fiction*. New York: Twayne, 1993. Makes a case for the technical skill, psychological depth, and thematic subtlety of Lawrence's short fiction.

Wagner-Martin, Linda, ed. *Hemingway: Seven Decades of Criticism*. East Lansing: Michigan State University Press, 1998. Includes essays ranging from Gertrude Stein's 1923 review of Hemingway's stories to recent responses to *The Garden of Eden* (1986).

THE LATE TWENTIETH CENTURY: 1960-2000

In the final decades of the twentieth century, the American short story enjoyed what many critics have called a renaissance of interest among both popular readers and professional critics. Stimulated partially by the popularity of such writers as Raymond Carver, who specialized in the short story, and the willingness of such editors as Gordon Lish, who encouraged short-story writers, a large number of short-story collections began to be published in the 1970's. So many have been published in the last few decades that this survey must focus only on the most representative and influential short-story writers of the period.

Because surveys of the short story in other countries are included elsewhere in *Critical Survey of Short Fiction*, this survey will focus only on writers in America and England; and since the short story has never been a popular form in England, whereas it has enjoyed burgeoning success in America, the focus will primarily be on the American short story. Also, since the short story as an expression of cultural diversity in America is admirably covered in special surveys on the African American, Native American, Asian American, and Latino short story elsewhere in *Critical Survey of Short Fiction*, this essay will not cover those areas.

Traditional Modernist Stories: 1960's

Several important American short-story writers of the 1960's, such as Flannery O'Connor, John Cheever, Bernard Malamud, and John Updike, who began their careers in the 1950's, represent the continuation of the traditional modern short story that originated with Sherwood Anderson, Ernest Hemingway, Katherine Anne Porter, and Eudora Welty earlier in the century.

Flannery O'Connor

Following her influential 1955 story collection *A Good Man Is Hard to Find*, startling readers and critics alike with its unique combination of complex Catholicism and simple southern fundamentalism, Flannery O'Connor's 1965 collection, *Everything That Rises Must Converge*, continued with similar rural characters and similar religious issues. Two of the most representative stories in this collection are "Greenleaf" and "Revelation," both of which focus on women who think they are "good country people," but who must face their true selves in violent religious visions.

"Revelation" focuses on Mrs. Turpin, who, while in a doctor's office with her husband, thinks of her superiority to those around her. When she shouts, "Thank you, Jesus," for not making her "a nigger or white-trash or ugly," one of O'Connor's physically unattractive but intellectually complex young women throws a book at her and calls her a warthog, telling her to "go back to hell" where she came from. Later, when Mrs. Turpin returns home, she stands by her hog pen asking God, "How am I saved and from hell too?" When she sees a vision of hordes of white trash, Negroes, freaks, and lunatics being led up to Heaven, while people like herself bring up the rear, she realizes the hard Christian truth that the last shall be first and all self-righteous virtue must be burned away by God's grace.

This final sacramental vision is even more difficult for Mrs. May in "Greenleaf," another of O'Connor's white middle-class southerners burdened by shiftless white trash. However, in spite of Mr. Greenleaf's laziness and Mrs. Greenleaf's prayer-healing, they hardly age at all, while Mrs. May is exhausted from overwork. Particularly galling to Mrs. May is a Greenleaf bull that is always on her land; she dreams of it devouring everything of hers until there is nothing left. The story ends when the bull comes into her pasture and gores her, not as an act of gratuitous violence, but as a symbol of being struck by the blinding light of revelation. Once again, O'Connor confronts her smug and sanctimonious character with the hard truth of Christian grace—that salvation is not earned nor easy but seizes one with the painful paradox of losing the self to find the self.

John Cheever

John Cheever first made his impact as a short-story writer in the 1950's with *The Enormous Radio and Other Stories* (1953). He continued to publish important stories for the next two decades, climaxing his career with his *The Stories of John Cheever* winning the Pulitzer Prize in 1978. The best-known story from Cheever's late collection *The Brigadier and the Golf Widow* (1964) is "The Swimmer," which combines a common theme of earlier Cheever stories—middle-aged men trying to hold on to youth and some meaningful place in life—with his penchant for the fantastic seen in such early stories as "The Enormous Radio." The complexity of this story of a man's decision to swim home from a party through his neighbors' swimming pools derives from its subtle combination of fantasy and reality. Although the action is presented as a real event, clues increasingly point to a distortion of time in the story. Because the protagonist must be allowed to believe that his metaphoric swim through the future and past is an actual swim in the present, the reader is never sure which events in the story are real and which are fantasy. The metaphoric nature of the swim is suggested by Cheever's presenting the protagonist as a legendary explorer and the pools as a "the river of life."

Bernard Malamud

Although Bernard Malamud is the best-known spokesman of the Jewish experience in American literature, the Jew in his short stories is an embodiment of the complex moral experience of universal human suffering, responsibility, and love, rather than a realistic representative of a particular ethnic or social situation. As the old tailor Manischevitz says in "Angel Levine," "Believe me, there are Jews everywhere." Indeed, in Malamud's worldview, all who suffer are Jews. The suffering that plagues Malamud's ghetto Jews is not the result of economics or politics or social injustice; it is the result of being merely human and thus ultimately alone in the world.

Although Malamud is a master of both the realistic and the fantastic, he is at his best when he mixes conventions of the two styles to establish a fictional world in which moral demands seem to force the supernatural into being from the psychic depths of the individual character's secret need. A number of Malamud stories focus on a mysterious stranger who makes demands on the central character which he cannot fulfill. The most famous such story is "The Last Mohican," which introduces the central character in the collection *Pictures of Fidelman: An Exhibition* (1969) who is set upon by beggar Susskind when he goes to Italy to study art. Although Susskind says all he wants is one of Fidelman's suits, what he really wants is Fidelman to come to some realization about the moral responsibility of art and the lack of authenticity of his own efforts. When Susskind burns the only copy of Fidelman's manuscript on Italian art, Fidelman is at first outraged. However, realizing Susskind's role at the end of the story, Fidelman chases him to give him the suit, crying all is forgiven, but Fidelman is unable to atone for his errors.

The most fantastic version of the alien stranger who demands acceptance, understanding, even love, in Malamud's fiction is the bedraggled Jewbird in the story of the same name who appears out of nowhere one day at Harry Cohen's window, seeking protection from "anti-Semeets" (*Idiots First*, 1963). Cohen puts up with the inconveniences of the Jewbird as long as he can and finally throws him out into the snow. When he is found in the spring by Cohen's son, who asks him who did this to him, the dying bird answers, "Anti-Semeets."

Malamud's stories suggest there is a powerful redemptive value in suffering. To truly find one's identity, especially in relation to the mysterious other, one must give more than one thought one could, endure more than one thought possible, and emerge with one's former false self burned away. More than any other modern practitioner of the genre, Malamud knows that the short story is both a very old and a very new form at once. He is able to focus on a powerful moment of time in which characters are caught in such complex moral dilemmas that no minister, no rabbi, no therapist, no law, no social policy can rescue them.

John Updike

No other living writer is so representative of that well-known brand of modern fiction known as *The*

New Yorker short story as John Updike. Updike's second collection of short fiction, *Pigeon Feathers and Other Stories*, which appeared in 1962, contains some of his most popular stories, including, in addition to the title story, "The Persistence of Desire," "A Sense of Shelter," "Wife-Wooing," "Lifeguard," and the anthology favorite, "A & P." Updike's collection of stories *The Afterlife and Other Stories* (1994) features a number of stories that focus on growing older.

What makes "A & P" Updike's most popular story is its presentation of the medieval notion of chivalric behavior in contemporary language. The young narrator Sammy is both a heroic figure and a childish grandstander. On one hand, his attitude toward the girls who come into the A & P store where he works seems morally superior to that of Lengel's Sunday-school-superintendent rigidity, but on the other hand he sees them only as three bodies. How the reader judges Sammy's character—which is revealed primarily through his language—determines how the reader reacts to his final chivalric gesture of quitting his job.

"Pigeon Feathers," one of the most explicit examples of Updike's Christian perspective, is a conventional, well-made story about a fourteen-year-old boy who confronts a challenge to his religious views. Visited by a vision of death and dissatisfied with his pastor's pragmatic interpretation of immortality, the boy feels that if there is nothing after death, then all of life is an ocean of horror. The epiphany of the story comes when, after shooting some troublesome pigeons and admiring the geometric lines of their feathers, he finally feels certain that the God who "lavished such craft upon these worthless birds would not destroy his whole Creation by refusing to let David live forever."

The title of Updike's 1994 collection of short fictions, *The Afterlife and Other Stories*, alludes not to life after death but to that ambiguous human condition just past middle age. Updike writes here about men, mostly in their fifties and sixties, who have entered such a state with, if not joy, at least graceful acceptance. Carter Billings, the fiftyish hero of the title story, is startled to discover that many of his friends are doing sudden surprising things in their middle age. When he and his wife go to visit one such couple who have moved to England, Billings has an incidental encounter that unsettles his settled ways. Thinking of his life as merely going through the motions and realizing with chagrin that there are vast areas of the world he no longer cares about, he flirts with the surprising and the unpredictable. "The Afterlife" is a typical delicate Updike story, lyrical and low-key but resonant with realization.

EXPERIMENTAL POSTMODERNIST STORIES: 1960'S

Partially in reaction to the traditional modernism of the stories of O'Connor, Cheever, Malamud, and Updike and partially a result of the invasion of European structuralism and deconstruction with their emphasis on the nature of fictionality, the most obvious shift in the short story in the 1960's was the introduction of experimental, metafictional short fiction by such writers as John Barth, Donald Barthelme, Robert Coover, and William H. Gass. Rather than presenting itself "as if" it were real—a mimetic mirroring of external reality—postmodernist short fiction makes its own artistic conventions and devices the subject of the story as well as its theme. The underlying assumption is that literary language is not a proxy for something else but rather an object of study itself. William H. Gass says that the fiction writer in the 1970's understands that his business is not to render a world but to make one from language.

JOHN BARTH

In 1968, John Barth surprised readers with his experimental collection of stories *Lost in the Funhouse*, in which fiction refused to focus on its so-called proper subject—the external world—and instead continually turned the reader's attention back to what Barth considered fiction's real subject—the process of fiction-making itself. Barth insists that the prosaic in fiction is only there to be transformed into fabulation. The artist's ostensible subject is not the main point, he argues; rather it is only an excuse or raw material for focusing on the nature of the fiction-making process. Great literature, says Barth, is almost always, regardless of what it seems to be about, about itself.

"Autobiography" is one of the most thoroughgoing self-reflexive fictions in *Lost in the Funhouse*, for it does not pretend, as conventional fictions do, that the voice of the fiction is the voice of a human being; rather it confronts directly the inescapable fact that what speaks to the reader is the story itself; thus, the only autobiography a story can present is a story of its own coming into being and its own mode of existence. Every statement in "Autobiography" is an assertion, in one way or another, about its own fictionality. Some of the key characteristics of narrative that the story foregrounds are that fictions have no life unless they are read, that fictions cannot know themselves, that fictions have no body, that fictions have one-track minds, that fictions can neither start themselves nor stop themselves, and that fictions reflect their authors in distorted ways.

ROBERT COOVER

Robert Coover's first collection of short stories, *Pricksongs and Descants* (1969), consists of a number of stories based on fairy tales, legends, folktales—all of which are made more earthy and "real" than their mythic originals. "The Door" is an erotic, self-reflexive retelling of "Little Red Riding Hood," while "The Magic Poker" is an elaborate exploration of fictional creation, reminiscent of William Shakespeare's *The Tempest* (pr. 1611), and "Seven Exemplary Fictions" is an homage to Miguel de Cervantes. However, the most popular story in the collection is "The Babysitter," a complex play with the shifting intermixture of fantasy and reality.

"The Babysitter" ultimately asks the basic question What actually happened? for the reader is never quite sure at any given point if he or she is reading a fantasy or a description of so-called reality. Although the story seems filled with ominous events, nothing actually happens, except in the sexual fantasies of the participants, which predominate over ordinary reality. At the end of the story, when a television program enters the mix of fantasies, it seems no less real than the character fantasies throughout. Few stories have gone as far as "The Babysitter" in undermining the easy assumption that reality refers merely to external events in the physical world.

DONALD BARTHELME

When Donald Barthelme's first collection of stories, *Come Back, Dr. Caligari*, appeared in 1964, critics complained that his work was without subject matter, without character, without plot, and without concern for the reader's understanding. For Barthelme, the problem of language is the problem of reality, for reality is the result of language processes. Because so much contemporary language has become trash, dreck, Barthelme takes as his primary task the recycling of language, making metaphor out of the castoffs of technological culture. For Barthelme, the task is to try to reach, through metaphor and the defamiliarization that results, that ineffable realm of knowledge which he says lies somewhere between mathematics and religion "in which what may fairly be called truth exists."

Barthelme has noted that since films tell a realistic narrative so well, the fiction writer must develop a new principle. Collage, says Barthelme, is the central principle of all art in the twentieth century, the point of which is that "unlike things are stuck together to make, in the best case, a new reality." One of the implications of this collage process is a radical shift from the usual, temporal, cause-and-effect process of fiction to the more spatial and metaphoric process of poetry.

The most basic example of Barthelme's use of this mode is "The Balloon," in which a large balloon has encompassed the city. The persona of the story says that it is wrong to speak of "situations, implying sets of circumstances leading to some resolution, some escape of tension." In this story there are no situations, only the balloon, a concrete particular thing which people react to and try to explain. The balloon is an extended metaphor for the Barthelme story, to which people try to find a means of access and which creates varied critical responses. To plunge into a Barthelme story is to immerse oneself in the flotsam and jetsam of contemporary society, for his stories are not so much plotted tales as they are parodies and satires based on the public junk and commercial media hype that clutter up and cover over a person's private life.

William H. Gass

A philosopher particularly interested in the fictional nature of reality, William H. Gass's contribution to the postmodernist short story came in his 1968 collection, *In the Heart of the Heart of the Country and Other Stories*. Gass, as well known for his philosophical literary essays as for his fiction, has always reminded readers that "stories and the places and people in them are merely made of words." A character in a story, Gass insists, is not an object of perception and "nothing whatever that is appropriate to persons can be said of him."

"Order of Insects," which Gass thinks is one of his best short fictions, charts the growth of a woman's obsession with a species of insect inhabiting her home. By limiting her vision obsessively, she transforms the insects into mythic creatures, ultimately feeling as though she has been entrusted with a kind of "eastern mystery, sacred to a dreadful god." As opposed to humans, the insects, whose skeletons are on the outside, retain their shape in death. They are beautiful in the ideal sense with a fierce joy in their very composition, a joy of stone that lives in its tomb like a stone lion. Never seeming to participate in decay, they are perfect geometric shapes representing pure order.

The title story of Gass's collection is a lyrical evocation of being in "retirement from love." The voice of the narrator, who has come to a small town in Indiana because he has "love left over," which he would like to lose, mixes his response to the inhabitants of the town with his meditations and memories of a past love, who was, as all romantic lovers are, a fiction. "In the Heart of the Heart of the Country" is the narrator's attempt to organize himself, pull himself together by means of the language of poetry.

Minimalist Stories: 1970's and 1980's

The term "minimalism," to characterize a type of fiction that sparked a new interest in the short story in the 1970's, has been widely rejected by writers and derided by critics. However, as innovated by Raymond Carver, Ann Beattie, Tobias Wolff, Mary Robison, Bobbie Ann Mason, and sometimes Richard Ford, Jayne Anne Phillips, and David Leavitt, the term gained enough critical currency in the 1980's to develop a consensus of characteristics: detached tone, elliptical style, no plot, no historical sense, mundane blue-collar subject matter, and little or no character development. John Barth called the new flowering of the American short story stimulated by minimalism "the most impressive phenomenon" on the literary scene in the early 1980's.

Raymond Carver

Raymond Carver was the leader of the revival of interest in the short story in the late 1970's and early 1980's which John Barth playfully termed "hyperrealistic minimalism," or the "less-is-more" school. Like the stories of his mentors, Anton Chekhov and Ernest Hemingway, Carver's stories communicate by indirection, suggesting much by saying little. Carver was proclaimed an overnight success in 1977 when he received a National Book Award nomination for his first major collection, *Will You Please Be Quiet, Please?* (1976). With his next collection, *What We Talk About When We Talk About Love* (1981), there was little doubt in anyone's mind that, as one critic said, Carver was a "full-blown" master.

"Neighbors" is typical of Carver's early fiction. The plot line of the story is simple: A young couple is asked to look after a neighbor couple's apartment while they are away, but the husband's visits to the apartment begin to affect him in a mysterious but powerful way. Each time he goes over he stays longer, rummaging through drawers, using the bathroom, trying on the neighbors' clothes. The story then reveals that his wife is similarly fascinated by the apartment, and they go over together, thinking in some fantastic way that the neighbors may not come back. When they lock the door after one such visit, they are horrified to discover that they have locked the key inside and cannot get back in. The story suggests not merely a simple kind of voyeurism but rather a subtle human desire to exchange lives with someone else and thus live life vicariously.

In "Why Don't You Dance?," from Carver's second collection, once again plot is minimal, the event is mysterious, and the characters are merely etched in outline. A man puts all of his furniture out in his front yard and runs an extension cord to the lamps, television, and phonograph so that they work as they did when they were inside. A young couple stop by, look at the furniture, try out the bed, have a drink, and the girl dances with the owner. The conversation is functional, devoted primarily to making purchases. The story has no conclusion but rather a sort of coda in which the girl tries to "talk out" the event, feeling there was more to it. However, as in most Carver stories, the problem cannot be "talked out" but can only be objectified in the story itself. The bare events communicate what no amount of exposition can: The man has externalized the secret life of his home on the lawn in a desperate metaphor of his broken marriage; the young couple play out a mock scenario of his marriage which presages their own.

"Cathedral," from Carver's 1983 collection of the same name, is his most frequently anthologized story. The narrator, whose wife is visited by a blind man for whom she once worked, has stereotyped views of the blind, is jealous of his wife's former friendship with the man, and is sarcastic about the visit. After the wife goes to sleep, the blind man asks the husband to describe a cathedral in a television show he is watching. When he cannot do it, the blind man suggests that they draw a cathedral together. As the man draws, with the blind man's hand on his own, a mysterious religious communion is established.

Carver's shift from so-called minimalism to a more "generous" and "moral fiction" in "Cathedral" can also be seen in his revision of two important early stories—"So Much Water Close to Home" and "The Bath" (revised as "A Small, Good Thing")—for his final collection, *Where I'm Calling From* (1988). Carver makes several stylistic changes to give the stories a more realistic texture and a more humanistic conclusion than in their original bare-bones versions. For example, both "The Bath" and "A Small, Good Thing" focus on a couple whose son is in a coma after being hit by a car on his eighth birthday and who receive annoying anonymous telephone calls from a baker from whom the wife had earlier ordered a custom-made birthday cake. However, whereas "The Bath" is a very brief story, told in Carver's early, neutralized style, the revision, five times longer, develops the emotional life of the couple in more sympathetic detail, suggesting that their prayers for their son bind them together in a genuine human communion they have never felt before. Moreover, whereas in the first version the child's death abruptly ends the story, in the second, the baker shares the couple's sorrow and they share his loneliness, ending in reconciliation rather than despair.

ANN BEATTIE

While Carver focused on the blue collar dispossessed, Ann Beattie zeroed in on the college-educated uncommitted. Critical reaction to her collections *Distortions* (1976), *Secrets and Surprises* (1978), *The Burning House* (1982), *Where You'll Find Me and Other Stories* (1986), and *What Was Mine and Other Stories* (1991) has been pretty much split between those who admire her pinpoint portraits of young adults of the 1960's and 1970's and those who accuse her of psychological vacuity and sociological indifference. Beattie's people seldom know what makes them do the things they do and have no real sense of purpose or destiny; thus instead of engaging in deliberate action, they more often seem acted upon. Some critics have argued that when purpose is eliminated, as it is in Beattie's stories, trivia fills the gap.

Beattie's characters seldom experience the kind of epiphany of awareness the reader is accustomed to in twentieth century short fiction from James Joyce and Sherwood Anderson up through Eudora Welty and Bernard Malamud. Moreover, since many of her stories are told in present tense, her characters seldom engage in meditation or attempt a search for meaning, and there is little cause for her narrators to indulge in exposition or exploration. Beattie, especially in her early stories, seems to follow the Chekhovian-inspired dictum in one of her own stories: "Any life will seem dramatic if you omit mention of most of it." Beattie's later collection, *Park City: New and Selected Stories* (1998), is a retrospective summation of her short-story career, containing many Beattie favorites, such as "Dwarf House," "A Vintage Thunderbird," "Shifting," "The Lawn Party," "Jacklighting," "Greenwich Time," "The Burning House," "Weekend," "Janus," and "What Was Mine." "Weekend," a typical early story, focuses on a fifty-five-year-old college professor who tries to deny aging by sexually exploiting college girls who look up to him and the thirty-four-year-old woman who lives with him and passively accepts the "sick game" that he plays. Characteristic of Beattie's technique, the story ends with an image of a past moment in the life of the couple, when things were somehow all right but which is now lost forever. In "A Vintage Thunderbird," the central character drifts through relationships, unable to commit himself to any of them because of a fantasy desire for the woman who owns a vintage Thunderbird, a metaphor for him of some inaccessible ideal. The central themes of the story—the inability to retrace and recapture old dreams and the realization that events have little significance—are typical of Beattie's short stories.

In "The Burning House," the central female character has fooled herself into thinking she knows the people around her just because she knows the small personal things about them; however, like many Beattie characters, she realizes she does not know them at all. She does understand, however, a central characteristic of male characters in Beattie stories—their vague, almost childlike longing for a lost dream, for all men, she says, think they are Spider Man or Buck Rogers, wishing to fly, to escape their limitations.

In "Janus," a classic of the so-called minimalist genre, the central character is a real-estate salesperson who uses an elegant bowl as a sort of trick to get buyers interested in a house. The bowl not only has a personal meaning for her because her lover gave it to her but also has a mysterious symbolic significance, for it seems to be both practical and spiritual at once. Every house she puts it in becomes the home that she and her lover never had. When she refuses to leave her husband, her lover asks, in an obvious reference to the title of the story, "Why be two-faced?" However, like most Beattie characters, she is unable to make a break, a decision, a commitment.

TOBIAS WOLFF

Author of the short-story collections *In the Garden of the North American Martyrs* (1981), *Back in the World* (1985), and *The Night in Question* (1996), Tobias Wolff is often aligned with his fellow writers and friends Raymond Carver and Richard Ford for his focus on the significance of the seemingly mundane. "Say Yes," in which the initiating situation is trivially domestic and the characters are ordinary people who are not particularly articulate, is a clear example of this similarity. As is often the case in Carver stories, the simple situation soon develops into a significant and universal conflict. The issue that creates the conflict—whether white people should marry black people—begins casually; for the man it seems to have nothing to do with himself personally. However, the issue becomes personalized when he says that people of different races could never really *know* each other, and the wife asks, "Like you know me?" What the story is about is not merely a minor conflict in the life of a particular couple but rather the realization of the ultimate strangeness of others, no matter how confident one is that one "knows" them. What the story suggests is that strangeness or difference is not skin-deep but profound.

MARY ROBISON

Like Raymond Carver and Ann Beattie, Mary Robison has been criticized for her so-called minimalism. Although critics such as John Aldridge complain that her characters have no motivation, no background, and no personality, "Pretty Ice" from her first collection *Days* (1979) is a clear representative of her subtle fictional technique. Nothing really happens in this very brief story, about a thirty-four-year-old single woman who goes with her mother to meet her fiancé at the train station and then says she is going to break up with him. The only clue the reader has to the motivation for the breakup is a huge billboard she and her mother pass that advertises a dance studio once operated by her father, who committed suicide when she was twenty. The sign, which shows a man in a tuxedo waltzing with a woman in an evening gown, has weathered into ghostly phantoms. At the end of the story, the mother says the ice storm they have just had is a beautiful thing, like a stage set, and the daughter agrees that "It is pretty." The fiancé's response is flat and practical, confirming her desire for something more beautiful and ephemeral than the world of everyday reality that he embodies.

"Coach," one of Robison's most popular and representative stories, from *An Amateur's Guide to the Night* (1983), seems to be all realistic surface with no significant thematic conflict, consisting primarily of a few conversations between the coach and his wife and daughter and a young man who comes to interview him for the school paper. However, gradually, the reader begins to sense a growing intensity of unarticulated problems that lie beneath the surface of the seemingly inconsequential dialogue, all of which subtly suggest the coach's loss of an irretrievable past and the family's fear of an unpredictable future. Robison knows that short stories may legitimately and sensitively deal with the seemingly ordinary reality of the everyday, under which lies the threats of human desire and disappointment.

Bobbie Ann Mason

Bobbie Ann Mason's short-story collections, *Shiloh and Other Stories* (1982) and *Love Life* (1989), popularized what became known as "K-Mart" fiction in the 1980's, primarily because of Mason's focus on working-class people in rural Western Kentucky and her frequent mention of brand name stores and products. Mason's best-known short fiction, the title story of her first collection, is highly representative of her themes and techniques. The central characters are truck driver Leroy Moffitt, stuck at home as a result of an accident, and his wife Norma Jean, who is trying to find new meaning in her life.

The gradual dissolution of the marriage is embodied in a symbolic gender-role-reversal in which Leroy takes up needlepoint and Norman Jean takes up weight lifting. While she learns how to play an organ he buys her, feeling she has missed something during the 1960's, he tries to organize his life in some meaningful way by building a log cabin from a kit. The story comes to a climax when, in an embodiment of their own civil conflict, the couple visit Shiloh, the site of the famous Civil War battle. Leroy comes to realize that just as he knows only the surface of the history that surrounds the place, he has only superficially participated in the history of their relationship.

"Big Bertha Stories," from Mason's second collection, centers on a Vietnam veteran who tells his children mythic stories about Big Bertha, a huge strip-mining machine he runs, which also remind him of his tour of duty in Vietnam, in which the Americans stripped off and destroyed the culture just as he destroys the topsoil of his native land. His wife neither understands his compulsion to tell stories of Vietnam nor his love of the giant machine. The story ends with him being treated for his post-war obsessions and his wife struggling to come to terms with the fact that something is missing in her husband.

Richard Ford

Richard Ford's *Rock Springs* (1987) contains a number of stories which focus on adolescent boys trying to find someone on whom to model their lives and displaced men unable to establish a sense of identity or stability. In the title story from this collection, the protagonist Earl Middleton drifts through life longing for some stability he can never quite achieve. When he and his girlfriend Edna and his small daughter Cheryl head for Tampa from Kalispell in a stolen Mercedes, they break down in Rock Springs, Wyoming, and Edna leaves him. One of the thematic keys to the story is Earl's inability to identify with Edna's guilt for a past misdeed. His visit to a nearby mobile home park attached to a gold mine suggests Earl's dreams of getting something for nothing, for he thinks of the gold mine as a place one could go and take whatever one wanted.

After Edna tells Earl she is going to leave him, he goes into the parking lot of the motel to find another car to steal, looking in the windows at sunglasses, books, kids' toys. The story ends with Earl asking what the reader would think if he or she saw a man looking in the windows of cars in the parking lot of the Ramada Inn. "Would you think he was trying to get his head cleared? Would you think he was trying to get ready for a day when trouble would come to him? . . . Would you think he was anybody like you?" Earl longs for the solidity of the families represented by the cars in the lot, but he does not seem to have either the energy or the responsibility to achieve it.

"Communist," another popular story in Ford's collection, focuses on a sixteen-year-old boy who is trying to create a relationship with Glen, the man his mother is dating after the death of his father. The central scene is a hunt on which Glen takes the boy and during which the two kill dozens of geese. When Glen refuses to go out and get a wounded goose on the lake and the boy's mother tells him he has no heart, he shoots the goose four times. The narrator, who relates the incident when he is forty-one, says he thinks Glen was the first man he ever saw scared, and he felt sorry for him as if he were already a dead man. The story ends with the narrator's realization that Glen was not a bad man, "only a man scared of something he'd never seen before . . . his life going a way he didn't like."

The adolescent boys who face identity crises in many of Ford's short stories become the middle-aged men who can never quite find a home in many others. Ford's adolescents seem at the mercy of the adults around them, but even though they seem to learn something from the pain this causes them, the adult men that they become somehow cannot accept responsibility and "grow up." The result is a gallery of males who are never able to be at home either with themselves or with others.

Jayne Anne Phillips

Jayne Anne Phillips's stories in her best-known collection, *Black Tickets* (1979), fall into three distinct categories: short lyrical prose poem pieces; on-the-road stories; and stories of a young woman who returns home to come to terms with her relationship with her parents. All three of the stories in this last group, which seem to have the most staying power, end in symbolic frozen moments: "Souvenir," with the mother and daughter suspended on the top of a Ferris wheel, "Heavenly Animal," in which the young narrator hits a deer with her car and remembers a Christmas day when she was a kid, and "Home," with the mother and daughter standing silently in front of a sink of steaming water.

"Home," which focuses on the tension between the mother's desire to forgo sexuality after her divorce and the narrator's inability to engage in sexuality easily, is structured around a number of contrasts between the way the mother looks at sexuality and the way the narrator does. At the end of "Heavenly Animal," when the narrator drives to visit a friend and hits a deer on the road, the deer takes on the significance of a spiritual animal, but like many of Phillips's young women, she realizes, "There was really nowhere to go."

"Lechery," the most sexually emphatic full-length story in *Black Tickets*, deals with an adolescent prostitute, abandoned as an infant, who has spent her childhood in a care facility; she describes in detail how she shows pornographic pictures to young boys and then masturbates them. Forced into prostitution when she is twelve by a female guardian and her lover, she unsuccessfully tries to get love from her guardians, who can only use her to support their drug habits. Jayne Anne Phillips creates a sometimes shocking world of pornographic peep shows, pimps, prostitutes, drug addicts, and drunks in a number of her stories, as well as the world of a transient young woman trying to find a stable role for herself and a tolerable relationship with her parents. Her stories have found a place in the American short story because of their subtle evocation of the post-1960's era when carefree transience gave way to the search for a home.

David Leavitt

David Leavitt's first collection of stories, *Family Dancing* (1984), focuses, as the title suggests, on family relationships, particularly relationships between young homosexual men and their mothers. In "Territory" the male persona is named Neil Campbell; his mother, still a peace-worker in the age of Ronald Reagan, has intellectually accepted his homosexuality but not emotionally. When Neil invites his lover Wayne to come home for a visit, the situation is much like that of a young man bringing his college girlfriend home for vacation with Neil worrying about whether they will make love in his house. The story is balanced between Neil's anguished inner guilt and the liberal tolerance of his mother, challenged by her son's homosexuality in a direct way.

In *A Place I've Never Been* (1990), Leavitt's second collection, his homosexual characters have pushed beyond the problem of self-acceptance or acceptance by others to confront the further implications of living with their sexual orientation. The clearest indication of Leavitt's shift from adolescent to more adult ramifications of the gay life can be seen in the title piece of the collection, which features two characters introduced in the story "Dedicated" from *Family Dancing*—Nathan, a young homosexual, and Celia, his female friend. In "Dedicated," Celia envied the gay men and admired them for their romantic difference; she yearned to put aside her fleshiness and put on their sleekness. In "A Place I've Never Been," the reunion of the two friends reveals how far both have developed and diverged since the period of the early story.

Non-Minimalist Storytellers: 1970's, 1980's, 1990's

A number of important short-story writers in the last three decades of the century cannot be classified as part of the minimalist renaissance, either because their talent is inimical to that trend or because they self-consciously rejected minimalism for a more positive moral stance or a narrative voice that favors plenitude rather than parsimony. Writers such as Lee K. Abbott and Andre Dubus openly acknowledged their resistance to the minimalist aesthetic, while such writers as Grace Paley and Cynthia Ozick developed their own communal or lyrical style. Barry Hannah and Thom Jones created a "pull-out-all-the-stops" narrative voice that stretched the seams of the well-made short story, and T. Coraghessan Boyle, Stephen Millhauser, and Stephen Dixon developed their own version of the fantastic experimentalism that characterized the 1960's.

Lee K. Abbott

When asked to comment on minimalism for a special issue of *The Mississippi Review*, Lee K. Abbott—who has specialized in the short story with such collections as *Love Is the Crooked Thing* (1986), *Strangers in Paradise* (1986), *Living After Midnight* (1991), and *Wet Places at Noon* (1997)—disavowed any relationship to that group, insisting he was a "mossback prose-writer who prefers stories with all the parts hanging out and whirling." Reese, the protagonist in one of Abbott's best-known "whirling" stories, "Living Alone in Iota," has been dumped by his woman and feels desolate. As a result he feels "love-sawed" and the drunk he seeks is "positively medieval." He tells the members of his crew, "Boys, I am being sand-bagged by memory." In this comic, rural romance, although Reese tries desperately to win his woman back, she remains as "distant from him as he from his ancestral fishes." Later, in a flash of unmotivated insight, he says "Boys I'm a fool." With its rough-neck Romeo full of poetry, "Living Alone in Iota" is one of Abbott's purest comic love stories.

Andre Dubus

Andre Dubus's short stories, from *Adultery and Other Choices* in 1977 to *Dancing After Hours* in 1996, have always manifested a hopeful spirituality and an optimistic humanism that has marked him as thematically old-fashioned and technically conservative. Many of the stories in *Dancing After Hours* are based on the conviction that most human beings are seeking love rather than sex, relationships rather than one-night-stands, and family rather than temporary thrills. The two most communal stories in the collection are "Blessings" and the title story. In the former, a family goes on a fishing trip, and the boat capsizes because of the captain's neglect. Told from the perspective of the mother one year after the family survived the accident, the story is about what gives people character and what holds them together. It ends with the husband and wife, in an intimate moment that no one can break through, agreeing that it was the worst day of their lives and yet the best day also.

In the title story, "Dancing After Hours," a forty-year-old female bartender who, because she is not pretty, still lives alone, finds renewed hope when she shares a communal party with a small group, including a man in a wheel chair who continues to live life with gusto in spite of his disability. A story of the stubbornness of the human heart in its refusal to surrender to loneliness, it is a fitting tribute to Dubus's career as a short-story writer.

Cynthia Ozick

Cynthia Ozick is a Jewish short-story writer in the tradition of Bernard Malamud, for her typical story, an almost magical blend of lyricism and realism, creates a world that is both mythically distant and socially immediate at the same time. In her powerful short story "The Shawl," the central character Rosa is a Polish refugee in a Nazi internment camp with her infant Magda and her fourteen-year-old niece Stella. They have been so brutalized that they are hardly recognizable as human. Since she can get no nourishment from Rosa's dried-up breasts, Magda sucks on the corner of a shawl, which magically comforts and sustains her. When Stella steals Magda's shawl to warm her own body, the child stumbles into the open camp yard crying out for it. In a horrifying poetic passage, with Rosa watching in anguish but unable to do anything, a Nazi guard throws Magda into an electrified fence, and she dies instantly.

The magic of the story "The Shawl" is largely due to its point of view which, although it remains with Rosa the mother and reflects her feelings, also exhibits the detached poetry of the nameless narrator. The perspective of this grotesque poetry reflects the extremity of horror of the Holocaust itself. When the reader sees the knees of Stella as "tumors of sticks," he or she sees the Holocaust has no ordinary imagery adequate to capture it, no ordinary voice capable of describing it. "The Shawl" leaves the reader stunned and breathless with its dumbfounding horror.

Grace Paley

Grace Paley once said in an interview that it was "the dark lives of women" that made her begin to write, adding that at the time she thought no one would be interested, "but I had to illuminate it anyway." Usually, the women in Paley's stories are either unwed, widowed, or divorced; although they have children, they are not defined either by marriage or the desire for marriage. Perhaps the first thing one notices about Paley's stories is the voice that tells them and the style in which they are told. It seems unmistakably a woman's voice talking to other women, and thus not a voice conditioned by the need to preserve a social image.

The most frequently anthologized story in *Enormous Changes at the Last Minute* (1974), "A Conversation with My Father," is also Paley's most explicit treatment of her view of story and its relationship to hope for the future of women. She says the father in the story, who asks his daughter to write a story for him and then sees the situation of the woman in the story-within-the-story as tragic, is right, from his point of view, for he came from a world where there was no choice, where one could not change careers at the age of forty-one.

Paley believes that women banding together and talking to one another, especially mothers, constitute a powerful political force for social change. However, although Paley's stories show a concern for social responsibility, they are far from solemn social tracts or feminist polemics. Instead, they are characterized by an earthy awareness of urban folk culture combined with an often bawdy sense of humor. Writing for Grace Paley is a collaborative, social act, not merely in the obvious sense of centering stories on social issues, but in the more complex and profound sense of writing as the creation of a community of speakers and listeners sharing the same values.

T. Coraghessan Boyle

T. Coraghessan Boyle's first collection *Descent of Man* (1979) features such absurd situations as Lassie leaving his master Timmy for a love affair with a coyote, a woman falling in love with a brilliant chimpanzee who is translating Charles Darwin and Friedrich Nietzsche into Yerkish, and a group of teenagers who are so stoned that they do not notice that it is literally raining blood. Boyle continued this kind of satire and parody in his second collection, *Greasy Lake and Other Stories* (1985), which contains parodies of Sherlock Holmes and Nikolai Gogol's famous story "The Overcoat," as well as stories about a secret love affair between Dwight D. Eisenhower and the wife of Nikita Krushchev and the mating of whales. It also contains such surrealistically sublime pieces as "The Hector Quesadilla Story," about a baseball game that goes on forever, and such classic comic-tragic nightmares as the title story, which confronts tough-talking young men with the reality of violence.

STEPHEN DIXON

The most frequent terms used to characterize the short fiction of Stephen Dixon, whose hefty collection *The Stories of Stephen Dixon* (1994) included thirty years of his work, are "experimental," "fabulous," "quirky," and "tour de force," for Dixon experiments with a wide range of narrative devices and fictional techniques. However, the problem with so many of his stories is that, as imaginative and inventive as they may be, they largely seem to be just that—bloodless experiments with devices and techniques rather than real human events. For example, "Man of Letters" makes use of the epistolary form in which a man named Newt, who features in a number of Dixon stories, writes a series of letters to a woman he has been seeing. Although he begins the first letter with the sentence, "I don't want to see you anymore," by the time he has verbally examined the relationship and justified his decision by writing a whole stack of letters, he ends by saying, "No matter what I'll be seeing you Friday night." It is as if the very act of writing has so self-consciously engaged the protagonist that he cannot state his feelings; he is too busy trying to impress instead of saying simply what he wants to express. Many of Dixon's stories convey this sense of being bogged down in verbal cleverness and thus never quite expressing a truly human experience.

STEVEN MILLHAUSER

Steven Millhauser's short fictions in *The Penny Arcade* (1986), *The Barnum Museum* (1990), and *The Knife Thrower and Other Stories* (1998) are basically "suppose" stories. Suppose someone built the ultimate shopping mall? Suppose adolescent female mystery was really caused by witches? Suppose there was an amusement park that opened the door to an alternate reality? However, Millhauser's most obsessive "suppose" is Suppose you took an ordinary entertainment, illusion, or metaphor and pushed it as far as it would go. One could say that all of Millhauser's stories go "too far," that is, if the intensive "too far" existed in his vocabulary. In the title story of his collection *The Knife Thrower and Other Stories*, for example, runner-up winner in the 1998 O. Henry Prize Awards, Millhauser takes the basis for the dangerous entertainment of knife-throwing—how close can the knife go?—to the next logical but incredible step.

While most short-story writers in the 1980's and 1990's have followed the realist rebellion against 1970's fabulism, Millhauser has stayed true to the fantastic tradition that extends from Scheherazade to Edgar Allan Poe and from Franz Kafka to Jorge Luis Borges, playfully exploring the freedom of the imagination to reject the ordinary world of the mundane and explore the incredible world of purely aesthetic creation. Whether his stories focus on magic carpets, men who marry frogs, automatons, balloon flights, or labyrinths that lie beneath everyday reality, Millhauser embodies one of the most powerful traditions of short fiction—the magical story of the reality of artifice.

BARRY HANNAH

Since his premier short-story collection *Airships* in 1979, Barry Hannah has made the so-called masculine dilemma his special territory. Hannah identifies with the image of the hard-talking barroom male, claiming that sex makes "death go away" and violence makes things "really meaningful come forth." Hannah's stories are filled with men trying to find ways to love women and be friends with men, while at the same time striving to come to terms with their sexual obsessiveness and their territorial possessiveness. Hannah's primary obsession, however, is not sex but storytelling; for Hannah, telling lies and getting at the truth often amount to the same thing.

Hannah's central story about the relationship between masculinity and telling lies is "Water Liars," which takes place at Farte Cove, a name suggestive of the gassy storytelling of old men who spend the last years of their lives fishing and spinning yarns about the ones that got away. The narrator is there because he has discovered that before they met his wife had about the same number of lovers he did, and it has driven him "wild." The very brief story concludes when a new man tells about catching his daughter having sex with a man on the river bank. The old men are appalled, telling him, "Tell your kind of story somewhere else." The narrator recognizes that he and the man are "both crucified by the truth."

Hannah's best-known story, "Testimony of Pilot," is about the difficulty men have in reconciling their limitations with their dreams. A "buddy" story about the narrator and a musician and fighter pilot named Quadberry, it focuses on the desire for the life of action. The narrator admires Quadberry for his uncanny ability to create a sound on the saxophone that has the erotic ability to go up the skirts of girls and envies his hold on Lilian, a majorette of faultless beauty. The story ends when Lilian is killed by a hijacker's bomb and vaporized into a cloud over the Gulf of Mexico and Quadberry dies in an operation meant to repair his injured back. The story is a parable about how men yearn for heroism, truth, and beauty, but often settle for something significantly less.

Thom Jones

Thom Jones's 1993 collection, *The Pugilist at Rest: Stories*, a finalist for the National Book Award, was greeted with rave reviews that compared his debut to that of Raymond Carver and called Jones an "impressive, audacious, powerful new talent." His second volume, *Cold Snap* (1995), contained ten stories in the same hyperadrenalized mode of his earlier pieces, featuring jive-talking marines, down-and-out prize-fighters, and manic-depressive doctors and writers who seemingly seek pain, dare death, and survive solely on demonic, drug-driven energy.

Jones says he wrote the story "The Pugilist at Rest" in a sort of "controlled ecstatic frenzy" and that "Way Down Deep in the Jungle" developed in his imagination "as if by magic." Many of his stories seem derived from a nonstop manic monologue that Jones overhears himself delivering and then transcribes. His persona for this possessed writing style is the character Ad Magic, featured in the story "The White Horse," from *The Pugilist at Rest*, and "Quicksand," from *Cold Snap*. In the first story, Ad Magic finds himself in India after a seizure of epileptic amnesia; in the second, he is a direct-mail wizard in Africa, writing fund appeal letters for the Global Aid Society hunger effort. Taking his name from an ability to lapse into a trancelike state and tap into a writing frenzy, Ad Magic is filled with existential angst and absurdity, feeling like a marionette in a Punch-and-Judy show and that life is nothing but a big cartoon. Jones's later book, *Sonny Liston Was a Friend of Minde* (1999), features stories that differ very little from those in his first two books.

Joyce Carol Oates

It is difficult to know where to place Joyce Carol Oates in any survey of modern fiction, for from her early collections–*By the North Gate* (1963), *Upon the Sweeping Flood* (1966), and *Where Are You Going, Where Have You Been?* (1974)—to her more recent, such as *Heat and Other Stories* (1990), she has experimented with and mastered every type of short story popular in the last forty years. The problem, however, with her short stories is that so many of them seem imitative of stories by stronger, more original writers. For example, her best-known story, "Where Are You Going, Where Have You Been?," highly imitative of Flannery O'Connor, is a classic example of the short-story convention of the ominous stranger who is ambiguous because one is never sure whether he is a realistic character or a hallucinatory internal force.

Perhaps the most obvious statement one can make about Joyce Carol Oates, and it has been made many times, is that she is extraordinarily prolific. With over fifty books to her credit she has already exceeded the production of such giants of literary productivity as Charles Dickens and Thomas Hardy. However, many of her stories seem to spring more from a dispassionate artistic "what if" than from a passionate involvement in the lives of her characters. Too many stories are derived from a purely intellectual motivation and too few spring from the raw emotion they are meant to evoke. Joyce Carol Oates's stories, while ostensibly visceral, are ultimately cerebral. Although Oates has sustained the short story over the past forty years, she has seldom innovated it.

The Short Story at the Turn of the Twenty-first Century

So many important short story collections have been published in the final years of the twentieth century that it is impossible to discuss them all. However, the following writers are among the most praised and the most promising.

CHRIS OFFUTT

The stories in Chris Offutt's first book, the well-received 1992 *Kentucky Straight*, are firmly situated in the mountains of Eastern Kentucky. In his second collection, *Out of the Woods* (1999), he has moved most of his characters out of the mountains, mainly to the wide-open spaces of the West. However, the Eastern Kentucky hills remain a central force in these stories, for no matter where Offutt's mountain men go, the hills haunt them.

The title story of Offutt's second collection is about a thirty-year-old man who has never been out of the county. To secure his position with his new wife and her family, he agrees to drive an old pickup two days to pick up his wife's brother who has been shot and is in a hospital in Wahoo, Nebraska. While this may seem like a simple task, for a mountain man it is fraught with unease; the land in Indiana and Illinois is as flat as a playing card with no place to hide, and at night the sky seems to press down on him in a threatening way. Heading back to Kentucky with his brother-in-law's body in the back of the pickup, he stops once to mound a pile of rich Illinois topsoil for his garden onto the body. This homey traveling grave becomes comically grotesque when he stops at a gas station and a dog starts to dig in the dirt; the smell is so bad a man thinks Gerald is taking a dead hog to the renderers. The story is a carefully controlled account of a simple man's homey, heroic management of an extraordinarily ordinary situation.

MICHAEL BYERS

The stories of Michael Byers, in his debut collection *The Coast of Good Intentions* (1998), affirm, in a seemingly simple, matter-of-fact way, the solid, unsentimental values of family, commitment, and hope for the future. Byers focuses primarily on men who, like the retired school teacher in "Settled on the Cranberry Coast," are still looking hopefully to the future, or, when they do look to the past, are like the elderly couple in "Dirigibles," reaffirmed rather than disappointed.

A satisfying story about second chances or the pleasant realization that it is never too late to live, "Settled on the Cranberry Coast" is narrated by Eddie, a bachelor who has just retired after teaching high school for twenty-seven years and has taken up part-time carpentry work. When Rosie, an old high school acquaintance, who has also never married, hires him to do some repairs, the story focuses on their inevitable gravitation toward each other. Not only does Rosie fill Eddie's need for a caring companion, but also her six-year-old granddaughter Hannah, who lives with her, gives him the child he has never had.

CHRISTOPHER TILGHMAN

The seven stories in Christopher Tilghman's *In a Father's Place* (1990) celebrate the solidity of place and the importance of community and family, defending the conservative values of working class men and landed gentry against any deviations from them or rebellions against them. In "Loose Reins," a young man returns to his Montana home to try to come to terms with the fact that his mother has married a former ranch hand; he decides that the hand, with his simple values, is superior to his businesslike and busy father. In the title story of the collection, the head of a well-established Maryland family drives out his son's iconoclastic and domineering girlfriend, thus asserting the superiority of family over her nihilistic postmodern views.

In the title story of Tilghman's second collection, *The Way People Run* (1999), the protagonist, driving across the country, on the way home to face his wife, his child, and numerous unpaid and unpayable bills, stops at a rundown Western town on the plains and becomes fascinated with the pull of permanence and place. The center of this magnetism is a beat-up café where he feels "utterly, extravagantly at home." The story ends with a haunting scene of a deserted school bus on the side of the road, and the protagonist standing on the vast "ownerless domain" of the prairie, wondering if this is "the way people run."

E. ANNIE PROULX

Although E. Annie Proulx's first collection, *Heart Songs and Other Stories* (1988), is relatively conventional in structure and language, the stories in her second collection, *Close Range: Wyoming Stories*

(1999), are compelling combinations of the grittily real and the magically mythical. Place is as important as people are in *Close Range*, for in the harsh but beautiful Wyoming landscape social props are worthless and folks are thrown back on their most basic instincts. "Brokeback Mountain," Proulx's most powerful tale, is a tragic love story of Jack Twist and Ennis del Mar, two country boys with no prospects who, while working alone on a sheep-herding operation on Brokeback Mountain, abruptly and silently engage in a sexual encounter, after which both immediately insist, "I'm not no queer."

Twenty years pass, and their infrequent encounters are combinations of sexual passion and personal concern. The story comes to a climax when Jack, who unsuccessfully tries to convince Ennis they can make a life together, is mysteriously killed on the roadside. Although officially it was an accident, Ennis sorrowfully suspects that Jack has been murdered after approaching another man. Proulx explores issues here more basic and primal than social homophobia; this straightforward love story elicits a genuine sympathy and understanding.

Andrea Barrett

The stories in Andrea Barrett's 1996 National Book Award winner, *Ship Fever*, focus on real people, such as Gregor Mendel and Carl Linnaeus, caught up in pursuits in the natural sciences, using scientific facts and historical events to throw light on basic human impulses and conflicts. "The Behavior of the Hawkweeds" is typical. Told by the wife of a mediocre twentieth century science professor who greatly admires the geneticist Gregor Mendel, it includes the historical account of how Mendel allowed himself to be misdirected from his valuable studies of the hybridization of the edible pea to a dead-end study of the hawkweed and the personal story of how the narrator's grandfather accidentally killed a man who he thought was trying to abuse her as a child. These stories from the past are paralleled by stories in the present in which the narrator finds herself leading a meaningless life at middle age.

The British Short Story: 1960-2000

It is a cultural fact that England, with its historical affiliation with the novel, has never been fertile soil for the short-story genre. However, although A. S. Byatt, Angela Carter, Graham Swift, Julian Barnes, and Ian McEwan are better known for their novels, their short stories in the past thirty years have made important contributions to the genre.

A. S. Byatt

A. S. Byatt's collections, *The Matisse Stories* (1993) and *Elementals: Stories of Fire and Ice* (1998), have received strong reviews from the critics. Byatt's most popular anthology piece, "Medusa's Ankles," is a well-made story about a middle-aged woman who rebels against the falsity of trying to look young while growing old. The protagonist, a university professor, who goes to a beauty salon because her hair has "grown old," recalls her mother looking artificial, coming out from under a hairdresser dome, which seemed "like some kind of electrically shocking initiation into womanhood."

While getting her hair done for a public presentation she must make, she looks in a mirror, wondering how her face could grow into the sag. She wants to accept her face but cannot. "What had left this greying skin, these flakes, these fragile stretches with no elasticity, was her, was her life, was herself." When the hairstylist says he has been talking with his girlfriend and has decided not to go back to his wife because "she's let her ankles get fat," the protagonist is sympathetic toward the wife. Remembering when she made love all day to an Italian student in Perugia, "rage rose in her, for the fat-ankled woman," and she starts throwing things in the shop until there is nothing left to hurl or to break. When she goes home to wash out her Medusa curls, her husband says that her hairdo takes twenty years off her and kisses her on the nape of her neck as he used to do.

Angela Carter

Angela Carter is best known for short stories that combine gothicism and eroticism with feminist critiques of legends and folktales derived from patriarchal culture. Her collected short stories, published under the title *Burning Your Boats* in 1995, included such early collections as *Fireworks: Nine Profane Pieces* (1974), *The Bloody Chamber and Other Stories* (1979), and *Black Venus* (1985). Her most popular story, "The Bloody Chamber," is a retelling of Bluebeard, the serial wifekiller of Charles Perrault's fairy tale. Often called a tour de force, the story documents an initiation into adult sexuality which suggests the sado-masochistic role that women play in male sexual aggressiveness. When the man looks at the narrator/protagonist with lust, she senses in herself for the first time "a potentiality for corruption" that takes her breath away.

"The Bloody Chamber" is like a catalog of all the traditional gothic pornographic paraphernalia: the brooding castle, the pale virgin, the Byronic husband/master, the sexual perversion. Ignoring the mythic paternalistic warning not to inquire into the sexual secrets of the husband, the bride discovers the "bloody chamber," where she finds the tortured and mutilated bodies of her predecessors. In the breathless climax of the story, as she prepares herself for martyrdom by decapitation, she is rescued by her mother who puts a bullet through her husband's head. The story has been the subject of some concern to feminist critics for inviting the reader to participate imaginatively in a masochistic fantasy.

GRAHAM SWIFT

Because Graham Swift believes that telling stories is a therapeutic means of coming to terms with the past, his short fictions in *Learning to Swim and Other Stories* (1982) focus on characters who try to come to terms with their personal pasts. The title story of the collection centers on a man teaching his six-year-old son Paul how to swim, but most of the story takes place in the memory of his wife as she recalls having thought about leaving him three times in the past primarily because of his lack of passion. The story then shifts to the two times he has thought of leaving his wife. Swimming is a central metaphor in the story, for in the Spartan purity of swimming the man feels superior to others who will "go under" in life. The undercurrent of marital conflict between the couple surfaces at the end of the story. She wants the kind of close relationship with her son typical of women who have rejected their husbands; he thinks that if the boy could swim he would be able to leave his wife. The story shifts finally to the boy, who fears that his mother will swallow him up and that he will not win the love of his father if he fails. Thus, he swims away from both, finding himself in a strange new element that seems all his own.

JULIAN BARNES

Because the stories in Julian Barnes's collection *Cross Channel* (1996) are all grounded as much in historical fact and cultural values as in individual characters, they focus more on social abstractions than on individuals. "Dragons," the most popular story in the collection, describes the occupation of a Protestant village in Southern France in the seventeenth century by paid dragonnades. Because the homeowner is a Protestant and thus considered an enemy of the king's religion, the soldiers burn the carpenter's fine wood, sell his tools, and make the members of his family recant their religion and return to the Church. The climax of the story comes when the reader learns that the dragons are Irish Catholics, who have become mercenaries for the French in revenge for Oliver Cromwell's Protestant atrocities against them many years before. "Dragons" is an ironic story about persecution and social intolerance, told in the formal language and tones of the folktale. The fact that the dragons are from Ireland seems a kind of poetic justice, since they have also been victims of religious persecution.

IAN MCEWAN

Ian McEwan's first short-story collection, *First Love, Last Rites* (1975), received mixed reviews when it first appeared because of its violence and sexuality. However, most critics agree that the title story of the collection, which McEwan once said he always thought of as an affirmative story, is his best. Focusing on a young couple who have run away together for a summer of complete sexual freedom, the story opens with their sense of an invisible creature scratching behind the wall of their hermitage. During sex, the boy has a fantasy of making the creature grow in her belly, although he has no desire to be a father. When she hears the creature, he knows it is a sound growing out of their lovemaking.

The couple grow increasingly unhappy, having sex less and less, while the rubbish accumulates around them. The girl begins to work in a factory, where she becomes indistinguishable from the four hundred other women who work there. When the boy kills the large rat living in the walls, it gives off a smell like that of the girl's monthly blood. A translucent purple bag with five little rats fall out and the girl kneels by it, "as if she had some special right," pushes the bag inside, and closes the fur over it. The story ironically suggests that to give in to the practical world of children, work, and everyday responsibility is to lose the fantasy of the endless summer of love and union.

Charles E. May

BIBLIOGRAPHY

Aldridge, John W. *Talents and Technicians: Literary Chic and the New Assembly-Line Fiction*. New York: Charles Scribner's Sons, 1992. A famous attack on many of the short-story writers of the 1970's and 1980's, such as Raymond Carver, Ann Beattie, Bobbie Ann Mason, Mary Robison, T. Coraghessan Boyle, and David Leavitt.

Herzinger, Kim. "Minimalism as a Postmodern: Some Introductory Notes." *New Orleans Review* 16 (Fall, 1989): 73-81. An important discussion of the basic characteristics and philosophic implications of minimalism.

Levy, Andrew. *The Culture and Commerce of the American Short Story*. Cambridge, England: Cambridge University Press, 1993. This study of the cultural development of the short story in America includes an important chapter about the influence of university creative writing programs on the contemporary short story.

May, Charles E. *The Short Story: The Reality of Artifice*. New York: Twayne Publishers, 1995. A critical/historical survey of the development of the short story as a genre that includes a chapter on the renaissance of the short story in America in the 1970's and 1980's.

"Special Section on 'Minimalist Fiction.'" *Mississippi Review*, nos. 40/41 (Winter, 1985). Features essays on the origins of minimalism, its basic characteristics, and what comes after it. Also includes brief essays by such writers as Raymond Carver, Lee K. Abbott, and Raymond Federman.

Style 27 (Fall, 1993). A special issue on the modern short story, with essays on the form by a number of critics such as Susan Lohafer and Charles May.

SHORT FICTION AROUND THE WORLD

AFRICAN SHORT FICTION

African short fiction comes in various forms: derivations of traditional tales, such as Jomo Kenyatta's "The Gentlemen of the Jungle" and Martha Mvungi's "Mwipenza the Killer"; narratives that are too compact to be novels, such as Alex La Guma's "A Walk in the Night"; and short narratives or stories ranging from a few pages to approximately ten pages. This body of writing can be appropriately considered a literature of neglect or a literature in search of critics. Unlike African long fiction, which has established a robust dialogue between writers and critics, African short fiction has received little critical attention. F. Odun Balogun's *Tradition and Modernity in the African Short Story: An Introduction to a Literature in Search of Critics*, published by Greenwood Press in 1991, is one of the only book-length studies on the subject. This anomaly cannot be attributed to a lack of production of short stories by Africans. While more of such stories could be published, African writers, both established ones and beginners, continue to express their conception of Africa through the short-story form. The neglect suffered by this genre can be partially attributed to its length, its brevity, which can easily lead to the misconception of a short story as an underdeveloped work in embryonic form, a stunted novel that has failed to reach fruition. Furthermore, most writers of short fiction have also turned their hands to writing longer fiction, thus making short-story writing appear as an apprenticeship, preparing one for a writing career in longer genres.

Nonetheless, short fiction defies narrow definition. It can claim the stature of other literary genres because it is endowed with the capacity, no matter how condensed, to illuminate the human condition by evoking a mood, state of mind, or condition, which can linger even after the narration itself has ended. It can bring about moments of epiphany, can depict one event or several closely related events, and has the capacity for great lyricism because, as a form, it compels scrupulous terseness. The compactness of the short-story form, its ability to promote greater artistic coherence than is possible with longer compositions, such as the novel, has made it a preferred vehicle for articulating many a human experience. In Africa, as in the West, most creative writers who have gained prominence working with other literary forms have also tried their hands at the short story with impressive results. These writers seem to have discovered in shorter fiction a form that best enables them to express what it means to be an African and a human being.

The African short story is extensive in the themes it covers, reflecting the problems of adjusting to life on a continent where the pace of change has been dizzying. Prominent among the themes of the African short story are critiques of colonialism, missionary activity, and religion (indigenous and foreign); the politics of independent Africa; the new ruling class; political and social corruption; apartheid and racial strife; economic and financial strife; indigenous culture, values, and village life; urban life and the lure of the city; the strain of growing up; old age, disease, and death; the sexual exploitation of women and prostitution; motherhood, childbearing, child rearing, and childlessness; the ravages of nature; and a search for a philosophy of life. There is also a considerable adaptation of traditional tales, which speaks to the blending of African oral narrative traditions with Western literary forms.

African writers have been recognized for doing exciting things with short fiction in their exploration and appraisal of indigenous African norms and values as well as the intricacies of life in contemporary Africa. In this quest, prominent African writers, such as Chinua Achebe, Ousmane Sembène, Ngugi wa Thiong'o, Grace Ogot, Flora Nwapa, Ama Ata Aidoo, and Bessie Head, who have all gained prominence in working with other genres, such as the novel, drama, and poetry, have all also authored short-story collections. Furthermore, African women writers have been quite prolific producers of short stories, with Nwapa and Aidoo each having two short-story collections to her credit. In fact, the stories of Aidoo, Head, and Ogot are quite widely anthologized.

While African short fiction dates back to the tail end of the nineteenth century, with the appearance of Cape Verdean Henrique de Vasconsellos's *A Mentira Vital* in 1896, most of the early works are out of print and extremely difficult to find. The proliferation of this art form, however, seems to have begun in the 1940's. Achebe notes in the introduction to *African Short Stories* (1985) that the short-story form has enjoyed the attention and patronage of African writers since Peter Abrahams's 1942 collection, *Dark Testament*. The short story continues to thrive among African writers, whether it is published in popular presses, journals and exclusive magazines, short-story collections, or anthologies of literature. A steady stream of single short stories in journals, literary magazines and newspapers, individual author collections, and multiple-author anthologies has continued to be published. Many aspiring African writers made their short-story debuts in campus magazines, such as *Penpoint*, *Sokoti*, *The Horizon*, and *Idoto*.

Charles Larson's *Under African Skies: Modern African Stories* (1997), translated from the French by Ellen Conroy Kennedy, is a multiple-author anthology. Most of the twenty-six stories in this collection, however, have been previously published in other anthologies. For instance, Achebe's "Girls at War," Bessie Head's "The Prisoner Who Wore Glasses," and Camara Laye's "The Eyes of the Statue" had appeared in *More Modern African Stories*, an earlier anthology, edited in 1975 by Larson. *Under African Skies* brings together stories from Anglophone, Francophone, and Lusophone Africa even though, as in most of the anthologies, selections from Anglophone writers dominate. Heinemann Educational Books, through its African Writers' Series, has one of the largest collections of both single-author collections and multiple-author anthologies of African short stories. The most popular multiple-author anthologies among these are *Unwinding Threads: Writing by Women in Africa* (1983), selected and edited by Charlotte H. Bruner, which comprises short stories and excerpts from longer fiction by African women writers, and *African Short Stories* (1985) and *The Heinemann Book of Contemporary African Short Stories* (1992), both edited by Achebe and C. L. Innes. The stories in these anthologies are selected from all over the continent and are organized by region. Heinemann also has regional anthologies such as *Africa South: Contemporary Writings* (1981), edited by Mothobi Mutloatse, and *Stories from Central and Southern Africa* (1983), edited by Paul A. Scanlon, which contains stories from Mozambique, Zimbabwe, Botswana, Lesotho, Swaziland, Malawi, Namibia, and South Africa.

Publishers other than Heinemann have also published anthologies of African short stories. A few are *Modern African Stories* (1966), edited by Ellis Ayitey Komey and Ezekiel Mphahlele and published by Faber and Faber; *Pan African Short Stories* (1965), edited by Neville Denny and published by Thomas Nelson and Sons; and *The Penguin Book of Southern African Stories* (1985), edited by Stephen Gray. There is also a considerable number of single-author collections of short stories. Prominent among these are Alex La Guma's *A Walk in the Night* (1962), Grace Ogot's *Land Without Thunder* (1968), Luís Bernardo Honwana's *We Killed Mangy-Dog and Other Mozambique Stories* (translated by Dorothy Guedes; 1969), Aidoo's *No Sweetness Here* (1970), Nwapa's *This Is Lagos: And Other Stories* (1971), Achebe's *Girls at War* (1972), Sembène's *Voltaïque* (1962; *Tribal Scars*, 1974), Ngugi's *Secret Lives* (1974), and Bessie Head's *The Collector of Treasures and Other Botswana Village Tales* (1977).

Lusophone Africa

Lusophone African writing is reputed to be the first to emerge in Africa. This primacy, coupled with the high esteem in which short fiction and poetry are regarded in Portuguese culture, has resulted in short fiction enjoying a long standing in Lusophone Africa, where the writer of the short story is regarded just as highly as the writer of longer fiction. Vasconsellos's *A Mentira Vital*, Mozambican João Albasini's *O livro da dor: Cartas de amor* (1925), and Angolan Castro Soromenho's *Nhari: O, Drama da gente negra* (1938) are among the earliest published volumes of African short stories. However, almost all of these works are either out of print or difficult to access in the English-speaking world. In the island of Cape

Verde, for example, short fiction has flowered in a manner in which longer fiction has not. Also, in Lusophone Africa, short-story anthologies have tended to be true short-story collections and not excerpts of longer fiction, as has been the case with some anthologies in Anglophone Africa. For instance, in the *Antologia da ficcao Cabo-Verdiana contemmporanea* (1960), edited by Baltasar Lopes and containing twenty-three entries covering works published between 1944 and 1959, as well as previously unpublished material, eighteen of the twenty-three entries are short stories (*contos*) and two are novellas (*noveletas*). Only three are excerpts from novels. In addition, writers who have been known to start their writing careers with longer fiction have later turned to short-story writing. In the case of the Angolan writer Oscar Ribas, who has published both long and short fiction, his various volumes of short fiction, beginning with *Flores e espinhos* (1948), started appearing twenty years after two longer works of fiction. Therefore, his reputation as a writer rests even more on his short-story collections.

The Mozambican Honwana is a Lusophone writer who is considered one of the foremost short-story writers of present-day Africa. His collection *We Killed Mangy-Dog and Other Mozambique Stories* is one of the few Lusophone collections that is available to English readers. In the collection is "We Killed Mangy-Dog" and six other stories, including the well-anthologized "Papa, Snake, and I" and "The Old Woman." "Papa, Snake, and I" is anthologized in *African Short Stories* and *Under African Skies*, and "The Old Woman" can be found in *Stories from Central and Southern Africa*. Honwana's collection is counted one of the best books of short stories. The title story and "Papa, Snake, and I," both of which are narrated by Ginho, a black youth, are coming-of-age stories involving a killing—the killing of Mangy-Dog in the former and the killing of a snake in the latter. In both, the killing serves as a ritual initiation of the young black adolescent narrator into manhood. "We Killed Mangy-Dog" initiates Ginho into a world of conflict between love and friendship, on one hand, and violence and inhumanity on the other. In "Papa, Snake, and I," the black youth is exposed both to racial oppression and to the subtle acts of resistance through which the oppressed reaffirm their constantly assaulted sense of humanity. Both stories, though contemporary narratives, rely on narrative techniques from the oral tradition through the interweaving of human and animal characters, with the animals endowed with human qualities. They are allegorical and lyrical, with the language bearing the stamp of simplicity of its youthful narrator.

"We Killed Mangy-Dog" is a story of failed leadership and callowness, a political allegory in which the plight of Mangy-Dog corresponds to the political and racial oppression as well as the outcast status of black people under Portuguese colonialism. The story focuses on a dozen young boys of various colors, whose schoolyard has become home to several dogs. One of the dogs, an old, feeble, sore-infested mutt, Mangy-Dog, who is despised by almost everybody except two outcasts, the black youth Ginho and a little girl believed to be crazy, is made a scapegoat and ordered to be taken into the fields and shot. Ironically, it is Senhor Duarte from the Veterinary Department who asks the boys to kill Mangy-Dog and presents the undertaking as recreation for the boys. Ginho, who considers Mangy-Dog an old friend, one whose pleading eyes appeal in vain to his killers' sense of humanity, is riddled with guilt and filled with sympathy for the dog but compelled to take the first shot because of his fear of being an outcast. Ginho's fear and sympathy, however, manifest his identification as a black "underdog" suffering along with Mangy-Dog under Portuguese imperialism.

"Papa, Snake, and I," is allegorical, with the snake symbolizing Portuguese colonialism and its preying on the Africans. This story depicts Portuguese oppression and African resistance. Papa represents the older generation of colonized Africans, who employ survival mechanisms, such as deference to whites, prayer, and even laughter, in order to counter the abuses perpetrated against them. In the story, Senhor Castro, Papa's Portuguese neighbor, is overbearing and abusive, his manner betraying the brutality of the Portuguese toward the Africans in the settlers' colonies. When the snake bites his dog, Wolf, he demands monetary compensation from Papa and threatens him with "a bloody good hiding." Papa, for his part, shows deference to his abuser. He calls Senhor Castro "son of a bitch" only when the latter has driven away in his car. Filled with anger on account of the abuse he suffers from the white colonizer, Papa turns to prayer. Significantly, Ginho, rather than Papa, is the one who kills the snake. When his wife shows Papa the havoc the snake is wreaking on the chickens, he tells her he will get help to kill the snake tomorrow. Tomorrow, of course, belongs to the new generation, symbolized here by Ginho, who is the one who kills the snake. Also, even though Ginho could have saved Senhor Castro's dog from being bitten by the snake, he chooses not to. Ginho's killing of the snake foreshadows the eventual overthrow of Portuguese imperialism that the younger generation of blacks will undertake. In spite of the humiliation of his father that Ginho witnesses, he gains an understanding of racial oppression and the mechanisms for survival to which the oppressed resort. The African youth learns that prayer and laughter are coping mechanisms in a system that shows no justice toward the oppressed blacks. He also comes to understand his not preventing the snake biting Senhor Castro's dog as an act of resistance.

Honwana's "The Old Woman," narrated by a young man, is a story of violence, rejection, and, at the same time, hope. The life depicted is a hard one. Life outside the home is highly alienating, marked by assaults, strange looks, and rejection. Life at home is characterized by meager meals and the squabbling and clamoring of children for food and attention. However, there is also the presence of maternal warmth, which brings a feeling of hope that things might change for the better.

Another Lusophone writer whose stories are available to English readers is Mozambican Mia Couto. His collection of short stories *Vozes anoitecidas*, published in 1986 in Mozambique and subsequently in Portugal and Italy, has been translated into English by David Brookshaw as *Voices Made Night*, published by Heinemann in 1990. Couto's "The Birds of God," anthologized in *Contemporary African Short Stories*, is a test of human endurance and sacrifice, a story of magic and harsh realism. In this story, Couto blends magical elements from the African folktale tradition with realism. The result is a parabolic rendering of colonialism and resistance as well as an interrogation of indigenous belief systems.

During a prolonged drought, a fisherman disillusioned about what his thirty years on the river has brought him makes what he considers a supreme sacrifice, which not only gives purpose to his life but also brings the much-needed rain to end the drought. Ernesto Timba, who has been bracing the river for thirty years in his dugout, has plenty of time to contemplate human suffering and the significance of faith. One day, he wishes for a majestic white bird flying above him to fall into his canoe, and it does. Shaken by the realization of his power, he is seized by the feeling that the bird is a sign from God, that God has chosen him to be his emissary on earth to remind his people that dispensing kindness in times of hardship is worth even more than it is in times of plenty. Rather than take the bird home for food, as he had originally intended, he builds a protective cage for it, despite the famine that has invaded the land. He feeds it the fish he has caught for his family as well as the family's other meager provisions. Upon Timba's wish, God gives the bird a mate, and they increase to five, living off the resources of the land, while the people starve. Caring only about the birds, Timba loses his family, and people become convinced he is mad.

Eventually, the people set fire to the bird cage. Timba, convinced that God will let his wrath loose on the people for failing his test of their kindness and endurance, sacrifices himself by drowning. Attempts to separate him from the river fail: "The body was stuck to the surface of the river." His death brings the much-needed rain to end the drought; his faith brings about the anticipated miracle that motivated his actions. On a symbolic level, however, the sudden descent of the white birds on the people and the birds' growing fat off the resources of the land, while the people suffer, is evocative of the coming of the Portuguese and their exploitation of the people and their land. The burning of the birds symbolizes the war for liberation, which eventually brought an end to Portuguese colonialism in Mozambique. Significantly, the demise of the white birds also brings an end to the drought.

Francophone Africa

Unlike the Lusophone African stories discussed above, which merely insinuate the theme of colonialism, Francophone African short stories often tackle colonialism head-on. The attack on French colonialism often takes the form of an attack on religion, particularly Catholicism. In Cameroonian Rene Philombe's "The True Martyr Is Me," included in Larson's *Under African Skies* and translated by Richard Bjornson, which was first published in *Tales from Cameroon* (1984), Christianity is exposed as an instrument for economic exploitation parading as a mechanism for spiritual salvation. In this story, African women, whose indigenous marriages are not recognized by the Catholic Church, are removed from their marital homes and kept for an indeterminate time at a secluded compound, the *sixa*, at the Catholic mission. The reason for keeping them at the *sixa* is ostensibly to give them moral and spiritual instruction to prepare them to receive the sacrament of marriage; however, it is evident that the exploitation of their labor is the real reason for their long seclusion. They are made to work in the fields owned by the Catholic mission. The song of the women as they work in the fields betrays their awareness of their plight. After Angoni, Edanga's wife, for whom he has "paid the bride price in front of witnesses," has been kept at the *sixa* for three years, forcing him to pine in celibacy, he becomes convinced the *sixa* is a slave camp and sets out to liberate his wife. In the process, he kills a Catholic priest who assaults him. After the priest announces that he is dying a martyr, Edanga is compelled to howl as he is being taken to the white commandant's jail: "The true martyr is me! The true martyr is me. . . ."

Ba'bila Mutia, another Cameroonian writer who writes in English, valorizes indigenous African beliefs over Christianity. In "The Miracle," published in *Contemporary African Short Stories*, Ba'mia, a fourteen-year-old cripple, born with a dead leg, is torn between his mother's Catholic beliefs and his father's belief that the son's place is with his ancestors. In the end, however, Ba'mia comes to accept that he is the reincarnation of his paternal grandfather, and that his place is in the family shrine rather than the Catholic Church. Convinced that a meeting with the Pope will bring about the desired healing to render Ba'mia's dead leg alive again, his mother takes him on a pilgrimage to meet the Pope. The encounter with the Pope fails to bring about the desired miracle. The story ends with Ba'mia handing to his mother a rosary that the Pope gave him and announcing that his place is with his ancestors. He is then ready to be initiated at the family shrine.

Senegalese writer Birago Diop's "Sarzan," in Larson's *Under African Skies*, was first published in *Les Contes d'Amadou Koumba* (*Tales of Amadou Koumba*, 1947). This story, like most of Diop's stories in the collection, taps the oral tradition of his Wolof people and explores the impact of the Islamic and French colonial experience. In "Sarzan," African ways are shown to be enduring in spite of the assaults by both Islam and Christianity. Diop's story advocates respect for ancestors and customary beliefs and an attention to the teachings of elders. The story is set in Dougouba, a place which, though at one time conquered by the Qur'anic Tukulor, at the time of the narration has regained its indigenous way of life. Dougouba "had long ago erased all traces of the Islamic hordes and returned to the teachings of the ancestors."

"Sarzan" shows what happens to people who turn their backs on the wisdom of their ancestors and the teachings of their elders. Thiemokho Keita, or rather Sarzan, a corruption of the French word "sergent," a son of Dougouba, returns from fighting for the French people filled with the white man's ways and beliefs and a civilizing mission. Part of his civilizing mission is positive: He extends the paved road all the way to his hometown. However, he also shows gross disrespect for indigenous beliefs and customs. He not only dismisses the customs of his people as savage but also desecrates their ways by publicly assaulting practitioners of indigenous rituals. In the end, Sarzan goes mad. The story is told in a manner that brings out the beauty, soundness, and virtue in indigenous ways. The civilizing mission championed by Sarzan, on the other hand, is shown to be insensitive to and disrespectful of the people. "Sarzan" is told in highly lyrical language, which captures the sonority and beauty of the rituals described in the story and the songs and incantations recited by the mad Sarzan.

Sembène, another Senegalese, is perhaps the most well-known of the Francophone African writers. Though he is best known for his pioneer filmmaking and for his novel *Les Bouts de bois de Dieu* (1960; *God's Bits of Wood*, 1962), stories out of his short-story collection *Voltaïque* (1962), translated into English by Len Ortzen as *Tribal Scars* (1974), have been quite widely anthologized. Sembène's works are marked by a strong social and political consciousness. He is the voice of the dispossessed, depicting with sympathy and realism often tinged with irony the lives of ordinary people in Senegal and France. He is one of the first writers to write about the plight of women among the polygamous Muslims of Senegal in stories such as "The *Bilal*'s Fourth Wife" and "Her Three Days."

Sembène's "The Promised Land," also translated as "Black Girl" by Kennedy, in Larson's *Under African Skies*, has been made into an award-winning film about the plight of an African girl who is lured by her French employers to France. Diouana accepts her white employers' invitation to go to France with them, believing she is going to the promised land, where she will luxuriate in beauty and high living and make her fortune. Once in France, she realizes that there is a big "difference between living in France and being a servant there." She discovers that the life of glamour that France represents is reserved for her white masters. For her, life is filled with constant toil and mistrust on the part of her white employers. Racism and the constant fetching and carrying make her feel like a slave. Feeling thoroughly dehumanized, Diouana kills herself at the end.

Another one of Sembène's anthologized stories is "The False Prophet," a story in which the author attacks, in a humorous way, those who hide behind religion in order to cheat. Mahmoud Fall, a charlatan, feigns being an Iman, using the Qur'an to lord over the believers and to cheat them out of their food and money. He collects their booty and leaves for the desert. He goes to bed believing he has hidden his stash in a safe place only to wake up and find his head shaved and his money gone. Angry at God for allowing this mishap, he vows never to pray again and realizes that he did not "need to believe in Allah in order to be a thief!" What stands out about this story is the humorous tone in which it is narrated and the elements of the mysterious that Sembène weaves into the narration.

"Tribal Scars," the story that gives its name to Sembène's collection, is a story of slavery in Africa told from the perspective of explaining a phenomenon: "Why do we have tribal scars?" The story is also narrated from the perspective of exploring the meaning of an indigenous practice, which is bound to lose its significance because people have lost sight of the reason for it. It is therefore a story of Africa's slave history, a part of African history that is not often discussed by Africans themselves. "Tribal Scars" is framed as a story within a story. The first part of the narrative deals with a group of men who gather on a regular basis to socialize and talk about matters of interest, such as politics and women. At one of their sessions, Saer raises a question about the origin of tribal scars, a question he explores rather intellectually. The second part of the story consists of Saer sharing his knowledge about the origin of tribal scars with his friends through storytelling. He tells about a raid for slaves in which a man, Amoo, who had killed his wife to save her from being captured, also seizes his daughter, makes cuts all over her body, and wraps her in leaves, which heal the cuts but leave scars. Slave traders "sought blacks who were strong and healthy and without blemish. . . . No one was inclined to buy merchandise which had any blemish or imperfection." The scars, therefore, save Amoo's daughter from being considered fit to be a slave. In Sembène's story, tribal scars, which are often perceived as a mark of African barbarism, are shown to be a vital aspect of Africa's resistance against enslavement.

Laye of Guinea is best known for his novel *L'Enfant noir* (1953; *The Dark Child*, 1954; also known as *The African Child*). His short story "The Eyes of the Statue," first published in *Black Orpheus*, is anthologized in Larson's *More Modern African Stories* and *Under African Skies*. This story is a philosophical exploration of the human condition of desolation, loneliness, and the enduring nature of art, explored through a woman's consciousness. The use of a woman as the central character in this story is highly innovative considering that women at the time were either completely left out of fictional depictions of the African experience or mostly limited to the domestic sphere. Contemplating the ruins of an ancient monument and the eyes of a fallen statue fills the female protagonist with an intense sadness, loneliness, and a recognition that artists do capture and reflect back to readers what is already inside them. The statue, made of stone, is without a doubt viewed as more than mere stone; it is an embodiment of human creativity that "would outlast man's life" itself. Laye's female protagonist is filled with an urge to venture out. The story is suffused with an element of the surreal; there is a hint at the end that everything that has transpired in the story has been a nightmare had by the woman, through whose consciousness the story unfolds. Ivorian Véronique Tadjo's story "The Magician and the Girl," translated from the French by the author herself, in *Under African Skies*, is from her *À Vol d'oiseau*, published in Paris in 1992, a work considered one of the most original pieces in Francophone writing. It defies easy classification, comprising ninety-two independent but related pieces, which can either stand on their own or combine into a unified piece of African social commentary. "The Magician and the Girl" taps into the African folktale tradition, combining elements of magic and mystery with realism. In this story of a magician of great power and renowned beauty, whose knowledge of secrets knows no boundaries, a female character is created whose capacities seem to equal or even surpass the magician's. The magician remains a mystery to everyone but the girl, who ventures to get to the root of his mystery. The girl is creative and courageous, one invested with life-engendering qualities.

Anglophone Africa

Most of the information available on African short fiction is from Anglophone Africa. The majority of stories in multiple-author anthologies as well as single-author collections are by Anglophone writers. Because of the constraints of space, this article will concentrate on a few writers who have gained international recognition and have their own collections of short stories, in addition to being anthologized in multiple-author collections. Writers from West Africa, East Africa, and Southern Africa will be discussed in that order. Achebe, who is best known for his novel *Things Fall Apart* (1958), has earned himself the unofficial title of "father of African fiction." His short-story collection *Girls at War* was first published by Heinemann in 1972. That collection comprises twelve stories spanning a twenty-year period beginning when he was a student at Ibadan right through to stories of the Nigerian civil war. Three of the stories in this collection, "The Voter," "Civil Peace," and "Girls at War," have been anthologized often. All three focus on the theme of political, social, and moral corruption, and all are told with considerable irony, with humor dominating the narration of "The Voter" and "Civil Peace." While the problems depicted in the stories are grave, the manner of treatment reflects Achebe's sensitivity to the human failings he delineates.

In "The Voter," which appears in *Pan African Short Stories* (1965), the lack of integrity on the part of the leaders and election tampering are central concerns. Proverbs and specially coined words are woven into the narrative to capture the sociocultural nuances. A son of Umuofia, "a not too successful mission school teacher," who is about to get into trouble for impregnating another teacher, runs for political office on the ticket of the People's Alliance Party and wins, becoming Chief the Honourable Marcus Ibe, Minister of Culture. With political power come two long automobiles, "the biggest [mansion] anyone had seen in these parts," and a private power plant to supply him with electricity while the rest of the town goes without. When election time comes around again, the elders refuse to give him their votes for free, in light of the fact that the candidate asking for them is now a visibly affluent man. Even Rufus Okeke, Marcus Ibe's chief campaigner, sells his vote to the opposition for five pounds. In the end, Rufus tears his ballot paper in two, putting half into the box of each candidate.

"Civil Peace," which appears in *African Short Stories*, depicts life following the Nigerian civil war. It is a story in which Achebe concentrates on the aftermath of war, showing that chaos and violence have become the order of the day, with life posing even more danger to civilians during peace time than during war. The blatant, calculated manner in which armed robbers go about the business of robbing reinforces the absolute breakdown of law and order. This story also valorizes the indigenous beliefs and values of unflinching faith in God, honest hard work, natural intelligence, and ingenuity. Jonathan Iwegbu, a man who is robbed at gunpoint after receiving his "eggrasher" (*ex gratia*) money from the Biafran government, manifests such qualities. Throughout the war, he works hard, making his money the old-fashioned way. After he is robbed, he wakes up the following morning ready to continue his hard work, going about life as if no adversity has befallen him, firm in his belief that "nothing puzzles God."

Achebe's "Girls at War," anthologized in *More Modern African Stories* and *Under African Skies*, the story that lends its title to the collection, is one of the most ironic in tone in the entire collection. It is a story about the tragic effects of the war on the civilian population and particularly its effects on one girl, Gladys, who starts with high ideals but loses them as the war drags on and survival becomes more precarious. The irony in the story is generated mainly through the discrepancy between perception and reality. Reginald Nwankwo perceives himself to be a highly principled, moral, and patriotic Biafran. He feels superior to those around him and pours scorn on them for compromising their integrity in the interest of survival, yet he is just a pompous self-seeker like the rest of them. He uses his connections to appropriate war relief supplies for himself and his loved ones, just as the other elites do. It is through Nwankwo's eyes that Gladys is unfolded to the reader. When the reader first encounters her, she is fully committed to the war effort. When the reader encounters her later, however, she is flagging cars down for a lift to go to the city, dressed in expensive clothes and "a high-tinted wig," which announces she must "be in the keep of some well-placed gentleman, one of those piling up money out of the war." Nwankwo, who picks her up and ends up spending a romantic weekend with her, is shocked at the transformation she has undergone. In the end, however, Gladys redeems herself, sacrificing her life during a raid to save a soldier crippled by war wounds. While Achebe minces no words about the corrupting effect of the war on people, he nonetheless depicts his characters, especially ordinary people like Gladys, with deep sympathy.

The collection of Ghana's Aidoo, *No Sweetness Here and Other Stories* (1970), is one of the finest African short-story collections dealing with the sociopolitical, economic, and developmental issues of Africa. This collection is a gallery of female portraits offering highly colorful and varied images of womanhood, covering everything from the growing girl to the grandmother. Aidoo's narratives are dramatic and have an aural quality to them. She prides herself on the fact that her "stories are written to be heard, primarily." "In the Cutting of a Drink" is constructed as a dialogue, a conversation between the protagonist/narrator and members of the extended family even though the protagonist/narrator's words are the only ones that are actually heard in the narrative.

In two of her most anthologized stories, "In the Cutting of a Drink" and "Two Sisters," Aidoo expresses great concern over the impact of modernization on Ghana's females. In both stories, the lure of the city and the peculiar ways in which it affects females with minimal Western education is explored. In "In the Cutting of a Drink," in *Pan African Short Stories*, also anthologized in *Modern African Stories* as "Cut Me a Drink," Mansa, who has a little schooling but not enough for a civil-service or teaching job, is sent to the city by her rural relatives to learn a trade to enhance her chances at a better economic life than is viable in the village. Considerable humor is generated in this story by revealing the city through the eyes of a visitor. After not visiting home for twelve years, Mansa's brother goes to the city to search for her and finds she has become a prostitute. Nonetheless, the narrative perspective is not condemnatory. Prostitution is portrayed as a way of making a living that is forced by the demands of modernization. As

Mansa tells her countrified brother, who meets her at a nightclub in Accra, "any form of work is work . . . is work . . . is work!"

Considerable cynicism is revealed in the narration of the story "Two Sisters" in *Under African Skies*, a story that exposes political and moral corruption. Attention in this story is focused on the females, particularly the unmarried younger sister, Mercy, who relies on her good looks to attract men with political power and money to maintain her high style of living, which she cannot support through her typing skills alone. Mercy takes on a politician boyfriend, who is old enough to be her father, because of the financial security he offers. When the civilian government is overthrown for political corruption and the politicians arrested, Connie, Mercy's older sister, breathes a sigh of relief, believing that her younger sister will give up her immoral ways. To her chagrin, Mercy shows up with a new boyfriend, one of the new military rulers who have overthrown the civilian government for corruption and mismanagement. Aidoo's Mercy reminds one of Nwapa's Soha in the story "This Is Lagos," in her collection bearing the same title. Soha has enough education to teach in a primary school but does not like it. She does not make enough from her teaching to live on her own, so she lives with an aunt and her aunt's family. Seeing her teaching job as a stepping stone to something better, she finds a man with a car and his own place so that she can move out of her aunt's house. The reason for seeking male companionship by females in the city, like Mercy and Soha, seems to be economic need rather than love.

Known as East Africa's most renowned and prolific writer, Ngugi wa Thiong'o, though best known for his novels and critical essays, also has a collection of short stories, *Secret Lives* (1974). "A Meeting in the Dark," his most anthologized story (*Pan African Short Stories*, *Modern African Stories*, *Under African Skies*), reflects the social consciousness for which Ngugi is well recognized. The story explores class divisions and hypocrisy, pitting moral against economic choices. John, a Western-educated, Christian young man, who is raised by a Pharisee-type father, becomes so morally stifled that when he impregnates Wamuhu, a local beauty, who is uneducated and circumcised, he is driven to commit murder out of fear of what may befall him should his father find out about it. Though his actions are compelled in part by economic considerations—he has gained admission to Makerere University, in Uganda, a prospect which opens the door for him to join the intellectual elite of his society, and marrying Wamuhu would put an end to that dream—the more compelling factor is his fear of being found out by the people and his father, who holds him to extremely high moral standards, standards that he himself has failed to meet. John has been conceived in "sin," an event that happened before his parents moved to their present community, where the father maintains his facade of a staunch Christian, one who does not condone the comingling of Christians and circumcised pagans. Ngugi makes masterful use of irony in this story, in which outward appearance assumes such importance that the young man's sense of his image in the community totally clouds his vision, making murder preferable to falling in stature.

The short-story collection of Kenya's Ogot, *Land Without Thunder* (1968), is among her best-known writings. Recognized for their fascinating yet critical depiction of old Africa's order, splendor, nobility, and simplicity, quite a number of stories out of the collection have been anthologized. "The Rain Came," the most anthologized of her stories, is a story that looks, with a critical eye, at the custom of human sacrifice. A king sacrifices his only daughter to the lake monster to bring much-needed rain to alleviate the hunger that threatens his people. This is not a story of mindless superstition but one of leadership, patriotism, heroism, courage, and selflessness, a story that reveals the nobility of the old Africa, which serves as a good foil to the new Africa, in which political leadership often comes with self-seeking and a lack of integrity. The father's selflessness is matched by the dignity and nobility of spirit with which his daughter responds to the call of duty. Even though the girl does not die in the end, the rains do come down profusely, showing that the spirit of action is what is important. The dignity of the characters depicted in Ogot's "The Rain Came" stands in stark contrast to the superficiality of the characters in Ngugi's "A Meeting in the

Dark." Ogot's "The Rain Came" is reminiscent of Ngugi's "The Fig Tree," in *More Modern African Stories* in which Mukami, a young woman who is shunned by her husband because she has proved barren, ventures into the deep forest in desperation to commune with the spirits of her ancestors, only to find that she is not barren after all. She goes back to the marriage she has left, with plans to prepare for the new life that is stirring inside of her. Both Ogot's and Ngugi's stories depict a people who live in close communion with the natural and spiritual worlds.

Southern Africa offers a wide array of short stories by both male and female writers. They dominate African short fiction, patronizing that genre more often than writers from other regions of the continent. Given the unstable situation in which the South African writers have had to operate under apartheid, the compact short-story form and poetry have suited their circumstances better than the more elaborate, extended form of the novel. Mphahlele, Can Themba, Nadine Gordimer, Richard Rive, Casey Motsisi, Head, Alex La Guma, James Matthews, Njabulo Ndebele, Mbulelo Nzamane, and Sindiwe Magona are some of the anthologized writers, some of whom also have individual-author collections.

Head, herself a victim of the oppressive system of South Africa, rejected that dehumanizing, alienating system by migrating to Botswana. While her works do not often deal overtly with apartheid, she does write metaphorically about it by focusing on issues of rejection, oppression (particularly women's oppression), superstition, and prejudice. Many of her stories in the collection *The Collector of Treasures and Other Botswana Village Tales* focus on local customs. In her stories, local customs and traditional beliefs seem to exert on people the same oppressive, debilitating constraints that apartheid exercises over the people in that system. Head's story "Witchcraft," which appears in *Stories from Central and Southern Africa*, is one that explores local beliefs regarding their confining impact on people. Her approach is anthropological, explaining witchcraft and its place in the society. She identifies witchcraft as one of the oldest beliefs coming down from ancestral times, a potent evil in the society, one that afflicts people and is often employed against one's enemies out of a feeling of jealousy. It is sad that people accept without question this supernatural force and its mysterious ability to destroy.

In Head's narrative "Witchcraft," she interrogates this belief system, raising questions about its efficacy. The protagonist, Mma-Mabele, who seems to be doing quite well in life, is suddenly stricken by what is believed to be witchcraft. She becomes very ill for quite some time and loses strength, nearly giving up her housekeeping job, which pays reasonably well. The job is a big strain on her, particularly during the time of her affliction. Just when she is expected to die from this evil force, however, she recovers. Her employer goes off on a month's holiday, offering Mma-Mabele the chance to rest well. She regains her appetite and her strength and resumes normal life. Head makes it evident that people are too quick to blame the things that confound them on the supernatural and do not pursue practical avenues for confronting their problems. There is little question that when life is hard—and the life Head's characters confront is filled with hardship—life can become confounding, making people prone to finding supernatural explanations efficacious. The traditional belief system dominates the lives of the people in Head's world in a manner similar to the way in which apartheid towers over the lives of black South Africans.

Alex La Guma's "A Walk in the Night," which in length is more of a novella and appears in his collection of the same name, is one of the best-known stories from South Africa. It reveals the evils of apartheid and the alienating, dehumanizing impact it has on its victims, with unnerving clarity. Apartheid is shown to be a legalized form of racial discrimination that considers whites to be superior to blacks and coloreds, upholds white privilege, exacts submission from nonwhites, and supports the entire dehumanizing system through rigid policing, which safeguards the rights of whites and terrorizes nonwhites. The blacks and coloreds, who are in the majority, are kept mostly in overcrowded, squalid places known as townships and are made to serve as cheap laborers and domestics, exploited by the rich, minority whites. Life for nonwhites is at best precarious, filled with fear, hunger, and frustration.

In the story, Micheal Adonis, the protagonist, loses his job for talking back to a white foreman, who criticizes him for taking a bathroom break. The frustration and oppression under which nonwhites constantly live engenders explosions of violence against innocent people. From being fired unjustly from his job and being terrorized by the police, Adonis harbors so much anger that he accidentally kills an Irishman who is trying to be neighborly. The wrong black man is hunted and gunned down for the murder. As far as the white apartheid police are concerned, blacks are faceless; a white man has been killed by a black man, and the crime must be avenged. In the end, Adonis is enticed to join a gang to rob people for a living, an act of resistance in a dehumanizing environment.

Given the pressures under which blacks live under apartheid, hemmed in like animals in a cage, it is not surprising that the oppressed often turn upon one another. Families become divided as the young identify themselves with radical groups intent on forcing change. Members of the older generation become bogged down with the business of seeking survival for themselves and their dependents the best way they know how. In Sindiwe Magona's "I'm Not Talking About That, Now," in *Under African Skies*, the impact of apartheid on an ordinary black South African family is explored. The young constitute a vigilante group, which is bent on ensuring that blacks engage in a consumer boycott they hope will bring down the white regime. In this endeavor, children turn against their parents, becoming a policing wing to punish those who do not observe the boycott. Mdlangathi witnesses some young people forcing their hands down the throat of a drunk to make him expel the white man's "poison."

The boycott has resulted in starvation, causing mothers to become desperate about how they are going to feed their families. Having run out of food and not willing to see her family starve, Mamvulane surreptitiously goes in search of food. In spite of the care she takes, she is discovered by the comrades, the vigilante group, among whom is her own son, and her provisions are trampled under foot. Having managed to secret a few items on her body, she succeeds in feeding her family except for Nteteli, who is in the streets doing his vigilante work. In the middle of the night, however, Nteteli arrives and demands his dinner. The father, who is outraged at his son for his role in humiliating his mother and depriving the family of direly needed provisions, grabs a stick to discipline the son and accidentally cracks his skull, causing him to bleed to death. Mamvulane loses both her son and husband, the first to death and the latter to imprisonment. In this story, the efforts of the oppressed are shown to make not even a dent in the apartheid system. What apartheid brings is further victimization of the oppressed. Nonetheless, it must be noted that the youth are the primary agents, whose hard-line, rebellious actions against apartheid finally lead to the revolution that brings an end to apartheid in South Africa. What Magona's story shows is the plight of the oppressed in the long struggle that eventually leads to the toppling of apartheid.

The short-story form is alive and active in Africa even though the criticism has yet to catch up with the production. Some of the finest stories are still coming out of Southern Africa, and West Africa also continues to stay strong in short-fiction writing. Women writers particularly are gaining more prominence than ever before. In addition to individual-author collections, anthologies of women's writing, most of them comprising poetry and short fiction, are often published by the women writers' organizations themselves. Examples are *Women in South Africa: From the Heart* (1988), *Zimbabwe Women Writers Anthology* (1994), and *Zimbabwe Women Writers: English Poetry and Short Stories* (1998). A few individual women's short-story collections from West Africa published in the 1990's are Aidoo's *The Girl Who Can and Other Stories* (1997), Chinyere Grace Okafo's *He Wants to Marry Me Again and Other Stories* (1996), Titilayo Ufomata's *Voices from the Marketplace* (1998), and Makuchi's *Your Madness, Not Mine: Stories of Cameroon* (1999). All of these works, with the exception of Makuchi's, have been published on the African continent.

Naana Banyiwa Horne

Anthologies

Achebe, Chinua, and C. L. Innes, eds. *African Short Stories*. London: Heinemann, 1985.

_______. *Contemporary African Short Stories*. London: Heinemann, 1992.

Brunner, Charlotte, ed. *Unwinding Threads: Writing by Women in Africa*. London: Heinemann, 1983.

Denny, Neville, ed. *Pan African Short Stories*. London: Thomas Nelson and Sons, 1965.

Gray, Stephen, ed. *The Penguin Book of Southern African Stories*. New York: Penguin Books, 1985.

Kitson, Norma, ed. *Zimbabwe Women Writers Anthology*. Harare, Zimbabwe: Zimbabwe Women Writers, 1994.

Komey, Ellis Ayitey, and Ezekiel Mphahlele, eds. *Modern African Stories*. London: Faber and Faber, 1964.

Larson, Charles R., ed. *Under African Skies: Modern African Stories*. New York: Farrar, Straus and Giroux, 1997.

Mutloatse, Mothobi, ed. *Africa South: Contemporary Writings*. London: Heinemann, 1981.

Scanlon, Paul A, ed. *Stories from Central and Southern Africa*. London: Heinemann, 1983.

Tsikang, Seageng, and Dinah Lefakane, eds. *Women in South Africa: From the Heart*. Johannesburg: Seriti sa Sechaba Publishers, 1988.

Bibliography

Balogun, F. Odun. *Tradition and Modernity in the African Short Story: An Introduction to a Literature in Search of Critics*. Westport, Conn.: Greenwood Press, 1991. Balogun seeks to bring a "neglected" body of work into the critical canon by appealing to a traditional set of standards.

Feuser, Willfried. "Aspects of the Short Story." In *European Language Writing in Sub-Saharan Africa*, edited by Albert Gerard. Budapest: Akadéémiai Kiadóó, 1986.

Horne, Naana Banyiwa. "Flora Nwapa's *This Is Lagos:* Valorizing the Female Through Narrative Agency." In *Emerging Perspectives on Flora Nwapa: Critical and Theoretical Essays*, edited by Marie Umeh. Trenton, N.J.: Africa World Press, 1998. This article forms part of a collection of critical/theoretical essays by some thirty writers and critics, each examining a different aspect of Nwapa's art.

Julien, Eileen. "Of Traditional Tales and Short Stories in African Literature." *Présence Africaine* 125 (1983): 146-165.

AFRICAN AMERICAN SHORT FICTION

Although it may be viewed as a modern genre, short fiction subsides into the mists of history in the form of fairy tales, anecdotes, myths, and historical legend. The form was known to the ancient Greeks. Actually, tales of *Alf layla wa-layla* (fifteenth century; *The Arabian Nights' Entertainments*, 1706-1708) and Geoffrey Chaucer's tales are classified as short stories. Besides the obvious difference in length, short fiction differs from longer fiction by focusing upon a single event occurring in one or two scenes and by including fewer characters. In addition, the compactness and unified effect of the literary form forces an economy of words, and setting is oftentimes simple. Edgar Allan Poe, who receives much credit for the development of the short story as a literary genre, remarked that the short story's primary distinguishing factor is the sense of aesthetic unity that can be read in one sitting. While the nineteenth century saw the development of the short story as it is understood today, the original form, passed down through oral tradition, predates recorded history and includes most cultures.

Oral tradition is especially important in African American literature. Many Africans, sold as slaves and forced into such places as Brazil, the Caribbean, and the United States, originated from cultures rich in oral traditions and oral literature. In an effort to preserve their group history, much of this spoken literature was later reworked and remade as written literature. Well-known American short-story writer John Cheever wrote: "So long as we are possessed by experience that is distinguished by its intensity and its episodic nature, we will have the short story in our literature." For African Americans, story telling especially in the form of folk culture, as critic John Edgar Wideman writes, "preserves and expresses an identity, a history, a self-evaluation apart from those destructive incarcerating images proliferated by mainline culture." African American writers drew on the universal black experience just like Sean O'Casey and Sholom Aleichem drew upon the Irish and Jewish experiences. Influential Irish short-story writer Frank O'Connor's suggestion that short fiction is a method for "submerged population groups" to address a dominant community would certainly hold true for African American short fiction. Often the African American short story has served as a vehicle for making short, to-the-point statements: social, cultural, economic, political, or otherwise. Although the short story deals primarily with racial pride and oppression, African American short fiction also celebrates survival and deliverance. From its inception, the African American short-story genre represents a range of styles, events, and experiences and draws upon the diversity of black lives within American history.

Nineteenth Century Short-Story Writers

Before their emergence as short-story writers, African Americans in the United States launched both an oral and a written tradition in the form of slave narratives which chronicled their harrowing experiences and their compelling, never-ceasing desire for freedom. During the nineteenth century African Americans were encouraged to write only autobiographies or slave narratives, such as Sojourner Truth's *Narrative of Sojourner Truth, a Northern Slave, Emancipated from Bodily Servitude by the State of New York, in 1828* (1850) and Frederick Douglass's *My Bondage and My Freedom* (1855), in an effort to propel the abolitionist movement. These narratives became the vehicle through which African Americans' gave voice to their experiences and entered American literature. The post-Civil War era saw the emergence of African American writers. Emancipation provided opportunities for education. In 1892 Anna Julia Cooper, a leading lecturer on black women's civil rights, who at one time shared a stage with the powerful black civil rights leader W. E. B. Du Bois, published *A Voice from the South: By a Black Woman of the South.* The daughter of a North Carolina slave and graduate of Oberlin College, Cooper encouraged women, both black and white, to seek education. In addition, when her work appeared the term "Negro" was in fashion and the term "Black Woman" in the title of her book surprised many. However, despite the fact that they wrote a great deal on a wide variety of subjects, black writers essentially remained ignored except for their slave narratives. It was not until the last quarter of the nineteenth century that Charles Waddell Chesnutt, Paul Laurence Dunbar, and his wife Alice Dunbar-Nelson, who utilized black tradition and myth to write remarkable short stories, were published—with one exception. Frances Ellen Watkins Harper's 1859 short story "The Two Offers" is recognized as the first ever published by a African American writer.

Harper was the child of free African Americans, who died when she was three. A poet, novelist, and social reformer, the youngster came under the guidance of her schoolteacher uncle. A novelist as well, Harper focused on slavery, motherhood, and Christianity and the role of the mulatto in society. American blacks, she said, "are homeless in the land of our births and worse than strangers in the land of our nativity." An active abolitionist for the Underground Railroad, which channeled slaves to freedom, Harper details the plight of a woman who goes against social conventions to advocate for the abolition of slavery in her story "The Two Offers." During an era which prescribed that women be angels in the house, Harper's story brings to light both black and white women's vulnerability, while it challenged the accepted social position of all American women.

Chesnutt, recognized primarily for his psychological realism, blazed a path for African American short-fiction writers. The son of free blacks, Chesnutt spent much of his early life teaching in North Carolina. Unable to cope with the South's harsh treatment of blacks, he moved to Cleveland, Ohio, where he became an attorney and established a law firm. Although writing was merely an avocation, he published more than fifty short stories and essays, two collections of short stories, a biography of Frederick Douglass, and three novels between 1885 and 1905. In 1885, he published his first notable short story, "Uncle Peter's House," for the S. S. McClure newspaper syndicate. The tale reflects the local color of its setting, a popular literary trend during the late 1800's. Historically significant and ironic, "The Goophered Grapevine" represents the first work by a black to be accepted by *The Atlantic Monthly.* Originating from an oral tale told by the family gardener, the narrative deals with the conjuration of black voodoo practices. Beyond this, however, the heroic narrator Uncle Julius displays an ability to utilize conjure stories to frighten his white employers and oftentimes to secure a financial advantage. "The Sheriff's Children," the first significant study of the mulatto in American life, was published in the fall of 1889 and deals with the repercussions of miscegenation, hatred, and violence in the postwar South. In "The Sheriff's Children," the illegitimate son of a North Carolina sheriff and a former slave is transported to his father's jail, where he has the opportunity to remind the sheriff (who fails to recognize him at first) of his parental shortcomings. While the sheriff experiences enlightenment and repents, the son ironically commits suicide in his father's jail. The tale amplified the era's social injustice.

Chesnutt is best known for his dialect short-fiction collection detailing incidents of slavery told by an old gardener, the trickster figure Uncle Julius, to his northern employers. *The Conjure Woman*, Chesnutt's first short-story collection, was published in 1899 and was critically well received. Unlike some period writers, Chesnutt does not romanticize the slavery practices of the Old South, describing instead a world of brutal masters whose sole focus is on profit. The author admirably describes the slaves' ingenious methods of retribution and their attempts at any cost to keep their families intact. Through the practice of conjuration, slaves in "Sis' Becky's Pickaninny," "Mars Jeems's Nightmare," and "Hot-Foot Hannibal" withstand and endure their dominant abusers. In addition, tales like "The Conjurer's Revenge" and "The Gray Wolf's Ha'nt," which illustrate the dark side of voodoo, demonstrate confrontations between slaves and free African Americans. Chesnutt oftentimes illustrates racial prejudice on both sides. In his second collection of nine short stories, *The Wife of His Youth and Other Stories of the Color Line* (1899), only one story, "The Passing of Grandison," presents the slave as trickster in a strategy to gain freedom. The rest of the stories occur after the Civil War and deal with social, psychological, and ethical implications of miscegenation. The title story, "The Wife of His Youth," deals with a free black's conflicting loyalties to the wife he married in slavery and the more refined women he meets years later. "A Matter of Principle" and "Her Virginia Mammy," drawn from Chesnutt's own experience, examine with great insight the racial prejudices of light-skinned, middle-class African Americans toward those of darker complexion. In "A Matter of Principle," the mulatto protagonist Cicero Clayton spoils his daughter's chance for happiness with a lighter-skinned congressman. In "Uncle Wellington's Wives," Chesnutt argues that southern men like Wellington, who believe they can gain equality by marrying white women, are irrational. Assimilation into mainstream American culture, Chesnutt argued, could come about only through education and hard work. The author requested that his publishers not mention his ethnicity in advertising his work because he desired to be judged strictly on literary merit. Many times compared to William Faulkner, Chesnutt remained the premier black writer until the 1930's when the Works Progress Administration (WPA) Federal Writers' Project (see below) provided a new route of emergence for African American writers. Through his indictment of racism, Chesnutt was viewed as a literary champion for the interests of middle- and working-class African Americans of the South, whom he had known growing up in North Carolina.

Pauline Elizabeth Hopkins counted herself a novelist, playwright, editor, actress, and singer in addition to short-fiction writer. Like many other female writers, Hopkins has been historically overlooked for her literary contributions until recently. Born in Portland, Maine, Hopkins had won a literary prize for an essay, "Evils of Intemperance and Their Remedies," by the time she was fifteen. In 1880, her first play, *Slaves' Escape: Or, The Underground Railroad* (retitled *Peculiar Sam: Or, The Underground Railroad*), was produced. Strongly influenced by W. E. B. Du Bois, founder and leader of the new National Association for the Advancement of Colored People, Hopkins utilized the romance model in the short-story form to explore racial violence and social themes such as the distress suffered by blacks after the Civil War. Actually, Hopkins single-handedly opened the door for black women's publishing with her 1900 novel *Contending Forces: A Romance Illustrative of Negro Life North and South*, published by the Boston Colored Co-operative Publishing Company, in which she was a shareholder. That same year, the Co-operative published the literary monthly *Colored American Magazine*, whose first issue featured Hopkins's first short story, "The Mystery Within Us," which she structured as a conversation between two men. In the time span of five years, Tom Underwood has moved from a state of down-and-out destitution to one of prosperity as a physician and author. Tom reminisces how, on the verge of suicide, a mysterious "Presence" appeared to him and encouraged him to change his way of life. The Presence interjects into Tom's mind the thoughts of Dr. Thorn, a notable physician, who unfortunately died before bringing his medical discoveries to public attention. Deeply concerned with metaphysics, Hopkins makes such mystical and spiritual phenomena the basis of many of her works. By the time the *Colored American Magazine* ceased publication in 1909, Hopkins had published six more short stories, including "Talma Gordon," "George Washington, a Christmas Story," "As the Lord Lives, He Is One of Our Mother's Children," and her powerful "A Dash for Liberty." In "A Dash for Liberty," which focuses on the theme of escape from slavery, the protagonist, Madison, although secure and sheltered in Canada, wishes to return to Virginia to free his wife Susan. Furthermore, as editor of the magazine, Hopkins focused on discovering and publishing short stories by black women. Contributors included Francis Ellen Watkins Harper. Hopkins denounced racist myths, demonstrated outrage of the role of women as victims, and stressed that black women must resist victimization whenever possible. She attempted to reify African American humanity and believed firmly that education was the key to conquering prejudice and attaining equality.

Paul Laurence Dunbar was born in Dayton, Ohio, the son of former slaves. A well-known poet and novelist, he authored four collections of short stories. With the encouragement of William Dean Howells, a well-known American novelist, Dunbar became one of the first African American writers to gain a large public following. In particular, his southern plantation stories were deeply admired by American readers. However, Dunbar, who worked as a reading-room assistant at the Library of Congress, has experienced recent attacks upon his literary reputation because of his use of southern dialect, his degrading stereotypes of black people, and his portrayal of the Old South in romantic terms. Many of the stories in Dunbar's four collections are free of these pejorative descriptions and deserve consideration on their literary merits. His stories (plantation tall tales, didactic stories warning his readers against weakness, narratives decrying southern social repression, and protest fiction) are oftentimes aimed directly against racism.

Dunbar's first collection of stories, *Folks from Dixie*, appeared in 1898 and is concerned with plantation tales depicting southern blacks who are fiercely loyal and religious. No doubt, the idea of slaves choosing loyalty to their masters over their own well-being can indeed be considered highly offensive. His story "The Colonel's Awakening," in *Folks from Dixie*, which portrays an old Virginia aristocrat, who after losing his two sons is unable to adjust to post-Civil War life, is recognized and praised as one of Dunbar's best-constructed stories. *The Strength of Gideon and Other Stories* (1900) remains Dunbar's most successful collection. Although it does present the South in sentimental terms, it additionally warns against the evils of northern vice. For instance, "The Trustfulness of Polly" describes the destruction of Polly Jackson's husband Sam as he falls prey to brothels. Dunbar's "The Tragedy at Three Forks" protests southern racism, and "The Ingrate" represents a fictionalized account of Dunbar's own father's escape on the Underground Railroad. The most bitter story Dunbar ever wrote, "One Man's Failure," addresses a black man's relationship to President Abraham Lincoln. His *In Old Plantation Days* (1903) makes up twenty-five short stories which unfortunately remain dependent on unpalatable stereotypes. The writer's 1904 short-story collection *The Heart of Happy Hollow* contains one of Dunbar's best short stories, "The Scapegoat," an ironic story of the political revenge that an angry black party boss takes upon the political establishment. In addition, Dunbar married Alice Ruth Moore, a writer and teacher who would achieve a measure of fame in her own right.

Alice Dunbar-Nelson, Paul Laurence Dunbar's wife, was also an early short-fiction writer. Born during Reconstruction and only a generation removed from slavery, Dunbar-Nelson felt a strong responsibility toward future generations of African Americans, and in this vein she attempted to share her knowledge and experience. Alice Ruth Moore was born in New Orleans, Louisiana. She received an M.A. from Cornell University. Incredibly versatile, she was a trained nurse, stenographer, and musician. Her first collection, *Violets and Other Tales*, which included poetry and essays in addition to short stories, was published in 1895. "Amid the Roses," "Love and the Butterfly," "At Eventide," and "Bay St. Louis" thematically center on racism, gender roles in society, and the importance of love, war, and death. The sentimental title story tells the story of a young girl in love, who dies within a year after placing a bouquet of violets, orange blossoms, and other flowers in a letter to her sweetheart. A teacher, the writer married author Paul Laurence Dunbar after accepting a teaching assignment in New York in 1898. Dunbar-Nelson was also a journalist and wrote for many black newspapers including the *Pittsburgh Courier* and the *Washington Eagle*, for which she wrote the column "As in a Looking Glass" from 1926 to 1930. In 1920 Dunbar-Nelson founded the *Wilmington Advocate*, a weekly newspaper. Her second collection of stories, *The Goodness of St. Rocque, and Other Stories* (1899), the first collection of short stories by a black woman, focuses on New Orleans Creole culture. In "La Juanita," which incorporates a blend of Catholic and black magic practices, beautiful Juanita loves the American Mercer, despite her grandfather's objections. Known as a transitional figure to the writers of the Harlem Renaissance, Dunbar-Nelson had a great influence on rising young writers of the period.

The Harlem Renaissance

After World War I, black soldiers returned to America having fought in Europe for the concepts of equality and freedom. The 369th Battalion, "The Harlem Hellfighters," was the most decorated American unit, and when they marched up Fifth Avenue to Harlem after the war's end, the black population felt part of a new beginning. This was the celebrated time for the "New Negro." The new black writers generated a powerful and refreshing voice which was heard with a great deal of respect by the white community. These writers, artists, intellectuals, and jazz musicians came to represent the Harlem Renaissance, one of the most fertile periods in America's literary history. The Harlem Renaissance not only exemplified the advancement of black arts but also staged the independence and liberty of African American writing and publishing. Two leading African American journals of the day, *Opportunity*, edited by Charles S. Johnson, which aimed to give voice to black culture hitherto neglected by mainstream American publishing, and the magazine of W. E. B. Du Bois's National Association for the Advancement of Colored People (NAACP), *The Crisis*, along with newspapers such as *Baltimore African American*, continued the fashion established by Pauline Hopkins of publishing and establishing black American writers and entered the short-story competition trend between 1920 and 1935. This publishing effort dispersed the Harlem Renaissance nationwide. Both periodicals and newspapers brought great attention to the black literary market, launching the careers of such writers as Zora Neale Hurston, Dorothy West, Gwendolyn Bennett, Claude McKay, Langston Hughes, and Countée Cullen, who made up the lively Harlem writers' group. Their works began to examine the stigmatizing stereotypes of African Americans that slavery and the post-Reconstruction period promoted in white American minds.

In the 1920's, the Harlem Renaissance, also called the New Negro Movement, burst into bloom, bringing a new creative energy to African American literature and changing forevermore what had earlier been viewed as folklore or imitation "white writing" into proud, complex investigations of black culture. Although the peak of this Renaissance era extended from 1921 to 1931, it remained influential throughout the 1930's. Centered on the black neighborhoods of Harlem, in New York City, and funded by philanthropic grants and scholarships, the movement cultivated and encouraged the hopeful young black writers who were central to the Harlem domain. Sadly, the Great Depression adversely affected this dynamic group of writers and many were ultimately forced to leave New York.

Jessie Redmon Fauset is said to be a focal figure of the Harlem Renaissance because of her extensive support of other black authors. Primarily a novelist, she also wrote numerous short stories as well as acting from 1919 to 1926 as the literary editor of the highly influential *Crisis* magazine. By confronting race and sex stereotyping, Fauset demonstrated a deep awareness of the unique situation of the American black woman. Born in Camden County, New Jersey, a suburb of Philadelphia, Pennsylvania, she came from a poor family who placed a premium on education. She received a scholarship to Cornell University and graduated in 1905; she remains possibly the first black woman to be elected to the academic honorary Phi Beta Kappa. During her tenure at *The Crisis*, she published a large number of women writers, black and white, who voiced convictions ranging from conservative to radical. After she left in 1926, the magazine never regained its former literary stature. In addition, she played a major influential role in the recognition and promotion of black art during the period of the Harlem Renaissance.

Zora Neale Hurston, a primary, influential African American folklorist and short-story writer, temporally captured and celebrated rural, black, southern American culture. Early in life she made her way to New York City during the Harlem Renaissance, where she associated with such writers as Langston Hughes, the prominent African American poet. Although she never finished grade school, she attended Howard University, going on to become a cultural anthropologist and ethnologist. In her scholarly endeavors, Hurston traveled to Haiti, where she researched voodoo. Hurston's first story, "John Redding Goes to Sea," was published in the literary magazine *Stylus* in

1921 and republished in 1926 in *Opportunity*, the leading periodical of the Harlem Renaissance. The story deals with young John Redding's incapacity to accomplish his goal of seeing the world (a desire brought about by a witch's spell) because the women in his life attempt to tie him down and encourage him instead to settle and marry rather than follow his dream. Throughout his life, John allows himself to be tied down and views the world only after he dies from drowning. This story set the themes Hurston was to develop throughout her career: the dream and the resistance against improving one's life and the strong, pervading sense of the supernatural.

"Drenched in Light" was published in *Opportunity* in 1924. The highly imaginative, eleven-year-old protagonist Isis (nicknamed Isie) Watts feels stifled by Grandmother Potts. Similar to the dreamer John Redding, young and impressionable Isis envisions wearing golden slippers and long princess robes while riding white horses to find the edge of the world. In vain, her grandmother disciplines the lively but mischievous girl and punishes her severely for merely whistling and playing with boys. After a white stranger, Helen, takes Isie to see a Gypsy dance performance, she is overwhelmed by the girl's exuberance and recognizes the emptiness of her own life. In what could be construed as an altruistic gesture, Helen attempts to take the youngster from her home. However, it becomes increasingly clear throughout the evolution of the story that Helen wants to absorb the child's energy only for her own delight. As one critic remarked, Helen's strategy is reminiscent of the whites who flocked to popular Harlem nightspots to be entertained by "primitive" black musicians. "Drenched in Light" describes the youthful effervescence Hurston herself exhibits in her autobiographical "How It Feels to Be Colored Me."

After moving to New York in 1925, Hurston quickly became known to and a central figure of Harlem Renaissance literary circles. Indeed, Langston Hughes found her the most amusing member of the writers' group. That year, Hurston also received a scholarship to Barnard College, where she entered as its first black student. Hurston's popular "Spunk" is a story about a giant man, Spunk Banks, who intentionally intimidates people. Using the black, central-Florida dialect and elements of the area's folklore, the tale is set in an area much like Hurston's hometown of Eatonville, Florida. The fearless Banks suffers a decline in pride which brings about his downfall when he courts Lena, another man's wife, in public. This prompts Joe Kanty, Lena's husband, to seek revenge. Kanty, however, is killed when Banks shoots him. After the murder trial, Spunk loses his courage, believing that he is haunted by Joe's ghost, and suffers a grisly death in a mysterious sawmill accident. The townspeople believe the death was caused by Joe's spirit, who assumed the form of a black panther. "Black Death" was also published in 1925 and highlights an Eatonville voodoo man named Old Man Morgan. Mrs. Boger consults him to seek revenge on the cold-hearted Beau Diddeley for refusing to marry her daughter Docia after impregnating her. While Beau courts another young girl, the conjure man casts his deadly spell, and soon Beau is found dead with an enigmatic powder burn found over his heart. In this tale, Hurston demonstrates her skill to connect folklore and fiction. In "Muttsy" Pinkie escapes her poverty-stricken, abusive southern home and moves to Harlem. Pinkie is directed to Ma Turner's place (a Harlem brothel and speakeasy), where she meets Muttsy Owens, a gambler who is smitten by her detached manner and superior beauty. Swearing his intentions are pure, he gives her a diamond ring, but she insists he give up gambling. Predictably, shortly after they marry, he resumes gambling.

Story Magazine published Hurston's most frequently anthologized story, "The Gilded Six-Bits," in 1933. Missie May and Joe Banks live happily together in wedded bliss in an edenic setting, as delighted and innocent as two candy-eating children, until the archetypal serpent, Otis D. Slemmons, a sly woman-chaser from Chicago with gold teeth, a gold stickpin, and a ten-dollar gold piece, intrudes into their perfect garden. Like Eve, Missie May is hypnotized by the newcomer's power and falls away from her loving husband Joe. Joe returns home unannounced one evening to find his wife in bed with Slemmons. Prostrate with grief, Missie May begs her crestfallen husband Joe for forgiveness. After three months, Joe relents and returns to her and after the birth of a son, the couple continue to love each other as before.

In the highly acclaimed *Mules and Men* (1935), her collection of folktales and humorous and tragic sketches, Hurston attempted to find a balance between the folk culture of her ethnic background and her development as an artist. For Hurston, it was paramount for readers "to realize that minorities do think, and think about something other than the race problem . . . that they are just like everyone else." Perhaps best known for her controversial 1937 novel *Their Eyes Were Watching God*, about an African American woman's search for love and identity, Hurston refused to see blacks as victimized. Indeed, Hurston celebrated her rural black heritage of Eatonville, Florida, a town founded by African Americans, and the first incorporated black town in the United States. In her autobiographical "How It Feels to Be Colored Me," Hurston declares "I am not tragically colored." Despite poverty, Hurston's characters, such as Missie and Joe in "The Gilded Six-Bits" and the aggrieved husband Joe Kanty, at odds with his manhood in "Spunk," live full-flowering lives. Her characters search for fulfillment not as African Americans but as women and men. Hurston's literary characteristics can later be seen in the works of Ralph Ellison and Toni Morrison. In her autobiography *Dust Tracks on a Road* (1942) Hurston comments that she "did not know how to be humble." Sadly, although Hurston published much more than any other African American woman of her time, she died in poverty: Her work was recovered by the women's movement. However, Hurston remains central to the Harlem Renaissance.

Langston Hughes is referred to by critics as the most influential black American writer of the twentieth century. Primarily a poet, Hughes recorded the black experience in the United States. A leading luminary in the Harlem Renaissance, during the early 1920's Hughes helped to open the doors of publishing houses to young black writers, prompting them to write with racial pride. His career stretched into the Black Arts movement of the late 1960's. Born in Joplin, Missouri, Hughes grew up in Lawrence, Kansas. One of America's best-known and best-loved poets, author in particular of the famous poem "The Negro Speaks of Rivers," Hughes was inspired by D. H. Lawrence to write short stories, which are not nearly as well known as his poetry. In his short fiction, Hughes sets an example of self-determination and artistic integrity. His book of short stories, *The Ways of White Folks*, was published in 1934. Hughes helped to inspire young writers, in particular James Baldwin and Alice Walker.

A Texas native, Gwendolyn Bennett, well recognized as a poet and essayist, also utilized the short-short form to project her literary voice. As the daughter of teacher-parents, Bennett grew up on a Nevada Indian reservation before her father brought her to live in Philadelphia. Educated at Columbia University, in New York City, Bennett drew on her African roots for inspiration. In her estimation, blacks in the United States were sad people "hidden by a minstrel smile." She became the editor of *Opportunity*, writing a popular literary news column and providing a historical account of the Harlem Renaissance. Her story "Wedding Day," a popularly anthologized piece, explores the question Who am I?, the universal conundrum every African American faces. Paul Watson, the protagonist, believes he can escape American racial prejudice by living an expatriate existence in Europe. He succeeds in Paris, becoming a well-known musician before he falls in love with a cruel white woman. His traumatic wedding day (hence the story's title) illustrates his loss of innocence when she abandons him, leaving him only a cruel note explaining that white women simply do not marry black men. "Tokens," which appeared in *Ebony* and *Topaz* in 1927, also centers on an American in Paris who remains in France after World War I. Jenks Barnett, dying from tuberculosis, recalls an earlier happier time, when he joyfully sang with other African American expatriate entertainers. Bennett strongly disputes the humiliating treatment of blacks by whites. Her best-known story, "To a Dark Girl," is often anthologized.

Dorothy West, also known as Mary Christopher, another member of the Harlem Renaissance, wrote and published the critically acclaimed novel *The Living Is Easy* (1948) along with forty short stories. The daughter of a former slave from Virginia, West studied journalism and philosophy at Columbia University. A writer from age seven, she published her first short story in the *Boston Post* when she was fifteen. West joined the Saturday Evening Quill Club, formed in 1925 by twenty burgeoning African American writers. *Opportunity* magazine published her "The Typewriter" in 1926. The story presents a spiritually bereft father who uses his daughter's typewriting lessons to gain a sense of individual worth. Imagining himself to be his daughter's successful businessman boss, when the father dictates a letter to his daughter he comes to embody the man he dreams of being, the man, ironically, that the dominant racist culture prevents him from becoming. By the story's end, this dire pretense causes the father's death. "The Typewriter" was included in Edward J. O'Brien's *The Best Short Stories of 1926*.

In Harlem, West worked initially as a social worker and traveled the Soviet Union in 1932, with Langston Hughes and other Harlem writers, as part of a writers' project. West founded and wrote for *Challenge*, a periodical that opposed fascism, published emerging black writers, and documented the black literary attitudes of the 1930's. She also took part in the Federal Writers' Project (see below). She wrote stories twice weekly for the *New York Daily News* until the late 1960's and was one of the earliest to explore the black urban lifestyle, which most short-story writers overlooked. West, strongly influenced by Fyodor Dostoevski, accentuates psychological and social confinement. The *Saturday Evening Quill* published "An Unimportant Man," which appeared in 1928 and addressed the irony of black urban existence. Zeb, another frustrated black man like the father in "The Typewriter," has a close relationship with his daughter Essie. Through her, Zeb vicariously strives to gain self-importance. He thinks of himself merely as a forty-year-old failure, a cook unable to take the bar exam for the fourth time. However, his daughter, he swears, will become a success. What remains unclear to him, however, is that his actions ironically parallel precisely how his mother treated him, pushing him against his will into difficult careers.

The end of the Harlem Renaissance represented the termination of a rich literary era and a turning point for African American writers. Simply put, black writers had to differentiate themselves from white writers because they had the twofold task of coming to terms with white American society and simultaneously opposing its inherent racism. In the process, they had to lend dignity to the African American community.

Federal Writers' Project

In 1935, the Works Progress Administration (WPA) developed the Federal Writers' Project as part of the New Deal struggle against the Great Depression. The project provided jobs for unemployed writers, editors, and research workers. Directed by Henry G. Alsberg, the program operated in all states and at one time employed sixty-six hundred men and women. In addition to producing guides for every state, the federal plan supported ethnic studies, folklore collections, and regional histories, producing ultimately more than one thousand publications and providing a means for such top African American writers as Richard Wright and Ralph Ellison to come to public attention.

Richard Wright, short-story writer and novelist, classified as an American modernist, was deeply influenced by the famous Russian short-fiction writer Anton Chekhov. Wright ingeniously explores the concept of the internalized plot that closely examines the inner emotions of characters. He endures as one of the first African American writers to protest white prejudice and violence against blacks. Born in Midland, Ontario, Wright moved to Toronto to pursue his education and a career in business.

In Wright's novel *Native Son* (1940) Bigger Thomas suffers at the hands of a rich white family. In Wright's autobiography *Black Boy* (1945), which details his childhood and young manhood in the South, the voice of protest that was to influence many post-World War II writers can also be heard. The grandchild of slaves and abandoned early on by his father, Wright grew up in poverty. The Federal Writers' Project provided him with the opportunity to write.

In 1937, he became Harlem editor of the communist publication *The Daily Worker*. His first short story, "Big Boy Leaves Home," appeared in the anthology *The New Caravan*. "The Ethics of Living John Crow: An Autobiographical Sketch" was published in 1937's *American Stuff: An Anthology of Prose and Verse by Members of the Federal Writers' Project*. A year later, after his first book, *Uncle Tom's Children* (1938, 1940), won a prize from *Story* magazine, Wright was catapulted into the public eye. Undoubtedly, in the genre of the short story, he was the most talented black male writer since Chesnutt. Unlike his predecessors, however, he was highly visible and received the attention and praise he richly deserved. In addition, Wright is credited with eliminating the barrier between black and white writers. In fact, he changed the tone of African American writing from one of placid petition to one of absolute insistence. In 1946, the author moved to Paris and never returned to the United States to live. After his death in 1960, a new generation of black writers, including James Baldwin, John Killens, Paule Marshall, Mary Elizabeth Vroman, London Brown, Albert Murray, William Melvin Kelley, Amiri Baraka (LeRoi Jones), Martin Hamer, and Ernest J. Gaines explored, questioned, and challenged what Ralph Ellison called "the full range of American Negro humanity."

The early years of Ralph Ellison were spent in poverty in Oklahoma City, Oklahoma, and prompted him to become an activist. An avid reader, Ellison early on set out "to look at [his] own life through the lives of fictional characters" and to connect his own world with the "worlds projected in literature." As a young adult in New York City, he met Langston Hughes and Richard Wright, who encouraged him in his efforts to become a writer. He served in the Merchant Marine during World War II. Immediately after the war, in 1945, he began work on his novel *Invisible Man*, which chronicles a young man's awakening to racial discrimination, and spent seven years writing it before it was published in 1952. The following year he won the National Book Award. Like Wright, Ellison's tone is insistent and demanding. "Battle Royal," Ellison's first short story and an excerpt which appeared a year before the novel, is frequently anthologized. In the story, Ellison insists that the narrator, although a man of substance, flesh, and bone, is invisible because people refuse to see him. The story details a painful episode in a young man's life; expecting a scholarship, the excited and proud youngster is invited to an elegant social function. However, instead of receiving the academic honors he expected, he is pitted against other teenage boys in a boxing match for the enjoyment of white male spectators. The broader context of the story illustrates the predictable rituals used to preserve racial lines. In "King of the Bingo Game" and "Flying Home" the main characters also undergo a trial by fire, which concludes in an elevated sense of self, a deeper maturity, and an ultimate responsibility to others. In the 1965 *Book Week* poll of two hundred writers and critics, Ellison was honored by being chosen above such black writers as Wright and Baldwin and such white writers as Ernest Hemingway, William Faulkner, J. D. Salinger, and John Steinbeck, for having penned the most celebrated novel written in the previous twenty years. However, Ellison suffered under the scathing critical scrutiny of the black nationalist writers of the Black Arts movement, such as Amiri Baraka (LeRoi Jones), who insisted Ellison "sold out" by being more concerned with style than with substance. Thus, racial allegiances became suspect.

World War II

Unlike many African American writers who focus on the South, Ann Petry focused upon black life in small-town New England. A pharmacist, Petry moved early on in life to New York, where she wrote for the *Peoples' Voice* of Harlem before studying creative writing at Columbia University (1944-1946). During World War II, Petry's stories began to appear in *The Crisis*. A novelist, who numbers among her best-selling highly acclaimed works *The Street* (1946), Petry first came to public notice through such short stories as "Like a Winding Street," a complex, forceful narrative of a couple's wartime struggle, and her heart-wrenching tale of domestic abuse "The Last Day of School," which deals with a young woman's attempt to leave Harlem. Her collection of short stories *Miss Muriel and Other Stories*, which contains

"Solo on the Drums" and "Has Anybody Seen Miss Dora Dean?," was published in 1971.

Although Frank Yerby authored thirty-three novels, his short story, "Health Card," which received the O. Henry Memorial Award for best first story in 1944, is his only highly acclaimed work. "Health Card," published in *Harper's* magazine, concerns the injustices inflicted by the military, which tended to view black women as prostitutes. The story brought Yerby to national attention.

Henry Dumas wrote about the clash between black and white cultures and captured in the process the psychological tone of the black southern experience. African American folklore and music and the Civil Rights movement, in which he was an active participant, remained important influences on all his writing. Born in Arkansas, Dumas migrated to Harlem at the age of ten, attended City College of New York, and served in the Air Force. His astute short stories draw on his own southern childhood experiences. "Rain God," which uses a stream-of-consciousness technique, was published in *Negro Digest* in 1968 and deals with three boys running home on the heels of a rainstorm. This tale, reminiscent of a folktale that pronounces that when sunshine and rain occur together, the Devil is beating his wife, projects the fear experienced by the narrator, young Blue, who fears the Devil. "The Crossing," in the collection *Ark of Bones and Other Stories* (1970), also deals with the sense of danger and fear inherent in the lives of southern blacks, particularly the vulnerability of black children amid the southern white lynch-mob mentality. Here again three young children, Jimmy, Bubba, and Essie, walk home from Sunday school, experience the fear of imminent danger, and tease one another until Bubba mentions Emmett Till, a teenager who was actually lynched in 1953. The tale of atrocity is repeated to Jimmy by Bubba. Again, the landscape figures profoundly in projecting and displacing the young characters' fear. Young sharecroppers encountering a civil rights worker and whites experiencing the mystical force of black music figure in the subject matter Dumas examined in his short stories, many of which were collected in *Ark of Bones and Other Stories* (1970) and *Rope of Wind and Other Stories* (1979).

Black Arts movement

The Black Arts movement, also called the Black Aesthetic movement, represented a literary advancement among black Americans in the 1960's and early 1970's. Based on the idea of black nationalism, the crusade sought to cultivate art forms that champion black separatism. Thus, the African American writer became activist. Using the black English vernacular, black writers discoursed on concerns of interracial tension and politics. Highly confrontational, many of these writers utilized African American history and culture to illustrate their apprehensions and anger. Brought about by such intellectual leaders as Houston A. Baker, Jr., and Henry Louis Gates, Jr., a trailblazing literary critic instrumental in recovering African American works such as Harriet E. Wilson's *Our Nig: Or, Sketches from the Life of a Free Black, in a Two-Story White House, North. Showing That Slavery's Shadow Falls Even There* (1859), the first known novel by a black American, the Black Arts movement developed theories of black literature. Utilizing critical methods such as semiotics and deconstruction, Baker proposed new standards, based on African American culture and values, for the interpretation and evaluation of literature and reconstructed the historical, social, political, and economic elements of African American culture.

His edited collections of poetry and essays by African Americans, such as Frederick Douglass, W. E. B. Du Bois, Booker T. Washington, Richard Wright, and Ralph Ellison, brought attention to African American literary works and demonstrated the verve and vigor of black culture and its intense desire to be heard. Tracing Caribbean and American culture back through slave narratives and folktales, Gates utilized fashionable critical theory to argue the term "signifyin'" as representative of black culture. Black writers, he claimed, are involved in an unbroken, interconnected conversation that reflects and interprets black social and cultural history. The inclusion of African American literature in the Western canon, Gates argues, cannot be ignored. Distinguished by intense self-scrutiny, the Black Arts movement was instrumental in producing such influential works as *The Autobiography of Malcolm X* (1965; with Alex

Haley) and Eldridge Cleaver's *Soul on Ice* (1968). This movement highly influenced novelist Toni Morrison, winner of the 1994 Nobel Prize in Literature. Amiri Baraka, also known as LeRoi Jones, founded the Black Arts Repertory Theatre in Harlem and emerged as a powerful playwright. When it comes to recognizing the black arts as a revolutionary concept, no African American writer has better articulated the alliance of art and politics. Although the bulk of his art encompassed drama, Baraka also produced a collection of short stories, *Tales* (1967), which documents the traumatic experiences, suppressed anger, and hostility of American blacks toward the dominant white culture.

James Alan McPherson's short stories examine love, universal pain, and racial tension. Often, his realistic characters face periods of isolation and the deep, longing pangs of love. Although it could be argued that McPherson's stories represent the Black Arts movement, there is little doubt his timeless tales move far beyond politics by appealing to all classes and both genders. McPherson, strongly influenced by Ralph Ellison, addresses age, race, and class in his first short story, "Gold Coast," for which he won a short-fiction contest in *The Atlantic Monthly* in 1968. In it, the author explores the relationship between Robert, a burgeoning black writer and Harvard University student, and James Sullivan, the older white janitor who searches merely for human fellowship. A highly skilled and intricate writer, McPherson sensitively perceives human nature in all its myriad light and dark manifestations. Regarding his popular short-story collection *Hue and Cry* (1969), McPherson, born in Savannah, Georgia, remarked "it is my hope that this collection of stories can be read as a book about people, all kinds of people: old, young, lonely, homosexual, confused, used, discarded, wronged."

Despite criticism during the revolutionary 1970's, McPherson received praise for his ability to see past the color line. In his "A Matter of Vocabulary" the writer draws upon his personal experience as a grocery store clerk. Similarly, in other stories he utilizes his own life experiences as a dining-car waiter, a law student, and a janitor for fictional fodder. His first collection of melancholy short stories, *Hue and Cry*, includes the title story about interracial relationships and "Solo Song: For Doc," which examines the life of an elderly dining-car waiter, Doc Craft, whose blood runs with the "the rhythm of the wheels." Never at "home on the ground," when Doc is forced into retirement he does not know how to cope. Ultimately, he freezes to death in the Chicago train yards. The author puts the American justice system under the microscope in "An Act of Prostitution." "On Trains" documents the life of a Pullman porter, a black servant serving out his days on trains during the time of transition from train travel to airline travel in American life. After forty-three years, the elderly porter still serves in the capacity of making passengers comfortable. Throughout the night he sits and waits until one evening a sleepless racist southern woman finally engages his awareness. The title story's protagonist Margot Payne, however, belongs to the younger generation of African Americans who refused to suffer quietly. McPherson's literary talent was recognized in 1978 with a Pulitzer Prize for his *Elbow Room* (1977), which illustrates the author's symmetrical division between dejection and hope. In twelve stories, McPherson explores the perplexity of individuality and diversity of American culture. In "A Loaf of Bread," Nelson Reed and his neighbors picket Harold Green for his unfair practice of charging higher food prices to the black community. While both men see themselves as good people, neither understands the other and thus look upon each other as evil enemies. In "Widows and Orphans," McPherson attains a similar level of understanding between communities.

The short stories of Alice Walker are noted for their thoughtful and insightful treatment of African American culture. As in her highly popular *The Color Purple* (1982), which won a Pulitzer Prize in 1983, Walker's work expresses with intense clarity the roles women play in the survival of the African American people. In this effort, she utilizes the history of black people in the United States, particularly in the South, where they were heartlessly enslaved. Walker grew up in Georgia and graduated from Sarah Lawrence College, in Bronxville, New York, in 1965, at which point she moved to Mississippi where she became an active participant in the Civil Rights movement. She also began teaching and publishing short fiction. Her short stories examine the relationships between black women and men and, while strongly engaging the deep spiritual tradition, center particularly on women. While African American men, Walker contends, have had to struggle with racism, black American women have to fight both racism and sexism. In 1973, the author published *In Love and Trouble: Stories of Black Women*, her first collection of short stories. This collection introduces Roselily, an impoverished mother of illegitimate children, who views her marriage to a black Muslim as a deliverance from poverty. Most of the female protagonists in this collection represent southern black women who challenge gender, race, and age. Because of its focus on the violence involved in sexism, some critics came to view it as dissident.

Walker's second collection of short stories, *You Can't Keep a Good Woman Down* (1981), her most outspoken feminist work, was also disliked by critics, who dismissed it as too controversial. In it, Walker addresses issues raised by feminists in the 1970's: abortion, sadomasochism, pornography, and rape, arguing that personal relationships reflect political issues. "Porn" examines the sexual relationship between a proud black man and an independent black woman who makes her own money. Walker explores how the male's pornographic fantasies and his need to prove himself through his sexuality inhibit him from truly loving and accepting the woman. When the woman realizes his dependence on pornography and the shallowness of their connection, their relationship is destroyed. Walker presents the stories in this collection as an ongoing process; they are not finished pieces. For example, "Advancing Luna" is a tale concerning a young southern woman's involvement in and her deepening understanding of interracial rape. The author maintains that, because of the historical alliance between lynching and rape, the story cannot be ended and thus Walker stylistically provides the tale with two conclusions. Although very different from her earlier short-story collection *In Love and Trouble: Stories of Black Women*, her second, more complex collection, *You Can't Keep a Good Woman Down* (1981), supports the Black Arts movement's impulse and establishes with certainty the freedom with which women pursue their individual selves. While the primary female characters in *In Love and Trouble* carry on and strive, the women in *You Can't Keep a Good Woman Down* are more heroic by intensely and openly confronting societal conventions.

Twentieth Century Women Writers

Women have from the beginning played a primary role in the growth of African American short fiction. In fact, more works of fiction by black women were published between 1890 and 1910 than black men had published in the previous fifty years. With the exception of Frances Ellen Watkins Harper's tale "The Two Offers," no short story by an African American woman appeared in print before 1895, when, at last, voices so long stifled were heard. In the outpouring of proud stories that followed, African American women shared their experiences, smashed stereotypes, and recorded the untold story of African American life. African American literature has further blossomed with black American women at the forefront as writers. Besides such immensely popular, award-winning novelists as Alice Walker and Toni Morrison, female short-story writers continue to proliferate. For African American women, storytelling between mothers and daughters, daughters and sisters, sisters and friends is what Paule Marshall metaphorically calls the "kitchen" of everyday experience in a world oblivious to black women's lives. As Alice Walker observed, the woman one shares one's story with as it is happening is someone who is implicitly trusted. African American female short-fiction writers demonstrate how they survived by listening and telling.

Alice Childress, a high school dropout, developed her distinct writing style by breaking rules. Born in Charleston, South Carolina, Childress was taken to New York at the age of five. An actor and director, the burgeoning author was a director of the American Negro Theatre (1914-1952). In fact, she won a Tony for her Broadway role in *Anna Lucasta* (1944) and became the first woman to win an Obie Award for best Off-Broadway play. Childress creates accurate depictions of black life and rejects black stereotypes, especially that black women are responsible for the problems of black men: "The Black writer explains pain to those who inflict it," she maintains. Best known for her novel directed at teenagers, *A Hero Ain't Nothin' but a Sandwich* (1978), she also gained much positive acclaim for her short-story collection *Like One of the Family: Conversations from a Domestic's Life* (1956), a series of vignettes told from the African domestic's point of view. The protagonist Mildred, a dayworker based on Childress's own Aunt Lorraine, refuses "to exchange dignity for pay," as she quietly battles for human dignity and civil rights. Although others consider her job menial, she heroically declines to be debased.

As a civil rights activist and teacher, Toni Cade Bambara wrote about the concerns of the African American community while attempting to raise black American consciousness. Born Miltona Mirkin Cade in New York City, she adopted the name Bambara in 1970 when she discovered it as a signature on a family sketchbook. Bambara published her first short story, "Sweet Town," in *Vendome* magazine in 1959, as Toni Cade. The author worked as a social worker for the Harlem Welfare Center between 1959 and 1960. In the 1960's, she was directly involved in the sociopolitical activities in American urban communities. She published her second story, "Mississippi Ham Rider," in 1960 in the distinguished *Massachusetts Review.* After receiving her master's degree, Bambara taught at the City College of New York from 1965 to 1969. Active during the 1970's in the black liberation and the women's rights movements, the writer submerged herself in civil rights issues by lecturing and helping to organize rallies within the black community, all the while utilizing her personal experiences in her writing. In 1970 she edited and published *The Black Woman*, an anthology designed to demonstrate the thoughts and actions of black women in the women's and Civil Rights movements. In 1971 Bambara edited her second anthology, entitled *Tales and Stories for Black Folks*, in which is included her own acclaimed "Raymond's Run." The author, who interjects black street dialect in her short fiction to create strong characters, sets her stories outside the home, where people are apt to mingle. Also, she sets her tales in both the American South and the North. Most of the stories Bambara wrote as Toni Cade between 1959 and 1970 were published in 1972 in her highly acclaimed collection *Gorilla, My Love*. The stories focus on the relationships among African Americans in both the urban North and the rural South. The title story, narrated by young Hazel, completely dissatisfied with grown-ups, describes the impact that careless adult words, particularly promises that cannot be kept, have on innocent children. In "Talkin' 'Bout Sonny," the author focuses on the coping mechanisms males utilize to maintain emotional equilibrium. Betty Butler, a social worker, dates Delauney, the father of two girls. At a local bar, Betty and Delauney discuss how their friend Sonny, while in a state of emotional collapse, stabbed his wife. Betty, appalled at first by Delauney's casual attitude, comes to realize how both men must work hard to repress and contain their sensation of free-floating rage. Delauney fully realizes that although he can understand Sonny, his own anger keeps him powerless. Bambara also published the novels *The Salt Eaters* (1980) and *If Blessing Comes* (1987).

Jamaica Kincaid was born in Antigua, in the West Indies. Finding her college experience to be a "dismal failure," the independent-minded Kincaid set about educating herself. Her early stories were published in *Rolling Stone*, *Paris Review*, and *The New Yorker.* Her first short-story collection, *At the Bottom of the River* (1983), which won the Morton Dauwen Zabel Award of the American Academy of Arts and Letters, features the much-anthologized, exceptional story "Girl." Although on the surface, the story reads principally like a list of rules any good mother would provide a daughter: "Don't walk barehead in the hot sun," the story also depicts maternal caution and counsel, particularly in the sexual arena. Much in keeping with the modernist movement, in which writers such as James Joyce redefined the borders and possibilities of the short-story form, this rhythmic, emotionally intense story details a young woman's life in a free-floating narrative without a conventional plot, characters, or dialogue. Kincaid's next "sister text" collection, *Annie John* (1985), contains eight stories that span Annie's childhood in Antigua to age seventeen. The poignant "The Circling Hand," portrays the author's theme of mother-child relationships. As a child, Annie trails her mother shopping, doing laundry, and cooking and experiences great anxiety when she wanders outside her mother's sphere. Ultimately, in the final chapter, Annie leaves her mother and home to take up nursing in England.

As compared to the novel, the short-story form receives much less critical notice and much of the criticism it garners deals with techniques of writing, rather than serious criticism of the literary work. However, for many readers, the short story, which often can be read in under an hour, represents a powerful, life-changing literary method that initiates and completes catharsis. The short story as a form is open-ended, ever-changing, and continuously vigorous.

M. Casey Diana

Bibliography

Andrews, William, ed. *Classic Fiction of the Harlem Renaissance.* New York: Oxford University Press, 1994. Includes a comprehensive collection of short stores by Langston Hughes, Zora Neale Hurston, Jessie Redmon Fauset, Gwendolyn Bennett, and many others.

Clarke, John Henrik, ed. *Black American Short Stories: One Hundred Years of the Best.* New York: Hill and Wang, 1993. A new introduction supplements this classic collection of stories by African Americans that features pieces by Charles Waddell Chesnutt, Zora Neale Hurston, Langston Hughes, Richard Wright, Frank Yerby, James Baldwin, Amiri Baraka, Alice Walker, and others.

Gates, Henry Louis, Jr. *The Signifying Monkey: A Theory of Afro-American Literary Criticism.* New York: Oxford University Press, 1988. Scholarly work that uses critical theory to interconnect such African American short-story writers as Ralph Ellison, Zora Neale Hurston, and Alice Walker.

Gayle, Addison, Jr., ed. *The Black Aesthetic.* Garden City, N.Y.: Doubleday, 1971. Provides excellent scholarly commentary and biographical notes for a number of African American authors.

Hughes, Langston, ed. *The Best Short Stories by Negro Writers: The Classic Anthology from 1899 to 1967.* Boston: Little, Brown, 1967. Features stories by outstanding African American writers that originally sold more than twenty-five thousand copies. An expanded edition with a new introduction offers a description of African American fiction from the nineteenth century to the present with new contributions by Alice Walker and James Alan McPherson.

Kanwar, Asha, ed. *The Unforgetting Heart: An Anthology of Short Stories by African American Women, 1859-1993.* San Francisco: Aunt Lute Books, 1993. Difficult to find but worth the effort. Contains very varied stories by well known and little know African American women writers.

Mullin, Bill, ed. *Revolutionary Tales: African American Women's Short Stories, from the First Story to the Present.* New York: Laurel, 1995. Containing forty four stories by thirty-six authors, this collection covers 150 years of the African American short story with stories by Alice Childress, Francis Ellen Watkins Harper, Zora Neale Hurston, Alice Walker, Dorothy West, and many others.

Naylor, Gloria, ed. *Children of the Night: The Best Short Stories by Black Writers, 1967 to the Present.* Boston: Little, Brown, 1995. Includes the works of leading African American short-story writers.

Pryse, Marjorie, and Hortense J. Spillers, eds. *Conjuring: Black Women, Fiction, and Literary Tradition.* Bloomington: Indiana University Press, 1985. Provides the historical and biographical background material for such short-story writers as Pauline Hopkins.

ASIAN AMERICAN SHORT FICTION

The period of the 1960's and 1970's was a significant time of social and political agitation and change in the United States. Among African Americans, Latinos, Native Americans, and Asian Americans, there was a growing racial-ethnic consciousness and anger concerning the long histories of racism these groups had encountered not only in the United States but also abroad in terms of colonialism and imperialism. The birth of the Civil Rights, Black power, Third World revolutionary and nationalist movements as well as the anti-Vietnam War, Free Speech, and the women's movements were part of this social and political turmoil. In recognizing the power of the dominant culture's influence in the shaping of their personal and collective identity, many racial-ethnic groups began to articulate the need to construct self-defined identities.

In this milieu, Asians in the United States sought to construct and define an "Asian American" racial-ethnic, cultural, and political identity for their ethnic communities, which had been long silenced, marginalized, or appropriated within mainstream American institutions and narratives. Working in alliance with community and political activists, Asian American cultural activists challenged the cultural, ideological, and psychosocial elements that were damaging to their communities from within and without.

In fashioning a new oppositional Asian American identity, cultural nationalists deconstructed the history of dehumanizing and debilitating representations of the "Oriental" in popular and elitist representations. They realized how privileged cultural narratives and representations contributed to the inequitable circulation of power within mainstream white society and within their own ethnic communities. At the same time, they sought to reconstruct the histories and literatures of Asians that had been erased from American historical and literary consciousness and records.

In the ruptured spaces created by these multiple challenges, cultural nationalists in the Asian American Movement urged writers to construct an Asian American sensibility and identity in their critical hybrid fictions. There was a strong desire to find more honest cultural representations and narratives of Asian American experience and history that could challenge the racist ideology and oppression Asians experienced in the United States. Early cultural nationalists formulated an Asian American cultural politics which assertively claimed roots in the United States, a contested and fragmented home ground in which young writers could nevertheless constructed their distinct, multiply situated cultural texts. Naming this as a site of struggle over cultural power and self-determination for Asian Americans in the United States, theirs was a substantial, trail-blazing contribution to the making of identity, culture, and community.

Aiiieeeee! Constructing an Asian American Cultural Politics

Some of the early critical voices who attempted to define a new Asian American aesthetic were Frank Chin, Jeffrey Paul Chan, Lawson Fusao Inada, and Shawn Wong. They assembled one of the first literary anthologies featuring the work of Asian American writers, *Aiiieeeee! An Anthology of Asian-American Writers* (1974, 1991). In this trailblazing anthology, the editors outlined in an introductory manifesto the long history of racism against Asians in the United States and discuss the erasure of "real," "more authentic" forms of Asian American history, literature, and culture by the publishing industry, by the Hollywood film industry, and by the educational and capitalist economic system in the United States.

The editors discuss how difficult it was to convince the white, male-dominated publishing industry to consider seriously the literature of Asian American writers. Their literary anthology was most likely perceived as too aggressively hostile, alien, and marginal to the interests of an American reading public. That is, it did not present the "Oriental" in ways that were accessible, familiar, and comfortable for mainstream white readers. In the volatile period of the 1960's and

1970's, *Aiiieeeee!* did not represent "similarity" and "difference" in "acceptable" or "tolerable" forms of cultural-political visibility and identity for subordinated racial-ethnic groups or general reading audiences. In their manifesto, the *Aiiieeeee!* editors remind writers and readers of the serious political implications and dilemmas in making choices about the style, language, and content by which one constructs and articulates alternative or oppositional forms of subjectivity against privileged cultural discourses and practices. They stress the need to interrogate and challenge how and why publishing institutions, cultural products, consumers, and critics might choose one text over another, one writer over another—sometimes for very racist and sexist reasons. The *Aiiieeeee!* anthology was repeatedly turned down by mainstream presses in the early 1970's, until it was finally published in 1974 by Howard University Press, an African American university press.

The editors urged writers to recover and articulate authenticating cultural identities, histories, and cultures that reflected voices and experiences not bounded by "white racist love." Such "love," they claimed, left Asian Americans not only marginalized and invisible within mainstream American culture but also in a "state of contempt, self-rejection, and disintegration." The *Aiiieeeee!* editors revealed how Asian Americans have been made invisible in society—how their history and voices are not represented in dominant discourses in society or, if represented, are often stereotypical, racist, sexist, and humiliating. They made clear the serious concerns about the damage these Orientalist images and discourses do to both Asian American and Anglo-American communities. They spoke to the need to recover the social and historical realities of Asian Americans as well as to know Asian cultural heritages and histories which have been inherited and continued in diasporic communities and imaginaries in the United States.

According to the editors, their anthology was for and by Asian Americans:

> That means Filipino, Chinese, and Japanese Americans, American-born and raised, who got their China and Japan from the radio, off the silver screen, from television, out of comic books, from the pushers of white American culture that pictured the yellow man as something that when wounded, sad, or angry, or swearing, or wondering whined, shouted, or screamed "aiiieeeee!" Asian America, so long ignored and forcibly excluded from creative participation in American culture, is wounded, sad, angry, swearing, and wondering, and this is his AIIIEEEEE! It is more than a whine, shout, or scream. It is fifty years of our whole voice.

The *Aiiieeeee!* anthology reclaimed a number of important writers who had been ignored or marginalized in mainstream American literature: Edith Eaton (Sui Sin Far), Louis Chu, Diana Chang, Carlos Bulosan, Toshio Mori, John Okada, Hisaye Yamamoto, and Wakako Yamauchi.

However, while calling for a radical redefinition of identity in terms of an Asian American sensibility and culture in this early manifesto, Frank Chin and his colleagues also discouraged a range of literary explorations of gender, sexuality, class, and other differences that would complicate their increasingly rigid, narrowly defined notion of "Asian American" culture, sensibility, and solidarity. That is, even as these writers were shaping an Asian American sensibility in literature, inspiring artists to articulate the experiences of Asian Americans in the United States during the 1960's and 1970's, their restrictive discourses were creating obstacles to understanding and appreciating the work of a number of writers. In the revised and expanded *The Big Aiiieeeee! An Anthology of Chinese American and Japanese American Literature* (1991), the editors restate their brand of oppositional Asian American canon formation. Significantly, in Chin's chapter entitled "Come All Ye Asian American Writers of the Real and the Fake," he singles out a number of well-known male and female writers as "fakes" and "white racists" who do not meet the editors' criteria for insertion into the first or latest edition of the *Aiiieeeee!* anthology. Though these male and female writers also worked to portray diversified and potentially resistant images of Asian Americans which could counter those stereotyped ones constructed within mainstream U.S. society, they were and are still condemned as unacceptable, inauthentic, and dishonest, not worthy to be claimed as "Asian American" writers.

For male and female writers, there may have been an early sense of exhilaration in the *Aiiieeeee!* call to create new narratives and images for our ethnic communities. The manifesto was indeed an assertive and fiery call to reclaim and contest the fields of cultural production, especially in its call to challenge the Eurocentric images and narratives of a decadent, effeminate East, of an apolitical model minority, of Asian American men as the emasculated Other and women as dragon ladies or passive sexualized and victimized lotus blossoms of men. However, the *Aiiieeeee!* editors' constitution of Asian American identity, sensibility, and solidarity increasingly operated as a dogmatic restriction on other Asian American male and female writers, who did not share their particular definitions of what constitutes "legitimate" or "authentic" Asian American literature or identity. As critics have noted, Chin's work, for example, seemed substantially vested within racial and masculine ideologies, representations, and institutions (see the section below on Frank Chin's short stories). Frank Chin and his allies, in effect, erased and marginalized important explorations of the significant differences and contradictions (such as class, gender, sexual orientation, and geopolitical locations) within emerging Asian American Movement politics that could also potentially destabilize a monolithic, narrowly defined conception of a cultural and ethnic identity in radical ways.

The following discussion of Asian American short fiction is meant to be an introductory survey. It is by no means an exhaustive list of Asian American writers or short stories. Readers must be aware that there is a very great diversity of voices, experiences, cultures, and histories that are usually categorized under the umbrella term "Asian American literature." Moreover, this introduction covers only short fiction written in English, which excludes the range of earlier fiction written in other languages and published in ethnic newspapers, journals, and other literary venues here and abroad.

Chinese American Short Stories

Edith Eaton, the Chinese American Lily, was one of the earliest Chinese American writers in the United States. She took the pen name Sui Sin Far. She was born in 1865 to an English father and Chinese mother—the eldest child in a family of fourteen surviving children. Her parents met in China, married, and returned to England. The family then moved to Montreal, Canada, where Eaton was educated. As a young woman, she worked as a traveling journalist. She finally settled in the United States (more specifically, in the San Francisco and Seattle areas) in 1898. Eaton's first collection of thirty-seven short stories and vignettes was published in 1912 (reissued 1995) as *Mrs. Spring Fragrance*, edited by Amy Ling and Annette White-Parks.

Eaton wrote in the late nineteenth and early twentieth centuries, when anti-Chinese hysteria was high. From the 1870's into the early 1900's, white-supremacist politicians, settlers, nativists, and craft and labor unionists agitated forcefully against the so-called hordes of coolie laborers, which they perceived as constituting a "Yellow Peril" competing for jobs with immigrant white European-Americans in an increasingly depressed economic market. As a result of this anti-Chinese hysteria, there was a great deal of racial violence against individual Chinese and their ethnic communities. They were harassed, burned out of town, murdered, and legally hounded by the government. In crowded Chinatowns, there was little freedom, safety, privacy, or peace to be found. More specifically, the Chinese, in their individual and communal lives, were governed by both federal and state laws concerning immigration, miscegenation, citizenship, and basic human rights. Regulations monitored and disciplined their work, hygiene, sexuality, behavior, everyday aesthetics, travel, and leisure.

Edith Eaton was deeply concerned by the representations and treatment of the Chinese in America. As a Eurasian, she understood racism and sexism from a personal perspective as well. She could not understand why her Chinese mother's ancestry was treated with such vicious contempt in comparison to her English father's. Throughout her life, she documented the racist and sexist encounters she experienced in her autobiographical article "Leaves from the Mental Portfolio of an Eurasian." Eaton was constantly an object of curiosity and disdain in British and American society.

Moreover, Asians were often portrayed in simplistic and dehumanizing images and stereotypes in popular American culture. These representations were often one-dimensional portrayals and stereotypes from the perspectives of white writers. In contrast, Sui Sin Far's *Mrs. Spring Fragrance* was one of the first attempts to explore Chinese American experiences by a woman with Chinese ethnic heritage. Eaton chose the pen name of Sui Sin Far (literally, "the narcissus flower") to indicate her solidarity and alliance with the Chinese. She died in 1914 and was memorialized by the Chinese American community that she loved.

Sui Sin Far's stories reverse the typical stereotypical images that suggested the criminality, cruelty, and inscrutability of the Chinese. In her short stories, Sui Sin Far set out to portray the Chinese and their ethnic communities in an empathetic and complex manner. Her stories advocated not only for Chinese and Chinese Americans but also for women's rights. Sui Sin Far herself remained a single, independent working woman, an unfashionable state for a woman in her time. In such stories as "The Inferior Woman" and "The Chinese Lily," she championed working-class women and women's rights.

Mrs. Spring Fragrance is divided into two sections: The first seventeen stories are categorized under "Mrs. Spring Fragrance" and include her more serious adult stories; the second section includes twenty stories categorized as "Tales of Chinese Children." In this collection, there are a range of human stories about love, family relationships, and male and female friendships, as well as betrayals and tragedies within the Chinese community and the white world. The relationships between women and men were sometimes interracial. For example, in "The Story of One White Woman Who Married a Chinese" and "Her Chinese Husband," Sui Sin Far forefronts the relationship between a white woman, abused by her former white husband, who befriends and marries a Chinese man named Liu Kanghi. He is portrayed lovingly in both his strengths and weaknesses as a man, husband, and father. Liu Kanghi is tragically murdered on his way home to his family.

The literary critic Annette White-Parks has analyzed the technical writing strategies of Sui Sin Far's short stories. She examines Sui Sin Far's desire to portray experiences and stories that were erased or marginalized in dominant Western portrayals of the Chinese in U.S. society. The Chinese and Chinese American characters become the "fictional center" of Sui Sin Far's stories, reversing more typical mainstream narrative structures and interpretations of Chinese experiences and culture:

> White Americans simultaneously shift to positions of 'Other-ness' or 'outsiders', appearing in this new light as antagonists to Chinese-Americans, and to the Chinatown community/culture. Frequently, Sui Sin Far's stylistic techniques also reverse the expected order of gender, as it is through the voices of the stereotypically silenced Chinese-American females that most viewpoints emerge.

Furthermore, the characters in Sui Sin Far's stories "are not valued by how closely they adhere to a 'white' standard, but by their assertion of individual and cultural integrity against the assimilative forces of North America." Other critics have also noted that in her mature stories, Sui Sin Far's narrative voice is refreshingly ironic, witty, charming, and incisive in its portrayals of the Chinese and Anglo-American communities.

Besides work on the *Aiiieeeee!* anthology, Frank Chin published a number of short stories, on which he had been working throughout the 1970's; they were later collected in *The Chinaman Pacific and Frisco R.R. Co.* (1988). In many of Chin's stories, Chinese American male protagonists are often portrayed as escaping pathologically dysfunctional Chinatown parents and family. In "The Only Real Day," "The Chinatown Kid," and "Railroad Standard Time," Chinese and Chinese American male characters, like Tampax, seek to escape the domestic and communal spaces that have defined their history of emasculation, humiliation, and cultural extinction in the United States. They are portrayed as trapped in and fleeing from Chinatown, sites of decay, despair, and death. In Chin's search for masculine heroic identities, he populates his frontier literary landscape with railroad men, old loners, virile macho types, Chinatown cowboys, boxers, and angry outlaws. They are also prominently represented in his essays, his plays *The Chickencoop Chinaman* (pr. 1972) and *The Year of the Dragon* (pr. 1974), and his novel *Gunga Din Highway* (1994).

A warrior language and writing style becomes, in Chin's stories, authenticating or legitimating enactments of the Asian American culture, history, and sensibility that the *Aiiieeeee!* editors were attempting to construct during the 1960's and 1970's. As writers they contributed to the verbal spectacle of refashioning a manhood that attempted to challenge racist "model minority" or effeminate stereotypes of Asian men:

> Language coheres the people into a community by organizing and codifying the symbols of their own common experience. Stunt the tongue and you've lopped off the culture and sensibility. On the simplest level, a man, in any culture, speaks for himself. Without a language of his own, he no longer is a man but a ventriloquist's dummy at worst and at best a parrot.

Language becomes a talking cure that reveals the self-contempt, rage, and disempowerment Chin's male characters feel within American society. At the same time, it is a way to speak and strut the language of the phallus—full of cocky streetwise rap, black, and working-class vernacular, bawdy sex-talk, and violence in order to wage war against the emasculation of Chinese men. In these stories, it seems that men, in order to be identified as "real" men, have to separate themselves from women or feminine-identified domestic culture. In many of Chin's stories, women are not portrayed with much complexity or depth; this is a critique that has often been made by critics of Chin's work.

In the 1970's, Jeffrey Chan, a coeditor of *Aiiieeeee!*, also published two short stories on similar themes of dying Chinatowns and male anger and humiliation, "Auntie Tsia Is Dying" and "Jackrabbit." "Jackrabbit" graphically situates the Chinese American male experience, identity, and sexuality of Frankie and Pete within the violent history of racism and sexism in the United States. In a more contemporary story, "The Chinese in Haifa," Jeffrey Chan portrays the life of a Chinese American character named Bill Wong, who lives in the suburbs, enjoys blintzes, and smokes marijuana. Wong is in the process of divorcing himself not only from his Chinese wife and children but also from a Chinese and Chinatown culture that he finds debilitating. As the house is vacated of furniture, family, and Chinese heritage, Wong contemplates an affair with his Jewish neighbor's blond wife.

David Wong Louie was born in 1954 in Rockville Center, New York, to first-generation Chinese immigrant parents who owned a family laundry. He attended Vassar College and in 1981 received a master's degree in fine arts from the University of Iowa. He taught at Vassar College and at various schools in Southern California, including the English Department and the Asian American Studies Department at the University of California at Los Angeles.

Louie won a *Los Angeles Times* Book Award for First Fiction and the Ploughshares John C. Zacharis First Book Award for *Pangs of Love* (1991). In this collection of eleven stories, Louie explores a number of alienated or marginalized characters (not all of whom are identifiably ethnic Chinese) moving through a disorienting American landscape.

The title story, "Pangs of Love," portrays a Chinese American son who is chosen by his family to care for his aging China-born mother, Mrs. Pang. The communications between mother and son are strained; he does not speak Mandarin or share her old-fashioned cultural values. He feels like "a linguistic dwarf" who is never adequate to the task of defining or communicating his sense of disorientation or the various inadequacies and frustrations in his life, especially those that deal with his manhood and sexuality, his job as a chemist, and his failed relationships with women. He has an even harder time explaining his brother Billy's homosexuality to his mother. He can barely mask his own darkly pessimistic frustration, anger, and yearning for nuclear extinction. At the same time, practical and assertive Mrs. Pang feels estranged from children who never seem to listen to her advice. She finds some superficial solace in watching Johnny Carson and wrestling on American television in a language and culture she cannot fully understand.

In another Louie story, "Displacement," Mrs. Chow, a former Chinese aristocrat, finds herself working as a caretaker for an abusive, elderly white woman; she feels displaced in her life in America. Nevertheless, she finds ways to survive and escape (even on a momentary roller-coaster ride) the routine drudgery and disappointments of her new life in America. This story was chosen for inclusion in *The Best American Short Stories 1989*. In another story, "Birthday," Louie portrays the frustration and displacement of Wallace Wong, who has been dumped by his white girlfriend. Her former husband wins custody of their little boy. Wong has grown to love this child as his own. He tries to make good on his earlier promise to take the boy to a baseball game on his birthday. However, the boy's biological father bars the heartbroken Wong from seeing or speaking to the boy.

Louie also has a number of inventive, humorous, and impressionistic stories, such as "Disturbing the Universe," in which baseball is invented by enslaved laborers building the Great Wall of China, "Bottles of Beaujolais," which involves the connections between an employee of a sushi eatery and a captive otter in a tank, and "One Man's Hysteria—Real and Imagined—in the Twentieth Century," which portrays a writer rewriting his life. One of Louie's quirkier stories concerns physics and is entitled "In a World Small Enough"; it was published in *The Big Aiiieeeee!*

The novelist Gish Jen, a second-generation Chinese American, published her first collection of short stories, *Who's Irish?*, in 1999. Her short stories have appeared in such prestigious publications as *The Atlantic Monthly*, *The Yale Review*, and *The New Yorker*. Her two novels *Typical American* (1991) and *Mona in the Promised Land* (1996) were favorably acclaimed for their witty and tragicomic explorations of the Chinese immigrant family in the United States during the period following World War II. In *Typical American*, for example, Ralph Chang and his sister Theresa and her friend Helen immigrate from China to the United States. For better and worse, they go through a roller coaster of transformations in their gradual acculturation and assimilation into "typical life" in America. Ralph seeks an engineering Ph.D. and finds himself owning a fried chicken palace. His wife Helen is in love with homes, success, and consumer culture. His doctor-sister Theresa keeps company with a married man. Each in his or her own way grapples with the American Dream in the seductive embrace of capitalist-consumer culture and values, which they had formally critiqued.

In the short stories collected in *Who's Irish?* Jen continues her critical and humorous explorations into what it means to be "American" and what it means to be "happy" and "successful" in contemporary American culture and society. In the title story "Who's Irish?" Jen critiques a supposedly happy and successful American family, from the viewpoint of the elderly immigrant Chinese mother, who baby-sits for her yuppie daughter and unemployed son-in-law. She is the outsider who gives the reader a biting comic and satiric look at daily routines, lifestyles, and pitfalls in upscale suburban American yuppiedom. In "Duncan in China," Jen explores an Asian American man's idealistic notions of China. "Birthmates" focuses on the consequences of racism, and "The Water Faucet" engages the topic of religion.

New Chinese American Short-Story Writers

The 1980's and 1990's have continued to produce a rich abundance of short-story writers and collections. The stories have an ever-increasing range of themes and are situated within more diversified social-economic, cultural, literary, historical, and geopolitical locations and traditions. Darrell Lum's *Sun: Short Stories and Drama* (1980) and *Pass On, No Pass Back!* (1990) explore the social interactions of the multicultural communities of Hawaii in local pidgin creole. His second collection of stories was awarded the 1992 Outstanding Book Award in Fiction from the Association for Asian American Studies and the 1991 Cades Award in Literature.

Shirley Geok-Lin Lim's *Two Dreams: New and Selected Stories* (1997) portrays the diasporic experiences and legacies of Chinese Malaysian characters moving through vast geopolitical spaces and imaginaries. Wang Ping's *American Visa* (1994) tracks the conflicted experiences of a young woman named Seaweed as she moves from a Chinese peasant village and the turmoil of the Cultural Revolution to the loneliness and uncertainties of New York.

Canadian Chinese writers and stories include Sky Lee, author of *Bellydancer: Stories* (1994); Evelyn Lau, author of *Fresh Girls and Other Stories* (1993); and Judy Fong Bates, who wrote *China Dog and Other Tales from the Chinese Laundry* (1997). Anthologies focusing on recent Chinese American or Chinese Canadian short stories include *Paké: Writings by Chinese in Hawai'i*, edited by Eric Chock and Darrell H. Y. Lum (1989), and *Many-Mouthed Birds*, edited by Bennett Lee and Jim Wong-Chu (1991).

Japanese American Short Stories

Japanese American writers have a vibrant literary history during the years leading up to World War II; they were producing a wide range of literary work in both Japanese and English. According to literary historian Stan Yogi, a number of Issei writers (first-generation Japanese born between 1885 and 1924) wrote in Japanese and composed in traditional Japanese literary forms in ethnic newspapers in Hawaii and in West Coast venues. The work in English by Japanese Americans was primarily produced by Nisei (second-generation Japanese Americans who were born between 1910 and 1924) and Sansei (third-generation Japanese Americans writing in the period of the 1960's and 1970's).

There were generational and intergenerational tensions in Japanese American communities. For example, the lives of Japanese Americans, especially the Issei, or first generation, were restricted by alien land laws, which prohibited Japanese ownership of land. They were also denied the rights to U.S. naturalization and citizenship. In contrast, the prewar American-born Nisei were not only affiliated with their Japanese American families and communities but also were acculturating and assimilating into mainstream American popular culture and society. In part as a result of this complicated history, Japanese Issei as well as their Nisei children grappled with a broad range of concerns and dilemmas in their ethnic families and communities, as well as in their interactions with mainstream Anglo-American society.

With the beginning of World War II, the lives of Nisei, who were coming to young adulthood in this period, were turned upside down. It was a traumatic experience, which forefronted serious questions and issues about identity, loyalty, U.S. citizenship, community, and nationality. In 1942, Executive Order 9066 authorized the military to prescribe military zones from which persons were excluded. Approximately 112,000 Japanese Americans were incarcerated in ten internment camps as a result.

Toshio Mori was one of the best-known Japanese American writers during the prewar period. He lived in San Leandro, California, working in his family's nursery business. At the age of twenty-two, he decided to become a writer. During the 1930's, his work was being recognized and published in literary journals such as *Writer's Forum*, *New Directions in Poetry and Prose*, *The Clipper*, and *Common Ground*. His collection of short stories *Yokohama, California* was originally scheduled for publication in 1942. With the start of World War II, Mori was interned at the Topaz internment camp, and his stories were not published until 1949. Though initial mainstream reviews were negative, suggesting his stories were maudlin and not grammatically correct or well plotted, the editors of the *Aiiieeeee!* anthology reclaimed Mori's work. Moreover, Lawson Fusao Inada's introduction to the 1985 edition of *Yokohama, California* positively reappraised Mori's work in terms of an Asian American literary aesthetic and sensibility.

Mori's collection provides an insider's view of a fictional Japanese American community across the San Francisco Bay. One of Mori's literary models for *Yokohama, California* was Sherwood Anderson's *Winesburg, Ohio* (1919). Mori charts this Japanese American community of the late 1930's and early 1940's with familiarity, respect, and affection. He has an insider's ear for the nuances of Japanese American

English. In his stories, Mori centralizes a Japanese American community—its individuals and daily routines of survival, struggle, and celebration. He does not romanticize or exoticize the lives of his characters. The Japanese American world functions within its own social, cultural and historical dynamics.

This is clear in a very short story, "She Makes Swell Doughnuts," which was originally meant to open Mori's collection of stories. It charts the daily routines of a hardworking wife and mother of six children, who has also toiled with her husband in the farm fields for forty years. She is content in her old age, now caring for grandchildren and "facing the summers and winters and also the springs and the autumns, running the household that is completely her world." "Mama," as she is called, offers to make doughnuts for her guest. He is filled with delight in her gracious hospitality and exuberance in the dailiness of life. The external plot action seems simple and routine; however, it is the social-emotional landscape that seems vibrantly alive in this simple story. He does not wish to wait for her death to conjure the meaning of her life or habit of being. As Inada states in the introduction:

> To say that the story is sentimental is not appropriate, is not the entire story. Rather, it might be said the story captures and conveys those qualities known as *yasashi*—a known, a given, but practically untranslatable. To say that a person, a story, is *yasashi*, is considerable. These terms come to mind: humility, respect, sweetness, devotion, caring, generosity, kindness, and warmth—the very essence of strength and wisdom. The best of humanity.

The characters in Mori's work have rich and complex inner lives. Philosophers or writers like Motoji Tsunoda, Toshio Mori, or Akira Yano long for communities or audiences in order to break their isolation and loneliness. They seek the company of friends and associates who understand them and their pursuits in life. Often, the characters are not fully able to communicate their idiosyncratic perspectives to the larger community. Nevertheless, they continue to articulate their ideas to anybody who will listen.

In Mori's short story "The Seventh Street Philosopher," Motoji Tsunoda is by day a quiet launderer who lives in the basement of a elderly woman's home. He lives in poverty and obscurity. When he ventures out, however, he tries to communicate his ideas to people, especially on his favorite topic: What is there for the individual to do today? His ideas are derived from a wide and eclectic range of readings: Shakyamuni, St. Shinran, Akegarasu, and Dewey. Tsunoda is disliked by some in the community; they find him boring or eccentric. Yet the narrator notices a special quality in Motoji Tsunoda: He is a man who needs to speak and takes a risk in order to communicate to his community. The narrator is in awe of the spectacle of the

> individual standing up and expressing himself. . . there was this man, standing up and talking to the world, and also talking to vindicate himself to people, trying as hard as he could so he would not be misunderstood. And as he faced the eleven people in the audience including the two babies, he did not look foolish, he was not just a bag of wind. Instead I am sure he had a reason to stand up and have courage and bravery to offset the ridicule, the nonsense, and the misunderstanding.

In stories like "The Trees" or "The Eggs of the World," Mori portrays philosopher-characters who struggle to communicate their often intuitive, Zen-like understanding of life to those who cannot hear or understand its contexts. The art of communicating is a tragicomic affair in a number of these stories. Mori's other stories are filled with characters who have rich inner worlds: Teruo, the flower-shop clerk who gives away flowers to customers; Sessue Matoi, the wit and drunkard, who expounds on his theory of eggs and people; Ishimoto-san, a truck grocer who can still woo his customers; Hatsuye, the plain girl who daydreams about Clark Gable and the glitz of Hollywood; and the truck driver Tsumura, who sits in the park "sad and alone but is laughing all the time." Each is an individual with a complex interior life that is tantalizing even in its incompleteness; the individual portrayals are not the stereotypical images of Asians that circulate in mainstream popular American culture.

POSTWAR NISEI WRITERS

Two well-known Japanese American Nisei short-story writers are Hisaye Yamamoto and Wakako Yamauchi. Their short stories sensitively chart lives of Japanese American individuals, families, and communities during the prewar period and through the war and postwar years. Yamamoto was born in 1921 in Redondo Beach, California, to Japanese immigrant parents. The family moved a great deal but finally settled in Oceanside, California, before their relocation to Poston, Arizona, after the bombing of Pearl Harbor in 1941. Yamamoto began writing in the 1930's for the Japanese American press. She continued to write for the internment camp newspaper *The Poston Chronicle*. There she befriended Wakako Yamauchi, a young artist, writer, and future playwright.

After World War II, Yamamoto settled in Los Angeles, where she worked on the African American weekly *The Los Angeles Tribune* from 1945 to 1948. In the late 1940's, Yamamoto's short stories about prewar life in Japanese American communities were making their way into national journals such as the *Kenyon Review, Harper's Bazaar*, and *Partisan Review*. They gained for her a national reputation as a fine American short-story writer. She won a John Hay Whitney Foundation Opportunity Fellowship in 1950. She married, had children, and spent a brief time working with the Catholic Workers of New York before returning to Los Angeles. Yamamoto's debut collection of short stories, entitled *Seventeen Syllables and Other Stories*, appeared in 1988.

She has been rightly lauded for her compassionate explorations of characters who have suffered loss or sorrow in the pursuit of love, beauty, art, and spirituality. Yamamoto's stories are also noted for their fine technical artistry. "Seventeen Syllables" and "Yoneko's Earthquake" are classic examples of her intricately developed double plots. Through the double plot, the reader sees the story from multiple perspectives—often from the eyes of young, naïve daughter-narrators who are just beginning to explore new experiences or awakenings, especially in love and sexuality. In contrast, their mothers' submerged stories hint at the darker, more traumatic aspects of adulthood: unfulfilled yearnings, alienation, loneliness, adultery, abortion, domestic violence, and loss of loved ones or of creativity. Yamamoto's stories portray a full range of generational and gender tensions, especially between mismatched Issei husbands and wives and between Issei parents and their Nisei children. In some of her stories, Yamamoto also explores interracial and cross-cultural relationships of women and men within Japanese American communities, expanding on multicultural themes and interactions in the United States.

In other finely crafted stories, including "The Legend of Ms. Sasagawara," "Wilshire Bus," and "Las Vegas Charley," Yamamoto explores the horrible toll of the internment on Japanese American individuals. In "Las Vegas Charley," Kazuyuki Matsumoto, better known as "Charley," lives in Las Vegas as a dishwasher. He is an alcoholic and a part-time gambler. A man who has tried to be a hardworking and loving husband and father to his two sons, he lost his sense of purpose after the death of his young wife. The aftermath of war, internment, death of a son, and daily racism have continued to break his spirit. In "The Legend of Miss Sasagawara," Yamamoto portrays the life of a Nisei ballet dancer-artist incarcerated in an internment camp. Mari Sasagawara is isolated from other internees, constantly an object of gossip and curiosity in the boring routine of the camp. She lives a maddening life with an otherworldly Buddhist minister-father, who does not understand his passionate daughter's needs and who has retreated from her life to pursue sainthood. "Wilshire Bus" tracks the interior tensions of Esther Kuroiwa, who fails to stand up against the racism she confronts on a routine bus ride. In "Life Among the Oilfields," Yamamoto portrays the life of a Japanese American family through a narrator recollecting the glamour, poverty, and racism of the Great Depression that followed the stock market crash of 1929.

Wakako Yamauchi was born in Westmoreland, California, in 1924. Her family lived in a Japanese American farming community in Southern California's Imperial Valley. The children attended rural schools, migrating from place to place as tenant farm workers because the California alien land laws prohibited Japanese aliens from owning land. Yamauchi's family finally settled in Oceanside, California, where they ran a boardinghouse for itinerant Japanese American farm workers. Like other American-born Nisei of her generation, Yamauchi juggled between Japanese traditions and cultural values inherited and practiced within her family and ethnic community and her acculturation into mainstream American culture. During World War II, while still in high school, Yamauchi was interned in the Poston Relocation Center in Arizona, where she worked with the writer Hisaye Yamamoto on the camp newspaper *The Poston Chronicle*.

After the war and an interim in Chicago, Yamauchi returned to California, more specifically to Los Angeles, where she again met Hisaye Yamamoto and attended art school. Yamauchi began to publish the stories she had been writing in the *Rafu Shimpo*, a bilingual Japanese daily, between 1960 and 1974. She was further encouraged by Frank Chin to publish her stories in his anthology *Aiiieeeee!* in 1974. A collection of her short stories is entitled *Songs My Mother Taught Me: Stories, Plays, and Memoir* (1994).

Yamauchi, well known as an Asian American playwright, transformed a number of her short stories into plays. For example, she converted her often anthologized short story "And the Soul Shall Dance" into a powerful drama about life in a prewar Japanese American agricultural community. This play launched her career as a playwright. In the story, Mr. and Mrs. Oka are a mispartnered pair, frustrated and disappointed in each other and their life in the United States. Emiko Oka, a former dancer in Japan, longs to return to Japan, back to the city, to her former life and lover. Instead, she is married by her family to her deceased sister's husband and is sent to America, to be a dutiful wife, stepmother, and farmworker. Emiko is obstinate in her desire to return to Japan and will not learn to adapt to married life in the farming community. She smokes, drinks, and dances; she does not behave like her more traditional next-door neighbor, Mrs. Murata. Emiko is abused by her husband and ostracized by her neighbors. She is considered a bad woman, or an eccentric and crazy one. In "The Soul Shall Dance," it is only the eleven-year-old narrator, Masako Murata, the young Nisei daughter of Mrs. Murata, who senses the desires of Emiko and bears witness to her sorrows and frustrations as an outcast woman. At the end of the story, Emiko, in a state of extreme isolation and despair, walks into the desert seeking return to a "home" where her thirsting body and spirit can finally be nourished. Yamauchi is sensitive, especially in her portrayals of the intense inner landscape of Japanese Issei women, who are often physically, emotionally, and imaginatively thwarted by the harsh realities of their lives.

In other stories, such as "That Was All," "Songs My Mother Taught Me," and "The Handkerchief," Yamauchi continues to use her evocative and lyrical style to explore her characters' submerged tragedies and private yearnings for love, beauty, passion, and freedom.

New Japanese American Short-Story Writers

A noteworthy group of Sansei (third-generation) short-story writers emerged between the 1970's and the 1990's, including David Masumoto. His *Silent Spring* (1984) explores life and racial-ethnic relations in Del Rey, a small farming town in the San Joaquin Valley in the California of the 1930's. Susan Nunes's *A Small Obligation and Other Stories of Hilo* (1982), Sylvia Watanabe's *Talking to the Dead and Other Stories* (1992), and Marie Hara's *Bananaheart and Other Stories* (1994) all portray the complex and rich interactions of Asians living in the local cultures of Hawaii. R. A. Sasaki's *The Loom and Other Stories* (1991) is a collection of interconnected short stories portraying lives of Sansei raised in the Richmond District of San Francisco during the 1950's and 1960's. Sasaki's stories show how the histories of racism and the Japanese American internment inform the individual experiences and collective interactions of the Sansei children, their parents, and contemporary communities.

Filipino American Short Stories

To understand Filipino American writing is to trace, in part, its links to nearly three centuries of Spanish colonialization, U.S. colonization (1902-1941), and neocolonial dependency (1946-1990's).

The early Filipino groups coming to the United States were mostly young male workers, who immigrated to the Hawaiian islands or to the mainland United States between 1902 and 1946. Within an exploitative transnational capitalist economy between the U.S. and its colony, many Filipino men found backbreaking work on plantations and low-paying domestic and factory work in cities. This first wave of immigration consisted of "American nationals" who were able to enter the United States without visas but were not granted the rights of citizenship, creating an ambiguous "in-between" status for Filipinos migrating between the Philippines and the United States. Included in this early wave were a more elite group of *pensionados*, the government-sponsored cohort of students studying in the U.S. who later returned to the Philippines after their educational internships in the United States. Later immigrant groups were veterans of World War II and their families and a post-1965 immigrant cadre of skilled professionals and family reunification immigrants.

Filipino writers who lived and wrote within and about the first broad waves to the United States include Bienvenido Santos (born 1910), José García Villa (born 1914), Carlos Bulosan (born 1911), and N. V. M. Gonazalez (born 1915). According to the literary critic Oscar Campomanes, the varying socioeconomic, cultural, and political circumstances of immigration produced a literature by Filipinos (political expatriates, exiles) and Filipino Americans that used recurring motifs such as "departure, nostalgia, incompletion, rootlessness, leavetaking, and dispossession, . . . with the Philippines as either the original or terminal reference point." Filipino literature, according to Campomanes, cannot be categorized simply as a "variant of the immigrant epic"; it is a

> literature of exile and emergence rather than a literature of immigration and settlement whereby life in the United States serves as the space for displacement, suspension, and perspective. Exile becomes a necessary, if inescapable, state for Filipinos in the United States—at once susceptible to the vagaries of the [neo]colonial U.S.-Philippine relationship and redeemable only by its radical restructuring.

Bienvenido Santos captured the anguish and loneliness of the earlier generations of Filipinos—the "hurt men"—in his *Scent of Apples* (1979). This collection brought together select stories from his earlier collections of short stories. Santos came to the United States in the 1940's as a student on fellowship at Columbia University. During World War II, he was stranded in the United States with other *pensionados*. Santos worked in the Information Division of the Commonwealth Building in Washington, D.C., where José García Villa, another writer (known for his collection *Footnote to Youth: Tales of the Philippines and Others*, 1933), also worked. Later, he spent time traveling and lecturing throughout the United States for the U.S. Office of Education. In this capacity, he found time to chart the lives of the stranded or temporarily exiled *pensionados* in San Francisco, New York, Washington, D.C., Chicago, and the Midwest. Some of these men were young students and others were older married men, temporarily exiled in the United States. They worried for their own uncertain circumstances as well as for the families and communities back home in the war-torn Philippines. These experiences are reflected in such stories as "The Hurt Men," "The Nightclub," and "Of Other Deaths."

Like other Filipino writers of this period, Santos discovered in his travels the groups of poor and working-class Pinoys or Manongs—the migrant farm workers, domestic workers, and factory workers—who labored in dehumanizing conditions in a racist America. Santos portrays their experiences of survival, despair, faith, and in some cases fierce resistance both for readers in the United States and, more so, for readers in the Philippines, especially those who have romanticized or idealized life in America for Filipinos. "Immigration Blues" portrays the tensions between aliens and permanent residents as a marriage is negotiated between a young woman and an older Pinoy. In often anthologized short stories such as "The Contender" or "The Day the Dancers Came," Santos poignantly represents the lives of two elderly Pinoys—the ailing Antonio Bataller, formerly a Pullman porter, and Filemon Acayan, a hospital menial. They form a unit for survival, comfort, and resistance. Antonio is the cynical one, while Filemon is the hopeful one. In his long and brutalizing homelessness through the landscapes of America, Filemon constructs a nostalgic diasporic image of a former homeland to sustain him through the despair and racism he is experiencing in America. Filemon hopes to make close contact with a troupe of Filipino and Filipina dancers who are visiting Chicago as part of a cultural exchange with the Philippines. Through contact with the dancers, he hopes to recapture the remembered remnants of the culture, language, and beauty of the people and country he left behind. However, he finds that the village culture, language, and civility that he has maintained over so many years of diasporic living have left him awkward and outcast in the presence of the sophisticated young dancers, who ignore or shun him as an old bum:

> I talked in the dialect, Ilocano, Tagalog, Bicol, but no one listened. They avoided me. They had been briefed too well: Do not talk to strangers. Ignore their invitations. Be extra careful in the big cities like New York and Chicago, beware of the old-timers, the Pinoys. Most of them are bums. Keep away from them. Be on the safe side—stick together, entertain only those who have been introduced to you properly.

Carlos Bulosan grew up in poverty in the Philippines. He developed a career as a prolific writer and labor unionist in America. Bulosan is most famous for his semiautobiographical novel *America Is in the Heart* (1946), which bears witness to his own hardships as well as those of his Filipino countrymen in the United States between the 1930's and the 1950's. He portrays the racism, loneliness, and violence he encountered through life while maintaining a belief in the possibility of a better America. He tracks Filipino union-organizing efforts throughout California and the Pacific Northwest and the ability of Pinoys to survive and resist dehumanizing experiences and violence. Among his better-known short-story collections are *The Laughter of My Father* (1944), *The Philippines Is in the Heart* (1978), and *If You Want to Know What We Are: A Carlos Bulosan Reader* (1983).

N. V. M. Gonzalez is an emeritus professor of English literature at California State University, Hayward, and a writer in residence at the University of the Philippines in Manila. His retrospective collection of short stories entitled *The Bread of Salt and Other Stories* (1993) looks back nostalgically to a native folk community living in the long-colonialized homeland of the Philippines. Gonzalez celebrates the survival and endurance of common folk—peasant farmers, fishermen, merchants, and teachers. He also portrays the exiles and expatriates who make their way to the United States, confronting another set of dilemmas and circumstances in naming identities and experiences. Gonzalez is known for a number of novels, including *A Season of Grace* and *The Bamboo Dancers*.

Flips and Expatriates

A generation of young writers coming of age during the 1960's and 1970's are known as the "Flips," who include Alfred Robles, Sam Tagatac, and Oscar Peñaranda. Besides this group, there emerged in the 1970's what Campomanes calls the "politically expatriated generation" of Epifanio San Juan, Linda Ty-Casper, Ninotchka Rosca, and Michelle Skinner.

The Filipino American writer Peter Bacho, a product of the 1960's and 1970's, won the American Book Award of the Before Columbus Foundation for his first novel, *Cebu* (1991). His first collection of short stories, *Dark Blue Suit and Other Stories* (1997), portrays life in a Filipino American community in Seattle and is partly semiautobiographical. He foregrounds familial struggles in the United States against racism, remembering efforts in union organizing and establishing ethnic communities. His stories bridge his father's early period (1920's through 1940's) within a predominantly migratory male society that circulated in the agricultural fields of California, in frontier towns, and in the salmon-canning factories of the Pacific Northwest, as well as the transitioning period of developing Filipino American families and communities (with the marriage of his father in the late 1940's).

Stories like "Dark Blue Suit," "The Wedding," "A Matter of Faith," and "A Family Gathering" memorialize the world of the Pinoys and the robust camaraderie they shared during the salmon-canning season and in bars, brothels, dance-halls, union meetings, and boxing rings. Bacho also charts their tearful returns to the Philippines to marry and to die. Buddy, the narrator, weaves the stories together, depicting Filipino American communities in the social ferment and influences of the 1960's and 1970's and in their interactions with African American culture and communities. Bacho also depicts the lives of their mixed-race children, the legitimate and illegitimate progeny of the Manongs. Two stories, "Home" and "Rico," feature a protagonist by the name of Rico Divina, the son of an Indian mother and a Filipino father. Rico is seen by the larger society as either vocational-school material or cannon fodder for the Vietnam War. The stories track the toll of the Vietnam War on those who fought and were changed by the violence and atrocities of the war and the ghetto, on one hand, and, on the other, those who remained behind to memorialize their friends, the contemporary "hurt men." The stories are written in bare and straightforward prose.

M. Evelina Galang, who teaches creative writing at Old Dominion University, is a relative newcomer. She debuted her first collection of short stories, *Her Wild American Self*, in 1996. Galang's earlier work appeared in *Amerasia Journal*, *American Short Fiction*, *Calyx*, *Quarterly West*, *Riksha*, and *New Voices*, and she won the Associated Writers Program Intro Award in Nonfiction for 1993. Her work speaks to the wide range of concerns in Filipino families and communities, which move back and forth (physically and imaginatively) between the United States and the Philippines. Stories such as "Rose Colored," "Talk to Me, Milagros," "Lectures on How You Never Lived Back Home," "Miss Teenage Sampaguita," and "Mix Like Stir Fry" engage a variety of themes: socioeconomic and cultural dislocation, generational and intergenerational tensions, racial-ethnic and gender identity, individual and communal responsibility, and the transnational bonding and networks within and among Filipino families and communities.

Joel Tan is a writer and poet who is also the director of the HIV Project at Asian Health Services in Oakland, California. His stories, poetry, and essays have appeared in anthologies such as *Asian American Sexualities* (1996) and *On a Bed of Rice* (1995). "In His Arms" and "Night Sweats" are two particularly powerful short stories concerning family, homosexuality, love, and death in the period of acquired immunodeficiency syndrome (AIDS).

Other Filipina and Filipino American short-story writers include Cecilia Manguerrra Brainard (*Woman with Horns and Other Stories*, 1987; *Acapulco at Sunset and Other Stories*, 1995), Jessica Hagedorn (*Dangerous Music*, 1975; *Pet Food and Tropical Apparitions*, 1981; *Danger and Beauty*, 1993), Ninotchka Rosca (*Bitter Country, and Other Stories*, 1970; *The Monsoon Collection*, 1983), Linda Ty-Casper (*The Transparent Sun and Other Stories*, 1963; *The Secret Runner and Other Stories*, 1974), Marianne Villanueva (*Ginseng and Other Tales from Manila*, 1991), and Michelle Cruz Skinner (*Balikbayan: A Filipino Homecoming*, 1988).

Anthologies of Filipino and Filipina American writing include *New Writing from the Philippines: A Critique and Anthology* (edited by Leonard Casper, 1966), *Asian American Authors* (edited by Kai-yu Hsu and Helen Palubinskas, 1972), *Fiction by Filipinos in America* (edited by Cecilia Manguerra Brainard, 1993), *Brown River, White Ocean: An Anthology of Twentieth-Century Philippine Literature in English* (edited by Luis H. Francia, 1993), and *Flippin': Filipinos on America* (edited by Luis H. Francia and Eric Gamalinda, 1996).

Korean American Short Stories

According to literary critic Elaine Kim, "published works written in English by Korean Americans are relatively few and were mostly brought to press after 1980." There are, however, two notable short-story writers to mention: Ty Pak and Gary Pak. Ty Pak published a collection of short stories entitled *Guilt Payment* (1983). He lived through the Japanese occupation of Korea until its liberation in 1945, as well as the trauma of the Korean War. He received a law degree from Seoul National University and worked as a reporter in Korea until 1965, when he came to the United States. He attended Bowling Green State University, receiving a Ph.D. in English. Ty Pak taught in the English Department at the University of Hawaii.

Like the stories of Korean American novelists and memoirists such as Richard Kim, Ronyoung Kim, Theresa Hak Kyung Cha, Sook Nyul Choi, and Nora Okja Keller, Ty Pak's short stories portray the effects of Japanese and Korean relations during World War II as well as the dislocation and relocation of Korean individuals, families, and communities in Korea and the United States. In the title story, "Guilt Payment," the narrator, a college teacher, recollects his traumatic personal experiences of the war (such as the violent death of his wife) and juxtaposes these experiences to his present life and relationship with his daughter Mira, who wants to go to Italy for music education. However, as noted by Kim,

> the stories in *Guilt Payment* are mostly male-centered war and adventure stories. Pak's female characters are often described as seductive objects of male desire. Many are cast as female avengers, . . . shrieking shrews, shamans possessed by spirits, and frightening vampires. In story after story, Pak imagines the woman' s body as raped, tortured, maimed, and mutilated.

A refreshingly original writer is Gary Pak, born in 1952 in Honolulu. He is the grandson of Korean immigrants, reared in Honolulu, attending college at Boston University, and returning to live, marry, and write in the Hawaiian islands. *The Watcher of Waipuna and Other Stories* (1992) is a wonderful debut collection, which won the Association for Asian American Studies 1993 National Book Award for Literature. He published his first novel, *A Ricepaper Airplane*, in 1998; it focuses specifically on his Korean American experience and history.

The Watcher of Waipuna and Other Stories engages with the diverse array of talk-story voices and experiences situated in the local communities of Hawaii where native pidgin creole is spoken. Pak's stories are rooted within the history of U.S. colonialism, racism (see "The Trial of Goro Fukushima"), Hawaiian sovereignty, and environmental social justice and land rights issues of concern to indigenous Hawaiians and local islanders. See, for example, "The Valley of Dead Air," "The Watcher of Waipuna" and "A Toast to Rosita"; the latter also addresses discrimination against homosexuals, or *mahus*, in the islands.

Voices Stirring: An Anthology of Korean American Writing, edited by Maria Hong and David Kim and appearing in *The Asian Pacific American Journal* (vol. 1, no. 2, 1992), is a fine anthology of Korean American writing, including short fiction.

South Asian American Short Stories

One of the best-known South Asian American novelists, essayists, and short-story writers is Bharati Mukherjee, who was born into a Hindu Bengali Brahman family and attended school in the United States, where she met and married her Canadian husband. In the 1970's, Mukherjee settled in Toronto, Canada, with her family. In 1980, disturbed by the racial prejudice against Indians that she encountered in Toronto, she decided to resettle with her family in the United States, a country that she asserts is more amenable to her claims on an American identity. She is known for such novels as *The Tiger's Daughter* (1972), *Wife* (1975), *Jasmine* (1989), *The Holder of the World* (1993), and *Leave It to Me* (1997). Her first collection of short stories, *Darkness* (1985), and her second collection of short stories, *The Middleman and Other Stories* (1988), portray both Indian and "Third World" immigrant women and men in the midst of self-inventing or refashioning their identities and social locations in the geopolitical and cultural landscapes of Canada and the United States. They come not only from India but also from such places as Iraq, Trinidad, Uganda, the Philippines, Vietnam, and Sri Lanka. Mukherjee depicts emergent, unstable, or suspended potential selves that are being negotiated in the rough-and-tumble process of acculturation and assimilation into American culture and society. These processes are interactive, changing her characters as well as the adopted country in which they live. In 1988, Mukherjee won the National Book Critics Circle Award for *The Middleman and Other Stories*.

In her stories, Mukherjee portrays not only the fascination and the potential for freedom but also the multiple tensions, ambiguities, and paralysis that are generated at these "in-between" sites of dislocation and relocation. In such often-anthologized stories as "A Wife's Story," "Jasmine," "The Management of Grief," and "The Tenant," Mukherjee's Third World women characters portray the serious obstacles, traumas, and excitements—the terrible beauty—of redefining themselves as more than wives, mothers, and daughters within patriarchal families, cultures, and communities. A number of her female characters experience tantalizing and empowering life options in American contexts that, at the same time, hint at sacrifice, risk, violence (both physical and psychic), and ambiguity. Mukherjee portrays the exploitative and gaudier sides of these new identities and worlds being birthed with, as she says, an immigrant's "hustlerish kind of energy."

Though Mukherjee does situate these transformations amid the harsh realities of socioeconomic exploitation, racism, sexism, and cultural discrimination in American society, some of her critics do not believe she addresses these aspects critically and systematically enough in her stories about becoming American. For example, Ketu Katrak and others critique Mukherjee's

> upper-class background and the classicist and elitist tone she adopts towards her characters. She overtly endorses the melting-pot concept and regards American society as the most welcoming of any in the world towards the "other." Even when racism is part of her exploration and critique, there is no attempt to place it within a larger political system of exploitation in the United States. . . . Mukherjee ignores the fact that to people of color of lower class and educational background than hers America is not always welcoming.

Chitra Banerjee Divarkaruni

Another South Asian writer is Chitra Banerjee Divarkaruni, an award-winning poet, novelist, and short-story writer. Her poetry and prose have been recognized by the Santa Clara Arts Council 1994 Award for Fiction and by the Wallace Alexander Gerbode Foundation's 1994 Award in Poetry. Her collection of eleven stories, *Arranged Marriage* (1995) won the 1996 American Book Award, the PEN Oakland Josephine Miles Award, and the Bay Area Book Reviewers Award for Fiction. The stories are about the immigrant experiences of Indian-born girls and women whose lives often bridge fascinatingly complex, and often conflicted, worlds in India and/or the United States. The stories engage with colonialism, geopolitical and cultural dislocation, and the changing gender interactions of men and women. The stories suggest the challenges and excitement in new possibilities in her female characters' lives and the harsh, painful realities, dilemmas, and compromises that are also encountered in India and the United States. See, for example, such short stories as "Clothes," "Silver Pavements, Golden Roofs," "The Word Love," "The Perfect Life," "The Disappearance," and "The Affair."

New South Asian American Short Fiction

Another original voice in South Asian American writing is Ginu Kamani, who was born in Bombay, India, and moved to the United States in 1962. She received an M.A. in creative writing from the University of Colorado, Boulder, in 1987. The eleven stories of her collection *Junglee Girl* (1995) are provocative and idiosyncratic in their explorations of sexual desires and sensual awakenings by female characters who challenge and subvert the oppressive traditions and taboos within culture and society. The word "junglee" is derived from a Sanskrit root, *jungle*, and refers in India to a wild and uncontrollable woman. Her short stories have also been published in the anthology *Our Feet Walk the Sky: Women of the South Asian Diaspora* (1993).

In addition, Jhumpa Lahiri's debut collection *Interpreter of Maladies* (1999) received praise for its finely nuanced stories. South Asian American short stories can also be located in *Contours of the Heart: South Asian Map North America* (edited by Sunaina Maira and Rajini Srikanth, 1996) and *Her Mother's Ashes Two: More Stories by South Asian Women in Canada and the United States* (edited by Nurjehan Aziz, 1998).

Vietnamese American Short Stories

Vietnamese American short stories in English are still emerging. According to Truong Vu, the term "Vietnamese Americans" refers to

> Americans of Vietnamese descent, including immigrants who may have arrived prior to 1975, refugees who started arriving in 1975, those who entered the United States as immigrants, starting in 1979 through the Orderly Departure Program, as well as the subsequent generations who have been and will be born in the United States.

The short stories of new Vietnamese and other Southeast American writers can be found in journals and anthologies such as *Viêt Nam Forum*, *The Other Side of Heaven: Postwar Fiction by Vietnamese and American Writers* (edited by Wayne Karlin, Le Minh Khue, and Truong Vu, 1995), *Amerasia Journal*, and *Asian Pacific American Journal*.

One upcoming Vietnamese American journalist, essayist, and short-story writer of note is Andrew Lam, who is also an associate editor with Pacific News Service in San Francisco. He has produced some delightful short stories, such as "She's in a Dance Frenzy" in *Once upon a Dream: The Vietnamese-American Experience* (edited by De Tran, Andrew Lam, and Hai Dai Nguyen, 1995), and "Grandma's Tales," in *Asian American Sexualities* (edited by Russell Leong, 1996). His stories portray the hybrid lives of young Vietnamese Americans who grow up in such places as the Tenderloin or the Mission District and develop their own pidgin creole and idiosyncratic perspectives on their border-crossings in culture, society, and history.

Wendy Ho

Anthologies

Chan, Jeffrey Paul, et al., eds. *The Big Aiiieeeee! An Anthology of Chinese American and Japanese American Literature*. New York: Meridian, 1991.

Chin, Frank, et al., eds. *Aiiieeeee! An Anthology of Asian-American Writers*. New York: Mentor, 1974, 1991.

Chock, Eric, et al., eds. *Growing Up Local: An Anthology of Poetry and Prose from Hawai'i*. Honolulu: Bamboo Ridge Press, 1998.

Chock, Eric, and Darrell H. Y. Lum, eds. *The Best of Bamboo Ridge*. Honolulu: Bamboo Ridge Press, 1986.

_______. *The Best of Honolulu Fiction: Stories from the "Honolulu" Magazine Fiction Contest*. Honolulu: Bamboo Ridge Press, 1999.

Hagedorn, Jessica, ed. *Charlie Chan Is Dead: An Anthology of Contemporary Asian American Fiction*. New York: Penguin, 1993.

Hong, Maria, ed. *Growing Up Asian American*. New York: William Morrow, 1993.

Lim, Shirley Geok-lin, ed. *Asian-American Literature: An Anthology*. Lincolnwood, Ill.: NTC Publishing Group, 2000.

Lim, Shirley Geok-lin, and Mayumi Tsutakawa, eds. *The Forbidden Stitch: An Asian American Women's Anthology*. Corvallis, Oreg.: Calyx Books, 1989.

Watanabe, Sylvia, and Carol Bruchac, eds. *Home to Stay: Asian American Women's Fiction*. Greenfield Center, N.Y.: Greenfield Review Press, 1990.

Wong, Shawn, ed. *Asian American Literature: A Brief Introduction and Anthology*. New York: HarperCollins, 1995.

Bibliography

Campomanes, Oscar V. "Filipinos in the United States." In *Reading the Literatures of Asian America*, edited by Shirley Geok-lin Lim and Amy Ling. Philadelphia: Temple University Press, 1992.

Cheung, King-Kok. *Articulate Silences: Hisaye Yamamoto, Maxine Hong Kingston, Joy Kogawa*. Ithaca, N.Y.: Cornell University Press, 1993. A critical study that analyzes Asian American literature, especially its nuanced and articulate silences.

Cheung, King-Kok, ed. *An Interethnic Companion to Asian American Literature*. Cambridge: Cambridge University Press, 1997. Excellent up-to-date and comprehensive introduction to different ethnic literatures, approaches, and themes.

Cheung, King-Kok, and Stan Yogi. *Asian American Literature: An Annotated Bibliography*. New York: Modern Language Association of America, 1988. Annotated bibliographic information on Asian American writers (by ethnicity and genre) and secondary critical sources and background readings.

Chin, Frank, et al., eds. *Aiiieeeee! An Anthology of*

Asian-American Writers. New York: Mentor, 1974, 1991.

Chin, Frank, and Jeffrey Paul Chan. "Racist Love." In *Seeing Through Shuck*, edited by Richard Kostelanetz. New York: Ballantine, 1972.

Ho, Wendy. *In Her Mother's House: The Politics of Asian American Mother-Daughter Writing*. Walnut Creek, Calif.: AltaMira Press, 1999. A critical study arguing for more radical and innovative approaches in reading literary texts by Asian American women writers, especially the mother-daughter writing by contemporary Chinese American writers.

Inada, Lawson Fusao. Introduction to *Yokohama, California*. Seattle: University of Washington Press, 1949, 1985.

Katrak, Ketu H. "South Asian American Literature." In *An Interethnic Companion to Asian American Literature*, edited by King-Kok Cheung. Cambridge, England: Cambridge University Press, 1997.

Kim, Elaine H. *Asian American Literature: An Introduction to the Writings and Their Social Context*. Philadelphia: Temple University Press, 1982. Classic, trailblazing introductory overview to the social-historical contexts of Asian American literature.

_______. "Korean American Literature." In *An Interethnic Companion to Asian American Literature*, edited by King-Kok Cheung. Cambridge, England: Cambridge University Press, 1997.

Li, David Leiwei. *Imagining the Nation: Asian American Literature and Cultural Consent*. Stanford, Calif.: Stanford University Press, 1998. Critical analysis of Asian American identity and literary formations in relation to the construction of nationhood and citizenship narratives and institutions.

Lim, Shirley Geok-lin, and Amy Ling, eds. *Reading the Literatures of Asian America*. Philadelphia: Temple University Press, 1992. Anthology of critical essays on Asian American ethnic literatures, approaches, and thematic concerns.

White-Parks, Annette. "A Reversal of American Concepts of 'Otherness' in the Fiction of Sui Sin Far." *MELUS* 20, no. 1 (1995): 17-34.

Wong, Sau-ling Cynthia. *Reading Asian American Literature: From Necessity to Extravagance*. Princeton, N.J.: Princeton University Press, 1993. An original literary study arguing for intertextual approaches in reading and analyzing Asian American texts by analyzing a variety of motifs.

Yamamoto, Traise. *Masking Selves, Making Subjects: Japanese American Women, Identity, and the Body*. Berkeley: University of California Press, 1999. A critical study of Japanese American women's literary texts in terms of identity and body themes.

Yogi, Stan. "Japanese American Literature." In *An Interethnic Companion to Asian American Literature*, edited by King-Kok Cheung. Cambridge, England: Cambridge University Press, 1997.

AUSTRALIA AND NEW ZEALAND SHORT FICTION

Frank O'Connor has suggested in *The Lonely Voice: A Study of the Short Story* (1963) that the short story flourishes best in an incompletely developed culture such as a regional culture. Existing outside the centers of society confers the status of outsider, which, O'Connor argues, characterizes modern short fiction. It is perhaps this reason that explains, more than any other, the fact that the short story has been claimed at various times as the paradigmatic prose form for both Australia and New Zealand. The sense of isolation and distance from the centers of culture that mark the development of the literature of both countries is served by the brevity and uncertainty inherent in the short-story form. In addition, particularly during the early period of colonization, writers have faced the difficulty of publishing longer works and have turned instead to the periodical as a means of publishing and distributing their writing.

The development of the short story in Australia and New Zealand has been motivated by a desire to distinguish the literature from that of Europe. This tendency to react against foreign forms is particularly noticeable in the work of Henry Lawson and Frank Sargeson. However, it would be a mistake to read the cultures and literatures of Australia and New Zealand as interchangeable or even as reflective of each other. While there has been some cross-fertilization, the development of the literatures of each country has been distinct and separate. Furthermore, a study that identifies the literatures closely with each other tends to obscure the influences of other cultures—European and American—which come into play in the development of a national literature.

The Short Story in Australia

The short story is frequently claimed to express something particularly Australian, as Marion Halligan and Roseanne Fitzgibbon have said in *The Gift of Story: Three Decades of UQP Short Stories* (1998): "a kind of sternness belonging to the frontier mentality which gave us our being, plain and no nonsense, or as a laconic but sensitive expression of pain." Alternatively, the aptness of the form has been traced back to the lifestyle of the early settlers and pioneers: telling yarns around the campfire, filling the cultural void with stories from the "old country." It has even been suggested that the origins of the Australian short story lie in the aboriginal oral tradition that was captured by bushmen and translated into an English speaking tradition. These explanations may be attractively mythic, but the real reasons for the dominance of the form in the early stages of Australia's literary history are more prosaic. The sense of cultural inauthenticity common to many colonial nations and a short history (at least in European terms) was conducive to the construction of short rather than lengthy narratives. Furthermore, by enabling the gathering of multiple stories into a single volume—in anthologies, collections or periodicals—a more complete sense of a new and unique culture could be created.

Although stories were published in Australia from early in the nineteenth century, it is the short fiction of the late nineteenth century that has been associated with the development of a certain vision of Australian national and literary identity. The *Bulletin* magazine, established in 1880 by J. F. Archibald, was at the heart of the development of an Australian national literary style.

With the institution in 1896 of the literary "Red Page," under the editorship of A. G. Stephens until 1906, the *Bulletin*'s influence on the development of a national literature was established. The magazine saw itself as "nurse and guardian of national literature" and was radical, republican, and very popular (it was known colloquially as the "bushman's bible"). In the buildup to Federation in 1901, both Archibald and Stephens were conscious of the need to generate a cultural narrative that was distinguishable from that of England and from Australia's convict past. They focused on the bush as an evocative image of that distinctly Australian and in doing so endeavored to develop an egalitarian and democratic vision of Australia. These stories privileged national unity, male solidarity, and the primacy of the bush, and adopted a laconic style, tinged with a certain grim humor and flashes of sentimentality. This portrait of Australia has been interpreted and reinterpreted in the intervening years, but there is no doubt that Henry Lawson played a pivotal role in its development and the resulting relationship between a national literary identity and the short story.

Henry Lawson

Henry Lawson's first publication was "A Song of the Republic," which appeared in the *Bulletin* in 1887 and began his long relationship with that publication. His stories focus on a drought-stricken and desperate rural landscape, alleviated only by the solidarity and sense of bush honor of his male characters, illustrated most famously in "The Bush Undertaker" and "The Union Buries Its Dead." This landscape is "no place for a woman" (the title of a Lawson story): Lawson's female characters are frequently deserted by their husbands, who are forced to seek seasonal shift work, or who disappear on alcoholic binges. Necessity breeds female resourcefulness, Lawson spoke of the courage of women in the "land where gaunt and haggard women live alone and work like men," but it also leads to unhappiness and even madness. His famous story "The Drover's Wife," in which a young woman defends her children against a snake, can be juxtaposed with the later "Water Them Geraniums," in which desertion, isolation, and desperate poverty finally drive Mrs. Spicer to her death. These stories epitomize his style: realistic and born of experience rather than imagination, laconic and spare, and something like a "yarn" but also redolent of a cynical humor and a quiet pathos which seem to coexist in his stories.

In his lifetime Lawson was claimed by A. G. Stephens as "the voice of the bush, and the bush is the heart of Australia," and his stories were immensely popular. Although Lawson's adoption of the short story coincided with the flowering of the short story in England and Europe in the 1890's, the movements do not seem to have been connected. Nevertheless, the interest in the short story indicates a desire to move away from the nineteenth century domestic novel, which had become the measure of literature during this period, with its emphasis on narrative causation reflecting a continuous and stable culture. For an Australian writer, in particular, the desire to deviate from a European literary model and establish a distinct voice and style would have pointed to the use of an alternative literary structure such as the short story.

Barbara Baynton

Henry Lawson outclassed the other writers of the period, with the exception of Barbara Baynton. Baynton was also associated with the *Bulletin*, although only one of her stories, "The Chosen Vessel," appeared in the magazine in 1896 and was heavily edited. This story appears in her collection *Bush Studies* (1902), on which her fame largely rests. The landscape of Baynton's stories resembles that of Lawson: It is a harsh and primitive rural environment in which survival is difficult, but for Baynton the violence of nature is reflected in man, and her female characters are its victims. In "Squeaker's Mate" the title character, paralyzed by a falling tree while doing the work of a man, must endure the neglect of her husband and the arrival of his new woman. In "The Chosen Vessel," a young woman, left alone by her cruel husband, barricades herself and her child against a swagman trying to force entry into her hut. Mistaking the sound of horses' hooves for possible salvation she escapes, only to be raped and murdered by her attacker. Like Lawson, Baynton uses the short story form to create vivid sketches of the Australian outback and its community, but her emphasis is on the way in which women are oppressed within that culture, thereby subverting the idealized images of the bush that were current in the *Bulletin* at the time.

Other writers who enjoyed considerable popularity during the period were the pseudonymous Price Warung and Steele Rudd. Price Warung, the pseudonym of William Astley, was the author of almost a hundred stories about the "System"—his term for the structures that enforced the convict system. Although he wrote after the period of transportation had ended (his first collection of stories was published by the *Bulletin* in 1892), his stories vividly and melodramatically reconstruct the brutality and evil of the convict period. Steele Rudd was the pen name used by Arthur Hoey Davis, a prolific story writer and playwright whose work first appeared in 1895. His famous Rudd family sketches, centering on "Dad and Dave," first appeared in the collection *On Our Selection!*, published by the *Bulletin* in 1899. Unlike Astley's visions of Hell, Davis's stories are comedies of defeat. His characters are none too bright, and their attempts to make a living from a harsh rural environment are both comic and slightly pathetic. Davis adopted the realist mode of Lawson's stories and contributed to the development of the archetypal Australian character, the laconic and stoic bushman. While the stories of Astley and Davis might appear to be completely different in style, they both associated the short story as a form with particularly Australian narratives.

THE 1920'S AND THE 1930'S

While the 1920's and 1930's did not produce a short fiction of the same national significance as that of the earlier period, there are a number of writers who published stories during this period that contributed importantly to the development of Australian short fiction: Henry Handel Richardson, Vance Palmer, Frank Dalby Davison, Marjorie Barnard, Christina Stead, and Katherine Susannah Prichard. While the emphasis in stories from the 1920's to the 1950's continued to be on nature, the idea of the story as just a yarn had given way to a desire to document and expose. Although the bulk of short fiction was written by men and had a rural focus, many of the most interesting stories of the period were written by women and focus on what O'Connor has called the "submerged population" of women and of disenfranchised female voices and on reinterpreting romantic conventions. Some of the most powerful of Richardson's stories, collected as *The End of a Childhood and Other Stories* (1934), focus on female characters approaching and in fear of sexual maturity, while Stead's much anthologized "My Friend, Lafe Tilly" and "A Harmless Affair" take an unconventional and critical approach to romantic love, passion, and marriage. Marjorie Barnard's evocative "The Persimmon Tree" belongs in this period as well, signaling the influence of modernism on the development of the Australian short story.

There was a second flowering of the short story during the postwar years. This was in large part facilitated by the development of a number of new journals: *Southerly*, *Meanjin*, *Angry Penguins*, and *Coast to Coast*. The postwar years were a period of national reevaluation, and the stories of this period move away from a preoccupation with the conquest of the landscape to a more internal examination of personality and relationships. As Vance Palmer stated in his introduction to the 1944 edition of *Coast to Coast:* "Nowadays a short story may be a dream, a dialogue, a study of character, a poetic reverie; anything that has a certain unity and the movement of life."

Social realist writers like Gavin Casey and John Morrison adopted the colloquial masculine narrative style of the traditional Lawson story, but their stories suggest the problems of communication. In Casey's "Short-Shift Saturday" the narrator can communicate easily with his mate but not with his wife, and the story ends (as does "The Last Night") with a missed opportunity for unity and understanding. These stories, like Morrison's frequently anthologized "The Incense-Burner," may not be about Australia in the way of a *Bulletin* story—with the landscape in the foreground—but they are vitally concerned with their place in that tradition. There is a sense that these writers are filling the gaps in the Lawson tradition; maintaining a masculine perspective while allowing their characters a greater introspection and emotional depth.

The realist stories of these writers and others such as Alan Marshall are matched during this period by an increase in the modernist influence on the short story in the work of writers such as Peter Cowan, Hal Porter, Dal Stivens, and Patrick White. Their stories indicate an increase in the confidence of Australian literature during this period which enabled writers to overturn Lawson's "bush realism" and adopt international styles without feeling that they would jeopardize or subsume local literary development. Stivens's "The Man Who Bowled Victor Trumper," for example, gives the Australian tall tale a modernist, fabulist dimension. White's "Clay" begins as social realism but ends with a sense of dreamlike distortion.

The 1960's and the 1970's

The late 1960's and early 1970's are often referred to as the renaissance of the short story in Australian literary historiography. Like the 1890's and the postwar years, this period was one of national self-examination and change. The late 1960's was marked by opposition to Australia's involvement in the Vietnam War, while at the same time attention was directed toward the United States and experimentation in American and South American literature. In the 1970's an increase in government subsidies to the arts made writing economically viable, while changes to censorship and pornography laws lifted restrictions on the publication of radical and controversial literature. Interestingly, the "new writing" of this period is confined to short fiction, indicating not only the primary role of the short story in the development of Australian literature but also the way in which short prose narrative lends itself to experimentation and reinvention. The writers of the period—in particular Frank Moorhouse, Michael Wilding, Murray Bail, Peter Carey, and Morris Lurie—built on the revolutionary foundations laid by Hal Porter and Patrick White, rejecting the Lawson tradition and nationalist preoccupations of the past and adopting American styles. They turned away from the rural environment and concentrated instead on urban settings, while at the same time rejecting the social realism and well-made story of the 1940's and 1950's. Their use of the short story can also be read as an ironic comment on the continued search for "the great Australian novel."

The "new" fiction is defined by its use of fantasy and surrealism, the breakdown of linear narrative, authorial self-consciousness and metafiction, and the exploration of the relationship between language and experience. In Bail's "Zoellner's Definition," a character sketch is broken up under headings—"man," "countenance," "age"—to suggest the limitations of description and of words. In Carey's famous "American Dreams" a small town is overrun with American tourists when one of its residents builds a model of the town that reveals its secrets. Not only does art reflect life, but also the model illustrates and mocks the way in which the people of the town look constantly toward America for entertainment, for culture, for "reality." This is a comment on the "cultural cringe"—the turn toward European and American culture and away from Australia's own—and a reflection of the forces that have influenced the development of the Australian literary identity.

The 1980's and the 1990's

In the 1980's and 1990's, development in the short story was marked by the writing of women, migrant writers, and aboriginal writers. To paraphrase O'Connor, "submerged populations" were finding their voices resonating clearly in the form of the short prose narrative. By the late 1970's women's writing was becoming more visible and more popular. Writers such as Elizabeth Jolley, Helen Garner, and Thea Astley were increasingly acclaimed for their stories as well as their novels. Each of these writers became vitally concerned with issues surrounding gender and power and quite literally the place of women within Australian society, from Helen Garner's overtly feminist stories set in the bohemia of 1970's Melbourne to Astley's acerbic stories—often told from a male point of view—about north Queensland and its stagnating communities of hippies and losers.

In the 1980's there was a modest explosion in the publication of women's writing and particularly anthologies of short stories by women. Stories by Olga Masters, Marion Halligan, Janette Turner Hospital, and Beverley Farmer were also included in anthologies of Australian short stories as emblematic of the current condition of the short story. There is a movement in these narratives back to realism after the surrealism of the early 1970's, but this is realism from a female perspective. Farmer, like Garner, is conscious of the need to bear witness to the lives of women. In the title story of her 1985 collection *Home Time* she suggests that men are fundamentally violent and that love cannot be trusted, themes disturbingly reminiscent of Baynton's stories written almost a century earlier. In Hospital's short stories she grapples with the difficulty of inserting the voices of women into a male-dominated literary history, just as she struggles to describe the intensity of the northern landscape of Australia. Astley and Hospital signal the use of the short story to express a particularly regional as well as female and feminist narrative.

Judah Waten is considered to be the first to write "from the inside" about non-English-speaking migrants in Australia. His autobiographical short-story cycle, *Alien Son* was published in 1952, and the final story, "The Mother," has been a staple of every self-respecting short-story anthology since. In this story the son of a Russian Jewish migrant family describes his non-English speaking, Eurocentric mother, and in doing so he articulates the interrelationship between foreignness and familiarity which characterizes both Australia and the "old country"—the inevitable split or hybridity of identity that can be a source of creativity (the stories that Waten tells) as well as of trauma or dislocation. More recent writers have explored this split in a structural way, using the experimental potential of the short story to transform and reinvent their adopted language of English and its narrative forms. Vicki Viidikas and Ania Walwicz are interested in finding new ways of expressing dislocation and alienation. Walwicz's style is particularly radical: Her unpunctuated pieces, such as "Australia" and "red sails," with their insistent, broken English and angry tone, offer a vision of Australia which is frightening, incomprehensible, and alien.

The aboriginal writer occupies a less privileged position in the culture than the Maori writer does in New Zealand. While aboriginals appear in the history of the short story in Australia, it has largely been as objects in colonial adventure stories that stressed the exoticism of the location. It was not until 1972 that the first collection of stories by an aboriginal writer appeared: Oodgeroo Noonuccal's collection for children, *Stradbroke Dreamtime*. The first collection of adult stories was Archie Weller's *Going Home* (1986). Despite Henrietta Drake-Brockman's assertion that the Australian short story can trace its roots to aboriginal oral narrative, the shape of aboriginal narrative does not seem to sit easily with short-story conventions, or perhaps it does not sit easily with publishing conventions. It was only in the 1980's, with the publication and popularity of fictive autobiographies and stories by aboriginal writers (and particularly female aboriginal writers, such as Sally Morgan and Ruby Langford Ginibi) that a market for such work was identified. Recent anthologies, such as *Paperbark: A Collection of Black Australian Writings* (1990) have been central to the recognition of aboriginal writing and have highlighted the distinctive use of forms associated with orality—such as storytelling and transcription—to disrupt and expand the conventional structure of the short narrative.

Contemporary Australian writers recognize the subversive potential of the short story. They are reacting against what has gone before, much as the writers of the *Bulletin* rejected the nineteenth century novel in their desire to develop a style definitive of the Australian literary identity. The realist stories of the 1940's and 1950's in turn altered the tradition to incorporate a greater sense of interiority and self-analysis. Then the "new" fiction of the 1960's and 1970's reacted against both the Lawsonian bush tradition and the realism of the postwar years, turning to stylistic experimentation and postmodernism. The reactive nature of the short story in Australian literary history is reflected in number of stories directly referring to "The Drover's Wife": Moorhouse's 1985 story, which also responds to Bail's 1975 story; Barbara Jefferis's story, written in 1980, which responds both to the Lawson story and to Baynton's "The Chosen Vessel" (as does Helen Garner's "What We Say"). In each case the writer is inserting a hitherto silenced or ignored narrative, but by invoking Lawson's story as symbolic of the Australian literary tradition, the writers are placing themselves and their stories within the continuum of Australian prose writing, dominated and defined by the short story.

The Short Story in New Zealand

The dominance of the short story in the development of prose literature in New Zealand is even more marked than it is in Australia. As Clare Hanson observes, the short story "seems to be the mode preferred by those writers who are not writing from within a fixed and stable cultural framework." The short story, with its brevity and ellipses, captures the uncertainties in national cultural identity. For New Zealand the difficulty of national self-definition is arguably greater than it is for Australia; the country must not only define itself against the colonizer Britain and increasingly America but also assert its cultural independence from Australia, looming large off its west coast.

Stories from the colonial period are largely tales and yarns. Writers such as Lady Barker, G. Born Lancaster, and Blanche Baughan are concerned primarily with documenting the new country. This documentary zeal was intended for a foreign audience at "home" in England, but it was also a way of making sense of a new and alien space. The desire to assert a unique literary voice strengthened in the late nineteenth century. As in Australia, this bid for literary identity was facilitated by a lively magazine culture. In particular, *Zealandia* was established by William Freeman in 1889 as a "distinctively national literary magazine." To foster the development of New Zealand literature he ensured that his contributors were all local and the magazine included a complete tale and an article descriptive of a part of New Zealand in each issue. In that way, the magazine perpetuated the documentary emphasis within the burgeoning literature and not only established the short story as a way to describe New Zealand but also made it a viable genre economically for local writers.

Katherine Mansfield

Katherine Mansfield is the writer who is most frequently associated with New Zealand and the short story, at least in the rest of the world. At the same time, there are problems associated with defining her as a New Zealand writer: Her stories are deeply imbued with the influence of European modernism and symbolism and the places she inhabited as an expatriate. Nevertheless, a large proportion (almost half) of her stories are set in New Zealand, in particular her two short-story sequences focusing on the Burnells and the Sheridans and including the famous "Prelude," "At the Bay," "The Doll's House," "The Garden-Party," and "Her First Ball." Mansfield published her first six stories in the New Zealand journals *Triad* and *The Native Companion*, but she left permanently for England in July, 1908. All her later New Zealand stories are written from memory and carry the patina conferred by distance and nostalgia. It is tempting to see in these stories and, indeed, in the gaps and ellipses in Mansfield's narrative style, references to the distant motherland and the repository of her childhood memories. Her New Zealand stories are remarkable for her evocative representation of space, emptiness, and silence, contrasting markedly with her representations of Europe in stories such as "The Daughters of the Late Colonel" and "Miss Brill" and indicating that New Zealand occupied a particular aesthetic and emotional place in her fiction.

At the same time, however, Mansfield's stories reveal her memories of a colonial, constrained, and class-bound culture—particularly "The Doll's House"—suggesting that distance did generate not only a romantic nostalgia but also a critical and possibly superior eye. Despite the sense of space and silence, there is also a great deal of human movement in these stories. In "Prelude" the Burnells are moving house, in "At the Bay" they are on holiday; "The Garden-Party" begins with the flurry of party preparations and ends with death. The representation of change and flux in these stories indicates that Mansfield's attitude to New Zealand was complex and ambivalent. There is a strong sense that she did not feel a strong cultural identification with her childhood home, and even her memories are tinged with the tone of impermanence and dislocation that marks the rest of her fiction.

Mansfield's stories brought literary modernism to New Zealand. Her emphasis on a disenfranchised community—she gave voice to women and children for whom she believed preexisting conventions did not speak—is a comment on her position as a colonial as well as a woman writer. Her gift for fragmentation, which enables her to "pronounce silence" and articulate what is inarticulate, transformed the short story (in New Zealand and elsewhere) from a documentary sketch or yarn to a complex evocation of a moment of revelation: what Nadine Gordimer has termed so elegantly the "flash of fireflies."

Frank Sargeson

Mansfield had an enduring impact on the development of the short story in English, but it is Frank Sargeson who is responsible for making the short story the paradigmatic New Zealand form, as it is so frequently described. His stories, peopled with laconic, working-class, rural men and using a vernacular style, first appeared in the journal *Tomorrow* in 1935 and dominated the development of the short story for decades. His stories include political comment—his characterization of New Zealand as puritanical and narrow-minded—but also focus on the difficulty of communication and the need to find a particularly distinctive national form of language (language which has many interesting similarities with the distinctively Australian language of Lawson's stories). Interestingly, in capturing the language of his characters, Sargeson utilizes a number of the techniques that Mansfield also uses: ellipsis and gaps, open-endedness. Like Mansfield, Sargeson frames and articulates silence, but while she does so to give voice to a silenced female population, the "submerged population" of Sargeson's stories is one of pakeha men, whose experience, he suggests, is not expressed through existing narrative structures.

In stories such as the early "Conversation with My Uncle" his use of an impoverished and repetitive idiom and the apparent banality of his subject matter only thinly disguises his preoccupation with identity: national identity, economic and social identity, and gender identity. In "The Making of a New Zealander" Sargeson juxtaposes his "ordinary New Zealand" narrator with Dalmation migrants in order to destabilize any certainty about what being a New Zealander means. In "The Hole That Jack Dug" a simple narrative about the speaker's friend Jack gives way to a far more complex discussion about the constraints and limitations of ordinary social relationships and a strong undercurrent of homosexual tension. Sargeson's subject matter and style have been deeply influential, ensuring that the focus of the New Zealand short story shifted to the world of men and in particular the pakeha, who inhabits a masculine, poor, and rural environment.

The many followers of the Sargesonian short story—such as A. P. Gaskell, G. R. Gilbert, Dan Davin, James Courage, O. E. Middleton, and Roderick Finlayson—have tended to mimic Sargeson's style as if he were a straightforward realist writer. In the best of these stories, one can see the effectiveness of Sargeson's minimalist and laconic language. In Davin's "Coming and Going" and "The Quiet One," for example, he uses silence and noncommunication to convey the pathos of the lives of isolated men. However, rather than challenge assumptions about New Zealand identity, as Sargeson does, these writers have accepted the community of his stories as "real," and likewise the language they use is presented as naturalistic rather than stylized, telling rather than revealing the truth. The working class, male, vernacular tradition spawned by Sargeson and entrenched by these writers has dominated the development of the New Zealand short story and contributed to the sense of a divided tradition: Mansfield versus Sargeson.

Janet Frame

The most significant writers of the short story after Sargeson are Janet Frame and Maurice Duggan. While both writers display the influence of the previous writers, they are more overtly engaged in manipulating language and short-story structure. Frame's first collection, *The Lagoon*, was published in 1951. These early stories illustrate her fascination with problems of meaning. She experiments with words and with reality until everything in her stories is uncertain, both familiar and unfamiliar, constantly changing and yet carrying the threat of impermanence. In her stories she creates an unlikely balance between realism and antirealism—the "penetration of the ordinary by the extraordinary" that characterizes Frame's portrayal of normality. Like Mansfield, Frame's stories—and particularly those in her first collection—evoke the voices of children and other lonely and isolated characters such as patients in psychiatric institutions (the publication of this collection freed Frame from a psychiatric hospital and a threatened leucotomy). Frame's stories give voice to the silence surrounding these characters and to their perceptions and understanding; this is reflected in her rejection of formal, official narrative language. A number of her stories are also about writing stories and, by extension, about the meaning and nature of storytelling. In "Jan Godfrey" story writing and personal identity are entwined. The confusion regarding the narrator's identity (is she Alison Hendry or Jan Godfrey or are they merely names that carry no significance?) is matched by confusion surrounding the nature of the story itself. In the final story in the collection, "My Last Story," Frame rejects the conventional way of telling stories, "I don't like putting he said she said he did she did," signaling her movement away from traditional narrative forms and representations of reality.

Maurice Duggan

Like Frame, Maurice Duggan manipulates the structure of the story and of language. As W. H. New writes, Duggan rejects "the realm of tight-lipped functional language." In "Along Rideout Road That Summer"—his most famous and commonly anthologized story—Duggan writes within and out of the Sargeson tradition of the laconic character, and he is clearly the inheritor of Sargeson's use of irony. Buster O'Leary's conversation with Fanny Hohepa is a parody of inarticulacy, but Buster's internal monologues are vivid, learned, and deeply intertextual. The problem is connection; there is no one with whom he can communicate, and so at the heart of the story is the split between the fictional world of Buster's narrative and the "real" world of the story that he is narrating. The metafictional aspect of Duggan's fiction, a feature also of Frame's stories, indicates the extent to which both writers grapple directly with storytelling and narrative point of view.

The stories of Frame and Duggan indicate a movement away from particular conventions of the New Zealand short story, but there is a common theme connecting them to Mansfield and Sargeson: the difficulty of communication associated with a sense of individual and cultural isolation and evocatively expressed in the short story with its gaps and silences. There is also a linkage between the stories of Frame and Duggan and those of more recent postmodern writers such as Russell Haley, Ian Wedde, Michael Gifkins, and John Cranna. Haley's playful distortions of narrative integrity and linearity in "Barbados—a Love Story," and Gifkins's matter-of-fact treatment of the mysterious and sinister in "After the Revolution" owe a great deal to the way in which Frame and Duggan moved the New Zealand short story away from the documentary sketch. The postmodern stories of the 1970's and 1980's (possibly influenced by the short-story renaissance in Australia at much the same time) exist alongside more conventional stories by writers such as Owen Marshall, Maurice Shadbolt, and Vincent O'Sullivan. The coexistence of the work of all these writers indicates a greater breadth within the short story and also indicates the dominance of the form by male pakeha writers.

Maori characters appeared in short stories during the colonial period. In Alfred Grace's *Maoriland Stories* (1895) and *Tales of a Dying Race* (1901) the Maori are portrayed in a sympathetic light, and Grace values their freedom from pakeha conventionalism and puritanism, but the stories nevertheless assert the superiority of pakeha culture. The Maori characters in these stories are childlike and mischievous, objects of fascination and remnants of a dying race. In Roderick Finlayson's stories the Maori are also presented as a dying race. Finlayson uses Maori/English idiomatic expressions and avoids sentimentalizing or reducing his characters. In "The Totara Tree," there is no sense of the superiority of one race over another. However, in his characterizations there is still a suggestion of the appropriation of one culture for the narrative purposes of the other.

The 1950's

In the 1950's the first stories in English by a Maori writer, J. C. Sturm, were published in literary periodicals. *Te Ao Hou*, the "Maori magazine," was established in 1952 with the express purpose of encouraging Maori writers and artists to produce texts that generate and affirm a positive collective identity among the magazine's readers and the community in general. This magazine, and its successors *Te Kaea*, *Te Maori*, and *Tu Tangata* became the publishing forum for new Maori writing. While the emphasis in the early stories was to increase the awareness of the reality of Maori life among the reading public, more recent stories by writers such as Patricia Grace, Witi Ihimaera, and Keri Hulme have revealed a desire to experiment with the conventions of the short-story narrative. Contemporary Maori writers combine English and Maori words to represent a cultural and linguistic fusion and, in some cases, deliberately to challenge the expectations of the pakeha reader. The construction of character is particularly important in the stories of Grace and Ihimaera. Grace's positive images of Maori women in stories such as "Between Earth and Sky"—a celebration of female fertility and Maori identity—are in response to their construction in pakeha literature as sexual objects. Similarly, Ihimaera's extended families and his description of the continuity of tribal life are ways of using a European literary form to express alternative experiences; in "A Game of Cards" Ihimaera's focus is on tribal unity and the dignity of his elderly Maori characters.

The 1960's

The 1960's was also a period of growth in the publication of migrant writers in New Zealand. Writers such as Amelia Batistich, Renato Amato, and Yvonne du Fresne have added their voices to the other writers who are adapting the traditional Sargesonian short story to their own ends. Like the work of the Maori writers who appeared at the same time (and the multicultural writers emerging in Australia), the presence of these narratives has highlighted and attempted to explode the myth of racial and cultural homogeneity circulating in New Zealand from the colonial period. The stories of these writers also offer a pluralistic approach to narrative within what has essentially been—with the Mansfield/Sargeson split—a binary tradition. In du Fresne's "The Morning Talk," Astrid's retelling of the myths of her family's Danish roots mingles with the reality of contemporary New Zealand, momentarily creating harmony in the divided and fractious classroom.

The more recent developments in the short story in New Zealand, as in Australia, can be illustrated by the large increase in the publication of short-story anthologies by women. Unlike the male pakeha writers, who have been drawn to postmodern narrative experimentation, recent female writers have tended to adopt a form of social realism concerned with investigating the female condition and their physical and emotional situation. Not surprisingly, many of their stories focus on the domestic sphere and the social roles women perform. Fiona Kidman's "The Tennis Player," Fiona Farrell's "The Gift," and Shonagh Koea's "Wednesdays," for example, are concerned with female power and self-definition.

However, the realist tendency within contemporary women's short fiction is being challenged by a more playful and experimental approach to narrative. Barbara Anderson's "Up the River with Mrs Gallant" uses a stream of dialogue, reported in all its banality and only briefly interspersed with description, to hint at the boredom and dissatisfaction of conventional relationships. Anne Kennedy's wonderfully whimsical story about angels, "An Angel Entertains Theatricals" and Emily Perkins's "Not Her Real Name" use metafiction and intertextuality to expand the conventional parameters of the short story. Yet many of the techniques they use are familiar: open-endedness, fragmentation, and irony. Indeed, while contemporary writers such as Ihimaera and Grace, du Fresne, Anderson and Kennedy are on one level doing something different, in many ways they are writing within the tradition of the New Zealand short story as it was developed by Mansfield, Sargeson, Duggan, and Frame. All these writers deliberately question and break conventions within their narratives, because they adapt language and structure to suit the particular submerged and silenced lives they wish to illuminate. All have recognized in the short story a form open to rupture and transformation, the best way to write about the silence and isolation that these writers identify in the lives of their characters and in their culture.

Selina Samuels

Bibliography

Bennett, Bruce. "Short Fiction and the Canon: Australia and Canada." *Antipodes* 7, no. 2 (1993): 109-114. A useful introductory essay, concentrating particularly on the "new" writing of the 1960's and 1970's.

Goldsworthy, Kerryn. "Short Fiction." In *The Penguin New Literary History of Australia*, edited by Laurie Hergenhan. Ringwood, Vic.: Penguin Australia, 1988. One of the few essays that covers the development of the short story from the 1890's to the 1980's in detail and with attention paid to the form and its relationship to the development of a national literary identity.

Goodwin, Ken. *A History of Australian Literature*. Basingstoke: Macmillan, 1986. A useful general text that covers the development of the short story from the 1890's to the 1980's, with particular attention paid to the social realist writers of the 1940's and 1950's and the "new" writing of the 1960's and 1970's.

Hadgraft, Cecil, ed. *The Australian Short Story Before Lawson*. Melbourne: Oxford University Press, 1986. A collection of early short stories with a comprehensive and entertaining introduction not only covering the early writing but also touching on the short story of the 1890's.

New, W. H. *Dreams of Speech and Violence: The Art of the Short Story in Canada and New Zealand*. Toronto: University of Toronto Press, 1987. An excellent analysis of the development of the short story and its relationship to the development of a New Zealand national literary identity. Not only does New provide an interesting general discussion of particular writers but also he provides close readings of stories by Katherine Mansfield, Frank Sargeson, Patricia Grace, and Maurice Duggan. The comparison between the short story in New Zealand and in Canada is interesting.

Wevers, Lydia. "The Short Story." In *The Oxford History of New Zealand Literature*, edited by Terry Sturm. Auckland: Oxford University Press, 1991. An excellent account of the development of the short story in New Zealand. It carries detailed discussions not only of the development of the form but also of individual writers and particular literary movements.

Williams, Mark. "Introduction: The Cultural Context." In *Leaving the Highway: Six Contemporary New Zealand Novelists*. Auckland: Auckland University Press, 1990. The introduction to this volume has an interesting discussion of New Zealand literary movements and nationalism.

CANADIAN SHORT FICTION

Short fiction was being written in Canada before there was a Canada. At the time of Confederation in 1867, short fiction already filled the magazines of the new country. These early stories, however, differed from the modern short story, often being closer in form and content to other prose genres such as the sketch, anecdote, editorial, and essay—all of which were popular in journals such as *The Literary Garland*, Rose-Belford's *Canadian Monthly, National Review*, and *The Week*. Today's definitions of short fiction must be relaxed when one surveys fiction of these earlier times, for the parameters defining what is good short fiction change over time. The sensibility of the late nineteenth century, for example, valued sentiment over realism; much that was then considered excellent writing, appears nauseatingly sweet to the twentieth century reader. When one surveys the past of a genre, one must be aware that one is looking from a particular point of view, that of scholars distanced from the dates and places of publication of the original fiction and necessarily seeing a literary landscape changed from that seen by the original writer, publisher, or even the critic of earlier decades.

Canadian and American short fiction

One feature of the Canadian cultural landscape that the writer of the millennium can see is its nearness to that of its neighbor, the United States. Canadian short fiction shares to some extent the history of the American genre. This survey will begin by establishing some of the basic points at which the two traditions run parallel or even converge. Later some points of divergence will be considered.

In both Canadian and American traditions, short fiction has its roots in sketch and anecdote and in the various prose forms that arose in the nineteenth century for the chronicling of personal experience. In both young countries short fiction found its initial home in magazines, sometimes in exciting, intellectual magazines, but often in cheap weeklies, tabloids, or Sunday-school papers. Not surprisingly, many writers of short fiction had previous or parallel careers as journalists, with the result that the demands of journalism (fact, brevity, popularity, and clarity) shaped early short fiction on both sides of the border. Developments in Canadian short fiction sometimes lagged behind those in American fiction, but in response to some trends, Canadian writers overcame the conservative influence of their colonial status to welcome similar literary innovations. Both Canadian and American short-story traditions, for instance, had strong local-color traditions in the last decades of the nineteenth century; these were regional in origin and very popular. Canada is and was a country divided into distinct regions—for example, the Maritimes, the Eastern Townships of Quebec, Southwestern Ontario, urban Montreal, the Prairie provinces, and so on. Short fiction from and about some of these regions developed just after its appearance south of the border, where writers such as Sarah Orne Jewett, Kate Chopin, and Mary E. Wilkins Freeman began to speak for and about distinct, marginalized parts of the continent in a new realistic voice. Such regional writing marked a stage in the development of the genre of short fiction toward naturalism and realism and has become a continuing, vital feature of Canadian short fiction, whose persistence has exerted a largely conservative influence on the development of the genre as a whole.

As the twentieth century unfolded, the international movement of modernism began to affect the writing of short fiction as well as poetry and the novel. Modernism is one area in the chronicle of North American short fiction where Canadian development temporarily parallels American. The friendship between Ernest Hemingway and Canada's Morley Callaghan was one factor ensuring that the revolution in writing begun by the older Hemingway would spread to the writing of the younger Callaghan. Later developments in short fiction, including the social realism of the 1930's, the minimalist fiction of the 1950's, the postmodern experimentation of the post-World War II era—all these affected both traditions, with the Canadian genre trailing by a few years. The distance between the two cultures closed up, however, in the mid-1960's, when Canadian cultural nationalism surged forward on the creativity of the newly adult baby boomers, and Canada enjoyed a bumper crop of new writers, for whom short fiction was a popular genre.

At the turn of the millennium, both short story traditions existed in a new era of internationalism, in which good writers belong to global, not national traditions. Both story traditions also exhibit strong representation by "niche" writing of various kinds. The publication of short story anthologies containing specialized kinds of subject matter, subject positions, or ideological commitments testifies to the vigor at the margin of the short fiction tradition.

In some respects the Canadian tradition in short fiction does diverge from the American. A major consideration is the presence of an early and continuing separate literature in French existing beside English-Canadian literature. Writers in French Canada (Quebec as well as French-speaking parts of Ontario, Manitoba, and New Brunswick) were producing short pieces as early as the 1830's, although recognizable short fiction really began with the Abbé Henri-Raymond Casgrain in the 1860's. Throughout this discussion it is important to remain aware of two traditions whose development is not always parallel. Another difference involves the lesser importance of the tall tale in early Canadian short fiction. When Mark Twain was harnessing the tall tale to create a new American voice in the humorous short tale, the Canadian short story was still in its parlor stage, still interested in morals, conduct, and gentility. The folksy voice of the tall tale never really entered mainstream Canadian short fiction, which vaulted this stage to embrace modernism. Neither did the English-Canadian short story owe much to the American tradition that produced Edgar Allan Poe: the detective, supernatural, or scientifically speculative tale never became popular. Also missing from the Canadian tradition is the contribution of African American storytellers and writers, such as the Americans had in Charles Waddell Chesnutt. Canada's smaller population of free black persons was perhaps not numerous or concentrated enough to establish and express a folk culture whose forms and subject material could influence Canadian short fiction. Both national traditions, however, share input from First Nations writers of short fiction: myth, folklore, and other features of oral story culture have been transformed by writers of various tribal allegiances into a significant factor in the present and future course of short fiction.

Early examples of short fiction in British North America did include humor, such as the satirical and descriptive sketches in Thomas Chandler Haliburton's Sam Slick stories. Appearing in *The Novascotian* between 1826 and 1835, the Sam Slick anecdotes demonstrate their author's vivid grasp of the society and politics of the Eastern seaboard and his talent for salty dialect, satirical portraiture, and national stereotypes. Sam Slick became for a time synonymous with a type of North American humor, and the collection *The Clockmaker: Or, The Sayings and Doings of Samuel Slick of Slickville* (1836) was enormously popular. Similar brief humorous pieces occur in the *Letters of Mephibosheth Stepsure* (1862) by Thomas McCulloch, whose original appearance in the *Acadian Recorder* (1821) make them among the earliest examples of Canadian short fiction. Like Haliburton, McCulloch relied on nuggets of anecdote, broad dialect effects, national stereotypes, and local political events for his comic effects.

The ancestry of nonhumorous short fiction in Canada begins in the pages of the early journals of Ontario and the Maritime provinces. Here one finds examples of short prose narratives, primarily realistic, whose plots endeavor to show character developed through events. Early stories in this mode often took as their focus courtship and marriage and maintained a tone of moral instruction. Stories by Mary Anne Sadlier, Harriet Cheney, and Eliza Lanesford Cushing often had European settings or generalized pastoral surroundings. New Brunswick's May Agnes Fleming published her early stories in the large magazines south of the border and went on to fame as a novelist. One writer whose career predates the Confederation and whose work is Canadian in setting, subject, and publication, is Rosanna Leprohon of Montreal. Her best story, "Alice Sydenham's First Ball," appearing first in the *Literary Garland* in 1849, transfers the Cinderella story to a contemporary ballroom, while teaching the folly of vanity and social pretension. Not a fairy tale despite its similar motifs, the story is handled with delicate irony; Leprohon's narrator enters into a conspiracy with the reader to wink at convention even while outwardly observing its dictates. This sophisticated, layered narrative technique was rare in early magazine fiction and sets Leprohon apart from other writers such as Susanna Moodie or Mary Herbert, both of whom were editors as well as writers of genteel moral fiction. Collections of short fiction published before 1900 tended to advertise their content as "tales": for example, Sadlier's *Tales of the Olden Times: A Collection of European Traditions* (1845), or a later book with local settings, *Acorn Leaves: A Series of Canadian Tales* (1873), by Nell Gwynne. Inexpertly edited, this volume contains one gem: "Miss Vandyke," which tells a realistic story of a young girl negotiating the boundary of puberty. Boggs's Nora chooses between possible female roles, including the traditional ones of suffering motherhood, bitter spinsterhood, and femme fatale, and arrives, after a sort illness, on the far shores of early adulthood, with the more realistic potential roles of teacher, mother, and sister clearly delineated.

The 1880's and the 1890's

It was not before the late 1880's and 1890's that good, nonhumorous short fiction began to appear in any quantity. The 1860's and 1870's belonged to the Sunday-school story and the women's magazine story, distinguished by their prominent didacticism and formulaic endings. Examples include Mary Herbert's "Light in The Darkness: A Sketch from Life," and May Agnes Fleming's "My Folly." Later, however, the decade of the "new" woman produced two good Canadian story writers: Sara Jeannette Duncan and Susie Frances Harrison, both of whom received recognition in literary circles in America as well as in Canada. Duncan, a well-traveled journalist, brought new ideas, both thematic and technical, to short fiction. Harrison, also a poet, experimented with narrative forms in her short fiction, with new settings, both generalized and local, and with the new ethos of the liberated woman, depicted independently of conventional roles of wife and mother (for example, "The Gilded Hammock"). In *Crowded Out! and Other Sketches* (1886), Harrison uses a frame story, in which a male narrator complains of being crowded out, perhaps indicating her own sense of the silencing of the woman's voice in literature, even in her own collection. From the same era comes Duncan, better known for her novels in the Jamesian international style. Like many post-Confederation story writers, Duncan exploited the new mobility of journalists by traveling, observing, and writing about experiences beyond the conventional women's sphere. Stories such as "A Mother in India" or "The Pool in the Desert" show more developed characterization than Harrison's, with more room for psychological roundness and a fine touch in depicting one of her favorite subjects: the hypocrisies of Anglo-Indian society.

Canada's main contribution to the development of short fiction at the beginning of the nineteenth century was the animal story. Neither the traditional, allegorized beast fable nor the sentimental pet story, this new naturalistic fiction depicting animals in their habitats drew on the post-Darwinian fascination with evolution. Sir Charles G. D. Roberts, a New Brunswick man of letters, wrote the first Canadian story in this genre—"Do Seek Their Meat from God." Balancing the lives of panther cubs against the life of a human child, Roberts's story takes a dispassionate stance which was revolutionary in its day. His collections of animal stories include *Earth's Enigmas: A Volume of Stories* (1896), *The Kindred of the Wild: A Book of Animal Life* (1902), and *The Watchers of the Trails: A Book of Animal Life* (1904). Another writer whose short fiction explores animal themes was Ernest Thompson Seton. Like many writers of this time, British born Seton lived in Ontario, where he became a skilled amateur naturalist and painter of animal subjects. His interest in the birds and small animals of Ontario, Manitoba, and New Mexico led to his first book of animal stories, *Wild Animals I Have Known* (1898), which uses American as well as Canadian animals and settings. Seton made his narrators into spokespersons for a varied palette of animals including wolves, crows, partridges, and rabbits, about all of whom Seton had made detailed observations. Seton saw himself as a mediator and translator of animal reality into human idiom, and his stories, including the famous wolf-hunting story "Lobo, the King of Currumpaw," often depend on anthropomorphic effects such as sentimental or heroic action.

In the 1890's popular short fiction continued to be written to various formulaic patterns of romance by Gilbert Parker, Edward William Thomson, and Alexander Fraser and, among women writers, by Isabella Valancy Crawford, Pauline Johnson, Lucy Maud Montgomery, and Nellie McClung. Each of these writers specialized in one area of experience, for instance, Johnson in the Native Canadian identity, Fraser in animal stories, Montgomery in comic analyses of Prince Edward Island society, and McClung in didactic temperance themes in prairie settings.

A writer less popular in his time but more esteemed now is Duncan Campbell Scott, whose *In the Village of Viger* (1896) has been chosen by W. H. New as marking a turning point in the history of Canadian short fiction. Its ten stories are reminiscent of the localized naturalism of the stories of Jewett to the south. Some of Scott's brief pictures of village tragedy and triumph nevertheless hark back to older models, Poe, for instance, or the French writers of the fabliau. Despite their village setting and Quebec location, Scott's stories can be seen as introducing a new era in Canadian short fiction, because they eschew nostalgia and folklore and concentrate instead on compressed studies of people and social structures of a small community at a time of change. Scott excelled his contemporaries in the depiction of character, especially of complex and abnormal psychological states. His best stories recall those of the American writer, Ambrose Bierce, and like his, foreshadow the changes that modernism would soon bring to fiction.

The early 1900's

Immediately after the turn of the century, humor was a dominant strain in Canadian short fiction. Stephen Leacock, an economics professor from Orillia, Ontario, began producing brief sketches, often monologues by a confident but misguided citizen, bent on misunderstanding the institutions of the new country and century. *Literary Lapses* (1910) contains the often-anthologized masterpiece "My Financial Career," which pits a befuddled little man of the twentieth century against the banking establishment of urban Canada. Shortly after, Leacock's *Sunshine Sketches of a Little Town* (1912), a collection of linked sketches unified by its setting, turned a gently satirical eye on the foibles of small-town Canada, while *Arcadian Adventures with the Idle Rich* (1914) displayed, in a connected series of stories, his criticism of an academic, urban world. Leacock epitomizes a movement in Canadian literature toward the subject of the small town, the voice of the little man, and a mood of sunny optimism mitigated by a quietly deprecating self-critical humor. Leacock's brand of light satire survives in the short fiction of contemporary writers such as Stuart McLean and Bill Richardson. Much recent humorous fiction originates from Canadian Broadcasting Corporation radio scripts, after the fashion of the mid-century classics, W. O Mitchell's Jake and the Kid stories. These were collected in 1961 and again twenty-eight years later (*According to Jake and the Kid*) in a volume which won the Stephen Leacock Award for Humor.

By the 1920's, short fiction moved in the new direction indicated by the fresh currents of modernism. Young writers such as Raymond Knister set out to get the country into and the parlor out of their fiction and to capture the mind in motion. Short fiction, like all literature in Canada at this time, was still intensely regional in flavor. However, Knister and Callaghan began to be published abroad; early stories of both writers appeared in Paris magazines. Although Knister died before he could produce a major body of work, Callaghan emerged into international prominence. His stories, though set in Toronto, were accepted as part of a new postwar literary movement. Callaghan is the premier short-story writer of the 1920's, the O. Henry of Canadian literature. The comparison with O. Henry may be misleading, as Callaghan is a sophisticated writer, with serious literary aims and complex philosophical positions. Like Henry, however, he was brief, pithy, and popular. He wrote of the urban world and of a new generation which worked in the factories of industrialized North America and found love in its streets and bars. Some of Callaghan's stories masquerade as American, but in his best he makes the landmarks of Toronto into the symbolic landscape of morally significant lives. In stories such as "A Girl with Ambition" and "A Predicament," Callaghan chronicles the struggle of the lower middle class to make money, keep respectable, and maintain a sense of themselves as moral agents in a chaotic modern world. Callaghan flirted with the symmetrical-twist action of surprise endings—for example, in "A Cap for Steve"—but never exalted coincidence or crossed lives as O. Henry did. Often compared with Hemingway, whose friend he became at the *Toronto Star* in the early 1920's, Callaghan has been overshadowed by the influential stylistic achievements of the better-known American. Hemingway spoke to and for the Lost Generation, whereas Callaghan, anchored by his Catholic faith in a country which found rather than lost itself in World War I, gives his characters the dignity of a meaningful universe, almost allegorical, in which to work out their minor daily dramas of moral action. Callaghan chooses closure over Hemingway's hanging endings, a landscape immanent with meaning rather than the blank hills like white elephants and a universe that substitutes willed human action for Hemingway's "nada."

Female modernist writers of short fiction include Jessie Sime, whose collection, *Sister Woman* (1919) combines urban realism with a nascent feminism that has recently brought renewed interest in her short fiction, despite the sentimentality of some stories. L. M. Montgomery, many of whose stories date from this period, seldom departs from the premodernist mode; collections such as *Further Chronicles of Avonlea* (1920) are remarkable for their warmth of character and setting, rather than for any narrative experiment.

Modernism in French Canadian short fiction had a later onset, for reasons that are not quite clear, but may have to do with a certain cultural isolation of this, the major non-English language group in North America. Short fiction in Quebec remained fascinated with the gothic and supernatural folktale well into the twentieth century, and many collections seem closer to folklore, as writers retained allegiance to the conte and fabliau of the European tradition. In so doing they created for Quebec a strong sense of its cultural past as a rural people. Major modernist writers in French include Yves Thériault (whose multiple collections cross three decades), Alain Grandbois, and Anne Hébert. Even writers who adapted some modernist techniques of point of view, however, still often used them to interpret older, semigothic subjects, as did Hébert in *Le Torrent* (1950). The achievements of Canadian short fiction were summed up by the appearance in 1928 of the first Canadian short-story anthology, *Canadian Short Stories*, edited by Raymond Knister, and published in Canada by Macmillan.

The mid-1900's

The middle decades of the twentieth century in Canadian short fiction were dominated by realism, in particular by the prairie realism of Frederick Philip Grove, Sinclair Ross, and W. O. Mitchell. Grove's stories of heroic battle with land and climate in *Over Prairie Trails* (1922) have a Manitoban setting, while Ross's more varied and human depictions of the difficulties of farm life are set farther west, on the Saskatchewan prairie. Both Ross and Grove set stylistic standards for natural description and content standards for gritty realism; together they laid to rest any lingering myth of the bountiful prairie farm. Another prairie writer however, W. O Mitchell, brought humor and a lively speaking voice to the realistic prairie story, while Margaret Laurence's later stories captured life in the fictional Manitoban prairie town of Manawaka. The linked stories in her collection *A Bird in the House* (1970) provide one of the best places to begin an acquaintance with Canadian short fiction.

An urban realism flourished too at this period, notably in the short fiction of Mordecai Richler, whose stories of a Jewish boyhood in Montreal are still often anthologized. On the West coast, Ethel Wilson wrote with sophisticated irony of the lives of middle-class people, avoiding a self-conscious Canadianness, while crafting exquisite dialogue and set pieces of natural description.

Several Canadian writers of midcentury began to write their short fiction both from and about life overseas. Europe was the chosen home of Mavis Gallant, whose stories of exile and alienation anatomized the clash between cultures and generations from Paris, through the Riviera to Eastern Europe. Residing in Paris, Gallant wrote prolifically, publishing most of her stories in *The New Yorker.* Her first collection, *The Other Paris* (1956) shows her command of an ironic, detached tone, her eagle eye for hypocrisies of language and action, and her uncompromising way with social and literary falsity. Several subsequent titles, *My Heart Is Broken: Eight Stories and a Short Novel* (1964), *The End of the World and Other Stories* (1974), *The Pegnitz Junction: A Novella and Five Short Stories* (1973), *From the Fifteenth District: A Novella and Eight Short Stories* (1979), and *Overhead in a Balloon: Stories of Paris* (1985), display Gallant's mastery of both very short stories (fifteen hundred words) and the longer genre of the novella. *Home Truths: Selected Canadian Stories* (1981), a Governor General's Award winner, brings Gallant's subject back to Canada. It contains a group of linked stories which are among her very best; the Linnet Muir stories tell of the growth to intellectual and artistic independence of a young woman in wartime Montreal. Her eleven collections and *The Collected Stories of Mavis Gallant* (1996) testify to her satirical touch, her fine control of nuance in tone and dialogue which give her stories a polish rare in previous fiction. Her internationalism and her historical perspective are also unusual and contribute to the power of her stories. Also writing from exile was Norman Levine, whose *One Way Ticket* (1961) speaks of the distortions implicit in writing from and about a condition of self-imposed artistic exile. Levine used fragmentary structures, fractured points of view, and a clipped prose style, whether in describing street life in Ottawa or cultural life in the hubs of Europe. His other collections are *Thin Ice* (1979) and *Champagne Barn* (1984).

Gallant became Canada's first international achievement in short fiction since Callaghan, and she was followed promptly by two other talented writers: Alice Munro and Margaret Atwood. Beginning with *Dance of the Happy Shades* (1968), Munro has produced multiple volumes of short fiction, including her *Selected Stories* of 1996. Her short fiction claims a new subject territory (small-town southwestern Ontario from the wrong side of the tracks) and a new narrative approach. Envisioning her fiction spatially, Munro sees her stories as rooms or houses, into which she invites her reader on leisurely narrative tours toward surprising closures. This digressive narrative technique has been a hallmark of her short fiction and is as visible in early stories, such as "How I Met My Husband" or "Something I've Been Meaning to Tell You," as in the title story from her 1998 collection "The Love of a Good Woman." In addition to nonlinear narration, Munro's fiction is also distinguished by its attention to domestic detail, to the small household and toilet objects that deck the lives of her female characters. In her hands, lamps, shoes, hats, potholders, and jelly jars are transformed by a scrutiny both relentless and compassionate into metaphorical keys to character and significance.

Atwood, better known for, first, her poetry and now, her novels, is another writer to emerge at midcentury and to be claimed by feminist readers and scholars. Atwood's stories inherit their enigmatically interior language from her poetry. Stories like "Giving Birth" foreground language itself and, in testing it, examining it for tricks and quicksand, finding it inevitably guilty. This self-consciousness is one feature which allies Atwood's fiction with that of the postmodern writers of the United States. Her fiction merges pop and high culture and seems capable of digesting comics, cartoons, or advertisement copy. A notable feature of her short fiction is her control of indirect interior monologue, as in "The Salt Garden" or "Hairball"; this technique accesses the flow of the character's conscious mind while remaining detached from both character and event. Many Atwood stories are a form of historiographical metafiction; that is, they make use of historical events and personages in such a way as to question the conventional truths of historical storytelling. In this mode Atwood uses both distant events such as the Franklin expedition to the Arctic ("The Age of Lead"), and more recent ones, such as the title event from "Hurricane Hazel." Many of Atwood's stories hover on the edge of the grotesque and offer a black humor that flouts many sacred subjects. In her short prose pieces from *Murder in the Dark* (1983; "Happy Endings," "Women's Novels"), Atwood uses humor to undermine the culture's most treasured assumptions about love, death, and the structure and content of fiction.

Among the finest writers of short fiction at this time is Alistair MacLeod. With only two collections, *The Lost Salt Gift of Blood* (1976) and *As Birds Bring Forth the Sun and Other Stories* (1986), MacLeod's output is less than that of the female storytellers of the 1960's and 1970's, but his tales of hard lives in the Cape Breton mining and fishing communities have a uniquely tough, lyrical quality that allies them with the Celtic revival in music. In structure, characterization, and control of techniques of reversal, contrast, and epiphany, Macleod is the current master of the classic well-made short story. His only rival in this territory is Margaret Laurence, already mentioned for her realistic prairie stories. She also wrote short fiction arising out of her experience in Africa; *The Tomorrow-Tamer* (1963) displays a meticulous balance of elements that recalls MacLeod's haunting tales of a similarly passing way of life.

Canada's one genuine movement in short fiction involved a group known as the Montreal Story Tellers, formed in the late 1960's in Montreal to promote the reading of short fiction to the general public at venues such as schools and community centers. Its members, John Metcalf, Clark Blaise, Ray Fraser, Ray Smith, and Hugh Hood, did much to raise the profile of short fiction. Four of these writers went on to publish individual types of short fiction: Smith in lively experimental stories, fabular and surreal (for example, "The Princess, the Boeing, and the Hot Pastrami Sandwich"); Hood in densely parabolic pieces grounded in the documentary reality of urban life in Montreal and Toronto (*Flying a Red Kite*, 1962; *You'll Catch Your Death*, 1992); Blaise in confessional fiction about a childhood and adolescence spent wandering in the no-man's land between French Canada, English Canada, and the United States (*A North American Education*, 1973; *Man and His World*, 1992).

Stories that exploit narrative technique to convey abnormal or altered mental states and to explore the human psyche are the forte of another group of short-fiction writers. Timothy Findley's work includes a novella (*You Went Away*, 1996) and two collections of stories, including a chilling psychological story called "Dreams." W. D. Valgardson's stories from northern Manitoba draw on mythical background to create tense dramas such as "Bloodflowers," a contemporary horror story and the title of his 1973 collection. Also from Manitoba, Sandra Birdsell writes of the difficulties of women's lives in rural settings. Her fictional location of Agassiz links the stories in *Night Travellers* (1982) and *Ladies of the House* (1984). From Saskatchewan comes Guy Vanderhaeghe's uncompromisingly realistic short fiction, collected in *Man Descending* (1982) and *Things as They Are?* (1992). Abnormal mental states and marginalized points of view are the main subject of Margaret Gibson's short fiction, from her early study of life on a mental ward "The Butterfly Ward," and her epistolary story "Making It," to more recent work such as *The Fear Room and Other Stories* (1996).

The 1970's and the 1980's

In the 1970's and 1980's it was popular to see all Canadian literature in terms of unifying thematic patterns, the most influential of which was Northrop Frye's template of the "garrison mentality," which became a symbol for the isolated, inward-looking, wilderness-fearing communities of early Canada. Together with Margaret Atwood's related concept of "survival," this term became for a while the touchstone of the good in short fiction as well as other genres. Short fiction whose plots conformed to this paradigm rose to the top, and other types of fiction were undervalued. Certainly many excellent Canadian short stories are illuminated by such readings: Frederick Philip Grove's Manitoba stories conform to the pattern. Atwood's own "The Age of Lead" (about the televised unearthing of the bodies and artifacts of the doomed Franklin expedition to the Arctic) repay interpretation as a conflict between human beings and an implacable wilderness. Thematic criticism offers a way of reading Sinclair Ross's "The Lamp at Noon,"

Joyce Marshall's "The Old Woman," Alice Munro's "Winter Wind," and Rudy Wiebe's "Oolulik" and "The Naming of Albert Johnson," but it excluded other types of fiction: the urban mythographers Morley Callaghan, Hugh Hood, and Hugh Garner, the ironic social anatomists Mavis Gallant, Mordecai Richler, Katherine Govier, John Metcalf, Carol Shields, and Janice Kulyk-Keefer—all are beyond the reach of the survival theme. Other thematic paradigms have been suggested, notably Constance Rooke's idea that "fear of the open heart" is the emotional and literary marker of a generation of Canadian writing.

After the definitive thematic statements of Laurence, Munro, Atwood, and Macleod, the focus in short fiction moved away from strict realism and the confining demands of national definition. Fiction writers whose works embraced postmodern modes and techniques include Leon Rooke, Jack Hodgins, George Bowering, Audrey Thomas, David Arnason, and Jane Urquhart. In his long writing career, Matt Cohen has produced short fiction in a variety of moods and styles, realistic as well as fabular (see *Columbus and the Fat Lady*, 1972), but his best-known stories, such as "The Sins of Tomas Benares," side with an experiential realism. Metafictional fabulation distinguishes the stories of W. P. Kinsella, especially in his popular baseball stories, such as "Shoeless Joe Jackson Comes to Iowa." Kinsella is as well known, however, for stories in a different genre: His humorous pieces about life on the Hobbema Reservation use Native Canadian characters presented through the voice and perspective of Silas Ermineskin. Despite the effervescence of his humor and his revelation of the resilience of native culture in changing times, Kinsella's Frank Fencepost stories, such as those in *Born Indian* (1981) and *Brother Frank's Gospel Hour and Other Stories* (1994) have been criticized as condescending to genuine speakers from Canada's First Nations.

Among these, the best writer of short fiction is Thomas King, who uses the motif of the aboriginal trickster, coyote, to challenge reader complacency about "Indian" subjects and narrative styles. In "The One About Coyote Going West" and "One Good Story, That One," King's deliberately sly narrator tricks the reader in his broken English, enmeshing the reader in the oral roots of narrative, in a place where practical joke meets story and the joke is on the reader. A different narrative focus marks his 1989 story "Borders," in which a preadolescent narrator struggles to understand the failed crossing of the Canada-U.S. border, when his Blackfoot mother refuses to answer queries about her nationality with any answer other than "Blackfoot." She and her son are stranded in the duty-free limbo between borders, trapped by a fatal clash between stubborn idealism and bureaucracy. This well-crafted story with its naïve narrator and pivotal subject matter may be one of the most important pieces of Canadian short fiction from the end of the twentieth century. Other native Canadian writers of short fiction include Daniel David Moses, whose "King of the Raft" is an often-anthologized lyrical story of adolescence. Less comfortable is the angry, radicalized prose of Lee Maracle (*Sojourner's Truth and Other Stories*, 1990).

In the 1980's, younger writers began to produce more daring stories, although Canadians never moved so far or so quickly toward the postmodern as their American peers. The Canadianness of these new stories was less self-conscious, expressed in self-reflexive and self-parodic ways. In this mode Diane Schoemperlen's story "Red Plaid Shirt" became an instant classic, and her collections *Hockey Night in Canada* (1987) and *The Man of My Dreams* (1990) held a playful, ironic mirror to the Canadian scene. A more recent collection, *Forms of Devotion*, which won the 1998 Governor General's Award, unites antique images of woodcut illustrations with self-reflexive fiction such as "How to Write a Serious Novel About Love."

Katherine Govier interpreted urban life in *Fables of Brunswick Avenue* (1985), then conducted more daring technical experiments in *Before and After* (1989) and *The Immaculate Conception Photography Gallery and Other Stories* (1994). Of particular note is "God Is Writing a Novel" a postmodern study of the metaphysics blending life and literature. Stories both shocking in subject matter and daring in execution constitute the oeuvre of Barbara Gowdy's urban gothic: *We So Seldom Look on Love* (1992). A good collection of contemporary urban stories is editor Barry Callaghan's *This Ain't No Healing Town: Toronto Stories* (1995). Linda Svendsen, in *Marine Life* (1992) introduced a new, spare prose in her short fiction. Reminiscent of both Hemingway and Flannery O'Connor, her British Columbia stories are flavored, nevertheless, with "Generation X" cynicism. The Generation X mood can also be sampled in the writing of Evelyn Lau (*Fresh Girls*, 1993) and Hiromi Goto.

Other writers contributing to the variety of voices heard in Canada came from immigrant writers, who wrote, not of assimilation but often of difference. An early contributor is Austin Clarke, originally from Barbados, who has written well for three decades of the dilemmas of immigrant life. His landmark early collection, *When He Was Free and Young and He Used to Wear Silks* (1971), analyzes the West Indian code of masculinity and its breakdown on the streets of Canada's big cities. Later collections–*Nine Men Who Laughed* (1986), *In This City* (1992), and *There Are No Elders* (1993) explore similar territory, with unusual prose rhythms in both dialogue and narrative voice. Other more recent writers include the acclaimed Neil Bissoondath, *Digging Up the Mountains* (1985) and *On the Eve of Uncertain Tomorrows* (1990), and Rohinton Mistry, whose *Tales from Firozsha Baag* (1987) chronicle life in the Parsi community in Bombay. Mistry's story "Swimming Lessons" and Himani Bannerji's "The Other Family" resemble Clarke's stories of immigrant life and together with them provide the finest work in this genre. Shyam Selvadurai (*Funny Boy*, 1994) also writes delicate, well-crafted, realistic stories of initiation and growing up in Sri Lanka. A different modern mood emerges from the short fiction of Dionne Brand (*Sans Souci and Other Stories*, 1988), whose use of a "tween-dialect," a merger of standard English and Trinidadian creole, animates her stories of immigrant struggle and violence. Brand's dark, dreamy vision of life on the seamy side is best sampled in "Blossom: Priestess of Oya, Goddess of Winds, Storms and Waterfalls."

Other short-fiction forms

There has also been a vital tradition of longer short fiction in Canada. The novella length has occurred in the writing of earlier writers such as Morley Callaghan (*A Native Argosy*, 1929, contains two novellas), Ethel Wilson ("Tuesday and Wednesday" and "Lilly's Story," in *The Equations of Love*, 1952), Mavis Gallant ("Potter" and "Its Image in the Mirror"), Malcolm Lowry ("The Forest Path to the Spring"), as well as in the exquisite prose pieces of John Metcalf ("Girl in Gingham" and "Private Parts: A Memoir"). Metcalf's novellas are collected in *Shooting the Stars* (1993). Also accomplished at this length is Keath Fraser, whose acclaimed *Foreign Affairs* (1985) and *Popular Anatomy* (1995) contain complex novellas. A collection of novellas, *On Middle Ground*, appeared in 1987, containing work by Clark Blaise, Keath Fraser, Mavis Gallant, Malcolm Lowry, John Metcalf, Audrey Thomas, and Ethel Wilson. Additionally, a novella prize is offered by the Malahat Review.

Another feature of current short fiction in Canada is its flirtation with the border between story and essay. Several fine pieces of writing refuse to declare full allegiance with either genre and exhibit the best features of both: the discursive meditation of the essay, as well as the particular event of the story. An early example is Roch Carrier's essay/story "The Hockey Sweater," one of the most anthologized pieces from Quebec, which speaks movingly of the anguish of a young fan stuck with a sweater from the opposing team. Drew Hayden Taylor's "Pretty Like a White Boy: The Adventures of a Blue-Eyed Ojibway" is a humorous anatomy of a hybrid existence; a similar topic in Makeda Silvera's "Her Head a Village" becomes an elegantly bitchy account of being a black Jamaican-Canadian lesbian mother and author. A more solemn tone distinguishes Rudy Wiebe's "Where Is the Voice Coming From?" which follows a writer in quest of any fact or artifact that will recapture the life and voice of the Cree warrior Big Bear. The quest leads through museums and archives but ends on a visionary note, as the 'voice' of the title comes unbidden to the writer.

An ongoing system of literary awards has helped to foster the boom in short fiction since the 1960's.

The country's premier literary award—the governor General's Literary Award—has often filled the fiction category with a volume of short fiction, thus giving a sales boost to a notoriously unprofitable genre. From *Hugh Garner's Best Stories* in 1963, two Alice Munro collections (*Dance of the Happy Shades*, 1968, and *The Progress of Love*, 1986), the 1995 award to Greg Hollingshead's robust absurdist tour de force *The Roaring Girl* (1995) and Schoemperlen's *Forms of Devotion* (1998), the award system has strongly supported short fiction. Other prizes also contribute to the genre, notably the Journey Prize (instituted by James Michener). The *Journey Prize Anthology* contains prize nominees from journals across the country, and its list of prize winners over the last ten years is a useful guide to the fund of new talent in short fiction.

The anthology enterprise keeps remaking the canon of good Canadian short fiction. Important series include *Canadian Short Stories* and the annual volume *The Best Canadian Short Stories*. Each of these recognizes established talent in the genre, as well as introducing new directions in short fiction, and are helpful resources for beginning an acquaintance with Canadian short fiction. Anthologists have also responded to the surge in writing from and of the cultural margins with many collections. *Other Solitudes: Canadian Multicultural Fictions* (1990) varies Hugh MacLennan's nation-defining formula of "two solitudes" to assert the plurality of experience in contemporary Canada. Also in this genre is *Making a Difference: Canadian Multicultural Literature* (1996—not exclusively short fiction).

An alternate way of getting to know Canadian short fiction is through film or video. The Canadian Short-Story Video Collection includes versions of about twenty-five stories by notable authors such as Sinclair Ross ("The Painted Door," "One's a Heifer"), Alice Munro "Connection"), Ernest Buckler, Margaret Laurence, Hugh Garner, Jack Hodgins, but also excellent adaptations of less well-known stories: Lois Simmie's "Red Shoes," David Billington's "Hotwalker," Isabel Huggan's "Jack of Hearts," and Guy Vanderhaeghe's "Cages."

Michelle Gadpaille

Bibliography

Gadpaille, Michelle. *The Canadian Short Story.* Toronto: Oxford University Press, 1988. In-depth discussions of individual stories by many of the authors mentioned above, including chapters on Mavis Gallant, Alice Munro, and Margaret Atwood.

New, W. H. *Canadian Short Fiction: From Myth to Modern*. Scarborough, Ontario: Prentice Hall, 1986. This is a comprehensive anthology with good representation of aboriginal work and nineteenth century writing, as well as sketches and tales. Excellent introduction including notes on short fiction forms, and a chronology. It has particularly good biographical introductions to individual writers.

_______. *Dreams of Speech and Violence: The Art of the Short Story in Canada and New Zealand*. Toronto: University of Toronto Press, 1987. Comparative study, including valuable material on the colonial contexts.

The New Oxford Book of Canadian Short Stories in English, edited by Margaret Atwood and Robert Weaver. Toronto: Oxford University Press, 1995. A selection of canonical short fiction, excluding that of the nineteenth century and beginning with earlier twentieth century writers such as Thomas Raddall and Ethel Wilson.

The Oxford Companion to Canadian Literature. Edited by Eugene Benson and William Toye. Toronto: Oxford University Press, 1997. Includes Robert Weaver's "Short Stories in English: To 1982"; Geoff Hancock's "Short Stories in English: 1983 to 1996"; Michel Lord's "Short Stories in French."

The Québec Anthology: 1830-1990, edited by Matt Cohen and Wayne Grady. Ottawa: Ottawa University Press, 1996. This is a good introduction to French Canadian short fiction.

Vauthier, Simone. *Reverberations: Explorations in the Canadian Short Story.* Concord, Ontario: Anansi, 1993. This is a full-length study of the genre.

Weiss, Allan. *A Comprehensive Bibliography of English-Canadian Short Stories: 1950-1983.* Toronto: ECW Press, 1988. This is still a good guide for those doing research on earlier Canadian writers and needing to find obscure stories, or dates of first publication.

CHINESE SHORT FICTION

The Chinese equivalent of "short fiction," "xiaoshuo," first appeared in *Han shu* (first century C.E.; *The History of the Former Han Dynasty*, 1938) as the heading of a section consisting of twenty-seven works. Although all these pieces have been lost, a large number of other collections of short fiction approximately from that period have survived. Among these collections are *Zhanguo ce* (*Chan-kuo ts'e*, 1970; intrigue of the warring states) by Liu Xiang, *Shiji* (c. 80 B.C.E.; partial translation as *Records of the Grand Historian of China*, 1961) by Si-ma Qian (*Xiao Lin*, c. 500; *The Forest of Smiles*) by Han-dan Chun, *Yu lin* (the forest of sayings) by Pei Chi, and (*Shi-shuo xinyu*, c. 430; *A New Account of Tales of the World*) by Liu Yiqing. In these collections are stories of famous statesmen and military figures, tales of historical events, political anecdotes, and popular jokes.

The Six Dynasties (220-589) witnessed a growing fascination with the fantastic and the supernatural in society. Narratives of miraculous phenomena and human encounters with ghosts and spirits flourished. Predominantly secularized versions of Daoist and Buddhist tales, these narratives were usually written in the official documentary style, for their authors believed that what they recorded were actual happenings rather than imagined realities. Some of the tales present Daoist believers attaining immortality through their religious practice. Others relate events of a fabulous or mythological nature, such as a return to life after a visit to death or human explorations into outer space with no special equipment. In the Tang Dynasty (618-907) a large number of these narratives were assiduously rewritten and refined. They were also further removed from their original religious sources, for Daoism, Buddhism, and Confucianism began to be integrated in the Tang Dynasty.

Of all the collections of stories of the strange and the supernatural, the largest is perhaps the *Taiping guangzhi* (assembled c. 976-983; extensive records from the reign of great tranquility), which preserves many important Tang-period classical-language works. Other collections include *Bowu zhi* (c. 270; account of wide-ranging matters) by Zhang Hua, the anonymous *Lie yi zhuan* (c. 320; strange tales), and *Sou shen zhi* (c. 320; *Search for the Supernatural*, 1958) by Gan Bao. There is also *Yijian zhi* (1166; record of yijian) by Hong Mai. Hong is the most prolific of all the authors of stories of the bizarre and fantastic; he wrote nearly all the twenty-seven hundred titles in *Record of Yi Jian*.

Stories of strange human encounters with supernatural beings as a genre was elevated to high art with the publication of *Liao-zhai's Record of Wonders* (Liao-zhai zhi-yi) by Pu Songling. All the Liao-zhai stories, written or edited by Pu himself, are exquisite and elegant, serving a clearly stated didactic purpose. In these stories male characters often unknowingly enter into a sexual relationship with ghosts and were-beasts disguised as beautiful females. What is amazing is that these males do not even show the slightest sign of shock or surprise when eventually facing the truth. These nonhuman beings often behave like humans, displaying the very admirable moral qualities that human characters profess to embrace yet fail to practice.

Vernacular Short Stories

The Song Dynasty (960-1279) saw the rise of stories written in the vernacular. Vernacular storytellers not only searched the treasure-house of the classical language stories for intriguing plots but also turned to various aspects of the Song society—the world of commerce, the judicial system, and courtesan romance—for new materials. In the Yuan (1279-1368) and Ming (1368-1644) Dynasties vernacular stories as a vehicle of popular culture gained unprecedented popularity and developed into a highly sophisticated medium of literary expression through the efforts of a number of masters. Among those masters are Feng Menglong, Lang Xian, and Ling Mengchu, all three being ardent collectors, skillful editors, and prolific writers.

Feng Menglong is best known for his three collections of short stories (Sanyan) entitled *Yushi mingyan* (c. 1620; illustrated words to instruct the world), *Jinghi tongyan* (c. 1624; common words to warn the world), and *Xinghi henyan* (c. 1627; constant words to awake the world). Feng's subject matter covers a wide range of social and moral issues: loyalty, patriotism, heroism, noble-minded leadership, scholars' active participation in politics, and the natural order of reward and retribution. Whatever its subject matter is, a story by Feng invariably concerns itself with a single character in a single action and begins with a preamble or prologue to direct his reader to a Confucian moral interpretation.

Lang Xian, author of *Shi dian tou* (c. 1628; the rocks nod their heads), displays a moral world somewhat different from Feng's. He doubts the validity of active participation in state affairs and advocates a Daoist's seclusion. He often presents scholar-officials and their lives as unpleasant and undesirable, while revealing his delight in nature and his fascination with the attainment of immortality. However, when it comes to filial duties, Lang is more of a Confucian disciple than a Daoist recluse. There is no lack of stories by him that commend children's avenging their parents' murder by whatever means available or their persistent search for their missing elders against all odds.

Unlike Feng Menglong and Lang Xian, Ling Mengchu shows little interest in a strict moral code whether it is Confucian or Daoist. As is indicated by his *Paian jingqi* (1628; striking the table in amazement) and *Erke paian jingqi* (1632; the second collection of striking the table in amazement), Ling likes reasonable behavior, attainable virtues, and practical morality. What he dislikes is human stupidity, ignorance, greed, and cruelty, and he shows his preferences and aversions with a voice that is unmistakably humorous, comical, or satirical.

Baihua Short Fiction Before 1949

Chinese short fiction underwent tremendous changes at the beginning of the twentieth century, when China was on the verge of total disintegration under the dual pressure of an incompetent government and Western and Japanese imperialists. Many writers used their pen as a powerful tool to mobilize the masses of people to save their ancient motherland and revitalize her. One prominent writer after another appeared on the scene: Lu Xun, Lao She, Mao Dun, Ba Jin, Ye Shengtao, Bin Xin, Ding Ling, Yu Dafu, and Qian Zhongshu, to name but a few. Ironically, the very artistic techniques and narrative structures they employed to accomplish their patriotic mission came from the Western world. The language they used to save their ancient land was not wen-yan, the classical literary language, but Baihua, the common spoken language, which overcame all the linguistic barriers created by numerous mutually unintelligible vernaculars or dialects.

One of the earliest and most influential writers in twentieth century China is Lu Xun, whose collections of short stories include *Nahan* (1923; *Call to Arms*, 1981), *Panghuang* (1926; *Wandering*, 1981), and *Gushi xinbian* (1935; *Old Tales Retold*, 1961). Realistic, indigenous, satirical, his stories serve to arouse the masses of people by relentlessly exposing their numbness and indifference, their ignorance and superstition, "My Native Place" and "Medicine" bring to light the sloth, superstition, cruelty, and hypocrisy of some small town residents. "The Diary of a Madman" details the protagonist's discovery of the two words "Eat men!" between the lines in a history book advocating benevolence, righteousness, truth, and virtue. "The True Story of Ah Q" portrays a character engaged in self-deception and self-aggrandizement under distressing and humiliating circumstances. Though many of his stories are based on people who lived in his native Shao-hsing, in Zhejiang, in the last decade or so of the Qing Dynasty (1644-1911), his careful choice of events and situations, his matter-of-fact narrative style, and his moral seriousness combine to make his stories mirror the general physical decay, emotional paralysis, and spiritual decline in China.

Like Lu Xun, Lao She saw all the ugliness and suffering in the lives of people tormented by brutal forces both domestic and foreign; however, he also saw the dignity and perseverance his people displayed in such adverse conditions. Therefore, he angrily denounces people's indifference to their own country's tragic fate in stories like "Getting a Prescription" and "Democratic World"; at the same time, he enthusiastically hails the heroism and self-sacrifice of all those resisting Japanese aggression in stories like "Of One Heart" and "Enemy and Friends." Lao She was also acutely aware of the innocence and spontaneity of his people as well as the deeply entrenched moral codes that aimed to suffocate these admirable attributes. However, he firmly believed that innocence and spontaneity would triumph and lead individuals to inner peace and contentment. This kind of awareness and belief is evident in many of the stories included in his collections under such titles as *Ganji* (1934), *Ying hai chi* (1935), *Huoche ji* (1941), and *Pinxue ji* (1945).

Mao Tun understood his people, especially the peasants and small town residents. He held that the root cause of his people's suffering was to be found in a corrupt government and imperialist aggression. He believed that his people had inherited such virtues as industry, endurance, fortitude, bravery, and a sense of justice. In his view, a people with these virtues, when led by a proletarian political party, would eventually win their struggle against their oppressors. Mao Tun gave his political belief rich artistic expression in many of his stories such as "Spring Silkworm," "Autumn Harvest," "Ruinous Winter," "The Lin's Family Store," and "The Struggle of Life."

A man with a broad worldview and an intense hatred for evil forces, Ba Jin is the author of more than ten collections of short stories including *Fuchou* (1931; *Revenge*, 1931), *Guangming* (1931; light), *Dianyi* (1932; electric chair), *Jiangjun* (1933; the general), and *Yingxiong de gushi* (1953; the story of heroes). Ba Jin's stories range from personal reminiscences at home and abroad to anarchistic or revolutionary figures in China, France, and Russia. Pa Chin insisted that art should never be an end in itself; instead, it should serve to bring some light to the masses and strike a blow at darkness. Some of his stories, like "The Antimony Miners," condemn the inhuman treatment of workers. Some of his stories, like "Dog," satirize the servitude of some of his countrymen to the Europeans in China. Other stories, like "The Dying Sun" and "The Story of Heroes," eulogize revolutionaries in their struggle against their oppressors.

Ye Shengtao showed great concern for the social problems faced by ordinary middle-class folk. He dwelt on the traditional indifference to child psychology and old peoples' loneliness, society's misunderstanding of female professionals and general apathy toward modern education, teachers' frustration and the urgent need to overcome the powerful forces of tradition and ignorance. His concern is brilliantly expressed in his short stories in *Pan xiansheng zanan zhong* (c. 1924; mr. pan in trouble). These stories demonstrate penetrating observations, realistic details, vivid descriptions with remarkable psychological precision, and a refined language and mature style emitting a genuine and warm humanity.

Two of the most prominent women writers in the first half of the twentieth century in China are Bing Xin and Ding Ling. Both are patriotic, and both are deeply concerned with the fate of women in a semifeudal, semicolonial society. Their early stories tell of dilemmas, agony, longings, and a sense of loss experienced by young women in a period of change and uncertainty. Bing Xin's first collection of short stories was published in 1923 under the title of *Chaoren* (superman), and Ding Ling's first collection of stories *zai hei'anzhong* (in darkness) came out in 1927. Both dedicated themselves to the course to save their country. Bin Xin participated in the anti-imperialist and antifeudal May Fourth Movement. Ding Ling joined in the resistance against Japanese aggression in Ya'an, where she began to depict the self-sacrifice of war heroes as well as their sufferings and internal conflict. In her collection of stories entitled *Wo zai xiachun de shihou* (1941; when I was in the village of Xia), she portrays a heroic female underground worker who has to endure brutal sexual assault and mental torture at the hands of the very enemy she determines to destroy for her country.

Yu Dafu not only wrote patriotic stories during World War II but also went to Singapore and the Island of Sumatra to carry out underground activities. Unfortunately, he was arrested and executed by the Japanese military police after Japan's surrender. As the author of a "Sinking" and "Silverygray Death,"

Yu is known for his bold use of individuals' suppressed sexuality as a metaphor for national humiliation, inaction, and shame.

Unlike many writers who focused their attention on other members of society, Qian Zhongshu turned inward into the world of writers themselves. Author of a collection of short stories entitled *Ren, shou, gui* (1946; men, beasts, ghosts), Qian saw some writers alienating themselves from the general public, found others vulgarizing contemporary letters, and resorted to satire as his weapon to protest such alienation and vulgarization.

Qian was also one of those writers who maintained a cool mind in a debate launched by the May Fourth Movement, a debate on the merits of the cultural traditions in China and in the West. Many writers participated in the debate, with quite a number of extremists on each side. Some advocated unconditional, complete westernization of China as the only road to national revival while others looked back to Confucian ideology as the only effective means to confront western invasion and restore China's former glory. Qian rejected both extreme views, holding that the two traditions should be complementary instead of antagonistic toward each other.

Baihua Short Fiction After 1949

After the founding of the People's Republic of China in 1949, all writers became members of writers' federations under the control of the ruling communist party. Paid fixed salaries as *ganbu* (cadres), they were required to follow the policy laid down by Mao Zedong: Art and literature should serve the party's political agenda and the broad masses of people—workers, peasants, soldiers. As a result, writers spent more time on ideological reform than on literary creation, and those who had established themselves before 1949 became very quiet.

Most of the short stories published by the party-controlled presses during the period of 1949 to 1976 were those glorifying Mao or revolutionaries under Mao's leadership. The only manner of representation writers were allowed to use was what Mao called "revolutionary realism combined with revolutionary romanticism." Both Lao She and Ba Jin wrote a few stories along the party line. Lao She's stories mostly focus on the heroes in the Korean War and a story by Ba Jin, "Song of Life," recounts the efforts to save a burned steelworker who dedicated his life to the building of socialism. Their stories were not as enthusiastically received by the party's propaganda department as was Ru Zhijuan's "Lilies." Ru's story presents the broad masses of people under Mao's judicious leadership in a life-or-death struggle against the nationalists in the civil war that followed immediately the defeat of the Japanese. It was hailed as a shining example of "realism combined with romanticism."

In the cultural revolution started by Mao in 1966, almost all writers were persecuted no matter how quiet they had been or how cautiously they had followed the party line. Quite a few did not survive the ten-year-long torment. Some of them, like Zhao Shuli, author of "Xiao er hei Got Married," were beaten to death by Mao's red guards; others like Lao She committed suicide to preserve their integrity and protest tyranny.

The rampage of Mao's revolution eventually came to an end with his death in 1976. Not long afterward, almost all the writers victimized by Mao's constant purges were rehabilitated. Literary creation resumed with a vengeance. Personal or family tragedies under Mao's tyranny became the logical and inevitable subject matter. The disparity between the ideals of socialism and the reality of brutality and corruption constituted the prevailing theme. New Realism emerged, with the publication of several explosive stories like Shen Rong's "Middle Age," Ru Zhijuan's "Sons and Successors," and Jiang Zilong's "Manager Qiao Assumes Office."

New Realism represents a daring and successful attempt to break away from the fetters imposed by Mao, thus paving the way for a new generation of writers who could afford to completely ignore what Mao had said about literature. Among these new writers are Cheng Naishan, Mo Yan, Deng Gang, and Zhan Kangkang. In her short stories, such as "The Blue House," Cheng presents the lives of upper-class, urban Chinese and deplores the loss of values and basic morality in a society still under the ruling communist party. Moreover, she expresses her Christian faith in "In My Heart There Is Room for You." Mo Yan, author of "Red Sorghum" and "Dry River," devotes himself to depicting life as lived by real ordinary peasants and their struggle against the foreign aggressors. He shows not just their strengths and moral aspirations but their sexual desires and weaknesses. Deng Gang, in stories such as "Flowers in the Heart," exposes the devastating Cultural Revolution and explores the lessons to be learned while Zhan Kangkang in her stories "Summer" and "Northern Light" asserts individuality and romantic love. Most of these writers are not *ganbu* with salaries paid by the government; for them, the manner of representation advocated by Mao has become only one choice among many.

Bibliography

Anderson, Jennifer, and Theresa Munford, trans. *Chinese Women Writers: A Collection of Short Stories by Chinese Women Writers of the 1920's and 30's*. Hong Kong: Joint Pub., 1985. Discusses the social life and customs of women in China during the 1920's and 1930's. Includes examination of selected stories by Ding Ling, Bing Xin, Luo Shu, Ling Shuhua, Wu Shutian, Lu Yin, Xiao Hong, Feng Keng, and Feng Yuanjun.

Bishop, John Lyman. *The Colloquial Short Story in China: A Study of the San-Yen Collections*. Cambridge, Mass.: Harvard University Press, 1956. History and criticism of Chinese short stories translated into English. Includes a bibliography.

Chao, Carolyn, and David Su Li-qun. *The Picador Book of Contemporary Chinese Fiction*. London: Picador, 1998. This anthology collection of twentieth century Chinese fiction translated into English includes a number of Chinese short stories.

Duke, Michael S. *Modern Chinese Women Writers: Critical Appraisals*. New York: M. E. Sharpe, 1989. The essays in this anthology employ particular literary-critical approaches to analyze a work or works by a particular writer or group of writers. Two deal with feminist literary criticism, three take the approach of fiction as autobiography, and seven are concerned with the complex relationships between narrative techniques and thematic statements in fiction.

Hanan, Patrick. *The Chinese Vernacular Story*. Cambridge, Mass.: Harvard University Press, 1981. Examines the *huaben*, or vernacular story, which was one of the most popular genres in Chinese literature, relating the stories and their authors to China's changing social and political life.

Hook, Brian, ed. *The Cambridge Encyclopedia of China*. New York: Cambridge University Press, 1991. Covers such diverse subjects as land and resources, people, society, art and architecture, and science and technology. Includes bibliographical references and an index.

Idema, Wilt, and Lloyd Haft. *A Guide to Chinese Literature*. Netherlands: Amsterdam University Press, 1996. A useful resource on Chinese history and literary criticism. Includes a bibliography.

Kao, Karl S. Y., ed. *Classical Chinese Tales of the Supernatural and the Fantastic: Selections from the Third to the Tenth Century*. Bloomington: Indiana University Press, 1985. This anthology collection covers all the prominent themes and motifs of the "supernatural and the fantastic" in Chinese fiction from the third to the tenth century. Describes the historical circumstances that induced the growth of this kind of narrative. Each entry is followed by an end note, which provides brief critical commentary.

Lee Yee, ed. *The New Realism: Writings from China after the Cultural Revolution*. New York: Hippocrene Books, 1983. Examines some of the more prominent Chinese fiction since 1978, including selected stories by Ru Zhijuan, Gao Xiaosheng, Jiang Zilong, Ye Wenfu, Wang Meng, Wang Jing, Shen Rong, Liu Binyan, Zhang Xian, Sha Yexin, Li Shoucheng, Yao Mingde, and Bai Hua.

Leung, Laifong. *Morning Sun: Interviews with Chinese Writers of the Lost Generation*. Armonk, N.Y.: M. E. Sharp, 1994. Interviews with twenty-six writers of the *zhiqing* generation, the urban secondary school and college students who on Mao's order were sent to the countryside during the Rustication Movement between the late 1960's and the mid-1970's.

Perkins, Dorothy. *Encyclopedia of China: The Essential Reference to China, Its History, and Culture*. New York: Facts on File, 1999. An all-around helpful source for students of Chinese culture. Includes bibliographical references and an index.

Roberts, Moss, ed. and trans. *Chinese Fairy Tales and Fantasies*. New York: Pantheon Books, 1979. This study examines a number of works of fiction and fairy tales translated into English.

Chenliang Sheng

IRISH SHORT FICTION

It is an undisputed fact of literary history that, whereas British writers and readers have always favored the novel over the short story, just the opposite has been the case for their Irish neighbors. Irish short-story writer Frank O'Connor has attributed this distinction to differences between national attitudes toward society. Whereas in England, O'Connor says, the intellectual's attitude toward society is, "It must work," in Ireland it is, "It can't work." The implication of O'Connor's remark, echoed by many critics since the 1963 publication of his well-known book on the short story, *The Lonely Voice*, is that, whereas the novel derives its subject matter from an organized society, the short story springs from an oral, anecdotal tradition. According to J. H. Delargy, in a frequently cited study of the Gaelic storyteller, ancient Ireland fostered an oral literature unrivaled in all of western Europe, a tradition that has influenced the growth of the modern Irish short story.

Delargy describes Irish storytelling as being centered on a gathering of people around the turf fire of a hospitable house on fall and winter nights. At these meetings, usually called a *céilidhe* (pronounced "kaylee"), a Gaelic storyteller, known as a *seanchaí* (pronounced "shanachie") if he or she specialized in short supernatural tales told in realistic detail, or a *sgéalaí* (pronounced "shagaylee") if he or she told longer fairy-tale stories focusing on a legendary hero, mesmerized the folk audience.

It is the shorter, realistic *seanchas* or *eachtra* (pronounced "achthrah") rather than the longer, epical fairy tales that have given rise to the Irish literary short story. This type of story, which usually featured supernatural events recounted with realistic detail suggesting an eyewitness account, has been described by late eighteenth and early nineteenth century German writers as the source of the *novelle* form, which usually featured a story striking enough to arouse interest in and of itself, without any connection to the society, the times, or the culture.

This view of short prose narrative as a form detached from any cultural background, drawing its interest from the striking nature of the event itself, has always been a central characteristic of short fiction. One of the most important implications of short fiction's detachment from social context and history, argued early theorists, was that, although the anecdote on which the story was based might be trivial and its matter slight, its manner or way of telling had to be appealing, thus giving the narrator a more important role than in other forms of fiction. The result was a shift in authority for the tale and thus a gradual displacement away from strictly formulaic structures of received story toward techniques of verisimilitude that create credibility. The displacement is from mythic authority to the authority of a single perspective that creates a unifying atmosphere or tone of the experience. It is this focus on a single perspective rather than on an organized social context that has made the Irish short story largely dependent on anecdote and the galvanizing voice of the storyteller.

Maria Edgeworth

The importance of the anecdote and the voice of the teller to the development of Irish short narrative can be seen most readily in a single work of fiction credited with beginning Irish literature in English—Maria Edgeworth's *Castle Rackrent*, published in 1800. Although usually characterized as a novel, the work is actually a novella focused more on regional particularities than on the social generalities that held together the heftier English novel. A number of critics have noted that the distinctive feature of *Castle Rackrent* is its imitation of a speaking voice telling a tale. What was new about *Castle Rackrent* was the colloquial voice of the teller of the story, the trusted retainer Thady Quirk, whose natural flow of talk created an ambiguous mixture of self-deception and self-revelation unmatched in England and not to be equaled in America until Mark Twain's *Adventures of Huckleberry Finn* (1884).

Although ostensibly *Castle Rackrent* is the history of four generations of the Rackrent family as told by the servant Thady, Edgeworth announces in the preface that her interest is not in epic history but on anecdotal revelation. She notes that although the public taste for anecdote has been ridiculed by critics, if considered properly, such a taste reflects the profound good sense of the times. However, in spite of Edgeworth's insistence that her storyteller is an illiterate but honest and innocent old retainer who tells the history of the drunken Sir Patrick, the litigious Sir Murtagh, the fighting Sir Kit, and the slovenly Sir Condy, many readers have always suspected that Thady is artful, shrewd, and calculating. By making Thady Quirk such an ambiguous point of view, Edgeworth created a new technique of fiction.

William Carleton

Prominent Irish literature critic Declan Kiberd has suggested that the short story has always flourished in countries where a "vibrant oral culture" was challenged by the "onset of a sophisticated literature tradition"; thus the short story, says Kiberd, is the natural result of a "fusion" between the folktale and modern literature. William Carleton is the most important Irish mediator between the folktale and the modern realistic story because of his attention to detail and his creation of the personality of the teller. His *Traits and Stories of the Irish Peasantry* (1830-1833) is an important early example of the transition from oral tale to modern short story. The purpose of the first-person narrator in romantic short fiction, as Carleton, and later Edgar Allan Poe and Nathaniel Hawthorne knew, is not only to verify the truth of the event being narrated but also to transform the event from an objective description to an individual perspective.

Critics of Irish fiction generally agree that Carleton's story "Wildgoose Lodge,"with its focus on the horrified emotions of the narrator, its terse style, and its suggestive detail, is his best, similar to the modern short story later developed by Poe and Hawthorne in America. "Wildgoose Lodge" recounts the revenge murder of an entire family by a Catholic secret society. Although ostensibly merely an eye-witness report by a former member of the society, the structure of the story reflects a self-conscious patterning of reality characteristic of the modern short story. A completed action, treated as if it were an action in process, "Wildgoose Lodge" is a classic example of how romantic short-story writers developed techniques to endow experience with thematic significance without using allegorical methods of symbolic characterization and stylized plot.

What makes "Wildgoose lodge" a modern story is the heightened perception of the engaged first-person narrator, who is both dramatically involved and self-consciously aware at once. Moreover, the story's selection of metaphoric detail with the potential for making an implied ironic moral judgment—the atmospheric weather, the ironic church setting, the physically isolated house, and the imagery of the leader as Satanic and his closest followers as fiendish—shift the emphasis in this story from a mere eyewitness account to a tight thematic structure. It is just this shift that signals the beginning of the modern short story most commonly attributed to Poe in the following decade.

Joseph Sheridan Le Fanu

Critic Harold Orel has suggested that by the time Joseph Sheridan Le Fanu appears in the 1850's, the oral tradition "has receded into the background," for the emphasis of La Fanu's stories is on a shaped fiction. Although Le Fanu did not create the horror story, says Orel, he developed ways to transform this popular narrative genre into "an artistically finished production, one worthy of the time of serious readers." In his best-known story, "Green Tea," first published in 1869 and reprinted in his collection *In a Glass Darkly* in 1872, Le Fanu blurs the line between the physical and the mental and in his narrator, Dr. Martin Hesselius, a "medical philosopher," creates a kind of psychoanalytic detective. On hearing the narrative of the Rev. Jennings, who is plagued by the appearance of an hallucinatory monkey, Hesselius seeks to solve the mystery and cure Jennings by applying his own theory about the nature of dual reality. The central focus of Hesselius's theory is that the natural world is only the expression of the spiritual world.

The monkey is the subject of most of the commentary on the story, with various critics calling it a Freudian animal or a manifestation of schizophrenia and repressed sexual desires and others suggesting that it is purposely open-ended to leave readers mystified and to create a Kafkaesque sense of generalized guilt. Hesselius's attributing the hallucination of the monkey to Rev. Jennings's drinking of green tea is not, most readers suspect, the true cause of the monkey's appearance. The actual details of the story suggest that the appearance of the creature results from Jennings's living alone and writing a book on the religious metaphysics of the ancients. Jennings says he was always thinking and writing on the subject and that it thoroughly "infected" him, drawing him into a purely mental world detached from physical reality. Indeed, Jennings's disease is not a physical one but rather an "artistic" one that can be cured only "critically." It represents the central problem that dominates the nineteenth century short story—the blurring of the lines between the psychical and the physical so that the psychical is projected outward and then responded to as if it were real.

George Moore

Many critics of the short story have suggested that the modern Irish short story begins in 1903 with the publication of George Moore's *The Untilled Field*, thus agreeing with Moore's own typically immodest assessment that the collection was a "frontier book, between the new and the old style" of fiction. Moore felt that *The Untilled Field* was his best work, boasting that he wrote the stories to be models for young Irish writers in the future. Indeed, as critics have suggested, the book had a significant effect on the collection of short stories that has become one of the most influential short-story collections in the twentieth century—James Joyce's *Dubliners* (1914).

In combining the coarse subject matter of the French naturalists with the polished style of the *fin-de-siècle* aesthetes, the stories in *The Untilled Field* seem unique for their time. However, they still maintain an allegiance to the folktale form and to the importance of story as a means of understanding reality. Moore's adherence to the folk tale form and the need to understand reality by means of story can be clearly seen in one of his best-known and most anthologized stories from *The Untilled Field*—"Julia Cahill's Curse." The story-within-the-story, told by a cart driver to the first-person narrator, recounts an event that took place twenty years earlier when a priest named Father Madden had Julia put out of the parish for what he considered unseemly behavior; in retaliation, Julia put a curse on the parish, prophesying that every year a roof would fall in and a family would go to America. The basic conflict in the tale is between Julia, who in her dancing and courting, represents free pagan values, and the priest, who, in his desire to restrain her, represents church restrictions.

The conflict between Julia and the priest is clear enough; however it is the relationship between the teller and the listener that constitutes the structural interest of the story, for what the tale focuses on is an actual event of social reality that has been mythicized by the teller and thus by the village folk both to explain and to justify the breakdown of Irish parish life in the late nineteenth century. Whereas the folk may believe such a tale literally, the modern listener believes it in a symbolic way. Indeed, what Moore does here is to present a story that is responded to within the story itself as both a literal story of magic and as a symbolic story to account for the breakdown of parish life.

"So on He Fares" is a more complex treatment of how story is used to understand a social situation. Moore himself had a high regard for this story, even going so far as to say in his boastful way that it was the best short story ever written. The basic situation is that of the loneliness of the child Ulick Burke who chaffs against the harsh control of his mother and dreams of his absent father and of running away from home. The story is very much like a fairy tale, complete with the evil parent, the absent soldier father, and the child's need to strike out and make his fortune. When Ulick becomes a man and returns home, he is met by a small boy, the same age as he when he left, whose name is also Ulick Burke.

"So on He Fares" is an interesting experiment with the nature of story as a projection of desire, in this case the basic desire of the child to escape his controlled situation. In one sense, it can be read literally; that is, that when Ulick returns he indeed finds a younger brother who has the love that he himself never had from his mother. In another sense, it can be read as a symbolic projection of the child, who throws himself into the river to escape his loneliness and then is reborn into a child the mother loves. Ultimately, it can be read as a projection of a child's desire to escape and still remain home at the same time; it is thus a story about story, about a childhood fantasy presented as if it really happened.

Frank O. Connor singles out Moore's "Home Sickness" as representative of the direction that the Irish short story would take in the twentieth century, arguing that it has the "absolute purity of the short story as opposed to the tale." The story seems simple enough. James Bryden, an Irish immigrant who works in a bar in the Bowery, goes back to Ireland "in search of health," and for a short time considers marrying a peasant girl and remaining there. What unifies the story beyond its simple narrative structure is the understated but sustained tone of Bryden's detachment from the reality of Irish life and his preference to live within a sort of nostalgic reverie, which he is disappointed to find remains unrealized.

Although Bryden longs for the Bowery as he contrasts the "weakness and incompetence" of the people around him with the "modern restlessness and cold energy" of the people in New York, and although he blames the ignorance and primitive nature of the folk who cling to religious authority as his reason for returning to America, the conclusion of the story suggests a more subtle and universal theme by counterpointing a detached dreamlike mood of reverie against Irish village reality. The story is about the unbridgeable gap between restless reality and dreamlike memory.

James Joyce

The most influential modern Irish short-story writer is James Joyce, although that influence is based on one slim volume, *Dubliners*. Joyce's most famous contribution to the theory and technique of modern short narrative is his notion of the "epiphany," which he defined in his early novel *Steven Hero* (1944): "By an epiphany he meant a sudden spiritual manifestation, whether in the vulgarity of speech or of gesture or in a memorable phrase of the mind itself. He believed that it was for the man of letters to record these epiphanies with extreme care, seeing that they themselves are the most delicate and evanescent of moments." In a Joyce story, an epiphany is a formulation through metaphor or symbol of some revelatory aspect of human experience, some highly significant aspect of personal reality, usually communicated by a pattern of what otherwise would be seen as trivial details and events. Joyce's technique is to transform the casual into the causal by repetition of seemingly trivial details until they are recognized as part of a significant pattern. Two of Joyce's best-known stories, "Eveline" and "Araby," end with decisions or revelations that seem unprepared for until the reader reflects back on the story and perceives the patterned nature of what at first seem only casual detail.

In "Eveline," the reader must determine how Eveline's thoughts of leaving in Part 1 inevitably lead to her decision to stay in Part 2. Most of the story takes place while Eveline is sitting at the window watching the evening "invade" the avenue. Nothing really "happens" in the present in the first part of the story, for her mind is on the past and the future, occupied with contrasting images of familiar/strange, duty/pleasure, earth/sea, entrapment/escape, death/life. It is the counterpoint pattern of these images that prepares the reader for the last section of the story when Eveline stands among the crowds and decides not to leave her father and Ireland.

The problem is how to understand how the first part of the story, which focuses primarily on the bleakness of Eveline's past life at home and thus seems to suggest that she will decide to go with Frank, manages at the same time to suggest that she will decide to stay. The basic tension is between the known and the unknown. Although Eveline does not have many happy memories of her childhood and family life, at least they are familiar and comfortable. Because these events have already happened, what "used to be" is still present and a part of her. However, life with Frank, because it has not yet happened, is tinged with fear of the unknown, in spite of the fact that it holds the promise of romance and respect. Thus, at the end, when she sets her face to him, passive, like a helpless animal, with no sign of love or farewell or recognition, we realize that her decision to stay is ultimately inexpressible.

What Joyce achieves in one of his most anthologized stories, "Araby," derives from Anton Chekhov's experiments with creating symbols out of objects by their role or context, not by their preexisting symbolic meaning. The primary counterpoint throughout the story consists of those images that suggest ordinary reality and those that suggest unknown romance. The result is a kind of realism that is symbolic at the same time, for the boy's spiritual romanticism is embodied in the realistic objects of his world. This is a story about the ultimate romantic projection, for the boy sees the girl as a religious object, a romantic embodiment of desire. Her name is like a "summons" to all his "foolish blood," yet it is such a sacred name that he cannot utter it. Her image accompanies him "even in places the most hostile to romance." Thus, when he visits Araby, a place he fancies the most sympathetic to romance, what he seeks is a sacred object capable of objectifying all his unutterable desires.

The conversation he overhears causes his realization precisely because of its trivial flirtatious nature, for what the boy discovers is that there is nothing so sacred that it cannot be made profane. To see his holy desire for Mangan's sister diminished to mere physical desire is to see a parody of himself. The result is the realization not only that he is driven and derided by vanity but also that all is vanity; there is no way for the sacred desires human beings store up in their ghostly hearts to be actualized and still retain their spiritual magic.

"The Dead" is the most subtle example of Joyce's innovative technique. The first two-thirds of the story reads as if it were a section from a novel, as numerous characters are introduced and the details of the party are reproduced in great detail. It is only in the last third, when Gabriel's life is transformed, first by his romantic and sexual fantasy about his wife and then by his confrontation with her secret life, that the reader reflects on the first two-thirds of the story and perceives that the earlier concrete details and the trivial remarks are symbolically significant. Thematically, the conflict that reflects the realistic/lyrical split in the story is the difference revealed to both Gabriel and the reader between public life and private life, between life as it is in actual experience and life perceived as desire.

The party portion of "The Dead" reflects Gabriel's public life; his chief interest is what kind of figure he is going to cut publicly. However, throughout the party period of the story, there are moments—particularly those moments that focus on the past, on music, and on marital union—when reality is not presented as here and now but as a mixture of memory and desire. During their short carriage ride to the hotel, he indulges in his own self-delusion about his relationship with his wife: "moments of their life together that no one knew of or would ever know of, broke upon and illuminated his memory."

When Gabriel discovers that Gretta has a secret life that has nothing to do with him, he sees the inadequacy of his public self. Michael Furey, who has been willing to sacrifice his life for love of another, challenges Gabriel's smug safety. In the much-discussed lyrical ending of "The Dead," Gabriel confronts the irony that the dead Michael is more alive than he is. "Generous tears" fill his eyes because he knows that he has never lived the life of desire, only the untransformed life of the everyday. At the end, awake and alone while his wife sleeps beside him, he loses his egoistic self and imaginatively merges into a mythic lyrical sense of oneness. "The Dead" is not a story that can be understood the way most novels are read—one thing after another—but the way the modern short story must be read—aesthetically patterned in such a way that only the end makes the rest of the story meaningful.

Seumas O'Kelly, James Stephens, Daniel Corkery

One of the most powerful post-Joycean Irish short stories, a story strikingly modern in its experimental use of a variety of stylistic modes, is Seumas O'Kelly's "The Weaver's Grave," which, while largely unknown among American readers, is appreciated by many Irish critics as a masterpiece of classical perfection. Although the story centers on the seemingly simple situation of two old men helping the weaver's young widow look for the grave plot of her recently deceased elderly husband, the symbolic structure of the story is elaborately complex. O'Kelly combines techniques of classical drama, poetry, painting, and philosophic discourse to create a story about aging, death, and rebirth that owes much to James Joyce, even as it anticipates the fiction of Samuel Beckett.

The most important symbolic elements in the story are the mazelike graveyard, the two grotesque old men, the handsome twin grave-diggers, the darkly beautiful widow, and the corpselike old cooper, Malachi Roohan. The thematic center occurs when the widow goes to the ancient cooper's house to see if he knows the location of her husband's grave site. A mummified figure, the cooper magically seems to come to life momentarily to tell her that she is a dream, that he is a dream, and that all the world is a dream.

When the widow returns to the graveyard, she has a epiphanic realization, a clear insight into something that had been obscure before. "And no sooner had the thing become definite and clear than a sense of the wonder of life came to her. It was all very like the dream Malachi Roohan had talked about." At the very moment she becomes aware of the individuality of one of the young gravediggers, they find the grave site. The story ends with the widow and the grave-digger standing across the grave from each other as she thinks that the man framed against the sky is a wonder, a poem, and the whole place swoons before her eyes. "Never was this world so strange, so like the dream that Malachi Rooham had talked about." The young man springs across the "open black mouth of the weaver's grave" to her, looks down into it and asks if she is satisfied. With this tableau, the curtain comes down as she says, in a voice like that of a young girl, "I'm satisfied." "The Weaver's Grave" is a masterpiece of narrative structure that focuses on the ultimate realities of death and rebirth occurring simultaneously, much like the mythic immolation and resurrection of the fabled phoenix.

James Stephens is another Irish short-story writer who bridges the gap between the modernism introduced by James Joyce and the experimentalism pushed to such extremes later on by Samuel Beckett. Of his two collections of stories, *Here Are Ladies* (1913), is the best known. Stephens's most anthologized story, "A Rhinoceros, Some Ladies, and a Horse." is also his most Beckett-like piece. The protagonist/narrator, a young man who works at a theatrical agency, encounters the rhinoceros, ladies, and horse in separate and seemingly unrelated events in the story. However, the encounters are related psychologically: First some boys push him into a rhinoceros cage, and the animal falls in love with his shoes. Second, a great music-hall lady comes into the theatrical office and looks at him the way the rhinoceros did; he wonders if she is going to smell him down one leg and up the other. Finally, when he is given letters to post, a man asks him to hold his horse, and the horse falls in love with him as if he had found his long-lost foal. The story ends with an encounter with a woman named Mary and her husband Joseph, a Christian reference further emphasized by the woman's referring to the protagonist as "Childagrace." The final comic scene centers on the pronunciation of "bosom" (introduced earlier by the music-hall woman who tells the boy to "come to my Boozalum, angel," echoed later by Joseph, who introduces Mary as "the wife of my bosum," and concluded when Mary calls to the narrator to "come to my boozalum, angel"). The absurd encounters of the narrator and the comic non-sequitur dialogue anticipate Beckett's *En attendant Godot* (pb. 1952; *Waiting for Godot*, 1954).

Another frequently anthologized Stephens story, "The Triangle," is an experiment with combining conventions of the essay with those of story, in which what little plot the story has centers on Mr. and Mrs. Morrissy and the visit of Mrs. Morrissy's cousin—all of whom create the triangularity of the story's title. The story moves from the stated platitude, "two is company and three is a crowd" through an exploration of how the introduction of the third party creates a plot and counterplot to bring some complication and thus life/story into the previously placid stasis of the Morrissy marriage. The story ends with Stephen's central thematic statement: "Fluidity is existence, there is no other, and for ever the chief attraction of

Paradise must be that there is a serpent in it to keep it lively and wholesome."

It is an unfortunate fact of literary history that the fiction of Daniel Corkery has been overshadowed by his mentoring of two younger writers, Frank O'Connor and Seán O'Faoláin. It is symbolically appropriate that Corkery's best-known collection, *A Munster Twilight*, was published in 1916, the year of the Easter Rising, since Corkery was a fervent nationalist who aligned himself with all things Irish: Catholicism, the Rising, the Gaelic language, and the rural Irish countryside. Typical of Corkery's affirmation of the mystical importance of rural place is his much-admired story, "The Ploughing of Leaca-na-Naomb," which begins appropriately with the question, "With which shall I begin—man or place?" Echoing the folktale magic of the "old times," the story centers on the basic conflict between the sacred and profane use of land and ends with a heroic gesture by the protagonist, who is seen as "the last of an immemorial line." However, Corkery is one of the last Irish writers to draw from the supernatural world of the old folk tellers, for, in the next generation, his two most famous students, O'Connor and Seán O'Faoláin, affirm the Joycean literary story of tight structure and realistic detail.

Seán O'Faoláin, Frank O'Connor, Liam O'Flaherty

Seán O'Faoláin has argued that the short story thrives best within a romantic framework; the more organized and established a country is, O'Faoláin claims, the less likely that the short story will flourish there. Although Ireland, a country that stubbornly sticks to its folk roots, has been a most hospitable place for the short-story form, O'Faolain seems to have constantly fought against the romanticism of the short story, yearning for the realism of the novel. Thus, his stories reveal a continual battle between his cultural predilection for the short story (with its roots in the folk and its focus on the odd and romantic slant) and his conviction that realism is the most privileged artistic convention.

O'Faoláin's eight separate collections of stories span the period from 1932 to 1976. In the thirteen-hundred-page single volume of his collected short stories, Seán O'Faoláin experiments with a wide range of generic types and language styles: from the romantic dreamlike narrative, "Fugue," to the allegorical satire, "The Man Who Invented Sin," and the social comedy, "The Faithful Wife," to the domestic comedy, "Childybawn."

"Fugue," an early O'Faoláin story, shows his self-conscious experimentation with narrative style. Although the plot focuses on a young Irish rebel trying to escape British soldiers, the heart of the story is his lyrically romantic encounter with a country girl. As the title suggests, what holds the story together is not linear plot but rather the polyphonic counterpoint of the threat of violence and death with the desire for the quiet rural life.

In "The Man Who Invented Sin," the focus is on the temporary escape of two young nuns and two young priests from the restrictions of the Church while on a summer program in the country to learn Irish. The idyllic retreat, filled with singing and dancing, is broken up by the local curate, who forces them back into religious reality like the serpent in the Garden of Eden. Over twenty years later, the narrator of the story meets the curate, who recalls the incident and laughs that he had to frighten the young innocents. As he walks away, however, the narrator sees his elongated shadow trailing behind him like a tail.

O'Faoláin's comic stories range from his domestic satire on the stereotype of the Irish male's relationship with his mother in "Childybawn" to the sophisticated satire of the Irish woman's relationship with the Catholic Church in "The Faithless Wife." In the first story, a man forgoes marriage to stay home to care for his mother, only to find out that she wishes he had married years ago, for he has limited her secret gambling and drinking. In the second, in the witty language and style of an Oscar Wilde comedy, a man pursues a young married woman, trying to break down the "formidable chastity" of the Irish woman. However, when her husband, a bore who reminds her of an unemptied ashtray, has a stroke, she refuses to leave him. The story ends with the man giving up on her and lamenting that Irish women are awful liars without a grain of romance in them.

O'Faoláin's stories reside uneasily between the romanticism to which he was born and the realism for which he yearned. His basic technique might be called "poetic realism," a kind of prose in which objects and events seem to be presented objectively, but yet are transformed by the unity of the form itself into meaningful metaphors. O'Faoláin is a craftsman with an accurate vision of his country and its people; however, he is a self-conscious imitator of more famous precursors, never quite able to find a distinctive voice that manifests his individual talent.

Although Frank O'Connor wrote poems, plays, novels, travel books, and literary criticism, his place in twentieth century literature is most assured by his work in the short-story genre. Of the nearly one hundred short stories he published in collections beginning with the 1931 *Guests of the Nation*, the best-known are "Guests of the Nation," "The Drunkard," "My Oedipus Complex," and "Judas." The first, published when O'Connor was a young man, is the stark and violent story about two British soldiers reluctantly executed by Irish rebels, whereas the other three are comic stories about a child's relationship with his parents and a young man's romantic love.

One of O'Connor's best-known books is his study of the short-story genre, *The Lonely Voice*, in which he argues that, as opposed to the novel, the short story takes as its primary subject the experiences of what he calls a "submerged population group," such as the peasants of Ivan Turgenev and Chekhov and the townsfolk of Sherwood Anderson and James Joyce. Although most critics agree that O'Connor never perfected the short story to the degree that Joyce did, his profound understanding of the secret of the short story's inherent difference from the novel, as well as his ability to capture what he called "The Irish middle-class Catholic way of life" in delightful little comic vignettes, has assured him a permanent place in the history of twentieth century Irish Literature.

Although the speaker in "Judas," one of O'Connor's best-known stories, is obviously older than the young boy in Joyce's "Araby," the conflict of the two stories is basically the same—the tension between a romanticized view of a young woman and a more realistic view. However, whereas the voice in Joyce's story is serious, the voice of O'Connor's young man is comically self-deprecating. One's first reaction may be that the Judas of the story is the boy himself, for he thinks he has betrayed his mother in some way. The conventional reference to the crowing of the cock after his sleepless night also suggests this. However, neither the action nor the imagery of the story indicates that the protagonist is the Judas betrayer. The real Judas in the story is the mother.

The mother, by instilling in the son an image of her own goodness and purity, betrays him into believing that all women, except the "bad women" he reads about in books, are like her. Thus, he feels guilty for the thoughts he has about "good girl" Kitty Doherty, thinking that she is "pure indeed." When Jerry finally confronts Kitty and hears her talk in "cold blood about 'spooning' with fellows all over the house," he feels "like a man who'd lived all his life in a dungeon getting into the sunlight for the first time." Thus resurrected from his guilt he goes home singing, "as if a stone had been lifted" from his heart. The mother's image has not been completely banished; he faces the silent reproach of her waiting in darkness, worrying about him. His cruel retort to her whimpering question is an expression of his anger at being betrayed now that he feels that he is a stranger to her.

Jerry, then, is not so much Judas as he is the ironic suffering Jesus Christ deceived by the mother into thinking that all women are pure. The final image in the story completes the terms of the ironic Mary-Christ parallel. When Jerry goes to the mother's room and sees her sitting in bed under the Sacred Heart Lamp, he bursts out crying, and she spreads her arms to hold him in the classic tableau of the Pieta. "All she could do was to try and comfort me for the way I'd hurt her, to make up to me for the nature she'd given me."

Liam O'Flaherty is most often described as a naturalist, like Émile Zola and Theodore Drieser, a writer who depicts the futile efforts of human beings in conflict with nature. In such stories as "Spring Sowing," which appeared in his collection of the same name in 1924, in spite of the lyrical love between the young Irish farm couple, their labor is menial and ultimately deadening, for they are controlled by the bleak landscape where they must spend their entire lives. A number of O'Flaherty's stories, such as "The Cow's Death" and "The Rockfish," are both poetic and primitive at once, depicting the natural cycle of animal life as simultaneously beautiful and frightening.

Two favorites with critics, because they are so Irish in subject matter, are "Going into Exile" and "The Two Lovely Beasts." The first falls into an Irish literary tradition of stories about young people leaving home for better prospects in America. "Going into Exile" quite simply focuses on a party on the night before the departure of a son and daughter in which, although little is said, much is felt about the loss of the children. The stoic restraint is broken only at the end when the cabin is filled with bitter wailing and the mother is left staring down an empty road. "The Two Lovely Beasts," from the collection *The Two Lovely Beasts and Other Stories* (1948), has been a favorite O'Flaherty story because it has been interpreted it as a clear attack on capitalism. Almost allegorical in its depiction of one man who gradually begins to acquire more and more wealth while his family suffers and his neighbors scorn him, the story is ultimately morally ambiguous, for even as the ambitious man is ruthless, his enemies seems stupid and malicious.

What makes the favorite anthology piece, "The Fairy Goose," a morally complex parable is its mixture of comic and tragic tone, as well as its thematic combination of the sacred and the profane. Although there is something comically absurd about transforming a goose into a sacred object with ribbons around its neck, at the same time there is something innocent and touching about the way O'Flaherty personalizes the goose as an embodiment of charm, innocence, and dignity. Moreover, although there is something foolish about the extreme reaction of the priest to the goose, at the same time there is something violent and vicious about this reaction as well.

Part of the power of O'Flaherty's satire is due to the fact that although Mrs. Wiggins has exploited the goose for her own profit, she has done no more than the Church itself. Although the priest's battle with his competition, the goose and the old woman, is comic, its result is, if not tragic, at least pathetic. The goose's death by stoning is a terrible indictment of the Church as a purveyor of fear and hate. Although the men who killed the goose take the advice of the priest to fear God, they are unable to love their neighbors. Their wives claim that the only time in the history of the village that there was peace and harmony was when they accepted the sacred nature of the goose. O'Flaherty's satire on the routing of the innocent religion of love by the avaricious religion of jealousy is given the authority of folktale.

Elizabeth Bowen, Mary Lavin, Edna O'Brien

Of the seventy-nine stories in *The Collected Stories of Elizabeth Bowen* (1981), published from the 1920's through the 1940's, less than ten percent center on Ireland. Instead, Bowen's best-known stories dramatize psychological states that hover somewhere between reality and hallucination. Such stories as "The Happy Autumn Fields" move so smoothly back and forth between the past and the present that distinctions between those two realms are meaningless. In "Her Table Spread," the real social world of the drawing room is invaded by romantic fantasy to such an extent that the relative reality of the two worlds is brought into question.

Bowen's most anthologized story, "The Demon Lover," is the most striking example of her fascination with a realm of reality that seems neither wholly phenomenal nor wholly hallucinatory. While some critics term the story a ghost tale, others argue that it is a story of psychological delusion. The problem centers on the mysterious letter the protagonist Mrs. Drover finds in her boarded-up London home when she visits it from the country where the family has retreated to escape World War II bombing. Bearing the current day's date, the letter is from a man that Mrs Drover knew twenty-five years before, who was reported missing during World War I. The letter reminds her of a promise she made to him and tells her to expect him on this day as they had arranged. The story makes use of the old legend of the demon lover, which usually focuses on a young woman's promise to love her young man forever and to await his return from battle. However, a few years after he is reported dead or missing she meets and plans to marry another man. Usually on the wedding day, the lost lover returns, sometimes as a rotting corpse, and carries the young bride away to join him in death.

Mrs. Drover is an example of a common short fiction protagonist whose life is so safe and comfortable that she must be invaded by some basic irrational force. Although her own feelings for the soldier were not passionate and she seemed relieved when he left, she did indeed make an "unnatural promise" that cuts her apart from the rest of human kind. Bowen's treatment of the demon lover myth largely depends on the residue of the past in the boarded-up house: a yellow smoke stain on the fireplace, a ring left by a vase on a table, the bruise in the wallpaper where the doorknob hit it, claw marks left by the piano on the parquet floor. These "traces" metaphorically bring the letter into existence, making a past promise a present reality. Bowen does not resolve the reader's uncertainty about the nature of Mrs. Drover's visitation, for what matters is the story's theme of the past's claim on the present.

Although Mary Lavin was born in Massachusetts, she lived in Ireland from the age of ten until her death in Dublin in 1996. Her first collection, *Tales from Bective Bridge* (1942) was very well received, garnering awards and prizes; she continued to publish important short stories up through the 1960's. One of her early stories, "Sarah," is still a reader favorite because it so economically and confidently explores a typical plight of young Irish womanhood. Sarah is a hard worker, but she has a bad reputation because she has had three sons out of wedlock. When she gets pregnant with a fourth child, this time by a married man for whom she works, her brothers throw her and the baby out. The story ends when the baby's father, who has denied any involvement with Sarah, is told that she and the baby have been found dead in a ditch by the side of the road. What makes the moral issues of the story complex and ambiguous is the fact that the wronged wife is maliciously responsible for Sarah's death. The story juxtaposes the two women—the respectable wife who holds back from life and the scorned Sarah who embraces it. Although social respectability triumphs over immorality in the story, it does so at the terrible price of loss of humanness.

Lavin's best-known story, published some forty years after "Sarah," is "The Great Wave," a harrowing tale about a terrible storm in which all the inhabitants of a small island except two young fishermen are killed in a giant tidal wave. The story is recalled by one of the young men, who is now a bishop on his way to the island many years later. What gives the story its power is Lavin's description of the wave which descends on the boys like a great green wall of water as if the whole sea has been stood up on its edge. The natural world takes on a mythic power in the story, as if the wave signals the end of the world.

Although best known for her *Country Girls Trilogy and Epilogue* (1986) and other novels, Edna O'Brien is the author of half a dozen short-story collections that have augmented her reputation as an Irish writer who has not been afraid to present Irish women as sexual human beings, who often find themselves caught in romantic fantasies. An early story by O'Brien, "Irish Revel," from her first collection *The Love Object* (1968) and a late story, "Lantern Slides," from the book of the same name published in 1990, both of which are anthology favorites, are good examples of her typical themes and her stylistic range.

"Irish Revel" centers on Mary, a seventeen-year-old village girl who has been invited to her first party in town. However, when she arrives in her best clothes, she discovers she has actually been invited to be a serving maid. Her head filled with romantic fantasies about life in town, she is surprised that so many people there are coarse and vulgar. When the men get drunk and start quarrels and one clumsily makes advances toward her, Mary loses all illusions about town life. Slipping out of the hotel before dawn, she goes home, but she has not given up her romantic hope for a handsome young man. The story ends with lines that echo the famous lyrical ending of Joyce's "The Dead": "Frost was general all over Ireland . . . frost on the stony fields, and on all the slime and ugliness of the world."

O'Brien's "Lantern Slides," the title story of her last collection, is also a tribute to "The Dead," for it recounts a contemporary Dublin party in which a number of characters tell their own stories of love and disappointment. Just as in Joyce's story, the focus here is on the ghostly nature of the past in which all have experienced the loss of romantic fantasies. However, the power of desire has such a hold on the characters that chivalric romance seems an attainable, yet not quite reachable, graillike goal. When the estranged husband of one of the women arrives, everyone hopes it is the wandering Odysseus returned home in search of his Penelope. "You could feel the longing in the room, you could touch it—a hundred lantern slides ran through their minds . . . It was like a spell . . . It was as if life were just beginning."

Brian Friel, John McGahern, William Trevor

Brian Friel has been criticized by some socially minded critics for writing stories in which the conflicts are more personal than political and the past more romantic than rebellious. His collection *The Saucer of Larks* (1962) is his most important collection; "Foundry House" is his best-known story, primarily because the dramatic oppositions in the story derive from Irish history and reflect a clearly defined class distinction that once was known as the "Big House" system, in which English Protestants lived in the large manor homes while Irish Catholic peasants were dependant on them. Friel symbolizes the difference between the dying old way and the competent new industrial world by making the "Big House" family aging and sterile and Joe, the working-class protagonist, a radio-television repairman. When Joe is called to the house to show the family how to play a tape recording from one of the daughters, the infirm father calls him "boy," as in the old days. However, when Joe returns home he can say only that they are a great, grand family.

The Irish stereotypes of the alcoholic husband and the shamed and embarrassed wife form the basis of Friel's "The Diviner." When Nelly Devenny is freed from her alcoholic husband by his death, after a suitable period of mourning, she remarries a respectable retired man from the West of Ireland, who is drowned in a lake three months later. After frogmen fail to find the body, a diviner is brought in, who, like a priest, can smell out the truth, which is two whisky bottles in the dead man's pocket. Nelly's final wail is not so much for the dead husband as it is for the respectability she had almost gained but which now is lost once again.

There are no sentimental images of the emerald isle in John McGahern's stories in his best-known collection *Nightlines*, published in 1970; many are darkly pessimistic. Moreover, it is not the speaking "voice" of the Irish storyteller that dominates his stories but the stylized tone of modern minimalism. Typical of the Joycean tradition, McGahern's stories are both realistic and lyrical at once. Also typical of that tradition, McGahern is not interested in confronting his characters with social abstractions but rather the universal challenges of guilt, responsibility, commitment, and death.

McGahern's best-known story, "The Beginning of an Idea," opens with the first sentences of Eva Lindberg's notebook, which describe how Chekhov was carried home to Moscow on an ice wagon with the word "Oysters" chalked on the side. Because the lines haunt her, she gives up her work as a theater director and her affair with a married man to go to Spain to write an imaginary biography of Chekhov. However, once there, she finds she cannot write. When a local policeman she befriends entraps her into having sex, she packs up and leaves, feeling rage about her own foolishness. On the train she has the bitter taste of oysters in her mouth, and when a wagon passes, she has a sudden desire to look and see if the word Oysters is chalked on it.

William Trevor is, without question, the most respected contemporary Irish short-story writer. Trevor has said that having been born Irish, he observes the world through "Irish sensibilities" and takes for granted an Irish way of doing things. However, as a writer he knows he has to "stand back" so far that he is "beyond the pale, outside the society he comments upon in order to get a better view of it." The result is that while most of Trevor's stories are not specifically Irish, even those that are centered in Ireland transcend limitations of time and place. Stories from such collections as *The Ballroom of Romance and Other Stories* (1972), *Angels at the Ritz and Other Stories* (1975), and *Beyond the Pale and Other Stories* (1982) have been republished in *The Stories of William Trevor*, published in 1983.

One of Trevor's most famous stories, "Beyond the Pale," is a powerful example of his treatment of an Irish theme. When two British couples make an annual visit to County Antrim, north of Belfast, there seems to be no sign of the so-called Troubles, violent skirmishes involving the Irish Republican Army. However, trouble in this story is submerged beneath the calm surface. The narrator, Milly, is having an affair with Dekko, whose wife Cynthia devours all the information she can find about Irish history and society. After a young man commits suicide at the hotel, Cynthia tells the others the story he told her before he died—a romantic fairy tale of two children who fall in love and live an idyll one summer at the hotel where the two British couples come for their own idyll. However, the young girl, becoming involved with political terrorism, is killed, after which the boy kills himself in despair. Cynthia uses the story, which everyone thinks she has invented, to represent all those put beyond the pale by violence and deception, ultimately relating it to the deception of her husband. Thus, although the story is an Irish parable in which romantic children grow into murdering riffraff, it is also a story of the deceiving British, who try to ignore their responsibility for the Troubles in Northern Ireland.

Trevor also juxtaposes Irish and British values in "Autumn Sunshine," this time in the person of an elderly Protestant cleric whose daughter has brought back a young man from England, who identifies with the Irish and wishes to align himself with rebels in the south. However, the cleric recognizes that the young man espouses the Irish cause only because it is one way the status quo in his own country can be damaged. Such men, the cleric thinks, deal out death and chaos, "announcing that their conscience insisted on it."

"Death in Jerusalem," which Trevor chose for his edition of *The Oxford Book of Irish Short Stories* (1989), focuses on Father Paul, an Irish priest who has gone away to America to become successful in the church and society, and his brother Francis, who has stayed home to care for their aging mother. When Father Paul finally convinces Francis to accompany him on a tour of Jerusalem, Francis is distressed that the actuality of what he sees does not match the idealized images of holy places he has in his imagination. The Via Dolorosa, for example, does not compare to his imaginative notion of Christ's final journey; he closes his eyes and tries to visualize it as he has seen it in his mind's eye. When Father Paul receives a telegram that their mother has died, he holds off telling his brother until he sees more of the Holy Land. However, Francis says Jerusalem does not feel as Jerusalem should; saying he will always hate the Holy Land, he insists on going home immediately. The story ends with an image of the priest, who does not look and act as observers think he should, smoking and drinking alone.

William Trevor is a master of the Irish short story, not because he writes stories about Ireland and the Irish, but because he has that fine artistic ability, like his most famous predecessor, James Joyce, to write about trivial, everyday experiences in such a way that they become resonant with universal significance. Trevor's stories seem to have deceptively simple realistic surfaces, until one begins to probe a bit more deeply to discover how tightly built and powerfully realized they are. In the short fiction of Trevor, the mere stuff of the world is transformed into artistic significance. Trevor has said that the artist "attempts to extract an essence from the truth by turning it into what John Updike has called 'fiction's shapely lies'."

Other Irish Short-Story Writers Since 1960

In addition to O'Brien, McGahern, and Trevor, several other Irish writers have excelled in the short story since the 1960's. The most frequently anthologized contemporary Irish stories range from the relatively simple "The Poteen Maker" by Michael McLaverty, "The Ring" by Bryan McMahon, and "Secrets" by Bernard McLaverty, to the more sophisticated "All Looks Yellow to the Jaundiced Eye" by William Plunkett, "An Occasion of Sin" by John Montague, and "Diamonds at the Bottom of the Sea" by Desmond Hogan.

Michael McLaverty's popular story, "The Poteen Maker" (*Collected Short Stories of Michael McLaverty*, 1978), is a relatively simple tale about a country school teacher. The central event, as recalled by a former student, deals with the teacher's demonstrating the process of distillation. It is only years later that the narrator realizes that the teacher was making poteen, a kind of Irish moonshine. The story simply and economically presents a nostalgic reminiscence reflecting the Irish fondness for drink and the camaraderie a "wee drop" encourages. Bryan MacMahon's "The Ring," from *The End of the World and Other Stories* (1978) is a brief pastoral parable about an elderly Irish widow who, having lost her wedding ring while harvesting hay, doggedly spends an entire week searching for it. The narrator, the old woman's grandson, who has always thought of her as "main hard," is struck by the one time he saw her express emotion, crying "like the rain" when she finds the ring. Bernard McLaverty's "Secrets," from his 1977 collection of the same name, is a somewhat more complex story about a young man's relationship with his maiden aunt. As a boy he read a batch of her love letters from a young soldier who later became a priest. Years later when he goes to visit her deathbed, he recalls her as his childhood teller of tales and weeps that she might forgive him.

Patrick Boyle's story, "All Looks Yellow to the Jaundiced Eye," from his 1971 collection of the same name, is an unsettling experimental story about a series of violent acts committed by a man who seemingly goes berserk for no apparent reason. The story explores the nature of unmotivated violence as presaged by an unarticulated sense of impending disaster. The day begins with mysterious portents sensed in the patterns of the flight of birds and the drumming of a rabbit's foot. Although the protagonist tries to remain calm, he seems driven to vicious behavior, wringing the necks of chickens, smashing the head of his dog, and finally strangling his wife, before shooting himself. It is a chilling story that makes no effort to provide psychological motivation for the man's behavior but rather suggests how such behavior is always a horrible human possibility.

John Montague's "An Occasion for Sin," from his *Death of a Chieftain and Other Stories* (1964), is a powerful story about Irish attitudes toward sexuality, told in an understated way from the perspective of a young French woman who has moved to the Dublin area with her new husband. While exploring the area, she finds a small beach south of the city, which she visits for sunbathing. What complicates this simple pleasure is the summer arrival of a number of clerical students who come to sunbathe on the beach and become friendly with the young woman. Although her conversations with the men are completely innocent, her Irish husband tells her she must be careful, for she might be classed as an "occasion for sin." Although she tries to ignore this warning, she discovers the basic truth of it when the young men begin to ask her about marriage because, as they say, "It's well known that French women think about nothing but love." She knows that she will probably not visit the beach the following summer.

Desmond Hogan's "Diamonds at the Bottom of the Sea," from his collection of the same name published in 1979, is a delicate love story about a man who, after living alone for many years, meets an old love who has lived in America. After the death of her husband, she returns to Ireland, and they both discover how little of their old love has died. The man seems dazed by this turn of events, as if it were all a dream. Indeed, the story is like an embodiment of a daydream fantasy of first love regained, aging forestalled, and old hopes rekindled. "Can't you see," the woman tells him, "it's the intense moments of youth. They won't leave, try as you will."

The main development of the Irish short story, from its roots in the rich folklore of the Irish people to its post-Joycean modernism, has been one in which the old local-color conventions and stereotypes of Ireland and its people have been replaced with an image of Ireland as a modern European country. Although many tourists may bemoan the loss of the old rural images, lamenting that Ireland and its literature is losing its distinctiveness, the fact is, most of those stereotypes were due to the biting poverty of many of the people, the harshness of British rule, and the despair and hopelessness that lead to the stereotypes of Irish immigration and drinking. The people of the new Ireland, the shining star of economic development in the European Union, are not sorry to see those myths laid to rest. The short story will probably always be a powerful literary form for Irish writers, but it will probably never again be a form that perpetuates the old local-color legends of the Emerald Isle.

Charles E. May

BIBLIOGRAPHY

Averill, Deborah M. *The Irish Short Story from George Moore to Frank O'Connor.* Washington: University Press of America, 1982. A helpful study of Moore, Corkery, O'Kelly, O'Flaherty, O'Faoláin, and O'Connor.

Delargy, J. H. "The Gaelic Story-Teller." *Proceedings of the British Academy* 31 (1945). An important study of the early Irish oral tradition of storytelling.

Kiberd, Declan. *Inventing Ireland: The Literature of the Modern Nation.* Cambridge, Mass.: Harvard University Press, 1996. An important study of the development of Irish literature from Oscar Wilde to the present day.

Kilroy, James, ed. *The Irish Short Story: A Critical History.* Boston: Twayne, 1984. A collection of five essays surveying the development of the Irish short story in the nineteenth and twentieth centuries.

Martin, Augustine, ed. *The Genius of Irish Prose.* Dublin: Mercier Press, 1985. Includes two relevant essays: "The Short-Story: 1900-1945" and "The Short Story After the Second World War."

Mercier, Vivian. "The Irish Short Story and Oral Tradition." In *The Celtic Cross: Studies in Irish Culture and Literature.* Edited by Ray B. Browne, William John Roselli, and Richard Loftus. West Lafayette, Ind.: Purdue University Studies, 1964. An influential essay that examines the relationship between the Irish folk tale and the modern Irish short story.

Orel, Harold. *The Victorian Short Story.* Cambridge: Cambridge University Press, 1986. A helpful historical study with important chapters on William Carleton and Sheridan Le Fanu.

Rafroidi, Patrick, ed. *The Irish Short Story.* Atlantic Highlands, N.J.: Humanities Press, 1979. An important collection of essays on both general historical/critical issues concerning the Irish short story and a number of important Irish short story writers from Carleton and Le Fanu to Patrick Boyle and John McGahern.

Thompson, Richard J. *Everlasting Voices: Aspects of the Modern Irish Short Story.* Troy, N.Y.: Whitston Publishing, 1989. A study of Moore's *The Untilled Field*, Joyce's *Dubliners*, and the stories of O'Connor, O'Faoláin, O'Flaherty, and Mary Lavin.

JAPANESE SHORT FICTION

People, it seems, cannot live without stories: Indeed, our need to construct narratives about our lives and the world around us is one of the things that make us human. Through stories we try to reach an understanding of who we are, individually and collectively, and of the various events that befall us. Where do we come from, and where do we end up? How can we control our passions, or endure the cares and woes of daily existence? Just as important, perhaps, how can we savor the comic, often ridiculous side of life? Through stories, people are able to share laughter and tears and confront an uncertain world.

Nevertheless, although all people live by narratives, not everyone tells, writes, or films them in exactly the same way. The shape of a narrative, for instance, and the way it is understood vary according to where and when it was fashioned. Japanese short fictions, as shall be seen, do not always fit neatly into the patterns that the modern, English-speaking readers expect. The first reaction may be that Japanese narratives do not end properly; yet on closer examination the reader finds that they do in fact resolve themselves through another kind of narrative logic, based more on the association of ideas and images than on a linear architectronic plan. Instead of a rising sea swell that propels the reader toward a final resolution—what might be called the Aristotelian pattern—one tends to find a series of smaller waves that carry the reader up and down, from one insight to the next. Though there are differences, however, Japanese short fictions are nevertheless fun and offer the reader a window into the imaginative sphere of one of the world's great literary cultures. To develop a fuller appreciation, this study will look at how this tradition evolved over the last eleven hundred years or so, focusing on the stories of a few selected authors, all available in translation. All the stories mentioned are available in English translation.

Early Short Fiction (900-1600 c.e.)

In ancient times, legends and folktales were assumed to be true, no matter how miraculous or weird they may seem to the modern reader. The local narratives that the Japanese wrote down in the seventh and eighth centuries, when they first adapted the Chinese writing system to fit their own very different language, generally belong in this category. Although they often make fascinating reading, they cannot really be called "fictions" since they were taken quite literally by their audience. By the late ninth and early tenth centuries, however, sophisticated and highly entertaining tales of the supernatural were making their way to Japan from Tang China, suggesting newer, more fictional forms of storytelling.

One of the best loved of the few Japanese stories that survive from this early period is "The Tale of the Bamboo Cutter." It tells of a tiny girl discovered by an old woodsman in the hollow stem of a bamboo, who quickly grows into a lovely young woman wooed by all the great lovers of the land. Although she shows not the slightest interest in any of them, five will not take no for an answer. She sets each of them an impossible task, demanding they bring her a jeweled branch from Paradise, for example, or the Buddha's own stone begging bowl. Then, when all have failed, revealing their weakness or dishonesty in the process, she returns to the moon from whence she came, despite the entreaties of the lovelorn emperor and the girl's aged parents. It is a wonderful tale, alternately amusing and touching, with the kind of highly structured plot that is rare in the short fictions that followed. In fact, it is likely that "The Tale of the Bamboo Cutter," although based on an existing story, creatively altered Chinese models to fit the Japanese context.

The Riverside Counselor's Stories

One of those creative alterations was the addition of fifteen thirty-one-syllable *waka* or *tanka* poems. These added beauty to "The Tale of the Bamboo Cutter" as well as a presumable touch of class, for "fiction" received very little respect from serious-minded individuals, who followed the Confucian line against such pursuits. Despite their lowly status, however, stories of various lengths thrived during the tenth and eleventh centuries, all mixing prose and poetry and often illustrations too. These reached their apex in Murasaki Shikibu's monumental *Genji monogatari* (c. 1004; *The Tale of Genji*, 1925-1933), which evoked the life and loves of the mythical Prince Genji and his descendants with extraordinary delicacy and insight. *The Tale of Genji* influenced all literature that followed, even short fiction, since despite the work's length (over a thousand pages in English translation), its episodic structure meant it could be read as a sequence of shorter narratives, each organized around *waka* poems.

Prominent among the few surviving works from that period is the *Tsutsumi chūnagon monogatari* (c. eleventh and twelfth century; *The Riverside Counselor's Stories*, 1985) a ten-story collection liberally sprinkled with *waka*. Its nameless authors were largely women of the upper classes who, like Murasaki, lived a sequestered life. Since their focus was the world around them, the material they had to work with was limited. Yet within that narrow range they moved adroitly and often to great effect. "The Lieutenant Plucks a Sprig of Flowering Cherry," for example, skewers the Genji-like "perfect lover" by having him accidentally abduct his beloved's grandmother for a romantic tryst (he follows through nonetheless), while "The Shell-Matching Contest" paints a portrait of innocent children at play with an unerring feel for setting and detail. Finally, "The Lady Who Admired Vermin" (or "The Lady Who Loved Insects"), most likely written by a man, introduces the thoroughly unforgettable character of a grown-up tomboy who scorns the primped and proper realm of femininity for the grubbier but more honest world of caterpillars and bugs.

Tale Literature

If aristocratic women writing for themselves and their immediate circle in a cloistered, hothouse environment shaped the type of short fictions found in *The Riverside Counselor's Stories*, then the public and male arena of Buddhist sermonizing gave birth to a very different kind of narrative, which spoke of and to common men and women. Beginning in the early ninth century, stories with religious themes were compiled and copied so that monks could use them to heighten their audience's awareness of Buddhism's long history, reminding them of the power of the Buddhas and bodhisattvas, and the efficacy of chanting the *sutras*. Yet, as time passed and Buddhism laid down roots in the local landscape, collections of such narratives came to include other types of folktales, some of which were secular in nature. By the mid-fourteenth century, at least forty-five anthologies of this sort of story—what the Japanese call *setsuwa bungaku* ("explained stories" or tale literature)— had been compiled for the pleasure of reading and listening as much as for religious instruction.

The most entertaining collection of tale literature in English, *Japanese Tales* (1987), selected, edited, and translated by Royall Tyler, draws heavily from two sources: the *Konjaku monogatari* (c. 1120; *Tales of Times Now Past*, 1979, partial translation), the most famous example of the genre, and the *Uji shūi monogatari* (*A Collection of Tales from Uji*, 1970), whose early thirteenth century compiler tells of collaring passersby both "high and low" to get them to add new examples to his collection. Thus it was that fearsome goblins, lustful snakes, and enchanted foxes came to take their place beside the assembled saints and sinners of Buddhist lore. Can one call these stories "short fictions"? Not really, perhaps, since the accounts are too brief to be fully developed (less than two pages on average), and the events they describe, however strange they may appear, were seen as factual at the time. Nevertheless, tale literature is crucially important since it was the inspiration for so many dramatic and short story masterpieces of later eras.

Medieval Short Stories

The fifteenth and sixteenth centuries were marked by civil warfare, which caused widespread suffering. Fortune was fickle in those violent years: Noble families might suddenly find themselves on the streets, while those of low birth, through luck or prowess, could rise to the very pinnacle of society. One diversion everyone could enjoy, however, was the *otogizōshi* (literally, companion stories), a form of popular story printed in hand-illustrated booklets or inscribed on scrolls. Traveling priests and storytellers drew from these medieval short stories, as they shall be called, in their work, which meant they were closely linked to the "vulgar" world of public performance. Thus, unlike the Noh theater and linked verse, elite pastimes whose texts were carefully preserved by later generations, medieval short stories were usually discarded.

Luckily, a few hundred examples managed to survive, which cover a remarkably wide range of subject matter. Some are confessional or revelatory tales (see the collection *Rethinking Sorrow: Revelatory Tales of Late Medieval Japan*, by Margaret Helen Childs, 1991) describing, often in heart-rending terms, events that provoked individuals to renounce the world for a life of Buddhist prayer and contemplation. Others, however, lean more toward the humorous and the romantic (see *Tales of Tears and Laughter: Short Fiction of Medieval Japan*, translated by Virginia Skord, 1991). Although the romantic kind are filled with *waka* poetry like their aristocratic predecessors *The Tale of Genji* and *The Riverside Counselor's Stories*, their style was more accessible to common people. Perhaps most entertaining are the humorous stories of lusty wives, lazy husbands, and an individual called the "King of Farts," whose famed ability to break wind tempts another, less talented man to imitate him, with disastrous results. While such stories can hardly be called great literature, they are fun and offer a glimpse into the lives of the peddlers and peasants, priests and samurai, who populated medieval Japan.

Short Fiction of the Edo Era (1600-1868)

If the fifteenth and sixteenth centuries were bloody and unstable, the period that followed was one of unprecedented peace. It was called either the Tokugawa, after the family name of the shoguns who ruled, or the Edo after their capital city, modern-day Tokyo. By world standards, Japan became an affluent, urban, and literate country during this time, with a public eager to buy books or, more likely, borrow them for a small fee. To meet this growing demand, publishers improved their printing techniques so that they could press hundreds of attractively illustrated volumes from a single set of carved wooden blocks. Readers were especially curious to know about the lives of the high-class courtesans, the kabuki actors, and the wealthy customers who populated the "floating world" of the pleasure district, as well as the samurai who populated the provincial castle towns and Edo estates of the great feudal lords, the *daimyō*.

It was under these conditions that Japan's first great short-story master, Saikaku Ihara, made his name. Like commercially successful authors everywhere, Saikaku was keenly aware of what his audience wanted to read and was able to write quickly, a skill he picked up as a rapid-fire composer of comic haiku verses (his record was 23,500 in twenty-four hours). One might think him a hack, but in fact Saikaku was a gifted storyteller who combined a scholar's knowledge of literature, a journalist's eye for concrete detail, and a most human sympathy for the foibles of his unforgettable characters. Four of the five heroines of *Kōshoku gonin onna* (1686; *Five Women Who Loved Love*, 1956), for example, are undone by disastrous love affairs, but there is something noble about their headstrong, impetuous behavior, even though it eventually leads to suicide, the execution grounds, or a nunnery.

The one exception is the fifteen-year-old heroine of the final story, "Gengobei, the Mountain of Love." She is able to seduce and marry the man of her dreams, the priest Gengobei, even though he has never even looked at a woman, preferring young men instead (her strategy is to pretend to be a boy until the crucial moment). Saikaku was hardly dismissive about male homosexual relationships, however, which were quite acceptable in Edo Japan: Indeed, he lauded them as the highest form of love in his *Nanshoku ōkagami* (1687; *The Great Mirror of Male Love*, 1990), a collection of forty stories whose teenage heroes are willing to sacrifice everything for the men to whom they are devoted. Whatever the interests or sexual preferences of his audience might be, Saikaku was wiling to meet them with short stories that entertained and enlightened.

Ueda Akinari

Enlightenment of a different sort was on the mind of Ueda Akinari when he wrote his great eighteenth century classic, *Ugetsu monogatari* (1776; *Tales of Moonlight and Rain*, 1974). Unlike Saikaku, who praised heterosexual love in one collection, homosexual in the next, Ueda sought less to please and more to "heal" his readers emotionally and spiritually, a fitting goal for a man who spent part of his life as a medical doctor. The sufferings of each of the nine heroes in the *Tales of Moonlight and Rain*, for example, represent the painful struggle to move from youthful passion and innocence (the "rain" in the title) to a higher state of wisdom and experience (the "moon"). In every story, moreover, this hard-won maturity is achieved through contact with what might be called the supernatural, which means that *Tales of Moonlight and Rain* is often enjoyed simply as a collection of spooky stories. Yet there is a lot more there than meets the eye. For not only did Ueda believe in his gods, ghosts, and spirits, but also did he use them to evoke a literary tradition that stretched back as far as *The Tale of Genji* and across the seas to China.

"The Lust of the White Serpent"—one of the two Ueda stories from which director Kenji Mizoguchi drew in his classic film *Ugetsu* (1953)—for example, is based on a Chinese story about a white snake who turns herself into a gorgeous young woman in order to bewitch and seduce an attractive young man. Ueda transposed the narrative, giving it Japanese characters and setting it in the poetic Yoshino area. He also added a few new twists. For instance, he linked his story to the well-known legend of the Dōjōji Temple (recorded in *Tales of Times Now Past* mentioned above) about a snake-girl who turns the man who jilted her into a pile of ashes. As in "Dōjōji" and earlier Chinese versions of the white serpent legend, Ueda's serpent actually kills people, instead of just threatening to do so. In another change, the figure of the Buddhist priest—who plays the role of the savior in the Chinese story—is made so old he cannot reach the hero in time to help him. Alone, the hero is able to defeat the serpent but loses his young wife (a new character created by Ueda) in the process. Through these stratagems, Ueda not only "Japanizes" the story but also moves it to a higher literary and psychological level by placing the onus of responsibility on the hero's shoulders and leaving him wiser but also inevitably sadder at the end of his rain-to-moon odyssey.

Masters of the Modern Short Story

As has been demonstrated, Japanese short fiction from "The Tale of the Bamboo Cutter" to *Tales of Moonlight and Rain* often drew inspiration from Chinese sources even as it developed its own styles, themes, and objectives. Once the modern period began in 1868 with the abolition of the Tokugawa shogunate and the "restoration" of the young Meiji emperor, however, inspiration was more likely to come from the literary traditions of the West. Yet this did not mean that the Japanese short story immediately flowered as a result; to the contrary, it took about thirty years for the reading public to adjust to stories without pictures written in a new "vernacular" style and for a new generation of university-educated authors to digest and reformulate what they had learned from their Western models.

Higuchi Ichiyō

Remarkably, the first great "modern" writer of the Meiji period, Higuchi Ichiyō, was no upper-class intellectual but an impoverished young woman ignorant of Western languages, whose main literary influences were classics like *The Tale of Genji* and the stories of Saikaku. Her enduring masterpiece "Growing Up" (also rendered as "Child's Play") in fact owes much to Saikaku in its command of detail and scene, yet Higuchi's delicate portrait of life in the pleasure quarters as seen through the eyes of its children is more poignant and affecting than anything the old master ever wrote. Indeed, her sensitive handling of her material makes one realize how much Japanese and, more generally, East Asian literature suffered from the Confucian dictum that women's activities should be confined to the household. Although Higuchi died young, worn out by poverty and overwork, she left behind a legacy for the many Japanese women writers who followed.

Mori Ōgai

Among Higuchi's many admirers in Japanese literary circles was Mori Ōgai. After four years of medical study in Germany, Ōgai returned to Japan armed with an arsenal of artistic and critical theories, which he quickly put to work in his own fiction. At first, this led to a highly romanticized, somewhat derivative type of writing, a famous example being "The Dancing Girl," Ōgai's semiautobiographical story of a love affair between a Japanese student and a young German woman. Gradually, however, Ōgai changed. He developed a more terse and vernacular style and shifted his attention to historical topics and the legends of the past. "Sanshō the Steward"—also rendered as *Sansho the Bailiff* in Kenji Mizoguchi's classic film (1954)—for instance, is an elaborated version of one of Japan's most beloved fairytales about a brother and sister torn from their mother and sold as slaves to an evil overseer. While Ōgai took pains to respect history "as it really was," "Sanshō" speaks to the spiritual crisis of his times, offering a vision of courage and self-sacrifice to a society reeling from the impact of wholesale modernization.

Ōgai's later works are quite unlike anything written before in either the West or Japan. Generally, they take the form of biographical sketches of relatively obscure historical figures, but their aesthetic structure and characterization clearly qualify them as short stories. Given Ōgai's mastery of Western literature, this move away from conventional forms was hardly a failing on the author's part. Rather, like the novelist Sōseki Natsume, the other great architect of Japan's modern literature, Ōgai had reached the point where a narrow adherence to Western models hindered rather than helped.

Ryūnosuke Akutagawa

The writers who followed Ōgai and Sōseki had it much easier. For one thing, although most could read a Western language, they did not have to be the linguists their elders had been, since so much of the best literature the West had to offer—including the short stories of authors like Guy de Maupassant, Anton Chekov, Edgar Allan Poe, and Hans Christian Anderson—had been well translated by the time their generation reached its maturity in the Taisho Period (1912-1926). For another, thanks to the efforts of Higuchi Ichiyō, Mori Ōgai, and many others, the Japanese short story was firmly established as a genre linked to but not synonymous with its Western cousins.

No single pattern characterized the fiction of this second generation of writers, probably the most gifted in Japan's modern literary history. Rather, their achievement is best appreciated by a consideration of their differences. Ryūnosuke Akutagawa, for example, wrote tightly constructed stories which often drew from old collections like *Tales of Times Now Past*, discussed above. Two such stories, "Rashōmon" and "In a Grove," were adapted by the director Akira Kurosawa in his famous 1950 film, *Rashomon* while another, the gripping "Hell Screen," paints a disturbing portrait of an artist who pays a terrible price to create "the perfect picture." All three stories examine philosophical issues such as the clash between morality and survival, the relativity of "truth," and the link between creativity and the darker side of the unconscious. Instead of helping Akutagawa, however, these inquiries only seem to have plunged him deeper into despair. When he finally put an end to his life on the eve of Japan's descent into militarism, his suicide was interpreted as a sad testimony to the limitations of rationality in a world increasingly ruled by nationalistic passions.

Shiga Naoya

Despite the gemlike brilliance of his elegantly crafted stories, Akutagawa was never satisfied with them. He preferred the "plotless stories" and robust approach to art and life of the other preeminent short-story writer of his time, Shiga Naoya, a master of the *shi-shōsetsu* ("I-novel") mode of autobiographical fiction. Shiga believed that art should follow the powerful, decidedly nonrational rhythms of the universe as embodied in the works of Saikaku or Auguste Rodin. Anything artificial or ornamental could only interfere with this rhythmic principle and had to be eliminated. As a result, Shiga's prose has a stripped-down, elemental quality, highly praised by Japanese critics but devilishly difficult to translate. His stories lack the kind of dramatic, architecturally structured plots found in most Western literary works and in those of writers like Akutagawa. Nevertheless, an outwardly simple story like "At Kinosaki," in which a man (presumably Shiga) recovering from a near-fatal accident meditates on the deaths of several small creatures, turns out to be surprisingly complex when examined closely. For if, as Shiga suggests, the key to life is learning to harmonize ourselves with the rhythms of nature, and the goal of art is to communicate that struggle, then the "structure" of serious fiction must follow the pattern of that healing process and of nature itself.

Jun'ichirō Tanizaki

Not everyone applauded Shiga Naoya's approach to art and life as Akutagawa did. Jun'ichirō Tanizaki, for example, bristled at the idea that "plot" was somehow a dirty word, nor did he think the pleasure of literature should take a back seat to its ostensible healing powers. Tanizaki was a great storyteller who enjoyed tantalizing and titillating his readers as he challenged their moral assumptions. A student of classical literature (he translated the lengthy *Tale of Genji* into modern Japanese several times), he often incorporated historical events and characters into his works. Whether set in the past or present, their subject matter consistently involved the clash between traditional and Western culture and the intricacies of sadomasochistic and incestuous relationships. In one of his last short stories, "The Bridge of Dreams," for example, Tanizaki transposes the love affair between Prince Genji and his stepmother into modern times, invoking the misty, indistinct realm of early childhood and the dangerous pleasures of forbidden love. As the story progresses, however, one gradually realizes that the narrator is not entirely forthcoming. Inevitably, this leads one to go back and read the story again, a common impulse when deciphering Tanizaki's deceptive fictions.

Yasunari Kawabata

If Jun'ichirō Tanizaki is Japan's most entertaining twentieth century author, then Yasunari Kawabata, who won the Nobel Prize for Literature in 1968, is the most poetic. Kawabata juxtaposed images in fresh and compelling ways, which gave his prose a traditional "haiku-like" aspect, yet he was a most modern and experimental writer. This is immediately evident in his *Palm-of-the-Hand Stories* (1988), a series of very short works, some barely a page in length, which he published intermittently over the course of his career. At first glance, these appear to be little more than dreams hastily jotted down or perhaps a writer's sketchbook for future reference. As one reads on, though, they begin to take on a character and a unity all their own. Entire worlds are compressed into small clusters of images: A dancing girl strolls by with a rooster under her arm, a bodhisattva's statue falls and shatters while trying to embrace a young man, a young woman posts packets of her dead baby's ashes to former lovers. Sometimes these crystallized stories grew into more substantial works; on occasion they distilled longer pieces already written. Above all they reveal the flexible narrative approach of a writer whose most famous novel *Yukiguni* (1935-1937, serial, 1947, book; *Snow Country*, 1956) was published in progressively longer versions three times in ten years. It could, he admitted, have been broken off at any point.

Yukio Mishima

Kawabata committed suicide in 1972, less than two years after the dramatic public *seppuku* of his illustrious protégé, Yukio Mishima. Although critics often link the two together by virtue of their aesthetic approach to art, Mishima, with his preternaturally structured mind, could never have composed in Kawabata's imagistic, open-ended way. Mishima, it seems, always knew exactly where he was going and never left anything to chance—even the circumstances of his death were plotted and rehearsed years in advance. The short story "Patriotism," for example, is a highly stylized depiction of the double suicide of a young army officer and his wife following an abortive army uprising in the 1930's. Mishima later made a short film of the story in the form of a modern Noh play, starring himself. "Patriotism" highlights the purity of the resolute, almost godlike young couple and draws a parallel between their suicide and the ritual love-making that precedes it. Eros and Death have been joined together in many interesting ways in Japanese literature, from *The Tale of Genji* to "The Lust of the White Serpent" to the novels of Tanizaki and Kawabata, but never in such a condensed and crystallized way as in Mishima's story.

Kōno Taeko

Like Mishima, Kōno Taeko was a young adult in August, 1945, when Japan's leaders surrendered their devastated country to the victorious Americans to end World War II. Unlike him, however, she felt no nostalgia for the patriotic samurai spirit of the militaristic old days. Forced to fend for herself and her family in the aftermath of the war, Kōno developed into a tough, resourceful woman able to eke out a living in a competitive, male-dominated world. As Japan regained its feet, opportunities increased for women of literary talent, and by the 1960's Kōno was recognized as a major author in the tradition of Jun'ichirō Tanizaki. Like many of Tanizaki's protagonists, for example, the childless heroine of her short story "Toddler-Hunting" is driven by her sadomasochistic impulses to seek the company of little boys, the unsuspecting objects of her fantasies, and to press her lover to use her more and more harshly. Yet, whereas Tanizaki discretely cloaks his characters' secret lives in layers of mist and unreliable narration, Kōno bares the shadowy side of hers for all to see, illuminating the dark and twisted underside of one of Japan's enduring archetypes, the all-providing, nurturing mother.

Haruki Murakami

Kōno's ability to deftly establish a believable and engaging narrator in the space of just a few lines is shared by Japan's premier storyteller of the 1980's and 1990's, Haruki Murakami. Yet there is a clear difference between the stories of Kōno, the doughty wartime survivor, and Murakami, the postwar baby boomer. Whereas Kōno's kinky characters are firmly rooted in reality, Murakami's outwardly normal heroes and heroines live in uneasy proximity to the realm of the absurd. The mundane protagonist of "TV People," for example, is beset by miniature television repairmen whom only he can see, who infiltrate his home and workplace for purposes that he can only guess at; while the equally uncharismatic hero of "The Elephant Vanishes" is obsessed by the sudden disappearance of an aged elephant and his trainer. Murakami's whimsical fictions make the reader smile, but they also suggest the spiritual vacuum that underlies "normal" daily life in affluent, postindustrial societies. Furthermore, given their broad popularity in China and Korea, they may herald the advent of what might be termed the "Asian postmodern" on the global literary stage.

Banana Yoshimoto

Like Murakami, Banana Yoshimoto is widely read in Asia and the West, but her readers are mostly young women in their teens and early twenties. Correspondingly, her stories focus on their concerns about things like growing up, parents, love affairs of various kinds, and, interestingly, death. Some have dismissed her as "a teen writer," but there is more to Yoshimoto—whose pen name plays on the "yellow on the surface, white underneath" taunt leveled at "Westernized" East Asians—than meets the eye. First and foremost she is an innovator, who has transposed some of the themes and conventions of Japanese *manga* (comics), in particular the *shojo manga* (romance comics) genre so popular in Japan, in a highly original way. The "unreal" element so apparent in her stories and novels derives from this influence. Parents, for example, die or disappear at an alarming rate, psychic healers abound, and love takes on an abstract, bisexual aura. In fact some Japanese have commented that they imagine cartoon characters, not real people, as they read along. Yet Yoshimoto's overseas readers also feel at home in her symbolic world and are warmed by her friendly, reassuring tone. Whether or not her art passes the test of time, Yoshimoto has succeeded in connecting not only *manga* and fiction but also groups of young women all over the world.

Bibliography

Backus, Robert L. *The Riverside Counselor's Stories*. Stanford, Calif.: Stanford University Press, 1985. A definitive translation, with notes and a helpful introduction.

Birnbaum, Alfred. *Monkey Brain Sushi*. New York:

Kodansha International, 1991. An entertaining collection of popular fiction of the 1980's, including "TV People" by Haruki Murakami.

Danly, Robert Lyons. *In the Shade of Spring Leaves*. Yale University Press, 1981. A beautiful evocation of Ichiyō Higuchi and her world, with translations that include "Child's Play."

Goossen, Theodore W. *The Oxford Book of Japanese Short Stories*. New York: Oxford University Press, 1997. The most recent of the comprehensive anthologies, it includes the following stories: "Sanshō the Steward" (Mori Ōgai), "In a Grove" (Ryūnosuke Akutagawa), "Toddler-Hunting" (Kōno Taeko), and "The Elephant Vanishes" (Haruki Murakami).

Hibbett, Howard. *Contemporary Japanese Literature*. New York: Alfred A. Knopf, 1977. A wide-ranging compendium of postwar writing including poetry, stories, and two screenplays. Includes a selection of Yasunari Kawabata's *Palm-of-the-Hand Stories* and Jun'ichirō Tanizaki's "Bridge of Dreams," discussed above.

Katō, Shūichi. *A History of Japanese Literature*. 3 vols. Tokyo: Kodansha International, 1979. A wide-ranging study that pays special heed to the sociohistorical background of Japan's literary development. A good counterbalance to Donald Keene's literary history.

Keene, Donald. *Dawn to the West: Japanese Literature in the Modern Era*. New York: Columbia University Press, 1984.

_______. *Modern Japanese Literature*. New York: Grove Press, 1956. A fine anthology that includes not only stories but also poetry and excerpts from longer works. Includes "Growing Up" (Ichiyō Higuchi), "At Kinosaki" (Shiga Naoya), and "Hell Screen" (Ryūnosuke Akutagawa).

_______. *Seeds in the Heart: Japanese Literature from the Earliest Times to the Late Sixteenth Century*. New York: Henry Holt, 1993. With the two following books, a three-volume history of Japanese literature up to Yukio Mishima.

_______. *World Within Walls: Japanese Literature of the Pre-Modern Era*. New York: Holt, Rinehart and Winston, 1976. Devoted to literature of the Tokugawa (Edo) period.

Miller, Stephen D. *Partings at Dawn: An Anthology of Japanese Gay Literature*. San Francisco: Gay Sunshine Press, 1996. Includes a number of short stories with gay themes.

Morris, Ivan. *Modern Japanese Stories*. Tokyo: Charles E. Tuttle, 1962. An excellent anthology which includes stories by most of the authors mentioned above.

Rimer, J. Thomas. *A Reader's Guide to Japanese Literature*. Rev. ed. New York: Kodansha International, 1999. An invaluable guide, which explores the connections between the classical and modern periods of Japanese literature. Includes the story "The Tale of the Bamboo Cutter."

Tanaka, Yukiko, and Elizabeth Hanson, eds. *This Kind of Woman: Ten Stories by Japanese Women Writers, 1960-1976*. Stanford, Calif.: Stanford University Press, 1982. Includes stories by Kōno Taeko and other major women authors.

Tsuruta, Kinya, and Thomas Swann, eds. *Approaches to the Modern Japanese Short Story*. Tokyo: Waseda University Press, 1982. A rare but immensely useful critical study of thirty-four stories, including seven of those discussed above.

Tyler, Royall. *Japanese Tales*. New York: Pantheon Books, 1987. An outstanding compilation of Japanese tales (*setsuwa bungaku*) collected in the twelfth and thirteenth centuries.

Zolbrod, Leon. *Ugetsu Monogatari (Tales of Moonlight and Rain)*. London: Allen & Unwin, 1974. With extensive footnotes and a fascinating introduction, perhaps the definitive translation of Akinari Ueda's classic collection.

Theodore W. Goossen

LATIN AMERICAN SHORT FICTION

As common and somewhat acceptable as the term "Latin American literature" is as a functional label for literature produced in the "Latin" countries of the Americas, most anthologists and scholars tend to take time to apologize for its usage or, at least, to justify its usage in the face of some opposition. The basic contention is valid: Latin America is not a distinctive geographical or geopolitical space. Nor is it a culturally homogenous space. The term is a convenience, but it is a convenience that is rooted in some basic facts of history. For the purposes of this survey, the term encompasses those countries in the "New World" formerly colonized by Portugal, Spain, and Italy. Included, therefore, are the countries that are located on the South American continent and those countries in the area that is now called Central America. Those islands in the Caribbean that share a history of colonization with the South American continent are also included. The functional languages of Latin American literature are Spanish and Portuguese. Spanish dominates. Without Brazil and its formidable tradition of literature, Latin America would be exclusively a Spanish domain. Very little exists in Latin America that pertains to Italy, even though Italians have had a significant presence in countries like Argentina and Bolivia, but then so have the English. English remains a distinct foil to the march of Latin American literature and culture.

The history of Latin America is a history which could have paralleled the history of North America and its increasingly homogenized single-nation identity. Like the American North, the South has had a strong imaginative sense of its unity. This imaginative identity dominated much of the seventeenth and eighteenth centuries largely because of the liberation efforts of individuals like Simón Bolívar. Bolívar imagined and wrote about a Latin American state that would share much of the sense of nationalism that would come to define the North. There is a reason for this development. As with the British empire, the Spanish empire was quite clearly understood to be an extension of the Spanish nation-state. Brazil remained a peculiar and massive interruption of the dominance of Spanish culture in the Americas. That dominance extended well into the North American continent until a century ago and has slowly begun to crawl its way back into that continent now through immigration and a redefining of cultural and racial demographics.

The Spanish colonial government understood its empire as a single force and a single protectorate and thus sought to conceive of a culture that was distinctive and somewhat homogeneous. The variations emerged through the peculiar dialogues and clashes that took place between these Spanish societies and the native communities that existed in the regions before the arrival of the Spanish. The Inca in eastern South America, the Aztec in Central America, and the Mayans in the rain forests of northeastern South America were large and dominant cultures before the arrival of the Spanish. Spanish colonialism forced these cultures to struggle for survival, but in their struggle they had lasting effect on the culture of the region—the understanding of landscape and the shaping of the imagination.

Latin American literature and, in many ways, Latin American short fiction emerge out of the strange contradictions between nationalism and empire that characterize the experience of the region. The movement toward independence in Latin America, as in all other formerly colonized states, entailed a cultural quest for a distinctive cultural and national identity. This identity would be found in the history and native presence of these nations and in the agendas for self-actualization that would emerge during the period leading toward independence and the demise of the Spanish empire's rule. Latin American identity is peculiarly defined by the tension between the colonial force of Spanish dominance, the spirit of discovery and the quest to found a new society with new values and a new understanding of landscape and individuality, and the presence of non-European cultures in the region. In Brazil, this pattern is very much a part of what has given a distinction to its cultural identity and to its literature. Brazil's distinction lies in the dialogue that the society has had with its racial complexity, particularly the presence of African slaves and freed people, especially from Nigeria, in the region. The religious and narrative experiences have given rise to a distinctive literary sensibility, which remains one of the more remarkable and fresh in the modern world.

Most scholars recognize in Latin American culture and literary practice the importance of history and the way that history has come to shape the way people see themselves. The question is, do Argentines see themselves as quite distinct from Colombians? Do Mexicans feel any affinity with Cubans? Do Peruvians believe that one can read their literature with the same lens that would be used to read Brazilian Literature? Nationalism has made it possible to recognize very peculiar and specific trends in Latin American writing that are specific to different regions and countries. The history of modern Latin American writing, like the history of Caribbean writing or African writing, has been one of balancing the pressures of the publishing industry, which has a tendency to homogenize and lump all countries into a single, manageable unit, and the desire for a distinctive nationalism that would recognize that the histories of these various countries, while intersecting at certain points, remain quite distinct.

This survey presents more similarities and patterns of Latin American literature than differences. It acknowledges also that the writers being discussed are themselves related to one another as part of a fraternity (or sorority) of like-minded artists working in a distinctive milieu. During the middle of the nineteenth century, a large contingent of Latin American writers found one another while studying in Paris. At the Parisian cafés, the talk was of politics, revolution, and the unification of Latin America. They found that they shared a language and a history of trying to break the shackles of the culture that undergirded their language. In Paris, they knew they were not Spanish or European writers—not in any useful political or cultural sense. They knew they were shaping a literature that was going to be uniquely birthed from the bloodied soil of Latin America. The shaping of a Latin American literary sensibility would grow out of the fact of language. Language helps to shape audience, and audience leads to the natural assumption of a literature—a national literature. The audience in this sense is an English-speaking audience that does presume the Latin American culture as a collective other. They share a language and, in time, have come to share certain distinctive traits in literary practice.

Most recently, the 1960's brought with it the work of Alejo Carpentier in Cuba, Gabriel García Márquez in Colombia, Jorge Luis Borges in Bolivia, and Mario Vargas Llosa in Peru what has been termed "Magical Realism" or "marvelous realism." This sometimes uncertainly and variously defined literary style came to shape much of the literature produced in the larger world in the last thirty years of the twentieth century. It is a remarkable phenomenon, but those who have been drawn to it have understood it in rather homogenized terms. There have been other trends, even if less influential, over the years. There was a period of Latin American writing in the 1930's when realist novelists, influenced by the Russian masters, were producing works of naturalism and political commitment. Brazilian writers wrote about the horrors of sugar plantation life, and those in the Spanish-speaking countries wrote of peasant life in the rural areas of these nations. These styles appeared in the many periodicals that would come to publish the work of the most important Latin American writers over the centuries.

In the late 1800's, Edgar Allan Poe supplied many Latin American writers with the grotesque sensibility that some have argued was the precursor of the magical side of Magical Realism. Latin writers encountered Poe's work while living in Paris. These writers were reading and translating the work of English and French writers and were bringing those sensibilities to bear on their own work. These patterns emerged in somewhat collective ways. Communication through periodicals, conferences, exile, and cross-country travel led to a situation in which these writers, while acknowledging their nationalist distinctions, also understood themselves to be part of a larger movement in literature. Philosophies therefore abound regarding the character of the Latin American aesthetic. The short story remains one of the most important forms of literary practice in Latin American literature because it has, whether by design or the accident of its length, been the laboratory of Latin American fictional writing. Any attempt to study the short story's peculiar history in Latin America amounts to a remarkable entry into the evolution of Latin American writing.

It would seem that a short story does, by its very nature, make certain aesthetic demands that have come to be accepted values or traits of the form. When does a short story become a novella, and when does a long short story become a novel? It is normally argued that the short story's popularity in Latin America emerges from the fact that the publishing industry there has been notoriously limited. The heart of fiction writing in the region has not been the novel-making of publishing houses (as has been the case in Britain and America, for instance) but has rested instead in the powerful and innovative works of periodicals and journals. These venues, the nature of their size, favored the short story. Others have argued that the short story is peculiarly popular and famous in Latin America because the aesthetics of the short story are closely tied to the narrative tradition of folklore and the oral tradition that have shaped the region over the years. Such scholars have linked the modern Latin American short story to the folktales of the Inca, Maya, Taino, and Aztec peoples; the oral epics of the Yoruba; and the detailed accounts of discovery and proselytizing that were written by conquerors and monks alike during the age of expansion. The idea is a compelling one but one that does not always explain some of the heavily Westernized qualities of the Latin American text. Others hold to the view that the short story developed well in Latin America because a few successful and sometimes exclusive short-story geniuses in the region (like Borges) made writing short stories a distinct cultural phenomenon. It forced all writers to take the perfection of the form seriously and to be venturesome in promoting it. Regardless of the reason, the short story is a major force in Latin American writing.

The short story is one way in which the literary developments of the region have been defined. There are hundreds of "groundbreaking" anthologies of the Latin American short story in translation emerging in the English-speaking parts of the world. These anthologies have also become one of the important vehicles by which the works of Latin American female writers are reaching the rest of the world. The short-story anthology is a convenient vehicle because it allows for the inclusion of many writers in a single volume and it serves as a splendid primer for university courses on Latin American writing.

This survey will examine some of the highlights of the development of Latin American writing and will draw attention to both the collective and shared sensibilities of the Latin American short story and the important nationalistic differences. It is more helpful, however, to examine these developments through the work of some of the most important writers of short fiction in the region.

THE COLONIAL PERIOD

Ascribing literary precedence to the colonial period in Latin American history is something that has been done increasingly by contemporary writers who have turned to the writings of that period for a tradition. They have, in effect, turned to the historical and bureaucratic documents of a massive and complex empire that established, in the middle of the sixteenth century, two major viceroyalties in Lima, Peru, and in Mexico City. These complex communities were shaped by the acts of the conquistadors, who marched through the continent transforming what had once been an empire of islands into a vast empire of lands and peoples, which stretched throughout the Americas, as far north as Texas and as far east as the Philippines. At first the island of Hispanola was the heart of the Spanish empire, but once Hernán Cortés had ransacked Mexico and had been followed first by an equally formidable army of monks and priests and later by a remarkably organized battalion of lawyers and bureaucrats, the Spanish empire was in full swing in the Americas.

For nearly two hundred years, the Spanish were the dominant force in the region. Havana remained an important Spanish American center and trade city, while Lima and Mexico City evolved as cultural hubs that in many ways challenged the ascendancy of Castille and Madrid. In these New World cities, there was a thriving artistic and literary community. The work produced by this community, however, was notably imitative of the work of the Golden Age in Spanish letters, and it produced a poet who is still recognized as one of the last of the great Golden Age poets, Sor Juana Inés de la Cruz. Modern Latin American writers have found greater affinity and relevance not in the literary output of the early colonials but in the historical documents of the great figures of that period.

Spain's government bureaucracies were, if nothing else, fascinated by the act of recording. Files upon files remain that detail the strange and vicious process of colonialization and the terrible anxiety and guilt that surrounded many of the actions of the colonizers in the region. The narratives of historians, governors, priests, and leaders of the evolving empire remain some of the most fascinating accounts of an emerging culture, an emerging identity that can now be regarded as distinctly Latin American.

Christopher Columbus himself began a trend in writing about the Indies that regards the apprehension of the new space as an act of "discovering" the other or coming to grips with the other. This otherness would come to influence the works of such Western artists as William Shakespeare, who in his play *The Tempest* (pr. 1611) echoed the fantastical narratives of the colonizing world in his construction of a play. The play is as much rooted in magic and the supernatural as it is in the celebration of colonial authority and the patriarchy of the colonialist agenda. Columbus told his tale and sought to reconstruct his tales of mystery and discovery. These tales, positioning the colonial space as a world of impossible and different happenings, can easily be seen as one of the important precursors to the Latin American text.

The political agenda of Columbus remained relevant to many who would follow him: a strong need to convince the rest of the world that a new space, a new sensibility, and a new world of powerful images and wealth had been found. It is not hard to see in much of the way that Latin American literature is apprehended today something of this quest. It is also not hard to see the inclination toward the magical as part of the larger project to create a sense of otherness, a sense of cultural removal in the work of contemporary writers.

Some of the important writers of histories and other fascinating narratives include seeming admonitions to pure and chaste life in bawdy stories that barely mask the relish that writers like Juan Rodríguez Freyle took in outlining some of the lewd acts of sinners. These writers remain the singular conduit by which the history of the Inca, Taino, Maya, and Aztec people of that continent have passed to the modern reader. Looming above all others is Bartolomé de Las Casas, who can be credited in many ways with defining the racial shape of the region in his many efforts to tackle the troubling question of the fate of the native peoples of the region. Las Casas's writings are peppered with detailed emblematic accounts of atrocities against native peoples. His efforts were to convince the Spanish crown of the need to treat the native peoples as humans, as worthy of the efforts of evangelism by the Catholic Church. Along with him were writers like Gonzalo Fernández de Oviedo, Francisco López de Gómara, and Bernal Díaz del Castillo.

There is no way to describe the works of these writers as short stories or even fictional narratives, but contemporary writers have shown again and again that there are, buried in these narratives, a series of shorter exemplary stories which have led to a tradition of aesthetics and narrative consistency in the work of the writers who came after them. The themes with which these writers grappled, the politics that shaped their existence, and the terrible conditions they witnessed, even as they enjoyed the excitement of establishing a whole new world, are elements that have come to shape the character of Latin American fiction in the last several hundred years.

It would therefore be a mistake to presume that the Latin American short story began in the nineteenth century. Indeed the Latin American tale, understood as emerging out of a larger tradition that was attempting to give names to a new space, began much earlier as part of the conflicted truth of the colonial agenda itself. Modern writers remain inscribed in the truth of this history and have, for years, been involved in restoring to the Latin American imagination the fact of these histories. In other words, it is impossible to read Carlos Fuentes, García Márquez, or Carpentier without reference to the writings of those figures of Latin American history listed above.

There exist several native narratives collected by priests and government officials that now form a part of the larger fabric of the Latin American text. No one can claim purity in these narratives, which were collected by colonizers and used for their own agendas, but many of these stories have somehow tallied with the oral narratives that have been passed down from generation to generation in the remote parts of Latin America.

Nationalism and the Emergence of the Short Story

The nineteenth century saw the continent-wide press toward nationalism. In many ways this pattern would not take root in Brazil in the same way because Brazil's position as the seat of the Portuguese empire was largely unassailable from the onset. In fact, much of the literature that has emerged in Brazil, while being rooted in the landscape and culture of the region, has so shaped and defined Portuguese letters that there is far less of a sense of inferiority and acquiescence to the metropolis or the mother country than has occurred in the literatures from the former English colonies and the Spanish colonial countries. The emergence of nationalism in the nineteenth century, however, played a major part in the shaping of a literary aesthetic. This aesthetic, influenced by the push for nationalism in such places as the United States, Haiti, and the march for revolution in France, generated, at first, works that sought to locate a literary tradition in the region. This attempt was not unlike the nineteenth century preoccupation with origins that characterized literary practice in Europe. In England, there was the championing of the Anglo-Saxon mythic narrative *Beowulf* (c. 1000), while in Germany numerous renderings of *Nibelungenlied* (c. 1200; *The Nibelungenlied*, 1848) served as foundation blocks for a nationalist aesthetic. In Chile, Diego Barros Arana produced a seminal edition of the epic poem by Fernando Álvarez de Toledo, *Purén Indómito* (1862), which would compete with the Argentine Juan María Gutiérrez's 1848 edition of Pedro de Oña's epic *Arauco domado* (*Aracuo Tamed*, 1948), which appeared in 1596.

It was also during this period that the first distinctive collections of short stories began to appear in Latin America. While some critics remain adamant that the "*cuadros de costumbres*" were in fact not quite short stories but narratives, which functioned as anecdotal tales with little of the structural unities normally associated with the short story as it emerged in the latter part of the nineteenth century. These narratives undeniably influenced the short-story movement that assumed full force at the beginning of the twentieth century.

The earlier part of the nineteenth century saw many examples of the long narrative. The novel was thriving, influenced largely by the massive efforts of writers like Charles Dickens, Nathaniel Hawthorne, Herman Melville, and other writers from outside the Latin American tradition. Significant epic novels would emerge as part of the articulation of nationalism. Postcolonial critic Homi Bhaba asserted that the novel is inextricably linked to the notion of nationalism. His belief was borne out in the literature produced in the early part of the century. Indeed this idea is the foundation of the work by Doris Sommer, *Foundational Fictions: The National Romances of Latin America* (1991), which argues convincingly that the shaping of the nationalism of the region was tied to the fiction generated during that time.

The *cuadros de costumbres* emerged out of a nineteenth century Latin American preoccupation with looking closely at the realities of the continent and the various societies that were emerging out of the colonial backdrop. Politics, sociological conditions, and a fascination with the flora and fauna of the region led to works that offered vignettes and narratives depicting the life of natives, Africans, and other peasant classes. The term *cuadros de costumbres* was coined in Colombia, where writers would submit these somewhat static and detailed accounts of Latin American culture to a select group of periodicals devoted to such narratives. *El Mosaico* (1858-1872) published the works of such writers as José Caicedo Rojas, Juan de Dios Restrepo, and José María Vergara y Vergara. The fascination with bizarre details and the focus on local experience would come to shape the work of writers that would follow them. Most importantly, however, they established in the imagination of Latin American readers and writers a language that was located in the region and that was involved with the casting of a reality that was distinctive and self-reflexive.

The true emergence of the modern short story—a genre in its own right—would not take place in Latin American letters until the latter half of the nineteenth century. At that time, the shared sense of a Latin American identity was taking shape. Periodicals throughout the region were publishing the writing of authors from all across the continent, and there was a growing sense that a distinctive sensibility was emerging. The next hundred and thirty years would see the emergence of some of the most important and gifted writers of the twentieth century. These writers evolved a nationalist agenda in their work—an agenda that would secure the nationalist identities of the various nations. They shaped an aesthetic that could be theorized as Latin American—an aesthetic emerging from a shared history, a shared political evolution, and a shared sense of literary antecedent.

Authors of what can be best termed *cuadros the costumbres*, such as Argentina's Esteban Echeverría, paved the way for writers such as Domingo Faustino Sarmiento, who has been described by Roberto González Echevarría as "one of the most prominent figures in nineteenth century Latin American literature, politics, social thought and education" largely on the strength of his sometimes-infamous *Civilización y barbarie: Vida de Juan Facundo Quiroga, y aspecto fisico, costumbres, y hábitos de la República Argentina* (commonly known as *Facundo*; 1845; *Life in the Argentine Republic in the Days of the Tyrants: Or, Civilization and Barbarism*, 1868), and the early feminist Juana Manuela Gorriti. Other notable nineteenth century authors include Ricardo Palma of Peru, and a writer who is quite decidedly one of the greatest writers of the last two hundred years, the mulatto Joaquim Maria Machado de Assis of Brazil. Machado published nine novels and more than two hundred short stories in his lifetime.

The Modern Short Story

There are several ways to talk about the Latin American short story. Some scholars have, in an attempt to underplay the regional distinctions of the genre, focused on a select number of stellar writers who have formed an impressive pantheon of Latin American giants stretching across the "cone" of South America and into the islands of the Caribbean archipelago. These writers all helped to shape a Latin American aesthetic that would give rise to even more cosmopolitan writers of the contemporary period. While movements are acknowledged, they are not defined by nationality but by literary trends and concerns. Others have sought more regional and nationalistic readings of the literature of the region. The distinctions that separate the Brazilian and Cuban literary traditions from those of the larger nation-states on the mainland of South America, for instance, are often cited as the basis for this approach. A number of short-story anthologies argue the case for a well-defined tradition by nationality, which must be identified, understood, and appreciated for any genuine understanding of the work of the region. These two approaches to the Latin American short story, however, cannot be seen as exclusive. Indeed, what is worth noting here is that the Latin American short story, like all of Latin American letters has, in the last century, been forced to define its relevance and strength in a milieu that lends itself to easy generalizations and the regionalism of the publishing world. In other words, for the last hundred years, Latin American literature has been perceived as a "new thing," a fantastic and unknown thing to be discovered. While literature from the region has never been obscure and inaccessible, it has been distant enough to make the discovery of a new voice an occasion for the celebration of otherness.

Many of the major writers of the region have, at some point in their careers, lived in extended exile from their home countries either in Latin American or Europe. This fact encourages a survey of the literature of the region through examination of the writers who have come to have an impact on the international stage. There are a number of indisputable giants of Latin American writing, figures who have been seen as representatives of the region and who have unquestionably influenced writers in the twentieth century. These stalwart figures have shaped the way in which the short story has been written in Latin America and around the world. They are influential writers, major figures of the century, and writers who should be studied carefully by anyone interested in examining Latin American literature. These writers, tellingly, have developed international reputations, but their lasting legacy is "local"—it rests in their success at establishing a tradition in Latin American writing.

Of this group of writers, Rubén Darío of Nicaragua is the least likely to be considered a master of the short story. He was better known as a poet. Darío is arguably the most important Spanish poet in centuries. His fresh modernism was, at its core, a rejection of the old literary traditions of Spain and an embrace of anything outside that sensibility. In a jazzlike openness to all other forms, Darío, on the strength of his first major success, *Azul* (1888), saw develop around him a movement that would be called *Modernismo*—a movement which would change the direction of Latin American writing. Dario's contributions were largely in poetry but he also wrote a series of very short, poetic narratives, which would influence the works of numerous short-story writers to come.

If Dario was a central influence, the person who would take Dario's ideas and transform them into the short-story genre, bringing to the form a perfection rarely surpassed since, was Horacio Quiroga, often labeled the father of the Latin American short story. His dispassionate rendering of narratives set in the jungles of Uruguay and his exploration of themes of violence and human abjection shaped an aesthetic which would come to be called Borges-like in the latter part of the twentieth century. Borges, along with García Márquez and Julio Cortázar, admitted an indebtedness to this writer of sublime tragedies.

During the early twentieth century, several important fiction writers emerged, many of them specializing in the short story. Their importance as writers rested largely on their international reputations. These writers included the Argentine Ricardo Güiraldes, author of *Cuentos de muerte y de sangre* (1915); Rómulo Gallegos of Venezuela, who, apart from writing one of the most important and definitive novels of Latin American letters, *Doña Bárbara* (1929; English translation, 1984), also published several short stories in the realist vein; and Luisa Mercedes Levinson, an Argentine who lived much of her life outside Argentina and who produced a small but significant body of stories and novels, which are notable for their striking comingling of the erotic and the violent.

It would be Jorge Luis Borges, however, her blind countryman and one of the first writers to declare exclusive loyalty to the short story (having found the novel to be far too long and flawed in its very essence), who has come to define the Latin American short story. Borges, in many ways, seems an unlikely spokesperson for a nationalist literary tradition since very little of his work is set in Latin America. Indeed, Borges was notorious for locating his narratives outside the region. Furthermore, Borges spent much of his writing life living outside Latin America. His literary style, rather than adhering to the stereotype established by other writers who focused so fully and passionately on the landscape and culture of the region, turned toward a more ironic and dispassionate tone. His devotion to German and English writers, whom he read in their original languages, is unquestionable, but he opened the Latin American text, allowing it to become more international in its vision. Borges also forced the artists of the region to seriously examine what an aesthetic truly is. Is an aesthetic defined by subject matter, by the use of local fauna and flora, or is an aesthetic related to literary style, having its shape and structure defined by a coherent and traceable tradition? Borges's narratives introduced certain critical features to the Latin American text. His *Ficciones, 1935-1944* (1944; English translation, 1962) can be called only seminal; it established his penchant for the use of fictionalized historical details, his fascination with the idea of the short story as a metaphysical essay—a polemical construct which never loses sight of the need for drama, tension, and conflict. Sentimentality was eschewed at all costs by Borges, and his work sought to stretch the narrative possibilities of the genre.

If Borges introduced the practice of irony and a dispassionate sensibility to the Latin American oeuvre, his Cuban contemporary Alejo Carpentier introduced a devotion to history that remains unchallenged. Carpentier's fiction is always fascinated by time, is always rooted in a strong sense of historical space, and always adheres to the notion that Latin American culture is shaped by a distinctive history that can be excavated for narrative possibilities. His ability to bring together a strong sense of history and a fascination with the magic of human experience and narrative is one of the reasons he is sometimes regarded as the first genuine practitioner of the Magical Realist approach to fiction. In his short-story collection *Guerra del tiempo* (1958; *War of Time*, 1970), Carpentier explores various narrative modes and thematic complexities, which have been extremely influential in modern Latin American fiction.

Miguel Ángel Asturias, the Guatemalan winner of the Nobel Prize for literature, may have been pivotal in alerting the Latin American literary world to the rich possibilities located in the native languages and cultures of the region. His short fictions, for years, seemed devoted to exploring the folk traditions of the Mayan tradition to which he belonged. Much of his early work involved the translation of these Mayan narratives into Spanish and the use of these tales to shape his novels and short stories. The incredible, mythic quality of these stories would serve as ample fodder for the "magical" side of the Magical Realist construct in Latin American writing.

The 1960's saw a seemingly sudden explosion of Latin American writing on the world stage and, in the process, led to the emergence of several figures who are now considered to be the stalwart figures of the modern Latin American short story. In 1960, Julio Cortázar published *Rayuela* (1963; *Hopscotch*, 1966) and in the process ushered in the careers of Carlos Fuentes, Gabriel García Márquez, and Vargas Llosa. Cortázar's short-story collections, which include the formidable *Bestiario* (1951) and the well-known *Todos los fuegos el fuego* (1966; *All Fires the Fire and Other Stories*, 1973), reflect his fascination with the extraordinary and the bizarre, a surrealist sensibility he honed while living in Paris.

Carlos Fuentes, a Mexican with a most cosmopolitan background, has published some of the more important novels in Latin American letters. Like Carpentier in Cuba, Fuentes has embarked on a journey to reconcile Mexico's violent and dichotomous past through sometimes conflicted but always probing narrative fiction. Fuentes's interest has always been to demonstrate that it is impossible to understand the Latin American sensibility without understanding both the native (in his case, the Aztec) and the colonial (Spanish) past and how these two pasts have intersected, clashed, and merged.

Gabriel García Márquez sets most of his narratives in his native Colombia. His fiction is fluent and remarkable for its capacity to balance his commitment to the exploration of political ideas and the study of human nature and human action. He remains, along with Borges, one of the best-known writers from Latin America, and he has always been a champion of writing from that region. While his output has been primarily in the form of the novel, he has published a number of remarkable short stories including the much-anthologized "A Very Old Man with Wings" and "Balthazar's Marvelous Afternoon," which reveal his interest in the surreal and supernatural and the uncannily deft way he excavates the foibles of the human condition. By locating the bulk of his narratives in his own region and by borrowing from such American writers as William Faulkner, García Márquez has effectively established one of the critical characteristics of the modern Latin American writer: an international bent that remains rooted in an understanding of the local. It is a balance that is not always achieved but one that many writers seek to accomplish.

Mario Vargas Llosa, like Marquez, has not published as widely as others in the area of the short story; however, like Marquez, Vargas Llosa has brought fame and some popularity to the Latin American literary world through the publication of several very important novels. Vargas Llosa, who was born in Peru, and who honed his craft in the region, published one collection of short stories, *Los jefes* (1959; *The Cubs and Other Stories*, 1979), which reflects some of the themes that would mark his work. Vargas Llosa's narratives are consistently preoccupied with guilt and regret—guilt shaped by the arrival of maturity and the capacity of an individual to view his or her sordid past with the hindsight of enlightenment. The horrors and failures of the past lead to intense guilt such that the narratives themselves tend to be extended acts of penance and expiation. It should not be lost on readers that this attempt to reconcile a past full of secrets and errors is quite emblematic of the Latin American text.

Beyond this grouping of important figures there are numerous other Latin American writers who have contributed significantly to the shaping of the Latin American short story. Each year new anthologies appear with translations of a "new wave" of narratives from Latin America. A significant development has been the appearance of many specialist anthologies, which have focused on the sometimes-ignored work of women writers from the region. These anthologies demonstrate that Latin American women have been writing stories for at least two centuries, and their work has proved as equally compelling and fascinating as the work of their male counterparts. At the same time, anthologies that focus on the work from specific countries continue to appear. Most of these anthologies attempt to justify the act of speaking about a national literature, but for the most part the act of collecting work from a given country is prompted by the pragmatics of publishing and the logistical nightmare that could come from other, more regional, anthologies.

Increasingly, the Latin American short story is expanding to include works by writers who were born and reared in the United States, some of whom are writing in English and others in Spanish. If nothing else, such developments show that Latin American writing is introducing more and more complex ways to view itself and is becoming a significant force in the evolution of the short-story genre. With the growth of a Latino population in North America, mass interest in Latin American authors has led to the emergence of many writers who have developed an international standing. These writers will form the core of a new generation, which will carry the Latin American short story into the twenty-first century.

THE CARIBBEAN SHORT STORY

Unlike Latin American literature, fiction from the English-speaking Caribbean remains a relatively new development. While there is a history of writing by colonial inhabitants of the islands, to a large extent this writing has been quite unremarkable and, more important, has not been part of the tradition that led to the developments in fiction in the twentieth century. The most useful writing of this type was travel writing—the work of travelers from Europe and the United States, who spent months traveling through the islands and writing accounts of their journeys. Filled with evidence of ignorance and arrogance, many of these narratives can be credited for the sometimes exotic and always negative image of the Caribbean that reached the rest of the world. For the most part, these writers, working either in response to the debate regarding slavery or as part of the mission to unearth salacious stories about the unruly and uncivilized world of the colonies, found the Caribbean to be a place of debauchery and license and the most consistent corrupter of good European youth in the prime of their lives.

While a number of poets found some desire to write about the Caribbean as home (see *The Penguin Book of Caribbean Verse in English*, 1986), for the most part the colonial period was not a time of intense literary progress among the educated people of the islands. It must be understood that the settlement of these islands was not driven by a desire to create new worlds of culture, satellite cultural havens that could serve as the alternate seats of the empire, as was the case in Latin America in the viceroyalties of Lima and Mexico City. The islands were quite simply lands to be exploited for whatever wealth they could generate. These islands served as factories of sugar and tobacco production, and the settlements reflected that purpose. Those who accused the islands of being void of any redeeming cultural values or ambitions could not be blamed for this perception, at least during the earliest days of colonialism. Indeed, the mother country was regarded as the seat of all culture and was the destination of children born in the islands to wealthy whites. Those who lived on the islands either had few other options in their home countries or were committed to the basic labor of plantation life. Unlike the settlers in North America and Latin America, many of whom had ambitions of creating a whole new society, there are few examples of such lofty aspirations among those who came to settle the islands. It would in fact take several generations of creolization for any kind of nationalism to take root. Only then would there be any interest in a literature rooted in the island communities.

It would be fair to say that Caribbean short fiction began to develop a tradition at the beginning of the nineteenth century. At about this time, the different islands were evolving a sense of national identity which, while not pressing for independence from the colonizing countries, at least understood a distinctive national sensibility as something worth writing about. Indeed, in his sometimes helpful *West Indian Narrative: An Introductory Anthology* (1966), Kenneth Ramchand is hard-pressed to find much of a narrative tradition in the West Indies before the work of H. G. De Lisser at the beginning of the nineteenth century. Ramchand includes only a handful of narrative writers, such as Aphra Behn, Olaudah Equiano, and Lady Nugent, all with rather tenuous connections to the West Indies. (Behn and Equiano may have been slaves briefly in the islands; Lady Nugent was the colonial governor's wife.) Ramchand's anthology, in fact, consists mostly of extracts from novels by the major writers of the region.

Short-story collections have been relatively rare in the region. Thus it makes sense to talk about West Indian short fiction beginning somewhere around 1900. The earliest writers of note in this category would be writers such as Tom Redcam, H. G. De Lisser, and Claude McKay, from Jamaica, and Jean Rhys, from Dominica. Both Redcam and De Lisser were light-skinned Jamaicans, who belonged to the elite upper classes. For the most part, the writing of these men reflected a fairly conservative view of the colonialized society to the extent that De Lisser, at least in his novels, could sometimes be accused of a certain reactionary affinity for and devotion to the principles of colonialism. De Lisser was, for years, the editor of the *Jamaica Daily Gleaner*, the national newspaper of the time, and he was responsible for publishing poetry and short stories by aspiring writers of the region. For the most part, De Lisser published work by writers who were largely conservative in their use of literary technique and quite derivative of European, and particularly British, literary styles and themes. Indeed, much of this writing was sometimes not discernibly Jamaican. The landscape might be suggested by a few details, but the themes, the language, and the very rhetorical construction of the narratives reflected the heavily instilled colonial bias.

McKay, of course, was an exception. His writing began to assume at least a thematic shift when he moved to the United States and became one of the leading figures of the Harlem Renaissance in the early part of the 1920's. The bulk of his short fiction, however, dealt with themes of race and identity in America. Some of his short stories explored the politics of race in Jamaica, but he was not especially interested in the themes that characterize the work of many of the writers that were to follow him in the 1930's and 1940's.

Rhys, arguably the most outstanding writer of the early period of West Indian writing, is noteworthy both for what she accomplished as a writer in an environment in which there was not a well-established writing tradition and for the way in which she has served as a model for many of the women writers who emerged since 1980. Rhys's writing did not focus on her West Indian experience but explored issues of identity and place that went beyond the limits of her island. She was one of the first cosmopolitan writers from the Caribbean, establishing her fame in France and England long before any Caribbean writer managed to achieve such status in English. Apart from novels, Rhys published a number of successful short stories well into the 1960's. However, her best-known work was published during the 1930's and 1940's.

The 1930's saw the emergence of writers who coincided with the movement toward nationalism and independence in the Caribbean. Many of these writers were associated with the important cultural and literary journals that emerged at that time. In Jamaica Edna Manley, a sculptor, spearheaded the publication of *Focus*, a magazine responsible for publishing the early work of some of the best writers on that island. In Trinidad the journals *Trinidad* and *Beacon* emerged. They published the works of Alfred Mendes and C. L. R. James, who would become some of the more prominent writers from the region. Other important voices from that period include the Guyanese Eric Walrond, who eventually moved to the United States, where he played a small but significant part in the Harlem Renaissance. In Barbados, *Bim* was started by Frank Collymore, and that journal would become one of the most important published in the region. *Bim* can claim to have introduced writers as diverse and significant as Derek Walcott, Kamau Brathwaite, George Lamming, and Samuel Selvon. It was complemented by writers who had moved to the United Kingdom to study and who found occasional work writing stories for the British Broadcasting Corporation's *Caribbean Voices* series. The stories aired on those programs were important models for many younger writers who would emerge in the 1960's and 1970's.

It is telling, though, that despite the presence of literary journals, newspapers, and periodicals, the publication of fiction by Caribbean writers was almost exclusively in the area of the novel. Much of the work published during the explosion in West Indian literature during the 1950's came from English publishers, who sought to promote fiction from the region. A number of writers would publish short-story collections, but few would claim to be exclusively short-story writers. Samuel Selvon published some early short-story collections that focused, in humorous ways, on the life and times of Indo-Caribbean people. Perhaps the most famous of short-story collections to emerge in the English-speaking Caribbean came from V. S. Naipaul, whose first book, *Miguel Street* (1959), though cast as an episodic novel (since it has a single narrator), was actually a collection of related stories that treat with wit and pathos the troubled world of colonial Caribbean society. Few of the short-story writers who followed these two major figures wrote in that form exclusively. Indeed, most of the short stories by these writers have appeared only in Caribbean literature anthologies. These writers include Edward Kamau Brathwaite, Neville Dawes, Orlando Patterson, Ismith Khan, John Wickham, Roger Mais, Roy A. K. Heath, Andrew Salkey, Paule Marshall, Michael Anthony, and Austin Clarke. Of this group, Salkey remains one of the few who devoted a great deal of attention to the short story. Salkey would publish collections for children, narratives exploring the trickster figure, while serving as one of the most indefatigable anthologists of Caribbean writing.

Because most of the English-speaking Caribbean islands received their independence from Britain after 1960, most of the writers normally seen as colonial have also been at the vanguard of the postcolonial writing that has emerged. What is significant about the developments since independence, however, is the emergence of women writers in the region. Most critics suggest that this development corresponds to the growth in the women's movement and is related to the emergence of African American women's voices during the same period. There are other factors as well. The initial wave of writers represented a cadre of mostly men, who had left the region to study in the United Kingdom. Much of their writing grew out of that exile, and the literary movement was inextricably linked to the pattern of their education. Typically, women were not encouraged to go away to study, and as a result few were drawn into the small clique of expatriate writers that formed in London during the 1950's and 1960's. The emergence of a stronger publishing interest in local writers, the return of the "exiled" writers to the Caribbean, and the increasing number of women attending university in the 1960's and 1970's led to the explosion in women's writing in the 1980's and 1990's.

Olive Senior stands out as one of the most important of this group largely because her preferred genre is the short story. She is also a poet, but she has not written any long fiction. She has published several important collections of short stories and leads a group that includes Velma Pollard, Lorna Goodison, Jean "Binta" Breeze, Christine Craig, Opal Palmer Adisa, Makeda Silvera, and Alecia McKenzie, all from Jamaica. Jamaica Kincaid, from Antigua, is probably the most famous of the short-story writers from the Caribbean, but her work remains rooted in the region despite the fact that she has built her career primarily in the United States. Other important women from the region include Merle Collins, Edwidge Danticat, Zoila Ellis, Pauline Melville, Miriam Warner-Vieyra, and Maryse Conde. This is a stunning group of female writers who have managed to establish a distinctive West Indian or pan-Caribbean voice, which is not preoccupied with the task of establishing its validity or place in the larger world market.

Of this generation, there are a number of male writers whose work stands out in the same regard. The short fiction of Lawrence Scott, from Trinidad, has joined the work of his compatriot Earl Lovelace in stretching the limits and shape of the short story in the English-speaking Caribbean. Jamaican poet and short-story writer Geofry Philp has published two collections of short stories. Jamaican novelist Colin Channer has published several of his short stories in various journals, works that explore the sensual and erotic in ways that few West Indian writers have done before him. In Canada, Guyana-born poet and novelist Cyril Dabydeen has published several collections with pieces set both in the Caribbean and in Canada. The Trinidad-born Neil Bisoondath is also based in Canada, and he too has published a significant number of short stories owing much of their style and complexity to the work of Naipaul. Patrick Chamoiseau, from Martinique, is proving to be, along with Trinidadian Robert Antoni, a voice of innovation and daring prose styling.

Despite this, it remains true that the short story of the region does not attract the kind of interest that the novel generates. This may be a condition of the publishing world, but it is exacerbated by the dearth of journals and periodicals dedicated to nurturing short fiction writing. There are few journals that appear regularly in the region, and so young writers are either forced to turn to international journals for publication or focus on longer forms of fiction to secure contracts with publishing houses. Many, no doubt, choose not to write at all.

Bim, *Caribbean Writer* (which is based in the U.S. Virgin Islands), and *Kunappippi*, are three of the more reliable journals that regularly publish short fiction. National newspapers on the various islands occasionally publish fiction, and there always arise several short-run journals that will publish the work of new writers. Most rely on contests and other such events to publish their work, but unlike in Latin America, where the short story is seen as a challenge to the hegemony of the long form, in the Caribbean the short story remains a modest and specialized genre.

Anthologies

Brown, Stewart, ed. *Caribbean New Wave: Contemporary Short Stories*. Portsmouth, N.H.: Heinemann, 1990. This anthology collection covers Caribbean short stories written in English and discusses Caribbean social life and customs.

Markham, E. A, ed. *The Penguin Book of Caribbean Short Stories*. Penguin, 1996. New York: Penguin Books, 1996. Covers Caribbean social life and customs and examines selected short stories. Includes bibliographical references.

Wickham, John, and Stewart Brown, eds. *The Oxford Book of Caribbean Short Stories*. New York: Oxford University Press, 1999. A pan-Caribbean collection, ranging beyond the Anglophone territories to include stories originally published in Spanish, French, and Dutch. Includes bibliographical references.

Bibliography

Arnold, A. James, Julio Rodríguez-Luis, and J. Michael Dash, eds. *A History of Literature in the Caribbean*. Philadelphia, Pa.: J. Benjamins, 1994. A historical and critical look at literature from the Caribbean. Includes bibliographical references and an index.

Balderston, Daniel, ed. *The Latin American Short Story: An Annotated Guide to Anthologies and Criticism*. Westport, Conn.: Greenwood Press, 1992. Organizes the enormous body of short-story anthologies from the nineteen countries of Spanish America and Brazil for systematic study. The main section comprises annotated listings of 1,302 short-story anthologies. A second section comprises annotated bibliographies of criticism of the short story. Includes bibliographical references and an index.

Bloom, Harold, ed. *Caribbean Women Writers*. Philadelphia, Pa.: Chelsea House, 1997. A thorough examination of contemporary, female Caribbean writers of English, including Jean Rhys, Jamaica Kincaid, Beryl Gilroy, and Edwidge Danticat. Includes bibliographical references and an index.

Echevarría, Roberto González, and Enrique Pupo-Walker, eds. *The Cambridge History of Latin American Literature*. 3 vols. New York: Cambridge University Press, 1996. Volume 1 covers the period from discovery to modernism, volume 2 covers the twentieth century, and volume 3 covers Brazilian literature. Includes bibliographical references and an index.

Erro-Peralta, Nora, and Caridad Silva-Núñez, eds. *Beyond the Border: A New Age in Latin American Women's Fiction*. Pittsburg, Pa.: Cleis Press, 1991. Covers works by Latin American female writers. Includes bibliographical references.

Foster, David William, ed. *Handbook of Latin American Literature*. New York: Garland Publishing, 1992. Offers separate essays on all Latin American countries, including French and Creole Haiti and Portuguese Brazil, written by scholars who focus on dominant issues and major movements, figures, and works, with emphasis on sociocultural and interpretive assessments. Includes bibliographical references and an index.

Moss, Joyce, and Lorraine Valestuk. *Latin American Literature and Its Times: Profiles of Notable Literary Works and the Historical Events That Influenced Them*. The fifty works included in this volume span a variety of genres and countries (including the United States) as well as historical periods. Includes bibliographical references and an index.

Partnoy, Alicia, ed. *You Can't Drown the Fire: Latin American Women Writing in Exile*. Pittsburg, Pa.: Cleis Press, 1988. Covers twentieth century female writers whose works have been translated into English. Includes bibliographical references.

Smith, Verity, ed. *Encyclopedia of Latin American Literature*. Chicago: Fitzroy Dearborn, 1997. Contains entries on writers, works, and topics relating to the literature of Latin America, including survey articles on all the continent's individual countries. Includes bibliographical references and an index.

Kwame Dawes

LATINO SHORT FICTION

While the popularity of short fiction in the twentieth century has been evidenced in the sheer volume of story anthologies, literary magazines, and copious production of collections by major artists, such as Joyce Carol Oates, John Updike, and Donald Barthelme, the short fiction of Latinos has rarely made an appearance. Large presses generally carried few or no works by Latino writers; mainstream and smaller literary magazines—primarily located on the East Coast and attuned to literature by Anglo men—believed there was no market for Latino stories. In fact, there was little appearance of Latino short fiction until mid-century; the genre began to create inroads into the Latino community (in fact, creating its own readership) only in the late 1960's and 1970's, and the publication of short stories by Latino authors became robust in the 1980's.

With the establishment of journals such as *Americas Review* (formerly *Revista Chicana-Riquena*) and of presses such as Arte Publico in Texas, which focus on writing by Latinos, a tradition of publication and distribution of short fiction began. As a result, the latter two decades of the twentieth century saw an explosion in the writing and publication of short fiction by Latinos and an exponential interest on the part of the public at large. Recently, several works of Chicano and Latino fiction have found their way into major literary anthologies and onto required reading lists in high school and college English classes. Despite the evidence of greater accessibility and acceptability into the literary world at large, Latino fiction is still, in many ways, a separate entity from Anglo-American, or "mainstream" literary studies. Latino fiction merits study as a serious field now, and with the emphasis on multicultural studies and the examination of historical and sociopolitical forces in literature, it can be informative and valuable to look at works from an ethnic perspective—to see, in other words, how specific ethnic or cultural identification affects literary trends and themes.

As literary production in the Latino community blossoms and as the U.S. Latino population increases—Latinos will be the largest minority group in the United States in the twenty-first century—there has been a significant increase in attention to "border" studies within the larger fields of American literature and cultural studies. Scholars and critics have begun to pay attention to the cultural dynamics of the U.S.-Mexican border, noting the exchange of influences and ideas. Prominent American studies and English professors such as Jose David Saldivar, Lois Parkinson Zamora, and Amy Kaplan have argued that scholars cannot consider the category "American literature" without taking into account all the Americas—North, South, and Central. At the same time, academic interest in the field of postcolonial studies requires a consideration of the relationship between the U.S. and its Caribbean neighbors, both in terms of considering the territory of each as colonized land following New World settlement and considering the participation of the United States in neocolonial relation to Puerto Rico, the Dominican Republic, and other Caribbean island nations. Among the results of this new focus is a fresh approach to a wide field of literature including fiction by Chicanos and Latinos living in the United States.

What is Latino Fiction?

Latino fiction includes works by writers in the United States who have either migrated from Latin America or are descendants of Latin Americans. Further, it can be argued that Latino writers are distinct in their linguistic, cultural, historical, and political sensibilities, and that their concerns frequently echo those of the community to which they belong. Still, the terms at times overlap and a word on usage is in order. While the term "Latino" is inclusive, meaning those from Mexico, Central and South America, and the Caribbean, the term "Chicano" is frequently employed when discussing those of Mexican or Mexican American heritage; Chicano/Latino is used when being both inclusive and mindful of distinctions therein. This article will avoid using the common term "Hispanic," which designates those whose linguistic origin is Spanish. This term is controversial, since many Latino groups claim that it is an outgrowth of U.S. governmental policies of foreign and domestic containment, overlooking the cultural diversity of the different Latino nations, and that, further, it inaccurately lays its claim in Spain and the Iberian peninsula, thereby eliding the history of colonization and its subsequent cultural manifestations. Therefore, "Latino/a" is preferred by many, being a reference to geographic origin, Latin America. While it is always problematic to assign a single term to a group that is far from homogeneous, it is the work of the scholar to locate the similarities that justify its usage, all the while attending to the cultural differences inherent in the field. Below, the aim is to do just that by tracing common themes, investigating their origins, and looking at particular authors and works that are notable for illustrating those themes.

The Latino Short-Story Form

Though not traditionally the dominant genre—novels and poetry have been more prevalent—the short-story form is particularly expressive for Chicano and Latino writers. The dramatic diversity and hybridity of Chicano and Latino life, and the tensions created by cultural flux, make apt material for the conventions of short fiction. It is no coincidence that some of the most influential works by Chicanos and Latinos are collections of short stories, such as experimental work by Tomás Rivera and the ground-breaking fiction of Sandra Cisneros. Rivera's and Cisneros's works are especially dependent on the accessibility and flexibility of the short-story genre, because both weave together a patchwork of narratives, a polymorphous collection of voices to articulate the lives of Latinos—an ethnic American group that is complex and varied. These and other writers have been able to express the complexities yet demonstrate the thematic concerns and stylistic sensibilities that make a particular work of short fiction distinctly Latino.

One of those distinctions is language. Many Chicanos and Latinos are fully bilingual or at least participate in more than one linguistic community. This Spanish-English bilingualism is directly addressed in many works of short fiction. While a few writers, such as Sabine Ulibarrí, were published in Spanish first, countless others demonstrate this bilingualism through the use of Spanish in the text via the insertion of "Spanglish," or anglicization of Spanish words, and frequent code-switching—that is, the act of alternating between or using the two languages at once, often in the same sentence or phrase. Although the English-language reader is usually able to fully comprehend these insertions through contextual clues or immediate translation, sometimes meaning is obscured for the readers who are not bilingual.

Customs and culture also play a large role in Latino short fiction. The inclusion of religious ritual, local legend, and popular folklore, much of which is unfamiliar to non-Latino or mainstream readers finds its way into a number of works. For the Latino writer, the delineations between fact and fantasy, dream and reality, legend and "truth" can sometimes be seen as arbitrary divisions, leading the work of writers such as Rudolfo Anaya to be labeled "Magical Realism." Many regional writers include particular myths, stories, and Catholic practices in their stories, as most of Latin America is Roman Catholic. Sandra Cisneros's story "Little Miracles, Kept Promises," for example, consists of a series of written thanks and descriptions of offerings, or *retablos* to various saints and the Virgin Mary, a custom particular to many Mexican Americans. Such customs and cultural practices, however, usually take place against the backdrop of a larger society, the United States, and so the stories at once represent cultural differences while negotiating the merging of Anglo-American U.S. and Latino cultures.

This negotiation leads to a preoccupation with geography in the literature. Latinos can be border-dwellers and border-crossers by virtue of the fact that they frequently have more than one national or cultural allegiance. Among these affiliations, Latinos are variously tied to New York, the Southwest, Chicago, or Texas in the United States and countries as culturally distinct as Cuba, the Dominican Republic, Mexico, or the United States territory of Puerto Rico. Additionally, Latino writers in the United States often write as exiles or as part of a larger diaspora, thereby evoking problematic sentiments of home, loyalty, cultural merging, and assimilation. For example, the Cubans, Dominicans and Puerto Ricans (or Nuyoricans) who have established themselves in the Northeast commonly write about the conflict between being part of the island culture, the land of their birth or ancestors, and life on the mainland. Different latitudes foster different attitudes, and these writers often contrast the harsh life in urban cities with tropical island living. The Chicanos of the Southwest integrate the landscape and its history of Anglo domination into the prose where it figures as either plot or character. Latino writers, therefore, are often deeply connected to the land they inhabit—either by native legacy or the attachments fostered by recent immigration—but cultural affiliations disrupt conventional national affiliations as regional terms like "Tejano" (a Mexican American from Texas) or "Californio" suggest, and so the site of Chicano/Latino narrative is physically and psychically shifting.

This continual shifting creates a tension in much of Latino short fiction, a tension that expresses itself in the duality of many of the characters as they struggle to be both Latino and North American, as they try to be at home in their barrios and comfortable in the world at large, and as they attempt to resist the pressures of an English-speaking world where racism still exists and cultural difference is not necessarily seen as an asset. Thus, assimilation and resistance to cultural dominance, along with themes of departure and return (and the migrant nature of culture) all play into the short fiction produced by Latinos in the United States. Clearly these are problems or issues that individuals encounter alone, and Chicano and Latino literature certainly portrays the single subject finding his or her way in two worlds, but these questions are vexing for the community at large; Latino characters are nearly always departing from or moving toward a reconciliation with a broader community. Indeed, perhaps the most notable and compelling feature of Chicano and Latino short fiction is the indelible sense of responsibility characters are shown to have for their respective communities.

Early Influences

While short fiction is a relatively recent phenomenon in Latino literature, it is useful to discuss the trajectory of the literature in general, before the appearance of the short story, in order to review the thematic concerns of Latino fiction and see how it is entwined with political history.

Latino literature in the United States—as with Latinos themselves—has a long history that is distinct from the Anglo-American tradition. In the early history of this country, Latino literature was written in Spanish and looked to Spanish-language traditions for literary inspiration. The literature of the sixteenth, seventeenth, and much of the eighteenth centuries, for example, mainly consisted of writings by the Spanish who settled in the New World and were chronicles of travels, memoirs, and letters, with some poetry and drama, as was typical of this time. Such works are now viewed as "American" works and are included in anthologies of U.S. literature, but set in context they stand out as antecedents to today's Latino fiction. A New World tradition of recounting and recording oral legends and myths, for example, combined with Spanish balladry prefigured much of the storytelling in forms such as the Mexican *corrido* that was to come.

It is during the nineteenth and early twentieth centuries that the territory now known as the United States began to take shape in what had been Hispanic territories. In 1821, Florida was ceded to the United States, and in 1848, with the treaty of Guadalupe Hidalgo, Mexico lost about a third of its territory including Alta California, Arizona, New Mexico, and Texas. Despite a great influx of Anglos to the region, Spanish remained the dominant language of the Southwest as the Mexican population struggled to remain in control of their property and culture. After the Spanish-American war of 1898, Cuba and Puerto Rico came under U.S. control, precipitating one of the first waves of Caribbean immigration into the Northeast and the South. Additionally, a wave of Mexican immigrants came into the country, concentrating in the Southwest after the Mexican revolution of 1910—some to escape the war, others in search of economic opportunities in the western United States.

During these turbulent decades the Latino literary world expanded tremendously and began to give voice to the concerns that are still being addressed in short fiction today. Fiction, however, was the slowest literary form to develop during this period, after memoirs, histories, chronicles, ballads, and poetry. According to Chicano literary scholar Raymund Paredes, "[the treaty of] Guadalupe Hidalgo had guaranteed Mexican-Americans frill rights as citizens but, in fact, they were frequently stripped of their property and subjected to severe discrimination. The Mexican-Americans expressed their resentment of this treatment in the large number of *corridos* that sprang from this region." The *corrido*, a border-based ballad form—became the preeminent narrative genre in the late nineteenth through mid-twentieth centuries along the border and was used to describe the sequence of domination and resistance between Mexicans and Anglos in the Southwest. Likewise, the Chicano fiction produced during this time took as its subject the land, its people, and its history. In California, Adolfo Carrillo published short stories and legends about the California missions and the gold rush. Eusebio Chacón, of New Mexico, published romantic novellas before the turn of the century. Urbano Chacón, and his son, Felipe Chacón, were newspaper editors in New Mexico. Felipe published a number of short stories in his newspaper and in books; however, this work was in Spanish as were many of the literary contributions around the turn of the century.

In fact, during this time, numerous Spanish-language newspapers were circulating, a large number of which carried poetry, stories, ballads, and serialized novels. *El Misisipi*, based in New Orleans, was probably the first Spanish-language newspaper in the United States. Other notable dailies and weeklies included *La Gaceta* of Santa Barbara, the literary magazine *Aurora*, and *La Prensa*, a newspaper which created its own weekly literary supplement. While much literary activity was centered on the Southwest and the former Mexican territories, in the Northeast, primarily New York, the *cronistas*, or newspaper columnists from Spanish-speaking communities, sought to nurture the cultural life of their groups of origin, most of which hailed from the Caribbean. Though there is little evidence that short fiction was produced by that community during the early part of the century, the seeds were sown for literary artistry in these newspapers.

The Advent of Latino Short Fiction

There are several authors from the first half of the twentieth century who have presaged the thematic concerns of Latino authors to follow and have received notice for their fiction. Josefina Niggli, who was born and lived in Mexico (though not to Mexican parents) is now generally considered one of the precursors of Chicano writers. Her best-selling story series of 1945, *Mexican Village*, charmingly and richly describes the Mexican town of Hidalgo and its people, yet at its center lies the issue of race: The reappearing protagonist of the stories is a half-Anglo, half-Mexican man who is rejected by his white father.

Mario Suárez is one of the first writers to use the term "Chicano" in print. His stories, many of which were published around mid-century, take Arizona as their scene; he describes the barrio in Tucson, replete with details about regional life, such as cultural customs that demonstrate the bridge between the ways of old Mexico and the U.S. Southwest. Though he did not publish abundantly, his realism and sympathetic portrayals of Chicanos have earned him respect as an early Chicano fiction writer.

A Franciscan priest born Manuel Chavez, Fray Angelico Chavez was a prolific writer who wrote historical narratives, as well as tracts on history and religion. The three stories that form *New Mexico Triptych* from 1940, combined with his other fictional works, have been compiled in *The Short Stories of Fray Angelico Chavez*, published in 1987. Chavez draws inspiration from traditional *hispano*—or Southwest Mexican and Mexican American Spanish-language stories. These stories are characterized by the use of provincial characters and situations, archetypal and religious narrative elements, and allegorical structures. The stories, considered by many to be quaint and charming renderings of the *Hispanos*, or Spanish-speakers of New Mexico, are currently the subject of much critical attention. While drawing upon the religious customs and folklore of the region,

Chavez takes on the social reality of the long process of transition from Mexican cultural norms in the Southwest and the inevitable cultural clashes that arose, illuminating the condescension of the Anglo-American toward the Mexican American. As the collection's editor, Genaro Padilla has put it, the stories present a "whimsical, romantic and mystic surface" to life in New Mexico, which is "quietly undermined by social criticism."

Américo Paredes, too, was writing about the American experience from a Mexican American perspective in the 1920's through 1950's. Paredes, who is best known for his ethnographic work on Mexican and Mexican American folklore, nonetheless published a number of short stories distinctive for their spare, realistic, and dialogic prose and contemporary contexts. Collected in *The Hammon and the Beans and Other Stories* (1994), these stories examine Chicano life from many social perspectives and take the reader from South Texas to Japan, from the Depression through World War II. The wide range of subjects and narrative points of view represent Paredes's view that the Chicano, no local or accidental cultural phenomenon, could be understood only in his or her relation to the United States and the world at large. According to literary critic Ramon Saldivar, *The Hammon and the Beans and Other Stories*, along with Paredes's scholarly work, constitute "a figural discourse of transnational epic proportions appropriate to the construction of a new narrative of a modern American social and cultural history."

The title piece of Paredes's collection, "The Hammon and the Beans," is set in the 1920's, takes place in a small town with a military base, and portrays the interweaving of the lives of sanctioned citizens, the military, with those marginalized on the border. In the story, a small Mexican-populated Texas town butts up against a U.S. military base. Focusing on the children of the town, the story shows the process by which the quotidian culture of Anglo-Americans is passed along to those on the margins. One little girl spies on the soldiers while they eat and steals their scraps for her family. Her playmates goad her into performing the banalities of the army mess hall with mock orations, at once for their own amusement and to master the discourse and interests of the dominant culture. The children realize they must learn English to survive in America but can do so only through subversion. In a telling episode, the young girl stands before her peers and mimics—with notable linguistic revision—the gruntings of hungry soldiers whom she has spied in the base mess hall: "Give me the *hammon* and the beans! give me the *hammon* and the beans!" The story ends with the narrator, now a young adult standing in food lines during the depression, thinking about the young girl and the (in)efficacy of her demand for food, which he now reads as a call for justice. The story is remarkable and characteristic of the collection as a whole in the way it represents the tangle of official vehicles of oppression—the military on the border—with quotidian lives, the lives of the hungry border-dwellers.

The short fiction of Paredes, along with that of Chavez, is preoccupied with life in the borderlands of the American Southwest during these decades, though in stylistically very different ways. However different the stories may read, they demonstrate that these concerns—those of geography, the concept of home, and social justice—are relevant to the Chicano/Latino community both then and now.

Contemporary Works and Authors

Contemporary Latino literature gains its unique voice from the civil-rights struggles in the 1960's in general and the academic protests by Chicanos and Latinos in the late 1960's and early 1970's in particular. The Chicano Movement, or "El Movemiento" as it is called in local circles, was a grassroots protest movement based in Texas and parts of the Southwest which called for equality and integration in schools, a fair language program that respected the primacy of Spanish in the homes of Chicano and Latino students, and a more balanced view of the history of the region. The Movement made strong political gains for Chicanos and Latinos, and it also sparked a social and cultural awakening, providing the inspiration and the symbolism for much of the literature that would follow. The Movement highlighted the rights of Chicanos and Latinos to their language, their cultural past, and their (symbolic) sovereignty over their land.

These themes show up in the efflorescence of literature and the deep commitment to artistic production and expression that followed. Chicano/Latino writers were less concerned during this time with the literary experimentation that was taking place among mainstream writers of the period and more concerned with thematic problems of identity, racial discrimination, immigration, and socioeconomic repression.

Tomás Rivera's works, *. . . y no se lo tragó la tierra . . . and the earth did not part* (1971) and *The Harvest: Short Stories* (1988), find a home in these thematic concerns. Considered a classic of Chicano fiction, *. . . y no se lo tragó la tierra* was published initially in Spanish and then as a bilingual work, with side-by-side English and Spanish versions of the text. This book consists of fourteen stories, twelve of which correspond to the months of the year, divided by thirteen vignettes. The stories piece together the life of a nameless boy over that year, a working-class character who embodies the collective voice of migrant workers—a group whose stories had rarely graced the pages of literature. A prayer for a son in Vietnam, a boy suffering from thirst in the fields, and the ostracization of migrant Mexican schoolchildren in the classroom are the focuses of some of the pieces. The short, fragmentary pieces that make up the whole, combined with the bilingual presentation of the text, echo the fragmentation of identity of people caught between two cultures. The work is considered to be a tremendous influence on Chicano/Latino writers who followed him, such as Sandra Cisneros.

The characters in Rivera's collection *The Harvest*, too, lead lives that mirror the experimental, minimalist prose. Rivera's stories, like his subjects' lives, are nonlinear, as characters migrate according to the season and live at the mercy of the growers who employ them. The characters are divested of conventional forms of agency, and so it is not their actions that determine the plot of the stories but the sudden and fatalistic whims of nature and economics. Rivera expresses the humanity of his subjects through their enduring commitment to one another and through their attempts to make meaning of their landscape and their lives. Again, and as will be seen with Cisneros, it is crucial to add that meaning itself is not achieved by any given story—Rivera's tales are not fables or allegories, and there are not always realizations for the reader—but the representation of a community attempting to understand their own lives is itself a meaningful act and the effect of much Chicano/Latino short fiction.

Another deeply influential author is Rudolfo Anaya, whose fiction has won numerous awards and much acclaim. In *The Silence of the Llano* (1982), Anaya takes as his subject the people of New Mexico and their lives in the rural areas of the state. Called a "Magical Realist," Anaya skillfully interweaves local belief and custom into his narratives, creating works that are steeped in the spiritual experiences that comprise the everyday lives of Chicanos and Mexicanos of that area. Sabine Reyes Ulibarrí also a New Mexican, has published short-story collections in both Spanish and English. *Tierra Amarilla: Cuentos de Nuevo Mexico* (1964; *Tierra Amarilla: Stories of New Mexico*, 1971) and *Mi abuela fumaba puros y otros cuentos de Tierra Amarilla/ My Grandma Smoked Cigars and Other Stories of Tierra Amarilla* (1977) were published with parallel texts in English and Spanish. Like the works of Anaya, Ulibarrí's stories are inspired by the landscape and people of New Mexico and draw upon local lore and oral tradition to portray the *hispano* communities there. Depicting a people who are deeply Catholic, Ulibarrí demonstrates the effect of lore on their lives, with stories such as "Mi caballo mago" about a magical stallion which recounts a version of *La llorona*, the Mexican tale of the legendary weeping woman who still travels the earth crying for her drowned children.

Though the authors mentioned above have received significant notice in journals and anthologies, there are still more Chicano writers whose work is less well-known but also deeply tied to regional concerns, describing life on the border and in the barrios, respectively. Genaro Gonzalez has published stories in a number of literary magazines. His collection *Only Sons* (1991) deals with living on the border in Texas and is concerned with the effect this political geography has on the people who inhabit this area. Nash Candelaria, Dagoberto Gilb, and Alberto Alvaro Rios have all published stories both in journals and in collections and have received critical attention for their work. Max Martinez's stories in *The Adventures of the Chicano Kid, and Other Stories* (1982) and *A Red Bikini Dream* (1990) depict the varied lives of Chicanos, from the poor of the barrio to upper-middle-class educated Chicanos in a frequently humorous vein.

Estela Portillo Trambley, from Texas, was the first Chicana to publish a book of short stories with *Rain of Scorpions and Other Writings* in 1975. Embodying feminist ideals of equality, women are the center of the narratives here, as Trambley decries the inequality and unjust treatment of women and celebrates their unique biology. In her fiction, Trambley proffers the belief that, because of the biological imperative of giving birth, women are by nature nurturing and sensitive to other beings. Common as they were in early 1970's mainstream feminist writing, these ideas also proliferated in early Chicana writing. Just as anti-essentialist feminist thought rebuffed the conundrum of biological essentialism, so too did early Chicana feminist fiction give way to a more sophisticated literary aesthetic, at once aware of the imperative to liberate Chicanas from the patriarchal representations of their bodies while able to represent the diversity among Chicanas' lives.

In the 1980's and 1990's there begins a renaissance of fiction by Chicana/Latina women in the United States. This has been an important cultural intervention into what has been a largely male-dominated ethnic literary movement. Many of these authors have taken on disrupting stereotypical constructions of gender through ethnic identification, satirizing and criticizing the portrayals of women as either wife/mother or sexually promiscuous vamp and interwoven the issues of immigration, work, love, identity, and self-realization. The interest in the writing of women such as Alicia Gaspar de Alba, Judith Oritz Cofer, and Roberta Fernandez has precipitated much of the current explosion in Latina fiction.

Probably the most popular and famous writer of this renaissance is the aforementioned Sandra Cisneros, author of *The House on Mango Street* (1984) and *Woman Hollering Creek and Other Stories* (1991). *The House on Mango Street* is a series of forty-four vignettes centered on a single protagonist, reminiscent of Tomás Rivera's *. . . y no se lo tragó la tierra*. Considered a feminist *Bildungsroman*, *The House on Mango Street* has enjoyed a popularity unprecedented in Latino fiction and is now widely used in high school and college literature classes. It is the collection *Woman Hollering Creek and Other Stories*, however, that solidifies Cisneros as a powerful writer of short fiction. The stories of this collection take place in Chicago (the city of Cisneros's birth, and home to a both a large Mexican American and Puerto Rican community), Mexico, and the American Southwest. Exemplifying the best of personal and political consciousness, Cisneros draws heavily on Mexican and Mexican American history and lore in many of these stories, such as "Eyes of Zapata," a tale told from the vantage point of Mexican revolutionary Emiliano Zapata's lover. The Virgin of Guadalupe, a Mexican icon who functions as symbol of inspirational womanhood, figures in a number of stories with settings on both sides of the border.

Written almost entirely from a first-person point of view, Cisneros's mostly female protagonists struggle with their Latina identity and the constraints and strengths that those identities confer upon the characters. These characters are varied in their life experiences and roles; some are mothers and wives, others are single females trying to find a place for themselves in a society which has presented them with few nontraditional options. Cisneros tackles issues as varied as spousal abuse ("Woman Hollering Creek"), acquired immunodeficiency syndrome ("Remember the Alamo"), and intracommunity racism ("Never Marry a Mexican"). The challenges that the protagonists take on—and that Cisneros takes on as a writer—exemplify the complexities of life as a Latina.

Cisneros has been a pioneer in the representation of the linguistic hybridity of border-based Chicanos and all Latinos. In her fiction there is frequently a strong emphasis on the verbal, expressed through long passages of dialogue, much of which is rapid and lively, and through the extensive use of interior monologues. The verbal quality is enhanced by continual infusions of "spanglish" and slang terms and almost constant cross-pollination, evident even in the titles of the stories, such as "Bien Pretty" or "My Tocaya." "The Marlboro Man" or "La Fabulosa," for example, consist of conversations between unnamed friends who create, through their dialogue, modern myths about people of their community, creating a contemporary version of traditional orality and popular legend that characterizes speech and storytelling in Latino communities.

Sandra Cisneros's narrative is in fact, often polyvocal, with the voice of a single protagonist displaced in favor of a community of (at times conflicting) voices. In "Little Miracles, Kept Promises," recitations of prayers and miracles formulate multiple narratives within a single tale. In the story "Woman Hollering Creek" the narrative voice shifts several times from the singular to the plural, from the protagonist to community members—at times echoing the shift in locality, as characters cross from the Mexican side of the border to the U.S. side and back again. These narrative voices combine not so much to plot the story as to represent the impact the main event of the story—already passed—has had on a neighborhood. Though it is not always clear *what* has happened, Cisneros shows *who* it has happened to and so gives expression to an otherwise underrepresented community of border-dwellers.

Writing in an accessible, lively style, Denise Chavez has authored the popular collection *The Last of the Menu Girls* (1986), a series of stories and vignettes narrated by a central character, Rocio Esquibel, who distributes menus to patients in a hospital. The highly verbal quality of these stories, along with Cisneros's, are representative of some of the best of Latina fiction. The stories are arranged not chronologically but thematically, dealing with such issues as the search for strong female role models, the value of women's work and daily tasks, and the role of memory, time, and communal and familial ties in the search for identity. Not coincidentally, the protagonist, Rocio, decides to become a writer and to chronicle the lives of friends and family in her community. Like several of the female protagonists of Cisneros's stories, Rocio finds strength and autonomy through artistic expression. Like Cisneros, Chavez's work has received much positive criticism: Selections from *The Last of the Menu Girls* have found their way into a number of anthologies of both Latino and mainstream American literature.

Helena María Viramontes is another major Chicana author who grapples with issues of ethnic identity and infuses them with feminist sensibilities, as in her collection *The Moths and Other Stories* (1985), her best-known work. The title story "The Moths" has been frequently anthologized in recent years, and the tragic story "The Cariboo Café" in particular has received considerable critical attention. In "The Cariboo Café" Viramontes narrates the experience of recent Mexican and Central American immigrants living in Los Angeles, weaving the lives of usually invisible characters into the fabric of the city as a whole. "The Cariboo Café," parsed in separate, disjointed sections, follows a series of characters whose lives become tragically tangled. In the first section Sonya (about six years old) and her baby brother Macky are inadvertently locked out of their apartment, somewhere north of the Mexican border. The parents, illegal immigrants, are both at work and have warned the children to never venture far from the apartment, never trust the "polie" for they are *la migra* (immigration) officials in disguise, and never talk to strangers. Section 1 ends with the children lost, wandering in a warehouse district, and approaching a strange lady who seems to offer help. Section 2 introduces the owner and operator of the Cariboo Café, a man down on his luck, unable to afford to hire any help, not even a dishwasher. Coping poorly with the recent breakup of his family, the café owner finds himself increasingly the peer of the junkies, drunks, and homeless who loiter in his cafe. Among the other liminal figures who enter are a strange woman and two children, clearly not her own. Watching the nightly news, the café owner learns that the children have been reported missing, possibly kidnapped, but upholding his own rule to never talk to the "polie," he declines to inform them of what he knows. In the final section, the putative kidnapper, a washerwoman by trade, narrates her own story in a hazy jumble of memory and motive. A native of Central America, the woman suffers the loss of her own child, probably a victim of the U.S.-sponsored Contra rebellion in the 1980's. Still suffering the trauma of loss, still in a haze of grief, the woman encounters the wandering Sonya and Macky and perceives the boy as her own lost son, attempting to bridge her trauma by taking him in. In her final and fatal confrontation with the police, she imagines she is back in Central America, fighting guerrilla forces.

Though "The Cariboo Café" ends with a determinedly heroic act, other stories in the collection are more ambivalently rendered, as Viramontes avoids the easy political dichotomies and portrays the complexity of Latino life. Her main characters are mostly women, and a common theme in her fiction is the struggle for women to recognize the source and means of their oppression, both by the majority culture and the patriarchal strictures of Mexican American culture. Plots turn on transitional moments for the women, as they build bridges across generations to other women ("The Moths") or come to recognize their loneliness ("The Neighbors"). A powerful theme in several stories is the Latina's developing relationship with her own sexuality, fraught by her family's prohibitions—for whom a woman's sexuality is a source of honor to be guarded—or by religious sanction. The ending passage of the story "Birthday," for example, narrates Alice's terrible confusion as she prepares to have an abortion. Here, Viramontes's prose style marks both the determined resolve of Alice's decision (a painful coming into womanhood) and the internal battle she still wages with her cultural upbringing:

> Now the doctor will insert . . . *the waves rock me into an anxious sleep. And i love. NO! I don't love you, not you, God, knotted ball. I hate you, Alice. . . .* Relax Alice, and try not to move again *reaching up to the vastness. calm. i relax under the fluids that thicken like jelly.* i am still; my body is transparent and light, and ounceless.

The oscillation between love and hate, faith and its rejection, occur simultaneously with the abortion, which is itself an ultimate action. Her decision renders her empty, or "ounceless," but she endures nonetheless; "i am still."

Puerto Rican, Cuban, and Dominican American Writers

For much of the Caribbean American community, concerns about space and place are every bit as important as they are for Chicano writers. With the movements to the mainland from Cuba and Puerto Rico, each wave of immigrants has created a new generation of writers.

Pedro Juan Soto and Luis Gonzalez, two Puerto Rican writers, were part of the "Generation of 1940" who wrote about life in New York at mid-century. Though he later returned to the island, Soto took as his subject the immigrant experience and barrio life. In *Spiks* (English translation, 1973), his collection of short stories published in 1956, Soto examined life on the streets. A heightened awareness of race, as indicated in the collection's title—"spik" being a derogatory term for Puerto Ricans—affects his acute portrayal of the difficulty of life in New York for the Puerto Rican community. *Spiks* is also noteworthy for its realism, extensive use of street slang, and code-switching—all fairly new techniques at the time. Gonzalez, too, was one of the first writers to discuss the exile of Puerto Ricans in the United States and the racial tensions and economic difficulties of the community in numerous short stories. These writers and others of the 1940's and 1950's influenced subsequent Puerto Rican and other Latino writers of the Northeast.

Just as the civil- and cultural-rights movements of the 1960's influenced Chicano literature, so too did the heightened awareness of cultural roots and political struggle affect Puerto Ricans on the mainland. This awareness manifested itself in the literary production of the "Nuyoricans," a term coined to describe the hybridity formed when island culture was imported to urban life. Early Nuyorican fiction prominently represented mostly male protagonists coming of age on the streets of New York. Consistently, the tension between life on the (Anglo-American) mainland and the persistence of native language, ethics and social mores, gave rise to a new ethnic sensibility. No longer Puerto Rican only, the Nuyorican writer reconceptualized identity and social landscape, writing into existence not only a new ethnicity, but also a new social construction of New York City.

While the difficulty of life in the United States and the racism of Anglo-American society were the focus of much fiction coming out of this period, it was accompanied by an idealized version of life on the island. A greater embrace of cultural difference began, a difference expressed in the writing through the extensive use of Spanish, frequent code-switching, and insertion of customs, practices, and terminologies particular to Puerto Ricans.

One such writer is Pin Thomas, whose autobiography *Down These Mean Streets* (1967) became widely popular; the tensions that arose for him, being a dark-skinned Puerto Rican in America, familiar with the ways of the streets, reveal themselves in his fiction and memoir alike. Yet his collection of short fiction, *Stories from El Barrio* (1978), does not dwell entirely upon the negative aspects of life in the barrio but affirms values such as male friendship and personal strength.

Ed Vega (Edgardo Vega Yunque), too, writes short stories that have their setting in the barrio. *Mendoza's Dreams* (1987) is a collection of stories linked through a narrator named Alberto Mendoza. Rather than a chronicle of difficulty and urban strife, Vega infuses these stories with humor. In this earlier work his characters are not suffering migrants but complexly rendered individuals who encounter success in unlikely but very American ways. His *Casualty Report* (1991), however, departs from the earlier works and focuses on the destruction wrought by violence and drugs in the Puerto Rican barrios.

Probably the most prolific Puerto Rican writer, Nicholasa Mohr, too, has been obsessed with the struggle of life between two cultures. Much of her writing has been for a young adult audience, including her *El Bronx Remembered* (1975), a novella with short stories, which was a finalist for the National Book Award. In this collection the stories span the years between 1946 and 1956, taking New York as the backdrop for Puerto Rican youth for whom the island life is distant but far from removed. Her *Rituals of Survival: A Woman's Portfolio* (1985) was her first work for adults, and in 1997 she published *A Matter of Pride and Other Stories*. Both these collections center on Puerto Rican women in New York struggling to cope with Latino machismo and break out of the barrio, and they highlight the poignancy of returning to the neighborhood of one's birth. Traditions and beliefs from the Caribbean still persist in these neighborhoods, despite the frequently hostile influence of "American" New York, a theme Mohr carries through all her works. In the story "Aunt Rosana's Rocker," for example, the female protagonist, Zoraida, is thought to be possessed, and a spiritualist is consulted and rituals performed to exorcize the invasive spirit.

Like Mohr, Judith Ortiz Cofer, in *An Island Like You* (1995), writes of young, contemporary protagonists who are Puerto Rican immigrants negotiating the space between the two cultures. Like her fellow Puerto Rican writers, the language and cultural particulars of the community figure here. Considered the most mainstream of Puerto Rican writers, Cofer markets both her poetry and young adult works to a wide audience and makes her work accessible and friendly.

In 1992, the young writer Abraham Rodriguez, Jr., published *The Boy Without a Flag*. These seven short stories center on Puerto Rican Americans—mainly adolescents—in the south Bronx and reflections of the alienation, rebellion, and submission experienced by that group in the United States. The title story is emblematic of the cultural collisions and confusion sometimes encountered when straddling a bifurcated identity. "Boy Without a Flag" tells of a boy who refuses to salute the American flag in school, after being told by his father that the United States is the enemy of the Puerto Rican people. The boy is sent to the principal, and his father is called in. Instead of denouncing the United States to the principal, as the boy expects, the father apologizes to the principal. The scene of capitulation is nearly archetypal in immigrant and ethnic fiction, and the collection received positive critical attention.

Cuban exiles and Cuban Americans form another vibrant sector of Latino short fiction. Roberto Fernandez, who came to the United States at eleven years of age, has written short-story collections in Spanish: *Cantos sin rumbos* (1975; directionless tales) and *El jardin de la luna* (1976; the garden of the moon). In the stories, Fernandez writes humorously about the Cuban community in the United

States and life in exile. Virgil Suarez, a Cuban American, writes about Cubans and their families who have left their island for life in the United States in *Welcome to the Oasis and Other Stories* (1992).

Junot Diaz, a Dominican American writer, seems poised to move Latino short fiction into the sights of mainstream readers and garner wide attention for his work and the work of other Latinos. Diaz has published stories in *The New Yorker, Story*, and *The Best American Short Stories 1996*, as well as mainstream magazines. In 1996 Diaz published a collection of his stories, entitled *Drown*, which was widely praised and quickly became a best-seller. With stories that take place in both the Dominican Republic and the northeastern United States, Diaz takes his place in the tradition of Caribbean writers who tell of the contrast between island and mainland life and all its attendant struggles. Like other Latino writers before him, Diaz employs extensive use of dialogue, using slang, anglicizations of English, and code-switching—yet manages a remarkably restrained style and lyricism that has won him much acclaim. *Drown* has been translated into Spanish as well, thereby widening his reading community and offering a literary link between mainland and Caribbean readers.

Junot Diaz is indicative of a trend. Latino fiction in the United States continues to explode, both in terms of volume and sales and in terms of the numbers of upcoming young authors. Michele Serros's *Chicana Falsa, and Other Stories of Death, Identity, and Oxnard* (1993) has received positive notices. Danny Romero, Veronica Gonzalez, and Sergio Troncoso are but a few of the up-and-coming names in Latino short fiction. There is increasing interest, too, in tracing the literary history of Latinos and creating a body of critical work to address the many issues imbedded in the fiction. As Latino short fiction gains prominence, it also gains gravity, drawing the attention of mainstream readers and presses. Indeed, it may be said that, as Latino fiction has shaped the landscape of Latino culture at large, so too has it helped reconstruct (along with other ethnic literatures) the broader American culture, thereby fully claiming a place in the American literary canon.

Adrienne Pilon and Dean Franco

Bibliography

Augenbraum, Harold, and Margarite Fernandez Olmos, eds. *The Latino Reader: An American Literary Tradition form 1542 to the Present*. New York: Houghton Mifflin, 1997. This collection provides historical background on writers and their sociopolitical context while featuring their works. A list of additional readings presents criticism and history for research on all periods.

Calderon, Hector, and Jose' David Saldivar, eds. *Criticism in the Borderlands: Studies in Chicano Literature, Culture and Ideology*. Durham: Duke University Press, 1991. This collection brings together some of the most compelling and important criticism on Chicano literature today by major Chicano scholars from around the country.

Cortina, Rodolfo, ed. *Hispanic American Literature: An Anthology*. Chicago: NTC, 1998. A comprehensive collection of Hispanic and Latino prose and poetry spanning from the sixteenth century to the present.

Luis, William. *Dance Between Two Cultures: Latino Caribbean Literature Written in the United States*. Nashville: Vanderbilt University Press, 1997. An historical overview of Puerto Rican, Dominican and Cuban literature in the United States along with critical essays.

Milligan, Bryce, Mary Guerrero Milligan, and Angela de Hoyos, eds. *Daughters of the Fifth Sun*. New York: Putnam, 1995. A feminist introduction starts off this collection of contemporary Latina short fiction and poetry.

Santiago, Roberto. *Boricuas: Influential Puerto Rican Writings—An Anthology*. New York: Ballantine, 1995. A good general reference on the subject, this text is comprehensive in its inclusion of a variety of genres.

Stavans, Ilan, ed. *New World: Young Latino Writers*. New York: Delta, 1997. Stavans has compiled twenty-three stories by some of the youngest and most exciting Latino writers working today.

Suarez, Virgil, and Delia Poey, eds. *Iguana Dreams: New Latino Fiction*. New York: Harper, 1992. The first anthology of contemporary Latino fiction, featuring twenty-nine different writers.

NATIVE AMERICAN SHORT FICTION

According to the conventional criteria used by literary scholars to define short fiction, the contributions of Native Americans to this genre are relatively recent. A consensus among commentators familiar with the field is that N. Scott Momaday's novel *House Made of Dawn* (1968) marked the beginning of a new phase of cultural expression in which First Nation people joined other ethnic groups in finding publishers for their writing. As Leslie Marmon Silko, whose novel *Ceremony* (1977) has been called the first written by a Native American woman, puts it somewhat sardonically, "the ignorant Anglo-Americans that suddenly let us publish our books" realized the growing interest in Native Americans had commercial possibilities. As Silko, in consort with many other accomplished First Nation novelists, has contended, this emergence into print is the latest and hardly most significant phase of a tradition of storytelling that reaches back to what might be called the dawn of human time. "From generation to generation the people had been telling stories," Silko explains, "and Scott Momaday could not have written the book if it not had been for the careful nurturing, for the care of the stories and his old grandmother he talks about." As she states in *Ceremony:*

> I will tell you something about stories,
> [he said]
> They aren't just entertainment.
> Don't be fooled.
> They are all we have, you see,
> all we have to fight off
> illness and death.

The "death" she speaks of is a death of the spirit, of a people's soul, of the culture that sustains a civilization, and the stories that she refers to have been an integral element of First Nations life and originate in the pre-Columbian distant past. Stories, or "short fiction," are a part of the oral tradition that preceded print, that continues coterminously with its invention, and that does not seem likely to be subverted or replaced entirely by written forms now that Native Americans have at least some access to the same media outlets as other citizens of the United States.

The Oral Tradition

Momaday (Kiowa), who calls himself a "man made of words," links the oral tradition with print work by saying "the writer, like the storyteller, I think, is concerned to create himself and his audience in language." Momaday sees the oral tradition not only as a part of a continuum spanning epochs but also as fundamental to the process of shaping language into meaning. By casting images into words at the moment of immediate response to a visual or aural stimuli, the storyteller (or poet/singer) can be working close to the point where consciousness and perception are linked in language. Simon Ortiz (Acoma Pueblo) connects the oral tradition to what he designates as "lifestyle," which he describes as the "whole process of that society in terms of its history, its culture, its language, its values, and subsequently its literature." Ultimately, he feels, "man exists because of language, consciousness comes about through language, or the world comes about through language. Life = language. Language is life, then."

In addition to the crucial link between written literature and the oral tradition, Ortiz, Momaday, and many other Native American writers have stressed the importance of a historical record which was preserved when the First Nation peoples were almost annihilated during the first two centuries of the American republic. Ortiz recalls his father "trying to express certain views about how important it was for him and for the people to retain their heritage." For Silko (Laguna Pueblo), storytelling was so much a part of her life that when she was a student at the University of New Mexico and was given an assignment to write a character sketch, she thought "I had thousands," and when she was told "We want a story," she thought, "Is he serious? Is this all it is? I just cashed in on all those things I heard." Emphasizing the commonality of stories in her life, she has observed "The best thing, I learned, the best thing you can have in life is to have someone tell you a story; they are physically with you." Gerald Vizenor (Chippewa) has developed the concept of the word as a weapon in his book *Wordarrows: Indians and Whites in the New Fur Trade* (1978), in which he says that "the arrowmakers and wordmakers survive in the word wars with sacred memories," and Paula Gunn Allen (Laguna-Lakota) has published a collection of stories by Native American women under the title *Spider Woman's Granddaughters: Traditional Tales and Comtemporary Writing by Native American Women* (1989) because, in a Cherokee account, Grandmother Spider brought "the light of intelligence and experience" to a people "who have been in a state of war for five hundred years."

SHAPING WORDS INTO TEXT

The sustaining power of the oral tradition is so strong that John Rouillard, a Santee Sioux and the director of a university Native American studies program, asked semiseriously at a meeting of the Modern Language Association, "Do Indians write novels?" His point was that perhaps it was "un-Indian" to be a published writer rather than a storyteller. Although his audience understood that he was setting up a false dichotomy, and Allen responded by saying that a novel is a long story weaving "a number of elements into a coherent whole," the relationship between the story as it existed through time—supple, flexible, and changing with each narration; shaped by the personality of the storyteller; altered by the experiences of the community; ordered by some aesthetic principles common to First Nation ways of thought—and the fixed form of the printed version raised some crucial issues that have had a significant impact on both spoken and written imaginative fiction.

Considering the enduring power of the oral tradition and the way in which some of its most accomplished practitioners have produced artifacts with some core similarities to the short story as it has existed in the United States at least since the work of Washington Irving and Edgar Allan Poe, it might seem that Native American artists would have been interested in and able to do some more formal work in that area before Momaday's Pulitizer Prize-winning novel. A review of the actual record of publication in various forms by First Nation writers does reveal some examples of short fictional narratives that reached printed form, but a devastating indictment by Allen of the obstacles that prevented more substantial contributions to the field makes the historical record clear. "Indian people didn't publish their work for the most part until this century," Allen states, because

> literacy as understood in modern America is not particularly useful to tribal peoples who were once able to survive and prosper without it. For another, instruction in literacy was accomplished through humiliation, beatings, and isolation in huts, dark closets, and tiny prisons. When students are force-taught, half-starved, dipped in sheep-dip, shorn, redressed, renamed, forbidden to see their families for years on end, given half-rotted and barely digestible alien food, shamed and humiliated publicly, forbidden to speak their native language, and indoctrinated to believe that their loved ones are naked, murderous, shameful savages, hardly on a par with beasts (who used to be friends and allies), their reluctance to take up pen and write is hardly surprising.

The anger and justifiable resentment running through this passage is both an explanation, and a revealing demonstration of one of the primary themes of Native American writing in the last decades of the twentieth century, and it offers a background against which the sporadic appearance of Indian writing in print can be assessed.

AMERICAN INDIANS IN PRINT: 1774-1900

The initial appearance in print of literary efforts by Native Americans was a result of the religious education they received in missionary schools. Samson Occom, a member of the Mohegan tribal grouping of the Hudson Valley in New York state, was a minister to several eastern tribes and published in 1774 *A Choice Collection of Hymns and Spiritual Songs*. David Cusick (Tuscarora) put together a history of his people based on stories from the oral tradition, *Sketches of Ancient History of the Six Nations* (1827). The section describing wars against fierce monsters has elements of the kind of folktale that often precedes a composed narrative. William Apes (Pequot) wrote a full-scale autobiography, *A Son of the Forest* (1829), in which he combined personal reminiscence with major historical events (for example, the War of 1812 in which he, among many other Indians, fought with Andrew Jackson's army). Elias Boudinot, known also by his Cherokee name—Galagina—translated into Cherokee a short fictional work called "Poor Sarah" in 1833. George Copway (Kahgegagahbowh; Objibwe) wrote an account of his travels in 1847–*The Life, History, and Travels of Kah-ge-ga-gah-bowh*—that went through six editions and contained vivid descriptions of Objibwe life, such as his family's near-starvation one winter, which approach the short story in form and effect. Copway's *The Traditional History and Characteristic Sketches of the Ojibway Nation* (1850) included some ancient myths and stories of hunting and game playing that placed material from the oral tradition in print for the first time.

The restrictions faced by Native American men applied to women as well, with the additional obstacle of patriarchial condescension that operated in both Anglo and First Nation societies, although not to the same degree. Sarah Winnemucca Hopkins's (Piute) book *Life Among the Piutes* (1883) is an imaginative personal and tribal history which included some intense descriptive passages quite similar to the short fiction published at the time. As the scholar A. Lavonne Brown Ruoff observes, "With a sharp eye for detail, Sarah re-creates scenes and dialogue that give her descriptions an immediacy missing in many other histories of the period." A Crow wise-woman known as Pretty-shield (born around 1858) was persuaded by the ethnographer Frank Linderman to tell him stories of her tribe, and she reluctantly agreed, partly to set the record straight (she "seemed to find his ignorance alarming and perhaps dangerous," Allen notes). "A Woman's Fight," published in 1932, has some of the qualities of a first-person, unfolding, present-tense narration that anticipates the modern short story. E. Pauline Johnson (Tehakionwake) born in 1861 in Canada, her father a Mohawk Nation activist, her English-descended mother a cousin of the prominent writer William Dean Howells, began to publish fiction in popular magazines and eventually gathered her stories in *The Moccasin Maker* (1913). "A Red Girl's Reasoning," which she published in 1906, uses the basic theme of an impending marriage to comment on the strained relationship between Native and Anglo Americans and to reflect on the basis for a harmonious joining. The use of dialogue, the development of a narrative thread and the depth of characterization are features of a literary work by an experienced and deft writer. Her *Legends of Vancouver* (1911) sprang from conversations with Chief Joe Capilano (Squamish) which initiate each retelling of an old legend and according to Ruoff is "among the most successful of the period in its reinterpretations of oral literature."

Native American Fiction in the Twentieth Century

Paula Gunn Allen, in her landmark edited collection *Song of the Turtle: American Indian Literature, 1974-1994* (1996) summarizes the writing of First Nations people in the twentieth century by dividing the era into three units, which she calls waves. The first wave, which covers the initial seven decades of the century, was marked by what Allen identifies as "issues of recovery and identity" resulting from the dispossession of Native Americans by "the alien nation that conquered them." The second wave, which Allen locates at the time in 1974 when Kenneth Rosen published the anthology *The Man to Send Rain Clouds*, continued and recapitulated the first wave themes while adding "a sense of renewal and hope" often reasserted with anger and pride. Conflict between cultures was a major subject of the collection, with many Native American protagonists victimized by an oppressive Anglo dominant society or destroyed in aggressive, violent attacks against it. As the second wave progressed through the 1970's and 1980's, a shift took place as the protagonists of novels and stories found ways to survive through the cultivation of a kind of ironic perspective that drew upon the revival or rediscovery of a cosmic vision grounded in the old ways of First Nations people. Notably, Abel in Momaday's *House Made of Dawn* literally becomes the mythic figure of a ritual that enables him to transcend the immediate reality of Indian life. In contrast to first wave fiction in which ritual was presented as withering away, Momaday, with Ortiz, Silko, and James Welch (Blackfeet), in particular, were inaugurating the third wave. Ritual in the second wave was often projected in stereotypical form—what some have called the "drums and feathers" school of Indianness—which did have the positive effect of introducing some aspects of a relatively authentic Native American experience to a much wider reading public but which Allen asserts was modeled on "works created or heavily edited by Anglo-Americans."

The crucial change from the second to the third wave involved a protagonist who not only could survive the difficult conditions of life on and off the reservation but also began a process of transcendence so that she or he could begin to learn and operate within a ceremonial (that is, recollectively historical) role which is nourishing and life-sustaining even amid a hostile, alien environment. During the last decade of the twentieth century, writers like Louise Erdrich and Sherman Alexie—enlarging the flow begun by Momaday, Silko, and Ortiz, among others—were instrumental in bringing what had been regarded as a separate subdivision of American writing into what the poet Ishmael Reed (Anglo-Irish/African/Cherokee) has called "the Ocean of American Literature."

The First Wave: 1900-1974

The best known and most widely read Native American writer of the first part of the twentieth century was Charles Eastman (Ohiyesa), who lived among nomadic Santee Sioux as they moved to avoid the encroachment of advancing cavalry units. When his father Jacob Eastman (Many Lightnings) was released from prison after participating in the 1862 Sioux uprising, he encouraged Eastman to attend Dartmouth College (B.A., 1887) and then Boston University Medical School (M.D., 1890). Working as an Indian Agency physician, Eastman tended the survivors of the massacre at Wounded Knee (1890) and began an autobiographical account of his experiences, which was published as *Indian Boyhood* in 1902. His work combined historical information, folktales, explanations of Sioux customs and sketches of people he knew, giving many Anglo readers their first sense of another cultural community living in the United States. In the area of short fiction, his *Red Hunters and the Animal People* (1904), ostensibly a book for younger readers, retold traditional legends previously preserved through oral transmission and animal stories based on the conversations of hunters. This book was very successful, and Eastman followed it with *Old Indian Days* (1907), which heightened his imaginative style of storytelling. "The War Maiden" from this collection was a ground-breaking account "of the Courageous and Womanly Indian woman" (in Eastman's words) in combat, tinged with humor and framed in a larger historical context by the first sentences: "The old man, Smoky Day, was for many years the best-known storyteller and historian of his tribe. He it was who told me the story of the War Maiden." This contextualization gives the story a resonance beyond its immediate occurrence and suggests by implication the much larger cultural pattern behind its creation.

Eastman's work stimulated the production of other autobiographical and historical writers, notably in the Sioux nation Luther Standing Bear (Ota K'te), who wrote a popular autobiography, political and philosophical tracts, and a collection *Stories of the Sioux* (1934) which were more formulaic than imaginative, of interest primarily as data concerning the efforts of the Carlisle Indian School to transform Native Americans into replicas of the "model" American citizen.

During the first decades of the twentieth century, the transition from the oral tradition of Native American literary expression toward the formal setting of printed matter took place sporadically, gaining momentum from 1900 to 1940, in Allen's estimation, and then dwindling for three decades due to what Allen calls "the bland and binding white cocoon of the 1950's, with its Red Scare, Cold War, and suburban fixations." One of the strongest limiting factors in the first half of the century was the estrangement of Native Americans from mainstream American society and a concomitant disinclination to share anything personal with the white world. Just as Frank

Linderman encouraged Pretty-shield to tell him (in sign language) about her culture, another anthropologist, Lucullus McWhorter, hired an Ocanogan woman, Humishuma (Mourning Dove), better known by her English name, Cristal Galler, to help him collect folktales. Her book *Coyote Stories* (1933) toned down some of the more provocative elements of the originals, as in "Coyote Juggles His Eyes," in which Bluebird and Bluejay, who are carrying the perennial trickster-diety/demon, keep dropping him. As Humishuma retold the story, Coyote kept shifting around so that he was difficult to hold. In the original, he was also sexually assaulting his bearers. This reduction may have been due to shyness before the eyes of a stranger but might also be a part of a protective preservation, an inclination to withhold the secrets of the sacred, or an assumption that an outsider from another cultural basis could not really understand all the implications of the story. The story deals with one of the most important figures in Native American mythology, Coyote the Trickster, who holds a degree of fascination that goes beyond the ceremonial practices of First Nation people and is also an echo of some of the motifs found in Euro-American children's literature, in which animals exhibit a satirical humor that comments on adult society.

From Speech to the Page

E. Pauline Johnson's ability to transfer told-to-people (from the oral tradition) stories into told-to-the-page stories was an anomaly dependent on her unique background in two cultures. Humishuma's collaboration with McWhorter was more typical. In spite of leaving school after the third or fourth grade, she was determined to write and to publish her work. Her novel *Cogewea, the Halfblood* was completed in 1916 but not published until 1927. It drew on the Chipmunk cycle of tales ("Cogewea" means "chipmunk"), linking separate short stories into a proto-novel, and required her to pay several hundred dollars to defray publication costs. Very few people had this kind of persistence. Estelle Armstrong, who also attended the Carlisle Indian School, wrote about young men from her Arizona tribal group in her short story "The Return" (1925), whose identity was severely compromised by their "education." During the second and third decades of the twentieth century, the predominant representations of Native American literature were novelistic in form, the work of men like John Oskison, one-eighth Cherokee and a Stanford University graduate (1898), whose story "Only the Master Shall Praise" won *Century* magazine's college prize award and whose novels *Brothers Three* (1935) and *Tecumseh and His Times* (1938) were indications of a growing interest in Native American heritage by the author and the public. The most famous writer of this era was D'Arcy McNickle (Anglo/Salish) whose novel *The Surrounded* (1936) dealt with the conflict between the two cultures of his protagonist, whose background was a mix of Hispanic and Salish similar to McNickle's. Nearly all of the First Nations writing during the 1930's and 1940's followed the now-acceptable path of ethnographic studies and took the form of historical chronicles or autobiographical declarations anticipating the modern memoir. They used the stories of the oral tradition to enliven their work, while keeping the stories surrounded by material that tended to obscure or diminish their literary power.

On isolated occasions, barely noticed when printed, overcoming all the obstacles to their publication, the stories themselves appeared. Zitkala-Sa (Yankton Sioux), also known as Gertrude Bonnin, published her versions of Sioux legends as *American Indian Stories* (1921). Her "A Warrior's Daughter" is a description of a woman attractive by conventional notions of femininity who also possesses the attributes of an independent and self-defined person. The third-person narration gives the account a feeling of historic gravity while also removing it to an extent from the reader, a result perhaps of Zitkala-Sa's lifelong commitment to the struggle for Indian rights which took precedence over her literary endeavors. Delia Oshogay's (Chippewa) "Oshkikiwe's Baby" is a more typical example of the oral tradition transferred to print. The story of two sisters, at least partly supernatural in essence, with elements of the occult not unusual in this genre, was told to Maggie Lamorie and placed in print by a collector in 1942. Almost nothing is known about Oshogay, since her personhood seemed unimportant to the anthropologists who often felt that they could explain the material from their academic perspective. This inclination was discussed and criticized by Vizenor, who observed, with respect to the misinterpretation of the trickster,

> Anthropology is a material creation; a trickster is a spiritual, imaginative act. Anthropologists have things; tricksters are; . . . an anthropologist records one version; an anthropologist/linguist translates it, and these translations unfortunately become objects, material objects. . . . that's not an idea of imagination and life.

The limitations of the as-told-to mode, plus the pressures placed on Native Americans during the decades that followed the defeat of the last Indian resistors in the late nineteenth century, resulted in a paucity of published short fiction during the first half of the twentieth century, especially in comparison to the huge hoard of stories that had been in circulation among First Nation peoples for many generations.

The Second Wave: 1974-1990

Leslie Marmon Silko generously credits Momaday's *House Made of Dawn* as the book that effectively opened the gates of the publishing mansion. It would be just as accurate to cite Silko's first published works of fiction, which appeared in Rosen's anthology in 1974 as equally important, one of the reasons that Allen chooses that date for the beginning of the "Second Wave" of Native American fiction. Silko's employment of traditional material—the stories told in the Laguna Pueblo that she heard in her youth—were fashioned into forms sufficiently recognizable to and accessible in the academic community so that "Lullaby" and "Yellow Woman" were included in prize-winning collections in 1975. While Allen's division of Native American writing in the twentieth century into three waves is very useful for understanding the cultural context that so heavily influenced the progress from a marginalized, compromised, nearly invisible subsection of American literature to a vibrant, accomplished force in the literary cosmos of the North American continent, the Second Wave is a genuine period of transition that is separated from the Third Wave not by a transformative event like Momaday's novel or Silko's short fiction but by the appearance of a mind-set that had been gradually developing throughout the time period.

As Allen describes it, "the proper attitude for authentic Native protagonists" of the Second Wave "was dispossession, anger, and internal conflict brought on by the opposing demands of a polarized culture. The second wave protagonist was portrayed by Native writers as a classic victim whose reaction to victimization was 1960's civil rights-type protest, with feathers, drums, and sweats added for flavor." In a fairly devastating dismissal, she summarizes, "In short, a protagonist modeled on the constructed Native character in works created or heavily edited by Anglo-Americans." This kind of characterization—noble, doomed, tragic—and "off the reservation" (that is, homeless in every sense) might be seen as a necessary step, or bridge, between the long history of periodic appearances in print of fragments of First Nations life and the robust, multi-voiced merging of Native American writing with the American literature of the last decade of the twentieth century. Just as Toni Morrison, Charles Johnson, or Amiri Baraka are not studied only in African American literature courses, Simon Ortiz, Joy Harjo, and Sherman Alexie are not confined to anthologies of Native American writers.

The Tribe of Pressed Trees

Louise Erdrich (Chippewa) developed her novel *Love Medicine* (1984) as a cycle of interlocking short stories which can stand separately as completed literary works, "a series of stories, many of which were published independently" as her collaborator Michael Dorris (Modoc) put it. The novel was designed to be the start of a tetralogy that expanded by structural design and was based on the inclusion of enduring traditional stories, told from diverse narrative viewpoints and gathered into an almost epic arrangement that moved back and forth across chronological time. This approach is indicative of the complex, sophisticated manner of presentation that Third Wave writers have devised to make use of the wealth of material available within the cultural community of First Nations people. In *Tracks* (1988), the second book of the tetralogy, Nanapush, Erdrich's "responsible storyteller and authorial ventriloquist who subtly instructs the reader in an ethics of 'listening'" (as the critic Catherine Rainwater perceptively describes him) laments the demise of the Chippewa by describing them as "a tribe of file cabinets and triplicates, a tribe of single-space documents, directives, policy. A tribe of pressed trees." Rainwater notes that Nanapush, another trickster figure, plays two parts, on one hand embodying literally the loss of power and sovereignty of native people, on the other demonstrating the power of print to replace those diminished strengths symbolized by the decimation of forest lands. Rainwater sees this "tribe of pressed trees"—that is, "the steadily increasing tribe of 'books' such as those by Erdrich and other Native American writers that aim to revise not simply the record of the past but the shape of the future," as the source of a new cultural paradigm in which an artist recovers a nation buried in silence and stereotype. Momaday's idea that "naming confers being," Vizenor's insistence that "story shapes reality," and Linda Hogan's theory that the phenomenal world is a story constantly under revision from other stories are at the center of the Third Wave position but have their origins in Second Wave writing. The Second Wave concentrated on the restoration of ceremonial practices; Third Wave writers carried these practices beyond "the Res," along the "Powwow highway," and into the world from which they had been exiled and estranged.

THE THIRD WAVE: AFTER 1990

The tripartite division of Native American writing is very useful in terms of clarifying the process of change that permitted an ancient manner of communication to enter and enliven what Marshall McLuhan called "The Gutenberg Galaxy." The landmark moment when Momaday's novel was published is a point in history that truly separates before and after, cited and acknowledged by writer after writer. Linda Hogan (Chickasaw), when asked about influences replied, "Momaday's *House Made of Dawn*—I thought it was for me the most important thing I had read." James Welch, an acclaimed novelist, says that after Momaday's book won the Pulitzer Prize "suddenly people started to notice Indian literature, that the way kind of opened for Indians; younger people too, younger people who didn't think that they had much of a chance as a writer, suddenly realized, well, an Indian can write." Ortiz observes, "There was really no Native American literature before the 1960's, which is true with some qualifications," and after a few isolated examples of pre-1960's (McNickle, Eastman) literature, explains, "Literature has always been there; it just hasn't been written with its more contemporary qualities and motives, nor has it been published." These qualities and motives are the distinguishing characteristics of the most interesting and accomplished Native American imaginative fiction and poetry of the last three decades of the twentieth century and are particularly evident in the short fiction of this era.

The profusion of capable, captivating Native American writers who have worked with short fiction during this time and the diversity of their styles and subjects makes it difficult, even deceptive, to generalize, suggesting that the range of writing can be reduced to formulas or conveyed by a generic outline. Still, some thematic patterns and some structural devices or techniques might be mentioned as a means of approaching the work of these authors. Allen identifies a number of these "contemporary qualities" in her survey, among them

> (1) A protagonist recognizes, accepts and then *becomes* a tradition—directed role within the *true*—that is, the ritual—life of their tribe. This is crucial in the alteration of portrayal from "genocided victim-cum-romantic martyr" to a person capable of directing their own destiny.
>
> (2) Traditional motifs—the trickster (i.e., Coyote, et al.); the warrior; the storyteller—are merged with images and devices from modern life.
>
> (3) Quests for identity (i.e., the totemic animal) include traditional strategies juxtaposed with contemporary American social concerns.

Clifford Trafzer (Anglo/Wyandot), in an introduction to *Earth Song, Sky Spirit* (1993), an anthology of short stories he collected "of the Contemporary Native American Experience," differentiates between conventional definitions of the short story and some variants in structural design that recur in the work of First Nation writers:

> Rather than focusing on one theme or character in a brief time frame, or using one geographical area, they often use multiple themes and characters with few boundaries of time or place. Their stories do not always follow a linear and clear path, and frequently the past and present, real and mythic, and conscious and unconscious are not distinguishable. Multidimensional characters are common, and involved stories usually lack absolute conclusions. Native American writers may also play tricks with language, deliberately misusing grammar, syntax and spelling.

One of the more striking aspects of Trafzer's description is how much it resembles descriptions of postmodern American fiction at the turn of the twenty-first century, indicating a diminishing degree of separation between what has been previously regarded as a ghetto subgenre and the fully national literature of which it was now becoming a crucial component. As Simon J. Ortiz said about his collection of short fiction *Fightin'* (1983), "My latest book . . . is a combination. There's nothing about being Indian in there. Just stories of people. Why shouldn't I write about non-Indians. I don't have to dress anybody in feathers." While the subjects and settings in the work of Native American writers are often drawn on a particular cultural community and its heritage, this is not a matter of confinement but enrichment.

Life on and off the Reservation

In his novel *Reservation Blues* (1996), Sherman Alexie (Spokane-Coeur d'Alene) describes his protagonist, Thomas Builds-the-Fire, as "the misfit storyteller of the Spokane Tribe" who had "caught some disease in the womb which forced him to tell stories. The weight of those stories bowed his legs and bent his spine a bit." His talent, like many gifts from higher powers, is a blessing and a burden; an obligation, a responsibility, a mystical urge, and a source of exaltation. The power of his stories is inescapable but not entirely welcome:

> Thomas Builds-the-Fire's stories climbed into your clothes like sand, and gave you itches that could not be scratched. If you repeated even a sentence from one of those stories, your throat was never the same again. The stories hung in your clothes and hair like smoke, and no amount of laundry soap or shampoo washed them out. Victor and Junior often tried to beat those stories out of Thomas, tied him down and taped his mouth shut. They pretended to be friendly and tried to sweet-talk Thomas into temporary silences, made promises of beautiful Indian women and cases of Diet Pepsi. But none of that stopped Thomas, who talked and talked.

The necessity underlying Thomas's compulsion—which Alexie characteristically expresses with a mixture of humor and seriousness—is a kind of fusion of the personal and the cultural. "Thomas looked around the little country he was trying to save, this reservation hidden away in a corner of the world." Preserving and proclaiming an often hidden heritage has been a core concern of American Indian artists, vital to the survival of First Nation people under assault since the arrival of Europeans on the North American continent. The shift of its written record from ethnographic transcription to imaginative expression in the last quarter of the twentieth century is manifest in the stories published by Thomas Builds-the-Fire's actual, virtual, and veritable peers.

The New Wave

One of the most striking stories in Erdrich's *Love Medicine* is the "chapter" called "Saint Marie" which plunges into the flow of narrative consciousness of a young Indian woman who has been placed in a convent school. Following the direction set by one of the teachers, Sister Leopolda (formerly Pauline), a half-white and mixed-blood Indian woman who is referred to earlier in the book as "an unknown mixture of ingredients," Marie Kashpaw ricochets between the lure of satisfying the demands of the Catholic disciples who run the school and her instinctive responses to the call of an Indian heritage which has been suppressed but not extinguished. In spite of all the tangible rewards that the Western religion and its acolytes seem to offer, Marie is prevented from making a full commitment to a conversion by the recurrent messages she senses from a source that Leopolda calls "the Dark one" but which is actually a mystical Indian spirit surfacing to assist Marie in maintaining an authentic identity. The story is a series of confrontations and clashes, projected through vivid imagery of a strongly physical nature that illustrates the connection between the body and the soul/spirit essence that is a precept of both the Anglo and Native American religious systems. The seemingly dormant power of the Old Ways and their manifestation in the modern world are aspects of Erdrich's exploration of a cultural heritage under siege, while the odd admixture of Indian and Western Catholic ideas acts as a forecast of future accommodations.

An oppositional attraction between realms of "reality"—Western theology and Indian Spirit Medicine in Erdrich's story—has been designated by Native American scholars as "liminality," which Allen defines as "a state of being on the threshold" and which she contends is the most essential condition of the ritual tradition. The potential for psychic disorder, as well as illuminating vision, is one of the exciting and alluring aspects of this experience. The trickster—exemplified by Coyote—is permanently located in this sphere and in Vizenor's story "The Baron of Patronia" the protagonist Luster Browne uses the wiles and wild spirit of an untamed and unconfined, independent Indian to resist the mendacity, spite, and pettiness of government bureaucrats. In an incident common to First Nations history, Browne, "son of a pagan mother and a mixed father," is given an allotment deemed worthless after he demonstrates that "he would never wait on a mission porch to have his mind mended." However, he thrives on "the wild outback of the reservation," comfortable in the landscape that Vizenor evokes with poetic fervor, at ease with the wilderness and its inhabitants. In an unusual but decorous courtship, he joins Novena Mae Ironmoccasin, a woman raised by nuns after her mother's death in childbirth, who politely rejects their invitation and joins "Lusterbow" Browne. They raise a family that Vizenor describes in a compact generational saga sketching the lives of an energetic, diverse clan who casually symbolize the various ways of Indian people across the previous 150 years. The story stretches on into time in accord with a mode that often has no specific closure and, as a portrait of a "compassionate tribal trickster," is a much more subtle employment of the classic figure than the "Coyote kitsch" that Vizenor has decried.

Vizenor has stated that one of his aims is to overturn or controvert a popular picture of Native Americans that has grown out of enforced silence and oppressive stereotypes. His use of humor is one of the more prevalent and effective practices in this regard, especially since previous portraits have been very short on comic styles. The mordant, self-aware edge of characters in Dan Crank's (Navajo) "Neon Powwow," who alternate between boozy self-pity and eloquent, ironic reflection; the dry, satiric wit of the Native men in Thomas King's (Cherokee/German/Irish) "A Seat in the Garden"; the direct, laconic take on modern warfare in Esther Belin's (Navajo) "indigenous irony"; the zaniness of Carter Revard's (Osage) "Never Quite a Hollywood Star," with its postmodern usage of metafictional tropes; the good-natured buffoonery in Gloria Bird's (Spokane) "Turtle Lake"; and the ingenious, often hilarious, very inventive stories in Alexie's landmark collection *The Lone Ranger and Tonto Fistfight in Heaven* (1994) are examples of a mode that has produced many entertaining and perceptive accounts of Indian life.

The Old Ways

The outpouring of fiction dealing with Native American life in the last decades of the twentieth century was an important corrective to the misrepresentations and insults of depictions by non-Native (and some Native) writers. This has meant a departure from the best side of earlier literature, the sensitive recreation of traditional stories from the oral tradition. However, the "talking leaves" (the title of an anthology edited by Craig Lesley) have not been superceded or silenced by "the tribe of pressed trees" and have continued to speak through an evolving interchange that confirms the ancient idea of a story "alive" to revise the record of the past and to shape the emerging "reality" of the future. Growing out of the storyteller's reactions to the responses of an audience during a performance, the mutability of the oral tradition is part of a philosophic system which maintains that participation affects the dimensions of the universe; that, as Rainwater phrases it, "humanity makes the world through the stories we tell" since "the American Indian concept of 'medicine' bears a notion of language as a powerful force of creation and destruction." Consequently, traditional themes and subjects have been regathered in new stories about old ways.

Allen's "Deer Woman" uses vernacular slang to introduce two men at a dance who offer rides to women they meet there. Captivated but unsettled by the strange beauty of the women (" . . . he saw the feet of both women as deer hooves. Man, he thought, I gotta lay off the weed."), the men are transported to a magical landscape where a stream becomes a grass path, a rock opens like a cabin door, and, in a strange place, the men are asked to take part in a baseball game controlled by the girl's uncle, who compliments them as worthy "snags"—the term they use to refer to women they hoped to meet. The next morning, one of the men finds himself on a familiar road and eventually settles in San Francisco. The other is mentioned in accounts of people who have seen him and is rumored to have died because he told forbidden secrets of their journey. The artful mix of mythic elements and contemporary details gives the story a resonance that reaffirms the validity of venerable phenomena and underscores Vizenor's contention that "ambivalence is a precise condition of Native American literature."

One of the most abiding subjects of Native American literature is the relationship of the people to the land, an area of perpetual fascination renewed by the increasing interest in environmental concerns in the latter decades of the twentieth century. Maurice Kenny (Mohawk), in his story "What's in a Song" follows a man into the woods where he hopes to hear the music of woodland creatures and to integrate it in his own compositions. A subject that might seem sentimental or juvenile is handled with seriousness and tonal control that gives it a dignity without making it solemn. The kind of contact with non-human living creatures that has been shunned by European civilizations is a crucial and plausible element in Kenny's story, as it is in numerous other works of fiction. The totemic emblem—especially with respect to an animal that corresponds to a person's inner nature—is registered by a name gained through the vision of an initiation ceremony, as in the characters Joe Bluesky in "Neon Powwow"or Tom Losteagle in Jason Edward's [Blackfeet] "Dreamland," or Vizenor's Saint Louis Bearheart, among many others. The protean Coyote, appearing in stories from almost every tribal group, is one of the most complex and variable animal spirits, available for many different narrative situations. Allen says that "no cycle of transformation stories can be complete without the Trickster," and Beth Brant (Bay Quinte Mohawk), in "Coyote Learns a New Trick," conceives of this transformation as one of gender—beginning as female, disguised as male—and then trying to trick Turtle, Hawk, and finally Fox. The deception misfires but leads to a satisfying conclusion, illustrating the capacity for change that is valued in First Nation societies. The sexual candor of the story is a part of the tradition that was often subdued or excised by cautious ethnographers acting on the values of their own culture.

Silko's Archetypal Storyteller

Just as Momaday's *House Made of Dawn* has been identified as the trailmaking act that opened the way for Native American literature to move into the realm of print, Silko's *Storyteller* (1981) could be regarded as the defining document which set the direction for the short fiction of the next decades. A multi-genre mix of prose and poetry, autobiographical recollection and historical evaluation, it set stories drawn from the oral tradition amid the cultural conditions that led to their creation and continued existence. Touching on many of the crucial concerns of First Nations people—including legends and myths of creation; power and medicine; communal stories of love, hunts, and heroic actions; poetic evocations of landscape and the inhabitants of the wilderness—stories like "Yellow Woman," "Lullaby," and the title piece carried the heritage and history of Native Americans through the arrival of European settlers and on to the end of the twentieth century. Silko's work stands as a testament to the power of the living tradition which she revitalizes and extends. As the opening lines of her poem "The Storyteller's Escape" have it,

The storyteller keeps the stories
all the escape stories
she says "With these stories of ours
we can escape almost anything
with these stories we will survive."

Leon Lewis

Bibliography

Alexie, Sherman. *The Lone Ranger and Tonto Fistfight in Heaven*. New York: Atlantic Monthly Press, 1993. An imaginative, original collection of linked short stories that reflect a contemporary sensibility in Native American life.

Allen, Paula Gunn, ed. *Song of the Turtle: American Indian Literature, 1974-1994*. New York: Ballantine Books, 1996. The complementary volume to *Voice of The Turtle*, another astute collection of short fiction, with an especially informative essay on the three "waves" of Native American writing, and additional material on the authors and other useful volumes on the subject.

_______, ed. *Spider Woman's Granddaughters: Traditional Tales and Contemporary Writing by Native American Women*. Boston: Beacon Press, 1989. A representative collection of the written work and oral expression of Native American women, with an illuminating introductory essay that covers the issues and circumstances of First Nations writing.

_______, ed. *Voice of the Turtle: American Indian Literature, 1900-1970*. New York: Ballantine Books, 1994. A very well-chosen collection of short stories and excerpts from longer works that demonstrate the range of Native American writing in the United States prior to the proliferation of published work in the 1970's. Gunn's introductory essay provides an historical overview of the material.

Coltelli, Laura. *Winged Words: American Indian Writers Speak*. Lincoln: University of Nebraska Press, 1990. Conversations with ten Native American writers. Intelligent, informative and accessible.

De Ramirez, Susan Berry Brill. *Contemporary American Indian Literatures and the Oral Tradition*. Tucson: University of Arizona Press, 1999. A "converse approach" for reading and understanding Native American literature, covering Silko, Alexis, and Momaday, among others.

Donovan, Kathleen. *Feminist Readings of Native American Fiction*. Tucson: University of Arizona Press, 1998. Probing considerations of the work of Momaday, Allen, Harjo and Mourning Dove, in conjunction with other writers and theorists whose work shares themes and ideas with theirs.

Lesley, Craig, ed. *Talking Leaves: Contemporary Native American Short Stories*. New York: Dell, 1991. Includes some of the same authors as the Allen anthologies, but with different selections and many additional writers.

Ortiz, Simon J. *Men on the Moon: Collected Short Stories*. Tucson: University of Arizona Press, 1999. The collected short stories of a poet whose craftsmanship and humanity is evident in the range of his writing.

Rainwater, Catherine. *Dreams of Fiery Stars: The Transformations of Native American Fiction*. Philadelphia: University of Pennsylvania Press, 1999. A very perceptive consideration of Native American fiction based on postmodern literary theory. Primarily for the serious scholar, but consistently interesting and provocative.

Silko, Leslie Marmon. *Storyteller.* New York: Grove Press, 1981. The book which compelled recognition of Native American short fiction as an important component of American literary experience.

Trafzer, Clifford, ed. *Blue Dawn, Red Earth: New Native American Storytellers*. New York: Anchor Books, 1996. An excellent sampling of the writing of both established and new Native American artists in the last decade of the twentieth century, with an evocative introduction that catches the spirit of the stories.

_______, ed. *Earth Song, Sky Spirit: Short Stories of the Native American Experience*. New York: Anchor Books, 1993. An informative introductory essay about the development of Native American literature, with incisive commentary on the selections, precedes stories that cover the range of Native American experience.

Vizenor, Gerald. *Fugitive Poses: Native American Indian Scenes of Absence and Presence*. Lincoln: University of Nebraska Press, 1998. Challenging and consistently interesting essays on many aspects of Native American literature. Intellectually stimulating, culturally comprehensive, stylishly engaging.

Weaver, Jace. *That the People Might Live: Native American Literatures and Native American Community*. New York: Oxford University Press, 1997. An historical survey and critical commentary, covering Silko, Vizenor, and other well-known authors, plus others recently receiving critical attention.

SOUTH ASIAN SHORT FICTION

Since what was once known simply as "India" now consists of a number of political entities, such as India, Pakistan, Bangladesh, Sri Lanka, Nepal, and Bhutan, the larger area is generally referred to either as "South Asia" or as "the Indian subcontinent." The writers who are classified as South Asian, however, may not have been born on the subcontinent or may have moved elsewhere. In a few cases, their connection to the continent is not by blood but through marriage to a South Asian.

Some very important South Asian writers spent their lives in the same area where they were born, Shashi Deshpande, Mrnala Pande, and R. K. Narayan, for example. However, when Partition and the violence that followed sent millions fleeing to safety, there were a number of writers among the refugees. For instance, Qurratulain Hyder left her longtime home in Lucknow, India, for Muslim Pakistan, where she lived for some years, eventually returning to India in order to escape Pakistan's increasing repression of women. Hyder became one of Bombay's most influential journalists, an authority on Urdu literature, and a prize-winning author, who in 1967 was awarded the prestigious Sahitya Akademi Award for her short-story collection in Urdu, *Patjhar ki Awaz*.

Expatriate South Asians

Other writers left the subcontinent, some for political reasons or for professional advancement, others because, as Salman Rushdie notes in his introduction to *Mirrorwork: Fifty Years of Indian Writing, 1947-1997* (1997), many of them are wanderers by nature. Among those who took up residence in the United States were Anjana Appachana, Chitra Banerjee Divakaruni, Bharati Mukherjee, and Padma Perera. Rohinton Mistry moved to Canada, while Attia Hosain and Salman Rushdie settled in England. Some had more than one home. Anita Desai divided her time between England and the United States; Vikram Chandra lived both in Washington, D.C., and his native Bombay; and after 1975 Ruth Prawer Jhabvala and her husband were commuting between New York and New Delhi.

As Rushdie points out, if one applied a residence test to writers, Ernest Hemingway and Henry James might not be considered American; Graham Greene, English; or James Joyce, Irish. The writers discussed in this essay are classified as South Asians because they all draw upon their experience of the Indian subcontinent for the characters, settings, and themes of their short fiction.

Shashi Tharoor and Jhumpa Lahiri

Given the broad definition above, a writer does not necessarily have to be a native of the subcontinent to be classified as a South Asian writer. For example, Shashi Tharoor was born in London, though he grew up in Bombay and Calcutta. Although his work for the United Nations has taken him all over the world, Tharoor's fiction reflects the experiences of his formative years.

Jhumpa Lahiri was also born in London, but she grew up in Rhode Island, seeing India only when her parents took her on visits to see her extended family. Although her parents always referred to India as "home," she has said that she felt like an outsider there fully as much as she did in the American small town where she lived. Lahiri's awareness of her cultural history, her perspective on the immigrant experience, and her preoccupation with alienation all justify her inclusion in this essay.

Robbie Clipper Sethi and Ruth Prawer Jhabvala

Robbie Clipper Sethi and Ruth Prawer Jhabvala are not South Asian by blood, but both are considered South Asian writers. Robbie Clipper Sethi is an American, reared in New Jersey, Indiana, and California, who met and married a Punjabi Sikh and at the time she published her first book was teaching in New Jersey. In *The Bride Wore Red: Tales of a Cross-Cultural Family* (1996), Sethi described three marriages, all between American women and South Asian men. However, one of the strengths of Sethi's book is her empathy with all her characters, not only the men, who by choosing their own wives defy their culture, but also their parents, who feel the loss of their ties to cultural tradition as well as their future as a family.

Ruth Prawer Jhabvala, too, is South Asian neither by birth nor by blood, but she is included in every list of major Indian fiction writers. Born in Germany to Jewish-Polish parents, then reared and educated in England, Jhabvala moved to India only after her marriage to an Indian architect in 1951. In "Introduction: Myself in India," which prefaces her volume *Out of India* (1986), Jhabvala insists that every year she is becoming less Indian. Nevertheless, India has so strong a claim on her that periodically she must leave if she is not to be swallowed up by it. Like Sethi, Jhabvala understands cross-cultural conflicts; like Lahiri, she understands alienation. However, while she is capable of empathy, Jhabvala distances herself from her subject more than either of them do and probably more than any other Indian writer. Her voice is one of the most distinctive in South Asian fiction.

One Subcontinent, Many Languages

Though Partition drove vast numbers of people to areas dominated by those of their faith, it did little to alter one of the basic characteristics of the subcontinent: its cultural and linguistic diversity. As A. K. Ramanujan points out in his introduction to *Folktales from India: A Selection of Oral Tales from Twenty-two Languages* (1991), the people of India alone speak one hundred different languages and sixteen hundred distinct dialects. In addition to Sanskrit, the language of ancient written texts, and English, which is read and spoken throughout the entire subcontinent, India has fifteen "major" vernacular languages, each of which is used by several million Indians. One of the most difficult decisions each South Asian writer must make is whether to write in one of the local languages or in English, which is familiar throughout the subcontinent.

The Argument for Writing in English

When India became independent from Great Britain, many nationalists felt that English was too tainted by colonialism to be appropriate for discourse, let alone for literary purposes. However, Salman Rushdie argues that, like Urdu, which came to India with earlier conquerors, the English used in the subcontinent should now be considered just another South Asian language.

Authors who write in English, Rushdie insists, are no less "Indian" in voice and perspective than those who utilize one of the native languages. Furthermore, if they are to reach a broad audience, works written in the vernacular must be translated into English, often suffering in the process. Rushdie contends that since independence the best works the subcontinent has produced have been written in English.

The Argument for the Vernacular

Aditya Behl and David Nicholls, editors of *The Penguin New Writing in India* (1994), disagree with Rushdie's assessment. They point out that, even if English-language authors produce some international bestsellers, their works are not necessarily better than those written in native languages. Behl and Nicholls offer the selections in their anthology as proof of the high quality of vernacular works and as evidence that any distrust of South Asian translators is unfounded. They are also convinced that, in an area where there are so many different cultures, only through vernacular literature can each of them be appreciated, understood, and perhaps even preserved.

A writer's decision about language is much more than a choice between nationalism, on one hand, or the hope of an international blockbuster, on the other. One of India's most respected playwrights and fiction writers, Mrinal Pande, was for many years a college English teacher, but she also served as editor of Hindi periodicals. She began writing in Hindi in order to reach more people and specifically more women. However, Pande changed to English for her short-story sequence, *Daughter's Daughter* (1993), so that she could distance herself from her autobiographical subject matter and even access lost memories from her past.

South Asian Writers and Genre

Though the short-fiction writers of the Indian subcontinent may be faced with more complex language issues than those in other parts of the world, they have the same problems when it comes to getting their works published. South Asian writers are only too aware of the facts. Most short stories are still published in periodicals; a few make it into anthologies, however, most publishers are hesitant to take a chance on a book-length collection of short fiction until an author has become established as a novelist.

Thus Ruth Prawer Jhabvala, Bharati Mukherjee, Salman Rushdie, and Vikram Chandra all published one or more successful novels before bringing out collections of short stories. Similarly, it was not until after the success of two novels, *The Great Indian Novel* (1989) and *Show Business* (1991), that Shashi Tharoor's early short fiction was accepted for publication. Although Tharoor warns readers that these stories were written when he was a relatively inexperienced writer and were designed for mass-circulation Indian magazines, reviewers found much to admire in *The Five-Dollar Smile: Fourteen Early Stories and a Farce in Two Acts* (1990; reissued in 1993 as *The Five-Dollar Smile and Other Stories*).

Sometimes, if a writer's long fiction captures the public's interest, critics will seek out earlier collections of short fiction by that writer. When Attia Hosain's novel *Sunlight on a Broken Column* (1961) was reissued in 1988, it almost immediately became the subject of scholarly studies. However, at least one reviewer pointed out the virtues of another volume by Hosain, which was reissued at the same time. *Phoenix Fled* (1953) was a collection of stories which originally appeared in Indian newspapers, and a good case can be made for its being superior to *Sunlight on a Broken Column*. Nevertheless, the scholarly community continued to focus almost exclusively on Hosain's novel, neglecting her fine short fiction.

Fiction Genres and the American Market

Because the American publishing industry found long fiction to be more marketable than short fiction, for a long time book-length collections by many of South Asia's finest short-story writers were unavailable in most American bookstores or even in many libraries. Krishna Baldev Vaid and the noted filmmaker Satyajit Ray, for example, were admired in India for their collections of beautifully crafted short fiction, but in the United States, one would have to look for their short stories either in anthologies or in an occasional issue of the *Chicago Review*.

This bias in favor of the novel meant that anyone who wrote long fiction as well as short was almost certain to be introduced to American readers as a novelist. The award-winning author Shashi Deshpande, for example, had published five collections of short stories in India, as well as several novels, before any of her fiction became available in the United States. Significantly, the work that was selected for her American debut was a novel, *A Matter of Time* (1999). As the twenty-first century began, American readers still had to depend on anthologies for examples of her short fiction.

Unlike Deshpande, many writers are comfortable only in one genre. For example, Anita Desai chose the novel form not because it was easier to market but because she did not really like writing short stories. Even though critics found much to admire in her collection *Games at Twilight and Other Stories* (1978), thereafter Desai published no more volumes of short fiction but turned her attention exclusively to the novel. She explained her reasons in an interview in *Literary India* (1995): Shorter forms, she said, such as poems and short stories, made her feel pressured, while the novel gave her ample time to develop her ideas and enough scope to explore all their complexities.

New Hope for Short Fiction

Late in the twentieth century, however, there seemed to be increased interest in short fiction. Critics were looking more closely at the genre. For example, Bharati Mukherjee had long been admired both for her novels and for her nonfiction publications, but it was her collection *The Middleman and Other Stories* (1988) that brought her the 1988 National Book Critics Circle Award for best fiction. Anjana Appachana, too, was gaining an international reputation on the basis of her short fiction. After winning the O. Henry Award in 1989 for a short story entitled "Her Mother," Appachana won high praise from the critics for her first book, *Incantations and Other Stories* (1991).

Now it was not just the novels of a few famous South Asian writers that were featured in bookstores; their short-story collections were also popular, and there was a marked proliferation of books by lesser-known writers. By the spring of 2000, one would have no difficulty buying paperback editions of Mukherjee's *The Middleman and Other Stories;* Jhabvala's *Out of India* and her *East into Upper East: Plain Tales from New York and New Delhi* (1998); Salman Rushdie's *East, West: Stories* (1994); Vikram Chandra's *Love and Longing in Bombay* (1997); and a number of R. K. Narayan's volumes, including *The Grandmother's Tale and Selected Stories* (1994).

Paperback Originals and a Pulitzer Prize

During the 1990's, some members of the publishing industry noticed that sales of short-story collections were increasing. They could only hypothesize about the cause. Perhaps the new young writers in the academic workshops were writing more short stories or more polished stories; perhaps they were submitting them in book form because there were fewer magazines in which their works could be placed. In any case, the publisher Houghton Mifflin decided to try an experiment. They would issue short-story collections by new or relatively unknown writers as paperback originals, reasoning that their customers would be more willing to take a chance on less expensive books. One of the collections selected by Houghton Mifflin for this experiment was Jhumpa Lahiri's *Interpreter of Maladies*. The volume appeared in 1999 as a Mariner Original; in 2000, it won the Pulitzer Prize for fiction.

As *Interpreter of Maladies* went into a second printing, Lahiri recalled the comment of an agent who had rejected it, suggesting that she come back when she had a novel, and a warning from the agent who did accept the book to the effect that short fiction did not sell well. According to conventional wisdom, both agents were right. Since *Interpreter of Maladies* was Lahiri's first book, she was not assured the audience that an earlier novel might have provided. Its success was clearly due to her very real talent. However, those who enjoy reading and writing short fiction hoped that it might also signal the arrival of a long-overdue renascence for short fiction.

The Storyteller and the Story

The people of the Indian subcontinent have one quality in common, a delight in storytelling. In *Gods, Demons, and Others* (1964), R. K. Narayan describes how a storyteller provided his village not only with entertainment but also with moral and religious instruction. As A. K. Ramanujan points out, folktales still permeate South Asian culture. They are familiar in cities as well as in villages, among those of every faith and every caste or class. Undoubtedly the subcontinent's receptivity to short fiction owes much to this ancient tradition.

By habitually describing himself as a storyteller, R. K. Narayan recognizes his indebtedness to the oral tradition. In Malgudi, the small fictional community where his works are set, Narayan shows human beings at their best and at their worst and dramatizes the cosmic conflict between good and evil.

The community where Rohinton Mistry set his *Tales from Firozsha Baag* (1987; published in the United States as *Swimming Lessons and Other Stories from Firozsha Baag*, 1989) is a Parsi housing complex in Bombay, but, like any village, it has a resident storyteller, Nariman Hansotia, who interprets events for his community and sometimes serves as its conscience. Subramaniam, the civil servant and teller of tales in Vikram Chandra's *Love and Longing in Bombay*, fulfills a similar function.

Traditions and Themes

A. K. Ramanujan classifies the folktales that pervade South Asian society by subject matter. Some feature strong men, others, strong women. Many deal with family relationships. There are stories of the supernatural and stories about animals, grim stories and humorous stories, and even stories about storytelling. Ramanujan's list could well be used as the basis of a study of subjects and themes in South Asian short fiction. For example, in *Love and Longing in Bombay* one finds family conflicts and conflicts between families, strong men and weak men, women who know how to play power games, violence and degradation, satire and humor, and even a ghost.

The old folktales in which human beings show themselves as animals or vice versa are obvious metaphors for issues of identity. In Ismat Chughtai's "Sacred Duty," from *The Quilt and Other Stories* (1994), a young couple attempt to placate their parents by being married in both Muslim and Hindu ceremonies, but when it becomes evident that their families will never let them be themselves, the newlyweds disappear. Naturally, the parents are devastated.

Throughout her works, this courageous writer called for an end to all forms of tyranny, including the patriarchal system, which she believed enslaved women and deprived them of their identities. Among the other South Asian female writers who focus on women's issues are Attia Hosain, Shashi Deshpande, Bharati Mukherjee, and Chitra Banerjee Divakaruni. In *Arranged Marriage* (1995), Divakaruni dramatizes the plight of women immigrants, bound to husbands they barely know and too fearful of their displeasure to venture into the new world outside the door. However, even if these women break free of their traditional prisons, they may not find happiness. As Mukherjee shows in works such as *The Middleman and Other Stories*, it is not easy for anyone to adapt to a strange land and an alien culture.

Given the multicultural nature of the subcontinent itself and the fact that so many of its people emigrate to other areas of the world, it is hardly surprising that the conflict of cultures continues to be a major theme in South Asian short fiction, as is evident in the titles of two volumes by major writers which appeared in the 1990's, *East into Upper East: Plain Tales from New York and New Delhi*, by Jhabvala, and *East, West: Stories*, by Salman Rushdie. In both books, there is one section for stories set in the East and another for those set in the West, though Rushdie does have a third group called "East, West." Nevertheless, the two worlds are not as separate as the divisions suggest, nor are the characters as different. While no good writer will ignore the influence of culture on one's life, in the end the best authors manage to transcend the particular. Tradition and change, rebellion and dislocation, conflicts within families and conflicts between cultures, and the yearning for spiritual certainty in an ever-changing world—these themes pervade South Asian short fiction just as they pervaded the storyteller's myths, because they affect not just one people or one part of the world but all of humanity.

Bibliography

Behl, Aditya, and David Nicholls, eds. *The Penguin New Writing in India*. London: Penguin, 1995. Originally published as a special issue of the *Chicago Review*, this useful anthology is made up primarily of works translated from a dozen different languages. Many of the writers will be new to English-speaking readers.

Gupta, R. K. "Trends in Modern Indian Fiction." *World Literature Today* 68 (Spring, 1994): 299-307. The author identifies six major themes in contemporary Indian fiction. Although he sometimes finds the writers' thinking simplistic, Gupta praises their technical skill and their "boundless creative energy."

Hogan, Patrick Colm, and Lalita Pandit, eds. *Literary India: Comparative Studies in Aesthetics, Colonialism, and Culture*.

Holmstrom, Lakshmi, editor. *The Inner Courtyard: Stories by Indian Women*. London: Virago, 1992. A wide-ranging collection of eighteen previously published works, each preceded by a brief introduction. Holmstrom's prefatory essay, "Indian Fiction in English," is also helpful, as is the glossary.

Kali for Women, eds. *Truth Tales: Contemporary Stories by Women Writers of India*. New York: Feminist Press, 1990.

Contains seven stories, each originally written in a different language. In her introduction, Meena Alexander considers issues of femininity and female power.

Modern Fiction Studies 39 (Spring, 1993). This issue, devoted to "Fiction on the Indian Subcontinent," contains essays on various subjects, including gender issues. There are also reviews, short fiction, and a photography-essay. Guest editor Aparajita Sagar's introduction is insightful.

Narayan, R. K. *Gods, Demons, and Others*. New York: Viking, 1964. Narayan's versions of major traditional myths. His introduction explains the importance of the storyteller in community life.

The New Yorker 73 (June 23, 30, 1997). This "special fiction issue" includes essays on a wide range of subjects, a profile of R. K. Narayan, and short fiction by Salman Rushdie, Kiran Desai, Vikram Chandra, and Ruth Prawer Jhabvala.

Ramanujan, A. K., ed. *Folktales from India: A Selection of Oral Tales from Twenty-two Languages.* New York: Pantheon, 1991. In a lengthy introduction, the editor maps the subcontinent linguistically and comments on the cultural significance of the folk tradition. Provides an essential context for the study of Indian fiction.

Rushdie, Salman, and Elizabeth West, eds. *Mirrorwork: Fifty Years of Indian Writing, 1947-1997.* New York: Henry Holt, 1997. Contains a number of short stories with biographical notes on the writers. Rushdie's introduction is excellent.

State University of New York. Albany: State University of New York Press, 1995. Essays by various scholars compare works from different literary traditions, considering such topics as caste and race, home and exile, political and social change, and language. Also contains an important interview with Anita Desai. Includes an index.

Rosemary M. Canfield Reisman

Research Tools

MAJOR AWARDS

These listings include only authors covered in this set.

The National Book Awards

Awarded annually since 1950 to books by U.S. citizens "that have contributed most significantly to human awareness, to the vitality of our national culture and to the spirit of excellence."

1950: Nelson Algren—*The Man with the Golden Arm*
1951: William Faulkner—*The Collected Stories of William Faulkner*
1953: Ralph Ellison—*Invisible Man*
1954: Saul Bellow—*The Adventures of Augie March*
1955: William Faulkner—*A Fable*
1956: John O'Hara—*Ten North Frederick*
1957: Wright Morris—*The Field of Vision*
1958: John Cheever—*The Wapshot Chronicle*
1959: Bernard Malamud—*The Magic Barrel*
1960: Philip Roth—*Goodbye, Columbus*
1963: J. F. Powers—*Morte D'Urban*
1964: John Updike—*The Centaur*
1965: Saul Bellow—*Herzog*
1966: Katherine Anne Porter—*The Collected Stories of Katherine Anne Porter*
1967: Bernard Malamud—*The Fixer*
1970: Joyce Carol Oates—*Them*
1971: Saul Bellow—*Mr. Sammler's Planet*
1972: Flannery O'Connor—*Flannery O'Connor: The Complete Stories*
1973: John Barth—*Chimera*
1974: Isaac Bashevis Singer—*A Crown of Feathers and Other Stories* and Thomas Pynchon—*Gravity's Rainbow*
1975: Robert Stone—*Dog Soldiers* and Thomas Williams— *The Hair of Harold Roux*
1977: Wallace Stegner—*The Spectator Bird*
1979: Tim O'Brien—*Going After Cacciato*
1981: Wright Morris—*Plains Song*
1982: John Updike—*Rabbit Is Rich*
1983: Alice Walker—*The Color Purple*
1984: Ellen Gilchrist—*Victory over Japan*
1990: Charles Johnson—*Middle Passage*
1993: E. Annie Proulx—*The Shipping News*
1995: Philip Roth—*Sabbath's Theater*
1996: Andrea Barrett—*Ship Fever and Other Stories*
1997: Charles Frazier—*Cold Mountain*
2000: Susan Sontag—*In America*

The Nobel Prize for Literature

Awarded annually since 1901, this award is generally regarded as the highest honor that can be bestowed upon an author for his or her total body of literary work.

1921: Anatole France
1923: William B. Yeats
1929: Thomas Mann
1932: John Galsworthy
1933: Ivan Bunin
1938: Pearl S. Buck
1946: Hermann Hesse
1949: William Faulkner
1951: Pär Lagerkvist
1954: Ernest Hemingway
1957: Albert Camus
1958: Boris Pasternak (declined)
1962: John Steinbeck
1964: Jean-Paul Sartre (declined)
1966: Shmuel Yosef Agnon (with Nelly Sachs)
1967: Miguel Angel Asturias
1968: Yasunari Kawabata
1969: Samuel Beckett
1970: Aleksandr Solzhenitsyn
1972: Heinrich Böll
1976: Saul Bellow
1978: Isaac Bashevis Singer
1982: Gabriel García Márquez
1988: Naguib Mahfouz
1991: Nadine Gordimer
1994: Kenzaburō Ōe

The PEN/Faulkner Award for Fiction

Awarded annually since 1981 to the most distinguished work of fiction by an American writer.

1984: John Edgar Wideman—*Sent for You Yesterday*
1985: Tobias Wolff—*The Barracks Thief*
1986: Peter Taylor—*The Old Forest*
1988: T. Coraghessan Boyle—*World's End*
1991: John Edgar Wideman—*Philadelphia Fire*
1993: E. Annie Proulx—*Postcards*
1996: Richard Ford—*Independence Day*
1997: Gina Berriault—*Women in Their Beds*

The Pulitzer Prize in Letters

Awarded annually since 1917, this award was given for novels only until 1948.

1921: Edith Wharton—*The Age of Innocence*
1923: Willa Cather—*One of Ours*
1932: Pearl S. Buck—*The Good Earth*
1940: John Steinbeck—*The Grapes of Wrath*
1942: Ellen Glasgow—*In This Our Life*
1947: Robert Penn Warren—*All the King's Men*
1949: James Gould Cozzens—*Guard of Honor*
1953: Ernest Hemingway—*The Old Man and the Sea*
1955: William Faulkner—*A Fable*
1958: James Agee—*A Death in the Family*
1963: William Faulkner—*The Reivers*
1965: Shirley Ann Grau—*The Keepers of the House*
1966: Katherine Ann Porter—*Collected Stories of Katherine Ann Porter*
1970: Jean Stafford—*Collected Stories*
1972: Wallace Stegner—*Angle of Repose*
1973: Eudora Welty—*The Optimist's Daughter*
1976: Saul Bellow—*Humboldt's Gift*
1978: James Alan McPherson—*Elbow Room*
1979: John Cheever—*The Stories of John Cheever*
1982: John Updike—*Rabbit Is Rich*
1983: Alice Walker—*The Color Purple*
1987: Peter Taylor—*A Summons to Memphis*
1989: Anne Tyler—*Breathing Lessons*
1991: John Updike—*Rabbit at Rest*
1992: Jane Smiley—*A Thousand Acres*
1993: Robert Olen Butler—*A Good Scent from a Strange Mountain*
1994: E. Annie Proulx—*The Shipping News*
1996: Richard Ford—*Independence Day*
1997: Steven Millhauser—*Martin Dressler: The Tale of an American Dreamer*
1998: Philip Roth—*American Pastoral*
2000: Jhumpa Lahiri—*Interpreter of Maladies*

The Rea Award

Awarded annually since 1986 to living American writers who have made a significant contribution to the short-story form.

1986: Cynthia Ozick
1987: Robert Coover
1988: Donald Barthelme
1989: Tobias Wolff
1990: Joyce Carol Oates
1991: Paul Bowles
1992: Eudora Welty
1993: Grace Paley
1994: Tillie Olsen
1995: Richard Ford
1996: Andre Dubus
1997: Gina Berriault
1998: John Edgar Wideman
1999: Joy Williams

THE BEST AMERICAN SHORT STORIES

Published annually since 1915, The Best American Short Stories reflects the best stories to appear in American magazines during the year. Selection for the volume is considered a high honor. Authors marked with an asterisk (*) are covered in this set.

The Best Short Stories of 1915, and the Yearbook of the American Short Story
***edited by* Edward J. O'Brien**

Burt, Maxwell Struthers—"The Water-Hole"
Byrne, Donn—"The Wake"
Comfort, Will Levington—"Chautonville"
Dwiggins, W. A.—"La Derniere Mobilisation"
Dwyer, James Francis—"The Citizen"
Gregg, Frances—"Whose Dog?"
Hecht, Ben—"Life"
Hurst, Fannie—"T. B."
Johnson, Arthur—"Mr. Eberdeen's House"
Jordan, Virgil—"Vengeance Is Mine"
Lyon, Harris Merton—"The Weaver Who Clad the Summer"
Muilenburg, Walter J.—"Heart of Youth"
Noyes, Newbold—"The End of the Path"
O'Brien, Seumas—"The Whale and the Grasshopper"
O'Reilly, Mary Boyle—"In Berlin"
Roof, Katharine Metcalf—"The Waiting Years"
Rosenblatt, Benjamin—"Zelig"
Singmaster, Elsie—"The Survivors"
Steele, Wilbur Daniel*—"The Yellow Cat"
Synon, Mary—"The Bounty-Jumper"

The Best Short Stories of 1916, and the Yearbook of the American Short Story
***edited by* Edward J. O'Brien**

Atherton, Gertrude—"The Sacrificial Altar"
Benefield, Barry—"Miss Willett"
Booth, Frederick—"Supers"
Burnet, Dana—"Fog"
Buzzell, Francis—"Ma's Pretties"
Cobb, Irvin S.—"The Great Auk"
Dreiser, Theodore*—"The Lost Phoebe"
Gordon, Armistead C.—"The Silent Infare"
Greene, Frederick Stuart—"The Cat of the Cane-Brake"
Hallet, Richard Matthews—"Making Port"
Hurst, Fannie—"'Ice water, Pl—!'"

The Best Short Stories of 1917, and the Yearbook of the American Short Story
***edited by* Edward J. O'Brien**

Babcock, Edwina Stanton—"Excursion"
Beer, Thomas—"Onnie"
Burt, Maxwell Struthers—"Cup of Tea"
Buzzell, Francis—"Lonely Places"
Cobb, Irvin S.—"Boys Will Be Boys"
Dobie, Charles Caldwell—"Laughter"
Dwight, H. G.—"Emperor of Elam"
Ferber, Edna—"Gay Old Dog"
Gerould, Katharine Fullerton—"Knight's Move"
Glaspell, Susan—"Jury of Her Peers"
Greene, Frederick Stuart—"Bunker Mouse"
Hallet, Richard Matthews—"Rainbow Pete"
Hurst, Fannie—"Get Ready the Wreaths"
Johnson, Fanny Kemble—"Strange Looking Man"
Kline, Burton—"Caller in the Night"
O'Sullivan, Vincent—"Interval"
Perry, Lawrence—"Certain Rich Man"
Pulver, Mary Brecht—"Path of Glory"
Steele, Wilbur Daniel*—"Ching, Ching, Chinaman"
Synon, Mary—"None So Blind"

The Best Short Stories of 1918, and the Yearbook of the American Short Story
edited by **Edward J. O'Brien**

Abdullah, Achmed—"A Simple Act of Piety"
Babcock, Edwina Stanton—"Cruelties"
Brown, Katharine Holland—"Buster"
Dobie, Charles Caldwell—"The Open Window"
Dudly, William—"The Toast to Forty-five"
Freedley, Mary Mitchell—"Blind Vision"
Gerould, Gordon Hall—"Imagination"
Gilbert, George—"In Maulmain Fever-Ward"
Humphrey, G.—"The Father's Hand"
Johnson, Arthur—"The Visit of the Master"
Kline, Burton—"In the Open Code"
Lewis, Sinclair—"The Willow Walk"
Moseley, Katharine Prescott—"The Story Vinton Heard at Mallorie"
Rhodes, Harrison—"Extra Men"
Springer, Fleta Campbell—"Solitaire"
Steele, Wilbur Daniel*—"The Dark Hour"
Street, Julian—"The Bird of Serbia"
Venable, Edward C.—"At Isham's"
Vorse, Mary Heaton—"De Vilmarte's Luck"
Wood, Frances Gilchrist—"The White Battalion"

The Best Short Stories of 1919, and the Yearbook of the American Short Story
edited by **Edward J. O'Brien**

Alsop, G. F.—"The Kitchen Gods"
Anderson, Sherwood*—"An Awakening"
Babcock, Edwina Stanton—"Willum's Vanilla"
Barnes, Djuna—"A Night Among the Horses"
Bartlett, Frederick Orin—"Long, Long Ago"
Brownell, Agnes Mary—"Dishes"
Burt, Maxwell Struthers—"The Blood-Red One"
Cabell, James Branch—"The Wedding-Jest"
Fish, Horace—"The Wrists on the Door"
Glaspell, Susan—"'Government Goat'"
Goodman, Henry—"The Stone"
Hallet, Richard Matthews—"To the Bitter End"
Hergesheimer, Joseph—"The Meeker Ritual"
Ingersoll, Will E.—"The Centenarian"
Johnston, Calvin—"Messengers"
Jones, Howard Mumford—"Mrs. Drainger's Veil"
La Motte, Ellen N.—"Under a Wine-Glass"
Lieberman, Elias—"A Thing of Beauty"
Vorse, Mary Heaton—"The Other Room"
Yezierska, Anzia—"'The Fat of the Land'"

The Best Short Stories of 1920, and the Yearbook of the American Short Story
edited by **Edward J. O'Brien**

Anderson, Sherwood*—"The Other Woman"
Babcock, Edwina Stanton—"Gargoyle"
Bercovici, Konrad—"Ghitza"
Bryner, Edna Clare—"The Life of Five Points"
Camp, Wadsroth—"The Signal Tower"
Crew, Helen Oale—"The Parting Genius"
Gerould, Katharine Fullerton—"Habakkuk"
Hartman, Lee Foster—"The Judgment of Vulcan"
Hughes, Rupert—"The Stick-in-the-Muds"
Mason, Grace Sartwell—"His Job"
Oppenheim, James—"The Rending"
Roche, Arthur Somers—"The Dummy-Chucker"
Sidney, Rose—"Butterflies"
Springer, Fleta Campbel—"The Rotter"
Steele, Wilbur Daniel*—"Out of Exile"
Storm, Ethel—"The Three Telegrams"
Wheelwright, John T.—"The Roman Bath"
Whitman, Stephen French—"Amazement"
Williams, Ben Ames—"Sheener"
Wood, Frances Gilchrist—"Turkey Red"

The Best Short Stories of 1921, and the Yearbook of the American Short Story
edited by **Edward J. O'Brien**

Anderson, Sherwood*—"Brothers"
Bercovici, Konrad—"Fanutza"
Burt, Maxwell Struthers—"Experiment"
Cobb, Irvin S.—"Darkness"
Colcord, Lincoln—"An Instrument of the Gods"
Finger, Charles J.—"The Lizard God"
Frank, Waldo—"Under the Dome"
Gerould, Katherine Fullerton—"French Eva"
Glasgow, Ellen*—"The Past"
Glaspell, Susan—"His Smile"
Hallet, Richard Matthews—"The Harbor Master"
Hart, Frances Noyes—"Green Gardens"
Hurst, Fannie—"She Walks in Beauty"
Komroff, Manuel—"The Little Master of the Sky"
Mott, Frank Luther—"The Man with the Good Face"
O'Sullivan, Vincent—"Master of Fallen Years"
Steele, Wilbur Daniel*—"The Shame Dance"
Thayer, Harriet Maxon—"Kindred"
Towne, Charles Hanson—"Shelby"
Vorse, Mary Heaton—"The Wallow of the Sea"

The Best Short Stories of 1922, and the Yearbook of the American Short Story
edited by **Edward J. O'Brien**

Aiken, Conrad*—"The Dark City"
Anderson, Sherwood*—"I'm a Fool"
Bercovici, Konrad—"The Death of Murdo"
Boogher, Susan M.—"An Unknown Warrior"
Booth, Frederick—"The Helpless Ones"
Bryner, Edna—"Forest Cover"
Cohen, Rose Gollup—"Natalka's Portion"
Finger, Charles J.—"The Shame of Gold"
Fitzgerald, F. Scott*—"Two for a Cent"
Frank, Waldo—"John the Baptist"
Freedman, David—"Mendel Marantz: Housewife"
Fullerton, Katharine—"Belshazzar's Letter"
Hecht, Ben—"Winkelburg"
Hergesheimer, Joseph—"The Token"
Jitro, William—"The Resurrection and the Life"
Lardner, Ring*—"The Golden Honeymoon"
Oppenheim, James—"He Laughed at the Gods"
Rosenblatt, Benjamin—"In the Metropolis"
Steele, Wilbur Daniel*—"From the Other Side of the South"
Wood, Clement—"The Coffin"

The Best Short Stories of 1923, and the Yearbook of the American Short Story
edited by **Edward J. O'Brien**

Adams, Bill—"Way for a Sailor"
Anderson, Sherwood*—"The Man's Story"
Babcock, Edwina Stanton—"Mr. Cardeezer"
Bercovici, Konrad—"Seed"
Burnet, Dana—"Beyond the Cross"
Clark, Valma—"Ignition"
Cobb, Irvin S.—"The Chocolate Hyena"
Cournos, John—"The Samovar"
Dreiser, Theodore*—"Reina"
Ferber, Edna—"Home Girl"
Goodman, Henry—"The Button"
Hemingway, Ernest*—"My Old Man"
Hurst, Fannie—"Seven Candles"
Montague, Margaret Prescott—"The Today Tomorrow"
Stewart, Solon K.—"The Contract of Corporal Twing"
Stimson, F. J.—"By Due Process of Law"
Sukow, Ruth—"Renters"
Toomer, Jean*—"Blood-Burning Moon"
Vorse, Mary Heaton—"The Promise"
Wilson, Harry Leon—"Flora and Fauna"

The Best Short Stories of 1924, and the Yearbook of the American Short Story
edited by Edward J. O'Brien

Burke, Morgan—"Champlin"
Cram, Mildred—"Billy"
Dell, Floyd—"Phantom Adventure"
Dobie, Charles Caldwell—"The Cracked Teapot"
Drake, Carlos—"The Last Dive"
Finger, Charles J.—"Adventures of Andrew Lang"
Gale, Zona—"The Biography of Blade"
Greenwald, Tupper—"Corputt"
Hervey, Harry—"The Young Men Go Down"
Hess, Leonard L.—"The Lesser Gift"
Hughes, Rupert—"Grudges"
Morris, Gouverneur—"A Postscript to Divorce"
Reese, Lizette Woodworth—"Forgiveness"
Sergel, Roger—"Nocturne: A Red Shawl"
Shiffrin, A. B.—"The Black Laugh"
Suckow, Ruth—"Four Generations"
Van den Bark, Melvin—"Two Women and Hog-Back Ridge"
Van Dine, Warren L.—"The Poet"
Wescott, Glenway*—"In a Thicket"
Wood, Frances Gilchrist—"Shoes"

The Best Short Stories of 1925, and the Yearbook of the American Short Story
edited by Edward J. O'Brien

Alexander, Sandra—"The Gift"
Anderson, Sherwood*—"The Return"
Asch, Nathan—"Gertude Donovan"
Benefield, Barry—"Guard of Honor"
Bercovici, Konrad—"The Beggar of Alcazar"
Cohen, Bella—"The Laugh"
Dobie, Charles Caldwell—"The Hands of the Enemy"
Fisher, Rudolph—"The City of Refuge"
Gerould, Katherine Fullerton—"An Army with Banners"
Gilkyson, Walter—"Coward's Castle"
Komroff, Manuel—"How Does It Feel to Be Free?"
Lardner, Ring*—"Haircut"
Robinson, Robert—"The Ill Wind"
Scott, Evelyn—"The Old Lady"
Stanley, May—"Old Man Ledge"
Steele, Wilber Daniel*—"Six Dollars"
Waldman, Milton—"The Home Town"
Wescott, Glenway*—"Fire and Water"
Willoughby, Barrett—"The Devil Drum"
Wylie, Elinor—"Gideon's Revenge"

The Best Short Stories of 1926, and the Yearbook of the American Short Story
edited by Edward J. O'Brien

Benefield, Barry—"Carrie Snyder"
Carver, Ada Jack—"Maudie"
Corley, Donald—"The Glass Eye of Throgmorton"
Crowell, Chester T.—"Take the Stand, Please"
Dingle, A. E.—"Bound for Rio Grande"
Dudley, Henry Walbridge—"Query"
Fauset, Arthur Huff—"Symphonesque"
Gale, Zona—"Evening"
Greenwald, Tupper—"Wheels"
Hemingway, Ernest*—"The Undefeated"
Komroff, Manuel—"The Christian Bite"
Krunich, Milutin—"Then Christs Fought Hard"
Lardner, Ring*—"Travelogue"
Mason, Grace Sartwell—"The First Stone"
Meriwether, Susan—"Grimaldi"
Morris, Ira V.—"A Tale from the Grave"
Sherwood, Robert E.—"'Extra! Extra!'"
Steele, Wilbur Daniel*—"Out of the Wind"
Strater, Edward L.—"The Other Road"
Tracy, Virginia—"The Giant's Thunder"

The Best Short Stories of 1927, and the Yearbook of the American Short Story
edited by **Edward J. O'Brien**

Anderson, Sherwood*—"Another Wife"
Bradford, Roark—"Child of God"
Brecht, Harold W.—"Vienna Roast"
Burman, Ben Lucien—"Minstrels of the Mist"
Finley-Thomas, Elisabeth—"Mademoiselle"
Hare, Amory—"Three Lumps of Sugar"
Hemingway, Ernest*—"The Killers"
Hergesheimer, Joseph—"Trial by Armes"
Heyward, DuBose—"The Half Pint Flask"
Hopper, James—"When it Happens"
La Farge, Oliver—"North is Black"
Lane, Rose Wilder—"Yarbwoman"
Le Sueur, Meridel—"Persephone"
Marquand, J. P.—"Good Morning, Major"
Saxon, Lyle—"Cane River"
Sexton, John S.—"The Pawnshop"
Shay, Frank—"Little Dombey"
Sullivan, Alan—"In Portofino"
Weeks, Raymond—"The Hound-Tuner of Callaway"
Wister, Owen—"The Right Honorable the Strawberries"

The Best Short Stories of 1928, and the Yearbook of the American Short Story
edited by **Edward J. O'Brien**

Brennan, Frederick Hazlitt—"The Guardeen Angel"
Bromfield, Louis—"The Cat That Lived at the Ritz"
Brush, Katharine—"Seven Blocks Apart"
Callaghan, Morley*—"A Country Passion"
Canfield, Dorothy—"At the Sign of the Three Daughters"
Chambers, Maria Cristina—"John of God, the Water Carrier"
Cobb, Irvin S.—"No Dam' Yankee"
Connolly, Myles—"The First of Mr. Blue"
Edmonds, Walter D.—"The Swamper"
Harris, Eleanor E.—"Home to Mother's"
Hughes, Llewellyn—"Lady Wipers—of Ypres"
Hurst, Fannie—"Give This Little Girl a Hand"
McKenna, Edward L.—"Battered Armor"
Parker, Dorothy*—"A Telephone Call"
Paul, L.—"Fences"
Roberts, Elizabeth Madox—"On the Mountain-side"
Seaver, Edwin—"The Jew"
Stevens, James—"The Romantic Sailor"
Suckow, Ruth—"Midwestern Primitive"
Ware, Edmund—"So-Long, Oldtimer"

The Best Short Stories of 1929, and the Yearbook of the American Short Story
edited by **Edward J. O'Brien**

Addington, Sarah—"'Hound of Heaven'"
Anderson, Sherwood*—"The Lost Novel"
Beede, Ivan—"The Country Doctor"
Bercovici, Konrad—"'There's Money in Poetry'"
Callaghan, Morley*—"Soldier Harmon"
Cather, Willa*—"Double Birthday"
Coates, Grace Stone—"Wild Plums"
Edmonds, Walter D.—"Death of Red Peril"
Glover, James Webber—"First Oboe"
Hall, James Norman—"Fame for Mr. Beatty"
Herald, Leon Srabian—"Power of Horizon"
Jenkins, MacGregor—"Alcantara"
Leech, Margaret—"Manicure"
McAlmon, Robert—"Potato Picking"
McCarty, Wilson—"His Friend the Pig"
McKenna, Edward L.—"I Have Letters for Marjorie"
Mullen, Robert—"Light Without Heat"
Patterson, Pernet—"'Cunjur'"
Wescott, Glenway*—"A Guilty Woman"
Williams, William Carlos*—"The Venus"

The Best Short Stories of 1930, and the Yearbook of the American Short Story
***edited by* Edward J. O'Brien**

Bishop, Ellen—"Along a Sandy Road"
Bragdon, Clifford—"Suffer Little Children"
Burnett, Whit—"Two Men Free"
Callaghan, Morley*—"The Faithful Wife"
Coates, Grace Stone—"The Way of the Transgressor"
Draper, Edythe Squier—"The Voice of the Turtle"
Furniss, Ruth Pine—"Answer"
Gilkyson, Walter—"Blue Sky"
Gordon, Caroline*—"Summer Dust"
Hahn, Emily—"Adventure"
Hartwick, Harry—"Happiness up the River"
Kittredge, Eleanor Hayden—"September Sailing"
Komroff, Manuel—"A Red Coat for Night"
Lewis, Janet—"At the Swamp"
March, William—"The Little Wife"
Parker, Dorothy*—"The Cradle of Civilization"
Paulding, Gouverneur—"The White Pidgeon"
Polk, William—"The Patriot"
Porter, Katherine Anne*—"Theft"
Upson, William Hazlett—"The Vineyard at Schloss Ramsburg

The Best Short Stories of 1931, and the Yearbook of the American Short Story
***edited by* Edward J. O'Brien**

Adamic, Louis—"The Enigma"
Barber, Solon R.—"The Sound That Frost Makes"
Bessie, Alvah C.—"Only We Are Barren"
Boyle, Kay*—"Rest Cure"
Bromfield, Louis—"Tabloid News"
Burnett, Whit—"A Day in the Country"
Caldwell, Erskine*—"Dorothy"
Callaghan, Morley*—"The Young Priest"
Edmonds, Walter D.—"Water Never Hurt a Man"
Faulkner, William*—"That Evening Sun Go Down"
Fitzgerald, F. Scott*—"Babylon Revisited"
Foley, Martha—"One with Shakespeare"
Gilpatric, Guy—"The Flaming Chariot"
Gowen, Emmett—"Fiddlers of Moon Mountain"
Herbst, Josephine—"I Hear You, Mr. and Mrs. Brown"
Horgan, Paul—"The Other Side of the Street"
March, William—"Fifteen from Company K"
Marquis, Don—"The Other Room"
Milburn, George—"A Pretty Cute Little Stunt"
Parker, Dorothy*—"Here We Are"
Read, Allen—"Rhodes Scholar"
Stevens, James—"The Great Hunter of the Woods"
Upson, William Hazlett—"The Model House"
Ward, Leo L.—"The Threshing Ring"
Wilson, Anne Elizabeth—"The Miracle"
Wimberly, Lowry Charles—"White Man's Town"

The Best Short Stories of 1932, and the Yearbook of the American Short Story
***edited by* Edward J. O'Brien**

Adams, Bill—"The Foreigner"
Bessie, Alvah C.—"Horizon"
Bragdon, Clifford—"Love's So Many Things"
Brennan, Louis—"Poisoner in Motley"
Burnett, Wanda—"Sand"
Burnett, Whit—"Sherrel"
Caldwell, Erskine*—"Warm River"
Callaghan, Morley*—"The Red Hat"
Caperton, Helena Lefroy—"The Honest Wine Merchant"
Cournos, John—"The Story of the Stranger"
DeJong, David Cornel—"So Tall the Corn"
Diefenthaler, Andra—"Hansel"
Faulkner, William*—"Smoke"
Komroff, Manuel—"Napoleon's Hat under Glass"
Le Sueur, Meridel—"Spring Story"
Lockwood, Scammon—"An Arrival at Carthage"

March, William—"Mist on the Meadow"
Milburn, George—"Heel, Toe, and a 1, 2, 3, 4"
Morris, Ira V.—"The Kimono"
Neagoe, Peter—"Shepherd of the Lord"
Schnabel, Dudley—"Load"
Stallings, Laurence—"Gentlemen in Blue"
Tuting, Bernhard Johann—"The Family Chronicle"
Villa, José García—"Untitled Story"
Ward, Leo L.—"The Quarrel"

The Best Short Stories of 1933, and the Yearbook of the American Short Story
edited by Edward J. O'Brien

Albee, George—"Fame Takes the J Car"
Bessie, Alvah C.—"A Little Walk"
Bishop, John Peale—"Toadstools Are Poison"
Boyd, Albert Truman—"Elmer"
Burnett, Whit—"Serenade"
Caldwell, Erskine*—"The First Autumn"
Callaghan, Morley*—"A Sick Call"
Cantwell, Robert—"The Land of Plenty"
Dobie, Charles Caldwell—"The Honey Pot"
Edmonds, Walter D.—"Black Wolf"
Farrell, James T.*—"Helen, I Love You!"
Fitzgerald, F. Scott*—"Crazy Sunday"
Flandrau, Grace—"What Was Truly Mine"
Foley, Martha—"Martyr"
Gowen, Emmett—"Fisherman's Luck"
Hale, Nancy*—"Simple Aveu"
Halper, Albert—"Going to Market"
Joffe, Eugene—"In the Park"
Lambertson, Louise—"Sleet Storm"
Leenhouts, Grant—"The Facts in the Case"
Milburn, George—"The Apostate"
Morris, Ira V.—"The Sampler"
Morris, Lloyd—"Footnote to a Life"
Porter, Katherine Anne*—"The Cracked Looking-Glass"
Reed, Louis—"Episode at the Pawpaws"
Shumway, Naomi—"Ike and Us Moons"
Steele, Wilbur Daniel*—"How Beautiful with Shoes"
Thomas, Dorothy—"The Joybell"
Villa, José García—"The Fence"

The Best Short Stories of 1934, and the Yearbook of the American Short Story
edited by Edward J. O'Brien

Appel, Benjamin—"Winter Meeting"
Bessie, Alvah C.—"No Final Word"
Burnett, Whit—"The Cats Which Cried"
Caldwell, Erskine*—"Horse Thief"
Callaghan, Morley*—"Mr. and Mrs. Fairbanks"
Childs, Marquis W.—"The Woman on the Shore"
Corle, Edwin—"Amethyst"
Corning, Howard McKinley—"Crossroads Woman"
Faulkner, William*—"Beyond"
Fisher, Rudolph—"Miss Cynthie"
Foley, Martha—"She Walks in Beauty"
Godin, Alexander—"My Dead Brother Comes to America"
Gordon, Caroline*—"Tom Rivers"
Goryan, Sirak—"The Broken Wheel"
Hall, James Norman—"Lord of Marutea"
Hughes, Langston*—"Cora Unashamed"
Joffe, Eugene—"Siege of Love"
Komroff, Manuel—"Hamlet's Daughter"
Lineaweaver, John—"Mother Tanner"
McCleary, Dorothy—"Winter"
Mamet, Louis—"The Pension"
March, William—"This Heavy Load"
Marshall, Alan—"Death and Transfiguration"
Ryan, Paul—"The Sacred Thing"
Sabsay, Nahum—"In a Park"
Sheean, Vincent—"The Hemlock Tree"
Sherman, Richard—"Now There Is Peace"
Tate, Allen—"The Immortal Woman"
Terrell, Upton—"Money at Home"
Zugsmith, Leane—"Home Is Where You Hang Your Childhood"

The Best Short Stories of 1935, and the Yearbook of the American Short Story
edited by **Edward J. O'Brien**

Appel, Benjamin—"Outside Yuma"
Benson, Sally—"The Overcoat"
Brace, Ernest—"The Party Next Door"
Brown, Carlton—"Suns That Our Hearts Harden"
Burnett, Whit—"Division"
Caldwell, Erskine*—"The Cold Winter"
Callaghan, Morley*—"Father and Son"
Cole, Madelene—"Bus to Biarritz"
Cooke, Charles—"Triple Jumps"
DeJong, David Cornel—"Home-Coming"
Faulkner, William*—"Lo!"
Godchaux, Elma—"Wild Nigger"
Haardt, Sara—"Little White Girl"
Haines, William Wister—"Remarks: None"
Hale, Nancy*—"The Double House"
Horgan, Paul—"A Distant Harbour"
McCleary, Dorothy—"Sunday Morning"
McHugh, Vincent—"Parish of Cockroaches"
Mamet, Louis—"Episode from Life"
Morang, Alfred—"Frozen Stillness"
Morris, Edita—"Mrs. Lancaster-Jones"
Saroyan, William*—"Resurrection of a Life"
Seager, Allan—"This Town and Salamanca"
Sylvester, Harry—"A Boxer: Old"
Thielen, Benedict—"Souvenir of Arizona"
White, Max—"A Pair of Shoes"
Wolfe, Thomas*—"The Sun and the Rain"

The Best Short Stories of 1936, and the Yearbook of the American Short Story
edited by **Edward J. O'Brien**

Burlingame, Roger—"In the Cage"
Callaghan, Morley*—"The Blue Kimono"
Canfield, Dorothy—"The Murder on Jefferson Street"
Carr, A. H. Z.—"The Hunch"
Cooke, Charles—"Catafalque"
Coombes, Evan—"The North Wind Doth Blow"
Faulkner, William*—"That Will Be Fine"
Fessier, Michael—"That's What Happened to Me"
Field, S. S.—"Torrent of Darkness"
Flannagan, Roy—"The Doorstop"
Foley, Martha—"Her Own Sweet Simplicity"
Gilkyson, Walter—"Enemy Country"
Hall, Elizabeth—"Two Words Are a Story"
Kelly, Frank K.—"With Some Gaiety and Laughter"
Kelm, Karlton—"Tinkle and Family Take a Ride"
Komroff, Manuel—"That Blowzy Goddess Fame"
Larsen, Erling—"A Kind of a Sunset"
Le Sueur, Meridel—"Annuciation"
McCleary, Dorothy—"The Shroud"
Maltz, Albert—"Man on a Road"
Porter, Katherine Anne*—"The Grave"
Richmond, Roaldus—"Thanks for Nothing"
Seager, Allan—"Fugue for Harmonica"
Slesinger, Tess—"A Life in the Day of a Writer"
Thomas, Elisabeth Wilkins—"Traveling Salesman"
Vines, Howell—"The Mustydines Was Ripe"
Whitehand, Robert—"American Nocturne"
Williams, Calvin—"On the Sidewalk"
Wilson, William E.—"The Lone Pioneer"
Wolfe, Thomas*—"Only the Dead Know Brooklyn"

The Best Short Stories of 1937, and the Yearbook of the American Short Story
edited by **Edward J. O'Brien**

Buckner, Robert—"The Man Who Won the War"
Burlingame, Roger—"The Last Equation"
Callaghan, Morley*—"The Voyage Out"
Cooke, Charles—"Enter Daisy; to Her, Alexandra"
Faulkner, William*—"Fool About a Horse"
Field, S. S.—"Goodbye to Cap'm John"
Foley, Martha—"Glory, Glory, Hallelujah!"
Godchaux, Elma—"Chains"

Halper, Albert—"The Poet"
Hemingway, Ernest*—"The Snows of Kilimanjaro"
Heth, Edward Harris—"Homecoming"
Horgan, Paul—"The Surgeon and the Nun"
Komroff, Manuel—"The Girl with the Flaxen Hair"
Krantz, David E.—"Awakening and the Destination"
Kroll, Harry Harrison—"Second Wife"
Linn, R. H.—"The Intrigue of Mr. S. Yamamoto"
MacDougall, Ursula—"Titty's Dead and Tatty Weeps"
McGinnis, Allen—"Let Nothing You Dismay"
March, William—"Maybe the Sun Will Shine"
Morris, Edita—"A Blade of Grass"
Morris, Ira V.—"Marching Orders"
Porter, Katharine Anne*—"The Old Order"
St. Joseph, Ellis—"A Passenger to Bali"
Saroyan, William*—"The Crusader"
Stuart, Jesse*—"Hair"
Thielen, Benedict—"Lieutenant Pearson"
Thompson, Lovell—"The Iron City"
Wright, Wilson—"Arrival on a Holiday"
Zugsmith, Leane—"Room in the World"

The Best Short Stories of 1938, and the Yearbook of the American Short Story
***edited by* Edward J. O'Brien**

Ayre, Robert—"Mr. Sycamore"
Benedict, Libby—"Blind Man's Buff"
Benét, Stephen Vincent*—"A Tooth for Paul Revere"
Bond, Nelson S.—"Mr. Mergenthwirker's Lobblies"
Callaghan, Morley*—"The Cheat's Remorse"
Cheever, John*—"The Brothers"
Cherkasski, Vladimir—"What Hurts Is That I Was in a Hurry"
Cook, Whitfield—"Dear Mr. Flessheimer"
Creyke, Richard Paulett—"Niggers Are Such Liars"
Di Donato, Pietro—"Christ in Concrete"
Fessier, Michael—"Black Wind and Lightning"
Hannum, Alberta Pierson—"Turkey Hunt"
Komroff, Manuel—"The Whole World Is Outside"
Le Sueur, Meridel—"The Girl"
Ludlow, Don—"She Always Wanted Shoes"
McCleary, Dorothy—"Little Bride"
March, William—"The Last Meeting"
Moll, Elick—"To Those Tho Wait"
Pereda, Prudencio de—"The Spaniard"
Prokosch, Frederic—"A Russian Idyll"
Rayner, George Thorp—"A Real American Fellow"
Roberts, Elizabeth Madox—"The Haunted Palace"
Schorer, Mark—"Boy in the Summer Sun"
Seager, Allan—"Pro Arte"
Steinbeck, John*—"The Chrysanthemums"
Stuart, Jesse*—"Huey, the Engineer"
Swados, Harvey—"The Amateurs"
Warren, Robert Penn*—"Christmas Gift"
Welty, Eudora*—"Lily Daw and the Three Ladies"
Wolfert, Ira—"Off the Highway"

The Best Short Stories of 1939, and the Yearbook of the American Short Story
***edited by* Edward J. O'Brien**

Beck, Warren—"The Blue Sash"
Caldwell, Ronald—"Vision in the Sea"
Callaghan, Morley*—"It Had to Be Done"
Cheever, John*—"Frère Jacques"
Clark, Gean—"Indian on the Road"
Coates, Robert M.—"Passing Through"
Cohn, David L.—"Black Troubadour"
Danielson, Richard Ely—"Corporal Hardy"
Ellson, Hal—"The Rat Is a Mouse"
Halper, Albert—"Prelude"
Horgan, Paul—"To the Mountains"
Jenison, Madge—"True Believer"
Komroff, Manuel—"What Is a Miracle?"
Le Sueur, Meridel—"Salutation to Spring"
MacDonald, Alan—"An Arm Upraised"
Maltz, Albert—"The Happiest Man on Earth"
St. Joseph, Ellis—"Leviathan"
Saroyan, William*—"Piano"
Schoenstedt, Walter—"The Girl from the River Barge"
Seager, Allan—"Berkshire Comedy"
Seide, Michael—"Bad Boy from Brooklyn"

Stuart, Jesse*—"Eustacia"
Sylvester, Harry—"The Crazy Guy"
Thielen, Benedict—"The Thunderstorm"
Warren, Robert Penn*—"How Willie Proudfit Came Home"
Welty, Eudora*—"A Curtain of Green"
Werner, Heinz—"Black Tobias and the Empire"
Wolfert, Ira—"The Way the Luck Runs"
Wright, Eugene—"The White Camel"
Wright, Richard*—"Bright and Morning Star"

The Best Short Stories of 1940, and the Yearbook of the American Short Story
***edited by* Edward J. O'Brien**

Boyle, Kay*—"Anschluss"
Caldwell, Erskine*—"The People vs. Abe Lathan, Colored"
Callaghan, Morley*—"Getting on in the World"
Eisenberg, Frances—"Roof Sitter"
Farrell, James T.*—"The Fall of Machine Gun McGurk"
Faulkner, William*—"Hand upon the Waters"
Fitzgerald, F. Scott*—"Design in Plaster"
Gordon, Caroline*—"Frankie and Thomas and Bud Asbury"
Hemingway, Ernest*—"Under the Ridge"
King, Mary—"The Honey House"
Komroff, Manuel—"Death of an Outcast"
Lull, Roderick—"That Fine Place We Had Last Year"
Lussu, Emilio—"Your General Does Not Sleep"
McCleary, Dorothy—"Something Jolly"
Morris, Edita—"Kullan"
Morris, Ira V.—"The Beautiful Fire"
Pasinetti, P. M.—"Family History"
Pereda, Prudencio de—"The Way Death Comes"
Pooler, James—"Herself"
Porter, Katherine Anne*—"The Downward Path to Wisdom"
Saroyan, William*—"The Presbyterian Choir Singers"
Seide, Michael—"Words Without Music"
Shaw, Irwin*—"Main Currents of American Thought"
Slocombe, George—"The Seven Men of Rouen"
Stern, Morton—"Four Worms Turning"
Storm, Hans Otto—"The Two Deaths of Kaspar Rausch"
Stuart, Jesse*—"Rich Men"
Sylvester, Harry—"Beautifully and Bravely"
Thielen, Benedict—"Night and the Lost Armies"
Welty, Eudora*—"The Hitch-Hikers"
Zara, Louis—"Resurgam"

The Best Short Stories of 1941, and the Yearbook of the American Short Story
***edited by* Martha Foley**

Ashton, E. B.—"Shadow of a Girl"
Benét, Stephen Vincent*—"All Around the Town"
Caldwell, Erskine*—"Handy"
Callaghan, Morley*—"Big Jules"
Coates, Robert M.—"The Net"
DeJong, David Cornel—"Mamma Is a Lady"
Exall, Henry—"To the Least . . ."
Fante, John—"A Nun No More"
Faulkner, William*—"Gold Is Not Always"
Garfinkel, Harold—"'Color Trouble'"
Gizycka, Felicia—"The Magic Wire"
Herman, Justin—"Smile for the Man, Dear"
Kees, Weldon—"The Life of the Mind"
King, Mary—"The White Bull"
Kober, Arthur—"Some People Are Just Plumb Crazy"
La Farge, Christopher—"Scorn and Comfort"
Levin, Meyer—"The System Was Doomed"
Lull, Roderick—"Don't Get Me Wrong"
Maltz, Albert—"Sunday Morning on Twentieth Street"
Neagoe, Peter—"Ill-Winds from the Wide World"
Saroyan, William*—"The Three Swimmers and the Educated Grocer"
Shaw, Irwin*—"Triumph of Justice"
Shore, Wilma—"The Butcher"

Stegner, Wallace*—"Goin' to Town"
Stuart, Jesse*—"Love"
Thielen, Benedict—"The Psychologist"
Weidman, Jerome*—"Houdini"
Weller, George—"Strip-Tease"
Wright, Richard*—"Almos' a Man"

The Best American Short Stories, 1942, and the Yearbook of the American Short Story
***edited by* Martha Foley**

Algren, Nelson*—"Biceps"
Bemelmans, Ludwig—"The Valet of the Splendide"
Benson, Sally—"Fifty-one Thirty-five Kensington: August, 1903"
Boyle, Kay*—"Nothing Ever Breaks Except the Heart"
Bryan, Jack Y.—"For Each of Us"
Clark, Walter Van Tilburg*—"The Portable Phonograph"
DeJong, David Cornel—"That Frozen Hour"
Eakin, Boyce—"Prairies"
Fineman, Morton—"Tell Him I Waited"
Gibbons, Robert—"A Loaf of Bread"
Hale, Nancy*—"Those Are as Brothers"
Kantor, MacKinlay—"That Greek Dog"
Knight, Eric—"Sam Small's Better Half"
Lavin, Mary*—"At Sallygap"
Medearis, Mary—"Death of a Country Doctor"
Morris, Edita—"Caput Mortuum"
O'Hara, Mary—"My Friend Flicka"
Peattie, Margaret Rhodes—"The Green Village"
Saroyan, William*—"The Hummingbird That Lived Through Winter"
Schulberg, Budd Wilson—"The Real Viennese Schmalz"
Seide, Michael—"Sacrifice of Isaac"
Shaw, Irwin*—"Search Through the Streets of the City"
Stegner, Wallace*—"In the Twilight"
Steinbeck, John*—"How Edith McGillcuddy Met R. L. Stevenson"
Stuart, Jesse*—"The Storm"
Taylor, Peter*—"The Fancy Woman"
Thomas, Dorothy—"My Pigeon Pair"
Thurber, James*—"You Could Look It Up"
Vatsek, Joan—"The Bees"
Worthington, Marjorie—"Hunger"

The Best American Short Stories, 1943, and the Yearbook of the American Short Story
***edited by* Martha Foley**

Baum, Vicki—"The Healthy Life"
Beck, Warren—"Boundary Line"
Boyle, Kay*—"Frenchman's Ship"
Cheever, John*—"The Pleasures of Solitude"
D'Agostino, Guido—"The Dream of Angelo Zara"
Dyer, Murray—"Samuel Blane"
Faulkner, William*—"The Bear"
Field, Rachel—"Beginning of Wisdom"
Fisher, Vardis—"A Partnership with Death"
Flandrau, Grace—"What Do You See, Dear Enid?"
Gibbons, Robert—"Time's End"
Gray, Peter—"Threnody for Stelios"
Hale, Nancy*—"Who Lived and Died Believing"
Horgan, Paul—"The Peach Stone"
Knight, Laurette MacDuffie—"The Enchanted"
Laidlaw, Clara—"The Little Black Boys"
Lavin, Mary*—"Love Is for Lovers"
Morris, Edita—"Young Man in an Astrakhan Cap"
Saroyan, William*—"Knife-like, Flower-like, Like Nothing at All in the World"
Schwartz, Delmore*—"An Argument in 1934"
Shaw, Irwin*—"Preach on the Dusty Roads"
Shedd, Margaret—"My Public"
Stegner, Wallace*—"Chip off the Old Block"
Stuart, Alison—"Death and My Uncle Felix"
Stuart, Jesse*—"Dawn of Remembered Spring"
Sullivan, Richard—"The Women"
Thurber, James*—"The Catbird Seat"
Treichler, Jessie—"Homecoming"
Weidman, Jerome*—"Philadelphia Express"
Welty, Eudora*—"Asphodel"

The Best American Short Stories, 1944, and the Yearbook of the American Short Story
***edited by* Martha Foley**

Alexander, Sidney—"The White Boat"
Barrett, William E.—"Señor Payroll"
Bellow, Saul*—"Notes of a Dangling Man"
Canfield, Dorothy—"The Knot Hole"
De Lanux, Eyre—"The SS Libertad"
Eastman, Elizabeth—"Like a Field Mouse over the Heart"
Eustis, Helen—"The Good Days and the Bad"
Fifield, William—"The Fishermen of Patzcuaro"
Fleming, Berry—"Strike up a Stirring Music"
Hawthorne, Hazel—"More Like a Coffin"
Houston, Noel—"A Local Skirmish"
Jackson, Shirley*—"Come Dance with Me in Ireland"
Johnson, Josephine W.—"The Rented Room"
Kaplan, H. J.—"The Mohammedans"
McCullers, Carson*—"The Ballad of the Sad Café"
March, William—"The Female of the Fruit Fly"
Meighan, Astrid—"Shoe the Horse and Shoe the Mare"
Mian, Mary—"Exiles from the Creuse"
Morris, Edita—"Heart of Marzipan"
Nabokov, Vladimir*—"'That in Aleppo Once . . .'"
Portugal, Ruth—"Neither Here Nor There"
Powers, J. F.*—"Lions, Harts, Leaping Does"
Schmitt, Gladys—"All Souls'"
Shaw, Irwin*—"The Veterans Reflect"
Stiles, George—"A Return"
Surmelian, Leon Z.—"My Russian Cap"
Trilling, Lionel—"Of This Time, of That Place"
Warner, Elizabeth—"An Afternoon"
West, Jessamyn*—"The Illumination"
Winters, Emmanuel—"God's Agents Have Beards"

The Best American Short Stories, 1945, and the Yearbook of the American Short Story
***edited by* Martha Foley**

Algren, Nelson*—"How the Devil Came Down Division Street"
Beck, Warren—"The First Fish"
Bromfield, Louis—"Crime Passionnel"
Bulosan, Carlos—"My Brother Osong's Career in Politics"
Deasy, Mary—"Harvest"
Fenton, Edward—"Burial in the Desert"
Fineman, Morton—"The Light of Morning"
Gerry, Bill—"Understand What I Mean?"
Gill, Brendan—"The Test"
Hagopian, Richard—"'Be Heavy'"
Hahn, Emily—"It Never Happened"
Hardy, W. G.—"The Czech Dog"
Johnson, Josephine W.—"Fever Flower"
McLaughlin, Robert—"Poor Everybody"
McNulty, John—"Don't Scrub off These Names"
Miller, Warren—"The Animal's Fair"
Panetta, George—"Papa, Mama, and Economics"
Pennell, Joseph Stanley—"On the Way to Somewhere Else"
Portugal, Ruth—"Call a Solemn Assembly"
Pratt, Theodore—"The Owl That Kept Winking"
Rosenfeld, Isaac—"The Hand That Fed Me"
Rowell, Donna—"A War Marriage"
Schmitt, Gladys—"The Mourners"
Shaw, Irwin*—"Gunners' Passage"
Stafford, Jean*—"The Wedding: Beacon Hill"
Tartt, Ruby Pickens—"Alabama Sketches"
Taylor, Peter*—"Rain in the Heart"
Warren, Robert Penn*—"Cass Mastern's Wedding Ring"
West, Jessamyn*—"First Day Finish"
Zugsmith, Leane—"This Is a Love Story"
Zukerman, William—"A Ship to Tarshish"

The Best American Short Stories, 1946, and the Yearbook of the American Short Story
***edited by* Martha Foley**

Angoff, Charles—"Jerry"
Beck, Warren—"Out of Line"
Berryman, John—"The Lovers"
Bradbury, Ray*—"The Big Black and White Game"
Breuer, Bessie—"Bury Your Own Dead"
Brown, T. K., III—"The Valley of the Shadow"
Burnett, W. R.—"The Ivory Tower"
Clark, Walter Van Tilburg*—"The Wind and the Snow of Winter"
Critchell, Laurence—"Flesh and Blood"
Deasy, Mary—"A Sense of Danger"
Elkin, Samuel—"In a Military Manner"
Gottlieb, Elaine—"The Norm"
Hardwick, Elizabeth—"The Mysteries of Eleusis"
Johnson, Josephine W.—"Story Without End"
Lampman, Ben Hur—"Old Bill Bent to Drink"
Liben, Meyer—"The Caller"
Liebling, A. J.—"Run, Run, Run, Run"
Mitchell, W. O.—"The Owl and the Bens"
Nabokov, Vladimir*—"Time and Ebb"
Petry, Ann*—"Like a Winding Sheet"
Ruml, Wentzle, III—"For a Beautiful Relationship"
Schmitt, Gladys—"The King's Daughter"
Stark, Irwin—"The Bridge"
Stern, James—"The Woman Who Was Loved"
Still, James—"Mrs. Razor"
Taylor, Peter*—"The Scout Master"
Trilling, Lionel—"The Other Margaret"
Weigel, Henrietta—"Love Affair"
West, Jessamyn*—"The Singing Lesson"
Woods, Glennyth—"Death in a Cathedral"

The Best American Short Stories, 1947, and the Yearbook of the American Short Story
***edited by* Martha Foley**

Broderick, Francis L.—"Return by Faith"
Canfield, Dorothy—"Sex Education"
Capote, Truman*—"The Headless Hawk"
Fontaine, Robert—"Day of Gold and Darkness"
Gerstley, Adelaide—"The Man in the Mirror"
Goodwin, John B. L.—"The Cocoon"
Goss, John Mayo—"Bird Song"
Griffith, Paul—"The Horse like September"
Guérard, Albert J.—"Turista"
Hardwick, Elizabeth—"The Golden Stallion"
Harris, Ruth McCoy—"Up the Road a Piece"
Heggen, Thomas—"Night Watch"
Heth, Edward Harris—"Under the Ginkgo Trees"
Humphreys, John Richard—"Michael Finney and the Little Men"
Lincoln, Victoria—"Down in the Reeds by the River"
Lowry, Robert—"Little Baseball World"
Martenet, May Davies—"Father Delacroix"
Mayhall, Jane—"The Darkness"
Powers, J. F.*—"Prince of Darkness"
Raphaelson, Samson—"The Greatest Idea in the World"
Schorer, Mark—"What We Don't Know Hurts Us"
Seager, Allan—"Game Chickens"
Shaw, Irwin*—"Act of Faith"
Shirley, Sylvia—"The Red Dress"
Stafford, Jean*—"The Interior Castle"
Stark, Irwin—"Shock Treatment"
Stegner, Wallace*—"The Women on the Wall"
Tucci, Niccolò—"The Seige"
Weaver, John D.—"Bread and Games"
Williams, Lawrence—"The Hidden Room"

The Best American Short Stories, 1948, and the Yearbook of the American Short Story
***edited by* Martha Foley**

Alexander, Sidney—"Part of the Act"
Bowles, Paul*—"A Distant Episode"
Bradbury, Ray*—"I See You Never"
Canfield, Dorothy—"The Apprentice"
Cheever, John*—"The Enormous Radio"
Clay, George R.—"That's My Johnny-Boy"

Clayton, John Bell—"Visitor from Philadelphia"
Cousins, Margaret—"A Letter to Mr. Priest"
Fisher, M. F. K.—"The Hollow Heart"
Garrigan, Philip—"'Fly, Fly, Little Dove'"
Gellhorn, Martha—"Miami-New York"
Grennard, Elliott—"Sparrow's Last Jump"
Gustafson, Ralph—"The Human Fly"
Hersey, John—"Why Were You Sent out Here?"
Jeffers, Lance—"The Dawn Swings In"
Lincoln, Victoria—"Morning, a Week Before the Crime"
Lowry, Robert—"The Terror in the Streets"
Lynch, John A.—"The Burden"
McHugh, Vincent—"The Search"
Morse, Robert—"The Professor and the Puli"
Portugal, Ruth—"The Stupendous Fortune"
Post, Mary Brinker—"That's the Man"
Root, Waverley—"Carmencita"
Sharp, Dolph—"The Tragedy in Jancie Brierman's Life"
Stegner, Wallace*—"Beyond the Glass Mountain"
Sulkin, Sidney—"The Plan"
Welty, Eudora*—"The Whole World Knows"
White, E. B.*—"The Second Tree from the Corner"

The Best American Short Stories, 1949, and the Yearbook of the American Short Story
***edited by* Martha Foley**

Albee, George—"Mighty, Mighty Pretty"
Biddle, Livingston, Jr.—"The Vacation"
Bishop, Elizabeth—"The Farmer's Children"
Bowles, Paul*—"Under the Sky"
Brookhouser, Frank—"My Father and the Circus"
Deal, Borden—"Exodus"
Dolokhov, Adele—"Small Miracle"
Dorrance, Ward—"The White Hound"
Felsen, Henry Gregor—"Li Chang's Million"
Gibbons, Robert—"Departure of Hubbard"
Griffith, Beatrice—"In the Flow of Time"
Hardwick, Elizabeth—"Evenings at Home"
Heller, Joseph—"Castle of Snow"
Herschberger, Ruth—"A Sound in the Night"
Hunter, Laura—"Jerry"
Kjelgaard, Jim—"Of the River and Uncle Pidcock"
Lull, Roderick—"Footnote to American History"
Mabry, Thomas—"The Vault"
Macdonald, Agnes—"Vacia"
Mayhall, Jane—"The Men"
Morgan, Patrick—"The Heifer"
Pfeffer, Irving—"All Prisoners Here"
Rogers, John—"Episode of a House Remembered"
Salinger, J. D.*—"A Girl I Knew"
Segre, Alfredo—"Justice Has No Number"
Shapiro, Madelon—"An Island for My Friends"
Stafford, Jean*—"Children Are Bored on Sunday"
West, Jessamyn*—"Road to the Isles"

The Best American Short Stories, 1950, and the Yearbook of the American Short Story
***edited by* Martha Foley**

Angoff, Charles—"Where Did Yesterday Go?"
Aswell, James—"Shadow of Evil"
Babb, Sanora—"The Wild Flower"
Beck, Warren—"Edge of Doom"
Bellow, Saul*—"A Sermon by Doctor Pep"
Bennett, Peggy—"Death Under the Hawthornes"
Bowles, Paul*—"Pastor Dowe at Tacaté"
Christopher, Robert—"Jishin"
Elliott, George P.*—"The NRACP"
Fiedler, Leslie A.—"The Fear of Innocence"
Gustafson, Ralph—"The Pigeon"
Hauser, Marianne—"The Mouse"
Johnson, Josephine W.—"The Author"
Kaplan, Ralph—"The Artist"
Karchmer, Sylvan—"'Hail Brother and Farewell'"
Lamkin, Speed—"Comes a Day"
Lincoln, Victoria—"The Glass Wall"
McCoy, Esther—"The Cape"
Maier, Howard—"The World Outside"
Newhouse, Edward—"My Brother's Second Funeral"
Norris, Hoke—"Take Her Up Tenderly"

Parker, Glidden—"Bright and Morning"
Putman, Clay—"The Old Acrobat and the Ruined City"
Rothberg, Abraham—"Not with Our Fathers"
Stewart, Ramona—"The Promise"
Still, James—"A Master Time"
Strong, Joan—"The Hired Man"
Taylor, Peter*—"A Wife of Nashville"

The Best American Short Stories, 1951, and the Yearbook of the American Short Story
***edited by* Martha Foley, assisted by Joyce F. Hartman**

Angell, Roger—"Flight Through the Dark"
Asch, Nathan—"Inland, Western Sea"
Bennett, Peggy—"A Fugitive from the Mind"
Bolté, Mary—"The End of the Depression"
Calisher, Hortense*—"In Greenwich There Are Many Gravelled Walks"
Casper, Leonard—"Sense of Direction"
Cassill, R. V.*—"Larchmoor Is Not the World"
Cheever, John*—"The Season of Divorce"
Downey, Harris—"The Hunters"
Enright, Elizabeth—"The Temperate Zone"
Gardon, Ethel Edison—"The Value of the Dollar"
Goodman, J. Carol—"The Kingdom of Gordon"
oyen, William—"Her Breath upon the Windowpane"
Jackson, Shirley*—"The Summer People"
Johnson, Josephine W.—"The Mother's Story"
Karmel, Ilona—"Fru Holm"
La Farge, Oliver—"Old Century's River"
Lanning, George—"Old Turkey Neck"
Lewis, Ethel G.—"Portrait"
Livesay, Dorothy—"The Glass House"
Macauley, Robie—"The Wishbone"
Malamud, Bernard*—"The Prison"
Patt, Esther—"The Butcherbirds"
Powers, J. F.*—"Death of a Favorite"
Rader, Paul—"The Tabby Cat"
Stafford, Jean*—"The Nemesis"
West, Ray B., Jr.—"The Last of the Grizzly Bears"
Williams, Tennessee*—"The Resemblance Between a Violin Case and a Coffin"

The Best American Short Stories, 1952, and the Yearbook of the American Short Story
***edited by* Martha Foley, assisted by Joyce F. Hartman**

Berge, Bill—"That Lovely Green Boat"
Bethel, Laurence—"The Call"
Bowen, Robert O.—"The Other River"
Boyle, Kay*—"The Lost"
Bradbury, Ray*—"The Other Foot"
Calisher, Hortense*—"A Wreath for Miss Totten"
Cardozo, Nancy—"The Unborn Ghosts"
Chaikin, Nancy G.—"The Climate of the Family"
Chidester, Ann—"Wood Smoke"
Eaton, Charles Edward—"The Motion of Forgetfulness Is Slow"
Elliott, George P.*—"Children of Ruth"
Enright, Elizabeth—"The First Face"
Garner, Hugh—"The Conversion of Willie Heaps"
Gellhorn, Martha—"Weekend at Grimsby"
Glen, Emilie—"Always Good for a Belly Laugh"
Hale, Nancy*—"Brahmin Beachhead"
Horton, Philip—"What's in a Corner"
Kuehn, Susan—"The Searchers"
Rooney, Frank—"Cyclists' Raid"
Saroyan, William*—"Palo"
Schulberg, Stuart—"I'm Really Fine"
Stafford, Jean*—"The Healthiest Girl in Town"
Stegner, Wallace*—"The Traveler"
Still, James—"A Ride on the Short Dog"
Swados, Harvey—"The Letters"
Van Doren, Mark—"Nobody Say a Word"
Waldron, Daniel—"Evensong"
Weston, Christine—"Loud Sing Cuckoo"
Yamamoto, Hisay—"Yoneko's Earthquake"

The Best American Short Stories, 1953, and the Yearbook of the American Short Story
edited by Martha Foley, assisted by Joyce F. Hartman

Agee, James*—"A Mother's Tale"
Ballard, James—"A Mountain Summer"
Becker, Stephen—"The Town Mouse"
Carroll, Joseph—"At Mrs. Farrelly's"
Cassill, R. V.*—"The Life of the Sleeping Beauty"
Coates, Robert M.—"The Need"
Deasy, Mary—"Morning Sun"
Downey, Harris—"Crispin's Way"
Duke, Osborn—"Struttin' with Some Barbecue"
Elliott, George P.*—"Faq'"
Froscher, Wingate—"A Death in the Family"
Gregory, Vahan Krikorian—"Athens, Greece, 1942"
Hall, James B.—"A Spot in History"
Jackson, Charles Tenney—"The Bullalo Wallow"
Jackson, Roberts—"Fly away Home"
Jones, Madison P., Jr.—"Dog Days"
Marsh, Willard—"Beachhead in Bohemia"
Marshall, Elizabeth—"The Hill People"
Noland, Felix—"The Whipping"
Pendergast, Constance—"The Picnic"
Purdy, Ken—"Change of Plan"
Putman, Clay—"Our Vegetable Love"
Shattuck, Roger—"Workout on the River"
Shultz, Henry—"Oreste"
Sultan, Stanley—"The Fugue of the Fig Tree"
Van Doren, Mark—"Still, Still So"
Wesely, Donald—"A Week of Roses"
Weston, Christine—"The Forest of the Night"
Williams, Tennessee*—"Three Players of a Summer Game"
Wincelberg, Simon—"The Conqueror"

The Best American Short Stories, 1954, and the Yearbook of the American Short Story"

Bush, Geoffrey—"A Great Reckoning in a Little Room"
Clay, Richard—"A Beautiful Night for Orion"
DeMott, Benjamin—"The Sense That in the Scene Delights"
Dorrance, Ward—"A Stop on the Way to Texas"
Doughty, LeGarde S.—"The Firebird"
Enright, Elizabeth—"Apple Seed and Apple Thorn"
Frazee, Steve—"My Brother Down There"
Gold, Ivan—"A Change of Air"
Heath, Priscilla—"Farewell, Sweet Love"
Hebert, Anne—"The House on the Esplanade"
Holwerda, Frank—"Char on Raven's Bench"
Jarrell, Randall—"Gertrude and Sidney"
Jenks, Almet—"No Way Down"
Loveridge, George—"The Latter End"
Patton, Frances Gray—"The Game"
Payne, Robert—"The Red Mountain"
Robinson, Rosanne Smith—"The Mango Tree"
Shaw, Irwin*—"In the French Style"
Stafford, Jean*—"The Shorn Lamb"
Taylor, Kressmann—"The Pale Green Fishes"
Traven, B.—"The Third Guest"
Weston, Christine—"The Man in Gray"
Wolfert, Ira—"The Indomitable Blue"
Yentzen, Vurell—"The Rock"

The Best American Short Stories, 1955, and the Yearbook of the American Short Story
edited by Martha Foley

Bowen, Robert O.—"A Matter of Price"
Cardozo, Nancy—"The Excursionists"
Chaikin, Nancy G.—"Bachelor of Arts"
Cheever, John*—"The Country Husband"
Connell, Evan S., Jr.*—"The Fisherman from Chihuahua"
Coogan, Joe—"The Decline and Fall of Augie Sheean"
Curley, Daniel—"The Day of the Equinox"
Eastlake, William—"Little Joe"
Elliott, George P.*—"Brother Quintillian and Dick the Chemist"
Hyman, Mac—"The Hundredth Centennial"

La Farge, Oliver—"The Resting Place"
Malumud, Bernard—"The Magic Barrel"
Merril, Judith—"Dead Center"
Middleton, Elizabeth H.—"Portrait of My Son as a Young Man"
Mudrick, Marvin—"The Professor and the Poet"
Nemerov, Howard—"Yore"
O'Connor, Flannery*—"A Circle in the Fire"
Shaw, Irwin*—"Tip on a Dead Jockey"
Stegner, Wallace*—"Maiden in a Tower"
Stuart, David—"Bird Man"
Swados, Harvey—"Herman's Day"
Van Doren, Mark—"I Got a Friend"
Vukelich, George—"The Scale Room"
Welty, Eudora*—"Going to Naples"

The Best American Short Stories, 1956, and the Yearbook of the American Short Story *edited by* Martha Foley

Angell, Roger—"In an Early Winter"
Brown, Morris—"The Snow Owl"
Clay, George R.—"We're All Guests"
Coates, Robert M.—"In a Foreign City"
Davis, Wesley Ford—"The Undertow"
Dorrance, Ward—"The Devil on a Hot Afternoon"
Downey, Harris—"The Hobo"
Eastlake, William—"The Quiet Chimneys"
Elliott, George P.*—"Is He Dead?"
Granit, Arthur—"Free the Canaries from Their Cages!"
Housepian, Marjorie—"How Levon Dai Was Surrendered to the Edemuses"
Jackson, Shirley*—"One Ordinary Day, with Peanuts"
Kerouac, Jack—"The Mexican Girl"
LaMar, Nathaniel—"Creole Love Song"
Lyons, Augusta Wallace—"The First Flower"
Molloy, Ruth Branning—"Twenty Below, at the End of a Lane"
O'Connor, Flannery*—"The Artificial Nigger"
Roth, Philip*—"The Contest for Aaron Gold"
Shepley, John—"The Machine"
Weston, Christine—"Four Annas"
Yellen, Samuel—"Reginald Pomfret Skelton"

The Best American Short Stories, 1957, and the Yearbook of the American Short Story *edited by* Martha Foley

Algren, Nelson*—"Beasts of the Wild"
Berriault, Gina*—"Around the Dear Ruin"
Betts, Doris*—"The Proud and Virtuous"
Blassingame, Wyatt—"Man's Courage"
Butler, Frank—"To the Wilderness I Wander"
Clemons, Walter—"The Dark Roots of the Rose"
Connell, Evan S., Jr.*—"Arcturus"
Downey, Harris—"The Song"
Eastlake, William—"The Unhappy Hunting Grounds"
Hale, Nancy*—"A Summer's Long Dream"
Langdon, John—"The Blue Serge Suit"
Mabry, Thomas—"Lula Borrow"
McClintic, Winona—"A Heart of Furious Fancies"
O'Connor, Flannery*—"Greenleaf"
Olsen, Tillie*—"I Stand Here Ironing"
Robinson, Anthony—"The Farlow Express"
Robinson, Rosanne Smith—"The Impossible He"
Smith, John Campbell—"Run, Run away, Brother"
Weigel, Henrietta—"Saturday Is a Poor Man's Port"
Woodward, Gordon—"Escape to the City"

The Best American Short Stories, 1958, and the Yearbook of the American Short Story
***edited by* Martha Foley and David Burnett**

Agee, James*—"The Waiting"
Baldwin, James*—"Sonny's Blues"
Bowles, Paul*—"The Frozen Fields"
Bradbury, Ray*—"The Day It Rained Forever"
Bradshaw, George—"'The Picture Wouldn't Fit in the Stove'"
Chester, Alfred—"As I Was Going up the Stair"
Grau, Shirley Ann*—"Hunter's Home"
Hill, Pati—"Ben"
Macauley, Robie—"Legend of Two Swimmers"
McCord, Jean—"Somewhere out of Nowhere"
Nemerov, Howard—"A Delayed Hearing"
O'Connor, Flannery*—"A View of the Woods"
Ostroff, Anthony—"La Bataille des Fleurs"
Parker, Dorothy*—"The Banquet of Crow"
Robin, Ralph—"Mr. Pruitt"
Scoyk, Bob Ban—"Home from Camp"
Stafford, Jean*—"A Reasonable Facsimile"
Swados, Harvey—"Joe, the Vanishing American"
Thurman, Richard—"Not Another Word"
White, Robin—"House of Many Rooms"
Wright, Richard*—"Big, Black, Good Man"

The Best American Short Stories, 1959, and the Yearbook of the American Short Story
***edited by* Martha Foley and David Burnett**

Berry, John—"Jawaharlal and the Three Cadavers"
Bingham, Sallie—"Winter Term"
Butler, Frank—"Amid a Place of Stone"
Cheever, John*—"The Bella Lingua"
Coates, Robert M.—"Getaway"
Finney, Charles G.—"The Iowan's Curse"
Gass, William H.*—"Mrs. Mean"
Geeslin, Hugh, Jr.—"A Day in the Life of the Boss"
Gold, Herbert*—"Love and Like"
Holwerda, Frank—"In a Tropical Minor Key"
Malamud, Bernard*—"The Last Mohican"
Nemerov, Howard—"A Secret Society"
Rosten, Leo—"The Guy in Ward Four"
Roth, Philip*—"The Conversion of the Jews"
Sayre, Anne—"A Birthday Present"
Swados, Harvey—"The Man in the Toolhouse"
Taylor, Peter*—"Venus, Cupid, Folly, and Time"
Updike, John*—"A Gift from the City"
Williams, Thomas—"The Buck in Trotevale's"
Wilson, Ethel—"The Window"

The Best American Short Stories, 1960, and the Yearbook of the American Short Story
***edited by* Martha Foley and David Burnett**

Babb, Sanora—"The Santa Ana"
Ellin, Stanley—"The Day of the Bullet"
Elliott, George P.*—"Words Words Words"
Fast, Howard—"The Man Who Looked like Jesus"
Gallant, Mavis*—"August"
Garrett, George*—"An Evening Performance"
Graves, John—"The Last Running"
Hall, Lawrence Sargent*—"The Ledge"
Hardwick, Elizabeth—"The Purchase"
MacDonald, Lachlan—"The Hunter"
Malamud, Bernard*—"The Maid's Shoes"
Miller, Arthur—"I Don't Need You Any More"
Nemerov, Howard—"Unbelievable Characters"
Roberts, Phyllis—"Hero"
Roth, Philip*—"Defender of the Faith"
Sturgeon, Theodore*—"The Man Who Lost the Sea"
Swados, Harvey—"A Glance in the Mirror"
Taylor, Peter*—"Who Was Jesse's Friend and Protector?"
Young, Elisabeth Larsh—"Counterclockwise"

The Best American Short Stories, 1961, and the Yearbook of the American Short Story
edited by **Martha Foley and David Burnett**

Baldwin, James*—"This Morning, This Evening, So Soon"
Berry, John—"The Listener"
Chester, Alfred—"Berceuse"
Gass, William H.*—"The Love and Sorrow of Henry Pimber"
Gold, Ivan—"The Nickel Misery of George Washington Carver Brown"
Goyen, William—"A Tale of Inheritance"
Harris, Mark—"The Self-Made Brain Surgeon"
Hurlbut, Kaatje—"The Vestibule"
Jacobs, Theodore—"A Girl for Walter"
Lavin, Mary*—"The Yellow Beret"
Ludwig, Jack—"Confusions"
McKelway, St. Clair—"First Marriage"
Marsh, Willard—"Mexican Hayride"
Olive, Jeannie—"Society"
Olsen, Tillie*—"Tell Me a Riddle"
Peden, William—"Night in Funland"
Pynchon, Thomas*—"Entropy"
Sandmel, Samuel—"The Colleagues of Mr. Chips"
Taylor, Peter*—"Miss Leonora When Last Seen"
White, Ellington—"The Perils of Flight"

The Best American Short Stories, 1962, and the Yearbook of the American Short Story
edited by **Martha Foley and David Burnett**

Arkin, Frieda—"The Light of the Sea"
Choy, Wayson S.—"The Sound of Waves"
Dahlberg, Edward—"Because I Was Flesh"
Deal, Borden—"Antaeus"
Elkin, Stanley*—"Criers and Kibbitzers, Kibbitzers and Criers"
Epstein, Seymour—"Wheat Closed Higher, Cotton Was Mixed"
Garrett, George*—"The Old Army Game"
Gass, William H.*—"The Pedersen Kid"
Gilbert, Sister Mary—"The Model Chapel"
Hall, Donald—"A Day on Ragged"
Karmel-Wolfe, Henia—"The Last Day"
Lavin, Mary*—"In the Middle of the Fields"
Leahy, Jack Thomas—"Hanging Hair"
Maddow, Ben—"'To Hell the Rabbis'"
McKenzie, Miriam—"Déjà vu"
Miller, Arthur—"The Prophecy"
Myers, E. Lucas—"The Vindication of Dr. Nestor"
O'Connor, Flannery*—"Everything That Rises Must Converge"
Selz, Thalia—"The Education of a Queen"
Shaw, Irwin*—"Love on a Dark Street"
Updike, John*—"Pigeon Feathers"

The Best American Short Stories, 1963, and the Yearbook of the American Short Story
edited by **Martha Foley and David Burnett**

Andersen, U. S.—"Turn Ever So Quickly"
Blattner, H. W.—"Sound of a Drunken Drummer"
Carter, John Stewart—"The Keyhole Eye"
Cheever, John*—"A Vision of the World"
Dawkins, Cecil—"A Simple Case"
Dickerson, George—"Chico"
Dikeman, May—"The Sound of Young Laughter"
Elkin, Stanley*—"I Look out for Ed Wolfe"
Godfrey, Dave—"Newfoundland Night"
Gordon, William J. J.—"The Pures"
Hermann, John—"Aunt Mary"
Loeser, Katinka—"Beggarman, Rich Man, or Thief"
McKelway, St. Clair—"The Fireflies"
Molinaro, Ursule—"The Insufficient Rope"
Oates, Joyce Carol*—"The Fine White Mist of Winter"
Phelan, R. C.—"Birds, Clouds, Frogs"
Richler, Mordecai*—"Some Grist for Mervyn's Mill"

Saroyan, William*—"What a World, Said the Bicycle Rider"
Sassoon, Babette—"The Betrayal"
Shaw, Irwin*—"Noises in the City"
Taylor, Peter*—"At the Drugstore"
Tucci, Niccolò—"The Desert in the Oasis"
West, Jessamyn*—"The Picnickers"

The Best American Short Stories, 1964, and the Yearbook of the American Short Story
edited by Martha Foley and David Burnett

Arkin, Frieda—"The Broomstick on the Porch"
Brown, Richard G.—"Mr. Iscariot"
Carter, John Stewart—"To a Tenor Dying Old"
Curley, Daniel—"A Story of Love, Etc."
Dikeman, May—"The Woman Across the Street"
Eastlake, William—"A Long Day's Dying"
Goyen, William—"Figure over the Town"
Horgan, Paul—"Black Snowflakes"
Humphrey, William*—"The Pump"
Jackson, Shirley*—"Birthday Party"
Konecky, Edith—"The Power"
Lolos, Kimon—"Mule No. 095"
Malamud, Bernard*—"The German Refugee"
McCullers, Carson*—"Sucker"
Moriconi, Virginia—"Simple Arithmetic"
Oates, Joyce Carol*—"Upon the Sweeping Flood"
Price, Reynolds*—"The Names and Faces of Heroes"
Randal, Vera—"Waiting for Jim"
Swados, Harvey—"A Story for Teddy"
Warren, Robert Penn*—"Have You Seen Sukie?"

The Best American Short Stories, 1965, and the Yearbook of the American Short Story
edited by Martha Foley

Amster, L. J.—"Center of Gravity"
De Paola, Daniel—"The Returning"
Elkin, Stanley*—"The Transient"
Gilchrist, Jack—"Opening Day"
Groshong, James W.—"The Gesture"
Hamer, Martin J.—"Sarah"
Howard, Maureen—"Sherry"
Hutter, Donald—"A Family Man"
Karmel-Wolfe, Henia—"The Month of His Birthday"
Lavin, Mary*—"Heart of Gold"
Lynds, Dennis—"A Blue Blonde in the Sky over Pennsylvania"
Morton, Frederic—"The Guest"
Neugeboren, Jay—"The Application"
Oates, Joyce Carol*—"First Views of the Enemy"
Robinson, Leonard Wallace—"The Practice of an Art"
Singer, Isaac Bashevis*—"A Sacrifice"
Somerlott, Robert—"Eskimo Pies"
Spencer, Elizabeth*—"The Visit"
Stafford, Jean*—"The Tea Time of Stouthearted Ladies"
Stein, Gerald—"For I Have Wept"
Taylor, Peter*—"There"
Yu-Hwa, Lee—"The Last Rite"

The Best American Short Stories, 1966, and the Yearbook of the American Short Story
edited by Martha Foley and David Burnett

Cady, Jack—"The Burning"
Dickerson, George—"A Mussel Named Ecclesiastes"
Downey, Harris—"The Vicar-General and the Wide Night"
Ely, David—"The Academy"
Faulkner, William*—"Mr. Acarius"
Grau, Shirley Ann*—"The Beach Party"
Hedin, Mary—"Places We Lost"
Hood, Hugh—"Getting to Williamstown"

Jackson, Shirley*—"The Bus"
Jacobsen, Josephine—"On the Island"
Kreisel, Henry—"The Broken Globe"
Lavin, Mary*—"One Summer"
Leviant, Curt—"Mourning Call"
Maxwell, William—"Further Tales About Men and Women"
O'Connor, Flannery*—"Parker's Back"
Rothberg, Abraham—"Pluto Is the Furthest Planet"
Terry, Walter S.—"The Bottomless Well"
Wakefield, Dan—"Autumn Full of Apples"
Whitehill, Joseph—"One Night for Several Samurai"
Wilner, Herbert—"Dovisch in the Wilderness"

The Best American Short Stories, 1967, and the Yearbook of the American Short Story
edited by Martha Foley and David Burnett

Ayer, Ethan—"The Promise of Heat"
Blake, George—"A Place Not on the Map"
Boyle, Kay*—"The Wild Horses"
Carver, Raymond*—"Will You Please Be Quiet, Please?"
Francis, H. E.—"One of the Boys"
Harris, MacDonald—"Trepleff"
Hazel, Robert—"White Anglo-Saxon Protestant"
Hunt, Hugh Allyn—"Acme Rooms and Sweet Marjorie Russell"
Lee, Lawrence—"The Heroic Journey"
Miller, Arthur—"Search for a Future"
Moore, Brian—"The Apartment Hunter"
Morgan, Berry—"Andrew"
Oates, Joyce Carol*—"Where Are You Going, Where Have You Been?"
Radcliffe, Donald—"Song of the Simidor"
Roth, Henry—"The Surveyor"
Rubin, David—"Longing for America"
Stuart, Jesse*—"The Accident"
Sturm, Carol—"The Kid Who Fractioned"
Travers, Robert—"The Big Brown Trout"
Wiser, William—"House of the Blues"

The Best American Short Stories, 1968, and the Yearbook of the American Short Story
edited by Martha Foley and David Burnett

Baldwin, James*—"Tell Me How Long the Train's Been Gone"
Bruce, Janet—"Dried Rose Petals in a Silver Bowl"
Deck, John—"Greased Samba"
Farrell, James T.*—"An American Student in Paris"
Freitag, George H.—"An Old Man and His Hat"
Gardner, Herb—"Who Is Harry Kellerman and Why Is He Saying Those Terrible Things About Me?"
Gass, William H.*—"In the Heart of the Heart of the Country"
Gavell, Mary Ladd—"The Rotifer"
Gropman, Donald—"The Heart of This or That Man"
Harrison, William—"The Snooker Shark"
Higgins, Judith—"The Only People"
Hudson, Helen—"The Tenant"
Litwak, Leo E.—"In Shock"
McKenna, Richard—"The Sons of Martha"
Moseley, William—"The Preacher and Margery Scott"
Ostrow, Joanna—"Celtic Twilight"
Parker, Nancy Huddleston—"Early Morning, Lonely Ride"
Phillips, John—"Bleat Blodgette"
Spingarn, Lawrence P.—"The Ambassador"
Weathers, Winston—"The Games That We Played"

The Best American Short Stories, 1969, and the Yearbook of the American Short Story
edited by Martha Foley and David Burnett

Brennan, Maeve—"The Eldest Child"
Cady, Jack—"Play Like I'm Sherrif"
Costello, Mark—"Murphy's Xmas"
Gerald, John Bart—"Walking Wounded"

Hughes, Mary Gray—"The Foreigner in the Blood"
Klein, Norma—"The Boy in the Green Hat"
Lavin, Mary*—"Happiness"
McGregor, Matthew W.—"Porkchops with Whiskey and Ice Cream"
MacLeod, Alistair—"The Boat"
McPherson, James Alan*—"Gold Coast"
Madden, David—"The Day the Flowers Came"
Malamud, Bernard*—"Pictures of Fidelman"
Milton, John R.—"The Inheritance of Emmy One Horse"
Oates, Joyce Carol*—"By the River"
Pansing, Nancy Pelletier—"The Visitation"
Plath, Sylvia*—"Johnny Panic and the Bible of Dreams"
Rugel, Miriam—"Paper Poppy"
Shipley, Margaret—"The Tea Bowl of Ninsei Nomura"
Singer, Isaac Bashevis*—"The Colony"
Winslow, Joyce Madelon—"Benjamen Burning"

The Best American Short Stories, 1970, and the Yearbook of the American Short Story
***edited by* Martha Foley and David Burnett**

Cady, Jack—"With No Breeze"
Cleaver, Eldridge—"The Flashlight"
Coover, Robert*—"The Magic Poker"
Davis, Olivia—"The Other Child"
Dubus, Andre*—"If They Knew Yvonne"
Gerald, John Bart—"Blood Letting"
Gillespie, Alfred—"Tonight at Nine Thirty-six"
Leffland, Ella—"The Forest"
Matthews, Jack—"Another Story"
Maxwell, William—"The Gardens of Mont-Saint-Michel"
Morris, Wright*—"Green Grass, Blue Sky, White House"
Oates, Joyce Carol*—"How I Contemplated the World from the Detroit House of Correction and Began My Life over Again"
Olsen, Paul—"The Flag Is Down"
Ozick, Cynthia*—"Yiddish in America"
Siegel, Jules—"In the Land of the Morning Calm, Déjà Vu"
Singer, Isaac Bashevis*—"The Key"
Stone, Robert*—"Porque no tiene, porque le falta"
Taylor, Peter*—"Daphne's Lover"
Weisbrod, Rosine—"The Ninth Cold Day"

The Best American Short Stories, 1971, and the Yearbook of the American Short Story
***edited by* Martha Foley and David Burnett**

Banks, Russell*—"With Che in New Hampshire"
Bennett, Hal—"Dotson Gerber Resurrected"
Blake, James—"The Widow, Bereft"
Cady, Jack—"I Take Care of Things"
Canzoneri, Robert—"Barbed Wire"
Drake, Albert—"The Chicken Which Became a Rat"
Eastlake, William—"The Dancing Boy"
Harvor, Beth—"Pain Was My Portion"
Madden, David—"No Trace"
Mitchell, Don—"Diesel"
Montgomery, Marion—"The Decline and Fall of Officer Fergerson"
Morris, Wright*—"Magic"
O'Connor, Philip F.—"The Gift Bearer"
Olsen, Tillie*—"Requa I"
Prashker, Ivan—"Shirt Talk"
Rush, Norman—"In Late Youth"
Santiago, Danny—"The Somebody"
Strong, Jonathan—"Xavier Fereira's Unfinished Book: Chapter One"
Tushnet, Leonard—"The Klausners"
Valgardson, W. D.—"Bloodflowers"
Woiwode, Larry*—"The Suitor"

The Best American Short Stories, 1972, and the Yearbook of the American Short Story
***edited by* Martha Foley**

Beal, M. F.—"Gold"
Brautigan, Richard*—"The World War I Los Angeles Airplane"
Cherry, Kelly—"Convenant"
Gold, Herbert*—"A Death on the East Side"
Greenberg, Joanne—"The Supremacy of the Hunza"
Heath, Mary—"The Breadman"
Holmes, Edward M.—"Drums Again"
Hughes, Mary Gray—"The Judge"
Jones, Ann—"In Black and White"
Just, Ward—"Three Washington Stories"
Kalechofsky, Roberta—"His Day Out"
Kavaler, Rebecca—"The Further Adventures of Brunhild"
L'Heureux, John*—"Fox and Swan"
Malony, Ralph—"Intimacy"
Mandell, Marvin—"The Aesculapians"
Ozick, Cynthia*—"The Dock-Witch"
Porter, Joe Ashby—"The Vacation"
Street, Penelope—"The Magic Apple"
Warren, Robert Penn*—"Meet Me in the Green Glen"
Weesner, Theodore—"Stealing Cars"
Yglesias, José—"The Guns in the Closet"

The Best American Short Stories, 1973, the Yearbook of the American Short Story
***edited by* Martha Foley**

Barthelme, Donald*—"A City of Churches"
Bromell, Henry—"The Slightest Distance"
Cheever, John*—"The Jewels of the Cabots"
Clayton, John J.—"Cambridge Is Sinking!"
Corrington, John William—"Old Men Dream Dreams, Young Men See Visions"
Davenport, Guy*—"Robot"
Eastlake, William—"The Death of Sun"
Greenberg, Alvin—"The Real Meaning of the Faust Legend"
Hayden, Julie—"In the Words Of"
Higgins, George V.—"The Habits of Animals: The Progress of the Seasons"
Just, Ward—"Burns"
Kenary, James S.—"Going Home"
Knight, Wallace E.—"The Way We Went"
Lardas, Konstantinos—"The Broken Wings"
McPherson, James Alan*—"The Silver Bullet"
Malamud, Bernard*—"God's Wrath"
Oates, Joyce Carol*—"Silkie"
Plath, Sylvia*—"Mothers"
Sandberg-Diment, Erik—"Come away, Oh Human Child"
Shetzline, David—"Country of the Painted Freaks"
Williams, Tennessee*—"Happy August the Tenth"

The Best American Short Stories, 1974, and the Yearbook of the American Short Story
***edited by* Martha Foley**

Boyer, Agnes—"The Deserter"
Bumpus, Jerry—"Beginnings"
Clark, Eleanor—"A Summer in Puerto Rico"
Esslinger-Carr, Pat M.—"The Party"
Horne, Lewis B.—"Mansion, Magic, and Miracle"
Ignatow, Rose Graubart—"Down the American River"
Kumin, Maxine—"Opening the Door on Sixty-second Street"
Levin, Mary—"Tom"
L'Heureux, John*—"A Family Affair"
Lopate, Phillip—"The Chamber Music Evening"
Minot, Stephen—"The Tide and Isaac Bates"
Mitchell, Beverly—"Letter from Sakaye"
Rothschild, Michael—"Dog in the Manger"
Sandberg, Peter L.—"Calloway's Climb"
Saroyan, William*—"Isn't Today the Day?"
Schneider, Philip H.—"The Gray"

Targan, Barry*—"Old Vemish"
Updike, John*—"Son"
Vivante, Arturo—"Honeymoon"
Walker, Alice*—"The Revenge of Hannah Kemhuff"

The Best American Short Stories, 1975, and the Yearbook of the American Short Story
***edited by* Martha Foley**

Banks, Russell*—"The Lie"
Barthelme, Donald*—"The School"
Brown, Rosellen—"How to Win"
Bumpus, Jerry—"Desert Matinee"
Busch, Frederick—"Bambi Meets the Furies"
Chaikin, Nancy G.—"Waiting for Astronauts"
Clearman, Mary—"Paths unto the Dead"
De Jenkins, Lyll Becerra—"Tyranny"
Dubus, Andre*—"Cadence"
Ford, Jesse Hill—"Big Boy"
Hoffman, William—"The Spirit in Me"
Hunter, Evan—"The Analyst"
Kaser, Paul—"How Jerem Came Home"
MacLeod, Alistair—"The Lost Salt Gift of Blood"
McNamara, Eugene—"The Howard Parker Montcrief Hoax"
Matthews, Jack—"The Burial"
Price, Reynolds*—"Night and Day at Panacea"
Rothberg, Abraham—"Polonaise"
Silko, Leslie Marmon*—"Lullaby"
Targan, Barry*—"The Who Lived"
Yglesias, José—"The American Sickness"

The Best American Short Stories, 1976, and the Yearbook of the American Short Story
***edited by* Martha Foley**

Adams, Alice*—"Roses, Rhododendron"
Battin, M. Pabst—"Terminal Procedure"
Briskin, Mae Seidman—"The Boy Who Was Astrid's Mother"
Chaikin, Nancy G.—"Beautiful, Helpless Animals"
Corrington, John William—"The Actes and Documents"
Francis, H. E.—"A Chronicle of Love"
Hagge, John—"Pontius Pilate"
Just, Ward—"Dietz at War"
McCluskey, John—"John Henry's Home"
Minot, Steven—"Grubbing for Roots"
Nelson, Kent—"Looking into Nothing"
Ozick, Cynthia*—"A Mercenary"
Price, Reynolds*—"Broad Day"
Rothschild, Michael—"Wondermonger"
Targan, Barry*—"Surviving Adverse Seasons"
Taylor, Peter*—"The Hand of Emmagene"
Updike, John*—"The Man Who Loved Extinct Mammals"

The Best American Short Stories, 1977, and the Yearbook of the American Short Story
***edited by* Martha Foley**

Busch, Frederick—"The Trouble with Being Food"
Caldwell, Price—"Tarzan Meets the Department Head"
Cheever, John*—"Falconer"
Copeland, Ann—"At Peace"
Corrington, John William—"Pleadings"
Damon, Philip—"Growing up in No Time"
Epstein, Leslie—"The Steinway Quintet"
Garber, Eugene K.—"The Lover"
Hampl, Patricia—"Look at a Teacup"
Kerr, Baine—"Rider"
Matthews, Jack—"A Questionnaire for Rudolph Gordon"
Minot, Stephen—"A Passion for History"
Newman, Charles—"The Woman Who Thought like a Man"

Oates, Joyce Carol*—"Gay"
O'Brien, Tim*—"Going After Cacciato"
Robbins, Tom—"The Chink and the Clock People"
Saroyan, William*—"A Fresno Fable"
Sayles, John*—"Breed"
Tyler, Anne*—"Your Place Is Empty"
Wilson, William S.—"Anthropology: What Is Lost in Rotation"

The Best American Short Stories, 1978: Selected from U.S. and Canadian Magazines, including the Yearbook of the American Short Story
***edited by* Ted Solotaroff, with Shannon Ravenel**

Baumbach, Jonathan—"The Return of Service"
Bowles, Jane*—"Two Scenes"
Brodky, Harold—"Verona: A Young Woman Speaks"
Cullinan, Elizabeth—"A Good Loser"
Elkin, Stanley*—"The Conventional Wisdom"
Epstein, Leslie—"Skaters on Wood"
Gardner, John*—"Redemption"
Helprin, Mark*—"The Schreuderspitze"
Kaplan, James—"In Miami, Last Winter"
McCarthy, Tim—"The Windmill Man"
McEwan, Ian*—"Psychopolis"
Marsh, Peter—"By the Yellow Lake"
Oates, Joyce Carol*—"The Translation"
Petesch, Natalie L. M.—"Main Street Morning"
Rishel, Mary Ann Malinchak—"Staus"
Schott, Max—"Murphy Jones: Pearblossom, California"
Schwartz, Lynne Sharon*—"Rough Strife"
Sintetos, L. Hluchan—"Telling the Bees"
Sorrells, Robert T.—"The Blacktop Champion of Ickey Honey"
Sorrentino, Gilbert—"Decades"
Taylor, Peter*—"In the Miro District"
Williams, Joy*—"Bromeliads"

The Best American Short Stories, 1979: Selected from U.S. and Canadian Magazines
***edited by* Joyce Carol Oates, with Shannon Ravenel**

Barthelme, Donald*—"The New Music"
Bellow, Saul*—"A Silver Dish"
Brown, Rosellen—"The Wedding Week"
Bowles, Paul*—"The Eye"
Coffin, Lyn—"Falling off the Scaffold"
Hedin, Mary—"The Middle Place"
Hurlbut, Kaatje—"A Short Walk into Afternoon"
Kumin, Maxine—"The Missing Person"
LaSalle, Peter—"Some Manhattan in New England"
McLaughlin, Ruth—"Seasons"
Malamud, Bernard*—"Home Is the Hero"
Munro, Alice*—"Spelling"
O'Connor, Flannery*—"An Exile in the East"
Phillips, Jayne Anne*—"Something That Happened"
Rubin, Louis D., Jr.—"Finisterre"
Sanford, Annette—"Trip in a Summer Dress"
Schwartz, Lynne Sharon*—"Plaisir D'amour"
Singer, Isaac Bashevis*—"A Party in Miami Beach"
Styron, William—"Shadrach"
Tennenbaum, Silvia—"A Lingering Death"
Thompson, Jean—"Paper Covers Rock"
Virgo, Sean—"Home and Native Land"
Wilner, Herbert—"The Quarterback Speaks to His God"
Wilson, Robley, Jr.—"Living Alone"
Yngve, Rolf—"The Quail"

The Best American Short Stories, 1980: Selected from U.S. and Canadian Magazines
***edited by* Stanley Elkin, with Shannon Ravenel**

Barthelme, Donald*—"The Emerald"
Busch, Frederick—"Long Calls"
Evanier, David—"The One-Star Jew"
Gallant, Mavis*—"The Remission; Speck's Idea"
Gass, William H.*—"The Old Folks"
Gertler, T.—"In Case of Survival"

Hardwick, Elizabeth—"The Faithful"
Heinemann, Larry—"The First Clean Fact"
Henderson, Robert—"Into the Wind"
Johnson, Curt—"Lemon Tree"
Paley, Grace*—"Friends"
Robison, James—"Home"
Rooke, Leon—"Mama Tuddi Done Over"
Sayles, John*—"At the Anarchist's Convention"
Singer, Isaac Bashevis*—"The Safe Deposit"
Stern, Richard*—"Dr. Cahn's Visit"
Targan, Barry*—"The Rags of Time"
Taylor, Peter*—"The Old Forest"
Updike, John*—"Gesturing"
Waksler, Norman—"Markowitz and the Gypsies"
Weaver, Gordon—"Hog's Heart"

The Best American Short Stories, 1981: Selected from U.S. and Canadian Magazines
***edited by* Hortense Calisher, with Shannon Ravenel**

Abish, Walter—"The Idea of Switzerland"
Apple, Max*—"Small Island Republics"
Beattie, Ann*—"Winter: 1978"
Coover, Robert*—"A Working Day"
Dethier, Vincent G.—"The Moth and the Primrose"
Dubus, Andre*—"The Winter Father"
Gallant, Mavis*—"The Assembly"
Hardwick, Elizabeth—"The Bookseller"
McElroy, Joseph—"The Future"
McGrath, Elizabeth—"Fogbound in Avalon"
Mason, Bobbie Ann*—"Shiloh"
Moseley, Amelia—"The Mountains Where Cithaeron Is"
Munro, Alice*—"Wood"
Oates, Joyce Carol*—"Presque Isle"
Ozick, Cynthia*—"The Shawl"
Rubin, Louis D., Jr.—"The St. Anthony Chorale"
Stern, Richard*—"Wissler Remembers"
Tallent, Elizabeth*—"Ice"
Updike, John*—"Still of Some Use"
Woiwode, Larry*—"Change"

The Best American Short Stories, 1982: Selected from U.S. and Canadian Magazines
***edited by* John Gardner, with Shannon Ravenel**

Baker, Nicholson—"K. 590"
Baxter, Charles*—"Harmony of the World"
Carver, Raymond*—"Cathedral"
Coggeshall, Rosanne—"Lamb Says"
Ferry, James—"Dancing Ducks and Talking Anus"
Freeman, Anne Hobson—"The Girl Who Was No Kin to the Marshalls"
Greenberg, Alvin—"The Power of Language Is Such That Even a Single Word Taken Truly to Heart Can Change Everything"
Gupta, Roberta—"The Cafe de Paris"
Hauptmann, William—"Good Rockin' Tonight"
Higgins, Joanna—"The Courtship of Widow Sobcek"
Johnson, Charles*—"Exchange Value"
Licht, Fred—"Shelter the Pilgrim"
McLaughlin, Lissa—"The Continental Heart"
MacMillan, Ian—"Proud Monster: Sketches"
Milton, Edith—"Coming Over"
Oates, Joyce Carol*—"Theft"
Renwick, Joyce—"The Dolphin Story"
Robison, Mary*—"Coach"
Rosner, Anne F.—"Prize Tomatoes"
Smith, R. E.—"The Gift Horse's Mouth"

The Best American Short Stories, 1983: Selected from U.S. and Canadian Magazines
***edited by* Anne Tyler, with Shannon Ravenel**

Barich, Bill—"Hard to be Good"
Bly, Carol—"The Dignity of Life"
Bond, James—"A Change of Season"
Carver, Raymond*—"Where I'm Calling From"

Chute, Carolyn—"'Ollie, Oh . . .'"
Colwin, Laurie—"My Mistress"
Epstein, Joseph—"The Count and the Princess"
Erdrich, Louise*—"Scales"
Le Guin, Ursula K.*—"The Professor's Houses; Sur"
Mason, Bobbie Ann*—"Graveyard Day"
Morris, Wright*—"Victrola"
Schumacher, Julie—"Reunion"
Stark, Sharon Sheehe—"Best Quality Glass Company, New York"
Taylor, Robert—"Colorado"
Thurm, Marian—"Starlight"
Updike, John*—"Deaths of Distant Friends"
Vanderhaeghe, Guy*—"Reunion"
Vreuls, Diane—"Beebee"
Woiwode, Larry*—"Firstborn"

The Best American Short Stories, 1984: Selected from U.S. and Canadian Magazines
***edited by* John Updike, with Shannon Ravenel (partial contents)**

Abbott, Lee K.*—"The Final Proof of Fate and Circumstance"
Bell, Madison Smartt*—"The Naked Lady"
Benedict, Dianne—"Unknown Feathers"
Bowles, Paul*—"In the Red Room"
Brown, Mary Ward—"The Cure"
DeMarinis, Rick—"Gent"
Dubus, Andre*—"A Father's Story"
Gallant, Mavis*—"Lena"
Hood, Mary—"Inexorable Progress"
Justice, Donald—"The Artificial Moonlight"
Kirk, Stephen—"Morrison's Reaction"
Minot, Susan*—"Thorofare"
Morris, Wright*—"Glimpse into Another Country"
Oates, Joyce Carol*—"Nairobi"
Ozick, Cynthia*—"Rosa"
Pei, Lowry—"The Cold Room"
Penner, Jonathan—"Things to Be Thrown Away"
Rush, Norman—"Bruns"
Salter, James—"Foreign Shores"
Schinto, Jeanne—"Caddie's Day"

The Best American Short Stories, 1985: Selected from U.S. and Canadian Magazines
***edited by* Gail Godwin, with Shannon Ravenel**

Banks, Russell*—"Sarah Cole: A Type of Love Story"
Bishop, Michael—"Dogs' Lives"
Canin, Ethan*—"Emperor of the Air"
Doctorow, E. L.—"The Leather Man"
Edwards, Margaret—"Roses"
Flythe, Starkey—"Walking, Walking"
Francis, H. E.—"The Sudden Trees"
Jafek, Bev—"You've Come a Long Way, Mickey Mouse"
L'Heureux, John*—"Clothing"
Meinke, Peter—"The Piano Tuner"
Morris, Wright*—"Fellow-Creatures"
Mukherjee, Bharati*—"Angela"
Nugent, Beth—"City of Boys"
Oates, Joyce Carol*—"Raven's Wing"
Rush, Norman—"Instruments of Seduction"
Sandor, Marjorie—"The Gittel"
Seabrooke, Deborah—"Secrets"
Smiley, Jane*—"Lily"
Stark, Sharon Sheehe—"The Johnstown Polka"
Williams, Joy*—"The Skater"

The Best American Short Stories, 1986: Selected from U.S. and Canadian Magazines
***edited by* Raymond Carver, with Shannon Ravenel**

Barthelme, Donald*—"Basil from Her Garden"
Baxter, Charles*—"Gryphon"
Beattie, Ann*—"Janus"
Burke, James Lee—"The Convict"

Canin, Ethan*—"Star Food"
Conroy, Frank*—"Gossip"
Ford, Richard*—"Communist"
Gallagher, Tess—"Bad Company"
Hempel, Amy*—"Today Will Be a Quiet Day"
Kaplan, David Michael*—"Doe Season"
Lipsky, David—"Three Thousand Dollars"
McGuane, Thomas—"Sportsmen"
McIlroy, Christopher—"All My Relations"
Munro, Alice*—"Monsieur Les Deux Chapeaux"
Neely, Jessica—"Skin Angels"
Nelson, Kent—"Invisible Life"
Paley, Grace*—"Telling"
Simpson, Mona*—"Lawns"
Williams, Joy*—"Health"
Wolff, Tobias*—"The Rich Brother"

The Best American Short Stories, 1987: Selected from U.S. and Canadian Magazines
***edited by* Ann Beattie, with Shannon Ravenel**

Abbott, Lee K.*—"Dreams of Distant Lives"
Baxter, Charles*—"How I Found My Brother"
Bell, Madison Smartt*—"Lie Detector"
Carlson, Ron—"Milk"
Carver, Raymond*—"Boxes"
Gallant, Mavis*—"Kingdom Come"
Haruf, Kent—"Private Debts/Public Holdings"
Lombreglia, Ralph—"Men Under Water"
Miller, Sue*—"Lover of Women"
Mukherjee, Bharati*—"Tenant"
Munro, Alice*—"Circle of Prayer"
Nova, Craig—"Prince"
O'Brien, Tim*—"Things They Carried"
Sontag, Susan*—"Way We Live Now"
Stern, Daniel—"Interpretation of Dreams by Sigmund Freud: A Story"
Tallent, Elizabeth*—"Favor"
Taylor, Robert—"Lady of Spain"
Updike, John*—"Afterlife"
Williams, Joy*—"Blue Men"
Wolff, Tobias*—"Other Miller"

The Best American Short Stories, 1988: Selected from U.S. and Canadian Magazines
***edited by* Mark Helprin, with Shannon Ravenel**

Bass, Rick*—"Cats and Students, Bubbles and Abysses"
Bausch, Richard*—"Police Dreams"
Blythe, Will—"Taming Power of the Small"
Carver, Raymond*—"Errand"
Currey, Richard—"Waiting for Trains"
Erdrich, Louise*—"Snares"
Gallant, Mavis*—"Dede"
Godshalk, C. S.—"Wonderland"
Goldman, E. S.—"Way to the Dump"
Honig, Lucy—"No Friends, All Strangers"
Jen, Gish—"Water-Faucet Vision"
Johnson, Hilding—"Victoria"
Kiteley, Brian—"Still Life with Insects"
Lacy, Robert—"Natural Father"
Lombreglia, Ralph—"Inn Essence"
Milton, Edith—"Entrechat"
Sandor, Marjorie—"Still Life"
Stone, Robert*—"Helping"
Taylor-Hall, Mary Ann—"Banana Boats"
Wolff, Tobias*—"Smorgasbord"

The Best American Short Stories, 1989: Selected from U.S. and Canadian Magazines
***edited by* Margaret Atwood, with Shannon Ravenel**

Baxter, Charles*—"Fenstad's Mother"
Bell, Madison Smartt*—"Customs of the Country"
Boswell, Robert—"Living to Be a Hundred"
Boyd, Blanche McCrary—"The Black Hand Girl"
Brown, Larry*—"Kubuku Riders (This Is It)"
Busch, Frederick—"Ralph the Duck"

Cunningham, Michael—"White Angel"
DeMarinis, Rick—"The Flowers of Boredom"
Doerr, Harriet*—"Edie: A Life"
Gallant, Mavis*—"The Concert Party"
Glover, Douglas—"Why I Decided to Kill Myself and Other Jokes"
Gowdy, Barbara—"Disneyland"
Hogan, Linda—"Aunt Moon's Young Man"
Louie, David Wong—"Displacement"
Mukherjee, Bharati*—"The Management of Grief"
Munro, Alice*—"Meneseteung"
Phillips, Dale Ray—"What Men Love For"
Richard, Mark—"Strays"
Robinson, Arthur—"The Boy on the Train"
Sharif, M. T.—"The Letter Writer"

The Best American Short Stories, 1990: Selected from U.S. and Canadian Magazines
***edited by* Richard Ford, with Shannon Ravenel**

Allen, Edward—"River of Toys"
Bausch, Richard*—"The Fireman's Wife"
Bausch, Richard*—"A Kind of Simple, Happy Grace"
Bell, Madison Smartt*—"Finding Natasha"
Godshalk, C. S.—"The Wizard"
Henley, Patricia—"The Secret of Cartwheels"
Houston, Pam*—"How to Talk to a Hunter"
Hustvedt, Siri—"Mr. Morning"
Johnson, Denis*—"Car-Crash While Hitchhiking"
McFarland, Dennis—"Nothing to Ask For"
Millhauser, Steven*—"Eisenheim the Illusionist"
Moore, Lorrie*—"You're Ugly, Too"
Munro, Alice*—"Differently"
Munro, Alice*—"Wigtime"
Powell, Padgett—"Typical"
Segal, Lore—"The Reverse Bug"
Tallent, Elizabeth*—"Prowler"
Tilghman, Christopher*—"In a Father's Place"
Wickersham, Joan—"Commuter Marriage"
Williams, Joy*—"The Little Winter"

The Best American Short Stories, 1991: Selected from U.S. and Canadian Magazines
***edited by* Alice Adams, with Katrina Kenison**

Bass, Rick*—"Legend of Pig-Eye"
Baxter, Charles*—"The Disappeared"
Bloom, Amy—"Love Is Not a Pie"
Braverman, Kate—"Tall Tales from the Mekong Delta"
Butler, Robert Olen*—"The Trip Back"
D'Ambrosio, Charles, Jr.—"The Point"
Dillon, Millicent—"Oil and Water"
Doerr, Harriet*—"Another Short Day in La Luz"
Eisenberg, Deborah—"The Custodian"
Gordon, Mary*—"Separation"
Graver, Elizabeth—"The Body Shop"
Hustvedt, Siri—"Houdini"
Iossel, Mikhail—"Bologoye"
Jauss, David—"Glossolalia"
Michaels, Leonard*—"Viva la Tropicana"
Moore, Lorrie*—"Willing"
Munro, Alice*—"Friend of My Youth"
Oates, Joyce Carol*—"American, Abroad"
Prose, Francine*—"Dog Stories"
Updike, John*—"A Sansstone Farmhouse"

The Best American Short Stories, 1992: Selected from U.S. and Canadian Magazines
***edited by* Alice Adams, with Katrina Kenison**

Adams, Alice*—"The Last Lovely City"
Bass, Rick*—"Days of Heaven"
Beller, Thomas—"A Different Kind of Imperfection"
Bloom, Amy—"Silver Water"
Butler, Robert Olen*—"A Good Scent from a Strange Mountain"

Gallant, Mavis*—"Across the Bridge"
Gautreaux, Tim*—"Same Place, Same Things"
Johnson, Denis*—"Emergency"
Jones, Thom—"The Pugilist at Rest"
Klimasewiski, Marshall N.—"JunHee"
Moore, Lorrie*—"Community Life"
Munro, Alice*—"Carried Away"
Oates, Joyce Carol*—"Is Laughter Contagious?"
Price, Reynolds*—"The Fare to the Moon"
Smith, Annick—"It's Come to This"
Tilghman, Christopher*—"The Way People Run"
Wallace, David Foster—"Forever Overhead"
Wheeler, Kate—"Under the Roof"
Winthrop, Elizabeth—"The Golden Darters"
Wolff, Tobias*—"Firelight"

The Best American Short Stories, 1993: Selected from U.S. and Canadian Magazines
***edited by* Louise Erdrich, with Katrina Kenison**

Berry, Wendell—"Pray Without Ceasing"
Dixon, Stephen*—"Man, Woman, and Boy"
Early, Tony—"Charlotte"
Edwards, Kim—"Gold"
Ellison, Harlan*—"The Man Who Rowed Christopher Columbus Ashore"
Fulton, Alice—"Queen Wintergreen"
Gaitskill, Mary*—"The Girl on the Plane"
Gordon, Mary*—"The Important Houses"
Johnson, Diane—"Great Barrier Reef"
Jones, Thom—"I Want to Live!"
Lee, Andrea—"Winter Barley"
Moore, Lorrie*—"Terrific Mother"
Munro, Alice*—"A Real Life"
Nelson, Antonya—"Naked Ladies"
Peery, Janet—"What the Thunder Said"
Power, Susan—"Red Moccasins"
Scott, Joanna—"Concerning Mold upon the Skin, Etc."
Shapiro, Jane—"Poltergeists"
Updike, John*—"Playing with Dynamite"
Woiwode, Larry*—"Silent Passengers"

The Best American Short Stories, 1994: Selected from U.S. and Canadian Magazines
***edited by* Tobias Wolff, with Katrina Kenison**

Alexie, Sherman*—"This Is What It Means to Say Phoenix, Arizona"
Anshaw, Carol—"Hammam"
Butler, Robert Olen*—"Salem"
Chang, Lan Samantha*—"Pipa's Story"
Cummins, Ann—"Where I Work"
Dark, Alice Elliott—"In the Gloaming"
Dybek, Stuart*—"We Didn't"
Earley, Tony—"The Prophet from Jupiter"
Ferrell, Carolyn—"Proper Library"
Gardiner, John Rolfe—"The Voyage Out"
Gates, David*—"The Mail Lady"
Hannah, Barry*—"Nicodemus Bluff"
Jones, Thom—"Cold Snap"
Keeble, John—"The Chasm"
Krusoe, Nancy—"Landscape and Dream"
Louis, Laura Glen—"Fur"
Offutt, Chris*—"Melungeons"
Robinson, Roxana—"Mr. Sumarsono"
Shepard, Jim—"Batting Against Castro"
Tilghman, Christopher*—"Things Left Undone"
Wilson, Jonathan—"From Shanghai"

The Best American Short Stories, 1995: Selected from U.S. and Canadian Magazines
***edited by* Jane Smiley, with Katrina Kenison**

Barrett, Andrea*—"The Behavior of the Hawkweeds"
Braverman, Kate—"Pagan Night"
Cornell, Jennifer C.—"Undertow"
Cozine, Andrew—"Hand Jive"
Davies, Peter Ho*—"The Ugliest House in the World"

Delaney, Edward J.—"The Drownings"
DeLillo, Don—"The Angel Esmeralda"
Doybyns, Stephen—"So I Guess You Know What I Told Him"
Falco, Edward—"The Artist"
Garland, Max—"Chiromancy"
Gilchrist, Ellen—"The Stucco House"
Gordon, Jaimy—"A Night's Work"
Jen, Gish—"Birthmates"
Jones, Thom—"Way down Deep in the Jungle"
Kincaid, Jamaica*—"Xuela"
Mandelman, Avner—"Pity"
Orozco, Daniel—"Orientation"
Polansky, Steven—"Leg"
Thon, Melanie Rae—"First, Body"
Williams, Joy*—"Honored Guest"

The Best American Short Stories, 1996: Selected from U.S. and Canadian Magazines
***edited by* John Edgar Wideman, with Katrina Kenison**

Adams, Alice*—"Complicities"
Bass, Rick*—"Fires"
Brown, Jason—"Driving the Heart"
Butler, Robert Olen*—"Jealous Husband Returns in Form of Parrot"
Chang, Lan Samantha*—"The Eve of the Spirit Festival"
Chaon, Dan—"Fitting Ends"
Davies, Peter Ho*—"The Silver Screen"
Díaz, Junot—"Ysrael"
Dixon, Stephen*—"Sleep"
Dybek, Stuart*—"Paper Lantern"
Galyan, Deborah—"The Incredible Appearing Man"
Gordon, Mary*—"Intertextuality"
Huddle, David—"Past My Future"
Keesey, Anna—"Bright Winter"
Kincaid, Jamaica*—"In Roseau"
Lewis, William Henry—"Shades"
Lychack, William—"A Stand of Fables"
Oates, Joyce Carol*—"Ghost Girls"
Patrinos, Angela—"Sculpture I"
Perabo, Susan*—"Some Say the World"
Schwartz, Lynne Sharon*—"The Trip to Halawa Valley"
Sharma, Akhil—"If You Sing Like That for Me"
Thompson, Jean—"All Shall Love Me and Despair"
Thon, Melanie Rae—"Xmas, Jamaica Plain"

The Best American Short Stories, 1997: Selected from U.S. and Canadian Magazines
***edited by* E. Annie Proulx, with Katrina Kenison**

Bausch, Richard*—"Nobody in Hollywood"
Bender, Karen E.—"Eternal Love"
Boyle, T. Coraghessan*—"Killing Babies"
Byers, Michael*—"Rites of Passage: Shipmates down Under"
Cliff, Michelle—"Identifying the Stranger: Transactions"
Cooke, Carolyn—"Bob Darling"
Davis, Lydia—"St. Martin"
Díaz, Junot—"Perceived Social Values: Fiesta, 1980"
Durban, Pam—"Soon"
Edgerton, Clyde—"Send Me to the Electric Chair"
Eugenides, Jeffrey—"Air Mail"
Franzen, Jonathan—"Chez Lambert"
Gautreaux, Tim*—"Little Frogs in a Ditch"
Hagy, Alyson—"Search Bay"
Hall, Donald—"From Willow Temple"
Jin, Ha—"Manners and Right Behavior: Saboteur"
Michaels, Leonard*—"A Girl with a Monkey"
Ozick, Cynthia*—"Save My Child!"
Spence, June—"Missing Women"
Stone, Robert*—"Under the Pitons"
Wolff, Tobias*—"Powder"

The Best American Short Stories, 1998: Selected from U.S. and Canadian Magazines
***edited by* Garrison Keillor, with Katrina Kenison**

Adrian, Chris—"Every Night for a Thousand Years"
Anshaw, Carol—"Elvis Has Left the Building"
Ballantine, Poe—"The Blue Devils of Blue River Avenue"
Broyard, Bliss*—"Mr. Sweetly Indecent"
Carter, Emily—"Glory Goes and Gets Some"
Chetkovich, Kathryn—"Appetites"
Crain, Matthew—"Penance"
Gautreaux, Tim*—"Welding with Children"
Kaplan, Hester—"Would You Know It Wasn't Love"
Larson, Doran—"Morphine"
Moore, Lorrie*—"People Like That Are the Only People Here"
Nelson, Antonya—"Unified Front"
Pearlman, Edith—"Chance"
Powell, Padgett—"Wayne in Love"
Proulx, Annie*—"The Half-Skinned Steer"
Schoemperlen, Diane—"Body Language"
Sharma, Akhil—"Cosmopolitain"
Swann, Maxine—"Flower Children"
Updike, John*—"My Father on the Verge"
Wolitzer, Meg—"Tea at the House"

The Best American Short Stories, 1999: Selected from U.S. and Canadian Magazines
***edited by* Amy Tan, with Katrina Kenison**

Bass, Rick*—"The Hermit's Story"
Díaz, Junot—"The Sun, the Moon, the Stars"
Divakaruni, Chitra—"Mrs. Dutta Writes a Letter"
Dobyns, Stephen—"Kansas"
Englander, Nathan—"The Tumblers"
Gautreaux, Tim*—"The Piano Tuner"
Hardy, Melissa—"The Uncharted Heart"
Harrar, George—"The Five Twenty-two"
Hemon, A.—"Islands"
Houston, Pam*—"The Best Girlfriend You Never Had"
Jin, Ha—"In the Kindergarten"
Julavits, Heidi—"Marry the One Who Gets There First"
Kaplan, Hester—"Live Life King-sized"
Kohler, Sheilia—"Africans"
Lahiri, Jhumpa*—"Interpreter of Maladies"
Moore, Lorrie*—"Real Estate"
Munro, Alice*—"Save the Reaper"
Proulx, Annie*—"The Bunchgrass Edge of the World"
Spencer, James—"The Robbers of Karnataka"
Upadhyay, Samrat—"The Good Shopkeeper"
Yarbrough, Steve—"The Rest of Her Life"

THE O. HENRY AWARDS, 1919-2000

The O. Henry Awards, published each year in a volume entitled Prize Stories, *were established in 1919. The volume features outstanding stories that appeared in American periodicals during the year. Authors marked with an asterisk (*) are covered in this set.*

1919

FIRST PRIZE

Montague, Margaret Prescott—"England to America"

SECOND PRIZE

Steele, Wilbur Daniel*—"For They Know Not What They Do"

OTHER SELECTED STORIES

Alsop, Guglielma—"The Kitchen Gods"
Cabell, James Branch—"Porcelain Cups"
Derieux, Samuel A.—"The Trial in Tom Belcher's Store"
Ferber, Edna—"April Twenty-fifth as Usual"
Hurst, Fannie—"Humoresque"
Marshall, Edison—"The Elephant Remembers"
Post, Melville D.—"Five Thousand Dollars Reward"
Ravenel, Beatrice—"The High Cost of Conscience"
Rice, Louise—"The Lubbeny Kiss"
Springer, Thomas Grant—"The Blood of the Dragon"
Terhune, Albert Payson—"On Strike"
Williams, Ben Ames—"They Grind Exceedingly Small"
Wood, Frances Gilchrist—"Turkey Red"

1920

FIRST PRIZE

Burt, Maxwell Struthers—"Each in His Generation"

SECOND PRIZE

Hart, Frances Noyes—"Contact!"

OTHER SELECTED STORIES

Fitzgerald, F. Scott*—"The Camel's Back"
Forbes, Esther—"Break-Neck Hill"
Gilpatric, Guy—"Black Art and Ambrose"
Hartman, Lee Foster—"The Judgement of Vulcan"
Hull, Alexander—"The Argosies"
Lewis, O. F.—"Alma Mater"
Miller, Alice Duer—"Slow Poison"
Pelley, William Dudley—"The Face in the Window"
Perry, Lawrence—"A Matter of Loyalty"
Robbins, L. H.—"Professor Todd's Used Car"
Rutledge, Maurice—"The Thing They Loved"
Sidney, Rose—"Butterflies"
Smith, Gordon Arthur—"No Flowers"
Steele, Wilbur Daniel*—"Footfalls"
Whitman, Stephen French—"The Last Room of All"

1921

FIRST PRIZE

Marshall, Edison—"The Heart of Little Shikara"

SECOND PRIZE

Jackson, Charles Tenney—"The Man Who Cursed the Lillies"

OTHER SELECTED STORIES

Allen, Maryland—"The Urge"
Beer, Thomas—"Mummery"
Chittenden, Gerald—"The Victim of His Vision"
Cooper, Courtney Ryley, and Lee F. Creagan—"Martin Gerrity Gets Even"
Cram, Mildred—"Stranger Things"
Derieux, Samuel A.—"Comet"
Heerman, Elizabeth Alexander—"Fifty-two Weeks for Florette"

Kerr, Sophie—"Wild Earth"
Kniffin, Harry Anable—"The Tribute"
Lewis, O. F.—"The Get-Away"
Mumford, Ethel Watts—"Aurore"

FIRST PRIZE
Cobb, Irvin S.—"Snake Doctor"

SECOND PRIZE
Lane, Rose Wilder—"Innocence"

BEST SHORT SHORT
Buckley, F. R.—"Gold-Mounted Guns"

OTHER SELECTED STORIES
Alexander, Charles—"As a Dog Should"
Barrett, Richmond Brooks—"Art for Art's Sake"
Beer, Thomas—"Tact"

FIRST PRIZE
Smith, Edgar Valentine—"Prelude"

SECOND PRIZE
Connell, Richard—"A Friend of Napoleon"

BEST SHORT SHORT
Folsom, Elizabeth Irons—"Towers of Fame"

OTHER SELECTED STORIES
Dell, Floyd—"Phantom Adventure"
Farogoh, Francis Edwards—"The Distant Street"
Glenn, Isa Urquhart—"The Wager"

FIRST PLACE
Irwin, Inez Haynes—"The Spring Flight"

SECOND PLACE
Crowell, Chester T.—"Margaret Blake"

BEST SHORT SHORT
Newman, Frances—"Rachel and Her Children"

Robbins, L. H.—"Mr. Downey Sits Down"
Steele, Wilbur Daniel*—"The Marriage in Kairwan"
Tupper, Tristram—"Grit"

1922

Bennett, James W.—"The Kiss of the Accolade"
Derieux, Samuel A.—"The Sixth Shot"
Horn, R. de S.—"The Jinx of the Shandon Belle"
Hull, Helen R.—"His Sacred Family"
Jackson, Charles Tenney—"The Horse of Hurricane Reef"
Lewis, O. F.—"Old Peter Takes an Afternoon Off"
Morris, Gouverneur—"Ig's Amock"
Steele, Wilbur Daniel*—"The Anglo-Saxon"
Terhune, Albert Payson—"The Writer-Upward"
Vorse, Mary Heaton—"Twilight of the God"

1923

Hopper, James—"Célestine"
Larsson, Genevieve—"Witch Mary"
Lemmon, Robert S.—"The Bamboo Trap"
Mahoney, James—"The Hat of Eight Reflections"
Mason, Grace Sartwell—"Home Brew"
Morris, Gouverneur—"Derrick's Return"
Synon, Mary—"Shadowed"
Tarkington, Booth—"The One Hundred Dollar Bill"
Watts, Mary S.—"Nice Neighbors"
Williams, Jesse Lynch—"Not Wanted"

1924

OTHER SELECTED STORIES
Benét, Stephen Vincent*—"Uriah's Son"
Connell, Richard—"The Most Dangerous Game"
Dobie, Charles Caldwell—"Horse and Horse"
Mirrielees, Edith R.—"Professor Boynton Rereads History"
Mosley, Jefferson—"The Secret at the Crossroads"
Pattullo, George—"The Tie That Binds"
Singmaster, Elsie—"The Courier of the Czar"

Smith, Edgar Valentine—"'Lijah"
Spears, Raymond S.—"A River Combine-Professional"
Steele, Wilbur Daniel*—"What Do You Mean—Americans?"
Stone, Elinore Cowan—"One Uses the Handkerchief"
Welles, Harriet—"Progress"

1925

FIRST PRIZE
Street, Julian—"Mr. Bisbee's Princess"

SECOND PRIZE
Williams, Wythe—"Splendid with Swords"

BEST SHORT SHORT
Austin, Mary—"Papago Wedding"

OTHER SELECTED STORIES
Anderson, Sherwood*—"The Return"
Babcock, Edwina Stanton—"Dunelight"
Brady, Mariel—"Peter Projects"
Brecht, Harold W.—"Two Heroes"
Carver, Ada Jack—"Redbone"
Eliot, Ethel Cook—"Maternal"
Hackett, Francis—"Unshapely Things"
Heyward, DuBose—"Crown's Bess"
Peterkin, Julia—"Maum Lou"
Steele, Wilbur Daniel*—"The Man Who Saw Through Heaven"—"Cornelia's Mountain"
Whitlock, Brand—"The Sofa"

1926

FIRST PRIZE
Steele, Wilbur Daniel*—"Bubbles"

SECOND PRIZE
Anderson, Sherwood*—"Death in the Woods"

BEST SHORT SHORT
Wetjen, Albert Richard—"Command"

OTHER SELECTED STORIES
Carver, Ada Jack—"Threeshy"
Detzer, Karl W.—"The Wreck Job"
Dobie, Charles Caldwell—"The Thrice Bereft Widow of Hung Gow"—"Symphonesque"
Goodloe, Abbie Carter—"Claustrophobia"
Graeve, Oscar—"A Death on Eighth Avenue"
Jacobs, Marguerite—"Singing Eagles"
Kelly, Eleanor Mercein—"Basquerie"
Saxon, Lyle—"Cane River"
Skinner, Constance Lindsay—"The Dew on the Fleece"
Tarkington, Booth—"Stella Crozier"
Vorse, Mary Heaton—"The Madelaine"
Williams, Ben Ames—"The Nurse"

1927

FIRST PRIZE
Bradford, Roark—"Child of God"

SECOND PRIZE
Hemingway, Ernest*—"The Killers"

BEST SHORT SHORT
Bromfield, Louis—"The Scarlet"

OTHER SELECTED STORIES
Adams, Bill—"Jukes"
Bellah, James Warner—"Fear"
Brush, Katherine—"Night Club"
Carver, Ada Jack—"Singing Woman"
Chapman, Elizabeth Cobb—"With Glory and Honor"
Daniels, Roger—"Bulldog"

Douglas, Marjory Stoneman—"He Man"
Ellerbe, Alma, and Paul Ellerbe—"Don Got Over"
Kelly, Eleanor Mercein—"Monkey Motions"
Sawyer, Ruth—"Four Dreams of Gram Perkins"
Suckow, Ruth—"The Little Girl from Town"
Taylor, Ellen Dupois—"Shades of George Sand"

1928

First Prize
Duranty, Walter—"The Parrot"

Second Prize
Douglas, Marjory Stoneman—"The Peculiar Treasure of Kings"

Best Short Short
Gale, Zona—"Bridal Pond"

Other Selected Stories
Adams, Bill—"Home Is the Sailor"
Aldrich, Bess Streeter—"The Man Who Caught the Weather"
Avery, Stephen Morehouse—"Never in This World"
Blackman, M. C.—"Hot Copy"
Bradford, Roark—"River Witch"
Brown, Cambray—"Episode in a Machine Age"
Cobb, Irvin S.—"An Episode at Pintail Lake"
Connell, Richard—"The Law Beaters"
Hartman, Lee Foster—"Mr. Smith" (or "Two Minutes to Live")
Johnson, Nunnally—"The Actor"
Marquis, Don—"O'Meara, the Mayflower—and Mrs. MacLirr"—"Lightning"
Tarleton, Fiswoode—"Curtains" (or "Bloody Ground")
Wescott, Glenway*—"Prohibition"

1929

First Prize
Parker, Dorothy—"Big Blonde"

Second Prize
Howard, Sidney—"The Homesick Ladies"

Best Short Short
Brush, Katherine—"Him and Her"

Other Selected Stories
Anderson, Sherwood*—"Alice"
Benét, Stephen Vincent*—"The King of the Cats"
Bromfield, Louis—"The Skeleton at the Feast"
Brush, Katherine—"Speakeasy"
Chapman, Maristan—"Treat You Clever"
Johnston, Mary—"Elephants Through the Country"
Leech, Margaret—"Manicure"
Marquis, Don—"The Red-Haired Woman"
Norris, Kathleen—"Sinners"
Patterson, Pernet—"Buttin' Blood"
Rushfeldt, Elise—"A Coffin for Anna"
Sanborn, Ruth Burr—"Professional Pride"
Slade, Caroline—"Mrs. Sabin"
Steele, Wilbur Daniel*—"The Silver Sword"

1930

First Prize
Burnett, W. R.—"Dressing-Up"

First Prize
John, William H.—"Neither Jew nor Greek"

Second Prize
Roberts, Elizabeth Madox*—"The Sacrifice of the Maidens"

Best Short Short
Connelly, Marc—"Coroner's Inquest"

Other Selected Stories
Bradford, Roark—"Careless Love"
Burt, Katherine Newlin—"Herself"
Cobb, Irvin S.—"Faith, Hope and Charity"
Cooper, Courtney Ryley—"The Elephant Forgets"
DeFord, Miriam Allen—"The Silver Knight"

Hallet, Richard Matthews—"Misfortune's Isle"
Held, John, Jr.—"A Man of the World"
Johnson, Nunnally—"Mlle. Irene the Great"
March, William—"The Little Wife"
Overbeck, Alicia O'Reardon—"Encarnatión"
Pelley, William Dudley—"The Continental Angle"
Peterkin, Julia—"The Diamond Ring"
Ryerson, Florence, and Colin Clements—"Lobster John's Annie"
Steele, Wilbur Daniel*—"Conjuh"
Street, Julian—"A Matter of Standards"
Thomason, Capt. John W., Jr.—"Born on an Iceberg"

1931

FIRST PRIZE
Steele, Wilbur Daniel*—"Can't Cross Jordan by Myself"

SECOND PRIZE
Swain, John D.—"One Head Well Done"

THIRD PRIZE
Bradley, Mary Hastings—"The Five-Minute Girl"

BEST SHORT SHORT
La Farge, Oliver—"Haunted Ground"

OTHER SELECTED STORIES
Beems, Griffith—"Leaf Unfolding"
Brush, Katharine—"Good Wednesday"
Chase, Mary Ellen—"Salesmanship"
Dobie, Charles Caldwell—"The False Talisman"
Faulkner, William*—"Thrift"
Hume, Cyril—"Forrester"
Loomis, Alfred F.—"Professional Aid"
Luhrs, Marie—"Mrs. Schwellenbach's Receptions"
March, William—"Fifteen from Company K"
Rice, Laverne—"Wings for Janie"
Ryerson, Florence, and Colin Clements—"Useless"
Smith, Edgar Valentine—"Cock-a-Doodle-Done!"
Tarkington, Booth—"Cider of Normandy"
Thorne, Crichton Alston—"Chimney City"

1932

FIRST PRIZE
Benét, Stephen Vincent*—"An End to Dreams"

SECOND PRIZE
Cozzens, James Gould*—"Farewell to Cuba"

BEST SHORT SHORT
Granberry, Edwin—"A Trip to Czardis"

OTHER SELECTED STORIES
Boone, Jack H.—"Big Singing"
Boyle, Kay*—"The First Lover"
Brush, Katherine—"Football Girl"
Canfield, Dorothy—"Ancestral Home"
Cobb, Irvin S.—"A Colonel of Kentucky"
Constiner, Merle—"Big Singing"
Coombes, Evan—"Kittens Have Fathers"
Edmonds, Walter D.—"The Cruise of the Cashalot"
Faulkner, William*—"Turn About"
Marquand, J. P.—"Deep Water"
Tarkington, Booth—"She Was Right Once"

1933

FIRST PRIZE
Rawlings, Marjorie Kinnan—"Gal Young Un"

SECOND PRIZE
Buck, Pearl S.*—"The Frill"

BEST SHORT SHORT
Hale, Nancy*—"To the Invader"

OTHER SELECTED STORIES
Adams, Bill—"The Lubber"
Aiken, Conrad*—"The Impulse"
Arnold, Len—"Portrait of a Woman"
Caldwell, Erskine*—"Country Full of Swedes"
Fitzgerald, F. Scott*—"Family in the Wind"
Frost, Francis M.—"The Heart Being Perished"

Haardt, Sarah—"Absolutely Perfect"
Lane, Rose Wilder—"Old Maid"
Robinson, Selma—"The Departure"
Smith, Robert—"Love Story"
Thomas, Dorothy—"The Consecrated Coal Scuttle"
Wilde, Hagar—"Little Brat"

1934

First Prize
Paul, Louis—"No More Trouble for Jedwick"

Second Prize
Gordon, Caroline*—"Old Red"

Third Prize
Saroyan, William*—"The Daring Young Man on the Flying Trapeze"

Other Selected Stories
Appel, Benjamin—"Pigeon Flight"
Buck, Pearl S.*—"Shanghai Scene"
Caldwell, Erskine*—"Maud Island"
Cole, Madelene—"Bus to Biarritz"
DeFord, Miriam Allen—"Pride"
Edmonds, Walter D.—"Honor of the County"
Faulkner, William*—"Wash"
Fisher, Vardis—"The Scarecrow"
Johnson, Josephine W.—"Dark"
Sherman, Richard—"First Flight"
Steinbeck, John*—"The Murder"
Stribling, T. S.—"Guileford"
Sylvester, Harry—"A Boxer: Old"
Wexley, John—"Southern Highway Fifty-one"
Wolfe, Thomas*—"Boom Town"
Zugsmith, Leane—"King Lear in Evansville"

1935

First Prize
Boyle, Kay*—"The White Horses of Vienna"

Second Prize
Thomas, Dorothy—"The Home Place"

Third Prize
Johnson, Josephine W.—"John the Six"

Other Selected Stories
Algren, Nelson*—"The Brother's House"
Benét, Stephen Vincent*—"The Professor's Punch"
Hamill, Katherine—"Leora's Father"
Kantor, MacKinlay—"Silent Grow the Guns"
McCleary, Dorothy—"Little Elise"
Mamet, Louis—"A Writer Interviews a Banker"
Marquis, Don—"Country Doctor"
O'Donnell, E. P.—"Jesus Knew"
Paul, Louis—"Lay Me Low!"
Santee, Ross—"Water"
Saroyan, William*—"Five Ripe Pears"
Shenton, Edward—"When Spring Brings Back . . ."
Sherman, Richard—"First Day"
Terrell, Upton—"Long Distance"
Weidman, Jerome*—"My Father Sits in the Dark"
Wolfe, Thomas*—"Only the Dead Know Brooklyn"

1936

First Prize
Cozzens, James Gould*—"Total Stranger"

Second Prize
Benson, Sally—"Suite Twenty Forty-nine"

Best Short Short
March, William—"A Sum in Addition"

Other Selected Stories
Bessie, Alvah C.—"A Personal Issue"
Bird, Virginia—"Havoc Is Circle"
Brace, Ernest—"Silent Whistle"
Cain, James M.*—"Dead Man"
Coatsworth, Elizabeth—"The Visit"
Colby, Nathalie—"Glass Houses"
Driftmier, Lucille—"For My Sister"

Edmonds, Walter D.—"Escape from the Mine"
Faulkner, William*—"Lion"
Gale, Zona—"Crisis"
Godchaux, Elma—"Chains"
Heth, Edward Harris—"Big Days Beginning"
Horgan, Paul—"The Trunk"
Katterjohn, Elsie—"Teachers"
Knight, Eric—"The Marne"
Owen, Janet Curren—"Afternoon of a Young Girl"

1937

FIRST PRIZE
Benét, Stephen Vincent*—"The Devil and Daniel Webster"

SECOND PRIZE
Moll, Elick—"To Those Who Wait"

THIRD PRIZE
Coates, Robert M.—"The Fury"

OTHER SELECTED STORIES
Appel, Benjamin—"Awroopdedoop!"
Bird, Virginia—"For Nancy's Sake"
DeJong, David Cornel—"The Chicory Neighbors"
Hale, Nancy*—"To the North"
Hilton, Charles—"Gods of Darkness"
Hunt, Hamlen—"The Saluting Doll"
McKeon, J. M.—"The Gladiator"
March, William—"The Last Meeting"
Martin, Charles—"Hobogenesis"
O'Hara, John*—"My Girls"
Patten, Katherine—"Man Among Men"
Pereda, Prudencio de—"The Spaniard"
Seager, Allan—"Pro Arte"
Still, James—"Job's Tears"
Stuart, Jesse*—"Whip-Poor-Willie"
Thibault, David—"A Woman Like Dilsie"
Warren, Robert Penn*—"Christmas Gift"
Weidman, Jerome*—"Thomas Hardy's Meat"

1938

FIRST PRIZE
Maltz, Albert—"The Happiest Man on Earth"

SECOND PRIZE
Wright, Richard*—"Fire and Cloud"

THIRD PRIZE
Steinbeck, John*—"The Promise"

OTHER SELECTED STORIES
Benét, Stephen Vincent*—"Johnny Pye and the Fool-Killer"
Bradley, Mary Hastings—"The Life of the Party"
Caldwell, Erskine*—"Man and Woman"
Daly, Maureen—"Sixteen"
Fuchs, Daniel—"The Amazing Mystery at Storick, Dorschi, Pflaumer, Inc."
Hale, Nancy*—"Always Afternoon"
Hunt, Hamlen—"Only by Chance Are Pioneers Made"
Moll, Elick—"Memoir of Spring"
Saroyan, William*—"The Summer of the Beautiful White Horse"
Still, James—"So Large a Thing as Seven"
Whitehand, Robert—"The Fragile Bud"

1939

FIRST PRIZE
Faulkner, William*—"Barn Burning"

SECOND PRIZE
Still, James—"Bat Flight"

THIRD PRIZE
DeJong, David Cornel—"Calves"

OTHER SELECTED STORIES
Baker, Dorothy—"Keeley Street Blues"

Boyle, Kay*—"Anschluss"
Brand, Millen—"The Pump"
Burt, Maxwell Struthers—"The Fawn"
Caldwell, Erskine*—"The People v. Abe Lathan, Colored"
Cooke, Charles—"Nothing Can Change It"
Foster, Joseph O'Kane—"Gideon"
Gordon, Caroline*—"Frankie and Thomas and Bud Asbury"
Shaw, Irwin*—"God on a Friday Night"
St. Joseph, Ellis—"A Knocking at the Gate"
Thielen, Benedict—"Silver Virgin"
Welty, Eudora*—"Petrified Man"

1940

First Prize
Benét, Stephen Vincent*—"Freedom's a Hard-Bought Thing"

Second Prize
Lull, Roderick—"Don't Get Me Wrong"

Third Prize
Havill, Edward—"The Kill"

Other Selected Stories
Boyle, Kay*—"Poor Monsieur Panalitus"
Brooks, Roy Patchen—"Without Hal"
Coates, Robert M.—"Let's Not Talk About It Now"
Faulkner, William*—"Hand upon the Waters"
Hale, Nancy*—"That Woman"
King, Mary—"Chicken on the Wind"
Lumpkin, Grace—"The Treasure"
McCleary, Dorothy—"Mother's Helper"
Porter, Katherine Anne*—"The Downward Path to Wisdom"
Rawlings, Marjorie Kinnan—"The Pelican's Shadow"
Robinson, Mabel L.—"Called For"
Saroyan, William*—"The Three Swimmers and the Educated Grocer"
Tracy, Tom—"Homecoming"
Wright, Richard*—"Almos' a Man"

1941

First Prize
Boyle, Kay*—"Defeat"

Second Prize
Welty, Eudora*—"A Worn Path"

Third Prize
Abbett, Hallie Southgate—"Eighteenth Summer"

Best First-Published Story
Logan, Andy—"The Visit"

Other Selected Stories
Aiken, Conrad*—"Hello, Tib"
Algren, Nelson*—"A Bottle of Milk for Mother (Biceps)"
Benson, Sally—"Retreat"
Cheever, John*—"I'm Going to Asia"
Clark, Walter Van Tilburg*—"Hook"
DeJong, David Cornel—"Seven Boys Take a Hill"
Faulkner, William*—"The Old People"
Gallico, Paul—"The Snow Goose"
Hale, Nancy*—"Those Are as Brothers"
Kunasz, Paul—"I'd Give It All up for Tahiti"
Maltz, Albert—"Afternoon in the Jungle"
Morris, Edita—"Caput Mortum"
O'Hara, Mary—"My Friend Flicka"
Sheean, Vincent—"The Conqueror"
Still, James—"The Proud Walkers"
Thomas, Dorothy—"My Pigeon Pair"

1942

First Prize
Welty, Eudora*—"The Wide Net"

Second Prize
Stegner, Wallace*—"Two Rivers"

Third Prize
Schramm, Wilbur L.—"Windwagon Smith"

Best First-Published Story
Wylie, Jeanne E.—"A Long Way to Go"

Other Selected Stories
Boyle, Kay*—"Their Name Is Macaroni"
Clark, Walter Van Tilburg*—"The Portable Phonograph"
Davis, Robert Gorham—"An Interval Like This"
DeJong, David Cornel—"Snow-on-the-Mountain"
Faulkner, William*—"Two Soldiers"
Green, Eleanor—"The Dear Little Doves"
Hale, Nancy*—"Sunday-1913"
Jaynes, Clare—"The Coming of Age"
Johnson, Josephine W.—"Alexander to the Park"
Laing, Alexander—"The Workmanship Has to Be Wasted"
McCullers, Carson*—"The Jockey"
Shuman, John Rogers—"Yankee Odyssey"
Steinbeck, John*—"How Edith McGillcuddy Met R. L. Stevenson"
Stuart, Alison—"The Yodeler"
Sullivan, Richard—"Feathers"
Weidman, Jerome*—"Basket Carry"
Worthington, Marjorie—"Hunger"

1943

First Prize
Welty, Eudora*—"Livvie Is Back"

Second Prize
Canfield, Dorothy—"The Knot Hole"

Third Prize
Fifield, William—"The Fisherman of Patzcuaro"

Best First-Published Story
Laidlaw, Clara—"The Little Black Boys"

Other Selected Stories
Boyle, Kay*—"The Canals of Mars"
Breuer, Bessie—"Pigeons en Casserole"
Buck, Pearl S.*—"The Enemy"
Clark, Walter Van Tilburg*—"The Ascent of Ariel Goodbody"
Cook, Whitfield—"The Unfaithful"
Grinnell, Sarah—"Standby"
Grossberg, Elmer—"Black Boy's Good Time"
Hale, Nancy*—"Who Lived and Died Believing"
Johnson, Josephine W.—"The Glass Pigeon"
Lampman, Ben Hur—"Blinker was a Good Dog"
McCullers, Carson*—"A Tree. A Rock. A Cloud"
Saroyan, William*—"Knife-like, Flower-like, Like Nothing at All in the World"
Smith, Margarita G.—"White for the Living"
Strong, Austin—"She Shall Have Music"
Stuart, Alison—"Death and My Uncle Felix"
Thurber, James*—"The Cane in the Corridor"
Von der Goltz, Peggy—"The Old She 'Gator"
White, William C.—"Pecos Bill and the Willful Coyote"

1944

First Prize
Shaw, Irwin*—"Walking Wounded"

Second Prize
Breuer, Bessie—"Home Is a Place"

Third Prize
Beems, Griffith—"The Stagecoach"

Best First-Published Story
Yerby, Frank G.—"Health Card"

Other Selected Stories
Clark, Walter Van Tilburg*—"The Buck in the Hills"
Eastman, Elizabeth—"Like a Field Mouse over the Heart"
Fineman, Morton—"Soldier of the Republic"
Fleming, Berry—"Strike up a Stirring Music"
Hope, Marjorie—"That's My Brother"
Johnson, Josephine W.—"Night Flight"
Knight, Ruth Adams—"What a Darling Little Boy"
Loveridge, George—"The Fur Coat"
Osborne, Margaret—"Maine"
Powers, J. F.*—"Lions, Harts, Leaping Does"
Roane, Marianne—"Quitter"
Schmitt, Gladys—"All Souls'"
Schorer, Mark—"Blockbuster"
Stuart, Alison—"Sunday Liberty"
Weston, Christine—"Raziya"
Wilcox, Wendall—"The Pleasures of Travel"
Young, Marguerite—"Old James"

1945

First Prize
Clark, Walter Van Tilburg*—"The Wind and the Snow of Winter"

Second Prize
Shaw, Irwin*—"Gunner's Passage"

Third Prize
Lampman, Ben Hur—"Old Bill Bent to Drink"

Other Selected Stories
Breuer, Bessie—"Bury Your Own Dead"
Critchell, Laurence—"Flesh and Blood"
Deasy, Mary—"Long Shadow on the Lawn"
Fenton, Edward—"Burial in the Desert"
Gerry, Bill—"Understand What I Mean"
Gordon, Ethel Edison—"War Front: Louisiana"
Hardwick, Elizabeth—"The People on the Roller Coaster"
Heyert, Murray—"The New Kid"
Hubbell, Catherine—"Monday at Six"
Lavin, Mary*—"The Sand Castle"
Martin, Hansford—"The Thousand-Yard Stare"
Patton, Frances Gray—"A Piece of Bread"
Portugal, Ruth—"Call a Solemn Assembly"
Powers, J. F.*—"The Trouble"
Seager, Allan—"The Conqueror"
Shattuck, Katharine—"Subway System"
Smith, Louise Reinhardt—"The Hour of Knowing"
West, Jessamyn*—"Lead Her Like a Pigeon"
Wilson, Michael—"Come Away Home"

1946

First Prize
Goss, John Mayo—"Bird Song"

Second Prize
Shedd, Margaret—"The Innocent Bystander"

Third Prize
Ullman, Victor—"Sometimes You Break Even"

Best First-Published Story
Meyer, Cord, Jr.—"Waves of Darkness"

Other Selected Stories
Berryman, John—"The Imaginary Jew"
Boyle, Kay*—"Winter Night"
Brookhouser, Frank—"Request for Sherwood Anderson"
Canfield, Dorothy—"Sex Education"
Capote, Truman*—"Miriam"
Enright, Elizabeth—"I Forgot Where I Was"
Hardwick, Elizabeth—"What We Have Missed"
Highsmith, Patricia*—"The Heroine"
Hutchins, M. P.—"Innocents"
Le Sueur, Meridel—"Breathe Upon These Slain"
Lytle, Andrew—"The Guide"
McCleary, Dorothy—"Not Very Close"
Rawlings, Marjorie Kinnan—"Black Secret"
Savler, David S.—"The Beggar"
Shaw, Irwin*—"Act of Faith"

Thielen, Benedict—"The Empty Sky"
Welty, Eudora*—"A Sketching Trip"
West, Jessamyn*—"The Blackboard"

1947

FIRST PRIZE
Clayton, John Bell—"The White Circle"

SECOND PRIZE
Burdick, Eugene L.—"Rest Camp on Maui"

THIRD PRIZE
Parsons, Elizabeth—"The Nightingales Sing"

BEST FIRST-PUBLISHED STORY
Lewis, Robert—"Little Victor"

OTHER SELECTED STORIES
Bowles, Paul*—"The Echo"
Bradbury, Ray*—"Homecoming"
Breuer, Bessie—"The Skeleton and the Easter Lily"
Cobb, Jane—"The Hot Day"
Deasy, Mary—"The Holiday"
DeJong, David Cornel—"The Record"
Elder, Walter—"You Can Wreck It"
Eustis, Helen—"An American Home"
Govan, Christine Noble—"Miss Winters and the Wind"
Kuehn, Susan—"The Rosebush"
Lynch, John A.—"The Burden"
Powers, J. F.*—"The Valiant Woman"
Shedd, Margaret—"The Great Fire of 1945"
Shorer, Mark—"What We Don't Know Hurts Us"
Smith, John Caswell, Jr.—"Fighter"
Stafford, Jean*—"The Hope Chest"
Thielen, Benedict—"Old Boy—New Boy"
Welty, Eudora*—"The Whole World Knows"
West, Jessamyn*—"Horace Chooney, M.D."

1948

FIRST PRIZE
Capote, Truman*—"Shut a Final Door"

SECOND PRIZE
Stegner, Wallace*—"Beyond the Glass Mountain"

THIRD PRIZE
Bradbury, Ray*—"Powerhouse"

BEST FIRST-PUBLISHED STORY
Grennard, Elliot—"Sparrow's Last Jump"

OTHER SELECTED STORIES
Brookhouser, Frank—"She Did Not Cry at All"
Gidney, James B.—"The Muse and Mr. Parkinson"
Gordon, Caroline*—"The Petrified Woman"
Greene, Mary Frances—"The Silent Day"
Hartley, Lodwick—"Mr. Henig's Wall"
Hauser, Marianne—"The Other Side of the River"
Ingles, James Wesley—"The Wind Is Blind"
Janeway, Elizabeth—"Child of God"
La Farge, Christopher—"The Three Aspects"
Malkin, Richard—"Pico Never Forgets"
Morse, Robert—"The Professor and the Puli"
Parsons, Elizabeth—"Welcome Home"
Shattuck, Katharine—"The Answer"
Shelton, William R.—"The Snow Girl"
Sorenson, Virginia—"The Talking Stick"
Sulkin, Sidney—"The Plan"
Terrett, Courtenay—"The Saddle"
Watson, John—"The Gun on the Table"
West, Ray B., Jr.—"The Ascent"

1949

FIRST PRIZE
Faulkner, William*—"A Courtship"

SECOND PRIZE
Van Doren, Mark—"The Watchman"

Third Prize
Dorrance, Ward—“The White Hound”

Other Selected Stories
Ashworth, John—“High Diver”
Bowles, Paul*—“Pastor Dowe at Tacate”
Calisher, Hortense*—“The Middle Drawer”
Coatsworth, Elizabeth—“Bremen’s”
Connell, Evan S., Jr.*—“I’ll Take You to Tennessee”
Conrad, Barnaby—“Cayetano the Perfect”
Cramer, Alice Carver—“The Boy Next Door”
Downey, Harris—“The Mulhausen Girls”
Enright, Elizabeth—“The Trumpeter Swan”
Goss, John Mayo—“Evening and Morning Prayer”
Jackson, Shirley*—“The Lottery”
Lavin, Mary*—“Single Lady”
Pierce, Phoebe—“The Season of Miss Maggie Reginald”
Plagemann, Bentz—“The Best Bread”
Rice, John Andrew—“You Can Get Just So Much Justice”
Salinger, J. D.*—“Just Before the War with the Eskimos”
Stafford, Jean*—“A Summer Day”
Weaver, John D.—“Meeting Time”
West, Jessamyn*—“Public Address System”
Wilson, Leon—“Six Months Is No Long Time”

1950

First Prize
Stegner, Wallace*—“The Blue-Winged Teal”

Second Prize
Leiper, Gudger Bart—“The Magnolias”

Third Prize
Lowry, Robert—“Be Nice to Mr. Campbell”

Other Selected Stories
Algren, Nelson*—“The Captain Is Impaled”
Bennett, Peggy—“Death Under the Hawthorns”
Berry, John—“New Shoes”
Boyle, Kay*—“Summer Evening”
Cheever, John*—“Vega”
Chidester, Ann—“Mrs. Ketting and Clark Gable”
Enright, Elizabeth—“The Sardillion”
Humphrey, William*—“The Hardy’s”
Justice, Donald—“The Lady”
Kuehn, Susan—“The Hunt”
Lamkin, Speed—“Comes a Day”
Newhouse, Edward—“Seventy Thousand Dollars”
Parsons, Elizabeth—“Not a Soul Will Come Along”
Putman, Clay—“The Wounded”
Robinson, Leonard Wallace—“The Ruin of Soul”
Salinger, J. D.*—“For Esmé—With Love and Squalor”
Switzer, Robert—“Death of a Prize Fighter”
Taylor, Peter*—“Their Losses”
Van Ness, Lilian—“Give My Love to Maggie”
Winslow, Anne Goodwin—“Seasmiles”

1951

First Prize
Downey, Harris—“The Hunters”

Second Prize
Welty, Eudora*—“The Burning”

Third Prize
Capote, Truman*—“The House of Flowers”

Other Selected Stories
Casper, Leonard—“Sense of Direction”
Cheever, John*—“The Pot of Gold”
Connell, Evan S., Jr.*—“I Came from Yonder Mountain”
Culver, Monty—“Black Water Blues”
Faulkner, William*—“A Name for the City”
Hall, James B.—“In the Time of Demonstrations”
Hersey, John—“Peggety’s Parcel of Shortcomings”
Kensinger, Faye Riter—“A Sense of Destination”
La Farge, Oliver—“Old Century’s River”
Love, Peggy Harding—“The Jersey Heifer”
Macauley, Robie—“The Invaders”

McCullers, Carson*—"The Sojourner"
Miller, Arthur—"Monte Saint Angelo"
Patt, Esther—"The Butcherbirds"
Patterson, Elizabeth Gregg—"Homecoming"
Phillips, Thomas Hal—"The Shadow of an Arm"
Rooney, Frank—"Cyclists' Raid"
Shirley, Sylvia—"Slow Journey"
Smith, John Campbell—"Who Too Was a Soldier"
Stafford, Jean*—"A Country Love Story"
Thompson, R. E.—"It's a Nice Day—Sunday"

1954

First Prize
Mabry, Thomas—"The Indian Feather"

Second Prize
Putman, Clay—"The News from Troy"

Third Prize
Wilbur, Richard—"A Game of Catch"

Other Selected Stories
Cassill, R. V.*—"The War in the Air"
Clay, Richard—"Very Sharp for Jagging"
Elliott, George P.*—"A Family Matter"
Gold, Herbert*—"The Witch"
Hall, James B.—"Estate and Trespass: A Gothic Story"
Harnden, Ruth—"Rebellion"
Justice, Donald—"Vineland's Burning"
Lowrey, P. H.—"Too Young to Have a Gun"
Maxwell, James A.—"Fighter"
O'Connor, Flannery*—"The Life You Save May Be Your Own"
Rugel, Miriam—"The Flower"
Stafford, Jean*—"The Shorn Lamb"
Stern, Richard G.*—"The Sorrows of Captain Schreiber"
Walker, Augusta—"The Day of the Cipher"
Wallace, Robert—"The Secret Weapon of Joe Smith"
West, Jessamyn*—"Breach of Promise"
Whitmore, Stanford—"Lost Soldier"
Whittemore, Reed—"The Stutz and the Tub"
Wilner, Herbert—"Whistle and the Heroes"
Worthington, Rex—"A Kind of Scandal"

1955

First Prize
Stafford, Jean*—"In the Zoo"

Second Prize
O'Connor, Flannery*—"A Circle in the Fire"

Third Prize
Buechner, Frederick—"The Tiger"

Other Selected Stories
Bingham, Robert—"The Unpopular Passenger"
Calisher, Hortense*—"A Christmas Carillon"
Cassill, R. V.*—"The Inland Years"
Cheever, John*—"The Five-forty-eight"
Elliott, George P.*—"Miss Cudahy of Stowes Landing"
Enright, Elizabeth—"The Operator"
Fowler, Mary Dewees—"Man of Distinction"
Fuchs, Daniel—"Twilight in Southern California"
Grau, Shirley Ann*—"Joshua"
Graves, John—"The Green Fly"
Powers, J. F.*—"The Presence of Grace"
Shultz, William Henry—"The Shirts off Their Backs"
Steele, Max—"The Wanton Troopers"
Stegner, Wallace*—"The City of the Living"
Wolfert, Ira—"The Indomitable Blue"

1956

First Prize
Cheever, John*—"The Country Husband"

Second Prize
Buechler, James—"Pepicelli"

Third Prize
Cassill, R. V.*—"The Prize"

Other Selected Stories
Bellow, Saul*—"The Gonzaga Manuscripts"
Calisher, Hortense*—"The Night Club in the Woods"
Carr, Archie—"The Black Beach"
Coates, Robert M.—"In a Foreign City"
Faulkner, William*—"Race at Morning"
Gold, Herbert*—"A Celebration for Joe"
Macauley, Robie—"The Chevigny Man"
Nemerov, Howard—"Tradition"
Stafford, Jean*—"Beatrice Trueblood's Story"
Steinbeck, John*—"The Affair at Seven, Rue de M—-"
Whitehill, Joseph—"Able Baker"
Yates, Richard—"The Best of Everything"

1957

First Prize
O'Connor, Flannery*—"Greenleaf"

Second Prize
Gold, Herbert*—"Encounter in Haiti"

Third Prize
Elliott, George P.*—"Miracle Play"

Other Selected Stories
Blassingame, Wyatt—"Man's Courage"
Cassill, R. V.*—"When Old Age Shall This Generation Waste"
Cheever, John*—"The Journal of an Old Gent"
Faulkner, William*—"By the People"
Granit, Arthur—"Free the Canaries from Their Cages!"
Langdon, John—"The Blue Serge Suit"
Liberman, M. M.—"Big Buick to the Pyramids"
McCarthy, Mary*—"Yellowstone Park"
Marsh, Willard—"Last Tag"
Miller, Nolan—"A New Life"
Rich, Cynthia Marshall—"My Sister's Marriage"
Settle, Mary Lee—"The Old Wives' Tale"
Shaw, Irwin*—"Then We Were Three"
Stafford, Jean*—"The Warlock"
Sunwall, Betty—"Things Changed"
Thurman, Richard Young—"The Credit Line"
Walter, Eugene—"I Love You Batty Sisters"

1958

First Prize
Gellhorn, Martha—"In Sickness as in Health"

Second Prize
Calisher, Hortense*—"What a Thing, to Keep a Wolf in a Cage!"

Third Prize
Steiner, George—"The Deeps of the Sea"

Other Selected Stories
Berriault, Gina*—"The Stone Boy"
Blanton, Lowell D.—"The Long Night"
Brown, T. K., III—"A Drink of Water"
Clemons, Walter—"A Summer Shower"
Enright, Elizabeth—"The Eclipse"
Granat, Robert—"My Apples"
Hale, Nancy*—"A Slow Boat to China"
Litwak, Leo—"The Making of a Clock"
Matthiessen, Peter—"Travelin' Man"
Newhouse, Edward—"The Ambassador"
Shore, Wilma—"A Cow on the Roof"
Stafford, Jean*—"My Blithe, Sad Bird"
White, Robin—"First Voice"
Wilner, Herbert—"The Passion for Silver's Arm"

1959

First Prize
Taylor, Peter*—"Venus, Cupid, Folly, and Time"

Second Prize
Elliott, George P.*—"Among the Dangs"

Third Prize
Turner, Thomas C.—"Something to Explain"

Other Selected Stories
Baldwin, James*—"Come out of the Wilderness"
Buchwald, Emilie Bix—"The Present"
Cheever, John*—"The Trouble of Marcie Flint"
Currie, Ellen—"Tib's Eve"
Eastlake, William—"Flight of the Circle Heart"
Filer, Tom—"The Last Voyage"
Harris, MacDonald—"Second Circle"
O'Connor, Flannery*—"A View of the Woods"
Sandburg, Helga—"Witch Chicken"
Stafford, Jean*—"A Reasonable Facsimile"
Stone, Alma—"The Bible Salesman"
Williams, Thomas—"Goose Pond"

1960

First Prize
Hall, Lawrence Sargent*—"The Ledge"

Second Prize
Roth, Philip*—"Defender of the Faith"

Third Prize
White, Robin—"Shower of Ashes"

Other Selected Stories
Berkman, Sylvia—"Ellen Craig"
Berriault, Gina*—"Sublime Child"
Enright, Elizabeth—"A Gift of Light"
Fowler, Janet—"A Day for Fishing"
Gold, Herbert*—"Love and Like"
Granat, Robert—"To Endure"
Henderson, Robert—"Immortality"
Kentfield, Calvin—"In the Cauldron"
Ogden, Maurice—"Freeway to Wherever"
Purdy, James—"Encore"
Spencer, Elizabeth*—"First Dark"
Swarthout, Glendon—"A Glass of Blessings"
Ziller, Eugene—"Sparrows"

1961

First Prize
Olson, Tillie—"Tell Me a Riddle"

Second Prize
Gold, Ivan—"The Nickel Misery of George Washington Carver Brown"

Third Prize
Price, Reynolds*—"One Sunday in Late July"

Other Selected Stories
Burgess, Jackson—"The Magician"
Currie, Ellen—"O Lovely Appearance of Death"
Ford, Jesse Hill—"How the Mountains Are Made"
Krause, Ervin D.—"The Quick and the Dead"
Ludwig, Jack—"Thoreau in California"
Miller, Arthur—"I Don't Need You Any More"
Shaber, David—"A Nous La Liberté"
Taylor, Peter*—"Heads of Houses"
Updike, John*—"Wife-Wooing"

1962

First Prize
Porter, Katherine Anne*—"Holiday"

Second Prize
Pynchon, Thomas*—"Under the Rose"

Third Prize
Cole, Tom—"Familiar Usage in Leningrad"

Other Selected Stories
Adams, Thomas E.—"Sled"
Deasy, Mary—"The People with the Charm"
Grau, Shirley Ann*—"Eight O'Clock One Morning"
Graves, John—"The Aztec Dog"
Howard, Maureen—"Bridgeport Bus"
Jackson, David—"The English Gardens"
McKenzie, Miriam—"Deja Vu"
Price, Reynolds*—"The Warrior Princess Ozimba"
Schoonover, Shirley W.—"The Star Blanket"
Shaber, David—"Professorio Collegio"
Updike, John*—"The Doctor's Wife"
Whitbread, Thomas—"The Rememberer"

1963

First Prize
O'Connor, Flannery*—"Everything That Rises Must Converge"

Second Prize
Krause, Ervin D.—"The Snake"

Third Prize
Selz, Thalia—"The Education of a Queen"

Other Selected Stories
Ansell, Helen Essary—"The Threesome"
Berkman, Sylvia—"Pontifex"
Cox, James Trammell—"That Golden Crane"
Douglas, Ellen*—"On the Lake"
Klein, Norma—"The Burglar"
McClure, J. G.—"The Rise of the Proletariat"
Maddow, Ben—"In a Cold Hotel"
Oates, Joyce Carol*—"The Fine White Mist of Winter"
Saroyan, William*—"Gaston"
Southern, Terry—"The Road Out of Axotle"
West, Jessamyn*—"The Picknickers"

1964

First Prize
Cheever, John*—"The Embarkment for Cythera"

Second Prize
Oates, Joyce Carol*—"Stigmata"

Third Prize
Shedd, Margaret—"The Everlasting Witness"

Other Selected Stories
Bingham, Sallie—"The Banks of the Ohio"
Calisher, Hortense*—"The Scream on Fifty-seventh Street"
Lanning, George—"Something Just for Me"
Malamud, Bernard*—"The Jewbird"
Ross, Lillian—"Night and Day, Day and Night"
Roth, Philip*—"Novotnoy's Pain"
Sara—"So I'm Not Lady Chatterly, So Better I Should Know It Now"
Schoonover, Shirley W.—"Old and Country Tale"
Shaw, Irwin*—"The Inhabitants of Venus"
Stacton, David—"The Metamorphosis of Kenko"
Stegner, Wallace*—"Carrion Spring"
Zorn, George A.—"Thompson"

1965

FIRST PRIZE
O'Connor, Flannery*—"Revelation"

SECOND PRIZE
Friedman, Sanford—"Ocean"

THIRD PRIZE
Humphrey, William*—"The Ballad of Jesse Neighbours"

OTHER SELECTED STORIES
Barthelme, Donald*—"Margins"
Beagle, Peter S.—"Come Lady Death"
Cavanaugh, Arthur—"What I Wish (Oh, I Wish) I Had Said"
Curley, Daniel—"Love in the Winter"
Ludwig, Jack—"A Woman of Her Age"
McCarthy, Mary*—"The Hounds of Summer"
McCullers, Carson*—"Sucker"
Manoff, Eva—"Mama and the Spy"
Mayer, Tom—"Homecoming"
Miller, Warren—"Chaos, Disorder, and the Late Show"
Oates, Joyce Carol*—"First Views of the Enemy"
Potter, Nancy A. J.—"Sunday's Children"
Rooke, Leon—"If Lost Return to the Swiss Arms"
Taylor, Peter*—"There"
Wolf, Leonard—"Fifty-Fifty"

1966

FIRST PRIZE
Updike, John*—"The Bulgarian Poetess"

SECOND PRIZE
Howard, Maureen—"Sherry"

THIRD PRIZE
Cole, Tom—"On the Edge of Arcadia"

OTHER SELECTED STORIES
Berriault, Gina*—"The Birthday Party"
Bingham, Sallie—"Bare Bones"
Davis, Christopher—"A Man of Affairs"
Ford, Jesse Hill—"To the Open Water"
Greene, Philip L.—"One of You Must Be Wendell Corey"
Hale, Nancy*—"Sunday Lunch"
McKinley, Georgia—"The Mighty Distance"
Michaels, Leonard*—"Sticks and Stones"
Petrakis, Harry Mark—"The Prison"
Randall, Vera—"Alice Blaine"
Spencer, Elizabeth*—"Ship Island"
Williams, Joy*—"The Roomer"
Zorn, George A.—"Mr. and Mrs. McGill"

1967

FIRST PRIZE
Oates, Joyce Carol*—"In the Region of Ice"

SECOND PRIZE
Barthelme, Donald*—"See the Moon?"

THIRD PRIZE
Strong, Jonathan—"Supperburger"

OTHER SELECTED STORIES
Buechler, James—"The Second Best Girl"
Finney, Ernest J.—"The Investigator"
Ford, Jesse Hill—"The Bitter Bread"
Jacobsen, Josephine—"On the Island"
Knickerbocker, Conrad—"Diseases of the Heart"
Kurtz, M. R.—"Waxing Wroth"
Macauley, Robie—"Dressed in Shade"
Mudrick, Marvin—"Cleopatra"
Oliver, Diane—"Neighbors"
Updike, John*—"Marching Through Boston"
Wheelis, Allen—"Sea-Girls"
Yates, Richard—"A Good and Gallant Woman"

1968

First Prize
Welty, Eudora*—"The Demonstrators"

Second Prize
Broner, E. M.—"The New Nobility"

Third Prize
Katz, Shlomo—"My Redeemer Cometh. . ."

Other Selected Stories
Branda, Eldon—"The Dark Days of Christmas"
Brower, Brock—"Storm Still"
Franklin, F. K.—"Nigger Horse"
Gration, Gwen—"Teacher"
Hale, Nancy*—"The Most Elegant Drawing Room in Europe"
Hall, James B.—"A Kind of Savage"
Harris, Marilyn—"Icarus Again"
Kentfield, Calvin—"Near the Line"
Klein, Norma—"Magic"
Neugeboren, Jay—"Ebbets Field"
Oates, Joyce Carol*—"Where Are You Going, Where Have You Been?"
Stacton, David—"Little Brother Nun"
Tyner, Paul—"How You Play the Game"
Updike, John*—"Your Lover Just Called"

1969

First Prize
Malamud, Bernard*—"Man in the Drawer"

Second Prize
Oates, Joyce Carol*—"Accomplished Desires"

Third Prize
Barth, John*—"Lost in the Funhouse"

Other Selected Stories
Corfman, Eunice Luccock—"To Be an Athlete"
Engberg, Susan—"Lambs of God"
Litwak, Leo—"In Shock"
Maddow, Ben—"You, Johann Sebastian Bach"
Michaels, Leonard*—"Manikin"
Mountzoures, H. L.—"The Empire of Things"
Packer, Nancy Huddleston—"Early Morning, Lonely Ride"
Paley, Grace*—"Distance"
Rubin, Michael—"Service"
Shefner, Evelyn—"The Invitations"
Steele, Max—"Color the Daydream Yellow"
Sterling, Thomas—"Bedlam's Rent"
Taylor, Peter*—"First Heat"
Tyler, Anne*—"The Common Courtesies"

1970

First Prize
Hemenway, Robert—"The Girl Who Sang with the Beatles"

Second Prize
Eastlake, William—"The Biggest Thing Since Custer"

Third Prize
Rindfleisch, Norval—"A Cliff of Fall"

Special Award for Continuing Achievement
Oates, Joyce Carol*—"How I Contemplated the World from the Detroit House of Correction and Began My Life Over Again" and "Unmailed, Unwritten Letters"

Other Selected Stories
Blake, George—"A Modern Development"
Buchan, Perdita—"It's Cold out There"
Cole, Tom—"Saint John of the Hershey Kisses: 1964"

Donahue, H. E. F.—"Joe College"
Griffith, Patricia Browning—"Nights at O'Rear's"
Grinstead, David—"A Day in Operations"
McPherson, James Alan*—"Of Cabbages and Kings"
Malamud, Bernard*—"My Son the Murderer"
Salter, James—"Am Strande Von Tanger"
Strong, Jonathan—"Patients"
Updike, John*—"Bech Takes Pot Luck"
Willard, Nancy—"Theo's Girl"

1971

FIRST PRIZE
Hecht, Florence M.—"Twin Bed Bridge"

SECOND PRIZE
Cardwell, Guy A.—"Did You Once See Shelley?"

THIRD PRIZE
Adams, Alice*—"Gift of Grass"

OTHER SELECTED STORIES
Cleaver, Eldridge—"The Flashlight"
Greene, Philip L.—"The Dichotomy"
Harter, Evelyn—"The Stone Lovers"
Hoagland, Edward—"The Final Fate of the Alligators"
Inman, Robert—"I'll Call You"
Jacobsen, Josephine—"The Jungle of Lord Lion"
Larson, Charles R.—"Up From Slavery"
Mazor, Julian—"The Skylark"
Michaels, Leonard*—"Robinson Crusoe Liebowitz"
Minot, Stephen*—"Mars Revisited"
Oates, Joyce Carol*—"The Children"
Parker, Thomas—"Troop Withdrawal: The Initial Step"
Price, Reynolds*—"Waiting at Dachau"
Taylor, Eleanor Ross—"Jujitsu"

1972

FIRST PRIZE
Batki, John—"Strange-Dreaming Charlie, Cow-Eyed Charlie"

SECOND PRIZE
Oates, Joyce Carol*—"Saul Bird Says: Relate! Communicate! Liberate!"

THIRD PRIZE
Rascoe, Judith—"Small Sounds and Tilting Shadows"

OTHER SELECTED STORIES
Adams, Alice*—"Ripped Off"
Barthelme, Donald*—"Subpoena"
Brown, Margery Finn—"In the Forests of the Riga the Beasts Are Very Wild Indeed"
Brown, Rosellen—"A Letter to Ismael in the Grave"
Eaton, Charles Edward—"The Case of the Missing Photographs"
Flythe, Starkey, Jr.—"Point of Conversion"
Gill, Brendan—"Fat Girl"
Gold, Herbert*—"A Death on the East Side"
Gottlieb, Elaine—"The Lizard"
Matthews, Jack—"On the Shore of Chad Creek"
McClatchy, J. D.—"Allonym"
Salter, James—"The Destruction of the Goetheanum"
Tyler, Anne*—"With All Flags Flying"
Zelver, Patricia—"On the Desert"

1973

FIRST PRIZE
Oates, Joyce Carol*—"The Dead"

SECOND PRIZE
Malamud, Bernard*—"Talking Horse"

THIRD PRIZE
Brown, Rosellen—"Mainlanders"

OTHER SELECTED STORIES
Adams, Alice*—"The Swastika on Our Door"

Bromell, Henry—"Photographs"
Carver, Raymond*—"What Is It?"
Cheever, John*—"The Jewels of the Cabots"
Jacobsen, Josephine—"A Walk with Raschid"
Johnson, Curt—"Trespasser"
Johnson, Diane—"An Apple, An Orange"
McPherson, James Alan*—"The Silver Bullet"
Malone, John—"The Fugitives"
Mayhall, Jane—"The Enemy"
Rascoe, Judith—"A Line of Order"
Reid, Randall—"Detritus"
Shaber, David—"Scotch Sour"
Sikes, Shirley—"The Death of Cousin Stanley"
Zelver, Patricia—"The Flood"

1974

First Prize
Adler, Renata—"Brownstone"

Second Prize
Henson, Robert—"Lizzie Borden in the p.m."

Third Prize
Adams, Alice*—"Alternatives"

Other Selected Stories
Busch, Frederick—"Is Anyone Left This Time of Year?"
Carver, Raymond*—"Put Yourself in My Shoes"
Clayton, John J.—"Cambridge Is Sinking!"
Davenport, Guy*—"Robot"
Eastlake, William—"The Death of Sun"
Fuller, Blair—"Bakti's Hand"
Gardner, John*—"The Things"
Hemenway, Robert—"Troy Street"
Hill, Richard—"Out in the Garage"
Hochstein, Rolaine—"What Kind of a Man Cuts His Finger Off"
Klein, Norma—"The Wrong Man"
Leach, Peter—"The Fish Trap"
McPherson, James Alan*—"The Faithful"
Salter, James—"Via Negativa"

1975

First Prize
Brodkey, Harold*—"A Story in an Almost Classical Mode"

First Prize
Ozick, Cynthia*—"Usurpation (Other People's Stories)"

Other Selected Stories
Arensberg, Ann—"Art History"
Arking, Linda—"Certain Hard Places"
Banks, Russell*—"With Che at Kitty Hawk"
Bayer, Ann—"Department Store"
Carver, Raymond*—"Are You a Doctor?"
Disch, Thomas M.*—"Getting into Death"
Doctorow, E. L.—"Ragtime"
Kotzwinkle, William—"Swimmer in the Secret Sea"
McCorkle, Susannah—"Ramona by the Sea"
McPherson, James Alan*—"The Story of a Scar"
Maxwell, William—"Over by the River"
Schell, Jessie—"Alvira, Lettie, and Pip"
Shelnutt, Eve—"Angel"
Updike, John*—"Nakedness"
Zelver, Patricia—"Norwegians"

1976

First Prize
Brodkey, Harold*—"His Son in His Arms, in Light, Aloft"

Second Prize
Sayles, John*—"I-80 Nebraska, M. 490-M. 205"

Third Prize
Adams, Alice*—"Roses, Rhododendrons"

Special Award for Continuing Achievement
Updike, John*—"Separating"

Other Selected Stories
Berryman, John—"Wash Far Away"
Brown, Rosellen—"Why I Quit the Gowanus Liberation Front"
Bumpus, Jerry—"The Idols of Afternoon"
Corrington, John William—"The Actes and Monuments"
Davenport, Guy*—"The Richard Nixon Freischutz Rag"
Francis, H. E.—"A Chronicle of Love"
Goyen, William*—"Bridge of Music, River of Sand"
Griffith, Patricia Browning—"Dust"
Halley, Anne—"The Sisterhood"
Helprin, Mark*—"Leaving the Church"
Hudson, Helen—"The Theft"
Jacobsen, Josephine—"Nel Bagno"
Oates, Joyce Carol*—"Blood-Swollen Landscape"
O'Brien, Tim*—"Night March"
Sadoff, Ira—"An Enemy of the People"
Shreve, Anita—"Past the Island, Drifting"

1977

First Prize
Hazzard, Shirley—"A Long Story Short"

First Prize
Leffland, Ella—"Last Courtesies"

Other Selected Stories
Adams, Alice*—"Flights"
Ballantyne, Sheila—"Perpetual Care"
Cheever, John*—"The President of the Argentine"
Colwin, Laurie—"The Lone Pilgrim"
Dixon, Stephen*—"Mac in Love"
Engberg, Susan—"A Stay by the River"
Fetler, Andrew—"Shadows on the Water"
Hedin, Mary—"Ladybug, Fly Away Home"
McCully, Emily Arnold—"How's Your Vacuum Cleaner Working?"
Minot, Stephen*—"A Passion for History"
Russ, Joanna—"Autobiography of My Mother"
Sayles, John*—"Breed"
Simmons, Charles—"Certain Changes"
Summers, Hollis—"A Hundred Paths"
Theroux, Paul—"The Autumn Dog"
Zelver, Patricia—"The Little Pub"

1978

First Prize
Allen, Woody*—"The Kugelmass Episode"

Second Prize
Schorer, Mark—"A Lamp"

Third Prize
Henson, Robert—"The Upper and the Lower Millstone"

Other Selected Stories
Adams, Alice*—"Beautiful Girl"
Apple, Max*—"Paddycake, Paddycake. . . A Memoir"
Brodkey, Harold*—"Verona: A Young Woman Speaks"
Clayton, John J.—"Bodies Like Mouths"
Engberg, Susan—"Pastorale"
Fuller, Blair—"All Right"
Helprin, Mark*—"The Schreuerspitze"
Jacobsen, Josephine—"Jack Frost"
Leviant, Curt—"Ladies and Gentlemen, The Original Music of the Hebrew Alphabet"
Oates, Joyce Carol*—"The Tattoo"
O'Brien, Tim*—"Speaking of Courage"
Pearlman, Edith—"Hanging Fire"
Schaeffer, Susan Fromberg—"The Exact Nature of Plot"
Schell, Jessie—"Undeveloped Photographs"
Schevill, James—"A Hero in the Highway"

1979

First Prize
Weaver, Gordon—"Getting Serious"

Second Prize
Bromell, Henry—"Travel Stories"

Third Prize
Hecht, Julie—"I Want You, I Need You, I Love You"

Other Selected Stories
Adams, Alice*—"The Girl Across the Room"
Baumbach, Jonathan—"Passion?"
Caputi, Anthony—"The Derby Hopeful"
Disch, Thomas M.*—"Xmas"
Gold, Herbert*—"The Smallest Part"
Goldberg, Lester—"Shy Bearers"
Heller, Steve—"The Summer Game"
Leaton, Anne—"The Passion of Marco Z—"
Molyneux, Thomas W.—"Visiting the Point"
Oates, Joyce Carol*—"In the Autumn of the Year"
Peterson, Mary—"Travelling"
Pfeil, Fred—"The Quality of Light in Maine"
Schwartz, Lynne Sharon*—"Rough Strife"
Smith, Lee*—"Mrs. Darcy Meets the Blue-eyed Stranger at the Beach"
Thomas, Annabel—"Coon Hunt"
Van Dyke, Henry—"Du Cote de Chez Britz"
Yates, Richard—"Oh, Joseph, I'm So Tired"
Zelver, Patricia—"My Father's Jokes"

1980

First Prize
Bellow, Saul*—"A Silver Dish"

Second Prize
Hallinan, Nancy—"Woman in a Roman Courtyard"

Third Prize
Michaels, Leonard*—"The Men's Club"

Other Selected Stories
Adams, Alice*—"Truth or Consequences"
Arensberg, Ann—"Group Sex"
Beattie, Ann*—"The Cinderella Waltz"
Chasin, Helen—"Fatal"
Dillon, Millicent—"All the Pelageyas"
Dubus, Andre*—"The Pitcher"
Dunn, Robert—"Hopeless Acts Performed Properly, with Grace"
Gertler, T.—"In Case of Survival"
Godwin, Gail*—"Amanuensis: A Tale of the Creative Life"
Krysl, Marilyn—"Looking for Mother"
L'Heureux, John*—"The Priest's Wife"
Phillips, Jayne Anne*—"Snow"
Rose, Daniel Asa—"The Goodbye Present"
Stafford, Jean*—"An Influx of Poets"
Sullivan, Walter—"Elizabeth"
Taggart, Shirley Ann—"Ghosts Like Them"
Targan, Barry*—"Old Light"
Taylor, Peter*—"The Old Forest"
Vaughn, Stephanie—"Sweet Talk"

1981

First Prize
Ozick, Cynthia*—"The Shawl"

Other Selected Stories
Adams, Alice*—"Snow"
Boyle, Kay*—"St. Stephen's Green"
Flowers, Sandra Hollin—"Hope of Zion"
Goodman, Ivy—"Baby"
Irving, John—"Interior Space"
L'Heureux, John*—"Brief Lives in California"
Matthews, Jack—"The Last Abandonment"
Novick, Marian—"Advent"
Oates, Joyce Carol*—"Mutilated Woman"

Packer, Nancy Huddleston—"The Women Who Walk"
Reid, Barbara—"The Waltz Dream"
Rottenberg, Annette T.—"The Separation"
Smith, Lee*—"Between the Lines"
Stern, Steve—"Isaac and the Undertaker's Daughter"
Tabor, James—"The Runner"
Theroux, Paul—"World's Fair"
Thomas, Annabel—"The Photographic Woman"
Walker, Alice*—"The Abortion"
Wetherell, W. D.—"The Man Who Loved Levittown"
Wolff, Tobias*—"In the Garden of North American Martyrs"

1982

First Prize
Kenney, Susan—"Facing Front"

Second Prize
McElroy, Joseph—"The Future"

Third Prize
Brooks, Ben—"A Postal Creed"

Special Award for Continuing Achievement
Adams, Alice*—"Greyhound People"—"To See You Again"

Other Selected Stories
Carkeet, David—"The Greatest Slump of All Time"
Dixon, Stephen*—"Layaways"
Gewertz, Kenneth—"I Thought of Chatterton, The Marvelous Boy"
Goodman, Ivy—"White Boy"
Holt, T. E.—"Charybdis"
Johnson, Nora—"The Jungle of Injustice"
Malone, Michael—"Fast Love"
Oates, Joyce Carol*—"The Man Whom Women Adored"
O'Brien, Tim*—"The Ghost Soldiers"
Smiley, Jane*—"The Pleasure of Her Company"
Taylor, Peter*—"The Gift of the Prodigal"
Trefethen, Florence—"Infidelities"
Wheeler, Kate—"La Victoire"
Wolff, Tobias*—"Next Door"

1983

First Prize
Carver, Raymond*—"A Small, Good Thing"

Second Prize
Oates, Joyce Carol*—"My Warsawa"

Third Prize
Morris, Wright*—"Victrola"

Other Selected Stories
Benedict, Elizabeth—"Feasting"
Bienen, Leigh Buchanan—"My Life as a West African Gray Parrot"
Faust, Irvin—"Melanie and the Purple People Eaters"
Gordon, Mary*—"The Only Son of a Doctor"
Jauss, David—"Shards"
Klass, Perri—"The Secret Lives of Dieters"
Lloyd, Lynda—"Poor Boy"
Meinke, Peter—"The Ponoes"
Norris, Gloria—"When the Lord Calls"
Plante, David—"Work"
Schwartz, Steven—"Slow-Motion"
Spencer, Elizabeth*—"Jeanne-Pierre"
Svendsen, Linda—"Heartbeat'
Updike, John*—"The City"
Van Wert, William F.—"Putting and Gardening"
Wetherell, W. D.—"If a Woodchuck Could Chuck Wood"
Whelan, Gloria—"The Dogs in Renoir's Garden"

1984

FIRST PRIZE
Ozick, Cynthia*—"Rosa"

OTHER SELECTED STORIES
Abbott, Lee K.*—"Living Alone in Iota"
Adams, Alice*—"Alaska"
Baumbach, Jonathan—"The Life and Times of Major Fiction"
Dickinson, Charles—"Risk"
Fetler, Andrew—"The Third Count"
Johnson, Willis—"Prayer for the Dying"
Justice, Donald—"The Artificial Moonlight"
Klass, Perri—"Not a Good Girl"
Leavitt, David*—"Counting Months"
Lish, Gordon—"For Jerome—with Love and Kisses"
Malamud, Bernard*—"The Model"
Menaker, Daniel—"The Old Left"
Norris, Gloria—"Revive Us Again"
Norris, Helen—"The Love Child"
Paley, Grace*—"The Story Hearer"
Pearlman, Edith—"Conveniences"
Pritchard, Melissa Brown—"A Private Landscape"
Salter, James—"Lost Sons"
Tallent, Elizabeth*—"The Evolution of Birds of Paradise"

1985

FIRST PRIZE
Dybek, Stuart*—"Hot Ice"

FIRST PRIZE
Smiley, Jane*—"Lily"

OTHER SELECTED STORIES
Beattie, Ann*—"In the White Night"
Cameron, Peter—"Homework"
Erdrich, Louise*—"Saint Marie"
Hamilton, R. C.—"Da Vinci Is Dead"
Heller, Steve—"The Crow Woman"
Hochstein, Rolaine—"She Should Have Died Hereafter"
Jacobsen, Josephine—"The Mango Community"
Just, Ward—"About Boston"
Koch, Claude—"Bread and Butter Questions"
McElroy, Joseph—"Daughter of the Revolution"
Minot, Susan—"Lust"
Morris, Wright*—"Glimpse into Another Country"
Norris, Helen—"The Quarry"
Oates, Joyce Carol*—"The Seasons"
Raymond, Ilene—"Taking a Chance on Jack"
Updike, John*—"The Other"
Wilson, Eric—"The Axe, the Axe, the Axe"
Wolff, Tobias*—"Sister"

1986

FIRST PRIZE
Walker, Alice*—"Kindred Spirits"

SPECIAL AWARD FOR CONTINUING ACHIEVEMENT
Oates, Joyce Carol*—"Master Race"

OTHER SELECTED STORIES
Adams, Alice*—"Molly's Dog"
Cameron, Peter—"Excerpts from Swan Lake"
DiFranco, Anthony—"The Garden of Redemption"
Dybek, Stuart*—"Pet Milk"
Eisenberg, Deborah—"Transactions in a Foreign Currency"
Faust, Irvin—"The Year of the Hot Jock"
Gerber, Merrill Joan—"I Don't Believe This"
Johnson, Greg—"Crazy Ladies"
Just, Ward—"The Costa Brava, 1959"
Kornblatt, Joyce R.—"Offerings"
L'Heureux, John*—"The Comedian"
Lish, Gordon—"Resurrection"
Mason, Bobbie Ann*—"Big Bertha Stories"
Meinke, Peter—"Uncle George and Uncle Stefan"
Norris, Gloria—"Holding On"
Spencer, Elizabeth*—"The Cousins"
Vaughn, Stephanie—"Kid MacArthur"
Wilmot, Jeanne—"Dirt Angel"

1987

First Prize
Erdrich, Louise*—"Fleur"

First Prize
Johnson, Joyce—"The Children's Wing"

Other Selected Stories
Adams, Alice*—"Tide Pools"
Barthelme, Donald*—"Basil from Her Garden"
Bausch, Richard*—"What Feels Like the World"
Berriault, Gina*—"The Island of Ven"
Boswell, Robert—"The Darkness of Love"
Dillon, Millicent—"Monitor"
Dybek, Stuart*—"Blight"
Home, Lewis—"Taking Care"
Lavers, Norman—"Big Dog"
Lott, James—"The Janeites"
Norris, Helen—"The Singing Well"
Oates, Joyce Carol*—"Ancient Airs, Voices"
Paley, Grace*—"Midrash on Happiness"
Pitzen, Jim—"The Village"
Robison, Mary—"I Get By"
Stern, Daniel—"The Interpretation of Dreams by Sigmund Freud: A Story"
Taylor, Robert, Jr.—"Lady of Spain"
Wallace, Warren—"Up Home"

1988

First Prize
Carver, Raymond*—"Errand"

Other Selected Stories
Adams, Alice*—"Ocrakoke Island"
Baumbach, Jonathan—"The Dinner Party"
Beattie, Ann*—"Honey"
Currey, Richard—"The Wars of Heaven"
Deaver, Philip F.—"Arcola Girls"
Dubus, Andre*—"Blessings"
Hazzard, Shirley—"The Place to Be"
Kohler, Sheila—"The Mountain"
La Puma, Salvatore—"The Gangster's Ghost"
LaSalle, Peter—"Dolphin Dreaming"
Mason, Bobbie Ann*—"Bumblebees"
Neugeboren, Jay—"Don't Worry About the Kids"
Oates, Joyce Carol*—"Yarrow"
Plant, Richard—"Cecil Grounded"
Sayles, John*—"The Halfway Diner"
Smiley, Jane*—"Long Distance"
Spencer, Elizabeth*—"The Business Venture"
Updike, John*—"Leaf Season"
Williams, Joy*—"Rot"

1989

First Prize
Finney, Ernest J.—"Peacocks"

Second Prize
Oates, Joyce Carol*—"House Hunting"

Third Prize
Doerr, Harriet*—"Edie: A Life"

Other Selected Stories
Adams, Alice*—"After You're Gone"
Bass, Rick*—"The Watch"
Boyle, T. Coraghessan*—"Sinking House"
Casey, John—"Avid"
Dickinson, Charles—"Child in the Leaves"
Dillon, Millicent—"Wrong Stories"
Harrison, Barbara Grizzuti—"To Be"
Herman, Ellen—"Unstable Ground"
Lary, Banning K.—"Death of a Duke"
Minot, Susan—"Île Séche"
Petroski, Catherine—"The Hit"
Ross, Jean—"The Sky Fading Upward to Yellow: A Footnote to Literary History"
Salter, James—"American Express"
Sherwood, Frances—"History"
Simmons, Charles—"Clandestine Acts"
Starkey, Flythe, Jr.—"CV Ten"
Wallace, David Foster—"Here and There"

1990

First Prize
Litwak, Leo—"The Eleventh Edition"

Second Prize
Matthiessen, Peter—"Lumumba Lives"

Third Prize
Segal, Lore—"The Reverse Bug"

Other Selected Stories
Ackerman, Felicia—"The Forecasting Game: A Story"
Adams, Alice*—"1940: Fall"
Blaylock, James P.—"Unidentified Objects"
Boyle, T. Coraghessan*—"The Ape Lady in Retirement"
Brinson, Claudia Smith—"Einstein's Daughter"
Eidus, Janice—"Vito Loves Geraldine"
Fleming, Bruce—"The Autobiography of Gertrude Stein"
Gillette, Jane Brown—"Sins Against Animals"
Greenberg, Joanne*—"Elizabeth Baird"
Jersild, Devon—"In Which John Imagines His Mind as a Pond"
Kaplan, David Michael*—"Stand"
McKnight, Reginald*—"The Kind of Light That Shines on Texas"
Oates, Joyce Carol*—"Heat"
Osborn, Carolyn—"The Grands"
Schumacher, Julie—"The Private Life of Robert Shumann"
Sides, Marilyn—"The Island of the Mapmaker's Wife"
Steinbach, Meredith—"In Recent History"

1991

Selected Stories
Updike, John*—"A Sandstone Farmhouse"
Adams, Alice*—"Earthquake Damage"
Averill, Thomas Fox—"During the Twelfth Summer of Elmer D. Peterson"
Baxter, Charles*—"Saul and Patsy Are Pregnant"
Broughton, T. Alan—"Ashes"
Dillon, Millicent—"Oil and Water"
Hall, Martha Lacy—"The Apple-Green Triumph"
Johnson, Wayne—"Hippies, Indians, Buffalo"
Klass, Perri—"For Women Everywhere"
Lear, Patricia—"Powwow"
Le Guin, Ursula K.—"Hand, Cup, Shell"
Levenberg, Diane—"The Ilui"
McFarland, Dennis—"Nothing to Ask For"
Norris, Helen—"Raisin Faces"
Oates, Joyce Carol*—"The Swimmers"
Stark, Sharon Sheehe—"Overland"
Sukenick, Ronald—"Ecco"
Swick, Marly—"Moscow Nights"
Walker, Charlotte Zoe—"The Very Pineapple"
Watanabe, Sylvia A.—"Talking to the Dead"

1992

First Prize
Ozick, Cynthia*—"Puttermesser Paired"

First Prize
Updike, John*—"A Sandstone Farmhouse"

Other Selected Stories
Adams, Alice*—"The Last Lovely City"
Barnes, Yolanda—"Red Lipstick"
Braverman, Kate—"Tall Tales from the Mekong Delta"
Chowder, Ken—"With Seth in Tana Toraja"
Dillon, Millicent—"Lost in L.A."
Doerr, Harriet*—"Way Stations"
Herrick, Amy—"Pinocchio's Nose"
Honig, Lucy—"English as a Second Language"
Klass, Perri—"Dedication"
Long, David—"Blue Spruce"
McNeal, Tom—"What Happened to Tully"
Meltzer, Daniel—"People"
Myers, Les—"The Kite"

Nelson, Antonya—“The Control Group”
Nelson, Kent—“The Mine from Nicaragua”
Oates, Joyce Carol*—“Why Don’t You Come Live with Me It’s Time”
Packer, Ann—“Babies”
Pomerance, Murray—“Decor”
Sherwood, Frances—“Demiurges”
Wagner, Mary Michael—“Acts of Kindness”

1993

FIRST PRIZE
Jones, Thom—“The Pugilist at Rest”

SECOND PRIZE
Lee, Andrea—“Winter Barley”

THIRD PRIZE
Van Wert, William F.—“Shaking”

OTHER SELECTED STORIES
Adams, Alice*—“The Islands”
Askew, Rilla—“The Killing Blanket”
Dixon, Stephen*—“The Rare Muscovite”
Eastman, Charles—“Yellow Flags”
Egan, Jennifer—“Puerto Vallerta”
Jacobsen, Josephine—“The Pier-Glass”
Johnson, Charles*—“Kwoon”
Levenberg, Diane—“A Modern Love Story”
Moore, Lorrie*—“Charades”
Nelson, Antonya—“Dirty Words”
Nixon, Cornelia—“Risk”
Oates, Joyce Carol*—“Goose-Girl”
Poverman, C. E.—“The Man Who Died”
Richardson, John H.—“The Pink House”
Schwartz, Steven—“Madagascar”
Stern, Daniel—“A Hunger Artist by Franz Kafka: A Story”
Svendsen, Linda—“The Edger Man”
Van Kirk, John—“Newark Job”
Weltner, Peter—“The Greek Head”
Wheeler, Kate—“Improving My Average”

1994

FIRST PRIZE
Baker, Alison—“Better Be Ready ‘Bout Half Past Eight”

SECOND PRIZE
Gardiner, John Rolfe—“The Voyage Out”

THIRD PLACE
Moore, Lorrie*—“Terrific Mother”

OTHER SELECTED STORIES
Bain, Terry—“Games”
Barton, Marlin—“Jeremiah’s Road”
Bloom, Amy—“Semper Fidelis”
Cherry, Kelly—“Not the Phil Donahue Show”
Cox, Elizabeth—“The Third of July”
Dybek, Stuart*—“We Didn’t”
Eidus, Janice—“Pandora’s Box”
Fox, Michael—“Rise and Shine”
Fremont, Helen—“Where She Was”
Graver, Elizabeth—“The Boy Who Fell Forty Feet”
Hester, Katherine L.—“Labor”
Kennedy, Thomas E.—“Landing Zone X-Ray”
McLean, David—“Marine Corps Issue”
Oness, Elizabeth—“The Oracle”
Ortiz Cofer, Judith—“Nada”
Richards, Susan Starr—“The Hanging in the Foaling Barn”
Tannen, Mary—“Elaine’s House”
Trudell, Dennis—“Gook”

1995

FIRST PRIZE
Nixon, Cornelia—“The Women Come and Go”

SECOND PRIZE
Clayton, John J.—“Talking to Charlie”

Other Selected Stories
Adams, Alice*—"The Haunted Beach"
Baker, Alison—"Loving Wanda Beaver"
Baxter, Charles*—"Kiss Away"
Bradford, Robin—"If This Letter Were a Beaded Object"
Byers, Michael*—"Settled on the Cranberry Coast"
Cameron, Peter—"Departing"
Cooper, Bernard—"Truth Serum"
Delaney, Edward J.—"The Drowning"
Eisenberg, Deborah—"Across the Lake"
Gates, David*—"The Intruder"
Gilchrist, Ellen*—"The Stucco House"
Goodman, Allegra—"Sarah"
Hardwick, Elizabeth—"Shot: A New York Story"
Klass, Perri—"City Sidewalks"
Krieger, Elliot—"Cantor Pepper"
Oates, Joyce Carol*—"You Petted Me and I Followed You Home"
Pierce, Anne Whitney—"Star Box"
Powell, Padgett—"Trick or Treat"
Updike, John*—"The Black Room"

1996

First Prize
King, Stephen*—"The Man in the Black Suit"

Second Prize
Sharma, Akhil—"If You Sing Like That for Me"

Other Selected Stories
Adams, Alice*—"His Women"
Baker, Alison—"Convocation"
Dillen, Frederick G.—"Alice"
Douglas, Ellen*—"Grant"
Graver, Elizabeth—"Between"
Hagenston, Becky—"'Til Death Do Us Part"
Hoffman, William—"Stones"
Honig, Lucy—"Citizens Review"
Kriegel, Leonard—"Players"
Lombreglia, Ralph—"Somebody Up There Likes Me"
McNally, T. M.—"Skin Deep"
Menaker, Daniel—"Influenza"
Mosley, Walter—"The Thief"
Oates, Joyce Carol*—"Mark of Satan"
Paine, Tom—"Will You Say Something Monsieur Eliot"
Schumacher, Julie—"Dummies"
Smiley, Jane*—"The Life of the Body"
Wiegand, David—"Buffalo Safety"

1997

First Prize
Gordon, Mary*—"City Life"

Second Prize
Saunders, George—"The Falls"

Third Prize
Abbott, Lee K.*—"The Talk Talked Between Worms"

Other Selected Stories
Barth, John*—"On with the Story"
Bradford, Arthur—"Catface"
Cooke, Carolyn—"The TWA Corbies"
Davenport, Kiana—"The Lipstick Tree"
Dubus, Andre*—"Dancing After Hours"
Eisenberg, Deborah—"Mermaids"
Gaitskill, Mary*—"Comfort"
Glave, Thomas—"The Final Inning"
Klam, Matthew—"The Royal Palms"
MacMillan, Ian—"The Red House"
Moody, Rick—"Demonology"
Morgan, Robert—"The Balm of Gilead Tree"
Munro, Alice*—"The Love of a Good Woman"
Ruff, Patricia Elam—"The Taxi Ride"
Schaeffer, Susan Fromberg—"The Old Farmhouse and the Dog-Wife"
Schutt, Christine—"His Chorus"
Shields, Carol—"Mirrors"

1998

FIRST PRIZE
Moore, Lorrie*—"People Like That Are the Only People Here"

SECOND PRIZE
Millhauser, Steven*—"The Knife Thrower"

THIRD PRIZE
Munro, Alice*—"The Children Stay"

OTHER SELECTED STORIES
Bass, Rick*—"The Myths of Bears"
Cooke, Carolyn—"Eating Dirt"
Davies, Peter Ho*—"Relief"
Erdrich, Louise*—"Satan: Hijacker of a Planet"
Evenson, Brian—"Two Brothers"
Heuler, Karen—"Me and My Enemy"
Jones, Thom—"Tarantula"
MacDonald, D. R.—"Ashes"
McKnight, Reginald*—"Boot"
Mehta, Suketu—"Gare du Nord"
Novakovich, Josip—"Crimson"
Proulx, Annie*—"Brokeback Mountain"
Saunders, George—"Winky"
Sharma, Akhil—"Cosmopolitan"
Swann, Maxine—"Flower Children"
Weltner, Peter—"Movietone: Detour"
Zancanella, Don—"The Chimpanzees of Wyoming Territory"

1999

FIRST PRIZE
Baida, Peter—"A Nurse's Story"

SECOND PRIZE
Holladay, Cary—"Merry-Go-Sorry"

THIRD PRIZE
Munro, Alice*—"Save The Reaper"

OTHER SELECTED STORIES
Benedict, Pinckney—"Miracle Boy"
Boyle, T. Coraghessan*—"The Underground Gardens"
Chabon, Michael*—"Son of the Wolfman"
Cunningham, Michael—"Mister Brother"
Davenport, Kiana—"Fork Used in Eating Reverend Baker"
Forbes, Charlotte—"Sign"
Houston, Pam—"Cataract"
Lahiri, Jhumpa*—"Interpreter of Maladies"
Potok, Chaim—"Moon"
Proulx, Annie*—"The Mud Below"
Reilly, Gerald—"Nixon Under the Bodhi Tree"
Saunders, George—"Sea Oak"
Schirmer, Robert—"Burning"
Schwartz, Sheila—"Afterbirth"
Wallace, David Foster—"The Depressed Person"
Wetherell, W. D.—"Watching Girls Play"
Whitty, Julia—"A Tortoise for the Queen of Tonga"

SHORT-FICTION CHRONOLOGY

Date	*Event*
B.C.E.	
c. 4000	*Tales of the Magicians* (Egyptian)
c. 2000	*The Epic of Gilgamesh* (Sumerian)
c. 750	Homer flourished
c. 564	Aesop died
c. 5th cent.	*Jatakas* (Indian)
c. 300	Theophrastus, *Characters*
c. 270	Theocritus, idylls, mimes
c. 100	Aristides, Milesian tales
	Tale of Daniel and Susanna (from the Apocrypha)
C.E.	
c. 8	Ovid, *Metamorphoses*
c. 1st cent.	Phaedrus, *Fabulae Aesopiae*
c. 400	*Vitae Patrum*
c. early 6th cent.	*Panchatantra* (Indian)
c. 6th cent.	Gregory the Great, *Dialogues*
c. late 8th cent.	*Fates of the Apostles*
c. 800	*The Thousand and One Nights* (in one form)
c. 9th cent.	*Romulus* (Latin)
c. 10th cent.	*Avian*
	Blickling Homilies (Anglo Saxon)
c. 990-997	Aelfric, *Sermones Catholici, passiones sanctorum*
c. 1000	*Beowulf*, manuscript written
c. 1100	*The Mabinogion* (Welsh), early tales written
	The Book of the Dun Cow (Irish)
	Chanson de Roland (The Song of Roland)
c. 1164-1180	Chrétien de Troyes, wrote earliest extant Arthurian romances in the vernacular
c. late 12th cent.	Marie de France, *Lais*
c. 1200	*The Thousand and One Nights*, has substantially taken shape
	Odo of Cheriton, *Fabuale*
c. early 13th cent.	Snorri Sturluson, *Prose Edda*
	Aucassin and Nicolette
c. 1250	*Dame Siriz*
c. 1275	*The Fox and the Wolf*
c. 13th cent.	*Gesta Romanorum*
	Ancren Riwle
c. 1280-1350	*South English Legendary*
c. 1303	Robert Mannyng of Brunne, *The Handlyng of Synne*
c. early 1300's	*Northern Homilies*
	Northern Legendary
1313	Giovanni Boccaccio born
1349-1351	Giovanni Boccaccio, *The Decameron*
1371-1372	*The Book of the Knight of La Tour Landry*
1375	Giovanni Boccaccio dies
c. 1383-1384	John Gower, *Confessio Amantis*
1387-1400	Geoffrey Chaucer, *The Canterbury Tales*
1485	Sir Thomas Malory, *Le Morte d'Arthur*
16th cent.	*The Thousand and One Nights* has taken final form
1526	Beatrice, *Hundred Mery Talys*
1550-1553	Giovan Francesco Straparola, *The Pleasureful Nights*
c. 1553	*Lazarillo de Tormes*
1558	Marguerite de Navarre, *Heptameron*
1566	William Painter, *The Palace of Pleasure*
1567	Geoffrey Fenton, *Tragical Discourses*
1568	*Lazarillo de Tormes* translated into English
1576	George Pettie, *A Petite Pallace of Pettie His Pleasure*
1579	John Lyly, *Euphues, The Anatomy of Wit*
1580	Michel Eyquem de Montaigne, *The Essays*
1581	Barnaby Riche, *Riche His Farewell to Militarie Profession*
1591	Robert Greene, *A Notable Discovery of Coosenage*

Date	Event
1593	Theophrastus's *Characters* translated into English
1597	Thomas Deloney, *The Gentle Craft*
1608	Joseph Hall, *Characters of Vices and Virtues*
1609	Thomas Dekker, *The Ravens Almanacke*
1613	Miguel de Cervantes, *The Exemplary Novels*
1614	Sir Thomas Overbury, *Characters*
1620	*Westward for Smelts*
1623	Charles Sorel, *Francion*
1628	John Earle, *Microcosmographie*
1664	Jean de La Fontaine, *Tales and Short Stories in Verse*
1688	Aphra Behn, *Oroonoko*
1691-1694	*The Gentleman's Journal*, edited by P. A. Motteux
1692	William Congreve, *Incognita*
1694	Voltaire born
1697	Charles Perrault, *Histories et contes du temps passé, avec des moralités*
1700	John Dryden, *Fables*
1704-1712	*The Thousand and One Nights*, first European translation (French) by Antoine Galland
1706	*The Thousand and One Nights*, partial translation of Galland's version into English
	Daniel Defoe, "The True Relation of the Apparition of One Mrs. Veal"
1709-1711	Joseph Addison and Richard Steele, *The Tatler*
1711-1712, 1714	Joseph Addison and Richard Steele, *The Spectator*
1720	Mrs. Manley, *The Power of Love: In Seven Novels*
1722	Benjamin Franklin, "Dogood Papers"
1725	Mrs. Haywood, *Secret Histories, Novels, and Poems* (2d ed.)
1732	Benjamin Franklin, "Alice Addertongue," "Celia Single," "Anthony Afterwit"
1739	Voltaire, "Voyage de Monsieur le Baron de Gangan"
1747	Voltaire, *Zadig*
1750-1752	Samuel Johnson, *The Rambler*
1752	Voltaire, "Micromégas"
1759	Voltaire, *Candide*
1762	Oliver Goldsmith, *The Citizen of the World*
1773	Ludwig Johann Tieck born
1776	E. T. A. Hoffmann born
1778	Voltaire dies
1795-1798	Hannah More, *Tracts*
1797	Ludwig Tieck, *Volksmärchen*
1799	Sir Walter Scott, *An Apology for Tales of Terror*
	Honoré de Balzac born
	Alexander Pushkin born
1801	Maria Edgeworth, *Moral Tales for Young People*
1804	Maria Edgeworth, *Popular Tales*
	Nathaniel Hawthorne born
1805	Hans Christian Andersen born
1807-1808	Washington Irving, *Salmagundi* ("Sketches from Nature" appeared in October, "The Little Man in Black" in November)
1809	Edgar Allan Poe born
	Nikolai Gogol born
1809-1812	Maria Edgeworth, *Tales of Fashionable Life*
1811	Théophile Gautier born
1812	Jacob and Wilhelm Grimm, *Grimm's Fairy Tales*
	Charles Dickens born
1812-1817	Ludwig Tieck, *Phantasus*
1814-1815	E. T. A. Hoffmann, *Fantasiestücke in Callots Manier*
1818	Ivan Turgenev born
1819	Leigh Hunt, "A Tale for a Chimney Corner"
	Herman Melville born
1819-1820	Washington Irving, *The Sketch Book of Geoffrey Crayon, Gent.* ("Rip Van Winkle," May, 1819; "The Spectre Bridegroom," November, 1819; "The Headless Horseman," March, 1820)
1819-1821	E. T. A. Hoffmann, *The Serapion Brethren*
1821	Fyodor Dostoevski born

Date	Event
1822	Charles Brockden Brown, *Carwin the Biloquist and Other American Tales and Pieces*
	Washington Irving, *Bracebridge Hall*
	Charles Lamb, "Dream Children"
	E. T. A. Hoffmann dies
1823	Charles Lamb, "Old China"
	Beginning of vogue in England of gift book annuals
1824	Washington Irving, *Tales of a Traveller* and letter to Henry Brevoort
	William Austin, "Peter Rugg, the Missing Man"
	Sir Walter Scott, "Wandering Willie's Tale" (in *Redgauntlet*)
1824-1832	Mary Russell Mitford, *Our Village*
1826	*The Atlantic Souvenir*, beginning of American gift book vogue
1827-1828	Sir Walter Scott, *Chronicles of the Canongate*, first series ("The Highland Widow," "The Two Drovers," "The Surgeon's Daughter")
1828	Leo Tolstoy born
1829	Sir Walter Scott, "My Aunt Margaret's Mirror," "The Tapestried Chamber"
	Prosper Mérimée, "Mateo Falcone"
1830	Nathaniel Hawthorne, "The Hollow of the Three Hills"
1831	Alexander Pushkin, *The Tales of the Late Ivan Petrovitch Belkin*
1831-1832	Nikolai Gogol, *Evenings on a Farm near Dikanka*
1831-1861	*The Spirit of the Times*
1832	Washington Irving, *The Alhambra*
	James Hall, *Legends of the West*
	J. P. Kennedy, *Swallow Barn*
	A. B. Longstreet begins publishing his sketches
	Nathaniel Hawthorne, "My Kinsman, Major Molineux"
	Edgar Allan Poe, "Metzengerstein"
	Honoré de Balzac, "La Grande Breteche"
1834	Albert Pike, *Prose Sketches and Poems Written in the Western Country*
	Alexander Pushkin, *The Queen of Spades*
1835	A. B. Longstreet, *Georgia Scenes*
	Nikolai Gogol, "The Diary of a Madman"
	Mark Twain born
1836	Charles Dickens, *Sketches by Boz*
	Nikolai Gogol, "The Nose," "The Carriage"
	Théophile Gautier, "Fortunato"
	Bret Harte born
1837	Nathaniel Hawthorne, *Twice-Told Tales* (first series)
	Charles Nodier, "Inez de las Sierras" (part 1)
	Alexander Pushkin dies
1838	Thomas De Quincey, "The Avenger"
1839	Edgar Allan Poe, "The Fall of the House of Usher"
1840	Edgar Allan Poe, *Tales of the Grotesque and Arabesque*
	Thomas Hardy born
1841	T. B. Thorpe, "The Big Bear of Arkansas"
1842	Nathaniel Hawthorne, *Twice-Told Tales* (second series)
	Edgar Allan Poe's first review of *Twice-Told Tales*
	Nikolai Gogol, "The Overcoat"
1843	Harriet Beecher Stowe, *The May Flower*
	Charles Dickens, *A Christmas Carol*
	William Makepeace Thackeray, "Dennis Haggarty's Wife"
	Henry James born
1845	Edgar Allan Poe, *Tales*
1846	Nathaniel Hawthorne, *Mosses from an Old Manse*
	Ivan Turgenev begins *A Sportsman's Sketches*
1847	Edgar Allan Poe's second review of Hawthorne's tales
1848	Joel Chandler Harris born

Date	Event
1849	Edgar Allan Poe dies
	Sarah Orne Jewett born
1850	Honoré de Balzac dies
	Robert Louis Stevenson born
	Guy de Maupassant born
1851	Nathaniel Hawthorne, *The Snow-Image and Other Twice-Told Tales*
1852	Ivan Turgenev, *A Sportsman's Sketches* (begun 1846)
	Nikolai Gogol dies
	Mary E. Wilkins Freeman born
1853	Ludwig Tieck dies
1855-1863	A. N. Afanasev, *Russian Folktales*
1856	Herman Melville, "Bartleby the Scrivener"
	Herman Melville, *The Piazza Tales*
	Wilkie Collins, *After Dark*
1857	Joseph Conrad born
1858	George Eliot, *Scenes of Clerical Life*
1859	Edward Bulwer-Lytton, "The House and the Brain"
1860	Anton Chekhov born
	Hamlin Garland born
1861	Rebecca Harding Davis, "Life in the Iron Mills"
1862	O. Henry (William Sidney Porter) born
1863-1864	Elizabeth Gaskell, *Cousin Phillis*
1864	Nathaniel Hawthorne dies
1865	Mark Twain, "The Celebrated Jumping Frog of Calaveras County"
	Rudyard Kipling born
1867	Mark Twain, *The Celebrated Jumping Frog of Calaveras County, and Other Sketches*
1868	Bret Harte, "The Luck of Roaring Camp"
1869	Alphonse Daudet, *Letters from My Mill*
1870	Bret Harte, *The Luck of Roaring Camp and Other Sketches*
	Charles Dickens dies
	Ivan Bunin born
1871	Henry Kingsley, "Our Brown Passenger"

Date	Event
	Stephen Crane born
	William Dean Howells, *Suburban Sketches*
	Théophile Gautier dies
1873	Thomas Bailey Aldrich, *Marjorie Daw and Other People*
1875	Henry James, *A Passionate Pilgrim*
	Hans Christian Andersen dies
	Thomas Mann born
1876	Fyodor Dostoevski, "The Peasant Marey"
	Friedrich Spielhagen, *Novellen*
	Sherwood Anderson born
1877	Sarah Orne Jewett, *Deephaven*
	Gustave Flaubert, *Three Tales*
1878	Henry James, *Daisy Miller*
1879	Henry James, *The Madonna of the Future*
	George Washington Cable, *Old Creole Days*
1880	Joel Chandler Harris, *Uncle Remus: His Songs and Sayings*
	Guy de Maupassant, "Boule de Suif"
1881	George Washington Cable, *Madame Delphine*
	Guy de Maupassant, *Madame Tellier's Establishment and Short Stories*
	Fyodor Dostoevski dies
1882	Frank R. Stockton, "The Lady, or the Tiger?"
	Robert Louis Stevenson, *The New Arabian Nights*
	Charles Reade, *Readiana*
	Virginia Woolf born
	James Joyce born
	Guy de Maupassant, *Mademoiselle Fifi and Other Stories*
1883	Ivan Turgenev dies
	Franz Kafka born
1884	Charles Egbert Craddock (Mary Noailles Murfree), *In the Tennessee Mountains*
	Guy de Maupassant, "The Necklace"
	Anton Chekhov, *Skazki Melpomeny*

Date	Event
1885	Brander Matthews, "The Philosophy of the Short-Story"
	D. H. Lawrence born
1886	Sarah Orne Jewett, *A White Heron*
	Robert Louis Stevenson, *The Strange Case of Dr. Jekyll and Mr. Hyde*
	Leo Tolstoy, *The Death of Ivan Ilyich*
	Anton Chekhov, *Pystrye rasskazy*
1887	Mary E. Wilkins Freeman, *A Humble Romance and Other Stories*
	Arthur Conan Doyle, *A Study in Scarlet*
	Anton Chekhov, *V sumerkakh* and *Nevinnye rechi*
1888	Rudyard Kipling, *Plain Tales from the Hills*
	Thomas Hardy, *Wessex Tales*
	Katherine Mansfield born
1890	Sarah Orne Jewett, *Tales of New England*
	Katherine Anne Porter born
1891	Hamlin Garland, *Main-Travelled Roads*
	Ambrose Bierce, *Tales of Soldiers and Civilians*
	William Dean Howells, *Criticism and Fiction*
	Herman Melville dies
1892	T. W. Higginson, "The Local Short-Story"
1893	Ambrose Bierce, *Can Such Things Be?*
	Guy de Maupassant dies
	Henry James, *The Real Thing*
1894	Luigi Pirandello, *Amori senza amore*
	Kate Chopin, *Bayou Folk*
	Robert Louis Stevenson dies
	Isaac Babel born
1896	Sarah Orne Jewett, *The Country of the Pointed Firs*
	Stephen Crane, *The Little Regiment and Other Episodes of the American Civil War*
1897	William Faulkner born
1898	Henry James, *The Turn of the Screw*
	Stephen Crane, "The Blue Hotel," *The Open Boat and Other Tales of Adventure*
	Anton Chekhov, "Gooseberries"
	Frederick Wedmore, "The Short Story"
	Charles R. Barrett, *Short Story Writing: A Practical Treatise on the Art of the Short Story*
	Anton Chekhov, "The Lady with the Dog"
	Stephen Crane, *The Monster and Other Stories*
1899	Edith Wharton, *The Greater Inclination*
	W. Somerset Maugham, *Orientations*
	Bret Harte, "The Rise of the Short Story"
	Ernest Hemingway born
	Vladimir Nabokov born
	Jorge Luis Borges born
1900	Stephen Crane, *Wounds in the Rain and Whilomville Stories*
	Jack London, *The Son of the Wolf*
	Stephen Crane dies
1902	Joseph Conrad, *Heart of Darkness*
	Bret Harte dies
1903	George Moore, *The Untilled Field*
	Thomas Mann, *Tonio Kröger*
1904	James Joyce, "The Sisters," "Eveline," "After the Race"
	Saki (H. H. Munro), *Reginald*
	Anton Chekhov dies
	Isaac Bashevis Singer born
	O. Henry, *Cabbages and Kings*
1905	Willa Cather, *The Troll Garden*
	Jean-Paul Sartre born
1906	O. Henry, *The Four Million*
1907	Alberto Moravia born
1908	O. Henry, *The Voice of the City*
	Joel Chandler Harris dies
1909	Henry S. Canby, *The Short Story in English*
	Sarah Orne Jewett dies
	Eudora Welty born

Date	Event
1910	O. Henry, "A Municipal Report"
	Joseph Conrad, "The Secret Sharer"
	Lord Dunsany, *A Dreamer's Tales*
	Mark Twain dies
	O. Henry dies
	Leo Tolstoy dies
1911	Katherine Mansfield, *In a German Pension*
	Saki (H. H. Munro), *The Chronicles of Clovis*
	E. M. Forster, *The Celestial Omnibus and Other Stories*
1912	Thomas Mann, *Death in Venice*
1913	Albert Camus born
1914	James Joyce, *Dubliners*
	D. H. Lawrence, *The Prussian Officer and Other Stories*
	Saki (H. H. Munro), *Beasts and Super-Beasts*
1915	Edward J. O'Brien, *The Best Short Stories of 1915* (annual volumes follow)
	Saul Bellow born
	Ivan Bunin, "The Gentleman from San Francisco"
	Franz Kafka, *The Metamorphosis*
	Ring Lardner, *You Know Me, Al*
1916	Lord Dunsany, *The Last Book of Wonder* (pb. in England as *Tales of Wonder*)
	Anton Chekhov, *The Tales of Chekhov* (English translation by Constance Garnett completed in 1922)
	Henry James dies
1918	Theodore Dreiser, *Free and Other Stories*
	Maxim Gorky, *Stories of the Steppe*
1919	Sherwood Anderson, *Winesburg, Ohio*
	Franz Kafka, "A Country Doctor" and "In the Penal Colony"
	First year of the annual O. Henry competition
1920	F. Scott Fitzgerald, *Flappers and Philosophers*
	Katherine Mansfield, *Bliss and Other Stories*
1921	Sherwood Anderson, *The Triumph of the Egg*
	Stephen Crane, *Men, Women, and Boats*
	W. Somerset Maugham, *The Trembling of a Leaf*
	A. E. Coppard, *Adam and Eve and Pinch Me*
1922	F. Scott Fitzgerald, *Tales of the Jazz Age*
	Katherine Mansfield, *The Garden Party and Other Stories*
1923	Ernest Hemingway, *Three Stories and Ten Poems*
	Sherwood Anderson, *Horses and Men*
	Katherine Mansfield, *The Doves' Nest and Other Stories*
	A. E. Coppard, *The Black Dog*
	Elizabeth Bowen, *Encounters*
	F. L. Pattee, *The Development of the American Short Story*
	Katherine Mansfield dies
1924	Ernest Hemingway, *In Our Time*
	Franz Kafka, "A Hunger Artist"
	Anton Chekhov, *Letters on the Short Story, the Drama, and Other Literary Topics* (in English)
	Joseph Conrad dies
	Franz Kafka dies
1925	Ernest Hemingway, *In Our Time* (enlarged edition)
	Flannery O'Connor born
	Yukio Mishima born
1926	F. Scott Fitzgerald, *All the Sad Young Men*
	Isaac Babel, *Red Cavalry*
1927	Ernest Hemingway, *Men Without Women*
1928	H. E. Bates, *Day's End and Other Stories*
	Thomas Hardy dies
	Gabriel García Márquez born
1930	Katherine Anne Porter, *Flowering Judas and Other Stories*
	Mary E. Wilkins Freeman dies
	D. H. Lawrence dies

Date	Event
1931	William Faulkner, *These Thirteen*
	Isaac Babel, *Tales of Odessa*
	Frank O'Connor, *Guests of the Nation*
1932	Conrad Aiken, "Mr. Arcularis," "Silent Snow, Secret Snow"
	Seán O'Faoláin, *Midsummer Night Madness and Other Stories*
	Marcel Aymé, *The Picture-Well*
1933	Sherwood Anderson, *Death in the Woods and Other Stories*
	Ernest Hemingway, *Winner Take Nothing*
1934	William Faulkner, *Doctor Martino and Other Stories*
	William Saroyan, *The Daring Young Man on the Flying Trapeze*
	D. H. Lawrence, *The Tales of D. H. Lawrence*
	Isak Dinesen, *Seven Gothic Tales*
	Marcel Aymé, *The Dwarf*
1935	F. Scott Fitzgerald, *Taps at Reveille*
	John O'Hara, *The Doctor's Son and Other Stories*
	Ignazio Silone, *Mr. Aristotle*
1936	Thomas Mann, *Stories of Three Decades*
	Rudyard Kipling dies
1938	Ernest Hemingway, *The Fifth Column and the First Forty-nine Stories*
	William Faulkner, *The Unvanquished*
	John Steinbeck, *The Long Valley*
	Richard Wright, *Uncle Tom's Children*
	Marcel Aymé, *Derriere Chez Martin*
1939	Katherine Anne Porter, *Pale Horse, Pale Rider*
	Jean-Paul Sartre, *The Wall and Other Stories*
1940	William Saroyan, *My Name Is Aram*
	Dylan Thomas, *Portrait of the Artist as a Young Dog*
	Hamlin Garland dies
1941	Eudora Welty, *A Curtain of Green and Other Stories*
	Jorge Luis Borges, "The Garden of Forking Paths"
	Sherwood Anderson dies
	James Joyce dies
	Virginia Woolf dies
	Isaac Babel dies
1942	William Faulkner, *Go Down, Moses*
	Mary McCarthy, *The Company She Keeps*
	Mary Lavin, *Tales from Bective Bridge*
	Isak Dinesen, *Winter's Tales*
1943	Eudora Welty, *The Wide Net and Other Stories*
	John Cheever, *The Way Some People Live*
	Virginia Woolf, *A Haunted House and Other Short Stories*
	Marcel Aymé, *The Walker Through Walls*
1944	Katherine Anne Porter, *The Leaning Tower and Other Stories*
	Frank O'Connor, *Crab Apple Jelly: Stories and Tales*
	Jorge Luis Borges, *Ficciones, 1935-1944*
1947	Vladimir Nabokov, *Nine Stories*
	J. F. Powers, *Prince of Darkness and Other Stories*
	Marcel Aymé, *Le vin de Paris*
1948	Truman Capote, *Other Voices, Other Rooms*
1949	William Faulkner, *Knight's Gambit*
	Eudora Welty, *The Golden Apples*
	Shirley Jackson, *The Lottery*
	Truman Capote, *A Tree of Night and Other Stories*
	Angus Wilson, *The Wrong Set*
1950	William Faulkner, *Collected Short Stories of William Faulkner*
	Mary McCarthy, *Cast a Cold Eye*
	Ray Bradbury, *The Martian Chronicles*
	Marcel Aymé, *En Arriere*

Date	*Event*
1951	Carson McCullers, *The Ballad of the Sad Café and Other Works*
	W. Somerset Maugham, *The Complete Short Stories of W. Somerset Maugham*
1952	Frank O'Connor, *The Stories of Frank O'Connor*
1953	J. D. Salinger, *Nine Stories*
	Jean Stafford, *Children Are Bored on Sunday*
	Erskine Caldwell, *Complete Stories*
	John Cheever, *The Enormous Radio and Other Stories*
	Yukio Mishima, *Death in Midsummer and Other Stories*
	Ivan Bunin dies
1955	Flannery O'Connor, *A Good Man Is Hard to Find*
	Eudora Welty, *The Bride of the Innisfallen and Other Stories*
	Dylan Thomas, *Adventures in the Skin Trade and Other Stories*
	Thomas Mann dies
1956	J. F. Powers, *The Presence of Grace*
1957	Isaac Bashevis Singer, *Gimpel the Fool and Other Stories*
	James Purdy, *Color of Darkness*
	Albert Camus, *Exile and the Kingdom*
	Isak Dinesen, *Last Tales*
1958	Vladimir Nabokov, *Nabokov's Dozen*
	Bernard Malamud, *The Magic Barrel*
	John Cheever, *The Housebreaker of Shady Hill and Other Stories*
	Isak Dinesen, *Anecdotes of Destiny*
	Samuel Beckett, *Stories and Texts for Nothing*
1959	Philip Roth, *Goodbye, Columbus*
	John Updike, *The Same Door*
	Alan Sillitoe, *The Loneliness of the Long-Distance Runner*
1960	Albert Camus dies
1961	Isaac Bashevis Singer, *The Spinoza of Market Street*
	Tillie Olsen, *Tell Me a Riddle*
	Richard Wright, *Eight Men*
	John Cheever, *Some People, Places, and Things That Will Not Appear in My Next Novel*
	J. D. Salinger, *Franny and Zooey*
	Ernest Hemingway dies
	James Purdy, *Children Is All*
1962	John Updike, *Pigeon Feathers and Other Stories*
	Jorge Luis Borges, *Labyrinths* (in English)
	William Faulkner dies
1963	Bernard Malamud, *Idiots First*
	J. D. Salinger, *Raise High the Roof Beam, Carpenters*, and *Seymour: An Introduction*
	Joyce Carol Oates, *By the North Gate*
	Doris Lessing, *A Man and Two Women*
1964	John Cheever, *The Brigadier and the Golf Widow*
	Doris Lessing, *African Stories*
	Jean Stafford, *Bad Characters*
	Donald Barthelme, *Come Back, Dr. Caligari*
	Flannery O'Connor dies
1965	Flannery O'Connor, *Everything That Rises Must Converge*
	James Baldwin, *Going to Meet the Man*
1966	John Updike, *The Music School*
	Joyce Carol Oates, *Upon the Sweeping Flood*
1968	Saul Bellow, *Mosby's Memoirs and Other Stories*
	Donald Barthelme, *Unspeakable Practices, Unnatural Acts*
	William H. Gass, *In the Heart of the Heart of the Country and Other Stories*
	John Barth, *Lost in the Funhouse*
1969	Bernard Malamud, *Pictures of Fidelman*
	James Alan McPherson, *Hue and Cry*
	Robert Coover, *Pricksongs and Descants*
	Peter Taylor, *The Collected Stories of Peter Taylor*

Date	Event
	Jean Stafford, *The Collected Stories*
	Frank O'Connor, *A Set of Variations*
1970	Isaac Bashevis Singer, *A Friend of Kafka and Other Stories*
	Donald Barthelme, *City Life*
	John Updike, *Bech: A Book*
	Joyce Carol Oates, *The Wheel of Love*
	Yukio Mishima dies
1972	Donald Barthelme, *Sadness*
	John Updike, *Museums and Women and Other Stories*
	John Barth, *Chimera*
	Joyce Carol Oates, *Marriages and Infidelities*
	Gabriel García Márquez, *Innocent Eréndira and Other Stories*
1973	Isaac Bashevis Singer, *A Crown of Feathers and Other Stories*
	Bernard Malamud, *Rembrandt's Hat*
1975	Isaac Bashevis Singer, *Passions and Other Stories*
1980	Eudora Welty, *The Collected Stories of Eudora Welty*
	Italo Calvino, *Italian Folktales*
	Katherine Anne Porter dies
	Jean-Paul Sartre dies
	George P. Elliott dies
	Samuel Beckett, *Company*
	John Collier dies
1981	Raymond Carver, *What We Talk About When We Talk About Love*
	Frank O'Connor, *Collected Stories*
	Caroline Gordon, *The Collected Stories of Caroline Gordon*
	Tobias Wolff, *In the Garden of the North American Martyrs*
	Donald Barthelme, *Sixty Stories*
	John L'Heureux, *Desires*
	Ellen Gilchrist, *In the Land of Dreamy Dreams*
	John Edgar Wideman, *Damballah*
	Mark Helprin, *Ellis Island*
1982	Isaac Asimov, *Foundation's Edge*
	Thomas M. Disch, *The Man Who Had No Idea*
	John Cheever dies
	John Gardner dies
	Bobbie Ann Mason, *Shiloh and Other Stories*
	Isaac Bashevis Singer, *The Collected Stories*
	Graham Swift, *Learning to Swim and Other Stories*
	Joy Williams, *Taking Care*
1983	Donald Barthelme, *Overnight to Many Distant Cities*
	Margaret Atwood, *Murder in the Dark*
	Truman Capote, *One Christmas*
	William Goyen dies
	Raymond Carver, *Cathedral*
	Seán O'Faoláin, *The Collected Stories*
	Frederick Barthelme, *Moon Deluxe*
	Mary Robison, *An Amateur's Guide to the Night*
	Elizabeth Tallent, *In Constant Flight*
1984	Saul Bellow, *Him with His Foot in His Mouth and Other Stories*
	Truman Capote dies
	Thomas Pynchon, *Slow Learner: Early Stories*
	Irwin Shaw dies
	Liam O'Flaherty dies
	David Leavitt, *Family Dancing*
	Ellen Gilchrist, *Victory over Japan*
	Jayne Anne Phillips, *Fast Tickets*
	Shūsaku Endō, *Stained Glass Elegies*
1985	Italo Calvino dies
	Stanley Elkin, *Early Elkin*
	Thomas M. Disch, *Torturing Mr. Amberwell*
	Shirley Ann Grau, *Nine Women*
	Heinrich Böll dies
	T. Coraghessan Boyle, *Greasy Lake and Other Stories*

Date	Event
	Tennessee Williams, *Collected Stories*
	Tobias Wolff, *Back in the World*
	Grace Paley, *Later the Same Day*
	Bharati Mukherjee, *Darkness*
	Peter Taylor, *The Old Forest and Other Stories*
	Richard Ford, *Rock Springs*
	Barry Hannah, *Captain Maximus*
	Steven Millhauser, *In the Penny Arcade*
	Angela Carter, *Black Venus*
	Muriel Spark, *The Stories of Muriel Spark*
	Mavis Gallant, *Overhead in a Balloon*
	Amy Hempel, *Reasons to Live*
1986	Bernard Malamud dies
	Jorge Luis Borges dies
	Truman Capote, *I Remember Grandpa: A Story*
	Lee K. Abbott, *Strangers in Paradise*
	Heinrich Böll, *The Stories of Heinrich Boll*
1987	Robert Coover, *A Night at the Movies*
	James Baldwin dies
	Erskine Caldwell dies
	Mary Gordon, *Temporary Shelter*
	Elizabeth Tallent, *Time With Children*
	Frederick Barthelme, *Chroma*
	Sue Miller, *Inventing the Abbotts*
1988	Raymond Carver, *Where I'm Calling From*
	Italo Calvino, *Under the Jaguar Sun*
	Paul Bowles, *Unwelcome Words*
	Mavis Gallant, *In Transit*
	Raymond Carver dies
	Nancy Hale dies
	Bharati Mukherjee, *The Middleman and Other Stories*
	Ethan Canin, *The Emperor of the Air*
	Larry Brown, *Facing the Music*
	Mary Robison, *Believe Them*
	A. S. Byatt, *Elementals: Stories of Fire and Ice*
	Isabelle Allende, *The Stories of Eva Luna*
	Mary Gaitskill, *Bad Behavior*
1989	Alice Adams, *After You've Gone*
	Samuel Beckett dies
	Ben Okri, *Stars of the New Curfew*
	Jane Smiley, *Ordinary Love and Good Will*
	Donald Barthelme dies
	Robert Penn Warren dies
	Mary McCarthy dies
	T. Coraghessan Boyle, *If the River Were Whiskey*
	Cynthia Ozick, *The Shawl*
	V. S. Pritchett, *Complete Collected Stories*
	Rick Bass, *The Watch*
	Bobbie Ann Mason, *Love Life*
	John Edgar Wideman, *Fever*
	Danilo Kiš, *The Encyclopedia of the Dead*
	Yukio Mishima, *Acts of Worship*
	Mary Robison, *An Amateur's Guide to the Night*
	Susan Minor, *Lust and Other Stories*
1990	J. G. Ballard, *War Fever*
	Alberto Moravia dies
	Arthur C. Clarke, *Tales from the Planet Earth*
	Patrick White dies
	Christopher Tilghman, *In A Father's Place*
	David Leavitt, *A Place I've Never Been*
	Larry Brown, *Big Bad Love*
	Richard Bausch, *The Fireman's Wife and Other Stories*
	Stuart Dybek, *The Coast of Chicago*
	Tim O'Brien, *The Things They Carried*
	Edna O'Brien, *Lantern Slides*
	Joy Williams, *Escapes*
	Steven Millhauser, *The Barnum Museum*
	Lee Smith, *Me and My Baby View the Eclipse*

Date	Event
	Amy Hempel, *At the Gates of the Animal Kingdom*
1991	Margaret Atwood, *Wilderness Tips*
	Ann Beattie, *What Was Mine and Other Stories*
	Saul Bellow, *Something to Remember Me By*
	Nadine Gordimer, *Crimes of Conscience*
	Joanne Greenberg, *With the Snow Queen and Other Stories*
	Graham Greene dies
	Isaac Bashevis Singer dies
	Seán O'Faoláin dies
	Wolfgang Hildesheimer dies
	Joyce Carol Oates, *Heat and Other Stories*
	Chris Offutt, *Kentucky Straight*
	Michael Chabon, *A Model World*
	Nadine Gordimer, *Jump and Other Stories*
	Sandra Cisneros, *Woman Hollering Creek*
	Lee K. Abbott, *Living After Midnight*
1992	Pam Houston, *Cowboys Are My Weakness*
	Robert Olmstead, *A Good Scent from a Strange Mountain*
	Denis Johnson, *Jesus' Son*
	Edward P. Jones, *Lost in the City*
	Tatyana Tolstaya, *Sleepwalker in a Fog*
	James Purdy, *Selected Stories*
	William Trevor, *Collected Stories*
1993	Reynolds Price, *The Collected Stories*
	Thom Jones, *The Pugilist at Rest*
	Amy Bloom, *Come to Me*
	Barry Hannah, *Bats out of Hell*
	John McGahern, *Collected Stories*
	A. S. Byatt, *The Matisse Stories*
	Stanley Elkin, *Van Gogh's Room at Arles*
	Gabriel García Márques, *Strange Pilgrims*
	John Edgar Wideman, *The Stories of John Edgar Wideman*
	Francine Prose, *A Peaceable Kingdom*
	Mavis Gallant, *Across the Bridge: Stories*
	Larry Woiwode, *Silent Passengers*
	Michael Dorris, *Working Men*
	W. P. Kinsella, *Shoeless Joe Comes to Iowa: Stories*
	John McKenna, *The Fallen and Other Stories*
1994	Ralph Ellison dies
	John Wain dies
	Peter Taylor dies
	Stephen Dixon, *The Stories of Stephen Dixon*
	Peter Carey, *Collected Stories*
	Alice Munro, *Open Secrets*
	Shūsaku Endō, *The Final Martyrs*
	John Updike, *The Afterlife and Other Stories*
	Antoyna Nelson, *Family Terrorists*
	Grace Paley, *Collected Stories*
	Frederick Busch, *The Children in the Woods*
1995	Stanley Elkin dies
	Mary Sarton dies
	Patricia Highsmith dies
	Harriet Doerr, *The Tiger in the Grass*
	Bruce Jay Friedman, *The Collected Stories*
	Thom Jones, *Cold Snap*
	Rick Moody, *The Ring of Brightest Angels Around Heaven*
	Salman Rushdie, *East, West*
	Helena Viramontes, *The Moths and Other Stories*
	Andrea Barrett, *Ship Fever and Other Stories*
	Evan S. Connell, *Collected Stories*
	William Maxwell, *All the Days and Nights*
	Janette Turner Hospital, *Collected Stories*
1996	Harold Brodkey dies
	José Donoso dies

Date	Event
	Michael M. Rea dies
	Mary Lavin dies
	Robie MacCauley dies
	Natalie Petesch, *The Immigrant Train and Other Stories*
	Andre Dubus, *Dancing After Hours*
	Tobias Wolff, *The Night in Question*
	William Trevor, *After Rain*
	Barry Hannah, *High Lonesome*
	Angela Carter, *Burning Your Boats: Collected Stories*
	Julian Barnes, *Cross Channel*
	Mavis Gallant, *Collected Stories*
	John Barth, *On with the Story*
1997	William Eastlake dies
	Michael Dorris dies
	Vladimir Soloukhin dies
	V. S. Pritchett dies
	William Humphrey dies
	Charles Baxter, *Believers: A Novella and Stories*
	Lee Smith, *News of the Spirit*
	Rick Bass, *The Sky, the Stars, the Wilderness*
	Yasunari Kawabata, *The Dancing Girl of Izu*
	Robert Stone, *Bear and His Daughters*
	Peter Ho Davies, *The Ugliest House in the World*
	Harold Brodkey, *The World is the Home of Love and Death*
	Carlos Fuentes, *The Crystal Frontier*
	Cynthia Ozick, *Puttermesser Papers*
	Richard Ford, *Women with Men*
	David Leavitt, *Arkansas*
	William Trevor, *After Rain*
1998	Jerome Weidman dies
	William Abrahams dies
	John Hawkes dies
	Wright Morris dies
	Brendhan Gill dies
	Alice Munro, *The Love of a Good Woman*
	Steven Millhauser, *The Knife Thrower and Other Stories*
	Lorrie Moore, *Birds of America*
	Judy Budnitz, *Flying Leap*
	Aimee Bender, *The Girl in the Flammable Skirt: Stories*
	Reginald McKnight, *White Boys*
	Ann Beattie, *Park City*
	Michael Byers, *The Coast of Good Intentions*
	William H. Gass, *Cartesian Sonata*
1999	J. F. Powers dies
	Alice Adams dies
	Andre Dubus dies
	E. Annie Proulx, *Close Range: Wyoming Stories*
	Julia Slavin, *The Woman Who Cut Off Her Leg at the Maidstone Club and Other Stories*
	David Gates, *The Wonders of the Invisible World*
	Jhumpa Lahiri, *Interpreter of Maladies*
	Pam Houston, *Waltzing the Cat*
	Thom Jones, *Sonny Liston Was a Friend of Mine*
	Chris Offutt, *Out of the Woods*
	Susan Perabo, *Who I Was Supposed to Be*
	Elwood Reid, *What Salmon Know*
	Stephen Dixon, *Sleep*
	Christopher Tilghman, *The Way People Run*
	Michael Chabon, *Werewolves in Their Youth*
	Lan Samantha Chang, *Hunger*
	Alice Adams, *The Last Lovely City*
	George Garrett, *Big Bad Blues*
	Bliss Broyard, *My Father, Dancing*
2000	William Trevor, *The Hill Bachelors*
	John Updike, *Licks of Love: Short Stories and a Sequel, "Rabbit Remembered"*
	Joy Harjo, *A Map to the Next World: Poetry and Tales*
	Ellen Gilchrist, *The Cabal and Other Stories*

TERMS AND TECHNIQUES

Aestheticism: The European literary movement, with its roots in France, that was predominant in the 1890's. It denied that art needed to have any utilitarian purpose and focused on the slogan "art for art's sake." The doctrines of aestheticism were introduced to England by Walter Pater and can be found in the plays of Oscar Wilde and the short stories of Arthur Symons. In American literature, the ideas underlying the aesthetic movement can be found in the short fiction of Edgar Allan Poe.

Allegory: A literary mode in which characters in a narrative personify abstract ideas or qualities and so give a second level of meaning to the work, in addition to the surface narrative. Two famous examples of allegory are Edmund Spenser's *The Faerie Queene* (1590, 1596) and John Bunyan's *The Pilgrim's Progress from This World to That Which Is to Come*, Part I (1678). Modern examples may be found in Nathaniel Hawthorne's story "The Artist of the Beautiful" and the stories and novels of Franz Kafka.

Allusion: A reference to a person or event, either historical or from a literary work, which gives another literary work a wider frame of reference and adds depth to its meaning. For example, Sylvia Townsend Warner's story "Winter in the Air" gains greater suggestiveness from the frequent allusions to William Shakespeare's play *The Winter's Tale* (c. 1610-1611), and her story "Swans on an Autumn River" is enriched by a number of allusions to the poetry of William Butler Yeats.

Ambiguity: Refers to the capacity of language to suggest two or more levels of meaning within a single expression, thus conveying a rich, concentrated effect. Ambiguity has been defined by William Empson in *Seven Types of Ambiguity* (1930) as "any verbal nuance, however, slight, which gives room for alternative reactions to the same piece of language." It has been suggested that because of the short story's highly compressed form, ambiguity may play a more important role in the form than it does in the novel.

Anachronism: An event, person, or thing placed outside—usually earlier than—its proper historical era. Shakespeare uses anachronism in *King John* (c. 1596-1597), *Antony and Cleopatra* (c. 1606-1607), and *Julius Caesar* (c. 1599-1600). Mark Twain employed anachronism to comic effect in *A Connecticut Yankee in King Arthur's Court* (1889).

Anecdote: The short narration of a single interesting incident or event. An anecdote differs from a short story in that it does not have a plot, relates a single episode, and does not range over different times and places.

Antagonist: A character in fiction who stands in opposition, or rivalry, to the protagonist. In Shakespeare's *Hamlet, Prince of Denmark* (c. 1600-1601), for example, King Claudius is the antagonist of Hamlet.

Anthology: A collection of prose or poetry, usually by various writers. Often serves to introduce the work of little-known authors to a wider audience.

Aphorism: A short, concise statement that states an opinion, precept, or general truth, such as Alexander Pope's "Hope springs eternal in the human breast."

Aporia: An interpretative point in a story that basically cannot be decided, usually as the result of some gap or absence.

Apostrophe: A direct address to a person (usually absent), inanimate entity, or abstract quality. Examples are the first line of William Wordsworth's sonnet "London, 1802," "Milton! Thou should'st be living at this hour," and King Lear's speech in Shakespeare's *King Lear* (c. 1605-1606), "Blow, winds, and crack your cheeks! rage! blow!"

Appropriation: The act of taking over part of a literary theory or approach for one's own ends, for example, male critics appropriating the approach of feminists.

Archetypal theme: Recurring thematic patterns in literature. Common archetypal themes include death and rebirth (Samuel Taylor Coleridge's *The Rime of the Ancient Mariner*, 1798), paradise-Hades (Coleridge's "Kubla Khan"), the fatal woman (Guy de Maupassant's "Doubtful Happiness"), the earth goddess ("Yanda" by Isaac Bashevis Singer), the scapegoat (D. H. Lawrence's "The Woman Who Rode Away"), and the return to the womb (Flannery O'Connor's "The River").

Archetype: The term was used by psychologist Carl Jung to describe what he called "primordial images," which exist in the "collective unconscious" of humankind and are manifested in myths, religion, literature, and dreams. Now used broadly in literary criticism to refer to character types, motifs, images, symbols, and plot patterns recurring in many different literary forms and works. The embodiment of archetypes in a work of literature can make a powerful impression on the reader.

Architectonics: A term borrowed from architecture to describe the structural qualities, such as unity and balance, of a work of literature. If the architectonics are successful, the work will give the impression of organic unity and balance, like a solidly constructed building in which the total value is more than the sum of the parts.

Asides: In drama, short passages generally spoken by one dramatic character in an undertone or directed to the audience, so as not to be heard by other characters on stage.

Atmosphere: The mood or tone of a work; it is often associated with setting but can also be established by action or dialogue. The opening paragraphs of Poe's "The Fall of the House of Usher" and James Joyce's "Araby" provide good examples of atmosphere created early in the works and pervading the remainder of the story.

Ballad: Popular ballads are songs or verse that tell dramatic, usually impersonal, tales. Supernatural events, courage, and love are frequent themes, but any experience that appeals to ordinary people is acceptable material. Literary ballads—narrative poems based on popular ballads—have frequently been in vogue in English literature, particularly during the Romantic period. One of the most famous is Samuel Taylor Coleridge's *The Rime of the Ancient Mariner.*

Black humor: A general term of modern origin that refers to a form of "sick humor" that is intended to produce laughter out of the morbid and the taboo. Examples are the works of Joseph Heller, Thomas Pynchon, Günter Grass, and Kurt Vonnegut.

Broadside ballad: A ballad printed on one side of a large, single sheet of paper and sung to a popular tune. Dating from the sixteenth century in England, the subject of the broadside ballad was a topical event or issue.

Burlesque: A work that, by imitating attitudes, styles, institutions, and people, aims to amuse. Burlesque differs from satire in that it aims to ridicule simply for the sake of amusement rather than for political or social change.

Canon: The standard or authoritative list of literary works that are widely accepted as outstanding representatives of their period and genre. In recent literary criticism, however, the established canon has come under fierce assault for its alleged culture and gender bias.

Canonize: The act of adding a literary work to the list of works that form the primary tradition of a genre or literature in general. For example, a number of stories by female and African American writers previously excluded from the canon of the short story, such as Charlotte Perkins Gilman's "The Yellow Wallpaper" and Charles Waddell Chesnutt's "The Sheriff's Children," have recently been canonized.

Caricature: A form of writing that focuses on unique qualities of a person and then exaggerates and distorts those qualities in order to ridicule the person and what he or she represents. Contemporary writers, such as Flannery O'Connor, have used caricature for serious and satiric purposes in such stories as "Good Country People" and "A Good Man Is Hard to Find."

Character type: The term can refer to the convention of using stock characters, such as the *miles gloriosus* (braggart soldier) of Renaissance and Roman comedy, the figure of vice in medieval morality plays, or the clever servant in Elizabethan comedy. It can also describe "flat" characters (the term was coined by E. M. Forster) in fiction who do not grow or change during the course of the narrative and who can be easily classified.

Chronicle: The precursors of modern histories, chronicles were written accounts of national or world events. One of the best known is the *Anglo-Saxon Chronicle*, begun in the reign of King Alfred in the late ninth century. Many chronicles were written in Elizabethan times, and these were used by Shakespeare as source documents for his history plays.

Classic/Classicism: A literary stance or value system consciously based on the example of classical Greek and Roman literature. While the term is applied to an enormous diversity of artists in many different periods and in many different national literatures, it generally denotes a cluster of values including formal discipline, restrained expression, reverence of tradition, and an objective rather than subjective orientation. Often contrasted to Romanticism.

Climax: Similar to crisis, the moment in a work of fiction at which the action reaches a turning point and the plot begins to be resolved. Unlike crisis, the term is also used to refer to the moment in which the reader's emotional involvement with the work reaches its point of highest intensity.

Comic story: Encompasses a wide variety of modes and inflections, such as parody, burlesque, satire, irony, and humor. Frequently, the defining quality of comic characters is that they lack self-awareness; the reader tends not to identify with them but perceives them from a detached point of view, more as objects than persons.

Conceit: A type of metaphor that makes highly intellectualized comparisons between seemingly disparate things. It is associated with the Metaphysical poets and the Elizabethan sonneteers; examples can also be found in the poetry of Emily Dickinson and T. S. Eliot.

Conflict: The struggle that develops as a result of the opposition between the protagonist and another person, the natural world, society, or some force within the self. In short fiction, the conflict is most often between the protagonist and some strong force either within the protagonist or within the given state of the human condition.

Connotation/Denotation: Denotation is the explicit, formal definition of a word, exclusive of its emotional associations. When a word takes on an additional meaning, other than its denotative one, it achieves connotation. For example, the word "mercenary" denotes a soldier who is paid to fight in an army not of his own region, but connotatively a mercenary is an unprincipled scoundrel who kills for money.

Conte: French for tale, a conte was originally a short adventure tale. In the nineteenth century, the term was used to describe a tightly constructed short story. In England, the term is used to describe a work longer than a short story and shorter than a novel.

Crisis: A turning point in the plot, at which the opposing forces reach the point that a resolution must take place.

Criticism: The study and evaluation of works of literature. Theoretical criticism, as for example in Aristotle's *De poetica*, c. 334-323 B.C.E. (*Poetics*, 1705) sets out general principles for interpretation. Practical criticism (Coleridge's lectures on Shakespeare, for example) offers interpretations of particular works or authors.

Deconstruction: A literary theory, primarily attributed to French critic Jacques Derrida, which has spawned a wide variety of practical applications, the most prominent being the critical tactic of laying bare a text's self-reflexivity, that is, showing how it continually refers to and subverts its own way of meaning.

Defamiliarization: A term coined by the Russian Formalists to indicate a process by which the writer makes the reader perceive the concrete uniqueness of an object, event, or idea that has been generalized by routine and habit.

Dénouement: Literally, "unknotting"; the conclusion of a drama or fiction, when the plot is unraveled and the mystery solved.

Detective story: The "classic" detective story (or "mystery") is a highly formalized and logically structured mode of fiction in which the focus is on a crime solved by a detective through interpretation of evidence and clever reasoning. Many modern practitioners of the genre, however, such as Raymond Chandler, Patricia Highsmith, and Ross Macdonald, have placed less emphasis on the puzzlelike qualities of the detective story and have focused instead on characterization, theme, and other elements of mainstream fiction. The form was first developed in short fiction by Edgar Allan Poe; Jorge Luis Borges has also used the convention in short stories.

Deus ex machina: Latin, meaning "god out of the machine." In the Greek theater, it referred to the use of a god lowered out of a mechanism onto the stage to untangle the plot or save the hero. It has come to signify any artificial device for the easy resolution of dramatic difficulties.

Device: Any technique used in literature in order to gain a specific effect. The poet uses the device of figurative language, for example, while the novelist may use the devices of foreshadowing, flashback, and so on, in order to create a desired effect.

Dialogics: The theory that fiction is a dialogic genre in which many different voices are held in suspension without becoming merged into a single authoritative voice. Developed by Russian critic Mikhail Bakhtin.

Didactic literature: Literature that seeks to instruct, give guidance, or teach a lesson. Didactic literature normally has a moral, religious, or philosophical purpose, or it will expound a branch of knowledge (as in Vergil's *Georgics*, c. 37-29 B.C.E.; English translation, 1589). It is distinguished from imaginative works, in which the aesthetic product takes precedence over any moral intent.

Diegesis: This term refers to the hypothetical world of a story, as if it actually existed in real space and time. It is the illusory universe of the story created by its linguistic structure.

Doggerel: Strictly speaking, doggerel refers to rough and jerky versification, but the term is more commonly applied to worthless verse that contains monotonous rhyme and rhythm and trivial subject matter.

Doppelgänger: A double or counterpart of a person, sometimes endowed with ghostly qualities. A fictional *Doppelgänger* often reflects a suppressed side of his or her personality, as in Fyodor Dostoevski's novella *Dvoynik* (1846; *The Double*, 1917) and the short stories of E. T. A. Hoffmann. Isaac Bashevis Singer and Jorge Luis Borges, among other modern writers, have also employed the *Doppelgänger* with striking effect.

Dream vision: An allegorical form common in the Middle Ages, in which the narrator or a character falls asleep and dreams a dream that becomes the actual framed story. Subtle variations of the form have been used by Hawthorne in "Young Goodman Brown" and by Poe in "The Pit and the Pendulum."

Dualism: A theory that the universe is explicable in terms of two basic, conflicting entities, such as good and evil, mind and matter, or the physical and the spiritual.

Eclogue: In Greek, the term means literally "selection." It is now used to describe a formal pastoral poem. Classical eclogues are constructed around a variety of conventional themes: the singing match, the rustic dialogue, the lament, the love lay, and the eulogy. During the Renaissance, eclogues were employed as veiled satires.

Écriture Féminine: French feminist Hélène Cixous argues for a unique female kind of writing, which in its fluidity disrupts the binary oppositions of male-dominated cultural structures.

Effect: The total, unified impression, or impact, made upon the reader by a literary work. Every aspect of the work—plot, characterization, style, and so on—is seen to directly contribute to this overall impression.

Elegy: A long, rhymed, formal poem whose subject is meditation upon death or a lamentation theme; Alfred, Lord Tennyson's *In Memoriam* (1850) is a well-known example. The pastoral elegy, such as Percy Bysshe Shelley's *Adonais: An Elegy on the Death of John Keats* (1821), uses a pastoral scene to express grief at the loss of a friend or important person.

Emotive meaning: The emotion that is commonly associated with a word. In other words, emotive meaning includes the connotations of a word, not merely what it denotes. Emotive meaning is contrasted with cognitive or descriptive meaning, in which neither emotions nor connotations are involved.

Epic: Although this term usually refers to a long narrative poem that presents the exploits of a central figure of high position, the term is also used to designate a long novel that has the style or structure usually associated with an epic. In this sense, for example, Herman Melville's *Moby Dick: Or, The Whale* (1851) and James Joyce's *Ulysses* (1922) may be called epics.

Epiphany: The literary application of this religious term was popularized by James Joyce in his book *Stephen Hero* (1944): "By an epiphany he meant a sudden spiritual manifestation, whether in the vulgarity of speech or of gesture or in a memorable phase of the mind itself." Many short stories since Joyce's collection *Dubliners* (1914) have been analyzed as epiphanic stories in which a character or the reader experiences a sudden revelation of meaning.

Episode: In Greek tragedy, the segment between two choral odes. Episode now refers to an incident presented as a continuous action. In a work of literature, many discrete episodes are woven together to form a more complex work.

Epistolary fiction: A work of fiction in which the narrative is carried forward by means of letters written by the characters. Epistolary novels were a quite popular form in the eighteenth century. Examples include Samuel Richardson's *Pamela: Or, Virtue Rewarded* (1740-1741) and *Clarissa: Or, The History of a Young Lady* (1747-1748). The form has not been much used in the twentieth century.

Essay: A brief prose work, usually on a single topic, that expresses the personal point of view of the author. The essay is usually addressed to a general audience and attempts to persuade the reader to accept the author's ideas.

Essay-sketch tradition: The first sketches can be traced to the Greek philosopher Theophrastus in 300 B.C.E., whose character sketches influenced seventeenth and eighteenth century writers in England, who developed the form into something close to the idea of character in fiction. The essay has an equally venerable history, and, like the sketch, had an impact on the development of the modern short story.

Euphony: Language that creates a harmonious and pleasing effect; the opposite of cacophony, which is a combination of harsh and discordant sounds.

Exemplum: A brief anecdote or tale introduced to illustrate a moral point in medieval sermons. By the fourteenth century these exempla had expanded into exemplary narratives. Geoffrey Chaucer's "The Nun's Priest's Tale" and "The Pardoner's Tale" are exempla.

Existentialism: A philosophy and attitude of mind that gained wide currency in religious and artistic thought after the end of World War II. Typical concerns of existential writers are human beings' estrangement from society, their awareness that the world is meaningless, and their recognition that one must turn from external props to the self. The novels of Albert Camus and Franz Kafka provide examples of existentialist beliefs.

Exposition: The part or parts of a work of fiction that provide necessary background information. Exposition not only provides the time and place of the action but also introduces readers to the fictive world of the story, acquainting them with the ground rules of the work. In the short story, exposition is usually elliptical.

Expressionism: Beginning in German theater at the start of the twentieth century, expressionism became the dominant movement in the decade following World War I. It abandoned realism and relied on a conscious distortion of external reality in order to portray the world as it is "viewed emotionally." The movement spread to fiction and poetry. Expressionism influenced the plays of Eugene O'Neill, Tennessee Williams, and Thornton Wilder and can be found in the novels of Franz Kafka and James Joyce.

Fable: One of the oldest narrative forms. Usually takes the form of an analogy in which animals or inanimate objects speak to illustrate a moral lesson. The most famous examples are the fables of Aesop, who used the form orally in 600 B.C.E.

Fabliau: A short narrative poem, popular in medieval French literature and during the English Middle Ages. Fabliaux were usually realistic in subject matter, bawdy, and made a point of satirizing the weaknesses and foibles of human beings. Perhaps the most famous are Geoffrey Chaucer's "The Miller's Tale" and "The Reeve's Tale."

Fabulation: A term coined by Robert Scholes and used in contemporary literary criticism to describe novels that are radically experimental in subject matter, style, and form. Like the Magical Realists, fabulators mix realism with fantasy. The works of Thomas Pynchon, John Barth, Donald Barthelme, and William Gass provide examples.

Fairy tale: A form of folktale in which supernatural events or characters are prominent. Fairy tales usually depict a realm of reality beyond that of the natural world and in which the laws of the natural world are suspended.

Fantastic: In his study *Introduction à la littérature fantastique*, 1970 (*The Fantastic: A Structural Approach to a Literary Genre*, 1973) the critic Tzvetan Todorov defines the fantastic as a genre that lies between the uncanny and the marvelous. Whereas the marvelous presents an event that cannot be explained by the laws of the natural world and the uncanny presents an event that is the result of hallucination or illusion, the fantastic exists as long as the reader cannot decide which of these two applies. Henry James's *The Turn of the Screw* (1898) is an example of the fantastic.

Figurative language: Any use of language that departs from the usual or ordinary meaning to gain a poetic or otherwise special effect. Figurative language embodies various figures of speech, such as irony, metaphor, simile, and many others.

Fin de siècle: Literally, "end of the century"; refers to the last decade of the nineteenth century, a transitional period in which artists and writers were aware that they were living at the close of a great age and deliberately cultivated a kind of languor, world weariness, and satiety. Associated with the period of aestheticism and the Decadent movement exemplified in Oscar Wilde.

Flashback: A scene that depicts an earlier event; it can be presented as a reminiscence by a character in a story, or it can simply be inserted into the narrative.

Folktale: A short prose narrative, usually handed down orally, found in all cultures of the world. The term is often used interchangeably with myth, fable, and fairy tale.

Form: The organizing principle in a work of literature, the manner in which its elements are put together in relation to its total effect. The term is sometimes used interchangeably with structure and is often contrasted with content: If form is the building, content is what is in the building and what the building is specifically designed to express.

Frame story: A story that provides a framework for another story (or stories) told within it. The form is ancient and is used by Geoffrey Chaucer in *The Canterbury Tales* (1387-1400). In modern literature, the technique has been used by Henry James in *The Turn of the Screw* (1898), Joseph Conrad in *Heart of Darkness* (1902), and John Barth in *Lost in the Funhouse* (1968).

Framework: When used in connection with a frame story, the framework is the narrative setting, within which other stories are told. The framework may also have a plot of its own. More generally, the framework is similar to structure, referring to the general outline of a work.

Gendered: When a work is approached as thematically or stylistically specific to male or female characteristics or concerns, it is said to be "gendered."

Genre study: The concept of studying literature by classification and definition of types or kinds, such as tragedy, comedy, epic, lyrical, and pastoral. First introduced by Aristotle in *Poetics*, the genre principle has been an essential concomitant to the basic proposition that literature can be studied scientifically.

Gothic genre: A form of fiction developed in the late eighteenth century which focuses on horror and the supernatural. Examples include Matthew Gregory Lewis's *The Monk: A Romance*, 1796 (also published as *Ambrosio: Or, The Monk*), Mary Wollstonecraft Shelley's *Frankenstein* (1818), and the short fiction of Edgar Allan Poe. In modern literature, the gothic genre can be found in the fiction of Truman Capote.

Grotesque: Characterized by a breakup of the everyday world by mysterious forces, the form differs from fantasy in that the reader is not sure whether to react with humor or horror. Examples include the stories of E. T. A. Hoffmann and Franz Kafka.

Gynocriticism: American feminist critic Elaine C. Showalter coined this term for her theory that women read and write differently than men do because of biological and cultural differences.

Hasidic tale: Hasidism was a Jewish mystical sect formed in the eighteenth century. The term "Hasidic tale" is used to describe some American short fiction, much of it written in the 1960's, which reflected the spirit of Hasidism, particularly the belief in the immanence of God in all things. Saul Bellow, Philip Roth, and Norman Mailer have been attracted to the genre, as has the Israeli writer Shmuel Yosef Agnon, who won the Nobel Prize in Literature in 1966.

Hegemony: Italian critic Antonio Gramsci maintains that capitalists create and sustain an ideology to support their dominance or hegemony over the working class. By maintaining economic and cultural power, capitalists receive the support of the working class, who adopt their values and beliefs, and thus control the ideology or social consciousness that in turn controls individual consciousness.

Historical criticism: In contrast to formalist criticism, which treats literary works as self-contained artifacts, historical criticism emphasizes the social and historical context of literature and allows itself to take into consideration the relevant facts and circumstances of the author's life. The method emphasizes the meaning that the work had in its own time rather than interpreting it for the present.

Hyperbole: The term is Greek for "overshooting" and refers to the use of gross exaggeration for rhetorical effect, based on the assumption that the reader will not be persuaded of the literal truth of the overstatement. Can be used for serious or comic effect.

Imagery: Often defined as the verbal stimulation of sensory perception. Although the word betrays a visual bias, imagery, in fact, calls on all five senses. In its simplest form, imagery re-creates a physical sensation in a clear, literal manner; it becomes more complex when a poet employs metaphor and other figures of speech to re-create experience.

In medias res: Latin phrase used by Horace, meaning literally "into the midst of things." It refers to a literary technique of beginning the narrative when the action has already begun. The term is used particularly in connection with the epic, which traditionally begins *in medias res*.

Initiation story: A story in which protagonists, usually children or young persons, go through an experience, sometimes painful or disconcerting, that carries them from innocence to some new form of knowledge and maturity. William Faulkner's "The Bear," Nathaniel Hawthorne's "Young Goodman Brown," Alice Walker's "To Hell with Dying," and Robert Penn Warren's "Blackberry Winter" are examples of the form.

Interior monologue: Defined as the speech of a character designed to introduce the reader directly to the character's internal life, the form differs from other monologues in that it attempts to reproduce thought before any logical organization is imposed upon it. An example is Molly Bloom's long interior monologue at the conclusion of James Joyce's *Ulysses*.

Interpretation: An analysis of the meaning of a literary work. Interpretation will attempt to explicate the theme, structure, and other components of the work, often focusing on obscure or ambiguous passages.

Irrealism: A term often used to refer to modern or postmodern fiction that is presented self-consciously as a fiction or fabulation rather than a mimesis of external reality. The best-known practitioners of irrealism are John Barth, Robert Coover, and Donald Barthelme.

Lai/Lay: A song or short narrative poem. The term was first applied to twelfth and thirteenth centuries French poems and to English poems in the fourteenth century that were based on them, including Geoffrey Chaucer's "The Franklin's Tale." In the nineteenth century, the term was applied to historical ballads such as Sir Walter Scott's *The Lay of the Last Minstrel* (1805).

Legend: A narrative that is handed down from generation to generation, usually associated with a particular place and a specific event. A legend may often have more historical truth than a myth, and the protagonist is usually a person rather than a supernatural being.

Leitmotif: From the German, meaning "leading motif." Any repetition—of a word, phrase, situation, or idea—that occurs within a single work or group of related works.

Literary short story: A term that was current in American criticism in the 1940's to distinguish the short fiction of Ernest Hemingway, Eudora Welty, Sherwood Anderson, and others from the popular pulp and slick fiction of the day.

Local color: Usually refers to a movement in literature, especially in the United States, in the latter part of the nineteenth century. The focus was on the environment, atmosphere, and milieu of a particular region. For example, Mark Twain wrote about the Mississippi region; Sarah Orne Jewett wrote about New England. The term can also be used to refer to any work that represents the characteristics of a particular region.

Logocentrism: Jacques Derrida argues that all Western thought is based on the quest for a nonexistent "transcendental signifier," a sort of primal origin that makes ultimate meaning possible. The Western assumption of some ultimate center, that it calls God, reason, truth, or essence, is what Derrida calls Logocentrism.

Lyric short story: A form in which the emphasis is on internal changes, moods, and feelings. The lyric story is usually open-ended and depends on the figurative language generally associated with poetry. Examples of lyric stories are the works of Ivan Turgenev, Anton Chekhov, Katherine Mansfield, Sherwood Anderson, Conrad Aiken, and John Updike.

Lyrical ballad: The term is preeminently associated with William Wordsworth and Samuel Taylor Coleridge, whose *Lyrical Ballads* (1798), which drew on the ballad tradition, was one of the seminal books of the Romantic age. *Lyrical Ballads* was a revolt against eighteenth century poetic diction; it was an attempt to create a new kind of poetry by using simple language and taking as subject the everyday lives of common folk and the strong emotions they experience.

Malaprop/Malapropism: A malapropism occurs when one word is confused with another because of a similarity in sound between them. The term is derived from the character Mistress Malaprop in Richard Brinsley Sheridan's *The Rivals* (1775), who, for example, uses the word "illiterate" when she really means "obliterate" and mistakes "progeny" for "prodigy."

Märchen: German fairy tales, as collected in the works of Wilhelm and Jacob Grimm or in the works of nineteenth century writers such as Novalis and E. T. A. Hoffmann.

Marginalization: The process by which an individual or a group is deemed secondary to a dominant group in power and thus denied access to the benefits enjoyed by the dominant group; for example, in the past women were marginalized by men and nonwhites were marginalized by whites.

Medieval romance: Medieval romances, which originated in twelfth century France, were tales of adventure in which a knight would embark on a perilous quest to win the hand of a lady, perform a service for his king, or seek the Holy Grail. He had to overcome many obstacles, including dragons and other monsters; magic spells and enchantments were prominent, and the romance embodied the chivalric ideals of courage, honor, refined manners, and courtly love. English romances include the anonymous *Sir Gawain and the Green Knight* and Sir Thomas Malory's *Le Morte d'Arthur* (1485).

Memoir: Usually written by people prominent in public life, memoirs are the authors' recollections of famous people they have known and great events they have witnessed. Memoir differs from autobiography, in that the emphasis in the latter is on the life of the author.

Metafiction: Refers to fiction that manifests a reflexive tendency, such as Vladimir Nabokov's *Pale Fire* (1962), and John Fowles's *The French Lieutenant's Woman* (1969). The emphasis is on the loosening of the work's illusion of reality to expose the reality of its illusion. Such terms as "irrealism," "postmodernist fiction," and "antifiction" are also used to refer to this type of fiction.

Metaphor: A figure of speech in which two dissimilar objects are imaginatively identified (rather than merely compared) on the assumption that they share one or more qualities: "She is the rose, the glory of the day" (Edmund Spenser). The term is often used in modern criticism in a wider sense to identify analogies of all kinds in literature, painting, and film.

Metonymy: A figure of speech in which an object that is closely related to a word comes to stand for the word itself, such as when one says "the White House" when meaning the "president."

Minimalist movement: A school of fiction writing that developed in the late 1970's and early 1980's and that John Barthes has characterized as the "less is more school." Minimalism attempts to convey much by saying little, to render contemporary reality in precise, pared-down prose that suggests more than it directly states. Leading minimalist writers are Raymond Carver and Ann Beattie. A character in Beattie's short story "Snow" (in *Where You'll Find Me*, 1986) seems to sum up minimalism: "Any life will seem dramatic if you omit mention of most of it."

Mise en abîme: A small story inside a larger narrative that echoes or mirrors the larger narrative, thus containing the larger within the smaller.

Modern short story: The modern short story dates from the nineteenth century and is associated with the names of Edgar Allan Poe (who is often credited with inventing the form) and Nathaniel Hawthorne in the United States, Honoré de Balzac in France, and E. T. A. Hoffmann in Germany. In his influential critical writings, Poe defined the short story as being limited to "a certain unique or single effect," to which every detail in the story should contribute.

Monologue: Any speech or narrative presented by one person. It can sometimes be used to refer to any lengthy speech, in which one person monopolizes the conversation.

Moral tract: A propaganda pamphlet on a political or religious topic, usually distributed free. The term is often associated with the Oxford Movement in nineteenth century England, which was a movement to reform the Church of England.

Motif: An incident or situation in a story that serves as the basis of its structure, creating by repetition and variation a patterned recurrence and consequently a general theme. Russian Formalist critics distinguish between bound motifs, which cannot be omitted without disturbing the thematic structure of the story, and unbound motifs, which serve merely to create the illusion of external reality. In this sense, motif is the same as leitmotif.

Myth: An anonymous traditional story, often involving supernatural beings or the interaction between gods and human beings and dealing with the basic questions of how the world and human society came to be as they are. Myth is an important term in contemporary literary criticism. Northrop Frye, for example, has said that "the typical forms of myth become the conventions and genres of literature." By this, he means that the genres of comedy, romance, tragedy, and irony (satire) correspond to seasonal myths of spring, summer, autumn, and winter.

Narrative: An account in prose or verse of an event or series of events, whether real or imagined.

Narrative persona: "Persona" means literally "mask": It is the self created by the author and through whom the narrative is told. The persona is not to be identified with the author, even when the two may seem to resemble each other. The narrative persona in George Gordon, Lord Byron's *Don Juan* (1819-1824), for example, may express many sentiments of which Byron would have approved, but he is nevertheless a fictional creation who is distinct from the author.

Narratology: The theoretical study of narrative structures and ways of meaning. Most all major literary theories have a branch of study known as narratology.

Narrator: The character who recounts the narrative. There are many different types of narrators: The first-person narrator is a character in the story and can be recognized by his or her use of "I"; third-person narrators may be limited or omniscient. In the former, the narrator is confined to knowledge of the minds and emotions of one or, at most, a few characters. In the latter, the narrator knows everything, seeing into the minds of all the characters. Rarely, second-person narration may be used. (An example can be found in Edna O'Brien's *A Pagan Place*, 1973.)

Novel: A fictional prose form, longer than a short story or novelette. The term embraces a wide range of types, but the novel usually includes a more complicated plot and a wider cast of characters than the short story. The focus is often on the development of individual characterization and the presentation of a social world and a detailed environment.

Novella, Novelette, Novelle, Nouvelle: These terms all refer to the form of fiction that is longer than a short story and shorter than a novel. *Novella*, the Italian term, is the term usually used to refer to American works in this genre, such as Joseph Conrad's *Heart of Darkness* (1902) and Henry James's *The Turn of the Screw* (1898). *Novelle* is the

German term; *nouvelle* the French; "novelette" the British. The term "novel" derived from these terms.

Objective correlative: A key concept in modern formalist criticism, coined by T. S. Eliot in *The Sacred Wood* (1920). An objective correlative is a situation, an event, or an object that, when presented or described in a literary work, expresses a particular emotion and serves as a precise formula by which the same emotion can be evoked in the reader.

Oral tale: A wide-ranging term that can include everything from gossip to myths, legends, folktales, and jokes. Among the terms used by Stith Thompson to classify oral tales (*The Folktale*, 1951) are *märchen*, fairy tale, household tale, *conte populaire*, novella, hero tale, local tradition, migratory legend, explanatory tale, humorous anecdote, and merry tale.

Oral tradition: Material that is transmitted by word of mouth, often through chants or songs, from generation to generation. Homer's epics, for example, were originally passed down orally and employ formulas to make memorization easier. Often, ballads, folklore, and proverbs are also passed down in this way.

Oriental tale: An eighteenth century form made popular by the translations of *Alf layla wa-layla* (fifteenth century; *The Arabian Nights' Entertainments*, 1706-1708) collected during the period. Oriental tales were usually solemn in tone, contained little characterization, and focused on improbable events and supernatural places.

Other: By a process of psychological or cultural projection, an individual or a dominant group accuses those of a different race or gender of all the negative qualities they themselves possess and then respond to them as if they were "other" than themselves.

Oxymoron: Closely related to paradox, an oxymoron occurs when two words of opposite meaning are placed in juxtaposition, such as "wise fool," "devilish angel," or "loving hate."

Parable: A short, simple, and usually allegorical story that teaches a moral lesson. In the West, the most famous parables are those told in the Gospels by Jesus Christ.

Paradox: A statement that initially seems to be illogical or self-contradictory yet eventually proves to embody a complex truth. In New Criticism, the term is used to embrace any complexity of language that sustains multiple meanings and deviates from the norms of ordinary language use.

Parataxis: The placing of clauses or phrases in a series without the use of coordinating or subordinating terms.

Parody: A literary work that imitates or burlesques another work or author for the purpose of ridicule. Twentieth century parodists include E. B. White and James Thurber.

Periodical essay/sketch: Informal in tone and style and applied to a wide range of topics, the periodical essay originated in the early eighteenth century. It is associated in particular with Joseph Addison and Richard Steele and their informal periodical, *The Spectator.*

Personification: A figure of speech which ascribes human qualities to abstractions or inanimate objects, as in these lines by W. H. Auden: "There's Wrath who has learnt every trick of guerrilla warfare,/ The shamming dead, the night-raid, the feinted retreat." Richard Crashaw's "Hope, thou bold taster of delight" is another example.

Plot: Plot refers to how authors arrange their material not only to create the sequence of events in a play or story but also to suggest how those events are connected in a cause-and-effect relationship. There is a great variety of plot patterns, each of which is designed to create a particular effect.

Point of view: The perspective from which a story is presented to the reader. In simplest terms, it refers to whether narration is first person (directly addressed to the reader as if told by one involved in the narrative) or third person (usually a more objective, distanced perspective).

Portmanteau words: The term was coined by Lewis Carroll to describe the creation of a new word by telescoping two existing words. In this way, "furious" and "fuming" can be combined to create "frumious." The works of James Joyce, as well as Carroll's *Through the Looking Glass and What Alice Found There* (1871), provide many examples of portmanteau words.

Postcolonial: A literary approach that focuses on

English-language texts from countries and cultures formerly colonized or dominated by the United States or the British Empire, and other European countries. Postcolonialists focus on the literature of such countries as Australia, New Zealand, Africa, South America, and such cultural groups as African Americans and Native Americans.

Postmodern: Although this term is so broad it is interpreted differently by many different critics, it basically refers to a trend by which the literary work calls attention to itself as an artifice rather than a mirror held up to external reality.

Prosody: The study of the principles of verse structure. Includes meter, rhyme, and other patterns of sound, such as alliteration, assonance, euphony and onomatopoeia, and stanzaic patterns.

Protagonist: Originally, in the Greek drama, the "first actor," who played the leading role. The term has come to signify the most important character in a drama or story. It is not unusual for a work to contain more than one protagonist.

Pun: A pun occurs when words that have similar pronunciations have entirely different meanings. The result may be a surprise recognition of an unusual or striking connection, or, more often, a humorously accidental connection.

Realism: A literary technique in which the primary convention is to render an illusion of fidelity to external reality. Realism is often identified as the primary method of the novel form; the realist movement in the late nineteenth century coincided with the full development of the novel form.

Reception Theory: Theorist Hans Robert Jauss argues that since readers from any historical milieu create their own criteria for judging a text, one should examine how a text was received by readers contemporary with it. Since every period creates its own "horizon of expectation," the meaning of a text changes from one period to another.

Reminiscence: An account, written or spoken, of remembered events.

Rhetorical device: Rhetoric is the art of using words clearly and effectively, in speech or writing, in order to influence or persuade. A rhetorical device is a figure of speech, or way of using language, employed to this end. It can include such elements as choice of words, rhythms, repetition, apostrophe, invocation, chiasmus, zeugma, antithesis, and the rhetorical question (a question to which no answer is expected).

Rogue literature: From Odysseus to Shakespeare's Autolocus to Huckleberry Finn, the rogue is a common literary type. He is usually a robust and energetic comic or satirical figure whose roguery can be seen as a necessary undermining of the rigid complacency of conventional society. The picaresque novel (*pícaro* is Spanish for "rogue"), in which the picaro lives by his wits, is perhaps the most common form of rogue literature.

Romance: Originally, any work written in Old French. In the Middle Ages, romances were about knights and their adventures. In modern times, the term has also been used to describe a type of prose fiction in which, unlike the novel, realism plays little part. Prose romances often give expression to the quest for transcendent truths. Examples of the form include Nathaniel Hawthorne's *The Scarlet Letter* (1850) and Herman Melville's *Moby Dick* (1851).

Romanticism: A movement of the late eighteenth and nineteenth centuries which exalted individualism over collectivism, revolution over conservatism, innovation over tradition, imagination over reason, and spontaneity over restraint. Romanticism regarded art as self-expression; it strove to heal the cleavage between object and subject and expressed a longing for the infinite in all things. It stressed the innate goodness of human beings and the evils of the institutions that would stultify human creativity.

Saga: Originally applied to medieval Icelandic and other Scandinavian stories of heroic exploits and handed down by oral tradition. The term has come to signify any tale of heroic achievement or great adventure.

Satire: A form of literature that employs the comedic devices of wit, irony, and exaggeration to expose, ridicule, and condemn human folly, vice, and stupidity. Justifying satire, Alexander Pope wrote that "nothing moves strongly but satire, and those who are ashamed of nothing else are so of being ridiculous."

Setting: The circumstances and environment, both

temporal and spatial, of a narrative. The term also applies to the physical elements of a theatrical production, such as scenery and properties. Setting is an important element in the creation of atmosphere.

Shishōsetsu: Literally translated as "I novel," *shishōsetsu* is a Japanese genre, a form of autobiographical or confessional writing used in novels and short stories. The protagonist and writer are closely identified. The genre originated in the early part of the twentieth century; a good example is *An'ya Koro* (1921-1928; *A Dark Night's Passing*, 1958) by Shiga Naoya.

Short story: A concise work of fiction, shorter than a novella, that is usually more concerned with mood, effect, or a single event than with plot or extensive characterization.

Signifier/Signified: Linguist Ferdinand de Saussure proposed that all words are signs made up of a "signifier," which is the written mark or the spoken sound of the word, and a "signified," which is the concept for which the mark or sound stands.

Simile: A type of metaphor in which two things are compared. It can usually be recognized by the use of the words "like," "as," "appears," or "seems": "Float like a butterfly, sting like a bee" (Muhammad Ali); "The holy time is quiet as a nun" (William Wordsworth).

Skaz: A term used in Russian criticism to describe a narrative technique that presents an oral narrative of a lowbrow speaker.

Sketch: A brief narrative form originating in the eighteenth century, derived from the artist's sketch. The focus of a sketch is on a single person, place, or incident; it lacks a developed plot, theme, or characterization.

Story line: The story line of a work of fiction differs from the plot. Story line is merely the events that happen; plot is how those events are arranged by the author to suggest a cause-and-effect relationship.

Stream of consciousness: A narrative technique used in modern fiction by which an author tries to embody the total range of consciousness of a character, without any authorial comment or explanation. Sensations, thoughts, memories, and associations pour out in an uninterrupted, prerational, and prelogical flow. Examples are James Joyce's *Ulysses* (1922), Virginia Woolf's *To the Lighthouse* (1927), and William Faulkner's *The Sound and the Fury* (1929).

Structuralism: Structuralism is based on the idea of intrinsic, self-sufficient structures that do not require reference to external elements. A structure is a system of transformations that involves the interplay of laws inherent in the system itself. The structuralist literary critic attempts, by using models derived from modern linguistic theory, to define the structural principles that operate intertextually throughout the whole of literature as well as principles that operate in genres and in individual works.

Style: Style is the manner of expression, or how the writer tells the story. The most appropriate style is that which is perfectly suited to conveying whatever idea, emotion, or other effect that the author wishes to convey. Elements of style include diction, sentence structure, imagery, rhythm, and coherence.

Subjective/Objective: Terms used in critical theory. Subjective refers to works that express the ideas and emotions, the values and judgments of the authors, such as William Wordsworth's *The Prelude* (1850). Objective works are those that appear to be free of the personal sentiments of authors, who take a detached view of the events they record.

Supplement: A term used by Jacques Derrida to refer to the unstable relationship between the two elements in a set of binary opposites. For example, in the opposition between truth and lies, although Western thought assumes that truth is superior to lies, closer study reveals that so-called lies frequently reveal profound truths.

Symbolism: A literary movement encompassing the work of a group of French writers in the latter half of the nineteenth century, a group that included Charles Baudelaire, Stéphane Mallarmé, and Paul Verlaine. According to Symbolism, a mystical correspondence exists between the natural and spiritual worlds.

Synesthesia: Synesthesia occurs when one kind of sense experience is described in terms of another. Sounds may be described in terms of colors, and so on. For example, these lines from Keats's poem

"Isabella," "O turn thee to the very tale,/ And taste the music of that vision pale," combine the senses of taste, hearing, and sight. Synesthesia was used especially by the nineteenth century French Symbolists.

Tale: A general term for a simple prose or verse narrative. In the context of the short story, a tale is a story in which the emphasis is on the course of the action rather than on the minds of the characters.

Tall-tale: A humorous tale popular in the American West; the story usually makes use of realistic detail and common speech, but it tells a tale of impossible events that most often focus on a single legendary, superhuman figure, such as Paul Bunyan or David Crockett.

Technique: Refers both to the method of procedure in creating an artistic work and to the degree of expertise shown in following the procedure.

Thematics: According to Northrop Frye, when a work of fiction is written or interpreted thematically, it becomes an illustrative fable. Murray Krieger defines thematics in *The Tragic Vision* (1960) as "the study of the experiential tensions which, dramatically entangled in the literary work, become an existential reflection of that work's aesthetic complexity."

Theme: Loosely defined as what a literary work means, theme is the underlying idea, the abstract concept, that the author is trying to convey: "the search for love," "the growth of wisdom," or some such formulation. The theme of William Butler Yeats's poem "Sailing to Byzantium," for example, might be interpreted as the failure of the attempt to isolate oneself within the world of art.

Tone: Strictly defined, tone is the authors' attitudes toward their subjects, their personas, themselves, their audiences, or their societies. The tone of a work may be serious, playful, formal, informal, morose, loving, ironic, and so on; it can be thought of as the dominant mood of a work, and it plays a large part in the total effect.

Trope: Literally "turn" or "conversion"; a figure of speech in which a word or phrase is used in a way that deviates from the normal or literal sense.

Vehicle: Used with the term "tenor" to understand the two elements of a metaphor. The tenor is the subject of the metaphor, and the vehicle is the image by which the subject is presented. The terms were coined by I. A. Richards. As an example, in T. S. Eliot's line, "The whole earth is our hospital," the tenor is "whole earth" and the vehicle is the "hospital."

Verisimilitude: When used in literary criticism, verisimilitude refers to the degree to which a literary work gives the appearance of being true or real, even though the events depicted may in fact be far removed from the actual.

Vignette: A sketch, essay, or brief narrative characterized by precision, economy, and grace. The term can also be applied to brief short stories, less than five hundred words long.

Yarn: An oral tale or a written transcription of what purports to be an oral tale. The yarn is usually a broadly comic tale, the classic example of which is Mark Twain's "Baker's Bluejay Yarn." The yarn achieves its comic effect by juxtaposing realistic detail and incredible events; tellers of the tale protest that they are telling the truth; listeners know differently.

Bryan Aubrey, updated by Charles E. May

BIBLIOGRAPHY

Adams, Alice. "The American Short Story in the Cybernetic Age." *Journal of the Short Story in English* 17 (Autumn, 1991): 9-22. After summarizing critical condemnation of the short story in the early twentieth century as mechanical and formulaic, Adams argues that the metafictional story of the 1960's and 1970's tries to reclaim the short story from its low-brow mechanistic state by making formula palpable.

Allen, Walter. *The Short Story in English*. Oxford, England: Clarendon Press, 1981. A historical study of the development of the form in England and the United States. Primarily a series of biographical discussions of authors and summary discussions of stories. Good for providing a framework for the development of the form.

Allende, Isabel. "The Short Story." *Journal of Modern Literature* 20 (Summer, 1996): 21-28. This personal account of storytelling makes suggestions about differences between the novel and the short story, the story's demand for believability, the story's focus on change, the story's relationship to dream, and the story as events transformed by poetic truth.

Averill, Deborah. *The Irish Short Story from George Moore to Frank O'Connor*. Washington, D.C.: University Press of America, 1982. An introductory study of the Irish short story intended primarily for teachers and students. Surveys historical conditions in the nineteenth and early twentieth centuries that contributed to the development of the Irish short story and discusses the major stories of George Moore, James Joyce, Seumas O'Kelly, Daniel Corkery, Liam O'Flaherty, Seán O'Faoláin, and Frank O'Connor. Discusses each writer's basic style or concept of form and recurrent themes.

Aycock, Wendell M., ed. *The Teller and the Tale: Aspects of the Short Story*. Lubbock: Texas Tech Press, 1982. A collection of papers presented at a scholarly conference focusing on various aspects of short fiction, including its oral roots, the use of silences in the text, and realism versus antirealism.

Bader, A. L. "The Structure of the Modern Short Story." *College English* 7 (1945): 86-92. Counters the charge that the short story lacks narrative structure by contrasting the traditional "plotted" story with the modern story, which is more suggestive, indirect, and technically patterned.

Baker, Falcon O. "Short Stories for the Millions." *Saturday Review*, December 19, 1953, 7-9, 48-49. Argues that as a result of formalist New Criticism, the short story has begun to ignore entertainment value and the ordinary reader.

Baldeshwiler, Eileen. "The Lyric Short Story: The Sketch of a History." *Studies in Short Fiction* 6 (1969): 443-453. A brief survey of the lyrical (as opposed to the epical) story from Ivan Turgenev to John Updike. The lyric story focuses on internal changes, moods, and feelings, utilizing a variety of structural patterns depending on the "shape of the emotion itself."

Baldwin, Dean. "The English Short Story in the Fifties." In *The English Short Story, 1945-1980*, edited by Dennis Vanatta. Boston: Twayne, 1985. Argues that after World War II, Great Britain experienced a bureaucratization of everyday life. Focuses on stories of social protest, especially those of Alan Sillitoe; the supernatural stories of Sylvia Townsend Warner and Muriel Spark; the mainstream writers H. E. Bates, V. S. Pritchett, Spark, and Rhys Davies; and the major writers Doris Lessing, Sillitoe, Roald Dahl, Angus Wilson, William Sansom, and Elizabeth Taylor.

Barth, John. "It's a Short Story" In *Further Fridays: Essays, Lectures, and Other Nonfiction, 1984-1994*. New York: Little, Brown and Company, 1995. A personal account by a "congenital novelist" of his brief love affair with the short story during the writing of *Chimera* (1972) and the stories in *Lost in the Funhouse* (1968).

Bates, H. E. *The Modern Short Story: A Critical Survey*. Boston: The Writer, 1941, 1972. A history of the major short-story writers and their work since Edgar Allan Poe and Nikolai Gogol. More focus on English and European short-story writers than most histories.

Bayley, John. *The Short Story: Henry James to Elizabeth Bowen*. New York: St. Martin's Press, 1988. A discussion of some of what Bayley calls the "special effects" of the short-story form, particularly its relationship to poetic techniques and devices. Much of the book consists of analyses of significant stories by Henry James, Ernest Hemingway, Rudyard Kipling, Anton Chekhov, D. H. Lawrence, James Joyce, and Elizabeth Bowen.

Beachcroft, T. O. *The Modest Art: A Survey of the Short Story in English*. London: Oxford University Press, 1968. A historical survey of the major figures of the English short story from Geoffrey Chaucer to Doris Lessing. The result of the basic difference between antique stories (listening) and modern stories (reading) is that modern short-story writers attempt to portray rather than expound. They remove their own personalities from the stories and present the flashes of insight through poetic needs.

Benjamin, Walter. "The Storyteller: Reflections on the Words of Nikolai Leskov." Reprinted in *Modern Literary Criticism: 1900-1970*, edited by Lawrence Lipking and A. Walton Litz. New York: Atheneum, 1972. Benjamin claims that the art of storytelling is coming to an end because of the widespread dissemination of information and explanation. The compactness of a story precludes analysis and appeals to readers through the rhythm of the work itself. For the storyteller, the old religious chronicle is secularized into an ambiguous network in which the worldly and the eschatological are interwoven.

Bierce, Ambrose. "The Short Story." In *The Collected Works of Ambrose Bierce*. New York: Gordian Press, 1966. Bierce criticizes William Dean Howells and the realistic school for their prosaic and pedestrian realism, which fails to perceive the mystery of human life.

Black, John, and Colleen M. Seifert. "The Psychological Study of Story Understanding." In *Researching Response to Literature and the Teaching of Literature*, edited by Charles R. Cooper. Norwood, N.J.: Ablex, 1985. Argues that when people read stories, they use the same psychological processes to comprehend the events in the story that they use to comprehend life. By studying how people respond to stories, psychologists can discover how people understand and remember. Cognitive research has shown that the knowledge of the world that readers bring to a story determines their understanding, whereas their memory of it is organized around schemata.

Blythe, Will, ed. *Why I Write: Thoughts on the Craft of Fiction*. Boston: Little, Brown, 1998. A collection of essays by various writers about writing fiction. The essays most relevant to the short story are those by Joy Williams, who says that writers must cherish the mystery of discovery in the process of writing; Thom Jones, who discusses his passionate engagement in the writing of short stories; and Mary Gaitskill, who calls stories the "rich, unseen underlayer of the most ordinary moments."

Bone, Robert, *Down Home: A History of Afro-American Short Fiction from Its Beginnings to the End of the Harlem Renaissance*. New York: Capricorn Books, 1975. Provides a background for the African-American folktale, the Brer Rabbit Tales, and the local-color writers; devotes a chapter each to Paul Laurence Dunbar, Charles Waddell Chesnutt, Jean Toomer, Langston Hughes, and Arna Bontemps. Also contains a chapter on the Harlem Renaissance, with mention of Zora Neale Hurston and others. Shows how the African-American short story is the child of a mixed heritage.

Bonheim, Helmut. *The Narrative Modes: Techniques of the Short Story*. Cambridge, England: D. S. Brewer, 1982. A systematic and statistical study of the short-story form, focusing on basic short-story techniques, especially short-story beginnings and endings. Argues that a limited set of techniques is used in story endings again and again. Discusses open and closed endings and argues that dynamic modes are more apt to be open, while static ones are more apt to be closed.

Boulanger, Daniel. "On the Short Story." *Michigan Quarterly Review* 26 (Summer, 1987): 510-514. A highly metaphoric and impressionistic study of the form, focusing primarily on the detached nature of the short story. Claims that there is a bit of Pontius Pilate in the short-story writer, for he or she is always removed from the tragic outcome. Points out how there are no class distinctions in the short story, no hierarchy.

Bowen, Elizabeth, ed. *The Faber Book of Modern Short Stories*. London: Faber & Faber, 1936. Bowen suggests that the short story, because it is exempt from the novel's often forced conclusiveness, more often approaches aesthetic and moral truth. She also suggests that the short story, more than the novel, is able to place the individual alone on that "stage which, inwardly, every man is conscious of occupying alone."

Boyce, Benjamin. "English Short Fiction in the Eighteenth Century: A Preliminary View." *Studies in Short Fiction* 5 (1968): 95-112. Discusses the types of short fiction found in periodicals and inserted in novels: character sketches, Oriental tales, stories of passion. Usually the purpose was didactic and the mode was either "hovering pathos" or "hovering irony." The most distinctive characteristic is the formal, even elegant language.

Brickell, Herschel. "What Happened to the Short Story?" *The Atlantic Monthly* 188 (September, 1951): 74-76. Argues that many modern writers have succeeded in breaking the short story away from its formal frame by drawing it nearer to poetry.

Broich, Ulrich. "Muted Postmodernism: The Contemporary British Short Story." *Zeitschrift für Anglistik und Amerikanistik* 41 (1993): 31-39. Analyzes the market conditions of contemporary British short fiction; argues that in spite of a remarkable number of excellent British short stories, the form is neglected by readers and critics; surveys three major types of British short story: feminist story, cultural conflict story, and experimental postmodernist story.

Brown, Suzanne Hunter. "The Chronotope of the Short Story: Time, Character, and Brevity." In *Creative and Critical Approaches to the Short Story*, edited by Noel Harold Kaylor, Jr. Lewiston, N.Y.: The Edwin Mellen Press, 1997. A survey and analysis of the frequent critical assumption that short stories deal with characters as eternal essence and that novels deal with characters who change over time. Argues that Mikhail Bakhtin's concept of "chronotrope," a literary work's projection of time and space, will help develop a generic theory of the short story that considers both historical and technical factors.

_______. "Discourse Analysis and the Short Story." In *Short Story Theory at a Crossroads*, edited by Susan Lohafer and Jo Ellyn Clarey. Baton Rouge: Louisiana State University Press, 1989. A helpful analytical survey of the research being carried on by psychologists into the nature of discourse, storyness, and cognitive response to narrative.

Brushwood, John S. "The Spanish American Short Story from Quiroga to Borges." In *The Latin American Short Story: A Critical History*, edited by Margaret Sayers Peden. Boston: Twayne, 1983. Horacio Quiroga was the first Spanish American writer to pay close attention to how a story is created. The late 1920's and early 1930's were characterized by innovative narration, a movement to regionalism took place in the mid-1930's, and a return to innovation and cosmopolitanism characterized the early 1940's.

Burgess, Anthony. "Anthony Burgess on the Short Story." *Journal of the Short Story in English*, no. 2 (1984): 31-47. Burgess admits that he disdains the short story because he cannot write it. He says that the novel presents an epoch, while the short story presents a revelation. Discusses different types of stories, distinguishing between the literary short story, which is patterned, and the commercial form, which is anecdotal.

Burgin, Mary. "The 'Feminine' Short Story: Recuperating the Moment." *Style* 27 (Fall, 1993): 380-386. Argues that there is a connection between so-called feminine writing that focuses on isolated moments and the concerns of women who have chosen the short story as a form. Claims that the twentieth century epiphanic short story is a manifestation of women's tradition of temporal writing as opposed to the spatial writing of men.

Campbell, Ewing. "How Minimal is Minimalism?" In *The Tales We Tell: Perspectives on the Short Story*, edited by Barbara Lounsberry, Susan Lohafer, Mary Rohrberger, Stephen Pett, and R. C. Feddersen. Westport, Conn.: Greenwood Press, 1998. A brief, suggestive essay which tries to define minimalist short fiction not in terms of length but in terms of the demands it makes on the reader. Argues that minimalist stories arrange significant details in such a way that the brain must supply missing information.

Canby, Henry S. *The Short Story in English*. New York: Holt, Rinehart, and Winston, 1909. Canby argues that the Romantic movement gave birth to the modern short story and that Edgar Allan Poe is its first important figure. The rest of the nineteenth century applied Poe's theory of single effect to new subjects, primarily the contrasts of civilization in flux.

Carens, James F. "In Quest of a New Impulse: George Moore's *The Untilled Field* and James Joyce's *Dubliners*." In *The Irish Short Story: A Critical History*, edited by James F. Kilroy. Boston: Twayne, 1984. Carens provides analyses of the major stories in these two most influential collections of Irish short fiction. Discusses the major contributions of the stories of Moore and Joyce responsible for creating the modern Anglo-Irish short story. Explains Moore's influence on Joyce, analyzing Joyce's "Counterparts" as a reworking of Moore's "The Clerk's Quest."

Chatman, Seymour. "New Ways of Analyzing Narrative Structure, with an Example from Joyce's *Dubliners*." *Language and Style* 2 (1969): 3-36. A "test" of the narrative theories of Ronald Barthes and Tzvetan Todorov, with a detailed analysis of James Joyce's "Eveline." The story is considered both in terms of the internal relations of the narrative and the external relations between narrator and reader.

Clark, Miriam Marty. "After Epiphany: American Stories in the Postmodern Age." *Style* 27 (Fall, 1993): 387-394. Argues that contemporary short stories can no longer be read in terms of epiphany. Claims that critics must develop a new reading strategy, shifting from metaphoric ways of meaning to metonymic ones to redefine the short story in its postmodern context.

Clarke, John H. "Transition in the American Negro Short Story." *Phylon* 21 (1960): 360-366. A shorter version of this article appears as the introduction to *American Negro Short Stories*, edited by John Henrik Clarke (1966). A brief historical survey of the African American short story from Paul Laurence Dunbar and Charles Waddell Chesnutt at the beginning of the twentieth century, through the Harlem Renaissance of the 1920's, to the emergence of Richard Wright, who marked the end of the double standard for black writers.

Connolly, Julian. "The Russian Short Story, 1880-1917." In *The Russian Short Story: A Critical History*, edited by Charles A. Moser. Boston: Twayne, 1986. Most of this essay focuses on Nikolai Leskov, Anton Chekhov, Maxim Gorky, Ivan Bunin, and Leonid Andreyev. Briefly discusses the Symbolist movement's influence on Russian literature at the end of the nineteenth century.

Coover, Robert. "Storying in Hyperspace: 'Linkages.'" In *The Tales We Tell: Perspectives on the Short Story*, edited by Barbara Lounsberry, Susan Lohafer, Mary Rohrberger, Stephen Pett, and R. C. Feddersen. Westport, Conn.: Greenwood Press, 1998. A discussion of the future of the short story in computerized hyperspace, as a form that is nonsequential, multidirectional, and interactive. Discusses linked short fictional pieces in the past in the Bible, in medieval romances, and by Giovanni Boccaccio, Miguel de Cervantes, and Geoffrey Chaucer.

Corey, Elsworth. "The Senility of the Short Story." *Dial* 62 (May 3, 1917): 379-381. Says the short story has become obsessed with a unity that is abnormally artificial and intense. Seldom attaining high seriousness, it is a literature of feverish excitement.

Cortázar, Julio. "Some Aspects of the Short Story."

Arizona Quarterly, Spring, 1982, 5-17. A discussion of the invariable elements that give a good short story its particular atmosphere. Says that the novel and the short story can be compared to the film and the photograph. The short story's most significant element is its subject, the act of choosing a real or imaginary happening that has the mysterious property of illuminating something beyond itself.

Curnutt, Kirk. *Wise Economies: Brevity and Storytelling in American Short Stories*. Moscow: University of Idaho Press, 1997. A historical analysis of the short story's development as the structuring of the tension between brevity and storytelling. Shows how stylistic brevity as an evolving aesthetic practice redefined the interpretative demands placed on readers.

Current-Garcia, Eugene. *The American Short Story, Before 1850*. Boston: Twayne, 1985. Focuses on the types of magazine fiction before 1820. Devotes individual chapters to Washington Irving, Nathaniel Hawthorne, and Edgar Allan Poe. Also includes a chapter on William Gilmore Simms and the frontier humorists, such as George Washington Harris. The shift toward realism in the last chapter is largely a result of the fiction of Herman Melville.

_______, and Walter R. Patrick. Introduction to *American Short Stories*. Rev. ed. Chicago: Scott, Foresman, 1964. A historical survey of the American short story through four periods: Romanticism, realism, naturalism, and the modern period of both traditionalists (those who have carried on the Poe/de Maupassant/James tradition) and experimentalists (those who have focused more on the fragmented inner world of the mind).

_______, eds. *What Is the Short Story?* Rev. ed. New York: Scott, Foresman, 1974. Although this volume is primarily a short-story anthology, it contains a generous selection of mostly American criticism on the short story, arranged in chronological order. Contains a four-page general bibliography on the short story.

Dawson, W. J. "The Modern Short Story." *North American Review* 190 (December, 1909): 799-810. Argues that a short story must be complete in itself and consist of a single incident. The finest writing in a short story, he says, is that which takes the reader most quickly to the very heart of the matter at hand.

Dollerup, Cay. "The Concepts of 'Tension,' 'Intensity,' and 'Suspense' in Short-Story Theory." *Orbis Litterarum* 25 (1970): 314-337. A heavily documented survey of critical theory in German, Danish, and English on the concepts of intensity or tension in the short story and how these terms have been applied to linguistic rhythm, contrast, character, structure, and reader suspense in the form.

Duncan, Edgar Hill. "Short Fiction in Medieval English: A Survey." *Studies in Short Fiction* 9 (1972): 1-28. A survey of short pieces in the Old English period, primarily in verse, that have in common the characteristic of "artfully telling a story in a relatively brief compass" and that focus on "singleness of character, of action, and/or impression." The fall of the angels and the fall of man in the *Genesis B*, the St. Guthlac poems, and *The Dream of the Rood* are analyzed.

_______. "Short Fiction in Medieval English: 2. The Middle English Period." *Studies in Short Fiction* 11 (1974): 227-241. A brief sampling of short fiction elements in the "shorter romance" form, the exemplary narrative, the beast tale, and the fabliau introduced to Middle English by the French. Also noted are paraphrases of biblical stories, saints' lives, the dream visions of *The Pearl* and Geoffrey Chaucer's "The Book of the Duchess" and the "Prologue to the Legend of Good Women."

Dunleavy, Janet Egleson. "Mary Lavin, Elizabeth Bowen, and a New Generation: The Irish Short Story at MidCentury." In *The Irish Short Story: A Critical History*, edited by James F. Kilroy. Boston: Twayne, 1984. Discusses Mary Lavin's art as economic, disciplined, and compressed; argues that she neither romanticizes nor trivializes Irish experience. Discusses the basic characteristics of the fiction of Elizabeth Bowen, Benedict Kiely, Michael McLaverty, and Bryan MacMahon.

Eichenbaum, Boris. *O. Henry and the Theory of the*

Short Story. Translated by I. R. Titunik. Michigan Slavic Contributions. Ann Arbor: University of Michigan, 1968. Originally published in 1925, this essay is a good example of the early Russian Formalist approach to fiction through a consideration of genre. Eichenbaum poses a generic distinction between the novel and the short story. Short stories are constructed on the basis of a contradiction, incongruity, error, or contrast, and, like the anecdote, build their weight toward the ending.

Eldred, Janet Carey. "Narratives of Socialization: Literacy in the Short Story." *College English* 53 (October, 1991): 686-700. Based on the critical assumption that all fiction historicizes problems of socialization; argues that the short story is a narrative of arrested socialization which ends with characters between two cultures who find their own speech inadequate but their new language problematic.

Elliott, George P. "A Defense of Fiction." *Hudson Review* 16 (1963): 9-48. Discusses the four basic impulses that mingle with the storytelling impulse: to dream, tell what happened, explain the sense of things, and make a likeness.

Engstrom, Alfred G. "The Formal Short Story in France and Its Development Before 1850." *Studies in Philology* 42 (1945): 627-639. After making distinctions between the *nouvelle* and the conte (a complex line of action versus a compressed one), Engstrom points out the lack of any significant examples of conte until Prosper Mérimée's "Mateo Falcone" (1829), the first formal short story in French literature. The only other significant contributors to the form before 1850 are Honoré de Balzac and Théophile Gautier.

Evans, Walter. "The English Short Story in the Seventies." In *The English Short Story, 1945-1980*, edited by Dennis Vanatta. Boston: Twayne, 1985. Focuses on new writers of the period, such as Susan Hill, Angela Carter, Gabriel Josipovici, and Christine Brooke-Rose. The emphasis here is on different themes: personal crises, the individual in conflict in society; briefly discusses the avant-garde, especially Josipovici and Brooke-Rose; claims the decade's finest collection of stories is *The Ebony Tower* (1974) by John Fowles.

Farrell, James T. *The League of Frightened Philistines and Other Papers*. New York: Vanguard Press, 1945. Ridicules the short-story handbooks published in the 1920's and 1930's and claims that in many contemporary short stories the revolutionary point of view appears more tacked on than integral to the story.

Ferguson, Suzanne C. "Defining the Short Story: Impressionism and Form." *Modern Fiction Studies* 28 (Spring, 1982): 13-24. Argues that there is no single characteristic or cluster of characteristics that distinguishes the short story from the novel; suggests that what is called the modern short story is a manifestation of impressionism rather than a discrete genre.

_______. "Local Color and the Function of Setting in the English Short Story." In *Creative and Critical Approaches to the Short Story*, edited by Noel Harold Kaylor, Jr. Lewiston, N.Y.: The Edwin Mellen Press, 1997. Ferguson argues that whereas the function of setting in early stories was to establish a degree of verisimilitude, greater emphasis on setting in later stories served to establish the emotional interaction of the characters with elements of the physical environment.

_______. "The Rise of the Short Story in the Hierarchy of Genres." In *Short Story Theory at a Crossroads*, edited by Susan Lohafer and Jo Ellyn Clarey. Baton Rouge: Louisiana State University Press, 1989. A historical/critical survey of the development of the English short story, showing how social factors influence the rise and fall of the prestige of the form.

Firchow, Peter E. "The Americaness of the American Short Story." *Journal of the Short Story in English* 10 (Spring, 1988): 45-66. Examines the common claim that the short story is a particularly American art form. Surveys and critiques a number of critics who have debated the issue; analyzes generic criteria for determining what is a short story, such as self-consciousness and length. Concludes that a short story is simply a story that is short and that the American short story is not unique to America but is merely a story that deals with American cultural contexts.

FitzGerald, Gregory. "The Satiric Short Story: A Definition." *Studies in Short Fiction* 5 (1968): 349-354. Defines the satiric short story as a subgenre that sustains a reductive attack upon its objects and conveys to its readers a significance different from its apparent surface meaning.

Flora, Joseph M., ed. *The English Short Story, 1880-1945*. Boston: Twayne, 1985. A collection of essays on a number of British short-story writers during the period, including Rudyard Kipling, D. H. Lawrence, Virginia Woolf, Saki, A. E. Coppard, P. G. Wodehouse, and V. S. Pritchett.

Fonlon, Bernard, "The Philosophy, the Science, and the Art of the Short Story, Part II." *Abbia* 34 (1979): 429-438. A discussion of the basic elements of a story, including character, conflict. Lists elements of intensity, detachment, skill, unity of effect. This essay presents primarily a set of rules aimed at inexperienced writers.

Friedman, Norman. "Recent Short Story Theories: Problems in Definition." In *Short Story Theory at a Crossroads*, edited by Susan Lohafer and Jo Ellyn Clarey. Baton Rouge: Louisiana State University Press, 1989. A critical review of major short-story critics, including Mary Rohrberger, Charles May, Susan Lohafer, John Gerlach, and others. Argues against those critics who support a deductive, single-term, mixed category approach to definition of the form. Urges that what is needed is a more inductive approach that follows the principle of suiting the definition to the facts rather than trying to suit the facts to the definition.

_______. "What Makes a Short Story Short?" *Modern Fiction Studies* 4 (1958): 103-117. Makes use of Neo-Aristotelian literary theory to determine the issue of the short story's shortness. To deal with the problem, Friedman says, one must ask the following questions: What is the size of the action? Is it composed of a speech, a scene, an episode, or a plot? Does the action involve a change? If so, is the change a major one or a minor one?

Fusco, Richard. *Maupassant and the American Short Story: The Influence of Form at the Turn of the Century*. University Park: Pennsylvania State University Press, 1994. Argues that Maupassant's influence on the twentieth century short story rivals that of Anton Chekhov. Discusses seven different short-story forms in Maupassant's stories: linear, ironic coda, surprise-inversion, loop, descending helical, contrast, and sinusoidal. Discusses Maupassant's influence on Ambrose Bierce, O. Henry, Kate Chopin, and Henry James.

Geismar, Maxwell. "The American Short Story Today." *Studies on the Left* 4 (Spring, 1964): 21-27. Criticizes J. D. Salinger, Philip Roth, Bernard Malamud, John Updike, and others for ignoring social realities of the time in their short stories.

Gerlach, John. "The Margins of Narrative: The Very Short Story, the Prose Poem, and the Lyric." In *Short Story Theory at a Crossroads*, edited by Susan Lohafer and Jo Ellyn Clarey. Baton Rouge: Louisiana State University Press, 1989. Explores the basic requirements of a story, focusing particularly on two minimalist stories by Enrique Anderson Imbert and Scott Sanders, as well as a short prose poem by W. S. Merwin. Argues that neither mere length nor fictionality is the principal constituent of story, but rather point.

_______. *Toward the End: Closure and Structure in the American Short Story*. Tuscaloosa: University of Alabama Press, 1985. A detailed theoretical study of the American short story, focusing particularly on the importance of closure, or the ending of the form; examines a number of stories in some detail in terms of the concept of closure.

Gerould, Katherine Fullerton. "The American Short Story." *Yale Review*, n.s. 13 (July, 1924): 642-663. Urges that the short story be read as critically as the novel. Argues that the short story must be well-made and must focus on a significant event that is either truly momentous for the individual character or typical of the lives of many people.

Goldberg, Michael E. "The Synchronic Series as the Origin of the Modernist Short Story." *Studies in Short Fiction* 33 (Fall, 1996): 515-527. Goldberg suggests that the cumulative power of modernist collections of stories such as James Joyce's

Dubliners (1914) and Ernest Hemingway's *In Our Time* (1924, 1925) is modeled after a synchronic series of stories innovated by Arthur Conan Doyle.

Gordimer, Nadine. "South Africa." *The Kenyon Review* 30 (1968): 457-461. The strongest convention of the novel, its prolonged coherence of tone, is false to the nature of what can be grasped as reality in the modern world. Short-story writers deal with the only thing one can be sure of—the present moment.

Gullason, Thomas A. "The 'Lesser' Renaissance: The American Short Story in the 1920's." In *The American Short Story: 1900-1945*, edited by Philip Stevick. Boston: Twayne, 1984. A historical survey of some of the major short-story writers of the 1920's in the United States. The essay analyzes briefly some of the best known stories of Sherwood Anderson, F. Scott Fitzgerald, Ring Lardner, Ernest Hemingway, Dorothy Parker, Katherine Anne Porter, and William Faulkner.

_______. "Revelation and Evolution: A Neglected Dimension of the Short Story." *Studies in Short Fiction* 10 (1973): 347-356. Challenges Mark Schorer's distinction between the short story as an "art of moral revelation" and the novel as an "art of moral evolution." Analyzes D. H. Lawrence's "The Horse Dealer's Daughter" and John Steinbeck's "The Chrysanthemums" to show that the short story embodies both revelation and evolution.

_______. "The Short Story: An Underrated Art." *Studies in Short Fiction* 2 (1964): 13-31. Points out the lack of serious criticism on the short story, suggests some of the reasons for this neglect, and concludes with an analysis of Anton Chekhov's "Gooseberries" and Nadine Gordimer's "The Train from Rhodesia" to disprove the charges that the short story is formulaic and lacks life.

Hallett, Cynthia J. "Minimalism and the Short Story." *Studies in Short Fiction* 33 (Fall, 1996): 487-495. A discussion of some of the characteristics of so-called minimalism based on analysis of stories by Raymond Carver, Mary Robison, and Amy Hempel. Argues that minimalism represents an intensification of some of the basic generic characteristics of the short story as a form.

Hanson, Clare, ed. Introduction to *Re-reading the Short Story*. New York: St. Martin's Press, 1989. Claims that the short story is a vehicle for different *kinds* of knowledge, knowledge that may be in some way at odds with the "story" of dominant culture. The formal properties of the short story—disjunction, inconclusiveness, obliquity—connect with its ideological marginality and with the fact that the form may be used to express something suppressed/repressed in mainstream literature.

_______. "The Lifted Veil: Women and Short Fiction in the 1880's and 1890's." *The Yearbook of English Studies* 26 (1996): 135-142. Argues that British women writers in the early modernist period chose the short story to challenge the existing dominant order. Shows how this challenge is embodied in such stories as Charlotte Mew's "Mark Stafford's Wife" as an encounter, presented in iconic, painterly terms, between a male protagonist and a woman, who is then unveiled.

_______. *Short Stories and Short Fictions, 1880-1980*. New York: St. Martin's Press, 1985. Argues that during this period, the authority of the teller, usually a first-person "framing" narrator who guaranteed the authenticity of the tale, was questioned by many modernist writers; argues that the movements from "teller" to indirect free narration, and from "tale" to "text" were part of a more general movement from "discourse" to "image" in the art and literature of the period. Chapters on Rudyard Kipling, Saki, W. Somerset Maugham, James Joyce, Virginia Woolf, Katherine Mansfield, Samuel Beckett.

_______. "Things out of Words: Towards a Poetics of Short Fiction." In *Re-reading the Short Story*, edited by Clare Hanson. New York: St. Martin's Press, 1989. Argues that the short story is a more literary form than the novel; also claims that short stories are framed, an aesthetic device that gives the sense of completeness, which allows gaps and absences to remain in the story; thus readers accept a degree of mystery or elision in the short story that they would not accept in the novel.

Hardy, Sarah. "A Poetics of Immediacy: Oral Narrative and the Short Story." *Style* 27 (Fall, 1993): 352-368. Argues that the oral-epic episode clarifies basic characteristics of the short story; it gives the reader a way to understand the density of meaning in the short story and provides a paradigm of the short-story audience as that of a participating community.

Harris, Wendell V. "Beginnings of and for the True Short Story in England." *English Literature in Transition* 15 (1972): 296-276. The true short story did not begin in England until Rudyard Kipling discovered the means to control the reader's angle of vision and establish a self-contained world within the story that keeps the reader at a distance. The externality of the reader to the story's participants is a basic characteristic of the short story.

_______. "English Short Fiction in the Nineteenth Century." *Studies in Short Fiction* 6 (1968): 1-93. After distinguishing between "short fiction" appearing before 1880 and "short story" after 1880, Harris surveys examples from both periods. The turning point was the definition posed by Brander Matthews, which first appeared in the *Saturday Review* in 1884.

_______. "Vision and Form: The English Novel and the Emergence of the Short Story." *Victorian Newsletter*, no. 47 (1975): 8-12. The short story did not begin in England until the 1880's because the presentation of isolated individuals, moments, or scenes was not considered a serious intellectual task for fiction to undertake. Only at the end of the century was reality perceived as congeries of fragments; the primary vehicle of this perception is the short story.

Head, Dominic. *The Modernist Short Story*. Cambridge: Cambridge University Press, 1992. An examination of the short story's formal characteristics from a theoretical framework derived from Louis Althusser and Bakhtin. Argues that the short story's stress on literary artifice lends itself to modernist experimentalism. Illustrates this thesis with chapters on Joyce, Tobias Woolf, Katherine Mansfield, and Wyndham Lewis.

Hedberg, Johannes. "What Is a 'Short Story?' and What Is an 'Essay'?" *Moderna Sprak* 74 (1980): 113-120. Reminds readers of the distinction between the Chekhovian story (lack of plot) and the Maupassant story (anecdotal and therefore commercial). Discusses basic characteristics of the essay and the story; claims they are similar in that they are both a whole picture in miniature, not merely a detail of a larger picture—a complete work, not an extract.

Hendricks, William O. "Methodology of Narrative Structural Analysis." In *Essays in Semiolinguistics and Verbal Art*. The Hague: Mouton, 1973. Structuralists, in the tradition of Vladimir Propp and Claude Levi-Strauss, usually bypass the actual sentences of a narrative and analyze a synopsis. This essay is a fairly detailed discussion of the methodology of synopsizing (using Faulkner's "A Rose for Emily" as an example), followed by a brief discussion of the methodology of structural analysis of the resultant synopsis.

Hesse, Douglas. "A Boundary Zone: First-Person Short Stories and Narrative Essays." In *Short Story Theory at a Crossroads*, edited by Susan Lohafer and Jo Ellyn Clarey. Baton Rouge: Louisiana State University Press, 1989. Argues that the precise boundary point between essays and short stories does not exist. Analyzes George Orwell's essay "A Hanging" as a short story and William Carlos Williams' short story "Use of Force" as an essay. Also discusses essays and stories that fall in a boundary zone between essay and story.

Hicks, Granville. "The Art of the Short Story." *Saturday Review* 41 (December 20, 1958): 16. Says that an emotional experience for the reader rather than character or plot is the focus of the modern short story.

Hogan, Robert. "Old Boys, Young Bucks, and New Women: The Contemporary Irish Short Story." In *The Irish Short Story: A Critical History*, edited by James F. Kilroy. Boston: Twayne, 1984. A general survey of contemporary Irish short-story writers such as old-guards Anthony C. West, James Plunkett, William Trevor, and Patrick Boyle; young buck writers Eugene McCabe, John Morrow, Bernard Mac Laverty, Desmond Hogan, and Gillman Noonan; and women writers such as Edna O'Brien, Maeve Kelly, Emma Cooke, Kate Cruise O'Brien, and Juanita Casey.

Holloway, John. "Identity, Inversion, and Density Elements in Narrative: Three Tales by Chekhov, James, and Lawrence." In *Narrative and Structure: Exploratory Essays*. Cambridge, England. Cambridge University Press, 1979. Holloway is concerned with looking at stories in which almost nothing happens. He says there is a distinctive kind of narrative episode introduced by an item that is then followed by another item in inverse relationship to the first, which cancels it out and brings the reader back to where he or she started.

Howe, Irving. "Tone in the Short Story." *Sewanee Review* 57 (Winter, 1949): 141-152. Says that because the short story lacks prolonged characterization and a structured plot, it depends mostly on tone to hold it together.

Howells, William Dean. "Some Anomalies of the Short Story." *North American Review* 173 (September, 1901): 422-432. Claims that when read in a volume each story requires so much of the reader's attention, he or she becomes exhausted. Argues that a defect of the short story is that it creates no memorable characters.

Iftekharuddin, Farhat, Mary Rohrberger, and Maurice Lee, eds. *Speaking of the Short Story: Interviews with Contemporary Writers*. Jackson: University Press of Mississippi, 1997. A collection of twenty-one interviews on the short story with short-story writers such as Isabel Allende, Rudolfo A. Anaya, Ellen Douglas, Richard Ford, Bharati Mukherjee, and Leslie Marmon Silko and short story critics such as Susan Lohafer, Charles May, and Mary Rohrberger.

Ingram, Forrest L. "The Dynamics of Short Story Cycles." *New Orleans Review* 2 (1979): 7-12. A historical and critical survey and analysis of short stories that form a single unit, such as James Joyce's *Dubliners* (1914), Ernest Hemingway's *In Our Time* (1924, 1925), and Sherwood Anderson's *Winesburg, Ohio* (1919). Suggests some of the basic devices used in such cycles.

"International Symposium on the Short Story" in *Kenyon Review*. Contributions from short-story writers from all over the world on the nature of the form, its current economic status, its history, and its significance. Part 1, vol. 30, no. 4, 1969: 443-490. Christina Stead (England), Herbert Gold (United States), Erih Koš (Yugoslavia), Nadine Gordimer (South Africa), Benedict Kiely (Ireland), Hugh Hood (Canada), Henrietta Drake-Brockman (Australia). Part 2, volume 31, issue 1, 1969, 58-94: William Saroyan (United States), Jun Eto (Japan), Maurice Shadbolt (New Zealand), Chanakya Sen (India), John Wain (England), Hans Bender (West Germany), and "An Agent's View" by James Oliver Brown. Part 3, volume 31, issue 4, 1969, 450-502. Ana María Matute (Spain), Torborg Nedreaas (Norway), George Garrett (United States), Elizabeth Taylor (England), Ezekiel Mphahlele (South Africa), Elizabeth Harrower (Australia), Mario Picchi (Italy), Junzo Shono (Japan), Khushwant Singh (India). Part 4, volume 32, issue 1, 1969, 78-108: Jack Cope (South Africa), James T. Farrell (United States), Edward Hyams (England), Luigi Barzini (Italy), David Ballantyne (New Zealand), H. E. Bates (England).

Jarrell, Randall. "Stories." In *The Anchor Book of Stories*. New York: Doubleday, 1958. Jarrell's introduction to this collection focuses on stories as being closer to dream reality than the waking world of everyday. There are two kinds of stories: stories-in-which-everything-is-a-happening (in which each event is so charged that the narrative threatens to disintegrate into energy) and stories-in-which-nothing-happens (in which even the climax may lose its charge and become one more portion of a lyric continuum).

Joselyn, Sister Mary. "Edward Joseph O'Brien and the American Short Story." *Studies in Short Fiction* 3 (1965): 1-15. Attempts a synthesis of O'Brien's philosophic and aesthetic attitudes, which may have determined his choices of "best stories." Discusses O'Brien's contribution to the history, theory, and growth of the American short story.

Jouve, Nicole Ward. "Too Short for a Book." In *Re-reading the Short Story*, edited by Clare Hanson. New York: St. Martin's Press, 1989. An impressionistic, noncritical essay about story length. Discusses *The Thousand and One Nights* as an archetypal model standing behind all stories, collections of stories, and storytelling. Makes a case for collections of stories that stand together as organic wholes rather than single individual stories that stand alone.

Kagan-Kans, Eva. "The Russian Short Story, 1850-1880." In *The Russian Short Story: A Critical History*, edited by Charles A. Moser. Boston: Twayne, 1986. Focuses primarily on Ivan Turgenev, Leo Tolstoy, Fyodor Dostoevski, and the radical, populist, and feminist writers of the period. Representative stories of the writers are discussed and analyzed in terms of their contributions to the form and their relationship to, or reflection of, Russian social life at the time.

Kennedy, J. Gerald, ed. *Modern American Short Story Sequences: Composite Fictions and Fictive Communities*. Cambridge: Cambridge University Press, 1995. An anthology of essays by various critics on short-story sequence collections such as Toomer's *Cane* (1923), Hemingway's *In Our Time* (1924, 1925), William Faulkner's *Go Down, Moses* (1942), Updike's *Olinger Stories: A Selection* (1964), Anderson's *Winesburg, Ohio* (1919), and several others. Kennedy's introduction provides a brief survey of the short-story cycle, a definition of the cycle, and a discussion of the short-story sequence's implications.

Kilroy, James F. Introduction to *The Irish Short Story: A Critical History*. Boston: Twayne, 1984. An abbreviated survey of the Irish short story, beginning with Maria Edgeworth's *Castle Rackrent* (1800). The focus is on the relationship between historical and social events in Ireland and the development of fiction in Ireland, including political conflicts and upheavals and the rise of periodical publication.

_______. "Setting the Standards: Writers of the 1920's and 1930's." In *The Irish Short Story: A Critical History*, edited by James F. Kilroy. Boston: Twayne, 1984. The major Irish writers who set the standards for short fiction in the 1920's and 1930's were Liam O'Flaherty, Frank O'Connor, and Seán O'Faoláin. Kilroy compares and contrasts the three writers by analyzing some of their best-known stories. The essay also includes brief discussions of Daniel Corkery and Seamus O'Kelley.

Kimbel, Ellen. "The American Short Story: 1900-1920." In *The American Short Story, 1900-1945*, edited by Philip Stevick. Boston: Twayne, 1984. A historical survey of the development of the short story in the first two decades of the twentieth century. Begins with Henry James and writers such as Edith Wharton and Willa Cather who were strongly influenced by his work. Discusses the innovations of Sherwood Anderson and points out how he differs from earlier writers in developing the modern short story.

Kostelanetz, Richard. "Notes on the American Short Story Today." *The Minnesota Review* 5 (1966): 214-221. Contemporary short-story writers focus on extreme rather than typical experiences and tend to emphasize the medium of language itself more than ever before. In a shift that pulls the genre farther away from narrative and pushes it closer to nonlinear forms of poetry, the contemporary short-story writer attempts to depict the workings of the mad mind, to simulate the feel of madness itself.

Leitch, Thomas M. "The Debunking Rhythm of the American Short Story." In *Short Story Theory at a Crossroads*, edited by Susan Lohafer and Jo Ellyn Clarey. Baton Rouge: Louisiana State University Press, 1989. Argues that a particular kind of closure is typical of the American short story. Uses the phrase "debunking rhythm" to characterize the kind of story in which a character realizes the falseness of one kind of knowledge but achieves no new kind of knowledge to take its place.

_______. "The *New Yorker* School." In *Creative and Critical Approaches to the Short Story*, edited by Noel Harold Kaylor, Jr. Lewiston, N.Y.: The Edwin Mellen Press, 1997. A brief history of the development of the so-called *New Yorker* story.

Charts the rise of the magazine as a powerful force in the modern short story. Argues that, much like the modern short story generally, the *New Yorker* story has defined itself in terms of its departure from its own norms.

Levy, Andrews. *The Culture and Commerce of the American Short Story.* Cambridge: Cambridge University Press, 1993. A historical survey showing how the short story became an image of American values through political movements, editorial policies, and changes in education. Devotes chapters to Poe's efforts to create a magazine that would accommodate his particular kind of story; summarizes short-story criticism and theory in the late nineteenth and early twentieth centuries; provides a brief history of creative writing programs and handbooks.

Lewis, C. S. "On Stories." In *Essays Presented to Charles Williams*. Grand Rapids, Mich.: Wm. B. Eerdmans, 1966. Although stories are series of events, this series, or what is called plot, is only a necessary means to capture something that has no sequence, something more like a state or quality. Thus, the means of "story" is always at war with its "end." This very tension, however, constitutes the story's chief resemblance to life. "We grasp at a state and find only a succession of events in which the state is never quite embodied."

Lindstrom, Naomi. "The Spanish American Short Story from Echeverria to Quiroga." In *The Latin American Short Story: A Critical History*, edited by Margaret Sayers Peden. Boston: Twayne, 1983. Discusses the first Latin American short story, Estaban Echeverría's 1838 "The Slaughtering Grounds." Discusses the movement from Romanticism to realism and naturalism and then to modernism; notes that whereas Edgar Allan Poe and Guy de Maupassant were not taken so seriously elsewhere, they were taken more seriously in Latin America. Latin American readers see them as providing channels to alternate realms of experience.

"Literary Magazine Editors on the State of the Short Story." *Literary Review* 37 (Summer, 1994): 619-649. Editors of a number of literary magazines that publish short fiction discuss future short-story trends, the importance of innovation to the short story, and the relationship between author vision and a good story. The editors discuss the short story's relationship to lyric poetry, the importance of a moral core, the lack of irony in the current short story, and the importance of language and form.

Lohafer, Susan. "A Cognitive Approach to Storyness." *Short Story*, Spring, 1990, 60-71. A study of what Lohafer calls "preclosure," those points in a story where it could end but does not. Studies the characters of such preclosure sentences—where they appear, what they signal—as part of a more general effort to clarify what constitutes storyness.

_______. *Coming to Terms with the Short Story.* Baton Rouge: Louisiana State University Press, 1983. A highly suggestive theoretical study of the short story that focuses on the sentence unit of the form as a way of showing how it differs from the novel.

_______. "Interdisciplinary Thoughts on Cognitive Science and Short Fiction Studies." In *The Tales We Tell: Perspectives on the Short Story*, edited by Barbara Lounsberry, Susan Lohafer, Mary Rohrberger, Stephen Pett, and R. C. Feddersen. Westport, Conn.: Greenwood Press, 1998. A brief summary of psychological approaches to cognitive strategies for reading short fiction. Makes a number of suggestions about the future of short-story criticism based on the cooperation between narrative theorists and cognitive scientists.

_______. "Preclosure and Story Processing." In *Short Story Theory at a Crossroads*, edited by Susan Lohafer and Jo Ellyn Clarey. Baton Rouge: Louisiana State University Press, 1989. Analysis of the responses to a story by Kate Chopin in terms of identifying those sentences that "could" end the story but do not. This essay is a continuation of Lohafer's study of what she has defined as preclosure in short fiction.

_______. "Preclosure in an 'Open' Story." In *Creative and Critical Approaches to the Short Story*, edited by Noel Harold Kaylor, Jr. Lewiston, N.Y.:

The Edwin Mellen Press, 1997. Presents the results of an experiment in preclosure studies in which 114 students were asked to read Julio Cortázar's story "Orientation of Cats" and report on their understanding of it. Lohafer asks the students to identify points at which the story might have ended—a preclosure procedure makes them more aware of reading tactics and their inherent sense of storyness.

_______. "Why the 'Life of Ma Parker' is Not So Simple: Preclosure in Issue-Bound Stories." *Studies in Short Fiction* 33 (Fall, 1996): 475-486. In this particular experiment with student reaction to preclosure markers in a story by Katherine Mansfield, Lohafer is interested in showing how attention to preclosure encourages readers to temporarily suppress their ready-made concepts and engage their story competence.

Luscher, Robert M. "The Short Story Sequence: An Open Book." In *Short Story Theory at a Crossroads*, edited by Susan Lohafer and Jo Ellyn Clarey. Baton Rouge: Louisiana State University Press, 1989. Discusses the need for readers of story cycles such as *Winesburg, Ohio* (1919) to extend their drive to find pattern to cover a number of individual sequences. Compares story cycles with mere aggregates of stories as well as with novelistic sequences.

McMurray, George R. "The Spanish American Short Story from Borges to the Present." In *The Latin American Short Story: A Critical History*, edited by Margaret Sayers Peden. Boston: Twayne, 1983. Discusses Jorge Luis Borges as a writer who ushered in a new literary era in South America and the shift to political and social problems during the 1950's. Argues that the most talented Spanish American writer since Borges is Julio Cortázar from Argentina. Also discusses José Donoso and Carlos Fuentes.

Marcus, Mordecai. "What Is an Initiation Story?" *The Journal of Aesthetics and Art Criticism* 14 (1960): 221-227. Distinguishes three types of initiation stories: those that lead protagonists only to the threshold of maturity, those that take the protagonists across the threshold of maturity but leave them in a struggle for certainty, and decisive initiation stories that carry protagonists firmly into maturity.

Marler, Robert F. "From Tale to Short Story: The Emergence of a New Genre in the 1850's." *American Literature: A Journal of Literary History, Criticism, and Bibliography* 46 (1974): 153-169. Using Northrop Frye's distinction between the tale (embodies "stylized figures which expand into psychological archetypes") and the short story (deals with characters who wear their "*personae* or social masks"), Marler surveys the critical condemnation of the tale form and the increasing emphasis on realism in the 1850's. The broad shift is from Edgar Allan Poe's overt romance to Herman Melville's mimetic portrayals, especially in "Bartleby the Scrivener."

Matthews, Brander. *The Philosophy of the Short-Story*. New York: Longmans, Green, 1901. An expansion of an 1882 article in which Matthews sets himself forth as the first critic (since Edgar Allan Poe) to discuss the short story (Matthews contributed the hyphen) as a genre. By asserting that the short story must have a vigorous compression, must be original, must be ingenious, must have a touch of fantasy, and so on, Matthews set the stage for a host of textbook writers on the short story who followed.

Maugham, W. Somerset. "The Short Story." In *Points of View: Five Essays*. Garden City, N.Y.: Doubleday, 1958. As might be expected, Maugham's preference is for the well-made story exemplified by Guy de Maupassant's "The Necklace." Most of the essay, however, deals with Chekhov and Mansfield biographical material.

May, Charles E. "Artifice and Artificiality in the Short Story." *Story* 1 (Spring, 1990): 72-82. Discusses the artificial and formalized nature of the endings of short stories, arguing that the short story is the most aesthetic narrative form; discusses the ending of several representative stories.

_______. "Chekhov and the Modern Short Story." In *A Chekhov Companion*, edited by Toby Clyman. Westport, Conn.: Greenwood Press, 1985. A detailed analysis of Anton Chekhov's influence on the development of the modern short story; isolates Chekhov's most important innovations in the form and then shows how these elements have been further used and developed by such modern writers as Katherine Mansfield, Ernest Hemingway, Bernard Malamud, Raymond Carver, and others.

_______. "HyperStory: Teaching Short Fiction with Computers." In *The Tales We Tell: Perspectives on the Short Story*, edited by Barbara Lounsberry, Susan Lohafer, Mary Rohrberger, Stephen Pett, and R. C. Feddersen. Westport, Conn.: Greenwood Press, 1998. Describes "HyperStory," a computer program developed by the author, which teaches students how to read short fiction more carefully and thoughtfully. Uses Poe's "The Cask of Amontillado" as an example; attempts to explain, with the help of student comments, the success of the program.

_______. "Metaphoric Motivation in Short Fiction: 'In the Beginning Was the Story.' " In *Short Theory at a Crossroads*, edited by Susan Lohafer and Jo Ellyn Clarey. Baton Rouge: Louisiana State University Press, 1989. A discussion of how short fiction moves from the "tale" form to the "short story" form through motivation by metaphor in "Fall of the House of Usher," "Bartleby the Scrivener," "The Legend of Sleepy Hollow," and "Young Goodman Brown."

_______. "The Nature of Knowledge in Short Fiction." *Studies in Short Fiction* 21 (Fall, 1984): 227-238. A theoretical study of the epistemological bases of short fiction. Argues that the short story originates as a primal mythic mode that develops into a metaphoric mode.

_______. "Obsession and the Short Story." In *Creative and Critical Approaches to the Short Story*, edited by Noel Harold Kaylor, Jr. Lewiston, N.Y.: The Edwin Mellen Press, 1997. An examination of the common charge that the short story is unhealthily limited and obsessed. Discusses the origins of the relationship between psychological obsession and aesthetic unity in the stories of Poe, Nathaniel Hawthorne, and Herman Melville; attempts to account for this relationship as a generic characteristic of the short story.

_______. "Prolegomenon to a Generic Study of the Short Story." *Studies in Short Fiction* 33 (Fall, 1996): 461-474. Tries to lay the groundwork for a generic theory of the short story in terms of new theories of genre. Discusses the short story's historical focus on the strange and unexpected and the formal demands made by this thematic focus. Argues for a mixed genre theory of the short story that can account for the form's essential as well as historically changing characteristics.

_______. "Reality in the Modern Short Story" *Style* 27 (Fall, 1993): 369-379. Argues that realism in the modern short story from Chekhov to Raymond Carver is not the simple mimesis of the realistic novel but rather the use of highly compressed selective detail configured to metaphorically objectify that which cannot be described directly. The result is a "hyperrealism" in which story is unified by tone, and meaning is created by aesthetic pattern.

_______. *Short Story Theories*. Athens: Ohio University Press, 1976. A collection of twenty previously published essays on the short story as a genre in its own right.

_______. "A Survey of Short Story Criticism in America." *The Minnesota Review*, Spring, 1973, 163-169. An analytical survey of criticism beginning with Edgar Allan Poe and focusing on the short story's underlying vision and characteristic mode of understanding and confronting reality.

_______. "The Unique Effect of the Short Story: A Reconsideration and an Example." *Studies in Short Fiction* 13 (1976): 289-297. An attempt to redefine Edgar Allan Poe's "unique effect" in the short story in terms of mythic perception. The short story demands intense compression and focusing because its essential subject is a manifestation of what philosopher Ernst Cassirer calls the "momentary deity." A detailed discussion of Stephen Crane's story "An Episode of War" illustrates the concept.

Menikoff, Barry. "The Problematics of Form: History and the Short Story." *Journal of the Short Story in English*, no. 2 (1984): 129-146. After a brief introduction on how the short story has been neglected, Menikoff comments briefly on the importance of Charles May's *Short Story Theories* (1976) and then discusses essays on the short story that appeared in *Critical Survey of Short Fiction* (1981) and a special issue of *Modern Fiction Studies* (1982). A sketchy and crotchety survey that adds little to an understanding of the short-story form.

Miall, David. "Text and Affect: A Model for Story Understanding." In *Re-reading the Short Story*, edited by Clare Hanson. New York: St. Martin's Press, 1989. A discussion of what readers are doing in emotional terms when they read, using the defamiliarization model of the Russian formalists. Focuses on three aspects of emotion: self-reference, domain crossing, and anticipation. Basically determines that whereas literary texts constrain response by means of their shared frames and conventions, their affective responses are highly divergent.

Mirrielees, Edith. "The American Short Story." *The Atlantic Monthly* 167 (June, 1941): 714-722. Complains that promising writers of the short story who succeed in the literary magazines decline in quality when they publish in the "slick" magazines.

Mish, Charles C. "English Short Fiction in the Seventeenth Century." *Studies in Short Fiction* 6 (1969): 223-330. Mish divides the period into two parts: 1600-1660, in which short fiction declined into sterile imitation and preciousness, and 1660-1700, in which it was revitalized by the French influence of such works as Madame de la Fayette's *La Princesse de Clèves* (1678; *The Princess of Clèves*, 1679). The French direction toward interiorization, psychological analysis and verisimilitude in action and setting, combined with the English style of the self-conscious narrator, moves fiction toward the novel of the eighteenth century.

Moffett, James. "Telling Stories: Methods of Abstraction in Fiction." *ETC*. 21 (1964): 425-50. Charts a sequence covering an "entire range" of ways in which stories can be told, from the most subjective and personal (interior monologue and dramatic monologue) to the most objective and impersonal (anonymous narration). Includes examples of each type.

Moravia, Alberto. "The Short Story and the Novel." In *Man as End: A Defense of Humanism*. Translated by Bernard Wall. New York: Farrar, Straus & Giroux, 1969. The basic difference between the novel and the short story is that the novel has a bone structure of ideological themes whereas the short story is made up of intuitions of feelings.

Moser, Charles A., ed. "Pushkin and the Russian Short Story." In *The Russian Short Story: A Critical History*. Boston: Twayne, 1986. Says that Pushkin reworked older tales, gave old plots a new twist, and "toyed with literary conventions." Argues that the short story might have developed as a genre that combined prose and verse. Discusses the brevity and surprise endings of the stories. Focuses on Pushkin's contribution to the short story as a genre: brevity, surprise endings, and self-consciousness of narrative technique. Discusses the innovations of Pushkin's stories as well as their influence on subsequent Russian writers.

Munson, Gorham. "The Recapture of the Storyable." *The University Review* 10 (Autumn, 1943): 37-44. Says that the best short-story writers are concerned with only three questions: whether they have found a storyable incident, how they should cast their characters, and who would best tell their story.

Neuhauser, Rudolf. "The Russian Short Story, 1917-1980." In *The Russian Short Story: A Critical History*, edited by Charles A. Moser. Boston: Twayne, 1986. Discussion of postrevolution writers in Russia such as Yevgeny Zamyatin, as well as the influence of Russian formalist critics and writers such as Viktor Shklovsky and Boris Eikhenbaum. A brief discussion of Isaac Babel is included here, although his influence on the short story as a form should probably make him loom higher than this. Separate sections are devoted to Russian literature and World War II, the thaw after the death of Joseph Stalin, the woman question, and science prose and village prose.

Oates, Joyce Carol. "Beginnings: The Origin and Art

of the Short Story." In *The Tales We Tell: Perspectives on the Short Story*, edited by Barbara Lounsberry, Susan Lohafer, Mary Rohrberger, Stephen Pett, and R. C. Feddersen. Westport, Conn.: Greenwood Press, 1998. Defines the short story as a form that represents an intensification of meaning rather than an expansion of the imagination; briefly discusses the importance of Poe's aesthetic and Mark Twain's oral tale to the development of the American short story.

_______. "The Short Story." *Southern Humanities Review* 5 (1971): 213-214. The short story is a "dream verbalized," a manifestation of desire. Its most interesting aspect is its "mystery."

O'Brien, Edward J. *The Advance of the American Short Story*. Rev. ed. New York: Dodd, Mead, 1931. A survey of the development of the American short story from Washington Irving to Sherwood Anderson. The focus is on contributions to the form by various authors: Irving's development of the story from the eighteenth century essay, Nathaniel Hawthorne's discovery of the subjective method for psychological fiction, Edgar Allan Poe's formalizing, Bret Harte's caricaturing, Henry James's development of the "central intelligence," and Anderson's freeing the story from O. Henry formalism.

_______. *The Dance of the Machines: The American Short Story and the Industrial Age*. New York: Macaulay, 1929. Chapter 4 of this rambling polemic against machinelike standardization of the industrial age describes thirty characteristics that the short story ("the most typical American form") shares with the machine: For example, it is patterned, impersonal, standardized, speeded-up, and cheap.

O'Connor, Flannery. "Writing Short Stories." In *Mystery and Manners*, edited by Sally and Robert Fitzgerald. New York: Farrar, Straus & Giroux, 1969. In this lecture at a southern writer' conference, O'Connor discusses the two qualities necessary for the short story: "sense of manners," which writers get from the texture of their immediate surroundings, and "sense of mystery," which is always the mystery of personality—"showing how some specific folks *will* do, in spite of everything."

O'Connor, Frank. *The Lonely Voice: A Study of the Short Story*. Cleveland: World Publishing, 1963. The introductory chapter contains extremely valuable "intuitive" criticism by an accomplished master of the short story. The basic difference between the novel and the short story is that in the latter one always finds an intense awareness of human loneliness. O'Connor believes that the protagonist of the short story is less an individual with whom the reader can identify than a "submerged population group"—that is, someone outside the social mainstream. The remaining chapters of the book treat this theme in the works of Ivan Turgenev, Anton Chekhov, Guy de Maupassant, Rudyard Kipling, James Joyce, Katherine Mansfield, D. H. Lawrence, A. E. Coppard, Isaac Babel, and Mary Lavin.

O'Faoláin, Seán. *The Short Story*. New York: Devin-Adair, 1951. This book on the technique of the short story claims that technique is the "least part of the business." O'Faoláin illustrates his thesis that personality is the most important element by describing the personal struggles of Alphonse Daudet, Anton Chekhov, and Guy de Maupassant. He does his duty to the assigned subject of the book by also discussing the technical problems of convention, subject, construction, and language.

Orel, Harold. *The Victorian Short Story: Development and Triumph of a Literary Genre*. Cambridge, England: Cambridge University Press, 1986. Contains chapters on Joseph Sheridan Le Fanu, Charles Dickens, Anthony Trollope, Thomas Hardy, Robert Louis Stevenson, Rudyard Kipling, H. G. Wells, and Joseph Conrad. Focuses on the relevant biographical and sociocultural factors and says something about writers' relationships with editors and periodicals. Does not attempt a formal history of the evolution of the genre.

O'Rourke, William. "Morphological Metaphors for the Short Story: Matters of Production, Reproduction, and Consumption." In *Short Story Theory at a Crossroads*, edited by Susan Lohafer and Jo

Ellyn Clarey. Baton Rouge: Louisiana State University Press, 1989. Explores a number of analogies drawn from the social and natural sciences to suggest ways of seeing how the short story is different from the novel: The novel has a structure like a vertebrate, whereas the short story is like an animal with an exoskeleton; the novel is a macro form, whereas the short story is a micro form.

O'Toole, L. Michael. *Structure, Style, and Interpretation in the Russian Short Story*. New Haven, Conn.: Yale University Press, 1982. An analysis of a few major stories by Nikolai Leskov, Nikolai Gogol, Alexander Pushkin, Maxim Gorky, Ivan Turgenev, and Anton Chekhov, in terms of the Formalist theories of Viktor Shklovsky, Boris Eikhenbaum, Boris Tomashevsky, Mikhail Bakhtin, and Vladimir Propp, and the structuralist theories of Roland Barthes and Tzvetan Todorov. The introduction provides a general methodological introduction to interpretation through structural analysis.

Overstreet, Bonaro. "Little Story, What Now?" *Saturday Review of Literature* 24 (November 22, 1941): 3-5, 25-26. Overstreet argues that as a result of a loss of faith in the old verities of the nineteenth century, the twentieth century short story is concerned with psychological materials, not with the events in the objective world

Pache, Walter. "Towards the Modern English Short Story." In *Modes of Narrative*, edited by Reingard M. Vischik and Barbara Korte. Wurzburg: Konigshausen and Neumann, 1990. A study of the relationship between the short fiction of the 1890's and the modern short story. Surveys changes in periodical publishing during the period, analyzes new directions in short story theory at the turn of the century, suggests some of the basic structural patterns of the end-of-the-century short story.

Pain, Barry. *The Short Story*. London: Martin Secker, 1916. Pain claims that the primary difference between the short story and the novel is that the short story, because of its dependence on suggestive devices, demands more of the reader's participation.

Palakeel, Thomas. "Third World Short Story as National Allegory?" *Journal of Modern Literature* 20 (Summer, 1996): 97-102. Argues against Frederic Jameson's claim that third-world fictions are always national allegories. Points out that this claim is even more damaging to the short story than to the novel because the short story is the most energetic literary activity in the Third World; argues that Jameson's theory cripples any non-Western literature that tries to deal with the psychological or spiritual reality of the individual.

Pasco, Allan H. "The Short Story: The Short of It." *Style* 27 (Fall, 1993): 442-451. Suggests a list of qualities of the short story generated by its brevity, such as the assumptions of considerable background on the part of the reader and that readers will absorb and remember all elements of the work. Claims that the short story shuns amplification in favor of inference, that it is usually single rather than multivalent, that it tends toward the general, and that it remains foreign to loosely motivated detail.

Patrick, Walton R. "Poetic Style in the Contemporary Short Story." *College Composition and Communication* 18 (1957): 77-84. The poetic style appears more consistently in the short story than in the novel because metaphorical dilations are essential to the writer who "strives to pack the utmost meaning into his restricted space."

Pattee, Fred Lewis. *The Development of the American Short Story*. New York: Harper & Row, 1923. The most detailed and historically full survey of the American short story from Washington Irving to O. Henry. Charts the changes in taste of the short-story reading public and indicates the major contributions to the form of such classic practitioners as Irving, Nathaniel Hawthorne, Edgar Allan Poe, and Bret Harte. Surveys the effect of the "Annuals," the "Ladies' Books," local color, Brander Matthews' *The Philosophy of the Short-Story* (1901), and the writing handbooks.

Peden, William. *The American Short Story: Continuity and Change, 1940-1975*, 2d ed. Boston: Houghton Mifflin, 1975. Includes chapters on publishing and the short story since 1940; the stories of suburbia by John Cheever, John Updike, and others; stories of physical illness and abnormality by James Purdy, Tennessee Williams, Flannery O'Connor, Joyce Carol Oates; stories by Jewish writers such as Bernard Malamud, Saul Bellow, J. D. Salinger, Grace Paley, Philip Roth, and Isaac Bashevis Singer; stories by black writers such as Langston Hughes, Richard Wright, Ann Petry, and Toni Cade Bambera.

_______. "The American Short Story During the Twenties." *Studies in Short Fiction* 10 (1973): 367-371. A highly abbreviated account of the causes of the explosion of short stories during the 1920's. Some of the causes discussed are the new freedom from plotted stories, new emphasis on "now-ness," the boom of little magazines, and the influence of cinematic techniques.

_______. *The American Short Story: Front Line in the National Defense of Literature*. Boston: Houghton Mifflin, 1964. A discussion of major trends in the American short story since 1940. The center of the book consists of a chapter on those writers who focus on everyday life in contemporary society (John Cheever, John O'Hara, Peter Taylor, John Updike, J. F. Powers, and J. D. Salinger) and a chapter on those who are preoccupied with the grotesque, abnormal, and bizarre (Carson McCullers, O'Connor, James Purdy, Truman Capote, and Tennessee Williams). An additional chapter surveys other short-story subjects such as the war, minorities, regions, and science fiction.

Penn, W. S. "The Tale as Genre in Short Fiction." *Southern Humanities Review* 15 (Summer, 1981): 231-241. Discusses the genre from the perspective of structure. Primarily uses suggestions made by Jonathan Culler in *Structuralist Poetics* for constructing a poetic persona in the lyric poem, what Culler calls an "enunciative posture"—that is, the detectable or intuited moral relation of the implied author to both the world at large and the world he or she creates. Develops two kinds of tales: the radical oral and the exponential oral.

Perry, Bliss. *A Study of Prose Fiction*. Boston: Houghton Mifflin, 1920. Perry claims that the short story differs from the novel by presenting unique and original characters, by focusing on fragments of reality, and by making use of the poetic devices of impressionism and symbolism.

Pickering, Jean. "The English Short Story in the Sixties." In *The English Short Story, 1945-1980*, edited by Dennis Vanatta. Boston: Twayne, 1985. Pickering says that few of the cultural developments in England in the 1960's were reflected in the short story and claims that the short story was in decline during the period. Focuses on short-story collections by Roald Dahl, William Sansom, Doris Lessing, V. S. Pritchett, and H. E. Bates.

_______. "Time and the Short Story." In *Re-reading the Short Story*, edited by Clare Hanson. New York: St. Martin's Press, 1989. A rehash of the old distinction between the short story as an art of revelation and the novel as an art of evolution. General implications that derive from this distinction are that short-story writers do not need to know all the details of their characters' lives and that the short story is doubly symbolic. Structure, theme, characterization, and language are influenced by the short story's particular relation to time as a moment of revelation.

Poe, Edgar Allan. Review of *Twice-Told Tales. Graham's Magazine*, May, 1842. The first critical discussion of the short story, or the "tale" as Poe terms it, to establish the genre as distinct from the novel. Because of its sense of totality, its single effect, and its patterned design, the short story is second only to the lyric in its demands on high genius and in its aesthetic beauty.

Pratt, Mary Louise. "The Short Story: The Long and the Short of It." *Poetics* 10 (1981): 175-194. A theoretical discussion of the form; presents eight ways that the short story is better understood if its dependence on the novel is understood.

Price, Kenneth M., and Susan Belasco Smith, eds. *Periodical Literature in Nineteenth-Century America*. Charlottsville: University Press of Virginia, 1995. A collection of essays by various scholars about how the periodical transformed the American literary marketplace between 1830 and 1890. Critics suggest how the development of the periodical as a market for short fiction had a powerful influence on the development of the form as a unique American genre.

Prince, Gerald. *A Grammar of Stories: An Introduction*. The Hague: Mouton, 1973. An attempt to establish rules to account for the structure of all the syntactical sets that we intuitively recognize as stories. The model used is Noam Chomsky's theories of generative grammar.

_______. "The Long and the Short of It." *Style* 27 (Fall, 1993): 327-331. Provides a definition of the short story as "an autonomous, short, fictional story written in prose and offered for display." Admits that such a definition has limited usefulness but argues that this is characteristic of generic definitions; says that texts belong not to one but to an indefinitely large number of textual families and use an indefinitely large number of clusters of features.

Pritchett, V. S. "Short Stories." *Harper's Bazaar* 87 (July, 1953): 31, 113. The short story is a hybrid, owing much to the quickness and objectivity of the cinema, much to the poet and the newspaper reporter, and everything to the "restlessness, the alert nerve, the scientific eye and the short breath of contemporary life." Makes an interesting point about the collapse of standards, conventions, and values which has so bewildered the impersonal novelist but has been the making of the story writer.

Propp, Vladimir. *Morphology of the Folktale*, edited by Svatava Pirkova-Jakovson. Translated by Laurence Scott. Bloomington: Indiana University Research Center, 1958. All Formalist and structuralist studies of narrative owe a debt to this pioneering early twentieth century study. Using one hundred fairy tales, Propp defines the genre itself by analyzing the stories according to characteristic actions or functions.

Pütz, Manfred. "The American Short Story: A Survey of Recent Publications in Germany. *Kritikon Litterarum* 4 (1975): 177-187. Surveys four collections of critical essays and two book-length studies of the American short story published in Germany in the early 1970's. The studies range from poetics and historical surveys to interpretation and analyses of structure and methodology. Most helpful is Theodore Wolper's theory of the short story's focus on ambiguity, paradox, and the enigmatic nature of concrete experience.

Reid, Ian. *The Short Story*. London: Methuen, 1977. A brief study in the Critical Idiom series. Deals with problems of definition, historical development, and related generic forms. Good introduction to the short story as a genre.

Rhode, Robert D. *Setting in the American Short Story of Local Color: 1865-1900*. The Hague: Mouton, 1975. A study of the various functions that setting plays in the local-color story in the late nineteenth century, from setting as merely background to setting in relation to character and setting as personification.

Rohrberger, Mary. "Between Shadow and Act: Where Do We Go from Here?" In *Short Story Theory at a Crossroads*, edited by Susan Lohafer and Jo Ellyn Clarey. Baton Rouge: Louisiana State University Press, 1989. A thought-provoking review of a number of modern short-story critics and theorists, largely by way of responding to, and disagreeing with, the strictly scientific and logical approach to definition of the form suggested by Norman Friedman. Also includes a restatement of the view that Rohrberger enunciated in her earlier book on Nathaniel Hawthorne, in which she argued for the essentially romantic nature of the short-story form.

_______. *Hawthorne and the Modern Short Story: A Study in Genre*. The Hague: Mouton, 1966. Attempts a generic definition of the short story as a form that derives from the romantic metaphysical view that there is more to the world than can be apprehended through the senses. Hawthorne is the touchstone for her definition, which she then applies to twentieth century stories by Eudora Welty, Ernest Hemingway, Sherwood Anderson, William Faulkner, and others.

_______. "The Question of Regionalism: Limitation and Transcendence." In *The American Short Story, 1900-1945*, edited by Philip Stevick. Boston: Twayne, 1984. This essay's focus is on such writers as Ruth Suckow, Jesse Stuart, Langston Hughes, and Jean Toomer. Calls Toomer's *Cane* (1923) the most significant work produced by the Harlem Renaissance and compares it with Sherwood Anderson's *Winesburg, Ohio*. Also discusses Ellen Glasgow, Sinclair Lewis, James T. Farrell, Erskine Caldwell, John O'Hara, and John Steinbeck.

Ross, Danforth. *The American Short Story*. Minneapolis: University of Minnesota Press, 1961. A sketchy survey that measures American stories since Edgar Allan Poe against Aristotelian criteria of action, unity, tension, and irony. Ends with the Beat writers who rebel against the Poe-Aristotle tradition by using shock tactics.

Ruthrof, Horst. "Bracketed World and Reader Construction in the Modern Short Story." In *The Reader's Construction of Narrative*. London: Routledge & Kegan Paul, 1981. Discusses the "boundary situation" as the basis for the modern short story. In the pure boundary situation, the reader's act of bracketing transforms the presented crisis into the existential experience of the reading act.

Schirmer, Gregory A. "Tales from Big House and Cabin: The Nineteenth Century." In *The Irish Short Story: A Critical History*, edited by James F. Kilroy. Boston: Twayne, 1984. Surveys the short fiction of Maria Edgeworth, William Carleton, and Joseph Sheridan Le Fanu, among others. Schirmer emphasizes the ironic voice of Edgeworth's *Castle Rackrent* (1800), the comic realism and the sophisticated use of narrative voice of Carleton, and the use of the gothic tradition and psychological complexity of Le Fanu.

Schlauch, Margaret. "English Short Fiction in the Fifteenth and Sixteenth Centuries." *Studies in Short Fiction* 3 (1966): 393-434. A survey of types of short fiction from the romantic *lai* to the exemplum, and from the bawdy fabliau to the novella. Schlauch's conclusions are that modern short-story writers are heirs both in subject matter (for example internal psychological conflict) and in technique (such as the importance of dialogue) to a long tradition that antedates the seventeenth century, a tradition that is still worth studying.

Senior, Olive. "Lessons from the Fruit Stand: Or, Writing for the Listener." *Journal of Modern Literature* 20 (Summer, 1996): 40-44. An account of one writer's development of the short story as a personal engagement between teller and listener. Discusses the relationship between the oral tradition of gossip and folklore and the development of short-story conventions. Claims that the short story is a form based on bits and pieces of human lives for which there is no total picture.

Shaw, Valerie. *The Short Story: A Critical Introduction*. London: Longman, 1983. A desultory discussion of the form, without a theoretical approach and little sympathy for a unified approach to the form. The focus is on British story writers primarily, with one chapter on the transitional figure Robert Louis Stevenson. Other chapters deal with the patterned form to the artless tale form, with chapters on character, setting, and subject matter. Shaw says that the short story cannot be defined by unity of effect or by a history of its "favorite devices and eminent practitioners."

Siebert, Hilary. "Did We Both Read the Same Story? Interpreting Cultural Contexts from Oral Discourses with the American Short Story." *Short Story* n.s. 6 (Spring, 1998). The history of the short story is one of many different types of discourses, both oral and written, blending together. The result of this textual tension and diversity is that educated readers may not be familiar with the variety of discourse conventions and thus read the stories incorrectly.

_______. "'Outside History': Lyrical Knowledge in the Discourse of the Short Story." In *Creative and Critical Approaches to the Short Story*, edited by Noel Harold Kaylor, Jr. Lewiston, N.Y.: The Edwin Mellen Press, 1997. A discussion of how readers of short stories must often shift from expectations of a revealed, discursive meaning typical of prose to a gradually apprehended suggestive meaning typical of lyric poetry.

Smith, Horatio E. "The Development of Brief Narrative in Modern French Literature: A Statement of the Problem." *PMLA* 32 (1917): 583-597. Surveys the confusion between the conte and *nouvelle* and calls for a critical investigation of the practice and theory of the French forms similar to those published on the American short story and the German *Nouvelle*.

Sodowsky, Roland. "The Minimalist Short Story: Its Definition, Writers, and (Small) Heyday." *Studies in Short Fiction* 33 (Fall, 1996): 529-540. A historical survey of minimalism's dominance of the short-story marketplace in the late 1970's and early 1980's in the United States. Based on an examination of short stories in such magazines as *The New Yorker*, *The Atlantic Monthly*, *Esquire*, and *Harper's* between 1975 and 1990, Sodowsky isolates and summarizes some of the basic characteristics of the minimalist short story.

Stanzel, Franz K. "Textual Power in (Short) Short Story and Poem." In *Modes of Narrative*, edited by Reingard M. Vischik and Barbara Korte. Wursburg: Konigshausen and Neumann, 1990. Argues that the modern short story and modern poetry, which at the turn of the century were far apart, have come closer together in both form and content. Suggests some of the similarities between the two forms, such as their focusing the reader's attention on beginnings and endings and their insistence on close readings of the structure of each line and sentence.

Steirle, Karl-Heinz. "Story as Exemplum—Exemplum as Story: On the Pragmatics and Poetics of Narrative Texts." In *New Perspectives in German Literary Criticism*, edited by Richard E. Amacher and Victor Lange. Translated by David Wilson et al. Princeton, N.J.: Princeton University Press, 1979. A generic discussion of how we move from exemplum, which is definite, to story, which is relativistic. Argues that if one wants to find the link between the short story and the exemplum, the answer must be found in Immanuel Kant's theory of discernment—that is, the ability to realize the particular as contained in the general.

Stevenson, Lionel. "The Short Story in Embryo." *English Literature in Transition* 15 (1972): 261-268. A discussion of the "agglomerative urge" in the English fiction of the eighteenth and nineteenth centuries that contributed to the undervaluing of the short story. Not until 1880, when the fragmentation of the well-integrated view of society began in England, did the short story come into its own in that country.

Stevick, Philip, ed. *Anti-Story: An Anthology of Experimental Fiction*. New York: Free Press, 1971. An influential collection of contemporary short fiction with a helpful introduction that characterizes antistory as against mimesis, reality, event, subject, the middle range of experience, analysis, and meaning.

________, ed. Introduction to *The American Short Story: 1900-1945*. Boston: Twayne, 1984. Stevick's extensive introduction to this collection of essays by various critics is a helpful historical overview of the development of the twentieth century short story. A good introduction to many of the features of the modern short story and how they came about at the beginning of the century.

Stinson, John J. "The English Short Story, 1945-1950." In *The English Short Story, 1945-1980*, edited by Dennis Vanatta. Boston: Twayne, 1985. Discusses some of the reasons why the short story was in decline in England during this period and claims there was no new direction in the form of the time. Discusses W. Somerset Maugham, A. E. Coppard, Graham Greene, Sylvia Townsend Warner, V. S. Pritchett, and Angus Wilson.

Stroud, Theodore A. "A Critical Approach to the Short Story." *The Journal of General Education* 9 (1956): 91-100. Makes use of American "New Criticism" to determine the pattern of the work—that is, why apparently irrelevant episodes are included and why some events are expanded and others excluded.

Suckow, Ruth. "The Short Story." *Saturday Review of Literature* 4 (November 19, 1927): 317-318. Suckow strongly argues that no one can define the short story, for it is an aesthetic method for dealing with diversity and multiplicity.

Sullivan, Walter. "Revelation in the Short Story: A Note of Methodology." In *Vanderbilt Studies in Humanities*, edited by Richard C. Beatty, John Philip Hyatt, and Monroe K. Spears. Vol. 1. Nashville: Vanderbilt University Press, 1951. The fundamental methodological concept of the short story is a change of view from innocence to knowledge. The change can be either "logical" (coming at the end of the story) or "anticipated" (coming near the beginning); it can be either "intraconcatinate" (occurring within the main character) or "extra-concatinate" (occurring within a peripheral character). Thus defined, the short story did not begin until the final years of the nineteenth century.

Summers, Hollis, ed. *Discussions of the Short Story.* Boston: D. C. Heath, 1963. The nine general pieces on the short story are the Poe and Bader essays listed above, Ray B. West's first chapter, Seán O'Faoláin's chapter on "Convention," a chapter each from Percy Lubbock's *Craft of Fiction* and Kenneth Payson Kempton's *The Short Story*, Bret Harte's "The Rise of the Short Story," and excerpts from Brander Matthews's book. Also includes seven additional essays on specific short-story writers.

Szávai, János. "Towards a Theory of the Short Story." *Acta Litteraria Academiae Scientiarum Hungariae, Tomus* 24 (1982): 203-224. Discusses the Boccaccio model as a genre that gives the illusion of reflecting reality directly and spontaneously, whereas it is actually a complex, structured entity that both retains and enriches the basic structure of the story. The enrichment resides, on the one hand, in the careful preparation of the *point* and its attachment to a key motif and, on the other, in the introduction of a new dimension in addition to the anecdote.

Terras, Victor. "The Russian Short Story: 1830-1850." In *The Russian Short Story: A Critical History*, edited by Charles A. Moser. Boston: Twayne, 1986. Points out that 1830 was a watershed in the history of Russian literature in that it marked the end of the golden age of poetry and the shift to prose fiction, particularly short fiction. Discusses the Romantic origins of short fiction in Russia with Alexander Pushkin, the transition to psychological realism with Mikhail Lermontov, the significant contributions of the stories of Nikolai Gogol, the transition to the so-called natural school, and the early works of Fyodor Dostoevski and Ivan Turgenev.

Thurston, Jarvis, O. B. Emerson, Carl Hartman, and Elizabeth Wright, eds. *Short Fiction Criticism: A Checklist of Interpretation Since 1925 of Stories and Novelettes (American, British, Continental), 1800-1958.* Denver: Alan Swallow, 1960. This checklist of interpretations of individual stories was brought up to date by Elizabeth Wright in the Summer, 1969, issue of *Studies in Short Fiction* and has been supplemented by Wright, George Hendrick, and Warren Walker in each summer issue thereafter.

Todorov, Tzvetan. "The Structural Analysis of Literature." In *Structuralism: An Introduction*, edited by David Robey. London: Clarendon Press, 1973. The "figure in the carpet" in Henry James's stories is the quest for an absolute and absent cause. The cause is either a character, an event, or an object; its effect is the story readers are told. Everything in the story owes its existence to this cause, but because it is absent, the reader sets off in quest of it.

Trask, Georgianne, and Charles Burkhart, ed. *Storytellers and Their Art.* New York: Doubleday Anchor, 1963. A valuable collection of comments on the short-story form by practitioners from Anton Chekhov to Truman Capote. Noteworthy in part 1 are "Definitions of the Short Story" and "Short Story vs. Novel."

Trussler, Michael. "The Short Story: Interview with Charles May and Susan Lohafer." *Wascana Review* 33 (Spring, 1998): 14-24. Interview with two well-known theorists of the short story, who discuss reasons for past critical neglect of the form, conditions of the recent renaissance of interest in the form by both critics and general readers, unique generic characteristics of the short story, and current and future trends in the short story and theoretical approaches to it.

_______. "Suspended Narratives: The Short Story and Temporality." *Studies in Short Fiction* 33 (Fall, 1996): 557-577. An analysis of the critical view that the short-story form focuses on atemporality. Synthesizes a number of theories that emphasize short fiction's focus on existential confrontations while refusing to mitigate such experiences with abstraction, context, or continuity.

Voss, Arthur. *The American Short Story: A Critical Survey*. Norman: University of Oklahoma Press, 1973. A comprehensive but routine survey of the major short-story writers in American literature. Valuable for an overview of the stories and criticism, but contains nothing original.

Wain, John. "Remarks on the Short Story." *Journal of the Short Story in English* 2 (1984): 49-66. Wain argues that the short story is a form of its own, with its own laws and logic, and that it is a modern form, beginning with Edgar Allan Poe. Says the novel is like a painting, whereas the short story is like a drawing, which catches a moment and is satisfying on its own grounds. He says there are perfectly successful short stories and totally unsuccessful ones, and nothing in between.

Watson, James G. "The American Short Story: 1930-1945." In *The American Short Story, 1900-1945*, edited by Philip Stevick. Boston: Twayne, 1984. Claims that the period between 1930 and 1945 had the most prolific outpouring of short fiction in the history of American literature. Focuses on the importance of the little magazines and discusses the contributions of Ernest Hemingway, William Faulkner, and F. Scott Fitzgerald.

Welty, Eudora. "The Reading and Writing of Short Stories." *The Atlantic Monthly*, February, 1949, 54-58; March, 1949, 46-49. An impressionistic but suggestive essay in two installments that focuses on the mystery of the story and the fact that one cannot always see the solid outlines of the story because of the atmosphere that it generates.

Werlock, Abby H. P., ed. *The Facts on File Companion to the American Short Story*. New York: Facts on File, 2000. Alphabetically arranged entries cover aspects of the American short story from the early nineteenth century to the 1990's. They include author biographies and bibliographies, plot synopses, character sketches, and major short-story analyses.

West, Ray B. "The American Short Story." In *The Writer in the Room*. Detroit: Michigan State University Press, 1968. Originally appeared as West's introduction to *American Short Stories* (Thomas Y. Crowell, 1959). Contrasts the short story's "microscopic" focus on inner motives with the novel's "telescopic" view of human beings from the outside. The novel is concerned with human beings' attempt to control nature through social institutions; the short story presents the individual's confrontation with nature as an indifferent force.

_______. "The Modern Short Story and the Highest Forms of Art." *English Journal* 46 (1957): 531-539. The rise of the short story in the nineteenth century is a result of the shift in narrative view from the "telescopic" (viewing nature and society from the outside) to the "microscopic" (viewing the unseen world of inner motives and impulses).

_______. *The Short Story in America: 1900-1950*. Chicago: Henry Regnery, 1952. Probably the most familiar and most often recommended history of the American short story. Takes up where Fred Lewis Pattee's book leaves off, but it lacks the completeness or the continuity necessary for an adequate history. Chapter 1, "The American Short Story at Mid-Century," is a short survey in itself of the development of the short story since Washington Irving, Nathaniel Hawthorne, and Edgar Allan Poe. Chapter 4 is devoted completely to Ernest Hemingway and William Faulkner.

Wharton, Edith. "Telling a Short Story." In *The Writing of Fiction*. New York: Charles Scribner's Sons, 1925. The chief technical difference between the novel and the short story is that the novel focuses on character while the short story focuses on situation; "and it follows that the effect produced by the short story depends almost entirely on its form."

Williams, William Carlos. *A Beginning on the Short Story: Notes*. Yonkers, N.Y.: The Alicat Bookshop Press, 1950. In these "Notes" from a writers' workshop session, Williams makes several interesting, if fragmentary and impressionistic, remarks about the form: the short story, as contrasted with the novel, is a brush-stroke instead of a picture. Stressing virtuosity instead of story structure, it is "one single flight of the imagination, complete: up and down." It is best suited to depicting the life of "briefness, brokenness, and heterogeneity."

Windholz, Anne M. "The American Short Story and Its British Critics: *Athenaeum* Reviews, 1880-1900." *Victorian Periodicals Review* 23 (Winter, 1990): 156-166. Argues that between 1880 and 1900, reviews of British and American short stories in the British journal *Athenaeum* helped establish an aesthetic that dominated critical analysis of the Anglo-American short story. Surveys reviewers' comments on American humor, dialect, and local color, as well as the importance of conciseness and unity of effect in both British and American short stories between 1880 and 1900.

Wright, Austin. *The American Short Story in the Twenties*. Chicago: University of Chicago Press, 1961. Using a canon of 220 stories, one set selected from the 1920's and the other from the period immediately preceding, Wright examines differing themes and techniques to test the usual judgments of what constitutes the "modern short story." The examination ends in proving only that the short story of the 1920's is different from the short story of the earlier period, that of the naturalists.

_______. "On Defining the Short Story: The Genre Question." In *Short Story Theory at a Crossroads*, edited by Susan Lohafer and Jo Ellyn Clarey. Baton Rouge: Louisiana State University Press, 1989. Discusses some of the theoretical problems involved in defining the short story as a genre. Argues for the formalist view of a genre definition as a cluster of conventions.

_______. "Recalcitrance in the Short Story." In *Short Story Theory at a Crossroads*, edited by Susan Lohafer and Jo Ellyn Clarey. Baton Rouge: Louisiana State University Press, 1989. A discussion of stories with endings that resist the reader's efforts to assimilate them and to make sense of them as a whole. Such final recalcitrance, Wright claims, is the extreme kind of resistance that the short story has developed to thwart final closure and reduce the complexity of the story to a conceptual understanding.

_______. "The Writer Meets the Critic on the Great Novel/Short Story Divide." *Journal of Modern Literature* 20 (Summer, 1996): 13-19. A personal account by a short-story critic and novelist of some of the basic differences between the critical enterprise and the writing of fiction, as well as some of the generic differences between the short story and the novel.

Charles E. May

CRITICAL SURVEY
OF
SHORT FICTION

GEOGRAPHICAL INDEX

AFRICA
Chinua Achebe, 4
Jane Bowles, 306
Paul Bowles, 311
Albert Camus, 429
Isak Dinesen, 737
Nadine Gordimer, 1039
Bessie Head, 1152
Doris Lessing, 1494
Ezekiel Mphahlele, 1717
Ben Okri, 1838
William Plomer, 1937

ALGERIA
Albert Camus, 429

ANTIGUA
Jamaica Kincaid, 1362

ARGENTINA
Jorge Luis Borges, 285
Julio Cortázar, 644
Juan Carlos Onetti, 1849
Horacio Quiroga, 2017
Luisa Valenzuela, 2386

AUSTRALIA
Peter Carey, 451
Janette Turner Hospital, 1228
Henry Lawson, 1458

AUSTRIA
Ilse Aichinger, 28
E. T. A. Hoffmann, 1216
Jakov Lind, 1513
Italo Svevo, 2269

BOHEMIA
Karel Čapek, 437

BOTSWANA
Bessie Head, 1152

BRAZIL
João Guimarães Rosa, 1092
Clarice Lispector, 1517
Joaquim Maria Machado de Assis, 1569

CANADA
Margaret Atwood, 108
Saul Bellow, 233
Morley Callaghan, 415
Mavis Gallant, 939
Janette Turner Hospital, 1228
W. P. Kinsella, 1382
Margaret Laurence, 1438
Wyndham Lewis, 1501
Bharati Mukherjee, 1721
Alice Munro, 1730
Mordecai Richler, 2036
Guy Vanderhaeghe, 2390

CHILE
Isabel Allende, 67
María Luisa Bombal, 278
José Donoso, 756

CHINA
Lu Xun, 1541
Pu Songling, 1984
Wang Anyi, 2443
Zhang Jie, 2578

COLOMBIA
Gabriel García Márquez, 950

CUBA
Alejo Carpentier, 460

CZECHOSLOVAKIA
Karel Čapek, 437
Franz Kafka, 1328
Milan Kundera, 1412

DENMARK
Hans Christian Andersen, 70
Isak Dinesen, 737

DOMINICA
Jean Rhys, 2031

EAST GERMANY. *See* **GERMANY**

ENGLAND
Joseph Addison, 14
Jane Austen, 123
J. G. Ballard, 141
Julian Barnes, 169
H. E. Bates, 197
Max Beerbohm, 225
Algernon Blackwood , 262
Elizabeth Bowen, 300
A. S. Byatt, 387
Angela Carter, 469
Geoffrey Chaucer, 518
G. K. Chesterton, 556
Agatha Christie, 572
Arthur C. Clarke, 590
John Collier, 605
William Congreve, 611
Joseph Conrad, 620
A. E. Coppard, 638
Roald Dahl, 664
Peter Ho Davies, 691
Rhys Davies, 694
Walter de la Mare, 704
Charles Dickens, 725
Arthur Conan Doyle, 775
Lord Dunsany, 797
Maria Edgeworth, 807
George Eliot, 816
E. M. Forster, 886
John Fowles, 891
John Galsworthy, 945
Penelope Gilliatt, 997
Oliver Goldsmith, 1033
Graham Greene, 1074
Robert Greene, 1081
Thomas Hardy, 1112

Bret Harte, 1133
John Hawkesworth, 1139
Lafcadio Hearn, 1156
Wolfgang Hildesheimer, 1201
Aldous Huxley, 1255
W. W. Jacobs, 1279
Henry James, 1283
Ruth Prawer Jhabvala, 1302
Samuel Johnson, 1314
Anna Kavan, 1339
Rudyard Kipling, 1388
Jhumpa Lahiri, 1424
D. H. Lawrence, 1449
Doris Lessing, 1494
Wyndham Lewis, 1501
Ian McEwan, 1562
Arthur Machen, 1574
Sir Thomas Malory, 1603
Katherine Mansfield, 1617
Marie de France, 1625
Adam Mars-Jones, 1630
W. Somerset Maugham, 1645
George Moore, 1695
Sylvia Plath, 1933
William Plomer, 1937
V. S. Pritchett, 1968
Jean Rhys, 2031
Salman Rushdie, 2068
Saki, 2072
William Sansom, 2084
Alan Sillitoe, 2142
Muriel Spark, 2196
Richard Steele, 2213
Graham Swift, 2272
Elizabeth Taylor, 2291
William Makepeace Thackeray, 2300
Dylan Thomas, 2306
William Trevor, 2340
Frank Tuohy, 2347
John Wain, 2424
Sylvia Townsend Warner, 2449
Denton Welch, 2466
Fay Weldon, 2472
H. G. Wells, 2476
Angus Wilson, 2535
Virginia Woolf, 2554

FRANCE
Honoré de Balzac, 147
Samuel Beckett, 218
Albert Camus, 429
Chrétien de Troyes, 567
Colette, 597
Julio Cortázar, 644
Alphonse Daudet, 676
Denis Diderot, 731
Gustave Flaubert, 872
Anatole France, 897
Mavis Gallant, 939
Théophile Gautier, 984
Hermann Hesse, 1187
Heinrich von Kleist, 1400
Milan Kundera, 1412
Marie de France, 1625
Guy de Maupassant, 1652
Prosper Mérimée , 1671
Gérard de Nerval, 1756
Anaïs Nin, 1760
Alain Robbe-Grillet, 2045
Jean-Paul Sartre, 2095
Voltaire, 2410
Émile Zola, 2584

GALICIA
Shmuel Yosef Agnon, 22

GERMANY
Heinrich Böll, 272
Bertolt Brecht, 348
Johann Wolfgang von Goethe, 1016
Brothers Grimm, 1086
Hermann Hesse, 1187
Wolfgang Hildesheimer, 1201
E. T. A. Hoffmann, 1216
Ruth Prawer Jhabvala, 1302
Denis Johnson, 1310
Franz Kafka, 1328
Heinrich von Kleist, 1400
Thomas Mann, 1607
Christoph Meckel, 1659

GREAT BRITAIN
Joseph Addison, 14
Jane Austen, 123
J. G. Ballard, 141
Julian Barnes, 169
H. E. Bates, 197
Samuel Beckett, 218
Max Beerbohm, 225
Algernon Blackwood, 262
Elizabeth Bowen, 300
A. S. Byatt, 387
William Carleton, 455
Angela Carter, 469
Geoffrey Chaucer, 518
G. K. Chesterton, 556
Agatha Christie, 572
Arthur C. Clarke, 590
John Collier, 605
William Congreve, 611
Joseph Conrad, 620
A. E. Coppard, 638
Roald Dahl, 664
Rhys Davies, 694
Walter de la Mare, 704
Charles Dickens, 725
Arthur Conan Doyle, 775
Lord Dunsany, 797
Maria Edgeworth, 807
George Eliot, 816
E. M. Forster, 886
John Fowles, 891
John Galsworthy, 945
Penelope Gilliatt, 997
Oliver Goldsmith, 1033
Graham Greene, 1074
Robert Greene, 1081
Thomas Hardy, 1112
Bret Harte, 1133
John Hawkesworth, 1139
Lafcadio Hearn, 1156
Wolfgang Hildesheimer, 1201
Aldous Huxley, 1255
W. W. Jacobs, 1279
Henry James, 1283
Ruth Prawer Jhabvala, 1302
Samuel Johnson, 1314
Anna Kavan, 1339
Rudyard Kipling, 1388
Jhumpa Lahiri, 1424
D. H. Lawrence, 1449
Doris Lessing, 1494
Wyndham Lewis, 1501
Ian McEwan, 1562
John McGahern, 1566
Arthur Machen, 1574
Sir Thomas Malory, 1603
Katherine Mansfield, 1617
Marie de France, 1625
Adam Mars-Jones, 1630
W. Somerset Maugham, 1645
George Moore, 1695
Edna O'Brien, 1780

Sylvia Plath, 1933
William Plomer, 1937
V. S. Pritchett, 1968
Jean Rhys, 2031
Salman Rushdie, 2068
Saki, 2072
William Sansom, 2084
Sir Walter Scott, 2120
Alan Sillitoe, 2142
Muriel Spark, 2196
Richard Steele, 2213
Robert Louis Stevenson, 2245
Graham Swift, 2272
Elizabeth Taylor, 2291
William Makepeace Thackeray, 2300
Dylan Thomas, 2306
William Trevor, 2340
Frank Tuohy, 2347
John Wain, 2424
Sylvia Townsend Warner, 2449
Denton Welch, 2466
Fay Weldon, 2472
H. G. Wells, 2476
Angus Wilson, 2535
Virginia Woolf, 2554

GREECE
Lafcadio Hearn, 1156
Homer, 1222

GUATEMALA
Miguel Ángel Asturias, 102

INDIA
Ruth Prawer Jhabvala, 1302
Rudyard Kipling, 1388
Bharati Mukherjee, 1721
R. K. Narayan, 1750
Salman Rushdie, 2068

IRELAND
Samuel Beckett, 218
Elizabeth Bowen, 300
William Carleton, 455
Lord Dunsany, 797
Maria Edgeworth, 807
Brian Friel, 920
Oliver Goldsmith, 1033
James Joyce, 1319
Benedict Kiely, 1356
Mary Lavin, 1443
Joseph Sheridan Le Fanu, 1469
John McGahern, 1566
George Moore, 1695
Edna O'Brien, 1780
Fitz-James O'Brien, 1786
Frank O'Connor, 1802
Seán O'Faoláin, 1816
Liam O'Flaherty, 1826
Richard Steele, 2213
William Trevor, 2340
William Butler Yeats, 2566

ISRAEL
Shmuel Yosef Agnon, 22
Wolfgang Hildesheimer, 1201
Amos Oz, 1860

ITALY
Giovanni Boccaccio, 266
Dino Buzzati, 381
Italo Calvino, 423
Dante, 670
Tommaso Landolfi, 1427
Alberto Moravia, 1702
Ovid, 1852
Cesare Pavese, 1893
Petronius, 1911
Luigi Pirandello, 1927
Italo Svevo, 2269
Giovanni Verga, 2393
Vergil, 2398

JAPAN
Ryūnosuke Akutagawa, 37
Osamu Dazai, 699
Shūsaku Endō, 841
Lafcadio Hearn, 1156
Ihara Saikaku, 1261
Yasunari Kawabata, 1344
Yukio Mishima, 1690
Kenzaburō Ōe, 1809
Jun'ichirō Tanizaki, 2283

KENYA
Isak Dinesen, 737

LATIN AMERICA
Isabel Allende, 67
Juan José Arreola, 89
Miguel Ángel Asturias, 102
María Luisa Bombal, 278
Jorge Luis Borges, 285
Julio Cortázar, 644
José Donoso, 756
Carlos Fuentes, 924
Gabriel García Márquez, 950
João Guimarães Rosa, 1092
Clarice Lispector, 1517
Joaquim Maria Machado de Assis, 1569
Juan Carlos Onetti, 1849
Horacio Quiroga, 2017
Juan Rulfo, 2064
Luisa Valenzuela, 2386

MEXICO
Juan José Arreola, 89
Carlos Fuentes, 924
Juan Rulfo, 2064

MOROCCO
Jane Bowles, 306
Paul Bowles, 311

MYANMAR
Saki, 2072

NEW ZEALAND
Katherine Mansfield, 1617

NIGERIA
Chinua Achebe, 4
Ben Okri, 1838

PANAMA
Carlos Fuentes, 924

PERU
Isabel Allende, 67

POLAND
Tadeusz Borowski, 295
Joseph Conrad, 620
Stanisław Lem, 1481
Rabbi Nahman of Bratslav, 1745
Isaac Leib Peretz, 1906
Bruno Schulz, 2106

PRUSSIA
E. T. A. Hoffmann, 1216
Heinrich von Kleist, 1400

RUSSIA
Sholom Aleichem, 50
Isaac Asimov, 95
Isaac Babel, 128
Ivan Bunin, 372
Anton Chekhov, 540
Fyodor Dostoevski, 760
Sergei Dovlatov, 769
Nikolai Gogol, 1022
Maxim Gorky, 1055
Nikolai Leskov, 1488
Rabbi Nahman of Bratslav, 1745
Boris Pasternak, 1887
Alexander Pushkin, 1997
Valentin Rasputin, 2023
Varlam Shalamov, 2126
Andrei Sinyavsky, 2165
Aleksandr Solzhenitsyn, 2187
Tatyana Tolstaya, 2320
Leo Tolstoy, 2326
Ivan Turgenev, 2352
Yevgeny Zamyatin, 2572
Mikhail Zoshchenko, 2589

SCOTLAND
Arthur Conan Doyle, 775
Sir Walter Scott, 2120
Muriel Spark, 2196
Robert Louis Stevenson, 2245

SERBIA
Danilo Kiš, 1397

SICILY
Giovanni Verga, 2393

SOUTH AFRICA
Nadine Gordimer, 1039
Bessie Head, 1152
Ezekiel Mphahlele, 1717
William Plomer, 1937

SOUTH ASIA
Ruth Prawer Jhabvala, 1302
Rudyard Kipling, 1388
Bharati Mukherjee, 1721
R. K. Narayan, 1750
Salman Rushdie, 2068

SOVIET UNION. *See also* **RUSSIA**
Isaac Babel, 128
Tadeusz Borowski, 295
Sergei Dovlatov, 769
Maxim Gorky, 1055
Boris Pasternak, 1887
Valentin Rasputin, 2023
Varlam Shalamov, 2126
Andrei Sinyavsky, 2165
Aleksandr Solzhenitsyn, 2187
Tatyana Tolstaya, 2320
Mikhail Zoshchenko, 2589

SPAIN
Pedro Antonio de Alarcón, 41
Miguel de Cervantes, 491
Juan Carlos Onetti, 1849
Emilia Pardo Bazán, 1878
Miguel de Unamuno y Jugo, 2371

SWEDEN
Pär Lagerkvist , 1420

SWITZERLAND
Hermann Hesse, 1187
Wolfgang Hildesheimer, 1201
Robert Walser, 2437

UKRAINE
Tadeusz Borowski, 295
Nikolai Gogol, 1022
Rabbi Nahman of Bratslav, 1745

UNITED STATES. *See also* **"Category Index": African American, Asian American, Chinese American, Jewish, Latino Culture**
Lee K. Abbott, 1
Alice Adams, 9
James Agee, 19
Conrad Aiken, 32
Thomas Bailey Aldrich, 46
Sholom Aleichem, 50
Sherman Alexie, 55
Nelson Algren, 58
Woody Allen, 62
Isabel Allende, 67
Sherwood Anderson, 76
Maya Angelou, 83
Max Apple, 86
Isaac Asimov, 95
Louis Auchincloss, 116
James Baldwin, 135
Toni Cade Bambara, 152
Melissa Bank, 156
Russell Banks, 160
Amiri Baraka, 165
Andrea Barrett, 173
John Barth, 176
Donald Barthelme, 182
Frederick Barthelme, 190
Rick Bass, 194
Richard Bausch, 203
Charles Baxter, 207
Ann Beattie, 210
Madison Smartt Bell, 230
Saul Bellow, 233
Aimee Bender, 239
Stephen Vincent Benét, 242
Gina Berriault, 248
Doris Betts, 252
Ambrose Bierce, 257
Arna Bontemps, 281
Jane Bowles, 306
Paul Bowles, 311
Kay Boyle, 317
T. Coraghessan Boyle, 325
Ray Bradbury, 331
Richard Brautigan, 341
Harold Brodkey, 354
Larry Brown, 360
Bliss Broyard, 363
Pearl S. Buck, 366
Robert Olen Butler, 377
Michael Byers, 390

George Washington Cable, 394
James M. Cain, 400
Erskine Caldwell, 404
Hortense Calisher, 409
Ethan Canin, 434
Truman Capote, 441
Orson Scott Card, 446
John Dickson Carr, 464
Raymond Carver, 472
R. V. Cassill, 481
Willa Cather, 485
Michael Chabon, 499
Raymond Chandler, 505
Lan Samantha Chang, 511
Fred Chappell, 514
John Cheever, 532
Charles Waddell Chesnutt, 549
Kate Chopin, 562
Sandra Cisneros, 579
Walter Van Tilburg Clark, 585
John Collier, 605
Evan S. Connell, Jr., 614
Frank Conroy, 628
Robert Coover, 632
James Gould Cozzens, 649
Stephen Crane, 654
Guy Davenport, 681
Peter Ho Davies, 691
Samuel R. Delany, 709
August Derleth, 714
Philip K. Dick, 719
Thomas M. Disch, 745
Stephen Dixon, 749
Harriet Doerr, 752
Ellen Douglas, 766
Sergei Dovlatov, 769
Theodore Dreiser, 783
Andre Dubus, 789
Paul Laurence Dunbar, 793
Stuart Dybek, 803
Stanley Elkin, 820
George P. Elliott, 825
Harlan Ellison, 831
Ralph Ellison, 837
Louise Erdrich, 847
James T. Farrell, 851
William Faulkner, 856
F. Scott Fitzgerald, 864
Richard Ford, 880
Benjamin Franklin, 903
Mary E. Wilkins Freeman, 908
Bruce Jay Friedman, 914
Ernest J. Gaines, 930
Mary Gaitskill, 936
John Gardner, 956
Hamlin Garland, 963
George Garrett, 969
William H. Gass, 975
David Gates, 980
Tim Gautreux, 988
Ellen Gilchrist, 991
Charlotte Perkins Gilman, 1003
Ellen Glasgow, 1007
Gail Godwin, 1013
Herbert Gold, 1030
Caroline Gordon, 1046
Mary Gordon, 1052
William Goyen, 1060
Shirley Ann Grau, 1065
Joanne Greenberg, 1069
Nancy Hale, 1096
Lawrence Sargent Hall, 1101
Dashiell Hammett, 1104
Barry Hannah, 1108
Joy Harjo, 1118
Joel Chandler Harris, 1121
Jim Harrison, 1127
Bret Harte, 1133
Nathaniel Hawthorne, 1143
Lafcadio Hearn, 1156
Robert A. Heinlein, 1159
Mark Helprin, 1164
Ernest Hemingway, 1172
Amy Hempel, 1180
O. Henry, 1183
Patricia Highsmith, 1193
Chester Himes, 1204
Edward Hoch, 1210
Janette Turner Hospital, 1228
Pam Houston, 1231
William Dean Howells, 1234
Langston Hughes, 1238
William Humphrey, 1243
Zora Neale Hurston, 1249
Aldous Huxley, 1255
Washington Irving, 1268
Shirley Jackson, 1274
Henry James, 1283
Sarah Orne Jewett, 1296
Ruth Prawer Jhabvala, 1302
Charles Johnson, 1306
Denis Johnson, 1310
David Michael Kaplan, 1336
Garrison Keillor, 1350
Jamaica Kincaid, 1362
Stephen King, 1368
Barbara Kingsolver, 1374
Maxine Hong Kingston, 1378
John Knowles, 1406
Jhumpa Lahiri, 1424
Ring Lardner, 1434
Mary Lavin, 1443
David Leavitt, 1463
Ursula K. Le Guin, 1476
John L'Heureux, 1509
Jack London, 1522
Augustus Baldwin Longstreet, 1527
Beth Lordan, 1531
H. P. Lovecraft, 1535
Mary McCarthy, 1551
Carson McCullers, 1556
Reginald McKnight, 1577
James Alan McPherson, 1581
Clarence Major, 1591
Bernard Malamud, 1595
Thomas Mann, 1607
Paule Marshall, 1634
Bobbie Ann Mason, 1639
Herman Melville, 1664
Leonard Michaels, 1675
Sue Miller, 1679
Steven Millhauser, 1682
Susan Minot, 1686
Lorrie Moore, 1699
Wright Morris, 1710
Bharati Mukherjee, 1721
Vladimir Nabokov, 1738
Anaïs Nin, 1760
Frank Norris, 1765
Joyce Carol Oates, 1771
Fitz-James O'Brien, 1786
Tim O'Brien, 1790
Flannery O'Connor, 1794
Chris Offutt, 1822
John O'Hara, 1832
Tillie Olsen, 1843
Cynthia Ozick, 1865
Grace Paley, 1872
Dorothy Parker, 1883
Susan Perabo, 1898
S. J. Perelman, 1901
Ann Petry, 1916
Jayne Anne Phillips, 1923
Sylvia Plath, 1933
Edgar Allan Poe, 1940
Katherine Anne Porter, 1949
J. F. Powers, 1957
Reynolds Price, 1961

Francine Prose, 1977
E. Annie Proulx, 1980
James Purdy, 1990
Thomas Pynchon, 2004
Ellery Queen, 2011
Elwood Reid, 2027
Tomás Rivera, 2041
Elizabeth Madox Roberts, 2049
Mary Robison, 2052
Philip Roth, 2059
J. D. Salinger, 2076
William Saroyan, 2090
John Sayles, 2102
Delmore Schwartz, 2112
Lynne Sharon Schwartz, 2117
Irwin Shaw, 2131
Leslie Marmon Silko, 2135
William Gilmore Simms, 2147
Mona Simpson, 2153
Julia Slavin, 2171
Jane Smiley, 2174
Lee Smith, 2182
Susan Sontag, 2193
Elizabeth Spencer, 2202
Jean Stafford, 2208
Wilbur Daniel Steele, 2217
Wallace Stegner, 2220
Gertrude Stein, 2225
John Steinbeck, 2233
Richard G. Stern, 2239
Frank R. Stockton, 2250
Robert Stone, 2254
Jesse Stuart, 2258
Theodore Sturgeon, 2264
Elizabeth Tallent, 2276
Amy Tan, 2279
Barry Targan, 2288
Peter Taylor, 2294
James Thurber, 2312
Christopher Tilghman, 2317
Jean Toomer, 2335
Mark Twain, 2359
Anne Tyler, 2365
John Updike, 2375
Helena María Viramontes, 2403
Gerald Vizenor, 2406
Kurt Vonnegut, 2416
Alice Walker, 2428
Robert Penn Warren, 2456
Jerome Weidman, 2462
Eudora Welty, 2482
Glenway Wescott, 2490
Jessamyn West, 2495
Edith Wharton, 2500
E. B. White, 2506
John Edgar Wideman, 2509
Marianne Wiggins, 2516
Joy Williams, 2520
Tennessee Williams, 2524
William Carlos Williams, 2530
Larry Woiwode, 2538
Thomas Wolfe, 2544
Tobias Wolff, 2549
Richard Wright, 2560

URUGUAY
Juan Carlos Onetti, 1849
Horacio Quiroga, 2017

WALES
Roald Dahl, 664
Rhys Davies, 694
Arthur Machen, 1574
Dylan Thomas, 2306

WEST GERMANY. *See* **GERMANY**

WEST INDIES
Alejo Carpentier, 460
Jamaica Kincaid, 1362
Jean Rhys, 2031

YUGOSLAVIA
Danilo Kiš, 1397

ZIMBABWE
Doris Lessing, 1494

CATEGORY INDEX

ABSURDISM
Ilse Aichinger, 28
John Barth, 176
Donald Barthelme, 182
Samuel Beckett, 218
T. Coraghessan Boyle, 325
Albert Camus, 429
Robert Coover, 632
Thomas M. Disch, 745
Bruce Jay Friedman, 914
John L'Heureux, 1509
Jakov Lind, 1513
Jean-Paul Sartre, 2095

ADVENTURE. *See also* **SCIENCE FICTION, SUSPENSE**
H. E. Bates, 197
Saul Bellow, 233
T. Coraghessan Boyle, 325
Joseph Conrad, 620
Stephen Crane, 654
Arthur Conan Doyle, 775
Robert Greene, 1081
Jim Harrison, 1127
Bret Harte, 1133
Homer, 1222
Pam Houston, 1231
Samuel Johnson, 1314
Ursula K. Le Guin, 1476
Petronius, 1911
Robert Louis Stevenson, 2245
H. G. Wells, 2476

AFRICAN AMERICAN CULTURE
Maya Angelou, 83
James Baldwin, 135
Toni Cade Bambara, 152
Amiri Baraka, 165
Arna Bontemps, 281
Charles Waddell Chesnutt, 549
Samuel R. Delany, 709
Paul Laurence Dunbar, 793
Ralph Ellison, 837
Ernest J. Gaines, 930
Joel Chandler Harris, 1121
Chester Himes, 1204
Langston Hughes, 1238
Zora Neale Hurston, 1249
Charles Johnson, 1306
Jamaica Kincaid, 1362
Joaquim Maria Machado de Assis, 1569
Reginald McKnight, 1577
James Alan McPherson, 1581
Clarence Major, 1591
Paule Marshall, 1634
Ann Petry, 1916
Jean Toomer, 2335
Alice Walker, 2428
John Edgar Wideman, 2509
Richard Wright, 2560

AFRICAN CULTURE
Bessie Head, 1152
Margaret Laurence, 1438
Ben Okri, 1838
William Plomer, 1937

ALLEGORY
Joseph Addison, 14
Ilse Aichinger, 28
John Barth, 176
Dino Buzzati, 381
William Carleton, 455
Angela Carter, 469
Miguel de Cervantes, 491
John Cheever, 532
Anton Chekhov, 540
Robert Coover, 632
A. E. Coppard, 638
Dante, 670
E. M. Forster, 886
Johann Wolfgang von Goethe, 1016
Thomas Hardy, 1112
John Hawkesworth, 1139
Nathaniel Hawthorne, 1143
Charles Johnson, 1306
Franz Kafka, 1328
Herman Melville, 1664
Rabbi Nahman of Bratslav, 1745
Joyce Carol Oates, 1771
Thomas Pynchon, 2004
Leslie Marmon Silko, 2135
Susan Sontag, 2193
Richard Steele, 2213
Robert Louis Stevenson, 2245
Edith Wharton, 2500

ANTISTORY. *See also* **IRREALISM, METAFICTION, POSTMODERNISM**
Donald Barthelme, 182
Heinrich Böll, 272
Jorge Luis Borges, 285
Raymond Carver, 472
Robert Coover, 632
Stuart Dybek, 803
John Fowles, 891
Barry Hannah, 1108
Vladimir Nabokov, 1738

ASIAN AMERICAN CULTURE
Lan Samantha Chang, 511
Maxine Hong Kingston, 1378
Jhumpa Lahiri, 1424
Bharati Mukherjee, 1721
Amy Tan, 2279

ASIAN CULTURE
Ryūnosuke Akutagawa, 37
Pearl S. Buck, 366
Osamu Dazai, 699
Shūsaku Endō, 841
John Hawkesworth, 1139
Lafcadio Hearn, 1156
Ihara Saikaku, 1261
Maxine Hong Kingston, 1378
Lu Xun, 1541
Yukio Mishima, 1690
Tim O'Brien, 1790
Kenzaburō Ōe, 1809
Pu Songling, 1984
Jun'ichirō Tanizaki, 2283
Wang Anyi, 2443

AUSTRALIAN CULTURE
Peter Carey, 451
Janette Turner Hospital, 1228
Henry Lawson, 1458

AUTOBIOGRAPHICAL STORIES
Isaac Babel, 128
Elizabeth Bowen, 300
Julio Cortázar, 644
Osamu Dazai, 699
Harriet Doerr, 752
Fyodor Dostoevski, 760
Louise Erdrich, 847
Hermann Hesse, 1187
Pam Houston, 1231
Ruth Prawer Jhabvala, 1302
Charles Johnson, 1306
Margaret Laurence, 1438
Mary Lavin, 1443
D. H. Lawrence, 1449
Leonard Michaels, 1675
Alberto Moravia, 1702
Gérard de Nerval, 1756
Seán O'Faoláin, 1816
William Plomer, 1937
Mordecai Richler, 2036
William Saroyan, 2090
John Sayles, 2102
Delmore Schwartz, 2112
Varlam Shalamov, 2126
Jean Stafford, 2208
Susan Sontag, 2193
James Thurber, 2312
Jerome Weidman, 2462
Marianne Wiggins, 2516
Tennessee Williams, 2524
William Carlos Williams, 2530
Larry Woiwode, 2538
Tobias Wolff, 2549

BLACK HUMOR
Margaret Atwood, 108
Ambrose Bierce, 257
Ray Bradbury, 331
John Collier, 605
Philip K. Dick, 719
Thomas M. Disch, 745
Stanley Elkin, 820
Bruce Jay Friedman, 914
Patricia Highsmith, 1193
Ben Okri, 1838
S. J. Perelman, 1901
Thomas Pynchon, 2004
Mordecai Richler, 2036
Jesse Stuart, 2258
James Thurber, 2312
Kurt Vonnegut, 2416
Fay Weldon, 2472
Angus Wilson, 2535

BRITISH CULTURE
Elizabeth Bowen, 300
Angela Carter, 469
A. E. Coppard, 638
Roald Dahl, 664
Rhys Davies, 694
Walter de la Mare, 704
Charles Dickens, 725
Arthur Conan Doyle, 775
George Eliot, 816
E. M. Forster, 886
John Fowles, 891
John Galsworthy, 945
George Garrett, 969
Graham Greene, 1074
Robert Greene, 1081
Thomas Hardy, 1112
Rudyard Kipling, 1388
D. H. Lawrence, 1449
Ian McEwan, 1562
Sir Thomas Malory, 1603
V. S. Pritchett, 1968
Saki, 2072
Alan Sillitoe, 2142
Muriel Spark, 2196
Elizabeth Taylor, 2291
William Makepeace Thackeray, 2300
John Wain, 2424
Sylvia Townsend Warner, 2449
Angus Wilson, 2535

CANADIAN CULTURE
Margaret Atwood, 108
Morley Callaghan, 415
W. P. Kinsella, 1382
Margaret Laurence, 1438
Bharati Mukherjee, 1721
Alice Munro, 1730
Mordecai Richler, 2036
Guy Vanderhaeghe, 2390

CHARACTER STUDIES
Joseph Addison, 14
Anton Chekhov, 540
Colette, 597
Benjamin Franklin, 903
Mary E. Wilkins Freeman, 908
Oliver Goldsmith, 1033
Nadine Gordimer, 1039
Caroline Gordon, 1046
Paule Marshall, 1634
Bobbie Ann Mason, 1639
J. D. Salinger, 2076
Richard Steele, 2213

CHINESE AMERICAN CULTURE
Lan Samantha Chang, 511
Maxine Hong Kingston, 1378
Amy Tan, 2279

CHINESE CULTURE
Maxine Hong Kingston, 1378
Lu Xun, 1541
Pu Songling, 1984
Wang Anyi, 2443

COLONIALISM
Chinua Achebe, 4
Joseph Conrad, 620
Carlos Fuentes, 924
Nadine Gordimer, 1039
Nathaniel Hawthorne, 1143
Bessie Head, 1152
Jamaica Kincaid, 1362
Rudyard Kipling, 1388
Margaret Laurence, 1438
W. Somerset Maugham, 1645
William Plomer, 1937
Salman Rushdie, 2068
Gerald Vizenor, 2406

COMIC REALISM
Saul Bellow, 233
Stanley Elkin, 820
William Faulkner, 856

CRIME. *See* **DETECTIVE AND MYSTERY**

DARK HUMOR. *See* **BLACK HUMOR**

DETECTIVE AND MYSTERY. *See also* **SUSPENSE**
Ryūnosuke Akutagawa, 37
Julian Barnes, 169
Jorge Luis Borges, 285
James M. Cain, 400
Karel Čapek, 437
John Dickson Carr, 464
Raymond Chandler, 505
G. K. Chesterton, 556
Agatha Christie, 572
Joseph Conrad, 620
Walter de la Mare, 704
August Derleth, 714
Charles Dickens, 725
Arthur Conan Doyle, 775
João Guimarães Rosa, 1092
Dashiell Hammett, 1104
Jim Harrison, 1127
Patricia Highsmith, 1193
Chester Himes, 1204
Edward Hoch, 1210
E. T. A. Hoffmann, 1216
Joseph Sheridan Le Fanu, 1469
Guy de Maupassant, 1652
Edgar Allan Poe, 1940
Ellery Queen, 2011

DIDACTIC STORIES
Joseph Addison, 14
Aimee Bender, 239
Pearl S. Buck, 366
Geoffrey Chaucer, 518
Dante, 670
Charles Dickens, 725
Paul Laurence Dunbar, 793
Maria Edgeworth, 807
Benjamin Franklin, 903
Charlotte Perkins Gilman, 1003
Oliver Goldsmith, 1033
Robert Greene, 1081
Brothers Grimm, 1086
John Hawkesworth, 1139
Robert A. Heinlein, 1159
Samuel Johnson, 1314
D. H. Lawrence, 1449
Naguib Mahfouz, 1586
Guy de Maupassant, 1652
Pu Songling, 1984
Alan Sillitoe, 2142
Richard Steele, 2213
James Thurber, 2312
Leo Tolstoy, 2326
Vergil, 2398

DOMESTIC REALISM
Lee K. Abbott, 1
Alice Adams, 9
Pedro Antonio de Alarcón, 41
Thomas Bailey Aldrich, 46
Isabel Allende, 67
Max Apple, 86
Toni Cade Bambara, 152
Melissa Bank, 156
Russell Banks, 160
Donald Barthelme, 182
Rick Bass, 194
H. E. Bates, 197
Saul Bellow, 233
Arna Bontemps, 281
Elizabeth Bowen, 300
Kay Boyle, 317
T. Coraghessan Boyle, 325
Harold Brodkey, 354
Larry Brown, 360
Bliss Broyard, 363
Morley Callaghan, 415
Albert Camus, 429
Truman Capote, 441
Raymond Carver, 472
John Cheever, 532
Kate Chopin, 562
Sandra Cisneros, 579
Isak Dinesen, 737
Theodore Dreiser, 783
Louise Erdrich, 847
William Faulkner, 856
F. Scott Fitzgerald, 864
Mary E. Wilkins Freeman, 908
Carlos Fuentes, 924
Mavis Gallant, 939
John Gardner, 956
Hamlin Garland, 963
Ellen Gilchrist, 991
Ellen Glasgow, 1007
Herbert Gold, 1030
Caroline Gordon, 1046
William Goyen, 1060
Nathaniel Hawthorne, 1143
Amy Hempel, 1180
Ruth Prawer Jhabvala, 1302
David Michael Kaplan, 1336
Barbara Kingsolver, 1374
David Leavitt, 1463
Katherine Mansfield, 1617
Bobbie Ann Mason, 1639
Lorrie Moore, 1699
Bharati Mukherjee, 1721
Alice Munro, 1730
Edna O'Brien, 1780
Frank O'Connor, 1802
Grace Paley, 1872
Jayne Anne Phillips, 1923
Francine Prose, 1977
Tomás Rivera, 2041
Lynne Sharon Schwartz, 2117
Mona Simpson, 2153
Jane Smiley, 2174
Elizabeth Tallent, 2276
Christopher Tilghman, 2317
Anne Tyler, 2365

EASTERN UNITED STATES
O. Henry, 1183
Sarah Orne Jewett, 1296

EGYPTIAN CULTURE
Naguib Mahfouz, 1586

EPIC
Dante, 670
Homer, 1222
James Joyce, 1319
Ovid, 1852
Vergil, 2398

EPIPHANY
Sherwood Anderson, 76
Frank Conroy, 628
James Joyce, 1319
Clarice Lispector, 1517

Bernard Malamud, 1595
V. S. Pritchett, 1968
Eudora Welty, 2482

EROTIC STORIES

Angela Carter, 469
Yasunari Kawabata, 1344
Leonard Michaels, 1675
Anaïs Nin, 1760

ESSAY-SKETCH TRADITION.
See also **SKETCHES**

Joseph Addison, 14
Benjamin Franklin, 903
Oliver Goldsmith, 1033
Nathaniel Hawthorne, 1143
Augustus Baldwin Longstreet, 1527
Richard Steele, 2213

EXEMPLUM

Giovanni Boccaccio, 266
Geoffrey Chaucer, 518
Charles Waddell Chesnutt, 549
Shūsaku Endō, 841

EXISTENTIALISM

Woody Allen, 62
Paul Bowles, 311
Dino Buzzati, 381
Hortense Calisher, 409
Albert Camus, 429
Fyodor Dostoevski, 760
Andre Dubus, 789
Franz Kafka, 1328
Tommaso Landolfi, 1427
Doris Lessing, 1494
Alberto Moravia, 1702
Flannery O'Connor, 1794
Cesare Pavese, 1893
Jean-Paul Sartre, 2095
John Edgar Wideman, 2509
Richard Wright, 2560

EXPERIMENTAL STORIES

Juan José Arreola, 89
J. G. Ballard, 141
John Barth, 176
Samuel Beckett, 218
Jorge Luis Borges, 285
Kay Boyle, 317
T. Coraghessan Boyle, 325
Richard Brautigan, 341
A. S. Byatt, 387
Peter Carey, 451
Sandra Cisneros, 579
Robert Coover, 632
Guy Davenport, 681
Stephen Dixon, 749
George P. Elliott, 825
John Fowles, 891
William H. Gass, 975
Penelope Gilliatt, 997
Jim Harrison, 1127
Denis Johnson, 1310
Yasunari Kawabata, 1344
Wyndham Lewis, 1501
Reginald McKnight, 1577
Clarence Major, 1591
Bernard Malamud, 1595
Christoph Meckel, 1659
Joyce Carol Oates, 1771
Sylvia Plath, 1933
Tomás Rivera, 2041
J. D. Salinger, 2076
William Saroyan, 2090
Jean-Paul Sartre, 2095
Bruno Schulz, 2106
Varlam Shalamov, 2126
Jane Smiley, 2174
Gertrude Stein, 2225
Frank R. Stockton, 2250
Graham Swift, 2272
Jun'ichirō Tanizaki, 2283
Jean Toomer, 2335
Robert Walser, 2437
Fay Weldon, 2472
Joy Williams, 2520
Larry Woiwode, 2538
Virginia Woolf, 2554

EXPRESSIONISM

James Joyce, 1319
Franz Kafka, 1328
Lu Xun, 1541
Bruno Schulz, 2106
Tennessee Williams, 2524
Yevgeny Zamyatin, 2572

FABLE

James Agee, 19
Ryūnosuke Akutagawa, 37
Hans Christian Andersen, 70
Juan José Arreola, 89
John Barth, 176
Donald Barthelme, 182
Charles Baxter, 207
Samuel Beckett, 218
Aimee Bender, 239
Stephen Vincent Benét, 242
Giovanni Boccaccio, 266
Heinrich Böll, 272
Jorge Luis Borges, 285
Paul Bowles, 311
Italo Calvino, 423
Albert Camus, 429
Miguel de Cervantes, 491
Geoffrey Chaucer, 518
John Cheever, 532
Anton Chekhov, 540
Walter Van Tilburg Clark, 585
Walter de la Mare, 704
Isak Dinesen, 737
Fyodor Dostoevski, 760
F. Scott Fitzgerald, 864
Gabriel García Márquez, 950
John Gardner, 956
Gail Godwin, 1013
Johann Wolfgang von Goethe, 1016
Brothers Grimm, 1086
Joel Chandler Harris, 1121
John Hawkesworth, 1139
Nathaniel Hawthorne, 1143
Lafcadio Hearn, 1156
Mark Helprin, 1164
Charles Johnson, 1306
W. P. Kinsella, 1382
Rudyard Kipling, 1388
Bernard Malamud, 1595
Marie de France, 1625
Herman Melville, 1664
Edgar Allan Poe, 1940
Pu Songling, 1984
Thomas Pynchon, 2004
Horacio Quiroga, 2017
Frank R. Stockton, 2250
James Thurber, 2312
Kurt Vonnegut, 2416
Zhang Jie, 2578

FAIRY TALE. *See also* **FABLE, FANTASY, FOLKTALES, MÄRCHEN, PARABLE, TALES**

Hans Christian Andersen, 70
A. S. Byatt, 387
Angela Carter, 469
Walter de la Mare, 704
Ellen Douglas, 766
Lord Dunsany, 797
Johann Wolfgang von Goethe, 1016
Brothers Grimm, 1086
Hermann Hesse, 1187
E. T. A. Hoffmann, 1216
Jakov Lind, 1513
Frank R. Stockton, 2250
James Thurber, 2312
Sylvia Townsend Warner, 2449
William Butler Yeats, 2566

FANTASY. *See also* **FABLE, FAIRY TALE, FOLKTALES, MAGICAL REALISM, MÄRCHEN, PARABLE, SUPERNATURAL STORIES, TALES**

Conrad Aiken, 32
Pedro Antonio de Alarcón, 41
Isabel Allende, 67
Max Beerbohm, 225
Madison Smartt Bell, 230
María Luisa Bombal, 278
Jorge Luis Borges, 285
T. Coraghessan Boyle, 325
Ray Bradbury, 331
Dino Buzzati, 381
A. S. Byatt, 387
Italo Calvino, 423
Truman Capote, 441
Orson Scott Card, 446
Peter Carey, 451
Alejo Carpentier, 460
Angela Carter, 469
John Cheever, 532
Walter Van Tilburg Clark, 585
Arthur C. Clarke, 590
Robert Coover, 632
A. E. Coppard, 638
Julio Cortázar, 644
Osamu Dazai, 699
Walter de la Mare, 704
Samuel R. Delany, 709
Denis Diderot, 731
Isak Dinesen, 737
Fyodor Dostoevski, 760
Lord Dunsany, 797
Harlan Ellison, 831
F. Scott Fitzgerald, 864
E. M. Forster, 886
Anatole France, 897
Gabriel García Márquez, 950
Théophile Gautier, 984
Nikolai Gogol, 1022
Joanne Greenberg, 1069
Joel Chandler Harris, 1121
Nathaniel Hawthorne, 1143
Lafcadio Hearn, 1156
Wolfgang Hildesheimer, 1201
E. T. A. Hoffmann, 1216
Charles Johnson, 1306
Franz Kafka, 1328
David Michael Kaplan, 1336
W. P. Kinsella, 1382
Rudyard Kipling, 1388
Ursula K. Le Guin, 1476
John L'Heureux, 1509
Jakov Lind, 1513
H. P. Lovecraft, 1535
Carson McCullers, 1556
Arthur Machen, 1574
Reginald McKnight, 1577
Bernard Malamud, 1595
Christoph Meckel, 1659
Leonard Michaels, 1675
Steven Millhauser, 1682
Vladimir Nabokov, 1738
Gérard de Nerval, 1756
Anaïs Nin, 1760
Flannery O'Connor, 1794
Juan Carlos Onetti, 1849
Cynthia Ozick, 1865
Grace Paley, 1872
Emilia Pardo Bazán, 1878
Edgar Allan Poe, 1940
Pu Songling, 1984
Tomás Rivera, 2041
William Sansom, 2084
Andrei Sinyavsky, 2165
Julia Slavin, 2171
Theodore Sturgeon, 2264
James Thurber, 2312
Ivan Turgenev, 2352
Mark Twain, 2359
Gerald Vizenor, 2406
Sylvia Townsend Warner, 2449

FARCE

Samuel Beckett, 218
Sergei Dovlatov, 769
Milan Kundera, 1412

FOLKTALES. *See also* **FABLE, FAIRY TALE, FANTASY, MÄRCHEN, PARABLE, TALES**

Pedro Antonio de Alarcón, 41
Hans Christian Andersen, 70
Miguel Ángel Asturias, 102
Julian Barnes, 169
Paul Bowles, 311
William Carleton, 455
Angela Carter, 469
Charles Waddell Chesnutt, 549
Robert Coover, 632
Benjamin Franklin, 903
Brian Friel, 920
Johann Wolfgang von Goethe, 1016
Nikolai Gogol, 1022
Brothers Grimm, 1086
Thomas Hardy, 1112
Joel Chandler Harris, 1121
Lafcadio Hearn, 1156
Zora Neale Hurston, 1249
Washington Irving, 1268
Charles Johnson, 1306
Augustus Baldwin Longstreet, 1527
Marie de France, 1625
Herman Melville, 1664
George Moore, 1695
Rabbi Nahman of Bratslav, 1745
Emilia Pardo Bazán, 1878
Isaac Leib Peretz, 1906
Edgar Allan Poe, 1940
Alexander Pushkin, 1997
Sir Walter Scott, 2120
Leslie Marmon Silko, 2135
William Gilmore Simms, 2147
Jesse Stuart, 2258
Luisa Valenzuela, 2386
William Butler Yeats, 2566

FRENCH CULTURE
Honoré de Balzac, 147
Chrétien de Troyes, 567
Colette, 597
Denis Diderot, 731
Anatole France, 897
Théophile Gautier, 984

GAY AND LESBIAN ISSUES
James Baldwin, 135
Samuel R. Delany, 709
E. M. Forster, 886
David Leavitt, 1463
Adam Mars-Jones, 1630
Yukio Mishima, 1690
Fitz-James O'Brien, 1786
James Purdy, 1990
Gertrude Stein, 2225
Denton Welch, 2466
Tennessee Williams, 2524
Virginia Woolf, 2554

GERMAN CULTURE
Heinrich Böll, 272
Bertolt Brecht, 348
Johann Wolfgang von Goethe, 1016
Wolfgang Hildesheimer, 1201

GHOST. *See also* **HORROR, SUPERNATURAL STORIES, SUSPENSE**
Nelson Algren, 58
Algernon Blackwood, 262
Arthur C. Clarke, 590
Walter de la Mare, 704
Charles Dickens, 725
William Goyen, 1060
E. T. A. Hoffmann, 1216
Henry James, 1283
Joseph Sheridan Le Fanu, 1469
H. P. Lovecraft, 1535
Sir Walter Scott, 2120
Edith Wharton, 2500

GOTHIC. *See also* **GHOST, GROTESQUE STORIES, HORROR, SUPERNATURAL STORIES**
Honoré de Balzac, 147
Ambrose Bierce, 257
George Washington Cable, 394
Erskine Caldwell, 404
Truman Capote, 441
Angela Carter, 469
Roald Dahl, 664
Walter de la Mare, 704
Isak Dinesen, 737
William Faulkner, 856
Théophile Gautier, 984
Nathaniel Hawthorne, 1143
Lafcadio Hearn, 1156
E. T. A. Hoffmann, 1216
Washington Irving, 1268
Tommaso Landolfi, 1427
Herman Melville, 1664
Edna O'Brien, 1780
Fitz-James O'Brien, 1786
Edgar Allan Poe, 1940

GROTESQUE STORIES. *See also* **GOTHIC, HORROR, SUPERNATURAL STORIES**
Franz Kafka, 1328
Jakov Lind, 1513
Carson McCullers, 1556
Edgar Allan Poe, 1940
Horacio Quiroga, 2017
William Sansom, 2084
Andrei Sinyavsky, 2165
Peter Taylor, 2294
Ivan Turgenev, 2352

HISTORICAL STORIES
Margaret Atwood, 108
Julian Barnes, 169
Andrea Barrett, 173
Saul Bellow, 233
Stephen Vincent Benét, 242
Alejo Carpentier, 460
Raymond Carver, 472
Willa Cather, 485
Guy Davenport, 681
Gustave Flaubert, 872
Amos Oz, 1860
Sir Walter Scott, 2120
William Gilmore Simms, 2147
Graham Swift, 2272
Vergil, 2398
Jessamyn West, 2495

HORROR. *See also* **GHOST, GROTESQUE STORIES, SUPERNATURAL STORIES**
Ambrose Bierce, 257
Algernon Blackwood, 262
Elizabeth Bowen, 300
Colette, 597
John Collier, 605
Walter de la Mare, 704
August Derleth, 714
Arthur Conan Doyle, 775
Lord Dunsany, 797
Nikolai Gogol, 1022
W. W. Jacobs, 1279
M. R. James, 1291
Stephen King, 1368
Rudyard Kipling, 1388
Joseph Sheridan Le Fanu, 1469
Jakov Lind, 1513
H. P. Lovecraft, 1535
Arthur Machen, 1574
Fitz-James O'Brien, 1786
Edgar Allan Poe, 1940
Horacio Quiroga, 2017
William Sansom, 2084
Robert Louis Stevenson, 2245

HUMANISM
Isaac Asimov, 95
Giovanni Boccaccio, 266
Heinrich Böll, 272
Ray Bradbury, 331
Morley Callaghan, 415
Italo Calvino, 423
Albert Camus, 429
Raymond Carver, 472
Miguel de Cervantes, 491
E. M. Forster, 886
Tim Gautreux, 988
Charlotte Perkins Gilman, 1003
Caroline Gordon, 1046
Zora Neale Hurston, 1249
Samuel Johnson, 1314
Stanisław Lem, 1481

Lu Xun, 1541
Ezekiel Mphahlele, 1717
Tillie Olsen, 1843
Lee Smith, 2182
Anne Tyler, 2365
Miguel de Unamuno y Jugo, 2371
Helena María Viramontes, 2403
Wang Anyi, 2443
Robert Penn Warren, 2456
Zhang Jie, 2578

HUMOR. *See* **BLACK HUMOR, COMIC REALISM, FARCE, IRONIC STORIES, PARODY, SATIRE, WIT AND HUMOR**

IMPRESSIONISM
Isaac Babel, 128
Willa Cather, 485
Anton Chekhov, 540
Stephen Crane, 654
Mary E. Wilkins Freeman, 908
Hamlin Garland, 963
Katherine Mansfield, 1617
Boris Pasternak, 1887
Edgar Allan Poe, 1940
William Saroyan, 2090
Giovanni Verga, 2393
Glenway Wescott, 2490

INDIAN CULTURE
Ruth Prawer Jhabvala, 1302
Rudyard Kipling, 1388
Bharati Mukherjee, 1721
R. K. Narayan, 1750
Salman Rushdie, 2068

IRISH CULTURE
Samuel Beckett, 218
Elizabeth Bowen, 300
William Carleton, 455
Lord Dunsany, 797
Maria Edgeworth, 807
Brian Friel, 920
James Joyce, 1319
Benedict Kiely, 1356
Mary Lavin, 1443
Joseph Sheridan Le Fanu, 1469
John McGahern, 1566
George Moore, 1695
Edna O'Brien, 1780
Frank O'Connor, 1802
Seán O'Faoláin, 1816
Liam O'Flaherty, 1826
William Butler Yeats, 2566

IRONIC STORIES
Sherman Alexie, 55
Ann Beattie, 210
Geoffrey Chaucer, 518
John Collier, 605
Louise Erdrich, 847
Bruce Jay Friedman, 914
Mavis Gallant, 939
Oliver Goldsmith, 1033
Thomas Hardy, 1112
Bret Harte, 1133
O. Henry, 1183
Hermann Hesse, 1187
Chester Himes, 1204
William Humphrey, 1243
Ring Lardner, 1434
Mary Lavin, 1443
Jack London, 1522
Lu Xun, 1541
Mary McCarthy, 1551
Bernard Malamud, 1595
Marie de France, 1625
Guy de Maupassant, 1652
Prosper Mérimée, 1671
Yukio Mishima, 1690
Vladimir Nabokov, 1738
R. K. Narayan, 1750
Flannery O'Connor, 1794
Grace Paley, 1872
Katherine Anne Porter, 1949
J. F. Powers, 1957
V. S. Pritchett, 1968
Mary Robison, 2052
Saki, 2072
William Saroyan, 2090
Julia Slavin, 2171
Muriel Spark, 2196
Frank R. Stockton, 2250
Peter Taylor, 2294
John Wain, 2424
Sylvia Townsend Warner, 2449
Eudora Welty, 2482
Tobias Wolff, 2549
Virginia Woolf, 2554

IRREALISM. *See also* **ANTISTORY, METAFICTION, POSTMODERNISM**
John Barth, 176
Donald Barthelme, 182
Robert Coover, 632
John Fowles, 891
Vladimir Nabokov, 1738

ITALIAN CULTURE
Giovanni Boccaccio, 266
Luigi Pirandello, 1927
Vergil, 2398

JAPANESE CULTURE
Ryūnosuke Akutagawa, 37
Osamu Dazai, 699
Shūsaku Endō, 841
Lafcadio Hearn, 1156
Ihara Saikaku, 1261
Yasunari Kawabata, 1344
Yukio Mishima, 1690
Kenzaburō Ōe, 1809
Jun'ichirō Tanizaki, 2283

JEWISH CULTURE
Shmuel Yosef Agnon, 22
Sholom Aleichem, 50
Nelson Algren, 58
Woody Allen, 62
Max Apple, 86
Isaac Asimov, 95
Isaac Babel, 128
Melissa Bank, 156
Saul Bellow, 233
Gina Berriault, 248
Harold Brodkey, 354
Hortense Calisher, 409
Stanley Elkin, 820
Bruce Jay Friedman, 914
Herbert Gold, 1030
Nadine Gordimer, 1039
Joanne Greenberg, 1069
Mark Helprin, 1164
Wolfgang Hildesheimer, 1201
Ruth Prawer Jhabvala, 1302
Franz Kafka, 1328
Stanisław Lem, 1481
Jakov Lind, 1513

Bernard Malamud, 1595
Leonard Michaels, 1675
Rabbi Nahman of Bratslav, 1745
Tillie Olsen, 1843
Amos Oz, 1860
Cynthia Ozick, 1865
Grace Paley, 1872
Isaac Leib Peretz, 1906
Francine Prose, 1977
Mordecai Richler, 2036
Philip Roth, 2059
Bruno Schulz, 2106
Delmore Schwartz, 2112
Lynne Sharon Schwartz, 2117
Richard G. Stern, 2239
Susan Sontag, 2193
Italo Svevo, 2269
Jerome Weidman, 2462

LATINO CULTURE
Isabel Allende, 67
Juan José Arreola, 89
Miguel Ángel Asturias, 102
María Luisa Bombal, 278
Jorge Luis Borges, 285
Alejo Carpentier, 460
Sandra Cisneros, 579
Julio Cortázar, 644
José Donoso, 756
Carlos Fuentes, 924
Gabriel García Márquez, 950
João Guimarães Rosa, 1092
Clarice Lispector, 1517
Joaquim Maria Machado de Assis, 1569
Horacio Quiroga, 2017
Tomás Rivera, 2041
Juan Rulfo, 2064
Luisa Valenzuela, 2386
Helena María Viramontes, 2403

LOCAL COLOR. *See also* **REGIONAL STORIES**
George Washington Cable, 394
Erskine Caldwell, 404
Shirley Ann Grau, 1065
Bret Harte, 1133
O. Henry, 1183
William Humphrey, 1243
Sarah Orne Jewett, 1296
Garrison Keillor, 1350
Prosper Mérimée , 1671
Chris Offutt, 1822
William Gilmore Simms, 2147
Jesse Stuart, 2258
Mark Twain, 2359
Eudora Welty, 2482

LYRICAL SHORT STORIES
Lee K. Abbott, 1
Shmuel Yosef Agnon, 22
Conrad Aiken, 32
Sherwood Anderson, 76
H. E. Bates, 197
John Cheever, 532
Anton Chekhov, 540
Fyodor Dostoevski, 760
Tim Gautreux, 988
Yasunari Kawabata, 1344
Jamaica Kincaid, 1362
D. H. Lawrence, 1449
Clarice Lispector, 1517
John McGahern, 1566
Clarence Major, 1591
Katherine Mansfield, 1617
Cynthia Ozick, 1865
Grace Paley, 1872
Boris Pasternak, 1887
Jayne Anne Phillips, 1923
Elizabeth Madox Roberts, 2049
John Steinbeck, 2233
Dylan Thomas, 2306
Ivan Turgenev, 2352
John Updike, 2375
Wang Anyi, 2443
Eudora Welty, 2482
Tobias Wolff, 2549
Virginia Woolf, 2554
Émile Zola, 2584

MAGICAL REALISM
Isabel Allende, 67
Rick Bass, 194
María Luisa Bombal, 278
Jorge Luis Borges, 285
Italo Calvino, 423
Alejo Carpentier, 460
Julio Cortázar, 644
Stuart Dybek, 803
Carlos Fuentes, 924
Gabriel García Márquez, 950
João Guimarães Rosa, 1092
Joy Harjo, 1118
Jamaica Kincaid, 1362
John L'Heureux, 1509
Beth Lordan, 1531
Julia Slavin, 2171
Luisa Valenzuela, 2386
Gerald Vizenor, 2406

MANNERS, FICTION OF. *See also* **SOCIAL REALISM, SOCIAL SATIRE**
Louis Auchincloss, 116
John Cheever, 532
Nancy Hale, 1096
Saki, 2072
Angus Wilson, 2535

MÄRCHEN. *See also* **FABLE, FAIRY TALE, FOLKTALES, PARABLE, TALES**
Johann Wolfgang von Goethe, 1016
Brothers Grimm, 1086
Hermann Hesse, 1187
E. T. A. Hoffmann, 1216

METAFICTION. *See also* **ANTISTORY, IRREALISM, POSTMODERNISM**
Thomas Bailey Aldrich, 46
Margaret Atwood, 108
John Barth, 176
Donald Barthelme, 182
Richard Brautigan, 341
Ethan Canin, 434
Truman Capote, 441
R. V. Cassill, 481
Walter Van Tilburg Clark, 585
Robert Coover, 632
John Fowles, 891
William H. Gass, 975
Henry James, 1283
W. P. Kinsella, 1382
John Knowles, 1406
Vladimir Nabokov, 1738
Juan Carlos Onetti, 1849
Grace Paley, 1872
Thomas Pynchon, 2004
Tennessee Williams, 2524

METAPHYSICAL STORIES
Jorge Luis Borges, 285
Dino Buzzati, 381
Karel Čapek, 437
Philip K. Dick, 719
Fyodor Dostoevski, 760
Denis Johnson, 1310
Tommaso Landolfi, 1427
Gérard de Nerval, 1756
Edgar Allan Poe, 1940

MIDWESTERN UNITED STATES
Garrison Keillor, 1350
Larry Woiwode, 2538

MINIMALISM
Lee K. Abbott, 1
Frederick Barthelme, 190
Ann Beattie, 210
Gina Berriault, 248
Raymond Carver, 472
Richard Ford, 880
Amy Hempel, 1180
David Leavitt, 1463
John McGahern, 1566
Bobbie Ann Mason, 1639
Lorrie Moore, 1699
Jayne Anne Phillips, 1923
Tomás Rivera, 2041
Alain Robbe-Grillet, 2045
Mary Robison, 2052
Mona Simpson, 2153
Gertrude Stein, 2225
Joy Williams, 2520
Tobias Wolff, 2549

MODERN SHORT STORY
Sherwood Anderson, 76
Honoré de Balzac, 147
Michael Byers, 390
Ethan Canin, 434
William Carleton, 455
Lan Samantha Chang, 511
John Cheever, 532
Anton Chekhov, 540
A. E. Coppard, 638
Stephen Crane, 654
Harriet Doerr, 752
Fyodor Dostoevski, 760
Shirley Ann Grau, 1065
Washington Irving, 1268
James Joyce, 1319
John Knowles, 1406
Katherine Mansfield, 1617
Herman Melville, 1664
Prosper Mérimée , 1671
George Moore, 1695
Alberto Moravia, 1702
Flannery O'Connor, 1794
John O'Hara, 1832
Susan Perabo, 1898
Edgar Allan Poe, 1940
Katherine Anne Porter, 1949
J. F. Powers, 1957
V. S. Pritchett, 1968
William Sansom, 2084
William Saroyan, 2090
Bruno Schulz, 2106
Sir Walter Scott, 2120
Wilbur Daniel Steele, 2217
Robert Louis Stevenson, 2245
Peter Taylor, 2294
John Updike, 2375
Giovanni Verga, 2393
Eudora Welty, 2482
E. B. White, 2506
Tobias Wolff, 2549

MODERNISM. *See also* **MODERN SHORT STORY, POSTMODERNISM**
Sherwood Anderson, 76
H. E. Bates, 197
Madison Smartt Bell, 230
Morley Callaghan, 415
John Cheever, 532
Anton Chekhov, 540
Guy Davenport, 681
George P. Elliott, 825
Ernest Hemingway, 1172
O. Henry, 1183
Pam Houston, 1231
Henry James, 1283
James Joyce, 1319
Wyndham Lewis, 1501
Bernard Malamud, 1595
Katherine Mansfield, 1617
Bruno Schulz, 2106
Jane Smiley, 2174
Italo Svevo, 2269
John Updike, 2375
Robert Walser, 2437
Edith Wharton, 2500
William Carlos Williams, 2530
Richard Wright, 2560

MORAL STORIES
Jane Austen, 123
Giovanni Boccaccio, 266
Raymond Carver, 472
Charles Dickens, 725
Ellen Douglas, 766
Maria Edgeworth, 807
George Eliot, 816
Gustave Flaubert, 872
Benjamin Franklin, 903
Tim Gautreux, 988
John Hawkesworth, 1139
Nathaniel Hawthorne, 1143
Mark Helprin, 1164
James Joyce, 1319
Ring Lardner, 1434
Nikolai Leskov, 1488
Bernard Malamud, 1595
Alberto Moravia, 1702
Dorothy Parker, 1883
Boris Pasternak, 1887
Katherine Anne Porter, 1949
J. F. Powers, 1957
Pu Songling, 1984
Horacio Quiroga, 2017
Shūsaku Endō, 841
William Gilmore Simms, 2147
Elizabeth Spencer, 2202
Robert Louis Stevenson, 2245
Theodore Sturgeon, 2264
Christopher Tilghman, 2317
Leo Tolstoy, 2326
Mark Twain, 2359
Miguel de Unamuno y Jugo, 2371
John Wain, 2424

MYSTERY. *See* **DETECTIVE AND MYSTERY**

MYTHIC STORIES
Jorge Luis Borges, 285
John Cheever, 532
Guy Davenport, 681

August Derleth, 714
Isak Dinesen, 737
William Faulkner, 856
William Goyen, 1060
E. T. A. Hoffmann, 1216
Homer, 1222
Jamaica Kincaid, 1362
D. H. Lawrence, 1449
Henry Lawson, 1458
Ovid, 1852
E. Annie Proulx, 1980
Leslie Marmon Silko, 2135
John Steinbeck, 2233
Vergil, 2398
Gerald Vizenor, 2406
William Butler Yeats, 2566

NATIVE AMERICAN CULTURE
Sherman Alexie, 55
Louise Erdrich, 847
Joy Harjo, 1118
Barbara Kingsolver, 1374
Leslie Marmon Silko, 2135
Gerald Vizenor, 2406

NATURALISM
Nelson Algren, 58
Elizabeth Bowen, 300
Morley Callaghan, 415
Willa Cather, 485
Kate Chopin, 562
Stephen Crane, 654
Alphonse Daudet, 676
Rhys Davies, 694
Theodore Dreiser, 783
Hamlin Garland, 963
Ernest Hemingway, 1172
Sarah Orne Jewett, 1296
D. H. Lawrence, 1449
Jack London, 1522
Frank Norris, 1765
Joyce Carol Oates, 1771
Liam O'Flaherty, 1826
Isaac Leib Peretz, 1906
Luigi Pirandello, 1927
Horacio Quiroga, 2017
John Steinbeck, 2233
John Edgar Wideman, 2509
Émile Zola, 2584

NEOREALISM
Frederick Barthelme, 190
Italo Calvino, 423
Cesare Pavese, 1893
Yevgeny Zamyatin, 2572

NIHILISM
Paul Bowles, 311
Bertolt Brecht, 348

NORTHEASTERN UNITED STATES
John Cheever, 532
Mary E. Wilkins Freeman, 908
Nathaniel Hawthorne, 1143

NORTHWESTERN UNITED STATES
Sherman Alexie, 55

OCCULT. *See also* **GHOST, GROTESQUE STORIES, SUPERNATURAL STORIES**
Algernon Blackwood , 262
Angela Carter, 469
Agatha Christie, 572
Carlos Fuentes, 924
Ellen Glasgow, 1007
E. T. A. Hoffmann, 1216
H. P. Lovecraft, 1535
Edgar Allan Poe, 1940

OLD WEST, THE. *See* **WESTERNS AND THE OLD WEST**

PARABLE. *See also* **FABLE, FAIRY TALE, FOLKTALES, MÄRCHEN, TALES**
Louise Erdrich, 847
Herbert Gold, 1030
Nathaniel Hawthorne, 1143

PARODY
Sherman Alexie, 55
Woody Allen, 62
Jane Austen, 123
Donald Barthelme, 182
Max Beerbohm, 225
Jorge Luis Borges, 285
T. Coraghessan Boyle, 325
Karel Čapek, 437
Anton Chekhov, 540
Robert Coover, 632
Stephen Crane, 654
Fyodor Dostoevski, 760
Lord Dunsany, 797
Stanley Elkin, 820
George P. Elliott, 825
F. Scott Fitzgerald, 864
Vladimir Nabokov, 1738
S. J. Perelman, 1901
Edgar Allan Poe, 1940
Thomas Pynchon, 2004
Saki, 2072
James Thurber, 2312
Mark Twain, 2359
E. B. White, 2506
Mikhail Zoshchenko, 2589

PHILOSOPHICAL STORIES
Ryūnosuke Akutagawa, 37
John Barth, 176
Samuel Beckett, 218
Saul Bellow, 233
Giovanni Boccaccio, 266
Jorge Luis Borges, 285
Dino Buzzati, 381
Morley Callaghan, 415
Albert Camus, 429
Karel Čapek, 437
Fyodor Dostoevski, 760
William Faulkner, 856
William H. Gass, 975
Oliver Goldsmith, 1033
Hermann Hesse, 1187
Janette Turner Hospital, 1228
Charles Johnson, 1306
Milan Kundera, 1412
Ursula K. Le Guin, 1476
Stanisław Lem, 1481
Thomas Mann, 1607
Guy de Maupassant, 1652
Flannery O'Connor, 1794
Cesare Pavese, 1893

Luigi Pirandello, 1927
Jean-Paul Sartre, 2095
Miguel de Unamuno y Jugo, 2371
Luisa Valenzuela, 2386
Guy Vanderhaeghe, 2390
Voltaire, 2410

POETIC SHORT STORIES

Geoffrey Chaucer, 518
Dante, 670
Homer, 1222
Yasunari Kawabata, 1344
Marie de France, 1625
Leonard Michaels, 1675
Ovid, 1852
Elizabeth Madox Roberts, 2049
Vergil, 2398
William Butler Yeats, 2566
Émile Zola, 2584

POSTMODERNISM. *See also* **ANTISTORY, IRREALISM, METAFICTION, MODERNISM**

Sherman Alexie, 55
Margaret Atwood, 108
Julian Barnes, 169
John Barth, 176
Donald Barthelme, 182
Stephen Vincent Benét, 242
John Cheever, 532
Robert Coover, 632
Peter Ho Davies, 691
Richard Ford, 880
John Fowles, 891
John Gardner, 956
William Gass, 975
David Gates, 980
Janette Turner Hospital, 1228
Maxine Hong Kingston, 1378
Carson McCullers, 1556
Ian McEwan, 1562
Steven Millhauser, 1682
Vladimir Nabokov, 1738
Juan Carlos Onetti, 1849
Cynthia Ozick, 1865
Thomas Pynchon, 2004
Irwin Shaw, 2131
Julia Slavin, 2171
Graham Swift, 2272
John Edgar Wideman, 2509

PSYCHOLOGICAL REALISM

Alice Adams, 9
Conrad Aiken, 32
Sherwood Anderson, 76
Margaret Atwood, 108
Isaac Babel, 128
James Baldwin, 135
Honoré de Balzac, 147
Melissa Bank, 156
Russell Banks, 160
Amiri Baraka, 165
Donald Barthelme, 182
Richard Bausch, 203
Charles Baxter, 207
Madison Smartt Bell, 230
Saul Bellow, 233
Gina Berriault, 248
Doris Betts, 252
Ambrose Bierce, 257
Elizabeth Bowen, 300
Paul Bowles, 311
Kay Boyle, 317
Harold Brodkey, 354
Bliss Broyard, 363
Michael Byers, 390
Hortense Calisher, 409
Morley Callaghan, 415
Albert Camus, 429
Ethan Canin, 434
Truman Capote, 441
Raymond Carver, 472
Willa Cather, 485
Michael Chabon, 499
Lan Samantha Chang, 511
Fred Chappell, 514
John Cheever, 532
Anton Chekhov, 540
Charles Waddell Chesnutt, 549
Kate Chopin, 562
Walter Van Tilburg Clark, 585
Colette, 597
Joseph Conrad, 620
A. E. Coppard, 638
Julio Cortázar, 644
Stephen Crane, 654
Peter Ho Davies, 691
Stephen Dixon, 749
José Donoso, 756
Fyodor Dostoevski, 760
Andre Dubus, 789
Stuart Dybek, 803
Ralph Ellison, 837
James T. Farrell, 851
William Faulkner, 856
F. Scott Fitzgerald, 864
Gustave Flaubert, 872
E. M. Forster, 886
Ernest J. Gaines, 930
Mary Gaitskill, 936
Mavis Gallant, 939
John Gardner, 956
Charlotte Perkins Gilman, 1003
Ellen Glasgow, 1007
Gail Godwin, 1013
Nadine Gordimer, 1039
Caroline Gordon, 1046
Joanne Greenberg, 1069
Graham Greene, 1074
Joy Harjo, 1118
Nathaniel Hawthorne, 1143
Amy Hempel, 1180
Chester Himes, 1204
Janette Turner Hospital, 1228
Henry James, 1283
Charles Johnson, 1306
Stephen King, 1368
Milan Kundera, 1412
Henry Lawson, 1458
David Leavitt, 1463
Doris Lessing, 1494
Clarice Lispector, 1517
Paule Marshall, 1634
Yukio Mishima, 1690
Bharati Mukherjee, 1721
Alice Munro, 1730
Joyce Carol Oates, 1771
Edna O'Brien, 1780
Tim O'Brien, 1790
Chris Offutt, 1822
Cynthia Ozick, 1865
Grace Paley, 1872
Isaac Leib Peretz, 1906
Ann Petry, 1916
Luigi Pirandello, 1927
Sylvia Plath, 1933
Edgar Allan Poe, 1940
Katherine Anne Porter, 1949
Reynolds Price, 1961
James Purdy, 1990
Lynne Sharon Schwartz, 2117
Leo Tolstoy, 2326
Wang Anyi, 2443

PSYCHOLOGICAL STORIES

Conrad Aiken, 32
Geoffrey Chaucer, 518
Joseph Conrad, 620
Isak Dinesen, 737
Johann Wolfgang von Goethe, 1016
William Goyen, 1060
Thomas Hardy, 1112
Patricia Highsmith, 1193
Anna Kavan, 1339
Joseph Sheridan Le Fanu, 1469
John L'Heureux, 1509
Guy de Maupassant, 1652
Gérard de Nerval, 1756
Joyce Carol Oates, 1771
Cesare Pavese, 1893
Thomas Pynchon, 2004
Andrei Sinyavsky, 2165
Julia Slavin, 2171
Muriel Spark, 2196
Italo Svevo, 2269
Luisa Valenzuela, 2386
Robert Walser, 2437
Eudora Welty, 2482

REALISM. *See also* **COMIC REALISM, DOMESTIC REALISM, IRREALISM, MAGICAL REALISM, NEOREALISM, PSYCHOLOGICAL REALISM, SOCIAL REALISM, SURREALISM, SYMBOLIC REALISM**

Lee K. Abbott, 1
Shmuel Yosef Agnon, 22
Thomas Bailey Aldrich, 46
Sherwood Anderson, 76
Isaac Babel, 128
Honoré de Balzac, 147
Melissa Bank, 156
Julian Barnes, 169
Andrea Barrett, 173
H. E. Bates, 197
Richard Bausch, 203
Samuel Beckett, 218
Madison Smartt Bell, 230
Gina Berriault, 248
Paul Bowles, 311
Kay Boyle, 317
A. S. Byatt, 387
James M. Cain, 400
Italo Calvino, 423
Truman Capote, 441
William Carleton, 455
Raymond Carver, 472
Miguel de Cervantes, 491
John Cheever, 532
Anton Chekhov, 540
Kate Chopin, 562
Evan S. Connell, Jr., 614
Frank Conroy, 628
A. E. Coppard, 638
Stephen Crane, 654
Kiš, Danilo, 1397
Alphonse Daudet, 676
Stephen Dixon, 749
Fyodor Dostoevski, 760
Ellen Douglas, 766
Theodore Dreiser, 783
Andre Dubus, 789
George P. Elliott, 825
William Faulkner, 856
F. Scott Fitzgerald, 864
Gustave Flaubert, 872
Richard Ford, 880
E. M. Forster, 886
Mary E. Wilkins Freeman, 908
Ernest J. Gaines, 930
Mavis Gallant, 939
David Gates, 980
Charlotte Perkins Gilman, 1003
Johann Wolfgang von Goethe, 1016
Nikolai Gogol, 1022
Shirley Ann Grau, 1065
Lawrence Sargent Hall, 1101
Mark Helprin, 1164
Hermann Hesse, 1187
Janette Turner Hospital, 1228
William Dean Howells, 1234
Henry James, 1283
Sarah Orne Jewett, 1296
Charles Johnson, 1306
Denis Johnson, 1310
James Joyce, 1319
Barbara Kingsolver, 1374
W. P. Kinsella, 1382
Ring Lardner, 1434
Margaret Laurence, 1438
Mary Lavin, 1443
D. H. Lawrence, 1449
Henry Lawson, 1458
Wyndham Lewis, 1501
Jakov Lind, 1513
Jack London, 1522
Lu Xun, 1541
Mary McCarthy, 1551
Carson McCullers, 1556
Ian McEwan, 1562
John McGahern, 1566
James Alan McPherson, 1581
Clarence Major, 1591
Bernard Malamud, 1595
Bobbie Ann Mason, 1639
W. Somerset Maugham, 1645
Guy de Maupassant, 1652
Christoph Meckel, 1659
Herman Melville, 1664
Prosper Mérimée, 1671
Leonard Michaels, 1675
George Moore, 1695
Alberto Moravia, 1702
Wright Morris, 1710
Ezekiel Mphahlele, 1717
Alice Munro, 1730
Vladimir Nabokov, 1738
Gérard de Nerval, 1756
Frank Norris, 1765
Joyce Carol Oates, 1771
Fitz-James O'Brien, 1786
Flannery O'Connor, 1794
Frank O'Connor, 1802
Kenzaburō Ōe, 1809
Seán O'Faoláin, 1816
John O'Hara, 1832
Juan Carlos Onetti, 1849
Cynthia Ozick, 1865
Grace Paley, 1872
Isaac Leib Peretz, 1906
Jayne Anne Phillips, 1923
Luigi Pirandello, 1927
Edgar Allan Poe, 1940
J. F. Powers, 1957
E. Annie Proulx, 1980
Pu Songling, 1984
Thomas Pynchon, 2004
Valentin Rasputin, 2023
Elwood Reid, 2027
Mordecai Richler, 2036
William Sansom, 2084
John Sayles, 2102
Bruno Schulz, 2106
Mona Simpson, 2153
Jane Smiley, 2174
Lee Smith, 2182
Aleksandr Solzhenitsyn, 2187

Gertrude Stein, 2225
John Steinbeck, 2233
Robert Stone, 2254
Jesse Stuart, 2258
Elizabeth Tallent, 2276
Barry Targan, 2288
Christopher Tilghman, 2317
Leo Tolstoy, 2326
William Trevor, 2340
Frank Tuohy, 2347
Ivan Turgenev, 2352
Guy Vanderhaeghe, 2390
Sylvia Townsend Warner, 2449
Jerome Weidman, 2462
Joy Williams, 2520
William Carlos Williams, 2530

REGIONAL STORIES. *See also* **LOCAL COLOR**
Sherwood Anderson, 76
George Washington Cable, 394
Kate Chopin, 562
Shirley Ann Grau, 1065
Janette Turner Hospital, 1228
William Humphrey, 1243
Sarah Orne Jewett, 1296
Garrison Keillor, 1350
Margaret Laurence, 1438
Henry Lawson, 1458
Augustus Baldwin Longstreet, 1527
Beth Lordan, 1531
Wright Morris, 1710
Chris Offutt, 1822
Liam O'Flaherty, 1826
Valentin Rasputin, 2023
Elizabeth Madox Roberts, 2049
William Gilmore Simms, 2147
Lee Smith, 2182
Jean Stafford, 2208
Wallace Stegner, 2220
Jesse Stuart, 2258
Guy Vanderhaeghe, 2390
Wang Anyi, 2443
Jessamyn West, 2495
Larry Woiwode, 2538

RELIGIOUS STORIES
James Agee, 19
Richard Bausch, 203
Giovanni Boccaccio, 266
G. K. Chesterton, 556
Dante, 670
Fyodor Dostoevski, 760
Ellen Douglas, 766
Andre Dubus, 789
George P. Elliott, 825
Tim Gautreux, 988
Mary Gordon, 1052
Graham Greene, 1074
John Hawkesworth, 1139
Nathaniel Hawthorne, 1143
Mark Helprin, 1164
Garrison Keillor, 1350
Pär Lagerkvist , 1420
Nikolai Leskov, 1488
John L'Heureux, 1509
Rabbi Nahman of Bratslav, 1745
Flannery O'Connor, 1794
Ovid, 1852
Amos Oz, 1860
J. F. Powers, 1957
Pu Songling, 1984
Shūsaku Endō, 841
Andrei Sinyavsky, 2165
Jesse Stuart, 2258
Leo Tolstoy, 2326
Larry Woiwode, 2538

ROMANCE
Chrétien de Troyes, 567
Sir Thomas Malory, 1603
Marie de France, 1625

ROMANTICISM
Dino Buzzati, 381
George Washington Cable, 394
Alphonse Daudet, 676
Théophile Gautier, 984
Oliver Goldsmith, 1033
Brothers Grimm, 1086
Bret Harte, 1133
Nathaniel Hawthorne, 1143
E. T. A. Hoffmann, 1216
Washington Irving, 1268
Thomas Mann, 1607
Prosper Mérimée, 1671
Gérard de Nerval, 1756
Fitz-James O'Brien, 1786
Boris Pasternak, 1887
Isaac Leib Peretz, 1906
Alexander Pushkin, 1997
Sir Walter Scott, 2120
William Gilmore Simms, 2147
John Steinbeck, 2233
Robert Louis Stevenson, 2245
Jesse Stuart, 2258
Ivan Turgenev, 2352

RUSSIAN CULTURE
Sholom Aleichem, 50
Ivan Bunin, 372
Anton Chekhov, 540
Fyodor Dostoevski, 760
Sergei Dovlatov, 769
Nikolai Gogol, 1022
Maxim Gorky, 1055
Isaac Babel, 128
Nikolai Leskov, 1488
Valentin Rasputin, 2023
Varlam Shalamov, 2126
Aleksandr Solzhenitsyn, 2187
Tatyana Tolstaya, 2320
Ivan Turgenev, 2352
Mikhail Zoshchenko, 2589

SATIRE. *See also* **MANNERS, FICTION OF, SOCIAL SATIRE**
Joseph Addison, 14
Max Apple, 86
Donald Barthelme, 182
Max Beerbohm, 225
Ambrose Bierce, 257
Giovanni Boccaccio, 266
Heinrich Böll, 272
T. Coraghessan Boyle, 325
Robert Olen Butler, 377
Truman Capote, 441
Willa Cather, 485
John Cheever, 532
Anton Chekhov, 540
John Collier, 605
Evan S. Connell, Jr., 614
Thomas M. Disch, 745
Stanley Elkin, 820
William Faulkner, 856
F. Scott Fitzgerald, 864
Anatole France, 897
Benjamin Franklin, 903
Nikolai Gogol, 1022
Nathaniel Hawthorne, 1143
Washington Irving, 1268

W. W. Jacobs, 1279
Ruth Prawer Jhabvala, 1302
W. P. Kinsella, 1382
Pär Lagerkvist, 1420
Ring Lardner, 1434
Wyndham Lewis, 1501
Jakov Lind, 1513
Lu Xun, 1541
Mary McCarthy, 1551
Leonard Michaels, 1675
R. K. Narayan, 1750
Flannery O'Connor, 1794
Cynthia Ozick, 1865
Grace Paley, 1872
Dorothy Parker, 1883
S. J. Perelman, 1901
Petronius, 1911
Edgar Allan Poe, 1940
J. F. Powers, 1957
Salman Rushdie, 2068
Saki, 2072
Lee Smith, 2182
Muriel Spark, 2196
Richard Steele, 2213
Frank R. Stockton, 2250
Elizabeth Taylor, 2291
William Makepeace Thackeray, 2300
Dylan Thomas, 2306
Mark Twain, 2359
Miguel de Unamuno y Jugo, 2371
Gerald Vizenor, 2406
Voltaire, 2410
Kurt Vonnegut, 2416
John Wain, 2424
Fay Weldon, 2472
E. B. White, 2506
Angus Wilson, 2535
Yevgeny Zamyatin, 2572
Zhang Jie, 2578
Mikhail Zoshchenko, 2589

SCIENCE FICTION

Isaac Asimov, 95
Margaret Atwood, 108
J. G. Ballard, 141
Stephen Vincent Benét, 242
Ray Bradbury, 331
Karel Čapek, 437
Orson Scott Card, 446
Peter Carey, 451
Arthur C. Clarke, 590
Samuel R. Delany, 709
Philip K. Dick, 719
Thomas M. Disch, 745
Arthur Conan Doyle, 775
Harlan Ellison, 831
E. M. Forster, 886
Robert A. Heinlein, 1159
Aldous Huxley, 1255
Anna Kavan, 1339
Ursula K. Le Guin, 1476
Stanisław Lem, 1481
Fitz-James O'Brien, 1786
Edgar Allan Poe, 1940
Frank R. Stockton, 2250
Theodore Sturgeon, 2264
Mark Twain, 2359
Kurt Vonnegut, 2416
H. G. Wells, 2476

SHORT SHORT STORY

Patricia Highsmith, 1193
Yasunari Kawabata, 1344

SKETCHES. *See also* **ESSAY-SKETCH TRADITION**

Joseph Addison, 14
Pedro Antonio de Alarcón, 41
Ambrose Bierce, 257
Tadeusz Borowski, 295
Ivan Bunin, 372
Morley Callaghan, 415
Anton Chekhov, 540
Sandra Cisneros, 579
Stephen Crane, 654
Charles Dickens, 725
Harriet Doerr, 752
Sergei Dovlatov, 769
Paul Laurence Dunbar, 793
Louise Erdrich, 847
Benjamin Franklin, 903
George Garrett, 969
Penelope Gilliatt, 997
Oliver Goldsmith, 1033
Caroline Gordon, 1046
Brothers Grimm, 1086
Aldous Huxley, 1255
Washington Irving, 1268
Henry James, 1283
Ruth Prawer Jhabvala, 1302
Jamaica Kincaid, 1362
Pär Lagerkvist, 1420
Doris Lessing, 1494
Augustus Baldwin Longstreet, 1527
Katherine Mansfield, 1617
R. K. Narayan, 1750
Joyce Carol Oates, 1771
Emilia Pardo Bazán, 1878
Reynolds Price, 1961
Richard Steele, 2213
William Makepeace Thackeray, 2300
James Thurber, 2312
Jean Toomer, 2335
Mark Twain, 2359
Mikhail Zoshchenko, 2589

SOCIAL CRITICISM

James Baldwin, 135
Toni Cade Bambara, 152
Russell Banks, 160
Bertolt Brecht, 348
Ivan Bunin, 372
Erskine Caldwell, 404
Sergei Dovlatov, 769
Paul Laurence Dunbar, 793
Anatole France, 897
John Galsworthy, 945
Nikolai Gogol, 1022
Nadine Gordimer, 1039
Maxine Hong Kingston, 1378
Guy de Maupassant, 1652
R. K. Narayan, 1750
Thomas Pynchon, 2004
Mary Robison, 2052
Elizabeth Taylor, 2291
Giovanni Verga, 2393
Helena María Viramontes, 2403
Voltaire, 2410
John Wain, 2424
Alice Walker, 2428
Yevgeny Zamyatin, 2572

SOCIAL REALISM. *See also* **MANNERS, FICTION OF**

Chinua Achebe, 4
Conrad Aiken, 32
Sherman Alexie, 55
Isabel Allende, 67
Maya Angelou, 83
Margaret Atwood, 108
Louis Auchincloss, 116

James Baldwin, 135
Honore de Balzac, 147
Toni Cade Bambara, 152
Frederick Barthelme, 190
Rick Bass, 194
Heinrich Böll, 272
Tadeusz Borowski, 295
Elizabeth Bowen, 300
Jane Bowles, 306
Kay Boyle, 317
Hortense Calisher, 409
Albert Camus, 429
William Carleton, 455
Willa Cather, 485
Michael Chabon, 499
Fred Chappell, 514
John Cheever, 532
Anton Chekhov, 540
Charles Waddell Chesnutt, 549
Kate Chopin, 562
Sandra Cisneros, 579
Colette, 597
James Gould Cozzens, 649
Alphonse Daudet, 676
Stuart Dybek, 803
Ralph Ellison, 837
F. Scott Fitzgerald, 864
Richard Ford, 880
Anatole France, 897
Mary E. Wilkins Freeman, 908
Ernest J. Gaines, 930
Mavis Gallant, 939
John Gardner, 956
Nadine Gordimer, 1039
Caroline Gordon, 1046
Maxim Gorky, 1055
Barry Hannah, 1108
Bessie Head, 1152
William Dean Howells, 1234
Aldous Huxley, 1255
Barbara Kingsolver, 1374
Milan Kundera, 1412
Pär Lagerkvist, 1420
Mary Lavin, 1443
Lu Xun, 1541
James Alan McPherson, 1581
Bobbie Ann Mason, 1639
Stephen Minot, 1686
George Moore, 1695
Lorrie Moore, 1699
Bharati Mukherjee, 1721
Joyce Carol Oates, 1771
Cynthia Ozick, 1865
Dorothy Parker, 1883
Ann Petry, 1916
Katherine Anne Porter, 1949
Reynolds Price, 1961
James Purdy, 1990
Valentin Rasputin, 2023
Mordecai Richler, 2036
Tomás Rivera, 2041
Philip Roth, 2059
Juan Rulfo, 2064
John Sayles, 2102
Aleksandr Solzhenitsyn, 2187
John Steinbeck, 2233
Guy Vanderhaeghe, 2390
Zhang Jie, 2578

SOCIAL SATIRE. *See also* **MANNERS, FICTION OF, SOCIAL REALISM**
James Alan McPherson, 1581
Grace Paley, 1872
Dorothy Parker, 1883
Voltaire, 2410
Kurt Vonnegut, 2416
Mikhail Zoshchenko, 2589

SOUTH AFRICAN CULTURE
Nadine Gordimer, 1039
Bessie Head, 1152
Doris Lessing, 1494
Ezekiel Mphahlele, 1717

SOUTHERN UNITED STATES
Lee K. Abbott, 1
James Agee, 19
Arna Bontemps, 281
Larry Brown, 360
George Washington Cable, 394
Erskine Caldwell, 404
Fred Chappell, 514
Kate Chopin, 562
Ralph Ellison, 837
William Faulkner, 856
Richard Ford, 880
Ernest J. Gaines, 930
Tim Gautreux, 988
Ellen Gilchrist, 991
Ellen Glasgow, 1007
Caroline Gordon, 1046
William Goyen, 1060
Shirley Ann Grau, 1065
Barry Hannah, 1108
William Humphrey, 1243
Zora Neale Hurston, 1249
Augustus Baldwin Longstreet, 1527
Carson McCullers, 1556
Bobbie Ann Mason, 1639
Flannery O'Connor, 1794
Chris Offutt, 1822
Katherine Anne Porter, 1949
Reynolds Price, 1961
Elizabeth Madox Roberts, 2049
William Gilmore Simms, 2147
Lee Smith, 2182
Elizabeth Spencer, 2202
Jesse Stuart, 2258
Peter Taylor, 2294
Anne Tyler, 2365
Robert Penn Warren, 2456
Eudora Welty, 2482

SOUTHWESTERN UNITED STATES
Barbara Kingsolver, 1374
Flannery O'Connor, 1794
Tomás Rivera, 2041

SPANISH CULTURE
Pedro Antonio de Alarcón, 41
Miguel de Cervantes, 491
Pardo Bazán, Emilia, 1878
Miguel de Unamuno y Jugo, 2371

SUPERNATURAL STORIES. *See also* **GHOST, GOTHIC, GROTESQUE STORIES, HORROR, MAGICAL REALISM, OCCULT, SUSPENSE**
Hans Christian Andersen, 70
J. G. Ballard, 141
Julian Barnes, 169
Ambrose Bierce, 257
Algernon Blackwood, 262
Elizabeth Bowen, 300
Paul Bowles, 311
John Cheever, 532
John Collier, 605

Charles Dickens, 725
Arthur Conan Doyle, 775
John Fowles, 891
Gabriel García Márquez, 950
Théophile Gautier, 984
Nikolai Gogol, 1022
Graham Greene, 1074
Thomas Hardy, 1112
Nathaniel Hawthorne, 1143
Patricia Highsmith, 1193
E. T. A. Hoffmann, 1216
Washington Irving, 1268
Shirley Jackson, 1274
Henry James, 1283
Franz Kafka, 1328
Stephen King, 1368
Rudyard Kipling, 1388
Heinrich von Kleist, 1400
Joseph Sheridan Le Fanu, 1469
Beth Lordan, 1531
H. P. Lovecraft, 1535
Arthur Machen, 1574
Marie de France, 1625
Guy de Maupassant, 1652
Prosper Mérimée, 1671
George Moore, 1695
R. K. Narayan, 1750
Gérard de Nerval, 1756
Fitz-James O'Brien, 1786
Ovid, 1852
Edgar Allan Poe, 1940
Pu Songling, 1984
Horacio Quiroga, 2017
Saki, 2072
Muriel Spark, 2196
Ivan Turgenev, 2352
Mark Twain, 2359
Edith Wharton, 2500
William Butler Yeats, 2566
Zhang Jie, 2578

SURREALISM
Ilse Aichinger, 28
Miguel Ángel Asturias, 102
Heinrich Böll, 272
María Luisa Bombal, 278
Dino Buzzati, 381
Peter Carey, 451
Angela Carter, 469
Miguel de Cervantes, 491
Julio Cortázar, 644
Guy Davenport, 681
Harlan Ellison, 831
Gabriel García Márquez, 950
Nikolai Gogol, 1022
Barry Hannah, 1108
Hermann Hesse, 1187
Denis Johnson, 1310
Franz Kafka, 1328
Anna Kavan, 1339
Jamaica Kincaid, 1362
W. P. Kinsella, 1382
Danilo Kiš, 1397
John Knowles, 1406
Tommaso Landolfi, 1427
Jakov Lind, 1513
Alberto Moravia, 1702
Joyce Carol Oates, 1771
Alain Robbe-Grillet, 2045
William Sansom, 2084
Bruno Schulz, 2106
Julia Slavin, 2171
Dylan Thomas, 2306
Joy Williams, 2520

SUSPENSE. *See also* **ADVENTURE, DETECTIVE AND MYSTERY**
Roald Dahl, 664
Dashiell Hammett, 1104
Stephen King, 1368

SYMBOLIC REALISM
Isaac Babel, 128
Joseph Conrad, 620
Stephen Crane, 654
Carlos Fuentes, 924
Gabriel García Márquez, 950

SYMBOLISM
Dino Buzzati, 381
Angela Carter, 469
Joseph Conrad, 620
Walter de la Mare, 704
Gustave Flaubert, 872
Johann Wolfgang von Goethe, 1016
Ernest Hemingway, 1172
James Joyce, 1319
D. H. Lawrence, 1449
Thomas Mann, 1607
Katherine Mansfield, 1617
Gérard de Nerval, 1756
Flannery O'Connor, 1794
Amos Oz, 1860
Isaac Leib Peretz, 1906
Katherine Anne Porter, 1949
Bruno Schulz, 2106
Elizabeth Tallent, 2276
Denton Welch, 2466
Tennessee Williams, 2524
Tobias Wolff, 2549

TALES. *See also* **FABLE, FAIRY TALE, FOLKTALES, MÄRCHEN, PARABLE**
Shmuel Yosef Agnon, 22
Pedro Antonio de Alarcón, 41
Miguel de Cervantes, 491
Arthur C. Clarke, 590
Paul Laurence Dunbar, 793
Henry James, 1283
Heinrich von Kleist, 1400
Augustus Baldwin Longstreet, 1527
H. P. Lovecraft, 1535
Rabbi Nahman of Bratslav, 1745
Isaac Leib Peretz, 1906
Petronius, 1911
Alexander Pushkin, 1997
William Gilmore Simms, 2147
William Makepeace Thackeray, 2300
Ivan Turgenev, 2352
Mark Twain, 2359
Voltaire, 2410
H. G. Wells, 2476
William Butler Yeats, 2566

UTOPIAN STORIES
Charlotte Perkins Gilman, 1003
Kurt Vonnegut, 2416
H. G. Wells, 2476
Zhang Jie, 2578

WAR
Isaac Babel, 128
H. E. Bates, 197
Ambrose Bierce, 257
Kay Boyle, 317
Robert Olen Butler, 377

Stephen Crane, 654
Roald Dahl, 664
Barry Hannah, 1108
Mark Helprin, 1164
Ernest Hemingway, 1172
Chester Himes, 1204
Homer, 1222
Bobbie Ann Mason, 1639
Guy de Maupassant, 1652
Tim O'Brien, 1790
Kenzaburō Ōe, 1809
Seán O'Faoláin, 1816
Cesare Pavese, 1893
Leo Tolstoy, 2326
H. G. Wells, 2476

WEST INDIAN CULTURE

Alejo Carpentier, 460
Jamaica Kincaid, 1362
Paule Marshall, 1634

WESTERN UNITED STATES

Lee K. Abbott, 1
Ambrose Bierce, 257
Willa Cather, 485
Stephen Crane, 654
Richard Ford, 880
Bret Harte, 1133
Barbara Kingsolver, 1374
Tomás Rivera, 2041
Wallace Stegner, 2220
Mark Twain, 2359

WESTERNS AND THE OLD WEST

Ambrose Bierce, 257
Willa Cather, 485
Stephen Crane, 654
Richard Ford, 880
Bret Harte, 1133
Wallace Stegner, 2220
Mark Twain, 2359

WIT AND HUMOR. *See also* **BLACK HUMOR, COMIC REALISM, FARCE, IRONIC STORIES, PARODY, SATIRE**

Lee K. Abbott, 1
Joseph Addison, 14
Sholom Aleichem, 50
Sherman Alexie, 55
Nelson Algren, 58
Woody Allen, 62
Melissa Bank, 156
Max Beerbohm, 225
Ambrose Bierce, 257
Giovanni Boccaccio, 266
Jorge Luis Borges, 285
T. Coraghessan Boyle, 325
Ray Bradbury, 331
Miguel de Cervantes, 491
G. K. Chesterton, 556
John Collier, 605
William Congreve, 611
Philip K. Dick, 719
Charles Dickens, 725
Thomas M. Disch, 745
Stanley Elkin, 820
Louise Erdrich, 847
Anatole France, 897
Benjamin Franklin, 903
Bruce Jay Friedman, 914
Penelope Gilliatt, 997
Nikolai Gogol, 1022
Oliver Goldsmith, 1033
Graham Greene, 1074
Jim Harrison, 1127
Bret Harte, 1133
O. Henry, 1183
Hermann Hesse, 1187
Patricia Highsmith, 1193
Ihara Saikaku, 1261
Washington Irving, 1268
Garrison Keillor, 1350
W. P. Kinsella, 1382
Ring Lardner, 1434
Henry Lawson, 1458
Stanisław Lem, 1481
Wyndham Lewis, 1501
Jakov Lind, 1513
Augustus Baldwin Longstreet, 1527
Adam Mars-Jones, 1630
W. Somerset Maugham, 1645
Guy de Maupassant, 1652
Leonard Michaels, 1675
Lorrie Moore, 1699
Wright Morris, 1710
R. K. Narayan, 1750
Flannery O'Connor, 1794
Frank O'Connor, 1802
Seán O'Faoláin, 1816
Ben Okri, 1838
Cynthia Ozick, 1865
Grace Paley, 1872
Dorothy Parker, 1883
S. J. Perelman, 1901
Petronius, 1911
Edgar Allan Poe, 1940
J. F. Powers, 1957
V. S. Pritchett, 1968
Thomas Pynchon, 2004
Mary Robison, 2052
Salman Rushdie, 2068
Saki, 2072
William Sansom, 2084
William Saroyan, 2090
Bruno Schulz, 2106
William Gilmore Simms, 2147
Julia Slavin, 2171
Lee Smith, 2182
Richard Steele, 2213
Richard G. Stern, 2239
Frank R. Stockton, 2250
Jun'ichirō Tanizaki, 2283
Barry Targan, 2288
Elizabeth Taylor, 2291
William Makepeace Thackeray, 2300
James Thurber, 2312
Tatyana Tolstaya, 2320
Mark Twain, 2359
Guy Vanderhaeghe, 2390
Gerald Vizenor, 2406
Voltaire, 2410
Kurt Vonnegut, 2416
Sylvia Townsend Warner, 2449
Jerome Weidman, 2462
Fay Weldon, 2472
H. G. Wells, 2476
Eudora Welty, 2482
E. B. White, 2506
Angus Wilson, 2535
Mikhail Zoshchenko, 2589

WOMEN'S ISSUES

Alice Adams, 9
Isabel Allende, 67
Maya Angelou, 83
Margaret Atwood, 108
Jane Austen, 123
Toni Cade Bambara, 152
Melissa Bank, 156

Ann Beattie, 210
Aimee Bender, 239
Gina Berriault, 248
Doris Betts, 252
María Luisa Bombal, 278
Elizabeth Bowen, 300
Jane Bowles, 306
Bliss Broyard, 363
Pearl S. Buck, 366
A. S. Byatt, 387
Hortense Calisher, 409
Angela Carter, 469
Kate Chopin, 562
Sandra Cisneros, 579
Isak Dinesen, 737
Ellen Douglas, 766
Maria Edgeworth, 807
George Eliot, 816
Louise Erdrich, 847
Mary E. Wilkins Freeman, 908
Mary Gaitskill, 936
Mavis Gallant, 939
Ellen Gilchrist, 991
Penelope Gilliatt, 997
Charlotte Perkins Gilman, 1003
Ellen Glasgow, 1007
Gail Godwin, 1013
Mary Gordon, 1052
Nancy Hale, 1096
Joy Harjo, 1118
Bessie Head, 1152
Amy Hempel, 1180
Janette Turner Hospital, 1228
Pam Houston, 1231
Zora Neale Hurston, 1249
Sarah Orne Jewett, 1296
Anna Kavan, 1339
Jamaica Kincaid, 1362
Barbara Kingsolver, 1374
Maxine Hong Kingston, 1378
Jhumpa Lahiri, 1424
Margaret Laurence, 1438
Mary Lavin, 1443
Ursula K. Le Guin, 1476
Clarice Lispector, 1517
Beth Lordan, 1531
Mary McCarthy, 1551
Naguib Mahfouz, 1586
Katherine Mansfield, 1617
Marie de France, 1625
Paule Marshall, 1634
Sue Miller, 1679
Susan Minot, 1686
Lorrie Moore, 1699
Bharati Mukherjee, 1721
Alice Munro, 1730
Anaïs Nin, 1760
Joyce Carol Oates, 1771
Edna O'Brien, 1780
Flannery O'Connor, 1794
Tillie Olsen, 1843
Cynthia Ozick, 1865
Grace Paley, 1872
Emilia Pardo Bazán, 1878
Dorothy Parker, 1883
Ann Petry, 1916
Jayne Anne Phillips, 1923
Sylvia Plath, 1933
Katherine Anne Porter, 1949
Jean Rhys, 2031
Lynne Sharon Schwartz, 2117
Shirley Jackson, 1274
Leslie Marmon Silko, 2135
Mona Simpson, 2153
Julia Slavin, 2171
Jane Smiley, 2174
Lee Smith, 2182
Susan Sontag, 2193
Muriel Spark, 2196
Elizabeth Spencer, 2202
Jean Stafford, 2208
Gertrude Stein, 2225
Elizabeth Tallent, 2276
Amy Tan, 2279
Elizabeth Taylor, 2291
Tatyana Tolstaya, 2320
Anne Tyler, 2365
Luisa Valenzuela, 2386
Helena María Viramontes, 2403
Alice Walker, 2428
Fay Weldon, 2472
Eudora Welty, 2482
Edith Wharton, 2500
Marianne Wiggins, 2516
Joy Williams, 2520
Virginia Woolf, 2554
Zhang Jie, 2578

SUBJECT INDEX

"A & P" (Updike), 2377, 2828
"A la deriva." *See* "Drifting"
"A. V. Laider" (Beerbohm), 2797
"Abbé Aubain, The" (Mérimée), 2769
Abbott, Lee K., 1-4, 2835; "Final Proof of Fate and Circumstance, The," 2; "Living Alone in Iota," 2, 2835; "Talk Talked Between Worms, The," 2
"Abduction of Bunny Steiner" (Disch), 747
Abel Sánchez (Unamuno y Jugo), 2372
"Aben." *See* "Monkey, The"
"About Loving Women" (Douglas), 768
"Abrazo de Vergara, El." *See* "Embrace at Vergara, The"
"Abroad" (Gordimer), 1042
"Absence of Mercy" (Stone), 2256
Abstractionism, 2229
"Accident" (Minot), 1688
"Accompagnatrice, La." *See* "Accompanist, The" (Colette)
"Accompanist, The" (Colette), 601
"Accompanist, The" (Pritchett), 1974
"Accountant" (Canin), 435
Achebe, Chinua, 4-9; "Civil Peace," 7, 2852; "Girls at War," 7, 2852; *Girls at War*, 2851; "Uncle Ben's Choice," 6; "Vengeful Creditor," 5; "Voter, The," 2851
Acquainted with the Night, and Other Stories (Schwartz, Lynn Sharon), 2118
Acres and Pains (Perelman), 1903
"Across the Bridge" (Gallant), 942
Actual, The (Bellow), 237
"Adam, One Afternoon" (Calvino), 425
Adams, Alice, 9-13; "Beautiful Girl," 12; "Greyhound People," 10; "Haunted Beach, The," 12; "Home Is Where," 10; *Last Lovely City, The*, 12; "Mexican Dust," 10; "Molly's Dog," 11; "Public Pool, A," 11; "To See You Again," 11; "You Are What You Own," 11
Addison, Joseph, 14-18; *Spectator, The*, 14, 2726, 2737-2738; *Tatler, The*, 14, 18, 2737-2738; *Tatler* 163, 16; "Vision of Mizrah, The," 15, 2727
"Admiral and the Nuns, The" (Tuohy), 2348
"Admiralty Spire, The" (Nabokov), 1742
"Adoration of the Magi, The" (Yeats), 2570
"Adore Her" (Robison), 2057
"Adrianna Takes a Trip" (Pirandello), 1930
"Adulterous Woman, The" (Camus, Albert), 430
"Adultery" (Dubus), 791
"Advanced Beginners" (Bank), 157
"Advancing Luna" (Walker), 2868
"Adventure of a Bather, The" (Calvino), 425
"Adventure of the Camberwell Beauty, The" (Derleth), 717
"Adventure of the Dancing Men, The" (Doyle), 781
"Adventure of the Empty House, The" (Doyle), 780
"Adventure of the Remarkable Worm, The" (Derleth), 716
"Adventure of the Rudberg Numbers, The" (Derleth), 716
"Adventure of the Speckled Band, The" (Doyle), 777
"Adventures of a Monkey, The" (Zoshchenko), 2592
Adventures of Ellery Queen, The (Queen), 2620
"Adventures of Lo Bun Sun, The" (Kingston), 1380
Aeneid (Vergil), 2399, 2663, 2665
"Aeroplanes at Brescia, The" (Davenport), 683
Aesop, 2626, 2661
Aesop (Caxton), 2628
Aestheticism, 3056
"Affair at the Bungalow, The" (Christie), 576
"Afonka Bida" (Babel), 132
Africa, 2845-2856. *See also* "Geographical Index"
African American culture, 2857-2870. *See also* "Category Index"
African culture, 2845-2856. *See also* "Category Index"
"African Traveller, The" (Queen), 2014
"After Holbein" (Wharton), 2503
"After Long Absence" (Hospital), 1229
"After Rain" (Trevor), 2345
After Rain (Trevor), 2345
"After the Ball" (Collier), 607
"Afterlife, The" (Updike), 2384
Afterlife and Other Stories, The (Updike), 2383, 2828
"Age of Analysis, The" (Schwartz, Lynne Sharon), 2118
Age of Grief, The (Smiley), 2176
"Age of Lead, The" (Atwood), 113
Age of Reason, 2726
Agee, James, 19-22; *Collected Short Prose of James Agee, The*, 20; "Death in the Desert," 21; *Death in the Family, A*, 19-20; "Dream Sequence," 21; "Knoxville," 20; *Morning Watch, The*, 19-20
"Aghwee the Sky Monster" (Ōe), 1812
"Agnes" (Gordon, Mary), 1053
Agnon, Shmuel Yosef, 22-28; "Book That Was Lost, A," 27; *Book That Was Lost and Other Stories, A*, 26; "Buczacz," 27; "Fable of the Goat," 24; "Kerchief, The," 25; "Tale of Menorah, The," 27; "Whole Loaf, A," 26
Agostino (Moravia), 2821
"Aguri" (Tanizaki), 2284
"Ah, the University!" (Collier), 609
Ai, shi buneng wangj de. See *Love Must Not Be Forgotten*
Aichinger, Ilse, 28-31; "Bound Man, The," 30; "Story in a Mirror," 29
Aickman, Robert, 2651

Aidoo, Ama Ata; "In the Cutting of a Drink," 2852; *No Sweetness Here and Other Stories*, 2852; "Two Sisters," 2853
Aiiieeeee!, 2871
Aiken, Conrad, 32-37; "Conversation, A," 35; "Silent Snow, Secret Snow," 32; "Strange Moonlight," 34; "Thistledown," 35; "Your Obituary, Well Written," 34
Airships (Hannah), 1109
Akutagawa, Ryūnosuke, 37-41, 2932; "Cogwheels," 40; "Hell Screen," 39, 2932; "In a Grove," 39, 2932; *Kappa*, 40; "Memories Sent to an Old Friend," 40; "Nose, The," 39; "Rashōmon," 38-39, 2932; "Spider's Thread, The," 39
Alarcón, Pedro Antonio de, 41-46; "Embrace at Vergara, The," 43; "Last Escapade, The," 44; "Nail, The," 43; "Nun, The," 44; "Prophecy, The," 43; "Stub-Book, The," 45
"Albatross, The" (Lem), 1486
Aldrich, Thomas Bailey, 46-49; "Marjorie Daw," 47, 2781; "Struggle for Life, A," 48
Aleichem, Sholom, 50-54
"ALĒTHIA" (Johnson, Charles), 1308
Alexie, Sherman, 55-58; "Because My Father Always Said He Was the Only Indian Who Saw Jimi Hendrix Play the Star-Spangled Banner at Woodstock," 56-57; "Drug Called Tradition, A," 57; "Every Little Hurricane," 57; *Lone Ranger and Tonto Fistfight in Heaven, The*, 56; "Only Traffic Signal on the Reservation Doesn't Flash Red Any More, The," 57; *Reservation Blues*, 2967
Alf layla wa-layla. See *Arabian Nights' Entertainments, The*
Alfonsi, Petrus; *Discipline clericalis*, 2701
Algren, Nelson, 58-61; "Bottle of Milk for Mother, A," 60; "Design for Departure," 59; "Face on the Barroom Floor, The," 60; "How the Devil Came Down Division Street," 60
Alguns Contos (Lispector), 1518
"Alice Addertongue" (Franklin), 905
"Alice Sydenham's First Ball" (Leprohon), 2899
"Alicia Who Sees Mice" (Cisneros), 581
"All Fires the Fire" (Cortázar), 646
"All He Needs Is Feet" (Himes), 1207
"All in a Maze" (Carr), 466
"All Looks Yellow to the Jaundiced Eye" (Boyle, Patrick), 2926
"All Sorts of Impossible Things" (McGahern), 1568
All Stories Are True (Wideman), 2514
"All Strange Away" (Beckett), 222
"All the Days of Our Lives" (Smith), 2183
"'All You Zombies'" (Heinlein), 1162
Allegory, 2625, 3056. *See also* "Category Index"
Allen, Paula Gunn, 2961-2962, 2966; "Deer Woman," 2969; *Song of the Turtle*, 2962
Allen, Walter Ernest, 2608
Allen, Woody, 62-66; "Condemned, The," 65; "Kugelmass Episode, The," 64; "Mr. Big," 63
Allende, Isabel, 67-70; "Camino hacia el norte, Un," 69; *Eva Luna*, 67; "Si me tocaras el corazón," 68; *Stories of Eva Luna, The*, 67; "Tosca," 68
"Alligators, The" (Updike), 2377
Allusion, 3056
"Almanac of Pain, An" (Dazai), 700
Almoran and Hamet (Hawkesworth), 1141
"Along Rideout Road That Summer" (Duggan), 2895
Alphabets and Birthdays (Stein), 2231
"Als der krieg zu ende war." *See* "As the War Ended"
"Altar of the Dead, The" (James, Henry), 1287
"Alternative, The" (Baraka), 167
"Amanuensis" (Godwin), 1015
"Amateur's Guide to the Night, An" (Robison), 2055
"Amazon, The" (Leskov), 1491
Ambiguity, 3056
"America! America!" (Schwartz, Delmore), 2115
America Is in the Heart (Bulosan), 2882
"American Couple, The" (Butler), 379
"American Dreams" (Carey), 454, 2891
American Ghosts and Old World Wonders (Carter), 471
American Indian Stories (Zitkala-Sa), 2964
American Visa (Ping), 2877
"Among the Dahlias" (Sansom), 2088
Among the Dahlias (Sansom), 2088
"Among the Impressionists" (Wiggins), 2517
"Among the Ruins" (Friel), 921
"Amos Barton" (Eliot), 817
"Amour." *See* "Love" (Colette)
"Amuck in the Bush" (Callaghan), 418
Amurath the Sultan (Hawkesworth), 1141
Anachronism, 3056
"Anaconda" (Quiroga), 2021
Anarchists' Convention, The (Sayles), 2104
Anaya, Rudolfo, 2950; *Silence of the Llano, The*, 2954
Ancient short fiction, 2657-2668
"And Both Shall Row" (Gates), 1533
. . . *And the earth did not part* (Rivera), 2042, 2954
"And the Rain Patters On" (Wang), 2444
"And the Soul Shall Dance" (Yamauchi), 2880
"And There Was the Evening and the Morning" (Böll), 274
Andersen, Hans Christian, 70-76; "Emperor's New Clothes, The," 74; "Nightingale, The," 74; "Shadow, The," 72; "Snow Queen, The," 71
Anderson, Sherwood, 76-82; "Book of the Grotesque, The," 78; "Death in the Woods," 80; "Egg, The," 81; "Godliness," 79; "Hands," 78; "I Am a Fool," 81; "Man Who Became a Woman, The," 80; "Paper Pills," 80; "Philosopher, The," 78; "Corn Planting, The," 81;

"Sophistication," 80; "Strength of God, The," 79; "Teacher, The," 79; *Winesburg, Ohio*, 77
"Andrea" (O'Hara), 1834
Andreas, 2687
"Andreuccio of Perugia" (Boccaccio), 269
Anecdote, 3056
"Angel Levine" (Malamud), 1598
"Angel of the Lord, The" (Howells), 1236
"Angelina: Or, L'Amie Inconnue" (Edgeworth), 811
"Angélique" (Nerval), 1757
Angelou, Maya, 83-86; "Reunion, The," 84; "Steady Going Up," 83
Anglophone African short fiction, 2851
Animal-Lover's Book of Beastly Murder, The (Highsmith), 1196
"Anitachi." *See* "My Older Brothers"
"Anna, Part I" (Gilchrist), 995
"Anonymiad" (Barth), 179
"Another Texas Ghost Story" (Brautigan), 346
"Another Time" (O'Brien, Edna), 1784
"Answer Is No, The" (Mahfouz), 1589
"Ant" (Dybek), 805
Antagonist, 3056
Anthology, 3056
"Anthony Afterwit" (Franklin), 904
"Antique Love Story, An" (Gilliatt), 1000
Antistory. *See* "Category Index"
Antologia da ficcao Cabo-Verdiana contemmporanea (Lopes), 2847
Apartheid, 2854
Apes, William, 2962
Aphorism, 3056
Aporia, 3056
Apostrophe, 3056
Apple, Max, 86-89; "Free Agents," 88; "Oranging of America, The," 87; "Selling Out," 87; "Walt and Will," 87
"Apple of Discord, The" (Humphrey), 1247
"Apple Tree, The" (Galsworthy), 946
Apples and Pears and Other Stories (Davenport), 687
Appropriation, 3056
"Approximations" (Simpson), 2155
"April" (Colette), 602
"Apropos of the Wet Snow" (Dostoevski), 2773
Apuleius, Lucius, 2664; *Metamorphoses*, 2664
"Aquatic Uncle, The" (Calvino), 426
"Arabesque: The Mouse" (Coppard), 642
Arabian Nights' Entertainments, The, 68, 2643, 2667, 2701, 2737
"Araby" (Joyce), 2918
Arbiter, Gaius Petronius. *See* Petronius
"Árbol, El." *See* "Tree, The" (Bombal)
Arcadia (Sidney), 2709, 2713
Archetectonics, 3057
Archetype, 3056-3057
"Arcturus" (Connell), 616
"Are You Too Late or Was I Too Early" (Collier), 609
"Area in the Cerebral Hemisphere, An" (Major), 1593
"Aren't You Happy for Me?" (Bausch), 204
"Argamak" (Babel), 132
Argentina. *See* "Geographical Index"
Argonautica (Rhodius), 2663
"Ark, The" (Zhang), 2581
Arkansas (Leavitt), 1467
Armstrong, Estelle; "Return, The," 2964
Arouet, François-Marie. *See* Voltaire
"Arrangement in Parents, An" (Hale), 1099
"Arrangements at the Gulf" (Stern), 2241
Arreola, Juan José, 89-95; "Baby H.P.," 93; "Bird Spider, The," 93; "Eve," 93; "Prodigious Milligram, The," 92; "Small Town Affair," 93; "Switchman, The," 92
Art of Living and Other Stories, The (Gardner), 961
"Artemis the Honest Well Digger" (Cheever), 534
"Artificial Nigger, The" (O'Connor, Flannery), 1797
"Artist at Work, The" (Camus, Albert), 432
"Aru kyuyu e okuru shuki." *See* "Memories Sent to an Old Friend"
Arvin, Newton, 2775
"As Fine as Melanctha" (Stein), 2229
"As Margens da Alegria." *See* "Thin Edge of Happiness, The"
"As the War Ended" (Böll), 274
"Ashikari" (Tanizaki), 2285
Asian American culture, 2871-2887. *See also* "Category Index"
Asian American Movement, 2871
Asian culture, 2908, 2928, 2935. *See also* "Category Index"
"Asian Shore, The" (Disch), 746
Aside, 3057
Asimov, Isaac, 95-102; "Dead Past, The," 99; "Liar!," 97; "Martian Way, The," 98; "Nightfall," 97, 2636
Aspects of the Novel (Forster), 2611
"Aspern Papers, The" (James, Henry), 1286
Assignation, The (Oates), 1777
"Dead Astronaut, The" (Ballard), 144
Astronomer and Other Stories, The (Betts), 253
Asturias, Miguel Ángel, 102-108, 2943; "Leyenda del sombrerón," 104; *Leyendas de Guatemala*, 104; *Men of Maize*, 104
"Asya" (Turgenev), 2356
"Asylum Piece" (Kavan), 1341
"At Kinosaki" (Shiga), 2933
"At Paso Rojo" (Bowles, Paul), 314
"At Sallygap" (Lavin), 1445

"At Sea" (Chekhov), 542
"At Sea" (Welch), 2467
"At the Anarchists' Convention" (Sayles), 2103
"At the Auction of the Ruby Slippers" (Rushdie), 2070
"At the Bay" (Mansfield), 1622
"At the Bottom of the Lake" (Broyard), 364
"At the Bottom of the River" (Kincaid), 1365
"At the Circus" (Sinyavsky), 2167
"At the Edge of the World" (Leskov), 1491
"At the Tolstoy Museum" (Barthelme, Donald), 187
"Athénaïse" (Chopin), 564
Atlakviða, 2686
Atmosphere, 3057
Atonement and Other Stories, The (Auchincloss), 122
"Atrocity Exhibition, The" (Ballard), 145
"Attack on the Mill, The" (Zola), 2587
"Attaque du Moulin, L'." *See* "Attack on the Mill, The"
Attila the Hun, 2685
Atwood, Margaret, 108-116, 2903; "Age of Lead, The," 113; "Bluebeard's Egg," 112; "Dancing Girls," 110; "Giving Birth," 111; *Good Bones and Simple Murders*, 114; "Man from Mars, The," 109; "Polarities," 111; "Significant Moments in the Life of My Mother," 112; "Unearthing Suite," 112; *Wilderness Tips*, 113
"Au Pair" (Weldon), 2474
Auchincloss, Louis, 116-123; *Atonement and Other Stories, The*, 122; *Fellow Passengers*, 121; *Injustice Collectors, The*, 118; *Partners, The*, 121; *Powers of Attorney*, 120; *Romantic Egoists, The*, 119; *Second Chance*, 121; *Tales of Manhattan*, 120
Auden, W. H., 2765
Audun and the Bear, 2678
"Augsburg Chalk Circle, The" (Brecht), 351
"August Eschenburg" (Millhauser), 1683
"Aunt Rosana's Rocker" (Mohr), 2958
Aura (Fuentes), 926
"Aurelia Frequenzia Reveals the Heart and Mind of the Man of Destiny" (Stern), 2242
"Auschwitz, Our Home (A Letter)" (Borowski), 296
Austen, Jane, 123-127; "Evelyn," 125; "Frederic and Elfrida," 125; *Lady Susan*, 125; *Love and Friendship*, 125
Australia, 2888-2889, 2897; 1920-1940, 2890; 1960-1980, 2891; 1980-2000, 2891. *See also* "Geographical Index"
Autobiographical stories. *See* "Category Index"
"Autobiography" (Barth), 2829
"Autumn Day" (Gallant), 941
"Autumn Sunshine" (Trevor), 2925
"Average Waves in Unprotected Waters" (Tyler, Anne), 2367
"Avril." *See* "April"
"Avventura di una bagnante, L'." *See* "Adventure of a Bather, The"
"Awakening" (Babel), 130
"Axolotl" (Cortázar), 646
"Aye, and Gomorrah" (Delany), 710
"Ayor" (Leavitt), 1465

Ba Jin, 2910
Babel, Isaac, 128-135, 2820; "Afonka Bida," 132; "Argamak," 132; "Awakening," 130; "Berestechko," 132; "Childhood: At Grandmother's," 129; "Crossing into Poland," 131; "Death of Dolgushov, The," 132, 2820; "Di Grasso," 130; "End of the Old Folks' Home, The," 131; "Father, The," 130; "First Love," 129; "Gedali," 131; "How It Was Done in Odessa," 130; "In the Basement," 130; "King, The," 130; "Letter, A," 131; "Lyubka the Cossack," 130; "Mama, Rimma, and Alla," 133; "My First Goose," 132, 2820; "Rabbi, The," 132; *Red Cavalry*, 131; "Salt," 132; "Sashka Khristov," 132; "Sin of Jesus, The," 133; "Story of My Dovecote, The," 129; "Tale of a Woman, The," 133; *Tales of Odessa*, 130; "Widow, The," 133
Babe's Bed, The (Wescott), 2493
"Babette's Feast" (Dinesen), 742
Babouc (Voltaire), 2412
Babrius, 2627
"Baby" (Sontag), 2195
"Baby H.P." (Arreola), 93
"Babylon Revisited" (Fitzgerald), 868
"Babyproofing" (Slavin), 2172
"Babysitter, The" (Coover), 2829
Bacho, Peter, 2882; *Dark Blue Suit and Other Stories*, 2882
"Back for Christmas" (Collier), 607
Back in the World (Wolff), 2552
"Backseat" (Wideman), 2514
"Bad Man Blues" (Garrett), 973
Bad Man Blues (Garrett), 972
Bader, Arno Lehman, 2607
"Bagatelles, The" (Franklin), 2730
Bagombo Snuff Box (Vonnegut), 2421
Baihua short fiction, 2909, 2911
"Bailbondsman, The" (Elkin), 823
Bailey, H. C., 2618
"Balaam and His Master" (Harris, Joel Chandler), 1125
Balaam and His Master and Other Sketches and Stories (Harris, Joel Chandler), 1125
Baldeshwiler, Sister Mary Joselyn, 2606
Baldwin, James, 135-140, 161; "Going to Meet the Man," 137; "Man Child, The," 136; "Sonny's Blues," 138
Baliverneries (Noël Du Fail), 2705
"Ball of Malt and Madame Butterfly, A" (Kiely), 1357
Ballad, 3057
"Ballad of the Flexible Bullet, The" (King), 1372
"Ballad of the Sad Café, The" (McCullers), 1560

Ballard, J. G., 141-147, 2639; "Atrocity Exhibition, The," 145; "Cage of Sand, The," 143, 2639; "Concentration City," 143; "Dead Astronaut, The," 144; "Enormous Space, The," 145; "Manhole Sixty-nine," 143; "Memories of the Space Age," 144; "Myths of the Near Future," 143; "Overloaded Man, The," 145; "Terminal Beach, The," 144; "War Fever," 146
"Balloon, The" (Barthelme, Donald), 185, 2829
"Balloons'n Tunes" (Wiggins), 2518
"Balthasar" (France), 899
Balzac, Honoré de, 147-152, 2750; *Droll Stories*, 149; "Facino Cane," 150; "Grande Bretèche, The," 149, 2750; "Unknown Masterpiece, The," 149
Bambara, Toni Cade, 152-156, 2869; "Gorilla, My Love," 154; *Gorilla, My Love*, 154, 2869; "Lesson, The," 155; "Medley," 155; "Raymond's Run," 154; "Talkin' 'Bout Sonny," 2869
"Bang-Bang You're Dead" (Spark), 2199
Bank, Melissa, 156-159; "Advanced Beginners," 157; "Girls' Guide to Hunting and Fishing, The," 158; "Worst Thing a Suburban Girl Could Imagine, The," 158
Banks, Russell, 160-165; "Conversion, The," 162; "Custodian, The," 162; *New World, The*, 162; "Queen for a Day," 164; "Sarah Cole: A Type of Love Story," 164; *Searching for Survivors*, 162; *Success Stories*, 164; *Trailerpark*, 163
Baotown (Wang), 2445
Baraka, Amiri, 165-169, 2867; "Alternative, The," 167; "Chase, A," 167; "Death of Horatio Alger, The," 167; *Native Son*, 167; "Screamers, The," 167; *Tales*, 166; "Uncle Tom's Cabin: Alternate Ending," 166
"Barbados" (Marshall), 1635
"Barbara of the House of Grebe" (Hardy), 1115
"Bardon Bus" (Munro), 1733
"Barishnya krestyanka." *See* "Squire's Daughter, The"
Barker, Clive, 2652
"Barn Burning" (Faulkner), 861
Barnes, Julian, 169-172, 2841; "Dragons," 170, 2841; "Evermore," 171; "Hermitage," 171; "Interference," 170; "Tunnel," 171
"Baron of Patronia, The" (Vizenor), 2968
Barrett, Andrea, 173-175, 2840; "Behavior of the Hawkweeds, The," 173, 2840; "Birds with No Feet," 174; "Littoral Zone, The," 174; "Ship Fever," 174
Barth, John, 176-181, 2828; "Anonymiad," 179; "Autobiography," 2829; "Lost in the Funhouse, 178; *Lost in the Funhouse*, 176; "Night-Sea Journey, 177; *On with the Story*, 180
Barthelme, Donald, 182-190, 2829; "At the Tolstoy Museum," 187; "Balloon, The," 185, 2829; "Glass Mountain, The," 188; "Indian Uprising, The," 185; "Leap, The," 187; "Me and Miss Mandible," 184; "New Music, The," 188; "Nothing: A Preliminary Account," 188; "Robert Kennedy Saved from Drowning," 186; "Sentence," 188; "Shower of Gold, A," 184; "Three Hermits, The," 187; "Views of My Father Weeping," 186
Barthelme, Frederick, 190-193; "Chroma," 192; "Driver," 192; "Safeway," 191; "Shopgirls," 191
"Bartleby the Scrivener" (Melville), 1666, 2629, 2775
"Base of the Wall, The" (Wang), 2445
"Basement Room, The" (Greene, Graham), 1077, 2814
Bass, Rick, 194-197; "Fires," 195; "In the Loyal Mountains," 195; "Myths of Bears, The," 196; "Watch, The," 195; "Wejumpka," 196
Bates, H. E., 197-203; *Black Boxer, The*, 200; *Colonel Julian and Other Stories*, 200; "Cowslip Field, The," 201; *Daffodil Sky, The*, 201; *Day's End and Other Stories*, 199; *Flying Goat, The*, 200; "Frontier, The," 201; "Maker of Coffins, The," 201; *My Uncle Silas*, 200; *Something Short and Sweet*, 200; *Watercress Girl and Other Stories, The*, 201
"Bath, The" (Carver), 2831
"Batorsag and Szerelem" (Canin), 436
Bats Out of Hell (Hannah), 1110
"Battle of Dorking, The" (Chesney), 2633
"Battle of Finney's Ford, The" (West), 2497
Battle of Maldon, 2686
"Battle Royal" (Ellison, Ralph), 2865
Bausch, Richard, 203-206; "Aren't You Happy for Me?," 204; "Brace, The," 205; "Not Quite Final," 204; "Valor," 205
Baxter, Charles, 207-210; *Believers*, 209; "Fensted's Mother," 208; *Harmony of the World*, 208; "Relative Stranger, A," 208; *Relative Stranger, A*, 208
Baynton, Barbara, 2889; "Chosen Vessel, The," 2889; "Squeaker's Mate," 2889
"Beach of Falesá, The" (Stevenson), 2248
"Beantwortung einer anfrage." *See* "Response to a Request"
"Bear, The" (Faulkner), 860, 2804
"Bear and His Daughter" (Stone), 2257
Bear and His Daughter (Stone), 2255
Beard, Thomas; *Theatre of Gods Judgements, The*, 2719
"Bearded Lady, The" (Queen), 2014
"Bears in Mourning" (Mars-Jones), 1632
"Beast, The" (Brecht), 349
"Beast in the Jungle, The" (James, Henry), 1288
Beasts and Super-Beasts (Saki), 2074
"Beating" (Gates), 982
Beattie, Ann, 210-217, 2831; "Burning House, The," 2832; "Cinderella Waltz, The," 213; "Dwarf House," 212; "Going Home With Uccello," 215; "Janus," 214, 2832; "Lifeguard, The," 212; "Park City," 215; "Snow," 214; "Vintage Thunderbird, A," 212; "Weekend," 2831;

"Windy Day at the Reservoir," 215; "Winter: 1978," 213
"Beautiful Girl" (Adams), 12
"Beautiful Stranger, The" (Jackson), 1275
"Beautiful Vampire, The" (Gautier), 985
"Because My Father Always Said He Was the Only Indian Who Saw Jimi Hendrix Play 'The Star-Spangled Banner' at Woodstock" (Alexie), 56-57
"Because They Wanted To" (Gaitskill), 937
Beckett, Samuel, 218-224; "All Strange Away," 222; *Company*, 222; "End, The," 221; "First Love," 220; "Imagination Dead Imagine," 222
Beckoning Fair One, The (Onions), 2649
Bede the Venerable, Saint, 2683; *Ecclesiastical History of the English People*, 2683
Beerbohm, Max, 225-229; "A. V. Laider," 2797; *Christmas Garland, Woven by Max Beerbohm, A*, 228; "Enoch Soames," 226; "Mote in the Middle Distance, H*nry J*m*s, The," 228; "'Savonarola' Brown," 227; *Seven Men*, 226
"Before His Time" (Oz), 1862
"Before the Law" (Kafka), 1332
"Beggar, The" (Chekhov), 544
"Beggars, The" (O'Flaherty), 1830
"Beggarwoman of Locarno, The" (Kleist), 1404
"Beginning, The" (Grau), 1068
"Beginning of an Idea, The" (McGahern), 1568, 2924
"Beginning of Grief, The" (Woiwode), 2540
"Beginning of Homewood, The" (Wideman), 2512
"Behavior of the Hawkweeds, The" (Barrett), 173, 2840
Behn, Aphra, 2723; *History of the Nun, The*, 2723
Beitong zhidi (Wang), 2447
Bela e a fera, A (Lispector), 1520
Believe Them (Robison), 2056
Believers (Baxter), 209
Bell, Madison Smartt, 230-233; "Customs of the Country," 231; "Dragon's Seed," 232; "Irene," 231; "Today Is a Good Day to Die," 231; "Triptych I," 230
"Bella-Vista" (Colette), 601
"Belle Zoraide, La" (Chopin), 564, 2787
Bellow, Saul, 233-239, 2812; *Actual, The*, 237; "Cousins," 237; "Gonzaga Manuscripts, The," 235; *Him with His Foot in His Mouth and Other Stories*, 236; "Looking for Mr Green," 234; "Mosby's Memoirs," 236; *Mosby's Memoirs and Other Stories*, 234; *Seize the Day*, 2812; "Silver Dish, A," 237; *What Kind of Day Did You Have?*, 237
"Belye nochi." *See* "White Nights"
"Ben ci lie che zhong dian zhan." *See* "Destination"
Bender, Aimee, 239-242; "Call My Name," 240; "Dreaming in Polish," 241; "Ring, The," 241; "Skinless," 241; "What You Left in the Ditch," 241
"Beneath the Shelter" (Mahfouz), 1588
Benét, Stephen Vincent, 242-248; "Devil and Daniel Webster, The," 244; "Freedom's a Hard-Bought Thing," 245; "Johnny Pye and the Fool-Killer," 246
Bennett, Gwendolyn, 2863; "Tokens," 2863; "Typewriter, The," 2864; "Wedding Day," 2863
"Benson Watts Is Dead and in Virginia" (Betts), 255
Benson, E. F., 2650
Bentley, E. C.; *Trent and the Last Case*, 2617; *Trent Intervenes*, 2618
Beowulf, 2663
"Berestechko" (Babel), 132
Berriault, Gina, 248-251; "Bystander, The," 249; "Death of a Lesser Man," 250; "Diary of K. W.," 250; "Infinite Passion of Expectation, The," 250; "Stone Boy, The," 250
"Bess" (Phillips), 1924
"Best Girlfriend You Never Had, The" (Houston), 1232
"Best Quality" (Tan), 2282
"Bestiary" (Cortázar), 645
Bet They'll Miss Us When We're Gone (Wiggins), 2517
Betrogene, Die. See *Black Swan, The*
"Bettelweib von Locarno, Das." *See* "Beggarwoman of Locarno, The"
Betts, Doris, 252-257; *Astronomer and Other Stories, The*, 253; "Benson Watts Is Dead and in Virginia," 255; *Gentle Insurrection and Other Stories, The*, 252; "Miss Parker Possessed," 253; "Spies in the Herb House, The," 255
"Between the Lines" (Smith, Lee), 2183
"Between Zero and One" (Gallant), 943
"Beverly Home" (Johnson, Denis), 1311
"Bewitched Jacket, The" (Buzzati), 384
"Beyond the Glass Mountain" (Stegner), 2222
"Beyond the Pale" (Kipling), 1390
"Beyond the Pale" (Trevor), 2925
"Bezhin Meadow" (Turgenev), 2355, 2772
Biafra, 5
Bible, 2626, 2658
"Biblioteca de Babel, La." *See* "Library of Babel, The"
Bierce, Ambrose, 257-262, 2601, 2649, 2758, 2788; "Chickamauga," 259, 2788; "Damned Thing, The," 260; "Death of Halprin Frayser, The," 2649; *Devil's Dictionary, The*, 258; "Inhabitant of Carcosa, An," 2649; "Man and the Snake, The," 2788; "Occurrence at Owl Creek Bridge, An," 258, 2788-2789; *Tales of Soldiers and Civilians*, 2649
Big Aiiieeeee!, The, 2872
Big Bad Love (Brown), 362
"Big Bertha Stories" (Mason), 1643, 2833
"Big Blonde" (Parker), 1885
"Big Garage, The" (Boyle, T. C.), 326
"Big Meeting" (Hughes), 1241
Big Sea, The (Hughes), 1238

"Biggest Band, The" (Cassill), 482
Bing Xin, 2910
"Bird in the House, A" (Laurence), 1441
Bird in the House, A (Laurence), 1441
"Bird Spider, The" (Arreola), 93
"Birds of God, The" (Couto), 2848
"Birds with No Feet" (Barrett), 174
"Birth" (Nin), 1762
"Birthday" (Louie), 2876
"Birthday" (Viramontes), 2957
"Birthmark, The" (Hawthorne), 1148
"Birthmark, The" (Kavan), 1340
"Bisclayret" (Marie de France), 1627
"Bishop's Fool, The" (Lewis), 1505
"Biter, The" (Steele), 2727
"Black Angels" (Friedman), 917
Black Arts movement, 2866
Black Boxer, The (Bates), 200
"Black Death" (Hurston), 2862
Black House, The (Highsmith), 1197
Black humor, 916, 3057
Black humor. *See* "Category Index"
"Black Is My Favorite Color" (Malamud), 1599
"Black Magic of Barney Haller, The" (Thurber), 2314
"Black Peril" (Plomer), 1939
Black Spirits and White (Cram), 2649
Black Swan, The (Mann), 1612
Black Venus (Carter), 471
"Black Winter" (Woiwode), 2542
"Blackberry Winter" (Warren), 2457
"Blackmailers Don't Shoot" (Chandler), 507
Blackwood, Algernon, 262-265, 2646, 2797; "Damned, The," 264; "Empty House, The," 263; *John Silence*, 264; "Man Whom the Trees Loved, The," 264; "Willows, The," 264, 2797
"Blank Page, The" (Dinesen), 2817
"Bleeding Heart, The" (Stafford), 2210-2211
"Blessings" (Dubus), 2835
"Blind Love" (Pritchett), 1973
"Blind Man, The" (Lawrence), 1452
"Blind Man's Tale, A" (Tanizaki), 2285
"Blinder" (Gordimer), 1044
"Blindness" (Woiwode), 2542
Blish, James, 2638; "Surface Tension," 2638
"Bliss" (Mansfield), 1619
"Blizzard, The" (Pushkin), 2000
Blonde Eckbert, Der. See *Fair Eckbert*
"Blood-Burning Moon" (Toomer), 2337
"Bloodfall" (Boyle, T. C.), 326
Bloodline (Gaines), 930, 933
"Bloody Chamber, The" (Carter), 2841
"Blow-Up" (Cortázar), 647
"Blowups Happen" (Heinlein), 2636
"Blue and Green" (Woolf), 2556
Blue City (Macdonald), 2621
"Blue Cross, The" (Chesterton), 558
"Blue Dive" (Chappell), 516
"Blue Hotel, The" (Crane), 659, 2790
"Blue Island" (Powers), 1959
"Blue Kimono, The" (Callaghan), 419
"Blue Lick" (Offutt), 1824
"Bluebeard's Egg" (Atwood), 112
"Bluebell Meadow" (Kiely), 1360
"Blundell's Improvement" (Jacobs), 1281
"Blush, The" (Taylor, Elizabeth), 2293
"Bob, A Dog" (Smith), 2184
Boccaccio, Giovanni, 266-271, 2702; "Andreuccio of Perugia," 269; "Cisti the Baker," 269; *Decameron, The*, 268, 2702; "Ser Cepparelo," 269
Bödeln. See *Hangman, The*
Bodkin, M. McDonnell, 2615
"Body, The" (King), 1371
Böll, Heinrich, 272-277; "And There Was the Evening and the Morning," 274; "As the War Ended," 274; "Breaking the News," 275; "Murke's Collected Silences," 274; "My Expensive Leg," 275; "Stranger, Bear Word to the Spartans We . . . ," 275; "Waiting-Room, The," 276
Bombal, María Luisa, 278-281; "Braids," 279; "Final Mist, The," 278; "New Islands," 280; "Tree, The," 279; "Unknown, The," 279
"Bones of Louella Brown, The" (Petry), 1921
Bontemps, Arna, 281-285; "Talk to the Music," 284
"Bontshe the Silent" (Peretz), 1908
"Book Buyers, The" (Kinsella), 1383
Book of Martyrs, The (Foxe), 2718
Book of Settlements (Thorgilsson), 2671
Book of the Duchess (Chaucer), 520
"Book of the Grotesque, The" (Anderson), 78
Book of the Icelanders (Thorgilsson), 2671
"Book That Was Lost, A" (Agnon), 27
Book That Was Lost and Other Stories, A (Agnon), 26
Borges, Jorge Luis, 285, 294, 2652, 2822, 2942; "Circular Ruins, The," 290; "Death and the Compass," 289; "Funes the Memorious," 2822; "Garden of Forking Paths, The," 290; "Library of Babel, The," 2823; "Pierre Menard, Author of the *Quixote*," 291, 2822; "South, The," 291; "Tlon, Uqbar, Orbis Tertius," 2823
"Boring Story, A" (Chekhov), 545
Borowski, Tadeusz, 295-299; "Auschwitz, Our Home (A Letter)," 296; "Day at Harmenz," 297; "Silence," 298; "Supper, The," 298; "This Way for the Gas, Ladies and Gentlemen," 297; "World of Stone," 298
Borrowed Time (Rasputin), 2025
"Boston" (Harjo), 1119
Boswell, James, 1314

"Botschaft, Die." *See* "Breaking the News"
"Bottle of Milk for Mother, A" (Algren), 60
"Bottle Party" (Collier), 609
Boudinot, Elias, 2962
"Boule de Suif" (Maupassant), 1655
"Bound Man, The" (Aichinger), 30
Bowen, Elizabeth, 300-306, 2605, 2922; *Collected Stories of Elizabeth Bowen, The*, 2922; "Demon Lover, The," 303, 2922; "Her Table Spread," 301, 2922; "Summer Night," 301
Bowles, Jane, 306-310; "Camp Cataract," 308; "Day in the Open, A," 307; "Everything Is Nice," 309; "Guatemalan Idyll, A," 307; "Plain Pleasures," 308; "Stick of Green Candy, A," 309
Bowles, Paul, 311-317, 2652; "At Paso Rojo," 314; "Delicate Prey, The," 314; "Distant Episode, A," 313; "Echo, The," 313; "Pages from Cold Point," 313; "Tapiama," 314; *Too Far from Home*, 315
"Bowmen, The" (Machen), 1576
"Box, The" (Endō), 845
"Box Seat" (Toomer), 2338
"Boxes" (Carver), 478
"Boy of Pergamum, The" (Petronius), 1912
Boy Without a Flag, The (Rodriguez), 2958
Boyle, Kay, 317-324; "Wedding Day," 319; "White Horses of Vienna, The," 320; "Winter Night," 322
Boyle, Patrick; "All Looks Yellow to the Jaundiced Eye," 2926
Boyle, T. Coraghessan, 325-330, 2836; "Big Garage, The," 326; "Bloodfall," 326; "Carnal Knowledge," 329; "Filthy with Things," 329; "Hector Quesadilla Story, The," 328; "Overcoat II, The, 327; "Sorry Fugu," 328; *T. C. Boyle Stories*, 329; "Two Ships," 327; *Without a Hero*, 329
"Brace, The" (Bausch), 205
Bradbury, Ray, 331-341, 2637, 2652; *Dark Carnival*, 335; *Golden Apples of the Sun, The*, 336; *I Sing the Body Electric!*, 338; *Illustrated Man, The*, 336; *Long After Midnight*, 338; *Machineries of Joy, The*, 337; *Martian Chronicles, The*, 335, 2637; *Medicine for Melancholy, A*, 337; "Next in Line, The," 335; *October Country, The*, 337; *Quicker than the Eye*, 339; *Stories of Ray Bradbury, The*, 338; "Third Expedition, The," 336; *Toynbee Convector, The*, 338
"Braids" (Bombal), 279
Bramah, Ernest, 2614
"Branch Road, A" (Garland), 966
Brant, Beth; "Coyote Learns a New Trick," 2969
Brautigan, Richard, 341-347; "Another Texas Ghost Story," 346; "Cleveland Wrecking Yard, The," 344; "Corporal," 345; "Kool-Aid Wino, The," 344; "Menu/1965, The," 346; "Revenge of the Lawn," 344; *Tokyo-Montana Express, The*, 345; *Trout Fishing in America*, 343; "Trout Fishing on the Bevel," 344; "Werewolf Raspberries," 346; "World War I Los Angeles Airplane, The," 345
"Brave and Cruel" (Welch), 2469
Brave Little Toaster, The (Disch), 747
Brave Little Toaster Goes to Mars, The (Disch), 747
"Brazil" (Marshall), 1636
Brazilian culture, 2936. *See also* "Geographical Index"
Bread of Salt and Other Stories, The (Gonzalez), 2882
"Breaking the News" (Böll), 275
Brecht, Bertolt, 348-354; "Augsburg Chalk Circle, The," 351; "Beast, The," 349; "Caesar and His Legionnaire," 350; "Wounded Socrates, The," 350
"Brethren" (Bunin), 374
"Breton Innkeeper, A" (Lewis), 1504
Briar Rose (Coover), 636
"Bride, The" (Chekhov), 547
"Bride Comes to Yellow Sky, The" (Crane), 659
"Bridge of Dreams, The" (Tanizaki), 2285, 2933
"Bridle, The" (Carver), 477
"Brief an einen besteller von novellen." *See* "Letter to a Commissioner of Novellas"
"Brief Fall, A" (Woiwode), 2541
"Brigadier and the Golf Widow, The" (Cheever), 538
"Brim Beauvais" (Stein), 2230
"British Guiana" (Marshall), 1636
"Britva." *See* "Razor, The"
"Broadsheet Ballad, A" (Coppard), 640
Broadside ballad, 3057
Brocade Valley (Wang), 2446
Brodkey, Harold, 354-359; "Bullies," 358; "Ceil," 357; *First Love and Other Sorrows*, 356; "Innocence," 356-357; "Sentimental Education," 356; "Waking," 358; *World Is the Home of Love and Death, The*, 358
"Brokeback Mountain" (Proulx), 1981, 2840
"Broken Homes" (Trevor), 2344
"Bromeliads" (Williams, Joy), 2522
"Brooklyn" (Marshall), 1636
Brooks, Cleanth; *Understanding Fiction*, 2607
"Brother Frank's Gospel Hour" (Kinsella), 1387
"Brother Jacob" (Eliot), 818
Brown, Larry, 360-363; *Big Bad Love*, 362; "End of Romance, The," 361; *Facing the Music*, 361; "Waiting for the Ladies," 362
Brown Dog (Harrison), 1130
Broyard, Bliss, 363-366; "At the Bottom of the Lake," 364; "Day in the Country, A," 365; "Loose Talk," 365; "Mr. Sweetly Indecent," 364; "My Father, Dancing," 364; *My Father, Dancing*, 364; "Snowed In," 365; "Trouble with Mr. Leopold, The," 365; "Ugliest Faces," 365
Brunetière, Ferdinand, 2749
"Brush Fire" (Cain), 401

"Brush-Wood Boy, The" (Kipling), 1391
"Bubba Stories, The" (Smith), 2185
Buck, Pearl S., 366-372; "Enemy, The," 368; "Good Deed, The," 369; "Hearts Come Home," 369
"Buck in the Hills, The" (Clark), 585
"Bucket Rider, The" (Kafka), 1332
"Buczacz" (Agnon), 27
"Bud Parrot" (Robison), 2054
Buddhism, 2908
Budō denraiki (Ihara Saikaku), 1265
"Buenaventura, Le." *See* "Prophecy, The"
"Buffalo" (Reid), 2029
"Bufords, The" (Spencer), 2205
Buke giri monogatari. See *Tales of Samurai Honor*
"Bull" (Kinsella), 1386
Bulletin, 2888
"Bullies" (Brodkey), 358
Bulosan, Carlos, 2882; *America Is in the Heart*, 2882
Bulwer-Lytton, Edward; "Haunted and the Haunters, The," 2770
"Bums in the Attic" (Cisneros), 581
Bunch, David R., 2640
"Bunchgrass Edge of the World, The" (Proulx), 1982
Bunin, Ivan, 372-377; "Brethren," 374; "Gentleman from San Francisco, The," 375; "Grammar of Love," 374; "Son, The," 374
"Burial" (Woiwode), 2541
Burlesque, 3057
"Burning House, The" (Beattie), 2832
"But at the Stroke of Midnight" (Warner), 2453
Butler, Robert Olen, 377-380; "American Couple, The," 379; "Crickets," 378; "Good Scent from a Strange Mountain, A," 379; *Tabloid Dreams*, 379; "*Titanic* Victim Speaks Through Waterbed," 379
Buzzati, Dino, 381-386; "Bewitched Jacket, The," 384; "Catastrophe," 384; "Colomber, The," 384; "Count's Wife, The," 385; "Scala Scare, The," 383; "Seven Floors," 383; "Seven Messengers," 383; "Suicidio al parco," 384
Byatt, A. S., 387-390, 2840; "Glass Coffin, The," 389; "Lamia in the Cévennes, A," 389; "Medusa's Ankles," 388, 2840; "Sugar," 388
Byers, Michael, 390-393, 2839; "Dirigibles," 391; "Fair Trade, A," 392; "In Spain, One Thousand and Three," 392; "Settled on the Cranberry Coast," 391, 2839; "Shipmates Down Under," 392
"Bystander, The" (Berriault), 249Cable, George Washington, 394-400, 2779; "Jean-ah Poquelin," 397, 2780; "Posson Jone," 2779; "'Sieur George," 395, 2780

Cadalso y Vásquez, José de; *Cartas marruecas*, 2733
"Caesar and His Legionnaire" (Brecht), 350
"Cage of Sand, The" (Ballard), 143, 2639
Cain, James M., 400-403; "Brush Fire," 401
Cakewalk (Smith), 2183
Caldwell, Erskine, 404-409; "Candy-Man Beechum," 407; "Growing Season, The," 406; "Kneel to the Rising Sun," 406; "Saturday Afternoon," 406
Calisher, Hortense, 409-415; "If You Don't Want to Live I Can't Help You," 411; "In Greenwich There Are Many Gravelled Walks," 410; "Middle Drawer, The," 412; Novellas of Hortense Calisher, The, 413
"Call My Name" (Bender), 240
"Call of Cthulhu, The" (Lovecraft), 1537
Callaghan, Morley, 415-422, 2901; "Amuck in the Bush," 418; "Blue Kimono, The," 419; "Cap for Steve, A," 421; "Cheat's Remorse, The," 420; "Country Passion, A," 417; "Escapade, An," 418; *In His Own Country*, 418; *Lost and Found Stories of Morley Callaghan, The*, 421; *Morley Callaghan's Stories*, 420; *Now That April's Here and Other Stories*, 419; "Predicament, A," 418; "Sick Call, A," 420; "Wedding Dress, A," 418
Calvino, Italo, 423-428; "Adam, One Afternoon," 425; "Adventure of a Bather, The," 425; "Aquatic Uncle, The," 426; "Crow Comes Last, The," 425; "Games Without End," 426
"Camberwell Beauty, The" (Pritchett) , 1974
"Cambio de armas." *See* "Other Weapons"
"Camino hacia el norte, Un" (Allende), 69
"Camionista, Il." *See* "Lorry Driver, The"
"Camp Cataract" (Bowles, Jane), 308
Campbell, John W., Jr., 2635, 2637
Campbell, Ramsey, 2652
Campomanes, Oscar, 2881
Camus, Albert, 429-433, 2819; "Adulterous Woman, The," 430; "Artist at Work, The," 432; "Growing Stone, The," 431; "Guest, The," 430, 2819; "Renegade, The," 432; "Silent Men, The," 432
Camus, Jean-Pierre; *Dorothée*, 2719; *Palombre*, 2719
Canada, 2898-2907; *1880-1900*, 2900; French speaking, 2899, 2902; early 1900's, 2901; mid-1900's, 2902; *1970-1990*, 2904. *See also* "Geographical Index"
Canby, Henry Seidel, 2600, 2603-2605; *Short Story in English, The*, 2600
Cancerqueen (Landolfi), 1430
Candide (Voltaire), 2412
"Candy-Man Beechum" (Caldwell), 407
Cane (Toomer), 2335-2339
Canin, Ethan, 434-437; "Accountant," 435; "Batorsag and Szerelem," 436; "City of Broken Hearts," 436; *Emperor of the Air*, 434; *Palace Thief, The*, 435; "Star Food," 435; "Year of Getting to Know Us, The," 435
Canon, 3057
Canonize, 3057
Cantar de ciegos (Fuentes), 926

Canterbury Tales, The (Chaucer), 524, 2704. *See also* "Knight's Tale, The," "Miller's Tale, The," and "Reeve's Tale, The"
Cantilena of St. Eulalia, 2688
"Cantleman's Spring-Mate" (Lewis), 1504, 1506
"Cap for Steve, A" (Callaghan), 421
Čapek, Karel, 437-441; *Fairy Tales*, 439; *Money and Other Stories*, 439; "Scandal and the Press, A," 439; "Tribunal," 439
Capellanus, 2696
"Capital Girl, A" (Fuentes), 927
Capote, Truman, 441-445; "Master Misery," 443; "Tree of Night, A," 442
Captain Maximus (Hannah), 1110
"Car Crash While Hitchhiking" (Johnson, Denis), 1311
Card, Orson Scott, 446-451; "Kingsmeat," 447; *Magic Mirror*, 449; "Porcelain Salamander, The," 448
Cardiff Team, The (Davenport), 689
Carey, Peter, 451-454; "American Dreams," 454, 2891; "Do You Love Me?," 452; "Fat Man in History,The," 453; "Kristu-Du," 452; "Withdrawal," 453
"Cariboo Café, The" (Viramontes), 2405, 2956
Caricature, 3057
Carleton, William, 455-460, 2915; "Lough Derg Pilgrim, The," 457; "Phelim O'Toole's Courtship," 457; "Three Tasks, The," 456; "Tubber Derg," 458; "Wildgoose Lodge," 2915
Carmen (Mérimée), 1673
"Carmilla" (Le Fanu), 1472
"Carnal Knowledge" (Boyle, T. C.), 329
Carpentier, Alejo, 460-464, 2943; "Like the Night," 461
Carr, John Dickson, 464-468; "All in a Maze," 466; "Door to Doom, The," 466; "Incautious Burglar, The," 467; "Invisible Hands," 467; "Shadow of the Goat, The," 466
Cartas marruecas (Cadalso y Vásquez), 2733
Carter, Angela, 469-472, 2652, 2840; *American Ghosts and Old World Wonders*, 471; *Black Venus*, 471; "Bloody Chamber, The," 2841; "Company of Wolves, The," 470; "Reflections," 470
Cartesian Sonata (Gass), 979
Carver, Raymond, 472-480, 2830; "Bath, The," 2831; "Boxes," 478; "Bridle, The," 477; "Cathedral," 2831; "Fat," 474; "Neighbors," 475, 2830; "Small, Good Thing, A," 2831; "Where I'm Calling From," 477; "Why Don't You Dance?," 476, 2830
"Case for Lombroso, A" (Norris), 1768
"Case of the Discontented Husband, The" (Christie), 576
"Case of the Discontented Soldier, The" (Christie), 576
"Case of the Missing Lady, The" (Christie), 576
Casey, Gavin, 2890; "Short-Shift Saturday," 2890
"Cask of Amontillado, The" (Poe), 2765
Cassill, R. V., 481-485; "Biggest Band, The," 482; "Crime of Mary Lynn Yager, The," 483; "Sunday Painter, The," 483
Cassirer, Ernst, 2759
Castle of Otranto, The (Walpole), 2643, 2729, 2756
Castle Rackrent (Edgeworth), 2914
"Casualty" (Lessing), 1499
"Catalogue of the Exhibition: The Art of Edmund Moorash (1810-1846)" (Millhauser), 1684
"Catastrophe" (Buzzati), 384
"Catch, The" (Ōe), 1811
"Cathedral" (Carver), 2831
Cather, Willa, 485-490; "Neighbor Rosicky," 488; "Paul's Case," 487, 2790; "Sculptor's Funeral, The," 486; "Uncle Valentine," 488
"Cavalleria rusticana." *See* "Rustic Chivalry"
"Cave, The" (Zamyatin), 2576
Caxton, William; *Aesop*, 2628
"Ceci n'est pas un conte." *See* "This Is Not a Story"
"Ceil" (Brodkey), 357
"Celebrated Jumping Frog of Calaveras County, The" (Twain), 2361
"Celestial Omnibus, The" (Forster), 889
"Celestina" (Moravia), 1706
Celestina, La (Rojas), 2720
"Celia Single" (Franklin), 904
Cena Trimalchionis (Petronius), 1912-1913
"Census Taker, The" (Oates), 1774
Cent nouvelles nouvelles, Les. See *One Hundred Merrie and Delightsome Stories*
Ceremony (Silko), 2960
Certain Tragical Discourses (Fenton), 2711
Cervantes, Miguel de, 491-499, 2706, 2721; "Colloquy of the Dogs," 494; *Exemplary Novels*, 493, 2706, 2720; "Glass Scholar, The," 496
Chabon, Michael, 499-505; "Little Knife, The," 503; "Model World, A," 501; "S ANGEL," 500; "Werewolves in Their Youth," 504
"Chac Mool" (Fuentes), 925
Chaereas and Callirhoe (Chariton), 2666
"Chain of Love, A" (Price), 1963
"Chair of Tears, The" (Vizenor), 2408
Chambers, Robert W., 2649; "Repairer of Reputations, The," 2649
"Chameleon, The" (Chekhov), 542
"Champion" (Lardner), 1435
Chan, Jeffrey, 2875; "Chinese in Haifa, The," 2875; "Jackrabbit," 2875
Chandler, Raymond, 505-510, 2617; "Blackmailers Don't Shoot," 507; "Guns at Cyrano's," 508; "Red Wind," 508
Chang, Lan Samantha, 511-514; "Eve of the Spirit Festival, The," 512; *Hunger*, 511; "Pippa's Story," 512; "Unforgetting, The," 512

"Chao-ch'âng hu." *See* "Tiger of Zhaochang, The"
Chappell, Fred, 514-518; "Blue Dive," 516; "Linnaeus Forgets," 517; "Lodger, The," 516; "Maker of One Coffin, The," 515; "Moments of Light," 516; *More Shapes than One*, 516; "Somewhere Doors, The," 517
Character type, 3057
Chariton; *Chaereas and Callirhoe*, 2666
"Chase (Alighieri's Dream), A" (Baraka), 167
"Chaser, The" (Collier), 607-608
Chaucer, Geoffrey, 518-531, 2628, 2704; *Book of the Duchess*, 520; *Canterbury Tales, The*, 524, 2704; "Clerk's Tale, The," 528; "Complaint of Mars, The," 519; "Franklin's Tale, The," 529; *Hous of Fame*, 520; "Knight's Tale, The," 525; *Legend of Good Women*, 522; "Merchant's Tale, The," 529; "Miller's Tale, The," 526; "Nun's Priest's Tale, The," 527; "Prioresss Tale, The," 527; "Reeve's Tale, The," 527; *Troilus and Criseyde*, 522
Chavez, Denise, 2956; *Last of the Menu Girls, The*, 2956
Chavez, Fray Angelico, 2952
"Chawdron" (Huxley), 1258
"Cheat's Remorse, The" (Callaghan), 420
Cheever, John, 532-540, 2810, 2827, 2857; "Artemis the Honest Well Digger," 534; "Brigadier and the Golf Widow, The," 538; "Country Husband, The," 537; "Death of Justina, The," 537; "Enormous Radio, The," 534, 2810; "Five-Forty-Eight, The," 536; "Goodbye, My Brother," 535; "Miscellany of Characters That Will Not Appear in My Next Novel, A," 533; "O Youth and Beauty," 536; "Swimmer, The," 538, 2827
"Chef-d'œuvre inconnu, Le." *See* "Unknown Masterpiece, The"
Chekhov, Anton, 540-549, 2606, 2794-2796; "At Sea," 542; "Beggar, The," 544; "Boring Story, A," 545; "Bride, The," 547; "Chameleon, The," 542; "Chorus Girl, The," 543; "Darling, The," 547; "Death of a Government Clerk, The," 542; "Duel, The," 545; "Fly, The," 2800; "Letter to a Learned Neighbor, A," 542; "Meeting, The," 544; "Melyuzga," 543; "Misery," 2795; "Night Before the Trial, The," 543; "Rothschild's Fiddle," 546; "Sergeant Prishibeev," 543; "Sleepy," 2795; "Steppe, The," 544
"Chelkash" (Gorky), 1057
Cheng Naishan, 2911
Chéri (Colette), 2818
Chesney, George T.; "Battle of Dorking, The," 2633
Chesnutt, Charles Waddell, 549-555, 2858; "Cicely's Dream," 554; *Conjure Woman, The*, 2858; "Conjurer's Revenge, The," 552; "Goophered Grapevine, The," 551, 2858; "Matter of Principle, A," 2859; "Passing of Grandison, The," 553; "Po' Sandy," 551; "Sheriff's Children, The," 2858; "Uncle Wellington's Wives," 553, 2859; "Wife of His Youth, The," 552
Chesterton, G. K., 556-562; "Blue Cross, The," 558; "Eye of Apollo, The," 558; "Hammer of God, The," 559; "Secret Garden, The," 559; "Secret of Father Brown, The," 558
"Chèvrefeuille." *See* "Honeysuckle, The"
Chicano, 2949. *See also* Latino culture, Hispanic
Chicano Movement, 2953
"Chickamauga" (Bierce), 259, 2788
"Child, The" (Walser), 2439
"Child of God, The" (O'Flaherty), 1828
"Child of Queen Victoria, The" (Plomer), 1938
"Child That Went with the Fairies, The" (Le Fanu), 2645
"Child Who Favored Daughter, The" (Walker), 2431
Childhood and Other Neighborhoods (Dybek), 804
"Childhood: At Grandmother's" (Babel), 129
"Childhood of a Boss" (Sartre), 2099
"Childhood of Luvers, The" (Pasternak), 1889
"Children of the Great" (Lewis), 1506
Childress, Alice, 2868; *Like One of the Family*, 2869
Childs, Margaret Helen; *Rethinking Sorrow*, 2930
"Child's Play" (Higuchi), 2931
"Childybawn" (O'Faoláin), 1818, 2920
Chin, Frank, 2872, 2874; *Chinaman Pacific and Frisco R.R. Co.*, 2874; "Come All Ye Asian American Writers of the Real and the Fake," 2872
China, 2908-2913. *See also* "Geographical Index"
"China" (Johnson, Charles), 1308
China Men (Kingston), 1380
"Chinaman, The" (Wideman), 2511
Chinaman Pacific and Frisco R.R. Co. (Chin), 2874
Chinese American culture, 2873, 2876. *See also* "Category Index"
"Chinese in Haifa, The" (Chan), 2875
"Chip of Glass Ruby, A" (Gordimer), 1042
Chopin, Kate, 562-567, 2787; "Athénaïse," 564; "Belle Zoraide, La," 564, 2787; "Désirée's Baby," 564, 2787; "Madame Celestin's Divorce," 2787; "Storm, The," 565; "Story of an Hour, The," 563
"Chorus Girl, The" (Chekhov), 543
"Chosen Vessel, The" (Baynton), 2889
Chrétien de Troyes, 567-572; *Cligés*, 570; *Erec et Enide*, 568; *Guillaume d'Angleterre*, 569; *Lancelot*, 569, 2695; *Perceval*, 570; *Yvain*, 569
Christ, Jesus, 2661
Christian Hero, The (Steele, Richard), 2216
"Christian Trevalga" (Symons), 2797
Christie, Agatha, 572-579, 2618; "Affair at the Bungalow, The," 576; "Case of the Discontented Husband, The," 576; "Case of the Discontented Soldier, The," 576; "Case of the Missing Lady, The," 576; "In a Glass Darkly," 575; *Labours of Hercules*, 2620; *Mr. Parker Pyne, Detective*, 2620; *Murder of Roger Ackroyd, The*, 2619; *Mysterious Mr. Quin, The*, 575, 2620; "Mystery

of the Blue Jar, The," 574; *Partners in Crime*, 576, 2619; *Poirot Investigates*, 2619; "Red Signal, The," 574; "Triangle at Rhodes," 577; "Where There's a Will," 575
Christmas Carol, A (Dickens), 729
"Christmas Client, The" (Hoch), 1214
Christmas Garland, Woven by Max Beerbohm, A (Beerbohm), 228
"Christmas Tree and a Wedding, A" (Dostoevski), 763
"Chroma" (Barthelme, Frederick), 192
Chronicle, 3057
Chronicle of a Death Foretold (García Márquez), 954
"Chrysanthemums (Steinbeck), 2236
Chughtai, Ismat, 2976
"Cicely's Dream" (Chesnutt), 554
"Cinderella" (Grimm), 1090
"Cinderella Waltz, The" (Beattie), 213
Cinnamon Shops (Schulz), 2108
"Circling Hand, The" (Kincaid), 2870
"Circular Ruins, The" (Borges), 290
"Circus, The" (Porter), 1953
"Circus in the Attic, The" (Warren), 2458
Cisneros, Sandra, 579-584, 2955; "Alicia Who Sees Mice," 581; "Bums in the Attic," 581; "Ednas Ruthie," 581; "Eleven," 582; "Eyes of Zapata," 2955; *House on Mango Street, The*, 580; "Little Miracles, Kept Promises," 2950; "Minerva Writes Poems," 581; "Never Marry a Mexican," 583; "One Holy Night," 582; "Red Clowns," 582; "Those Who Don't," 581; "Three Sisters, The," 582; "Woman Hollering Creek," 583, 2956; *Woman Hollering Creek and Other Stories*, 582, 2955
"Cisti the Baker" (Boccaccio), 269
Citizen of the World, The (Goldsmith), 1034
"City, The" (Updike), 2383
"City Boy" (Michaels), 1677
"City of Broken Hearts" (Canin), 436
"City of the Dead, a City of the Living, A" (Gordimer), 1044
City of the Living and Other Stories, The (Stegner), 2222
"Civil Peace" (Achebe), 7, 2852
Clarey, Jo Ellyn; *Short Story Theory at a Crossroads*, 2608
Clark, Walter Van Tilburg, 585-590; "Buck in the Hills, The," 585; "Hook," 588; "Indian Well, The," 588; "Portable Phonograph, The," 587; *Track of the Cat, The*, 588
Clarke, Arthur C., 590-596; "Hammer of God, The," 594; "Meeting with Medusa, A," 593; "Nine Billion Names of God, The," 593; "Rescue Party," 591; "Sentinel, The," 592; "Star, The," 593
Classic, 3058
Classicism, 3058
Clavijo y Fajardo, José; *Pensador, El*, 2732
"Clavo, El." *See* "Nail, The"
Clemens, Samuel Langhorne. *See* Twain, Mark
"Clerk's Quest, The" (Moore, George), 2801
"Clerk's Tale, The" (Chaucer), 528
"Cleveland Wrecking Yard, The" (Brautigan), 344
Cligés (Chrétien de Troyes), 570
Climax, 3058
Close Range: Wyoming Stories (Proulx), 1981
"Closed Door, The" (Donoso), 758
"Cloud, The" (Fowles), 895
"Cloud, Castle, Lake" (Nabokov), 1742
"Clouk" (Colette), 599
"Clytie" (Welty), 2808
"Coach" (Robison), 2055
Coast of Chicago, The (Dybek), 804
"Cock Robin, Beale Street" (Hurston), 1253
"Code of a Herdsman, The" (Lewis), 1506
"Cœur simple, Un." *See* "Simple Heart, A"
Cofer, Judith Ortiz, 2958
"Coffin on the Hill, The" (Welch), 2467
Cogewea, the Halfblood (Humishuma), 2964
"Cogwheels" (Akutagawa), 40
"Cohorts" (Gold), 1032
"Cold Ground Was My Bed Last Night" (Garrett), 970
Coleridge, Samuel Taylor, 2757, 2786
Colette, 597-604, 2818; "Accompanist, The," 601; "April," 602; "Bella-Vista," 601; *Chéri*, 2818; "Clouk," 599; "Fenice, La," 601; "Kepi, The," 602; *Last of Chéri, The*, 2818; "Lola," 601; "Love," 600; "Matinée," 601; "Misfit, The," 601; "Monsieur Maurice," 601; "Sick Child, The," 602; "Tender Shoot, The," 600; "Tendrils of the Vine, The," 600
"Collaboration" (Collier), 609
Collected Ancient Greek Novels (Reardon), 2665
Collected Short Prose of James Agee, The (Agee), 20
Collected Stories, The (Paley), 1875
Collected Stories, The (Price), 1966
Collected Stories of Elizabeth Bowen, The (Bowen), 2922
Collected Stories of Evan S. Connell, The (Connell), 618
Collected Stories of Jean Stafford, The (Stafford), 2209
Collected Stories of Mavis Gallant, The (Gallant), 942
Collection of Tales from Uji, A, 2929
"Collector of Treasures, The" (Head), 1153
Collector of Treasures and Other Botswana Village Tales, The (Head), 1153, 2854
Collier, John, 605-611, 2650; "After the Ball," 607; "Ah, the University!," 609; "Are You Too Late or Was I Too Early," 609; "Back for Christmas," 607; "Bottle Party," 609; "Chaser, The," 608; "Collaboration," 609; "De Mortuis," 607; *Devil and All, The*, 606; "Evening Primrose," 608; *Fancies and Goodnights*, 608; "Frog Prince, The," 609; "Gavin O'Leary," 608; "Green

Thoughts," 608; "Halfway to Hell," 606, 609; "Incident on a Lake," 607; "Invisible Dove Dancer of Strathpheen Island, The," 609; "Lady on the Grey, The," 608; "Little Momento," 608; "Matter of Taste, A," 607; "Midnight Blue," 609; "Old Acquaintance," 609; "Over Insurance," 607; *Pictures in the Fire*, 607; "Possession of Angela Bradshaw, The," 606; "Right Side, The," 606; "Seasons of Mists," 609; "Steel Cat, The," 609; "Think No Evil," 608; "Three Bears Cottage," 607; "Touch of Nutmeg Makes It, The," 610; "Variation on a Theme," 609; "Without Benefit of Galsworthy," 608
Collins, Wilkie; "Traveler's Story of a Terribly Strange Bed, The," 2770
"Colloquy of the Dogs" (Cervantes), 494
Colomba (Mérimée), 1672
"Colomber, The" (Buzzati), 384
Colonel Julian and Other Stories (Bates), 200
"Colonel's Awakening, The" (Dunbar), 2860
Colonialism, 2849, 2936, 2938, 2940, 2944-2945, 2973. *See also* "Category Index"
"Color of Darkness" (Purdy), 1993
Color of Darkness (Purdy), 1993
Color Purple, The (Walker), 2867
Colored American Magazine, 2859
Columbus, Christopher, 2939
"Come All Ye Asian American Writers of the Real and the Fake" (Chin), 2872
"Come on Back" (Gardner), 961
"Come On, Ye Sons of Art" (Ozick), 1874
"Comedian, The" (L'Heureux), 1512
"Comendadora, La." *See* "Nun, The"
"Comfort" (Kaplan), 1337
Comic story, 3058
"Coming Attractions" (Wolff), 2552
"Coming of the Christ-Child, The" (Head), 1154
Coming to Terms with the Short Story (Lohafer), 2608
Command and I Will Obey You (Moravia), 1707
"Communist" (Ford), 2833
Company (Beckett), 222
"Company of the Dead, The" (Price), 1966
"Company of Wolves, The" (Carter), 470
"Complaint of Mars, The" (Chaucer), 519
"Completed" (Williams, Tennessee), 2527
Compromise, The (Dovlatov), 773
Conceit, 3058
"Concentration City" (Ballard), 143
"Condemned, The" (Allen), 65
"Condemned Librarian, The" (West), 2498
"Confessionals" (Woiwode), 2542
"Confessions of Fitz-Boodle" (Thackeray), 2303
"Confidences de Nicolas, Les" (Nerval), 1757
Conflict, 3058
Congreve, William, 611-614; *Incognita*, 612, 2724
Conjure Woman, The (Chesnutt), 2858
"Conjurer's Revenge, The" (Chesnutt), 552
Connell, Evan S., Jr., 614-619; "Arcturus," 616; *Collected Stories of Evan S. Connell, The*, 618; "Fisherman from Chihuahua, The," 616; "Mountains of Guatemala, The," 618; "Otto and the Magi," 618; "Palace of the Moorish Kings, The," 616; "Saint Augustine's Pigeon," 617; "Walls of Avila, The," 616
Connotation, 3058
Conrad, Joseph, 620-628, 2799; "Duel, The," 625; "Gaspar Ruiz," 625; *Heart of Darkness*, 623, 2755; "Lagoon, The," 622; "Outpost of Progress, An," 622; "Secret Sharer, The," 626, 2799; "Typhoon," 624; "Youth," 623
Conroy, Frank, 628-631; "Gossip," 630; "Midair," 629; "Sense of the Meeting, The," 629-630
Conte, 2749, 3058
"Contender, The" (Santos), 2881
Contes du lundi. See *Monday Tales*
Contest of Ladies, A (Sansom), 2088
"Contraband" (Jacobs), 1280
"Conversation, A" (Aiken), 35
"Conversation with My Father, A" (Paley), 2836
Conversations of German Emigrants (Goethe), 2731
"Conversion, The" (Banks), 162
"Conversion of an English Courtizan, The" (Greene, Robert), 1084
"Red Convertible, The" (Erdrich), 848
Cooper, Anna Julia, 2857
Coover, Robert, 632-638, 2829; "Babysitter, The," 2829; *Briar Rose*, 636; "Inside the Frame," 636; "Intermission," 636; *Night at the Movies, A*, 635; "Phantom of the Movie Palace, The," 636; *Pricksongs and Descants*, 634; "Shootout at Gentry's Junction," 635; "You Must Remember This," 636
"Cop and the Anthem, The" (Henry), 2791
Coppard, A. E., 638-644; "Arabesque: The Mouse," 642; "Broadsheet Ballad, A," 640; "Field of Mustard, The," 639; "Higgler, The," 641; "Lucy in Her Pink Jacket," 643
Copway, George, 2962; *Traditional History and Characteristic Sketches of the Ojibway Nation*, 2962
"Cords" (O'Brien, Edna), 1781
Corey, Elsworth, 2604
Corkery, Daniel, 2920
Corkery, James; "Ploughing of Leaca-na-Naomb, The," 2920
"Corn Planting, The" (Anderson), 81
Coronel no tiene quien le escriba, El. See *No One Writes to the Colonel*
"Corpo, O" (Lispector), 1520
"Corporal" (Brautigan), 345

Cortázar, Julio, 644-649, 2612; "All Fires the Fire," 646; "Axolotl," 646; "Bestiary," 645; "Blow-Up," 647; "Letter to a Young Lady in Paris," 646
"Cortes Island" (Munro), 1735
"Councillor Krespel" (Hoffmann), 1219
"Counterfactual Proposal, A" (Stern), 2241
"Counting the Ways" (Perabo), 1899
"Country Doctor, A" (Kafka), 1333
"Country Doctor, The" (Turgenev), 2771
"Country Funeral, The" (McGahern), 1567
"Country Husband, The" (Cheever), 537
"Country of the Blind, The" (Wells), 2479
Country of the Pointed Firs, The (Jewett), 1297-1298
"Country Passion, A" (Callaghan), 417
"Count's Wife, The" (Buzzati), 385
"Course of English Studies, A" (Jhabvala), 1304
"Courter, The" (Rushdie), 2070
Courtly love, 2696, 2715
"Cousin Theresa" (Saki), 2073
"Cousins" (Bellow), 237
Couto, Mia; "Birds of God, The," 2848; *Voices Made Night*, 2848
"Coventry" (Heinlein), 2636
Coverley, Sir Roger de, 17
"Cow in the House, A" (Kiely), 1357
"Cow Story, The" (Gates), 1532
"Cowslip Field, The" (Bates), 201
Cox, William Trevor. *See* Trevor, William
"Coyote Juggles His Eyes" (McWhorter), 2964
"Coyote Learns a New Trick" (Brant), 2969
"Coyotes" (Mason), 1642
Cozzens, James Gould, 649-654; "Eyes to See," 652; "Farewell to Cuba," 651; "Total Stranger," 650
"Cracked Looking-Glass, The" (Porter), 1951
"Crainquebille" (France), 901
Cram, Ralph Adams, 2649; *Black Spirits and White*, 2649
Crane, Stephen, 654-663; "Blue Hotel, The," 659, 2790; "Bride Comes to Yellow Sky, The," 659; "Death and the Child," 661; "Experiment in Misery, An," 656; "Four Men in a Cave," 656; "Open Boat, The," 657
Crawford, F. Marion; *Wandering Ghosts*, 2649
"Crazy Thought, The" (Gates), 982
Cress Delahanty (West), 2497
"Crickets" (Butler), 378
"Crime at the Tennis Club" (Moravia), 1705
"Crime do professor de matemática, O." *See* "Crime of the Mathematics Professor, The"
"Crime of Mary Lynn Yager, The" (Cassill), 483
"Crime of the Mathematics Professor, The" (Lispector), 1519
Crimson Ramblers of the World, Farewell (West), 2498
Crisis, 3058
Criticism, 3058
"Croeso i Gymru" (Wiggins), 2518
Crónica de una muerte anunciada. See *Chronicle of a Death Foretold*
"Crossing, The" (Dumas), 2866
"Crossing into Poland" (Babel), 131
"Crow, The" (Meckel), 1662
"Crow Comes Last, The" (Calvino), 425
"Crown, The" (Lawrence), 1454
"Cruel and Barbarous Treatment" (McCarthy), 1552
"Cruise of the Idlewild, The" (Dreiser), 785
"Crusade" (Oz), 1863
Crystal Frontier, The (Fuentes), 927-928
Cuadros de costumbres, 2940-2941
Cuba, 2957-2958. *See also* "Geographical Index"
Cuban American culture, 2958
Cuentos de Amor (Pardo Bazán), 1880
Cuentos de Marineda (Pardo Bazán), 1880
Culhwch ac Olwen, 2694
Cumpleaños (Fuentes), 926
Curnutt, Kirk; *Wise Economies*, 2610
"Currency" (Dazai), 702
"Curtain Blown by the Breeze, A" (Spark), 2198
Cusick, David, 2961
"Custodian, The" (Banks), 162
"Customs of the Country" (Bell), 231
"Cutting Edge" (Purdy), 1993
Cyberiad, The (Lem), 1486
Cyberpunk, 2641
"Cynthia" (Huxley), 1258

"Daddy Garbage" (Wideman), 2512
Daffodil Sky, The (Bates), 201
Dahl, Roald, 664-669; "Lamb to the Slaughter," 665; "Man from the South," 666; "Neck," 667; "Royal Jelly," 666
Daisy Miller (James, Henry), 1285, 2783
"Daisy's Valentine" (Gaitskill), 936
Daly, John Carroll, 2616
"Damballah" (Wideman), 2512
Damballah (Wideman), 2511
"Damned, The" (Blackwood), 264
"Damned Thing, The" (Bierce), 260
"Dance of the Happy Shades" (Munro), 1731
"Dancing After Hours" (Dubus), 2835
"Dancing Girl, The" (Mori, Ōgai), 2932
"Dancing Girls" (Atwood), 110
Dangerous Visions (Ellison), 2640
Dannay, Frederic. *See* Queen, Ellery
Dante, 670-675; *Divine Comedy, The*, 670-671
Daoism, 2908-2909
"Daphne" (Ovid), 1855
Daphnis and Chloë (Longus), 2666
"Dare's Gift" (Glasgow), 1010

"Daring Young Man on the Flying Trapeze, The" (Saroyan), 2092
Darío, Rubén, 2942
Dark Blue Suit (Bacho), 2882
Dark Carnival (Bradbury), 335
Darkness (Mukherjee), 1723
"Darkness Box" (Le Guin), 1478
"Darling, The" (Chekhov), 547
"Date with a Bird" (Tolstaya), 2322
Daudet, Alphonse, 676-681; *Fédor, La*, 680; "Last Class, The," 679; "Legend of the Man with the Golden Brain, The," 679; *Letters from My Mill*, 678; "M. Seguin's Goat," 678; *Monday Tales*, 679; "Pope's Mule, The," 679; "Reverend Father Gaucher's Elixir, The," 678; *Trésor d'Arlatan, Le*, 680
"Daughters of the Late Colonel, The" (Mansfield), 1620
Davenport, Guy, 681-691; "Aeroplanes at Brescia, The," 683; *Apples and Pears and Other Stories*, 687; *Da Vinci's Bicycle*, 685; "Dawn in Erewhon, The," 684; "Death of Picasso, The," 686; *Drummer of the Eleventh North Devonshire Fusiliers, The*, 689; *Eclogues*, 686; *Jules Verne Steam Balloon, The*, 688; "Mesoroposthonippidon," 687; "On Some Lines of Virgil," 687; "Robot," 684; "Tatlin!," 684
David, 2658
Davies, Peter Ho, 691, 694; "Hull Case, The," 693; "Small World," 693; "Ugliest House in the World, The," 692; *Union, A*, 692
Davies, Rhys, 694-698; "Dilemma of Catherine Fuchsias, The," 697; "Nightgown, The," 696; "Revelation," 697; "Trip to London, The," 696
Da Vinci's Bicycle (Davenport), 685
"Dawn" (Purdy), 1994
"Dawn in Erewhon, The" (Davenport), 684
"Dawn of Remembered Spring" (Stuart), 2259
Dawson, William James, 2603
"Day at Harmenz" (Borowski), 297
"Day Before, The" (Endō), 844
"Day He Himself Shall Wipe My Tears Away, The" (Ōe), 1812
"Day He Left, The" (Simpson), 2155
"Day in the Country, A" (Broyard), 365
"Day in the Open, A" (Bowles, Jane), 307
"Day the Dancers Came, The" (Santos), 2881
Day's End and Other Stories (Bates), 199
"Dayspring Mishandled" (Kipling), 1394
Dazai, Osamu, 699-703; "Almanac of Pain, An," 700; "Currency," 702; "Eight Views of Tokyo," 701; *Eight Views of Tokyo*, 700; "Gemeine, Das" 702; "Island of Monkeys, The," 701; "Mound of the Monkey's Grave, The," 701; "My Older Brothers," 701; "Putting Granny Out to Die," 701; "Recollections," 700; *Return to Tsugaru*, 700; "Taking the Wen Away," 702; "Toys," 701; "Transformation," 701
De Lisser, H. G., 2945
"De Mortuis" (Collier), 607
"De noche soy tu caballo." *See* "I'm Your Horse in the Night"
"Dead, The" (Joyce), 1322-1323, 1326, 2801, 2918
"Dead as They Come" (McEwan), 1565
"Dead Man, The" (Quiroga), 2020
"Dead Past, The" (Asimov), 99
"Dead Ringer" (Queen), 2014
"Deal, The" (Michaels), 1676
"Deal in Wheat, A" (Norris), 1768
"Dean of Men" (Taylor, Peter), 2296
"Dear Phil Donahue" (Smith), 2183
"Death and the Child" (Crane), 661
"Death and the Compass" (Borges), 289
"Death and the Single Girl" (Disch), 746
"Death in Jerusalem" (Trevor), 2925
Death in Midsummer and Other Stories (Mishima), 1691
"Death in the Desert" (Agee), 21
Death in the Family, A (Agee), 19-20
"Death in the Woods" (Anderson), 80
Death in Venice (Mann), 1611
"Death of a Government Clerk, The" (Chekhov), 542
"Death of a Lesser Man" (Berriault), 250
"Death of a Traveling Salesman" (Welty), 2484
"Death of Dolgushov, The" (Babel), 132, 2820
"Death of Halprin Frayser, The" (Bierce), 2649
Death of Hind Legs and Other Stories (Wain), 2426
"Death of Horatio Alger, The" (Baraka), 167
Death of Ivan Ilyich, The (Tolstoy), 2331, 2794
"Death of Justina, The" (Cheever), 537
"Death of King Arthur, The" (Malory), 1605
"Death of Olivier Bécaille, The" (Zola), 2586
"Death of Picasso, The" (Davenport), 686
"Death the Proud Brother" (Wolfe), 2547
"Deathless Lovers" (Woiwode), 2540
"Debriefing" (Sontag), 2194
Decameron, The (Boccaccio), 268, 2702
"Decapitated Chicken, The" (Quiroga), 2019
Deconstruction, 3058
"Dedicated" (Leavitt), 1464, 2835
"Dedicated Man, A" (Taylor, Elizabeth), 2292
"Deeds of Light" (Price), 1966
Deeds of the Kings of the English, The (William of Malmesbury), 2693
"Deer Woman" (Allen), 2969
Defamiliarization, 3058
"Defeated, The" (Gordimer), 1044
"Defender of the Faith" (Roth), 2062, 2813
Defoe, Daniel; *True Relation of the Apparition of One Mrs Veal*, 2728

"Degradation of Tenderness, The" (Stern), 2243
De la Mare, Walter, 704-708, 2650, 2798; "Ideal Craftsman, An," 707; "In the Forest," 706; "Orgy, The," 705; "Riddle, The," 705
Delany, Samuel R., 709-714; "Aye, and Gomorrah," 710; "Driftglass," 711; "Tale of Dragons and Dreamers, The," 712; "Tale of Gorgik, The," 712; "Tale of Old Venn, The," 712; "Tale of the Small Sarg, The," 711; *Tales of Nevèrÿon*, 712; "Time Considered as a Helix of Semiprecious Stones," 711; *We, in Some Strange Power's Employ Move on a Rigorous Line*, 711
"Delia" (Gordon, Mary), 1053
"Delicate Prey, The" (Bowles, Paul), 314
"Delitto al circolo di tennis." *See* "Crime at the Tennis Club"
"Demon Lover, The" (Bowen), 303, 2922
Deng Gang, 2912
Denotation, 3058
Dénouement, 3058
"Dentophilia" (Slavin), 2173
"Departures" (L'Heureux), 1511
Derleth, August, 714-719, 2651; "Adventure of the Camberwell Beauty, The," 717; "Adventure of the Remarkable Worm, The," 716; "Adventure of the Rudberg Numbers, The," 716; *Three Problems for Solar Pons*, 717
"Dernière Classe, La." *See* "Last Class, The"
Desai, Anita, 2974
"Descendant of El Cid, A" (Pardo Bazán), 1879
"Descent into the Maelström, A" (Poe), 1942
Desengaños amorosos (Zayas y Sotomayor), 2706
"Desert Breakdown, 1968" (Wolff), 2552
Deshpande, Shashi, 2974
"Design for Departure" (Algren), 59
"Desire and the Black Masseur" (Williams, Tennessee), 2527
"Désirée's Baby" (Chopin), 564, 2787
"Despicable Bastard" (Endō), 844
"Desquite." *See* "Revenge, The"
"Destination" (Wang), 2444
"Destiny" (Erdrich), 849
"Destructors, The" (Greene, Graham), 1078, 2815
Detective and mystery, 2613-2624, 2797, 3058. *See also* "Category Index"
"Detective's Wife, The" (Hoch), 1214
"Detroit Skyline, 1949" (Mason), 1641
"Detstvo: U babushki." *See* "Childhood: At Grandmother's"
Deus ex machina, 3059
"Deux Amis de Bourbonne, Les." *See* "Two Friends from Bourbonne, The"
Devatero pohádek. See *Fairy Tales*
Device, 3059
Devil and All, The (Collier), 606
"Devil and Daniel Webster, The" (Benét), 244
"Devil Was the Joker, The" (Powers), 1958
Devil's Dictionary, The (Bierce), 258
"Dhoya" (Yeats), 2567
"Di Grasso" (Babel), 130
Diagnosis: Impossible (Hoch), 1212
Dialogi. See *Dialogues*
Dialogics, 3059
Dialogues (Gregory the Great), 2682
"Diamond Badge, The" (Welch), 2470
"Diamond Lens, The" (O'Brien, Fitz-James), 1787
"Diamonds at the Bottom of the Sea" (Hogan), 2926
Diary of a Mad Old Man (Tanizaki), 2286
"Diary of a Madman" (Gogol), 1027
"Diary of a Madman, The" (Lu), 1545
"Diary of a Sixteen-Year-Old" (Kawabata), 1346
"Diary of a Superfluous Man, The" (Turgenev), 2355
"Diary of K. W." (Berriault), 250
Diaz, Junot, 2959; *Drown*, 2959
Dick, Philip K., 719-725, 2637; "Little Black Box, The," 723; "Mold of Yancy, The," 722; "Project: Earth," 722; "Rautavaara's Case," 721; "Roog," 721; "Second Variety," 723; "Small Town," 722; "Trouble with Bubbles, The," 722
Dickens, Charles, 725-731, 2613, 2644; *Christmas Carol, A*, 729; *George Silverman's Explanation*, 728; "Haunted Man, The," 729; "History of a Self-Tormentor, The," 727; *Pickwick Papers*, 726; "Queer Client," 727; "Signalman, The," 2770; "Sketches by Boz," 2745; "Story of the Goblins Who Stole a Sexton, The," 729
Didactic, 2626, 2628, 2701, 2728, 3059. *See also* "Category Index"
Diderot, Denis, 731-737; "Madame de la Carlière," 734; *Supplement to Bougainville's Voyage*, 735; "This Is Not a Story," 734; "Two Friends from Bourbonne, The," 733
Diegesis, 3059
"Difference, The" (Glasgow), 1009
"Difficult Case, A" (Howells), 1235
"Difficulty with a Bouquet" (Sansom), 2087
"Dilemma of Catherine Fuchsias, The" (Davies, Rhys), 697
"Diles que no me maten!" *See* "Tell Them Not to Kill Me"
"Dimond Cut Dimond" (Thackeray), 2302
Dinesen, Isak, 737-744, 2816; "Babette's Feast," 742; "Blank Page, The," 2817; "Heroine, The," 742; "Monkey, The," 738; "Sailor-Boy's Tale, The," 741, 2817; "Sorrow-Acre," 740, 2817; "Young Man with the Carnation, The," 740
Ding Ling, 2910
Diop, Birago; "Sarzan," 2849

"Dirigibles" (Byers), 391
"Dirty Wedding" (Johnson, Denis), 1312
"Disabled Soldier, The" (Goldsmith), 2728
Disch, Thomas M., 745-749, 2640; "Abduction of Bunny Steiner," 747; "Asian Shore, The," 746; *Brave Little Toaster, The*, 747; *Brave Little Toaster Goes to Mars, The*, 747; "Death and the Single Girl," 746; "Getting into Death," 746; "Joycelin Shrager Story, The," 747; "Let Us Quickly Hasten to the Gate of Ivory," 746; "Man Who Had No Idea, The," 747
Disciplina clericalis (Alfonsi), 2701
Discourse of the Adventures Passed by Master F. J., The (Gascoigne), 2712
"Disorder and Early Sorrow" (Mann), 2816
Displaced Person, The (O'Connor, Flannery), 1798
"Displacement" (Louie), 2876
Disputation Between a Hee Conny-Catcher and a Shee Conny-Catcher, A (Greene, Robert), 1084
"Distant Episode, A" (Bowles, Paul), 313
"Distracted Preacher, The" (Hardy), 1114
"District in the Rear, A" (Pasternak), 1891
Divarkaruni, Chitra Banerjee, 2885
"Diver, The" (Pritchett), 1974
"Dividends" (O'Faoláin), 1820
Divine Comedy, The (Dante), 670-671. See also *Inferno, The*
"Diviner, The" (Friel), 921, 2924
"Divorce" (Lu), 1548
Dixon, Stephen, 749-752, 2837; *Frog*, 751; "Intruder, The," 751; "Last May," 750; "Man of Letters," 750, 2837; "Man, Woman and Boy," 751; "Signing, The," 750
"Dnevnik lishnega cheloveka." *See* "Diary of a Superfluous Man, The"
"Do Seek Their Meat from God" (Roberts), 2900
"Do You Love Me?" (Carey) , 452
Doce cuentos peregrinos. See *Strange Pilgrims*
"Doctor, The" (Gallant), 943
"Dr. Murkes gesammeltes Schweigen." *See* "Murke's Collected Silences"
"Doctor's Son, The" (O'Hara), 1836
"Dodu" (Narayan), 1753
Dodu and Other Stories (Narayan), 1752
"Doe Season" (Kaplan), 1337
Doerr, Harriet, 752-755; "Edie: A Life," 753; "Mexico," 754; "Tiger in the Grass, The," 754
"Doge and Dogaressa" (Hoffmann), 1220
Doggerel, 3059
"Doll's House, The" (Mansfield), 1622
"Domestic Dilemma, A" (McCullers), 1558
Dominican American culture, 2959
Dominican Republic, 2957
"Dominion" (Targan), 2289
"Don Juan's Last Illusion" (Pardo Bazán), 1880
"Donde viven las águilas." *See* "Up Among the Eagles"
Donoso, José, 756-760; "Closed Door, The," 758; *Gaspard de la nuit*, 758; *Green Atom Number Five*, 759; "Güero, The," 757; "Lady, A," 757; "Santelices," 757; *Still Life with Pipe*, 759; "Walk, The," 758
"Don't Call Me by My Right Name" (Purdy), 1993
"Door, The" (White), 2507
"Door in the Wall, The" (Wells), 2479
"Door to Doom, The" (Carr), 466
"Doorbell, The" (Nabokov), 1740
Doppelgänger, 3059
"Doppelganger" (Lewis), 1506
"Doppioni." *See* "Doubles"
"Dorothea." *See* "Confessions of Fitz-Boodle"
Dorothée (Camus, Jean-Pierre), 2719
"Dos Elenas, Las." *See* "Two Elenas, The"
"Dos madres." *See* "Two Mothers"
Dostoevski, Fyodor, 760-765; "Apropos of the Wet Snow," 2773; "Christmas Tree and a Wedding, A," 763; "Dream of a Ridiculous Man, The," 763; *Notes from the Underground*, 2794; "Peasant Marey, The," 2774; "White Nights," 762
"Double Admiral, The" (Metcalfe), 2650
"Double Charley" (Stern), 2241
"Double Happiness Bun, The" (Gilchrist), 993
"Doubles" (Moravia), 1707
Douglas, Ellen, 766-769; "About Loving Women," 768; *Hold On*, 767; "I Just Love Carrie Lee," 767; *Truth*, 768
"Dove of the East, A" (Helprin), 1167
Dove of the East and Other Stories, A (Helprin), 1166
Dovlatov, Sergei, 769-775; *Compromise, The*, 773; "Mother," 771; "My First Cousin," 772; "Photo Album, The," 774; "Uncle Aron," 771; "Uncle Leopold," 772; *Zone, The*, 773
"Down at the Dollhouse" (Gilchrist), 996
"Down Then by Derry" (Kiely), 1360
"Downward Path to Wisdom, The" (Porter), 1954
Dowson, Ernest; "Dying of Francis Donne, The," 2797
Doyle, Arthur Conan, 775-783, 2613, 2633, 2648; "Adventure of the Speckled Band, The," 777; "Adventure of the Dancing Men, The," 781; "Adventure of the Empty House, The," 780; "Final Problem, The," 779; "Red-Headed League, The," 778; "Scandal in Bohemia, A," 778
"Dragon's Seed" (Bell), 232
"Dragons" (Barnes), 170, 2841
"Dream Children" (Lamb), 2745
"Dream Come True, A" (Onetti), 1850
"Dream of a Ridiculous Man, The" (Dostoevski), 763
"Dream Sequence" (Agee), 21
Dream vision, 3059

"Dreaming in Polish" (Bender), 241
Dreiser, Theodore, 783-788; "Cruise of the Idlewild, The," 785; "Khat," 785; "Lost Phoebe, The," 787; "McEwen of the Shining Slave Makers," 785; "Nigger Jeff," 785; "Old Neighborhood, The," 786; "Prince Who Was a Thief, The," 785; "St. Columba and the River," 787; "Sanctuary," 785; *Sister Carrie*, 784; "Story of Stories, A," 785; "When the Old Century Was New," 785
"Drenched in Light" (Hurston), 2862
"Dressmaker's Dummy, The" (Robbe-Grillet), 2046
"Driftglass" (Delany), 711
"Drifting" (Quiroga), 2020
"Driver" (Barthelme, Frederick), 192
Droll Stories (Balzac), 149
"Drover's Wife, The" (Lawson), 1460
Drown (Diaz), 2959
"Drug Called Tradition, A" (Alexie), 57
"Drummer Boy, The" (Trevor), 2343
"Drummer of All the World, The" (Laurence), 1441
Drummer of the Eleventh North Devonshire Fusiliers, The (Davenport), 689
Drunk with Love (Gilchrist), 994
"Drunkard, The" (O'Connor, Frank), 1806, 2815
Dualism, 3059
Dubliners (Joyce), 1321, 2801
Dubus, Andre, 789-793, 2835; "Adultery," 791; "Blessings," 2835; "Dancing After Hours," 2835; "Father's Story, A," 791; "Finding a Girl in America," 791; "If They Knew Yvonne," 790; "Intruder, The," 789; "Pretty Girl, The," 790
"Duel, The" (Chekhov), 545
"Duel, The" (Conrad), 625
"Duellists, The." *See* "Duel, The"
Du Fresne, Yvonne; "Morning Talk, The," 2896
Duggan, Maurice, 2895; "Along Rideout Road That Summer," 2895
Duke Humphrey's Dinner (O'Brien, Fitz-James), 1789
Dumas, Henry, 2866; "Crossing, The," 2866
"Dummy, The" (Sontag), 2195
"Dun, The" (Edgeworth), 813
Dunbar-Nelson, Alice, 2860; "Violets," 2860
Dunbar, Paul Laurence, 793-797, 2859; "Colonel's Awakening, The," 2860; *Folks from Dixie*, 795, 2860; *Heart of Happy Hollow, The*, 796; *In Old Plantation Days*, 796; *Strength of Gideon and Other Stories, The*, 795
Dunsany, Lord, 797-802, 2648; "Ghosts, The," 2797; "Idle Days on the Yann," 800; "Sword of Welleran, The," 799; "What Jorkens Has to Put Up With," 801
"Dunwich Horror, The" (Lovecraft), 1538
Dupin, C. Auguste, 777, 1944-1945
"Dushechka." *See* "Darling, The"
"Dva gusara." *See* "Two Hussars"
"Dva pomeshchika." *See* "Two Landowners"
"Dvadtsat'shest' i odna." *See* "Twenty-six Men and a Girl"
"Dwarf House" (Beattie), 212
Dybek, Stuart, 803-806; "Ant," 805; *Childhood and Other Neighborhoods*, 804; *Coast of Chicago, The*, 804
"Dying" (Stern), 2242
"Dying of Francis Donne, The" (Dowson), 2797
"Dymchurch Flit" (Kipling), 1392
"Dynamite" (Smiley), 2177
"Dzień na Hermenzach." *See* "Day at Harmenz"

"Early One Morning" (Warner), 2453
Early Sorrows (Kiš), 1398
Earthdivers (Vizenor), 2408
"Earthquake in Chile, The" (Kleist), 1401
East into Upper East (Jhabvala), 2976
East, West: Stories (Rushdie), 2976
Eastman, Charles, 2963
Eastman, Jacob; *Indian Boyhood*, 2963; *Red Hunters and the Animal People*, 2963; *Stories of the Sioux*, 2963; "War Maiden, The," 2963
Eaton, Edith. *See* Sui Sin Far
"Ebony Tower, The" (Fowles), 893
Ecclesiastical History of the English People (Saint Bede the Venerable), 2683
"Echo, The" (Bowles, Paul), 313
"Echo and the Nemesis, The" (Stafford), 2210
Eclogue, 3059
Eclogues (Davenport), 686
Écriture Féminine, 3059
Edgeworth, Maria, 807-816, 2914; "Angelina or L'Amie Inconnue," 811; *Castle Rackrent*, 2914; "Dun, The," 813; *Frank, I-IV*, 810; "Good Aunt, The," 811; "Lottery, The," 812; "Mademoiselle Panache," 811; *Modern Griselda, The*, 813; *Parent's Assistant, The*, 809; *Popular Tales*, 811; "Prussian Vase, The," 810; "Purple Jar, The," 809; "Simple Susan," 809; *Tales of Fashionable Life*, 813
"Edie: A Life" (Doerr), 753
"Editha" (Howells), 1236, 2787
"Ednas Ruthie" (Cisneros), 581
Edo era, 2930
"Education of Mingo, The" (Johnson, Charles), 1307
"Edward and God" (Kundera), 1416
Effect, 3059
Egan, Greg, 2641
"Egg, The" (Anderson), 81
"Egg Race, The" (Updike), 2382
Egil's saga, 2674
Egyptian culture, 2659. *See also* "Geographical Index"
"Eight Views of Tokyo" (Dazai), 701
Eight Views of Tokyo (Dazai), 700
Eighteenth century, 2726-2735

"Eighty-Yard Run, The" (Shaw), 2132
"Eileen" (Gordon, Mary), 1054
"Eine seele aus holz." *See* "Soul of Wood"
"Einfahrt, Die" (Walser), 2440
Ejxenbaum, B. M., 2752-2753, 2762
El Bronx Remembered (Mohr), 2958
Elbow Room (McPherson), 2867
"Electioneering on Big Injun Mountain" (Murfree), 2780
Elegy, 3059
Elene (Cynewulf), 2687
"Elephant Vanishes, The" (Murakami), 2934
"Eleven" (Cisneros), 582
"Eli, the Fanatic" (Roth), 2060
"Eliduc" (Fowles), 894
"Eliduc" (Marie de France), 1628
Eliot, George, 816-820; "Amos Barton," 817; "Brother Jacob," 818; "Janet's Repentance," 818; "Mr. Gilfil's Love Story," 817; "Lifted Veil, The," 818
Eliot, T. S., 2795
"Elisabetta, Carlotta, Catherine" (Kaplan), 1337
"Elixir de Révérend Père Gaucher, L'." *See* "Reverend Father Gaucher's Elixir, The"
Elizabethan romance, 2710
"Elka i svad'ba." *See* "Christmas Tree and a Wedding, A"
Elkin, Stanley, 820-825; "Bailbondsman, The," 823; "Everything Must Go!," 821; "In the Alley," 822; *Van Gogh's Room at Arles*, 823
Ellin, Stanley; "Specialty of the House, The," 2621
Elliott, George P., 825-830, 2607; *Hour of Last Things and Other Stories, An*, 828; "Into the Cone of Cold," 828; "Miss Cudahy of Stowe's Landing," 829; "NRACP, The," 827
Ellis Island and Other Stories (Helprin), 1168
Ellison, Harlan, 831-836; *Dangerous Visions*, 2640; "Face of Helene Bournouw, The," 834; "Jeffty Is Five," 835; "On the Downhill Side," 834; "Shattered Like a Glass Goblin," 832
Ellison, Ralph, 837-841, 2865; "Battle Royal," 2865; "Flying Home," 839; *Flying Home and Other Stories*, 838; "In a Strange Country," 839; *Invisible Man*, 2865; "King of the Bingo Game," 839
"Embrace at Vergara, The" (Alarcón), 43
"Emerald" (Zhang), 2580
"Emergency" (Johnson, Denis), 1311
Emotive meaning, 3059
Emperor of the Air (Canin), 434
"Emperor's New Clothes, The" (Andersen), 74
Empress's Ring, The (Hale), 1097
"Empty House, The" (Blackwood), 263
"Enciklopedija mrtvih." *See* "Encyclopedia of the Dead"
"Encyclopedia of the Dead" (Kiš), 1399
"End, The" (Beckett), 221
"End of a World, The" (Hildesheimer), 1203
"End of August, The" (Pavese), 1897
"End of Romance, The" (Brown), 361
"End of the Old Folks' Home, The" (Babel), 131
"Ende einer welt, Das." *See* "End of a World, The"
"Ending" (Grau), 1068
Endō, Shūsaku, 841-847; "Box, The," 845; "Day Before, The," 844; "Despicable Bastard," 844; "Final Martyrs, The," 845; "Forty-Year-Old Man, A," 843; "Incredible Voyage," 844; "Retreating Figures," 843; "Shadow Figure, The," 844
"Enemy, The" (Buck), 368
"Enfance d'un chef." *See* "Childhood of a Boss"
"Enfant malade, Le." *See* "Sick Child, The"
England, 2726; 1880-1920, 2796; and medieval romance, 2695; modern short story and, 2744. *See also* "Geographical Index"
"Enigma, The" (Fowles), 895
Enlightenment, 2726, 2732, 2734
"Enoch Soames" (Beerbohm), 226
"Enormous Door" (Price), 1966
"Enormous Radio, The" (Cheever), 534, 2810
"Enormous Space, The" (Ballard), 145
"Entered as Second-Class Matter" (Perelman), 1904
"Entrance into Life" (Hale), 1098
"Entropy" (Pynchon), 2007
"Ephemera, The" (Franklin), 906
Epic, 2661, 2685, 3059. *See also* "Category Index"
Epidemia, L' (Moravia), 1706
"Epilogue II" (Mansfield), 1619
Epiphany, 1321, 1518-1519, 2917, 3060. *See also* "Category Index"
Episode, 3060
"Episode at Gastein" (Sansom), 2088
Epistolary fiction, 3060
"Epitaph, An" (Shalamov), 2129
"Epstein" (Roth), 2061
"Erdbeben in Chili, Das." *See* "Earthquake in Chile, The"
Erdrich, Louise, 847-850; "Destiny," 849; "Fleur," 849; *Love Medicine*, 2965; "Matchimanito," 849; "Red Convertible, The," 848; "Saint Marie," 849, 2967; *Tracks*, 2965
Erec et Enide (Chrétien de Troyes), 568
Ermanaric, 2684
"Ermolai and Miller's Wife" (Turgenev), 2354
"Ermolai i mel'nichikha." *See* "Ermolai and Miller's Wife"
"Erostrate." *See* "Erostratus"
"Erostratus" (Sartre), 2098
Erotic Tales (Moravia), 1708
"Es lebe die freiheit." *See* "Hurrah for Freedom"
"Es que somos muy pobres." *See* "We're Very Poor"
"Escapade, An" (Callaghan), 418

"Escapes" (Williams, Joy), 2522
Escapes (Williams, Joy), 2521
"Esperanto" (Shalamov), 2128
Espurgatoire Saint Patriz (Marie de France), 1628
Essais. See *Essays, The*
Essay, 3060
Essay-sketch tradition, 2737-2739, 2744, 3060. *See also* "Category Index"
Essays, The (Montaigne), 2737
"Esther" (Toomer), 2336
Etchison, Dennis, 2652
"Eterna" (Lavin), 1447
"Eternal Moment, The" (Forster), 888
Eternal Smile, The (Lagerkvist), 1421
"Ethan Brand" (Hawthorne), 1149
Ethiopian History, An (Heliodorus), 2666
Euphony, 3060
Euphues, the Anatomy of Wit (Lyly), 2714
Europe; and science fiction, 2633; and the supernatural, 2645
"Eva." *See* "Eve"
Eva Luna (Allende), 67
"Evangeline's Mother" (Kinsella), 1383
"Eve" (Arreola), 93
"Eve of the Spirit Festival, The" (Chang), 512
"Eveline" (Joyce), 2917
"Evelyn" (Austen), 125
"Evening in Connecticut" (Tuohy), 2349
"Evening Primrose" (Collier), 608
"Evening with Dr. Faust, An" (Hesse), 1190
"Evening with John Joe Dempsey, An" (Trevor), 2342
"Eventide" (Purdy), 1996
"Evermore" (Barnes), 171
"Every Little Hurricane" (Alexie), 57
"Everybody Knew Bubba Riff" (Wideman), 2514
"Everyday Disorders" (Prose), 1977
"Everyday Use" (Walker), 2434
"Everything Is Nice" (Bowles, Jane), 309
"Everything Must Go!" (Elkin), 821
"Everything That Rises Must Converge" (O'Connor, Flannery), 1799
Everything That Rises Must Converge (O'Connor, Flannery), 1799
"Everything Under the Sun" (Purdy), 1994
Eviga leendet, Det. See *Eternal Smile, The*
"Ex Parte" (Lardner), 1436
Executioner, The. See *Hangman, The*
"Executor, An" (Mars-Jones), 1632
Exemplary Novels (Cervantes), 493, 2706, 2720
Exemplum, 2701, 2939, 3060. *See also* "Category Index"
Exile of the Sons of Uisliu, 2688
Existentialism, 3060. *See also* "Category Index"
"Expatriates' Party, The" (Vanderhaeghe), 2392
"Experiment in Misery, An" (Crane), 656
Experimental, 2828. *See also* "Category Index"
Exposition, 3060
Expressionism, 3060. *See also* "Category Index"
"Extract from an Account of the Captivity of William Henry" (Franklin), 906
"Eye of Apollo, The" (Chesterton), 558
"Eyes, The" (Wharton), 2502
"Eyes of the Statue, The" (Laye), 2850
"Eyes of Zapata" (Cisneros), 2955
"Eyes to See" (Cozzens), 652
Eyrbggja saga, 2674

Fable, 2625-2631, 2658, 2660, 2736, 3060; eighteenth century, 2629; medieval, 2626, 2628; nineteenth century, 2629; seventeenth century, 2629; twentieth century, 2630. *See also* "Category Index"
"Fable of the Goat" (Agnon), 24
Fables of a Jewish Aesop (Natronai ha-Nakdan), 2628
Fabliau, 3060
Fabulation, 3060
"Face of Helene Bournouw, The" (Ellison, Harlan), 834
"Face of Stone, A" (Williams, William Carlos), 2532
"Face on the Barroom Floor, The" (Algren), 60
Facing the Music (Brown), 361
"Facino Cane" (Balzac), 150
"Facts Concerning the Recent Carnival of Crime in Connecticut, The" (Twain), 2361
Fair Eckbert (Tieck), 2731
"Fair Trade, A" (Byers), 392
"Fairy Goose, The" (O'Flaherty), 1828, 2922
Fairy tale, 2658, 2736-2737, 3060. *See also* "Category Index"
"Fairy Tale, The" (Goethe), 1019
Fairy Tales (Čapek), 439
"Fall of the House of Usher, The" (Poe), 1276, 1945, 2644, 2743, 2767
"Falling Free" (Targan), 2289
"False Dawn" (Mahfouz), 1589
"False Lights" (Godwin), 1014
"False Prophet, The" (Sembène), 2850
"Fame" (Walker), 2433
"Family, The" (Pavese), 1895
Family Happiness (Tolstoy), 2330
Family Ties (Lispector), 1519
"Famous Poll at Jody's Bar, The" (Gilchrist), 993
Fanatic Heart, A (O'Brien, Edna), 1784
Fancies and Goodnights (Collier), 608
"Fangzhou." *See* "Ark, The"
Fantastic, 3061. *See also* "Category Index"
Fantastics and Other Fancies (Hearn), 1157
"Far och jag" (Lagerkvist), 1422
"Fard" (Huxley), 1258

"Fare to the Moon" (Price), 1965
"Farewell to Cuba" (Cozzens), 651
Farewell to Matyora (Rasputin), 2025
Farewell to Militarie Profession (Rich), 2711
"Farmers' Daughters, The" (Williams, William Carlos), 2533
Farrell, James T., 851-856; "Fastest Runner on Sixty-first Street, The," 854; "When Boyhood Dreams Come True," 852
"Fastest Runner on Sixty-first Street, The" (Farrell), 854
"Fat" (Carver), 474
"Father, The" (Babel), 130
"Father, A" (Mukherjee), 1725
"Father's Last Escape" (Schulz), 2110
"Father's Story, A" (Dubus), 791
Faulkner, William, 856-864, 2804; "Barn Burning," 861; "Bear, The," 860, 2804; "Rose for Emily, A," 858, 2805; "That Evening Sun," 2805
Fauset, Jessie Redmon, 2861
"Feather in the Toque, The" (Minot), 1688
"Feather Pillow, The" (Queen), 2019
Fédor, La (Daudet), 680
Felicidade clandestina (Lispector), 1519
"Feliz aniversário." *See* "Happy Birthday"
Fellow Passengers (Auchincloss), 121
Feng Menglong, 2908
"Fenice, La" (Colette), 601
"Fensted's Mother" (Baxter), 208
Fenton, Geoffrey; *Certain Tragical Discourses*, 2711
Fernandez, Roberto, 2958
Fetish, The (Moravia), 1707
"Fever" (Wideman), 2513
Fever (Wideman), 2513
"Few Crusted Characters, A" (Hardy), 1115
Ficciones, 1935-1944, 2942
"Fiddler, The" (Melville), 1669
"Fiddler of the Reels, The" (Hardy), 1114
Fiddler on the Roof (film), 50
"Fidelity" (Jhabvala), 1305
"Field Guide to the Western Birds" (Stegner), 2222
"Field of Mustard, The" (Coppard), 639
"Fifteen-Dollar Eagle, The" (Plath), 1935
"Fifteen: Spring" (West), 2497
"Fig Tree, The" (Ngugi), 2854
"Fig Tree, The" (Porter), 1954
"Fight, The" (Thomas), 2309
Fightin' (Ortiz), 2967
Figurative language, 3061
"Figure in the Carpet, The" (James, Henry), 1287
Figure on the Boundary Line, The (Meckel), 1662
Filipino American culture, 2880, 2882
"Filthy with Things" (Boyle, T. C.), 329
Fin de Chéri, La. See *Last of Chéri, The*
Fin de siècle, 3061
"Final Martyrs, The" (Endō), 845
"Final Mist, The" (Bombal), 278
"Final Problem, The" (Doyle), 779
"Final Proof of Fate and Circumstance, The" (Abbott), 2
"Finding a Girl in America" (Dubus), 791
"Findling, Der." *See* "Foundling, The"
"Fine Accommodations" (Hughes), 1241
"Fingers in the Door" (Tuohy), 2349
Finlayson, Roderick; "Totara Tree, The," 2895
Firdusi; *Shahnamah*, 2664
"Fire and Cloud" (Wright, Richard), 2561
"Fire in the Wood, The" (Welch), 2470
Fireman Flower (Sansom), 2085
"Fires" (Bass), 195
"First Communion" (Rivera), 2043
"First Confession" (O'Connor, Frank), 1806
"First Dark" (Spencer), 2204
"First Death of Her Life, The" (Taylor, Elizabeth), 2292
"First Love" (Babel), 129
"First Love" (Beckett), 220
"First Love" (Pavese), 1896
"First Love" (Turgenev), 2357
First Love and Other Sorrows (Brodkey), 356
First Love, Last Rites (McEwan), 1564, 2841
"First Seven Years, The" (Malamud), 1597
"First Year of My Life, The" (Spark), 2199
"Firstborn" (Woiwode), 2541
"Fisherman and His Wife, The" (Grimm), 1087
"Fisherman from Chihuahua, The" (Connell), 616
Fisherman of the Inland Sea, A (Le Guin), 1479
Fitzgerald, F. Scott, 864-871; "Babylon Revisited," 868; "Last Kiss," 869; "Rich Boy, The," 867; "Winter Dreams," 867
Fitzgibbon, Roseanne, 2888
"Five-Forty-Eight, The" (Cheever), 536
Five Women Who Loved Love (Ihara Saikaku), 1263, 2930
Flashback, 3061
Flaubert, Gustave, 872-879, 2792; "Hérodias," 877; "Legend of St. Julian, Hospitaler, The," 876, 2792; "Simple Heart, A," 873, 2782
"Fleur" (Erdrich), 849
"Flight" (Grau), 1068
"Flight" (Steinbeck), 2237
"Flight" (Updike), 2377
Flights of Angels (Gilchrist), 995
"Flights of Fancy" (Trevor), 2344
"Flood, The" (Harjo), 1119
"Flood, The" (Zamyatin), 2576
"Flowering Judas" (Porter), 1951, 2807
"Fly, The" (Chekhov), 2800
"Fly, The" (Mansfield), 1621

Flying Goat, The (Bates), 200
"Flying Home" (Ellison, Ralph), 839
Flying Home and Other Stories (Ellison, Ralph), 838
"Fog, The" (Kavan), 1342
Folks from Dixie (Dunbar), 795, 2860
Folktale, 2657, 2745, 2975, 3061. *See also* "Category Index"
"For Esmé—with Love and Squalor" (Salinger), 2078
"For Real" (Robison), 2057
"For the Good of the Cause" (Solzhenitsyn), 2190
Ford, Richard, 880-885, 2833; "Communist," 2833; "Great Falls," 882; "Optimists," 881; "Rock Springs," 882, 2833; "Sweethearts," 883; *Wildlife*, 883; *Women with Men*, 884
Foreign Legion, The (Lispector), 1519
Foreseeable Future, The (Price), 1965
"Forest in Full Bloom, The" (Mishima), 1691
"Foring Parts" (Thackery), 2302
"Forks, The" (Powers), 1958
Form, 3061
Forster, E. M., 886-891; *Aspects of the Novel*, 2611; "Celestial Omnibus, The," 889; "Machine Stops, The," 887; "Eternal Moment, The," 888; "Other Kingdom," 887, 889; "Road from Colonus, The," 889; "Story of a Panic, The," 887
Fortune, Reggie, 2618
"Forty-Year-Old Man, A" (Endō), 843
"Forty-five a Month" (Narayan), 1753
"Foundling, The" (Kipling), 1403
"Foundry House" (Friel), 922, 2924
"Four Men in a Cave" (Crane), 656
Fowles, John, 891-897; "Cloud, The," 895; "Ebony Tower, The," 893; "Eliduc," 894; "Enigma, The," 895; "Poor Koko," 894
Fox, The (Lawrence), 2814
"Fox and Swan" (L'Heureux), 1511
Foxe, John; *Book of Martyrs, The*, 2718
"Fragment of the Lives of Three Friends, A" (Hoffmann), 1219
Frame, Janet, 2894-2895; *Lagoon, The*, 2894; "My Last Story," 2895
Frame story, 3061
Framework, 3061
France, 2730; 1880-1920, 2792; and medieval romance, 2692; modern short story and, 2749; novella and, 2704. *See also* "Geographical Index"
France, Anatole, 897-902; "Balthasar," 899; "Crainquebille," 901; "Juggler of Our Lady, The," 900; "M. Pigeonneau," 900; "Procurator of Judea, The," 900; "Putois," 901
Francis, Dick, 2622
Francophone African short fiction, 2849
Frank, I-IV (Edgeworth), 810
Franklin, Benjamin, 903-908; "Alice Addertongue," 905; "Anthony Afterwit," 904; "Bagatelles, The," 2730; "Celia Single," 904; "Ephemera, The," 906; "Extract from an Account of the Captivity of William Henry," 906; "Letter from China, A," 906; *Reflections on Courtship and Marriage*, 2730; "Silence Dogood Essays," 2730; "Speech of Polly Baker," 905
"Franklin's Tale, The" (Chaucer), 529
"Franny" (Salinger), 2080
Franny and Zooey (Salinger), 2080
"Fräulein von Scudéri, Das." *See* "Mademoiselle de Scudéry"
"Fred and Arthur" (Gilliatt), 999
"Frederic and Elfrida" (Austen), 125
"Free Agents" (Apple), 88
Free Joe and Other Georgian Sketches (Harris, Joel Chandler), 1124
"Free Joe and the Rest of the World" (Harris, Joel Chandler), 1124
"Free Will" (Pavese), 1896
"Freedom's a Hard-Bought Thing" (Benét), 245
Freeman, Mary E. Wilkins, 908-914, 2787; "New England Nun, A," 910, 2787; "Poetess, A," 911; "Revolt of 'Mother,' The," 909
Freeman, R. Austin, 2615
"French Lessons" (Rasputin), 2024
"French Poodle, The" (Lewis), 1505
"Fresh Snow, A" (Humphrey), 1246
Friedman, Bruce Jay, 914-920; "Black Angels," 917; "Good Time, The," 917; "Lady," 918; "Partners, The," 918; "Pitched Out," 919; "Punch, The," 917; "Trip, The," 917; "When You're Excused You're Excused," 918
Friedman, Norman, 2607
Friel, Brian, 920-923, 2924; "Among the Ruins," 921; "Diviner, The," 921, 2924; "Foundry House," 922, 2924; "My Father and the Sergeant," 922; "Saucer of Larks, The," 922
Friendly Persuasion, The (West), 2496
Fritz Kochers Aufsätze (Walser), 2439
Frog (Dixon), 751
"Frog Prince, The" (Collier), 609
"From the Journal of a Leper" (Updike), 2381
Frontera de cristal, La. See *Crystal Frontier, The*
"Frontier, The" (Bates), 201
Frye, Northrop; *Words with Power*, 2659
Fuentes, Carlos, 924-929, 2943; *Aura*, 926; *Cantar de ciegos*, 926; "Capital Girl, A," 927; "Chac Mool," 925; *Crystal Frontier, The*, 927-928; *Cumpleaños*, 926; *Holy Place*, 926; "Old Morality, The," 926; "Pain," 927; "Two Elenas, The," 926
"Fugue" (O'Faoláin), 2920
Fun and Games (Major), 1592

Funerales de la Mamá Grande, Los (García Márquez), 953
"Funes the Memorious" (Borges), 2822
"Fur Coat, The" (O'Faoláin), 1819
Further Confessions of Zeno (Svevo), 2271
"Further Reminiscences of Ijon Tichy: IV" (Lem), 1485
Fūten rōjin nikki. See *Diary of a Mad Old Man*
Futrelle, Jacques, 2614
Futurians, 2638

Gaines, Ernest J., 930-935; *Bloodline*, 930, 933; "Just Like a Tree," 934; "Long Day in November, A," 932; "Sky Is Gray, The," 932; "Three Men," 933
Gaitskill, Mary, 936-938; "Because They Wanted To," 937; "Daisy's Valentine," 936; "Girl on the Plane, The," 937; "Something Nice," 937; "Tiny, Smiling Daddy," 937
Galang, M. Evelina, 2883
Gallant, Mavis, 939-944, 2903; "Across the Bridge," 942; "Autumn Day," 941; "Between Zero and One," 943; *Collected Stories of Mavis Gallant, The*, 942; "Doctor, The," 943; "In Youth Is Pleasure," 943; "Moslem Wife, The," 942; "Other Paris, The," 940; "Poor Franzi," 941
Galsworthy, John, 945-950; "Apple Tree, The," 946; "Indian Summer of a Forsyte, The," 947; *On Forsyte 'Change*, 947; "Salvation of a Forsyte, The," 947; "Spindleberries," 948
"Game of Clue, A" (Millhauser), 1684
"Games Without End" (Calvino), 426
"Gamlet Shchigrovskogo uezda." *See* "Prince Hamlet of Shchigrovo"
"Gander-Pulling, The" (Longstreet), 1528
"Gangu." *See* "Toys"
García Márquez, Gabriel, 950-956, 2943; *Chronicle of a Death Foretold*, 954; *Funerales de la Mamá Grande, Los*, 953; *Innocent Eréndira and Other Stories*, 954; *No One Writes to the Colonel*, 953; *Ojos de perro azul*, 952; *Strange Pilgrims*, 954
"Garden of Forking Paths, The" (Borges), 290
"Garden Party, The" (Mansfield), 1623
Gardner, John, 956-963; *Art of Living and Other Stories, The*, 961; "Come on Back," 961; "John Napper Sailing Through the Universe," 959; "King's Indian, The," 960; *King's Indian, The*, 958; "Midnight Reader, The," 958; "Pastoral Care," 958; "Ravages of Spring, The," 958; "Redemption," 961; "Tales of Queen Louisa," 960; "Temptation of St. Ivo, The," 959; "Warden, The," 959
Garland, Hamlin, 963-969, 2789; "Branch Road, A," 966; "Lucretia Burns," 965; "Return of a Private, The," 967; "Sociable at Dudleys, A," 965; "Under the Lion's Paw," 965
Garrett, George, 969-974; *Bad Man Blues*, 972-973; "Cold Ground Was My Bed Last Night," 970; "Genius Baby," 972; "Going to See the Elephant," 973; "Magic Striptease, The," 971; "Wreath for Garibaldi, A," 971
Gascoigne, George; *Discourse of the Adventures Passed by Master F. J., The*, 2712
"Gaspar Ruiz" (Conrad), 625
Gaspard de la nuit (Donoso), 758
Gass, William H., 975-980, 2830; *Cartesian Sonata, The*, 979; "In the Heart of the Heart of the Country," 978; "Mrs. Mean," 978; "Order of Insects," 977, 2830; "Pederson Kid, The," 977
Gates, David, 980-983; "Beating," 982; "Crazy Thought, The," 982; "Intruder, The," 982; "Mail Lady, The," 982; "Saturn," 982; "Star Baby," 981; "Vigil," 982; "Wonders of the Invisible World, The," 981; *Wonders of the Invisible World, The*, 981; "Wronged Husband, A," 981
Gautier, Théophile, 984-987, 2750; "Beautiful Vampire, The," 985; "King Candaules," 986; "Mummy's Foot, The," 2768; "Omphale," 985; "One of Cleopatra's Nights," 986
Gautreux, Tim, 988-991; "Little Frogs in a Ditch," 989; "Piano Tuner, The," 990; "Same Place, Same Things," 988; "Welding with Children," 989
"Gavin O'Leary" (Collier), 608
"Gedali" (Babel), 131
Geismar, Maxwell, 2604
"Gemeine, Das" (Dazai), 702
Gendered, 3061
"General's Day, The" (Trevor), 2342
"Generous Wine" (Svevo), 2271
"Gengobei, the Mountain of Love" (Ihara Saikaku), 2930
"Genius Baby," (Garrett), 972
Genji monogatari. See *Tale of Genji, The*
Genre study, 3061
Genre theory, 2610
Gentle Grafter, The (Henry), 1186
Gentle Insurrection and Other Stories, The (Betts), 252
"Gentleman from Cracow, The" (Singer), 2818
"Gentleman from San Francisco, The" (Bunin), 375
Geoffrey of Monmouth; *History of the Kings of Britain*, 2694
George Silverman's Explanation (Dickens), 728
"Georgia Theatrics" (Longstreet), 1528
"Geranium, The" (O'Connor, Flannery), 1796
"German Refugee, The" (Malamud), 1600
Germany, 2731; 1880-1920, 2793; modern short story and, 2747. *See also* "Geographical Index"
"Germinal" (Æ), 1078
Gerould, Katherine Fullerton, 2755
"Get on with the Sleeping" (Zoshchenko), 2591
"Getting into Death" (Disch), 746
"Ghost Girls" (Oates), 1778
"Ghostly Kiss, The" (Hearn), 1157

"Ghosts, The" (Dunsany), 2797
"Giacca stregata, La." *See* "Bewitched Jacket, The"
"Giacchetta di cuoio, La." *See* "Leather Jacket, The"
"Gift of the Magi, The" (Henry), 1184, 2791
Gilchrist, Ellen, 991-997; "Anna, Part I," 995; "Double Happiness Bun, The," 993; "Down at the Dollhouse," 996; *Drunk with Love*, 994; "Famous Poll at Jody's Bar, The," 993; *Flights of Angels*, 995; "Have a *Wonderful* Nice Walk," 996; *I Cannot Get You Close Enough*, 995; "Jade Buddhas, Red Bridges, Fruits of Love," 993; "Light Can Be Both Wave and Particle," 995; *Light Can Be Both Wave and Particle*, 995; "Mexico," 995; "Miss Crystal Confronts the Past," 995; "Mississippi," 996; "Music," 994; "Rich," 993; "Sordid Tale," 996; "Traceleen at Dawn," 995; "Tree to Be Desired, A," 996; *Victory over Japan*, 993
"Gilded Six-Bits, The" (Hurston), 1253, 2862
"Giles and Penelope" (Wain), 2426
Gilgamesh, 2661
Gilliatt, Penelope, 997-1003; "Antique Love Story, An," 1000; "Fred and Arthur," 999; *Lingo*, 1001; "Living on the Box," 999; *Nobody's Business*, 1000; *Quotations from Other Lives*, 1000; "Redhead, The," 999, 1002; *Splendid Lives*, 1000; "Staying in Bed," 1000; "Stephanie, Stephen, Steph, Steve," 1002; *They Sleep Without Dreaming*, 1001; "What's It Like Out?," 999; *What's It Like Out?*, 999
Gilman, Charlotte Perkins, 1003-1007; "Making a Change," 1005; "Mr. Peebles' Heart," 1006; "When I Was a Witch," 1006; "Yellow Wallpaper, The," 1005
"Gimpel Tam." *See* "Gimpel the Fool"
"Gimpel the Fool" (Singer), 2161, 2818
"Giochi senza fine." *See* "Games Without End"
"Girders, The" (Lavin), 1448
"Girl" (Kincaid), 1364, 2869
"Girl on the Bus, The" (Sansom), 2087
"Girl on the Plane, The" (Gaitskill), 937
"Girls at War" (Achebe), 7, 2852
Girls at War (Achebe), 2851
"Girls in Their Summer Dresses, The" (Shaw), 2133
"Girls' Guide to Hunting and Fishing, The" (Bank), 158
Gissing, George; "House of Cobwebs," 2797
"Give It Up!" (Kafka), 1331
"Giving Birth" (Atwood), 111
Glasgow, Ellen, 1007-1012; "Dare's Gift," 1010; "Difference, The," 1009; "Jordan's End," 1011; "Romance and Sally Byrd," 1009
"Glass Coffin, The" (Byatt), 389
"Glass Family Cycle, The" (Salinger), 2079
"Glass Mountain, The" (Barthelme, Donald), 188
"Glass Scholar, The" (Cervantes), 496
"Glimpse into Another Country" (Morris), 1713
"Go-Away Bird, The" (Spark) , 2199
"Go Back to Your Precious Wife and Son" (Vonnegut), 2420
"Go South in the Winter" (Spencer), 2206
"Godfather Death" (Grimm), 1088
"Godliness" (Anderson), 79
"God's World" (Mahfouz), 1587
"God's Wrath" (Malamud), 1601
Godwin, Gail, 1013-1016; "Amanuensis," 1015; "False Lights," 1014; "Legacy of the Motes, The," 1015; "Nobody's Home," 1014
Goethe, Johann Wolfgang von, 1016-1022; *Conversations of German Emigrants*, 2731; "Fairy Tale, The," 1019; *Novelle*, 1020; *Sorrows of Young Werther, The*, 1018
Gogol, Nikolai, 1022-1029, 2645, 2748-2749; "Diary of a Madman," 1027; "Ivan Fyodorovich Shponka and His Aunt," 1025; "May Night, A," 1025; "Nevsky Prospect," 1026; "Overcoat, The," 1027; "Tale of How Ivan Ivanovich Quarreled with Ivan Nikiforovich, The," 1026; "Taras Bulba," 1026; "Viy," 1026
"Gogol's Wife" (Landolfi), 1431
"Going After Cacciato" (O'Brien, Tim), 1792
"Going Home With Uccello" (Beattie), 215
"Going into Exile" (O'Flaherty), 2922
"Going to Meet the Man" (Baldwin), 137
"Going to See the Elephant (Garrett), 973
"Going Up in the World" (Kavan), 1340
Gold, Herbert, 1030-1033; "Cohorts," 1032; "Heart of the Artichoke, The," 1031; "Love and Like," 1032; *Lovers and Cohorts*, 1031
"Gold Coast" (McPherson), 1582, 2867
"Golden Apple of Eternal Desire, The" (Kundera), 1417
Golden Apples of the Sun, The (Bradbury), 336
"Golden Child" (Price), 1966
Golden Flower Pot, The (Hoffmann), 1219
"Golden Girl" (Hospital), 1229
"Golden Honeymoon" (Lardner), 1436
Goldsmith, Oliver, 1033-1039; *Citizen of the World, The*, 1034; "Disabled Soldier, The," 2728
"Gololeditsa." *See* "Icicle, The"
"Gonzaga Manuscripts, The" (Bellow), 235
Gonzalez, Genaro, 2954
Gonzalez, Luis, 2957
Gonzalez, N. V. M., 2882; *Bread of Salt and Other Stories*, 2882
"Good Advice Is Rarer than Rubies" (Rushdie), 2069
"Good Aunt, The" (Edgeworth), 811
Good Bones and Simple Murders (Atwood), 114
"Good Country People" (O'Connor, Flannery), 1798
"Good Deed, The" (Buck), 369
"Good Man Is Hard to Find, A" (O'Connor, Flannery), 2809
Good Man Is Hard to Find, A (O'Connor, Flannery), 1797
"Good Morrow, Swine" (Stern), 2240

"Good Scent from a Strange Mountain, A" (Butler), 379
"Good Time, The" (Friedman), 917
Good Will (Smiley), 2179
"Good Women, The" (Sillitoe), 2145
"Goodbye and Good Luck" (Paley), 1873
"Goodbye, My Brother" (Cheever), 535
Good-bye, Wisconsin (Wescott), 2492
"Goophered Grapevine, The" (Chesnutt), 551, 2858
Gordimer, Nadine, 1039-1046, 2603; "Abroad," 1042; "Blinder," 1044; "Chip of Glass Ruby, A," 1042; "City of the Dead, a City of the Living, A," 1044; "Defeated, The," 1044; "Soldier's Embrace, A," 1043; "Intruder, The," 1042; "Is There Nowhere Else Where We Can Meet?," 1041; "Sins of the Third Age," 1044; "Six Feet of the Country," 1041; *Something Out There*, 1043
Gordon, Caroline, 1046-1051; "Ice House, The," 1050; "Last Day in the Field, The," 1048; "One Against Thebes," 1049
Gordon, Mary, 1052-1055; "Agnes," 1053; "Delia," 1053; "Eileen," 1054; *Rest of Life, The*, 1054
"Gorilla, My Love" (Bambara), 154
Gorilla, My Love (Bambara), 154, 2869
Gorky, Maxim, 1055-1060; "Chelkash," 1057; "In the Steppe," 1058; "Makar Chudra," 1057; "Man Is Born, A," 1057; "Old Woman Izergil," 1057; "On the Rafts," 1058; "One Autumn Night," 1058; "Orlov Married Couple," 1058; "Song of the Falcon, The," 1057; "Twenty-six Men and a Girl," 1057; "Varenka Olesova," 1058
"Gospodin iz San Frantsisko." *See* "Gentleman from San Francisco, The"
"Gossip" (Conroy), 630
Gothic, 2643, 2729, 2734, 2748, 3061. *See also* "Category Index"
Goyen, William, 1060-1064; "Shape of Light, A," 1062; "White Rooster, The," 1061
"Grabezh." *See* "Robbery, A"
"Grace" (Joyce), 1323
Grace, Alfred; *Maoriland Stories*, 2895; *Tales of a Dying Race*, 2895
"Grammar of Love" (Bunin), 374
"Grammatika liubvi." *See* "Grammar of Love"
Grand parangon des nouvelles nouvelles, Le (Nicolas de Troyes), 2705
"Grande Bretèche, The" (Balzac), 149, 2750
"Grandfather and Grandson" (Singer), 2162
"Grandmother's Tale, The" (Narayan), 1754
Grandmother's Tale and Selected Stories, The (Narayan), 1754
Grau, Shirley Ann, 1065-1069; "Beginning, The," 1068; "Ending," 1068; "Flight," 1068; "Home," 1068; "Housekeeper," 1067; "Hunter," 1067; "Joshua," 1066; "Letting Go," 1068; "Man Outside, The," 1067; "Miss Yellow-Eyes," 1065; *Nine Women*, 1067; "Summer Shore," 1067; "Way Back, The," 1067; "Widow's Walk," 1068; *Wind Shifting West, The*, 1066
"Grave, The" (Porter), 1954, 2807
"Grayling" (Simms), 2150
Great Britain; and medieval romance, 2693; 1920-1960, 2813; and science fiction, 2638; and the supernatural, 2647, 2650. *See also* "Geographical Index"
"Great Falls" (Ford), 882
Great God Pan, The (Machen), 1575
Great Mirror of Male Love, The (Ihara Saikaku), 1265, 2930
"Great Wave, The" (Lavin), 2923
"Greater Grace of Carlisle, The" (Perabo), 1900
Greek myth, 2660
Green Atom Number Five (Donoso), 759
"Green Hills of Earth, The" (Heinlein), 1161
"Green Park" (Wiggins), 2517
"Green Tea" (Le Fanu), 2645, 2915
"Green Thoughts" (Collier), 608
"Green Tunnels" (Huxley), 1258
Greenberg, Joanne, 1069-1074; *High Crimes and Misdemeanors*, 1072; "Hunting Season," 1071; "Supremacy of the Hunza, The," 1070; "Things in Their Season," 1072; *With the Snow Queen*, 1073
Greene, Graham, 1074-1080, 2814; "Basement Room, The," 1077, 2814; "Destructors, The," 1078, 2815; "Germinal," 1078; "Hint of an Explanation, The," 1075; "Lost Childhood, The," 1075
Greene, Robert, 1081-1085, 2714; "Conversion of an English Courtizan," 1084; *Disputation Between a Hee Conny-Catcher and a Shee Conny-Catcher, A*, 1084; *Greene's Groats-worth of Witte Bought with a Million of Repentance*, 1082; *Menaphon*, 1082; *Notable Discovery of Cozenage, A*, 1083; *Pandosto*, 1082
Greene's Groats-worth of Witte Bought with a Million of Repentance (Greene, Graham), 1082
"Greenleaf" (O'Connor, Flannery), 1799, 2826
Gregory of Tours; *Historia Francorum*, 2682
Gregory the Great, 2682; *Dialogues*, 2682
Grettis saga, 2674
"Greyhound People" (Adams), 10
Gridr's Fosterling, Illugi, 2678
"Grieg on a Stolen Piano" (Mphahlele), 1718
Griffith, George, 2634
Grimm, Brothers, 1086-1092, 2658; "Cinderella," 1090; "Fisherman and His Wife, The," 1087; "Godfather Death," 1088; *Grimm's Fairy Tales*, 1086; "Lady and the Lion, The," 1088; "Little Farmer, The," 1089; "Rapunzel," 1088; "Singing Bone, The," 1090; "Six Soldiers of Fortune," 1087; "Sleeping Beauty," 1089; "Snow White," 1090; "Violence," 1090; "Wonderful Glass, The," 1088

Grimm's Fairy Tales (Grimm), 1086
Grobnica za Borisa Davidovi a. See *Tomb for Boris Davidovich, A*
"Grobovshchik." *See* "Undertaker, The"
"Grocer's Daughter" (Wiggins), 2518
"Grosse Fifi, La" (Rhys), 2032
Grotesque, 3061. *See also* "Category Index"
"Growing Season, The" (Caldwell), 406
"Growing Stone, The" (Camus, Albert), 431
"Growing Up" (Higuchi), 2931
"Guardagujas, El." *See* "Switchman, The"
"Guardapelo, El." *See* "Locket, The"
Guardian, The (Steele, Richard), 2214-2216
"Guatemalan Idyll, A" (Bowles, Jane), 307
"Güero, The" (Donoso), 757
"Guest, The" (Camus, Albert), 430, 2819
Guests of Mrs. Timms, The (Jewett), 1301
"Guests of the Nation" (O'Connor, Frank), 1804, 2815
"Guided Tours of Hell" (Prose), 1977, 1979
Guillaume d'Angleterre (Chrétien de Troyes), 569
Guilt Payment (Pak, Ty), 2884
Guilty vicarage crime fiction, 2617
"Guilty Woman, A" (Wescott), 2492
Guimarães Rosa, João, 1092-1095; "Thin Edge of Happiness, The," 1093
"Gulfport" (Smith), 2184
Gulistan. See *Rose Garden, The*
Gullason, Thomas, 2759
"Guns at Cyrano's" (Chandler), 508
Gwynne, Nell; "Miss Vandyke," 2900
Gynocriticism, 3061
"Gyofukuki." *See* "Transformation"
"Gypsy Delegate, The" (Hoch), 1214

"Haguruma." *See* "Cogwheels"
"Haircut" (Lardner), 1435
Hale, Edward Everett; "Man Without a Country, The," 2777
Hale, Nancy, 1096-1101; "Arrangement in Parents, An," 1099; *Empress's Ring, The*, 1097; "Entrance into Life," 1098; *Heaven and Hardpan Farm*, 1098; "Journeys," 1099; *Life in the Studio, The*, 1099; "Miss August," 1097; "On the Beach," 1097; "Pattern of Perfection, The," 1098; *Pattern of Perfection, The*, 1098; *Realities of Fiction, The*, 1099; "Rich People," 1098; *Secrets*, 1099; "Through the Dark Glass to Reality," 1100; "Two Way Imagination, The," 1100
"Half-Holiday" (Huxley), 1258
"Half-Skinned Steer, The" (Proulx), 1982
"Halfway to Hell" (Collier), 606, 609
Haliburton, Thomas Chandler, 2899
Hall, Lawrence Sargent, 1101-1104; "Ledge, The," 1102; "Sequel, The," 1103; "Twenty-three, Please," 1103
Halligan, Marion, 2888
Hamðismál, 2684
"Hammer of God, The" (Chesterton), 559
"Hammer of God, The" (Clarke), 594
Hammett, Dashiell, 1104-1108, 2616; "House in Turk Street, The," 1106
"Hammon and the Beans, The" (Paredes), 2953
Hammon and the Beans and Other Stories, The (Paredes), 2953
Hams al-junūn (Mahfouz), 1587
"Hana." *See* "Nose, The"
"Right Hand, The" (Solzhenitsyn), 2190
"Hands" (Anderson), 78
"Handsome Is as Handsome Does" (Pritchett), 1971
Hangman, The (Lagerkvist), 1422
Hangman's Holiday (Sayers), 2618
Hannah, Barry, 1108-1111, 2837; *Airships*, 1109; *Bats Out of Hell*, 1110; *Captain Maximus*, 1110; *High Lonesome*, 1110; "Testimony of Pilot," 2838; "Water Liars," 2837
"Happily Ever After" (Huxley), 1257
"Happiness" (Lavin), 1447
"Happiness of Others, The" (Price), 1964
"Happy Birthday" (Lispector), 1519
"Happy Death, A" (Lavin), 1445
"Happy Memories Club" (Smith), 2186
Happy to Be Here (Keillor), 1353
"Hapworth 16, 1924" (Salinger), 2082
Hara, Marie, 2880
"Hard Candy" (Williams, Tennessee), 2526
Hard Time to Be a Father, A (Weldon), 2474
Hardy, Thomas, 1112-1118; "Barbara of the House of Grebe," 1115; "Distracted Preacher, The," 1114; "Few Crusted Characters, A," 1115; "Fiddler of the Reels, The," 1114; "Withered Arm, The," 1113
"Hardys, The" (Humphrey), 1246
Harjo, Joy, 1118-1121; "Boston," 1119; "Flood, The," 1119; "Northern Lights," 1119; "Warrior Road," 1120; "Woman Who Fell from the Sky, The," 1120
Harlem Renaissance, 281, 1238, 1249, 2861
Harley Quin stories, 575
Harmony of the World (Baxter), 208
Harper, Frances Ellen Watkins, 2858; "Two Offers, The," 2858
Harris, George Washington; "Mrs. Yardley's Quilting," 2779; "Sicily Burns's Wedding," 2779; *Sut Lovingood*, 2779
Harris, Joel Chandler, 1121-1127, 2780; "Balaam and His Master," 1125; *Balaam and His Master and Other Sketches and Stories*, 1125; *Free Joe and Other Georgian Sketches*, 1124; "Free Joe and the Rest of the World," 1124; "How Mr. Rabbit Saved His Meat," 1123; "Mingo," 1124; *Mingo and Other Sketches in*

Black and White, 1124; "Mr. Rabbit Meets His Match Again," 1123; "Mr. Rabbit Meets His Match at Last," 1123; "Mr. Rabbit Nibbles Up the Butter," 1123; *Nights with Uncle Remus*, 1124; "Sad Fate of Mr. Fox, The," 1123; *Uncle Remus*, 1123; "Where's Duncan?," 1125; "Wonderful Tar-Baby Story, The," 1123
Harris, Wendell, 2601, 2796
Harrison, Jim, 1127-1133; *Brown Dog*, 1130; *Julip*, 1131; *Man Who Gave Up His Name, The*, 1129; *Revenge*, 1128; *Woman Lit by Fireflies, The*, 1131
"Harrison Bergeron" (Vonnegut), 2419
"Harry Belten and the Mendelssohn Violin Concerto" (Targan), 2288
Harte, Bret, 1133-1138; "Outcasts of Poker Flat, The," 1135; "Tennessee's Partner," 2777
"Harvest, The" (Hempel), 1181
Harvest, The (Rivera), 2954
Hasidic tale, 3061
"Hateful Word, The" (Welch), 2470
"Haunted and the Haunters, The" (Bulwer-Lytton), 2770
"Haunted Beach, The" (Adams), 12
"Haunted House, A" (Woolf), 2557
"Haunted Man, The" (Dickens), 729
"Haunted Palace, The" (Roberts), 2050
"Have a *Wonderful* Nice Walk" (Gilchrist), 996
Havelok the Dane, 2696
Hawkesworth, John, 1139-1143; *Almoran and Hamet*, 1141
Hawthorne, Nathaniel, 1143-1152, 2600, 2632, 2644, 2741, 2758, 2761-2762; "Birthmark, The," 1148; "Ethan Brand," 1149; "May-Pole of Merrymount, The," 1147; "Minister's Black Veil, The," 1146, 2763; "My Kinsman, Major Molineux," 1144-1145, 2741, 2763; "Rappaccini's Daughter," 1148, 2764; "Roger Malvin's Burial," 1145; "Young Goodman Brown," 1147, 2644, 2741, 2762
Hawthorne and the Modern Short Story (Rohrberger), 2758
"He" (Porter), 1951
Head, Bessie, 1152-1155; "Collector of Treasures, The," 1153; *Collector of Treasures and Other Botswana Village Tales, The*, 1153, 2854; "Coming of the Christ-Child, The," 1154; "Life," 1154; "Lovers, The," 1154; "Prisoner Who Wore Glasses, The," 1154; "Witchcraft," 2854
Head, Dominic, 2612; *Modernist Short Story, The*, 2610
"Headwaiter" (Himes), 1206
"Health" (Williams), 2522
"Health Card" (Yerby), 2866
Hearn, Lafcadio, 1156-1159; *Fantastics and Other Fancies*, 1157; "Ghostly Kiss, The," 1157; "In a Cup of Tea," 1158; *Kotto*, 1158; *Kwaidan*, 1158; *Some Chinese Ghosts*, 1157; "Soul of the Great Bell, The," 1157; *Stray Leaves from Strange Literature*, 1158; "Vision of the Dead Creole, The," 1157
"Heart" (Robison), 2055
Heart of Darkness (Conrad), 623, 2755
Heart of Happy Hollow, The (Dunbar), 796
"Heart of Stone, A" (Zoshchenko), 2592
"Heart of the Artichoke, The" (Gold), 1031
"Hearts Come Home" (Buck), 369
"Heat Lightning" (Smith), 2184
Heaven and Hardpan Farm (Hale), 1098
"Hector Quesadilla Story, The" (Boyle, T. C.), 328
"*Hee-Haw!*" (Warner), 2450
Hegemony, 3062
Heinlein, Robert A., 1159-1164; "'All You Zombies'," 1162; "Blowups Happen," 2636; "Coventry," 2636; "Green Hills of Earth, The," 1161; "Menace from Earth, The," 1162; "Requiem," 2636; "—We Also Walk Dogs," 1160
Heliodorus; *Ethiopian History, An*, 2666
"Hell Most Feared" (Onetti), 1850
"Hell Screen" (Akutagawa), 39, 2932
"Hellgraue frühjahrsmantel, Der." *See* "Light Gray Spring Coat, The"
"Heloise." *See* "Heroine, The"
"Helping" (Stone), 2256
Helprin, Mark, 1164-1171; "Dove of the East, A," 1167; *Dove of the East and Other Stories, A*, 1166; *Ellis Island and Other Stories*, 1168; "Home Front, The," 1166; "Jew of Persia, A," 1167; "Katherine Comes to Yellow Sky," 1166; "Katrina, Katrin'," 1166; "Last Tea with the Armorers," 1170; "Letters from the *Samantha*", 1168; "North Light," 1169; "Palais de Justice," 1169; "Room of Frail Dancers, A," 1169; "Schreuderspitze, The," 1168
Hemingway, Ernest, 1172-1179, 2606, 2805; "Hills Like White Elephants," 1174; "In Another Country," 1174; "Killers, The," 1175, 2806; "Short Happy Life of Francis Macomber, The," 1176; "Snows of Kilimanjaro, The," 1176, 2806; "Soldier's Home," 1175
Hempel, Amy, 1180-1183; "Harvest, The," 1181; "In the Cemetery Where Al Jolson Is Buried," 1180; "Most Girl Part of You, The," 1182; "Sportsman," 1182; "Today Will Be a Quiet Day," 1181; *Tumble Home*, 1182
Henry, O., 1183-1187, 2791; "Cop and the Anthem, The," 2791; *Gentle Grafter, The*, 1186; "Gift of the Magi, The," 1184, 2791; "Past One at Rooney's," 1185; "Ransom of Red Chief, The," 1186; *Roads of Destiny*, 1185; "Shearing the Wolf, The," 1186; "Trimmed Lamp, The," 1185; "Unfinished Story, An ", 1185
Henryson, Robert; *Morall Fabillis of Esope, the Phrygian, The*, 2628
Heptameron, The (Marguerite de Navarre), 2705

"Her Table Spread" (Bowen), 301, 2922
"Her Whole Existence" (Himes), 1206
"Here Come the Maples" (Updike), 2381
Hermetics, 1428
"Hermitage" (Barnes), 171
"Hérodias" (Flaubert), 877
"Heroine, The" (Dinesen), 742
Hesiod; *Works and Days*, 2626
Hesse, Hermann, 1187-1193; "Evening with Dr. Faust, An," 1190; "Man by the Name of Ziegler, A," 1188; "Poet, The," 1190; "Walter Kömpff," 1189
"Hey Sailor, What Ship?" (Olsen), 1845
Hichens, Robert S., 2648
Hicks, Granville, 2607
"Hiding" (Minot), 1687
"Higgler, The" (Coppard), 641
High Crimes and Misdemeanors (Greenberg), 1072
High Lonesome (Hannah), 1110
"Highland Widow, The" (Scott), 2122
Highsmith, Patricia, 1193-1200; *Animal-Lover's Book of Beastly Murder, The*, 1196; *Black House, The*, 1197; *Little Tales of Misogyny*, 1195; *Mermaids on the Golf Course and Other Stories*, 1198; "Quest for *Blank Claveringi*, The," 1195; *Slowly Slowly in the Wind*, 1196; *Snail-Watcher and Other Stories, The*, 1194; *Tales of Natural and Unnatural Catastrophe*, 1198; "Terrapin, The," 1195
Higuchi Ichiyō, 2931; "Child's Play," 2931; "Growing Up," 2931
"Hijo." *See* "Son, The"
Hildebrandslied, The, 2685
Hildesheimer, Wolfgang, 1201-1204; "End of a World, The," 1203; "I Am Not Writing a Book on Kafka," 1202; "Light Gray Spring Coat, The," 1202; "Sleep," 1203
"Hill of Evil Counsel, The" (Oz), 1862
"Hills Like White Elephants" (Hemingway), 1174
Him with His Foot in His Mouth and Other Stories (Bellow), 236
Himes, Chester, 1204-1209; "All He Needs Is Feet," 1207; "Headwaiter," 1206; "Her Whole Existence," 1206; "His Last Day," 1206; "Lunching at the Ritzmore," 1207; "Nigger, A," 1206; "So Softly Smiling," 1207; "Tang," 1207
"Hint of an Explanation, The" (Greene, Graham), 1075
Hiraoka, Kimitake. *See* Mishima, Yukio
"His Last Day" (Himes), 1206
"His Wife's Deceased Sister" (Stockton), 2253
Hispanic, 2949. *See also* Latino culture, Chicano
Historia Brittonum (Nennius), 2693
Historia ecclesiastica gentis Anglorum. See *Ecclesiastical History of the English People*
Historia Francorum (Gregory of Tours), 2682
Historical criticism, 3062
"History of a Self-Tormentor, The" (Dickens), 727
History of the Kings of Britain (Geoffrey of Monmouth), 2694
History of the Nun, The (Behn), 2723
"Hitchhiking Game, The" (Kundera), 1415
Hoax, The (Svevo), 2270
Hoch, Edward D., 1210-1216; "Christmas Client, The," 1214; "Detective's Wife, The," 1214; *Diagnosis: Impossible*, 1212; "Gypsy Delegate, The," 1214; "I'd Know You Anywhere," 1212; *Leopold's Way*, 1213; "Problem of the General Store, The," 1213; *Quests of Simon Ark, The*, 1211; "Sacajawea's Gold," 1212; *Spy and the Thief, The*, 1212; "Sweating Statue, The," 1214; "Theft of the General's Trash, The," 1213
Hodgson, William Hope, 2648; "Voice of the Night, The," 2634
Hoffmann, E. T. A., 1216-1222, 2643; "Councillor Krespel," 1219; "Doge and Dogaressa," 1220; "Fragment of the Lives of Three Friends, A," 1219; *Golden Flower Pot, The*, 1219; "Interrupted Cadence, An," 1220; "Mademoiselle de Scudéry," 1219; "Mines of Falun, The," 1219; "New Year's Eve Adventure, A," 1220; *Princess Brambilla*, 1220; "Sandman, The," 1220; *Signor Formica*, 1220; "Story of Serapion, The," 1218
"Hoffmeier's Antelope" (Swift), 2273
Hogan, Desmond; "Diamonds at the Bottom of the Sea," 2926
"Hokuro no Tegami." *See* "Mole, The"
Hold On (Douglas), 767
"Hole in the Day" (Tilghman), 2318
"Hole That Jack Dug, The" (Sargeson), 2894
"Holiday" (Porter), 1955
"Holidays" (Kincaid), 1365
"Hollow Stone, A" (Oz), 1863
Holmes, Sherlock, 776-777, 2613, 2615
Holy Place (Fuentes), 926
"Hombre muerto, El." *See* "Dead Man, The"
Hombres de maíz. See *Men of Maize*
"Home" (Grau), 1068
"Home" (Phillips), 2834
"Home Front, The" (Helprin), 1166
"Home Is Where" (Adams), 10
"Home Sickness" (Moore, George), 2917
"Homeland" (Kingsolver), 1376
Homeland and Other Stories (Kingsolver), 1376
Homer, 1222-1227, 2661; *Iliad*, 1223, 2661-2662; *Odyssey*, 1225, 2661-2663
Homewood Trilogy, The. See *Damballah*
Honchō nijū fukō (Ihara Saikaku), 1265
"Honey" (Tallent), 2278
"Honeysuckle, The" (Marie de France), 1627

Honwana, Luís Bernardo; "Old Woman, The," 2848; "Papa, Snake, and I," 2847; "We Killed Mangy-Dog," 2847; *We Killed Mangy-Dog and Other Mozambique Stories*, 2847
Hood, Hugh, 2754
"Hook" (Clark), 588
Hopkins, Pauline Elizabeth, 2859; "Mystery Within Us, The," 2859
Hopkins, Sarah Winnemucca, 2962
Horace, 2661; *Satires*, 2627
"Horla, The" (Maupassant), 1657, 2793
Hornung, E. W., 2615
Horse and Two Goats and Other Stories, A (Narayan), 1753
"Horse Dealer's Daughter, The" (Lawrence), 1453, 2813
"Horse That Could Whistle 'Dixie,'" The" (Weidman), 2464
Hosain, Attia, 2974
Hospital, Janette Turner, 1228-1231; "After Long Absence," 1229; "Golden Girl," 1229; "Litany for the Homeland," 1229; "Unperformed Experiments Have No Results," 1230; "You Gave Me Hyacinths," 1229
"Hostages" (Wideman), 2513
"Hôte, L'." *See* "Guest, The"
Hour of Last Things and Other Stories, An (Elliott), 828
"Hour of Letdown, The" (White), 2508
Hous of Fame (Chaucer), 520
"House in Turk Street, The" (Hammett), 1106
House Made of Dawn (Momaday), 2960, 2962
"House of Cobwebs" (Gissing), 2797
House of Sleep, The (Kavan), 1342
House of the Sleeping Beauties (Kawabata), 1348
House on Mango Street, The (Cisneros), 580
"Housekeeper" (Grau), 1067
"Houses" (Leavitt), 1466
Houston, Pam, 1231-1233; "Best Girlfriend You Never Had, The," 1232; "Moving from One Body of Water to Another," 1233; "Waltzing the Cat," 1233; *Waltzing the Cat*, 1232
"How Beautiful with Shoes" (Steele, Wilbur Daniel), 2219
"How I Became a Holy Mother" (Jhabvala), 1304
"How I Finally Lost My Heart" (Lessing), 1497
"How It Feels to Be Colored Me" (Hurston), 2863
"How It Was Done in Odessa" (Babel), 130
"How Mr. Rabbit Saved His Meat" (Harris, Joel Chandler), 1123
"How Sharp Snaffles Got His Capital and His Wife" (Simms), 2148
"How the Devil Came Down Division Street" (Algren), 60
"How to Tell a Story" (Twain), 2778
Howard, Elizabeth Jane, 2652
Howard, Robert E., 2651
Howe, Irving, 2605
Howells, William Dean, 1234-1237, 2604, 2787; "Angel of the Lord, The," 1236; "Difficult Case, A," 1235; "Editha," 1236, 2787; "Magic of a Voice, The," 1235
Hrafnkel's Saga, 2676
Hreidar the Fool, 2677
"Hua ma." *See* "Picture Horse, The"
"Hua p'i." *See* "Painted Skin, The"
"Hubert and Minnie" (Huxley), 1258
"Hue and Cry" (McPherson), 1583
Hue and Cry (McPherson), 2867
Hughes, Langston, 1238-1243, 2863; "Big Meeting," 1241; *Big Sea, The*, 1238; "Fine Accommodations," 1241; "Little Dog," 1239; "Professor," 1240; "Thank You Ma'am," 1240
"Hull Case, The" (Davies, Peter Ho), 693
"Human Element, The" (Maugham), 1649
Humishuma, 2964; *Cogewea, the Halfblood*, 2964
Humphrey, William, 1243-1249; "Apple of Discord, The," 1247; "Fresh Snow, A," 1246; "Hardys, The," 1246; "Last Husband, The," 1246; *Last Husband and Other Stories, The*, 1245; "Mouth of Brass," 1246; "Quail for Mr. Forester," 1246; *September Song*, 1247; *Time and a Place, A*, 1246; "Voice from the Woods, A," 1246
Hunger (Chang), 511
"Hunger" (Rhys), 2032
"Hunter" (Grau), 1067
"Hunters in the Snow" (Wolff), 2551
"Hunting Season" (Greenberg), 1071
"Hurrah for Freedom" (Lind), 1514
Hurston, Zora Neale, 1249-1255, 2861; "Black Death," 2862; "Cock Robin, Beale Street," 1253; "Drenched in Light," 2862; "Gilded Six-Bits, The," 1253, 2862; "How It Feels to Be Colored Me," 2863; "John Redding Goes to Sea," 1252, 2861; *Mules and Men*, 2863; "Muttsy," 2862; "Spunk," 1252, 2862; "Sweat," 1253
Huxley, Aldous, 1255-1260; "Chawdron," 1258; "Cynthia," 1258; "Fard," 1258; "Green Tunnels," 1258; "Half-Holiday," 1258; "Happily Ever After," 1257; "Hubert and Minnie," 1258; "Little Mexican," 1259; "Portrait, The," 1258; "Rest Cure, The," 1258; "Uncle Spencer," 1258; "Young Archimedes," 1259
Hyder, Qurratulain, 2972
"Hymeneal" (O'Faoláin), 1820
Hyperbole, 3062

"'I Always Wanted You to Admire My Fasting'" (Roth), 2063
"I Am a Fool" (Anderson), 81
I Am Lazarus (Kavan), 1341
"I Am Not Writing a Book on Kafka" (Hildesheimer), 1202
"I Am Twenty-One" (Robison), 2056
I Cannot Get You Close Enough (Gilchrist), 995

"I Do What I Can and I Am What I Am" (Weldon), 2474
"I-80 Nebraska, m. 490-m. 205" (Sayles), 2104
"I Just Love Carrie Lee" (Douglas), 767
"I Knew What I Was Doing" (Weidman), 2464
I-novel, 2932
"I See London, I See France" (Leavitt), 1465
I Sing the Body Electric! (Bradbury), 338
"I Stand Here Ironing" (Olsen), 1845
"I Used to Live Here Once" (Rhys), 2034
"Iazvitel'nyi." *See* "Stinger, The"
"Ice" (Tallent), 2277
"Ice House, The" (Gordon, Caroline), 1050
Icelandic culture, 2669-2670
"Ich schreibe kein buch über Kafka." *See* "I Am Not Writing a Book on Kafka"
"Icicle, The" (Sinyavsky), 2168
"I'd Know You Anywhere" (Hoch), 1212
Idea-as-hero story, 2634, 2636
"Ideal Craftsman, An" (de la Mare), 707
"Idiots First" (Malamud), 1599
"Idle Days on the Yann" (Dunsany), 800
Idrimi, 2658
"If Not Higher" (Peretz), 1909
"If They Knew Yvonne" (Dubus), 790
"If You Don't Want to Live I Can't Help You" (Calisher), 411
Ihara Saikaku, 1261-1267, 2930; *Budō denraiki*, 1265; *Five Women Who Loved Love*, 1263, 2930; "Gengobei, the Mountain of Love," 2930; *Great Mirror of Male Love, The*, 1265, 2930; *Honchō nijū fukō*, 1265; *Japanese Family Storehouse, The*, 1265; *Saikaku okimiyage*, 1266; *Saikaku shokoku-banashi*, 1265; *Tales of Samurai Honor*, 1265; *Worldly Mental Calculations*, 1266
"Iisusov grekh." *See* "Sin of Jesus, The"
Il Novellino: The Hundred Old Tales, 2701
Iliad (Homer), 1223, 2661-2662
Illustrated Man, The (Bradbury), 336
Im Land der Umbramauten (Meckel), 1661
"I'm Not Talking About That, Now" (Magona), 2855
"I'm Your Horse in the Night" (Valenzuela), 2387
"Image-Vendor, The" (Okri), 1840
Imagery, 3062
"Imagination Dead Imagine" (Beckett), 222
Impressionism, 2787, 2790, 2796, 2801. *See also* "Category Index"
In a Café (Lavin), 1447
"In a Café" (Mansfield), 1619
"In a Cup of Tea" (Hearn), 1158
"In a Father's Place" (Tilghman), 2318
"In a Glass Darkly" (Christie), 575
In a Glass Darkly (Le Fanu), 1472
"In a Grove" (Akutagawa), 39, 2932
"In a Strange Country" (Ellison, Ralph), 839
"In a Thicket" (Wescott), 2492
"In a Word, Trowbridge" (Stern), 2243
"In Another Country" (Hemingway), 1174
"In Between the Sheets" (McEwan), 1564
"In Corner B" (Mphahlele), 1719
"In Darkness and Confusion" (Petry), 1919
"In Dreams Begin Responsibilities" (Schwartz, Delmore), 2113
"In Greenwich There Are Many Gravelled Walks" (Calisher), 410
"In guter hut." *See* "Waiting-Room, The"
In His Own Country (Callaghan), 418
"In Jewel" (Robison), 2056
In Love and Trouble (Walker), 2430, 2868
In medias res, 3062
In Old Plantation Days (Dunbar), 796
"In Old Russia" (Zamyatin), 2575
"In Spain, One Thousand and Three" (Byers), 392
"In the Alley" (Elkin), 822
"In the Autumn of the Year" (Oates), 1776
"In the Basement" (Babel), 130
"In the Cemetery Where Al Jolson Is Buried" (Hempel), 1180
"In the City of Red Dust" (Okri), 1841
"In the Cutting of a Drink" (Aidoo), 2852
"In the Forest" (de la Mare), 706
"In the Garden" (Paley), 1875
"In the Garden of the North American Martyrs" (Wolff), 2551
In the Garden of the North American Martyrs (Wolff), 2551
"In the Heart of the Heart of the Country" (Gass), 978
"In the Loyal Mountains" (Bass), 195
In the Midst of Life. See *Tales of Soldiers and Civilians*
"In the Realm of the Heron" (Kaplan), 1336
"In the Region of Ice" (Oates), 1775
"In the Steppe" (Gorky), 1058
"In the Train" (O'Connor, Frank), 1804
In the Village of Viger (Scott), 2901
"In Youth Is Pleasure" (Gallant), 943
Inada, Lawson Fusao, 2877
"Incautious Burglar, The" (Carr), 467
"Incident at Krechetovka Station" (Solzhenitsyn), 2189
"Incident on a Lake" (Collier), 607
Incidents at the Shrine (Okri), 1839
Incognita (Congreve), 612, 2724
"Incredible Voyage" (Endō), 844
Increíble y triste historia de la Cándida Eréndira y de su abuela desalmada, La. *See* "New Islands"
"Ind Aff or Out of Love in Sarajevo" (Weldon), 2474
Indian Boyhood (Eastman), 2963

Indian culture, 2972. *See also* "Category Index"; "Geographical Index"
"Indian Summer of a Forsyte, The" (Galsworthy), 947
"Indian Uprising, The" (Barthelme, Donald), 185
"Indian Well, The" (Clark), 588
Industrial Age, 2726
"Infant Prodigy, The" (Mann), 1611
Inferno, The (Dante), 672
"Infinite Passion of Expectation, The" (Berriault), 250
"Inhabitant of Carcosa, An" (Bierce), 2649
Initiation story, 3062
Injustice Collectors, The (Auchincloss), 118
"Inkle and Yarico" (Steele, Richard), 2215
"Innocence" (Brodkey), 356-357
Innocent and the Guilty, The (Warner), 2453
Innocent Eréndira and Other Stories (García Márquez), 954
Innocent Eréndira Islas nuevas, Las. See "New Islands"
"Inside the Frame" (Coover), 636
"Interference" (Barnes), 170
Interior monologue, 3062
"Intermission" (Coover), 636
Interpretation, 3062
"Interpreter of Maladies, The" (Gates), 1425
Interpreter of Maladies (Lahiri), 2975
"Interrupted Cadence, An" (Hoffmann), 1220
"Into the Cone of Cold" (Elliott), 828
"Intruder, The" (Dixon), 751
"Intruder, The" (Dubus), 789
"Intruder, The" (Gates), 982
"Intruder, The" (Gordimer), 1042
"Inventing the Abbotts" (Miller), 1681
"Inverno di malato" (Moravia), 1705
"Invisible Dove Dancer of Strathpheen Island, The" (Collier), 609
"Invisible Hands" (Carr), 467
"Invisible Lover, The" (Queen), 2015
Invisible Man (Ellison), 2865
Ireland, 2914-2927; 1880-1920, 2800; 1920-1960, 2815. *See also* "Geographical Index"
"Irene" (Bell), 231
Irish Literary Revival, 1322
"Irish Revel, The" (O'Brien, Edna), 2923
"Iron Will" (Leskov), 1492
Irrealism, 3062. *See also* "Category Index"
Irving, Washington, 1268-1273, 2600, 2643, 2738, 2756; "Legend of Sleepy Hollow, The," 1271; "Little Man in Black, The," 1269, 2738; "Rip Van Winkle," 1270, 2738-2740; *Sketch Book of Geoffrey Crayon, Gent., The*, 2644; "Sketches from Nature," 1269; "Spectre Bridegroom, The," 1270
"Is There Nowhere Else Where We Can Meet?" (Gordimer), 1041
"Island, The" (Jackson), 1275
Island Like You, An (Ortiz), 2958
"Island of Monkeys, The" (Dazai), 701
Islanders, The (Zamyatin), 2574
"Islands on the Moon" (Kingsolver), 1377
Íslendingabók. See *Book of the Icelanders*
Issei, 2877
"Istoriia moei golubiatni." *See* "Story of My Dovecote, The"
Italian culture, 2702. *See also* "Category Index"
Italy, 2733. *See also* "Geographical Index"
"Ivan Fyodorovich Shponka and His Aunt" (Gogol), 1025
Ivar's Story, 2678
"Izu Dancer, The" (Kawabata), 1346

"Jackrabbit" (Chan), 2875
Jackson, Shirley, 1274-1279; "Beautiful Stranger, The," 1275; "Island, The," 1275; "Little House, The," 1275; "Lottery, The," 1277; "Louisa, Please," 1275; "Pillar of Salt," 1276; "Tooth, The," 1275; "Visit, The," 1276
Jacobs, W. W., 1279-1282, 2648; "Blundell's Improvement," 1281; "Contraband," 1280; "Monkey's Paw, The," 1281
"Jade Buddhas, Red Bridges, Fruits of Love" (Gilchrist), 993
"Jakarta" (Munro), 1736
James, Henry, 1283-1291, 2649, 2789; "Altar of the Dead, The," 1287; "Aspern Papers, The," 1286; "Beast in the Jungle, The," 1288; *Daisy Miller*, 1285, 2783; "Figure in the Carpet, The," 1287; "Jolly Corner, The," 1289; "Real Thing, The," 1286, 2789
James, M. R., 1291-1296, 2647; "Lost Hearts," 1293; "Oh, Whistle, and I'll Come to You, My Lad," 1294
"Janet's Repentance" (Eliot), 818
"Janus" (Beattie), 214, 2832
Japan, 2928-2935; medieval, 2929; 1600-1868, 2930; modern, 2931; 900-1600, 2928; 1920-1960, 2821. *See also* "Geographical Index"
Japanese American culture, 2877, 2880. *See also* "Category Index"
Japanese Family Storehouse, The (Ihara Saikaku), 1265
Japanese Tales (Tyler, Royall), 2929
"Jasmine" (Mukherjee), 1726
"Je Ne Parle Pas Français" (Mansfield), 1619
"Je Suis le Plus Malade des Surrealistes" (Nin), 1762
"Jean Beicke" (Williams, William Carlos), 2532
"Jean-Pierre" (Spencer), 2206
"Jean-ah Poquelin" (Cable), 397, 2780
Jeannot and Colin (Voltaire), 2413
"Jeffrey, Believe Me" (Smiley), 2177
"Jeffty Is Five" (Ellison, Harlan), 835
Jen, Gish; *Who's Irish?*, 2876
"Jerusalem's Lot" (King), 1370

Jest-books, 2718
"Jew of Persia, A" (Helprin), 1167
"Jewbird, The" (Malamud), 1600
Jewett, Sarah Orne, 1296-1302; *Country of the Pointed Firs, The*, 1297-1298; *Guests of Mrs. Timms, The*, 1301; "Martha's Lady," 1300; "Only Rose, The," 1299; "White Heron, A," 1298
Jewish culture, 2811, 2827, 2836. *See also* "Category Index"; "Geographical Index"
Jhabvala, Ruth Prawer, 1302-1306, 2972-2973, 2976; "Course of English Studies, A," 1304; *East into Upper East*, 2976; "Fidelity," 1305; "How I Became a Holy Mother," 1304; "Old Lady, The," 1304
"Jockey, The" (McCullers), 1557
"John Napper Sailing Through the Universe" (Gardner), 959
"John Redding Goes to Sea" (Hurston), 1252, 2861
"John Sherman" (Yeats), 2568
John Silence (Blackwood), 264
"Johnny Panic and the Bible of Dreams" (Plath), 1934
"Johnny Pye and the Fool-Killer" (Benét), 246
Johnson, Charles, 1306-1309; "ALĒTHIA," 1308; "China," 1308; "Education of Mingo, The," 1307; "Kwoon," 1308
Johnson, Denis, 1310-1313; "Beverly Home," 1311; "Car Crash While Hitchhiking," 1311; "Dirty Wedding," 1312; "Emergency," 1311
Johnson, E. Pauline, 2962; *Legends of Vancouver*, 2962; "Red Girl's Reasoning, A," 2962
Johnson, Samuel, 1314-1319; *Rasselas*, 1316
"Jolly Corner, The" (James, Henry), 1289
Jones, Edith Newbold. *See* Wharton, Edith
Jones, Everett LeRoi. *See* Baraka, Amiri
Jones, Thom, 2838; "White Horse, The," 2838
"Jongleur de Notre-Dame, Le." *See* "Juggler of Our Lady, The"
"Jordan's End" (Glasgow), 1011
Joseph Conrad (O'Flaherty), 1827
"Joshua" (Grau), 1066
"Journey Through the Night" (Lind), 1515
"Journey to Petrópolis" (Lispector), 1519
"Journey to the Seven Streams, A" (Kiely), 1357
"Journeys" (Hale), 1099
"Joy Luck Club, The" (Tan), 2281
Joy Luck Club, The (Tan), 2281
Joyce, James, 1319-1327, 2801, 2917; "Araby," 2918; "Dead, The," 1322-1323, 1326, 2801, 2918; *Dubliners*, 1321, 2801; "Eveline," 2917; "Grace," 1323; "Painful Case, A," 1323
"Joycelin Shrager Story, The" (Disch), 747
"Juan Darién" (Quiroga), 2021
"Judas" (O'Connor, Frank), 2921
"Judas Tree, The" (Welch), 2468
"Judgement Day" (O'Connor, Flannery), 1800
"Judgment, The" (Kafka), 1330
"Juggler of Our Lady, The" (France), 900
Jules Verne Steam Balloon, The (Davenport), 688
"Julia and the Bazooka" (Kavan), 1342
Julia and the Bazooka and Other Stories (Kavan), 1342
"Julia Cahill's Curse" (Moore, George), 2800, 2916
Julip (Harrison), 1131
Junglee Girl (Kamani), 2885
"Junior" (Lewis), 1506
"Junius Maltby" (Steinbeck), 2236
"Jūrokusai no nikki." *See* "Diary of a Sixteen-Year-Old"
"Just Like a Tree" (Gaines), 934
Just So Stories (Kipling), 1392

"Kabnis" (Toomer), 2338
Kafka, Franz, 1328-1335, 2646; "Before the Law," 1332; "Bucket Rider, The," 1332; "Country Doctor, A," 1333; "Give It Up!," 1331; "Judgment, The," 1330; *Metamorphosis, The*, 2794
"Kafkas" (Wiggins), 2517
"Kak eto delalos v Odesse." *See* "How It Was Done in Odessa"
Kamani, Ginu, 2885; *Junglee Girl*, 2885
"Kamennoe serdtse." *See* "Heart of Stone, A"
"Kamienny świat." *See* "World of Stone"
Kaplan, David Michael, 1336-1339; "Comfort," 1337; "Doe Season," 1337; "Elisabetta, Carlotta, Catherine," 1337; "In the Realm of the Heron," 1336; "Love, Your Only Mother," 1336; "Skating in the Dark," 1338; *Skating in the Dark*, 1338; "Summer People," 1336
Kappa, 40
"Kataude." *See* "One Arm" (Kawabata)
"Katherine Comes to Yellow Sky" (Helprin), 1166
"Katrina, Katrin'" (Helprin), 1166
Kavan, Anna, 1339-1344; "Asylum Piece," 1341; "Birthmark, The," 1340; "Fog, The," 1342; "Going Up in the World," 1340; *House of Sleep, The*, 1342; *I Am Lazarus*, 1341; "Julia and the Bazooka," 1342; *Julia and the Bazooka and Other Stories*, 1342; *My Soul in China*, 1343; "Old Address, The," 1342; "Palace of Sleep, The," 1341; "There Is No End," 1341; "World of Heroes, The," 1342
Kawabata, Yasunari, 1344-1349, 2933; "Diary of a Sixteen-Year-Old," 1346; *House of the Sleeping Beauties*, 1348; "Izu Dancer, The," 1346; "Man Who Did Not Smile, The," 1347; "Mole, The," 1347; "Moon on the Water, The," 1347; "Of Birds and Beasts," 1347; "One Arm," 1348; *Palm-of-the-Hand Stories*, 2933; *Snow Country*, 2933
"Keela, the Outcast Indian Maiden" (Welty), 2484
Keillor, Garrison, 1350-1356; *Happy to Be Here*, 1353; *Lake Wobegon Days*, 1353; *Leaving Home*, 1353;

Prairie Home Companion, A, 1354; "Wake, The," 1354; *We Are Still Married*, 1354
Kenny, Maurice; "What's in a Song," 2969
"Kepi, The" (Colette), 602
"Kerchief, The" (Agnon), 25
"Kew Gardens" (Woolf), 2557
"Khat" (Dreiser), 785
"Kholstomer." *See* "Strider"
"Khor and Kalynich" (Turgenev), 2354
"Khor'i Kalynich." *See* "Khor and Kalynich"
Kibert, Declan, 2915
"Kid in the Stove, The" (Kinsella), 1386. *See also* Silas Ermineskin stories
Kiely, Benedict, 1356-1362; "Ball of Malt and Madame Butterfly, A," 1357; "Bluebell Meadow," 1360; "Cow in the House, A," 1357; "Down Then by Derry," 1360; "Journey to the Seven Streams, A," 1357; "Maiden's Leap," 1359
"Killers, The" (Hemingway), 1175, 2806
"Killing of Colin Moosefeathers, The" (Kinsella), 1385. *See also* Silas Ermineskin stories
Kincaid, Jamaica, 1362-1367, 2869, 2947; "At the Bottom of the River," 1365; "Circling Hand, The," 2870; "Girl," 1364, 2869; "Holidays," 1365; "Letter from Home, The," 1365; "My Mother," 1365; "What I Have Been Doing Lately," 1365; "Xuela," 1366
"Kind of Light That Shines on Texas, The" (McKnight), 1579
"King, The" (Babel), 130
King, Stephen, 1368-1374, 2652; "Ballad of the Flexible Bullet, The," 1372; "Body, The," 1371; "Jerusalem's Lot," 1370; "Man in the Black Suit, The," 1372; "Mangler, The," 1370; "Monkey, The," 1370; "One for the Road," 1370; "Trucks," 1370; "Woman in the Room, The," 1371
King, Thomas, 2905
"King Caliban" (Wain), 2426
"King Candaules" (Gautier), 986
"King Lear of the Steppes" (Turgenev), 2356
"King of the Bingo Game" (Ellison, Ralph), 839
"King of the Trenches, The" (Lewis), 1507
Kingdoms of Elfin (Warner), 2454
"King's Ankus, The" (Kipling), 1392
"King's Indian, The" (Gardner), 960
King's Indian, The (Gardner), 958
"Kingsmeat" (Card), 447
Kingsolver, Barbara, 1374-1377; "Homeland," 1376; *Homeland and Other Stories*, 1376; "Islands on the Moon," 1377
Kingston, Maxine Hong, 1378-1381; "Adventures of Lo Bun Sun, The," 1380; *China Men*, 1380; "Laws, The," 1380; "No Name Woman," 1379; "On Discovery," 1380; "White Tigers," 1380
"Kinjū." *See* "Of Birds and Beasts"
Kinsella, W. P., 1382-1388; "Book Buyers, The," 1383; "Brother Frank's Gospel Hour," 1387; "Bull," 1386; "Evangeline's Mother," 1383; "Kid in the Stove, The," 1386; "Killing of Colin Moosefeathers, The," 1385; "Last Pennant Before Armageddon, The," 1384; "Thrill of the Grass, The," 1384
"Kinsman of His Blood, A" (Wolfe), 2546
Kipling, Rudyard, 1388-1396, 1646, 2606, 2798; "Beyond the Pale," 1390; "Brush-Wood Boy, The," 1391; "Dayspring Mishandled," 1394; "Dymchurch Flit," 1392; *Just So Stories*, 1392; "King's Ankus, The," 1392; "Love-o'-Women," 1390; "Man Who Would Be King, The," 2799; "Mary Postgate," 1394; "Mrs. Bathurst," 1392; "Phantom 'Rickshaw, The," 1391; *Puck of Pook's Hill*, 1392; "They," 1394; "Wish House, The," 1391
Kiš, Danilo, 1397-1400; *Early Sorrows*, 1398; "Encyclopedia of the Dead," 1399; "Knife with the Rosewood Handle, The," 1399; "Pages from a Velvet Album," 1398; "Sow That Eats Her Farrow, The," 1399; *Tomb for Boris Davidovich, A*, 1398
"Kite and Paint" (Robison), 2054
Klausner, Amos. *See* Oz, Amos
Klein, T. E. D., 2652
"Kleine Herr Friedemann, Der." *See* "Little Herr Friedemann"
Kleist, Heinrich von, 1400-1406; "Beggarwoman of Locarno, The," 1404; "Earthquake in Chile, The," 1401; "Foundling, The," 1403; "Marionette Theater, The," 1402; *Michael Kohlhaas*, 1403; *Prince of Homburg, The*, 1400; "St. Cecilia," 1404
"Kneel to the Rising Sun" (Caldwell), 406
"Knife Thrower, The" (Millhauser), 1685
Knife Thrower and Other Stories, The (Millhauser), 1684
"Knife with the Rosewood Handle, The" (Kiš), 1399
Knight, Damon, 2638
"Knight's Tale, The" (Chaucer), 525
"Knights and Dragons" (Spencer), 2205
"Knight's Tale, The" (Chaucer), 525
"Knot, The" (Minot), 1688
Knowles, John, 1406-1411; "Phineas," 1409; *Phineas*, 1407; "Turn with the Sun, A," 1408
"Knoxville" (Agee), 20
"Kobutori." *See* "Taking the Wen Away"
"Kohei." *See* "Currency"
"Kolacje." *See* "Supper, The"
Kompromiss. See *Compromise, The*
"Konets bogadel'ni." *See* "End of the Old Folks' Home, The"
"Kong yiji" (Lu), 1545
Konjaku monogatari. See *Tales of Times Now Past*
Kōno Taeko, 2934; "Toddler-Hunting," 2934

"Kool-Aid Wino, The" (Brautigan), 344
"Korea" (McGahern), 1567
Korean American culture, 2883
Kornbluth, Cyril M., 2637
Kōshoku gonin onna. *See Five Women Who Loved Love*
Kotto (Hearn), 1158
Kreutzer Sonata, The (Tolstoy), 2332
"Kristu-Du" (Carey) , 452
"Kübelreiter, Der" *See* "Bucket Rider, The"
"Kugelmass Episode, The" (Allen), 64
"Kumo no ito." *See* "Spider's Thread, The"
Kundera, Milan, 1412-1419; "Edward and God," 1416; "Golden Apple of Eternal Desire, The," 1417; "Hitchhiking Game, The," 1415; *Laughable Loves*, 1414; "Let the Old Dead Make Room for the Young Dead," 1416; "Nobody Will Laugh," 1414; "Symposium," 1416
"Kuno no nenkan." *See* "Almanac of Pain, An"
Kurosawa, Akira, 39
"Kvartiranty." *See* "Tenants"
Kwaidan (Hearn), 1158
"Kwoon" (Johnson, Charles), 1308
Kyng Alisaunder, 2692
"Kyōfu." *See* "Terror"

"Labor Day Dinner" (Munro), 1734
Labours of Hercules (Christie), 2620
"Lady, A" (Donoso), 757
"Lady" (Friedman), 918
"Lady and the Lion, The" (Grimm), 1088
"Lady Macbeth of the Mtsensk District" (Leskov), 1491
"Lady on the Grey, The" (Collier), 608
Lady Susan (Austen), 125
La Fontaine, Jean de, 2629
Lagerkvist, Pär, 1420-1423; *Eternal Smile, The*, 1421; "Far och jag," 1422; *Hangman, The*, 1422; "Lilla fälttåget, Det," 1422
"Lagoon, The" (Conrad), 622
Lagoon, The (Frame), 2894
La Guma, Alex; "A Walk in the Night," 2854
Lahiri, Jhumpa, 1424-1427, 2972, 2975; "Interpreter of Maladies, The," 1425, 2975; "Temporary Matter, A," 1425; "Third and Final Continent, The," 1426; *When Mr. Pirzada Came to Dinner*, 1425
Lai, 3062
Lais (Marie de France), 1625
"Laissé-pour-compte, Le." *See* "Misfit, The"
Lake Wobegon Days (Keillor), 1353
Lake Wobegon stories (Keillor), 1352
Lamb, Charles; "Dream Children," 2745
"Lamb to the Slaughter" (Dahl), 665
"Lame Shall Enter First, The" (O'Connor, Flannery), 1799
"Lamia in the Cévennes, A" (Byatt), 389
Lancelot (Chrétien de Troyes), 569, 2695
"Land of Exile" (Pavese), 1894
Land Without Thunder (Ogot), 2853
"Landarzt, Ein." *See* "Country Doctor, A"
"Landfill Meditation" (Vizenor), 2407
Landnámabók. See *Book of Settlements*
Landolfi, Tommaso, 1427-1433; *Cancerqueen*, 1430; "Gogol's Wife," 1431; "Mute, The," 1431; *Two Old Maids, The*, 1429
Landwirth, Heinz. *See* Lind, Jakov
Lang Xian, 2909
"Lantern Slides" (O'Brien, Edna), 2923
"Lanval" (Marie de France), 1626
Lao She, 2909, 2911
"Lappin and Lapinova" (Woolf), 2557
Lapse of Time (Wang), 2445
Lardner, Ring, 1434-1438; "Champion," 1435; "Ex Parte," 1436; "Golden Honeymoon," 1436; "Haircut," 1435; "Some Like Them Cold," 1436
Larson, Charles; *Under African Skies*, 2846
Las Casas, Bartolomé de, 2939
"Las Vegas Charley" (Yamamoto), 2879
"Last Class, The" (Daudet), 679
"Last Day, The" (Verga), 2396
"Last Day in the Field, The" (Gordon, Caroline), 1048
"Last Escapade, The" (Alarcón), 44
"Last Frontier, The" (Schwartz, Lynne Sharon), 2119
"Last Husband, The" (Humphrey), 1246
Last Husband and Other Stories, The (Humphrey), 1245
"Last Kiss" (Fitzgerald), 869
Last Lovely City, The (Adams), 12
"Last May" (Dixon), 750
"Last Mohican, The" (Malamud), 1598, 2827
Last of Chéri, The (Colette), 2818
Last of the Menu Girls, The (Chavez), 2956
"Last Pennant Before Armageddon, The" (Kinsella), 1384
"Last Tea with the Armorers" (Helprin), 1170
"Late Love" (Oz), 1863
Latin America, 2822, 2936-2948. *See also* "Geographical Index"
Latino culture, 2936, 2944, 2949-2959. *See also* "Category Index"
Laughable Loves (Kundera), 1414
"Laura Borealis" (Reid), 2029
Laurence, Margaret, 1438-1442; "Bird in the House, A," 1441; *Bird in the House, A*, 1441; "Drummer of All the World, The," 1441; "Perfume Sea, The," 1440; "Tomorrow-Tamer, The," 1440; *Tomorrow-Tamer, The* (Laurence), 1440; "Voices of Adamo, The," 1440
"Laüstic" (Marie de France), 1627
Lavin, Mary, 1443-1449, 2923; "At Sallygap," 1445; "Eterna," 1447; "Girders, The," 1448; "Great Wave, The," 2923; "Happiness," 1447; "Happy Death, A,"

1445; *In a Café*, 1447; "Miss Holland," 1444; "Sarah," 2923; "Say Could That Lad Be I," 1446; "Senility," 1446; *Tales from Bective Bridge*, 2923; "Tom," 1446
"Law of Life" (London), 1524
Lawley Road (Narayan), 1753
"Lawns" (Simpson), 2155
Lawrence, D. H., 1449-1457, 2813; "Blind Man, The," 1452; "Crown, The," 1454; *Fox, The*, 2814; "Horse Dealer's Daughter, The," 1453, 2813; *Man Who Died, The*, 1455; "Odour of Chrysanthemums," 1451; "Princess, The," 1455; "Prussian Officer, The," 1453, 2814; *St. Mawr*, 1455; "Shades of Spring, The," 1452; "Shadow in the Rose Garden, The," 1452; "Tickets, Please," 2813; "Woman Who Rode Away, The," 1455; "You Touched Me," 1453
"Laws, The" (Kingston), 1380
Lawson, Henry, 1458-1462, 2889; "Drover's Wife, The," 1460; "Song of the Republic, A," 2889; "Union Buries Its Dead, The," 1460; "'Water Them Geraniums,'" 1461
Laxdœla Saga, 2674
Lay, 3062
Laye, Camara; "Eyes of the Statue, The," 2850
Leacock, Stephen, 2901
"Leaning Tower, The" (Porter), 1954
"Leap, The" (Barthelme, Donald), 187
"Learning to Swim" (Swift), 2272
Learning to Swim and Other Stories (Swift), 2841
"Leather Jacket, The" (Pavese), 1895
"Leaves from the Mental Portfolio of an Eurasian" (Sui Sin Far), 2874
Leaving Home (Keillor), 1353
"Leaving Home" (Miller), 1680
"Leaving One, The" (Offutt), 1824
Leavitt, David, 1463-1469, 2834; *Arkansas*, 1467; "Ayor," 1465; "Dedicated," 1464, 2835; "Houses," 1466; "I See London, I See France," 1465; "Lost Cottage, The," 1466; "My Marriage to Vengeance," 1466; "Place I've Never Been, A," 1465; *Place I've Never Been, A*, 2834; "Saturn Street," 1468; "Spouse Night," 1467; "Term Paper Artist, The," 1467; "Territory," 1465, 2834; "When You Grow to Adultery," 1465; "Wooden Anniversary, The," 1468
"Lechery" (Phillips), 2834
"Ledge, The" (Hall), 1102
"Ledi Makbet Mtsenskogo uezda." *See* "Lady Macbeth of the Mtsensk District"
Lee, Manfred Bennington. *See* Queen, Ellery
Le Fanu, Joseph Sheridan, 1469-1475, 2645, 2915; "Carmilla," 1472; "Child That Went with the Fairies, The," 2645; "Green Tea," 2645, 2915; *In a Glass Darkly*, 1472; "Madame Crowl's Ghost," 2645; "Schalken the Painter," 1471
Left Bank and Other Stories, The (Rhys), 2031
"Legacy, The" (Spencer), 2206
"Legacy of the Motes, The" (Godwin), 1015
Legend, 3062
Legend of Good Women (Chaucer), 522
"Legend of Miss Sasagawara, The" (Yamamoto), 2879
"Legend of St. Julian, Hospitaler, The" (Flaubert), 876, 2792
"Legend of Sleepy Hollow, The" (Irving), 1271
"Legend of the Man with the Golden Brain, The" (Daudet), 679
"Legend of Tularecito, The" (Steinbeck), 2236
"Légende de l'homme à la cervelle d'or, La." *See* "Legend of the Man with the Golden Brain, The"
"Légende de Saint Julien l'Hospitalier, La." *See* "Legend of St. Julian, Hospitaler, The"
Legends of Vancouver (Johnson, E. Pauline), 2962
Le Guin, Ursula K., 1476, 1481, 2641; "Darkness Box," 1478; *Fisherman of the Inland Sea, A*, 1479; "Ones Who Walk Away from Omelas, The," 1479
Leiber, Fritz, 2640, 2651
Leiden des jungen Werthers, Die. See *Sorrows of Young Werther, The*
Leitmotif, 3062
Lem, Stanisław, 1481-1488, 2640; "Albatross, The," 1486; *Cyberiad*, 1486; "Further Reminiscences of Ijon Tichy: IV," 1485; *Memoirs of a Space Traveler*, 1484; *Mortal Engines*, 1486; "Patrol, The," 1485; *Perfect Vacuum, A*, 1483; *Tales of Pirx the Pilot*, 1485; "Test, The," 1485
Leopold's Way (Hoch), 1213
Lepofsky, Manfred. *See* Queen, Ellery
Leprohon, Rosanna; "Alice Sydenham's First Ball," 2899
Leskov, Nikolai, 1488-1494; "Amazon, The," 1491; "At the Edge of the World," 1491; "Iron Will," 1492; "Lady Macbeth of the Mtsensk District," 1491; "March Hare, The," 1493; "Musk-Ox, The," 1490; "Night Owls," 1493; "Robbery, A," 1493; "Sealed Angel, The," 1491; "Sentry, The," 1492; "Stinger, The," 1490; "Toupee Artist, The," 1492; "Winter's Day, A," 1493
Lessing, Doris, 1494-1501; "Casualty," 1499; "How I Finally Lost My Heart," 1497; "Man and Two Women, A," 1498; "New Café, The," 1498; "Sparrows," 1499; "Storms," 1499; "Two Old Women and a Young One," 1499
Lessing, Gotthold, 2629
"Lesson, The" (Bambara), 155
"Let the Old Dead Make Room for the Young Dead" (Kundera), 1416
"Let Us Quickly Hasten to the Gate of Ivory" (Disch), 746
"Letter, A" (Babel), 131
"Letter from China, A" (Franklin), 906
"Letter from Home, The" (Kincaid), 1365
"Letter to a Commissioner of Novellas " (Walser), 2442
"Letter to a Learned Neighbor, A" (Chekhov), 542

"Letter to a Young Lady in Paris" (Cortázar), 646
Letters de mon moulin. See *Letters from My Mill*
Letters from My Mill (Daudet), 678
"Letters from the *Samantha*" (Helprin), 1168
"Letters from Tula" (Pasternak), 1889
"Letting Go" (Grau), 1068
Leucippe and Clitophon (Tatius), 2666
Levine, Norman, 2903
Lew Archer, Private Investigator (Macdonald), 2621
Lewis, C. S., 2611
Lewis, Wyndham, 1501-1509; "Bishop's Fool, The," 1505; "Breton Innkeeper, A," 1504; "Cantleman's Spring-Mate," 1504, 1506; "Children of the Great," 1506; "Code of a Herdsman, The," 1506; "Doppelganger," 1506; "French Poodle, The," 1505; "Junior," 1506; "King of the Trenches, The," 1507; "Man Who Was Unlucky with Women, The," 1505; "Room Without a Telephone, The," 1504; "Rot, The," 1505; *Rotting Hill*, 1505; "Time the Tiger," 1505; "Unlucky for Pringle," 1504; "War Baby, The," 1504, 1506; *Wild Body, The*, 1503
"Leyenda del sombrerón" (Asturias), 104
Leyendas de Guatemala (Asturias), 104
L'Heureux, John, 1509-1513; "Comedian, The," 1512; "Departures," 1511; "Fox and Swan," 1511; "Priest's Wife, The," 1511
"Liar!" (Asimov), 97
"Library of Babel, The" (Borges), 2823
Licht (Meckel), 1662
"Life" (Head), 1154
"Life Among the Oilfields" (Yamamoto), 2879
"Life Guard, The" (Wain), 2426
Life in the Studio, The (Hale), 1099
"Life of Engineer Kipreev, The" (Shalamov), 2128
Life of St. Alexis, 2688
"Life of the Body, The" (Wolff), 2553
"Life on the Moon" (Smith), 2185
"Life You Save May Be Your Own, The" (O'Connor, Flannery), 1797
"Life, Death" (Sansom), 2088
"Lifeguard, The" (Beattie), 212
"Lifted Veil, The" (Eliot), 818
"Light Can Be Both Wave and Particle" (Gilchrist), 995
Light Can Be Both Wave and Particle (Gilchrist), 995
"Light Gray Spring Coat, The" (Hildesheimer), 1202
"Like a Lover" (Wescott), 2492
"Like a Winding Sheet" (Petry), 1919
"Like Argus of Ancient Times" (London), 1525
Like One of the Family (Childress), 2869
"Like the Night" (Carpentier), 461
"Lilla fälttåget, Det" (Lagerkvist), 1422
"Lily's Party" (Purdy), 1995
Lim, Shirley Geok-Lin; *Two Dreams*, 2877
Limitação da rosa, A (Lispector), 1520
"Limpopo" (Tolstaya), 2324
Lind, Jakov, 1513-1516; "Hurrah for Freedom," 1514; "Journey Through the Night," 1515; "Soul of Wood," 1514; "Stove, The," 1515; *Stove, The*, 1515
Linderman, Frank, 2962; "Woman's Fight, A," 2962
Ling Mengchu, 2909
Lingo (Gilliatt), 1001
"Linnaeus Forgets" (Chappell), 517
"Lions, Harts, Leaping Does" (Powers), 1960
Lispector, Clarice, 1517-1522; *Alguns Contos*, 1518; *Bela e a fera, A*, 1520; "Corpo, O," 1520; "Crime of the Mathematics Professor, The," 1519; *Family Ties*, 1519; *Felicidade clandestina*, 1519; *Foreign Legion, The*, 1519; "Happy Birthday," 1519; "Journey to Petrópolis," 1519; *Limitação da rosa, A*, 1520; "Love," 1518; "Miss Ruth Algrave," 1520; "Preciousness," 1519; "Procura de uma dignidade, A," 1520; *Via crucis do corpo, A*, 1520
"Litany for the Homeland" (Hospital), 1229
Literary short story, 3062
"Little Black Box, The" (Dick), 723
"Little Brown Girl, The" (Spencer), 2204
Little Disturbances of Man, The (Paley), 1873
"Little Dog" (Hughes), 1239
"Little Farmer, The" (Grimm), 1089
"Little Frogs in a Ditch" (Gautreaux), 989
"Little Herr Friedemann" (Mann), 1609
"Little House, The" (Jackson), 1275
Little Jinx (Sinyavsky), 2169
"Little Kingdom of Franklin J. Payne, The" (Millhauser), 1684
"Little Knife, The" (Chabon), 503
"Little Man in Black, The" (Irving), 1269, 2738
"Little Mexican" (Huxley), 1259
"Little Miracles, Kept Promises" (Cisneros), 2950
"Little Momento" (Collier), 607-608
Little Novels of Sicily (Verga), 2396
Little Tales of Misogyny (Highsmith), 1195
"Littoral Zone, The" (Barrett), 174
"Liubish'—ne liubish'." *See* "Loves Me, Loves Me Not"
"Liubka Kazak." *See* "Lyubka the Cossack"
Live and Remember (Rasputin), 2025
Live Bait and Other Stories (Tuohy), 2349
"Live Bottomless" (Smith), 2185
"Live Life Deeply" (West), 2498
"Lives of the Invertebrates" (Slavin), 2173
"Living Alone in Iota" (Abbott), 2, 2835
"Living on the Box" (Gilliatt), 999
"Livvie" (Welty), 2485
"Lizabeth: The Caterpillar Story" (Wideman), 2512
"Loaf of Bread, A" (McPherson), 1584, 2867
Local color, 2786, 2788, 3062. *See also* "Category Index"
"Locket, The" (Pardo Bazán), 1881

"Locura del doctor Montarco, La." *See* "Madness of Doctor Montarco, The"
"Lodger, The" (Chappell), 516
"Lodging for the Night, A" (Stevenson), 2246, 2798
Logocentrism, 3063
Lohafer, Susan; *Coming to Terms with the Short Story*, 2608; *Short Story Theory at a Crossroads*, 2608
"Lola" (Colette), 601
London, Jack, 1522-1526; "Law of Life," 1524; "Like Argus of Ancient Times," 1525; "To Build a Fire," 1524
Lone Ranger and Tonto Fistfight in Heaven, The (Alexie), 56
"Loneliness of the Long-Distance Runner, The" (Sillitoe), 2144
Lonely Voice, The (O'Connor, Frank), 1807, 2753, 2914
Long After Midnight (Bradbury), 338
"Long Day in November, A" (Gaines), 932
"Long Distance" (Smiley), 2177
"Long-Distance Runner, The" (Paley), 1876
"Long Road to Ummera, The" (O'Connor, Frank), 1805
Long Valley, The (Steinbeck), 2236
"Longing" (Oz), 1862
Longstreet, Augustus Baldwin, 1527-1531, 2743; "Gander-Pulling, The," 1528; "Georgia Theatrics," 1528; "Shooting-Match, The," 1529
Longus; *Daphnis and Chloë*, 2666
"Looking for Mr. Green" (Bellow), 234
Loom and Other Stories, The (Sasaki), 2880
"Loon Point" (O'Brien, Tim), 1793
"Loose Reins" (Tilghman), 2318, 2839
"Loose Talk" (Broyard), 365
Lopes, Baltasar; *Antologia da ficcao Cabo-Verdiana contemmporanea*, 2847
Lord Love Us (Sansom), 2088
"Lord of the Dynamos, The" (Wells), 2478
Lordan, Beth, 1531-1534; "And Both Shall Row," 1533; "Cow Story, The," 1532; "Widow, The," 1532
"Lorry Driver, The" (Moravia), 1706
Lost and Found Stories of Morley Callaghan, The (Callaghan), 421
"Lost Battle, The" (Mansfield), 1620
"Lost Childhood, The" (Greene, Graham), 1075
"Lost Cottage, The" (Leavitt), 1466
"Lost Hearts" (James, M. R.), 1293
"Lost in the Funhouse" (Barth), 178
Lost in the Funhouse (Barth), 176
"Lost Phoebe, The" (Dreiser), 787
"Lost Princess, The" (Nahman), 1746
"Lottery, The" (Edgeworth), 812
"Lottery, The" (Jackson), 1277
"Lotus, The" (Rhys), 2032
"Lough Derg Pilgrim, The" (Carleton), 457
Louie, David Wong, 2875; "Birthday," 2876; "Displacement," 2876; "Pangs of Love," 2875; *Pangs of Love*, 2875
"Louisa, Please" (Jackson), 1275
"Love" (Colette), 600
"Love" (Lispector), 1518
Love and Friendship (Austen), 125
"Love and Like" (Gold), 1032
Love in a Small Town (Wang), 2446
Love Life (Mason), 1642
"Love Match, A" (Warner), 2451
Love Medicine (Erdrich), 2965
Love Must Not Be Forgotten (Zhang), 2580
"Love-o'-Women" (Kipling), 1390
Love of a Good Woman, The (Munro), 1735
Love on a Barren Mountain (Wang), 2446
"Love, Your Only Mother" (Kaplan), 1336
Lovecraft, H. P., 1535-1541, 2650; "Call of Cthulhu, The," 1537; "Dunwich Horror, The," 1538; "Nameless City, The," 1536; "Outsider, The," 1536
"Lovely Beasts, The" (O'Flaherty), 1829
"Lovers, The" (Head), 1154
Lovers and Cohorts (Gold), 1031
"Lovers of Their Time" (Trevor), 2343
"Love's Lesson" (O'Brien, Edna), 1784
"Loves Me, Loves Me Not" (Tolstaya), 2322
"Low-Lands" (Pynchon), 2006
Lu Hsün. *See* Lu Xun
Lu Xun, 1541-1550, 2909; "Diary of a Madman, The," 1545; "Divorce," 1548; "Kong yiji," 1545; "Medicine," 1546; "New Year's Sacrifice, The," 1547; *True Story of Ah Q, The*, 1546; "Upstairs in a Wineshop," 1548; *Wandering*, 1547
"Lucretia Burns" (Garland), 965
"Lucy in Her Pink Jacket" (Coppard), 643
Ludwig, Otto, 2793
Lukács, Georg; *Theory of the Novel, The*, 2753
"Lullaby" (Robison), 2137
"Lulu" (Williams, Joy), 2522
"Luminous Thighs: *Mythic Tropisms*" (Vizenor), 2408
"Lunching at the Ritzmore" (Himes), 1207
"Lupa, La." *See* "She-Wolf, The"
Lusophone African short fiction, 2846
"Lust" (Minot), 1688
Lust and Other Stories (Minot), 1688
"Lust of the White Serpent, The" (Ueda), 2931
"Luvina" (Rulfo), 2066
Lyly, John, 2714; *Euphues, the Anatomy of Wit*, 2714
Lyrical, 3063. *See also* "Category Index"
"Lyubka the Cossack" (Babel), 130

"M. Pigeonneau" (France), 900
"M. Seguin's Goat" (Daudet), 678

McCarthy, Mary, 1551-1555; "Cruel and Barbarous Treatment," 1552; "Man in the Brooks Brothers Shirt, The," 1553
McCullers, Carson, 1556-1562; "Ballad of the Sad Café, The," 1560; "Domestic Dilemma, A," 1558; "Jockey, The," 1557; "Madame Zilensky and the King of Finland," 1557; "Tree. A Rock. A Cloud, A," 1558, 2809; "Wunderkind," 1557
Macdonald, Ross, 2621; *Blue City*, 2621; *Lew Archer, Private Investigator*, 2621
McEwan, Ian, 1562-1566, 2841; "Dead as They Come," 1565; *First Love, Last Rites*, 1564, 2841; "In Between the Sheets," 1564; "Psychopolis," 1565
"McEwen of the Shining Slave Makers" (Dreiser), 785
McGahern, John, 1566-1569, 2924; "All Sorts of Impossible Things," 1568; "Beginning of an Idea, The," 1568, 2924; "Country Funeral, The," 1567; "Korea," 1567; *Nightlines*, 2924; "Peaches," 1567
Machado de Assis, Joaquim Maria, 1569-1574; "Singular Event, A," 1570
Machen, Arthur, 1574-1577, 2646; "Bowmen, The," 1576; *Great God Pan, The*, 1575; "N," 1576; *Three Impostors, The*, 1575; "White People, The," 1576
"Machine Stops, The" (Forster), 887
Machineries of Joy, The (Bradbury), 337
McKay, Claude, 2945
McKnight, Reginald, 1577-1580; "Kind of Light That Shines on Texas, The," 1579; "Quitting Smoking," 1579; "Uncle Moustapha's Eclipse," 1578; "White Boys, The," 1580
McLaverty, Bernard; "Secrets," 2926
McLaverty, Michael; "Poteen Maker, The," 2925
MacLeod, Alistair, 2904
MacMahon, Bryan; "Ring, The," 2926
MacNickle, D'Arcy; *Surrounded, The*, 2964
McPherson, James Alan, 1581-1585, 2867; "Elbow Room," 2867; "Gold Coast," 1582, 2867; "Hue and Cry," 1583; *Hue and Cry*, 2867; "Loaf of Bread, A," 1584, 2867; "On Trains," 2867; "Solo Song: For Doc, A," 1583; "Why I Like Country Music," 1583
McWhorter, Lucullus, 2964; "Coyote Juggles His Eyes," 2964
"Madame Celestin's Divorce" (Chopin), 2787
"Madame Crowl's Ghost" (Le Fanu), 2645
Madam Crowl's Ghost and Other Tales of Mystery (James, M. R.), 1292
"Madame de la Carlière" (Diderot), 734
"Madame Tellier's Establishment" (Maupassant), 1656
"Madame Zilensky and the King of Finland" (McCullers), 1557
"Mademoiselle de Scudéry" (Hoffmann), 1219
"Mademoiselle Panache" (Edgeworth), 811
"Madness of Doctor Montarco, The" (Unamuno y Jugo), 2372
"Madwoman, The" (Maupassant), 1654
"Maggie Meriwether's Rich Experience" (Stafford), 2210
"Magic Barrel, The" (Malamud), 1598, 2812
"Magic Egg, The" (Stockton), 2251
Magic Mirror (Card), 449
"Magic of a Voice, The" (Howells), 1235
"Magic Striptease, The" (Garrett), 971
Magical Realism, 2937, 2943. *See also* "Category Index"
"Magician and the Girl, The" (Tadjo), 2851
Magona, Sindiwe; "I'm Not Talking About That Now," 2855
Mahabharata, 2664
Mahfouz, Naguib, 1586-1591; "Answer Is No, The," 1589; "Beneath the Shelter," 1588; "False Dawn," 1589; "God's World," 1587; *Hams al-junūn*, 1587; "Min taht ila Fawq," 1589; "Sa'iq al-qitar," 1588; *Taḥta al-miẓalla*, 1589; "Zaabalawi," 1588
"Maiden in a Tower" (Stegner), 2222
"Maiden's Leap" (Kiely), 1359
"Mail Lady, The" (Gates), 982
Major, Clarence, 1591-1594; "Area in the Cerebral Hemisphere, An," 1593; *Fun and Games*, 1592; "My Mother and Mitch," 1592; "Scat," 1593; "Ten Pecan Pies," 1593
"Makar Chudra" (Gorky), 1057
"Maker of Coffins, The" (Bates), 201
"Maker of One Coffin, The" (Chappell), 515
"Making a Change" (Gilman), 1005
"Making of a New Zealander, The" (Sargeson), 2894
Malamud, Bernard, 1595-1602, 2811, 2827; "Angel Levine," 1598; "Black Is My Favorite Color," 1599; "First Seven Years, The," 1597; "German Refugee, The," 1600; "God's Wrath," 1601; "Idiots First," 1599; "Jewbird, The," 1600; "Last Mohican, The," 1598, 2827; "Magic Barrel, The," 1598, 2812; "Notes from a Lady at a Dinner Party," 1601; "Rembrandt's Hat," 1600
Malaprop, 3063
Malapropism, 3063
Malgudi Days (Narayan), 1752
Malory, Sir Thomas, 1603-1606; "Death of King Arthur, The," 1605; *Morte d'Arthur, Le*, 2695; "Quest of the Holy Grail, The," 1604; "Tale of Balin, The," 1604; "Tale of King Arthur, The," 1603
Malzberg, Barry N., 2640
"Mama, Rimma, and Alla" (Babel), 133
"Mamay" (Zamyatin), 2576
"Man and the Character, The" (Moravia), 1707
"Man and the Snake, The" (Bierce), 2788
"Man and Two Women, A" (Lessing), 1498
"Man and Wife" (Purdy), 1996

"Man by the Name of Ziegler, A" (Hesse), 1188
"Man Child, The" (Baldwin), 136
Man Descending (Vanderhaeghe), 2391
"Man from Mars, The" (Atwood), 109
"Man from the South" (Dahl), 666
"Man in the Black Suit, The" (King), 1372
"Man in the Brooks Brothers Shirt, The" (McCarthy), 1553
"Man Is Born, A" (Gorky), 1057
Man Must Live, and Other Stories (Mphahlele), 1718
"Man of Letters" (Dixon), 750, 2837
"Man Outside, The" (Grau), 1067
"Man That Corrupted Hadleyburg, The" (Twain), 2362
"Man Who Became a Soprano, The" (Updike), 2383
"Man Who Became a Woman, The" (Anderson), 80
"Man Who Could Work Miracles, The" (Wells), 2478
"Man Who Did Not Smile, The" (Kawabata), 1347
Man Who Died, The (Lawrence), 1455
Man Who Gave Up His Name, The (Harrison), 1129
"Man Who Had No Idea, The" (Disch), 747
"Man Who Invented Sin, The" (O'Faoláin), 2920
"Man Who Lived Underground, The" (Wright, Richard), 2562
"Man Who Lost the Sea, The" (Sturgeon), 2267
"Man Who Saw Through Heaven, The" (Steele, Wilbur Daniel), 2219
"Man Who Was Unlucky with Women, The" (Lewis), 1505
"Man Who Would Be King, The" (Kipling), 2799
"Man Whom the Trees Loved, The" (Blackwood), 264
"Man Without a Country, The" (Hale), 2777
"Man Without a Temperament, The" (Mansfield), 1621
"Man, Woman and Boy" (Dixon), 751
"Mangler, The" (King), 1370
"Manhole Sixty-nine" (Ballard), 143
Mann, Thomas, 1607-1616, 2793, 2816; *Black Swan, The*, 1612; *Death in Venice*, 1611; "Disorder and Early Sorrow," 2816; "Infant Prodigy, The," 1611; "Little Herr Friedemann," 1609; *Mario and the Magician*, 1612, 2816; "Railway Accident," 2816; *Tonio Kröger*, 1610; *Transposed Heads, The*, 1612
Mansfield, Katherine, 1617-1624, 2605, 2800, 2893; "At the Bay," 1622; "Bliss," 1619; "Daughters of the Late Colonel, The," 1620; "Doll's House, The," 1622; "Epilogue II," 1619; "Fly, The," 1621; "Garden Party, The," 1623; "In a Café," 1619; "Je Ne Parle Pas Français," 1619; "Lost Battle, The," 1620; "Man Without a Temperament, The," 1621; "Marriage à la Mode," 1620; "Miss Brill," 1620; "Ole Underwood," 1621; "Prelude," 1622; "Psychology," 1619; "Woman at the Store, The," 1621; "Young Girl, The," 1620
"Manuscript, The" (Singer), 2162
Mao Tun, 2910
Maori, 2895
Maoriland Stories (Grace), 2895
"March Hare, The" (Leskov), 1493
Märchen, 3063
"Märchen, Das." *See* "Fairy Tale, The"
Märchen. *See* "Category Index": Märchen
Mare, Walter de la. *See* De la Mare, Walter
Marginalization, 3063
Marguerite de Navarre, 2705; *Heptameron, The*, 2705
"María Concepción" (Porter), 1951
"Marie" (Woiwode), 2541
Marie de France, 1625-1630, 2628, 2697; "Bisclayret," 1627; "Eliduc," 1628; *Espurgatoire Saint Patriz*, 1628; "Honeysuckle, The," 1627; *Lais*, 1625; "Lanval," 1626; "Laüstic," 1627; *Medieval Fables*, 1628
Mario and the Magician (Mann), 1612, 2816
"Marionette Theater, The" (Kleist), 1402
"Marjorie Daw" (Aldrich), 47, 2781
"Mark of Apelles, The" (Pasternak), 1888
"Mark of Satan" (Oates), 1778
"Markheim" (Stevenson), 2247
"Marleen American Horse" (Vizenor), 2407
Marler, Robert, 2775
"Marmalade Bird, The" (Sansom), 2089
Marmalade Bird, The (Sansom), 2089
Maro, Publius Vergilius. *See* Vergil
"Marriage à la Mode" (Mansfield), 1620
Mars-Jones, Adam, 1630-1633; "Bears in Mourning," 1632; "Executor, An," 1632; "Remission," 1632; "Slim," 1631; "Small Spade, A," 1632; "Summer Lightning," 1632
Marshall, Alan, 2890
Marshall, Paule, 1634-1638; "Barbados," 1635; "Brazil," 1636; "British Guiana," 1636; "Brooklyn," 1636; *Merle*, 1637; "Reena," 1637; *Reena and Other Stories*, 1636; *Soul Clap Hands and Sing*, 1635; "To Da-duh, in Memoriam," 1637; "Valley Between, The," 1636
"Martha's Lady" (Jewett), 1300
Martian Chronicles, The (Bradbury), 335, 2637
"Martian Way, The" (Asimov), 98
"Mary Postgate" (Kipling), 1394
Mason, Bobbie Ann, 1639-1644; "Big Bertha Stories," 1643, 2833; "Coyotes," 1642; "Detroit Skyline, 1949," 1641; *Love Life*, 1642; *Midnight Magic*, 1643; "Nancy Culpepper," 1643; "Offerings," 1641; "Private Lies," 1643; "Residents and Transients," 1641; "Shiloh," 1640, 2833; *Shiloh and Other Stories*, 1640; "State Champions," 1642
"Masque of the Red Death, The" (Poe), 2766
"Master and Man" (Tolstoy), 2332
"Master Misery" (Capote), 443
"Master of Prayers, The" (Nahman), 1747
"Master Richard" (Wain), 2425

Masumoto, David, 2880; *Silent Spring*, 2880
"Matchimanito" (Erdrich), 849
"Matchmaker, The" (Steele, Richard), 2727
"Mateo Falcone" (Mérimée), 1672, 2750
"Matinée" (Colette), 601
"Matryona's House" (Solzhenitsyn), 2190
"Matter of Chance, A" (Nabokov), 1741
"Matter of Principle, A" (Chesnutt), 2859
"Matter of Taste, A" (Collier), 607
Matthews, Brander, 2599, 2758, 2790
Maugham, W. Somerset, 1645-1651, 2604; "Human Element, The," 1649; "Rain," 1648; "Red," 1647; *Six Stories Written in the First Person Singular*, 1649; *Trembling of a Leaf, The*, 1646
Maupassant, Guy de, 1652-1659, 2792; "Boule de Suif," 1655; "Horla, The," 1657, 2793; "Madame Tellier's Establishment," 1656; "Madwoman, The," 1654; "Necklace, The," 2793
May, Charles E.; *New Short Story Theories, The*, 2610; *Short Story Theories*, 2607
"May Night, A" (Gogol), 1025
"May-Pole of Merrymount, The" (Hawthorne), 1147
"May Queen" (Robison), 2055
"Mayskaya Noch." *See* "May Night, A"
"Me and Miss Mandible" (Barthelme, Donald), 184
"Me and My Baby View the Eclipse" (Smith), 2185
Me and My Baby View the Eclipse (Smith), 2184
"Measure of Devotion, The" (Perabo), 1899
Meckel, Christoph, 1659-1664; "Crow, The," 1662; *Figure on the Boundary Line, The*, 1662; *Im Land der Umbramauten*, 1661; *Licht*, 1662; *Noticen des Feuerwerkers Christopher Magalan, Die*, 1662; *Plunder*, 1663; *Suchbild*, 1663; *Tullipan*, 1662; *Wahre Muftoni, Der*, 1663
"Medea" (Ovid), 1855
"Medicine" (Lu), 1546
Medicine for Melancholy, A (Bradbury), 337
Medieval fables, 2626, 2628
Medieval Fables (Marie de France), 1628
Medieval romance, 2691-2699, 3063
Medieval short fiction, 2669, 2672; early, 2680-2690
"Medley" (Bambara), 155
"Medusa's Ankles" (Byatt), 388, 2840
"Meeting, The" (Chekhov), 544
"Meeting in the Dark, A" (Ngugi), 2853
"Meeting with Medusa, A" (Clarke), 593
"Mein teures bein." *See* "My Expensive Leg"
Melting Pot and Other Subversive Stories, The (Schwartz, Lynn Sharon), 2119
Melville, Herman, 1664-1670; "Bartleby the Scrivener," 1666, 2629, 2775; "Fiddler, The," 1669
"Melyuzga" (Chekhov), 543
Memnon (Voltaire), 2413
Memoir, 3063
Memoirs of a Space Traveler (Lem), 1484
"Memories of the Space Age" (Ballard), 144
"Memories Sent to an Old Friend" (Akutagawa), 40
Men of Maize (Asturias), 104
"Menace from Earth, The" (Heinlein), 1162
Menachem-Mendl letters (Aleichem), 53
Menaphon (Greene, Robert), 1082
"Menu/1965, The" (Brautigan), 346
"Merchant's Tale, The" (Chaucer), 529
Mérimée, Prosper, 1671-1675, 2750; "Abbé Aubain, The," 2769; *Carmen*, 1673; *Colomba*, 1672; "Mateo Falcone," 1672, 2750; *Venus of Ille, The*, 1673
Merle (Marshall), 1637
Mermaids on the Golf Course and Other Stories (Highsmith), 1198
Merril, Judith, 2638
Mesopotamian culture, 2659
"Mesoroposthonippidon" (Davenport), 687
"Message from the Pig-Man, A" (Wain), 2425
Metafiction, 3063. *See also* "Category Index"
Metamorphoses (Apuleius), 2664
Metamorphoses (Ovid), 1853, 2643, 2660
Metamorphosis, The (Kafka), 2794
Metaphor, 3063
Metcalfe, John, 2650; "Double Admiral, The," 2650
"Metel." *See* "Blizzard, The"
Metonymy, 3063
"Mexican Dust" (Adams), 10
Mexican Village (Niggli), 2952
"Mexico" (Doerr), 754
"Mexico" (Gilchrist), 995
"Miaomiao" (Wang), 2447
Michael Kohlhaas (Kleist), 1403
Michaels, Leonard, 1675-1678; "City Boy," 1677; "Deal, The," 1676; "Murderers," 1676
"Microcosmic God" (Sturgeon), 2265
"Midair" (Conroy), 629
"Middle Classes, The" (Schwartz, Lynne Sharon), 2118
"Middle Drawer, The" (Calisher), 412
Middleman and Other Stories, The (Mukherjee), 1725
Middleton, Richard, 2648
Middleton-Murry, John, 2639
"Middling Type, A" (Moravia), 1707
"Midnight Blue" (Collier), 609
Midnight Magic (Mason), 1643
"Midnight Reader, The" (Gardner), 958
"Miel silvestre, La" (Quiroga), 2020
"Migala, La." *See* "Bird Spider, The"
"Migraine Workers, The" (Paley), 1922
"Milczenie." *See* "Silence"
Miller, Sue, 1679-1682; "Inventing the Abbotts," 1681; "Leaving Home," 1680; "Tyler and Brina," 1680

"Miller's Tale, The" (Chaucer), 525-526
Millhauser, Steven, 1682-1685, 2837; "August Eschenburg," 1683; "Catalogue of the Exhibition: The Art of Edmund Moorash," 1684; "Game of Clue, A," 1684; "Knife Thrower, The," 1685; *Knife Thrower and Other Stories, The*, 1684; "Little Kingdom of Franklin J. Payne, The," 1684; "New Automaton Theater, The," 1685; "Paradise Park," 1685
"Min taht ila Fawq" (Mahfouz), 1589
"Minerva Writes Poems" (Cisneros), 581
"Mines of Falun, The" (Hoffmann), 1219
"Mingo" (Harris, Joel Chandler), 1124
Mingo and Other Sketches in Black and White (Harris, Joel Chandler), 1124
Minimalism, 2830-2831, 2833, 3063. *See also* "Category Index"
"Minister's Black Veil, The" (Hawthorne), 1146, 2763
Minot, Susan, 1686-1689; "Accident," 1688; "Feather in the Toque, The," 1688; "Hiding," 1687; "Knot, The," 1688; "Lust," 1688; *Lust and Other Stories*, 1688; *Monkeys*, 1687; "Navigator, The," 1688; "Party Blues," 1688; "Thorofare," 1688; "Thrilling Life, A," 1689
"Miracle, The" (Mutia), 2849
Mirrielees, Edith R., 2605
Mirror in the Roadway, The (O'Connor, Frank), 1807
"Misanthrope, The" (Moravia), 1707
"Miscellany of Characters That Will Not Appear in My Next Novel, A" (Cheever), 533
Mise en abîme, 3064
"Miserere" (Stone), 2255
"Misery" (Chekhov), 2795
"Misfit, The" (Colette), 601
Mishima, Yukio, 1690-1695, 2821, 2933; *Death in Midsummer and Other Stories*, 1691; "Forest in Full Bloom, The," 1691; "Patriotism," 1693, 2822, 2933; "Priest of Shiga Temple and His Love, The," 1692
Mishle shu'alim. See *Fables of a Jewish Aesop*
"Miss August" (Hale), 1097
"Miss Brill" (Mansfield), 1620
"Miss Crystal Confronts the Past" (Gilchrist), 995
"Miss Cudahy of Stowe's Landing" (Elliott), 829
"Miss Holland" (Lavin), 1444
"Miss Leonora When Last Seen" (Taylor, Peter), 2297
"Miss Loewe." *See* "Confessions of Fitz-Boodle"
Miss Marple stories, 576
"Miss Muriel" (Petry), 1920
Miss Muriel and Other Stories (Petry), 1919
"Miss Parker Possessed" (Betts), 253
"Miss Ruth Algrave" (Lispector), 1520
"Miss Shum's Husband" (Thackeray), 2301
"Miss Vandyke" (Gwynne), 2900
"Miss Yellow-Eyes" (Grau), 1065
"Mississippi" (Gilchrist), 996
Mo Yan, 2912
Mochulsky, Konstantin, 2773
"Model World, A" (Chabon), 501
Modern Griselda, The (Edgeworth), 813
Modern short story, 1998, 2121, 2397, 2599, 2612, 2941, 3064; definition, 2738-2739; England and, 2744, 2798; France and, 2749; Germany and, 2747, 2794; Ireland and, 2800; Latino, 2938; 1960, 2826; Russia and, 2748, 2794-2795; United States and, 2790, 2792. *See also* "Category Index"
Modernism, 2782, 2796, 2802, 2826, 2902. *See also* "Category Index"
Modernist Short Story, The (Head), 2610
"Moglie conle ali, La." *See* "Count's Wife, The"
"Mohican, The" (Nin), 1761
Mohr, Nicholasa, 2958; "Aunt Rosana's Rocker," 2958; El Bronx Remembered, 2958
"Moi pervyi gus'." *See* "My First Goose"
"Mold of Yancy, The" (Dick), 722
"Mole, The" (Kawabata), 1347
"Molly's Dog" (Adams), 11
Momaday, N. Scott, 2960; *House Made of Dawn*, 2960, 2962
"Moments of Light" (Chappell), 516
"Mōmoku monogatari." *See* "Blind Man's Tale, A"
"Monday or Tuesday" (Woolf), 2556
Monday Tales (Daudet), 679
Money and Other Stories (Čapek), 439
Money for Maria (Rasputin), 2025
"Monkey, The" (Dinesen), 738
"Monkey, The" (King), 1370
Monkeys (Minot), 1687
"Monkey's Paw, The" (Jacobs), 1281
Monologue, 3064
"Monsieur Maurice" (Colette), 601
Montague, John; "Occasion for Sin, An," 2926
Montaigne, Michel Eyquem de; *Essays, The*, 2737
Montesquieu, 2730
Montreal Story Tellers, 2904
"Moon Came Out, The" (Tolstaya), 2324
"Moon Lake" (Welty), 2486
"Moon on the Water, The" (Kawabata), 1347
"Moon Over Minneapolis" (Weldon), 2474
Moon Over Minneapolis (Weldon), 2473
"Moonshine War, The" (Sturgeon), 2261
Moorcock, Michael, 2639
Moore, George, 1695-1699, 2916; "Clerk's Quest, The," 2801; "Home Sickness," 2917; "Julia Cahill's Curse," 2800, 2916; "Sarah Gwynn," 1697; "So on He Fares," 1697, 2916; *Story-Teller's Holiday, A*, 1698; *Untilled Field, The*, 2800, 2916; "Wilfrid Holmes," 1696

Moore, Lorrie, 1699-1702; "People Like That Are the Only People Here," 1701; "Real Estate," 1700; "Terrific Mother," 1701; "You're Ugly Too," 1701
Moral tract, 3064. *See also* "Category Index"
Morall Fabillis of Esope, the Phrygian, The (Henryson), 2628
Moravia, Alberto, 1702-1710, 2603, 2821; *Agostino*, 2821; "Celestina," 1706; *Command and I Will Obey You*, 1707; "Crime at the Tennis Club," 1705; "Doubles," 1707; *Epidemia, L*, 1706; *Erotic Tales*, 1708; *Fetish, The*, 1707; "Inverno di malato," 1705; "Lorry Driver, The," 1706; "Man and the Character, The," 1707; "Middling Type, A," 1707; "Misanthrope, The," 1707; *Paradise and Other Stories*, 1707; "Primo rapporto sulla terra dell' Inviato speciale della luna," 1706; "Products," 1708
More, Hannah, 2728
More Shapes than One (Chappell), 516
Mori, Toshio, 2877; "Seventh Street Philosopher," 2878; "She Makes Swell Doughnuts," 2878; *Yokohama, California*, 2877
Mori Ōgai, 2931; "Dancing Girl, The," 2932; "Sanshō the Steward," 2932
Morkinskinna, 2671-2672
Morley Callaghan's Stories (Callaghan), 420
"Morning of the Day They Did It, The" (White), 2508
"Morning Talk, The" (du Fresne), 2896
Morning Watch, The (Agee), 19-20
Morris, Wright, 1710-1717; "Glimpse into Another Country," 1713; "Origin of Sadness, The," 1714; "Ram in the Thicket, The," 1712; "Safe Place, The," 1712; "Uno Más," 1715
Morrison, Arthur, 2615
Morrison, John, 2890
"Mort d'Olivier Bécaille, La." *See* "Death of Olivier Bécaille, The"
Mortal Engines (Lem), 1486
"Mortality and Mercy in Vienna" (Pynchon), 2006
"Morte amoureuse, La." *See* "Beautiful Vampire, The"
Morte d'Arthur, Le (Malory), 2695
Mortimer, John, 2622; *Rumpole à la Carte*, 2623
"Mosby's Memoirs" (Bellow), 236
Mosby's Memoirs and Other Stories (Bellow), 234
Moses, 2658
"Moslem Wife, The" (Gallant), 942
"Most Beloved" (Tolstaya), 2323
"Most Girl Part of You, The" (Hempel), 1182
"Mote in the Middle Distance, H*nry J*m*s, The" (Beerbohm), 228
"Moth and the Star, The" (Thurber), 2315
"Mother" (Dovlatov), 771
"Mother Africa" (Paley), 1922
"Mothers" (Plath), 1935
"Moths, The" (Viramontes), 2404, 2956
Motif, 3064
"Mound of the Monkey's Grave, The" (Dazai), 701
"Mountain Tavern, The" (O'Flaherty), 1830
"Mountains of Guatemala, The" (Connell), 618
"Mouth of Brass" (Humphrey), 1246
"Moving from One Body of Water to Another" (Houston), 1233
Mphahlele, Ezekiel, 1717-1720; "Grieg on a Stolen Piano," 1718; "In Corner B," 1719; *Man Must Live, and Other Stories*, 1718; "Mrs. Plum," 1719; *Renewal Time*, 1719
"Mr. and Mrs. Frank Berry" (Thackeray), 2303
"Mr. Big" (Allen), 63
"Mr. Gilfil's Love Story" (Eliot), 817
"Mr. Levi" (Oz), 1862
"Mr. McMillan" (Spencer), 2206
Mr. Parker Pyne, Detective (Christie), 2620
"Mr. Peebles' Heart" (Gilman), 1006
"Mr. Rabbit Meets His Match Again" (Harris, Joel Chandler), 1123
"Mr. Rabbit Meets His Match at Last" (Harris, Joel Chandler), 1123
"Mr. Rabbit Nibbles Up the Butter" (Harris, Joel Chandler), 1123
"Mr. Sweetly Indecent" (Broyard), 364
"Mrs. Bathurst" (Kipling), 1392
"Mrs. Mean" (Gass), 978
"Mrs. Plum" (Mphahlele), 1719
Mrs. Reinhardt and Other Stories (O'Brien, Edna), 1783
Mrs. Spring Fragrance (Sui Sin Far), 2873-2874
"Mrs. Yardley's Quilting" (Harris, George Washington), 2779
"Mud Below, The" (Proulx), 1982
"Muerte y la brújula, La." *See* "Death and the Compass"
Mukherjee, Bharati, 1721-1730, 2884, 2974; *Darkness*, 1723; "Father, A," 1725; "Jasmine," 1726; *Middleman and Other Stories, The*, 1725; "Nostalgia," 1724; "Tamurlane," 1724; "Tenant, The," 1727; "World According to Hsu, The," 1724
"Mule du Pape, La." *See* "Pope's Mule, The"
Mules and Men (Hurston), 2863
"Mummy's Foot, The" (Gautier), 2768
"Mumu" (Turgenev), 2356
Munderic, 2682
Munro, Alice, 1730-1737; "Bardon Bus," 1733; "Cortes Island," 1735; "Dance of the Happy Shades," 1731; "Jakarta," 1736; "Labor Day Dinner," 1734; *Love of a Good Woman, The*, 1735; "Peace of Utrecht, The," 1732; "Tell Me Yes or No," 1734
Munro, Hector Hugh. *See* Saki
Munson, Gorham Bert, 2604
"Mur, Le." *See* "Wall, The" (Sartre)

Murakami, Haruki, 2934; "Elephant Vanishes, The," 2934; "TV People," 2934
Murasaki Shikibu; *Tale of Genji, The*, 2667, 2929
Murder of Roger Ackroyd, The (Christie), 2619
"Murderers" (Michaels), 1676
"Murders in the Rue Morgue, The" (Poe), 2613
Murfree, Mary; "Electioneering on Big Injun Mountain," 2780
"Murke's Collected Silences" (Böll), 274
Museums and Women and Other Stories (Updike), 2379
"Music" (Gilchrist), 994
"Music on the Muscatatuck" (West), 2496
Music School, The (Updike), 2379
"Musk-Ox, The" (Leskov), 1490
"Muta, La." *See* "Mute, The"
"Mute, The" (Landolfi), 1431
"Mute Companions, The" (Narayan), 1752
Mutia, Ba'bila; "Miracle, The," 2849
"Muttsy" (Hurston), 2862
"My Expensive Leg" (Böll), 275
"My Father and the Sergeant" (Friel), 922
"My Father Is an Educated Man" (Sturgeon), 2262
"My Father Sits in the Dark" (Weidman), 2463
"My Father, Dancing" (Broyard), 364
My Father, Dancing (Broyard), 364
"My First Cousin" (Dovlatov), 772
"My First Goose" (Babel), 132, 2820
"My First Tooth" (Shalamov), 2129
"My Kinsman, Major Molineux" (Hawthorne), 1144-1145, 2741, 2763
"My Last Story" (Frame), 2895
"My Marriage to Vengeance" (Leavitt), 1466
"My Mother" (Kincaid), 1365
"My Mother and Mitch" (Major), 1592
My Name Is Aram (Saroyan), 2093
"My Oedipus Complex" (O'Connor, Frank), 1806
"My Older Brothers" (Dazai), 701
My Soul in China (Kavan), 1343
My Uncle Silas (Bates), 200
Mysterious Mr. Quin, The (Christie), 575, 2620
"Mystery of the Blue Jar, The" (Christie), 574
"Mystery Within Us, The" (Hopkins), 2859
Myth, 3064
Mythic, 2659. *See also* "Category Index"
"Myths of Bears, The" (Bass), 196
"Myths of the Near Future" (Ballard), 143

"N" (Machen), 1576
"NRACP, The" (Elliott), 827
"Na kraiu sveta." *See* "At the Edge of the World"
"Na plotakh." *See* "On the Rafts"
"Na zolotom kryl'tse sideli." *See* "On the Golden Porch"
"Nabeg: Razskaz volontera." *See* "Raid: A Volunteer's Story, The"
Nabokov, Vladimir, 1738-1745, 2821; "Admiralty Spire, The," 1742; "Cloud, Castle, Lake," 1742; "Doorbell, The," 1740; "Matter of Chance, A," 1741; "Razor, The," 1740; "Scoundrel, The," 1741; "Signs and Symbols," 1743, 2821; "Spring in Fialta," 1742
Nahman of Bratslav, Rabbi, 1745-1750; "Lost Princess, The," 1746; "Master of Prayers, The," 1747; "Tale of the Seven Beggars, The," 1748
"Nail, The" (Alarcón), 43
"Nameless City, The" (Lovecraft), 1536
Names and Faces of Heroes, The (Price), 1963
"Nancy Culpepper" (Mason), 1643
Nanshoku ōkagami. See *Great Mirror of Male Love, The*
Narayan, R. K., 1750-1755, 2975; "Dodu," 1753; *Dodu and Other Stories*, 1752; "Forty-five a Month," 1753; "Grandmother's Tale, The," 1754; *Grandmother's Tale and Selected Stories, The*, 1754; *Horse and Two Goats and Other Stories, A*, 1753; *Lawley Road*, 1753; *Malgudi Days*, 1752; "Mute Companions, The," 1752; "Salt and Sawdust," 1754; *Under the Banyan Tree and Other Stories*, 1753
Narrative, 3064
Narrative persona, 3064
Narratology, 3064
Narrator, 3064
Nashe, Thomas; *Unfortunate Traveller, The*, 2716
Naso, Publius Ovidius. *See* Ovid
Nathan, Daniel. *See* Queen, Ellery
National Association for the Advancement of Colored People, 2861
Native American culture, 2960-2971. *See also* "Category Index"
Native Argosy, A. See *In His Own Country*
Native Son (Wright), 167
Natronai ha-Nakdan, Rabbi Berechiah ben; *Fables of a Jewish Aesop*, 2628
Naturaleza muerta con cachimba. See *Still Life with Pipe*
Naturalism, 2789. *See also* "Category Index"
"Nature of Almost Everything, The" (Robison), 2055
"Navigator, The" (Minot), 1688
"Navodnenie." *See* "Flood, The" (Zamyatin)
"Necessary Knocking on the Door, The" (Paley), 1921
"Neck" (Dahl), 667
"Necklace, The" (Maupassant), 2793
"Neighbor Rosicky" (Cather), 488
"Neighbors" (Carver), 475, 2830
"Neighbors" (Viramontes), 2405
"Neighbors" (West), 2498
Nennius; *Historia Brittonum*, 2693
Nerval, Gérard de, 1756-1759; "Angélique," 1757; "Confidences de Nicolas, Les," 1757; "Pandora," 2768;

"Sylvie," 1757; "Tale of the Queen of the Morning and Soliman the Prince of the Genii, The," 1758
Neumiller Stories, The (Woiwode), 2539
"Never Marry a Mexican" (Cisneros), 583
"Nevesta." *See* "Bride, The"
"Nevsky Prospect" (Gogol), 1026
"New Automaton Theater, The" (Millhauser), 1685
"New Café, The" (Lessing), 1498
New Criticism, 2607
"New England Nun, A" (Freeman), 910, 2787
New Gods Lead, The (Wright, S. Fowler), 2639
"New Islands" (Bombal), 280
"New Mirror, The" (Petry), 1920
"New Music, The" (Barthelme, Donald), 188
New Novel, 460, 2045-2047, 2193
New Realism, 2911
New Short Story Theories, The (May), 2610
New World, The (Banks), 162
"New Year's Eve Adventure, A" (Hoffmann), 1220
"New Year's Sacrifice, The" (Lu), 1547
New Zealand, 2888, 2892-2895, 2897; and the Maori, 2895; 1950-1950, 2895; 1960-1970, 2896. *See also* "Geographical Index"
"Newborn Thrown in Trash and Dies" (Wideman), 2514
News of the Spirit (Smith), 2185
"Next Door" (Wolff), 2551
"Next in Line, The" (Bradbury), 335
Ngugi wa Thiong'o; "Fig Tree, The," 2854; "Meeting in the Dark, A," 2853
Nibelungenlied, 2675
"Nice Day at School" (Trevor), 2342
Nice Old Man and the Pretty Girl and Other Stories, The (Svevo), 2270
Nicolas de Troyes; *Grand parangon des nouvelles nouvelles, Le*, 2705
"Nigger, A" (Himes), 1206
"Nigger Jeff" (Dreiser), 785
Niggli, Josefina, 2952; *Mexican Village*, 2952
Night at the Movies, A (Coover), 635
"Night Before the Trial, The" (Chekhov), 543
"Night in Question, The" (Wolff), 2553
Night in Question, The (Wolff), 2552
"Night of the Great Season, The" (Schulz), 2109
"Night of the Iguana, The" (Williams, Tennessee), 2525
"Night Owls" (Leskov), 1493
"Nightfall" (Asimov), 97, 2636
"Nightgown, The" (Davies, Rhys), 696
"Nightingale, The" (Andersen), 74
Nightlines (McGahern), 2924
Nights with Uncle Remus (Harris, Joel Chandler), 1124
"Night-Sea Journey" (Barth), 177
Nin, Anaïs; "Birth," 1762; "Je Suis le Plus Malade des Surrealistes," 1762; "Mohican, The," 1761; "Ragtime," 1762; *Under a Glass Bell and Other Stories*, 1761
Nin, Anaïs, 1760-1764
"Nine Ball" (Offutt), 1824
"Nine Billion Names of God, The" (Clarke), 593
Nine Women (Grau), 1067
"Nineteen Fifty-Five" (Walker), 2433
Nineteenth century; and African American writers, 2857; Canada, 2900; 1800-1840, 2736-2751; 1840-1880, 2752-2785; 1880-1920, 2786
"99.6" (West), 2496
Nippon eitaigura: Daifuku shin chōja-kyō. See *Japanese Family Storehouse, The*
Nisei, 2877, 2879
"No Door" (Wolfe), 2546
"No Name Woman" (Kingston), 1379
No One Writes to the Colonel (García Márquez), 953
"No One's a Mystery" (Tallent), 2277
No Sweetness Here and Other Stories (Aidoo), 2852
"Nobby's Run of Luck" (Zhang), 2582
"Nobody Will Laugh" (Kundera), 1414
Nobody's Business (Gilliatt), 1000
"Nobody's Home" (Godwin), 1014
"Noc wielkiego sezonu." *See* "Night of the Great Season, The"
Noël Du Fail; *Baliverneries*, 2705
"Nomad and Viper" (Oz), 1863
"Noon Wine" (Porter), 1952
Norris, Frank, 1765-1770; "Case for Lombroso, A," 1768; "Deal in Wheat, A," 1768; "Reversion to Type, A," 1767; "Third Circle, The," 1767
"North, The" (Zamyatin), 2575
"North Light" (Helprin), 1169
"Northern Lights" (Harjo), 1119
"Nose, The" (Akutagawa), 39
"Nostalgia" (Mukherjee), 1724
"Not Quite Final" (Bausch), 204
Notable Discovery of Cozenage, A (Greene, Robert), 1083
"Notes from a Lady at a Dinner Party" (Malamud), 1601
Notes from the Underground (Dostoevski), 2794
"Nothing: A Preliminary Account" (Barthelme, Donald), 188
Noticen des Feuerwerkers Christopher Magalan, Die (Meckel), 1662
Nouvelle, 2749, 3064
Novel, 3064
Novelas amorosas y exemplares (Zayas y Sotomayor), 2706
Novelas ejempalares. See *Exemplary Novels*
Novelette, 3064
Novella, 2711, 2731, 2747, 2906, 3064; Renaissance, 2700-2707

Novellas of Hortense Calisher, The (Calisher), 413
Novelle, 3064
Novelle (Goethe), 1020
Novelle rusticane. See *Little Novels of Sicily*
Novellino, Il. See *Il Novellino: The Hundred Old Tales*
"Novotny's Pain" (Roth), 2062
Now That April's Here and Other Stories (Callaghan), 419
"Nuit de Cléopâtre, Une." *See* "One of Cleopatra's Nights"
"Nun, The" (Alarcón), 44
"Nun's Priest's Tale, The" (Chaucer), 527
Nuyorican, 2957
Nwapa, Flora; "This Is Lagos," 2853

"O Yes" (Olsen), 1845
"O Youth and Beauty" (Cheever), 536
Oates, Joyce Carol, 1771-1779, 2838; *Assignation, The*, 1777; "Census Taker, The," 1774; "Ghost Girls," 1778; "In the Autumn of the Year," 1776; "In the Region of Ice," 1775; "Mark of Satan," 1778; "Raven's Wing," 1777; "Scream, The," 1776; "Where Are You Going, Where Have You Been?," 1775; *Will You Always Love Me?*, 1777
Objective, 3067
Objective correlative, 3065
"Oblako, ozero, bashnya." *See* "Cloud, Castle, Lake"
O'Brien, Edna, 1780-1786, 2923; "Another Time," 1784; "Cords," 1781; *Fanatic Heart, A*, 1784; "Irish Revel, The," 2923; "Lantern Slides," 2923; "Love's Lesson," 1784; *Mrs. Reinhardt and Other Stories*, 1783; *Returning*, 1783; "Savages," 1783; "Scandalous Woman, A," 1782
O'Brien, Edward Joseph Harrington, 2600
O'Brien, Fitz-James, 1786-1790; "Diamond Lens, The," 1787; *Duke Humphrey's Dinner*, 1789; "What Was It?," 1789, 2774; "Wondersmith, The," 1788
O'Brien, Tim, 1790-1793; "Going After Cacciato," 1792; "Loon Point," 1793; "Things They Carried, The," 1792; *Things They Carried, The*, 1792
"Occasion for Sin, An" (Montague), 2926
Occom, Samson, 2961
"Occurrence at Owl Creek Bridge, An" (Bierce), 258, 2788-2789
O'Connor, Flannery, 1794-1802, 2601, 2808, 2826; "Artificial Nigger, The," 1797; *Displaced Person, The*, 1798; "Everything That Rises Must Converge," 1799; *Everything That Rises Must Converge*, 1799; "Geranium, The," 1796; "Good Country People," 1798; "Good Man Is Hard to Find, A," 2809; *Good Man Is Hard to Find, A*, 1797; "Greenleaf," 1799, 2826; "Judgement Day," 1800; "Lame Shall Enter First, The," 1799; "Life You Save May Be Your Own, The," 1797; "Parker's Back," 1800; "Revelation," 1800, 2826; "Turkey, The," 1797
O'Connor, Frank, 1802-1809, 2603, 2606, 2755, 2761, 2815, 2888, 2914, 2921; "Drunkard, The," 1806, 2815; "First Confession," 1806; "Guests of the Nation," 1804, 2815; "In the Train," 1804; "Judas," 2921; *Lonely Voice, The*, 1807, 2753, 2914; "Long Road to Ummera, The," 1805; *Mirror in the Roadway, The*, 1807; "My Oedipus Complex," 1806; "Overcoat, The," 2761; "Story by Maupassant, A," 1806
October Country, The (Bradbury), 337
"Odnazhdy osen'iu." *See* "One Autumn Night"
O'Donovan, Michael Francis. *See* O'Connor, Frank
"Odour of Chrysanthemums" (Lawrence), 1451
Odyssey (Homer), 1225, 2661-2663
Ōe, Kenzaburō, 1809-1816; "Aghwee the Sky Monster," 1812; "Catch, The," 1811; "Day He Himself Shall Wipe My Tears Away, The," 1812; *Teach Us to Outgrow Our Madness*, 1814
"Of Birds and Beasts" (Kawabata), 1347
O'Faoláin, Seán, 1816-1822, 2603, 2920; "Childybawn," 1818, 2920; "Dividends," 1820; "Fugue," 2920; "Fur Coat, The," 1819; "Hymeneal," 1820; "Man Who Invented Sin, The," 2920; "Old Master, The," 1818; "Patriot, The," 1821; "Sugawn Chair, The," 1819
Ofen, Der. See *Stove, The*
"Offerings" (Mason), 1641
"Office Romances" (Trevor), 2343
Offutt, Chris, 1822-1825, 2839; "Blue Lick," 1824; "Leaving One, The," 1824; "Nine Ball," 1824; "Out of the Woods," 2839; *Out of the Woods*, 1825; "Sawdust," 1823
O'Flaherty, Liam, 1826-1832, 2921; "Beggars, The," 1830; "Child of God, The," 1828; "Fairy Goose, The," 1828, 2922; "Going into Exile," 2922; *Joseph Conrad*, 1827; "Lovely Beasts, The," 1829; "Mountain Tavern, The," 1830; "Post Office, The," 1830; "Red Barbara," 1829; "Red Petticoat, The," 1829; "Spring Sowing," 2921; "Two Lovely Beasts, The," 2922
Ogot, Grace; *Land Without Thunder*, 2853; "The Rain Came," 2853
"Oh, Whistle, and I'll Come to You, My Lad" (James, M. R.), 1294
O'Hara, John, 1832-1838; "Andrea," 1834; "Doctor's Son, The," 1836; "You Can Always Tell Newark," 1835
Ohrfeige und Sonstiges, Eine. See *Slap in the Face Et Cetera, A*
Ojos de perro azul (García Márquez), 952
O'Kelly, Seumas, 2918; "Weaver's Grave, The," 2918
Okri, Ben, 1838-1843; "Image-Vendor, The," 1840; "In the City of Red Dust," 1841; *Incidents at the Shrine*, 1839; "Stars of the New Curfew," 1841; *Stars of the New Curfew*, 1841; "What the Tapster Saw," 1842; "When the Lights Return," 1842; "Worlds That Flourish," 1841

"Old Acquaintance" (Collier), 609
"Old Address, The" (Kavan), 1342
"Old Doc Rivers" (Williams, William Carlos), 2531
"Old Forest, The" (Taylor, Peter), 2298
"Old Halvorson Place, The" (Woiwode), 2541
"Old Lady, The" (Jhabvala), 1304
"Old Master, The" (O'Faoláin), 1818
"Old Morality, The" (Fuentes), 926
"Old Mortality" (Porter), 1952, 2807
"Old Neighborhood, The" (Dreiser), 786
"Old Order, The" (Porter), 1953
"Old Woman, The" (Honwana), 2848
"Old Woman Izergil" (Gorky), 1057
Oldest Olafs saga helga, 2671
"Ole Underwood" (Mansfield), 1621
Olsen, Tillie, 1843-1848; "Hey Sailor, What Ship?," 1845; "I Stand Here Ironing," 1845; "O Yes," 1845; "Tell Me a Riddle," 1846
"Omoide." *See* "Recollections"
"Omphale" (Gautier), 985
"On Discovery" (Kingston), 1380
On Forsyte 'Change (Galsworthy); , 947
"On Saturday Afternoon" (Sillitoe), 2144
"On Some Lines of Virgil" (Davenport), 687
"On the Beach" (Hale), 1097
"On the Downhill Side" (Ellison, Harlan), 834
"On the Edge of the Cliff" (Pritchett), 1975
"On the Golden Porch" (Tolstaya), 2321
On the Golden Porch (Tolstaya), 2322
On the Gulf (Spencer), 2206
"On the Mountainside" (Roberts), 2050
"On the Rafts" (Gorky), 1058
"On the Rivershore" (Tilghman), 2318
"On Trains" (McPherson), 2867
On with the Story (Barth), 180
"One Against Thebes" (Gordon, Caroline), 1049
"One Arm" (Kawabata), 1348
"One Arm" (Williams, Tennessee), 2528
"One Autumn Night" (Gorky), 1058
"One for the Road" (King), 1370
"One Holy Night" (Cisneros), 582
One Hundred Merrie and Delightsome Stories, 2704
"£1,000,000 Bank-Note, The" (Twain), 2362
"One of Cleopatra's Nights" (Gautier), 986
"Ones Who Walk Away from Omelas, The" (Le Guin), 1479
Onetti, Juan Carlos, 1849-1852; "Dream Come True, A," 1850; "Hell Most Feared," 1850; "Welcome, Bob," 1850
Onions, Oliver; *Beckoning Fair One, The*, 2649
"Only Rose, The" (Jewett), 1299
"Only the Master Shall Praise" (Oskison), 2964
"Only Traffic Signal on the Reservation Doesn't Flash Red Any More, The" (Alexie), 57
"Open Boat, The" (Crane), 657
Open to the Public (Spark), 2200
"Open Window, The" (Saki), 2074, 2798
"Optimists" (Ford), 881
Oral tale, 3065
Oral tradition, 2137, 2407, 2657, 2662, 2667, 2857, 3065; Native American, 2960-2961
"Oranging of America, The" (Apple), 87
"Orchards, The" (Thomas), 2310
Orczy, Baroness, 2616
"Order of Insects" (Gass), 977, 2830
Ordinary Love (Smiley), 2178
Orel, Harold, 2915
"Orgy, The" (de la Mare), 705
Oriental tale, 3065
"Origin of Sadness, The" (Morris), 1714
"Orlov Married Couple" (Gorky), 1058
"Orpheus" (Ovid), 1857
Ortiz, Simon, 2960; *Fightin'*, 2967
"Oshkikiwe's Baby" (Oshogay), 2964
Oshogay, Delia; "Oshkikiwe's Baby," 2964
"Oskar" (Walser), 2440
Oskison, John; "Only the Master Shall Praise," 2964
"Ostatnia ucleczka ojca." *See* "Father's Last Escape"
Ostrovityane. See *Islanders, The*
"Otec." *See* "Father, The"
Other, 3065
"Other Kingdom" (Forster), 887, 889
"Other Miller" (Wolff), 2552
"Other Paris, The" (Gallant), 940
"Other Weapons" (Valenzuela), 2388
"Other World, The" (Zhang), 2581
Otogi-zōshi, 2929
"Ottilia." *See* "Confessions of Fitz-Boodle"
"Otto and the Magi" (Connell), 618
Otuel, 2693
"Our Story Begins" (Wolff), 2550
"Out of the Woods" (Offutt), 2839
Out of the Woods (Offutt), 1825
"Outcasts of Poker Flat, The" (Harte), 1135
"Outpost of Progress, An" (Conrad), 622
"Outsider, The" (Lovecraft), 1536
"Over Insurance" (Collier), 607
"Overcoat, The" (Gogol), 1027, 2761
"Overcoat II (Boyle, T. C.), 327
"Overloaded Man, The" (Ballard), 145
Overstreet, Bonaro Wilkinson, 2602, 2792
"Overtime" (Reid), 2029
Ovid, 1852-1860; "Medea," 1855; *Metamorphoses*, 1853, 2643, 2660; "Orpheus," 1857; "Pan and Syrinx," 1856; "Python," 1855

"Ovtsebyk." *See* "Musk-ox, The"
"Owen's Father" (Woiwode), 2542
"Oxenhope" (Warner), 2453
Oxymoron, 3065
Oz, Amos, 1860-1865; "Before His Time," 1862; "Crusade," 1863; "Hill of Evil Counsel, The," 1862; "Hollow Stone, A," 1863; "Late Love," 1863; "Mr. Levi," 1862; "Nomad and Viper," 1863; "Setting the World to Rights," 1863; "Strange Fire," 1862; "Trappist Monastery, The," 1863; "Upon This Evil Earth," 1863; "Way of the Wind," 1862; *Where the Jackals Howl and Other Stories*, 1862
Ozick, Cynthia, 1865-1871, 2836; "Pagan Rabbi, The," 1866; "Puttermesser and the Muscovite Cousin," 1869; "Puttermesser in Paradise," 1869; "Puttermesser Paired," 1869; *Puttermesser Papers, The*, 1869; "Rosa," 1868; "Shawl, The," 1868, 2836

Pa Jin, 2911
"Pagan Rabbi, The" (Ozick), 1866
"Pages from a Velvet Album" (Kiš), 1398
"Pages from Cold Point" (Bowles, Paul), 313
"Pain" (Fuentes), 927
Pain, Barry, 2603
"Painful Case, A" (Joyce), 1323
"Pains" (Weldon), 2474
"Painted Skin, The" (Pu), 1987
Painter, William; *Palace of Pleasure*, 2711
"Pair of Tickets, A" (Tan), 2282
Pak, Gary, 2884; *Watcher of Waipuna and Other Stories*, 2884
Pak, Ty, 2883; *Guilt Payment*, 2884
Palace of Pleasure (Painter), 2711
"Palace of Sleep, The" (Kavan), 1341
"Palace of the Moorish Kings, The" (Connell), 616
Palace Thief, The (Canin), 435
"Palais de Justice" (Helprin), 1169
"Pale Horse, Pale Rider" (Porter), 1953
"Pale Pink Roast, The" (Paley), 1874
Paley, Grace, 1872-1877, 2836; *Collected Stories, The*, 1875; "Come On, Ye Sons of Art," 1874; "Conversations with My Father, A," 2836; "Goodbye and Good Luck," 1873; "In the Garden," 1875; *Little Disturbances of Man, The*, 1873; "Long-Distance Runner, The," 1876; "Pale Pink Roast, The," 1874; "Wants," 1874
Palm-of-the-Hand Stories (Kawabata), 2933
Palombe (Camus, Jean-Pierre), 2719
"Pan" (Schulz), 2108
"Pan and Syrinx" (Ovid), 1856
Panchatantra, 2700
"Pandora" (Nerval), 2768
Pandosto (Greene, Robert), 1082
"Pangs of Love" (Louie), 2875
Pangs of Love (Louie), 2875
"Papa, Snake, and I" (Honwana), 2847
"Paper Pills" (Anderson), 80
Parable, 2660-2661, 3065. *See also* "Category Index"
Paradise and Other Stories (Moravia), 1707
"Paradise Lounge, The" (Trevor), 2344
"Paradise Park" (Millhauser), 1685
Paradox, 3065
Parataxis, 3065
Pardo Bazán, Emilia, 1878-1883; *Cuentos de Amor*, 1880; "Descendant of El Cid, A," 1879; "Don Juan's Last Illusion," 1880; "Locket, The," 1881; "Revenge, The," 1881; "White Lock of Hair," 1880
Paredes, Américo, 2953; "Hammon and the Beans, The," 2953; *Hammon and the Beans and Other Stories, The*, 2953
Paredes, Raymund, 2952
Parent's Assistant, The (Edgeworth), 809
"Park City" (Beattie), 215
Parker Pyne Investigates. See *Mr. Parker Pyne, Detective*
Parker Pyne stories, 575
Parker, Dorothy, 1883-1887; "Big Blonde," 1885; "Telephone Call, A," 1884; "Waltz, The," 1884
"Parker's Back" (O'Connor, Flannery), 1800
Parlement of Foules (Chaucer), 521
Parody, 3065. *See also* "Category Index"
Partners, The (Auchincloss), 121
"Partners, The" (Friedman), 918
Partners in Crime (Christie), 576, 2619
"Party Blues" (Minot), 1688
Pasco, Allan H., 2608
"Paseo." *See* "Walk, The" (Donoso)
"Passenger" (Wolff), 2552
"Passing of Grandison, The" (Chesnutt), 553
Passionate North, The (Sansom), 2087
"Past One at Rooney's" (Henry), 1185
Pasternak, Boris, 1887-1892; "Childhood of Luvers, The," 1889; "District in the Rear, A," 1891; "Letters from Tula," 1889; "Mark of Apelles, The," 1888; *Safe-Conduct, A*, 1889; *Second Birth*, 1891; "Story, The," 1890; "Story of a Contraoctave, The," 1888; "Without Love," 1889
"Pastoral Care" (Gardner), 958
Pastures of Heaven, The (Steinbeck), 2235
"Patricia, Edith and Arnold" (Thomas), 2308
"Patriot, The" (O'Faoláin), 1821
"Patriotism" (Mishima), 1693, 2822, 2933
"Patrol, The" (Lem), 1485
Pattee, Fred Lewis, 2600, 2606, 2757
"Pattern of Perfection, The" (Hale), 1098
Pattern of Perfection, The (Hale), 1098
"Paul's Case" (Cather), 487, 2790

"Paura alla Scala." *See* "Scala Scare, The"
Pavese, Cesare, 1893-1898; "End of August, The," 1897; "Family, The," 1895; "First Love," 1896; "Free Will," 1896; "Land of Exile," 1894; "Leather Jacket, The," 1895; "Suicides," 1895; "Summer Storm," 1895; "Wedding Trip," 1895
"Pawnbroker's Wife, The" (Spark), 2198
"Payoff" (Queen), 2015
"Peace of Utrecht, The" (Munro), 1732
Peaceable Kingdom, The (Prose), 1978
"Peaches" (McGahern), 1567
"Peaches, The" (Thomas), 2307
"Peasant Marey, The" (Dostoevski), 2774
"Pederson Kid, The" (Gass), 977
Pensador, El (Clavijo y Fajardo), 2732
"People Like That Are the Only People Here" (Moore, Lorrie), 1701
"People Who Don't Know the Answers" (Tyler, Anne), 2368
Peoples Redemption Party (Nigeria), 5
Per le vie (Verga), 2396
Perabo, Susan, 1898-1901; "Counting the Ways," 1899; "Greater Grace of Carlisle, The," 1900; "Measure of Devotion, The," 1899; "Rocks over Kyburz, The," 1900; "Thick as Thieves," 1899
Perceval (Chrétien de Troyes), 570
"Perekhod cherez Zbruch." *See* "Crossing into Poland"
Perelman, S. J., 1901-1906; *Acres and Pains*, 1903; "Entered as Second-Class Matter," 1904; "Tomorrow—Fairly Cloudy," 1903
Peretz, Isaac Leib, 1906-1910; "Bontshe the Silent," 1908; "If Not Higher," 1909; "Three Gifts, The," 1909
"Perfect Day for Bananafish, A" (Salinger), 2080
Perfect Vacuum, A (Lem), 1483
"Perfume Sea, The" (Laurence), 1440
Periodical essay/sketch, 3065
Perl, Arnold; *World of Sholom Aleichem, The*, 50
Permanent Errors (Price), 1964
Perry, Bliss, 2601; *Study of Prose Fiction, A*, 2758
Personification, 3065
"Pervaia liubov." *See* "First Love" (Babel)
"Pervaya lyubov." *See* "First Love" (Turgenev)
"Perviy zub." *See* "My First Tooth"
"Pesn' torzhestvuiushchei liubvi." *See* "Song of Triumphant Love, The"
"Pesnia o sokole." *See* "Song of the Falcon, The"
"Peters" (Tolstaya), 2323
Petite Pallace of Pettie His Pleasure, A (Pettie), 2711
Petronius, 1911-1916, 2664; "Boy of Pergamum, The," 1912; *Cena Trimalchionis*, 1912-1913; *Satyricon, The*, 1911, 2664; "Widow of Ephesus, The," 1913
Petry, Ann, 1916-1923, 2865; "Bones of Louella Brown, The," 1921; "In Darkness and Confusion," 1919; "Like a Winding Sheet," 1919; "Migraine Workers, The," 1922; "Miss Muriel," 1920; *Miss Muriel and Other Stories*, 1919; "Mother Africa," 1922; "Necessary Knocking on the Door, The," 1921; "New Mirror, The," 1920; "Witness, The," 1921
Pettie, George; *Petite Pallace of Pettie His Pleasure, A*, 2711
"Pevtsy." *See* "Singers, The"
Phaedrus, 2627
"Phantom of the Movie Palace, The" (Coover), 636
"Phantom 'Rickshaw, The" (Kipling), 1391
"Pheasants" (Woiwode), 2540
"Phelim O'Toole's Courtship" (Carleton), 457
Phillips, Jayne Anne, 1923-1926, 2834; "Bess," 1924; "Home," 2834; "Lechery," 2834; "Something That Happened," 1925
Philombe, Rene; "The True Martyr Is Me," 2849
"Philosopher, The" (Anderson), 78
"Phineas" (Knowles), 1409
Phineas (Knowles), 1407
"Photo Album, The" (Dovlatov), 774
"Piano Tuner, The" (Gautreaux), 990
"Piano Tuner's Wife, The" (Trevor), 2345
Pickwick Papers (Dickens), 726. *See also* "Queer Client"
"Picture Horse, The" (Pu), 1987
Pictures in the Fire (Collier), 607
"Pierre Menard, Author of the *Quixote*" (Borges), 291, 2822
"Pigeon Feathers" (Updike), 2828
Pigeon Feathers and Other Stories (Updike), 2377
Pilgrim Hawk: A Love Story, The (Wescott), 2493
"Pillar of Salt" (Jackson), 1276
Ping, Wang; *American Visa*, 2877
"Pippa's Story" (Chang), 512
Pirandello, Luigi, 1927-1933; "Adrianna Takes a Trip," 1930; "Signora Frola and Her Son-in-Law, Signor Ponza," 1930; "Sunlight and Shadow," 1929
"Pisma iz Tuly." *See* "Letters from Tula"
"Pis'mo." *See* "Letter, A"
"Pit and the Pendulum, The" (Poe), 2766
"Pit Strike" (Sillitoe), 2145
"Pitched Out" (Friedman), 919
"Pkhentz" (Sinyavsky), 2169
"Place I've Never Been, A" (Leavitt), 1465
Place I've Never Been, A (Leavitt), 2834
"Plain Pleasures" (Bowles, Jane), 308
Plath, Sylvia, 1933-1936; "Fifteen-Dollar Eagle, The," 1935; "Johnny Panic and the Bible of Dreams," 1934; "Mothers," 1935; "Sunday at the Mintons'," 1934
"Playing Ball on Hampstead Heath" (Richler), 2039
"Pleasure of Her Company, The" (Smiley), 2177
Plomer, Franklyn, 1937-1939

Plomer, William, 1940; "Black Peril," 1939; "Child of Queen Victoria, The," 1938; "Ula Masonda," 1938; "When the Sardines Came," 1938
Plot, 3065
"Ploughing of Leaca-na-Naomb, The" (Corkery, James), 2920
Plunder (Meckel), 1663
"Po' Sandy" (Chesnutt), 551
"Poaching" (Wolff), 2552
"Podlets." *See* "Scoundrel, The"
Poe, Edgar Allan, 1940-1948, 2599-2600, 2604, 2611, 2613, 2632-2633, 2644, 2741, 2759, 2796, 2857; "Cask of Amontillado, The," 2765; "Descent into the Maelström, A" , 1942; "Fall of the House of Usher, The," 1276, 1945, 2644, 2743, 2767; "Masque of the Red Death, The," 2766; "Murders in the Rue Morgue, The," 2613; "Pit and the Pendulum, The," 2766; "Purloined Letter, The," 1944; "Raven, The," 2791; "Tell-Tale Heart, The," 2767
"Poet, The" (Hesse), 1190
"Poetess, A" (Freeman), 911
Poetic Edda, 2670
Poetic realism, 2793
Pohl, Frederik, 2637
Point of view, 3065
Poirot, Hercule, 2620
Poirot Investigates (Christie), 2619
Poirot stories, 576
"Polarities" (Atwood), 111
"Polunoshchniki." *See* "Night Owls"
"Pomegranate Trees" (Saroyan), 2093
"Pomeriggio, Adamo, Un." *See* "Adam, One Afternoon"
"Poor Franzi" (Gallant), 941
"Poor Koko" (Fowles), 894
"Poor Little Rich Town" (Vonnegut), 2420
"Poor Thing, The" (Powers), 1959
"Pope's Mule, The" (Daudet), 679
Popular Tales (Edgeworth), 811
"Porcelain Salamander, The" (Card), 448
"Porn" (Walker), 2868
"Portable Phonograph, The" (Clark), 587
Porter, Katherine Anne, 1949-1956; "Circus, The," 1953; "Cracked Looking-Glass, The," 1951; "Downward Path to Wisdom, The," 1954; "Fig Tree, The," 1954; "Flowering Judas," 1951, 2807; "Grave, The," 1954, 2807; "He," 1951; "Holiday," 1955; "Leaning Tower, The," 1954; "María Concepción," 1951; "Noon Wine," 1952; "Old Mortality," 1952, 2807; "Old Order, The," 1953; "Pale Horse, Pale Rider," 1953; "Rope," 1951; "Theft," 1952
Porter, William Sydney. *See* Henry, O.
Portmanteau words, 3065
"Portobello Road, The" (Spark), 2199
"Portrait, The" (Huxley), 1258
"Portrait of Shunkin, A" (Tanizaki), 2285
Portrait of the Artist as a Young Dog (Thomas), 2307
Portuguese African short fiction, 2846
"Possession of Angela Bradshaw, The" (Collier), 606
"Posson Jone" (Cable), 2779
Post, Melville Davisson, 2616
"Post Office, The" (O'Flaherty), 1830
Postcolonial, 3065
Postmodernism, 2828, 3066. *See also* "Category Index"
"Poteen Maker, The" (McLaverty), 2925
Potocki, Count Jan, 2643; *Saragossa Manuscript, The*, 2643
"Pourriture Noble, La" (Stern), 2242
"Povest o tom, kak possorilsya Ivan Ivanovich s Ivanom Nikiforovichem *See* "Tale of How Ivan Ivanovich Quarreled with Ivan Nikiforovich, The"
Powers, J. F., 1957-1961; "Blue Island," 1959; "Devil Was the Joker, The," 1958; "Forks, The," 1958; "Lions, Harts, Leaping Does," 1960; "Poor Thing, The," 1959; "Prince of Darkness," 1958; "Valiant Woman, The," 1959
Powers of Attorney (Auchincloss), 120
Pozhar (Rasputin), 2026
Prairie Home Companion, A (Keillor), 1354
Pratt, Mary Louise, 2608
"Preciosidade." *See* "Preciousness"
"Preciousness" (Lewis), 1519
"Predicament, A" (Callaghan), 418
"Prelude" (Mansfield), 1622
"Premier amour." *See* "First Love" (Beckett)
"President Regrets, The" (Queen), 2015
"Pretty Girl, The" (Dubus), 790
"Pretty Ice" (Robison), 2054
Price, Reynolds, 1961-1968; "Chain of Love, A," 1963; *Collected Stories, The*, 1966; "Company of the Dead, The," 1966; "Deeds of Light," 1966; "Enormous Door," 1966; "Fare to the Moon," 1965; *Foreseeable Future, The*, 1965; "Golden Child," 1966; "Happiness of Others, The," 1964; *Names and Faces of Heroes, The*, 1963; *Permanent Errors*, 1964; "Truth and Lies," 1967
Pricksongs and Descants (Coover), 634
"Priest of Shiga Temple and His Love, The" (Mishima), 1692
"Priest's Wife, The" (L'Heureux), 1511
"Prikliucheniia obeziany." *See* "Adventures of a Monkey, The"
"Prime Leaf" (Warren), 2458
"Primo amore." *See* "First Love" (Pavese)
"Primo rapporto sulla terra dell' Inviato speciale della luna" (Moravia), 1706
"Prince Hamlet of Shchigrovo" (Turgenev), 2355

"Prince of Darkness" (Powers), 1958
Prince of Homburg, The (Kipling), 1400
"Prince Who Was a Thief, The" (Dreiser), 785
"Princess, The" (Lawrence), 1455
Princess Brambilla (Hoffmann), 1220
Prinz Friedrich von Homburg. See *Prince of Homburg, The*
"Prioresss Tale, The" (Chaucer), 527
"Prisoner Who Wore Glasses, The" (Head), 1154
Pritchett, V. S., 1968-1976, 2604; "Accompanist, The," 1974; "Blind Love," 1973; "Camberwell Beauty, The" , 1974; "Diver, The," 1974; "Handsome Is as Handsome Does," 1971; "On the Edge of the Cliff," 1975; "Sense of Humour," 1971; "Skeleton, The," 1973; "When My Girl Comes Home," 1972
"Private Lies" (Mason), 1643
"Problem of the General Store, The" (Hoch), 1213
Problems and Other Stories (Updike), 2380
"Probuzhdenie." *See* "Awakening"
"Procura de uma dignidade, A" (Lispector), 1520
"Procurator of Judea, The" (France), 900
"Prodigious Milligram, The" (Arreola), 92
"Products" (Moravia), 1708
"Professor" (Hughes), 1240
"Project: Earth" (Dick), 722
"Project for a Trip to China" (Sontag), 2194
"Promised Land, The" (Sembène), 2850
Pronzini, Bill, 2621
"Property" (Verga), 2396
"Prophecy, The" (Alarcón), 43
"Prophet's Hair, The" (Rushdie), 2070
Prose, Francine, 1977-1980; "Everyday Disorders," 1977; "Guided Tours of Hell," 1977, 1979; *Peaceable Kingdom, The*, 1978
Prose Edda (Sturluson), 2670, 2672
Prosody, 3066
"Prospect of the Sea, A" (Thomas), 2309
"Proszę państwa do gazu." *See* "This Way for the Gas, Ladies and Gentlemen"
Protagonist, 3066
"Proud Costello, MacDermot's Daughter, and the Bitter Tongue" (Yeats), 2568
Proulx, E. Annie, 1980-1983, 2839; "Brokeback Mountain," 1981, 2840; "Bunchgrass Edge of the World, The," 1982; *Close Range: Wyoming Stories*, 1981; "Half-Skinned Steer, The," 1982; "Mud Below, The," 1982
"Prowler" (Tallent), 2276
"Prussian Officer, The" (Lawrence), 1453, 2814
"Prussian Vase, The" (Edgeworth), 810
"Psychology" (Mansfield), 1619
"Psychopolis" (McEwan), 1565
"Psychotaxidermist, The" (Vizenor), 2407
Pu Songling, 1984-1990; "Painted Skin, The," 1987; "Picture Horse, The," 1987; "Pupils of the Eyes That Talked, The," 1986; "Tiger of Zhaochang, The," 1986
"Public Pool, A" (Adams), 11
Puck of Pook's Hill (Kipling), 1392
"Pueblerina." *See* "Small Town Affair"
"Puerta cerrada, La." *See* "Closed Door, The"
Puerto Rico, 2957
Pulp magazines, 1535, 2616, 2634
Pun, 3066
"Punch, The" (Friedman), 917
"Pupils of the Eyes That Talked, The" (Pu), 1986
Purdy, James, 1990-1997; "Color of Darkness," 1993; *Color of Darkness*, 1993; "Cutting Edge," 1993; "Dawn," 1994; "Don't Call Me by My Right Name," 1993; *Dream Palace*, 1995; "Eventide," 1996; "Everything Under the Sun," 1994; "Lily's Party," 1995; "Man and Wife," 1996; "Rapture," 1994; "Sleep Tight," 1993; "Some of These Days," 1994; "Sound of Talking," 1996; "Summer Tidings," 1994; "Why Can't They Tell You Why?," 1993
"Purloined Letter, The" (Poe), 1944
"Purple Jar, The" (Edgeworth), 809
Pushkin, Alexander, 1997-2004, 2748; "Blizzard, The," 2000; *Queen of Spades, The*, 2001, 2748-2749; "Shot, The," 1999; "Squire's Daughter, The," 2001; "Undertaker, The," 2000
"Putois" (France), 901
"Puttermesser and the Muscovite Cousin" (Ozick), 1869
"Puttermesser in Paradise" (Ozick), 1869
"Puttermesser Paired" (Ozick), 1869
Puttermesser Papers, The (Ozick), 1869
"Putting Granny Out to Die" (Dazai), 701
Pynchon, Thomas, 2004-2010; "Entropy," 2007; "Low-Lands," 2006; "Mortality and Mercy in Vienna," 2006; "Secret Integration, The," 2008; *Slow Learner*, 2009; "Small Rain, The," 2005; "Under the Rose," 2008
"Python" (Ovid), 1855

Qian Zhongshu, 2911
"Quail for Mr. Forester" (Humphrey), 1246
"Qualcosa era successo." *See* "Catastrophe"
"Queen for a Day" (Banks), 164
Queen of Spades, The (Pushkin), 2001, 2748-2749
Queen, Ellery, 2011-2017, 2620; *Adventures of Ellery Queen, The*, 2620; "African Traveller, The," 2014; "Bearded Lady, The," 2014; "Dead Ringer," 2014; "Invisible Lover, The," 2015; "Payoff," 2015; "President Regrets, The," 2015
"Queer Client" (Dickens), 727
"Quest for *Blank Claveringi*, The" (Highsmith), 1195
"Quest of the Holy Grail, The" (Malory), 1604
Quests of Simon Ark, The (Hoch), 1211

Quicker than the Eye (Bradbury), 339
Quiller-Couch, Arthur, 2648
Quiroga, Horacio, 2017-2022, 2942; "Anaconda," 2021; "Dead Man, The," 2020; "Decapitated Chicken, The," 2019; "Drifting," 2020; "Feather Pillow, The," 2019; "Juan Darién," 2021; "Miel silvestre, La," 2020; "Son, The," 2020
"Quitting Smoking" (Oates), 1579
"Quo Vadimus" (White), 2508
Quotations from Other Lives (Gilliatt), 1000

"Rabbi, The" (Babel), 132
"Ragtime" (Nin), 1762
"Raid: A Volunteer's Story, The" (Tolstoy), 2329
"Railway Accident" (Mann), 2816
"Rain" (Maugham), 1648
"Rain Came, The" (Ogot), 2853
Rain of Scorpions and Other Writings (Trambley), 2955
Rainwater, Catherine, 2966
"Rainy Season, A" (Tuohy), 2351
"Raise High the Roof Beam, Carpenters" (Salinger), 2079
"Ram in the Thicket, The" (Morris), 1712
Rambler, The (Johnson, Samuel), 1315
Rani jadi. See *Early Sorrows*
"Ransom of Red Chief, The" (Henry), 1186
"Rappaccini's Daughter" (Hawthorne), 1148, 2764
"Rapture" (Purdy), 1994
"Rapunzel" (Grimm), 1088
"Rashōmon" (Akutagawa), 38-39, 2932
Rasputin, Valentin, 2023-2027; *Borrowed Time*, 2025; *Farewell to Matyora*, 2025; "French Lessons," 2024; *Live and Remember*, 2025; *Money for Maria*, 2025; *Pozhar*, 2026; "Vasily and Vasilisa," 2024
Rasselas (Johnson, Samuel), 1316
"Rasskaz o samom glavnom." *See* "Story About the Most Important Thing, A"
"Rautavaara's Case" (Dick), 721
"Ravages of Spring, The" (Gardner), 958
"Raven, The" (Poe), 2791
"Raven's Wing" (Oates), 1777
"Raymond's Run" (Bambara), 154
"Razor, The" (Nabokov), 1740
"Real Estate" (Moore, Lorrie), 1700
"Real Thing, The" (James, Henry), 1286, 2789
Realism, 2739, 2774, 2786, 2788, 2792, 2801, 2937, 3066. *See also* "Category Index"
Realities of Fiction, The (Hale), 1099
"Realpolitik" (Wilson), 2536
Reardon, B. P.; *Collected Ancient Greek Novels*, 2665
Reception theory, 3066
"Recital for the Pope, A" (Stern), 2242
"Recollections" (Dazai), 700
"Red" (Maugham), 1647
"Red Barbara" (O'Flaherty), 1829
Red Cavalry (Babel), 131
"Red Clowns" (Cisneros), 582
"Red Girl's Reasoning, A" (Johnson, E. Pauline), 2962
Red Hunters and the Animal People (Eastman), 2963
"Red-Letter Day, A" (Taylor, Elizabeth), 2292
"Red Petticoat, The" (O'Flaherty), 1829
"Red Signal, The" (Christie), 574
"Red Wind" (Chandler), 508
"Redemption" (Gardner), 961
"Redhead, The" (Gilliatt), 999, 1002
"Red-Headed League, The" (Doyle), 778
"Reena" (Marshall), 1637
Reena and Other Stories (Marshall), 1636
"Reeve's Tale, The" (Chaucer), 526-527
"Reflections" (Carter), 470
"Reflections on Courtship and Marriage" (Franklin), 2730
Reid, Elwood, 2027-2030; "Buffalo," 2029; "Laura Borealis," 2029; "Overtime," 2029; "What Salmon Know," 2028
"Reine du Matin et Soliman, Prince des Génies, La." *See* "Tale of the Queen of the Morning and Soliman the Prince of the Genni, The"
"Reise durch die nacht." *See* "Journey Through the Night"
"Relative Stranger, A" (Baxter), 208
Relative Stranger, A (Baxter), 208
Religious, 2658, 2670. *See also* "Category Index"
"Rembrandt, The" (Wharton), 2501
"Rembrandt's Hat" (Malamud), 1600
Reminiscence, 3066
"Remission" (Mars-Jones), 1632
Renaissance, 2700-2709, 2711, 2715-2716, 2718-2720, 2722, 2724
"Renegade, The" (Camus, Albert), 432
"Renegade, The" (Jackson), 1275
Renewal Time (Mphahlele), 1719
"Repairer of Reputations, The" (Chambers), 2649
"Requiem" (Heinlein), 2636
"Rescue Party" (Clarke), 591
"Resemblance Between a Violin Case and a Coffin, The" (Williams, Tennessee), 2526
Reservation Blues (Alexie), 2967
"Residents and Transients" (Mason), 1641
"Response to a Request" (Walser), 2440
"Rest Cure, The" (Huxley), 1258
Rest of Life, The (Gordon, Mary), 1054
Rethinking Sorrow (Childs), 2930
"Retreating Figures" (Endō), 843
"Return, The" (Armstrong), 2964
"Return of a Private, The" (Garland), 967
Return to Tsugaru (Dazai), 700
Returning (O'Brien, Edna), 1783

"Reunion, The" (Angelou), 84
"Revelation" (Davies, Rhys), 697
"Revelation" (O'Connor, Flannery), 1800, 2826
Revenge (Harrison), 1128
"Revenge, The" (Pardo Bazán), 1881
"Revenge of Hannah Kemhuff, The" (Walker), 2431
"Revenge of the Lawn" (Brautigan), 344
"Reverend Father Gaucher's Elixir, The" (Daudet), 678
"Reversion to Type, A" (Norris), 1767
"Revolt of 'Mother,' The" (Freeman), 909
"Revolver, The" (Pardo Bazán), 1881
Reynolds, John; *Triumphs of Gods Revenge, Against the Crying, and Execrable Sinne of Murther, The*, 2719
Rhetorical device, 3066
"Rhinoceros, Some Ladies, and a Horse, A" (Stephens), 2919
Rhodius, Apollonius; *Argonautica*, 2663
Rhys, Jean, 2031-2035, 2945; "Grosse Fifi, La," 2032; "Hunger," 2032; "I Used to Live Here Once," 2034; *Left Bank and Other Stories, The*, 2031; "Lotus, The," 2032; "Sleep It Off, Lady," 2033; *Sleep It Off, Lady*, 2033; "Till September Petronella," 2032
Ribas, Oscar, 2847
"Rich" (Gilchrist), 993
Rich, Barnaby; *Farewell to Militarie Profession*, 2711
"Rich Boy, The" (Fitzgerald), 867
"Rich Brother, The" (Wolff), 2552
"Rich People" (Hale), 1098
Richler, Mordecai, 2036-2041; "Playing Ball on Hampstead Heath," 2039; "Some Grist for Mervyn's Mill," 2038; "Summer My Grandmother Was Supposed to Die, The," 2037
"Riddle, The" (de la Mare), 705
"Right Side, The" (Collier), 606
"Ring, The" (Bender), 241
"Ring, The" (MacMahon), 2926
"Rip Van Winkle" (Irving), 1270, 2738-2740
Rivera, Tomás, 2041-2044, 2954; . . . *And the earth did not part*, 2042, 2954; "First Communion," 2043; *Harvest, The*, 2954; "Salamanders, The," 2043; "Zoo Island," 2043
Riverside Counselor's Stories, The, 2928-2929
"Road from Colonus, The" (Forster), 889
Roads of Destiny (Henry), 1185
Robbe-Grillet, Alain, 2045-2048; "Dressmaker's Dummy, The," 2046; "Secret Room, The," 2046-2047; "Shore, The," 2046; "Way Back, The," 2046
"Robbery, A" (Leskov), 1493
"Robert Kennedy Saved from Drowning" (Barthelme, Donald), 186
Roberts, Elizabeth Madox, 2049-2052; "Haunted Palace, The," 2050; "On the Mountainside," 2050; "Sacrifice of the Maidens, The," 2050; "Scarecrow, The," 2051
Roberts, Sir Charles G. D.; "Do Seek Their Meat from God," 2900
Robison, Mary, 2052-2059, 2832; "Adore Her," 2057; "Amateur's Guide to the Night, An," 2055; *Believe Them*, 2056; "Bud Parrot," 2054; "Coach," 2055; "For Real," 2057; "Heart," 2055; "I Am Twenty-One," 2056; "In Jewel," 2056; "Kite and Paint," 2054; "May Queen," 2055; "Nature of Almost Everything, The," 2055; "Pretty Ice," 2054; "Seizing Control," 2056; "Trying," 2057; "Yours," 2056
"Robot" (Davenport), 684
"Rock Springs" (Ford), 882, 2833
"Rocks over Kyburz, The" (Perabo), 1900
Rodriguez, Abraham, Jr.; *Boy Without a Flag, The*, 2958
"Roger Malvin's Burial" (Hawthorne), 1145
Rogue literature, 3066
Rohrberger, Mary, 2601; *Hawthorne and the Modern Short Story*, 2758
"Roi Candaule, Le." *See* "King Candaules"
Rojas, Fernando de; *Celestina, La*, 2720
Roland and Vernagu, 2693
Roman de Brut (Wace), 2694
Romance, 2665, 2729, 3066; Elizabethan, 2710; medieval, 2691-2699. *See also* "Category Index"
"Romance and Sally Byrd" (Glasgow), 1009
Romantic Egoists, The (Auchincloss), 119
Romanticism, 2731-2732, 2756, 2768, 2786, 2788, 2801, 3066. *See also* "Category Index"
Rome, 2692
"Roog" (Dick), 721
"Room for Mistakes" (Tilghman), 2318
"Room of Frail Dancers, A" (Helprin), 1169
"Room Without a Telephone, The" (Lewis), 1504
"Rope" (Porter), 1951
"Rosa" (Ozick), 1868
"Rose for Emily, A" (Faulkner), 858, 2805
Rose Garden, The (Saʿdi of Shiraz), 2661
"Roselily" (Walker), 2430
Ross, Danforth, 2604
"Rot, The" (Lewis), 1505
"Rot" (Williams, Joy), 2522
Roth, Philip, 2059-2064, 2813; "Defender of the Faith," 2062, 2813; "Eli, the Fanatic," 2060; "Epstein," 2061; "'I Always Wanted You to Admire My Fasting'," 2063; "Novotny's Pain," 2062
"Rothschild's Fiddle" (Chekhov), 546
Rotting Hill (Lewis), 1505
Rousseau, Jean-Jacques, 2731
"Royal Jelly" (Dahl), 666
"Rozhdenie cheloveka." *See* "Man Is Born, A"
Rudd, Steele, 2889
"Ruinas circulares, Las." *See* "Circular Ruins, The"
"Rules of the Game" (Tan), 2281

Rulfo, Juan, 2064-2068; "Luvina," 2066; "Talpa," 2066; "Tell Them Not to Kill Me," 2066; "We're Very Poor," 2065
Rumpole, Horace, 2622
Rumpole à la Carte (Mortimer), 2623
"Rus." *See* "In Old Russia"
Rushdie, Salman, 2068-2071, 2973, 2976; "At the Auction of the Ruby Slippers," 2070; "Courter, The," 2070; *East, West: Stories*, 2976; "Good Advice Is Rarer than Rubies," 2069; "Prophet's Hair, The," 2070; "Vina Divina," 2070
Russ, Joanna, 2641
Russia; 1880-1920, 2794; modern short story and, 2748. *See also* "Geographical Index"
"Rustic Chivalry" (Verga), 2395

"S ANGEL" (Chabon), 500
Saʿdi of Shiraz; *Rose Garden, The*, 2661
"Sabbatha and Solitude" (Williams, Tennessee), 2527
"Sacajawea's Gold" (Hoch), 1212
"Sacrifice of the Maidens, The" (Roberts), 2050
"Sad Fate of Mr. Fox, The" (Harris, Joel Chandler), 1123
Safe-Conduct, A (Pasternak), 1889
"Safe Place, The" (Morris), 1712
"Safeway" (Barthelme, Frederick), 191
Saga, 2669-2676, 2679, 2700, 3066; Family, 2672, 2675-2676; Kings', 2671-2672; Past Times, 2675
Saga of Gisli, The, 2674
Saga of the Volsungs, The, 2675
Saikaku okimiyage (Ihara Saikaku), 1266
Saikaku shokoku-banashi (Ihara Saikaku), 1265
"Sailor, The" (Wescott), 2492
"Sailor-Boy's Tale, The" (Dinesen), 741, 2817
"Sailor off the Bremen" (Shaw), 2131
"Saint Augustine's Pigeon" (Connell), 617
"St. Cecilia" (Kleist), 1404
"St. Columba and the River" (Dreiser), 787
"Saint Manuel Bueno, Martyr" (Unamuno y Jugo), 2373
"Saint Marie" (Erdrich), 849, 2967
St. Mawr (Lawrence), 1455
"Saint Paul" (Smith), 2184
"Sa'iq al-qitar" (Mahfouz), 1588
Saki, 2072-2076, 2648, 2797; *Beasts and Super-Beasts*, 2074; "Cousin Theresa," 2073; "Open Window, The," 2074, 2798; "Sredni Vashtar," 2074; *When William Came*, 2075
"Salamanders, The" (Rivera), 2043
Saldivar, Ramon, 2953
Salinger, J. D., 2076-2083; "For Esmé—with Love and Squalor," 2078; "Franny," 2080; *Franny and Zooey*, 2080; "Glass Family Cycle,The," 2079; "Hapworth 16, 1924," 2082; "Raise High the Roof Beam, Carpenters," 2079; "Seymour: An Introduction," 2082; "Uncle Wiggily in Connecticut," 2079; "Zooey," 2080
Salinger, J.D.; "Perfect Day for Bananafish, A," 2080
Salkey, Andrew, 2946
"Salt" (Babel), 132
"Salt and Sawdust" (Narayan), 1754
"Salvation of a Forsyte, The" (Galsworthy), 947
"Samaia liubimaia." *See* "Most Beloved"
Same Door, The (Updike), 2377
"Same Place, Same Things" (Gautreaux), 988
"San Manuel Bueno, mártir." *See* "Saint Manuel Bueno, Martyr"
Sanatorium Under the Sign of the Hourglass (Schulz), 2110
"Sanctuary" (Dreiser), 785
"Sandman, The" (Hoffmann), 1220
"Sandstone Farmhouse, A" (Updike), 2383
Sansei, 2877
"Sanshō the Steward" (Mori, Ōgai), 2932
Sansom, William, 2084-2090; "Among the Dahlias," 2088; *Among the Dahlias*, 2088; *Contest of Ladies, A*, 2088; "Difficulty with a Bouquet," 2087; "Episode at Gastein," 2088; *Fireman Flower*, 2085; "Girl on the Bus, The," 2087; "Life, Death," 2088; *Lord Love Us*, 2088; "Marmalade Bird, The," 2089; *Marmalade Bird, The*, 2089; *Passionate North, The*, 2087; "Something Terrible, Something Lovely," 2086; *Something Terrible, Something Lovely*, 2086; *South*, 2087; "Three Dogs of Siena," 2087; *Touch of the Sun, A*, 2088; "Tutti-Frutti," 2087; "Various Temptations," 2089; "Vertical Ladder, The," 2086; "Wall, The," 2085; "Witness, The," 2086
"Santelices" (Donoso), 757
Santos, Bienvenido, 2881; "Contender, The," 2881; "Day the Dancers Came, The," 2881
Saragossa Manuscript, The (Potocki), 2643
"Sarah" (Lavin), 2923
"Sarah Cole: A Type of Love Story" (Banks), 164
"Sarah Gwynn" (Moore, George), 1697
Sargeson, Frank, 2893; "Hole That Jack Dug, The," 2894; "Making of a New Zealander, The," 2894
Sarmiento, Domingo Faustino, 2941
Saroyan, William, 2090-2095; "Daring Young Man on the Flying Trapeze, The," 2092; *My Name Is Aram*, 2093; "Pomegranate Trees," 2093; "Summer of the Beautiful White Horse, The," 2093
Sartre, Jean-Paul, 2095-2102, 2818; "Childhood of a Boss," 2099; "Erostratus," 2098; "Wall, The," 2097, 2819
"Sarugashima." *See* "Island of Monkeys, The"
"Saruzuka." *See* "Mound of the Monkey's Grave, The"
"Sarzan" (Diop), 2849
Sasaki, R. A., 2880; *Loom and Other Stories, The*, 2880
"Sashka Khristov" (Babel), 132

Satire, 2637, 2664, 3066. *See also* "Category Index"
Satires (Horace), 2627
"Saturday Afternoon" (Caldwell), 406
"Saturn" (Gates), 982
"Saturn Street" (Leavitt), 1468
Satyricon, The (Petronius), 1911, 2664
"Saucer of Larks, The" (Friel), 922
"Savages" (O'Brien, Edna), 1783
Save Every Lamb (Sturgeon), 2262
"'Savonarola' Brown" (Beerbohm), 227
"Sawdust" (Offutt), 1823
"Say Could That Lad Be I" (Lavin), 1446
"Say Yes" (Wolff), 2832
Sayers, Dorothy L., 2618; *Hangman's Holiday*, 2618
Sayles, John, 2102-2105; *Anarchists' Convention, The*, 2104; "At the Anarchists' Convention," 2103; "I-80 Nebraska, m. 490-m. 205," 2104; "Schiffman's Ape," 2104; "Tan," 2104
"Scala Scare, The" (Buzzati), 383
"Scandal and the Press, A" (Čapek), 439
"Scandal in Bohemia, A" (Doyle), 778
"Scandalous Woman, A" (O'Brien, Edna), 1782
"Scarecrow, The" (Roberts), 2051
"Scat" (Major), 1593
Scenes of Childhood (Warner), 2454
"Schalken the Painter" (Le Fanu), 1471
"Schiffman's Ape" (Sayles), 2104
"Schläferung." *See* "Sleep"
Schlegel, Friedrich, 2599
"Schloimele" (Singer), 2163
Schorer, Mark, 2754
"Schreuderspitze, The" (Helprin), 1168
Schulz, Bruno, 2106-2112; *Cinnamon Shops*, 2108; "Father's Last Escape," 2110; "Night of the Great Season, The," 2109; "Pan," 2108; *Sanatorium Under the Sign of the Hourglass*, 2110
Schwartz, Delmore, 2112-2117; "America! America!," 2115; "In Dreams Begin Responsibilities," 2113
Schwartz, Lynne Sharon, 2117-2120; *Acquainted with the Night, and Other Stories*, 2118; "Age of Analysis, The," 2118; "Last Frontier, The," 2119; *Melting Pot and Other Subversive Stories, The*, 2119; "Middle Classes, The," 2118; "So You're Going to Have a New Body," 2119; "What I Did for Love," 2118-2119
Science ficion, 2632-2642
Science fiction; avant-garde, 2640; contemporary, 2640; eighteenth century, 2632; pulp, 2634. *See also* "Category Index"
Scott, Duncan Campbell; *In the Village of Viger*, 2901
Scott, Sir Walter, 2120-2125; "Highland Widow, The," 2122; "Two Drovers, The," 2123; "Wandering Willie's Tale," 2122, 2745
"Scoundrel, The" (Nabokov), 1741
"Scream, The" (Oates), 1776
"Screamers, The" (Baraka), 167
"Sculptor's Funeral, The" (Cather), 486
"Sealed Angel, The" (Leskov), 1491
Searching for Survivors (Banks), 162
"Seasons of Mists" (Collier), 609
"Sebastopol in August" (Tolstoy), 2329
"Sebastopol in December" (Tolstoy), 2329
"Sebastopol in May" (Tolstoy), 2329
Sebastopol sketches (Tolstoy), 2329
Second Birth (Pasternak), 1891
Second Chance (Auchincloss), 121
"Second Tree from the Corner, The" (White), 2507
"Second Variety" (Dick), 723
"Secret Garden, The" (Chesterton), 559
"Secret Integration, The" (Pynchon), 2008
"Secret Life of Walter Mitty, The" (Thurber), 2314
"Secret of Father Brown, The" (Chesterton), 558
"Secret Room, The" (Robbe-Grillet), 2046-2047
"Secret Sharer, The" (Conrad), 626, 2799
"Secreto, Lo." *See* "Unknown, The"
Secrets (Hale), 1099
"Secrets" (McLaverty), 2926
Seize the Day (Bellow), 2812
"Seizing Control" (Robison), 2056
Seken munezan'y. See *Worldly Mental Calculations*
Seldes, Gilbert, 2791
"Selling Out" (Apple), 87
"Seltsame stadt." *See* "Strange City, A"
Sembène, Ousmane; "False Prophet, The," 2850; "Promised Land, The," 2850; *Tribal Scars*, 2850
Sembène, Ousmane; "Tribal Scars," 2850
"Semejante a la noche." *See* "Like the Night"
Semeynoye schast'ye. See *Family Happiness*
"Senility" (Lavin), 1446
Senior, Olive, 2946
"Señora, Una." *See* "Lady, A"
"Sense of Humour" (Pritchett), 1971
"Sense of the Meeting, The" (Conroy), 629-630
"Sentence" (Barthelme, Donald), 188
"Sententious" (Shalamov), 2128
"Sentimental Education" (Brodkey), 356
"Sentinel, The" (Clarke), 592
"Sentry, The" (Leskov), 1492
"Separating" (Updike), 2380
September Song (Humphrey), 1247
"Sequel, The" (Hall), 1103
"Ser Cepparelo" (Boccaccio), 269
"Seraph and the Zambesi, The" (Spark), 2198
"Sergeant Prishibeev" (Chekhov), 543
Sethi, Robbie Clipper, 2972
Seton, Ernest Thompson, 2900
Setsuwa bungaku, 2929

"Sette messaggeri, I." *See* "Seven Messengers"
"Sette piani." *See* "Seven Floors"
Setting, 3066
"Setting the World to Rights" (Oz), 1863
"Settled on the Cranberry Coast" (Byers), 391, 2839
"Sevastopol v dekabre." *See* "Sebastopol in December"
"Sevastopol v mae." *See* "Sebastopol in May"
Sevastopolskiye rasskazy. See *Sebastopol*
"Seven Floors" (Buzzati), 383
Seven Men (Beerbohm), 226
"Seven Messengers" (Buzzati), 383
Seventeenth century, 2708, 2718-2720, 2722, 2724
"Seventh Street Philosopher, The" (Mori, Tashio), 2878
"Seymour: An Introduction" (Salinger), 2082
Shadbolt, Maurice, 2606
"Shades of Spring, The" (Lawrence), 1452
"Shadow, The" (Andersen), 72
"Shadow Figure, The" (End[omacr}), 844
"Shadow in the Rose Garden, The" (Lawrence), 1452
"Shadow of the Goat, The" (Carr), 466
Shah, Indries, 2754
Shahnamah (Firdusi), 2664
Shalamov, Varlam, 2126-2130; "Epitaph, An," 2129; "Esperanto," 2128; "Life of Engineer Kipreev, The," 2128; "My First Tooth," 2129; "Sententious," 2128
"Shame Dance, The" (Steele, Wilbur Daniel), 2218
"Shape of Light, A" (Goyen), 1062
"Shares: A Novel in Ten Pieces" (Stern), 2243
Shares and Other Fictions (Stern), 2243
"Shattered Like a Glass Goblin" (Ellison, Harlan), 832
Shaw, Irwin, 2131-2135; "Eighty-Yard Run, The," 2132; "Girls in Their Summer Dresses, The," 2133; "Sailor off the Bremen," 2131; "Tip on a Dead Jockey," 2133
"Shawl, The" (Ozick), 1868, 2836
"She" (Woiwode), 2541
"She Makes Swell Doughnuts" (Mori, Tashio), 2878
"She-Wolf, The" (Verga), 2395
"Shearing the Wolf, The" (Hemingway), 1186
Shelley, Mary, 2756
Shelley, Percy Bysshe, 2761
"Shepherd" (Williams, Joy), 2521
"Sheriff's Children, The" (Chesnutt), 2858
Shiel, M. P., 2647
Shiga Naoya, 2932; "At Kinosaki," 2933
"Shigadera Shōnin no Koi." *See* "Priest of Shiga Temple and His Love, The"
"Shiloh" (Mason), 1640, 2833
Shiloh and Other Stories (Mason), 1640
"Shinel." *See* "Overcoat, The"
"Ship Fever" (Barrett), 174
"Ship Island" (Spencer), 2205
"Shipmates Down Under" (Byers), 392
"Shisei." *See* "Tattooer, The"
Shishōsetsu, 3067
Shi-shōsetsu. See I-novel
"Shooting-Match, The" (Longstreet), 1529
"Shootout at Gentry's Junction" (Coover), 635
"Shopgirls" (Barthelme, Frederick), 191
"Shore, The" (Robbe-Grillet), 2046
"Short Happy Life of Francis Macomber, The" (Hemingway), 1176
Short Sentimental Journey and Other Stories (Svevo), 2271
"Short-Shift Saturday" (Casey), 2890
Short story, 3067
Short Story in English, The (Canby), 2600
Short Story Theories (May), 2607
Short Story Theory at a Crossroads (Lohafer and Clarey), 2608
"Shot, The" (Pushkin), 1999
"Shower of Gold, A" (Barthelme, Donald), 184
Shu-jên, Chou. *See* Lu Xun
Shushu de gushi (Wang), 2447
"Si me tocaras el corazón" (Allende), 68
"Sicily Burns's Wedding" (Harris, George Washington), 2779
"Sick Call, A" (Callaghan), 420
"Sick Child, The" (Colette), 602
Sidney, Sir Philip, 2713; *Arcadia*, 2713
"'Sieur George" (Cable), 395, 2780
"Signalman, The" (Dickens), 2770
"Significant Moments in the Life of My Mother" (Atwood), 112
Signified, 3067
Signifier, 3067
"Signing, The" (Dixon), 750
Signor Formica (Hoffmann), 1220
"Signora Frola and Her Son-in-Law, Signor Ponza" (Pirandello), 1930
"Signora Frola e il signor Ponza, suo genero, La." *See* "Signora Frola and Her Son-in-Law, Signor Ponza"
"Signs and Symbols" (Nabokov), 1743, 2821
Silas Ermineskin stories (Kinsella), 1385
"Silence" (Borowski), 298
"Silence Dogood Essays" (Franklin), 2730
Silence of the Llano, The (Anaya), 2954
"Silent Men, The" (Camus, Albert), 432
"Silent Passengers" (Woiwode), 2542
Silent Passengers (Woiwode), 2542
"Silent Snow, Secret Snow" (Aiken), 32
Silent Spring (Masumoto), 2880
Silko, Leslie Marmon, 2135-2142, 2960; *Ceremony*, 2960; "Lullaby," 2137; "Storyteller," 2138; *Storyteller*, 2969; *Yellow Woman*, 2139
Sillitoe, Alan, 2142-2147; "Good Women, The," 2145; "Loneliness of the Long-Distance Runner, The," 2144;

"On Saturday Afternoon," 2144; "Pit Strike," 2145; "Uncle Ernest," 2143
"Silver Dish, A" (Bellow), 237
Silverberg, Robert, 2640
"Simetrías." *See* "Symmetries"
Simile, 3067
Simms, William Gilmore, 2147-2153; "Grayling," 2150; "How Sharp Snaffles Got His Capital and His Wife," 2148; "Snake of the Cabin, The," 2150
"Simple Heart, A" (Flaubert), 873, 2782
"Simple Susan" (Edgeworth), 809
Simpson, Mona, 2153-2156; "Approximations," 2155; "Day He Left, The," 2155; "Lawns," 2155; "Victory Mills," 2156; "What My Mother Knew," 2154
"Sin of Jesus, The" (Babel), 133
Singer, Isaac Bashevis, 2157-2165, 2817; "Gentleman from Cracow, The," 2818; "Gimpel the Fool," 2161, 2818; "Grandfather and Grandson," 2162; "Manuscript, The," 2162; "Schloimele," 2163; "Smuggler, The," 2163; "Spinoza of Market Street, The," 2161; "Taibele and Her Demon," 2160; "Two Corpses Go Dancing," 2160; "Zeitl and Rickel," 2161
"Singers, The" (Turgenev), 2355
"Singing Bone, The" (Grimm), 1090
"Singular Event, A" (Machado de Assis), 1570
"Singular occurrência." *See* "Singular Event, A"
"Sins of the Third Age" (Gordimer), 1044
Sinuhe, 2657
Sinyavsky, Andrei, 2165-2171; "At the Circus," 2167; "Icicle, The," 2168; *Little Jinx*, 2169; "Pkhentz," 2169; "Tenants," 2167; "You and I," 2168
Sister Carrie (Dreiser), 784
"Six Feet of the Country" (Gordimer), 1041
"Six Soldiers of Fortune" (Grimm), 1087
Six Stories Written in the First Person Singular (Maugham), 1649
Sixteenth century, 2705, 2708, 2710, 2713, 2715-2716, 2722, 2724
Sixty-three: Dream Palace (Purdy), 1995
Skallagrimsson, Egill, 2671
"Skandál a žurnalistika." *See* "Scandal and the Press, A"
"Skater, The" (Williams, Joy), 2522
"Skating in the Dark" (Kaplan), 1338
Skating in the Dark (Kaplan), 1338
Skaz, 3067
"Skazka pro babu." *See* "Tale of a Woman, The"
"Skeleton, The" (Pritchett), 1973
Sketch, 2737-2739, 2744, 3067. *See also* "Category Index"
Sketch Book of Geoffrey Crayon, Gent., The (Irving), 2644
Sketches by Boz (Dickens), 2745
"Sketches from Nature" (Irving), 1269
"Skibsdrængens fortælling." *See* "Sailor-Boy's Tale, The"
"Skinless" (Bender), 241
Skord, Virginia; *Tales of Tears and Laughter*, 2930
"Skripka Rotshil'da." *See* "Rothschild's Fiddle"
"Skuchnaia istoriia." *See* "Boring Story, A"
"Sky Is Gray, The" (Gaines), 932
Slap in the Face Et Cetera, A (Walser), 2441
Slavin, Julia, 2171-2174; "Babyproofing," 2172; "Dentophilia," 2173; "Lives of the Invertebrates," 2173; "Swallowed Whole," 2172
"Sleep" (Hildesheimer), 1203
"Sleep It Off, Lady" (Rhys), 2033
Sleep It Off, Lady (Rhys), 2033
"Sleep Tight" (Purdy), 1993
"Sleeping Beauty" (Grimm), 1089
Sleepwalker in a Fog (Tolstaya), 2323
"Sleepy" (Chekhov), 2795
"Slim" (Mars-Jones), 1631
"Slippage" (Updike), 2382
Slow Learner (Pynchon), 2009
"Slow Sculpture" (Sturgeon), 2267
Slowly Slowly in the Wind (Highsmith), 1196
"Sluchainost." *See* "Matter of Chance, A"
"Small Rain, The" (Pynchon), 2005
"Small Spade, A" (Mars-Jones), 1632
"Small Town" (Dick), 722
"Small Town Affair" (Arreola), 93
"Small World" (Davies, Peter Ho), 693
"Small, Good Thing, A" (Carver), 2831
"Smert' Dolgushova." *See* "Death of Dolgushov, The"
Smert' Ivana Il'icha. See *Death of Ivan Ilyich, The*
Směšne lásky. See *Laughable Loves*
Smiley, Jane, 2174-2181; *Age of Grief, The*, 2176; "Dynamite," 2177; *Good Will*, 2179; "Jeffrey, Believe Me," 2177; "Long Distance," 2177; *Ordinary Love*, 2178; "Pleasure of Her Company, The," 2177
Smith, Clark Ashton, 2651
Smith, Lee, 2182-2187; "All the Days of Our Lives," 2183; "Between the Lines," 2183; "Bob, A Dog," 2184; "Bubba Stories, The," 2185; *Cakewalk*, 2183; "Dear Phil Donahue," 2183; "Gulfport," 2184; "Happy Memories Club," 2186; "Heat Lightning," 2184; "Life on the Moon," 2185; "Live Bottomless," 2185; "Me and My Baby View the Eclipse," 2185; *Me and My Baby View the Eclipse*, 2184; *News of the Spirit*, 2185; "Saint Paul," 2184; "Southern Cross," 2186
"Smuggler, The" (Singer), 2163
Snail-Watcher and Other Stories, The (Highsmith), 1194
"Snake, The" (Steinbeck), 2809
"Snake of the Cabin, The" (Simms), 2150
"Snapshots" (Viramontes), 2404
"Snow" (Beattie), 214
Snow Country (Kawabata), 2933
"Snow Queen, The" (Andersen), 71

"Snow White" (Grimm), 1090
"Snowed In" (Broyard), 365
"Snows of Kilimanjaro, The" (Hemingway), 1176, 2806
"So." *See* "Salt"
"So on He Fares" (Moore, George), 1697, 2916
"So Softly Smiling" (Himes), 1207
"So ward abend und morgen." *See* "And There Was the Evening and the Morning"
"So You're Going to Have a New Body" (Schwartz, Lynne Sharon), 2119
"Sociable at Dudleys, A" (Garland), 965
"Soldier's Embrace, A" (Gordimer), 1043
"Soldier's Home" (Hemingway), 1175
"Sole e ombra." *See* "Sunlight and Shadow"
"Solid Objects" (Woolf), 2557
"Solo Song: For Doc, A" (McPherson), 1583
Solzhenitsyn, Aleksandr, 2187-2192; "For the Good of the Cause," 2190; "Right Hand, The," 2190; "Incident at Krechetovka Station," 2189; "Matryona's House," 2190
Some Chinese Ghosts (Hearn), 1157
"Some Grist for Mervyn's Mill" (Richler), 2038
"Some Like Them Cold" (Lardner), 1436
"Some of These Days" (Purdy), 1994
"Something Else" (Zhang), 2582-2583
"Something Nice" (Gaitskill), 937
Something Out There (Gordimer), 1043
Something Short and Sweet (Bates), 200
"Something Terrible, Something Lovely" (Sansom), 2086
Something Terrible, Something Lovely 2 (Sansom), 2086
"Something That Happened" (Phillips), 1925
"Somewhere Doors, The" (Chappell), 517
"Son, The" (Bunin), 374
"Son, The" (Quiroga), 2020
"Son smeshnogo cheloveha." *See* "Dream of a Ridiculous Man, The"
"Song of the Falcon, The" (Gorky), 1057
"Song of the Republic, A" (Lawson), 2889
Song of the Turtle (Allen), 2962
"Song of Triumphant Love, The" (Turgenev), 2357
"Songs of Reba Love Jackson, The" (Wideman), 2512
"Sonny's Blues" (Baldwin), 138
Sontag, Susan, 2193-2196; "Baby," 2195; "Debriefing," 2194; "Dummy, The," 2195; "Project for a Trip to China," 2194
"Sophistication" (Anderson), 80
"Sordid Tale" (Gilchrist), 996
"Sorg-agre." *See* "Sorrow-Acre"
"Sorrow-Acre" (Dinesen), 740, 2817
Sorrows of Young Werther, The (Goethe), 1018
"Sorry Fugu" (Boyle, T. C.), 328
Soto, Pedro Juan, 2957; *Spiks*, 2957
Soul Clap Hands and Sing (Marshall), 1635
"Soul of the Great Bell, The" (Hearn), 1157
"Soul of Wood" (Lind), 1514
"Sound of Talking" (Purdy), 1996
"Source" (Walker), 2434
"South, The" (Borges), 291
South (Sansom), 2087
South Asia, 2972-2977
South Asian American culture, 2884
"Southern Cross" (Smith), 2186
"Southern Landscape, A" (Spencer), 2204
Southern Renaissance, 1047
Southern United States, 2806. *See also* "Category Index"
Southwestern United States, 2744. *See also* "Category Index"
"Sow That Eats Her Farrow, The" (Kiš), 1399
Sowdone of Babylone, The, 2693
Spain, 2732. *See also* "Geographical Index"
Spanish culture, 2706. *See also* "Category Index"
Spark, Muriel, 2196-2202; "Bang-Bang You're Dead," 2199; "Curtain Blown by the Breeze, A," 2198; "First Year of My Life, The," 2199; "Go-Away Bird, The" , 2199; *Open to the Public*, 2200; "Pawnbroker's Wife, The," 2198; "Portobello Road, The," 2199; "Seraph and the Zambesi, The," 2198
"Sparrows" (Lessing), 1499
"Specialty of the House, The" (Ellin), 2621
Spectator, The (Addison and Steele), 14, 18, 2213-2214, 2216, 2726, 2737-2738
"Spectre Bridegroom, The" (Irving), 1270
"Speech of Polly Baker" (Franklin), 905
Spencer, Elizabeth, 2202-2208; "Bufords, The," 2205; "First Dark," 2204; "Go South in the Winter," 2206; "Jean-Pierre," 2206; "Knights and Dragons," 2205; "Legacy, The," 2206; "Little Brown Girl, The," 2204; "Mr. McMillan," 2206; *On the Gulf*, 2206; "Ship Island," 2205; "Southern Landscape, A," 2204
"Spi skorei." *See* "Get on with the Sleeping"
"Spider's Thread, The" (Akutagawa), 39
"Spies in the Herb House, The" (Betts), 255
Spiks (Soto), 2957
"Spindleberries" (Galsworthy), 948
"Spinoza of Market Street, The" (Singer), 2161
"Spinster's Tale, A" (Taylor, Peter), 2296
Splendid Lives (Gilliatt), 1000
"Sportsman" (Hempel), 1182
Sportsman's Sketches, A (Twain), 2353
"Spouse Night" (Leavitt), 1467
"Spring in Fialta" (Nabokov), 1742
"Spring Sowing" (O'Flaherty), 2921
"Spunk" (Hurston), 1252, 2862
Spy and the Thief, The (Hoch), 1212
"Squeaker's Mate" (Baynton), 2889
"Squire's Daughter, The" (Pushkin), 2001
"Sredni Vashtar" (Saki), 2074

Stafford, Jean, 2208-2212; "Bleeding Heart, The," 2210; *Collected Stories of Jean Stafford, The*, 2209; "Echo and the Nemesis, The," 2210; "Healthiest Girl in Town, The," 2211; "Liberator, The," 2211; "Maggie Meriwether's Rich Experience," 2210
"Star, The" (Clarke), 593
"Star Baby" (Gates), 981
"Star Food" (Canin), 435
"Stars of the New Curfew" (Okri), 1841
Stars of the New Curfew (Okri), 1841
"Starukha Izergil." *See* "Old Woman Izergil"
"State Champions" (Mason), 1642
"State Fair" (Keillor), 1352
"Staying in Bed" (Gilliatt), 1000
Stead, Christina, 2754
"Steady Going Up" (Angelou), 83
"Steel Cat, The" (Collier), 609
Steele, Richard, 2213-2217; "Biter, The," 2727; *Christian Hero, The*," 2216; *Guardian, The*, 2214-2216; "Inkle and Yarico," 2215; "Matchmaker, The," 2727; *Spectator, The*, 14, 2213-2214, 2216, 2726, 2737-2738; *Tatler, The*, 14, 18, 2213-2214, 2216, 2737-2738
Steele, Wilbur Daniel, 2217-2220; "How Beautiful with Shoes," 2219; "Man Who Saw Through Heaven, The," 2219; "Shame Dance, The," 2218; "When Hell Froze," 2219
Stegner, Wallace, 2220-2224; "Beyond the Glass Mountain," 2222; *City of the Living and Other Stories, The*, 2222; "Field Guide to the Western Birds," 2222; "Maiden in a Tower," 2222; "Two Rivers," 2222; *Women on the Wall, The*, 2221-2222
Stein, Gertrude, 2225-2233; *Alphabets and Birthdays*, 2231; "As Fine as Melanctha," 2229; "Brim Beauvais," 2230; *Tender Buttons*, 2228
Steinbeck, John, 2233-2238; "Chrysanthemums, The, 2236; "Flight," 2237; "Junius Maltby," 2236; "Legend of Tularecito, The," 2236; *Long Valley, The*, 2236; *Pastures of Heaven, The*, 2235; "Snake, The," 2809; "White Quail, The," 2236
Steinhöwel, Heinrich, 2628
"Stephanie, Stephen, Steph, Steve" (Gilliatt), 1002
Stephens, James, 2919; "Triangle, The," 2919
"Stepnoi Korol' Lir." *See* "King Lear of the Steppes"
"Steppe, The" (Chekhov), 544
Stern, Richard G., 2239-2244; "Arrangements at the Gulf," 2241; "Aurelia Frequenzia Reveals the Heart and Mind of the Man of Destiny," 2242; "Counterfactual Proposal, A," 2241; "Degradation of Tenderness, The," 2243; "Double Charley," 2241; "Dying," 2242; "Good Morrow, Swine," 2240; "In a Word, Trowbridge," 2243; "Pourriture Noble, La," 2242; "Recital for the Pope, A," 2242; "Shares: A Novel in Ten Pieces," 2243; *Shares and Other Fictions*, 2243; *Understanding Fiction*, 2240; "Veni, Vidi . . . Wendt," 2241; "Wissler Remembers," 2242
Stevenson, Lionel, 2796
Stevenson, Robert Louis, 2245-2250, 2798; "Beach of Falesá, The," 2248; "Lodging for the Night, A," 2246, 2798; "Markheim," 2247
"Stick of Green Candy, A" (Bowles, Jane), 309
Still Life with Pipe (Donoso), 759
"Still Moment, A" (Welty), 2486
"Stinger, The" (Leskov), 1490
Stockton, Frank R., 2250-2254; "His Wife's Deceased Sister," 2253; "Magic Egg, The," 2251
Stone, Robert, 2254-2257; "Absence of Mercy," 2256; "Bear and His Daughter," 2257; *Bear and His Daughter*, 2255; "Helping," 2256; "Miserere," 2255; "Under the Pitons," 2256
"Stone Boy, The" (Berriault), 250
Stories of Eva Luna, The (Allende), 67
Stories of Ray Bradbury, The (Bradbury), 338
Stories of Red Hanrahan (Yeats), 2569
Stories of the Sioux (Eastman), 2963
"Storm, The" (Chopin), 565
"Storms" (Lessing), 1499
"Story, The" (Pasternak), 1890
"Story About the Most Important Thing, A" (Zamyatin), 2576
"Story by Maupassant, A" (O'Connor, Frank), 1806
"Story of Serapion, The" (Hoffmann), 1218
"Story in a Mirror" (Aichinger), 29
Story line, 3067
"Story of a Contraoctave, The" (Pasternak), 1888
"Story of a Panic, The" (Forster), 887
"Story of an Hour, The" (Chopin), 563
Story of Burnt Njal, The, 2675
"Story of My Dovecote, The" (Babel), 129
"Story of Stories, A" (Dreiser), 785
"Story of the Goblins Who Stole a Sexton, The" (Dickens), 729
"Storyteller" (Silko), 2138
Storyteller (Silko), 2969
Story-Teller's Holiday, A (Moore, George), 1698
"Stove, The" (Lind), 1515
Stove, The (Lind), 1515
"Strange City, A" (Walser), 2440
"Strange Fire" (Oz), 1862
"Strange Moonlight" (Aiken), 34
Strange Pilgrims (García Márquez), 954
"Stranger, Bear Word to the Spartans We . . ." (Böll), 275
Stray Leaves from Strange Literature (Hearn), 1158
Stream of consciousness, 3067
Strength of Gideon and Other Stories, The (Dunbar), 795
"Strength of God, The" (Anderson), 79
"Strider" (Tolstoy), 2330

Stroud, Theodore Albert, 2607
Structuralism, 3067
"Struggle for Life, A" (Aldrich), 48
Stuart, Jesse, 2258-2263; "Dawn of Remembered Spring," 2259; "Moonshine War, The," 2261; "My Father Is an Educated Man," 2262; *Save Every Lamb*, 2262; "Sunday Afternoon Hanging," 2261; "Sylvania Is Dead," 2260
"Stub-Book, The" (Alarcón), 45
Study of Prose Fiction, A (Perry), 2758
Sturgeon, Theodore, 2264-2268, 2637; "Man Who Lost the Sea, The," 2267; "Microcosmic God," 2265; "Slow Sculpture," 2267; "World Well Lost, The," 2266
Sturluson, Snorri, 2672; *Prose Edda*, 2670, 2672
Style, 3067
Suárez, Mario, 2952
"Subject to Diary" (Weldon), 2474
Subjective, 3067
"Sublimating" (Updike), 2380
Success Stories (Banks), 164
Suchbild (Meckel), 1663
Suckow, Ruth, 2755
"Sugar" (Byatt), 388
"Sugawn Chair, The" (O'Faoláin), 1819
Sui Sin Far, 2873; "Leaves from the Mental Portfolio of an Eurasian," 2874; *Mrs. Spring Fragrance*, 2873-2874
"Suicides" (Pavese), 1895
"Suicidio al parco" (Buzzati), 384
"Suigetsu." *See* "Moon on the Water, The"
"Beautiful Suit, The" (Wells), 2479
Sullivan, John Walter, 2607
"Summer Lightning" (Mars-Jones), 1632
"Summer My Grandmother Was Supposed to Die, The" (Richler), 2037
"Summer Night" (Bowen), 301
"Summer of the Beautiful White Horse, The" (Saroyan), 2093
"Summer People" (Kaplan), 1336
"Summer Shore" (Grau), 1067
"Summer Storm" (Parvese), 1895
"Summer Storms" (Woiwode), 2542
"Summer Tidings" (Purdy), 1994
"Summer Tragedy, A" (Bontemps), 283
"Sunday Afternoon Hanging" (Sturgeon), 2261
"Sunday at the Mintons'" (Plath), 1934
"Sunday Painter, The" (Cassill), 483
"Sunlight and Shadow" (Pirandello), 1929
Supernatural, 2643-2653, 2745, 2797, 2908, 2943. *See also* "Category Index"
"Supper, The" (Borowski), 298
Supplement, 3067
Supplement to Bougainville's Voyage (Diderot), 735
"Supremacy of the Hunza, The" (Greenberg), 1070
"Suprugi Orlovy." *See* "Orlov Married Couple"
"Sur, El." *See* "South, The"
"Surface Tension" (Blish), 2638
"Surfiction" (Wideman), 2513
Surrealism, 2943. *See also* "Category Index"
Surrounded, The (McNickle), 2964
"Survivor in Salvador, A" (Tuohy), 2348
Sut Lovingood (Harris, George Washington), 2779
Svevo, Italo, 2269-2272; *Further Confessions of Zeno*, 2271; "Generous Wine," 2271; *Hoax, The*, 2270; *Nice Old Man and the Pretty Girl and Other Stories, The*, 2270; *Short Sentimental Journey and Other Stories*, 2271
"Svidanie s ptitsei." *See* "Date with a Bird"
"Swallowed Whole" (Slavin), 2172
"Swans on an Autumn River" (Warner), 2452
"Sweat" (Hurston), 1253
"Sweating Statue, The" (Hoch), 1214
"Sweethearts" (Ford), 883
Swift, Graham, 2272-2275, 2841; "Hoffmeier's Antelope," 2273; "Learning to Swim," 2272; *Learning to Swim and Other Stories*, 2841; "Tunnel, The," 2273; "Watch, The," 2274
"Swimmer, The" (Cheever), 538, 2827
"Switchman, The" (Arreola), 92
"Sword of Welleran, The" (Dunsany), 799
"Sylvania Is Dead" (Sturgeon), 2260
"Sylvie" (Nerval), 1757
Symbolism, 2796, 2799, 3067. *See also* "Category Index"
"Symmetries" (Valenzuela), 2388
Symons, Arthur; "Christian Trevalga," 2797
"Symposium" (Kundera), 1416
Synesthesia, 3067

"Tables of the Law, The" (Yeats), 2569
Tabloid Dreams (Butler), 379
Tadjo, Véronique; "Magician and the Girl, The," 2851
Taḥta al-miẓalla (Mahfouz), 1589
"Taibele and Her Demon" (Singer), 2160
"Taking Care" (Williams, Joy), 2521
"Taking the Wen Away" (Dazai), 702
Tale, 2736, 2929, 3068. *See also* "Category Index"
"Tale of a Woman, The" (Babel), 133
"Tale of Balin, The" (Malory), 1604
"Tale of Dragons and Dreamers, The" (Delany), 712
Tale of Genji, The (Murasaki), 2667, 2929
"Tale of Gorgik, The" (Delany), 712
"Tale of How Ivan Ivanovich Quarreled with Ivan Nikiforovich, The" (Gogol), 1026
"Tale of King Arthur, The" (Malory), 1603
"Tale of Menorah, The" (Agnon), 27
"Tale of Old Venn, The" (Delany), 712
"Tale of the Bamboo Cutter, The," 2928

"Tale of the Queen of the Morning and Soliman the Prince of the Genii, The" (Nerval), 1758
"Tale of the Seven Beggars, The" (Nahman), 1748
"Tale of the Small Sarg, The" (Delany), 711
Tales (Baraka), 166
Tales from Bective Bridge (Lavin), 2923
Tales of a Dying Race (Grace), 2895
Tales of Fashionable Life (Edgeworth), 813
Tales of Manhattan (Auchincloss), 120
Tales of Moonlight and Rain (Ueda), 2931
Tales of Natural and Unnatural Catastrophe (Highsmith), 1198
Tales of Nevèrÿon (Delany), 712
Tales of Odessa (Babel), 130
Tales of Pirx the Pilot (Lem), 1485
"Tales of Queen Louisa" (Gardner), 960
Tales of Samurai Honor (Ihara Saikaku), 1265
Tales of Soldiers and Civilians (Bierce), 2649
Tales of Tears and Laughter (Skord), 2930
Tales of Times Now Past, 2929
"Talk Talked Between Worms, The" (Abbott), 2
"Talk to the Music" (Bontemps), 284
"Talkin' 'Bout Sonny" (Bambara), 2869
Tallent, Elizabeth, 2276-2279; "Honey," 2278; "Ice," 2277; "No One's a Mystery," 2277; "Prowler," 2276
Tall-tale, 3068
"Talpa" (Rulfo), 2066
"Tamurlane" (Mukherjee), 1724
"Tan" (Sayles), 2104
Tan, Amy, 2279-2282; "Best Quality," 2282; "Joy Luck Club, The," 2281; *Joy Luck Club, The*, 2281; "Pair of Tickets, A," 2282; "Rules of the Game," 2281; "Two Kinds," 2281
Tan, Joel, 2883
"Tang" (Himes), 1207
Tanizaki, Jun'ichirō, 2283-2287, 2933; "Aguri," 2284; "Ashikari," 2285; "Blind Man's Tale, A," 2285; "Bridge of Dreams, The," 2285, 2933; *Diary of a Mad Old Man*, 2286; "Portrait of Shunkin, A," 2285; "Tattooer, The," 2284; "Terror," 2284; "Thief, The," 2284
Tanka poems, 2928
Tantalus, 2660
"Tapiama" (Bowles, Paul), 314
"Taras Bulba" (Gogol), 1026
Targan, Barry, 2288-2291; "Dominion," 2289; "Falling Free," 2289; "Harry Belten and the Mendelssohn Violin Concerto," 2288
Tatius; *Leucippe and Clitophon*, 2666
Tatler, The (Addison and Steele), 14, 16, 18, 2213-2214, 2216, 2737-2738
Tatler 163 (Addison), 16
"Tatlin!" (Davenport), 684
"Tattooer, The" (Tanizaki), 2284
Taylor, Elizabeth, 2291-2294, 2606; "Blush, The," 2293; "Dedicated Man, A," 2292; "First Death of Her Life, The," 2292; "Red-Letter Day, A," 2292
Taylor, Peter, 2294-2299; "Dean of Men," 2296; "Miss Leonora When Last Seen," 2297; "Old Forest, The," 2298; "Spinster's Tale, A," 2296; "What You Hear from 'Em?," 2297; "Wife of Nashville, A," 2297
T. C. Boyle Stories (Boyle, T. C.), 329
Teach Us to Outgrow Our Madness (Ōe), 1814
"Teacher, The" (Anderson), 79
Technique, 3068
"Teenage Wasteland" (Tyler, Anne), 2368
"Telephone Call, A" (Parker), 1884
"Tell Me a Riddle" (Olsen), 1846
"Tell Me Yes or No" (Munro), 1734
"Tell-Tale Heart, The" (Poe), 2767
"Tell Them Not to Kill Me" (Rulfo), 2066
"Temporary Matter, A" (Gates), 1425
"Temporate d'estate." *See* "Summer Storm"
"Temptation of St. Ivo, The" (Gardner), 959
"Ten Pecan Pies" (Major), 1593
"Tenant, The" (Mukherjee), 1727
"Tenants" (Sinyavsky), 2167
Tender Buttons (Stein), 2228
"Tender Shoot, The" (Colette), 600
"Tendrils of the Vine, The" (Colette), 600
"Tendron, Le." *See* "Tender Shoot, The"
"Tennessee's Partner" (Harte), 2777
"Term Paper Artist, The" (Leavitt), 1467
"Terminal Beach, The" (Ballard), 144
"Terra d'esilio." *See* "Land of Exile"
"Terrapin, The" (Highsmith), 1195
"Terrific Mother" (Moore, Lorrie), 1701
"Territory" (Leavitt), 1465, 2834
"Terror" (Tanizaki), 2284
"Test, The" (Lem), 1485
"Testimony of Pilot" (Hannah), 2838
Tevye stories (Aleichem), 52
Thackeray, William Makepeace, 2300-2305; "Confessions of Fitz-Boodle," 2303; "Dimond Cut Dimond," 2302; "Foring Parts," 2302; "Miss Shum's Husband," 2301; "Mr. and Mrs. Frank Berry," 2303
"Thank You Ma'am" (Hughes), 1240
Tharoor, Shashi, 2972
"That Evening Sun" (Faulkner), 2805
Tháttr, 2669-2670, 2672, 2677-2679
"The Fat Man in History" (Carey) , 453
"Theater" (Toomer), 2337
Theatre of Gods Judgements, The (Beard), 2719
"Theft" (Porter), 1952
"Theft of the General's Trash, The" (Hoch), 1213
Thematics, 3068
Theme, 3068

Theory of Literature (Wellek and Warren), 2752
Theory of short fiction, 2599, 2612
Theory of the Novel, The (Lukács), 2753
"There Is No End" (Kavan), 1341
"They" (Kipling), 1394
They Sleep Without Dreaming (Gilliatt), 1001
"Thick as Thieves" (Perabo), 1899
"Thief, The" (Tanizaki), 2284
"Thin Edge of Happiness, The" (Guimarães Rosa), 1093
"Things in Their Season" (Greenberg), 1072
"Things They Carried, The" (O'Brien, Tim), 1792
Things They Carried, The (O'Brien, Tim), 1792
"Think No Evil" (Collier), 608
"Third and Final Continent, The" (Gates), 1426
"Third Circle, The" (Norris), 1767
"Third Expedition, The" (Bradbury), 336
"This Is Lagos" (Nwapa), 2853
"This Is Not a Story" (Diderot), 734
"This Way for the Gas, Ladies and Gentlemen" (Borowski), 297
"Thistledown" (Aiken), 35
Thomas, Dylan, 2306-2312; "Fight, The," 2309; "Orchards, The," 2310; "Patricia, Edith and Arnold," 2308; "Peaches, The," 2307; *Portrait of the Artist as a Young Dog*, 2307; "Prospect of the Sea, A," 2309; "Tree, The," 2310; "Visitor, The," 2310
Thomas, Pin, 2958
Thorgilsson, Ari; *Book of Settlements*, 2671; *Book of the Icelanders*, 2671
"Thorofare" (Minot), 1688
"Those Who Don't" (Cisneros), 581
"Three Bears Cottage" (Collier), 607
"Three Dogs of Siena" (Sansom), 2087
"Three Gifts, The" (Peretz), 1909
"Three Hermits, The" (Barthelme, Donald), 187
Three Impostors, The (Machen), 1575
Three Loves trilogy. *See Brocade Valley, Love in a Small Town*, and *Love on a Barren Mountain*
"Three Men" (Gaines), 933
"Three Players of a Summer Game" (Williams, Tennessee), 2526
Three Problems for Solar Pons (Derleth), 717
"Three Sisters, The" (Cisneros), 582
"Three Tasks, The" (Carleton), 456
"Three-Two Pitch" (Weidman), 2463
"Thrill of the Grass, The" (Kinsella), 1384
"Thrilling Life, A" (Minot), 1689
"Through the Dark Glass to Reality" (Hale), 1100
Thurber, James, 2312-2317; "Black Magic of Barney Haller, The," 2314; "Moth and the Star, The," 2315; "Secret Life of Walter Mitty, The," 2314; *White Deer, The*, 2315
"Tickets, Please" (Lawrence), 2813
Tieck, Ludwig, 2599, 2731; *Fair Eckbert*, 2731
"Tiger in the Grass, The" (Doerr), 754
"Tiger of Zhaochang, The" (Pu), 1986
Tilghman, Christopher, 2317-2320, 2839; "Hole in the Day," 2318; "In a Father's Place," 2318; "Loose Reins," 2318, 2839; "On the Rivershore," 2318; "Room for Mistakes," 2318; "Way People Run, The," 2319, 2839
"Till September Petronella" (Rhys), 2032
Time and a Place, A (Humphrey), 1246
"Time Considered as a Helix of Semiprecious Stones" (Delany), 711
"Time of Learning, A" (West), 2497
"Time the Tiger" (Lewis), 1505
"Tiny, Smiling Daddy" (Gaitskill), 937
"Tip on a Dead Jockey" (Shaw), 2133
"Tipo medio." *See* "Middling Type, A"
"*Titanic* Victim Speaks Through Waterbed" (Butler), 379
"Tlön, Uqbar, Orbis Tertius" (Borges), 2823
"To Build a Fire" (London), 1524
"To Da-duh, in Memoriam" (Marshall), 1637
"To Hell with Dying" (Walker), 2432
"To See You Again" (Adams), 11
"Today Is a Good Day to Die" (Bell), 231
"Today Will Be a Quiet Day" (Hempel), 1181
"Today's Agenda" (Zhang), 2582
"Toddler-Hunting" (Kōno), 2934
"Todos los fuegos el fuego." *See* "All Fires the Fire"
"Tokens" (Bennett), 2863
Tokugawa era, 2930
"Tokyo Hakkei." *See* "Eight Views of Tokyo"
Tokyo-Montana Express, The (Brautigan), 345
Tolstaya, Tatyana, 2320-2325; "Date with a Bird," 2322; "Limpopo," 2324; "Loves Me, Loves Me Not," 2322; "Moon Came Out, The," 2324; "Most Beloved," 2323; "On the Golden Porch," 2321; *On the Golden Porch*, 2322; "Peters," 2323; *Sleepwalker in a Fog*, 2323
Tolstoy, Leo, 2326-2335; *Death of Ivan Ilyich, The*, 2331, 2794; *Family Happiness*, 2330; *Kreutzer Sonata, The*, 2332; "Master and Man," 2332; "Raid: A Volunteer's Story, The," 2329; *Sebastopol* sketches, 2329; "Sebastopol in August," 2329; "Sebastopol in December," 2329; "Sebastopol in May," 2329; "Strider," 2330; "Two Hussars," 2330
"Tom" (Lavin), 1446
Tomb for Boris Davidovich, A (Kiš), 1398
Tommy and Tuppence Beresford stories, 576
"Tomorrow—Fairly Cloudy" (Perelman), 1903
"Tomorrow-Tamer, The" (Laurence), 1440
Tomorrow-Tamer, The (Laurence), 1440
Tone, 3068
Tonio Kröger (Mann), 1610
Too Far from Home (Bowles, Paul), 315

Toomer, Jean, 2335-2340; "Blood-Burning Moon," 2337; "Box Seat," 2338; *Cane*, 2335-2339; "Esther," 2336; "Kabnis," 2338; "Theater," 2337
"Tooth, The" (Jackson), 1275
"Tosca" (Allende), 68
"Total Stranger" (Cozzens), 650
"Totara Tree, The" (Finlayson), 2895
"Totentanz" (Wilson), 2536
"Touch of Nutmeg Makes It, The" (Collier), 610
Touch of the Sun, A (Sansom), 2088
"Toupee Artist, The" (Leskov), 1492
Toynbee Convector, The (Bradbury), 338
"Toys" (Dazai), 701
"Traceleen at Dawn" (Gilchrist), 995
Track of the Cat, The (Clark), 588
Tracks (Erdrich), 2965
Traditional History and Characteristic Sketches of the Ojibway Nation, The (Copway), 2962
Trailerpark (Banks), 163
Trambley, Estela Portillo; *Rain of Scorpions and Other Writings*, 2955
"Transaction" (Updike), 2381
"Transformation" (Dazai), 701
Transposed Heads, The (Mann), 1612
Trapné povídky. See *Money and Other Stories*
"Trappist Monastery, The" (Oz), 1863
"Traveler's Story of a Terribly Strange Bed, The" (Collins), 2770
"Traveling to Pridesup" (Williams, Joy), 2521
"Tree, The" (Bombal), 279
"Tree, The" (Thomas), 2310
"Tree. A Rock. A Cloud, A" (McCullers), 1558, 2809
"Tree of Night, A" (Capote), 442
"Tree to Be Desired, A" (Gilchrist), 996
Trembling of a Leaf, The (Maugham), 1646
Trent and the Last Case (Bentley), 2617
Trent Intervenes (Bentley), 2618
"Trenzas." *See* "Braids"
Trésor d'Arlatan, Le (Daudet), 680
Trevor, William, 2340-2347, 2924; "After Rain," 2345; *After Rain*, 2345; "Autumn Sunshine," 2925; "Beyond the Pale," 2925; "Broken Homes," 2344; "Death in Jerusalem," 2925; "Drummer Boy, The," 2343; "Evening with John Joe Dempsey, An," 2342; "Flights of Fancy," 2344; "Lovers of Their Time," 2343; "Nice Day at School," 2342; "Office Romances," 2343; "Paradise Lounge, The," 2344; "Piano Tuner's Wife, The," 2345
"Triangle, The" (Stephens), 2919
"Triangle at Rhodes" (Christie), 577
"Tribal Scars" (Sembène), 2850
Tribal Scars (Sembène), 2850
"Tribunal" (Čapek), 439
"Trimmed Lamp, The" (Henry), 1185
"Trip, The" (Friedman), 917
"Trip to London, The" (Davies, Rhys), 696
"Triptych I" (Bell), 230
"Triumph of Reason, The" (Gilchrist), 996
Triumphs of Gods Revenge, Against the Crying, and Execrable Sinne of Murther, The (Reynolds), 2719
Troilus and Criseyde (Chaucer), 522
Trope, 3068
"Trouble with Bubbles, The" (Dick), 722
"Trouble with Mr. Leopold, The" (Broyard), 365
Trout Fishing in America (Brautigan), 343
"Trout Fishing on the Bevel" (Brautigan), 344
"Trucks" (King), 1370
"True Martyr Is Me, The" (Philombe), 2849
True Relation of the Apparition of One Mrs. Veal, A (Defoe), 2728
"True Story, A" (Twain), 2361
True Story of Ah Q, The (Lu), 1546
"Trust Me" (Updike), 2382
Truth (Douglas), 768
"Truth and Lies" (Price), 1967
"Trying" (Robison), 2057
Tsutsumi Chūnagon monogatari. See *Riverside Counselor's Stories, The*
"Tubber Derg" (Carleton), 458
Tullipan (Meckel), 1662
Tumble Home (Hempel), 1182
"T'ung-jân yü." *See* "Pupils of the Eyes That Talked, The"
"Tunnel" (Barnes), 171
"Tunnel, The" (Swift), 2273
Tuohy, Frank, 2347-2351; "Admiral and the Nuns, The," 2348; "Evening in Connecticut," 2349; "Fingers in the Door," 2349; *Live Bait and Other Stories*, 2349; "Rainy Season, A," 2351; "Survivor in Salvador, A," 2348
"Tupeinyi khudozhnik." *See* "Toupee Artist, The"
Turgenev, Ivan, 2352-2359; "Asya," 2356; "Bezhin Meadow," 2355, 2772; "Country Doctor, The," 2771; "Diary of a Superfluous Man, The," 2355; "Ermolai and Miller's Wife," 2354; "First Love," 2357; "Khor and Kalynich," 2354; "King Lear of the Steppes," 2356; "Mumu," 2356; "Prince Hamlet of Shchigrovo," 2355; "Singers, The," 2355; "Song of Triumphant Love, The," 2357; *Sportsman's Sketches, A*, 2353; "Two Landowners," 2354
"Turkey, The" (O'Connor, Flannery), 1797
"Turn with the Sun, A" (Knowles), 1408
"Tutti-Frutti" (Sansom), 2087
"TV People" (Murakami), 2934
Twain, Mark, 2359-2364; "Celebrated Jumping Frog of Calaveras County, The," 2361; "Facts Concerning the Recent Carnival of Crime in Connecticut, The," 2361; "How to Tell a Story," 2778; "Man That Corrupted

Hadleyburg, The," 2362; "£1,000,000 Bank-Note, The," 2362; "True Story, A," 2361
Twentieth century; and African American women writers, 2868; and African American writers, 2865; Canada, 2901-2902; 1880-1920, 2786; 1920-1960, 2803-2825; 1960-2000, 2826-2842
"Twenty-six Men and a Girl" (Gorky), 1057
"Twenty-three, Please" (Hall), 1103
"Twisting of the Rope, The" (Yeats), 2569
"Two Corpses Go Dancing" (Singer), 2160
Two Dreams: New and Selected Stories (Lim), 2877
"Two Drovers, The" (Scott), 2123
"Two Elenas, The" (Fuentes), 926
"Two Friends from Bourbonne, The" (Diderot), 733
"Two Hussars" (Tolstoy), 2330
"Two Kinds" (Tan), 2281
"Two Landowners" (Turgenev), 2354
"Two Lovely Beasts, The" (O'Flaherty), 2922
"Two Mothers" (Unamuno y Jugo), 2373
"Two Offers, The" (Harper), 2858
Two Old Maids, The (Landolfi), 1429
"Two Old Women and a Young One" (Lessing), 1499
"Two Rivers" (Stegner), 2222
"Two Ships" (Boyle, T. C.), 327
"Two Sisters" (Aidoo), 2853
"Two Way Imagination, The" (Hale), 1100
"Ty i ya." *See* "You and I"
"Tyler and Brina" (Miller), 1680
Tyler, Anne, 2365-2370; "Average Waves in Unprotected Waters," 2367; "People Who Don't Know the Answers," 2368; "Teenage Wasteland," 2368; "Your Place Is Empty," 2367
Tyler, Royall, 2929; *Japanese Tales*, 2929
"Typewriter, The" (Bennett), 2864
"Typhoon" (Conrad), 624

"U nas, w Auschwitzu." *See* "Auschwitz, Our Home (A Letter)"
"Ubasute." *See* "Putting Granny Out to Die"
"Über das Marionettentheater." *See* "Marionette Theater, The"
Ueda Akinari, 2930; "Lust of the White Serpent, The," 2931; *Tales of Moonlight and Rain*, 2931
Ugetsu monogatari. See *Tales of Moonlight and Rain*
"Ugliest Faces" (Broyard), 365
"Ugliest House in the World, The" (Davies, Peter Ho), 692
"Ula Masonda" (Plomer), 1938
Ulibarrí, Sabine Reyes, 2954
"Ultima giornata, L'." *See* "Last Day, The"
"Última ilusión de Don Juan, La." *See* "Don Juan's Last Illusion"
"Última niebla, La." *See* "Final Mist, The"
"Ultimo viene il corvo." *See* "Crow Comes Last, The"
Unamuno y Jugo, Miguel de, 2371-2374; *Abel Sánchez*, 2372; "Madness of Doctor Montarco, The," 2372; "Saint Manuel Bueno, Martyr," 2373; "Two Mothers," 2373
"Uncle Aron" (Dovlatov), 771
"Uncle Ben's Choice" (Achebe), 6
"Uncle Ernest" (Sillitoe), 2143
"Uncle Leopold" (Dovlatov), 772
"Uncle Moustapha's Eclipse" (McKnight), 1578
Uncle Remus (Harris, Joel Chandler), 1123
"Uncle Spencer" (Huxley), 1258
"Uncle Tom's Cabin: Alternate Ending" (Baraka), 166
"Uncle Valentine" (Cather), 488
"Uncle Wellington's Wives" (Chesnutt), 553, 2859
"Uncle Wiggily in Connecticut" (Salinger), 2079
Under a Glass Bell and Other Stories (Nin), 1761
Under African Skies (Larson), 2846
Under the Banyan Tree and Other Stories (Narayan), 1753
"Under the Jaguar Sun" (Calvino), 427
"Under the Lion's Paw" (Garland), 965
"Under the Pitons" (Stone), 2256
"Under the Rose" (Pynchon), 2008
Under the Shadow of Etna (Verga), 2395-2396
Understanding Fiction (Brooks and Warren), 2240, 2607
"Undertaker, The" (Pushkin), 2000
"Une Nuit de Cléopâtre." *See* "One of Cleopatra's Nights"
"Unearthing Suite" (Atwood), 112
"Unfinished Story, An " (Henry), 1185
"Unforgetting, The" (Chang), 512
Unfortunate Traveller, The (Nashe), 2716
"Unge mand med nelliken, Den" *See* "Young Man with the Carnation, The"
"Unimportant Man, An" (West), 2864
Union, A (Davies, Peter Ho), 692
"Union Buries Its Dead, The" (Lawson), 1460
United States, 2729; 1820-1920, 2786; 1920-1960, 2803; 1660-2000, 2826; and science fiction, 2632; and the supernatural, 2643, 2649-2650. *See also* "Geographical Index"
"Unknown, The" (Bombal), 279
"Unknown Masterpiece, The" (Balzac), 149
"Unlucky for Pringle" (Lewis), 1504
"Uno Más" (Morris), 1715
"Unperformed Experiments Have No Results" (Hospital), 1230
Unterhaltungen deutscher Ausgewanderten. See *Conversations of German Emigrants*
Untilled Field, The (Moore, George), 2800, 2916
"Uomo e il personaggio, Il." *See* "Man and the Character, The"
"Up Among the Eagles" (Valenzuela), 2387
Updike, John, 2375-2385, 2827; "A & P," 2377, 2828; "Afterlife, The," 2384; *Afterlife and Other Stories, The,*

2383, 2828; "Alligators, The," 2377; "City, The," 2383; "Egg Race, The," 2382; "Flight," 2377; "From the Journal of a Leper," 2381; "Here Come the Maples," 2381; "Man Who Became a Soprano, The," 2383; *Museums and Women and Other Stories*, 2379; *Music School, The*, 2379; "Pigeon Feathers," 2828; *Pigeon Feathers and Other Stories*, 2377; *Problems and Other Stories*, 2380; *Same Door, The*, 2377; "Sandstone Farmhouse, A," 2383; "Separating," 2380; "Slippage," 2382; "Sublimating," 2380; "Transaction," 2381; "Trust Me," 2382; "When Everyone Was Pregnant," 2379; "Wife-Wooing," 2378
"Upon This Evil Earth" (Oz), 1863
"Upstairs in a Wineshop" (Lu), 1548
"Uroki francuzskogo." *See* "French Lessons"
"Urteil, Das." *See* "Judgment, The"
Utopian, 2633. *See also* "Category Index"

"V podvale." *See* "In the Basement"
"V stepi." *See* "In the Steppe"
"Valaida" (Wideman), 2513
Valenzuela, Luisa, 2386-2389; "I'm Your Horse in the Night," 2387; "Other Weapons," 2388; "Symmetries," 2388; "Up Among the Eagles," 2387
"Valiant Woman, The" (Powers), 1959
"Valley Between, The" (Marshall), 1636
"Valor" (Bausch), 205
Van Gogh, Vincent, 823
Van Gogh's Room at Arles (Elkin), 823
Vanderhaeghe, Guy, 2390-2393; "Expatriates' Party, The," 2392; *Man Descending*, 2391; "Watcher, The," 2391
Vapnfjord Men, The, 2676
"Varenka Olesova" (Gorky), 1058
Vargas Llosa, Mario, 2943
"Variation on a Theme" (Collier), 609
"Various Temptations" (Sansom), 2089
"Vasily and Vasilisa" (Rasputin), 2024
"Vdova" *See* "Widow, The" (Babel)
Vega, Ed, 2958
Vehicle, 3068
"Vengeful Creditor" (Achebe), 5
"Veni, Vidi . . . Wendt" (Stern), 2241
Venus of Ille, The (Mérimée), 1673
Verga, Giovanni, 2393-2398; "Last Day, The," 2396; *Little Novels of Sicily*, 2396; *Per le vie*, 2396; "Property," 2396; "Rustic Chivalry," 2395; "She-Wolf, The," 2395; *Under the Shadow of Etna*, 2395-2396
Vergil, 2398-2403; *Aeneid*, 2399, 2663, 2665
Verisimilitude, 3068
Verism, 2790
"Vertical Ladder, The" (Sansom), 2086
Verwandlung, Die. See *Metamorphosis, The*
"Vesna v Fialte." *See* "Spring in Fialta"
Via crucis do corpo, A (Lispector), 1520
"Viaggio, La." *See* "Adrianna Takes a Trip"
"Viaggio di nozze." *See* "Wedding Trip"
"Victory Mills" (Simpson), 2156
Victory over Japan (Gilchrist), 993
Vidocq, François-Eugène, 2613
"Vieja moralidad." *See* "Old Morality, The"
Vietnamese American culture, 2885
"Views of My Father Weeping" (Barthelme, Donald), 186
"Vigil" (Gates), 982
Vignette, 3068
Villon, 2798
"Vina Divina" (Rushdie), 2070
"Vintage Thunderbird, A" (Beattie), 212
"Violence" (Grimm), 1090
"Violets" (Dunbar-Nelson), 2860
Viramontes, Helena María, 2403-2406, 2956; "Birthday," 2957; "Cariboo Café, The," 2405, 2956; "Moths, The," 2404, 2956; "Neighbors," 2405; "Snapshots," 2404
"Vision of Mizrah, The" (Addison), 15, 2727
"Vision of the Dead Creole, The" (Hearn), 1157
"Visit, The" (Jackson), 1276
"Visitation, The" (Woiwode), 2540
"Visitor, The" (Thomas), 2310
Vita dei campi. See *Under the Shadow of Etna*
"Viy" (Gogol), 1026
Vizenor, Gerald, 2406-2409, 2961; "Baron of Patronia, The," 2968; "Chair of Tears, The," 2408; *Earthdivers*, 2408; "Landfill Meditation," 2407; "Luminous Thighs: *Mythic Tropisms*," 2408; "Marleen American Horse," 2407; "Psychotaxidermist, The," 2407; *Wordarrows*, 2407
"Voice from the Woods, A" (Humphrey), 1246
"Voice of the Night, The" (Hodgson), 2634
Voices Made Night (Couto), 2848
"Voices of Adamo, The" (Laurence), 1440
Völsunga Saga. See *Saga of the Volsungs, The*
Voltaire, 2410-2416, 2730; *Babouc*, 2412; *Candide*, 2412; *Jeannot and Colin*, 2413; *Memnon*, 2413; *Zadig*, 2412
Vonnegut, Kurt, 2416-2423; *Bagombo Snuff Box*, 2421; "Go Back to Your Precious Wife and Son," 2420; "Harrison Bergeron," 2419; "Poor Little Rich Town," 2420; "Welcome to the Monkey House," 2418
"Vor dem Gesetz." *See* "Before the Law"
Vorticism, 1501
"Voter, The" (Achebe), 2851
Voyage of St. Brendan, 2687
Vtoroye rozhdeniye. See *Second Birth*
"Vystrel." *See* "Shot, The"

Wace; *Roman de Brut*, 2694
Wahre Muftoni, Der (Meckel), 1663

Wain, John, 2424-2428; *Death of Hind Legs and Other Stories*, 2426; "Giles and Penelope," 2426; "King Caliban," 2426; "Life Guard, The," 2426; "Master Richard," 2425; "Message from the Pig-Man, A," 2425; "While the Sun Shines," 2426
"Waiting for the Ladies" (Brown), 362
"Waiting-Room, The" (Böll), 276
Waka poems, 2928
"Wake, The" (Keillor), 1354
Wakefield, H. Russell, 2650
"Waking" (Brodkey), 358
"Wald, Der" (Walser), 2439-2440
Waldo, Edward Hamilton. *See* Sturgeon, Theodore
Waldrop, Howard, 2641
"Walk, The" (Donoso), 758
"Walk, The" (Walser), 2440
"Walk in the Night, A" (La Guma), 2854
Walker, Alice, 2428-2437, 2867; "Advancing Luna," 2868; "Child Who Favored Daughter, The," 2431; *Color Purple, The*, 2867; "Everyday Use," 2434; "Fame," 2433; *In Love and Trouble*, 2430, 2868; "Nineteen Fifty-Five," 2433; "Porn," 2868; "Revenge of Hannah Kemhuff, The," 2431; "Roselily," 2430; "Source," 2434; "To Hell with Dying," 2432; *You Can't Keep a Good Woman Down*, 2432, 2868
"Wall, The" (Sansom), 2085
"Wall, The" (Sartre), 2097, 2819
"Walls of Avila, The" (Connell), 616
Walpole, Horace; *Castle of Otranto, The*, 2643, 2729, 2756
Walser, Martin, 2606
Walser, Robert, 2437-2443; "Child, The," 2439; "Einfahrt, Die," 2440; *Fritz Kochers Aufsätze*, 2439; "Letter to a Commissioner of Novellas," 2442; "Oskar," 2440; "Response to a Request," 2440; *Slap in the Face Et Cetera, A*, 2441; "Strange City, A," 2440; "Wald, Der," 2439-2440; "Walk, The," 2440
"Walt and Will" (Apple), 87
"Walter Kömpff" (Hesse), 1189
Waltharius, 2685
"Waltz, The" (Parker), 1884
"Waltzing the Cat" (Houston), 1233
Waltzing the Cat (Houston), 1232
Walwicz, Ania, 2892
"Wanderer, kommst du nach spa . . ." *See* "Stranger, Bear Word to the Spartans We . . ."
Wandering (Lu), 1547
Wandering Ghosts (Crawford), 2649
"Wandering Willie's Tale" (Scott), 2122, 2745
Wandrei, Donald, 2651
Wang Anyi, 2443-2449; "And the Rain Patters On," 2444; *Baotown*, 2445; "Base of the Wall, The," 2445; *Beitong zhidi*, 2447; *Brocade Valley*, 2446; "Destination," 2444; *Lapse of Time*, 2445; *Love in a Small Town*, 2446; *Love on a Barren Mountain*, 2446; "Miaomiao," 2447; *Shushu de gushi*, 2447; *Xianggang de qing yu ai*, 2447
"Wants" (Paley), 1874
War. *See* "Category Index"
"War Baby, The" (Lewis), 1504, 1506
"War Fever" (Ballard), 146
"War Maiden, The" (Eastman), 2963
"Warawanu otoko." *See* "Man Who Did Not Smile, The"
Ward, Alfred, 2757
"Warden, The" (Gardner), 959
Warner, Sylvia Townsend, 2449-2455; "But at the Stroke of Midnight," 2453; "Early One Morning," 2453; "*Hee-Haw!*," 2450; *Innocent and the Guilty, The*, 2453; *Kingdoms of Elfin*, 2454; "Love Match, A," 2451; "Oxenhope," 2453; *Scenes of Childhood*, 2454; "Swans on an Autumn River," 2452; "Winter in the Air," 2451
Warren, Austin; *Theory of Literature*, 2752
Warren, Robert Penn, 2456-2461; "Blackberry Winter," 2457; "Circus in the Attic, The," 2458; "Prime Leaf," 2458; *Understanding Fiction*, 2607; "When the Light Gets Green," 2457
"Warrior Road" (Harjo), 1120
"Warrior's Daughter, A" (Zitkala-Sa), 2964
Warung, Price, 2889
"Watakushi." *See* "Thief, The"
"Watch, The" (Bass), 195
"Watch, The" (Swift), 2274
"Watcher, The" (Vanderhaeghe), 2391
Watcher of Waipuna and Other Stories, The (Pak, Gary), 2884
"Watching Me, Watching You" (Weldon), 2473
Waten, Judah, 2892
"Water Liars" (Hannah), 2837
"'Water Them Geraniums'" (Lawson), 1461
Watercress Girl and Other Stories, The (Bates), 201
"Way Back, The" (Grau), 1067
"Way Back, The" (Robbe-Grillet), 2046
"Way of the Wind" (Oz), 1862
"Way People Run, The" (Tilghman), 2319, 2839
"—We Also Walk Dogs" (Heinlein), 1160
We Are Still Married (Keillor), 1354
We, in Some Strange Power's Employ Move on a Rigorous Line (Delany), 711
"We Killed Mangy-Dog" (Honwana), 2847
We Killed Mangy-Dog and Other Mozambique Stories (Honwana), 2847
"Weaver's Grave, The" (O'Kelly), 2918
"Wedding Day" (Bennett), 2863
"Wedding Day" (Boyle, Kay), 319
"Wedding Dress, A" (Callaghan), 418
"Wedding Trip" (Pavese), 1895
"Weekend" (Beattie), 2831

Weidman, Jerome, 2462-2465; "Horse That Could Whistle 'Dixie,'" The," 2464; "I Knew What I Was Doing," 2464; "My Father Sits in the Dark," 2463; "Three-Two Pitch," 2463
"Wejumpka" (Bass), 196
Welch, Denton, 2466-2471; "At Sea," 2467; "Brave and Cruel," 2469; "Coffin on the Hill, The," 2467; "Diamond Badge, The," 2470; "Fire in the Wood, The," 2470; "Hateful Word, The," 2470; "Judas Tree, The," 2468; "When I Was Thirteen," 2468
"Welcome to the Monkey House" (Vonnegut), 2418
"Welcome, Bob" (Onetti), 1850
"Welding with Children" (Gautreaux), 989
Weldon, Fay, 2472-2476; "Au Pair," 2474; *Hard Time to Be a Father, A*, 2474; "I Do What I Can and I Am What I Am," 2474; "Ind Aff or Out of Love in Sarajevo," 2474; "Moon Over Minneapolis," 2474; *Moon Over Minneapolis*, 2473; "Pains," 2474; "Subject to Diary," 2474; "Watching Me, Watching You," 2473
Wellek, René; *Theory of Literature*, 2752
Wells, H. G., 2476-2481, 2633; "Country of the Blind, The," 2479; "Door in the Wall, The," 2479; "Lord of the Dynamos, The," 2478; "Man Who Could Work Miracles, The," 2478; "Beautiful Suit, The," 2479
Welty, Eudora, 2482-2489, 2605, 2808; "Clytie," 2808; "Death of a Traveling Salesman," 2484; "Keela, the Outcast Indian Maiden," 2484; "Livvie," 2485; "Moon Lake," 2486; "Still Moment, A," 2486; "Where Is the Voice Coming From?," 2488; "Whole World Knows, The," 2487; "Why I Live at the P.O.," 2484, 2808; "Wide Net, The," 2485; "Worn Path, A," 2484
Wen-Amon , 2658
"We're Very Poor" (Rulfo), 2065
"Werewolf Raspberries" (Brautigan), 346
"Werewolves in Their Youth" (Chabon), 504
Wescott, Glenway, 2490-2494; *Babe's Bed, The*, 2493; *Good-bye, Wisconsin*, 2492; "Guilty Woman, A," 2492; "In a Thicket," 2492; "Like a Lover," 2492; *Pilgrim Hawk: A Love Story, The*, 2493; "Sailor, The," 2492; "Whistling Swan, The," 2492
West Indian culture, 2944, 2957. *See also* "Category Index"; "Geographical Index"
West, Dorothy, 2863; "Unimportant Man, An," 2864
West, Jessamyn, 2495-2499; "Battle of Finney's Ford, The," 2497; "Condemned Librarian, The," 2498; *Cress Delahanty*, 2497; *Crimson Ramblers of the World, Farewell*, 2498; "Fifteen: Spring," 2497; *Friendly Persuasion, The*, 2496; "Live Life Deeply," 2498; "Music on the Muscatatuck," 2496; "Neighbors," 2498; "99.6," 2496; "Time of Learning, A," 2497
West, Ray Benedict, 2602
Western United States, 2744. *See also* "Category Index"
Wharton, Edith, 2500-2505, 2602, 2649; "After Holbein," 2503; "Eyes, The," 2502; "Rembrandt, The," 2501
"What Do Hippos Eat?" (Wilson), 2536
"What I Did for Love" (Schwartz, Lynne Sharon), 2118-2119
"What I Have Been Doing Lately" (Kincaid), 1365
"What Jorkens Has to Put Up With" (Dunsany), 801
What Kind of Day Did You Have? (Bellow), 237
"What My Mother Knew" (Simpson), 2154
"What Salmon Know" (Reid), 2028
"What the Tapster Saw" (Okri), 1842
"What Was It?" (O'Brien, Fitz-James), 1789, 2774
What We Talk About When We Talk About Love (Cheever), 475
"What You Hear from 'Em?" (Taylor, Peter), 2297
"What You Left in the Ditch" (Bender), 241
"What's in a Song" (Kenny), 2969
"What's It Like Out?" (Gilliatt), 999
What's It Like Out? (Gilliatt), 999
"What's Wrong with Him?" (Zhang), 2581
"When Boyhood Dreams Come True" (Farrell), 852
"When Everyone Was Pregnant" (Updike), 2379
"When Hell Froze" (Steele, Wilbur Daniel), 2219
"When I Was a Witch" (Gilman), 1006
"When I Was Thirteen" (Welch), 2468
When Mr. Pirzada Came to Dinner (Gates), 1425
"When My Girl Comes Home" (Pritchett), 1972
"When the Light Gets Green" (Warren), 2457
"When the Lights Return" (Okri), 1842
"When the Old Century Was New" (Dreiser), 785
"When the Sardines Came" (Plomer), 1938
When William Came (Saki), 2075
"When You Grow to Adultery" (Leavitt), 1465
"When You're Excused You're Excused" (Friedman), 918
"Where Are You Going, Where Have You Been?" (Oates), 1775
"Where I'm Calling From" (Carver), 477
"Where Is the Voice Coming From?" (Welty), 2488
Where the Jackals Howl and Other Stories (Oz), 1862
"Where There's a Will" (Christie), 575
"Where's Duncan?" (Harris, Joel Chandler), 1125
"While the Sun Shines" (Wain), 2426
"Whistling Swan, The" (Wescott), 2492
"White" (Williams, Joy), 2522
"White Boys, The" (Oates), 1580
White Deer, The (Thurber), 2315
"White Heron, A" (Jewett), 1298
"White Horse, The" (Jones), 2838
"White Horses of Vienna, The" (Boyle, Kay), 320
"White Lock of Hair, The" (Pardo Bazán), 1880
"White Nights" (Dostoevski), 762
"White People, The" (Machen), 1576
"White Quail, The" (Steinbeck), 2236

"White Rooster, The" (Goyen), 1061
"White Tigers" (Kingston), 1380
White, E. B., 2506-2509; "Door, The," 2507; "Hour of Letdown, The," 2508; "Morning of the Day They Did It, The," 2508; "Quo Vadimus," 2508; "Second Tree from the Corner, The," 2507
White, Edward Lucas, 2650
Whitehead, Henry S., 2651
"Whole Loaf, A" (Agnon), 26
"Whole World Knows, The" (Welty), 2487
Who's Irish? (Jen), 2876
"Why Can't They Tell You Why?" (Purdy), 1993
"Why Don't You Dance?" (Carver), 476, 2830
"Why I Like Country Music" (McPherson), 1583
"Why I Live at the P.O." (Welty), 2484, 2808
"Wide Net, The" (Welty), 2485
Wideman, John Edgar, 2509-2515, 2857; *All Stories Are True*, 2514; "Backseat," 2514; "Beginning of Homewood, The," 2512; "Chinaman, The," 2511; "Daddy Garbage," 2512; "Damballah," 2512; *Damballah*, 2511; "Everybody Knew Bubba Riff," 2514; "Fever," 2513; *Fever*, 2513; "Hostages," 2513; "Lizabeth: The Caterpillar Story," 2512; "Newborn Thrown in Trash and Dies," 2514; "Songs of Reba Love Jackson, The," 2512; "Surfiction," 2513; "Valaida," 2513
"Widow, The" (Babel), 133
"Widow of Ephesus, The" (Petronius), 1913
"Widow's Walk" (Grau), 1068
Wieland, Christopher Martin, 2747
"Wife of Bath's Tale, The" (Chaucer), 528
"Wife of His Youth, The" (Chesnutt), 552
"Wife of Nashville, A" (Taylor, Peter), 2297
"Wife-Wooing" (Updike), 2378
Wiggins, Marianne, 2516-2519; "Among the Impressionists," 2517; "Balloons'n Tunes," 2518; *Bet They'll Miss Us When We're Gone*, 2517; "Croeso i Gymru," 2518; "Green Park," 2517; "Grocer's Daughter," 2518; "Kafkas," 2517
Wild Body, The (Lewis), 1503
Wilderness Tips (Atwood), 113
"Wildgoose Lodge" (Carleton), 2915
Wildlife (Ford), 883
"Wilfrid Holmes" (Moore, George), 1696
Will You Always Love Me? (Oates), 1777
William of Malmesbury; *Deeds of the Kings of the English, The*, 2693
Williams, Ella Gwendolen Rees. *See* Rhys, Jean
Williams, Joy, 2520-2524; "Bromeliads," 2522; "Escapes," 2522; *Escapes*, 2521; "Health," 2522; "Lulu," 2522; "Rot," 2522; "Shepherd," 2521; "Skater, The," 2522; "Taking Care," 2521; "Traveling to Pridesup," 2521; "White," 2522; "Winter Chemistry," 2521
Williams, Tennessee, 2524-2530; "Completed," 2527; "Desire and the Black Masseur," 2527; "Hard Candy," 2526; "Night of the Iguana, The," 2525; "One Arm," 2528; "Resemblance Between a Violin Case and a Coffin, The," 2526; "Sabbatha and Solitude," 2527; "Three Players of a Summer Game," 2526
Williams, William Carlos, 2530-2534; "Face of Stone, A," 2532; "Farmers' Daughters, The," 2533; "Jean Beicke," 2532; "Old Doc Rivers," 2531
"Willows, The" (Blackwood), 264, 2797
"Wilshire Bus" (Yamamoto), 2879
Wilson, Angus, 2535-2538; "Realpolitik," 2536; "Totentanz," 2536; "What Do Hippos Eat?," 2536
Wilson, Edmund, 2799
Wimsey, Lord Peter, 2618
Wind Shifting West, The (Grau), 1066
"Widow, The" (Gates), 1532
"Windy Day at the Reservoir" (Beattie), 215
Winesburg, Ohio (Anderson), 77
"Winter Chemistry" (Williams, Joy), 2521
"Winter Dreams" (Fitzgerald), 867
"Winter in the Air" (Warner), 2451
"Winter Night" (Boyle, Kay), 322
"Winter: 1978" (Beattie), 213
"Winter's Day, A" (Leskov), 1493
"Wireless." *See* "Where There's a Will"
Wise Economies (Curnutt), 2610
"Wish House, The" (Kipling), 1391
"Wissler Remembers" (Stern), 2242
Wit and humor, 2664, 2744. *See also* "Category Index"
"Witchcraft" (Head), 2854
With the Snow Queen (Greenberg), 1073
"Withdrawal" (Carey), 453
"Withered Arm, The" (Hardy), 1113
Without a Hero (Boyle, T. C.), 329
"Without Benefit of Galsworthy" (Collier), 608
"Without Love" (Pasternak), 1889
"Witness, The" (Sansom), 2086
"Witness, The" (Petry), 1921
Woiwode, Larry, 2538-2543; "Beginning of Grief, The," 2540; "Black Winter," 2542; "Blindness," 2542; "Brief Fall, A," 2541; "Burial," 2541; "Confessionals," 2542; "Deathless Lovers," 2540; "Firstborn," 2541; "Marie," 2541; *Neumiller Stories, The*, 2539; "Old Halvorson Place, The," 2541; "Owen's Father," 2542; "Pheasants," 2540; "She," 2541; "Silent Passengers," 2542; *Silent Passengers*, 2542; "Summer Storms," 2542; "Visitation, The," 2540
Wolfe, Thomas, 2544-2548; "Death the Proud Brother," 2547; "Kinsman of His Blood, A," 2546; "No Door," 2546
Wolff, Tobias, 2549-2554, 2832; *Back in the World*, 2552; "Coming Attractions," 2552; "Desert Breakdown,

1968," 2552; "Hunters in the Snow," 2551; "In the Garden of the North American Martyrs," 2551; *In the Garden of the North American Martyrs*, 2551; "Life of the Body, The," 2553; "Next Door," 2551; "Night in Question, The," 2553; *Night in Question, The*, 2552; "Other Miller," 2552; "Our Story Begins," 2550; "Passenger," 2552; "Poaching," 2552; "Rich Brother, The," 2552; "Say Yes," 2832
"Woman at the Store, The" (Mansfield), 1621
"Woman Hollering Creek" (Cisneros), 583, 2956
Woman Hollering Creek and Other Stories (Cisneros), 582, 2955
"Woman in the Room, The" (King), 1371
Woman Lit by Fireflies, The (Harrison), 1131
"Woman Who Fell from the Sky, The" (Harjo), 1120
"Woman Who Rode Away, The" (Lawrence), 1455
"Woman's Fight, A" (Linderman), 2962
Women on the Wall, The (Stegner), 2221-2222
Women with Men (Ford), 884
Women's issues, 2638, 2946, 2976. *See also* "Category Index"
"Wonderful Glass, The" (Grimm), 1088
"Wonderful Tar-Baby Story, The" (Harris, Joel Chandler), 1123
"Wonders of the Invisible World, The" (Gates), 981
Wonders of the Invisible World, The (Gates), 981
"Wondersmith, The" (O'Brien, Fitz-James), 1788
"Wooden Anniversary, The" (Leavitt), 1468
Wooing of Etain, 2689
Woolf, Virginia, 2554-2560; "Blue and Green," 2556; "Haunted House, A," 2557; "Kew Gardens," 2557; "Lappin and Lapinova," 2557; "Monday or Tuesday," 2556; "Solid Objects," 2557
Wordarrows (Vizenor), 2407
Words with Power (Frye), 2659
Wordsworth, William, 2757, 2786
Works and Days (Hesiod), 2626
Works Progress Administration, 2864
"World According to Hsu, The" (Mukherjee), 1724
World Is the Home of Love and Death, The (Brodkey), 358
"World of Heroes, The" (Kavan), 1342
World of Sholom Aleichem (Perl), 50
"World of Stone" (Borowski), 298
"World War I Los Angeles Airplane, The" (Brautigan), 345
"World Well Lost, The" (Sturgeon), 2266
Worldly Mental Calculations (Ihara Saikaku), 1266
"Worlds That Flourish" (Okri), 1841
"Worn Path, A" (Welty), 2484
"Worst Thing a Suburban Girl Could Imagine, The" (Bank), 158
"Wounded Socrates, The" (Brecht), 350
"Wreath for Garibaldi, A" (Garrett), 971
Wright, Austin McGiffert, 2602
Wright, Richard, 2560-2565, 2864; "Fire and Cloud," 2561; "Man Who Lived Underground, The," 2562
Wright, S. Fowler; *New Gods Lead, The*, 2639
"Wronged Husband, A" (Gates), 981
"Wunderkind, Das." *See* "Infant Prodigy, The"
"Wunderkind" (McCullers), 1557

Xianggang de qing yu ai (Wang), 2447
"Xuela" (Kincaid), 1366

. . . Y no se lo tragó la tierra. See *. . . And the earth did not part*
"Yabu no naka." *See* "In a Grove"
Yamamoto, Hisaye, 2879; "Legend of Miss Sasagawara, The," 2879; "Life Among the Oilfields," 2879; "Wilshire Bus," 2879
Yamauchi, Wakako, 2879; "And the Soul Shall Dance," 2880
"Yao." *See* "Medicine"
Yarn, 3068
Ye Shengtao, 2910
"Year of Getting to Know Us, The" (Canin), 435
Yeats, William Butler, 2566-2571; "Adoration of the Magi, The," 2570; "Dhoya," 2567; "John Sherman," 2568; "Proud Costello, MacDermot's Daughter, and the Bitter Tongue," 2568; *Stories of Red Hanrahan*, 2569; "Tables of the Law, The," 2569; "Twisting of the Rope, The," 2569
"Yellow Wallpaper, The" (Gilman), 1005
Yellow Woman (Silko), 2139
Yerby, Frank; "Health Card," 2866
Yokohama, California (Mori, Tashio), 2877
"Yōkoku." *See* "Patriotism"
Yoshimoto, Banana, 2934
"You and I" (Sinyavsky), 2168
"You Are What You Own" (Adams), 11
"You Can Always Tell Newark" (O'Hara), 1835
You Can't Keep a Good Woman Down (Walker), 2432, 2868
"You Gave Me Hyacinths" (Hospital), 1229
"You Must Remember This" (Coover), 636
"You Touched Me" (Lawrence), 1453
"Young Archimedes" (Huxley), 1259
"Young Girl, The" (Mansfield), 1620
"Young Goodman Brown" (Hawthorne), 1147, 2644, 2741, 2762
"Young Man with the Carnation, The" (Dinesen), 740
"Your Obituary, Well Written" (Aiken), 34
"Your Place Is Empty" (Tyler, Anne), 2367
"You're Ugly Too" (Moore, Lorrie), 1701
"Yours" (Robison), 2056

"Youth" (Conrad), 623
Yu Dafu, 2910
Yukiguni. See *Snow Country*
"Yume no ukihashi." *See* "Bridge of Dreams, The"
Yvain (Chrétien de Troyes), 569

"Zaabalawi" (Mahfouz), 1588
Zadig (Voltaire), 2412
Zakani, ʿUbaid, 2661
Zamyatin, Yevgeny, 2572-2578; "Cave, The," 2576; "Flood, The," 2576; "In Old Russia," 2575; *Islanders, The*, 2574; "Mamay," 2576; "North, The," 2575; "Story About the Most Important Thing, A," 2576
"Zapechatlennyi angel." *See* "Sealed Angel, The"
Zapiski iz podpolya. See *Notes from the Underground*
Zapiski okhotnika. See *Sportsman's Sketches, A*
"Zapiski sumasshedshego." *See* "Diary of a Madman"
Zayas y Sotomayor, María de; *Desengaños amorosos*, 2706; *Novelas amorosas y exemplares*, 2706
"Ze wspomnień Ijona Ticheyo IV." *See* "Further Reminiscences of Ijon Tichy: IV"
Zealandia, 2893
"Zeitl and Rickel" (Singer), 2161
Zhan Kangkang, 2912
Zhang Jie, 2578-2584; "Ark, The," 2581; "Emerald," 2580; *Love Must Not Be Forgotten*, 2580; "Nobby's Run of Luck," 2582; "Other World, The," 2581; "Something Else," 2582-2583; "Today's Agenda," 2582; "What's Wrong with Him?," 2581
"Zheleznaia volia." *See* "Iron Will"
"Zhitie inzhenera Kipreeva." *See* "Life of Engineer Kipreev, The"
"Zio acquatico, Lo." *See* "Aquatic Uncle, The"
Zitkala-Sa; *American Indian Stories*, 2964; "Warrior's Daughter, A," 2964
Zola, Émile, 2584-2588; "Attack on the Mill, The," 2587; "Death of Olivier Bécaille, The," 2586
Zona sagrada. See *Holy Place*
Zone, The (Dovlatov), 773
"Zoo Island" (Rivera), 2043
"Zooey" (Salinger), 2080
Zoshchenko, Mikhail, 2589-2595; "Adventures of a Monkey, The," 2592; "Get on with the Sleeping," 2591; "Heart of Stone, A," 2592
"Zum lu." *See* "Emerald"
"Zvonok." *See* "Doorbell, The"